UNIVERSITY CASEBOOK SERIES®

CONTRACTS

CASES AND COMMENTS

ELEVENTH EDITION

JOHN P. DAWSON
Late Charles Stebbins Fairchild Professor of Law
Harvard University

WILLIAM BURNETT HARVEY
Late Professor of Law and Political Science
Boston University

STANLEY D. HENDERSON
F.D.G. Ribble Professor of Law Emeritus
University of Virginia

DOUGLAS G. BAIRD
Harry A. Bigelow Distinguished Service Professor
The University of Chicago

FOUNDATION PRESS

444 Cedar Street, Suite 700
St. Paul, MN 55101
1-877-888-1330

Printed in the United States of America

ISBN: 978-1-68328-649-3

PREFACE TO THE ELEVENTH EDITION

With the appearance of the Eleventh Edition, the book finds itself well into its sixth decade. More than a thousand teachers and hundreds of thousands of law students across the country have subjected the book to the scrutiny of the classroom. This edition, the eighth for one of us and the third for the other, carries forward the main themes put in place by Jack Dawson and Burnett Harvey. We remain committed to preserving and building upon the book's distinctive character, especially its use of canonical cases, its sensitivity to the history and evolution of doctrine, and its close attention to the legal consequences of breach.

This is a teaching book, a vehicle for the formal study of contract law's rules and processes and the values they are supposed to serve. There is an informational base and a culture to be passed on, a critical and inquiring element to be shared. Every case tells a story, and every story presents a problem rooted in a particular context. Having entered the realm of legal rules, a territory containing an assortment of landmarks, many blurred or at odds with one or more others, students must consider the possible ways of handling a problem, and defend choices when alternative outcomes are possible by reason of competing facts or principles. It is a range of possibilities, not facile answers to hard questions, that one must master.

Since the beginning, the editors of this book have believed that contract law is best understood—the broad conceptions as well as the formal rules and technical formulations—by beginning with a focus on the nature of the legally enforceable promise. The underlying purposes of contract law (what it seeks to protect, and how it hopes to accomplish its aims) are revealed most clearly when problems are looked at from a perspective of taking care of harms or losses, or gains held unjustly. Students must see that the limitations of contract in our society are no small part of the story of its functions, and that the business of "enforcing" (perhaps dismantling) unkept bargains has much to contribute in the fixing of those limits and, accordingly, the forming of a working understanding of the law of contract as a whole. In a word, when a dispute over an obligation voluntarily assumed ends up in court, the great question of "when" to enforce cannot be detached from the also-great question of "how" to enforce.

There are a few additional introductory points. One is that the materials used to educate law students—particularly students in their first year—typically focus on the past, on disputes courts have already considered and decided, often long ago. But there is a larger sense in which history, long a particular emphasis of this book, is important, indeed indispensable. Legal rules and standards, if they are to attract a following in law offices and courts, must be explained, which is to say, understood. And if we are to truly understand where we are in contracts today, we need to have a feel for where we once were, and how and why it happened that there was movement from one rule or doctrine to another, from one dividing line to a different test altogether for division. It is therefore no surprise that many of the opinions new to this edition rely so heavily on the canonical opinions that have long been at this book's core.

A number of the problems raised in this book are unlikely to come through the door of today's practicing commercial lawyer. In the year 1869 an uncle rises to speak at a joyous family occasion, promising a favored nephew (then fifteen) a very large sum of money if the nephew, in the six years left before his twenty-first birthday, gives up alcohol, tobacco, swearing, and gambling. The nephew agrees and remains true to his word, presumably at some cost, but the uncle dies many years later (eighteen in fact) without having kept his side of the bargain. Even earlier in the 1800s, a farmer, learning of his brother's death in the farm country some seventy miles distant, writes to his brother's widow saying that he has more land than he can tend and that he wants her and her children "to do well." The letter concludes: "If you will come down and see me, I will let you have a place to raise your family." The widow and children make the move, again presumably at some cost, emotional as well as financial. They are given land to work, plus a house, but it all ends abruptly a year or two later, when they are evicted (we are not told why).

In both cases, we want to know whether the promises are legally enforceable, whether the victim of the broken promise can call upon the state to hold the other to it, by force if necessary. Each is an artifact of its own time and place. No giant corporation, no sophisticated bargain, is involved. Nevertheless, such situations provide excellent vehicles for exploring basic principles—such as the extent to which the law should enforce any promise seriously made and reasonably relied upon. Mastery of these and other cases that have become part of the canon increase our confidence in distinguishing between the hard and easy cases. Even more telling, they guide our deliberations in classifying the vast expanse of cases that properly fall somewhere between hard and easy. It is no small matter that the term "artifact," as commonly defined, denotes a thing "showing human workmanship or modification, a product of civilization or artistic endeavor." Again, it is the collective yield of cases litigated by many courts over many decades that gives "commonness" to our common law.

Those familiar with the book will see that this edition's general order of march is largely unchanged. Nevertheless, times of economic dislocation create their share of important legal disputes, and the last several years have been no exception. This edition introduces several dozen new principal cases. As always, we have attempted to keep the materials to manageable length, and notwithstanding the addition of the new cases, this edition is about the same length as the previous one. (The number of pages has increased, but this is the result of a larger font size.)

Much of the newly-added material is designed to further consolidate topics within the book's customary structure and headings. The effort to reduce the number of ancillary cases has continued. The text remains on as objective a level as possible, and this edition again seeks to accommodate differing conceptions and modes of analysis of contract, as well as divergent views of legal method. Students should understand that a single book in the hands of different teachers can be a quite different thing. Through classroom approach and emphasis, aided by handouts and assigned readings, every teacher makes choices with a view to "personalizing" the course in Contracts. A particular challenge in organizing any casebook—especially one aimed at a national audience—is to steer a sufficiently "center-lane" path so as to allow the instructor room to provide the ultimate "take" on what it is that the book puts before the students.

We acknowledged in previous editions the contributions and support of many law teachers, now a list too long to repeat here. We are especially indebted to those in the academy who continue to offer suggestions (and criticisms). A special word of gratitude is again due Harvard's Clark Byse. His help and advice given over many years, first to his colleague and devoted friend Jack Dawson, and then to us, reaches far beyond contracts and the covers of this book.

Jack Dawson and Burnett Harvey are no longer here, but teachers who know about the study of contract in our nation's law schools will also know that Jack and Burnett created something worth preserving. We are privileged to be able to carry that tradition forward.

STANLEY D. HENDERSON
DOUGLAS G. BAIRD

Charlottesville, Virginia
Chicago, Illinois
January 2019

JOHN P. DAWSON
1902–1985

WILLIAM BURNETT HARVEY
1922–1999

ACKNOWLEDGMENTS

We are indebted to the following authors and publishers for permission to reprint excerpts from copyrighted material:

Charny, Hypothetical Bargains: The Normative Structure of Contract Interpretation, 89 Mich.L.Rev. 1815 (1991). Reprinted with permission of the Michigan Law Review.

Cohen, The Basis of Contract, 46 Harv.L.Rev. 553 (1933). Reprinted with permission of the Harvard Law Review Ass'n.

Corbin, Conditions in the Law of Contracts, 28 Yale L.J. 739 (1919). Reprinted with permission of the author, the Yale Law Journal Co., and Fred B. Rothman & Co.

A. Corbin, Corbin on Contracts, vols. 3, 3A (1960). Reprinted with permission of Yale University Law School.

Dawson, Economic Duress—An Essay in Perspective, 45 Mich.L.Rev. 253 (1947). Reprinted with permission of the Michigan Law Review.

Dawson, Judicial Revision of Frustrated Contracts: The United States, 64 B.U.L.Rev. 1 (1984). Reprinted with permission of the Boston University Law Review.

Dawson, Unconscionable Coercion: The German Version, 89 Harv.L.Rev. 1041 (1976). Reprinted with permission of the Harvard Law Review Ass'n.

J. Dawson, Gifts and Promises 216–218 (1980). Reprinted with permission of the Yale University Press.

Fuller, Consideration and Form, 41 Colum.L.Rev. 799 (1941). Reprinted with permission of the author and the Columbia Law Review.

Fuller & Perdue, The Reliance Interest in Contract Damages (pt. 1), 46 Yale L.J. 52 (1936). Reprinted with permission of the authors, the Yale Law Journal Co., and Fred B. Rothman & Co.

Gilmore, Law, Logic, and Experience, 3 How.L.J. 26 (1957). Reprinted with permission of the Howard Law Journal.

Goetz & Scott, Enforcing Promises: An Examination of the Basis of Contract, 89 Yale L.J. 1261 (1980). Reprinted with permission of the authors, the Yale Law Journal Co., and Fred B. Rothman & Co.

Henderson, Promises Grounded in the Past: The Idea of Unjust Enrichment and the Law of Contracts, 57 Va.L.Rev. 1115 (1971). Reprinted with permission of the Virginia Law Review Ass'n and Fred B. Rothman & Co.

Holmes, The Path of the Law, 10 Harv.L.Rev. 457 (1987). Reprinted with permission of the Harvard Law Review Ass'n.

Kessler, Contracts of Adhesion—Some Thoughts About Freedom of Contract, 43 Colum.L.Rev. 628 (1943). Reprinted with permission of the author and the Columbia Law Review.

Konefsky, How to Read, or at Least Not Misread, Cardozo in the *Allegheny College* Case, 36 Buffalo L.Rev. 645 (1988). Reprinted with permission of the author and the Buffalo Law Review.

Kull, Mistake, Frustration, and the Windfall Principle of Contract Remedies, 43 Hastings L.J. 1 (1991). Reprinted with permission of the author and the Hastings College of the Law.

Llewellyn, What Price Contract?—An Essay in Perspective, 40 Yale L.J. 704 (1931). Reprinted with permission of the author and the Yale Law Journal Co.

K. Llewellyn, The Bramble Bush (1951). Reprinted with permission of Oceana Publications, Inc.

Patterson, An Apology for Consideration, 58 Colum.L.Rev. 929 (1958). Reprinted with permission of the Columbia Law Review.

Patterson, Constructive Conditions in Contracts, 42 Colum.L.Rev. 903 (1942). Reprinted with permission of the author and the Columbia Law Review.

Posner, The Law and Economics of Contract Interpretation, 83 Tex. L. Rev. 1581 (2005). Reprinted with permission of the author and the Texas Law Review Association.

Rakoff, Good Faith in Contract Performance: Market Street Associates Ltd. Partnership v. Frey, 120 Harv. L. Rev. 1187 (2007). Reprinted with permission of the Harvard Law Review Association; permission conveyed through Copyright Clearance Center, Inc.

Schwartz & Scott, Precontractual Liability and Preliminary Agreements, 120 Harv. L. Rev. 661, 662–65 (2007). Reprinted with permission of the Harvard Law Review Association; permission conveyed through Copyright Clearance Center, Inc.

Shapiro, Courts, Legislatures, and Paternalism, 74 Va.L.Rev. 519 (1988). Reprinted with permission of the author, the Virginia Law Review Ass'n, and Fred B. Rothman & Co.

Sharp, Pacta Sunt Servanda, 41 Colum.L.Rev. 783 (1941). Reprinted with permission of the Columbia Law Review.

Sharp, Promissory Liability (pts. 1 & 2), 7 U.Chi.L.Rev. 1, 250 (1939–1940). Reprinted with permission of the University of Chicago Law Review.

A.W.B. Simpson, A History of the Common Law of Contract (1975). Reprinted with permission of the author and Oxford University Press.

Whittier, The Restatement of Contracts and Mutual Assent, 17 Calif.L.Rev. 441 (1929). Reprinted with permission of the California Law Review.

S. Williston, A Treatise on the Law of Contracts, vol. 6 (3d ed. 1962). Reprinted with permission of Baker, Voorhis & Co., Inc.

Wormser, The True Conception of Unilateral Contracts, 26 Yale L.J. 136 (1916). Reprinted with permission of the Yale Law Journal Co. and Fred B. Rothman & Co.

The photo of Chief Justice Roger J. Traynor is reproduced with the permission of the Traynor Family, as well as the copyright holder, Moulin Studios of San Francisco. The photos of John Dawson, Oliver Wendell Holmes, Learned Hand, and Benjamin Cardozo are courtesy of Historical and Special Collections, Harvard Law School Library. Burnett Harvey's photo is from the collection of Boston University, and the photo of Karl Llewellyn is from Special Collections, University of Chicago Library.

We remain indebted to the American Law Institute for permission to quote from the Restatement (First) of Contracts, copyright © 1932 by The American Law Institute; the Restatement (Second) of Contracts, copyright © 1981 by The American Law Institute; the Restatement of Restitution, copyright © 1937 by The American Law Institute; the Restatement (Second) of Trots, copyright © 1965 by The American Law Institute; and ALI Proceedings, copyright © 1926, 1965, 1967, and 1971 by The American Law Institute; all excerpts from which are reprinted with the permission of The American Law Institute.

Once again, we acknowledge permission to reprint provisions of the Uniform Commercial Code, copyright © 1991 by The American Law Institute and the National Conference of Commissioners on Uniform State Laws. Reprinted with permission of the Permanent Editorial Board for the Uniform Commercial Code.

SUMMARY OF CONTENTS

PART THREE. THE BOUNDARIES OF CONTRACT

TABLE OF CONTENTS

PART THREE. THE BOUNDARIES OF CONTRACT

TABLE OF CASES

The principal cases are in bold type.

TABLE OF CITATIONS TO THE RESTATEMENT OF CONTRACTS

TABLE OF CITATIONS TO THE UNIFORM COMMERCIAL CODE (2002 OFFICIAL TEXT)

UNIVERSITY CASEBOOK SERIES®

CONTRACTS

CASES AND COMMENTS

ELEVENTH EDITION

PART ONE

THE CORE PRINCIPLES OF CONTRACT LAW

INTRODUCTORY NOTE

Much of what happens Anglo-American courts in contract cases seems straightforward. Contracts are enforced according to their terms. In this respect, our contract law is indistinguishable from virtually any other in the developed world. But identifying the precise contours of any given set of contractual obligations and establishing exactly what it means to enforce it turn on the distinctive features of each legal system. In the case of the Anglo-American system, locating the domain of contract law requires making sense of hundreds of years of case law precedent. Recognizing this need, at the end of the nineteenth century a small group of lawyers and academics—most prominently Christopher Columbus Langdell, Oliver Wendell Holmes, Jr., and Samuel Williston—took on the task. They attempted to capture contract law as it had developed over time. Their work has cast a long shadow over contract law ever since.

Langdell, Holmes, and Williston believed that the vast number of decided cases revolved around just three core principles. They focused first on what it meant—the consequence or remedy—when a promise is legally enforceable. Anglo-American law, in contrast to civil law systems, provides compensatory money damages as its principal remedy for breach of contract. To say that a promise is legally enforceable is, with only a few qualifications, to say that the victim of a particular promise can recover an amount of money that will put her in the same position she would have been in had the promise been kept—no more and no less. As a general matter, she is without other remedy. Someone who breaks her promise is neither forced to keep it nor punished for breaking it.

The contours and various qualifications to this idea—the expectation damages principle—are the focus of the first chapter. Requiring the breacher to pay might seem sometimes too little and at other times too much. If one merchant promises to sell goods to another merchant at the market price and then fails to keep the promise, she is liable only for whatever it costs the second merchant to obtain them from someone else. This might be only the cost of a phone call. On the other hand, if someone makes a legally enforceable promise and immediately realizes that it is a bad deal only a few seconds after she has signed the contract, major consequences still follow. The other party remains entitled to the full benefit of the promise, even though she is no worse off than she was a few moments before.

There are exceptions to the expectation damages principle. In some cases, the victim will be entitled to force the breacher to disgorge whatever the breacher has been given. In other cases, the victim of a breach of promise can compel performance or enjoin the breacher from taking advantage of the opportunities that the breach made possible. Understanding when these other remedies are available is also a critical part of what it means to say that a promise is legally enforceable.

The second chapter of the book examines the second core principle: the problem of distinguishing promises that are legally enforceable from those that are not. People, of course, should keep their promises. But whether promises should be kept is not the question that contract law asks. Contract law asks instead whether redressing a breach of a particular promise is so important that the state should intervene. This question is radically different from the question of whether someone is morally bound to keep her promises.

When a judge awards money damages, it is not just so much talk. The judgment entitles the prevailing party to a writ of execution, an order that compels the sheriff to seize property of the person who broke the promise, using force if necessary. Allowing a private actor to call upon the coercive hand of the state is a serious business. There is a big difference between saying that, as an ethical matter, someone should keep her promise and saying that, if she does not, the sheriff should be able to break into her house and take her property to make things right.

Some line needs to be drawn between those promises that are enforceable and those that are not. Most of us share the intuition that the state has an interest in ensuring that markets work but that it does not have a similar interest in enforcing ordinary social promises (such as a promise to take a friend for drinks). The difference between the two, however, is sometimes elusive.

Langdell, Holmes, and Williston extracted from the case law the idea that what sets legally enforceable promises apart is that they are part of a bargained-for exchange. Merchants strike bargains with one another. Friends in their ordinary social interactions do not. For much of the twentieth century, successive generations of judges, lawyers, and academics pushed back against this idea that legal enforceability does or should revolve exclusively around the existence of a bargained-for exchange. These successors to Langdell, Holmes, and Williston discovered another idea in the case law: legally enforceable promises should also include those that are seriously made and reasonably and foreseeably relied upon. This idea, grounded on reliance on the promise, has supplemented the traditional focus on the bargained-for exchange. It is still evolving.

The third chapter concludes the first part of this book and explores the last of the three core principles Langdell, Holmes, and Williston identified. By their account, contractual liability was an objective, on/off affair: there is a single identifiable moment when a merchant goes from being able to walk away from the bargaining table with utterly no liability to being liable to perform the promise or pay whatever it takes to put the other person in the position she would have been in had the promise been kept. Nineteenth century traditionalists believed that there needed to be, and that there were, objective benchmarks that allowed parties to know where they stood.

This idea that the decision to enter into a contract has such hard edges stands in tension with the realities of commercial life. Parties are separated by time and space. Sometimes there are long discussions and a commitment on the part of both parties becomes manifest only gradually. There are also bargains struck through an exchange of boilerplate forms that have never been read. In neither case is there a single moment at which there is a meeting of the minds. Setting out the rules that determine exactly when parties in various environments become legally bound, and to what, is the focus of the third chapter.

Before examining these themes in detail, read the following opinion closely. The judge who wrote it learned contracts from Samuel Williston while he was his student at Harvard. Williston's influence is manifest. It epitomizes the style and approach to contract law set in motion at the end of the nineteenth century.

Hawkins v. McGee

Supreme Court of New Hampshire, 1929.
84 N.H. 114, 146 A. 641.

Assumpsit against a surgeon for breach of an alleged warranty of the success of an operation. Trial by jury. Verdict [of $3,000] for the plaintiff. The writ also contained a count in negligence upon which a nonsuit was ordered, without exception.

Defendant's motions for a nonsuit and for a directed verdict on the count in assumpsit were denied, and the defendant excepted. During the argument of plaintiff's counsel to the jury, the defendant claimed certain exceptions, and also excepted to the denial of his requests for instructions and to the charge of the court upon the question of damages, as more fully appears in the opinion. The defendant seasonably moved to set aside the verdict upon the grounds that it was (1) contrary to the evidence; (2) against the weight of the evidence; (3) against the weight of the law and evidence; and (4) because the damages awarded by the jury were excessive. The court denied the motion upon the first three grounds, but found that the damages were excessive, and made an order that the verdict be set aside, unless the plaintiff elected to remit all in excess of $500. The plaintiff having refused to remit, the verdict was set aside "as excessive and against the weight of the evidence," and the plaintiff excepted.

The foregoing exceptions were transferred by Scammon, J. The facts are stated in the opinion.

BRANCH, J. The operation in question consisted in the removal of a considerable quantity of scar tissue from the palm of the plaintiff's right hand and the grafting of skin taken from the plaintiff's chest in place thereof. The scar tissue was the result of a severe burn caused by contact with an electric wire, which the plaintiff received about nine years before the time of the transactions here involved. There was evidence to the effect that before the operation was performed the plaintiff and his father went to the defendant's office, and that the defendant, in answer to the question, "How long will the boy be in the hospital?" replied, "Three or four days, not over four; then the boy can go home and it will be just a few days when he will go back to work with a good hand." Clearly this and other testimony to the same effect would not justify a finding that the doctor contracted to complete the hospital treatment in three or four days or that the plaintiff would be able to go back to work within a few days thereafter. The above statements could only be construed as expressions of opinion or predictions as to the probable duration of the treatment and plaintiff's resulting disability, and the fact that these estimates were exceeded would impose no contractual liability upon the defendant. The only substantial basis for the plaintiff's claim is the testimony that the defendant also said before the operation was decided upon, "I will guarantee to make the hand a hundred per cent perfect hand or a hundred per cent good hand." The plaintiff was present when these words were alleged to have been spoken, and, if they are to be taken at their face value, it seems obvious that proof of their utterance would establish the giving of a warranty in accordance with his contention.

The defendant argues, however, that, even if these words were uttered by him, no reasonable man would understand that they were used with the intention of entering "into any contractual relation whatever," and that they could reasonably be understood only "as his expression in strong language that he believed and expected that as a result of the operation he would give the plaintiff a very good hand." It may be conceded, as the defendant contends, that, before the question of the making of a contract should be submitted to a jury, there is a preliminary question of law for the trial court to pass upon, i.e. "whether the words could possibly have the meaning imputed to them by the party who founds his case upon a certain interpretation," but it cannot be held that the trial court decided this question erroneously in the present case. It is unnecessary to determine at this time whether the argument of the defendant, based upon "common knowledge of the uncertainty which attends all surgical operations," and the improbability that a surgeon would ever contract to make a damaged part of the human body "one hundred per cent perfect" would, in the absence of countervailing considerations, be regarded as conclusive, for there were other factors in the present case which tended to support the contention of the plaintiff. There was evidence that the defendant repeatedly solicited from the plaintiff's father the opportunity to perform this operation, and the theory was advanced by plaintiff's counsel in cross-examination of defendant that he sought an opportunity to "experiment on skin grafting," in which he had little previous experience. If the jury accepted this part of plaintiff's contention, there would be a reasonable basis for the further conclusion that, if defendant spoke the words attributed to him, he did so with the intention that they should be accepted at their face value, as an inducement for the granting of consent to the operation by the plaintiff and his father, and there was ample evidence that they were so accepted by them. The question of the making of the alleged contract was properly submitted to the jury.

The substance of the charge to the jury on the question of damages appears in the following quotation: "If you find the plaintiff entitled to anything, he is entitled to recover for what pain and suffering he has been made to endure and for what injury he has sustained over and above what injury he had before." To this instruction the defendant seasonably excepted. By it, the jury was permitted to consider two elements of damage: (1) Pain and suffering due to the operation; and (2) positive ill effects of the operation upon the plaintiff's hand. Authority for any specific rule of damages in cases of this kind seems to be lacking, but, when tested by general principle and by analogy, it appears that the foregoing instruction was erroneous.

"By 'damages,' as that term is used in the law of contracts, is intended compensation for a breach, measured in the terms of the contract." Davis v. New England Cotton Yarn Co., 77 N.H. 403, 92 A. 732. The purpose of the law is "to put the plaintiff in as good a position as he would have been in had the defendant kept his contract." 3 Williston Cont. § 1338; Hardie-Tynes Mfg. Co. v. Eastern Cotton Oil Co., 150 N.C. 150, 63 S.E. 676. The measure of recovery "is based upon what the defendant should have given the plaintiff, not what the plaintiff has given the defendant or otherwise expended." 3 Williston Cont. § 1341. . . .

The present case is closely analogous to one in which a machine is built for a certain purpose and warranted to do certain work. In such cases, the usual rule of damages for breach of warranty in the sale of chattels is applied, and it is held that the measure of damages is the difference between the value of the machine, if it had corresponded with the warranty and its actual value, together with such incidental losses as the parties knew, or ought to have known, would probably result from a failure to comply with its terms. . . .

The rule thus applied is well settled in this state. "As a general rule, the measure of the vendee's damages is the difference between the value of the goods as they would have been if the warranty as to quality had been true, and the actual value at the time of the sale, including gains prevented and losses sustained, and such other damages as could be reasonably anticipated by the parties as likely to be caused by the vendor's failure to keep his agreement, and could not by reasonable care on the part of the vendee have been avoided." Union Bank v. Blanchard, 65 N.H. 21, 18 A. 90; . . . P.L. ch. 166, § 69, subd. 7. We therefore conclude that the true measure of the plaintiff's damage in the present case is the difference between the value to him of a perfect hand or a good hand, such as the jury found the defendant promised him, and the value of his hand in its present condition, including any incidental consequences fairly within the contemplation of the parties when they made their contract. 1 Sutherland, Damages (4th Ed.) § 92. Damages not thus limited, although naturally resulting, are not to be given.

The extent of the plaintiff's suffering does not measure this difference in value. The pain necessarily incident to a serious surgical operation was a part of the contribution which the plaintiff was willing to make to his joint undertaking with the defendant to produce a good hand. It was a legal detriment suffered by him which constituted a part of the consideration given by him for the contract. It represented a part of the price which he was willing to pay for a good hand, but it furnished no test of the value of a good hand or the difference between the value of the hand which the defendant promised and the one which resulted from the operation.

It was also erroneous and misleading to submit to the jury as a separate element of damage any change for the worse in the condition of the plaintiff's hand resulting from the operation, although this error was probably more prejudicial to the plaintiff than to the defendant. Any such ill effect of the operation would be included under the true rule of damages set forth above, but damages might properly be assessed for the defendant's failure to improve the condition of the hand, even if there were no evidence that its condition was made worse as a result of the operation.

It must be assumed that the trial court, in setting aside the verdict, undertook to apply the same rule of damages which he had previously given to the jury, and, since this rule was erroneous, it is unnecessary for us to consider whether there was any evidence to justify his finding that all damages awarded by the jury above $500 were excessive.

Defendant's requests for instructions were loosely drawn, and were properly denied. A considerable number of issues of fact were raised by the evidence, and it would have been extremely misleading to instruct the jury in accordance with defendant's request No. 2, that "the only issue on which you have to pass is whether or not there was a special contract between the plaintiff and the defendant to produce a perfect hand." Equally inaccurate was defendant's request No. 5, which reads as follows: "You would have to find, in order to hold the defendant liable in this case, that Dr. McGee and the plaintiff both understood that the doctor was guaranteeing a perfect result from this operation." If the defendant said that he would guarantee a perfect result, and the plaintiff relied upon that promise, any mental reservations which he may have had are immaterial. The standard by which his conduct is to be judged is not internal, but external. . . . Defendant's request No. 7 was as follows: "If you should get so far as to find that there was a special contract guaranteeing a perfect result, you would still have to find for the defendant unless you also found that a further operation would not correct the disability claimed by the plaintiff." In view of the testimony that the defendant had refused to perform a further operation, it would clearly have been erroneous to give this instruction. The evidence would have justified a verdict for an amount sufficient to cover the cost of such an operation, even if the theory underlying this request were correct. . . .

New trial.

NOTE

On the eve of the new trial ordered in the case reported above, Dr. McGee paid Hawkins $1,400 and settled the lawsuit. McGee then sued his liability insurance carrier in the federal district court for New Hampshire to recover that sum and an additional $2,850 in expenses, mostly attorneys' fees. (Counsel for the insurance company had participated in the trial of Hawkins v. McGee, assisting Dr. McGee's lawyer throughout, even though the insurance company had notified McGee at an early point in the proceedings that it disclaimed any liability, under its policy, because of McGee's alleged guaranty of the results of the operation.) The federal court denied McGee's claim, holding that the policy in question did not cover the "special contract" made with Hawkins but was limited by its terms to liabilities "in consequence of any malpractice, error, or mistake." Since the negligence count had been dismissed from the *Hawkins* litigation, McGee's insurer was therefore free to deny all liability under its policy.

This ruling was affirmed in McGee v. United States Fidelity & Guaranty Co., 53 F.2d 953 (1st Cir. 1931), where the court's opinion reveals that Hawkins' complaint in the original suit against McGee (the case reported above) had alleged that Hawkins had been hospitalized for three months at the time of the operation, and that "the new tissue grafted upon said hand became matted, unsightly, and so healed and attached to said hand as to practically fill the hand with an unsightly growth, restricting the motion of the plaintiff's hand so that said hand has become useless to the plaintiff wherein, pre–vious to said operation[,] [it] was a practical, useful hand." Additional information derived from later interviews with family members and Hawkins' lawyer can be found in Roberts, Hawkins Case: A Hair-Raising Experience, 66 Harv. L. Rec. 1 (1978). It seems the $1,400 settlement was used to take George to Montreal to determine whether another operation might reduce the hand's deformity. Doctors there concluded that nothing could be done for him. A comprehensive review of the trial itself and the competing accounts of Hawkins and McGee respectively can be found in O'Gorman, Expectation Damages, the Objective Theory of Contracts, and the "Hairy Hand" Case: A Proposed Modification to the Effect of Two Classical Contract Law Axioms in Cases Involving Contractual Misunderstandings, 99 Ky. L.J. 327 (2010).

Much of the *Hawkins v. McGee* trial court opinion above focuses on the first core principle of contract law that Langdell, Holmes, and Williston identified—that when a promise is legally enforceable, the victim of a breach of that promise is entitled to compensatory damages. The challenge the court faced is making sense of this idea when the promise concerns a deformed hand rather than a broken machine.

The two other core ideas of traditional contract law are present in the case as well. When Dr. McGee agreed to do the operation, he may not have charged Hawkins anything. By the traditional account, courts enforce promises only if they are part of a bargained-for exchange. It might seem that if Hawkins promised Dr. McGee nothing, Dr. McGee's promise of a perfect hand would not be legally enforceable. The reasoning of the court, however, makes it plain that whether McGee was paid for performing the operation is irrelevant. Dr. McGee wanted to "experiment on skin grafting." For this reason, Dr. McGee did receive something—an opportunity to experiment—in return for performing the operation. Hawkins's consent to the operation therefore provided a benefit to him. This benefit is enough to constitute consideration and was sufficient to make the promise legally enforceable. Each was doing something in exchange for something from the other. Hawkins was getting the operation; in exchange, McGee was getting the opportunity to practice a new skill.

The court also rejected Dr. McGee's claim that he never intended to make a guarantee. As the materials in the third chapter show, subjective intent is not relevant in determining whether a contract is formed. In assessing whether a contract is formed, it is not the subjective intent of the parties that matters, but rather what is objectively manifest. What Dr. McGee thought to himself is not relevant. What matters is what a reasonable person in Hawkins's position would understand him to have said. As the court explained, "[t]he standard by which his conduct is to be judged is not internal, but external."

CHAPTER 1

THE CONSEQUENCES OF LEGAL ENFORCEABILITY: THE EXPECTATION DAMAGES PRINCIPLE AND ITS LIMITS

Before one can assess whether it makes sense to hold a particular promise enforceable, it is useful to know the stakes. One should know the consequences that follow when a court finds a promise is enforceable. Determining when the law's intervention into voluntary exchanges is appropriate cannot be separated from the problem of setting sanctions when promises are broken. Moreover, what contract law is attempting to accomplish—that is to say, its underlying premises and objectives, and recurrent themes—is revealed most clearly in its approach to remedies and measures of recovery.

In one of the best known lectures on the common law, Holmes, The Path of the Law, 10 Harv. L. Rev. 457, 458–469 (1897), Oliver Wendell Holmes gave the following account of what it meant to say that a promise was legally enforceable:

> The duty to keep a contract at common law means a prediction that you must pay damages if you do not keep it—and nothing else. If you commit a tort, you are liable to pay a compensatory sum. If you commit a contract, you are liable to pay a compensatory sum unless the promised event comes to pass, and that is all the difference.

Holmes captures in this passage the idea that someone who breaks a legally enforceable promise is, in the usual case, obliged only to pay compensation. The person is neither punished nor forced to perform. Holmes, however, offers no justification for the rule, identifies no qualifications or exceptions, and does not explain what it means "to pay a compensatory sum." We explore all of these questions in this chapter, beginning with the question of how this "compensatory sum" is measured.

SECTION 1. MEASURING EXPECTATION DAMAGES

Understanding the interests protected by these ideas lies at the heart of understanding the consequences that follow from making a promise legally enforceable at common law. We need to understand why the compensation principle makes sense, how one goes about implementing it, and what limits need to be placed upon it.

Groves v. John Wunder Co.

Supreme Court of Minnesota, 1939.
205 Minn. 163, 286 N.W. 235.

STONE, J. Action for breach of contract. Plaintiff got judgment for a little over $15,000. Sorely disappointed by that sum, he appeals.

In August, 1927, S.J. Groves & Sons Co., a corporation (hereinafter . . . Groves), owned a tract of 24 acres of Minneapolis suburban real estate. It was served or easily could be reached by railroad trackage. It is zoned as heavy industrial property. But for lack of development of the neighborhood its principal value thus far may have been in the deposit of sand and gravel which it carried. The Groves company had a plant on the premises for excavating and screening the gravel. Nearby defendant owned and was operating a similar plant.

In August, 1927, Groves and defendant made the involved contract. For the most part it was a lease from Groves, as lessor, to defendant, as lessee; its term seven years. Defendant agreed to remove the sand and gravel and to leave the property "at a uniform grade, substantially the same as the grade now existing at the roadway . . . on said premises, and that in stripping the overburden . . . it will use said overburden for the purpose of maintaining and establishing said grade."

Under the contract defendant got the Groves screening plant. The transfer thereof and the right to remove the sand and gravel made the consideration moving from Groves to defendant, except that defendant incidentally got rid of Groves as a competitor. On defendant's part it paid Groves $105,000. So that from the outset, on Groves' part the contract was executed except for defendant's right to continue using the property for the stated term. (Defendant had a right to renewal which it did not exercise.)

Defendant breached the contract deliberately. It removed from the premises only "the richest and best of the gravel" and wholly failed, according to the findings, "to perform and comply with the terms, conditions, and provisions of said lease [respecting] the condition in which the surface of the demised premises was required to be left." Defendant surrendered the premises, not substantially at the grade required by the contract "nor at any uniform grade." Instead, the ground was "broken, rugged, and uneven." Plaintiff sues as assignee and successor in right of Groves.

As the contract was construed below, the finding is that to complete its performance 288,495 cubic yards of overburden would need to be excavated, taken from the premises, and deposited elsewhere. The reasonable cost of doing that was found to be upwards of $60,000. But, if defendant had left the premises at the uniform grade required by the lease, the reasonable value of the property on the determinative date would have been only $12,160. The judgment was for that sum, including interest, thereby nullifying plaintiff's claim that cost of completing the contract rather than difference in value of the land was the measure of damages. The gauge of damage adopted by the decision was the difference between the market value of plaintiff's land in the condition it was when the contract was made and what it would have been if defendant had performed.[1] The one question for us arises upon plaintiff's assertion that he was entitled, not to that difference in value, but to the reasonable cost to him of doing the work called for by the contract which defendant left undone.

1. Defendant's breach of contract was willful. There was nothing of good faith about it. Hence, that the decision below handsomely rewards bad faith and deliberate breach of contract is obvious. That is not allowable. Here the rule is well settled, and has been since Elliott v. Caldwell, 43 Minn. 357, 45 N.W. 845, that where the contractor willfully and fraudulently varies from the terms of a construction contract he cannot sue thereon and have the benefit of the equitable doctrine of substantial performance. That is the rule generally. . . .

Jacob & Youngs, Inc. v. Kent, 230 N.Y. 239, 129 N.E. 889, is typical. It was a case of substantial performance of a building contract. (This case is distinctly the opposite.) Mr. Justice Cardozo, in the course of his opinion, stressed the distinguishing features. "Nowhere," he said, "will change be tolerated, however, if it is so dominant or pervasive as in any real or substantial measure to frustrate the purpose of the contract." Again, "the willful transgressor must accept the penalty of his transgression."

2. In reckoning damages for breach of a building or construction contract, the law aims to give the disappointed promisee, so far as money will do it, what he was promised. (9 Am.Jur., § 152.) It is so ruled by a long line of decisions in this state, beginning with Carli v. Seymour, Sabin & Co., 26 Minn. 276, 3 N.W. 348, where the contract was for building

---

[1] [It appears this statement contains an error. The trial judge (jury trial having been waived by the parties) in fact described the damage formula as "the difference between the reasonable value of the property in the condition in which it was left by the defendant and what would be its reasonable market value had the defendant complied in all respects with the grading provisions of the contract." (Record, p. 258).

The trial judge had found (Record, p. 241) that the land was "without any value" on May 1, 1934, the date it was surrendered to Groves. This finding was based on the testimony of two witnesses who had testified at the trial in early December 1936. One of them, a real estate broker specializing in business and industrial properties, had stated (Record, p. 189): "You couldn't sell it now for any purpose; the value of real estate is the use to which it can be put, and I can't conceive of any use to which this property could be put in its condition, with the economical conditions as they were as of May 1st, 1934."—Eds.]

a road. There was a breach. Plaintiff was held entitled to recover what it would cost to complete the grading as contemplated by the contract. . . .

Never before, so far as our decisions show, has it even been suggested that lack of value in the land furnished to the contractor who had bound himself to improve it [provides] any escape from the ordinary consequences of a breach of the contract.

A case presently as interesting as any of our own is Sassen v. Haegle, 125 Minn. 441, 147 N.W. 445. The defendant, lessee of a farm, had agreed to haul and spread manure. He removed it, but spread it elsewhere than on the leased farm. Plaintiff had a verdict, but a new trial was ordered for error in the charge as to the measure of damages. The [court said], 125 Minn. 443, 147 N.W. [at] 446: "But it is also true that the landlord had a perfect right to stipulate as to the disposal of the manure or as to the way in which the farm should be worked, and the tenant cannot evade compliance by showing that the farm became more valuable or fertile by omitting the agreed work or doing other work. . . . The question is not whether plaintiff made a wise or foolish agreement. He had a right to have it performed as made, and the resulting damage, in case of failure, is the reasonable cost of performance. Whether such performance affects the value of the farm was no concern of defendant."

Even in case of substantial performance in good faith, the resulting defects being remediable, it is error to instruct that the measure of damage is "the difference in value between the house as it was and as it would have been if constructed according to contract." The "correct doctrine" is that the cost of remedying the defect is the "proper" measure of damages. Snider v. Peters Home Bldg. Co., 139 Minn. 413, 167 N.W. 108.

Value of the land (as distinguished from the value of the intended product of the contract, which ordinarily will be equivalent to its reasonable cost) is no proper part of any measure of damages for willful breach of a building contract. The reason is plain.

The summit from which to reckon damages from trespass to real estate is its actual value at the moment. The owner's only right is to be compensated for the deterioration in value caused by the tort. That is all he has lost. But not so if a contract to improve the same land has been breached by the contractor who refuses to do the work, especially where, as here, he has been paid in advance. The summit from which to reckon damages for that wrong is the hypothetical peak of accomplishment (not value) which would have been reached had the work been done as demanded by the contract.

The owner's right to improve his property is not trammeled by its small value. It is his right to erect thereon structures which will reduce its value. If that be the result, it can be of no aid to any contractor who declines performance. As said long ago in Chamberlain v. Parker, 45 N.Y. 569, 572: "A man may do what he will with his own, . . . and if he chooses to erect a monument to his caprice or folly on his premises, and employs and pays another to do it, it does not lie with a defendant who had been so employed and paid for building it, to say that his own performance would not be beneficial to the plaintiff." To the same effect is Restatement, Contracts, § 346, Illustrations of Subsection (1), par. 4.

Suppose a contractor were suing the owner for breach of a grading contract such as this. Would any element of value or lack of it, in the land, have any relevance in reckoning damages? Of course not. The contractor would be compensated for what he had lost, i.e., his profit. Conversely, in such a case as this, the owner is entitled to compensation for what he has lost, that is, the work or structure which he has been promised, for which he has paid, and of which he has been deprived by the contractor's breach.

To diminish damages recoverable against him in proportion as there is presently small value in the land would favor the faithless contractor. It would also ignore and so defeat plaintiff's right to contract and build for the future. . . . This factor is important when the subject matter is trackage property in the margin of such an area of population and industry as that of the Twin Cities. . . .

The genealogy of the error pervading the argument contra is easy to trace. It begins with Seely v. Alden, 61 Pa. 302, a tort case for pollution of a stream. Resulting depreciation in value of plaintiff's premises, of course, was the measure of damages. About 40 years later, in Bigham v. Wabash-Pittsburg T.R. Co., 223 Pa. 106, 72 A. 318, the measure of damages of the earlier tort case was used in one for breach of contract, without comment or explanation to show why. That case was followed [in cases decided in the states of Washington and Kentucky], with no thought given to the anomaly of using in a case in contract a standard ordinarily applicable only in cases of tort. . . .

The objective of this contract of present importance was the improvement of real estate. That makes irrelevant the rules peculiar to damages to chattels, arising from tort or breach of contract. . . . In tort, the thing lost is money value, nothing more. But under a construction contract, the thing lost by a breach such as we have here is a physical structure or accomplishment, a promised and paid for alteration in land. That is the "injury" for which the law gives him compensation. Its only appropriate measure is the cost of performance.

It is suggested that because of little or no value in his land the owner may be unconscionably enriched by such a reckoning. The answer is that there can be no unconscionable enrichment, no advantage upon which the law will frown, when the result is but to give one party to a contract only what the other has promised; particularly where, as here, the delinquent has had full payment for the promised performance.

3. It is said by the Restatement, Contracts, § 346, Comment b: "Sometimes defects in a completed structure cannot be physically reme-

died without tearing down and rebuilding, at a cost that would be imprudent and unreasonable. The law does not require damages to be measured by a method requiring such economic waste. If no such waste is involved, the cost of remedying the defect is the amount awarded as compensation for failure to render the promised performance."

The "economic waste" declaimed against by the decisions applying that rule has nothing to do with the value in money of the real estate, or even with the product of the contract. The waste avoided is only that which would come from wrecking a physical structure completed, or nearly so, under the contract. The cases applying that rule go no further. . . . Absent such waste, as it is in this case, the rule of the Restatement, Contracts, § 346, is that "the cost of remedying the defect is the amount awarded as compensation for failure to render the promised performance." That means that defendants here are liable to plaintiff for the reasonable cost of doing what defendants promised to do and have willfully declined to do. . . .

The judgment must be reversed with a new trial to follow.

OLSON, J. (dissenting). . . . [The] premises were to be used by defendant "for the purpose of removing the sand and gravel therefrom." The cash consideration was $105,000, plus defendant's covenant to level and grade the premises to a specified base. There was no segregation or allocation of the cash consideration made applicable to any of the various items going into the deal, and the instrument does not suggest any sum as being representative of the cost of performance by defendant of the leveling and grading process. Nor is there any finding that the contractor "willfully and fraudulently" violated the terms of its contract. All that can be said is that defendant did nothing except to mine the sand and gravel purchased by it and deemed best suited to its own interest and advantage. No question of partial or substantial performance of its covenant is involved since it did nothing in that behalf. The sole question here is whether the rule adopted by the court respecting recoverable damages is wrong. . . . [Plaintiff's] sole contention before the trial court and here is that upon [the] findings the court, as a matter of law, should have allowed him the cost of performance, $60,893.28, plus interest since date of the breach, May 1, 1934, amounting to more than $76,000.

Since there is no issue of fact, we should limit our inquiry to the single legal problem presented: What amount in money will adequately compensate plaintiff for his loss caused by defendant's failure to render performance? . . .

We have here then a situation where, concededly, if the contract had been performed, plaintiff would have had property worth, in round numbers, no more than $12,000. If he is to be awarded damages in an amount exceeding $60,000 he will be receiving at least 500 percent more than his property, properly leveled to grade by actual performance, was intrinsically worth when the breach occurred. To so conclude is to give him something far beyond what the parties had in mind or contracted for. There is no showing made, nor any finding suggested, that this property was unique, specially desirable for a particular or personal use, or of special value as to location or future use different from that of other property surrounding it. . . . [I]t seems clear that what the parties contracted for was to put the property in shape for general sale. . . .

The theory upon which plaintiff relies for application of the cost of performance rule must have for its basis cases where the property or the improvement to be made is unique or personal instead of being of the kind ordinarily governed by market values. His action is one at law for damages, not for specific performance. As there was no affirmative showing of any peculiar fitness of this property to a unique or personal use, the rule to be applied is, I think, the one applied by the [trial] court. . . . Damages recoverable for breach of a contract to construct is the difference between the market value of the property in the condition it was when delivered to and received by plaintiff and what its market value would have been if defendant had fully complied with its terms. . . . Sandy Valley & Elkhorn Ry. Co. v. Hughes, 175 Ky. 320, 194 S.W. 344. It is interesting to note that in the Kentucky case the court reversed its former opinion, [saying] (175 Ky. 320, 321, 194 S.W. 344):

". . . From plaintiffs' avowal on the first trial it appears that it would cost at least $15,000 to do the work required by the contract, and from other testimony in the record it is by no means improbable that the cost would be far in excess of that sum. If this be true, the cost would far exceed the market value of the entire farm. If the contract had been performed, plaintiff would have had a farm with the place from which the earth and stone were taken reduced to the level of the railroad grade and in condition for building purposes. As the case stands, this provision of the contract has not been complied with. What, then, was plaintiff's damage? *Manifestly, not what it would cost to do the work, for, if the work had been done, plaintiff would not have received the cost of the work, but would have been benefited only to the extent that the work increased the market value of his land.* We, therefore, conclude that the measure of damages is the difference between the market value of the farm in its present condition and what its market value would have been if the land from which the earth and stone were removed had been reduced to the level of the railroad grade and left in condition for building purposes." (Italics supplied.)

The principle for which I contend is not novel in construction contract cases. It is well stated in McCormick, Damages, § 168, pp. 648, 649: "In whatever way the issue arises, the generally approved standards for measuring the owner's loss from defects in the work are two: First, in cases where the defect is one that can be repaired or cured without undue expense, so as to make the building conform to the agreed plan, then the owner recovers such amount as he has reasonably expended, or will reasonably have to spend, to remedy the defect. Second, if, on the other hand, the defect in material or construction is one that cannot be remedied without an expenditure for reconstruction disproportionate to the end to be attained, or without endangering unduly other parts of the building, then the damages will be measured not by the cost of remedying the defect, but by the difference between the value of the building as it is and what it would have been worth if it had been built in conformity with the contract." . . .

In 1 Restatement, Contracts, § 346, Illustrations of Subsection (1), par. 3, reads: "A contracts with B to sink an oil well on A's own land adjacent to the land of B, for development and exploration purposes. Other exploration wells prove that there is no oil in that region; and A breaks his promise to sink the well. B can get judgment for only nominal damages, not the cost of sinking the well." And in Guardian Trust Co. v. Brothers (Tex.Civ.App.) 59 S.W.2d 343, a case in substance much like ours, the court said: "The loss or injury actually sustained by the obligee, rather than the cost of performance by the obligor, is the proper measure of damages for the breach of a contract. . . ."

If this were a case to recover damages for tortious injury the applicable rule is the difference in the market value and not the cost of restoring the premises to the former condition if such exceeds the diminution in value. . . . If, then, the landowner received full compensation by this measure, why is he not also fully compensated by receiving the same amount in the case before us? Once it has been held that the market value wholly restores the landowner when his property is permanently damaged, it must be held that he is also entirely repaid by the same measure in our present situation. So it would seem that whether plaintiff's damages are to be measured by the rule applicable to the theory of breach of contract cases or that of tortious conduct the extent of his recovery can be no greater than his actual loss. In either case he may not be heard to complain that because the equivalent to defendant's performance will cost a larger amount than that, therefore he should receive such greater amount rather than his real loss. . . .

No one doubts that a party may contract for the doing of anything he may choose to have done (assuming what is to be done is not unlawful) "although the thing to be produced had no marketable value." (45 N.Y. 572.) In 1 Restatement, Contracts, § 346, Illustrations of Subsection (1), par. 4, the same thought is thus stated:

"A contracts to construct a monumental fountain in B's yard for $5,000, but abandons the work after the foundation has been laid and $2,800 has been paid by B. The contemplated fountain is so ugly that it would decrease the number of possible buyers of the place. The cost of completing the fountain would be $4,000. B can get judgment for $1,800, the cost of completion less the part of price unpaid."

But that is not what plaintiff's predecessor in interest contracted for. Such a provision might well have been made, but the parties did not. They could undoubtedly have provided for liquidated damages for nonperformance, . . . or they might have determined in money what the value of performance was considered to be and thereby have contractually provided a measure for failure of performance.

The opinion also suggests that this property lies in an area where the owner might rightly look for future development, being in a so-called industrial zone, and that as such he should be privileged to so hold it. This he may of course do. But let us assume that on May 1, 1934, condemnation to acquire this area had so far progressed as to leave only the question of price (market value) undetermined; that the area had been graded in strict conformity with the contract but that the actual market value of the premises was only $12,160, as found by the court and acquiesced in by plaintiff, what would the measure of his damages be? Obviously, the limit of his recovery could be no more than the then market value of his property. . . . In what manner has plaintiff been hurt beyond the damages awarded? As to him "economic waste" is not apparent. Assume that defendant abandoned the entire project without taking a single yard of gravel therefrom but left the premises as they were when the lease was made, could plaintiff recover damages upon the basis here established? The trouble with the prevailing opinion is that here plaintiff's loss is not made the basis for the amount of his recovery but rather what it would cost the defendant. No case had been decided upon that basis until now.

Plaintiff asserts that he knows of no rule "giving a different measure of damages for public contracts and for private contracts in case of nonperformance." It seems to me there is a clear distinction to be drawn with respect to the application of the rule for recoverable damages in case of breach of a public works contract from that applicable to contracts between private parties. The construction of a public building, a sewer, drainage ditch, highway, or other public work, permits of no application of the market value doctrine. There simply is and can be no "market value" as to such. And for this cogent reason there can be but one rule of damages to apply, that of cost of completion of the thing contracted to be done. I think the judgment should be affirmed.

[One judge joined in the dissent; two others did not participate. The vote was 3 to 2. Not quite 20 years later, the Supreme Court of Minnesota, in discussing Groves v. John Wunder Co., commented that "[t]he majority opinion is based, at least in part, on the fact that the breach of contract was willful and in bad faith"—a deliberate "failure to perform at all," distinguished from a situation where a defective performance is accompanied by a "substantial good-faith effort" to fulfill the contract. H.P. Droher & Sons v. Toushin, 250 Minn. 490, 85 N.W.2d 273 (1957).]

NOTE

Counsel in the *Groves* case have provided some later history of the Groves tract. After the decision reported above, the case was compromised and defendant paid $55,000 in a cash settlement. The land remained in the same condition until 1951, when a corporation controlled by Frank Groves, to which he had meanwhile transferred it, leveled a portion of the surface without removing any of the overburden. In 1953, approximately three-fifths of the tract was sold for $45,000. The cost of leveling this portion had been about $6,000. The purchaser bought with the intention of using the land for the erection of factories that required railroad trackage. The leveling done rendered the land suitable for this purpose, though the grade and elevation remained higher than they would have been if the overburden had been removed in accordance with the lease to the Wunder Co.

Peevyhouse v. Garland Coal & Mining Co.

382 P.2d 109 (Okl. 1962), cert. denied, 375 U.S. 906 (1963)

Plaintiffs leased 60 acres of their 120-acre farm, which contained coal deposits, to defendant for a period of five years. It was understood that defendant would extract the coal from the leased premises by strip mining. The lease expressly provided that defendant, at the conclusion of its operations, would fill in all pits and smooth the surface. Defendant performed none of these remedial measures, which, the evidence at trial showed, would have required moving "many thousand cubic yards" of dirt at a cost estimated by the plaintiffs' expert witness to be $29,000. The defendant introduced evidence showing that these measures would increase the value of the farm by not more than $300. Plaintiffs sued for $25,000 damages and in the trial court recovered a judgment (based on a jury verdict) for $5,000. The Oklahoma Supreme Court (4 to 3) modified the judgment, reducing it to $300. The majority opinion pointed out that $5,000 was more than the value of the farm had the remedial work been done, that the primary object of the contract was "the economical recovery and marketing of coal from the premises, to the profit of all the parties," and that the remedial work promised was merely "incidental." The majority also relied on an Oklahoma statute providing that "no person can recover a greater amount in damages for breach of an obligation than he would have gained by the full performance thereof on both sides." In the court's view, this statute limited plaintiffs' damages to diminution in value "in spite of the agreement of the parties."

The majority dealt with the relevant case law in this manner: "Groves v. John Wunder Co. is the only case . . . in which the [cost] rule has been followed [where] the cost of performance greatly exceeded the diminution in value resulting from the breach. . . . [T]hree out of four appellate courts have followed the diminution in value rule [in such] circumstances. . . . We do not think either [the building and construction contract analogy used in *Groves* or the grading and excavation analogy used by the other courts] is strictly applicable [here]. The primary purpose of the lease contract [was neither construction nor grading but] merely to accomplish the economical recovery and marketing of coal from the premises. The . . . remedial work [was] incidental to the main object involved.

"Even in the case of . . . building and construction contracts, the authorities are not in agreement as to the factors to be considered in determining whether the [cost] or value rule should be applied. [The court here quotes Restatement of Contracts § 346(1)(a), which is reproduced infra p. 21.] [T]he

Restatement makes it clear that the 'economic waste' referred to consists of the destruction of a substantially completed [structure]. . . . [N]o such destruction is involved [here]. On the other hand, in McCormick, Damages, § 168, it is said with regard to [building] contracts that '. . . where the defect is one that can be repaired or cured without *undue expense*' the cost of performance is the proper measure of damages, but where [the defect] 'is one that cannot be remedied without *an expenditure for reconstruction disproportionate to the end to be attained*' (emphasis supplied) the value rule should be followed. The same idea was expressed in Jacob & Youngs, Inc. v. Kent, 230 N.Y. 239, 129 N.E. 889, as follows: 'The owner is entitled to the money which will permit him to complete, unless the costs of completion is grossly out of proportion to the good to be attained. When that is true, the measure is the difference in value.' . . .

"In view of the unrealistic fact situation in the instant case [an outlay of $29,000 for improvements to property that would increase its value about $300], and [the Oklahoma statute which bars a plaintiff from receiving greater damages for a breach than would have been realized from a contract's full performance], we are of the opinion that the 'relative economic benefit' is a proper consideration here. . . . We therefore hold that where, in a coal mining lease, . . . the [agreed] remedial work is not done, the measure of damages . . . is ordinarily the reasonable cost of performance of the work; however, where the contract provision breached was merely incidental to the main purpose in view, and where the economic benefit . . . to the lessor by full performance of the work is grossly disproportionate to the cost of performance, the damages . . . are limited to the diminution in value [of the premises]."

The dissenting opinion argued that all the costs and difficulties in performing defendant's promise could have been foreseen when the contract was made and that, by defendant's own admission, the plaintiffs had insisted on inclusion of the remedial provision and had indicated that without it they would not sign the lease. The dissent urged that the cost of the promised performance should have been awarded, as in Groves v. John Wunder Co., and that the majority's solution "completely rescinds and holds for naught" the solemn contract of the parties, "taking from the plaintiffs the benefits of the contract and placing those benefits in defendant." [The factual background of the case is examined in great depth in Maute, The Unearthed Facts of *Peevyhouse v. Garland Coal & Mining Co.*, in Contracts Stories 265–303 (2007). Professor Maute points out that the Peevyhouses, in insisting on remediation, gave up a $3,000 payment the coal company typically gave to landowners. She also suggests that their lawyer, who was used to handling tort cases, exaggerated the costs of remediation and that these may in fact have been close to the jury verdict of $5,000. Do either of these facts change the way you look at the case? In the decades after the lawsuit, the Peevyhouses continued to live on the farm.

COMMENT: COST OR VALUE IN GENERAL CONTRACT LAW

The Restatement of Contracts, to which both *Groves* and *Peevyhouse* refer, was issued by the American Law Institute (ALI), a private organization whose elected membership includes prominent lawyers, judges, and law teachers interested in improving the law and its administration. The group was formed in 1923, as a result of a study reporting that the two chief defects in our law were its uncertainty and its complexity. Accordingly, over the years the ALI has prepared and published in condensed form "Restatements"—now in a third series—of the principal subject-matter areas of American private law (it has also undertaken numerous codification projects, model acts, and studies).

The first of these projects was the Restatement of Contracts, which was completed in 1932. Its purpose was "to state clearly and precisely in the light of the decisions the principles and rules of the common law," including "the law which has grown from the application by the courts of generally and long adopted statutes." Work on a revised contracts Restatement was begun in the early 1960s and completed in 1979. One particular aim of the Restatement, Second, of the Law of Contracts, was to take account of the formulations of contract principles appearing in Article 2 (Sales) of the Uniform Commercial Code (UCC), a comprehensive statute on commercial law which was also sponsored (in part) by the Institute and which has been adopted in all of our states except Louisiana.

There will be many occasions ahead for referring to both the UCC and the contracts Restatements. Both provide useful ways of accessing the common law of contracts. At the same time, both have significant limitations. The UCC, when adopted by a legislature, becomes a set of fully authoritative rules, binding on the courts. Article 2, however, only applies to contracts involving the sale of goods. Many, indeed perhaps most, of the contracts that the practicing lawyer encounters—from merger agreements to real estate transactions to employment contracts—do not involve goods. Article 2 applies in these cases only by analogy. Article 2 itself is now more than fifty years old. The ALI engaged in a large-scale effort to revise it in the 1990s, but the revised version did not win any adoptions.

The Restatements, in contrast, aspire to apply to contracts of every type, but they are not law and, technically speaking, not binding on anyone. Courts generally have accorded to the Restatements a status of "persuasive" authority, commensurate with the Institute's claim, made in the first Restatement of Contracts, that its formulations of rule and doctrine "may be regarded as . . . the product of expert opinion as well as the expression of the law by the legal profession." It is accurate to say that the influence of the ALI's work is widespread, and that many of its Restatements have been accorded an authority greater than that of any legal treatise.

Section 346 of the first Restatement, on which both opinions in *Groves* rely in drawing their opposing conclusions, stated the principles that were believed to be appropriate for calculating damages for breach of construction contracts. Section 346(1)(a) provides that for "defective and unfinished construction," the aggrieved party can get judgment for either:

> (i) the reasonable cost of construction and completion in accordance with the contract, if this is possible and does not involve unreasonable economic waste; or
>
> (ii) the difference between the value that the product contracted for would have had and the value of the performance that has been received by the plaintiff, if construction and completion in accordance with the contract would involve unreasonable economic waste. . . .

It then gives several illustrations, of which we repeat the two quoted by the dissenter in *Groves*:

> 3. A contracts with B to sink an oil well on A's land adjacent to the land of B, for development and exploration purposes. Other exploration wells prove that there is no oil in that region; and A breaks his promise to sink the well. B can get judgment for only nominal damages, not for the cost of sinking the well.
>
> 4. A contracts to construct a monumental fountain in B's yard for $5000, but abandons the work after the foundation has been laid and $2800 has been paid by B. The contemplated fountain is so ugly that it would decrease the number of possible buyers of the place. The cost of completing the fountain would be $4000. B can get judgment for $1800, the cost of completion less the part of the price unpaid.

The general principles stated in § 346 of the first Restatement are preserved in the second Restatement §§ 347 and 348, with some changes in terminology—most notably abandonment of talk of "economic waste." Thus, § 348(2), which replaces former § 346 on breaches resulting in defective or unfinished construction, recognizes the customary alternative bases for calculating the injured party's loss in value, but in these terms: "diminution in the market price of the property" or "the reasonable cost of completing performance or of remedying the defects if that cost is not clearly disproportionate to the probable loss in value to him."

Landis v. William Fannin Builders, Inc.

Court of Appeals of Ohio, 2011.
193 Ohio App. 3d 318, 951 N.E.2d 1078.

KLATT, J. . . . In 2004, Landis and his wife, Weidman, decided to build a custom home on land that Landis owned in Pleasantville, Ohio. After interviewing three builders, they chose Fannin Builders to construct their home. On May 4, 2004, appellees signed a contract with Fannin Builders, in which Fannin Builders agreed to construct appellees' home in accordance with the plans and specifications attached to the contract for $356,750.

The specifications for appellees' home called for T1-11 exterior siding covered with two coats of stain in a color of appellees' choice. T1-11 siding is a plywood siding with one-inch-deep vertical grooves spaced 11 inches apart. Appellees chose T1-11 siding for their home because it provided a more natural, rustic look than other types of siding. Before signing the construction contract, appellees sought, and received, assurances from Fannin Builders that it had experience with installing and staining T1-11 siding.

For the most part, the contract specifications indicated certain types of materials appellees wanted (i.e., ceramic tile floors or marble countertops), but did not list specific brands, designs, or colors of the materials. Throughout construction, Fannin Builders would request that appellees choose the brands, designs, or colors as the home progressed to the point where Fannin Builders needed to install the materials. When the time came to apply the stain to the exterior siding, Fannin Builders provided appellees with a brochure entitled "Semi-Transparent & Semi-Solid Color Palettes for all Cabot Colors." The brochure depicted stains in over 30 colors, each available in two different pigment levels: semitransparent (lightly pigmented) or semisolid (extra pigment). Appellees chose a semitransparent stain in a green color, which Cabot, the stain manufacturer, named "allagash." Landis communicated his and his wife's choice to Fannin Builders in a September 2, 2004 e-mail.

Fannin Builders subcontracted with 84 Lumber for the procurement and installation of the T1-11 siding. Unfortunately, 84 Lumber underestimated the amount of siding needed to completely clad appellees' home. Consequently, the company 84 Lumber hired to stain the T1-11 siding, Precision Applied Coating Enterprises ("PACE"), stained the 19 additional sheets separately from the majority of the siding. Although PACE stained both batches of siding with Cabot semitransparent allagash stain, one batch of siding turned out a noticeably darker hue than the other batch.

Weidman visited the construction site after 84 Lumber delivered the siding, and she saw that one stack of siding appeared darker in shade than the other stack. Weidman asked Jeff Klinger, Fannin Builder's field superintendent, if the different color would be a problem. According to Weidman, Klinger answered "no" and assured her that a second coat of stain, applied after the siding was in place, would blend the two shades so that they would match.

When installing the siding, 84 Lumber did not attempt to group same-colored siding together. Instead, 84 Lumber placed darker and lighter siding at random intervals around the perimeter of the house and unattached garage. As a result, appellees' home acquired a striped or patchwork appearance.

The closing on appellees' home was scheduled for January 4, 2005. While Fannin Builders had substantially completed construction by that date, certain tasks remained undone. One of these tasks was the application of the second coat of stain on the siding. Fannin Builders told appellees that the stain should not be applied in temperatures below 50 degrees Fahrenheit, so appellees consented to delay application of the second coat of stain until spring 2005.

At the closing, appellees paid Fannin Builders almost the entire contract price, withholding only $2,000 in escrow to be paid out once Fannin Builders finished all work on the house. During the closing, appellees received from Fannin Builders a number of documents, including a homeowner's manual, a 20-year limited warranty on the home's structural components, and a one-year limited warranty on various aspects of the home's materials and construction.

Shortly after they moved into their new house, appellees observed workers applying a second coat of stain to the exterior siding outside their dining room. Appellees contend that eventually, the whole house and the garage received a second coat of stain. Although appellees did not see the entire staining process, they base their contention on the fact that green stain appears on all the grey trim that edges the siding. Because PACE stained the trim at its facility, the green stain on the trim could have come only from the sloppy application of a second coat of stain after both the siding and trim were installed.

Contrary to Klinger's earlier assurances, the second coat of stain did not improve the patchwork appearance of the siding. Appellees and Fannin Builders discussed various ways in which to fix the patchwork appearance. In spring 2005, appellees allowed Fannin Builders to remove siding from the back of the garage in order to try stain matching. The attempt was unsuccessful in producing a uniform color.

On June 14, 2005, representatives from Fannin Builders, 84 Lumber, and PACE met at appellees' home to confer about the siding problem. At that meeting, 84 Lumber agreed to provide and install new siding, and PACE agreed to stain the new siding. . . .

84 Lumber delivered the replacement siding to appellees' home in early September 2005. When appellees examined the siding, they discovered that it was yellow, not green. Appellees contacted Fannin Builders immediately, explained that the siding was the wrong color, and stated that they did not want the siding installed without discussion of the problem.

When subsequent communication with PACE revealed that PACE had, indeed, stained the replacement siding with the correct stain, appellees and Fannin Builders disagreed about the appropriate next course of action. Fannin Builders wanted to restain the siding on the house, while appellees advocated restaining the replacement siding. Landis told Fannin to delay any additional staining until they could arrive at a mutually agreeable solution. Despite Landis's instruction, a Fannin Builders' subcontractor attempted to blend the two stain colors on the siding on the front of the garage. Both appellees and Fannin Builders agree that the result looked horrible.

The same day that the subcontractor tried to fix the siding with additional stain, Fannin Builders had 84 Lumber remove the replacement siding from appellees' property. As Fannin later explained, he had 84 Lumber remove the replacement siding because appellees "rejected the color of the new siding [and] it makes no sense to put a siding on [the] home with a color [appellees] do not like and hope we can re-stain it to something acceptable." However, Fannin Builders did not inform appellees of its decision to recall the replacement siding or the reasoning behind that decision before implementing it.

After discovering the botched fix and the absence of the siding, Landis e-mailed Fannin Builders instructing it not to do any additional work relative to the siding problem without appellees' prior notice and approval. In a telephone call following that e-mail, Scott Gramke, owner and general manager of PACE, suggested that a solid stain in the allagash color would cover the patchwork appearance of the siding. Appellees were reluctant to use a solid stain because it could not render the natural, rustic look that appellees wanted. Unlike a semitransparent stain, a solid stain masked, rather than highlighted, the grain and natural imperfections of the T1-11 siding. Nevertheless, Landis agreed to test the solid stain by applying it to a sheet of siding that appellees had taken from the replacement batch of siding. Unfortunately, appellees were displeased with both the color and opacity of the solid stain.

Over the next year and a half, appellees and Fannin Builders periodically discussed potential solutions for fixing the patchwork appearance of the siding, but they could not come to any agreement. . . .

The trial court determined that appellees' damages amounted to $66,906.24, and after setting off the $3,908.98 that appellees owed Fannin Builders under the construction contract, the trial court awarded appellees $62,997.26. . . .

In the case at bar, the parties do not dispute that the evidence establishes that Fannin Builders fell below local industry standards in constructing a house with siding of such disparate color. Fannin admitted that the siding is unacceptable under industry standards. The BIA report states that the color variance in the siding "does not comply with professional standard's [sic] in the residential construction industry." Finally, appellees' expert witness testified that the patchwork appearance of the siding does not meet industry standards. Given this evidence, we conclude that the trial court did not err in finding that Fannin Builders' failure to provide siding in a uniform color amounted to a breach of contract. Because the siding does not conform to industry standards, Fannin Builders breached its implied duty to perform in a workmanlike manner. . . .

Fannin Builders argues that the trial court erred in awarding appellees damages based on the cost to replace the mismatched siding instead of the difference in the market value of the house as contracted for and as received. We disagree.

Generally, the appropriate measure of damages in an action for a breach of a construction contract is the cost to repair the deficient work, that is, the cost of placing the building in the condition contemplated by the parties at the time they entered into the contract. Some Ohio courts subscribe to an exception to this general measure of damages. Although never adopted by this court, various other Ohio appellate courts have applied the economic-waste rule to determine damages for the breach of a construction contract. Under the economic-waste rule, if repair of a construction defect "will involve unreasonable economic waste, damages are measured by the difference between the market value that the structure contracted for would have had and that of the imperfect structure received by the plaintiff." Ohio Valley Bank v. Copley (1997), 121 Ohio App.3d 197, 210, 699 N.E.2d 540. Economic waste arises when the total cost to remedy a construction defect is grossly disproportionate to the good to be attained. . . .

The economic-waste rule emanates from courts' disinclination to award windfalls. Sometimes, the owner of a defective structure receives sufficient value from the builder's work that he or she will decide not to fix the defect, and instead, will pocket any damages awarded based on the cost of repairs. . . .

Similar concerns about unjust enrichment underlie the rule establishing the measure of damages for temporary injury to real property. In Ohio Collieries v. Cocke (1923), 107 Ohio St. 238, 248–249, 140 N.E. 356, the Supreme Court of Ohio held that if wrongful injury to real property can be repaired, then:

> [T]he measure of damages is the reasonable cost of restoration, plus reasonable compensation for the loss of the use of the property between the time of the injury and the restoration, unless such cost of restoration exceeds the difference in the market value of the property before and after the injury, in which case the difference in market value becomes the measure.

Like the economic-waste rule, this rule seeks to preclude the injured party from receiving a monetary windfall. In the case of temporary injury to real property, the injured party achieves this windfall by choosing to sell the property rather than restore it, resulting in a profit to the extent that the restoration costs exceed the diminution in market value.

Recently, in *Martin v. Design Constr. Servs., Inc.*, 121 Ohio St. 3d 66, 2009-Ohio-1, 902 N.E.2d 10, the Supreme Court of Ohio limited the rule enunciated in *Ohio Collieries*. The court recognized the relevance of evidence regarding the diminution in market value of injured property in setting a damage award. However, the court abjured *Ohio Collieries'* automatic limitation of damages to the loss of market value when the cost of restoration exceeded that loss. In the place of the *Ohio Collieries* rule, the court imposed a reasonableness test. While diminution in market value remains a consideration, "the essential inquiry is whether the damages sought are reasonable." Id. at ¶ 25.

The economic-waste rule and the rule expressed in *Ohio Collieries* developed in different contexts. The economic-waste rule restricts the damages recoverable for breach of contract. The rule governing imposition of damages for the temporary injury to real property originated from, and is generally applied to, tort cases. Nevertheless, we conclude that the reasonableness test announced in *Martin* precludes a strict application of the economic-waste rule.

"The fundamental rule of the law of damages is that the injured party shall have compensation for all of the injuries sustained." Fantozzi v. Sandusky Cement Prods. Co. (1992), 64 Ohio St.3d 601, 612, 597 N.E.2d 474. Thus, in both contract and tort actions, the appropriate measure of damages is that which will make the injured party whole. Consequently, both the economic-waste rule and the rule governing temporary injury to real property share the same objective. Moreover, as we explained above, both rules emerged from a desire to prevent the injured party from receiving a windfall. Given the rules' identical purpose and origin, we conclude that the economic-waste rule, like the *Ohio Collieries* rule, must cede in favor of the reasonableness test.

Therefore, in a case involving a breach of a construction contract where the breaching party seeks to limit damages to the diminution in value, a fact-finder must determine whether under the facts of that case, it is more reasonable to award damages based on the cost of the remedy or based on the diminution in value. Although a fact-finder may consider whether the cost of the remedy grossly exceeds the difference in the value of the structure with and without the defect, that consideration will not necessarily control the amount of the damage award. Since the goal of any damage award is to make a party whole, a fact-finder must determine which measure of damage best accomplishes that goal without exceeding the bounds of reasonableness.

Here, the trial court awarded appellees the cost to replace the siding because it determined that damages based on loss of market value could not fully compensate appellees. Because the purpose of the contract was the construction of a custom-built home with the aesthetics appellees desired, Fannin Builders' failure to achieve those aesthetics warranted an award of damages that would allow appellees to correct the defect. We find the trial court's decision to award appellees the cost of replacement, rather than the loss of market value, reasonable in this case.

As appellees testified, they contracted for the construction of a custom-built home. Appellees decided to build such a home because they wanted a particular house design and the ability to choose any material and finish they liked. Appellees explained to Fannin Builders that they wanted their house to have a natural, rustic look and that to achieve this look, they wanted T1-11 exterior siding stained with a semitransparent stain. Although the contract did not designate any particular stain opacity, Fannin conceded in his trial testimony that under the contract, Fannin Builders was obligated to apply stain with the opacity that appellees chose. Indisputably, appellees chose a semitransparent stain.

Because appellees placed such importance on the natural appearance of their home, they repeatedly rebuffed Fannin Builders' suggestion that they accept a solid stain. Appellees hired Fannin Builders to construct their "dream home," in which they planned to live many years. Consequently, appellees vigorously opposed Fannin Builders' attempts to get them to compromise on their desire to have T1-11 siding with a semitransparent stain.

According to 84 Lumber's expert witness, the market value of appellees' home is $8,500 less than it would be if it was stained a uniform color. The expert witness arrived at this valuation because the cost to apply two coats of solid stain to the siding is $8,500. Under the economic-waste rule, appellees' damages might have amounted to only $8,500, as opposed to the $66,906.24 necessary to replace the siding.[2] We, however, concur with the trial court that $8,500 could not fully compensate appellees. Given that appellees contracted for a custom home and that appellees place a high value on the rustic look, the cost to achieve the rustic look is the only reasonable measure of damages. Thus, the trial court did not err in awarding appellees damages based on the cost to replace the siding. . . .

Acme Mills & Elevator Co. v. Johnson

Court of Appeals of Kentucky, 1911.
141 Ky. 718, 133 S.W. 784.

CLAY, COMMISSIONER. On April 26th, 1909, appellee J.C. Johnson executed and delivered to appellant Acme Mills & Elevator Co. the following contract:

"April 26th, 1909.

"I have this day sold to Ernest W. Steger, for Acme Mills & Elevator Co., 2,000 bushels No. 2 merchantable wheat, mill scale to apply, sacks

---

[2] We question the likelihood of this outcome. Courts outside of Ohio exempt cases from the economic-waste rule and award damages based on the cost of remedy when aesthetic values make correction of the defect particularly important to a homeowner. As one court observed:

> If a proud householder, who plans to live out his days in the home of his dreams, orders a new roof of red barrel tile and the roofer instead installs a purple one, money damages for the reduced value of his house may not be enough to offset the strident offense to aesthetic sensibilities, continuing over the life of the roof.

Gory Assoc. Indus., Inc. v. Jupiter Roofing & Sheet Metal, Inc. 358 So. 2d 93, 95 (Fla. App. 1978).

to be furnished, to be paid for on delivery at Hopkinsville, Kentucky, at $1.03 per bushel, to be delivered from thresher 1909."

Appellee failed to deliver the wheat at the time agreed upon, and appellant brought this action to recover damages in the sum of $240 and for the further sum of $80, being the value of 1,000 sacks which appellant had furnished to appellee for his use in delivering the wheat. Appellee admitted the execution and breach of the contract, but denied that appellant was damaged. He further pleaded that he threshed his wheat after the 25th of July; that this was the time fixed for delivery, and wheat was then worth only about 97½ cents per bushel. He also pleaded that, at the time fixed for the delivery of the wheat, appellant had suspended business, was unable to comply with its contract, and had no money to pay for the wheat. In another paragraph he admitted his indebtedness for the item of $80 covering the sacks furnished him by appellant, and offered to confess judgment for that amount. The allegations of the answer were denied by reply. Subsequently appellant tendered and offered to file an amended reply, wherein it pleaded that on the 13th day of July, 1909, appellee, of his own wrong and without right or legal authority or the consent of appellant, sold his wheat to the Liberty Mills at Nashville, Tennessee, at the price of $1.16 per bushel, and that by reason of this fact he was estopped to plead in his answer that his wheat was not threshed until after the 25th of July, or that the market price for said wheat at the date of said threshing did not exceed $1 per bushel. The court declined to permit this amended reply to be filed, but entered an order making it a part of the record. The trial resulted in a verdict for appellant in the sum of $80 for the sacks, whereupon judgment was entered against appellee for $80 and costs. From that judgment this appeal is prosecuted.

The evidence for appellee is to the effect that he did not begin threshing his wheat until after the 25th of July; he completed his threshing about the 29th. . . . This fact is established by appellee and his brother and the testimony of two or three other witnesses who passed appellee's field while he was engaged in the work of threshing. There is no evidence to the contrary. At the time he finished threshing, wheat of the kind which he had contracted to sell appellant was not worth over $1 per bushel. This fact is established by the evidence of several witnesses, and there is practically no evidence to the contrary. Appellee attempted to justify his conduct in breaching the contract by certain rumors to the effect that appellant had suspended business and was unable to pay for the wheat. While there may have been rumors to this effect, the evidence fails to establish the fact that appellant had suspended business. About the 14th or 15th of July, appellee sold his wheat to the Liberty Mills at Nashville for $1.16 per bushel. On the 24th of July the price of wheat began to fall, until it reached about $1 per bushel on the 29th.

[Appellant's evidence] is devoted, chiefly, to establishing the fact that appellant did not suspend business and was fully able to pay for the wheat contracted for. While their evidence tends to show that the price of wheat, from the 14th or 15th of July to the 24th, was far in excess of the contract price, they practically admit that wheat was not worth more than a dollar per bushel at the time appellee claims he finished threshing.

One of the errors relied upon is the failure of the court to permit appellant's amended reply to be filed, wherein it attempted to plead that appellee was estopped by his conduct, in selling the wheat, from claiming that he threshed it at a later date or that appellant was not damaged by reason of the breach of the contract. In this connection it is insisted that appellee had no right to violate his contract by selling the wheat to another at a price far in excess of the contract price, using for that purpose the sacks appellant had furnished, and then claim that as a matter of fact he had not threshed the wheat until a later date, and at that time the market price of wheat was below the contract price.

In contracts for the delivery of personal property at a fixed time and at a designated place, the vendee is entitled to damages against the vendor for a failure to comply and the measure of damages is the difference between the contract price and the market price of the property at the place and time of delivery. (Miles v. Miller, 12 Bush 134). This principle of law is so well settled . . . that it is no longer open to discussion. There is no reason why this rule should not apply [here]. The evidence clearly established the fact that the threshing was not completed until about the 29th of July. There is nothing in the evidence tending to show that appellee fraudulently delayed the threshing of the wheat for the purpose of permitting the market price . . . to go down. Indeed, all the circumstances pointed to an advance rather than a decline in the price, and appellee had no reason to anticipate that the market would decline. As he finished threshing on the 29th of July, and the wheat was to be delivered from the thresher, and appellant was not to accept and pay for the wheat until the time fixed for the delivery, that is the time which determines whether or not appellant was damaged. If appellee had sold his wheat on July 14th or 15th, at $1.16 and the price on July 29th was $1.50 per bushel, appellant would not be contending that the measure of his damages was the difference between the contract price and the price appellee received for it on July 14th or 15th, but would insist that he was entitled to the difference between the contract price and $1.50 per bushel. Besides, appellee was not required by his contract, to deliver to appellant any particular wheat. Had he delivered other wheat of like quantity and quality, he would have complied with the contract. When he sold his wheat on July 14th or 15th, for a price in excess of the contract price, and, therefore, failed to deliver to appellant wheat of the quantity and quality contracted for, he took the chances of being mulcted in damages for the breach of the contract. Estoppel can only be invoked where a party by his conduct has led another to act to his prejudice. There is nothing in the facts of this case to justify the application of that doctrine.

. . . As stated before, the evidence overwhelmingly established the fact—indeed, it is practically admitted—that the market price of wheat of the kind and quality contracted to be delivered at the time and place designated in the contract did not exceed $1 per bushel. That being true, appellant, instead of being damaged by the breach of the contract, was actually benefited to the extent of about three cents per bushel. Had the jury upon this state of facts found anything for the appellant, it would have been the duty of this court to reverse the judgment because the verdict was flagrantly against the evidence. . . .

Judgment affirmed.

QUESTIONS

(1) Suppose in *Acme Mills* the market price of wheat had been $1.16 on July 29, and that Liberty Mills appeared for the first time as Johnson was finishing up the threshing that day. If Liberty Mills offered $1.16 for the wheat, should Johnson sell?

(2) Some breaches of contract are "opportunistic," meaning, as one court put it, "the promisor wants the benefit of the bargain without bearing the agreed-upon cost, and exploits the inadequacies of purely compensatory damages." Patton v. Mid-Continent Systems, 841 F.2d 742, 751 (7th Cir. 1988). Such breaches presumably are to be deterred. How are we to determine whether a breach such as Johnson's sale to Liberty Mills is to be characterized as "opportunistic"?

Laurin v. DeCarolis Constr. Co., Inc.

372 Mass. 688, 363 N.E.2d 675 (1977)

Plaintiffs purchased from defendant a wooded lot on which a dwelling was then under construction. During the finishing of construction and prior to the closing of the transaction, defendant removed gravel from the property without plaintiffs' approval. Plaintiffs sought and were awarded damages of $6,480 for the fair market value of the gravel removed—360 truckloads found to have an average fair market value of $18 per load. An intermediate appellate court reversed the judgment on the ground that the court below had improperly awarded the value of the gravel on a tort theory of "conversion." Since plaintiffs were not in (or entitled to) possession at the time the gravel was removed, this court reasoned that plaintiffs had no action in tort for conversion but were limited to contract damages measured by the diminution in the value of the premises. On further appeal, *held*, damages measured by the fair market value of the gravel removed are proper here.

Justice Braucher spoke for the court: The rights of a land purchaser are contract rights. The case must be decided not as a tort action for injury to or conversion of property, but "as a claim for a deliberate and willful breach of contract." Plaintiffs make no claim to recover the cost of restoring the premises to the bargained-for condition, nor do they seek the net proceeds of wrongful sales of gravel made by defendant. "In similar cases involving a tortious conversion of property, we have held that the diminution in the value of the premises is a proper measure of damages; alternatively, at the owner's election, we have upheld the award of the fair market value of the material removed. . . . Here the gravel was actually removed, and proof of its value is not confusing or speculative. Particularly where the defendant's breach is deliberate and willful, we think damages limited to diminution in value of the premises may sometimes be seriously inadequate. 'Cutting a few trees on a timber tract, or taking a few hundred tons of coal from a mine, might not diminish the market value of the tract, or of the mine, and yet the value of the wood or coal, severed from the soil, might be considerable. The wrongdoer would in such cases be held to pay the value of the wood and coal, and he could not shield himself by showing that the property from which it was taken was, as a whole, worth as much as it was before.' . . . This reasoning does not depend for its soundness on the holding of a property interest, as distinguished from a contractual interest, by the plaintiffs. Nor is it punitive; it merely deprives the defendant of a profit wrongfully made, a profit which the plaintiff was entitled to make." But a recovery in contract should not include the value added by defendant's labor in severing the gravel and loading it on trucks. Since the lower court determined the value of the gravel loaded on trucks rather than its value as it lay in the land, the case must be remanded for a redetermination of damages.

[Another court has said: "Since the purpose of [contract] damages is to compensate the injured party for the loss caused by the breach, those damages are generally measured by the plaintiff's actual loss. While on occasion the defendant's profits are used as the measure[,] . . . this generally occurs when those profits tend to define the plaintiff's loss, for an award of defendant's profits when they greatly exceed plaintiff's loss and there has been no tortious conduct [by defendant] would tend to be punitive, and punitive damages are not part of the law of contract damages." U.S. Naval Inst. v. Charter Commc's, Inc., 936 F.2d 692 (2d Cir. 1991).]

NOTE: THE CONCEPT OF ESTOPPEL

The term "estoppel" mentioned in *Acme Mills* describes a general and most flexible doctrine of American law; it will be encountered in various contexts, in this course and others. Literally, to estop is to stop, to bar or prevent. What may seem to be a simple misspelling is the product of a period in history (reaching into the seventeenth century) when the language of the English common law was French of a peculiar hybrid type. The English verb "stop" was Gallicized and in the process became a term of art.

In the law of property one encounters "estoppel by deed," which rests on the principle that a party to a deed cannot contradict or disprove a statement contained in the deed, especially if that party is a grantor seeking to diminish or destroy the language of the grant. Also much used in our law is "estoppel in pais," usually called "equitable estoppel," which operates similarly to prevent a litigant from repudiating a representation that has reasonably induced reliance by the person to whom it was made. It is commonly said that the party to be estopped must intend or reasonably expect that his representations will be acted upon by the party asserting the estoppel; if foreseeable reliance follows, the maker of the representation is forbidden to deny it in court, that is, "turn the tables" on the unsuspecting party. There is, on its face, a tort-like quality to such a doctrine. A classic example of "ordinary" estoppel resting on a false representation of fact can be found in the next chapter (Am. Nat'l Bank v. A.G. Sommerville, Inc., *infra* p. 412). Much attention also will be given in this book to so-called "promissory estoppel," which involves application of the estoppel principle not to a factual representation about the past or present, but to a promise of future action.

It appears that Acme Mills was invoking standard equitable estoppel against the defaulter Johnson. Note the reason the Kentucky court gave for refusing to apply estoppel.

COMMENT: DAMAGES AS PUNISHMENT FOR CONTRACT BREACH

A tort obligation is commonly described as a duty imposed by law to avoid causing injury to others. A person may therefore be liable in tort when there is no contract in the picture at all, as well as when there has been a breach of a duty of reasonable care distinct from contractual obligations. There are, in addition, some kinds of aggravated misconduct for which so-called "exemplary" or "punitive" damages may be awarded under the law of torts (only a few states fail to recognize a common law right to seek punitive damages, requiring instead a statute authorizing their award). Such awards are determined not by the extent of a victim's injury but by the desire to punish (and thus deter) misconduct deemed highly offensive. Standard examples would be deliberate fraud, assault and battery, defamation, or intentional destruction of property. Often the intention to cause harm is very clear and the misconduct so destructive that the legislature has been moved to make it a crime.

In such situations, one objection to punitive damages being awarded in civil actions is that the defendant is denied the safeguards applicable in a criminal prosecution—proof beyond a reasonable doubt, the privilege against self-incrimination, and so on. Another more general objection to punitive damages is that jurors will be left free to award money in amounts that are measured only by the degree of their disapproval of the defendant's conduct. Likewise, judges, exercising the powers of review described earlier, will have no basis in the evidence and no standard derived from some external source to use in determining whether the penalty and its amount are justified.

The arguments to the contrary, in favor of punitive damages, are that public prosecutors are usually too preoccupied to deal with criminal prosecutions of relatively minor offenses and that public prosecutions, even when they are brought and are successful, aim only to vindicate the public interest and seldom include any indemnity to those injured. And so, the argument proceeds, because punitive damages encourages those who have been injured to sue, it serves the double purpose of reimbursing private parties for their losses (including litigation costs) and deterring misconduct by others. These dual goals of compensation and deterrence provide much of the thinking behind our system of tort law.

It is usually said in tort actions that punitive damages are available only in limited circumstances. Negligence, even "gross" negligence, or a barebones intentional act, will not be enough to justify such damages. Instead, to justify such awards, the misconduct must be "outrageous," "wanton," or at least "malicious"—i.e., particularly objectionable in nature (in the words of many courts, "morally reprehensible"). A special money sanction, one exceeding the actual injury suffered, is therefore thought necessary if aggravated forms of otherwise wrongful acts are to be deterred.

In light of the considerations used to justify punitive damages in tort law, are they appropriate as a sanction for breach of contract? It is, of course, quite possible for a breach of contract to be accomplished by conduct that is "outrageous" and independently wrongful—for example, an employee of a common carrier evicts a ticket-carrying passenger and in the process injures the passenger in an unprovoked and violent assault. In almost all of the contract cases in which an award of punitive damages has been sustained, there has been this combination of contract breach and independent tort accompanied by some element of aggravation.

But where the tort element is missing altogether, modern decisions overwhelmingly assert that neither punishment of the breacher nor "setting an example" for others can justify a damage award that is isolated and identified as serving only these purposes. E.g., Morrow v. L.A. Goldschmidt Assoc., 112 Ill. 2d 87, 492 N.E.2d 181 (1986) ("tort and contract law are founded on different policies which justify separate rules" respecting punitive damages); Paiz v. State Farm Fire & Cas. Co., 118 N.M. 203, 880 P.2d 300 (1994) ("the amount of recovery should not depend on the manner in which the contract was breached, and the nonbreaching party should not be able to extract an extra bonus from a breach characterized by a high degree of fault or resulting from a low degree of care"). Even the court that produced Groves v. John Wunder Co. has adhered to the view that a willful, malicious, or bad-faith breach of contract is itself neither tortious—that is to say, independently unlawful—nor a proper basis for imposing punitive damages. See Barr/Nelson, Inc. v. Tonto's, Inc., 336 N.W.2d 46 (Minn. 1983); Wild v. Rarig, 302 Minn. 419, 234 N.W.2d 775 (1975).

One question today is whether there has been a shift in direction—whether, as some have claimed, there exists a greater willingness by courts to award punitive damages in actions that appear to be primarily contractual. It is true that a fair number of our state legislatures have passed "unfair and deceptive trade practices" acts, applicable generally to consumer transactions, that provide for punitive awards in the private causes of action created. There are, in addition, modern statutes providing for the "doubling" and "tripling" of any compensatory damages awarded for certain types of conduct (e.g., trespass to land and unauthorized removal of timber). Also, beginning in earnest in the 1970s, courts have significantly expanded liability for punitive damages in insurance disputes, holding that a company's unjustified refusal to pay or settle a claim can constitute the tort of "bad faith breach of contract." See, e.g., Gruenberg v. Aetna Ins. Co., 9 Cal. 3d 566, 108

Cal. Rptr. 480, 510 P.2d 1032 (1973). In the employment area, expanded tort theories have similarly been used by the courts to reexamine, and break down, the longstanding at-will doctrine, as we shall see later (Sheets v. Teddy's Frosted Foods, Inc., p. 869).

With the gradual expansion of tort liability, presumably more types of conduct, including conduct relating to bargains, will come to be viewed as independently wrongful. But the bone of contention is whether punitive damages will be awarded directly in noninsurance cases when the breach of a contract is found to be objectionable in a moral or ethical sense, but not tortious. It appears only a very small number of courts have taken that step.

The reluctance of courts to depart from the "independent tort" requirement in contract actions is discussed in Sullivan, Punitive Damages in the Law of Contract: The Reality and the Illusion of Legal Change, 61 Minn. L. Rev. 207 (1977). For the story of the general refusal of courts to extend the tort doctrine of "bad faith" breach beyond the insurance cases in California (the initiating state) and elsewhere, see Seaman's Direct Buying Service, Inc. v. Standard Oil Co., 36 Cal. 3d 752, 206 Cal. Rptr. 354, 686 P.2d 1158 (1984), and Freeman & Mills, Inc. v. Belcher Oil Co., 11 Cal. 4th 85, 44 Cal. Rptr. 2d 420, 900 P.2d 669 (1995) (overruling *Seaman's* and approving rule precluding tort recovery for noninsurance contract breach, absent violation of independent tort duty other than "bad faith denial of the existence of, or liability under, the breached contract").

Missouri Furnace Co. v. Cochran

United States Circuit Court, W.D. Pennsylvania, 1881.
8 F. 463.

ACHESON, DISTRICT JUDGE. This suit, brought February 26, 1880, was to recover damages for the breach by Cochran of a contract for the sale and delivery by him to the plaintiff of 36,621 tons of standard Connellsville coke, at the price of $1.20 per ton, . . . deliverable on cars at his works, at the rate of nine cars of 13 tons each per day on each working day during the year 1880. After 3,765 tons were delivered, Cochran, on February 13, 1880, notified the plaintiff that he had rescinded the contract, and thereafter delivered no coke. After Cochran's refusal further to deliver coke, the plaintiff made a substantially similar contract with one Hutchinson for the delivery during the balance of the year of 29,587 tons of Connellsville coke at four dollars per ton, which was the market rate for such a forward contract, and rather below the market price for present deliveries on February 27, the date of the Hutchinson contract. The plaintiff claimed to recover the difference between the price stipulated in the contract sued on, and the price which the plaintiff agreed to pay Hutchinson under the contract of February 27. But the court refused to adopt this standard of damages, and instructed the jury that the plaintiff was "entitled to recover, upon the coke which Cochran contracted to deliver and refused to deliver to the plaintiff the sum of the difference between the contract price—that is, the price Cochran was to receive—and the market price of standard Connellsville coke, at the price of delivery, at the several dates when the several deliveries should have been made under the contract." Under this instruction there was a verdict for the plaintiff for $22,171.49. . . .

The plaintiff moved the court for a new trial. . . . But we are not convinced that the instruction complained of was erroneous.

Undoubtedly it is well settled . . . that when contracts for the sale of chattels are broken by the vendor failing to deliver, the measure of damages is the difference between the contract price and the market value of the article at the time it should be delivered. Sedgwick on the Measure of Damages (7th Ed.) 552. In Shepherd v. Hampton, 3 Wheat. 200, this rule was distinctly sanctioned[:] . . . "[T]he price of the article at the time it was to be delivered is the measure of damages." Nor does the case of Hopkins v. Lee, 6 Wheat. 118, promulgate a different doctrine; for, clearly, "the time of the breach" there spoken of is the time when delivery should have been made under the contract.

It is said in Sedgwick [(7th Ed.) 558]: "Where delivery is required to be made by instalments, the measure of damages will be estimated by the value at the time each delivery should have been made." In accordance with this principle the damages were assessed in Brown v. Muller, Law Rep., 7 Ex. 319, and Roper v. Johnson, Law Rep., 8 C.P. 167, which were suits by vendee against vendor for damages for failure to deliver iron, in the one case, and coal, in the other, deliverable in monthly instalments. In one of these cases suit was brought after the contract period had expired; in the other case before its expiration; but in both cases the vendor had given notice to the plaintiff that he did not intend to fulfill his contract. To the argument, there urged on behalf of the vendor, that upon receiving such notice it is the duty of the vendee to go into the market and provide himself with a new forward contract, Kelly, C.B., in Brown v. Muller, said: "He is not bound to enter into such a contract, which might be to his advantage or detriment, according as the market might fall or rise. If it fell, the defendant might fairly say that the plaintiff had no right to enter into a speculative contract, and insist that he was not called upon to pay a greater difference than would have existed had the plaintiff held his hand." . . .

In this case I fail to perceive anything to call for a departure from that standard. There was no evidence of any special damage to the plaintiff by the stoppage of its furnaces or otherwise. Furthermore, the contract with Hutchinson . . . was made at a time when the coke market was excited and in an extraordinary condition. Unexpectedly and suddenly coke had risen to the unprecedented price of four dollars per ton; but this rate was of brief duration. The market declined about May 1, 1880, and by the middle of that month the price had fallen to one dollar and thirty cents per ton. The good faith of the plaintiff in entering into the new contract cannot be questioned, but it proved a most unfortunate venture. By the last of May the plaintiff had in its hands more coke than was required in its business, and it procured—at what precise loss does not clearly appear—the cancellation of contracts with Hutchinson to the extent of 20,000 tons. As the plaintiff was not bound to enter into the new forward contract, it seems to me it did so at its own risk, and cannot fairly claim that the damages chargeable against the defendant shall be assessed on the basis of that contract.

The motion for a new trial is denied.

NOTE

The sudden rise in the price of coke in the early months of 1880 may have been due to an agreement among Pennsylvania producers to cut coal production, by closing down three days a week, in order to raise prices (this was before the passage of antitrust legislation such as the Sherman Act). This agreement was reported in the New York Times for Saturday, February 14, 1880, but with no specific reference to coke, of which Connellsville, Pa., was a well-known source. It may also be that the rise in the price of coke was due to the prospect of strikes that might affect supply. On Sunday, February 15, 1880, the New York Times reported that the coal miners of the Cumberland region, numbering some 20,000, had given notice on February 13 that they would strike ten days later unless their wage demands were met; and most of them did strike accordingly on February 23 (Boston Herald, February 23, 1880). There was no nation-wide strike of the miners during the late winter and early spring of 1880, since a union capable of conducting such a strike had not yet been organized. In various places in Pennsylvania, however, there were local strikes that had begun in the last two weeks of February (New York Times, March 7, 1880).

COMMENT: THE BUYER'S DAMAGES ON BREACH BY ANTICIPATORY REPUDIATION

The day before the breach, Missouri Furnace had Cochrane's promise to take care of all its needs for coke for the whole year in exchange for its promise to pay $1.20 a ton. After the breach, Missouri Furnace had to promise to pay $4 a ton to get someone else to promise to do the same thing—to satisfy its need for coke for the entire year. To put Missouri Furnace in the same position it had been in before Cochrane broke its promise, it would seem Missouri Furnace needed damages based on the difference between $4 and $1.20.

Missouri Furnace entered into its contract with Cochrane in the first place because it had decided not to buy on the spot market. Missouri Furnace bargained for the benefit of a forward contract. Missouri Furnace did not want to buy on the spot market. It wanted to pay a fixed price for the coke. For that reason Missouri Furnace bargained for a forward contract with

Cochrane, and it is this benefit that it lost when Cochrane broke his contract. To be made whole Missouri Furnace needs the amount it would cost to enter into another forward contract.

This reasoning suggests that, contrary to the conclusion that the court reached in Missouri Furnace, awarding the forward price would be consistent with the expectation damages principle. But is there anything the matter with the legal rule the court adopted? It would seem that providing the nonbreaching party with the spot price might be easier to apply. The spot price is usually readily available, while in many cases there will not be a forward market that the buyer can reenter. Once a spot-market rule is in place, Missouri Furnace can just buy coke in the spot market and send Cochrane the bill. It is not any worse off. Even if the forward contract measure is conceptually correct, is there anything the matter with the spot price measure? The price could prove higher or lower after the fact, but is there anything systematically wrong with it? In an interesting article, Thomas Jackson argues that the spot market measure is indeed wrong. Although such a remedy is worse for the innocent party in Missouri Furnace itself, over the course of many cases this measure is overcompensatory. Using this measure tends to give the nonbreaching party more than it needs to be put back in the position it would have been in had there been performance. See Jackson, "Anticipatory Repudiation" and the Temporal Element of Contract Law: An Economic Inquiry into Contract Damages in Cases of Prospective Nonperformance, 31 Stan. L. Rev. 69 (1978).

Neri v. Retail Marine Corp.

Court of Appeals of New York, 1972.
30 N.Y.2d 393, 334 N.Y.S.2d 165, 285 N.E.2d 311.

GIBSON, J. The appeal concerns the right of a retail dealer to recover loss of profits and incidental damages upon the buyer's repudiation of a contract governed by the Uniform Commercial Code. This is, indeed, the correct measure of damage in an appropriate case and to this extent the code (§ 2–708(2)) effected a substantial change from prior law, whereby damages were ordinarily limited to "the difference between the contract price and the market or current price." . . . [T]he courts below erred in declining to give effect to the new statute and so the order appealed from must be reversed.

The plaintiffs contracted to purchase from defendant a new boat of a specified model for the price of $12,587.40, against which they made a deposit of $40. They shortly increased the deposit to $4,250 in consideration of the defendant dealer's agreement to arrange with the manufacturer for immediate delivery on the basis of "a firm sale," instead of the delivery within approximately four to six weeks originally specified. Some six days after the date of the contract plaintiffs' lawyer sent to defendant a letter rescinding the sales contract for the reason that plaintiff Neri was about to undergo hospitalization and surgery, in consequence of which, according to the letter, it would be "impossible for Mr. Neri to make any payments." The boat had already been ordered from the manufacturer and was delivered to defendant at or before the time the attorney's letter was received. Defendant declined to refund plaintiffs' deposit and this action to recover it was commenced. Defendant counterclaimed, alleging plaintiffs' breach of the contract and defendant's resultant damage in the amount of $4,250, for which sum defendant demanded judgment. Upon motion, defendant had summary judgment on the issue of liability tendered by its counterclaim; and Special Term directed an assessment of damages, upon which it would be determined whether plaintiffs were entitled to the return of any portion of their down payment.

[I]t was shown [at trial] that the boat ordered and received by defendant in accordance with plaintiffs' contract of purchase was sold some four months later to another buyer for the same price as that negotiated with plaintiffs. From this proof the plaintiffs argue that defendant's loss on its contract was recouped, while defendant argues that but for plaintiffs' default, it would have sold two boats and have earned two profits instead of one. Defendant proved, without contradiction, that its profit on the sale under the contract in suit would have been $2,579 and that during the period the boat remained unsold incidental expenses aggregating $674 for storage, upkeep, finance charges and insurance were incurred. Additionally, defendant proved and sought to recover attorneys' fees of $1,250.

The trial court found "untenable" defendant's claim for loss of profit, inasmuch as the boat was later sold for the same price that plaintiffs had contracted to pay; found, too, that defendant had failed to prove any incidental damages; further found "that the terms of [UCC 2–718(2)(b)] are applicable and same make adequate and fair provision to place the sellers in as good a position as performance would have done" and, in accordance with [2–718(2)(b)], awarded defendant $500 upon its counterclaim and directed that plaintiffs recover the balance of their deposit, amounting to $3,750. The ensuing judgment was affirmed, without opinion, at the Appellate Division, and defendant's appeal to this court was taken by our leave.

The issue is governed in the first instance by [UCC] 2–718 which provides, among other things, that the buyer, despite his breach, may have restitution of the amount by which his payment exceeds: (a) reasonable liquidated damages stipulated by the contract or (b) absent such stipulation, 20% of the value of the buyer's total performance or $500, whichever is smaller (§ 2–718(2), pars. a, b). As above noted, the trial court awarded defendant an offset in the amount of $500 under paragraph (b) and directed restitution to plaintiffs of the balance. Section 2–718, however, establishes, in paragraph [(3)(a)] an alternative right of offset in favor of the seller, as follows: "(3) The buyer's right to restitution under subsection (2) is subject to offset to the extent that the seller establishes (a) a right to recover damages under the provisions of this Article other than subsection (1)."

Among "the provisions of this Article other than subsection (1)" are those to be found in § 2–708, which the courts below did not apply. [Section 2–708(1)] provides that "the measure of damages for non-acceptance or repudiation by the buyer is the difference between the market price at the time and place for tender and the unpaid contract price together with any incidental damages provided in this Article (§ 2–710), but less expenses saved in consequence of the buyer's breach." However, this provision is made expressly subject to subsection (2), providing: "(2) If the measure of damages provided in subsection (1) is inadequate to put the seller in as good a position as performance would have done then the measure of damages is the profit (including reasonable overhead) which the seller would have made from full performance by the buyer, together with any incidental damages provided in this Article (§ 2–710), due allowance for costs reasonably incurred and due credit for payments or proceeds of resale."

The provision of the code upon which the decision at Trial Term rested [§ 2–718(2)(b)] does not differ greatly from the corresponding provisions of the prior statute (Personal Property Law, § 145–a(1)(b)), except as the new act includes the alternative remedy of a lump sum award of $500. Neither does the present reference [in § 2–718(3)(a)] to the recovery of damages pursuant to other provisions of the article differ from a like reference in the prior statute (§ 145–a(2)(a)) to an alternative measure of damages under § 145 of that act; but § 145 made no provision for recovery of lost profits as does [UCC 2–708(2)]. The new statute is thus innovative and significant and its analysis is necessary to the determination of the issues here presented.

Prior to the code, the New York cases "applied the 'profit' test, contract price less cost of manufacture, only in cases where the seller was a manufacturer or an agent for a manufacturer" (1955 Report of N.Y. Law Rev. Comm., vol. 1, p. 693). Its extension to retail sales was "designed to eliminate the unfair and economically wasteful results arising under the older law when fixed price articles were involved. This section permits the recovery of lost profits in all appropriate cases, which would include all standard priced goods." (Official Comment 2, [UCC] § 2–708.) Additionally, and "in all cases the seller may recover incidental damages" (id., Comment 3). The buyer's right to restitution was established at Special Term upon the motion for summary judgment, as was the seller's right to proper offsets, in each case pursuant to § 2–718; and, as the parties concede, the only question before us, following the assessment of damages at Special Term, is that as to the proper measure of damage to be applied. The conclusion is clear from the record—indeed with mathematical certainty—that "the measure of damages provided in subsection (1) is inadequate to put the seller in as good a position as performance would have done" ([UCC] § 2–708(2)) and hence—again under subsection (2)—that the seller is entitled to its "profit (including reasonable overhead) . . . together with any incidental damages[,] . . . due allowance for costs reasonably incurred and due credit for payments or proceeds of resale."

It is evident, first, that this retail seller is entitled to its profit and, second, that the last sentence of subsection (2), as hereinbefore quoted, referring to "due credit for payments or proceeds of resale" is inapplicable to this retail sales contract.[2] Closely parallel to the factual situation now before us is that hypothesized by Dean Hawkland as illustrative of the operation of the rules: "Thus, if a private party agrees to sell his automobile to a buyer for $2,000, a breach by the buyer would cause the seller no loss (except incidental damages, i.e., expense of a new sale) if the seller was able to sell the automobile to another buyer for $2000. But the situation is different with dealers having an unlimited supply of standard-priced goods. Thus, if an automobile dealer agrees to sell a car to a buyer at the standard price of $2000, a breach by the buyer injures the dealer, even though he is able to sell the automobile to another for $2000. If the dealer has an inexhaustible supply of cars, the resale to replace the breaching buyer costs the dealer a sale, because, had the breaching buyer performed, the dealer would have made two sales instead of one. The buyer's breach, in such a case, depletes the dealer's sales to the extent of one, and the measure of damages should be the dealer's profit on one sale. Section 2–708 recognizes this, and it rejects the rule developed under the Uniform Sales Act by many courts that the profit cannot be recovered in this case." (Hawkland, Sales and Bulk Sales 1958 ed., pp. 153–154. . . .)

The record which in this case establishes defendant's entitlement to damages in the amount of its prospective profit, at the same time confirms defendant's cognate right to "any incidental damages provided in this Article (§ 2–710)"[3] ([UCC], § 2–708(2)). . . . [I]t is too clear to require discussion that the seller's right to recover loss of profits is not exclusive and that he may recoup his "incidental" expenses as well. . . . Although the trial court's denial of incidental damages in the uncontroverted amount of $674 was made in the context of its erroneous conclusion that [§ 2–718(2)(b)] was applicable and was "adequate . . . to place the sellers in as good a position as performance would have done," the denial seems not to have rested entirely on the court's mistaken application of the law, as there was an explicit finding "that defendant completely failed to show

---

[2] The concluding clause, "due credit for payments or proceeds of resale," is intended to refer to "the privilege of the seller to realize junk value when it is manifestly useless to complete the operation of manufacture". . . . The commentators who have considered the language have uniformly concluded that "the reference is to a resale as scrap under . . . Section 2–704" (1956 Report of N.Y. Law Rev. Comm., p. 397 . . .). Another writer, reaching the same conclusion, after detailing the history of the clause, says that " 'proceeds of resale' previously meant the resale value of the goods in finished form; now it means the resale value of the components on hand at the time plaintiff learns of breach" (Harris, Seller's Damages, 18 Stan.L.Rev. 66, 104).

[3] "Incidental damages to an aggrieved seller include any commercially reasonable charges, expenses or commissions incurred in stopping delivery, in the transportation, care and custody of goods after the buyer's breach, in connection with return or resale of the goods or otherwise resulting from the breach" ([UCC], § 2–710).

that it suffered any incidental damages." We find no basis for the court's conclusion . . . inasmuch as the proper items of the $674 expenses (being for storage, upkeep, finance charges and insurance for the period between the date performance was due and the time of the resale) were proven without objection and were in no way controverted, impeached or otherwise challenged, at the trial or on appeal. Thus the court's finding of a failure of proof cannot be supported upon the record and, therefore, and contrary to plaintiffs' contention, the affirmance at the Appellate Division was ineffective to save it.

The trial court correctly denied defendant's claim for recovery of attorney's fees incurred by it in this action. Attorney's fees incurred in an action such as this are not in the nature of the protective expenses contemplated by the statute ([UCC], § 1–106(1); § 2–710; § 2–708(2)). . . .

It follows that plaintiffs are entitled to restitution of the sum of $4,250 . . . less an offset to defendant in the amount of $3,253 on account of its lost profit of $2,579 and its incidental damages of $674.

The order of the Appellate Division should be modified, with costs in all courts, in accordance with this opinion, and, as so modified, affirmed.

NOTE

A detailed analysis of the UCC sections bearing on the question of damages for a lost-volume seller can be found in R.E. Davis Chem. Corp. v. Diasonics, Inc., 826 F.2d 678 (7th Cir. 1987), including a discussion of whether 2–708 should be "relegated to a role inferior to that of 2–706 and 2–709 and [whether] one can turn to 2–708 only after [it is] concluded that neither 2–706 nor 2–709 is applicable." The court rejected that latter view, at least as concerns 2–706, concluding, in line with most courts, that a reselling lost-volume seller is free to bypass 2–706's damage measure and to proceed under 2–708. The *R.E. Davis* court, however, questioned Neri's conclusion that market-based damages are inadequate in these cases "with mathematical certainty."

> [U]nder some circumstances, the measure of damages provided under 2–708(1) will not put a reselling seller in as good a position as it would have been in had the buyer performed because the breach resulted in the seller losing sales volume. However, we disagree with the definition of "lost volume seller" adopted by other courts. Courts awarding lost profits to a lost volume seller have focused on whether the seller had the capacity to supply the breached units in addition to what it actually sold. In reality, however, the relevant questions include, not only whether the seller could have produced the breached units in addition to its actual volume, but also whether it would have been profitable for the seller to produce both units. . . . As one commentator has noted, under "the economic law of diminishing returns or increasing marginal costs[,] . . . as a seller's volume increases, then a point will inevitably be reached

> where the cost of selling each additional item diminishes the incremental return to the seller and eventually makes it entirely unprofitable to conclude the next sale." (Shanker, [The Case for a Literal Reading of UCC Section 2–708(2) One Profit for the Reseller), 24 Case W.Res.L.Rev. 697 (1973)] at 705. Thus, under some conditions, awarding a lost volume seller its presumed lost profit will result in overcompensating the seller, and 2–708(2) would not take effect because the damage formula provided in 2–708(1) does place the seller in as good a position as if the buyer had performed. Therefore, on remand, [plaintiff] must establish, not only that it had the capacity to produce the breached unit in addition to the unit resold, but also that it would have been profitable for it to have produced and sold both.

On remand, plaintiff met this burden. See R.E. Davis Chem. Corp. v. Diasonics, Inc., 924 F.2d 709 (7th Cir. 1991). There is an abundance of law-journal writing on lost-volume damage claims, including a most helpful discussion in Goldberg, An Economic Analysis of the Lost-Volume Retail Seller, 57 So. Cal. L. Rev. 283 (1984).

Illinois Central R.R. Co. v. Crail

Supreme Court of the United States, 1930.
281 U.S. 57, 50 S.Ct. 180.

STONE, J. . . . Respondent, plaintiff below, a coal dealer in Minneapolis, purchased, while in transit, a carload of coal weighing at shipment 88,700 pounds. On delivery at destination, the respondent's industrial siding, there was a shortage of 5,500 pounds. At the time of arrival, respondent had not resold any of the coal. It was intended to be, and was, added to his stock of coal for resale, but the shortage did not interfere with the maintenance of his usual stock. He lost no sales by reason of it, and purchased no coal to replace the shortage, except in carload lots. In the course of his business, respondent could and did, both before and after the present shipment, purchase coal of like quality in carload lots of 60,000 pounds or more, delivered at his siding, at $5.50 per ton, plus freight. The market price in Minneapolis for like coal sold at retail in less than carload lots was $13 per ton including $3.30 freight. . . .

It is not denied that a recovery measured by the wholesale market price of the coal would fully compensate the respondent, or that the retail price, taken as the measure of the recovery allowed below, includes costs of delivery to retail consumers which respondent did not incur, and a retail profit which he had not earned by any contract of resale. But respondent contends, as was held below, that the established measure of damage for nondelivery of a shipment of merchandise is the sum required to replace the exact amount of the shortage at the stipulated time and place of delivery, which, in this case, would be its retail value, and that convenience and the necessity for a uniform rule require its application here.

This contention ignores the basic principle underlying common-law remedies that they shall afford only compensation for the injury suffered, and [give] only a right of recovery for "actual loss." The rule urged by respondents was applied below in literal accordance with its conventional statement. As so stated, when applied to cases as they usually arise, it is a convenient and accurate method of arriving at an amount of recovery which is compensatory. As so stated, it would have been applicable here if there had been a failure to deliver the entire carload of coal, since the wholesale price, at which a full carload could have been procured at point of destination, would have afforded full compensation, or, in some circumstances, if respondent had been under any constraint to purchase less than a carload lot to repair his loss or carry on his business, for in that event the measure of his loss would have been the retail market cost of the necessary replacement. But in the actual circumstances the cost of replacing the exact shortage at retail price was not the measure of the loss, since it was capable of replacement, and was, in fact, replaced in the course of respondent's business from purchases made in carload lots at wholesale market price without added expense.

There is no greater inconvenience in the application of the one standard of value than the other, and we perceive no advantage to be gained from an adherence to a rigid uniformity, which would justify sacrificing the reason of the rule, to its letter. The test of market value is at best but a convenient means of getting at the loss suffered. It may be discarded and other more accurate means resorted to, if, for special reasons, it is not exact or otherwise not applicable. In the absence of special circumstances, the damage for shortage in delivery by the seller of fungible goods sold by quantity is measured by the bulk price rather than the price for smaller quantities. . . Likewise, we think that the wholesale market price is to be preferred as a test over the retail when, in circumstances like the present, it is clearly the more accurate measure. . . .

Reversed.

NOTE

Does the principle underlying *Crail* apply in contexts other than the sale of goods? Louise Caroline Nursing Home, Inc. v. Dix Constr. Corp., 362 Mass. 306, 285 N.E.2d 904 (1972), involved breach of a contract to build a nursing home. Part way through construction, defendant contractor halted its work without justification. An auditor found, however, that plaintiff nursing home suffered no compensable damages as a result, since the cost to complete the structure at the time of the breach was less than the contract price minus what had already been paid to defendant. Plaintiff appealed the denial of its motion to recommit the auditor's report, arguing that it was entitled to "the difference between the value of the building as left by Dix and the value it would have had if the contract had been fully performed." The reviewing court rejected this argument, upholding the auditor's findings. The court reasoned that compensation is the fundamental principle of damages. "Compensation," the court explained, "is the value of the performance of the contract, that is, what the plaintiff would have made had the contract been performed. . . . The plaintiff is entitled to be made whole and no more." Accordingly, in failure-to-complete cases such as this, "[t]he measure of the plaintiff's damages . . . can be only in the amount of the reasonable cost of completing the contract and repairing the defendant's defective performance less such part of the contract price as has not been paid."

Watt v. Nevada Central R.R. Co.

23 Nev. 154, 44 P. 423 (1896)

Defendant's locomotive, through what was found to be negligence in its operation, set fire in October 1893 to a hay stack and hay press on plaintiff's ranch. The hay had been produced on the ranch and was stored there as a reserve supply to feed plaintiff's cattle in the event of a recurrence of the severe winter that, in 1889–1890, had caused plaintiff to lose $100,000 worth of cattle through starvation. Plaintiff testified that half of these cattle could have been saved if, at the time, he had had on hand the quantity of hay (700 tons) that defendant's locomotive destroyed. He also testified that he had no other use whatever for the hay and had used none of it since he began storing hay in 1890, four years before. There was no market for hay nearer than Austin, Nevada, which was 37 miles distant by rail. Hay of the quality of that destroyed, when baled, sold in Austin for $10 to $12 a ton. The cost of baling was $2 a ton and the cost of transportation by rail between plaintiff's ranch and the Austin market was $6.50 a ton. The trial judge (jury trial being waived) gave plaintiff a judgment for the hay valued at $10 a ton. On defendant's appeal, this judgment was reversed and judgment was entered for the lost hay valued at $3.50 a ton, the top Austin price of $12 less $8.50 baling and transportation costs. On plaintiff's own testimony, said the court, the hay had no value for use as feed. Whether it would be used on the ranch in the future was so uncertain and so conjectural that no estimate of its value for this purpose could provide a basis for damage recovery. Plaintiff contended that the cost of baling and transportation between Austin and the ranch should be added to, not subtracted from, the Austin price, but the court rejected this claim, commenting that such a recovery would give plaintiff a sum far in excess of his loss and that the fire would then be a "source of great profit." Plaintiff did not buy any hay in Austin to replace the hay destroyed, "evidently for the reason that the cost would have greatly exceeded the value of the hay." Nor had plaintiff introduced at trial any evidence showing his costs of growing and storing the hay. But as to the hay press, plaintiff can recover the purchase price of another press, $80 in Lake Valley, plus the $30 cost of transporting it to the ranch, or $110.

QUESTIONS

(1) Although the damages in this case arise out of a tort, they could easily arise out of a breach of contract action. Under the expectation damages principle, we would look for a way to measure how much the hay was worth

to Watt. What if Watt had replaced the hay promptly by purchasing an equal quantity in Austin? What if he regularly sold hay in Austin?

(2) The court noted that Watt had failed to offer any evidence of the cost of producing and storing the destroyed hay. What if he had shown these costs to be $5 per ton?

SECTION 2: RELIANCE: A PRINCIPLE OR A PROXY?

In thinking about the question of how to measure compensation, consider the possible alternatives to expectation damages. In a path-breaking article published in 1936, Lon Fuller and William Perdue set out a taxonomy of possible approaches to contract damages. Fuller & Perdue, The Reliance Interest in Contract Damages (pt. 1), 46 Yale L.J. 52, 56–57 (1936). Fuller and Perdue presented three different foundations on which to base contract remedies. The terms they used to describe each—expectation, reliance, and restitution—are now an essential part of the law and the literature of contract.

We have already encountered the expectation interest. In their paper, Fuller and Perdue coined the term "expectation interest" to describe the interest of a party in realizing the value created by the other's promise. By seeking to give the promisee the value of the expectancy that the promise created, the aim is to put the promisee "in as good a position as [she] would have occupied had the defendant performed [her] promise." "Reliance" and "restitution" capture two other ideas.

Fuller and Perdue used the term "reliance interest" to describe a party's interest in recovering losses suffered by virtue of reliance on the contract. They used the term "restitution interest" to describe the interest of a party in recovering value conferred on the other party. When damages are awarded to reimburse the promisee for a change of position in reliance on the contract, the object is to put the promisee "in as good a position as [she] was in before the promise was made." The restitution interest prevents the defaulting promisor from profiting at the expense of the promisee—i.e., "the prevention of unjust enrichment."

As we shall see in the third section of this chapter, restitution stands as an independent principle of Anglo-American contract law. Someone who breaches a contract cannot keep what she has received from the other party. These are ill-gotten gains. This remedy is always available as an alternative to expectation damages. In most cases, the availability of this additional remedy is of no consequence. Expectation damages are usually greater than restitution damages, and an injured party is entitled only to a single remedy. Restitution damages do take center stage, however, in those exceptional cases in which the contract would have been a losing one for the victim of the breach and expectation damages are smaller than restitution damages.

We turn first, though, to reliance damages, the focus of this section. We examine whether allowing reliance damages, like allowing restitution damages, also stands as an independent principle of the law of contracts. We ask whether someone who is the victim of a breach of contract should be able to insist on being returned to where she was before she entered the contract, regardless of how the contract would have turned out. Just as someone who commits a tort is obliged to restore the status quo ante, the law might hold that the contract breacher is responsible for the injury she caused. Even if the deal would have proved a losing one, the victim of a breach of contract might be entitled to be restored to her starting position when the other party breaches.

Consider Restatement (Second) of Contracts § 349:

> As an alternative to the measure of damages stated in § 347, the injured party has a right to damages based on his reliance interest, including expenditures made in preparation for performance or in performance, less any loss that the party in breach can prove with reasonable certainty the injured party would have suffered had the contract been performed.

Section 349 suggests that the victim of a breach of contract can recover her costs (and hence insist on being returned to her starting position) even when she cannot prove that she would have benefitted if the promise had been kept. It does not necessarily follow, however, that this provision is grounded in the idea that reliance is an independent principle.

A presumption in favor of awarding reliance damages might simply be a proxy—a way to estimate expectation damages when they cannot readily be measured directly. Parties, after all, do not willingly enter losing deals. Hence, even if a party cannot identify exactly how the contract would have benefited her, it may make sense to presume that the deal, when completed, would have provided her with *some* benefit. Unless things changed unexpectedly, it should not have left her worse off; otherwise, she would not have entered in to the deal in the first place.

To be sure, things do not always work out as planned. The deal might have been a losing one, and reliance damages might in any particular case not be a good way to measure expectation damages. If awarding expectation damages was the goal, the person who breached the contract should not have had to pay damages because the contract, if had it been performed, would have left the victim worse off. But the victim should not have to bear the burden of showing such unusual conditions did not exist. Instead, if the case was one of those rare ones in which the contract breacher, by virtue of the breach, left the innocent party better off, the burden should be on the breacher to show it.

Reliance damages, in sum, might not rightly be considered an independent principle for determining the amount of damages. Instead, presuming innocent parties would recover at least their out-of-pocket costs is a way of measuring expectation damages indirectly when direct measures are not available. Precisely because it is serving only as a proxy for expectation damages, reliance damages are only presumptively available. The breaching party can overcome the presumption if she can show that the contract would have been a losing one.

Chicago Coliseum Club v. Dempsey

Appellate Court of Illinois, First District, 1932.
265 Ill. App. 542.

WILSON, J. [The plaintiff] brought its action against William Harrison Dempsey, known as Jack Dempsey, to recover damages for breach of a written contract executed March 13, 1926, but bearing date of March 6 of that year.

Plaintiff was incorporated as an Illinois corporation for the promotion of general pleasure and athletic purposes and to conduct boxing, sparring and wrestling matches and exhibitions for prizes or purses. The defendant . . . was well known in the pugilistic world, and, at the time of [the] contract in question, held the title of world's Champion Heavy Weight Boxer.

Under [the] written agreement, the plaintiff was to promote a public boxing exhibition in Chicago, or some suitable place to be selected by the promoter, and had engaged the services of one Harry Wills, another well known boxer and pugilist, to engage in a boxing match with the defendant Dempsey for the championship of the world. By the terms of the agreement Dempsey was to receive $10, receipt of which was acknowledged, and the plaintiff further agreed to pay Dempsey the sum of $300,000 on the 5th day of August 1926,—$500,000 in cash at least 10 days before the date fixed for the contest, and a sum equal to 50 percent of the net profits over and above the sum of $2,000,000 in the event the gate receipts should exceed that amount. In addition the defendant was to receive 50 percent of the net revenue derived from moving picture concessions or royalties received by the plaintiff, and defendant agreed to have his life and health insured in favor of the plaintiff in a manner and at a place to be designated by the plaintiff. Defendant further agreed not to engage in any boxing match after the date of the agreement and prior to the date on which the contest was to be held. . . .

March 6, 1926, the plaintiff entered into an agreement with Harry Wills [to engage in] a boxing match with [Dempsey]. Under this agreement the plaintiff . . . was to deposit $50,000 in escrow in the National City Bank of New York City, . . . to be paid over to Wills on the 10th day prior to the date fixed for the holding of the boxing contest. . . . There is no evidence in the record showing that the $50,000 was deposited nor that it has ever been paid. . . . This contract between the plaintiff and Wills appears to have been entered into several days before the contract with Dempsey.

March 8, 1926, the plaintiff entered into a contract with one Andrew C. Weisberg, under which it appears that it was necessary for the plaintiff to have the services of an experienced person skilled in promoting boxing exhibitions. . . . It appears further from the agreement that it was necessary to incur expenditures in the way of traveling expenses, legal services and other costs in and about the promotion of the boxing match, and Weisberg agreed to investigate, canvass and organize the various hotel associations and other business organizations for the purpose of securing accommodations for spectators and to procure subscriptions and contributions from such hotels and associations and others for the erection of an arena and other necessary expense in order to carry out the enterprise and to promote the boxing match. . . . Weisberg was to furnish the funds for such purposes and was to be reimbursed out of the receipts from the sale of tickets for the expenses incurred by him, together with a certain amount for his services.

Both the Wills contract and the Weisberg contract are referred to at some length, inasmuch as claims for damages by plaintiff are predicated upon these two agreements. Under the terms of the contract between the plaintiff and Dempsey and the plaintiff and Wills, the contest was to be held during the month of September, 1926.

July 10, 1926, plaintiff wired Dempsey at Colorado Springs, Colorado, stating that representatives of life and accident insurance companies would call on him for the purpose of examining him for insurance in favor of the Chicago Coliseum Club, in accordance with the terms of his contract, and also requesting the defendant to begin training for the contest not later than August 1, 1926. In answer to this communication plaintiff received a telegram from Dempsey, as follows:

BM Colorado Springs Colo July 10th 1926
B.E. Clements
President Chicago Coliseum Club Chgo

> Entirely too busy training for my coming Tunney match to waste time on insurance representatives stop as you have no contract suggest you stop kidding yourself and me also

Jack Dempsey.

We are unable to conceive upon what theory the defendant could contend that there was no contract, as it appears to be admitted in the proceeding here and bears his signature and the amounts involved are sufficiently large to have created a rather lasting impression on the mind of anyone signing such an agreement. It amounts, however, to a repudiation of the agreement and from that time on Dempsey refused to take any steps to carry out his undertaking. It appears that Dempsey at this time was engaged in preparing himself for a contest with Tunney to be held at Philadelphia sometime in September, and on August 3, 1926, plaintiff, as complainant, filed a bill in the superior court of Marion county, Indiana, asking to have Dempsey restrained and enjoined from engaging in the contest with Tunney, which complainant was informed and believed was to be held on the 16th day of September, and which contest would be in violation of [the] agreement entered into between the plaintiff and defendant [on March 13].

Personal service was had upon the defendant Dempsey in the proceeding in the Indiana court and on August 27, 1926, he entered his general appearance, by his attorneys, and filed his answer in said cause. September 13, a decree was entered in the [Indiana] superior court, finding that the contract was a valid and subsisting contract between the parties, and that the complainant had expended large sums of money in carrying out [the] agreement, and entering a decree that Dempsey be perpetually restrained and enjoined from in any way, wise, or manner, training or preparing for or participating in any contracts or engagements in furtherance of any boxing match, . . . and particularly from engaging or entering into any boxing match with one Gene Tunney, or with any person other than the one designated by plaintiff.

It is insisted . . . that the costs incurred by the plaintiff in procuring the [Indiana] injunctional order were properly chargeable against Dempsey for his breach of contract and recoverable in this proceeding. Under the evidence in the record . . . there appears to have been a valid subsisting agreement between the plaintiff and Dempsey [that Dempsey has refused to perform], and the plaintiff, as a matter of law, was entitled at least to nominal damages. For this reason, if for no other, judgment should have been for the plaintiff.

During [this proceeding] it was sought to introduce evidence for the purpose of showing damages, other than nominal damages, and in view of the fact that the case has to be retried, this court is asked to consider the various items of expense claimed to have been incurred and various offers of proof made to establish damages. . . . Under the proof offered, the question of damages naturally divides itself into the four following propositions:

1st. Loss of profits which would have been derived by the plaintiff in the event of the holding of the contest in question;

2nd. Expenses incurred by the plaintiff prior to the signing of the agreement between the plaintiff and Dempsey;

3rd. Expenses incurred in attempting to restrain the defendant from engaging in other contests and to force him into a compliance with the terms of his agreement with the plaintiff; and

4th. Expenses incurred after the signing of the agreement and before the breach of July 10, 1926.

Proposition 1: Plaintiff offered to prove by one Mullins that a boxing exhibition between Dempsey and Wills held in Chicago on September 22, 1926, would bring a gross receipt of $3,000,000, and that the expense incurred would be $1,400,000, leaving a net profit to the promoter of

$1,600,000. The court properly sustained an objection to this testimony. The character of the undertaking was such that it would be impossible to produce evidence of a probative character sufficient to establish any amount which could be reasonably ascertainable by reason of the character of the undertaking. The profits from a boxing contest of this character, open to the public, is dependent upon so many different circumstances that they are not susceptible of definite legal determination. The success or failure of such an undertaking depends largely upon the ability of the promoters, the reputation of the contestants and the conditions of the weather at and prior to the holding of the contest, the accessibility of the place, the extent of the publicity, the possibility of other and counter attractions and many other questions which would enter into consideration. Such an entertainment lacks utterly the element of stability which exists in regular organized business. This fact was practically admitted by the plaintiff by the allegation of its bill filed in the [Indiana court] asking for an injunction against Dempsey [and charging]: "That by virtue of the premises aforesaid, the plaintiff will, unless it secures the injunctive relief herein prayed for, suffer great and irreparable injury and damages, not compensable by any action at law in damages, the damages being incapable of commensuration, and plaintiff, therefore, has no adequate remedy at law."

Compensation for damages for a breach of contract must be established by evidence from which a court or jury are able to ascertain the extent of such damages by the usual rules of evidence and to a reasonable degree of certainty. . . . [T]he performance in question is not susceptible of proof sufficient to satisfy [these] requirements[;] the damages, if any, are purely speculative. . . .

Proposition 2: Expenses incurred by the plaintiff prior to the signing of the agreement between the plaintiff and Dempsey.

The general rule is that in an action for a breach of contract a party can recover only on damages which naturally flow from and are the result of the act complained of. O'Conner v. Nolan, 64 Ill.App. 357. The Wills contract was entered into prior to the contract with the defendant and was not made contingent upon the plaintiff's obtaining a similar agreement with the defendant Dempsey. Under the circumstances the plaintiff speculated as to the result of his efforts to procure the Dempsey contract. It may be argued that there had been negotiations pending between plaintiff and Dempsey which clearly indicated an agreement between them, but the agreement in fact was never consummated until sometime later. The action is based upon the written agreement which was entered into in Los Angeles. Any obligations assumed by the plaintiff prior to that time are not chargeable to the defendant. Moreover, . . . the $50,000 named in the contract with Wills, which was to be payable upon a signing of the agreement, was not and never has been paid. There is no evidence in the record showing that the plaintiff is responsible financially, and even though there were, we consider that it is not an element of damage which can be recovered for breach of the contract in question.

Proposition 3: Expenses incurred in attempting to restrain the defendant from engaging in other contests and to force him into a compliance with [his] agreement with the plaintiff.

After the repudiation of the agreement by the defendant, plaintiff was advised of defendant's match with Tunney which . . . was to take place in Philadelphia in the month of September and was in direct conflict with [the] agreement entered into between plaintiff and defendant. Plaintiff's bill, filed in the superior court of [Indiana], was an effort on the part of the plaintiff to compel defendant to live up to the terms of his agreement. The chancellor in the Indiana court entered his decree, which apparently is in full force and effect, and the defendant in violating the terms of that decree, after personal service, is answerable to that court. . . . The expenses incurred, however, by the plaintiff in procuring that decree are not collectible in an action for damages in this proceeding; neither are such similar expenses as were incurred in the trips to Colorado and Philadelphia, nor the attorney's fees and other expenses thereby incurred. Cuyler Realty Co. v. Teneo Co., 188 N.Y.S. 340. The plaintiff having been informed that the defendant intended to proceed no further under his agreement, took such steps at its own financial risk. There was nothing in the agreement regarding attorney's fees and there was nothing in the contract in regard to the services of the defendant from which it would appear that the action for specific performance would lie. After the clear breach of contract by the defendant, the plaintiff proceeded with this character of litigation at its own risk. . . . [T]he trial court properly held that this was an element of damages which was not recoverable.

Proposition 4: Expenses incurred after the signing of the agreement and before the breach of July 10, 1926.

After the signing of the agreement plaintiff attempted to show expenses incurred by one Weisberg in and about the furtherance of the project. Weisberg testified that he . . . was in the employ of the Chicago Coliseum Club under [the March 8, 1926] contract during all of the time that his services were rendered in furtherance of this [contract]. Under its terms Weisberg was to be reimbursed out of the gate receipts and profits derived from the performance. His compensation depended entirely upon the success of the exhibition. Under his agreement with the plaintiff there was nothing to charge the plaintiff unconditionally with the costs and expenses of Weisberg's services. The court properly ruled against the admissibility of the evidence.

HARRY WILLS

We find in the record, however, certain evidence which should have been submitted to the jury on the question of damages. . . . The contract on which the breach of the action is predicated shows a payment of $10 by the plaintiff to the defendant and the receipt acknowledged. It appears that the stadium . . . known as Soldier Field was considered as a site for the holding of the contest and plaintiff testified that it paid $300 to an architect for plans in the event the stadium was to be used for the performance. This item of damage . . . was sufficient to go to the jury. There were certain elements in regard to wages paid assistant secretaries which may be substantiated by evidence showing that they were necessary in furtherance of the undertaking. If these expenses were incurred they are recoverable if in furtherance of the general scheme. The defendant should not be required to answer in damages for salaries paid regular officials of the corporation who were presumed to be receiving such salaries by reason of their position, but special expenses incurred are recoverable. The expenses of Hoffman in going to Colorado for the purpose of having Dempsey take his physical examination for insurance, if before the breach and reasonable, are recoverable. The railroad fares for those who went to Los Angeles for the purpose of procuring the signing of the agreement are not recoverable as they were incurred in a furtherance of the procuring of the contract and not after the agreement was entered into. The services of Shank in looking after railroad facilities and making arrangements with the railroad for publicity and special trains and accommodations were items which should be considered and if it develops that they were incurred in a furtherance of the general plan and properly proven, are items for which the plaintiff should be reimbursed.

The items recoverable are such items of expense as were incurred between the date of the signing of the agreement and the breach of July 10, 1926, by the defendant and such as were incurred as a necessary expense in furtherance of the performance. . . .

For the reasons stated in this opinion the judgment of the circuit court is reversed and the cause remanded for a new trial.

NOTE

Jack Dempsey fought Gene Tunney in Philadelphia on September 23, 1926, losing the heavyweight title. The injunction against Dempsey issued by the Indiana court operated only for the month of September 1926. Dempsey appealed from this decree, but the appeal was dismissed in 1928 (on mootness grounds), without a determination of the propriety of the injunction. Dempsey v. Chicago Coliseum Club, 88 Ind. App. 251, 162 N.E. 237. Apparently no contempt proceedings were ever started against Dempsey in Indiana.

The gate receipts of the Dempsey-Tunney fight in Philadelphia on September 23, 1926, were reported to be $1,895,000. On September 22, 1927, Tunney again defeated Dempsey at Soldier Field in Chicago, in a fight whose gate receipts were reported to be $2,658,000. Would evidence of the gate receipts from these two fights dispose of the court's objection that the anticipated profits of the Dempsey-Wills fight were too uncertain?

Security Stove & Mfg. Co. v. American Ry. Express Co.

227 Mo. App. 175, 51 S.W.2d 572 (1932)

Security Stove brought an action for damages against the Express Co. for its failure to transport from Kansas City to Atlantic City, for exhibition at a gas association convention, a combination oil and gas burner that plaintiff had designed. The burner was not intended to be sold at the convention; plaintiff's object was to interest a particular company that distributed such equipment. Plaintiff wrote to the Express Co. on September 18, 1926, stating that it had engaged a booth at the convention for the week beginning October

11, and that "in order to get this exhibit in place on time it should be in Atlantic City not later than October the 8th." An agent of the Express Co. stated that, to meet that deadline, it would need to have the shipment in its hands by October 4; plaintiff actually delivered the burner to the Express Co. on October 2. Plaintiff's president went to Atlantic City to install the exhibit and found there, properly delivered, all but one of the twenty-one packages into which the shipment had been divided. The missing package was the part that controlled the flow of gas into the burner, the most important part and irreplaceable. A tracer was sent out for the missing package but it did not arrive in Atlantic City until the convention had closed. Plaintiff sued for and recovered: (1) $147 charges paid to the Express Co. for shipment of the exhibit; (2) $45.12 freight on the return shipment of the exhibit to Kansas City; (3) $101.39 railroad and pullman fares to and from Atlantic City, for plaintiff's president and an employee who had accompanied him; (4) $48 hotel costs for the two; (5) $150 for the president's time; (6) $40 for the wages of the accompanying employee; and (7) $270 for rental of the booth, which plaintiff had been unable to use.

Judgment for plaintiff for these sums was affirmed on appeal. Plaintiff had informed defendant of the necessity of prompt delivery of the shipment. "It is no doubt the general rule that where there is a breach of contract the party suffering the loss can recover only that which he would have had, had the contract not been broken. . . . But this is merely a general statement of the rule and is not inconsistent with the holdings that, in some instances, the injured party may recover expenses incurred in relying upon the contract, although such expenses would have been incurred had the contract not been breached." No profits were contemplated here, but "there is no contention that the exhibit would have been entirely valueless and whatever it might have accomplished, defendant knew of the circumstances and ought to respond for whatever damages the plaintiff suffered. In cases of this kind the method of estimating the damages should be adopted which is the most definite and certain and which best achieves the fundamental purpose of compensation." Even though the booth space had been rented before plaintiff contracted with defendant, plaintiff had arranged for the exhibit knowing that it could call on defendant to perform its common law duty to accept and transport the shipment with reasonable dispatch. The whole damage, therefore, was suffered in contemplation of defendant's performing its contract, which it failed to do, and all of plaintiff's losses were caused by defendant's breach.

COMMENT: EQUITY RELIEF IN ADVANCE OF TRIAL

The purpose of the Indiana proceeding initiated by the Coliseum Club was to obtain a court order restraining Dempsey from engaging in the match with Tunney. This type of remedy, aimed at compelling a party to do (or not do) something, rather than at compensating in money for an injury already inflicted, is called "equitable." We will consider such remedies later in this chapter. For now, it is necessary to note a striking feature of such relief—its availability in some circumstances in advance of a trial on the merits.

Such orders fall into two categories: temporary restraining orders and temporary injunctions (also sometimes called preliminary or interlocutory injunctions or injunctions pendente lite). A temporary restraining order may be issued without any notice to the defendant, or opportunity to be heard, if the plaintiff's need is sufficiently compelling to warrant restraint for a brief period (usually not more than ten days). Before a temporary restraining order terminates, or, if such ex parte relief could not be justified initially, the plaintiff may seek a preliminary injunction, after notice to the defendant and a hearing, typically abbreviated and perhaps simply on the basis of affidavits submitted. The standards for granting preliminary relief have been stated in various forms (e.g., plaintiff must show a reasonable likelihood of success on the merits), but the basic idea is to preserve the suit for an *effective decision* after a full trial. Therefore, where the harm to the plaintiff would be irreparable if preliminary relief were withheld, and such relief would not be irreversible so as to make a later decision against the plaintiff ineffective, the court may appropriately act before a full trial. Where the consequences of granting or withholding preliminary relief seem irreversible and not clearly compensable in money, the court must balance the hardships to the parties in reaching its decision. In the end, the benefits to the plaintiff from the injunction must be found to outweigh the injury that the defendant might suffer. Most temporary relief is cast in a negative form to prevent some prejudicial change in the existing situation, but mandatory injunctions ordering affirmative action can be issued.

Since preliminary relief necessarily involves some impingement on due process values, special procedural safeguards have been introduced. For example, it is customary to require from the plaintiff an injunction bond to indemnify the defendant if the injunction is later found to have been improvidently issued. Also, some procedural systems permit an appeal from the decision on a motion for a preliminary injunction, even though it is not a "final order," and the operative effect of the injunction may be stayed pending appeal, particularly if it is mandatory.

The power to issue preliminary injunctions in equity cases obviously adds to the remedial resources available to trial judges. Even with the safeguard of an injunction bond, the power may be exercised so as to bear down heavily on the party enjoined. It will usually be difficult to organize any effective review by appellate courts, if only because the time factor will be crucial, and it is recognized everywhere that the terms, scope, and conditions of the preliminary injunction are left largely to trial court discretion. Appellate courts often exhort trial judges to use their powers with restraint.

Again, the primary purpose of a temporary injunction is to preserve the *status quo*. The difficulty in defining this elusive phrase is illustrated by the injunction issued by the Indiana court against Dempsey's fighting Tunney in Philadelphia. If the injunction had been enforceable and compliance had been compelled, it would have given the Coliseum Club a much firmer grip on Dempsey, but it would also, no doubt, have caused severe losses and a considerable change in the situation for the promoters of the Philadelphia fight.

Yet the basic assumption is that the interlocutory injunction, "temporary" or "preliminary" though it be, must be obeyed and that a court, if it has means to do so, not only can but properly should punish any disobedience. If Dempsey had ventured back into Indiana before the case was formally held to be moot (so that the injunction was dissolved), the Indiana court clearly had power to punish him for contempt and might well have levied at least a money fine for his disobedience. The disabilities of the Indiana court were due to (1) the basic limitation that the process of a state court has no legal effect outside the boundaries of the state in which it sits, and (2) the conception of contempt as an offense against the court issuing the order, so that that court alone can punish. Such limitations might lead a court in its discretion not to enter on so difficult an enterprise, but they did not mean that the Indiana court, if proper service in Indiana of a summons on Dempsey had been secured, lacked power or acted improperly in giving this "interlocutory" relief.

L. Albert & Son v. Armstrong Rubber Co.

United States Court of Appeals, Second Circuit, 1949.
178 F.2d 182.

L. HAND, CIRCUIT JUDGE. Both sides appeal from the judgment in an action brought by the Albert Co., which we shall speak of as the Seller, against the Armstrong Co., which we shall call the Buyer. The action was to recover the agreed price of four "Refiners," machines designed to recondition old rubber; the contract of sale was by an exchange of letters in December, 1942, and the Seller delivered two of the four "Refiners" in August, 1943, and the other two on either August 31st or September 8th, 1945. Because of the delay in delivery of the second two, the Buyer refused to accept all four in October, 1945—the exact day not being fixed—and it counterclaimed for the Seller's breach. The judge dismissed both the complaint and the counterclaim; but he gave judgment to the Seller for the value without interest on a part of the equipment delivered—a 300 horse-power motor and accessories—which the Buyer put into use on February 20th, 1946. . . .

[In an omitted passage, the court held that the seller was entitled to recover from the buyer the fair market value of the equipment and accessories actually delivered (an amount set at $4,590) along with interest. The court went on to conclude that the buyer had justifiably rejected the four refiners, and thus affirmed dismissal of the seller's complaint for the price. Judge Hand then turned to the buyer's appeal.]

[Buyer] does not claim any loss of profit, but it does claim the expenses which it incurred in reliance upon the Seller's promise. These were of three kinds: its whole investment in its "reclaim department,"

$118,478; the cost of its "rubber scrap," $27,555.63; the cost of the foundation which it laid for the "Refiners," $3,000. The judge in his opinion held that the Buyer had not proved that "the lack of production" of the reclaim department "was caused by the delay in delivery of plaintiffs' refiners"; but that that was "only one of several possible causes. Such a possibility is not sufficient proof of causation to impose liability on the plaintiffs for the cost of all machinery and supplies for the reclaim department." The record certainly would not warrant our holding that this holding was "clearly erroneous"; indeed, the evidence preponderates in its favor. The Buyer disposed of all its "scrap rubber" in April and May, 1945; and, so far as appears, until it filed its counterclaim in May, 1947, it never suggested that the failure to deliver two of the four "Refiners" was the cause of the collapse of its "reclaim department." The counterclaim for these items has every appearance of being an afterthought, which can scarcely have been put forward with any hope of success.

The claim for the cost of the foundation which the Buyer built for the "Refiners," stands upon a different footing. Normally a promisee's damages for breach of contract are the value of the promised performance, less his outlay, which includes, not only what he must pay to the promisor, but any expenses necessary to prepare for the performance; and in the case at bar the cost of the foundation was such an expense. The sum which would restore the Buyer to the position it would have been in, had the Seller performed, would therefore be the prospective net earnings of the "Refiners" while they were used (together with any value they might have as scrap after they were discarded), less their price—$25,500—together with $3,000, the cost of installing them. The Buyer did not indeed prove the net earnings of the "Refiners" or their scrap value; but it asserts that it is nonetheless entitled to recover the cost of the foundation upon the theory that what it expended in reliance upon the Seller's performance was a recoverable loss. In cases where the venture would have proved profitable to the promisee, there is no reason why he should not recover his expenses. On the other hand, on those occasions in which the performance would not have covered the promisee's outlay, such a result imposes the risk of the promisee's contract upon the promisor. We cannot agree that the promisor's default in performance should under this guise make him an insurer of the promisee's venture; yet it does not follow that the breach should not throw upon him the duty of showing that the value of the performance would in fact have been less than the promisee's outlay. It is often very hard to learn what the value of the performance would have been; and it is a common expedient, and a just one, in such situations to put the peril of the answer upon that party who by his wrong has made the issue relevant to the rights of the other. On principle therefore the proper solution would seem to be that the promisee may recover his outlay in preparation for the performance, subject to the privilege of the promisor to reduce it by as much as he can show that the promisee would have lost, if the contract had been performed. . . .

[I]t appears to us . . . that the reported decisions leave it open to us to adopt the rule we have stated. Moreover, there is support for this result in the writings of scholars. The Restatement of Contracts [§ 333(d)] allows recovery of the promisee's outlay "in necessary preparation" for the performance, subject to several limitations, of which one is that the promisor may deduct whatever he can prove the promisee would have lost, if the contract had been fully performed. Professor McCormick thinks, [McCormick on Damages, § 142] that "the jury should be instructed not to go beyond the probable yield" of the performance to the promisee, but he does not consider the burden of proof. Much the fullest discussion of the whole subject is Professor Fuller's in the Yale Law Journal [46 Yale L.J. 52, 75–80]. The situation at bar was among those which he calls cases of "essential reliance," and for which he favors the rule we are adopting. It is one instance of his "very simple formula: We will not in a suit for reimbursement of losses incurred in reliance on a contract knowingly put the plaintiff in a better position than he would have occupied, had the contract been fully performed." . . .

. . . To the allowance for the motor and accessories will be added interest from February 20th, 1946. The Buyer will be allowed to set off $3,000 against the Seller's recovery with interest from October, 1945, subject to the Seller's privilege to deduct from that amount any sum which upon a further hearing it can prove would have been the Buyer's loss upon the contract, had the "Refiners" been delivered on [time]. Judgment [affirmed] as so modified.

NOTE

This contractual dispute should be seen against the background of the Second World War. The war cut off many sources of rubber to the United States at the same time the demand for rubber grew dramatically. As a result, the market for reconditioned rubber grew. Once the war ended, rubber could once again be imported, and the business of reconditioning rubber suddenly became far less attractive.

World of Boxing LLC v. King

United States District Court, Southern District of New York, 2014.
107 F. Supp. 3d 265, rev'd in part on other grounds, 634 Fed. Appx. 1.

SCHEINDLIN, DISTRICT JUDGE. [Plaintiffs Vladimir Hrunov and Andrey Ryabinskiy are Russian boxing promoters who do business as World of Boxing ("WOB"). Defendant Don King ("King") is an American boxing promoter who does business as Don King Productions. King and WOB entered into an agreement in which King promised to produce Guillermo Jones ("Jones") for a bout against Denis Lebedev ("Lebedev") on April 25, 2014. The day the bout was supposed to take place, Jones tested positive for furosemide, an illicit, performance-enhancing diuretic. The positive drug test precluded Jones from competing, and the bout was called off.

The Agreement required King to "cause [Jones] to participate in a 12 Round WBA Cruiserweight World Title match [against Lebedev]." Under WBA rules—which the Agreement incorporated by reference—any boxer who tested positive for a banned, performance-enhancing substance was disqualified from WBA-sponsored bouts for no less than six months. Both parties agreed that Jones ingested furosemide, and there was no question that having tested positive for furosemide, Jones could not participate in the bout.

The judge reasoned that, if Jones could not participate in the bout, King could not keep his promise to have Jones fight. Because the event was not the unexpected event of the sort that would excuse nonperformance, King therefore breached the contract. The judge then turned to the question of damages.]

. . . Because WOB's "lost profits"—*i.e.,* its expectation damages—"cannot be reasonably quantified," it seeks instead to recover the costs it incurred in anticipation of the bout. . . .

New York courts have long distinguished between two different forms of redress in breach of contract suits: "expectation damages" and "reliance damages." Expectation damages provide the injured party with the benefit she would have enjoyed had no breach occurred—*i.e.,* they aim to fulfill the injured party's *expectations* from the contract. Reliance damages, by contrast, seek to restore the injured party to the position she was in before the contract was formed. They allow for recovery of "expenditures [the injured party] made in reliance on defendant's representations and that he otherwise would not have made." Farash v. Sykes Datatronics, 59 N.Y.2d 500, 465 N.Y.S.2d 917, 919, 452 N.E.2d 1245 (1983). Under New York law, when expectation damages defy precise calculation, reliance damages are the appropriate remedy. That is what WOB seeks.

To calculate reliance damages, courts must assess the costs that "a plaintiff [incurred from] . . . 'expenditures made in preparation for performance or in performance, less any loss that . . . the injured party would have suffered had the contract been performed.' " St. Lawrence Factory Stores v. Ogdensburg Bridge & Port Auth., 13 N.Y.3d 204, 208, 889 N.Y.S.2d 534, 918 N.E.2d 124 (2009). The purpose of offsetting reliance damages against anticipated losses is to ensure that contract damages do no more than make an injured party whole—*i.e.,* to ensure that damages do not "put the plaintiff [ ] in a better position than he would have occupied had the contract been fully performed." Bausch & Lomb, Inc. v. Bressler, 977 F.2d 720, 729 (2d Cir. 1992). Thus, "[i]f the breaching party establishes that the plaintiff's losses upon full performance would have equaled or exceeded its reliance expenditures, the plaintiff will recover nothing under a reliance theory." Id.

Typically, the party who moves for summary judgment bears the burden of demonstrating that no material dispute of fact exists. In this context, however, it is the party *in breach*—in this case, King—that bears the burden of "prov[ing] with reasonable certainty" what losses the "injured party would have suffered" in the event that all contractual obligations had been properly discharged. St. Lawrence Factory Stores, 13 N.Y.3d at 208, 889 N.Y.S.2d 534, 918 N.E.2d 124. . . .

King does not argue that WOB's preparatory expenditures are improperly calculated. Nor does he claim that any of WOB's preparatory expenditures were not reasonable or foreseeable. Instead, King invokes the principle that reliance damages should be offset against losses that WOB "reasonabl[y] certain[ly]" would have incurred, and he argues that WOB's damages should therefore be capped at $98,607—the value of the tickets that WOB had to refund as a consequence of the bout's cancellation.

King's argument rests on the premise that WOB stood to derive only one type of benefit from the bout, had the bout gone forward—revenue already realized from ticket sales prior to the breach. This premise is erroneous. In fact, there are (at least) two other types of benefits that WOB might have enjoyed in connection with the bout.

First, WOB might well have realized revenue during and after the bout. Maxim Kopylkov, custodian of financial records for the WOB, testified that WOB "expected to receive an undetermined amount of revenue from the television broadcast of [the bout] and from business generated by promotional and advertising activity during [the bout]." King complains—correctly—that WOB has not provided a rigorous accounting of the post-bout revenue it expected to receive. But that is not surprising. The whole reason that WOB is seeking reliance damages rather than expectation damages is that its projected profits (and losses) from the bout are a matter of speculation. To fault WOB for failing to offer concrete projections of post-bout profit would reverse the burden of proof. It is not WOB's burden to prove how much profit it stood to gain. Rather, because King seeks to reduce the amount of preparatory costs that WOB can recover—costs that King admits WOB would not have incurred had no agreement existed—King has the burden to prove with certainty that WOB would *not* have made further revenue.

King has not sustained his burden. He has offered no theory—much less any factual material—to suggest that WOB would have seen no financial upside from the television broadcasting of such a hotly anticipated match. The lack of supporting evidence is not surprising, because King's economic analysis makes little sense. If King is right, WOB's revenue from the bout would have been less than the amount it pledged to King as a signing bonus, even putting *every other preparatory cost* to one side. That hypothesis is implausible. This was no small-time bout; it was the Cruiserweight World Title match. Furthermore, WOB and King are both sophisticated parties, with proven track records in the boxing world.

Although it is certainly *possible* that WOB agreed to underwrite a bout of this import without realizing how drastically its costs would outstrip its gains, that explanation seems very unlikely. And King has given the Court no reason to think it more likely on the specific facts of this case.

Second, WOB might have expected to derive future benefits from the bout—benefits that would not be manifest in immediate revenue, but that would nevertheless make the bout a worthwhile investment for WOB. Indeed, this possibility underscores the conceptual error at the heart of King's position. It disregards the fact that businesses can—and often do—engage in rational loss-leading. There are numerous ways that WOB might have derived value from the bout after the fact. Post-event gains might have included, for example, profit from future re-broadcasting; the benefit of a continued business relationship with Lebedev (the boxer whom WOB was promoting); or simply the creation of a positive track-record within the boxing world.

By way of analogy, imagine if a young art dealer, eager to promote her first gallery, entered into the following arrangement with a famous artist—she will pay him $5,000, and he will visit the gallery to give a lecture about this work. Having scheduled the event, the gallery owner sends out invitations, and she hires caterers, a live band, and security personnel—all of which costs her (a non-refundable) $10,000. The night before he is supposed to speak, the artist backs out, forcing the gallery owner to cancel the event. She sues him for breach of contract, seeking $10,000 in reliance damages. In response, the artist argues that the gallery owner stood to derive no profit from the event—indeed, she stood to lose $15,000—so any reliance damages should be offset to zero.

The artist's logic, which is also King's logic, is flawed. It misses the point—even if it is accurate—to say that the gallery owner was not going to derive an immediate financial benefit from the event. That was not the event's purpose. Rather, the event was a capital investment, which the gallery owner thought would pay off in the future. In the real world, many investments are made without a guarantee of return, and some are even made with the explicit *intention* of losing money—at least in the short-term. A theory of contract damages that fails to account for this reality cannot be right.

Indeed, this is exactly why a breaching party bears the burden of "prov[ing] with reasonable certainty" that losses would have occurred absent a breach. To cap reliance damages, a breaching party must show, in effect, that losses were inevitable. In *St. Lawrence Factory Stores v. Ogdensburg Bridge & Port Authority*, for example, the Third Department held that an offset was appropriate when a construction project was simply "not feasible," because plaintiff was bound by covenant to build a retail factory outlet but was not able to secure adequate financing for the project. In light of this, the court reasoned that plaintiff should not be able to recover preparatory expenditures—because the project was doomed. Here, it is far from clear that WOB's investment in the bout was fated to be a losing proposition. Kopylkov's testimony suggests otherwise. As does common sense.

Ultimately, King has extrapolated the wrong principle from the case law. In his view, if a breached contract was not going to yield an immediate and direct financial benefit, no reliance damages should be awarded. But the correct principle is narrower, and—as one might expect—more favorable to injured parties. Plaintiffs who prevail on breach of contract claims may recover full reliance damages *unless* there is evidence that completion of the contract could not possibly have resulted in gain. Here, that is plainly not the case. WOB is entitled to recover its preparatory costs. . . .

Putting the foregoing analysis to one side, King is certainly right about one thing. Reliance damages are about restoration. They strive to "place [injured parties] in the same position as they were prior to the execution of the contract," not to work a "windfall" for injured parties. In this case, WOB retained approximately $75,000 in revenue from ticket sales, notwithstanding the breach. This amount should be deducted from the final judgment. Otherwise, WOB would recover its preparatory costs *and* see the upside of ticket sales that never would have been earned absent the contract. . . .

Merry Gentleman, LLC v. George and Leona Productions, Inc.

United States Court of Appeals, Seventh Circuit, 2015.
799 F.3d 827.

HAMILTON, CIRCUIT JUDGE. Plaintiff Merry Gentleman, LLC produced the motion picture *The Merry Gentleman,* which was released in 2009. Despite some critical acclaim, the film was a commercial flop. Merry Gentleman blames defendant Michael Keaton, the film's lead actor and director, for the bust. It brought this breach of contract action against Keaton and defendant George and Leona Productions, Inc., Keaton's "loan-out company" that he uses for professional contracting, alleging that Keaton violated his directing contract by (1) failing to prepare the first cut of the film in a timely fashion, (2) submitting a first cut that was incomplete, (3) submitting a revised cut that was not ready for the producers to watch, (4) communicating directly with officials at the Sundance Film Festival and threatening to boycott the festival if they did not accept his director's cut instead of the producers' preferred cut, (5) failing to cooperate with the producers during the post-production process, and (6) failing to promote the film adequately.

If the case were to go to trial, one might expect Keaton to dispute that any of these alleged breaches actually violated the directing contract. After all, Keaton completed the movie. It was accepted at the prestigious Sundance Film Festival. It received critical praise—Roger Ebert, for example, gave it 3.5 stars out of 4 and called it "original, absorbing and curiously moving." And the film's executive producer, Paul Duggan, admitted during his deposition that he was unaware of any director who did more publicity than Keaton did for a movie with a comparable budget.

Keaton moved for summary judgment, however, on the narrow ground that Merry Gentleman had failed to produce sufficient evidence that his alleged breaches of the directing contract caused it damages. For purposes of deciding this appeal, we must therefore assume as the district court did that Keaton in fact breached the contract.

Illinois law governs the directing contract. Under Illinois law, a "party injured by another's breach or repudiation of a contract usually seeks recovery in the form of damages based on his 'expectation interest,' which involves obtaining the 'benefit of the bargain,' or his 'reliance interest,' which involves reimbursement for loss caused by reliance on a contract." MC Baldwin Financial Co. v. DiMaggio, Rosario & Veraja, LLC, 845 N.E.2d 22, 30 (Ill. App. 2006). The district court granted Keaton's motion for summary judgment, concluding that Merry Gentleman had failed to present a genuine issue of material fact on either damages theory. . . .

Illinois follows the approach of § 349 of the Restatement (Second) of Contracts (1981), which provides that as an alternative to expectation damages, "the injured party has a right to damages based on his reliance interest, including expenditures made in preparation for performance or in performance, less any loss that the party in breach can prove with reasonable certainty the injured party would have suffered had the contract been performed."

Merry Gentleman argues that the district court required too much when it held that Merry Gentleman failed to establish a causal connection between its expenditures on the film and Keaton's alleged breaches. The causation standard is minimal when the injured party seeks reliance damages under § 349, Merry Gentleman contends, and it cleared this low hurdle when it submitted an affidavit from Duggan stating that the production company spent over $5 million in reliance on the directing contract. Once it produced that evidence, Merry Gentleman continues, the burden shifted to Keaton to prove that the production company would have suffered the alleged losses even if Keaton had fully performed. And because Keaton did not submit evidence with his motion for summary judgment showing beyond reasonable dispute that these losses were inevitable, summary judgment against Merry Gentleman was improper. Or so goes the argument.

We agree with Merry Gentleman that a party seeking reliance damages under § 349 has a relatively low bar to clear to establish causation and that once it makes this showing, the burden shifts to the breaching party to prove any reduction in those damages. This causation threshold is low because the injured party is forced to prove a counterfactual: what would have happened if the contract had not been signed in the first place. Proving this kind of counterfactual is difficult because the value of performance can be so difficult to establish. That is especially true in cases where the injured party is seeking reliance damages. If damages were easy to calculate, the injured party likely would have sought expectation damages to begin with on a benefit-of-the-bargain theory under § 347. Reliance damages are appropriate precisely because the injured party is at an evidentiary disadvantage. That is why courts use the burden-shifting framework of § 349. As Judge Hand explained long ago:

> It is often very hard to learn what the value of the performance would have been; and it is a common expedient, and a just one, in such situations to put the peril of the answer upon that party who by his wrong has made the issue relevant to the rights of the other. On principle therefore the proper solution would seem to be that the promisee may recover his outlay in preparation for the performance, subject to the privilege of the promisor to reduce it by as much as he can show that the promisee would have lost, if the contract had been performed.

L. Albert & Son v. Armstrong Rubber Co., 178 F.2d 182, 189 (2d Cir. 1949).

The burden does not shift to the breaching party until the injured party first satisfies this threshold showing of causation, however. And just because the causation threshold under § 349 is low does not mean it is not there, as Merry Gentleman seems to suggest. To oppose summary judgment on this point, the injured party must still produce evidence sufficient to permit a reasonable trier of fact to find that the losses claimed were caused by the breach.

In the typical case where reliance damages are sought, the defendant has simply repudiated the contract and walked away from the deal. This causal link will be straightforward in those cases. As the district court explained, in such cases the non-breaching plaintiff is left "holding the bag after having made its expenditures." In those cases, it is appropriate for the injured party to claim as damages all expenditures it made in preparation for performance because the other side failed to perform at all. In such cases, the complete loss of investment will often be the proximate result of the breach.

But in cases like this one, where the breaching party has substantially performed and the alleged breaches have to do with the quality of the final product, the causal link between reliance damages and the breach is not so direct. An injured party cannot reasonably claim that *all* of its expenditures were caused by the other party's breach without some reason to think the breach destroyed the entire value of the breaching party's performance. In this context, the breach does not cause the complete loss of investment.

Take this case, for example. Who can say why a critically praised movie did not make money? Merry Gentleman claims as damages all $5.5

million it spent to produce the movie. If Keaton had somehow prevented completion of the movie, Merry Gentleman might well have been entitled to all expenditures made in preparation for his performance (subject, of course, to the "losing contract" limitation in § 349). But here, Keaton actually made the movie. Merry Gentleman complains that Keaton slowed down the production process and failed to publicize the movie adequately after it was finished. No doubt, these services have economic value and, on a proper showing, Merry Gentleman might have been entitled to recover damages for these shortcomings. (Imagine, for instance, if Keaton's tardiness in submitting the first cut forced Merry Gentleman to pay the film editors for a longer period. Or, to take a more extreme example, imagine if Keaton had publicly criticized the film released to theaters so harshly that no one bought tickets to see it.) But no reasonable trier of fact could find that Merry Gentleman lost its entire investment of $5.5 million because Keaton failed to submit his first cut on time or failed to publicize the movie better. Merry Gentleman entered the directing contract to have Keaton deliver a finished movie, and he delivered one that showed well at Sundance and won some critical praise. The breaches by Keaton that Merry Gentleman alleges cannot reasonably be said to have rendered the investment completely worthless.

The fundamental problem we have been describing is that Merry Gentleman's damages theory is completely insensitive to the importance and severity of Keaton's alleged breaches. This is how Merry Gentleman explained its damages theory in opposing summary judgment:

> Keaton's actions were in breach of his contract, and caused damage to MG LLC in that it was unable to screen and market the film of its choosing (as was its contractual right); in that it endured substantial additional costs; and in that in reliance on its expectation that Keaton would satisfy his contractual obligations, it spent millions of dollars to finance Keaton's temper tantrum, money it never would have expended if it had been aware of Keaton's unwillingness to conform his behavior to his contractual obligations.

That's it. Merry Gentleman did not explain how Keaton's cut differed from "the film of its choosing." Nor did it explain how that difference caused it damage. It did not identify what it meant by "substantial additional costs." And the last claim—that it never would have signed the contract if it had known that Keaton would breach—is something almost any plaintiff can say in a breach-of-contract dispute. . . .

We agree with the district court that Merry Gentleman, in seeking $5.5 million in reliance damages, "effectively wants to shift the entire cost—and risk—of producing *The Merry Gentleman* to Keaton for his alleged breaches, giving it a windfall and placing it in a *better* position than it would have been in had the contract never been signed." Reliance damages are not insurance. . . .

As noted, we must assume here that Keaton breached the $100,000 contract as alleged, but these alleged breaches did not render his performance completely worthless. He directed the movie, it was accepted by Sundance, and it was released to the public. Reimbursing Merry Gentleman for all $5.5 million it spent, even though it received from Keaton a finished film praised by critics, would put it in a better position than if the contract had not been made. . . .

COMMENT: THE ECONOMICS OF CONTRACT REMEDIES

The compensation principle does not punish those who break their promises. As Holmes characterized the law (recall the Introductory Note, supra p. 1), it gives those who make promises a choice to perform or pay a compensatory sum, but takes no position on whether keeping promises is either good or bad. He explained as follows (The Path of the Law, 10 Harv. L. Rev. 457, 458–469 (1897)):

> The first thing for a business-like understanding of the matter is to understand its limits, and therefore I think it desirable at once to point out and dispel a confusion between morality and law, which sometimes rises to the height of conscious theory, and more often and indeed constantly is making trouble in detail without reaching the point of consciousness. You can see very plainly that a bad man has as much reason as a good one for wishing to avoid an encounter with the public force, and therefore you can see the practical importance of the distinction between morality and law. A man who cares nothing for an ethical rule which is believed and practised by his neighbors is likely nevertheless to care a good deal to avoid being made to pay money, and will want to keep out of jail if he can.
>
> I take it for granted that no hearer of mine will misinterpret what I have to say as the language of cynicism. The law is the witness and external deposit of our moral life. Its history is the history of the moral development of the race. The practice of it, in spite of popular jests, tends to make good citizens. . . . When I emphasize the difference between law and morals I do so with reference to a single end, that of learning and understanding the law. For that purpose you must definitely master its specific marks, and it is for that I ask you for the moment to imagine yourselves indifferent to other and greater things.
>
> I do not say that there is not a wider point of view from which the distinction between law and morals becomes of secondary or no importance, as all mathematical distinctions vanish in presence of the infinite. But I do say that that distinction is of the first importance for the object which we are here to consider,—a right study and mastery of the law as a business with well understood limits, a body of dogma enclosed within definite lines. I have just shown the practical reasoning for saying so.

> If you want to know the law and nothing else, you must look at it as a bad man, who cares only for the material consequences which such knowledge enables him to predict, not as a good one, who finds his reason for conduct, whether inside the law or outside of it, in the vaguer sanctions of conscience. The theoretical importance of the distinction is no less, if you would reason on your subject aright. The law is full of phraseology drawn from morals, and by the mere force of language continually invites us to pass from one domain to the other without perceiving it, as we are sure to do unless we have the boundary constantly before our minds. . . .
>
> The confusion with which I am dealing besets confessedly legal conceptions. Take the fundamental question, What constitutes the law? You will find some text writers telling you that it is something different from what is decided by the courts of Massachusetts or England, that it is a system of reason, that it is a deduction from principles of ethics or admitted axioms or what not, which may or may not coincide with the decisions. But if we take the view of our friend the bad man we shall find that he does not care two straws for the axioms or deductions, but that he does want to know what the Massachusetts or English courts are likely to do in fact. I am much of his mind. The prophecies of what the courts will do in fact, and nothing more pretentious, are what I mean by the law. . . .
>
> Nowhere is the confusion between legal and moral ideas more manifest than in the law of contract. Among other things, here again the so called primary rights and duties are invested with a mystic significance beyond what can be assigned and explained.

Holmes was a legal pragmatist. His project was to describe the world. He ignored the moral underpinnings because they tended to obscure an understanding of the law; so he took no view on whether keeping promises was good or bad. In our own time, Richard Posner is the judge/scholar who has thought most explicitly—and controversially—about the compensation principle. In his view, expectation damages are to be preferred to reliance damages because protecting expectancies forces those who make promises to internalize the costs the breach imposes on the other party. Someone who makes a promise in an expectation damages regime has no incentive to break the promise unless he has better opportunities elsewhere. And—and this is the controversial point—if he has better opportunities elsewhere, it is desirable that he take advantage of them. Holmes made no judgment about whether keeping a promise was good or bad; Posner appears to take the view that what he calls "efficient" breach is normatively desirable.

OLIVER WENDELL HOLMES, JR.
1841–1935

The following example generally captures Posner's notion of efficient breach. I promise to mow your lawn on Saturday for $10. It will cost you $15 to have someone else do it, once the aggravation and inconvenience are taken into account. If I must pay you $5 damages in the event that I breach, I have no reason to breach unless I have an opportunity that brings me a benefit of more than $15. The expectation damages rule is thus uniquely sensible. If damages were less, I would have an incentive to breach even when my time was best spent mowing your lawn. If damages were greater, I would sometimes still mow your lawn, even though my time was better spent elsewhere. Only expectation damages ensure that the promise is kept if and only if keeping the promise remains mutually beneficial.

Law and economics scholars who built on Posner's insight looked at other ways in which contract remedies affected the incentives of both parties.

Ensuring that the promisor internalize the costs of breach is not the only objective of contract law. The remedy imposed in the event of breach also affects the behavior of the beneficiary of the promise. As noted above, the virtue of enforcing promises derives in large measure from allowing the other party to rely on the promise. But there can be too much of a good thing. A world in which the innocent party recovers full expectation damages induces overreliance.

Imagine that a homeowner contemplates adding a driveway and a garage to her house. Because the driveway is not worth as much without the garage, she would, other things being equal, prefer to build the garage at the same time as the driveway. But there is an offsetting consideration. Only after construction of the driveway begins will the underlying conditions of the soil be fully known. Bad soil conditions would increase the cost of the driveway, and there is a chance that these costs will be so high that the owner is better off cutting her losses by abandoning the project and living without either the driveway or the garage. Because of this possibility, it makes sense to wait until the soil conditions are known before starting on the garage. The homeowner will therefore choose to forgo the benefit of having both the garage and driveway completed early because of the risk that she would incur the cost of building part of the garage only to discover that, because of bad soil conditions, it did not make sense to complete the driveway that would be needed to make the garage useful.

The incentives of the homeowner would change, however, if she were to hire a third party to build the driveway. Once she enters into such a contract, she no longer has a reason to wait before building the garage. If the conditions of the soil are good, the homeowner will enjoy the benefit of having the garage ready as soon as the driveway is finished. If bad soil conditions make construction of the driveway so expensive that the third party decides to breach, expectation damages will still leave the homeowner in the same position she would have been in had the driveway been built as promised.

In this example, the prospect of expectation damages allows the beneficiary of a promise to treat the promisor's performance as sure-fire even though it is not. Unless the contract provides otherwise, the homeowner is under no obligation to hold off on the construction of the garage. If the soil conditions prove to be bad, the third party will breach, calculating that it is cheaper to pay expectation damages than to spend what it would take to complete the driveway under those conditions. With the prospect of expectation damages, the homeowner will thus have an incentive to build the garage too soon. As a general matter, expectation damages give the innocent party an incentive to ignore the reality that sometimes it makes sense to call deals off. This is the problem of "overreliance."

Of course, if the parties were to anticipate the risk of bad soil conditions, they could write a contract that would excuse the third party's obligation to perform if the soil conditions proved worse than expected. But the builder of the driveway may not know enough to insist on such a clause.

In a competitive market, of course, the cost of this overreliance will not fall entirely on the contractor. Parties negotiate in the shadow of the legal rule. We should expect that the promisor will demand a price for the driveway contract that takes into account the possibility of bad soil conditions, breach, and the obligation to pay expectation damages. But readjusting the price does not cure the underlying distortion. Sometimes the homeowner will still build a useless garage. Resources are wasted relative to what would have happened if the homeowner built both the garage and the driveway. We shall see a number of doctrines in the expectation context that limit the most egregious cases. But not all forms of overreliance can be specified in detail.

The overreliance that expectation damages induce, however, does not mean that reliance damages are to be preferred. Merely capping damages at the homeowner's reliance costs does not induce the homeowner's to build the garage at the right time. Indeed, it increases the likelihood of building early.

In a reliance regime, in fact, the homeowner has an incentive to build the garage early even if doing so brings her no benefit at all. Assume that the homeowner receives no benefit from building the garage before the driveway. In this event, if she were building both, she would wait until she knew about the soil conditions. But with reliance damages, she will build the garage as soon and as quickly as she can in order to provide a spur to the builder of the driveway. Building the garage increases the amount of the reliance damages that the builder must pay if she breaches. The more she spends, the more reluctant the builder will be to breach. Consequently, soil conditions will have to be even worse relative to an expectation damages regime before the builder will breach.

In a reliance damages regime, the builder has to weigh the costs of finishing the job against the amount the homeowner has spent on the garage. The more the homeowner spends, the more likely the builder is to complete the job. The builder may be better off completing the driveway after bad soil conditions are discovered, given the costs that have been sunk in building the garage. A project that never would have been done if a sole owner were bearing all the costs is done anyway.

In a reliance-based world, the innocent party is not indifferent as between breach and performance. She prefers performance, and she is willing to spend resources to induce performance, even if having the garage done early provides no other benefit. This situation is worse than in an expectation damages regime, where the homeowner builds the garage early only to the extent doing so provides her with some benefit. Steven Shavell, Damage Measures for Breach of Contract, 11 Bell J. Econ. 466 (1980). Because of the overreliance problem, an expectation damages scheme is unambiguously better than a reliance damages scheme. Expectation damages force you to internalize the costs of breaking your promise, and although I incur inefficient expenses as a result of having your promise, I do not incur as many as I do in a reliance-based regime.

Law and economics scholars must be cautious about overemphasizing the importance of a rule that induces efficient breach and optimal reliance. The value of such a rule is necessarily tempered by the costs of renegotiation at the time of performance. See Richard Craswell, Contract Remedies, Renegotiation, and the Theory of Efficient Breach, 61 S.Cal.L.Rev. 629 (1988). If

I have an opportunity that is worth more than performing my promise to you, you and I should be able to renegotiate our contract and reach a deal that will leave us both better off.

Suppose you promise to sell me a unique machine for $1 million that will give me $200,000 in additional profit. Before you deliver it to me, you find someone for whom it will generate $500,000 in additional profit. It might seem that a damage rule allowing you to breach your contract with me and pay me $200,000 is socially desirable. After all, the third party values the machine more than I do. But things are not so simple. Instead of using the machine myself, I might have been able to sell it to a third party. More to the point, once you find the other buyer, you can always renegotiate with me and the machine will end up in that person's hands regardless of what the damage remedy is. The costs of renegotiation limit the benefits of an optimal damage remedy.

In short, the importance of a contract damages rule that promotes efficient breach turns largely on the costs of renegotiation. When these are low, the problem of inefficient breach is not that serious. Indeed, in a world in which it is costly to search for potential buyers, it may make sense to have a legal rule that requires specific performance so that at a given moment only one of us has the incentive to look for buyers. Negotiation is costly, but so too is the implementation of expectation damages.

In addition to uncertainties respecting transaction costs, the cases and examples we have seen—the "scarred land," the "ugly fountain," the "perfect hand"—suggest the hazards of analyzing breach of contract as if a market value were always readily accessible. One concern, evident in the trial court's findings in *Groves* (and underscored ahead in Vines v. Orchard Hills, Inc., p. 171) is the inherent limitation any judge or juror faces in estimating damages. A true expectation damages remedy requires identifying the amount of money that would have made the plaintiff indifferent to whether the promise had been kept. In many situations—such as the value of the "perfect hand" in *Hawkins*—this value is inherently subjective and cannot be measured precisely. Invocations of economic language and markets in such circumstances may imply a precision that is illusory. Moreover, for the defendant to internalize properly the costs of the breach to the plaintiff, expectation damages must reflect the value the plaintiff himself attaches to the promise, not the value others put upon it. For this reason, a focus on markets may lead to damage awards that are undercompensatory. The Peevyhouses may put a much higher value on having their land fully restored than would be reflected in the market price.

We shall return to Holmes's "bad man" conception of the common law and the contributions of Richard Posner and other law-and-economics scholars. Many question whether Holmes' figure of the "bad man" is the appropriate starting place for understanding contract law. In particular, such an account of contract may slight the moral dimension of the law. A modern exemplar is Charles Fried, Contract as Promise: A Theory of Contractual Obligation (1981). See also Shiffrin, The Divergence of Contract and Promise, 120 Harv.L.Rev. 708 (2007). As Lon Fuller observed, The Law in Quest of Itself 92–95 (1940), "it is a peculiar sort of bad man who is worried about judicial decrees and is indifferent to extra-legal penalties, who is concerned about a fine of two dollars but apparently not about the possible loss of friends and customers."

SECTION 3. THE DUTY TO MITIGATE AND OTHER LIMITATIONS ON EXPECTATION DAMAGES

Rockingham County v. Luten Bridge Co.

United States Court of Appeals, Fourth Circuit, 1929.
35 F.2d 301.

[The Luten Bridge Co. sued to recover the sum alleged to be due under a contract with Rockingham County for the construction of a bridge. On January 7, 1924, the board of commissioners of the county, by a vote of 3 to 2, awarded the contract to the plaintiff. As a result of continuing dissension over the issue, Pruitt, one of the commissioners who had voted in the affirmative, on February 11, 1924, sent a letter of resignation to the county's clerk of the superior court. The clerk immediately accepted the resignation and noted his acceptance on the letter. Later that same day, Pruitt telephoned the clerk and withdrew his resignation and subsequently confirmed this in writing, but the clerk ignored the withdrawal and appointed one Hampton as Pruitt's replacement. Hampton took an oath of office and thereafter attended the advertised meetings of the commissioners. Neither Pruitt nor the other two commissioners who had voted for the construction of the bridge attended any further advertised meetings of the commissioners.

On February 21, 1924, three commissioners (two holdovers and Hampton), at a regularly advertised meeting, unanimously adopted a resolution, of which a copy was sent to the plaintiff, to the effect that the contract for the construction of the bridge was not valid and that plaintiff should proceed no further under it. At the same meeting, the three commissioners rescinded action previously taken looking to the construction of a hard surface road for which the bridge was to be a connecting link. By February 21, plaintiff had expended in labor and materials a sum estimated at $1,900. After receiving the notice of the votes at the February 21 meeting, plaintiff proceeded to construct the bridge. On November 24, 1924, plaintiff brought the present action claiming $18,301.07 as the contract price for the bridge. Three days later, on November 27, Pruitt and the other two commissioners who had voted for the construction of the bridge but who, unlike Pruitt, had not attempted to resign, met with an attorney and prepared an answer to plaintiff's suit which admitted the county's liability. A newly-elected board of commissioners took office on December 1, 1924. It voted to repudiate this answer by Pruitt and his two colleagues and also to contest the county's liability under the contract with the plaintiff.

"Fishing Creek Bridge"—Built by Luten Bridge Co., 1924

The trial judge ruled that the answer filed by Pruitt and his colleagues was a valid answer by a majority of the commissioners and was binding on the county. The judge therefore directed the jury to render a verdict for the plaintiff and the jury complied. In passages here omitted, the Court of Appeals held this instruction to be erroneous on two grounds. First, though North Carolina statutes made no provision for the resignation of county commissioners, a public officer under common law rules had a power to resign if the resignation was accepted by the proper authority, which in this case was the clerk of the superior court. Second, the November 27 meeting of Pruitt and his two colleagues had not been advertised so that the three, even if they had constituted a majority of the board, were not empowered to bind the county at this informal meeting.]

PARKER, CIRCUIT JUDGE. . . . Coming, then, to the third question—i.e., as to the measure of plaintiff's recovery—we do not think that, after the county had given notice, while the contract was still executory, that it did not desire the bridge built and would not pay for it, plaintiff could proceed to build it and recover the contract price. It is true that the county had no right to rescind the contract, and the notice given plaintiff amounted to a breach on its part; but, after plaintiff had received notice of the breach, it was its duty to do nothing to increase the damages flowing therefrom. If A enters into a binding contract to build a house for B, B, of course, has no right to rescind the contract without A's consent. But if, before the house is built, he decides that he does not want it, and notifies A to that effect, A has no right to proceed with the building and thus pile up damages. His remedy is to treat the contract as broken when he receives the notice, and sue for the recovery of such damages as he may have sustained from the breach, including any profit which he would have realized upon performance, as well as any other losses which may have resulted to him. [Here,] the county decided not to build the road of which the bridge was to be a part, and did not build it. The bridge, built in the midst of the forest, is of no value to the county because of this change of circumstances. When, therefore, the county gave notice to the plaintiff that it would not proceed with the project, plaintiff should have desisted from further work. It had no right thus to pile up damages by proceeding with the erection of a useless bridge.

The contrary view was expressed by Lord Cockburn in Frost v. Knight, L.R. 7 Ex. 111, but, as pointed out by Prof. Williston (Williston on Contracts, vol. 3, p. 2347), it is not in harmony with the decisions in this country:

> There is a line of cases running back to 1845 which holds that, after an absolute repudiation or refusal to perform by one party to a contract, the other party cannot continue to perform and recover damages based on full performance. This rule is only a particular application of the general rule of damages that a plaintiff cannot hold a defendant liable for damages which need not have been incurred; or, as it is often stated, the plaintiff must, so far as he can without loss to himself, mitigate the damages caused by the defendant's wrongful act. . . . If a man engages to have work done, and afterwards repudiates his contract before the work has been begun or when it has been only partially done, it is inflicting damage on the defendant without benefit to the plaintiff to allow the latter to insist on proceeding with the contract. The work may be useless to the defendant, and yet he would be forced to pay the full contract price. On the other hand, the plaintiff is interested only in the profit he will make out of the contract. If he receives this it is equally advantageous for him to use his time otherwise.

The leading case on the subject [is] Clark v. Marsiglia, 1 Denio (N.Y.) 317. . . . [D]efendant had employed plaintiff to paint certain pictures for him, but countermanded the order before the work was finished. Plaintiff, however, went on and completed the work and sued for the contract price. In reversing a judgment for plaintiff, the court said: "The defendant, by requiring the plaintiff to stop work upon the paintings, violated his contract, and thereby incurred a liability to pay such damages as the plaintiff should sustain. Such damages would include a recompense for the labor done and materials used, and such further sum in damages as might, upon legal principles, be assessed for the breach of the contract; but the plaintiff had no right, by obstinately persisting in the work, to make the penalty upon the defendant greater than it would otherwise have been."[2]

---

[2] [The court in Clark v. Marsiglia also stated: "To hold that one who employs another to do a piece of work is bound to suffer it to be done at all events, would sometimes lead to great injustice. A man may hire another to labor for a year, and within the year his situation may be

We have carefully considered the cases . . . upon which plaintiff relies; but we do not think that they are at all in point. Roehm v. Horst [178 U.S. 1] merely follows the rule of Hochster v. De La Tour, 2 El. & Bl. 678, to the effect that where one party to any executory contract refuses to perform in advance of the time fixed for performance, the other party, without waiting for the time of performance, may sue at once for damages occasioned by the breach. . . . [I]n none of [these cases] was the point involved which is involved here, viz. whether, in application of the rule which requires that the party to a contract who is not in default do nothing to aggravate the damages arising from breach, he should not desist from performance of an executory contract for the erection of a structure when notified of the other party's repudiation, instead of piling up damages by proceeding with the work. As stated above, we think that reason and authority require that this question be answered in the affirmative. It follows that there was error in directing a verdict for plaintiff for the full amount of its claim. The measure of plaintiff's damage, upon its appearing that notice was duly given not to build the bridge, is an amount sufficient to compensate plaintiff for labor and materials expended and expense incurred in the part performance of the contract, prior to its repudiation, plus the profit which would have been realized if it had been carried out in accordance with its terms. . . .

Our conclusion, on the whole case, is that there was error in failing to strike out the answer of Pruitt, Pratt, and McCollum, [and] in directing a verdict for plaintiff. The judgment below will accordingly be reversed, and the case remanded for a new trial.

Leingang v. City of Mandan Weed Board

468 N.W.2d 397 (N.D. 1991)

The city's Weed Board awarded Leingang a contract to cut weeds on municipal lots of more than 10,000 square feet in size. Another contractor was given a contract to cut smaller lots. Leingang brought suit upon discovering that the Weed Board had improperly assigned large lots to the small-lot contractor. The city admitted its breach at trial, conceding that the contract price for the work that should have gone to Leingang was $1,933. Leingang urged that his damages should be $1,722, calculated by subtracting from $1,933 the further sum of $211, which, he testified, represented the total of gas, oil, repair, and blade-replacement expenses he had avoided by not performing the work wrongfully taken from him. The city argued that only "net profits" were recoverable, and that, in calculating such profits, some of Leingang's overhead expenses—items beyond those he testified he had avoided—should be attributed to the contract in question and deducted

---

such as to render the work entirely useless to him. . . . In all such cases the just claims of the party employed are satisfied when he is fully recompensed for his part performance and indemnified for his loss in respect to the part left unexecuted; and to persist in accumulating a larger demand is not consistent with good faith towards the employer."—Eds.]

from the contract price of the lost work. The trial court adopted this approach. By subtracting four categories of expenses reported on the business schedule of Leingang's tax returns (insurance, repairs, supplies, and vehicle expenses) from the weed-cutting income reported on those returns, the court arrived at "a profit margin of 20 percent." Accordingly, the court awarded Leingang 20 percent of the price of the lost work, or $386. *Held*, this was error; there must be a new trial on damages. A plaintiff is to be compensated for all the detriment caused by the breach. "Where the contract is for service and the breach prevents performance of that service, the value of the contract consists of two items: (1) the party's reasonable expenditures toward performance, including costs paid, material wasted, and time and service spent on the contract, and (2) the anticipated profits." A plaintiff ordinarily proves profits "by reducing the contract price by the [total] amount it would have spent to perform." But "constant overhead expenses" are not included as a cost of performance because a plaintiff must pay them whether or not the contract was breached. In fact, a plaintiff is compensated for overhead by recovering "the contract price, reduced only by expenses saved because the contract did not have to be performed." It was therefore error to calculate a "net profit margin" by deducting Leingang's general costs of doing business "without determining whether these costs remained constant" regardless of the city's breach. "The reduction from the contract price of a portion of the 'fixed,' or constant expenses, effectively required Leingang to pay that portion twice."

Kearsarge Computer, Inc. v. Acme Staple Co.

116 N.H. 705, 366 A.2d 467 (1976)

Kearsarge performed data-processing services for Acme under a one-year contract. About halfway through the year Acme terminated the contract on the ground that Kearsarge's performance was unsatisfactory. Kearsarge sued for damages. The trial court adopted a master's report which found for Kearsarge on all issues and awarded damages for the full balance of the contract price, $12,313.22, with no reductions. On appeal, Acme contended that the recovery of the contract price should have been reduced in the amount of (1) "certain savings" realized by Kearsarge as a result of the breach, and (2) "income from new business" generated by Kearsarge after termination of the contract. *Held*, there was no error in the master's denial of Acme's claims for reduction of damages. The breach did not produce "substantial savings." Kearsarge "would not have spent significantly more on salaries, machine rental, or other overhead expenses if it continued to provide Acme with data processing services. With respect to labor costs, if a plaintiff cannot reduce his work force because of the breach, no savings result. . . . No layoffs were possible in this case because each of Kearsarge's three employees performed separate functions. . . . Kearsarge's operating costs—notably the rentals on computers and other equipment—were substantially fixed. The reduction of output due to the breach did not result in savings. R. Posner, Economic Analysis of the Law 59 n.7 (1972)." Moreover, Kearsarge's only remaining performance was the running of equipment and the delivery of the results to Acme.

"The cost of performance was the cost of paper, electricity and transportation of data to and from the offices of the parties. . . . The costs of performance were trivial in relation to the contract price. Because the breach did not relieve Kearsarge of a costly burden, the master did not err in awarding Kearsarge the full contract price. . . . The fact that plaintiff did not introduce evidence of the cost of paper, electricity and delivery of data does not bar recovery because the defendant has the burden of proving savings."

Nor is there evidence that Kearsarge could not have serviced its "new" (i.e., post-breach) clients "but for" Acme's breach. "The general rule is that 'gains made by the injured party on other transactions after the breach are never to be deducted from the damages that are otherwise recoverable, unless such gains could not have been made, had there been no breach.' . . . In contrast to an employee's suit for breach of a personal services contract, no deduction is allowed if the plaintiff sells to a third party a product that can be produced according to demand. The theory is that the second sale would have occurred even if the defendant did not breach this contract. See Locks v. Wade, 36 N.J.Super. 128, 114 A.2d 875 (App.Div. 1955)." The contract here is neither purely for personal services nor the sale of goods. It involves "a combination of personal skills and labor, materials, equipment and time. In these respects, a contract for data processing services is similar to a construction contract. . . The builder's profits on contracts entered into after the breach do not mitigate the damages unless the first contract required the builder's personal services to such an extent that concurrent performance of another contract would be impossible. . . . The reason is that, like manufacturing, these businesses are deemed to be expandable. The law presumes that they can accept a virtually unlimited amount of business so that income generated from accounts acquired after the breach does not mitigate the plaintiff's damages. . . . We hold that in the absence of evidence to the contrary a data processing contract does not involve unique personal services to such an extent that when the provider of such services seeks new business after a breach of contract, the income from such new business mitigates the damages owed to him by the breaching party."

QUESTION

The *Leingang* and *Kearsarge* cases illustrate the problems that can arise in applying the *Luten Bridge* damage formula, including the problem of distinguishing overhead or "fixed" costs from "variable" costs, which are said to vary with the plaintiff's business activity. The nonbreaching parties stand in a position different from that of the builder in *Luten Bridge*. The issue is not whether they should be paid for expenses they incurred on the contract after the breach, but rather what damages they should be able to enjoy when they ceased performing and turned to work elsewhere. Judge Cudahy, writing in Hallmark Ins. Adm'rs v. Colonial Penn Life, 990 F.2d 984, 990 (7th Cir. 1993), offered this analysis:

> . . . [A] party harmed by another's breach of contract is entitled to collect those lost net revenues that would have helped defray fixed costs and contributed to profit. [The amount by which revenue net of variable costs exceed fixed costs is "profit" in the sense that term

is commonly understood.] A central element in making this calculation . . . is the ascertainment of which costs vary with output and which do not (i.e., are truly fixed). . . . If a business operates more than one activity [is a multiple-activity firm], fixed costs are not usually deducted from gross revenues since the business would be expected to continue operating [despite one broken contract] and "fixed" costs would continue to be incurred. The owner would be entitled, in this situation, to collect the contribution toward fixed expenses that it would have received but for the breach.

Had the bridge company stopped work upon receiving notice of the county's repudiation, diverting its workers and equipment to other bridge jobs, what deductions would have been proper in figuring the plaintiff's damages?

Parker v. Twentieth Century-Fox Film Corp.

Supreme Court of California, 1970.
3 Cal. 3d 176, 89 Cal. Rptr. 737, 474 P.2d 689.

BURKE, J. Defendant Twentieth Century-Fox Film Corp. appeals from a summary judgment granting to plaintiff the recovery of agreed compensation under a written contract for her services as an actress in a motion picture. . . . [W]e have concluded that the trial court correctly ruled in plaintiff's favor and that the judgment should be affirmed.

Plaintiff is well known as an actress,[3] and in the contract between plaintiff and defendant is sometimes referred to as the "Artist." Under the contract, dated August 6, 1965, plaintiff was to play the female lead in defendant's contemplated production of a motion picture entitled "Bloomer Girl." The contract provided that defendant would pay plaintiff a minimum "guaranteed compensation" of $53,571.42 per week for 14 weeks commencing May 23, 1966, for a total of $750,000. Prior to May 1966 defendant decided not to produce the picture and by a letter dated April 4, 1966, it notified plaintiff of that decision and that it would not "comply with our obligations to you under" the written contract.

By the same letter and with the professed purpose "to avoid any damage to you," defendant instead offered to employ plaintiff as the leading actress in another film tentatively entitled "Big Country, Big Man" (hereinafter, "Big Country"). The compensation offered was identical, as were 31 of the 34 numbered provisions or articles of the original contract.[1] Unlike Bloomer Girl, however, which was to have been a musical production, Big Country was a dramatic western type movie. Bloomer

[3] [Better known under the name Shirley MacLaine.—Eds.]

[1] Among the identical provisions was the following found in the last paragraph of Article 2 of the original contract: "We [defendant] shall not be obligated to utilize your [plaintiff's] services in or in connection with the Photoplay hereunder, our sole obligation, subject to the terms and conditions of this Agreement, being to pay you the guaranteed compensation herein provided for."

Girl was to have been filmed in California; Big Country was to be produced in Australia. Also, certain terms in the proffered contract varied from those of the original.[2] Plaintiff was given one week within which to accept; she did not and the offer lapsed. Plaintiff then commenced this action seeking recovery of the agreed guaranteed compensation.

The complaint sets forth two causes of action. The first is for money due under the contract; the second, based upon the same allegations as the first, is for damages resulting from defendant's breach of contract. Defendant in its answer admits the existence and validity of the contract, that plaintiff complied with all the conditions, covenants, and promises and stood ready to complete the performance, and that defendant breached and "anticipatorily repudiated" the contract. It denies, however, that any money is due to plaintiff either under the contract or as a result of its breach, and pleads as an affirmative defense to both causes of action plaintiff's allegedly deliberate failure to mitigate damages, asserting that she unreasonably refused to accept its offer of the leading role in "Big Country."

Plaintiff moved for [summary judgment], the motion was granted, and summary judgment for $750,000 plus interest was entered in plaintiff's favor. This appeal by defendant followed.

The familiar rules are that the matter to be determined by the trial court on a motion for summary judgment is whether facts have been presented which give rise to a triable factual issue. The court may not pass upon the issue itself. Summary judgment is proper only if the affidavits or declarations in support of the moving party would be sufficient to sustain a judgment in his favor and his opponent does not by affidavit show

---

[2] Article 29 of the original contract specified that plaintiff approved the director already chosen for "Bloomer Girl" and that in case he failed to act as director plaintiff was to have approval rights of any substitute director. Article 31 provided that plaintiff was to have the right of approval of the "Bloomer Girl" dance director, and Article 32 gave her the right of approval of the screenplay.

Defendant's letter of April 4 to plaintiff, which contained both defendant's notice of breach of the "Bloomer Girl" contract and offer of the lead in "Big Country," eliminated or impaired each of those rights. It read in part as follows: "The terms and conditions of our offer of employment are identical to those set forth in the 'Bloomer Girl' Agreement, Articles 1 through 34 and Exhibit A to the Agreement, except as follows:

> "1. Article 31 of said Agreement will not be included in any contract of employment regarding 'Big Country, Big Man' as it is not a musical and it thus will not need a dance director.
>
> "2. In the 'Bloomer Girl' Agreement, in Articles 29 and 32, you were given certain director and screenplay approvals and you had preapproved certain matters. Since there simply is insufficient time to negotiate with you regarding your choice of director and regarding the screenplay and since you already expressed an interest in performing the role in 'Big Country, Big Man,' we must exclude from our offer of employment in 'Big Country, Big Man' any approval rights as are contained in said Articles 29 and 32; however, we shall consult with you respecting the director to be selected to direct the Photoplay and will further consult with you with respect to the screenplay and any revisions or changes therein, provided, however, that if we fail to agree . . . the decision of . . . defendant with respect to the selection of a director and to revisions and changes in the said screenplay shall be binding upon the parties to said Agreement."

facts sufficient to present a triable issue of fact. The affidavits of the moving party are strictly construed and doubts as to the propriety of summary judgment should be resolved against granting the motion. Such summary procedure is drastic and should be used with caution so that it does not become a substitute for the open trial method of determining facts. . . .

The general rule is that the measure of recovery by a wrongfully discharged employee is the amount of salary agreed upon for the period of service, less the amount which the employer affirmatively proves the employee has earned or with reasonable effort might have earned from other employment. . . . However, before projected earnings from other employment opportunities not sought or accepted by the discharged employee can be applied in mitigation, the employer must show that the other employment was comparable, or substantially similar, to that of which the employee has been deprived; the employee's rejection of or failure to seek other available employment of a different or inferior kind may not be resorted to in order to mitigate damages. . . .

[D]efendant has raised no issue of *reasonableness of efforts* by plaintiff to obtain other employment; the sole issue is whether plaintiff's refusal of defendant's substitute offer of "Big Country" may be used in mitigation. Nor, if the "Big Country" offer was of employment different or inferior when compared with the original "Bloomer Girl" employment, is there an issue as to whether or not plaintiff acted reasonably in refusing the substitute offer. . . . [N]o case cited . . . holds or suggests that reasonableness is an element of a wrongfully discharged employee's option to reject, or fail to seek, different or inferior employment lest the possible earnings therefrom be charged against him in mitigation of damages.[5]

Applying the foregoing rules[,] . . . with all intendments in favor of the party opposing the summary judgment motion—here, defendant—it is clear that the trial court correctly ruled that plaintiff's failure to accept defendant's tendered substitute employment could not be applied in mitigation of damages because the offer of the "Big Country" lead was of employment both different and inferior, and that no factual dispute was presented on that issue. The mere circumstance that "Bloomer Girl" was to be a musical review calling upon plaintiff's talents as a dancer as well as an actress, and was to be produced in Los Angeles, whereas "Big Country" was a straight dramatic role in a "Western Type" story taking place

[5] Instead, in each case the reasonableness referred to was that of the *efforts* of the employee to obtain other employment that was not different or inferior; his right to reject the latter was declared as an unqualified rule of law. Thus, Gonzales v. Internat. Assn. of Machinists, 213 Cal.App.2d 817, holds that the trial court correctly instructed the jury that plaintiff union member, a machinist, was required to make "such *efforts* as the average member of his union desiring employment would make at that particular time and place" (italics added); but, further, that the court *properly rejected* defendant's *offer of proof of the availability of other kinds of employment* at the same or higher pay than plaintiff usually received and all outside the jurisdiction of his union, as plaintiff could not be required to accept different employment or a nonunion job. . . .

in an opal mine in Australia, demonstrates the difference in kind between the two employments; the female lead as a dramatic actress in a western style motion picture can by no stretch of imagination be considered the equivalent of or substantially similar to the lead in a song-and-dance production.

Additionally, the substitute "Big Country" offer proposed to eliminate or impair the director and screenplay approvals accorded to plaintiff under the original "Bloomer Girl" contract, and thus constituted an offer of inferior employment. No expertise or judicial notice is required in order to hold that [the] infringement of an employee's rights held under an original employment contract converts the available "other employment" relied upon by the employer to mitigate damages, into inferior employment which the employee need not seek or accept. (See Gonzales v. Internat. Assn. of Machinists, fn. 3, supra.) . . .

In view of the determination that defendant failed to present any facts showing the existence of a factual issue with respect to its sole defense—plaintiff's rejection of its substitute employment offer in mitigation of damages—we need not consider plaintiff's further contention that for various reasons, including the provisions of the original contract set forth in footnote 1, ante, plaintiff was excused from attempting to mitigate damages.

The judgment is affirmed.

SULLIVAN, ACTING C.J. (dissenting). The basic question [is] whether or not plaintiff acted reasonably in rejecting defendant's offer of alternate employment. The answer depends upon whether that offer (starring in "Big Country, Big Man") was an offer of work that was substantially similar to her former employment (starring in "Bloomer Girl") or of work that was of a different or inferior kind. . . . [T]his is a factual issue which the trial court should not have determined on a motion for summary judgment. . . .

The familiar rule requiring a plaintiff in a tort or contract action to mitigate damages embodies notions of fairness and socially responsible behavior which are fundamental to our jurisprudence. Most broadly stated, it precludes the recovery of damages which, through the exercise of due diligence, could have been avoided. Thus, in essence, it is a rule requiring reasonable conduct in commercial affairs. This general principle governs the obligations of an employee after his employer has wrongfully repudiated or terminated the employment contract. Rather than permitting the employee simply to remain idle during the balance of the contract period, the law requires him to make a reasonable effort to secure other employment.[1] He is not obliged, however, to seek or accept any

[1] The issue is generally discussed in terms of a duty on the part of the employee to minimize loss. The practice is long-established and there is little reason to change despite Judge Cardozo's observation of its subtle inaccuracy. "The servant is free to accept employment or reject it according to his uncensored pleasure. What is meant by the supposed duty is merely this, that if he unreasonably reject, he will not be heard to say that the loss of wages from then

and all types of work which may be available. Only work which is in the same field and which is the same quality need be accepted.

Over the years the courts have employed various phrases to define the type of employment which the employee, upon his wrongful discharge, is under an obligation to accept. Thus in California alone it has been held that he must accept employment which is "substantially similar," . . . "comparable employment," . . . employment "in the same general line of the first employment," . . . "equivalent to his prior position," . . . "employment in a similar capacity," . . . employment which is "[not] of a different or inferior kind. . . ."

For reasons which are unexplained, the majority . . . select from among the various judicial formulations [one] particular phrase, "Not of a different or inferior kind," with which to analyze this case. I have discovered no historical or theoretical reason to adopt this phrase, which is simply a negative restatement of the affirmative standards set out in the [cases], as the exclusive standard. . . . However, the phrase is a serviceable one and my concern is not with its use as the standard but rather with what I consider its distortion.

The relevant language excuses acceptance only of employment which is of a *different kind*. . . . It has never been the law that the mere existence of *differences between two jobs in the same field* is sufficient, as a matter of law, to excuse an employee wrongfully discharged from one from accepting the other in order to mitigate damages. Such an approach would effectively eliminate any obligation of an employee to attempt to minimize damage arising from a wrongful discharge. The only alternative job offer an employee would be required to accept would be an offer of his former job by his former employer.

Although the majority appear to hold that there was a difference "in kind" between the employment offered plaintiff in "Bloomer Girl" and that offered in "Big Country," an examination of the opinion makes crystal clear that the majority merely point out differences between the two *films* (an obvious circumstance) and then apodictically assert that these constitute a difference in the *kind of employment*. The entire rationale of the majority boils down to this: that the *"mere circumstances"* that "Bloomer Girl" was to be a musical review while "Big Country" was a straight drama "demonstrates the difference in kind" since a female lead in a western is not "the equivalent of or substantially similar to" a lead in a musical. This is merely attempting to prove the proposition by repeating it. . . .

---

on shall be deemed the jural consequence of the earlier discharge. He has broken the chain of causation, and loss resulting to him thereafter is suffered through his own act." (McClelland v. Climax Hosiery Mills, 252 N.Y. 347, 169 N.E. 605 (1930), concurring opinion.)

SHIRLEY MacLAINE

. . . The inquiry in cases such as this should not be whether differences between the two jobs exist (there will always be differences) but whether the differences which are present are substantial enough to constitute differences in the *kind* of employment or, alternatively, whether they render the substitute work employment of an *inferior kind*. . . .

It is not intuitively obvious, to me at least, that the leading female role in a dramatic motion picture is a radically different endeavor from the leading female role in a musical comedy film. Nor is it plain to me that the rather qualified rights of director and screenplay approval contained in the first contract are highly significant matters either in the entertainment industry in general or to this plaintiff in particular. . . .

Nevertheless, the trial court granted the motion, declaring that these approval rights were "critical" and that their elimination altered "the essential nature of the employment." . . .

[T]he relevant question in such cases is whether or not a particular contract provision is so significant that its omission creates employment of an inferior kind. This question is, of course, intimately bound up in what I consider the ultimate issue: whether or not the employee acted reasonably. This will generally involve a factual inquiry to ascertain the importance of the particular contract term and a process of weighing the absence of that term against the countervailing advantages of the alternate employment. In the typical case, this will mean that summary judgment must be withheld. . . .

Billetter v. Posell

94 Cal. App. 2d 858, 211 P.2d 621 (1949)

Defendants employed plaintiff to work in defendants' store from July 1, 1946, to June 30, 1947, as "floor lady and designer," at a salary of $75 a week plus a Christmas bonus of $500. This contract had been proposed by defendants to counter a similar offer made to plaintiff by another employer. During the Christmas holidays, defendants notified plaintiff that they had decided to employ another designer and to have plaintiff take the place of another floor lady at $55 a week, a sum they later offered to raise to $60 a week. Unwilling to accept these terms, plaintiff left defendants' employment on December 31, 1946. Plaintiff then sued for her salary of $75 a week from January 1 to June 30, 1947, and for $300 unpaid on the promised $500 Christmas bonus. Judgment for plaintiff for these amounts affirmed. (1) Defendants are not entitled to credit for the unemployment compensation that plaintiff received from the state unemployment compensation fund during the ensuing six months. "Such funds are not deductible as compensation received from other employment in mitigation of damages. Benefits of this character are intended to alleviate the distress of unemployment and not to diminish the amount which an employer must pay as damages for the wrongful discharge of an employee." (2) Nor are defendants entitled to credit for the $60 a week they offered to pay her for serving as floor lady. An employee is not required to perform the same work for less pay in mitigation of damages. Moreover, the offer of $60 was not qualified by any protective condition saving her rights to be paid $75 a week under the original contract, so that if she had accepted the offer she would have lost her right to a higher wage. "An employee, upon wrongful discharge [that prevents the employee from performing], should not be required to accept a new employment under circumstances which permit the claim that [she] consents to a modification of the original contract and an abandonment of her right of action under it."

QUESTIONS

(1) What if defendants on December 30 had offered plaintiff a position as sales clerk in the appliance department, at $75 a week?

(2) What if plaintiff on January 2 had been offered a position as waitress at the Star Restaurant, one block away, at $90 a week?

(3) What if plaintiff accepted the Star Restaurant position and held it until June 30?

(4) What if plaintiff on January 2 had learned that a store in a town 30 miles from her home was advertising a position of "floor lady and designer" at $75 a week?

(5) What if defendants on December 30 had offered plaintiff her old job on the exact same terms?

Metoyer v. Auto Club Family Insurance Company

536 F. Supp. 2d 664 (E.D. La. 2008)

Metoyer sustained damage to his New Orleans home as a result of Hurricane Katrina and filed suit on March 1, 2007 to recover sums alleged due under his insurance contract with Auto Club. Additionally, he was awarded a $150,000 grant from the Louisiana Recovery Authority to rebuild his home and a $10,000 grant from the U.S. Small Business Association. Autocredit argued that it should be able to credit these recoveries against its obligation to pay damages. Metoyer argued that the grants were "collateral sources." In tort actions, courts have usually found that damages should not take into account recoveries from a "collateral source" such as an insurance policy. Courts, however, have only infrequently confronted the question whether such a "collateral source" rule applied in contracts cases, and they have not provided consistent answers. See John G. Fleming, The Collateral Source Rule and Contract Damages, 71 Cal. L. Rev. 56, 56 & n. 1 (1983); Richard C. Witzel, Jr., The Collateral Source Rule and State-Provided Special Education and Therapy, 75 Wash. U. L.Q. 697, 703 n.27 (1997). There is dictum in some cases to the effect that the collateral source rule does not apply in contract cases and that damages are therefore reduced by recoveries from third parties, but there are few holdings to that effect. See Joseph M. Perillo, The Collateral Source Rule in Contract Cases, 46 San Diego L. Rev. 705 (2009).

The most common reason put forward in tort cases for not taking the collateral source into account is that a defendant should not be allowed to profit from the outside benefits provided to the plaintiff. The classic formulation of the rule is that a tortfeasor's liability should be the same, regardless of whether the plaintiff had the foresight to buy insurance. But there is an element of punitive damages to a collateral source award and in general the law "prohibits punitive or exemplary damages in contract actions." In contract law there is a concern that allowing the nonbreaching party to recover from a collateral source and also collect damages is overcompensatory. The court in *Metoyer* concluded, however, "There cannot be a blanket prohibition of the application of the collateral source rule" in contract cases. First, even in contract cases, the innocent party with insurance should not have a lower recovery than one who did not. Allowing a party to recover damages as well as collect on the insurance policy recognizes that the insured party has paid insurance premiums. Moreover, in many cases, including the one before the court, "there is no danger of a double recovery or windfall." The Louisiana Recovery Authority required that, when it awards a grant, it will be subrogated to the rights of the homeowner with regard to insurance payments. The LRA will have the right to step into the shoes of any recipient and assert whatever rights it has. This "subrogation right negates the negative effects of the collateral source rule in a contract claim." Thus, "if the Defendant's position is adopted, it will amount to a windfall, not for plaintiffs, but for [the defendants]."

In re WorldCom, Inc.

United States Bankruptcy Court, Southern District of New York, 2007.
361 Bankr. 675.

GONZALEZ, BANKRUPTCY JUDGE. . . . On or about July 10, 1995, Jordan and the Debtors entered into an endorsement agreement (the "Agreement"). At that time, Jordan was considered to be one of the most popular athletes in the world. The Agreement granted MCI a ten-year license to use Jordan's name, likeness, "other attributes," and personal services to advertise and promote MCI's telecommunications products and services beginning in September 1995 and ending in August 2005. The Agreement did not prevent Jordan from endorsing most other products or services, although he could not endorse the same products or services that MCI produced. In addition to a $5 million signing bonus, the Agreement provided an annual base compensation of $2 million for Jordan. The Agreement provided that Jordan would be treated as an independent contractor and that MCI would not withhold any amount from Jordan's compensation for tax purposes. The Agreement provided that Jordan was to make himself available for four days, not to exceed four hours per day, during each contract year to produce television commercials and print advertising and for promotional appearances. The parties agreed that the advertising and promotional materials would be submitted to Jordan for his approval, which could not be unreasonably withheld, fourteen days prior to their release to the general public. From 1995 to 2000, Jordan appeared in several television commercials and a large number of print ads for MCI.

On July 1, 2002, MCI commenced a case under chapter 11 of title 11 of the United States Code (the "Bankruptcy Code") in the Bankruptcy Court for the Southern District of New York. [T]he Debtors rejected the Agreement . . . pursuant to § 365 of the Bankruptcy Code. Following that rejection of the Agreement, Jordan filed Claim No. 36077 (the "Claim") in the amount of $8 million . . . .

MCI argues that Jordan had an obligation to mitigate his damages and failed to do so. MCI argues that . . . the Claim should be reduced to $4 million. MCI argues that it is under no obligation to pay Jordan for contract years 2004 and 2005.

Jordan argues for summary judgment allowing the Claim in full and overruling and dismissing MCI's objections to the Claim. . . . Jordan argues that the objection should be overruled and dismissed for three independent reasons (1) Jordan was a "lost volume seller" and thus mitigation does not apply, (2) there is no evidence that Jordan could have entered into a "substantially similar" endorsement agreement, and (3) Jordan acted reasonably when he decided not to pursue other endorsements after MCI's rejection of the Agreement. . . .

The doctrine of avoidable consequences, which has also been referred to as the duty to mitigate damages, "bars recovery for losses suffered by a non-breaching party that could have been avoided by reasonable effort and without risk of substantial loss or injury." Edward M. Crough, Inc. v. Dep't of Gen. Servs., 572 A.2d 457, 466 (D.C. 1990). The burden of proving that the damages could have been avoided or mitigated rests with the party that committed the breach. The efforts to avoid or mitigate the damages do not have to be successful, as long as they are reasonable. . . .

Jordan argues that MCI's mitigation defense does not apply here because Jordan is akin to a "lost volume seller." Jordan points to testimony demonstrating that he could have entered into additional endorsement contracts even if MCI had not rejected the Agreement. Thus, he argues, any additional endorsement contracts would not have been substitutes for the Agreement and would not have mitigated the damages for which MCI is liable.

"A lost volume seller is one who has the capacity to perform the contract that was breached in addition to other potential contracts due to unlimited resources or production capacity." Precision Pine & Timber, Inc. v. United States, 72 Fed. Cl. 460, 490 (Fed. Cl. 2006). A lost volume seller does not minimize its damages by entering into another contract because it would have had the benefit of both contracts even if the first were not breached. The lost volume seller has two expectations, the profit from the breached contract and the profit from one or more other contracts that it could have performed at the same time as the breached contract. "The philosophical heart of the lost volume theory is that the seller would have generated a second sale irrespective of the buyer's breach" and that "[i]t follows that the lost volume seller cannot possibly mitigate damages." D. Matthews, Should the Doctrine of Lost Volume Seller Be Retained? A Response to Professor Breen, 51 U. Miami L. Rev. 1195, 1214 (July 1997).

The lost volume seller theory is recognized in the Restatement (2d) of Contracts, §§ 347, 350 (1981) (the "Restatement (2d)"). The lost volume seller theory applies to contracts for services as well as goods. See Restatement (2d), § 347, ill. 16.

This case offers a twist on the typical lost volume seller situation. In what the Court regards as the typical situation, the non-breaching seller has a near-inexhaustible supply of inventory. In the typical situation, when a buyer breaches an agreement to buy a good or service from the seller, the item is returned to inventory and the lost volume seller continues in its efforts to sell its goods or services. However, the transactions that occur following the breach are not necessarily the result of the breach but fundamentally the result of the seller continuing efforts to market its goods and services. It is this continuous effort coupled with a virtually limitless supply that warrants the lost volume exception to mitigation. As stated above, the transactions that may occur after the breach would in the context of the lost volume seller have occurred independent of the breach. Here, Jordan lacked a nearly limitless supply and had no intention of continuing to market his services as a product endorser . . . .

In his arguments, Jordan focuses primarily on his *capacity* to enter subsequent agreements, arguing that the loss of MCI's sixteen-hour annual time commitment hardly affected his ability to perform additional endorsement services. On this prong alone, Jordan likely would be considered a lost volume seller of endorsement services because he had sufficient time to do multiple endorsements. Although he does not have the "infinite capacity" that some cases discuss, a services provider does not need unlimited capacity but must have the requisite capacity and intent to perform under multiple contracts at the same time.

Contrary to Jordan's analysis, courts do not focus solely on the seller's capacity. The seller claiming lost volume status must also demonstrate that it *would* have entered into subsequent transactions. Jordan has not shown he could and *would have* entered into a subsequent agreement. Rather, the evidence shows that Jordan did not have the "subjective intent" to take on additional endorsements. The testimony from Jordan's representatives establishes that although Jordan's popularity enabled him to obtain additional product endorsements in 2003, Jordan desired to scale back his level of endorsements. Jordan's financial and business advisor, Curtis Polk ("Polk"), testified that at the time the Agreement was rejected, Jordan's desire was "not to expand his spokesperson or pitchman efforts with new relationships." Polk testified that had Jordan wanted to do additional endorsements after the 2003 rejection, he could have obtained additional deals. Jordan's agent, David Falk ("Falk"), testified that "there might have been twenty more companies that in theory might have wanted to sign him" but that Jordan and his representatives wanted to avoid diluting his image. Jordan's Memorandum for Summary Judgment stated that at the time the Agreement was rejected, Jordan had implemented a strategy of not accepting new endorsements because of a belief that new deals would jeopardize his ability to achieve his primary goal of National Basketball Association ("NBA") franchise ownership. . . .

Because the evidence establishes, among other things, that Jordan would not have entered into subsequent agreements, Jordan has not established that he is a lost volume seller. This theory thus does not relieve Jordan from the duty to mitigate damages. . . .

Jordan argues at length that MCI must show that Jordan could have entered a "substantially similar" endorsement contract in order to mitigate damages. However, this is not the law of the mitigation of damages or the avoidable consequences theory. This language stems from federal employment cases concerning back pay and mitigation, which this case, while similar in many respects, is not. . . .

Several of the justifications for the "substantially similar or equivalent" standard of employment law, aside from the general remedial policy of making the non-breaching party whole for losses caused by the breaching party, show why there is less concern here regarding a "substantially equivalent" opportunity as Jordan was not an employee of MCI. For one, the standard exists in part to ensure the employee's future advancement by mandating that the employee's promotional opportunities and status should be virtually identical to the prior position. Since Jordan was never an employee of MCI, this is not relevant. Second, to require acceptance of inferior employment can mean "that one who has been discriminated against would be obliged, in order to mitigate damages, to submit to the very discrimination of which he complains." This, obviously, has no application here. Finally, the employee's duty to make reasonable efforts in finding substantially equivalent employment is "based both on the doctrine of mitigation of damages and on the policy of promoting production and employment." See N.L.R.B. v. Miami Coca-Cola Bottling Co., 360 F.2d 569, 575 (5th Cir. 1966).

The main case relied on by Jordan for this argument regarding a "substantially similar" opportunity is a case analyzed under employment law and one that presented a completely different factual and procedural background. See Parker v. Twentieth Century-Fox Film Corp., 3 Cal. 3d 176, 89 Cal.Rptr. 737, 474 P.2d 689 (1970). In *Parker*, the plaintiff, a leading movie actress, agreed to perform in a musical-type film in California. The employer studio later decided not to make the movie and offered to the plaintiff as a substitute the leading role in a dramatic "western type" movie set in an opal mine and to be filmed in Australia. The plaintiff turned down that offer, sued for damages on the original agreement, and the trial court ruled on a summary judgment motion that the earnings from this substitute employment that the plaintiff refused could not be applied in mitigation because the second offer was "different" and "inferior." The California Supreme Court affirmed.

More accurately, MCI must show the absence of reasonable efforts by Jordan to avoid consequences or minimize his damages. . . .

Since "reasonable efforts in the form of *affirmative steps* are required to mitigate damages," see Robinson v. United States, 305 F.3d 1330, 1334 (Fed. Cir. 2002) (emphasis added) (citing Restatement (2d) § 350), MCI carries its burden by showing that Jordan has not taken affirmative steps to mitigate damages. Jordan admits in his brief that at the time of the rejection of the Agreement, "Jordan had already implemented a business strategy of not accepting new endorsements." Falk testified that a replacement telecommunications company was not approached. Polk testified that Jordan did not return to the endorsement marketplace to try and replace the revenue he was to be paid under the Agreement. Polk explained that Jordan did not wish to expand his "pitchman efforts with new relationships" because of his primary goal of becoming the owner of an NBA team. Although Jordan points to his discussions with another company, Nextel, as showing that he was willing to listen to endorsement agreements after MCI's bankruptcy, MCI effectively responds that responding to an inquiry by giving them contact information and indicating a willingness to respond to another call "is not trying to find an alternative" agreement—it is, in effect, "doing nothing." Based on the foregoing, and drawing all permissible factual inferences in favor of Jordan, the Court determines that MCI has established that Jordan did not take affirmative steps to mitigate damages. . . .

Jordan cites the risk that entering another endorsement contract could dilute his impact as an endorser or damage his reputation or business interests. . . .

Jordan's dilution argument is not convincing. Jordan's agent Falk testified that although there were no "fixed numbers" for the amount of endorsements, Jordan and his representatives were wary about dilution and sensitive about "protecting the brand" of Jordan. Jordan does not set forth any facts showing that Jordan's image was at risk of dilution. MCI convincingly responds that adding an agreement to replace a lost one is merely maintaining the status quo, not a dilution of Jordan's impact by addition. MCI's expert stated that Jordan had previously had sixteen endorsement agreements in place, which further weakens Jordan's dilution argument and casts doubt on Falk's statement that Jordan and his advisors "always felt that less is more" in terms of endorsements. While the Court recognizes that Jordan's image is the true commodity here and its market value could be diluted from overexposure, MCI has shown that Jordan's image was not at risk of dilution by replacing the MCI endorsement agreement with another one. The only statements Jordan offers to support his argument that he behaved reasonably by not seeking another endorsement in 2003 because of a concern with diluting his image are conclusory in nature and contradicted by the available evidence. The contention that pursuing an endorsement opportunity would dilute the image Jordan wished to cultivate as one befitting an NBA team owner . . . may well raise factual issues regarding the impact an endorsement may have on a team owner's image but that impact is irrelevant to Jordan's duty to mitigate damages for his "rejected" endorsement contract. There is no genuine issue of material fact that dilution did not excuse Jordan's duty to mitigate damages. . . .

Under the risk to reputation theory Jordan cites, an injured party is not allowed to recover from a wrongdoer those damages that the injured party "could have avoided without undue risk, burden or humiliation."

See Restatement (2d), § 350(1). Jordan's "harm to reputation" argument is flawed because the envisioned harm to Jordan's reputation does not rise to the level of harm found in the cited case law.

The cases cited by Jordan illustrate the harm to reputation that will excuse a party's duty to mitigate. In Eastman Kodak Co. v. Westway Motor Freight, Inc., 949 F.2d 317 (10th Cir. 1991), Kodak shipped a load of sensitized photographic material on a truck operated by the defendant. Most of the material was destroyed in transit because of the defendant's mishandling. The Tenth Circuit held that Kodak was not required to sell the damaged merchandise to mitigate damages, stating that the record revealed that Kodak's reputation, which it spent considerable resources in developing, "could be harmed if it was required to sell damaged merchandise in order to mitigate damages." *Id.* at 320.

Another case cited by Jordan is similar to *Eastman Kodak.* In Sony Magnetic Products, Inc. of America v. Merivienti O/Y, 668 F. Supp. 1505 (S.D. Ala. 1987), the plaintiff's merchandise, cassette tapes, had been damaged while it was being loaded onto a ship. The plaintiff refused to allow the cassettes to be marketed as "seconds" with only a non-warranty sticker on them and without removal of the marks identifying the cassettes as plaintiff's products. The court stated it was "convinced that as a matter of public policy a manufacturer which has spent years and millions of dollars developing a reputation in the marketplace should not be required to jeopardize that reputation under [those] circumstances." *Id.* at 1515.

Those cases show the uncontroversial maxim that a plaintiff faced with the choice of (1) selling a sub-standard product to the public to mitigate damages caused by the breach of another and (2) doing nothing—can choose to do nothing, but Jordan was not confronted with those circumstances. While Jordan's reputation is considerable and obviously the result of careful development, there are no factual assertions that support the proposition that Jordan's choosing another endorsement opportunity is akin to being forced to sell damaged goods, as was the case in *Eastman Kodak* and *Sony Magnetic Products.*

Jordan also cites District Concrete Co. v. Bernstein Concrete Corp., 418 A.2d 1030, 1037 (D.C. 1980), for the proposition that it is not unreasonable for a plaintiff "to take into consideration . . . consequences such as injury to reputation" as a factor in post-breach decisions. Bernstein had sued its concrete supplier, District Concrete, for breach of a requirements contract. Bernstein was the sub-contractor for a construction project building an apartment complex. After the complex's roof was poured with concrete, defects in the concrete were found. Bernstein considered two approaches to cure the problem (1) tearing out the slab and replacing it, or (2) building a "composite slab" over the defective area. Bernstein estimated the cost of each approach to be about $100,000 but considered that the highly visible "tear-out method" could damage Bernstein's and the general contractor's reputations. Although the chosen "composite slab" approach ended up costing more than anticipated, the court held that the choice of this method was reasonable when made, given that the "costs and time involved" for each were comparable *and also* considering the consequences of possible reputation damage.

That case is of little help to Jordan. For one, any harm to Jordan's reputation arising from MCI's bankruptcy is not comparable to the reputation damage a construction contractor faces from building a defective roof. As MCI's expert testified, consumers do not believe that celebrity endorsers are experts in the products they endorse, while a consumer would expect a builder to build a defective-free roof. If the roof fails, consumers would blame the builder. If a company fails, consumers do not blame the company's celebrity endorsers. Also, Jordan has not shown that he faced two reasonable approaches to mitigate his damages, with one of those approaches carrying a risk to his reputation. Jordan has stated that he was faced with two choices (1) mitigate damages, which he alleges could harm his reputation, or (2) concentrate on a venture that has no connection to the mitigation of damages. This situation is thus not comparable to *District Concrete.*

The above analysis also applies to Jordan's cited case of Citizens Fed. Bank v. United States, 66 Fed. Cl. 179 (Fed. Cl. 2005). There, the court held that the breaching party cannot engage in "Monday-morning quarterbacking" to criticize the wronged party's choice of mitigation. *Id.* at 185. "Where a choice has been required between two reasonable courses, the person whose wrong forced the choice cannot complain that one rather than the other was chosen." *Id.* Here, MCI is not complaining about the choice between "two reasonable courses" of mitigation. MCI is arguing that choosing to take no steps to mitigate is not a reasonable course.

In arguing that Jordan acted reasonably by avoiding further endorsements based on a belief that those efforts would harm his business interests or reputation, Jordan argues essentially that he would be harmed by doing precisely what he originally contracted to do under the Agreement and what he has been doing for other clients for a number of years—endorsing products and services. The Court recognizes the possibility of Jordan's market saturation being a valid concern but Jordan's argument that he wanted to get out of endorsements to pursue other ventures does not relieve the duty to mitigate. Furthermore, MCI's expert stated that an additional endorsement agreement would not have harmed Jordan's reputation by either diminishing Jordan's image in the endorsement marketplace or harming Jordan's goal of becoming an NBA team owner. Jordan has not asserted any facts to refute those assertions nor did he undermine the credibility of the expert making such assertions. Based on the foregoing, there is a no genuine issue of material fact as to whether reasonable endorsement efforts done to mitigate damages would have harmed Jordan's reputation. The Court notes that even if there were a genuine issue of material fact as to whether another endorsement would negatively impact his becoming an NBA team owner, for the reasons set forth below, such would be irrelevant to the issue of mitigation regarding his endorsement contract. . . .

In this case, there has been no determination and no evidence presented of what Jordan could have reasonably earned had he fulfilled his obligation to mitigate damages by entering the endorsement marketplace following MCI's rejection of the Agreement. It is not clear that Jordan could have found an endorsement agreement in 2003 that paid him $2 million a year for the contract years 2004 and 2005. It is also unlikely that Jordan would have been obligated to accept a large number of endorsements of smaller value to make up the $2 million, due to the dilution effect such a number would have, because such efforts would likely be unreasonable. However, the facts may reveal that one or more endorsements could have been found without "diluting" his image and partially or completely mitigating the damages. Although MCI's expert stated that he believed that Jordan could have easily earned $2 million from an additional endorsement in 2003, that opinion was not presented with any objective evidence of the marketplace, such as what other celebrity endorsers of Jordan's stature earned that year and which companies were in the market for an endorser of Jordan's stature. Although the Court finds that as a matter of law Jordan has not mitigated damages, there must be an evidentiary hearing on how much his claim should be reduced to reflect what portion would have been mitigated had he used reasonable efforts to do so. . . .

NOTE

The advertising campaign at issue in *WorldCom* focused on MCI's consumer telephone services. The ads featured Michael Jordan and co-stars from the movie *Space Jam*. These advertisements can still be found on-line. See, e.g., http://www.youtube.com/watch?v=BV0yQcOXc_Y. By the time that its parent company found itself in bankruptcy, MCI had discontinued its consumer phone business. It had no further need for Jordan's services. It therefore wanted to terminate its contract with him. The breach in bankruptcy, as outside, gives the nonbreaching party a claim for damages. The bankruptcy lawyer must apply the common law of contract damages in the same fashion as every other lawyer. Because of the bankruptcy, Jordan might not be able to collect in full, but this is no different from having a claim against someone outside of bankruptcy who lacks the assets to satisfy a judgment.

In considering how these damages might be calculated, consider how Jordan's work with MCI had foreclosed and limited his other opportunities. While Jordan might have the ability to endorse many products, his work for MCI may have made him less attractive to other telecommunications companies. Similarly, his ability to run ads with his *Space Jam* co-stars might be compromised as well. The novelty of seeing him with Daffy Duck might wear thin.

Hadley v. Baxendale

Court of Exchequer, 1854.
9 Exch. 341.

At the trial before Crompton, J., at the last Gloucester Assizes, it appeared that the plaintiffs carried on an extensive business as millers at Gloucester; and that, on the 11th of May, their mill was stopped by a breakage of the crank shaft by which the mill was worked. The steam-engine was manufactured by Messrs. Joyce & Co., the engineers, at Greenwich, and it became necessary to send the shaft as a pattern for a new one to Greenwich. The fracture was discovered on the 12th, and on the 13th, the plaintiffs sent one of their servants to the office of the defendants, who are the well known carriers trading under the name of Pickford & Co., for the purpose of having the shaft carried to Greenwich. The plaintiffs' servant told the clerk that the mill was stopped, and that the shaft must be sent immediately; and in answer to the inquiry when the shaft would be taken, the answer was, that if it was sent up by twelve o'clock any day, it would be delivered at Greenwich on the following day. On the following day the shaft was taken by the defendants, before noon, for the purpose of being conveyed to Greenwich, and the sum of £2. 4s. was paid for its carriage for the whole distance; at the same time the defendants' clerk was told that a special entry, if required, should be made to hasten its delivery. The delivery of the shaft at Greenwich was delayed by some neglect; and the consequence was, that the plaintiffs did not receive the new shaft for several days after they would otherwise have done, and the working of their mill was thereby delayed and they thereby lost the profits they would otherwise have received.

[The defendants] objected that these damages were too remote, and that the defendants were not liable with respect to them. The learned Judge left the case generally to the jury, who found a verdict with £25 damages beyond the amount paid into Court.

Whateley, in last Michaelmas Term, obtained a rule nisi for a new trial, on the ground of misdirection.

Keating and Dowdeswell (Feb. 1) showed cause.—The plaintiffs are entitled to the amount awarded by the jury as damages. These damages are not too remote, for they are not only the natural and necessary consequence of the defendants' default, but they are the only loss which the plaintiffs have actually sustained. The principle upon which damages are assessed is founded upon that of rendering compensation to the injured party. . . . [PARKE, B.—The sensible rule appears to be that which has been laid down in France, and which is declared in their code [and] translated in Sedgwick: "The damages due to the creditor consist in general of the loss that he has sustained, and the profit which he has been prevented from acquiring. . . . The debtor is only liable for the damages foreseen, or which might have been foreseen, at the time of the execution of the contract, when it is not owing to his fraud that the agreement has been violated. Even in the case of non-performance of the contract, resulting from the fraud of the debtor, the damages only comprise so much of the loss sustained by the creditor, and so much of the profit which he has been prevented from acquiring, as directly and immediately results from the non-performance of the contract."] If that rule is to be adopted, there was ample evidence in the present case of the defendants' knowledge of such a state of things as would necessarily result in the damage the plaintiffs suffered through the defendants' default. . . .

ALDERSON, B. We think that there ought to be a new trial in this case; but, in so doing, we deem it to be expedient and necessary to state explicitly the rule which the Judge, at the next trial, ought, in our opinion, to direct the jury to be governed by when they estimate the damages. It is, indeed, of the last importance that we should do this; for if the jury are left without any definite rule to guide them, it will, in such cases as these, manifestly lead to the greatest injustice. . . .

Now we think the proper rule in such a case as the present is this:—Where two parties have made a contract which one of them has broken, the damages which the other party ought to receive in respect of such breach of contract should be such as may fairly and reasonably be considered either arising naturally, i.e., according to the usual course of things, from such breach of contract itself, or such as may reasonably be supposed to have been in the contemplation of both parties, at the time they made the contract, as the probable result of the breach of it. Now, if the special circumstances under which the contract was actually made were communicated by the plaintiffs to the defendants, and thus known to both parties, the damages resulting from the breach of such a contract, which they would reasonably contemplate, would be the amount of injury which would ordinarily follow from a breach of contract under these special circumstances so known and communicated. But, on the other hand, if these special circumstances were wholly unknown to the party breaking the contract, he, at the most, could only be supposed to have had in his contemplation the amount of injury which would arise generally, and in the great multitude of cases not affected by any special circumstances, from such a breach of contract. For, had the special circumstances been known, the parties might have specially provided for the breach of contract by special terms as to the damages in that case; and of this advantage it would be very unjust to deprive them. Now the above principles are those by which we think the jury ought to be guided in estimating the damages arising out of any breach of contract. It is said, that other cases such as breaches of contract in the nonpayment of money, or in the not making a good title to land,[4] are to be treated as exceptions from this, and as governed by a conventional rule. But as, in such cases, both parties must be supposed to be cognisant of that well-known rule, these cases may, we think be more properly classed under the rule above enunciated

[4] [The court is referring to the doctrine of Flureau v. Thornhill, 2 WM.Bl. 1078 (1776)—Eds.]

as to cases under known special circumstances, because there both parties may reasonably be presumed to contemplate the estimation of the amount of damages according to the conventional rule.

Now, in the present case, if we are to apply the principles above laid down, we find that the only circumstances here communicated by the plaintiffs to the defendants at the time the contract was made, were, that the article to be carried was the broken shaft of a mill, and that the plaintiffs were the millers of that mill. But how do these circumstances show reasonably that the profits of the mill must be stopped by an unreasonable delay in the delivery of the broken shaft by the carrier to the third person? Suppose the plaintiffs had another shaft in their possession put up or putting up at the time, and that they only wished to send back the broken shaft to the engineer who made it; it is clear that this would be quite consistent with the above circumstances, and yet the unreasonable delay in the delivery would have no effect upon the intermediate profits of the mill. Or, again, suppose, that, at the time of the delivery to the carrier, the machinery of the mill had been in other respects defective, then, also, the same results would follow. Here it is true that the shaft was actually sent back to serve as a model for a new one, and that the want of a new one was the only cause of the stoppage of the mill, and that the loss of profits really arose from not sending down the new shaft in proper time, and that this arose from the delay in delivering the broken one to serve as a model. But it is obvious that, in the great multitude of cases of millers sending off broken shafts to third persons by a carrier under ordinary circumstances, such consequences would not, in all probability, have occurred; and these special circumstances were here never communicated by the plaintiffs to the defendants. It follows, therefore, that the loss of profits here cannot reasonably be considered such a consequence of the breach of contract as could have been fairly and reasonably contemplated by both the parties when they made this contract. For such loss would neither have flowed naturally from the breach of this contract in the great multitude of such cases occurring under ordinary circumstances, nor were the special circumstances, which, perhaps, would have made it a reasonable and natural consequence of such breach of contract, communicated to or known by the defendants. The Judge ought, therefore, to have told the jury that, upon the facts then before them, they ought not to take the loss of profits into consideration at all in estimating the damages. There must therefore be a new trial in this case.

Rule absolute.

NOTE

In Black v. Baxendale, 1 Exch. 410 (1847), an action brought seven years earlier against the same carrier, it appeared that defendant had undertaken to transport haycloths from London to Bedford and that through delay in shipment plaintiff had been unable to sell the cloths in Bedford and had had to reship them to another town for sale. In an action for the expense of reshipment and for the personal expenses of plaintiff's employee who had been sent to Bedford to receive and sell the cloths, all the judges agreed that whether these expenses were "reasonable" was entirely for the jury. One of the judges was Baron Alderson, who wrote the opinion in Hadley v. Baxendale; another *Hadley* judge, Baron Parke, was also on the panel. Chief Baron Pollock added that notice to defendant that delivery was required at a particular time might perhaps increase defendant's liability for expenses incurred by plaintiff, "but whether any particular class of expense is reasonable or not depends upon the usage of trade, and other circumstances. It is not a question for the Judge, but for the jury, to decide what are reasonable expenses."

Globe Refining Co. v. Landa Cotton Oil Co.

Supreme Court of the United States, 1903.
190 U.S. 540, 23 S.Ct. 754.

HOLMES, J. This is an action of contract brought by the plaintiff in error, a Kentucky corporation, against the defendant in error, a Texas corporation, for breach of a contract to sell and deliver crude oil. The defendant excepted to certain allegations of damage, and pleaded that the damages had been claimed and magnified fraudulently for the purpose of giving the United States circuit court jurisdiction, when in truth they were less than $2,000. The judge sustained the exceptions. He also tried the question of jurisdiction before hearing the merits, refused the plaintiff a jury, found that the plea was sustained, and dismissed the cause. The plaintiff excepted to all the rulings. . . . If the rulings and findings were right, there is no question that the judge was right in dismissing the suit but the grounds upon which he went are re-examinable here.

The contract was made through a broker . . . in the following letter:

Dallas, Texas, 7/30/97.

Landa Oil Company,
New Braunfels, Texas.

Gentlemen:

Referring to the exchange of our telegrams to-day, we have sold for your account to the Globe Refining Co., Louisville Kentucky, ten (10) tanks prime crude C/S oil at the price of 15¾ cents per gallon of 7½ pounds, f.o.b. buyers' tank at your mill. Weights and quality guaranteed.

Terms: Sight draft without exchange b/ldg. attached. Sellers paying commission.

Shipment: Part last half August and balance first half September. Shipping instructions to be furnished by the Globe Refining Co.

Yours truly,
Thomas & Green, as *Broker*.

Having this contract before us, we proceed to consider the allegations of special damage over and above the difference between the contract price of the oil and the price at the time of the breach, which was the measure adopted by the judge. These allegations must be read with care, for it is obvious that the pleader has gone as far as he dared to go, and to the verge of anything that could be justified under the contract, if not beyond.

It is alleged that it was agreed and understood that the plaintiff would send its tank cars to the defendant's mills, and that the defendant promptly would fill them with oil (so far, simply following the contract), and that the plaintiff sent tanks. "In order to do this, the plaintiff was under the necessity of obligating itself unconditionally to the railroad company (and of which the defendant had notice) to pay to it for the transportation of the cars from said Louisville to said New Braunfels in the sum of $900," which sum plaintiff had to pay, "and was incurred as an advancement on said oil contract." This is the first item. The last words quoted mean only that the sum paid would have been allowed by the railroad as part payment of the return charges had the tanks been filled and sent back over the same road.

Next it is alleged that the defendant, contemplating a breach of the contract, caused the plaintiff to send its cars a thousand miles, at a cost of $1,000; that defendant canceled its contract on the 2d of September, but did not notify the plaintiff until the 14th, when, if the plaintiff had known of the cancelation, it would have been supplying itself from other sources; that [defendant] did so wilfully and maliciously, causing an unnecessary loss of $2,000.

Next it is alleged that, by reason of the breach of contract and want of notice, plaintiff lost the use of its tanks for thirty days—a loss estimated at $700 more. Next it is alleged that the plaintiff had arranged with its own customers to furnish the oil in question within a certain time, which contemplated sharp compliance with the contract by the defendant; "all of which facts, as above stated, were well known to the defendant, and defendant had contracted to that end with the plaintiff." This item is put at $740, with $1,000 more for loss of customers, credit, and reputation. Finally, at the end of the petition, it is alleged generally that it was known to defendant, and in contemplation of the contract, that plaintiff would have to send tanks at great expense from distant points, and that plaintiff "was required to pay additional freight in order to rearrange the destination of the various tanks and other points." Then it is alleged that by reason of the defendant's breach, the plaintiff had to pay $350 additional freight.

Whatever may be the scope of the allegations which we have quoted, it will be seen that none of the items was contemplated expressly by the words of the bargain. Those words . . . go no further than to contemplate that when the deliveries were to take place the buyer's tanks should be at the defendant's mill. Under such circumstances the question is suggested how far the express terms of a writing, admitted to be complete, can be enlarged by averment and oral evidence; and, if they can be enlarged in that way, what averments are sufficient. When a man commits a tort, he incurs, by force of the law, a liability to damages, measured by certain rules. When a man makes a contract, he incurs, by force of the law, a liability to damages, unless a certain promised event comes to pass. But, unlike the case of torts, as the contract is by mutual consent, the parties themselves, expressly or by implication, fix the rule by which the damages are to be measured. The old law seems to have regarded it as technically in the election of the promisor to perform or to pay damages. It is true that, as people when contracting contemplate performance, not breach, they commonly say little or nothing as to what shall happen in the latter event, and the common rules have been worked out by common sense, which has established what the parties probably would have said if they had spoken about the matter. But a man never can be absolutely certain of performing any contract when the time of performance arrives, and, in many cases, he obviously is taking the risk of an event which is wholly, or to an appreciable extent, beyond his control. The extent of liability in such cases is likely to be within his contemplation, and, whether it is or not, should be worked out on terms which it fairly may be presumed he would have assented to if they had been presented to his mind. For instance, in the present case, the defendant's mill and all its oil might have been burned before the time came for delivery. Such a misfortune would not have been an excuse, although probably it would have prevented performance of the contract. If a contract is broken, the measure of damages generally is the same, whatever the cause of the breach. We have to consider, therefore, what the plaintiff would have been entitled to recover in that case, and that depends on what liability the defendant fairly may be supposed to have assumed consciously, or to have warranted the plaintiff reasonably to suppose that it assumed, when the contract was made.

This point of view is taken by implication in the rule that "a person can only be held to be responsible for such consequences as may be reasonably supposed to be in the contemplation of the parties at the time of making the contract." [Hadley v. Baxendale, 9 Exch. 341, 354.] The suggestion thrown out . . . in Gee v. Lancashire & Y. R. Co., 6 Hurlst. & N. 211, 218, that perhaps notice after the contract was made and before breach would be enough, is not accepted by the later decisions. The consequences must be contemplated at the time of the making of the contract.

The question arises, then, What is sufficient to show that the consequences were in contemplation of the parties, in the sense of the vendor taking the risk? It has been held that it may be proved by oral evidence when the contract is in writing. But, in the language quoted, with seeming approbation, by Blackburn, J., from Mayne on Damages, 2d ed. 10, in Elbinger Actien-Gesellschafft v. Armstrong, L. R. 9 Q. B. 473, 478, "it may be asked, with great deference, whether the mere fact of such consequences being communicated to the other party will be sufficient, without going on to show that he was told that he would be answerable for them, and consented to undertake such a liability." Mr. Justice Willes answered this question . . . in British Columbia & V. I. Spar, Lumber, & Saw-Mill Co. v. Nettleship, L. R. 3 C. P. 499, 500: "I am disposed to take the narrow view that one of two contracting parties ought not to be allowed to obtain an advantage which he has not paid for. . . . If that [a liability for the full profits that might be made by machinery which the defendant was transporting, if the plaintiff's trade should prove successful and without a rival] had been presented to the mind of the ship owner at the time of making the contract, as the basis upon which he was contracting, he would at once have rejected it. And though he knew, from the shippers, the use they intended to make of the articles, it could not be contended that the mere fact of knowledge, without more, would be a reason for imposing upon him a greater degree of liability than would otherwise have been cast upon him. To my mind, that leads to the inevitable conclusion that the mere fact of knowledge cannot increase the liability. The knowledge must be brought home to the party sought to be charged, under such circumstances that he must know that the person he contracts with reasonably believes that he accepts the contract with the special condition attached to it." . . . See also Benjamin, Sales, 6th Am. ed. § 872.

It may be said with safety that mere notice to a seller of some interest or probable action of the buyer is not enough necessarily and as matter of law to charge the seller with special damage on that account if he fails to deliver the goods. With that established, we recur to the allegations. With regard to the first, it is obvious that the plaintiff was free to bring its tanks from where it liked,—a thousand miles away or an adjoining yard,—so far as the contract was concerned. The allegation hardly amounts to saying that the defendant had notice that the plaintiff was likely to send its cars from a distance. It is not alleged that the defendant had notice that the plaintiff had to bind itself to pay $900, at the time when the contract was made, and it nowhere is alleged that the defendant assumed any liability in respect of this uncertain element of charge. The same observations may be made with regard to the claim for loss of use of the tanks and to the final allegations as to sending the tanks from distant points. It is true that this last was alleged to have been in contemplation of the contract, if we give the plaintiff the benefit of the doubt in construing a somewhat confused sentence. But, having the contract before us, we can see that this ambiguous expression cannot be taken to mean more than notice, and notice of a fact which would depend upon the accidents of the future.

It is to be said further, with regard to the foregoing items, that they were the expenses which the plaintiff was willing to incur for performance. If it had received the oil, these were deductions from any profit which the plaintiff would have made. But, if it gets the difference between the contract price and the market price, it gets what represents the value of the oil in its hands, and to allow these items in addition would be making the defendant pay twice for the same thing.

It must not be forgotten that we are dealing with pleadings, not evidence, and with pleadings which, as we have said, evidently put the plaintiff's case as high as it possibly can be put. There are no inferences to be drawn. . . . It is a simple question of allegations which, by declining to amend, the plaintiff has admitted that it cannot reinforce. This consideration applies with special force to the attempt to hold the defendant liable for the breach of the plaintiff's contract with third persons. The allegation is that the fact that the plaintiff had contracts over was well known to the defendant, and that "defendant had contracted to that end with the plaintiff." Whether, if we were sitting as a jury, this would warrant an inference that the defendant assumed an additional liability, we need not consider. It is enough to say that it does not allege the conclusion of fact so definitely that it must be assumed to be true. With the contract before us it is in a high degree improbable that any such conclusion could have been made good.

The only other allegation needing to be dealt with is that the defendant maliciously caused the plaintiff to send the tanks a thousand miles, contemplating a breach of its contract. So far as this item has not been answered by what has been said, it is necessary only to add a few words. The fact alleged has no relation to the time of the contract. Therefore it cannot affect the damages, the measure of which was fixed at that time. The motive for the breach commonly is immaterial in an action on the contract. It is in this case. Whether, under any circumstances, it might give rise to an action of tort, is not material here. . . .

Judgment affirmed.

NOTE

For an incisive critique of Globe Refining, see Larry T. Garvin, *Globe Refining Co. v. Landa Cotton Oil Co.* and the Dark Side of Reputation, 12 Nev. L.J. 659 (2012).

Lamkins v. International Harvester Co.

207 Ark. 637, 182 S.W.2d 203 (1944)

The dispute grew out of a sale of a farm tractor. The buyer had told the seller at the time of the contract that he wanted lighting equipment so that he could use the tractor at night. The tractor was delivered on May 1, 1942, without lighting equipment, and the seller's agent promised that lighting equipment would be supplied within three weeks; it was not supplied until nearly a year later. The buyer alleged that without lights he could not work the tractor at night and therefore was unable to plant and harvest a 25-acre tract on his farm, on which he would have grown soy beans if the tractor had had lights. The court quoted from an earlier Arkansas case: "Where the damages arise from special circumstances, and are so large as to be out of proportion to the consideration agreed to be paid for the services to be rendered under the contract, it raises a doubt at once as to whether the party would have assented to such liability had it been called to his attention at the making of the contract unless the consideration to be paid was also raised so as to correspond in some respect to the liability assumed." In the present case, even if the buyer's testimony were believed, "there is nothing in the testimony showing circumstances surrounding and connected with the transaction which were calculated to bring home to the dealer knowledge that appellant expected him to assume liability for a crop loss which might amount to several hundreds of dollars, if he should fail to deliver a $20 lighting accessory. There was, of course, no such express contract on the dealer's part, and the facts and circumstances are not such as to make it reasonable for the trier of facts to believe that the dealer at the time tacitly consented to be bound for more than ordinary damages in case of default on his part." [The "tacit agreement" test embraced by the *Lamkins* court is usually attributed to Justice Holmes' rationalization of *Hadley* in *Globe Refining*.]

Bi-Economy Market, Inc. v. Harleysville Ins. Co.

New York, Court of Appeals, 2008.
10 N.Y.3d 187, 856 N.Y.S.2d 505, 886 N.E.2d 127.

PIGOTT, J. . . . Bi-Economy Market, a family-owned wholesale and retail meat market located in Rochester, New York, suffered a major fire in October 2002, resulting in the complete loss of food inventory and heavy structural damage to the building and business-related equipment. At the time of the fire, Bi-Economy was insured by defendant Harleysville Insurance Company under a "Deluxe Business Owners" policy that provided replacement cost coverage on the building as well as business property or "contents" loss coverage.

The policy also provided coverage for lost business income, what is commonly referred to as "business interruption insurance," for up to one year from the date of the fire. Specifically, the contract stated that Harleysville would "pay for the actual loss of Business Income . . . sustain[ed] due to . . . the necessary suspension of [Bi-Economy's] 'operations' during the 'period of restoration.'" Business income is defined as the "(1) Net Income (Net Profit *or Loss* before income taxes) that would have been earned or incurred; and (2) Continuing normal operating expenses incurred, including payroll." "Period of restoration" is defined as the period of time that "[b]egins with the date of direct physical loss or damage" and "[e]nds on the date when the property . . . should be repaired, rebuilt or replaced with reasonable speed and similar quality."

Following the fire, Bi-Economy submitted a claim to Harleysville pursuant to the terms of the contract. Harleysville disputed Bi-Economy's claim for actual damages, and advanced only the sum of $163,161.92. More than a year later, following submission of their dispute to alternative dispute resolution, Bi-Economy was awarded the additional sum of $244,019.88. During all this time, Harleysville offered to pay only seven months of Bi-Economy's claim for lost business income, despite the fact that the policy provided for a full 12 months. Bi-Economy never resumed business operations. . . .

It is well settled that in breach of contract actions "the nonbreaching party may recover general damages which are the natural and probable consequence of the breach" Kenford Co. v. County of Erie, 73 N.Y.2d 312, 319, 540 N.Y.S.2d 1, 537 N.E.2d 176 (1989). Special, or consequential damages, which "do not so directly flow from the breach," are also recoverable in limited circumstances American List Corp. v. U.S. News & World Report, 75 N.Y.2d 38, 43, 550 N.Y.S.2d 590, 549 N.E.2d 1161 (1989). In *Kenford,* we stated that

> [i]n order to impose on the defaulting party a further liability than for damages [which] naturally and directly [flow from the breach], i.e., in the ordinary course of things, arising from a breach of contract, such unusual or extraordinary damages must have been brought within the contemplation of the parties as the probable result of a breach at the time of or prior to contracting.

73 N.Y.2d at 319. We later explained that "[t]he party breaching the contract is liable for those risks foreseen or which should have been foreseen at the time the contract was made" Ashland Mgt. v. Janien, 82 N.Y.2d 395, 403, 604 N.Y.S.2d 912, 624 N.E.2d 1007 (1993). It is not necessary for the breaching party to have foreseen the breach itself or the particular way the loss occurred, rather, "[i]t is only necessary that loss from a breach is foreseeable and probable"

To determine whether consequential damages were reasonably contemplated by the parties, courts must look to "the nature, purpose and particular circumstances of the contract known by the parties . . . as well as 'what liability the defendant fairly may be supposed to have assumed consciously, or to have warranted the plaintiff reasonably to suppose that it assumed, when the contract was made' " (Kenford, 73 N.Y.2d at 319, 540 N.Y.S.2d 1, 537 N.E.2d 176, quoting Globe Refining Co. v. Landa Cotton Oil Co., 190 U.S. 540, 544 (1903)). Of course, proof of consequential damages cannot be speculative or conjectural . . . .

The purpose served by business interruption coverage cannot be clearer—to ensure that Bi-Economy had the financial support necessary to sustain its business operation in the event disaster occurred. Certainly, many business policyholders, such as Bi-Economy, lack the resources to continue business operations without insurance proceeds. Accordingly, limiting an insured's damages to the amount of the policy, i.e., money which should have been paid by the insurer in the first place, plus interest, does not place the insured in the position it would have been in had the contract been performed.

Thus, the very purpose of business interruption coverage would have made Harleysville aware that if it breached its obligations under the contract to investigate in good faith and pay covered claims it would have to respond in damages to Bi-Economy for the loss of its business as a result of the breach.

Furthermore, . . . the purpose of the contract was not just to receive money, but to receive it promptly so that in the aftermath of a calamitous event, as Bi-Economy experienced here, the business could avoid collapse and get back on its feet as soon as possible. Thus, this insurance contract included an additional performance-based component: the insurer agreed to evaluate a claim, and to do so honestly, adequately, and—most importantly—promptly. The insurer certainly knew that failure to perform would (a) undercut the very purpose of the agreement and (b) cause additional damages that the policy was purchased to protect against in the first place. Here, the claim is that Harleysville failed to promptly adjust and pay the loss, resulting in the collapse of the business. When an insured in such a situation suffers additional damages as a result of an insurer's excessive delay or improper denial, the insurance company should stand liable for these damages. This is not to punish the insurer, but to give the insured its bargained-for benefit. . . .

Sunnyland Farms, Inc. v. Central New Mexico Electric Cooperative, Inc.

Supreme Court of New Mexico, 2013.
301 P.3d 387.

CHÁVEZ, JUSTICE. . . . Sunnyland purchased its electricity from CNMEC. On September 8, 2003, CNMEC shut off electrical service to Sunnyland. Prior to disconnecting electricity for nonpayment, CNMEC ordinarily gives its customers notice that they have fifteen days to pay their overdue bills before service is suspended. It did not give Sunnyland this fifteen-day notice. The trial court record indicates a confusing array of possible billing irregularities, but it is not necessary to address them here because CNMEC does not contest the trial court's findings that it was negligent and that it breached its duty to Sunnyland.

On the morning of September 9, 2003, before electrical service was restored, several Sunnyland employees engaged in arc welding near flammable materials, including cardboard boxes. In doing so, they started a fire that ultimately consumed Sunnyland Farms' packhouse and operations building. When Sunnyland's employees initially discovered the fire, they attempted to put it out using ordinary hoses, but without electricity, the Sunnyland facility had no running water, and the fire grew. Sunnyland does not contest that its employees were negligent both in starting the fire and in reacting to it, for example, by failing to use a fire extinguisher.

Someone living on Sunnyland's property called the fire department. Fire trucks arrived, but they were unable to access well water for firefighting because there was no electricity to power the pumps. Sunnyland had also failed to make alternative arrangements for emergency water in the event that power failed. Firefighters attempted to contact CNMEC to restore electricity to the water sources, but CNMEC employees expressed reservations to the emergency dispatcher, and the firefighters interpreted their statements as a threat that the fire department would have to assume liability. Firefighters attempted to use reservoir water and to preserve water by using foam and smaller hoses, but the buildings were nonetheless destroyed.

Sunnyland sued CNMEC in contract and tort, among other causes of action, for damages resulting from the fire, alleging that if CNMEC had taken adequate care prior to disconnecting Sunnyland's electrical service, firefighters and Sunnyland employees would have had access to water and the fire could have been contained. The trial court found CNMEC liable both in contract and in tort. It calculated total consequential damages of over $21 million, of which $13.7 million was the net value of lost crops that the facility would have been able to grow in the absence of the fire. The trial court reduced the damages in tort by 80% to account for Sunnyland's comparative fault; however, in contract, the trial court awarded the entire almost $21.4 million. The trial court allowed plaintiffs to elect a remedy in contract or tort after the resolution of their appeals. . . .

This Court has previously stated that in an action for breach of contract, the breaching party "is justly responsible for all damages flowing naturally from the breach." *Camino Real Mobile Home Park P'ship v. Wolfe,* 119 N.M. 436, 443, 891 P.2d 1190, 1197 (1995). Damages "that arise naturally and necessarily as the result of the breach" are "general damages," which give the plaintiff whatever value he or she would have obtained from the breached contract. In some circumstances, the plaintiff can also recover for "consequential damages" or "special damages," which "are not based on the capital or present value of the promised performance but upon benefits it can produce or losses that may be caused by its absence."

The classic test for whether a plaintiff may recover consequential damages comes from *Hadley v. Baxendale,* 156 Eng. Rep. 145, 9 Ex. 341 (1854). . . .

The *Hadley* standard has been interpreted as an objective foreseeability test: A defendant is liable for losses that were foreseeable at the time of contracting, regardless of whether the defendant actually contemplated or foresaw the loss. This foreseeability standard is more stringent than "proximate cause" in tort law; the loss must have been foreseeable as the *probable* result of breach, not merely as a possibility. *Hadley,* 156 Eng. Rep. at 151, 9 Ex. at 354; Restatement (Second) of Contracts § 351(1), § 351 cmt. a. The Restatement asks whether there were "special circumstances, beyond the ordinary course of events, that the party in breach had reason to know." Id. § 351(2)(b). In the absence of such circumstances, the breaching party is liable only for general damages.

This Court has cited the *Hadley* standard approvingly and described it as the appropriate rule of analysis in New Mexico cases dealing with consequential damages. However, we have also stated that "the foreseeability . . . rule anticipates an explicit or tacit agreement by the defendant" that he or she will assume particular damages if he or she breaches. *Camino Real*, 119 N.M. at 446, 891 P.2d at 1200; see also *Wall v. Pate*, 104 N.M. 1, 2, 715 P.2d 449, 450 (1986) (suggesting that the conditions required for an award of special damages must include a "tacit agreement" (citing Globe Ref. Co. v. Landa Cotton Oil Co., 190 U.S. 540, 543–44 (1903))). . . .

We now abandon the "tacit agreement" test. While we suspect that there may not, in fact, be much space between a "tacit agreement" and the special circumstances required to render a defendant liable for consequential damages, our previous emphasis on the tacit agreement test from *Globe Refining* is confusing and antiquated. We hold that the proper test for consequential damages in New Mexico is the *Hadley* standard as interpreted in Restatement (Second) of Contracts § 351. In a contract action, a defendant is liable only for those consequential damages that were objectively foreseeable as a probable result of his or her breach when the contract was made. To the extent our earlier cases suggest a different standard, they are overruled. . . .

Sunnyland suggests that it was sufficient that CNMEC knew that Sunnyland was a for-profit enterprise and it depended on electricity. Both of these factual statements are supported by the trial court's findings of fact and by the evidence presented at trial. The trial court found that "CNMEC [e]mployees . . . testified that it was well known within the community that [the Sunnyland] facility was a hydroponic tomato facility." Furthermore, the trial court found that prior to disconnecting electricity, a CNMEC employee allowed a Sunnyland employee to open the windows in the greenhouse to allow venting, which suggests that CNMEC might have known that cutting off electricity could harm Sunnyland's tomato crop.

Taking these findings of fact to indicate the presence of special circumstances is problematic for three reasons. First, although this Court indulges reasonable inferences in favor of the trial court's judgment, this is simply too speculative. This Court does not speculate about what the fact-finder might have meant to say but did not.

Second, Sunnyland's injury was not directly caused by the lack of electricity. The actual harm was more attenuated: the lack of electricity interrupted Sunnyland's water supply, which, in conjunction with Sunnyland's lack of backup firefighting options, made it difficult for Sunnyland to respond to the fire its employees negligently started. There were no findings that CNMEC should have known that Sunnyland was likely to start fires or was depending on electricity in order to fight any fires that occurred. Even if some damage to the tomato crop was foreseeable from the disconnection of electricity, the particular damage that occurred was not, and consequential damages are only permissible if the particular damage that actually occurred was foreseeable. "The mere circumstance that some loss was foreseeable, or even that some loss of the same general kind was foreseeable, will not suffice if the loss that actually occurred was not foreseeable." Restatement (Second) of Contracts § 351 cmt. (a).

Third, even if CNMEC had reason to know that Sunnyland depended on its electricity to power water in the event of a fire, CNMEC would still not be liable without the presence of additional special circumstances. *Hadley* provides a good example of what does and does not qualify as "special circumstances." In *Hadley,* the defendant knew that the crankshaft it was carrying was a broken part of a for-profit mill. However, the plaintiff never told the defendant exactly what was at stake, i.e., that there was no backup shaft or other alternative plan to keep the mill running. Similarly, in this case, CNMEC would have needed to know not only that Sunnyland depended on its electricity for access to water, but that there was no backup power source, or that there was a particularized need for uninterrupted water or power. There is no evidence that CNMEC had reason to know any of this. In particular, CNMEC could not have been expected to know that Sunnyland did not have a separate power source, independent of the power for the main building, for the well that was to be used in the event of a fire. A firefighter's trial testimony agreed that "if it's going to be an approved firefighting source of water, it has to have two separate sources of electricity . . . [a]nd one of them cannot come through the building that's being . . . protected by the pump," and the trial court found that "Sunnyland Farms was negligent in having only one source of power which ran through the support building to energize the exterior well pump." CNMEC cannot have been expected to anticipate Sunnyland's negligence in this regard.

Langley v. Pacific Gas & Electric Co., 41 Cal.2d 655, 262 P.2d 846 (1953) (in bank), provides an instructive example of what a utility company would need to know to render it liable for consequential damages in the event of a power shutoff. The plaintiff ran a trout hatchery that required electricity to oxygenate the water and keep the trout alive. If power was shut off, the fish could survive for only three and a half hours.

The plaintiff purchased electricity from the utility and explained his situation to its employees, asking whether the utility had 24-hour monitoring and would always be able to tell him before power was shut off. The plaintiff told the utility that if it was not able to make this guarantee, he would put in a backup pump. The utility's employees assured the plaintiff that he would be notified any time the power was shut off. Several years later, power to the fish hatchery was shut off for several hours, and the utility failed to warn or inform the plaintiff. Nearly all of the plaintiff's fish died. The plaintiff sued the utility for breach of contract, and the California Supreme Court upheld a jury verdict in his favor, apparently including full consequential damages. The court found that the utility "knew that a continuous supply of electric current to plaintiff was imperative," and the utility had an obligation either to provide it or to give the plaintiff notice so that he could make alternative arrangements.

The facts in *Langley* are starkly different from the facts in the present case. In *Langley,* the plaintiff had an unusual and pressing need for uninterrupted service, and he took steps to notify the utility of that need. He also relied on the utility's assurances by choosing not to install backup power, and the utility knew of that fact as well. Unlike in *Hadley* and the present case, the utility in *Langley* understood the particular consequences that would result from a breach, and it accepted the contract anyway.

There were no findings in this case that CNMEC should have known of a particular vulnerability to fire on Sunnyland's part, or that Sunnyland had no backup source of power or water. With neither findings nor evidence of special circumstances, we cannot uphold a judgment for consequential damages. Accordingly, we affirm the Court of Appeals' reversal of the trial court's award of contract damages to Sunnyland. . . .

NOTE: HADLEY'S FORESEEABILITY TEST

Hadley holds that a party is not entitled to recover all consequential damages that flow from a breach of contract. The innocent party can recover only those damages that are reasonably foreseeable. Under tort law, you are liable for all the damages proximately caused by your negligence. Under contract law, you are liable only for the reasonably foreseeable damages that flow from the breach. The basic logic is straightforward. A tort victim has no way to let the tortfeasor know of her special needs, but a party to a contract stands in a different position. She can communicate her special circumstances, and the other can take precautions accordingly. The *Hadley* rule encourages such communication.

But should it be enough for the innocent party merely to put the potential breacher on notice? *Hadley* suggests that once someone tells her contracting opposite of her special circumstances, she is entitled to all the damages that flow from the breach. By virtue of the communication, the other party knows what will happen in the event of breach. This would seem to make the victim's damages in the event of breach "reasonably foreseeable." Once Baxendale knows that the mill will remain shut down until the shaft is returned, he knows that Hadley will lose profits each day the shipment of the shaft is delayed.

In *Globe Refining Co. v. Landa Cotton Oil*, 190 U.S. 540 (1903), Justice Holmes rejects this idea. He holds that merely informing the other party about the consequences of breach is not enough. In his view, a breaching party is liable for unusual damages, even when communicated to her, only if this additional liability is something to which the parties would have agreed had they bargained over the matter explicitly. One needs to ask, in other words, whether assuming liability under special circumstances was part of a "tacit agreement" between the parties.

Courts in New York have accepted Holmes's gloss on *Hadley*. Courts elsewhere, however, have shown little enthusiasm for it. Many courts, such as the one in *Sunnyland*, have resisted *Globe Refining*'s "tacit agreement" test, and offer formulations of *Hadley* that seem to suggest that, when a party will suffer unusually high damages in the event of breach, mere communication is enough to ensure that they can be recovered. It is irrelevant whether the breaching party would have accepted such a risk had there been explicit bargaining over the question.

But one needs to be cautious about taking these opinions at face value. Return to the facts of *Sunnyland*. Would the case in fact have come out differently if Sunnyland had merely told CNMEC that it depended upon electricity for access to water, that it had no back-up generator, and that it therefore depended upon electricity from CNMEC in the event of fire? And what are those people who are told the information supposed to do with it? In an industrialized economy, the person who is given the relevant information (the customer service representative who oversees the account) may not even have the power to ensure that the promisor changes its behavior to account for the unusual risk. Large organizations simply are not structured in a way that allows this. Moreover, making a case turn on what was communicated imposes additional factfinding burdens on the court. As in *Hadley* itself, there will be some ambiguity about what was actually said. We do not know in *Hadley* if the agent was told that the mill would be shut until a new shaft could be made.

For decades, when students take the standard formulations of *Hadley* in subsequent cases at face value, law professors have confronted them with what they call among themselves the "hop-in-buddy" hypothetical. An entrepreneur is rushing to the airport to close a big deal. She hails a cab. She tells the cabdriver that she must catch an airplane or she will lose a million dollar deal. She asks the cabdriver if she will get her to the airport in half an hour in return for an extra $20. The cabdriver confidently says, "Hop in, buddy!" Is the driver liable for a million dollars in damages if, notwithstanding her best efforts, the entrepreneur misses her flight?

Formulations of *Hadley* that make everything turn on foreseeability suggest that courts would hold the cabdriver liable, but, of course, the reality is quite different. It would be an exceedingly odd law of contracts that held a cabdriver fully liable for a rich entrepreneur's failure to get to the airport on time. It is much more plausible to think that her failure leaves her only without the $20 bonus. She should not be responsible for the loss of the deal. The entrepreneur could have prevented the trouble from arising in the first place by planning her day so that she had more time to get to the airport.

Holmes's thought experiment solves the "hop-in-buddy" problem. It takes little imagination to see that there is not the remotest chance any sane cabdriver would agree to pay the entrepreneur a million dollars for failing to get her to the airport in half an hour in exchange for an extra $20. Courts that resist the tacit agreement test do not think otherwise, notwithstanding what their formulations might seem to suggest.

Even when the breaching party is aware of the other's special circumstances, courts usually put limits on the innocent party's ability to recover damages. When the promisee gives notice of special circumstances, the promisor becomes liable only for the reasonably foreseeable damages that can be calculated with certainty and only if the promisee could not have avoided the damages. Moreover, the promisee's damages cannot be grossly disproportionate to the amount paid to the promisor.

The Restatement, Second tracks the Code in formulating the *Hadley* requirement. But observe the limitation in subsection (3), one not found in the first Restatement:

§ 351. Unforeseeability and Related Limitations on Damages

(1) Damages are not recoverable for loss that the party in breach did not have reason to foresee as a probable result of the breach when the contract was made.

(2) Loss may be foreseeable as a probable result of a breach because it follows from the breach

(a) in the ordinary course of events, or

(b) as a result of special circumstance, beyond the ordinary course of events, that the party in breach had reason to know.

(3) A court may limit damages for foreseeable loss by excluding recovery for loss of profits, by allowing recovery only for loss incurred in reliance, or otherwise if it concludes that in the circumstances justice so requires in order to avoid disproportionate compensation.

The *Lamkins* case, among others, is cited to illustrate § 351(3). More on the power of exclusion granted courts by § 351(3) can be found in Harvey, Discretionary Justice Under the Restatement (Second) of Contracts, 67 Cornell L. Rev. 666 (1982). Guidance on the general question of reducing the extent of a promisor's risk is provided in Garvin, Disproportionality and the Law of Consequential Damages: Default Theory and Cognitive Reality, 59 Ohio St. L.J. 339 (1998).

The distinction between "general" and "consequential" damages, though clear in principle, can be elusive at times. Similarly, the line between "incidental" and "consequential" damages is occasionally blurred. Locating that line in goods cases can matter a good deal, for under the UCC consequential damages are a buyer's, not a seller's, remedy. See UCC §§ 2–710 and 2–715.

This has led to disputes over whether a particular item claimed by a seller is properly classified as "incidental" rather than "consequential" damage—e.g., additional interest expense incurred in the interval between the breach and the seller's cover sale, deemed incidental in Afram Export Corp. v. Metallurgiki Halyps, S.A., 772 F.2d 1358 (7th Cir. 1985), in disagreement with the district judge.

Valentine v. General American Credit, Inc.

Supreme Court of Michigan, 1984.
420 Mich. 256, 362 N.W.2d 628.

LEVIN, J. Sharon Valentine seeks to recover mental distress damages arising out of the alleged breach of an employment contract. Valentine claims that, under the contract, she was entitled to job security and the peace of mind that is associated with job security. Because an employment contract providing for job security has a personal element, and breach of such a contract can be expected to result in mental distress, Valentine argues that she should be able to recover mental distress damages. She also asks for exemplary damages.

The Court of Appeals affirmed the decision of the trial court dismissing the claims for mental distress and exemplary damages. We affirm. . . .

Employers and employees [are] free to provide, or not to provide, for job security. Absent a contractual provision for job security, either the employer or the employee may ordinarily terminate an employment contract at any time for any, or no, reason. The obligation which gave rise to this action is based on the agreement of the parties; it is not an obligation imposed on the employer by law. This is an action for breach of contract and not a tort action.

Valentine may not recover mental distress damages for breach of the employment contract, although such damages may have been foreseeable and she might not be "made whole" absent an award of mental distress damages.

Valentine relies on the rule of Hadley v. Baxendale. . . . [T]hat rule has not been applied scrupulously. As stated by Professor Dobbs in his treatise on remedies, a "difficulty in the *Hadley* type case is that the test of foreseeability [i.e., whether damages 'arise naturally'] has little or no meaning. The idea is so readily subject to expansion or contraction that it becomes in fact merely a technical way in which the judges can state their conclusion."[7]

Under the [*Hadley*] rule, literally applied, damages for mental distress would be recoverable for virtually every breach of contract. . . . In

---

[7] Dobbs, Remedies, § 12.3, p. 814. See also Dobbs, § 12.3, p. 804; 5 Corbin, Contracts, § 1007, pp. 70–71.

Stewart v. Rudner, 349 Mich. 459, 84 N.W.2d 816 (1957), this Court said that "all breaches of contract do more or less" cause "vexation and annoyance"; similarly, see Kewin v. Massachusetts Mut. Life Ins. Co., 409 Mich. 401, 295 N.W.2d 50 (1980).

Yet the general rule, with few exceptions, is to "uniformly den[y]" recovery for mental distress damages although they are "foreseeable within the rule of Hadley v. Baxendale." The rule barring recovery of mental distress damages—a gloss on the generality of the [*Hadley*] rule—is fully applicable to an action for breach of an employment contract.

The denial of mental distress damages, although the result is to leave the plaintiff with less than a full recovery, has analogy in the law. The law does not generally compensate for all losses suffered. Recovery is denied for attorney's fees, for mental anguish not accompanied by physical manifestation, and "make-whole" or full recovery has been denied where the cost of performance exceeds the value to the promisee. The courts have not, despite "make whole" generalizations regarding the damages recoverable, attempted to provide compensation for all losses. Instead, specific rules have been established that provide for the calculation of the damages recoverable in particular kinds of actions. In contract actions, the market price is the general standard.

. . . [T]he courts of this state have qualified the general rule, pursuant to which mental distress damages for breach of contract are not recoverable, with a narrow exception. Rather than look to the foreseeability of loss to determine the applicability of the exception, the courts have considered whether the contract "has elements of personality"[19] and whether the damage suffered upon the breach of the agreement is capable of adequate compensation by reference to the terms of the contract. [*Kewin*, 409 Mich. [at] 417, 295 N.W.2d 50.]

The narrow scope of those verbal formulas appears on consideration of the limited situations in which this Court has allowed the recovery of mental distress damages for breach of contract. In Vanderpool v. Richardson, 52 Mich. 336, 17 N.W. 936 (1883), recovery was allowed for breach of a promise to marry. In Stewart v. Rudner, a doctor who failed to fulfill his promise to deliver a child by caesarean section was required to pay mental distress damages. In Miholevich v. Mid-West Mut. Auto Ins. Co., 261 Mich. 495, 246 N.W. 202 (1933), the plaintiff, who was jailed for failure to pay a liability judgment, recovered mental distress damages from an insurer who had failed to pay the judgment.[21]

---

[19] *Stewart*, supra, 349 Mich. [at] 471, 84 N.W.2d 816. In *Stewart*, the Court also said that mental distress damages are recoverable in cases "where a contract is *made* to secure relief from a particular inconvenience or annoyance, or to confer a particular enjoyment." (Emphasis supplied.) See also *Kewin*, supra, in which the Court emphasized that, for mental distress damages to be recoverable, the parties must have formed "a contract *meant* to secure [the] protection" of personal interests. (Emphasis supplied.)

[21] Humphrey v. Michigan United R. Co., 166 Mich. 645, 132 N.W. 447 (1911), concerned the duty of a common carrier to a passenger. This duty is imposed by law without regard to contract.

Loss of a job is not comparable to the loss of a marriage or a child and generally results in estimable monetary damages. In *Miholevich*, the breach resulted in a deprivation of personal liberty.

An employment contract will indeed often have a personal element. Employment is an important aspect of most persons' lives, and the breach of an employment contract may result in emotional distress. The primary purpose in forming such contracts, however, is economic and not to secure the protection of personal interests. The psychic satisfaction of the employment is secondary.

Mental distress damages for breach of contract have not been awarded where there is a market standard by which damages can be adequately determined. Valentine's monetary loss can be estimated with reasonable certainty according to the terms of the contract and the market for, or the market value of, her service. . . . [B]ecause an employment contract is not entered into primarily to secure the protection of personal interests and pecuniary damages can be estimated with reasonable certainty, . . . a person discharged in breach of an employment contract may not recover mental distress damages.

Valentine has not separately argued her exemplary damage claim. In *Kewin*, this Court said that "absent allegation and proof of tortious conduct existing independent of the breach [citation omitted], exemplary damages may not be awarded in common-law actions brought for breach of a commercial contract." Valentine failed to plead the requisite purposeful tortious conduct, and therefore she may not recover exemplary damages.

Affirmed.

Hancock v. Northcutt

808 P.2d 251 (Alaska 1991)

"The view that contracts pertaining to one's dwelling are not among those contracts which, if breached, are particularly likely to result in serious emotional disturbance is reflected in numerous cases. . . . [B]reach of a house construction contract is . . . not so highly personal and laden with emotion as contracts where emotional damages have typically been allowed to stand on their own. . . . Further, the typical damages for breach of house construction contracts can appropriately be calculated in terms of monetary loss. By contrast, the damages in contracts of a more personal nature in which emotional disturbance damages are allowed are usually intangible. Thus, there would ordinarily be only a nominal recovery unless emotional disturbance damages were allowed." [California's highest court, endorsing the *Hancock* position in Erlich v. Menezes, 21 Cal.4th 543, 87 Cal.Rptr.2d 886, 981 P.2d 978 (1999), added: "[T]o permit emotional distress damages [on a contract claim for] negligent construction of a personal residence [would] make the financial risks of construction agreements difficult to predict. Contract damages must be clearly ascertainable in both nature and origin. . . . Moreover, adding an emotional distress component to recovery for construction defects could increase the already prohibitively high cost of housing in California, affect the availability of insurance for builders, and greatly diminish the supply of affordable housing. . . . [And] [p]ermitting damages for emotional distress on the theory that certain contracts carry a lot of emotional freight provides no useful guidance. Courts have carved out a narrow range of exceptions . . . where emotional tranquility is the contract's essence. [This] reflects a fundamental policy choice. A rule which focuses not on the risks contracting parties voluntarily assume but on one party's reaction to inadequate performance, cannot provide any principled limit on liability."]

NOTE: EMOTIONAL DISTRESS DAMAGES

Sharon Valentine had included in her complaint a claim for intentional infliction of mental or emotional distress, which is either an independent tort (indeed, a very young tort in some states, dating from the 1970s) or, if it will not support a recovery "on its own," a standard element of tort damages in limited types of negligence cases—e.g., the mental anguish that accompanies a physical injury caused by another's tortious act. In any case, Valentine apparently did not pursue a tort theory on appeal.

The practice of adding the separate tort of intentional (or, alternatively, negligent) infliction of emotional distress to what is essentially a contract action has increased considerably in recent times. An example is provided by Brown v. Fritz, 108 Idaho 357, 699 P.2d 1371 (1985), where a vendor contracted to sell land a portion of which he had previously sold to another—inadvertently, the vendor claimed, though the jury apparently thought otherwise. The purchaser's recovery below included damages of $2,100 for misrepresentation of the condition of the property (insulation, septic tanks, and boundary lines) and $15,000 for negligent infliction of emotional distress. The trial judge had permitted the latter issue to go to the jury, but refused to let the jury hear the purchaser's claim for punitive damages. Only the award for emotional distress was appealed. The court reversed, holding emotional distress damages unrecoverable in a suit for breach of a contractual relationship:

> [I]t is clear that any damage, pecuniary or emotional, which fell upon [the purchaser] resulted from the negotiations for and the consummation of a contract to convey real property. The damage did not result from an "independent" tort involving a physical or a constructive contact between two parties who were not in a contractual relationship. It did not involve the harassment of another or the libeling or slandering of another. . . . The distinction is far from clear [between] an action based upon breach of contract and an action for tortious breach of contract. . . . [O]ur allowance of an action . . . for negligent infliction of emotional distress resulting from a breach of contract can do little except muddy the already murky waters.

> We note the close parallel between allowable damages for breach of contract under the terminology of "emotional distress" and for punitive damages. . . . We hold that there is no significant, if in fact any, difference between conduct of a defendant which may be seen to justify an award of punitive damages, and conduct which may justify an award of damages for emotional distress. Justification for [emotional distress damages, like punitive damages,] seems to lie in the quantum of outrageousness of the defendant's conduct. . . . We also suggest that the enormous differences that exist between individuals as to their ability to withstand mental stress, frustration, embarrassment or humiliation make next to impossible the application of a reasonableness standard as to plaintiffs whom defendants must expect to encounter in contractual dealings. While we have stated that in tort cases a defendant must take a plaintiff as he is found, including excessive fragility and the like, we know of no such standard applicable to the psychological state of a [contract] plaintiff which a defendant might encounter.

In reversing, the Idaho court concluded that the trial judge should have the benefit of its views on plaintiff's emotional distress claim (again, the only issue appealed). The case was therefore remanded for a new trial solely on the question of punitive damages.

The Restatement, Second § 353 provides: "Recovery for emotional disturbance will be excluded unless the breach also caused bodily harm or the contract or the breach is of a kind that serious emotional disturbance was a particularly likely result." As *Valentine* indicates, exceptions to the general rule against recovery for mental distress have been limited, usually involving contracts between carriers and innkeepers and their passengers and guests, contracts for the carriage and disposition of dead bodies, and contracts for the delivery of messages concerning death. McAfee v. Wright, 651 A.2d 371 (Me. 1994). Under § 353, would George Hawkins have been entitled to emotional distress damages from Dr. McGee? What of a contract to care for one's child or elderly parent?

MindGames, Inc. v. Western Publishing Co.

United States Court of Appeals, Seventh Circuit, 2000.
218 F.3d 652.

POSNER, CHIEF JUDGE. This is a diversity suit for breach of contract, governed by Arkansas law because of a choice of law provision in the contract. The plaintiff, MindGames, was formed in March of 1988 by Larry Blackwell to manufacture and sell an adult board game, "Clever Endeavor," that he had invented. The first games were shipped in the fall of 1989 and by the end of the year, 75 days later, 30,000 had been sold. In March of 1990, MindGames licensed the game to the defendant, Western, a major marketer of games. Western had marketed the very successful adult board games "Trivial Pursuit" and "Pictionary" and thought

"Clever Endeavor" might be as successful. The license contract, on which this suit is premised, required Western to pay MindGames a 15 percent royalty on all games sold. The contract was by its terms to remain in effect until the end of January of 1993, or for another year if before then Western paid MindGames at least $1.5 million in the form of royalties due under the contract or otherwise, and for subsequent years as well if Western paid an annual renewal fee of $300,000.

During the first year of the contract, Western sold 165,000 copies of "Clever Endeavor" and paid MindGames $600,000 in royalties. After that, sales fell precipitously (though we're not told by how much) but the parties continued under the contract through January 31, 1994, though Western did not pay the $900,000 ($1.5 million minus $600,000) that the contract would have required it to pay in order to be entitled to extend the contract for a year after its expiration. In February of 1994 the parties finally parted. Later that year MindGames brought this suit, which seeks $900,000, plus lost royalties of some $40 million that MindGames claims it would have earned had not Western failed to carry out the promotional obligations that the contract imposed on it, plus $300,000 on the theory that Western renewed the contract for a third year, beginning in February of 1994; Western sold off its remaining inventory of "Clever Endeavor" in that year.

The district court granted summary judgment for Western, holding that the contract did not entitle MindGames to a renewal fee and that Arkansas's "new business" rule barred any recovery of lost profits. 944 F.Supp. 754 (E.D.Wis. 1996); 995 F.Supp. 949 (E.D.Wis. 1998). Although the victim of a breach of contract is entitled to nominal damages, MindGames does not seek them; and so if it is not entitled to either type of substantial damages that it seeks, judgment was correctly entered for Western. By not seeking nominal damages, incidentally, MindGames may have lost a chance to obtain significant attorneys' fees, to which Arkansas law entitles a prevailing party in a breach of contract case.

The rejection of MindGames' claim to the renewal fee for the second year (and *a fortiori* the third) was clearly correct. . . .

The more difficult issue is MindGames' right to recover lost profits for Western's alleged breach of its duty to promote "Clever Endeavor." A minority of states have or purport to have a rule barring a new business, as distinct from an established one, from obtaining damages for lost profits as a result of a tort or a breach of contract. The rule of Hadley v. Baxendale often prevents the victim of a breach of contract from obtaining lost profits, but that rule is not invoked here. Neither the "new business" rule nor the rule of [*Hadley*] stands for the *general* proposition that lost profits are never a recoverable item of damages in a tort or breach of contract case.

Arkansas is said to be one of the "new business" rule states on the strength of a case decided by the state's supreme court many years ago. The appellants in Marvell Light & Ice Co. v. General Electric Co., 162

Ark. 467, 259 S.W. 741 (1924), sought to recover the profits that they claimed to have lost as a result of a five and a half month delay in the delivery of icemaking machinery; the delay, the appellants claimed, had forced them to delay putting their ice factory into operation. The court concluded, however, that because there was no indication "that the manufacture and sale of ice by appellants was an established business so that proof of the amount lost on account of the delay . . . might be made with reasonable certainty," "the anticipated profits of the new business are too remote, speculative, and uncertain to support a judgment for their loss." It quoted an earlier decision in which another court had said that "he who is prevented from embarking in [*sic*—must mean 'on'] a new business can recover no profits, because there are no provable data of past business from which the fact that anticipated profits would have been realized can be legally deduced." Central Coal & Coke Co. v. Hartman, 111 Fed. 96, 99 (8th Cir. 1901). That quotation is taken to have made Arkansas a "new business" state, although the rest of the *Marvell* opinion indicates that the court was concerned that the anticipated profits of the *particular* new business at issue, rather than of every new business, were too speculative to support an award of damages. On its facts, moreover, *Marvell* was a classic [*Hadley*] type of case—in fact virtually a rerun of *Hadley*, except that the appellants alleged that they had notified the seller of the icemaking machinery of the damages that they would suffer if delivery was delayed, and the seller had agreed to be liable for those damages. The decision is puzzling in light of that allegation; it is doubly puzzling because, assuming that by the time of the trial the ice factory was up and running, it should not have been difficult to compute the damages that the appellants had lost by virtue of the five and a half month delay in placing the factory in operation. Presumably it would have had five and a half months of additional profits.

Marvell has never been overruled; and federal courts ordinarily take a nonoverruled decision of the highest court of the state whose law governs a controversy by virtue of the applicable choice of law rule to be conclusive on the law of the state. But this is a matter of practice or presumption, not of rule. The rule is that in a case in federal court in which state law provides the rule of decision, the federal court must predict how the state's highest court would decide the case, and decide it the same way. Law, Holmes said, in a controversial definition that is, however, a pretty good summary of how courts apply the law of other jurisdictions, is just a prediction of what the courts of that jurisdiction would do with the case if they got their hands on it. Holmes, "The Path of the Law," 10 Harv.L.Rev. 457, 461 (1897). Since state courts like federal courts do occasionally overrule their decisions, there will be occasional, though rare, instances in which the best prediction of what the state's highest court will do is that it will *not* follow its previous decision.

That is the best prediction in this case. *Marvell* was decided more than three quarters of a century ago, and the "new business" rule which it has been thought to have announced has not been mentioned in a published Arkansas case since. The opinion doesn't make a lot of sense on its facts, as we have seen, and the Eighth Circuit case on which it relied has long been superseded in that circuit. The Arkansas cases decided since *Marvell* that deal with damages issues exhibit a liberal approach to the estimation of damages that is inconsistent with a flat rule denying damages for lost profits to all businesses that are not well established. Jim Halsey Co. v. Bonar, 284 Ark. 461, 683 S.W.2d 898, 902–03 (1985); Tremco, Inc. v. Valley Aluminum Products Corp., 38 Ark.App. 143, 831 S.W.2d 156, 158 (1992); Ozark Gas Transmission Systems v. Barclay, 10 Ark.App. 152, 662 S.W.2d 188, 192 (1983). The *Ozark* decision, for example, allowed an orchard farmer to recover for the damages to a *new* orchard. The "new business" rule has, moreover, been abandoned in most states that once followed it, and it seems to retain little vitality even in states like Virginia, which purport to employ the hard-core per se approach.

Western tries to distinguish *Ozark* by pointing to the fact that the plaintiff there was an established orchard farmer, albeit the particular orchard represented a new venture for him. This effort to distinguish that case brings into view the primary objection to the "new business" rule, an objection of such force as to explain its decline and make it unlikely that Arkansas would follow it if the occasion for its supreme court to choose arose. The objection has to do with the difference between *rule* and *standard* as methods of legal governance. A rule singles out one or a few facts and makes it or them conclusive of legal liability; a standard permits consideration of all or at least most facts that are relevant to the standard's rationale. A speed limit is a rule; negligence is a standard. Rules have the advantage of being definite and of limiting factual inquiry but the disadvantage of being inflexible, even arbitrary, and thus overinclusive, or of being underinclusive and thus opening up loopholes (or of being *both* over-and underinclusive!). Standards are flexible, but vague and open-ended; they make business planning difficult, invite the sometimes unpredictable exercise of judicial discretion, and are more costly to adjudicate—and yet when based on lay intuition they may actually be more intelligible, and thus in a sense clearer and more precise, to the persons whose behavior they seek to guide than rules would be. No sensible person supposes that rules are always superior to standards, or vice versa, though some judges are drawn to the definiteness of rules and others to the flexibility of standards. But that is psychology; the important point is that some activities are better governed by rules, others by standards. States that have rejected the "new business" rule are content to control the award of damages for lost profits by means of a standard—damages may not be awarded on the basis of wild conjecture, they must be proved to a reasonable certainty—that is applicable to proof of damages generally. The "new business" rule is an attempt now widely regarded as failed to control the award of such damages by means of a rule.

The rule doesn't work because it manages to be at once vague and arbitrary. One reason is that the facts that it makes determinative, "new," "business," and "profits," are not facts, but rather are the conclusions of a reasoning process that is based on the rationale for the rule and that as a result turns the rule into an implicit standard. What, for example, is a "new" business? What, for that matter, is a "business"? And are royalties what the rule means by "profits"? MindGames was formed more than a year before it signed the license agreement with Western, and it sold 30,000 games in the six months between the first sales and the signing of the contract. MindGames' only "business," moreover, was the licensing of intellectual property. An author who signs a contract with a publisher for the publication of his book would not ordinarily be regarded as being engaged in a "business," or his royalties or advance described as "profits." He would be surprised to learn that if he sued for unpaid royalties he could not get them because his was a "new business." Suppose a first-time author sued a publisher for an accounting, and the only issue was how many copies the publisher had sold. Under the "new business" rule as construed by Western, the author could not recover his lost royalties even though there was no uncertainty about what he had lost. So construed and applied, the rule would have no relation to its rationale, which is to prevent the award of speculative damages.

Western goes even further, arguing that even if it, Western, a well-established firm, were the plaintiff, it could not recover its lost profits because the sale of "Clever Endeavor" was a new business. On this construal of the rule, "business" does not mean the enterprise; it means any business activity. So Western's sale of a new game is a new business, yet we know from the *Ozark* decision that an orchard farmer's operation of a new orchard is an old business.

The rule could be made sensible by appropriate definition of its terms, but we find it hard to see what would be gained, given the existence of the serviceable and familiar standard of excessive speculativeness. The rule may have made sense at one time; the reduction in decision costs and uncertainty brought about by avoiding a speculative mire may have swamped the increased social costs resulting from the systematically inadequate damages that a "new business" rule decrees. But today the courts have become sufficiently sophisticated in analyzing lost-earnings claims, and have accumulated sufficient precedent on the standard of undue speculativeness in damages awards, to make the balance of costs and benefits tip against the rule. In any event we are far in this case, in logic as well as time, from the ice factory whose opening was delayed by the General Electric Co. We greatly doubt that there is a "new business" rule in the common law of Arkansas today, but if there is it surely does not extend so far beyond the facts of the only case in which the rule was ever invoked to justify its invocation here. There is no authority for, and no common sense appeal to, such an extension.

But that leaves us with the question of undue speculation in estimating damages. Abrogation of the "new business" rule does not produce a free-for-all. What makes MindGames' claim of lost royalties indeed dubious is not any "new business" rule but the fact that the success of a board game, like that of a book or movie, is so uncertain. Here newness enters into judicial consideration of the damages claim not as a rule but as a factor in applying the standard. Just as a start-up company should not be permitted to obtain pie-in-the-sky damages upon allegations that it was snuffed out before it could begin to operate (unlike the ice factory in *Marvell*, which did begin production, albeit a little later than planned), capitalizing fantasized earnings into a huge present value sought as damages, so a novice writer should not be permitted to obtain damages from his publisher on the premise that but for the latter's laxity he would have had a bestseller, when only a tiny fraction of new books achieve that success. . . .

This is not to suggest that damages for lost earnings on intellectual property can never be recovered; that "entertainment damages" are not recoverable in breach of contract cases. That would just be a variant of the discredited "new business" rule. What is important is that Blackwell had no track record when he created "Clever Endeavor." He could not point to other games that he had invented and that had sold well. He was not in the position of the bestselling author who can prove from his past success that his new book, which the defendant failed to promote, would have been likely—not certain, of course—to have enjoyed a success comparable to that of the average of his previous books if only it had been promoted as promised. That would be like a case of a new business launched by an entrepreneur with a proven track record.

In the precontract sales period and the first year of the contract a total of 195,000 copies of "Clever Endeavor" were sold; then sales fizzled. The public is fickle. It is possible that if Western had marketed the game more vigorously, more would have been sold, but an equally if not more plausible possibility is that the reason that Western didn't market the game more vigorously was that it correctly sensed that demand had dried up.

Even if that alternative is rejected, we do not see how the number of copies that would have been sold but for the alleged breach could be determined given the evidence presented in the summary judgment proceedings (a potentially important qualification, of course); and so MindGames' proof of damages is indeed excessively speculative. Those proceedings were completed with no evidence having been presented from which a rational trier of fact could conclude *on this record* that some specific quantity, or for that matter some broad but bounded range of alternative estimates, of copies of "Clever Endeavor" would have been sold had Western honored the contract. MindGames obtained $600,000 in royalties on sales of 165,000 copies of the game, implying that Western would have had to sell more than 10 million copies to generate the $40 million in lost royalties that MindGames seeks to recover.

When the breach occurred, MindGames should have terminated the contract and sought distribution by other means. The fact that it did not do so—that so far as appears it has made no effort to market "Clever Endeavor" since the market for the game collapsed in 1991—is telling evidence of a lack of commercial promise unrelated to Western's conduct.

Although Western in its brief in this court spent most of its time misguidedly defending the "new business" rule, clinging to *Marvell* for dear life (a case seemingly on point, however vulnerable, is a security blanket that no lawyer feels comfortable without), it did argue that in any event MindGames' claim for lost royalties was too speculative to ground an award of damages for that loss. The argument was brief but not so brief as to fail to put MindGames on notice of a possible alternative ground for upholding the district court's judgment; we may of course affirm an award of summary judgment on any ground that has not been forfeited or waived in the district court. MindGames did not respond to the argument in its reply brief. It pointed to no evidence from which lost royalties could be calculated to even a rough approximation. We find its silence eloquent and Western's argument compelling, and so the judgment in favor of Western is

Affirmed.

ASK Chemicals, LP v. Computer Packages, Inc.

United States Court of Appeals, Sixth Circuit, 2014.
593 Fed. Appx. 506.

BOGGS, CIRCUIT JUDGE. . . . In 1997, Ashland, a chemical company, applied for a Japanese patent [the '168 patent] to protect the method by which it produced a particular type of riser sleeve that was unique in its employment of a "cold-box" manufacturing process. Riser sleeves are used throughout the foundry industry to improve the quality of metal castings. As the liquid metal cools in the hollow of a casting, it solidifies and shrinks. The last part of the casting to cool within the hollow will often form a void where remaining shrinkage occurs. The result is a defective metal casting. Riser sleeves, essentially metal reservoirs external to the casting, prevent this potential defect by providing additional liquid metal during cooling so that voids form in the riser, not in the casting itself.

The '168 patent issued on April 30, 2002 and was assigned by Ashland to ASK on November 30, 2010.

A version of the riser sleeve, ASK's "Exactcast" riser sleeve, is covered by a number of European and American patents. Although Exactcast riser sleeves have sold successfully in both the Americas and Europe, ASK's (and its predecessor's) efforts in Japan were less fruitful: a factory fire in 2003 put an end to its initial penetration of the Japanese market and ASK did not again focus on Japan until 2008, when it began developing Japanese clients, a long and arduous process requiring the commitment of significant time, effort, and money. At the time the '168 patent lapsed, ASK had no sales of related technology in Japan. . . .

Ashland, while still the holder of the '168 patent, had hired CPI to pay the annual fees due on its patents in Japan. After the assignment of the '168 patent to ASK, CPI continued in its role maintaining the patent. Had the patent been properly maintained under Japanese law, it would have expired on March 21, 2017. But the patent was not maintained. CPI failed to make the ninth necessary payment, due in January 2010. Six months later, at the end of Japan's statutory grace period, the patent lapsed irretrievably.

On July 20, 2012, ASK filed a complaint against CPI in the United States District Court for the Southern District of Ohio, requesting compensatory, direct, expectancy, and prospective damages under two counts: breach of contract and breach of implied-in-fact contract. CPI filed an answer on April 5, 2012, in which it admitted that it had failed to pay the required fees and that, as a result of its failure, the patent lapsed. . . .

Under Ohio law, consequential damages, including damages for lost profits, are available in suits for breach of contract. A plaintiff can recover lost profits if it can show that "(1) profits were within the contemplation of the parties at the time the contract was made, (2) the loss of the profits is the probable result of the breach of contract, and (3) the profits are not remote and speculative and may be shown with reasonable certainty." City of Gahanna v. Eastgate Props., Inc., 36 Ohio St.3d 65, 521 N.E.2d 814, 817 (1988). However, in order for a plaintiff to recover lost profits, "the *amount* of the lost profits, as well as their existence, must be demonstrated with reasonable certainty." Id. at 818 (emphasis added). In other words, damages are not awarded merely on a plaintiff's assertion "that it would have made a particular amount of profits, but [the plaintiff] must prove lost profits with calculations based on facts." UZ Engineered Prods. Co. v. Midwest Motor Supply Co., Inc., 147 Ohio App.3d 382, 770 N.E.2d 1068, 1083 (2001).

We do not address the question of whether lost-profits damages *never* may be proven by comparison to a plaintiff's performance in an existing market. But in the case of ASK's complaint, neither of the first two elements is in doubt. Profits were certainly in the contemplation of the parties at the time the contract was made—CPI was, after all, in the business of administering the patent-management programs of intellectual-property owners. Similarly, there is no dispute over the second element, causation. If ASK had suffered lost profits as the result of the lapse of the '168 patent, it would have been because of CPI's (admitted) failure to pay the required annual payment.

The parties dispute only the final requirement, that the lost profits be shown to a "reasonable certainty." In demonstrating lost profits, Ohio law does not require plaintiffs to prove the amounts lost with absolute precision. The evidence "need only be reasonable, not specific." Charles R. Combs Trucking, Inc. v. Int'l Harvester Co., 12 Ohio St.3d 241, 466 N.E.2d 883, 887 (1984). But demonstrating lost profits to a reasonable certainty requires the use of detailed evidence, for example, "expert testimony, economic and financial data, market surveys and analyses, business records of similar enterprises, and the like." AGF, Inc. v. Great Lakes Heat Treating Co., 51 Ohio St.3d 177, 555 N.E.2d 634, 640 (1990). The evidence submitted must be sufficient to support calculations establishing the amount of lost profits: "Unless the figure is supported by calculations based on facts available or in evidence, the courts will properly reject it as speculative or uncertain." Endersby v. Schneppe, 73 Ohio App.3d 212, 596 N.E.2d 1081, 1084 (1991).

A review of four Ohio cases—one of which established lost profits and three of which did not—demonstrates what constitutes non-speculative, reasonably certain lost profits. First, lost profits were awarded under Ohio law in Michigan Millers Mut. Ins. Co. v. Christian, 153 Ohio App.3d 299, 794 N.E.2d 68 (2003), a case in which the evidence demonstrated the amount of lost profits to a reasonable certainty. Among the types of evidence were testimony regarding market conditions, records of company earnings during the time period in question, records of company earnings during identical periods in the preceding years, and compilations of customer receipts and business transaction records. From this evidence, a simple computation comparing the profits of one period with the profits of another period at the same time of year in the same location in the same enterprise allowed the establishment of lost profits to a reasonable certainty.

Second, and in contrast, in *Homes by Calkins,* the plaintiff failed to demonstrate lost profits to a reasonable certainty because the claim was necessarily unprovable and speculative. In a suit for damages based on a vendor's failure to have a deed restriction removed, the plaintiff, a real-estate developer, was delayed in building a development by the eleven months necessary to clear the property's title following sale. Reviewing his evidence, the trial court found, and the Court of Appeals of Ohio affirmed, that since neither the plaintiff nor the court "could reasonably estimate how many units [the plaintiff] could have sold, if it could have sold any," the plaintiff failed to demonstrate lost profits to a reasonable certainty. Homes by Calkins, Inc. v. Fisher, 92 Ohio App.3d 262, 634 N.E.2d 1039, 1045 (1993). Since the demonstration of lost profits in a new business is necessarily more speculative, such demonstrations "*receive greater scrutiny* because there is no track record upon which to base an estimate." Andrew v. Power Mktg. Direct, Inc., ___ Ohio App. ___, 978 N.E.2d 974, 992 (2012).

Third, in Ace Vending Co. v. Davidson, 8 Ohio App.3d 328, 457 N.E.2d 341 (1982), the plaintiff failed to demonstrate its lost profits to a reasonable certainty because the evidence it submitted was based on an inapposite comparison. Ace Vending had several vending machines that were unlawfully detained after the closing of the pizzeria in which they were installed. The evidence submitted consisted of little more than the testimony of Ace Vending's office manager as to the average amount of money per week made by the machines during the last two months the pizzeria was open. Since the pizzeria had gone out of business, however, the court rejected this evidence because, following the pizzeria's closing, the lost profits would necessarily have been limited to the amount of money that the machines would have made *at another location* had they been timely returned.

Finally, in Kosier v. DeRosa, 169 Ohio App.3d 150, 862 N.E.2d 159 (2006), the court found that the plaintiff failed to demonstrate lost profits where his calculations lacked necessary data. In a suit for breach of contract to install new flooring into a house, the plaintiff submitted evidence as to his labor costs, but provided no information as to how many hours of work would have been required to complete the contract. The Ohio Court of Appeals held that, in the absence of such evidence, it was not possible to establish the amount of profits lost to a reasonable certainty.

In this case, ASK's evidentiary submissions suffer from each of the defects outlined in the three Ohio cases above. Like the plaintiff in *Homes by Calkins,* ASK had no track record of riser-sleeve sales in Japan aside from the decade-old effort that had been abandoned following the factory fire. The lack of any reliable track record subjects ASK's lost-profits calculations to stricter inquiry and increases the difficulty of determining a reasonably accurate figure for lost profits. Though ASK had again taken the initial steps necessary to reintroduce their riser sleeves into Japan (they sought certification from several potential clients and sold test products), they still had almost no sales history and thus any attempt to demonstrate lost profits using riser-sleeve sale projections alone would suffer from a lack of hard data.

ASK's evidence was also like that in *Ace Vending* because it sought to establish profits in the Japanese market based on an inapposite comparison with sales in Europe and North America. Having provided sales figures only for North America and Europe and providing virtually no relevant market research on Japan, ASK sought to establish potential future sales and profits by analogizing sales in one region of the world with potential sales in another. Such extrapolation, without more, is insufficient to establish lost profits to a reasonable certainty.

Lastly, ASK's evidentiary submissions appear to suffer from the same basic fault as in *Kosier* because the submissions lacked necessary data. As the plaintiff in *Kosier* failed to provide one of the basic elements necessary to its calculations (the number of hours of labor performed), ASK has failed to give basic data about the Japanese market that would be necessary to make reasonably certain projections of potential future profits. As the district court pointed out, without data on the size of the Japanese market or ASK's sales and direct costs, it would be virtually impossible to settle on a figure for ASK's lost profits.

Were the demonstration of the *existence* of lost profits all that was necessary to overcome a motion for summary judgment, ASK may have had success. Based on the evidence submitted, a jury could very well find that ASK had lost profits because of CPI's breach. On appeal, ASK provides a painstaking roster of all the evidence placed in the record, including marketing surveys, its 1998 marketing plan, its regional market-share calculations, European and American licenses, and projections of capital costs for the building of a new factory. However, since there is no way that the evidence submitted could lead a court to determine the *amount* of lost profits to a reasonable certainty, there is no genuine dispute of material fact for a jury. ASK's evidentiary submissions, even though voluminous, do little to establish a specific sum necessary to meet the standard of a "reasonable certainty."

Freund v. Washington Square Press, Inc.

34 N.Y.2d 379, 357 N.Y.S.2d 857, 314 N.E.2d 419 (1974)

Plaintiff author and college teacher granted defendant exclusive rights to publish and sell in book form a manuscript on modern drama. The agreement called for Publisher to pay Author a $2,000 advance plus royalties. In addition, publisher agreed to publish a hardbound edition if it did not terminate the agreement within sixty days of receipt of the manuscript. Publisher paid the advance in full but merged thereafter with another company and ceased publishing hardbound books altogether. Though it never terminated the agreement as the contract allowed, Publisher refused to publish the book in any form. Author sued, seeking damages and specific performance. The trial court denied the request for specific performance but identified three categories of damages possibly arising from the breach: (1) delay in academic promotion; (2) loss of royalties that would have been earned; and (3) the cost of publication if plaintiff had made his own arrangements to publish. Ultimately, it found no delay in advancement and denied recovery of lost royalties without discussion. The court ruled, however, that plaintiff was entitled to that amount of money that would allow him to publish the manuscript, which it assessed at $10,000. The intermediate appellate court affirmed (3 to 2), and Publisher appealed. *Held*, plaintiff may recover nominal damages only. The law, so far as is possible, "attempts to secure to the injured party the benefit of his bargain. . . ." The lower court's analogy to a breach of construction contract was therefore inapposite. In that case, "[t]he value of the promised performance to the owner is the properly constructed building." But here, "unlike the typical construction contract, the value to the plaintiff of the promised performance—publication—was a percentage of sales of the books published and not the books themselves. Had the plaintiff contracted for the printing, binding and delivery of a number of hardbound copies of his manuscript, to be sold or disposed of as he wished, then perhaps the construction analogy, and measurement of damages by the cost of replacement or completion, would have some application." Because the royalties plaintiff would have realized were not ascertained with adequate certainty, "the order of the Appellate Division should be modified to the extent of reducing the damage award of $10,000 for the cost of publication to six cents, but with costs and disbursements to the plaintiff."

Fera v. Village Plaza, Inc.

396 Mich. 639, 242 N.W.2d 372 (1976)

Plaintiffs signed a 10-year lease for a "book and bottle" shop in defendants' proposed shopping center; the rent was a monthly minimum of $1,000, plus a percentage of annual receipts exceeding $240,000. The center eventually opened despite problems and delays, but plaintiffs' space was given to another tenant. Defendants' offer of alternative space was refused by plaintiffs as unsuitable for their planned venture. In the suit that followed, a jury awarded plaintiffs $200,000 for profits prevented by the breach. An intermediate appellate court, believing that a new business is barred from recovering lost profits and finding that plaintiffs' proofs of anticipated profits were "entirely speculative," ordered a new trial on damages. *Held*, the trial court's judgment based on the jury's verdict should be reinstated. Earlier decisions indicating reluctance to award an untried business lost profits "should not be read as stating a rule of law which prevents *every* new business from recovering" such damages. As Corbin has observed, the problem is not with profits as such but with the requirement that damages be proved with "certainty," that a plaintiff "lay a basis for a reasonable estimate of the extent of [harm], measured in money." Here, "there were days and days of testimony. . . The proofs ranged from no profits to [plaintiffs' own testimony of $270,000] over a ten-year period. . . . The weaknesses of plaintiffs' specially prepared budget were thoroughly explored on cross-examination. . . . The jury weighed the conflicting testimony and determined that plaintiffs were entitled to damages of $200,000. . . . 'Where injury to some degree is found, we do not preclude recovery for lack of precise proof. We do the best we can with what we have. . . . Particularly is this true where it is defendant's own act or neglect that has caused the imprecision.' While we might have found plaintiffs' proofs lacking had we been [the jury], that is not the standard of review we employ."

Restatement of Contracts, Second

§ 352. Uncertainty as a Limitation on Damages

Comment: . . .

b. Proof of profits. The difficulty of proving lost profits varies greatly with the nature of the transaction. If, for example, it is the seller who claims lost profit on the ground that the buyer's breach has caused him to lose a sale, proof of lost profit will ordinarily not be difficult. If, however, it is the buyer who claims lost profit on the ground that the seller's breach has caused him loss in other transactions, the task of proof is harder. Furthermore, if the transaction is more complex and extends into the future, as where the seller agrees to furnish all of the buyer's requirements over a period of years, proof of the loss of profits caused by the seller's breach is more difficult. If the breach prevents the injured party from carrying on a well-established business, the resulting loss of profits can often be proved with sufficient certainty. Evidence of past performance will form the basis for a reasonable prediction as to the future. . . . However, if the business is a new one or if it is a speculative one that is subject to great fluctuations in volume, costs or prices, proof will be more difficult. Nevertheless, damages may be established with reasonable certainty with the aid of expert testimony, economic and financial data, market surveys and analyses, business records of similar enterprises, and the like.

SECTION 4. THE RESTITUTION ALTERNATIVE

INTRODUCTORY NOTE

The prevailing theory of contract damages aims to give the injured party the money equivalent of the promised performance. This means that damage rules, as they are usually phrased, protect both the expectation and the reliance interests; the defaulter, it is commonly said, must account for "gains prevented" as well as "losses caused," the latter because the nondefaulter normally will have acted in reliance on the contract. Thus, the court in Rockingham County v. Luten Bridge Co. embraced familiar doctrine in measuring damages by "labor and materials expended and expense incurred in the part performance of the contract, prior to its repudiation, plus the profit which would have been realized if it had been carried out in accordance with its terms."

The question raised by the present section is whether there are alternatives to the full enforcement of expectations through a money substitute for the promised performance.

Boone v. Coe

Court of Appeals of Kentucky, 1913.
153 Ky. 233, 154 S.W. 900.

CLAY, C. Plaintiffs, W.H. Boone and J.T. Coe, brought this action against defendant, J.F. Coe, to recover certain damages, alleged to have resulted from defendant's breach of a parol contract of lease for one year to commence at a future date. . . [D]efendant was the owner of a large and valuable farm in Ford County, Tex. Plaintiffs were farmers, and were living with their families in Monroe County, Ky. In the fall of 1909 defendant made a verbal contract with plaintiffs, whereby he rented to them his farm in Texas for a period of 12 months, to commence from the date of plaintiffs' arrival at defendant's farm. Defendant agreed that if plaintiffs would leave their said homes and businesses in Kentucky, and with their families, horses, and wagons, move to defendant's farm in Texas, and take charge of, manage, and cultivate same in wheat, corn, and cotton for the 12 months next following plaintiffs' arrival at said farm, the defendant would have a dwelling completed on said farm and ready for occupancy upon their arrival, which dwelling plaintiffs would occupy as a residence during the period of said tenancy. Defendant also agreed that he would furnish necessary material at a convenient place on said farm out of which to erect a good and commodious stock and grain barn, to be used by plaintiffs. The petition further alleges that plaintiffs were to cultivate certain portions of the farm, and were to receive certain portions of the crops raised, and that plaintiffs, in conformity with their said agreement, did move from Kentucky to the farm in Texas, and carried with them their families, wagons, horses, and camping outfit, and in going to Texas they traveled for a period of 55 days. It is also charged that defendant broke his contract, in that he failed to have ready and completed on the farm a dwelling house in which plaintiffs and their families could move, and also failed to furnish the necessary material for the erection of a suitable barn; that on December 6th defendant refused to permit plaintiffs to occupy the house and premises, and failed and refused to permit them to cultivate the land or any part thereof, that on the ___ day of December, 1909, they started for their home in Kentucky, and arrived there after traveling for a period of 4 days. It is charged that plaintiffs spent in going to Texas, in cash, the sum of $150; that the loss of time to plaintiffs and their teams in making the trip to Texas was reasonably worth $8 a day for a period of 55 days, or the sum of $440; that the loss of time to them and their teams during the period they remained in Texas was $8 a day for 22 days, or $176; that they paid out in actual cash for transportation for themselves, families, and teams from Texas to Kentucky the sum of $211.80; that the loss of time to them and their teams in making the last-named trip was reasonably worth the sum of $100; that in abandoning and giving up their homes and business in Kentucky they had been damaged in the sum of $150, making a total damage of $1,387.80 for which judgment was asked. Defendant's demurrer to the petition was sustained and the petition dismissed. Plaintiffs appeal. . . .

The statute of frauds (§ 470, sub-secs. 6 & 7 (Ky. Statutes)) provides as follows: "No action shall be brought to charge any person: 6. Upon any contract for the sale of real estate, or any lease thereof, for longer term than one year; nor 7. Upon any agreement which is not to be performed within one year from the making thereof, unless the promise, contract, agreement, representation, assurance or ratification, or some memorandum or note thereof be in writing, and signed by the party to be charged therewith, or by his authorized agent; but the consideration need not be expressed in the writing; it may be proved when necessary, or disproved by parol or other evidence." A parol lease of land for one year, to commence at a future date, is within the statute. Greenwood v. Strother, 91 Ky. 482, 16 S.W. 138.

The question sharply presented is: May plaintiffs recover for expenses incurred and time lost on the faith of a contract that is unenforceable under the statute of frauds? . . . It is the general rule that damages cannot be recovered, for violation of a contract within the statute of frauds. . . .

To this general rule there are certain well-recognized exceptions. . . . [I]t has been held that, where services have been rendered during the life of another, on the promise that the person rendering the service should receive at the death of the person served a legacy, and the contract so made is within the statute of frauds, a reasonable compensation may be recovered for the services actually rendered. It has also been held that the vendee of land under a parol contract is entitled to recover any portion of the purchase money he may have paid, and is also entitled to compensation for improvements. . . .

And under a contract for personal services within the statute an action may be maintained on a quantum meruit. [Myers v. Korb, 50 S.W. 1108, 21 Ky.Law Rep. 163.] The doctrine of these cases proceeds upon the theory that the defendant has actually received some benefits from the acts of part performance; and the law therefore implies a promise to pay. In 29 Am. & Eng. Ency. 836, the rule is thus stated: "Although part performance by one of the parties to a contract within the statute of frauds will not, at law, entitle such party to recover upon the contract itself, he may nevertheless recover for money paid by him, or property delivered, or services rendered in accordance with and upon the faith of the contract. The law will raise an implied promise on the part of the other party to pay for what has been done in the way of part performance. But this right of recovery is not absolute. The plaintiff is entitled to compensation only under such circumstances as would warrant a recovery in case there was no express contract; and hence it must appear that the defendant has actually received, or will receive, some benefit from the acts of part performance. It is immaterial that the plaintiff may have suffered a loss because he is unable to enforce his contract." . . .

In the case under consideration the plaintiffs merely sustained a loss. Defendant received no benefit. Had he received a benefit, the law would imply an obligation to pay therefor. Having received no benefit, no obligation to pay is implied. The statute says that the contract defendant made with plaintiffs is unenforceable. Defendant therefore had the legal right to decline to carry it out. To require him to pay plaintiffs for losses and expenses incurred on the faith of the contract, without any benefit accruing to him, would, in effect, uphold a contract upon which the statute expressly declares no action shall be brought. The statute was enacted for the purpose of preventing frauds and perjuries. That it is a valuable statute is shown by the fact that similar statutes are in force in practically all, if not all, of the states of the Union. Being a valuable statute, the purposes of the lawmakers in its enactment should not be defeated by permitting recoveries in cases to which its provisions were intended to apply.

The contrary rule was announced by this court [in] McDaniel v. Hutcherson, 136 Ky. 412, 124 S.W. 384. There the plaintiff lived [in] Illinois. The defendant owned a farm in Mercer County, Ky. The defendant agreed with plaintiff that if plaintiff and his family would come to Kentucky and live with defendant the defendant would furnish the plaintiff a home during defendant's life, and upon his death would give plaintiff his farm. It was held that, although the contract was within the statute of frauds, plaintiff could recover his reasonable expenses in moving to Kentucky, and reasonable compensation for loss sustained in giving up his business elsewhere. Upon reconsideration of the question involved, we conclude that the doctrine announced in that case is not in accord with the weight of authority, and should be no longer adhered to. It is therefore overruled.

Judgment affirmed.

NOTE

In all of our states there are statutes modeled on the English Statute of Frauds of 1677. The key phrases in the original statute were that "no action shall be brought . . . whereby to charge the defendant . . . unless the agreement upon which such action shall be brought, or some memorandum or note thereof, shall be in writing, and signed by the party to be charged therewith, or some other person thereunto by him lawfully authorized." There are five classes of agreements for which this requirement is commonly imposed:

(1) contracts for the sale of an interest in land;

(2) contracts for the sale of goods for a price exceeding a specified amount ($500 or more in the Uniform Commercial Code, § 2–201);

(3) promises "to answer for the debt, default or miscarriage of another" (i.e., suretyship or guaranty);

(4) contracts "not to be performed within one year";

(5) contracts in consideration of marriage.

A discussion of the history and the general scope and operation of the statute of frauds can be found in the Appendix. The general aim of the statute, it seems, is to encourage parties to memorialize certain types of agreements by putting them in writing. The court in Boone v. Coe appears to have concluded that the lease agreement in question fell within the "not-to-be-performed-within-one-year" clause of the Kentucky statute, if not the land clause, which included long-term leases, as well. You should consult the Appendix on these two clauses generally.

Mobil Oil Exploration & Producing Southeast, Inc. v. United States

Supreme Court of the United States, 2000.
530 U.S. 604, 120 S.Ct. 2423.

BREYER, J. Two oil companies, petitioners here, seek restitution of $156 million they paid the Government in return for lease contracts giving them rights to explore for and develop oil off the North Carolina coast. The rights were not absolute, but were conditioned on the companies' obtaining a set of further governmental permissions. The companies claim that the Government repudiated the contracts when it denied them certain elements of the permission-seeking opportunities that the contracts had promised. We agree that the Government broke its promise; it repudiated the contracts; and it must give the companies their money back. . . .

A description at the outset of the few basic contract law principles applicable to this action will help the reader understand the significance of the complex factual circumstances that follow. "When the United States enters into contract relations, its rights and duties therein are governed generally by the law applicable to contracts between private individuals." United States v. Winstar Corp., 518 U.S. 839, 895, 116 S.Ct. 2432, 135 L.Ed.2d 964 (1996) (plurality opinion) (internal quotation marks omitted). The Restatement of Contracts reflects many of the principles of contract law that are applicable to this action. As set forth in the Restatement of Contracts, the relevant principles specify that, when one party to a contract repudiates that contract, the other party "is entitled to restitution for any benefit that he has conferred on" the repudiating party "by way of part performance or reliance." Restatement (Second) of Contracts § 373 (1979) (hereinafter Restatement). The Restatement explains that "repudiation" is a "statement by the obligor to the obligee indicating that the obligor will commit a breach that would of itself give the obligee a claim for damages for total breach." Id., § 250. And "total breach" is a breach that "so substantially impairs the value of the contract to the injured party at the time of the breach that it is just in the

rental, maintaining that it was not obligated to do so under the subcontract. Because of Blair's failure to make payments for crane rental, and after completion of approximately 28 percent of the subcontract, Coastal terminated its performance. Blair then proceeded to complete the job with a new subcontractor. Coastal brought this action to recover for labor and equipment furnished.

The district court found that the subcontract required Blair to pay for crane use and that Blair's refusal to do so was such a material breach as to justify Coastal's terminating performance. This finding is not questioned on appeal. The court then found that under the contract the amount due Coastal, less what had already been paid, totaled approximately \$37,000. Additionally, the court found Coastal would have lost more than \$37,000 if it had completed performance. Holding that any amount due Coastal must be reduced by any loss it would have incurred by complete performance of the contract, the court denied recovery to Coastal. While the district court correctly stated the " 'normal' rule of contract damages," we think Coastal is entitled to recover in quantum meruit.

In United States for Use of Susi Contracting Co. v. Zara Contracting Co., 146 F.2d 606 (2d Cir. 1944), a Miller Act action, the court was faced with a situation similar to that involved here—the prime contractor had unjustifiably breached a subcontract after partial performance by the subcontractor. The court stated [at 610]:

> For it is an accepted principle of contract law, often applied in the case of construction contracts, that the promisee upon breach has the option to forego any suit on the contract and claim only the reasonable value of his performance.

. . . [T]he right to seek recovery under quantum meruit in a Miller Act case is clear. Quantum meruit recovery is not limited to an action against the prime contractor but may also be brought against the Miller Act surety, as in this case. Further, that the complaint is not clear in regard to the theory of a plaintiff's recovery does not preclude recovery under quantum meruit. Narragansett Improvement Co. v. United States, 290 F.2d 577 (1st Cir. 1961). A plaintiff may join a claim for quantum meruit with a claim for damages from breach of contract.

In the present case, Coastal has, at its own expense, provided Blair with labor and the use of equipment. Blair, who breached the subcontract, has retained these benefits without having fully paid for them. On these facts, Coastal is entitled to restitution in quantum meruit.

> The 'restitution interest,' involving a combination of unjust impoverishment with unjust gain, presents the strongest case for relief. If, following Aristotle, we regard the purpose of justice as the maintenance of an equilibrium of goods among members of society, the restitution interest presents twice as strong a claim to judicial intervention as the reliance interest, since if A

> not only causes B to lose one unit but appropriates that unit to himself the resulting discrepancy between A and B is not one unit but two.

Fuller & Perdue, The Reliance Interest in Contract Damages, 46 Yale L.J. 52, 56 (1936).

The impact of quantum meruit is to allow a promisee to recover the value of services he gave to the defendant irrespective of whether he would have lost money on the contract and been unable to recover in a suit on the contract. Scaduto v. Orlando, 381 F.2d 587 (2d Cir. 1967). The measure of recovery for quantum meruit is the reasonable value of the performance, Restatement of Contracts § 347 (1932); and recovery is undiminished by any loss which would have been incurred by complete performance. 12 Williston on Contracts § 1485 (3d ed. 1970). While the contract price may be evidence of reasonable value of the services, it does not measure the value of the performance or limit recovery. Rather, the standard for measuring the reasonable value of the services rendered is the amount for which such services could have been purchased from one in the plaintiff's position at the time and place the services were rendered.

Since the district court has not yet accurately determined the reasonable value of the labor and equipment use furnished by Coastal to Blair, the case must be remanded for those findings.[9] When the amount has been determined, judgment will be entered in favor of Coastal, less payments already made under the contract. . . . [T]he decision of the district court is [r]eversed and remanded with instructions.

NOTE

The sub, Coastal, was permitted to disregard terms of the contract by claiming "quantum meruit." What justifies this? Judge Learned Hand, faced with a similar claim in Schwasnick v. Blandin, 65 F.2d 354 (2d Cir. 1933), considered just ahead, p. 168, remarked: "When [the promisee] has fulfilled the condition [of the promise], and the promisor has broken his promise, he [the promisee] sues upon that wrong. True, he does not seek the equivalent in money of what was promised; but it is the breach which gives him the power to call off the contract and raises the obligation to restore him to the status quo ante. The action is therefore a remedy for the breach, though it requires the equivalent of something which the promisor has never undertaken to perform." Judge Hand's last observation underscores the power of restitution in the setting of total breach. It is no objection that the remedy requires the defendant to do something that was never promised.

---

[9] Under the view of the case taken by the district court it was unnecessary to precisely appraise the value of services and materials rendered; an approximation was thought to suffice because the hypothetical loss had the contract been fully performed was greater in amount.

Kearns v. Andree

107 Conn. 181, 139 A. 695 (1928)

Plaintiff owned land on which stood a house then under construction but almost finished. Plaintiff contracted to sell the property to defendant for $8,500, of which $4,000 was to be paid in cash and the balance of $4,500 by the defendant's assumption of a first mortgage in that amount. There was no mortgage on the property at the time, but plaintiff undertook to find a lender and to execute a mortgage which defendant could then assume. Defendant thereafter became dissatisfied with the contract, but finally agreed to go through with it if plaintiff would make certain alterations and finish the house with paint and wallpaper chosen by defendant. Plaintiff did these things. Then defendant refused to complete the purchase. The way in which the house had been finished at defendant's urging made the property less saleable, but plaintiff finally succeeded in reselling the house and lot to another purchaser for $8,250, after repainting and repapering to meet that purchaser's objections. Plaintiff sued to recover (1) expenses incurred in finishing the house as defendant had requested, (2) repapering and repainting expenses to adapt it to the second purchaser's desires, and (3) the difference between the contract and resale prices. *Held*, the written contract was fatally indefinite as to the mortgage that defendant was to assume, since the identity of the mortgagee and the terms of payment were left undetermined. The contract was therefore wholly unenforceable. But there are cases where a plaintiff who cannot bring an action on the contract for some reason other than his own default is permitted a recovery for the reasonable value of his services, without regard to whether those services have benefitted the other party. These are situations where "the law [will] imply an agreement" to make reasonable compensation. "The basis of that implication is that the services have been requested [by the defendant] and have been performed by the plaintiff in the known expectation that he would receive compensation, and neither the extent nor the presence of benefit to the defendant . . . is of controlling significance." The principle applies where, as here, the attempted contract, unenforceable though it was, showed the parties' expectation that compensation was to be made.

Accordingly, "the sums . . . for the repapering and repainting, which was done after the defendant refused to purchase [item (2)], do not fall within the [applicable] principles. . . . To allow them in this action would be, in effect, to permit a recovery upon an unenforceable contract, which may not be done. But, if the work done on the property to adapt it to the desires of the defendant [item (1)] was done under the terms of an oral agreement for the sale of the premises, in good faith, and in the honest belief that the agreement was sufficiently definite to be enforced, the plaintiff is entitled to recover reasonable compensation therefor. In fixing the amount of that compensation, however, a proper deduction must be made for any benefit that has accrued to the plaintiff himself by reason of the work he did upon the premises at the defendant's request."

NOTE

A situation similar to Kearns v. Andree was presented in Farash v. Sykes Datatronics, Inc., 59 N.Y.2d 500, 465 N.Y.S.2d 917, 452 N.E.2d 1245 (1983). Plaintiff claimed that the parties had entered into an agreement whereby defendant would lease for two years a building owned by plaintiff, who was to modify the building in certain respects and complete its renovation. Plaintiff made the modifications, but no agreement was ever signed and defendant refused to occupy the building. Plaintiff's suit survived defendant's motions in the trial court but was dismissed by the Appellate Division for failure to state a cause of action. The Court of Appeals (4–2), invoking *Kearns*, thought otherwise:

> Plaintiff pleaded three causes of action. . . . The first was to enforce an oral lease for a term longer than one year. This is clearly barred by the Statute of Frauds (Gen. Obligs. Law, § 5–703). The third cause of action is premised on the theory that the parties contracted by exchanging promises that plaintiff would perform certain work in his building and defendant would enter into a lease for a term longer than one year. This is nothing more than a contract to enter into a lease; it is also subject to the Statute of Frauds . . . [and] was properly dismissed.
>
> Plaintiff's second cause of action, however, is not barred by the Statute of Frauds. It merely seeks to recover for the value of the work performed by plaintiff in reliance on statements by and at the request of defendant. This is not an attempt to enforce an oral lease or an oral agreement to enter a lease, but is in disaffirmance of the void contract and so may be maintained. . . . That defendant did not benefit from plaintiff's efforts does not require dismissal; plaintiff may recover for those efforts that were to his detriment and that thereby placed him in a worse position (see Kearns v. Andree, 107 Conn. 181, 139 A. 695 . . .).

In pleading the second cause of action, plaintiff's complaint had alleged that "[p]laintiff, in reliance on statements made [by] the defendant and at its request, performed work, provided labor and material to the defendant," and that "[d]efendant has failed to compensate the plaintiff for monies and other expenses incurred by the plaintiff in preparing the property . . . to the defendant's needs," resulting in damages of $400,000. It seems plaintiff's third cause of action also sought $400,000 damages, which sum, the dissenting judge pointed out, happened to be the annual rent allegedly agreed upon by the parties.

The dissent made two arguments to show that plaintiff's second cause of action was also barred by the statute of frauds. One was that quasi-contract was not available because the plaintiff had failed to demonstrate any "unjust enrichment." The other, premised on plaintiff's failure to allege a specific promise of compensation for the work to be performed, was that the second cause of action was nothing more than a rephrasing of the third—i.e., a claim for damages for defendant's alleged breach of an oral agreement to enter into a two-year lease. Accordingly, plaintiff should not be permitted to do indirectly what it cannot do directly.

Did the dissent have the better of the argument? It seems not, if the *Kearns* line of authority is to be believed.

A student commentator, writing long ago about recoveries for part performance of a contract (Note, 44 Harv.L.Rev. 623, 627 (1930)), concluded: "The true concept underlying the decisions seems to be not one of restitution based on quasi-contractual principles, but rather one of indemnification sounding in tort." Does that characterization fit cases such as *Algernon Blair*, *Kearns*, and *Farash*?

Olsson v. Moore

590 N.E.2d 160 (Ind. Ct. App. 1992)

Plaintiffs, the Moores, answered defendant Olsson's advertisement of a house and lot for sale. Plaintiffs indicated their willingness to buy the property, but because the Olsson house was unsuitable for winter habitation and the closing on the sale of their current home was imminent, plaintiffs asked permission to begin renovations on the house immediately. Olsson agreed, and by mid-December 1988, after placing the utility services in their name, plaintiffs had repaired the kitchen floor, renovated a total of four rooms, and reroofed the entire house. Throughout this period the parties were negotiating the purchase price of the property. Plaintiffs wanted more land than the one acre offered in the original advertisement. Forrest Moore testified he thought the deal was the house and 40 acres for $70,000; though Olsson had a survey drawn up for a sale of the house and five acres, he conceded there had been no definite agreement about acreage or price; Nancy Moore testified that the price changed so often she "couldn't keep track of it." On December 16, the day after plaintiffs closed on the sale of their home, the Olsson house was totally destroyed by a fire of accidental origin. Olsson was insured and collected $40,000 under his policy; no part of this payment was for the Moores' improvements. Plaintiffs then tendered a bill for $5,000 to Olsson, for labor and materials supplied, but Olsson refused to pay. Plaintiffs thereupon filed suit and, following a bench trial, were awarded a $4,800 judgment for their labor and materials. The judgment was affirmed on appeal.

Judge Baker, for the Court of Appeals, reasoned as follows: No contract of sale, written or oral, existed at the time of the fire; the parties' minds did not "meet" as required by standard contract doctrines. The fact neither party requested specific performance is further proof that, at most, negotiations produced only "an agreement to agree." Yet Olsson is wrong in contending "he received no benefit" from plaintiffs' improvements. Even if it be granted that plaintiffs' work was intended and understood to be for their own benefit, not Olsson's, "the fact remains that Olsson was the legal and equitable owner [on] the day of the fire" and, as Olsson concedes, "The Moores' work increased the value of the home." Thus, the conclusion that Olsson benefited from the improvements "is inescapable." Moreover, Olsson "consented to" and "sanction[ed]" the improvements, since he told plaintiffs they could do "whatever they needed to do" to make the house habitable when he might have stopped the work simply by giving notice. It is critical here that no contract of sale was made. Absent such a contract, the property remained exclusively Olsson's—because it cannot be said that "equitable ownership" passed to plaintiffs under the prevailing rule, followed in Indiana, that upon entry into a real estate contract the purchaser becomes the "equitable owner" who must assume the risk of loss from destruction of buildings or other improvements on the land. Olsson therefore "bear[s] the cost of the benefits he [received and] ratified," where there was "the opportunity to decline." The trial court's award of "the cost of [plaintiffs'] labor and expenses in bestowing the benefits" is proper.

COMMENT: THE "DOING AND GIVING" PROBLEM

An illustration accompanying Restatement, Second § 370 states: "A contracts to sell B a machine for $100,000. After A has spent $40,000 on the manufacture of the machine but before its completion, B repudiates the contract. A cannot get restitution of the $40,000 because no benefit was conferred on B." This illustration is intended to pose the so-called "doing and giving" problem, where, as concerns the restitution remedy, much depends on a determination of what it was that the party in breach "requested" and agreed to pay for. The grand case of Curtis v. Smith, 48 Vt. 116 (1874), is representative of the considerable authority that was the basis for the conclusion given by the restaters.

Plaintiff had contracted in writing to build stone "wing walls" around defendant's bakery, at a stipulated price for each completed yard of wall. Defendant repudiated before any installation had begun, though plaintiff had already quarried stone from his own quarry for use in building the walls. Plaintiff sued to recover the value of his work in quarrying the stone. The Vermont high court, reversing a judgment for plaintiff entered below on a jury verdict, held that the suit on the common counts for the value of plaintiff's work in quarrying the stone must fail. There simply was no ground for a recovery in restitution:

> If the completed work is not delivered so that the defendant receives a benefit from it, the plaintiff, by his work and material, does not lay the foundation for a recovery under the common counts, however wrongfully the defendant may have prevented the completion and delivery of such perfected work. . . . The defendants did not contract with the plaintiff for his labor, but for the wing walls completed. The plaintiff, in quarrying stone from his own quarry, was not at work for the defendants, but was at work for himself, getting out material that he might or might not use in the erection of the wing walls. The stone when quarried belonged to the plaintiff, and he could put [it] to any use he saw fit. The plaintiff had performed no labor for the defendants, or that had enured to their benefit. . . . The gravamen of his complaint [is] that he has not been allowed to realize this expectation by reason of the act of the

> defendants in wrongfully terminating the contract. If he would recover for this, he should declare upon the contract specially, and for the breach thereof of which he now complains.

The wall builder's remedy, the court noted, was a suit for damages ("he should declare upon the contract specially"). Note also that the result stated in the Rest.2d § 370 illustration quoted above is that the seller "cannot get restitution." Nothing is said about damages. The emergence of the alternative *Dempsey* theory of recovery—damages measured by loss through reliance on the contract, not the expected profit—has no doubt meant that the need for the restitution remedy is greatly lessened. Still, as *Boone*, *Kearns*, and *Farash* all illustrate, a fair number of the "preparation" cases will involve agreements that are unenforceable for some reason, often because a writing was not made. A damage remedy is therefore unavailable, even one restricted to reliance loss. The well-known case of Santoro v. Mack, 108 Conn. 683, 145 A. 273 (1929), provides another example of the consequences when contractual efforts fall short of the bargained exchange. The purchaser, relying on an oral contract for the sale of land, employed an architect to draw plans for improvements and an electrician to give cost estimates for wiring. Recovery for these expenditures was denied, since the agreement was within the statute of frauds and the sums expended were not "at the request" of the defaulting seller.

The most troubling cases remain those found in the Restatement's illustration reproduced above—substantial outlays to produce something that, by virtue of the defendant's substantial breach, is never delivered or installed. The product may have been planned with the special needs of the defendant in mind. In Curtis v. Smith, for example, the activity required to produce the specified "wing walls"—the quarrying and the shaping of the stone—may have rendered the stone of little use for other building projects. What should be the function of the restitution remedy in such cases? Can the bargain itself—the terms of the exchange—provide a satisfactory basis for answering that question?

PROBLEM

B contracts with S to buy S's used car for $900, paying $100 down. S repudiates before the deal is carried through. The market value of the car at the time of S's repudiation is proved to be $700. Is B entitled to restitution of the $100 payment?

Oliver v. Campbell

43 Cal. 2d 298, 273 P.2d 15 (1954)

Plaintiff, a lawyer, agreed in writing to represent defendant in a pending action brought by defendant's wife for separate maintenance, later changed by amendment to an action for divorce. The contract provided for a total fee of $850. The divorce trial, at which plaintiff represented defendant, lasted 29 days. After the trial ended, the court indicated its intention to give defendant's wife a divorce, but before the court's findings were signed defendant dismissed plaintiff from the case and thereafter represented himself in the proceeding. The court then filed its findings in favor of the wife, and (by implication) it appears that a decree of divorce was entered. In this action based on the employment contract, the reasonable value of plaintiff's services was found to be $5,000. *Held*, plaintiff can recover only $300, the unpaid balance of the $850 contract fee. Where an employment contract is terminated by wrongful discharge before performance is completed, the contract does not operate as a limit on recovery. "Inasmuch as the contract has been repudiated by the employer before its term is up and after the employee has partly performed and the employee may treat the contract as 'rescinded,' there is no longer any contract upon which the employer can rely as fixing conclusively the limit of the compensation—the reasonable value of services recoverable by the employee for his part performance." But here the trial was at an end, the court had indicated its intention to give judgment for the wife, and all that remained was the signing of findings and judgment. Plaintiff had "in effect" performed and was therefore limited to the contract price, in accordance with the settled rule of Restatement, Contracts § 350: "The remedy of restitution in money is not available to one who has fully performed[,] . . . if the only part of the agreed exchange for such performance that has not been rendered by the defendant is a sum of money constituting a liquidated debt."

NOTE: DISCONTINUITY AT FULL PERFORMANCE

In *Algernon Blair*, had Coastal not stopped work when the general contractor refused to pay for crane rentals, but completed performance in full before bringing suit, would Coastal still recover in quantum meruit? Oliver v. Campbell provides a reliable guide as to the authorities.

One court has offered the following explanation for the rule applied in Oliver v. Campbell: "There is excellent reason to look to the terms of a contract . . . to govern the measure of compensation. The contract provisions will disclose, as they do in the instant case, what the contracting parties thought was appropriate, thus obviating an extended inquiry into external sources of information as to what may be fair compensation." Fay, Spofford & Thorndike, Inc. v. Massachusetts Port Authority, 7 Mass.App.Ct. 336, 387 N.E.2d 206 (1979). Another court has said that remedial rights in the event of a plaintiff's full performance are "rooted in the nature of the remedy that restitution affords," adding: "[B]ecause the remedy in restitution is designed to prevent unjust enrichment of the party responsible for a material breach of an enforceable contract, the remedy is measured not by the loss suffered by the *injured* party but by the gain received by the party in breach." John T. Brady & Co. v. City of Stamford, 220 Conn. 432, 447, 599 A.2d 370, 377 (1991). Is there in fact "excellent reason" (perhaps "reasons") for limiting a party who has fully performed to a remedy "on the contract" when the other party's breach is a failure to pay the money price of that performance?

sale of goods—after title had passed but before possession had been delivered. The writ that most nearly approached a generalized contract remedy was the writ of *debt*, which was not limited to liabilities arising from contract but could be used to collect a sum of money due for any reason, including contract, statute, or local custom. The most serious defect of the action of debt was that the defendant could escape liability altogether by "waging his law," that is, by securing twelve persons who were willing to swear that they believed the defendant told the truth in denying that the debt was owed. It is easy to understand the desire of litigants for an improved remedy by which they could escape from this archaism, whose main effect was to give incentives to perjury.

The escape route from the procedural inadequacies and hazards of the action of debt followed a tortuous course, becoming entangled along the way with the evolution of *trespass*—the form of action that always showed the greatest capacity for growth and change—and with the damage remedy that was to become the standard sanction of the common law for breach of contract. We make a giant leap over years of development during which the trespass action—originally designed to deal with violent breaches of the peace—had been extended to deal with miscellaneous wrongs that we would now call torts. This extended form of trespass acquired its own name—*trespass on the case*—and was gradually extended to provide a damage remedy for negligent acts that also involved breaches of promises, e.g., driving a nail too far into a horse's hoof while performing a promise to shoe the horse. In the early development, the action would lie only where a promisor performed negligently and caused injury ("misfeasance"); it was unavailable if the promisor failed to perform at all. In the sixteenth century, however, a major transition occurred when relief became available for "nonfeasance," failures to act as promised. With this transition accomplished, the breach of promise remedy through trespass on the case came to be recognized as sufficiently distinct to have a title of its own, *assumpsit* ("he undertook" or "he promised").

The action of trespass on the case and its offspring assumpsit could be brought in either the Court of King's Bench or the Court of Common Pleas; the older action of debt could be brought only in the Common Pleas. Since judges derived their income from litigants' fees, it is not surprising that competition for judicial business developed between these two central courts. The economic interest of the judges, combined with whatever attraction they found in law reform, led the King's Bench first to permit assumpsit to be used in any case where a new promise was made to pay a debt already due. An illustration would be a simple contract to sell goods—say, a horse for a £10 price. If the horse had been delivered to the buyer, the seller could sue in debt (Common Pleas) and recover £10. But if the buyer, having received the horse, had made a second promise to pay the overdue debt, the seller could sue in assumpsit (Common Pleas or King's Bench). A pleading form reflecting this extension developed, called *indebitatus assumpsit* ("being indebted, he promised"). You will see this phrase often, even today.

Indebitatus assumpsit (often called general assumpsit) was transformed into a complete substitute for debt, available whenever debt would lie, by the decision in Slade's Case, 4 Coke 926 (1602). This was a simple suit involving an express contract for the sale of a specific quantity of grain for £16. Plaintiff, the seller, alleged that the buyer, after the debt arose, had made a second promise to pay the £16 price. But plaintiff was unable to prove this. All the judges of England were assembled in solemn conclave; after extensive debate, they decided that the second promise did not have to be proved. The judges understood that by this pleading fiction they were making available to litigants a remedy to collect debts in which disputes over facts would be decided by juries, so that debtors could not escape payment by the wager of law, that is, simply by finding twelve friends willing to perjure themselves on the debtor's behalf. Thereafter, debt remained available, but it was a poor competitor with assumpsit and its more rational procedure. Eventually, debt faded out as a contract remedy and assumpsit occupied the field, with its "counts" or pleading forms becoming "common" indeed.

We must pursue the development of assumpsit a bit further. Consider the following situations:

> Case 1. Debtor borrows $3,000 from Creditor and promises repayment at the rate of $200 on the first of each month until the whole sum is paid. Debtor makes 10 payments (totaling $2,000) on time and at midpoint in the series also makes one extra prepayment of $500; the balance due is therefore $500. Forgetting about this extra $500 payment and calculating the balance to be $1,000, Debtor pays Creditor $1,000. Can Debtor recover the $500 overpayment made through mistake?
>
> Case 2. Owner of a car delivers it to Repairshop under an agreement calling for specified repairs for a price of $425. The repairs completed, Owner tenders $425 and demands the car. Repairshop refuses to return it unless paid $600. Owner pays this sum. Can Owner recover the $175 over-payment exacted by "duress"?
>
> Case 3. Jay Walker is run over in a street accident and lies unconscious on the curb. Dr. Smith, a physician, is called to the scene, renders services, and accompanies Walker in an ambulance to the hospital. There Dr. Smith administers further treatment but without success; Walker dies without ever regaining consciousness. Though no contract was ever made, should Dr. Smith be allowed to recover the reasonable value of the medical services from Walker's estate?

In the years after Slade's Case, while assumpsit was establishing itself as the principal remedy for breach of an express contract, the English courts began to hold that claims like these could be brought in general or indebitatus assumpsit. The appeal of claims of this type was that the defendant had been enriched by something the plaintiff had provided or done; allowing the defendant to retain the benefit without payment seemed unjust. It therefore mattered not in the least that the defendant had made no promise to repay the mistaken or coerced payment, or pay for unrequested services, for the English courts (and much later, the American courts) explained the result—recovery in assumpsit—by saying that a promise by the defendant to pay should be "implied." This fiction of a contract to ground assumpsit helped to popularize the term "quasi-contract" to describe a basis for restitution in law actions, ordinarily leading to money judgments, that has been greatly expanded in modern American law. The "quasi" is meant to indicate that liability does not rest on contract after all, and that, like other restitution remedies, the aim is to prevent the alleged unjust enrichment of one person at the expense of another. Such an objective indeed has broad dimensions, and a wide appeal. The suit by Dr. Smith against Jay Walker's estate (Case 3 above) illustrates quasi-contract in its most obvious form—a recovery resting on an implication of law in circumstances wholly lacking any basis for finding an actual contract. To be sure, use of the term "quasi-contract" and talk of promises "implied in law" in such noncontractual settings produce confusion and, occasionally, unwarranted results. The failure of courts and commentators to settle on a common language to describe the restitutionary claim—especially when it arises in the absence of any semblance of promissory obligation—is no small part of the problem. But the historical terminology remains in use today, and you must be familiar with it.

We must emphasize again that the pleading forms of the "common counts" are entirely neutral and disclose nothing at all as to the source from which the debt arose, except the type of performance the plaintiff had supplied (rendering services, delivering goods, paying money). The counts also can be used to enforce a liability that arises through and is measured by the terms of an express contract, as in Slade's Case itself. How is this possible? As we have said, general assumpsit developed as a full substitute for the action of debt. It was only natural that courts and litigants, through use of the pleading forms of the common counts, should think the assumpsit action available to collect the "debt" arising through full performance of a contract to perform services or deliver goods in return for the payment of money. In Oliver v. Campbell, then, where the recovery was precisely the sum promised by express contract, a count for work and labor done (quantum meruit) would have been entirely suitable. This, of course, is not quasi-contract; plaintiff's recovery was limited to the contract price. The phrases quantum meruit and quantum valebat are probably most often used, however, to suggest a recovery that does not aim at all at enforcing a contract but, quite the contrary, at recovering the value of a performance rendered—enforcing restitution. This was the sense in which quantum meruit was used by Judge Craven in imposing on Algernon Blair, Inc. what was clearly viewed as quasi-contractual liability. It is the standard work of the restitution remedy where performance of a contract has been brought to a halt by one party's substantial breach.

We will not be concerned in general with the grounds for restitution, other than those that arise following a disruption (e.g., unforeseen events) or a substantial breach of an actual or supposed contract. The breach can be by the recipient of a requested performance (as in *Algernon Blair*) or by the performing party, who usually seeks restitution because a substantial default bars recovery on the contract. Because the common counts are used frequently in actions to enforce a contract, as well as to claim restitution in the absence of an enforceable contract, we stress again that you cannot reliably identify the basis of the action from the pleading form used. The problem is compounded by the great variety and irregularity of bargaining transactions that become derailed and require unwinding. It should be added that the law of restitution that emerged in the course of the nineteenth century has produced an assortment of remedies, many of which award not a money judgment but specific relief in one form or another (and thus are conceived of as "equitable"). We will see only a few of these remedies in this book. The point to be clear about at this stage is that restitution is not exclusively a "legal" or an "equitable" remedy; it is both, and it is routinely ordered in law and equity proceedings alike. Whether it is properly viewed as one or the other in a given case depends mainly on what is being sought by a claimant, money or something else.

It must also be said, however, that restitution's association with unjust enrichment—the origins of which, as the basis for an independent cause of action, lie largely in equity—invites talk of "equitable" factors and considerations, whatever the type of restitution claim. Since the restitution remedy is often focused on whether, in light of circumstances and the parties' conduct, a particular outcome is "fair" or "just," "equitable" or "inequitable," "conscionable" or "unconscionable," courts commonly speak of restitution as "equitable in nature." Kull, Rationalizing Restitution, 83 Cal. L.Rev. 1191 (1995), is helpful on these characterization questions.

The benefits that the breaching party enjoys as a result of the breach are ordinarily irrelevant. The focus is either, in the case of expectation damages, on making the innocent party whole or, in the case of a restitution action, retrieving from the breaching party whatever she received from the innocent one. It is possible, however, for the conduct of the breaching party to be sufficiently egregious that the profits she enjoyed from breach, even if not from the innocent party, are found to be ill-gotten gains that the victim of a breach of promise can recover in a restitution action. This idea is set out in § 39 of the Restatement (Third) of Restitution.

Restatement (Third) of Restitution and Unjust Enrichment

§ 39. Profit From Opportunistic Breach

(1) If a deliberate breach of contract results in profit to the defaulting promisor and the available damage remedy affords inadequate protection to the promisee's contractual entitlement, the promisee has a claim to restitution of the profit realized by the promisor as a result of the breach. Restitution by the rule of this section is an alternative to a remedy in damages.

(2) A case in which damages afford inadequate protection to the promisee's contractual entitlement is ordinarily one in which damages will not permit the promisee to acquire a full equivalent to the promised performance in a substitute transaction.

(3) Breach of contract is profitable when it results in gains to the defendant (net of potential liability in damages) greater than the defendant would have realized from performance of the contract. Profits from breach include saved expenditure and consequential gains that the defendant would not have realized but for the breach, as measured by the rules that apply in other cases of disgorgement.

Comment:

a. General principles and scope; relation to other sections. In exceptional cases, a party's profitable breach of contract may be a source of unjust enrichment at the expense of the other contracting party. The law of restitution treats such cases in the same way that it treats other instances of intentional and profitable interference with another person's legally protected interests, authorizing a claim by the injured party to the measurable benefit realized as a result of the defendant's wrong. The claim described in this section is accordingly an instance of restitution for benefits wrongfully obtained. . . .

Judged by the usual presumptions of contract law, a recovery for breach that exceeds the plaintiff's provable damages is anomalous on its face. A breach of contract—whatever the actor's state of mind—is not usually treated in law as a wrong to the injured party of a sort comparable to a tort or breach of equitable duty. There is substantial truth, though not of course the whole story, in the Holmesian paradox according to which the legal obligation imposed by contract lies in a choice between performance and payment of damages. But the observation is most accurate where it matters least: in those transactional contexts where damages can be calculated with relative confidence as a full equivalent of performance.

By contrast, there are numerous legal relations—including some created by contract—in which a legal entitlement receives insufficient protection when the remedy for violation is limited to compensation in the form of damages. The traditional "inadequacy" test for the availability of equitable remedies may be largely a historical artifact, but it appropriately emphasizes this vital justification for supplemental relief. It is not generally the case, in short, that a person is free to choose whether to respect another's legal entitlement or pay damages for interference. It is precisely where a potential damage claim affords inadequate protection to a recognized entitlement that a court will enjoin a threatened interference. If a profitable interference has already occurred, the law of restitution allows a claim to disgorgement of profits, as an alternative to damages, in cases of intentional interference with legal entitlements of any kind.

Compared to other forms of legal entitlement, contract rights may often be easier to value in money; but they would be vulnerable to the same risks of underenforcement if the exclusive remedy for breach were an action for money damages. Where a party's contractual entitlement would be inadequately protected by the legal remedy of damages for breach, a court will often reinforce the protection given to the claimant by an order of injunction or specific performance. Restitution affords comparable protection after the fact, awarding the gains from a profitable breach of a contract that the defendant can no longer be required to perform.

The restitution claim described in this section is infrequently available, because a breach of contract that satisfies the cumulative tests of § 39 is rare. At the same time, the cases in which such a remedy is appropriate are generally uncontroversial and in some instances even well known. The innovation of the present section consists, not in proposing that defendants in such cases be liable to disgorge profits derived from a deliberate breach, but in stating a rule to generalize these commonly accepted outcomes. . . .

Kansas v. Nebraska

135 S.Ct. 1042 (2015)

Cases in which the Supreme Court is the court of first impression are rare. The Supreme Court has heard fewer than two hundred such original jurisdiction cases in its history. The most common are disputes between states, such as controversies over boundaries or water rights. In resolving these, the Court must turn, in addition to the small number of its own precedents, to common law principles.

In this case, Kansas and Nebraska had a dispute over water rights. They eventually settled the dispute. Their settlement agreement, like any other settlement agreement, was a legally enforceable contract. When Nebraska broke it by diverting water, Kansas asked the Supreme Court to award it damages for the breach. A dispute then arose over how to measure damages. The benefit Nebraska enjoyed from diverting the water was greater than the harm that Kansas suffered from its loss. Kansas argued that it should recover the amount of this benefit rather than expectation damages, the amount that would put it in the same position it would have been in had Nebraska kept its promise. Justice Kagan, writing for the Court, awarded Kansas this greater amount. In addition to invoking a variety of principles of federalism, Justice Kagan pointed to the Restatement (Third) of Restitution § 39.

Justice Thomas, in dissent, argued that Nebraska's conduct was not sufficiently culpable to justify using a disgorgement remedy rather than ordinary expectation damages. For his part, Justice Scalia argued that it was a mistake to pay much heed to section 39:

> I write separately to note that modern Restatements—such as the Restatement (Third) of Restitution and Unjust Enrichment (2010), which both opinions address in their discussions of the disgorgement remedy—are of questionable value, and must be used with caution. The object of the original Restatements was "to present an orderly statement of the general common law." Restatement of Conflict of Laws, Introduction, p. viii (1934). Over time, the Restatements' authors have abandoned the mission of describing the law, and have chosen instead to set forth their aspirations for what the law ought to be. Section 39 of the Third Restatement of

Restitution and Unjust Enrichment is illustrative .... Restatement sections such as that should be given no weight whatever as to the current state of the law, and no more weight regarding what the law ought to be than the recommendations of any respected lawyer or scholar. And it cannot safely be assumed, without further inquiry, that a Restatement provision describes rather than revises current law.

Enslin v. The Coca-Cola Company

United States District Court, Eastern District of Pennsylvania, 2015.
136 F. Supp. 3d 654.

LEESON, UNITED STATES DISTRICT JUDGE. . . . This action arises out of the theft of fifty-five laptops allegedly containing the personal identification information ("PII") of Plaintiff and 74,000 other current and former employees of the Coke Defendants.

Plaintiff was hired by Defendant Keystone Coca-Cola Bottling Company ("Keystone Coke") in 1996 as a service technician assigned to the Poconos region of Pennsylvania. As part of his employment, Plaintiff was required to provide Keystone Coke with his PII. This PII included Plaintiff's Social Security number ("SSN"), address, bank account information, credit card numbers, driver's license information, and motor vehicle records. Plaintiff's PII was stored by Keystone Coke on one or more laptop computers in an unencrypted format. During his term of employment, the Coke Defendants represented to Plaintiff that, in exchange for his employment, his PII would be securely retained. In 2007, after eleven years of employment, Plaintiff left his job at Keystone Coke.

On December 31, 2007, Defendant Coca-Cola Enterprises ("CCE") acquired Keystone Coke as a subsidiary of CCE. In 2010, The Coca-Cola Company ("Coca-Cola Co.") acquired CCE. While it is unclear which Coke Defendant controlled Plaintiff's PII at each of the relevant times in Plaintiff's complaint, eventually "laptops assigned to current CCR and former CCE users" containing the PII of Plaintiff and relevant class members made their way into the possession of CCE.

Over a nearly six-year period, beginning in January 2007 and continuing through November 2013, approximately fifty-five of these laptop computers were stolen from CCE. The stolen laptops allegedly contained the PII of over 74,000 people, including Plaintiff. On November 17, 2013, the Coke Defendants discovered that the theft had occurred and undertook efforts to recover the stolen laptops. By December 10, 2013, the Coke Defendants had recovered all fifty-five stolen laptops.

The Coke Defendants determined that Thomas William Rogers, an employee of CCE responsible for retaining or destroying the laptops, was responsible for the theft of the laptops. Rogers was arrested on June 14,

2014, by Cobb County police and stands charged with felony and misdemeanor theft by taking. Plaintiff alleges that, from these stolen laptops, various, unknown identity thieves were able to gain access to Plaintiff's PII.

On February 23, 2014, CCE and Coca-Cola Co. sent a letter to Plaintiff, notifying him of the theft of the laptops and informing him that these laptops may have contained his PII. The letter also offered Plaintiff a one-year subscription [to a] credit monitoring service.

A few months after receiving this notification letter, Plaintiff alleges he began to experience unauthorized uses of his finances and identity by unknown persons ("Identity thieves"). . . . Plaintiff has sufficiently pled damages as a result of this breach due to the costs Plaintiff incurred in connection with the migration of his banking from one account to another. . . .

Plaintiff alleges that "[by deliberately breaching their contract with Plaintiff] the Coke Defendants have been knowingly enriched by the savings in costs that should have been reasonably expended to protect the PII of the Plaintiff and the Class." That claims sounds in the "opportunistic breach" theory of restitution, which supports a claim for relief when "a deliberate breach of contract results in profit to the defaulting promisor and the available damage remedy affords inadequate protection to the promisee's contractual entitlement," measured by the profit realized by the defaulting promisor. In re 400 Walnut Associates, L.P., 506 B.R. 645, 668 (E.D. Pa. 2014) (quoting Restatement (Third) of Restitution and Unjust Enrichment § 39(1)).

At this procedural stage, the Court need not precisely sketch the boundaries of this claim but takes this opportunity to observe that the circumstances affording relief under this theory are narrow. Integral to the claim is that the breach must be deliberate. The breach must not merely have been efficient or advantageous for the breaching party, but must have been the result of "conscious advantage-taking" or "opportunistic calculation." The breach must also be profitable, such that "the gain to the defendant as a result of the default will exceed the injury to the plaintiff from the same cause." Restatement (Third) of Restitution and Unjust Enrichment § 39(3) & cmt. f.

Finally, and vitally, the contractual damage remedy must "afford inadequate protection to the promisee's contractual entitlement," for the essence of the claim is the need to "reinforce[ ] . . .an entitlement that would be inadequately protected if liability for interference were limited to provable damages." See id. § 39(2) & cmt. b. Understood by its purpose, this claim embraces those circumstances where "the promisee's contractual position is vulnerable to abuse" in order to prevent an inadequate damage remedy from "undermin[ing] the stability of any contractual exchange in which one party's performance may neither be easily compelled nor easily valued." See id. § 39 cmt. b.

These requirements serve to distinguish this claim from those circumstances where it is improper to assert a claim in restitution in a contractual setting. Contracting parties sometimes seek to wield a claim in restitution to disgorge a benefit from a counterparty when a contractual benefit, usually unforeseen by the contracting party at the time the bargain was struck, accrues to the counterparty during the course of performance. Such was the case in *Wilson Area School District v. Skepton*, where a school district, which had invited bids for the construction of a new school, sought to disgorge from the contractor certain cost savings the contractor was able to secure during the course of construction. See 586 Pa. 513, 895 A.2d 1250, 1251–53 (2006). The bid terms required that the contractors secure and pay for all necessary permits, governmental fees, and licenses. After paying the permit fees assessed by the local borough, the contractors, through suit in state court, were able to obtain a refund of those fees when the fees were found to have violated a provision of the borough's code. The school district sought to disgorge the refunded fees from the contractors, arguing that "a mistake of law" entitled them to a claim in restitution. The Supreme Court of Pennsylvania rejected this claim, stating that "it has long been held in this Commonwealth that the doctrine of unjust enrichment is inapplicable when the relationship between the parties is founded upon a written agreement or express contract, regardless of how harsh the provisions of such contracts may seem in the light of subsequent happenings." See id. at 1254. Put another way, the benefit obtained by the contractors was not "without adequate legal ground," because the risk associated with the calculation of the fees that the borough would ultimately assess was contractually allocated to the contractors. The line of cases cited in *Wilson* affirm the basic principle that no claim in restitution arises when a contracting party obtains a contractually-allocated benefit.

By contrast, Plaintiff is not attempting to use the vehicle of restitution to rewrite the terms of an agreement the parties allegedly made. Rather, the claim that another engaged in an opportunistic breach of a contract is "the equivalent, in the contractual context, of an intentional and profitable tort," and "it is properly understood and delimited" by analogy to claims in restitution that arise when one engages in an "intentional and profitable interference with another person's legally protected interests." See Restatement (Third) of Restitution and Unjust Enrichment § 39 cmts. a & b. Plaintiff has stated a claim in restitution, and Defendants' motion to dismiss this claim at this juncture is denied.

Hoffman v. L & M Arts

United States Court of Appeals, Fifth Circuit, 2016.
838 F.3d 568.

ELROD, CIRCUIT JUDGE. . . . Dallas arts patron Marguerite Hoffman purchased Mark Rothko's *Untitled* 1961 ("the Red Rothko") in 1998. Hoffman later bequeathed the Red Rothko to the Dallas Museum of Art, of which she was a major supporter, and it hung there from November 2006 through April 2007 as part of an exhibit called "Fast Forward" that showcased future additions to the museum's collections. The painting had been publicly associated with Hoffman on the front page of the Dallas Morning News and in other media. Nevertheless, in the wake of her husband's death in 2006, Hoffman decided to sell the Red Rothko. Although the sale was permitted under the terms of the bequest, Hoffman was eager to avoid the publicity that would likely result from a public sale and decided to sell the Red Rothko privately.

For help finding a buyer, Hoffman and family friend John Van Doren reached out to Robert Mnuchin, a long-time friend and an expert in the market for Rothkos. Mnuchin, along with Dominique Levy, was the co-principal of defendant L & M Arts, an art gallery. Through Van Doren, Hoffman conveyed to L & M her concern for confidentiality. To maintain the secrecy of the sale, Mnuchin agreed to approach only a single buyer and assured Van Doren that the buyer would be an individual.

L & M approached defendant David Martinez, an art collector, to discuss purchasing the Red Rothko. On several previous occasions, both Levy and Mnuchin had transacted with Martinez. Martinez would acquire art sometimes on his own behalf and other times on behalf of Studio Capital, a Belize corporation with which he was involved. From L & M's perspective when transacting with Martinez, he and Studio Capital were one and the same.

Martinez's and Studio Capital's identities remained undisclosed to Hoffman, but Mnuchin assured Van Doren that the buyer was a "very private" "single individual" and that the painting would "disappear" into that buyer's collection based in Europe. In early 2007, Martinez flew with Levy to Dallas to view the Red Rothko, which was still hanging in the Dallas Museum of Art. Negotiations began over the sale, with L & M communicating offers and counteroffers back and forth between Van Doren and Martinez.

The parties eventually agreed to a sale price of $17.6 million (excluding commissions) and memorialized the terms of the sale in a February 2007 letter agreement ("the February Agreement"). The agreement contained a specific confidentiality provision, which provided that "[i]t is the specified wish of the seller that the sale and terms of the sale remain confidential," and that "[i]t is requested that confidentiality be maintained indefinitely." In March 2007, however, Christie's auction house contacted Hoffman to discuss her plans to sell the Red Rothko. Christie's had learned the Red Rothko was for sale because Martinez, in the midst of negotiations, had consulted with the chairman of Christie's International for his advice on an appropriate price. Hoffman immediately canceled the sale and conveyed to Martinez and Studio Capital ("the Martinez defendants") and to L & M her sense that there had been a breach of confidentiality.

In April 2007, Van Doren and Mnuchin executed a new letter agreement for the sale of the Red Rothko ("the Agreement"). The Agreement reflected the same sale price as the February Agreement, $17.6 million excluding commissions, but differed from the February Agreement in two notable respects. First, the Agreement contained several new commitments by the buyer: to anonymously donate $500,000 to the Dallas Museum of Art on behalf of an entity of Hoffman's choosing; to allow Hoffman to retain possession of the painting for six months after closing; and to refrain from hanging or displaying the painting for an additional six months thereafter. Second, the Agreement contained modified confidentiality language: "All parties agree to make maximum efforts to keep all aspects of this transaction confidential indefinitely." The entire Agreement fit on a single page.

The Agreement closed, Martinez paid the purchase price, and title for the Red Rothko passed from Hoffman to Studio Capital. As agreed, the painting remained in Hoffman's possession for six months and was subsequently shipped to Studio Capital. After attempting to privately resell the Red Rothko with the aid of L & M for a year spanning March 2009 to March 2010, Martinez moved the Red Rothko to L & M's gallery in New York and decided to sell it at public auction at Sotheby's. L & M shipped the Red Rothko to Sotheby's on Martinez's instructions. During this time and until May 15, 2010—three days after it was ultimately auctioned—the Red Rothko was the subject of a consignment agreement between Studio Capital and L & M that entitled L & M to possess it.

In May 2010, the Red Rothko appeared on the cover of the Sotheby's catalog. The catalog entry for the Red Rothko, as to which L & M had input with Sotheby's, referenced the "Fast Forward" exhibit at the Dallas Museum of Art that had been dedicated to Hoffman and two other benefactors. The entry specifically referenced pages in the "Fast Forward" exhibit catalog that contained pictures of Hoffman and her late husband posing in front of the Red Rothko and of the Red Rothko hanging in their home. In the lead-up to the auction, an art blogger referenced the Red Rothko's previous appearance in the "Fast Forward" exhibit and named the exhibit's three benefactors, including Hoffman.

Mnuchin reached out to Hoffman in mid-March 2010 and informed her of the impending auction. Through Van Doren, Hoffman asked Mnuchin if she could buy back the painting and was rebuffed. On May 12, 2010, Sotheby's auctioned the Red Rothko for approximately $31 million, including commissions.

Hoffman sued the Martinez defendants and L & M for breach of contract in Texas state court in May 2010, and the defendants removed the case to federal court shortly thereafter based on diversity. The defendants moved to dismiss, arguing in part that there had been no breach because the confidentiality provision in the Agreement governed disclosures about the terms of the 2007 private sale, but not about the fact of the sale itself. In denying the motion, the district court held that the confidentiality provision was enforceable as a best-efforts clause, and that the fact of the sale was among the "aspects of the transaction" that the parties were obligated to make best efforts to keep confidential.

At the conclusion of discovery, all defendants moved for summary judgment, arguing that there was insufficient evidence of breach and no triable issue on damages. In denying summary judgment, the district court specifically upheld Hoffman's proposed damages measure based on an "auction premium" theory. Per the district court, the value of the allegedly breached confidentiality provision—*i.e.* the benefit of the bargain that Hoffman did not receive—could be measured by "the difference between $17.6 million [the sale price in the Agreement excluding commissions] and what the painting would have sold for at public auction on or around April 24, 2007." . . .

L & M first argues that it is entitled to judgment as a matter of law on Hoffman's breach-of-contract claim because the evidence did not support a finding that the confidentiality clause, properly construed, had been breached. The confidentiality clause provided that "All parties agree to make maximum effort to keep all aspects of this transaction confidential indefinitely." . . .

The language of the Agreement indicates that the confidentiality clause does not require secrecy as to the fact of the sale. By its own terms, the confidentiality clause requires maximum effort to keep secret "all aspects of th[e] transaction." References to an object's "aspects" generally describe features of the object rather than the object itself. *See The American Heritage Dictionary of the English Language* (5th ed. 2016) (defining "aspect" as "[a] characteristic or feature of something"). As most naturally understood, the fact that the 2007 sale occurred is not an "aspect" of that transaction subject to the confidentiality clause.

Other provisions of the Agreement also indicate that the confidentiality clause does not require secrecy as to the fact of the 2007 sale. Immediately after the confidentiality clause, the Agreement provided: "In addition, the buyer agrees not to hang or display the work for six months following receipt of the painting." This specific, express prohibition on displaying the Red Rothko for a fixed period of time "raises an inference," per "[t]he maxim *expressio unius est exclusio alterius*," that the parties did not intend to forbid the buyer from displaying the painting once that fixed period had passed. . . .

We accordingly hold that L & M was entitled to judgment as a matter of law on Hoffman's breach-of-contract claim. . . .

Even were we to conclude that a reasonable jury could have found that L & M breached the agreement, L & M would nevertheless be entitled to judgment as a matter of law because the jury's damages award rested on a legally non-viable measure of damages. . . .

Typical contract damages calculate the benefit of the bargain by subtracting the value of the performance actually received by the non-breaching party from the value of the performance contracted for. Where the dollar value of the contracted-for performance is difficult to ascertain, a benefit-of-the-bargain jury question can permissibly use the value of the non-breaching party's performance as a proxy in appropriate circumstances. In all circumstances, however, a benefit-of-the-bargain damages question must encapsulate the difference between what was bargained for and what was received. Restatement (Second) of Contracts § 347.

Question 3(A) did not properly encapsulate the lost benefit of Hoffman's bargain. Because the parties agree that the defendants performed all of their duties under the Agreement with the exception of the duty of confidentiality, a proper benefit-of-the-bargain question should have captured the value to Hoffman of the performance of that duty, standing alone. Instead, Question 3(A) measured the difference "between the *sum of money for which Hoffman sold the painting* in the transaction in question and what she could have sold the painting for at public auction on or around April 24, 2007," the date the Agreement was signed. . . .

Question 3(C) asked for "[t]he value of the benefits that [each defendant] received in connection with the transaction." The district court concluded that Question 3(C) elicited a disgorgement remedy and made an *Erie* guess that the Supreme Court of Texas would not allow a disgorgement remedy for a breach-of-contract claim. We agree.

In Texas, "[t]he universal rule for measuring damages for the breach of a contract is just compensation for the loss or damage *actually sustained.*" CQ, Inc. v. TXU Min. Co., L.P., 565 F.3d 268, 278 (5th Cir. 2009). Though benefit-of-the-bargain damages are not the *only* proper measure of the plaintiff's losses, the other permissible measures—including reliance and restitution damages—also focus squarely on the plaintiff's actual losses. Unlike these permissible damages remedies, equitable disgorgement focuses on divesting the wrongdoer of its ill-gotten gains rather than making the victim whole.

Because Question 3(C) asked for "the value of the benefits that [each defendant] received" rather than the value of the benefits conferred on each defendant by Hoffman, we hold that it reflected a disgorgement remedy that the Supreme Court of Texas would reject. Several Texas intermediate courts have held disgorgement to be an unavailable remedy under Texas contract law. . . .

Against these authorities, Hoffman highlights section 39 of the Restatement (Third) of Restitution and Unjust Enrichment, which "describes a *disgorgement* remedy" in the event of a profitable opportunistic breach. Cmt. a. Hoffman also notes that the Supreme Court of the United States recently endorsed a disgorgement remedy for breach of an agreement between two states as a matter of federal common law, with extensive reference to section 39 of the Restatement. Kansas v. Nebraska, ___ U.S. ___, 135 S.Ct. 1042, 1056–58, 191 L.Ed.2d 1 (2015). Nevertheless, given Texas courts' singular focus on compensating a plaintiff for its losses, we conclude that the Supreme Court of Texas would not follow this approach in a Texas breach-of-contract case, at least absent a fiduciary relationship between the parties.

Because neither Question 3(A), on which the district court awarded judgment for Hoffman, nor Question 3(C), on which Hoffman seeks to recover, awarded a legally valid measure of damages for any breach of the Agreement by the defendants, we conclude that the defendants are entitled to judgment as a matter of law even if such a breach occurred. . . .

NOTE: RESTITUTION FOR THE PARTY IN BREACH

In the restitution cases considered up to this point, restitution served as an alternative path to recovery for the nonbreaching party. Cases also arise in which the breaching party asserts a restitution action. Notwithstanding the breach, this party attempts to recover the benefits that have been bestowed upon its contracting opposite. The two cases that follow present contrasting approaches. While the view put forward in the second case has largely prevailed, the view presented in the first remains an undercurrent in the law.

Stark v. Parker

Supreme Judicial Court of Massachusetts, 1824.
19 Mass. (2 Pick.) 267.

This was an action of *indebitatus assumpsit* brought to recover the sum of [$27.33], as a balance due for services rendered by the plaintiff on the defendant's farm. . . .

At the trial, . . . the defendant admitted that the plaintiff had performed the service set forth in the declaration, and for the price therein stated, and that he, the defendant, had paid him from time to time, before he left the defendant's service, money amounting in the whole to about [$36], and on account of his labor, but the defendant proved that the plaintiff agreed to work for him a year, for the sum of [$120], and that he, the defendant, agreed to pay him that sum for his labor. He also proved that the plaintiff voluntarily left his service before the expiration of the year, and without any fault on the part of the defendant, and against his consent.

The judge thereupon instructed the jury, that the plaintiff would be entitled to recover in this action a sum in proportion to the time he had served, deducting therefrom such sum, if any, as the jury might think the defendant had suffered by having his service deserted; and if such sum should exceed the sum claimed by the plaintiff, they might find a verdict for the defendant. The jury having returned a verdict for the plaintiff, the defendant filed his exceptions to this instruction. . . .

LINCOLN, J. This case comes before us upon exceptions filed. . . . The exceptions present a precise abstract question of law for consideration, namely, whether upon an entire contract for a term of service for a stipulated sum, and a part-performance, without any excuse for neglect of its completion, the party guilty of the neglect can maintain an action against the party contracted with, for an apportionment of the price, or a *quantum meruit*, for the services actually performed. . . . The direction to the jury was, "that although proved to them, that the plaintiff agreed to serve the defendant for an agreed price for a year, and had voluntarily left his service before the expiration of that time, and without the fault of the defendant, and against his consent, still the plaintiff would be entitled to recover of the defendant, in this action, a sum in proportion to the time he had served, deducting therefrom such sum, (if any,) as the jury might think the defendant had suffered by having his service deserted." If this direction was wrong, the judgment must be reversed, and the case sent to a new trial. . . .

It cannot but seem strange to those who are in any degree familiar with the fundamental principles of law, that doubts should ever have been entertained upon a question of this nature. . . . The true ground of legal demand in all cases of contracts between parties is, that the party claiming has done all which on his part was to be performed *by the terms of the contract*, to entitle him to enforce the obligation of the other party. It is not sufficient that he has given to the party contracted with, a right of action against him . . . .

Upon examining the numerous authorities, . . . it will be found, that a distinction has been uniformly recognised in the construction of contracts, between those in which the obligation of the parties is reciprocal and independent, and those where the duty of the one may be considered as a condition precedent to that of the other. In the latter cases, it is held, that the performance of the precedent obligation can alone entitle the party bound to it, to his action. It is assumed by [plaintiff's counsel], that the service of the plaintiff for a year was not a condition precedent to his right to a proportion of the stipulated compensation for that entire term of service, but that upon a just interpretation of the contract, it is so far divisible, as that consistently with the terms of it, the plaintiff, having labored for any portion of the time, may receive compensation *pro tanto*. That this was the intention of the parties is said to be manifest from the fact found in the case, that the defendant from time to time did in fact make payments expressly toward this service. [However] the parties may have intended between themselves, we are to look to the construction given to the contract by the court below. The jury were . . . instructed, that if the contract was entire, in reference alike to the service and the compensation, still by law it was so divisible in the remedy, that the party might recover an equitable consideration for his labor, although the engagement to perform it had not been fulfilled. The contract itself was not discharged; it was considered as still subsisting, because the loss sustained by the defendant in the breach of it was to be estimated in the assessment of damages to the plaintiff. A proposition apparently more objectionable in terms can hardly be stated. . . . The plaintiff sues in *indebitatus assumpsit* as though there was no special contract, and yet admits the existence of the contract to affect the amount he shall recover. The defendant objects to the recovery of the plaintiff [on] the express contract which has been broken, and is himself charged with damages for the breach of an implied one which he never entered into. The rule that *expressum facit cessare tacitum*, is as applicable to this, as to every other case. If the contract is entire and executory, it is to be declared upon. Where it is executed and a mere duty to pay the stipulated compensation remains, a general count for the money is sufficient. Numerous instances are indeed to be found in the books, of actions being maintained where the specific contract has not been executed by the party suing for compensation, but in every case it will be seen that the precise terms of the contract have been first held, either to have been expressly or impliedly waived, or the non-execution excused upon some known and settled principle of law. . . . Nothing can be more unreasonable than that a man, who deliberately and wantonly violates an engagement, should be permitted to seek in a court of justice an indemnity from the consequences of his voluntary act; and we are satisfied that the law will not allow it.

That such a contract as is supposed in the exceptions before us, expresses a condition to be performed by the plaintiff precedent to his right of action against the defendant, we cannot doubt. The plaintiff was to labor one year for an agreed price. The money was to be paid in compensation for the service, and not as a consideration for an engagement to serve. Otherwise, as no precise time was fixed for payment, it might as well be recovered before the commencement of the labor or during its progress, as at any subsequent period. While the contract was executory and in the course of execution and the plaintiff was in the employ of the defendant, it would never have been thought an action could be maintained for the precise sum of compensation agreed upon for the year. The agreement of the defendant was as entire on his part to pay, as that of the plaintiff to serve. The latter was to serve *one year*, the former to pay *one hundred and twenty dollars*. Upon the construction contended for by the plaintiff's counsel, . . . there is no rule by which the defendant's liability can be determined. The plaintiff might as well claim his wages by the month as by the year, by the week as by the month, and by the day or hour as by either. The responsibility of the defendant would thus be affected in a manner totally inconsistent with the terms of his agreement to pay for a year's service in one certain and entire amount. Besides, a construction to this effect is utterly repugnant to the general understanding of the nature of such engagements. The usages of the country and common opinion upon subjects of this description are especially to be regarded. . . . [I]n no case has a contract in the terms of the one under consideration, been construed by practical men to give a right to demand the agreed compensation, before the performance of the labor, and that the employer and employed alike universally so understand it. The rule of law is in entire accordance with this sentiment. . . .

The performance of a year's service was in this case a condition precedent to the obligation of payment. The plaintiff must perform the condition, before he is entitled to recover any thing under the contract, and he has no right to renounce his agreement and recover upon a *quantum meruit*. . . . The decisions in the English cases express the same doctrine, and the principle is fully supported by all the elementary writers.

But it has been urged, that whatever may be the principle of the common law, and the decisions in the courts of New York on this subject, a different rule of construction has been adopted in this commonwealth; and we are bound to believe that such has sometimes been the fact, from the opinion of the learned and respectable judge who tried this cause, and from instances of similar decisions cited at the bar, but not reported. The occasion of so great a departure from ancient and well established principles cannot well be understood. It has received no sanction at any time from the judgment of this Court within the period of our Reports. . . . The law indeed is most reasonable in itself. It denies only to a party an advantage from his own wrong. It requires him to act justly by a faithful performance of his own engagements, before he exacts the fulfilment of dependent obligations on the part of others. It will not admit of the monstrous absurdity, that a man may voluntarily and without cause violate his agreement, and make the very breach of that agreement the foundation of an action which he could not maintain under it. Any apprehension that this rule may be abused to the purposes of oppression, by holding out an inducement to the employer, by unkind treatment near the close of a term of service, to drive the laborer from his engagement, to the sacrifice of his wages, is wholly groundless. It is only in cases where the desertion is voluntary and without cause on the part of the laborer, or fault or consent on the part of the employer, that the principle applies. Wherever there is a reasonable excuse, the law allows a recovery. To say that this is not sufficient protection, that an excuse may in fact exist in countless secret and indescribable circumstances, which from their very nature are not susceptible of proof, or which, if proved, the law does not recognise as adequate, is to require no less than that the law should *presume* what can never legally be established, or should admit that as *competent*, which by positive rules is held to be wholly *immaterial*. We think well established principles are not thus to be shaken, and that in this commonwealth more especially, where the important business of husbandry leads to multiplied engagements of precisely this description, it should least of all be questioned, that the laborer is worthy of his hire, only upon the performance of his contract, and as the reward of fidelity.

The judgment of the Court of Common Pleas is reversed, and a new trial granted at the bar of this Court.

Britton v. Turner

Supreme Court of New Hampshire, 1834.
6 N.H. 481.

[Plaintiff agreed to work on defendant's farm for one year, from March 1831 to March 1832, at a wage of $120 for the year. After working until December 27, 1831, just over 9½ months, plaintiff abandoned performance. Plaintiff's suit in assumpsit included a count in quantum meruit alleging the worth of the work done to be $100. The defense was that the work had been done under a "special contract" which was unfulfilled, though defendant offered no evidence of damages resulting from plaintiff's departure.

The trial judge instructed the jury that plaintiff was entitled to recover under the quantum meruit count what his labor "was reasonably worth," even though he had left the job without defendant's consent and without good cause. The jury gave plaintiff a verdict for $95.]

PARKER, J. . . . It may be assumed, that the labor performed by the plaintiff, and for which he seeks to recover a compensation in this action, was commenced under a special contract to labor for the defendant the term of one year, for the sum of one hundred and twenty dollars, and that the plaintiff has labored but a portion of that time, and has voluntarily failed to complete the entire contract. It is clear, then, that he is not entitled to recover upon the contract itself. . . But the question arises, can the plaintiff . . . recover a reasonable sum for the service he has actually performed, under the count in *quantum meruit*. Upon this, and questions of a similar nature, the decisions to be found in the books are not easily reconciled.

It has been held, upon contracts of this kind for labor to be performed at a specified price, that the party who voluntarily fails to fulfil the contract by performing the whole labor contracted for, is not entitled to recover any thing for the labor actually performed, however much he may have done towards the performance, and this has been considered the settled rule of law upon this subject. [Stark v. Parker, 2 Pick. 267] That such rule in its operation may be very unequal, not to say unjust, is apparent.

A party who contracts to perform certain specified labor, and who breaks his contract in the first instance, without any attempt to perform it, can only be made liable to pay the damages which the other party has sustained by reason of such non performance, which in many instances may be trifling—whereas a party who in good faith has entered upon the performance of his contract, and nearly completed it, and then abandoned the further performance—although the other party has had the full benefit of all that has been done, and has perhaps sustained no actual damage—is in fact subjected to a loss of all which has been performed, in the nature of damages for the non fulfilment, of the remainder, upon the technical rule, that the contract must be fully performed in order to a recovery of any part of the compensation. By the operation of this rule, then, the party who attempts performance may be placed in a much worse situation than he who wholly disregards his contract, and the other party may receive much more, by the breach of the contract, than the injury which he has sustained by such breach, and more than he could be entitled to were he seeking to recover damages by an action.

The case before us presents an illustration. Had the plaintiff in this case never entered upon the performance of his contract, the damage could not probably have been greater than some small expense and trouble incurred in procuring another to do the labor which he had contracted to perform. But having entered upon the performance, and labored nine and a half months, the value of which labor to the defendant as found by the jury is $95, if the defendant can succeed in this defence, he in fact receives nearly five sixths of the value of a whole year's labor, by reason of the breach of contract by the plaintiff, a sum not only utterly disproportionate to any probable, not to say possible damage which could have resulted from the neglect of the plaintiff to continue the remaining two and an half months, but altogether beyond any damage which could have been recovered by the defendant, had the plaintiff done nothing towards the fulfilment of his contract.

[In an omitted passage, the court noted the leading case of Lantry v. Parks, 8 Cow. 63 (N.Y. 1827), which held that an employee who left a job after completing just over 10 months of a one-year contract could recover nothing for his labor.]

There are other cases, however, in which principles have been adopted leading to a different result. It is said, that where a party contracts to perform certain work, and to furnish materials, as, for instance, to build a house, and the work is done, but with some variations from the mode prescribed by the contract, yet if the other party has the benefit of the labor and materials he should be bound to pay so much as they are reasonably worth. . . . It is in truth virtually conceded in such cases that the work has not been done, for if it had been, the party performing it would be entitled to recover upon the contract itself. . . .

Those cases are not to be distinguished, in principle, from the present, unless it be in the circumstance, that where the party has contracted to furnish materials, and do certain labor, as to build a house in a specified manner, if it is not done according to the contract, the party for whom it is built may refuse to receive it—elect to take no benefit from what has been performed—and therefore if he does receive, he shall be bound to pay the value—whereas in a contract for labor, merely, from day to day, the party is continually receiving the benefit of the contract under an expectation that it will be fulfilled, and cannot, upon the breach of it, have an election to refuse to receive what has been done, and thus discharge himself from payment. But we think this difference in the nature of the contracts does not justify the application of a different rule in relation to them.

The party who contracts for labor merely, for a certain period, does so with full knowledge that he must, from the nature of the case, be accepting part performance from day to day, if the other party commences the performance, and with knowledge also that the other may eventually fail of completing the entire term. If under such circumstances he actually receives a benefit from the labor performed, over and above the damage occasioned by the failure to complete there is as much reason why he should pay the reasonable worth of what has thus been done for his benefit, as there is when he enters and occupies the house which has been built for him, but not according to the stipulations of the contract, and which he perhaps enters, not because he is satisfied with what has been done, but because circumstances compel him to accept it such as it is. . . .

If on [a] failure to perform the whole, the nature of the contract be such that the employer can reject what has been done, and refuse to receive any benefit from the part performance, he is entitled so to do, and in such case is not liable to be charged, unless he has before assented to and accepted of what has been done, however much the other party may have done towards the performance. He has in such case received nothing, and having contracted to receive nothing but the entire matter contracted for, he is not bound to pay, because his express promise was only to pay on receiving the whole, and having actually received nothing the law cannot and ought not to raise an implied promise to pay. But where the party receives value—takes and uses the materials, or has advantage from the labor, he is liable to pay the reasonable worth of what he has received. 1 Camp. 38, Farnsworth v. Garrard. And the rule is the same whether it was received and accepted by the assent of the party prior to the breach, under a contract by which, from its nature, he was to receive labor, from time to time until the completion of the whole contract; or whether it was received and accepted by an assent subsequent to the performance of all which was in fact done. If he received it under such circumstances as precluded him from rejecting it afterwards, that does not alter the case—it has still been received by his assent.

In fact we think the technical reasoning, that the performance of the whole labor is a condition precedent, and the right to recover any thing dependent upon it—that the contract being entire there can be no apportionment—and that there being an express contract no other can be implied, even upon the subsequent performance of service—is not properly applicable to this species of contract, where a beneficial service has been actually performed; for we have abundant reason to believe, that the general understanding of the community is, that the hired laborer shall be entitled to compensation for the service actually performed, though he do not continue the entire term contracted for, and such contracts must be presumed to be made with reference to that understanding, unless an express stipulation shows the contrary. . . .

It is easy, if parties so choose, to provide by an express agreement that nothing shall be earned, if the laborer leaves his employer without having performed the whole service contemplated, and then there can be no pretence for a recovery if he voluntarily deserts the service before the expiration of the time.

The amount, however, for which the employer ought to be charged, where the laborer abandons his contract, is only the reasonable worth, or the amount of advantage he receives upon the whole transaction, . . . and, in estimating the value of the labor, the contract price for the service cannot be exceeded. . . . If a person makes a contract fairly he is entitled to have it fully performed, and if this is not done he is entitled to damages. He may maintain a suit to recover the amount of damage sustained by the non performance.

The benefit and advantage which the party takes by the labor, therefore, is the amount of value which he receives, if any, after deducting the amount of damage; and if he elects to put this in defence he is entitled so to do, and the implied promise which the law will raise, in such case, is to pay such amount of the stipulated price for the whole labor, as remains after deducting what it would cost to procure a completion of the residue of the service, and also any damage which has been sustained by reason of the non fulfilment of the contract.

If in such case it be found that the damages are equal to, or greater than the amount of the labor performed, so that the employer, having a right to the full performance of the contract, has not upon the whole case received a beneficial service, the plaintiff cannot recover.

This rule, by binding the employer to pay the value of the service he actually receives, and the laborer to answer in damages where he does not complete the entire contract, will leave no temptation to the former to drive the laborer from his service, near the close of his term, by ill treatment, in order to escape from payment; nor to the latter to desert his service before the stipulated time, without a sufficient reason; and it will in most instances settle the whole controversy in one action, and prevent a multiplicity of suits and cross actions. . . .

Applying the principles thus laid down, . . . the plaintiff is entitled to judgment on the verdict. The defendant . . . does not appear to have offered evidence to show that he was damnified by [the] breach, or to have asked that a deduction should be made upon that account. The direction to the jury was therefore correct, that the plaintiff was entitled to recover as much as the labor performed was reasonably worth, and the jury appear to have allowed a *pro rata* compensation, for the time which the plaintiff labored in the defendant's service. . . . Judgment on the verdict.

NOTE

Should the restitution claim of the employee who quits without legal justification be affected by the moral quality of the employee's conduct? For a long, long time in this country, employees who abandoned employment contracts without compelling reason were refused relief in restitution, even though in other settings—e.g., a purchaser's default under a land contract—the character or quality of the breach might well be accorded less weight by the courts. Where the employee, discharged for "cause" (a good reason), had nevertheless made an effort to perform, courts adhering to the strict view occasionally softened their resistance to quasi-contractual relief. Today, though prediction is not easy (i.e., cases granting an employee restitution, without much attention given the reasons why performance was abandoned or proved defective, continue to appear regularly in the reports), the strictest tests probably are still applied to defaulters under service contracts not involving the construction or repair of buildings. See, e.g., Bright v. Ganas, 171 Md. 493, 189 A. 427 (1937) (misconduct amounting to "moral depravity"—here, revealing a fixation on the employer's spouse—bars all recovery, on an express contract and in quantum meruit for work already done); Stiff v. Associated Sewing Supply Co., 436 N.W.2d 777 (Minn. 1989) ("gross misconduct" involving dishonesty and disloyalty triggers common law's longstanding "forfeiture doctrine," under which employer owes employee nothing).

NOTE: THE "GRAND TRADITION"

The opinion in Britton v. Turner warrants a brief word on judicial style. As Stark v. Parker suggests, the great weight of authority was contrary to the *Britton* result. Justice Parker's effort, under any test of balloting, surely qualifies for the Contracts Hall of Fame. It seems appropriate to recall the following passage from Professor Karl Llewellyn's memorable discussion of judges and judging (The Bramble Bush 157–158 (1951)):

> But I am concerned here with one special phase of the conditioning machinery of judges which goes not only unplanned but substantially unnoticed: that of the period-style of the law-crafts. It seems to me essential to health of our law and legal work that student, bar and bench should know that the Grand Tradition of the Common Law is our rightful heritage and needs complete and conscious recapture. They should read enough in the reports of the 1830's or 1840's (and a single volume read in sequence is commonly enough) to recognize as a prevailing style a handling of material as essentially made up of principle rather than of mere precedent, and of that finer type of principle which has perceptible reason and makes perceptible sense in life. They should come to recognize the court's steady quest for rules which satisfy the needs of the Grand

Tradition—each rule with a singing reason apparent on its face, each rule a rule whose reason guides and often even controls application according to the double maxim: *the rule follows where its reason leads; where the reason stops, there stops the rule.* They should come to recognize the steady and open checking of results against sense and decency as an of-courseness of our system of precedent when that system is working right; to recognize as of the essence a following because reason dictates following, a distinguishing or developing or shift in direction because reason dictates as the case may be distinction or development or shift.

Only then can student or bar or bench perceive that the conceptions of precedent as a static something, of movement as queer or improper or "departure," of figuring a court's prospective result without taking full account of the guidance the court rightly seeks also from its sense of decency and sense—that such conceptions are an aberration which crept upon and into lawyers' thinking in those least happy days of our legal system, the 80's and 90's of the Nineteenth Century. Not every court fell prey to the new formal style of work at the same time. . . . But the thinking of the whole bar about the proper way of judicial work had taken shape by 1910 as if the Grand Tradition had never been. It is against a rediscovery of the latter that student, bar and bench can then come, and come at once, to recognize that the picture of our appellate courts over the past thirty years, and increasingly with each of the decades, is one not of departing from the "good" old ways but rather of a groping, almost instinctive struggle to recapture the truly good and older ways which to the discredit of the work of law had slid into the bog.

Of course there is confusion when courts seek to work in the Grand Manner but still seek to write in the Formal Style. For esthetic comfort, work and opinion should match in style. For clarity of mind in judging, a man's verbal tools should fit comfortably into the jobs he is seeking to do with them. For consistency of results, a man needs conscious knowledge of the kind of result he has the job of gunning for—else again and again, and quite unpredictably, he fails to aim or aims in the wrong direction. Finally, for the sure pride of craft and craftsmanship which comforts and strengthens, which gives courage and infuses beauty and vision, for that a man needs not only personal knowledge of his finer craft traditions, but recognition by his fellows that he has such knowledge and that he works with it in the little as in the large.

Pinches v. Swedish Evangelical Lutheran Church

Supreme Court of Errors of Connecticut, 1887.
55 Conn. 183, 10 A. 264.

BEARDSLEY, J. The plaintiff claims to recover upon the counts for work and materials furnished in the erection of a church edifice for the defendants. A written contract was entered into by the parties, providing that the plaintiff should erect the edifice upon the land of the defendants, in accordance with certain plans and specifications. The plaintiff completed the building on the twenty-first day of January, 1885, when the defendants entered into the full possession and occupancy of the same. The building varies from the requirements of the contract in several material particulars. The ceiling is two feet lower, the windows are shorter and narrower, and the seats are narrower than the specifications require, and there are some other variations and omissions. The defect in the height of the ceiling is due to the combined error of the plaintiff and the defendants' architect. The other changes and omissions occurred through the inadvertence of the plaintiff and his workmen. The defendants knew of the change in the height of the ceiling when they took possession of the building, and of the changes in the windows and seats shortly afterwards, and objected to the changes as soon as they discovered them.

The plaintiff, in doing the work and furnishing the materials, acted in good faith, and the building, as completed, is reasonably adapted to the wants and requirements of the defendants, and its use is beneficial to them. It would be practically impossible to make the building conform to the contract without taking it partially down and rebuilding it. The defendants . . . offered evidence to prove the amount it would cost to make the building conform to the contract; claiming that they were entitled to such sum as damages. The court excluded the evidence, and the only error assigned is the exclusion of that evidence. The defendants' claim rests upon the assumption that the liability of the plaintiff to damages is not affected by the fact that his deviation from the contract was unintentional, nor by the advantageous use of the building, but that it is the same as it would have been if he had willfully departed from the contract, and they had rejected the building, and received no benefit from it.

The defendants' claim is undoubtedly supported by decisions of courts of eminent authority in England and this country, which hold that no recovery can be had for labor or materials furnished under a special contract, unless the contract has been performed, or its performance has been dispensed with by the other party.

The hardship of this rule upon the contractor who has undesignedly violated his contract, and the inequitable advantage it gives to the party who receives and retains the benefit of his labor and materials, has led to its qualification; and the weight of authority is now clearly in favor of allowing compensation for services rendered and materials furnished under a special contract, but not in entire conformity with it, provided that the deviation from the contract was not willful, and the other party has availed himself of and been benefited by such labor and materials, and, as a general rule, the amount of such compensation is to depend upon the extent of the benefit conferred, having reference to the contract price for the entire work. . . . In cases where only some additions to the work are required to finish it according to the contract, or where . . . the defects in it may be remedied at a reasonable expense, it seems proper to deduct from the contract price the sum which it would cost to complete it, as was done in that case.

In the present case the result of the plaintiff's labor and materials is a structure adapted to the purpose for which it was built, and of which the defendants are in the use and enjoyment, but which cannot be made to conform to the special contract, except by an expenditure which would probably deprive the plaintiff of any compensation for his labor.

We think that the court below properly deducted from the contract price the amount of the diminution in the value of the building by reason of the plaintiff's deviation from the contract. There is no error.

PARK, C.J., and CARPENTER, J., concurred. PARDEE and LOOMIS, JJ., dissented.

NOTE

Judge Learned Hand's analysis in Schwasnick v. Blandin, 65 F.2d 354 (2d Cir. 1933), may be helpful here. A lumberman who had contracted to cut timber on defendant's land left the job when defendant, claiming the work was defective, refused to pay a salary installment. The lumberman then sued on the common counts and recovered a judgment based on a jury's verdict.

Judge Hand reversed and remanded the case for a new trial. The trial court's charge to the jury was found to be erroneous in that the jury was told that (1) if plaintiff had failed to perform the work in a workmanlike manner, even in "bad faith," he might nevertheless recover the reasonable value of his services; and (2) defendant had the burden of proving that the plaintiff had broken the contract. Observing also that the "whole action was misconceived" below (the case apparently was tried as one in special assumpsit for damages, when in fact it "could be nothing else" but on the counts for restitution), Judge Hand declared:

> When the promisee has not performed, he obviously cannot recover on the [defendant's] promise. . . . Yet when the default is not willful and deliberate, it is generally agreed that he may recover so much as his efforts have actually benefited the promisor. [Citing cases, including Pinches.] The theory is that it is unjust for the promisor to profit, even though his promise has never become absolute. Furthermore, if the promisee has performed so far as he has gone, and the promisor breaks his promise, the promisee may abandon the contract and sue for restitution, in which he can recover the reasonable value of his services, measured by what he could have got for them in the market, and not by their benefit to the promisor. . . .
>
> This difference in the recovery is in accord with principle. When the promisee has not fulfilled the condition of the promise, and cannot charge the promisor with a breach, he may invoke only the equitable intervention of a court, though the remedy is legal in

form. Justice demands no more than that the promisor shall not profit at the promisee's expense. . . .

The charge upon the burden of proof was [also wrong], because if the plaintiff wished . . . to recover on the theory that though he had not performed, he was not in willful and deliberate default, he was . . . bound to prove that he was not, since that too was a condition upon the implied obligation to restore any benefits received. . . . [T]he burden was on him to prove the amount of that benefit; that is, by how much the defendants were enriched, notwithstanding any injuries done to their [land, tools, or timber]. [T]he jury should have been told to find the net benefit of the plaintiff's services to the defendant after deducting any injuries so done by defective work.

Observe Judge Hand's assertion that the law's different treatment of the restitution recovery when it is the plaintiff, not the defendant, who is in substantial default is "in accord with principle." Is it difficult to find the "principle" for defining the objective of restitution differently in cases like *Britton* or *Schwasnick*?

Putting the willfulness disqualification aside, it is fair to say that courts have not been in agreement on the principles for determining whether the plaintiff's own nonperformance precludes a restitution remedy. In some places (the state of New York, for one), courts have found that a building contractor whose work fails to add up to "substantial performance" is denied relief in quasi-contract altogether. Steel Storage & Elevator Constr. Co. v. Stock, 225 N.Y. 173, 121 N.E. 786 (1919), remains the leading authority. The view with a much larger following holds that a contractor who fails to satisfy the test of substantial performance may recover in quasi-contract for the value of work done (less, of course, the other's damages). E.g., Levan v. Richter, 152 Ill.App.3d 1082, 504 N.E.2d 1373 (1987). We will see more of these doctrines in this book, especially "substantial performance."

Kelley v. Hance

108 Conn. 186, 142 A. 683 (1928)

Plaintiff agreed to excavate to the proper level and construct a concrete sidewalk and curb in the front of defendant's property, for a price of $420. Plaintiff removed a strip of earth, 12 feet wide and 8 feet deep, then left the premises and did not return. Defendant notified plaintiff that the contract was cancelled. Plaintiff sued to recover the reasonable value of the work done, which was found to be $158.60, and in the trial court recovered judgment for that amount minus $25, the value of earth removed by plaintiff. *Held*, reversed. In a construction contract like this a contractor who has deviated slightly from the contract, not willfully but in good faith, can recover if there has been a "substantial performance" (citing *Pinches*). Even where the performance is not substantial but the breach is merely negligent, recovery can be allowed, not on the contract but in quasi-contract. Also, a voluntary acceptance of benefits may raise an implied promise, but acceptance will not be implied from a mere retention of possession of land on which work has been done where the benefit cannot be returned. Here, however, plaintiff abandoned the work without justification before any part of the sidewalk and curb was built and no acceptance by defendant has been shown. Plaintiff can recover nothing.

NOTE: "WILLFUL" BREACH

As Learned Hand noted in *Schwasnick*, a "willful and deliberate" breach—this phrase was written into the first Restatement, § 357—is commonly said to preclude restitution (indeed, all relief). An "intentional" deviation from a contract, particularly a construction contract, may be given the effect of willfulness. E.g., Material Movers, Inc. v. Hill, 316 N.W.2d 13 (Minn. 1982). See also Smedley v. Walden, 246 Mass. 393, 141 N.E. 281 (1923) (disapproving jury instruction distinguishing good faith from intentional breach, because "an intentional departure [in performance] is in itself such bad faith as bars recovery, regardless of the presence or absence of an intent to gain or obtain some advantage thereby"). If the many stern denials found in the opinions are to be believed, one would expect to find that restitution is withheld regardless of the size of the forfeiture. Yet a search of the restitution cases—even a search limited to the construction cases, one of the most active groupings—fails to reveal many instances of judicial tolerance of clearly severe forfeiture.

The court that decided Britton v. Turner has invoked that decision to cast doubt on the customary view that "willful" conduct bars a restitution recovery. See, e.g., R.J. Berke & Co., Inc. v. J.P. Griffin, Inc., 116 N.H. 760, 367 A.2d 583 (1976) ("[t]he quality of the breach bears no logical relationship to the theory of quantum meruit recovery"). The court that in the 1920s decided Kelley v. Hance has, a half-century later, cited that decision as evidence of Connecticut's approval of the proposition that "a contractor who is guilty of a 'wilful' breach cannot maintain an action upon the contract." Vincenzi v. Cerro, 186 Conn. 612, 442 A.2d 1352 (1982). Still, that court was quick to add:

> The contemporary view, however, is that even a conscious and intentional departure from the contract specifications will not necessarily defeat recovery, but may be considered as one of the several factors involved in deciding whether there has been full performance. 3A Corbin, Contracts § 707; 2 Rest.2d, Contracts § 237, comment d. The pertinent inquiry is not simply whether the breach was "wilful" but whether the behavior of the party in default "comports with standards of good faith and fair dealing." 2 Rest.2d, Contracts § 241(e); see comment f. Even an adverse conclusion on this point is not decisive but is to be weighed with other factors, such as the extent to which the owner will be deprived of a reasonably expected benefit and the extent to which the builder may suffer forfeiture, in deciding whether there has been substantial performance.

In keeping with this approach, the Restatement, Second's provision on restitution for a party in breach, § 374, drops any mention of willfulness, explaining in a Reporter's Note that the section is intended to be "more liberal in allowing recovery in accord with the policy behind UCC § 2–718(2)."

We shall return to the factor of willfulness or bad faith in Chapter 5. That issue, as well as restitution for defaulters generally, is discussed fully in 1 G. Palmer, The Law of Restitution §§ 5.1–5.15 (1978).

Vines v. Orchard Hills, Inc.

Supreme Court of Connecticut, 1980.
181 Conn. 501, 435 A.2d 1022.

PETERS, J.[6] This case concerns the right of purchasers of real property, after their own default, to recover moneys paid at the time of execution of a valid contract of sale. The plaintiffs, Euel D. Vines and his wife Etta Vines, contracted, on July 11, 1973, to buy Unit No. 10, Orchard Hills Condominium [in] New Canaan, from the defendant Orchard Hills, Inc. for $78,800. On or before that date, they had paid the defendant $7880 as a down payment toward the purchase. Alleging that the sale of the property was never consummated, the plaintiffs sought to recover their down payment. The trial court [overruled] the defendant's demurrer to the plaintiffs' amended complaint [and], after a hearing, . . . rendered judgment for the plaintiffs for $7880 plus interest. The defendant's appeal maintains that its demurrer should have been sustained, that its liquidated damages clause should have been enforced, and that evidence of the value of the property at the time of the trial should have been excluded.

. . . When the purchasers contracted to buy their condominium in July, 1973, they paid $7880, a sum which the contract of sale designated as liquidated damages.[1] The purchasers decided not to take title to the condominium because Euel D. Vines was transferred by his employer to New Jersey; the Vines so informed the seller by a letter dated January 4, 1974. There has never been any claim that the seller has failed, in any respect, to conform to his obligations under the contract, nor does the

---

[6] [Ellen Ash Peters was a member of the Connecticut high court from 1978 to 2000; she served as Chief Justice from 1984 to 1996. Prior to her appointment to the bench, she was the Southmayd Professor of Law at the Yale Law School, teaching and writing in the field of commercial law. Justice Peters' scholarly works include a highly influential article that remains a classic today, Remedies for Breach of Contracts Relating to the Sale of Goods Under the Uniform Commercial Code: A Roadmap for Article Two, 73 Yale L.J. 199 (1963).—Eds.]

[1] Paragraph 9 of the contract of sale provided: "DEFAULT: In the event Purchaser fails to perform any of the obligations herein imposed on the Purchaser, the Seller performing all obligations herein imposed on the Seller, the Seller shall retain all sums of money paid under this Contract, as liquidated damages, and all rights and liabilities of the parties hereto shall be at an end."

complaint allege that the purchasers are legally excused from their performance under the contract. In short, it is the purchasers and not the seller whose breach precipitated the present cause of action.

. . . [T]he purchasers established that the value of the condominium that they had agreed to buy for $78,800 in 1973 had, by the time of the trial in 1979, a fair market value of $160,000. The trial court relied on this figure to conclude that, because the seller had gained what it characterized as a windfall of approximately $80,000, the purchasers were entitled to recover their down payment of $7880. Neither the purchasers nor the seller proffered any evidence at the trial to show the market value of the condominium at the time of the purchasers' breach of their contract or the damages sustained by the seller as a result of that breach. . . .

The ultimate issue on this appeal is the enforceability of a liquidated damages clause as a defense to a claim of restitution by purchasers in default on a land sale contract. Although the parties, both in the trial court and here, have focused on the liquidated damages clause per se, we must first consider when, if ever, purchasers who are themselves in breach of a valid contract of sale may affirmatively invoke the assistance of judicial process to recover back moneys paid to, and withheld by, their seller.

The right of a contracting party, despite his default, to seek restitution for benefits conferred and allegedly unjustly retained has been much disputed in the legal literature and in the case law. See 5A Corbin, Contracts §§ 1122–1135 (1964); Dobbs, Remedies § 12.14 (1973); 1 Palmer, Restitution, c. 5 (1978). . . . Although earlier cases often refused to permit a party to bring an action that could be said to be based on his own breach, see, e.g., [Ketchum & Sweet v. Evertson, 13 Johns. 359, 365 (N.Y. 1816)],[7] many of the more recent cases support restitution in order to prevent unjust enrichment and to avoid forfeiture. See, e.g., [Freedman v. Rector, Wardens & Vestrymen of St. Mathias Parish, 37 Cal.2d 16, 230 P.2d 629 (1951); De Leon v. Aldrete, 398 S.W.2d 160 (Tex.Civ.App. 1965)].

A variety of considerations, some practical and some theoretical, underlie this shift in attitude toward the plaintiff in breach. As Professor Corbin pointed out in his seminal article, "The Right of a Defaulting Vendee to the Restitution of Installments Paid," 40 Yale L.J. 1013 (1931), the anomalous result of denying any remedy to the plaintiff in breach is to punish more severely the person who has partially performed, often in good faith, than the person who has entirely disregarded his contractual obligations from the outset. Only partial performance triggers a claim for restitution, and partial performance will not, in the ordinary course of

---

[7] [The *Ketchum* court denied defaulting vendees recovery of a $700 down payment on a farm, saying: "It would be an alarming doctrine to hold that the plaintiffs might violate the contract and, because they chose to do so, make their own infraction of the agreement the basis of an action for money had and received. Every man who makes a bad bargain, and has advanced money upon it, would have the right to recover it back that the plaintiffs have."—Eds.]

events, have been more injurious to the innocent party than total nonperformance. Recognition of a claim in restitution is, furthermore, consistent with the economic functions that the law of contracts is designed to serve. . . . The principal purpose of remedies for the breach of contract is to provide compensation for loss, . . . and therefore a party injured by breach of contract is entitled to retain nothing in excess of that sum which compensates him for the loss of his bargain. Indeed, there are those who argue that repudiation of contractual obligations is socially desirable, and should be encouraged, whenever gain to the party in breach exceeds loss to the party injured by breach. Birmingham, "Breach of Contract, Damage Measures, and Economic Efficiency," 24 Rut.L.Rev. 273, 284 (1970); Posner, Economic Analysis of Law § 4.9, pp. 89–90 (2d Ed. 1977). To assign such primacy to inferences drawn from economic models requires great confidence that the person injured by breach will encounter no substantial difficulties in establishing the losses for which he is entitled to be compensated. It is not necessary to push the principle of compensatory damages that far, or to disregard entirely the desirability of maintaining some incentives for the performance of promises. A claim in restitution, although legal in form, is equitable in nature, and permits a trial court to balance the equities, to take into account a variety of competing principles to determine whether the defendant has been unjustly enriched. . . .

In this state, at the turn of the century, in Pierce v. Staub, 78 Conn. 459, 62 A. 760 (1906), this court acknowledged the equitable claim of a purchaser in breach to recover moneys paid under a contract to purchase real property. Pierce v. Staub is distinguishable from the case before us, because the court there found that the parties had, after the buyer's breach, rescinded the contracts in question. In view of this rescission, the purchaser's widow was held to be entitled to a return of the $60,000 paid on the purchase price of $150,000. . . . Apart from Pierce v. Staub, we have never directly decided whether a purchaser of real estate may, despite his breach, recover payments made to his seller. But Pierce v. Staub is an impressive, and an impressively early, guidepost toward permitting such a cause of action. The court's narrow reliance on the possibly artificial conclusion of mutual rescission should not obscure the breadth of its language deploring forfeiture. . . . We therefore conclude that a purchaser whose breach is not willful has a restitutionary claim to recover moneys paid that unjustly enrich his seller. In this case, no one has alleged that the purchasers' breach, arising out of a transfer to a more distant place of employment, should be deemed to have been willful. The trial court was therefore not in error in initially overruling the seller's demurrer and entertaining the purchasers' cause of action.

> a deposit in real estate transactions when the buyer defaults cannot be blindly applied to non-real estate contracts without an examination of the relevant contract at issue. In the context of a real estate transaction, the amount of actual damages or net benefit conferred upon a seller as a result of a breach by the buyer and subsequent sale by the seller may be difficult to determine depending upon the real estate market, the seller's personal situation and the costs that may be incurred in remarketing the property and delaying the sale. A liquidated damages provision may be a practical estimate of the amount of actual damages in these situations. In the context of an auction sale, as in the case before this Court, parties participate knowing that they would be bound by their bids. There is generally a successful bidder and next successful bidder and the amount of their bids are known. While it is not often that the successful bidder fails to close, when this does occur, the next successful bidder is in place for closing to occur quickly without the need for further marketing of the assets and uncertainty on the part of the seller. Even rarer is a scenario where the ultimate purchase price from the next successful bidder would be greater than that of the original successful bid. Nevertheless, the difference between the original successful bid and the final purchase price is capable of a determination as to value whereas that may not be the case in a real estate transaction.

In re Brown Publishing Co., 486 B.R. 46, 58 (Bankr. E.D.N.Y. 2013).

SECTION 5. CONTRACTUAL CONTROLS ON THE DAMAGE REMEDY

INTRODUCTORY NOTE

The doctrines examined in this section say that a contract clause fixing damages in the event of breach is enforceable only if it constitutes a reasonable forecast of the injury resulting from breach, and then only if the injury is difficult to measure. A damages clause that is found to do something else will be classified as a "penalty" and held unenforceable.

The case of Pacheco v. Scoblionko, 532 A.2d 1036 (Me. 1987), provides a starting place. Plaintiff had for several years sent his child to defendant's summer camp. Since early payment of fees entitled a camper to a tuition reduction, plaintiff registered his child before February 1, paying in full the reduced charge of $3,100. The contract plaintiff signed was on a preprinted form supplied by defendant; it included a paragraph on "refunds" and "liquidated damages," as follows:

> The $500 deposit will be refunded if a request is received by the camp prior to February 1st, less a $25 administrative processing fee. If a refund request is received on or after February 1st and prior to May 1st, then no refund of the $500 deposit will be

made. If a refund request is received on or after May 1st, the entire sum then paid to date shall be retained by the camp. The parties agree that any deposit so retained would constitute liquidated damages for cancellation of the contract.

The camp season was to commence in July. On June 14, plaintiff was informed that his child, a high school student, had failed a final exam in Spanish and would be required to attend summer school. That same day plaintiff telephoned defendant, saying that his child would be unable to attend camp and asking for return of the fee paid. When defendant refused to refund any portion of the $3,100, plaintiff sued to recover it.

What was defendant's purpose in putting the "refund/liquidated damages" clause in the contract? Does a clause of this type serve any substantial and legitimate business interest?

The Maine Supreme Court, affirming a judgment for plaintiff for the full $3,100, agreed with the trial court that the clause in question was an "unenforceable penalty." The test of enforceability, said the court, is two-pronged: whether damages are "difficult to estimate accurately" and whether the amount fixed is a "reasonable forecast" of what is required to "justly compensate" the injured party. Here, defendant, who as the proponent of the clause bore the burden of proof of its validity, had failed to offer evidence as to what damages, if any, were anticipated or actually suffered as a result of plaintiff's cancellation. The amount declared forfeited was therefore "excessive" and "disproportionate to the contract price," suggesting that the clause was placed in the contract "for its in terrorem effect."

Is *Pacheco* an "easy" case to decide? Do you suppose that parents' last-minute withdrawals of their children is a recurring problem for summer-camp operators? Absent such a clause, how would a camp operator's damages be measured?

In approaching the materials that follow, it may be helpful to consider two differing perspectives:

> The rationale for the rule against enforcing penalties in contract cases is not crystal clear. But it is not hard to imagine why a court might be loath to enforce a contract provision specifying a disproportionately large sum—which courts call a penalty—for breach of the contract. The parties may make such an agreement far in advance of the dispute and may not appreciate the full impact if the unlikely breach does occur. Contract damages, broadly speaking, aim at compensation, not at punishment. Finally, courts do not like results that appear unjust. Xerox Fin. Serv. Life Ins. v. High Plains, 44 F.3d 1033 (1st Cir. 1995) (Boudin, J.).

> Parties are more likely to make a reasonable estimate of the harm from a breach of contract than judges are—it is the parties' money that is on the line, after all—even though the parties are making it in advance whereas the judges would be assessing harm after it had occurred as a result of the breach. If the parties make a mistake they have only themselves to blame; why should the courts get involved? Of course it is settled doctrine . . . that a party

that the party in whose favor the penalty or forfeiture exists must prove his damage.

can complain that a liquidated damages provision to which it freely

> futures market during the period beginning with the date of breach or default by the Grower (taking into account the grade, staple, and micronaire of such cotton) and ending with the final delivery by the Association of cotton sold during that year, and (b) the highest price per pound received by the Association for the membership cotton (of the same or nearest grade, staple, and micronaire) sold by it from the same year's crop.

The May 2011 letter didn't demand a specific liquidated-damages sum; rather, it stated that Autauga hoped to avoid a lawsuit and urged CCCC to "take prompt action to resolve this matter in a way that satisfies [Autauga]." Nearly three years later, Autauga's attorney sent a second letter that, for the first time—and purporting to use the formula set out in the agreement—calculated the liquidated damages to be $1,305,397. The second letter included an offer to settle for less if the Crosbys paid within 30 days; otherwise, it said, Autauga would be "forced to initiate a lawsuit." . . .

The Crosbys didn't pay, and Autauga sued. Claiming that the Crosbys had breached the marketing agreement by failing to deliver their pledged cotton for the 2010 crop year, Autauga asserted that it was entitled to liquidated damages. Having initially calculated the liquidated-damages sum to be $1,305,397, Autauga increased the amount to $1,340,225 when it filed its complaint—and then later revised it upward to $1,660,857, and then upward again to $1,712,846, and then downward to $1,696,610. . . .

The general common-law rules regarding liquidated damages are well-settled. Under Alabama law, bona fide liquidated-damages provisions—which prescribe "a sum to be paid in lieu of performance"—are enforceable, but "penalty" clauses—which impose "a security for the performance of the agreement or . . . a punishment for default"—are void. Camelot Music, Inc. v. Marx Realty & Imp. Co., 514 So.2d 987, 990 (Ala. 1987). The trick, of course, is distinguishing between the two. Helpfully, Alabama courts have identified three essential markers of a valid liquidated-damages provision: "First, the injury caused by the breach must be difficult or impossible to accurately estimate; second, the parties must intend to provide for damages rather than for a penalty; and, third, the sum stipulated must be a reasonable pre-breach [estimate] of the probable loss." If any one of these three criteria isn't satisfied, "the clause must fail as a penalty." Milton Const. Co. v. State Highway Dep't, 568 So.2d 784, 790 (Ala. 1990), overruled on other grounds by Ex parte Alabama Dep't of Transp., 978 So.2d 17, 23 (Ala. 2007). . . .

The Crosbys insist that the formula can't survive Camelot's three-part test. They attack the formula as unreasonable and punitive, criticizing its ambiguity and the grossly disproportionate results that it produces. We agree. Faithful application of Camelot requires us to conclude that the provision at issue here is an unenforceable penalty rather than a valid liquidated-damages clause. . . .

To begin, *Camelot's* first prong is easily satisfied—the injury caused by the Crosbys' alleged breach is "difficult or impossible to accurately estimate." 514 So.2d at 990. Indeed, although Autauga devotes the bulk of its briefing to arguing prong one, the Crosbys don't even dispute that it is met. The problem for Autauga isn't prong one, but rather prongs two and three. . . .

Camelot's second prong—whether the parties "intend[ed] to provide for damages rather than for a penalty"—weighs heavily against enforceability. We find two pieces of evidence particularly indicative of an intent to penalize rather than to compensate.

First, there is the text of the agreement itself. As a benchmark for measuring damages—*i.e.*, as the top number in what amounts to a subtraction equation—the liquidated-damages provision's formula uses the "highest price per pound received" by Autauga for cotton at any time during the relevant crop year, no matter how small the amount. That "highest price" factor certainly doesn't evidence an intent to reasonably estimate Autauga's actual loss. Indeed, so far as we can tell, it bears no necessary (or even probable) relationship to actual loss, or to the real world more generally. Why the "highest price," as opposed to the "average," "median," or even "lowest"? That question seems to us to answer itself—in order to pump up the prescribed damages and thereby maximally deter breaches of the agreement.

Second, Autauga's own damages expert confirmed what the agreement itself indicates when he repeatedly testified during his deposition—both on direct and on cross—that the liquidated-damages provision's formula was intended not to estimate actual loss, but rather to discourage breach. Asked point-blank initially, "What purpose does th[e] formula serve?" he answered, three separate times, "there's a disincentive for a farmer . . . to not perform and not deliver his cotton," "it's a disincentive to not perform, to breach the contract," and "it's a disincentive for anybody to breach the contract." When asked later if he wanted to clarify or add any nuance, Autauga's expert doubled down:

> Q: "I know you said that this formula is supposed to be a disincentive. But is it also supposed to approximate some loss to Autauga Quality Cotton Association?"
>
> A: "Yeah. I wouldn't agree with that. I would say it should have some attempt toward making Autauga whole, but I don't know that it is trying to approximate actual loss."

Finally, asked by Autauga's own lawyer, the expert reiterated that the liquidated-damages provision is "not a make-Autauga-whole" remedy, but rather a "disincentive for a farmer to not perform."

The evidence thus strongly indicates that the agreement's liquidated-damages provision was designed to deter breaches, not to estimate and compensate losses. Under longstanding Alabama law, a provision that is intended to serve as a disincentive to breach or a security for performance is void as a penalty. Accordingly, the formula fails *Camelot's* second factor. . . .

The formula also fails the third *Camelot* criterion because "the sum stipulated" isn't "a reasonable pre-breach [estimate] of the probable loss." 514 So.2d at 990.

As an initial matter, the liquidated-damages provision is fatally ambiguous. . . . [A]lthough the formula requires that the "price" be determined, in part, by reference to the "date of breach," it never defines that term—and perhaps not surprisingly, in offering a wide variety of damages calculations, Autauga has used as many as *eight* different breach dates, each presumably tied to some different alleged act or omission of CCCC. A formula plagued with such pervasive ambiguity doesn't—and can't—provide a reasonable pre-breach estimate of probable loss.

Finally, and separately. . . *Camelot's* third prong requires a hindsight comparison of actual harm to the damages prescribed by the contract. In this case, that comparison yields a grossly disproportionate number. Autauga is a non-profit association that recoups only its operating and marketing expenses before distributing earnings to its members. Here, the Crosbys (as members of the association) would have received the bulk of any sales revenue from their cotton. But the liquidated-damages sum that Autauga is seeking—now calculated to be $1,696,610—is more than 80% of the total sales value of CCCC's entire 2010 crop ($2,092,015.89) and nearly three times CCCC's 2010 net earnings ($592,015.89). The liquidated-damages figure vastly exceeds anything that Autauga could even possibly have lost as a result of the Crosbys' alleged breach. . . .

Put simply, there's just no evidence that the liquidated-damages formula here bears any relation to Autauga's probable loss. By contrast, the contractual language, Autauga's own expert's testimony, and the grossly disproportionate sum that Autauga claims combine to demonstrate that the agreement's liquidated-damages provision was intended as "a security for the performance of the agreement or as a punishment for default"—precisely what Alabama courts have forbidden. Accordingly, under the usual common-law rules, the liquidated-damages clause is a void and unenforceable penalty. . . .

Yockey v. Horn

880 F.2d 945 (7th Cir. 1989)

Two former business partners entered into a settlement agreement intended to resolve all disputes arising from their failed relationship. The settlement included a promise by Horn not to "voluntarily participate in any litigation against Frank Yockey" for events up to the date of the agreement (Yockey gave Margaret Horn a similar promise), as well as a clause fixing liquidated damages of $50,000 for either's breach by "voluntary participation in any lawsuit by anyone" against the other. A few months after signing the settlement, Horn, apparently disturbed by Yockey's business practices, contacted one Schrock, a business acquaintance who had invested money with Yockey. Although the substance of the Horn-Schrock conversations was not revealed, Schrock thereafter successfully sued Yockey for fraud and securities violations, recovering damages of $111,000. It was in that litigation that Horn, not under subpoena or other court process, gave a deposition which was received into evidence at the Schrock-Yockey trial. Yockey then sued Horn for breach of the settlement agreement, alleging that Horn, by giving the deposition, had violated her "covenant not to voluntarily participate" in litigation against Yockey. The trial court found a breach and awarded Yockey $50,000 in liquidated damages. *Held*, judgment affirmed "despite the rather harsh result." In the absence of clear Illinois precedent, we rely on general principles, notably Rest.2d § 356 [reproduced infra p. 189], which calls for enforcement of a liquidated damages clause if the amount estimated is reasonable either at the time of contracting or at the time of injury—provided the nonbreaching party has suffered some actual damage. On one view, it appears that Yockey suffered no injury by virtue of Horn's breach. Even if Horn had refused to testify without a subpoena, she could easily have been subpoenaed to give the same testimony. Moreover, Yockey concedes that Schrock's judgment against him was in no part based on Horn's deposition. But "[t]his analysis fails to account for other types of damage that Horn's breach might have caused. . . . Yockey's business reputation might have been significantly damaged in the eyes of investors or lenders when Horn, his former [partner], participated in litigation against him." Such damages are "difficult to evaluate" and, accordingly, the "proper subject" for a contract clause; they are also "what was anticipated." It follows that the $50,000 estimate was reasonable when made. "[A] great deal of damage might have been caused by Horn's breach."

QUESTION

What if the delay in completion of the work in *Muldoon* had been only 10 days?

COMMENT: THE PENAL BOND

In the early stages of the common law's development, the recovery of a penalty was a frequently used sanction for nonperformance of a contract. For planned transactions in which there was much at stake, it became customary to use the so-called "penal bond," which was a promise under seal to pay a specified sum of money if by a certain date a particular event did not occur—e.g., a sum of money was not paid, a house under construction was not completed, services promised were not rendered. The penalty—often a sum twice the amount of the actual obligation owed—was recoverable in the common law action of covenant. By the sixteenth century, however, the Chancery, concerned about oppression and extortion, had established the practice of intervening, regularly and predictably, to enjoin the collection of penal sums promised in bonds under seal. The underlying Chancery attitudes of disapproval were in time absorbed by the common law, aided by an English statute of 1687, and these have influenced our modern attitudes toward contractual penalties, as was noted in Muldoon v. Lynch. The interplay of ideas in this development has been summarized by Professor A.W.B. Simpson (A History of the Common Law of Contract 123–125 (1975)):

> [T]here existed for many centuries a divorce between contractual theory and contractual practice. This divorce can in its turn be understood if it is seen as reflecting a tension between two ideas. On the one hand we have the idea that the real function of contractual institutions is to make sure, so far as possible, that agreements are performed; the institution of the penal bond and the practice of the courts in upholding such bonds exemplified this idea. On the other hand we have the idea that it suffices for the law to provide compensation for loss suffered by failure to perform agreements. This second idea is not, of course, necessarily incompatible with the pursuit of the aim of encouraging contractual performance, but it is bound to impose a limitation upon the enthusiasm with which that aim is pursued, and there can well be contexts (for example, contracts for personal service) in which a positive value is attached to the right to break the contract so long as the defaulting party is made to pay compensation. Now if securing performance is the aim to be pursued, the use of penalties *in terrorem* of the party from whom performance is due is the natural and obvious technique. Thus today the decree of specific performance is given teeth by the threat of imprisonment for contempt, and in the criminal courts we are familiar with such institutions as the granting of bail and the entry into recognizances to keep the peace, which institutions, to those who are not over-impressed by labels, are nothing more than modern versions of the conditioned bond used to bind persons to the performance of contracts. What has happened is not that contracts *in terrorem* have been outlawed, or that the use of penal mechanisms no longer plays any part in contract law, but only that the courts have come to acquire a monopolistic control over the use of terror. It is today the courts which may do things which in former ages private citizens might do. Nobody who is familiar with the modern practice of hire-purchase, or other forms of usury could doubt that there is still a demand for private trafficking in penalties; the general trend is, however, to resist this demand.
>
> In early law this demand is not resisted; hence the prevalence in more or less primitive communities of the use of the pledge or hostage, at least in the case of important contracts, as a device for securing performance; where men cannot trust each other, and the machinery of the law is weak, the contracting party must place some important stake at the mercy of the other party. The penal bond for securing performance was a sophisticated form of self-pledge, and Shylock's bond with its forfeit of a pound of flesh neatly

illustrates the fact that the best pledge of all is the body of the contractor, which in early law he could have used as security. The provision of security for performance is still a common practice today, but the general triumph of the compensatory principle has radically altered its character; so far as the law is concerned, security has come to be non-penal where the device is used by private persons. The decline in the use of the penal bond, and the corresponding shift in the centre of gravity of contract law from the law of debt *sur obligation* to the law of the action on the case upon an assumpsit represents a major step in social evolution.

It would be a mistake, however, to suppose either that the decline in the popularity of the bond was rapid, or that the granting of relief against penalties deprived it of all usefulness. Commercial and legal habits do not change overnight, and even if the law only permits contracting parties to stipulate for liquidated damages of a compensatory character there can still be advantages in adopting this course rather than leaving the question open to later settlement in litigation or negotiation—for example, in contracts where the determination of compensatory damages is necessarily speculative. Furthermore there can be exceptions to the general principle, and ways of getting round it. Thus even today the use of the penal bond is not wholly obsolete in private transactions.

For some purposes, the practice of expressing formal obligations in the form of the ancient penal bond (a promise of a sum of money, followed by an express condition discharging the promisor in the event stated obligations are performed) is common even now. But the operative effect of such instruments—for example, a surety bond of the type sued on in *Algernon Blair*—is much different from that of its remote ancestor. As we shall see later, the conventional "interpretation" of the surety bond today converts what is stated as a condition of defeasance into a promise, with the sum promised functioning as an upper limit of liability and the principle of compensation measuring actual liability. Stated differently, a term fixing a flat sum as a penalty for the nonoccurrence of the condition of the bond is deemed unenforceable to the extent it exceeds the actual loss caused by such nonoccurrence.

Restatement of Contracts, Second

§ 356. Liquidated Damages and Penalties

(1) Damages for breach by either party may be liquidated in the agreement but only at an amount that is reasonable in the light of the anticipated or actual loss caused by the breach and the difficulties of proof of loss. A term fixing unreasonably large liquidated damages is unenforceable on grounds of public policy as a penalty.

Comment: . . .

b. *Test of penalty.* . . . [T]wo factors combine in determining whether an amount of money fixed as damages is so unreasonably large as to be a penalty. The first factor is the anticipated or actual loss caused by the breach. The amount fixed is reasonable to the extent that it approximates the actual loss that has resulted from the particular breach, even though it may not approximate the loss that might have been anticipated under other possible breaches. . . . [Alternatively,] the amount fixed is reasonable to the extent that it approximates the loss anticipated at the time of the making of the contract, even though it may not approximate the actual loss. . . . The second factor is the difficulty of proof of loss. The greater the difficulty either of proving that loss has occurred or of establishing its amount with the requisite certainty . . ., the easier it is to show that the amount fixed is reasonable. . . . If the difficulty of proof of loss is great, considerable latitude is allowed in the approximation of anticipated or actual harm. [If] the difficulty of proof of loss is slight, less latitude is allowed in that approximation. If, to take an extreme case, it is clear that no loss at all has occurred, a provision fixing a substantial sum as damages is unenforceable.

NOTE: ONE LOOK OR TWO?

The first Restatement of Contracts § 339 embraced the historical "time of contracting" test of validity (the reasonableness of the forecast when made, taking account of the difficulty of accurate estimation); any "hindsight" inquiry in light of actual damages caused by the breach was rejected. The Reporter's Note to § 356(1) of the second Restatement, reproduced above, states that the section "has been redrafted to harmonize with Uniform Commercial Code § 2–718(1)," with only slight changes in terminology. The UCC's 2–718(1), calling for greater flexibility in the evaluation of damage clauses, was before the New York's high court in Equitable Lumber Corp. v. IPA Land Dev. Corp., 38 N.Y.2d 516, 381 N.Y.S.2d 459, 344 N.E.2d 391 (1976). That court said:

> The first sentence of § 2–718(1) focuses on the situation of the parties both at the time of contracting and at the time of breach. Thus, a liquidated damages provision will be valid if reasonable with respect to *either* (1) the harm which the parties anticipate will result from the breach at the time of contracting or (2) the actual damages suffered by the non-defaulting party at the time of breach (see *Hawkland*, A Transactional Guide to the [UCC], § 1.–280101). Interestingly, § 2–718(1) does, in some measure, signal a departure from prior law which considered only the anticipated harm at the time of contracting. . . . Thus, decisions which have restricted their analysis of the validity of liquidated damages clauses solely to the anticipated harm at the time of contracting have, to this extent, been abrogated by the [UCC] in cases involving transactions in goods. . . . Having satisfied the test set forth in the first part of § 2–

718(1), a liquidated damages provision may nonetheless be invalidated under the last sentence of the section if it is so unreasonably large that it serves as a penalty rather than a good faith attempt to pre-estimate damages. . . .

It is clear that the law of liquidated damages has evolved over time. Assessing "reasonableness" at either the time of contract formation or at the time of the breach (a "second look") presumably means there is to be a larger role for damage clauses. Indeed, a leading decision asserts broadly that, in commercial transactions between parties with comparable bargaining power, the "modern trend" is toward enforcing stipulated damages clauses. Wasserman's Inc. v. Middletown, 137 N.J. 238, 645 A.2d 100 (1994) (reserving the issue of validity as concerns consumer contracts). Nevertheless, some courts (by one count, perhaps as many as 22), at least in the common law (non-UCC) cases, many involving real estate contracts, continue to adhere to the first Restatement's time-of-formation test. E.g., Watson v. Ingram, 124 Wash.2d 845, 881 P.2d 247 (1994) ("the prospective approach [of § 339] better fulfills the underlying purposes of liquidated damages clauses and gives greater weight to the parties' expectations"). One such case, Kelly v. Marx, 428 Mass. 877, 705 N.E.2d 1114 (1999), involved facts similar to Vines v. Orchard Hills, supra p. 171, in that the seller, within weeks of the breach, resold the property for $5,000 more than the contract price. The breached agreement had included this clause: "If the BUYER shall fail to fulfill the BUYER'S agreements herein, all deposits made hereunder by the BUYER shall be retained by the SELLER as liquidated damages." The court, limiting inquiry to a prospective or "single look," permitted the seller to keep the buyer's five percent deposit, explaining:

> [A] damages clause in a purchase and sale agreement will be enforced where, at the time the agreement was made, potential damages were difficult to determine and the clause was a reasonable forecast of damages expected to occur in the event of a breach. . . In addition to meeting the parties' expectations, the "single look" approach helps resolve disputes efficiently by making it unnecessary to wait until actual damages from a breach are proved. By reducing challenges to a liquidated damages clause, the "single look" approach eliminates uncertainty and tends to prevent costly future litigation. The "second look," by contrast, . . . increases the potential for litigation by inviting the aggrieved party to attempt to show evidence of damage when the contract is breached. . . . The plaintiffs argue that application of a "second look" approach would allow the court to guard against undue windfalls, such as the one the defendants would receive here if they were to keep the deposit, because the defendants suffered no loss from the breach of the sale. We disagree. In essence, the plaintiffs want to undo the agreement between the parties, who expect to receive stipulated damages, not damages resolved by a court examining postbreach circumstances. The parties agreed to the extent of their damages when they agreed on a liquidated damages clause. . . .

The Kelly v. Marx court, addressing Rest.2d § 356(1) specifically, made two points worth noting. One was a reiteration of agreement with the section's second sentence—a term fixing "unreasonably large" damages is an unenforceable penalty. The second was a flat rejection of any suggestion that § 356(1)'s comments and illustrations mean that a clause found "reasonable in light of anticipated loss" could, nevertheless, be unenforceable if the nonbreacher does not suffer a loss. Consider whether there is any inconsistency here.

Wilt v. Waterfield

273 S.W.2d 290 (Mo. 1954)

Plaintiffs' complaint alleged that defendant, owner of an 825-acre farm, had contracted to sell it to them for $19,000; that they had paid defendant $1,900 on the purchase price; and that defendant, in breach of contract, then sold the farm to someone else. The lower court entered judgment for plaintiffs for $7,000 damages. Defendant appealed, urging that plaintiffs' recovery was limited by a printed clause in the contract, providing: "If either party hereto fails or neglects to perform his part of this agreement, he shall forthwith pay and forfeit as liquidated damages to the other party a sum equal to ten percent of the agreed price of sale." The evidence showed that after signing the contract with plaintiffs, defendant had conveyed the farm to one Windon for $26,000 and had paid $1,900 to the agent who arranged the second sale. Plaintiffs contended that the quoted clause was a penalty and did not limit their recovery of actual damages. *Held*, plaintiffs are correct. The parties' intention, drawn from their words, governs the construction of clauses fixing damages. To arrive at that intention, a court "may consider whether the agreement contains various stipulations of various degrees of importance, the breaches of which would be easy to calculate in damages as to some and difficult as to others, in which event the sum specified would be construed as a penalty and not as liquidated damages. . . . [U]nder [this] contract defendant was bound to convey the full 825 acres; to share the 1951 crops of corn, oil beans and hay; to hold plaintiffs' check until September 19; to cut none of the lespedeza crop; to furnish abstract of title, to deliver deed and possession by February 20. [Plaintiffs say] these are of varying degrees of importance and would each give cause to a different amount of damages in case of failure to perform, bearing no relation to the amount fixed by the contract. . . . It seems apparent that if the defendant . . . had failed or neglected to perform [any part of any one of these duties], the damages accruing thereby to the plaintiffs might in some of such instances be entirely disproportionate to the $1,900 stipulated in the contract. Being so, such arbitrary amount would constitute a penalty. . . ." Given the proofs of the farm's value, the verdict of $7,000 was well within the difference between the purchase and market prices.

COMMENT: APPLYING DAMAGE CLAUSES

The *Wilt* case raises the problem of the "undifferentiated" clause. The conventional view is that a damage formula that "is invariant to the gravity of the breach," that is, applies to a variety of breaches of varying degrees of importance, is not a reasonable effort to estimate damages. Lake River Corp. v. Carborundum Co., 769 F.2d 1284 (7th Cir. 1985). This is especially true when the fixed sum greatly exceeds losses likely to flow from minor breaches. It should be obvious that the doctrines operating here require careful attention, else the loophole of escape from agreed terms will be too readily accessible. One might ask why it is not a good idea to limit the "reasonableness" test to the breach that actually occurred and is sued upon, or why a defaulter should escape a contract term by drawing attention to "what might have been" had a different breach occurred.

These problems serve as a reminder of the overriding importance of "interpretation," determining what the parties intended a given clause to do or to be. If a contract term on remedies does not reach a dispute at all, there is of course no occasion to confront the term's "reasonableness" in the circumstances.

Consider the following situations:

(1) Plaintiff, a city, contracted with a contractor (defendant) for the construction of a parking garage. Various disputes arose during construction, including the question of defendant's entitlement to progress payments. As a result, defendant left the job some five months before the designated completion date (a breach, said the trial court). Plaintiff was forced to retain another contractor to finish the project, which delayed the garage's opening. Plaintiff's suit against the contractor included a claim for liquidated damages, under the following clause: "As actual damages for any delay in completing the work . . . are impossible to determine, the Contractors and their Sureties shall be liable for [the sum of $1,000] as fixed, agreed and liquidated damages for each calendar day of delay from the above stipulated completion date until such work is satisfactorily completed and accepted." At trial, plaintiff recovered only actual damages. On appeal, the denial of liquidated damages was affirmed. The damage clause, by its terms, dealt only with "delay"; the language used failed to clearly indicate that the parties also intended to cover "abandonment" of the work, "an entirely separate eventuality." It followed that liability under the clause did not attach "until the contractor had fulfilled its agreement." Plaintiff's contention that the court's reading of the clause would encourage contractors to abandon projects in order to avoid contractual delay damages was found unavailing, since owners were always free to negotiate for delay damages even in the event of abandonment. City of Elmira v. Larry Walter, Inc., 76 N.Y.2d 912, 563 N.Y.S.2d 45, 564 N.E.2d 655 (1990).

Would the result have been different had the clause provided for liquidated damages until "the entire completion of the work"? At least one court has given a "yes" answer. City of Boston v. New England Sales & Mfg. Corp., 386 Mass. 820, 438 N.E.2d 68 (1982) (liquidated damages recoverable beyond date of abandonment but time taken to complete work with another contractor must be "reasonable"; the injured party must act promptly to complete work).

(2) Plaintiff contractor sued to recover $21,300 withheld by the defendant city from the price it agreed to pay plaintiff for constructing four piers for a bridge across the Mississippi River. The contract fixed a time limit of 350 days for completion of the piers. A clause in the contract stated that the bridge was to be operated as a toll bridge, and that "delay in completion will cause interference with the traffic and losses, such as lost earnings, interest on investment, administration expenses and other tangible and intangible loss" and will inconvenience the public. To partially cover such losses and expenses, the city was given the right to deduct as liquidated damages $250 for each day that completion of the piers was delayed. Plaintiff was late by 96½ days. For access to the western end of the bridge, which was on the Arkansas shore, the state of Arkansas had agreed to construct a highway. Because of that state's delay in constructing the highway, the entire bridge was completed at least 30 days before the bridge could be used, since there was no access at the western end. Under these circumstances, a deduction of $250 a day for the 96½ day period would, said the court, be "inequitable and unreasonable and would amount to the infliction of a penalty." The parties intended to provide for losses "caused by a delay in completion," that is, their purpose was to guard against losses caused by delay in completing the bridge when this delay was due to plaintiff's delay in building the four piers. Here the bridge could not be used anyway. "[I]f the contingency upon which the presupposition [of the damages a breach would incur] is based never happens, the presupposition must vanish." Massman Constr. Co. v. City Council of Greenville, Miss., 147 F.2d 925 (5th Cir. 1945).

Is this "interpretation"? The Rest.2d § 356(1) , through comment and illustration, indicates that the *Massman* clause, in the circumstances of that case, is "unenforceable on grounds of public policy," a penalty.

(3) A farmer contracted to sell to a canning company all the tomatoes grown on the farmer's six-acre farm during the 1944 season, for a price of $28 a ton. The contract provided in Clause 12:

> [I]f Grower shall fail to deliver to the Company any part or all of the Tomatoes herein contracted for, . . . the Company will sustain substantial damages, uncertain in amount, and not readily susceptible of proof under the rules of evidence, and great and irreparable damage to the Company will result from a breach of this agreement on the part of the Grower, and Grower hereby covenants and agrees with the Company that in case of such failure on Grower's part Grower shall and will pay to the Company the sum of $300 as liquidated damages and not as a penalty.

After delivering 10.99 tons of tomatoes to the company, the farmer sold the balance of the crop (about 44 tons) on the open market at prices varying between $33 and $36 a ton. A vice-president of the company testified that, from past experience, the company had learned that it would normally be advantageous to a grower to deliver one-third of the crop under contract during the "glut" period when tomato prices were low, and to sell two-thirds in the open market when prices had risen; and that the $300 figure in this contract was based on an estimate of $50 an acre as the company's loss in such a case, through calculation of the average yield per acre of this grower's six-acre farm and the range of tomato prices the previous year. On motion, the trial judge struck out this testimony. The appellate court held this was not error. The sum fixed was the same for both total and partial breach. Furthermore, "the specified damages are in no way proportionate to the possible extent of the prospective breach, nor do we find that the prospective damages for failure to deliver tomatoes having a ready market are incapable or difficult of ascertainment. . . . [C]lause 12 of the contract is a penalty and hence unenforceable." H.J. McGrath Co. v. Wisner, 189 Md. 260, 55 A.2d 793 (1947).

Can this be right? Observe that the court appears to treat the difficulty of estimating possible damages as a requirement or test with independent significance. Further, absent explicit language, should it be presumed that contracting parties intend a damages provision to apply only to "material" and not "partial" breaches? Cases illustrating one state's consistent position on nonmaterial breaches are collected in United Air Lines, Inc. v. Austin Travel Corp., 867 F.2d 737 (2d Cir. 1989).

PROBLEM

Company breached a vice-president's two-year employment contract by discharging the officer without cause. The contract provided: "Should this Agreement be terminated by Company without cause and prior to its expiration date, Company will be responsible for fulfilling the entire unpaid salary obligation of this Agreement for the full period of two years." The vice-president is entitled to $75,000 under this provision. Shortly after the dismissal, the vice-president went to work for another firm, in a similar position, and was paid $50,000 for the balance of the term of the breached contract.

(1) Is evidence of the $50,000 earnings relevant on the issue of the validity of the clause in question?

(2) Will the vice-president recover $75,000 from Company?

(3) Would your answers change if the vice-president had been paid $150,000 by the second employer?

Samson Sales, Inc. v. Honeywell, Inc.

Supreme Court of Ohio, 1984.
12 Ohio St.3d 27, 465 N.E.2d 392.

[Plaintiff, operator of a pawn shop, contracted with Morse Signal for a burglar alarm system, agreeing to pay $1,500 at the installation and $150 a month thereafter for five years. Defendant Honeywell subsequently acquired Morse Signal, assuming the contract with plaintiff. A burglary occurred at plaintiff's shop, but defendant refused to pay more than $50 for the loss. Plaintiff sued, seeking $68,303 for merchandise lost in the burglary; it alleged that defendant's negligent failure to transmit the alarm signal to the police, as the agreement required, was a breach of contract. Defendant invoked the following provision of the agreement:

> It is agreed by and between the Parties that Company is not an insurer; and that this Agreement in no way binds Company as an insurer of the premises or of the property of the Subscriber, and that all charges are based solely on the value of the service, maintenance and installation of the system. In the event of loss or damage to Subscriber resulting by reason of failure of the performance of such service or the failure of the system to properly operate, Company's liability, if any, shall be limited to the sum of Fifty Dollars ($50.00) as liquidated damages and not as a penalty and this liability shall be exclusive.

The trial court awarded plaintiff summary judgment, but limited damages to $50. An intermediate appellate court reversed on the ground the contract clause was an unenforceable penalty.]

KERNS, J. The only issue of any consequence in this appeal is whether the exculpatory clause limiting Honeywell's liability to $50 is valid and enforceable.

While some jurisdictions have rejected such contract provisions on policy grounds, clauses in contracts providing for reasonable liquidated damages are recognized in Ohio as valid and enforceable. Jones v. Stevens, 112 Ohio St. 43, 146 N.E. 894 (1925). However, reasonable compensation for actual damages is the legitimate objective of such . . . provisions and where the amount specified is manifestly inequitable and unrealistic, courts will ordinarily regard it as a penalty. Hence, Honeywell's standard reference "to the sum of Fifty Dollars ($50.00) as liquidated damages and not as a penalty" is by no means conclusive or controlling in this case.

Whether a particular sum specified in a contract is intended as a penalty or as liquidated damages depends upon the operative facts and circumstances surrounding each particular case, but time has apparently had no undermining influence upon the guiding principles initially set forth in Jones v. Stevens, supra[:]

> Where the parties have agreed on the amount of damages, ascertained by estimation and adjustment, and have expressed this agreement in clear and unambiguous terms, the amount so fixed should be treated as liquidated damages and not as a penalty, if the damages would be (1) uncertain as to amount and difficult of proof, and if (2) the contract as a whole is not so manifestly unconscionable, unreasonable, and disproportionate in amount as to justify the conclusion that it does not express the true intention of the parties, and if (3) the contract is consistent

with the conclusion that it was the intention of the parties that damages in the amount stated should follow the breach thereof.

With reference to the initial test suggested in *Jones*, the court of appeals expressly noted that "the damages here are patently estimable," and this finding is attuned to the indisputable fact that the damages in this case would be as readily ascertainable as the damages in a multitude of other conceivable situations involving negligence and/or breach of contract. As to the second guideline recommended by this court, the stated sum of $50 in the contract involved in this case is manifestly disproportionate to either the consideration paid by Samson or the possible damage that reasonably could be foreseen from the failure of Honeywell to notify the police of the burglary. And with particular emphasis upon the third condition proposed in [*Jones*], it is beyond comprehension that the parties intended that damages in the amount of $50 should follow the negligent breach of the contract.

In other words, an examination of the minute type used in the standard contract issued by Morse, as well as a fair construction of the contract provision as a whole, fails to evince a conscious intention of the parties to consider, estimate, or adjust the damages that might reasonably flow from the negligent breach of the agreement. Surely, Samson, which apparently had some business experience, did not pay $10,500 for the mere possibility of recouping $50 if Honeywell provided no service at all under the terms of the contract. Characteristically, therefore, and by way of analysis, the nominal amount set forth in the contract between Samson and Honeywell has the nature and appearance of a penalty.

Accordingly, the judgment of the court of appeals is affirmed.

NOTE

Courts regularly assert that liquidated damage provisions are unenforceable if they lead to awards that are unreasonably small as well as too large, but cases such as *Samson* in which a court actually holds liquidated damages unreasonably low are rare. It would be odd if things were otherwise. Contracting parties often agree to waive consequential damages, and such waivers are routinely enforced. Limitations on damages seem the same. Moreover, instead of limiting damages, a contracting party can merely limit its obligations under the contract in the first instance. How is an artificially low liquidated damages clause any different from an exceedingly modest promissory undertaking? Even on its facts, *Samson* is an unusual case. The majority of suits against suppliers of alarm systems come out the other way. See, e.g., Fretwell v. Protection Alarm Co., 764 P.2d 149 (1988) (*Samson*-type clause which "makes no attempt to reasonably forecast just compensation for the harm caused, [but] is clearly an attempt to limit damages, is neither unconscionable nor against public policy"); Better Food Markets v. American Dist. Tel. Co., 40 Cal.2d 179, 253 P.2d 10 (1953) (clause akin to that in *Samson* is a provision for liquidated damages and valid in circumstances). Parties bringing these suits against alarm companies often employ a tort theory (perhaps joining a contract claim with the tort claim). The tort commonly asserted is negligence. Language often will be decisive here; a failure to include the terms "negligence" or "tort" has led to the conclusion that an intention to limit noncontractual liability has not been sufficiently demonstrated. Compare Schrier v. Beltway Alarm Co., 73 Md.App. 281, 533 A.2d 1316 (1987), with DCR Inc. v. Peak Alarm Co., 663 P.2d 433 (Utah 1983). Often the cases that sound in contract in which courts refuse to enforce clauses with low liquidated damages are cases in which the breach is willful and wanton. See, e.g., Core-Mark Midcontinent, Inc. v. Sonitrol Corp., 300 P.3d 963 (Colo. App. 2012); ADT Security. Services., Inc. v. Swenson, 276 F.R.D. 278, 301 (D. Minn. 2011); Fed. Ins. Co. v. Honeywell, Inc., 641 F. Supp. 1560, 1562 (S.D.N.Y. 1986).

COMMENT: THE PENALTY RULE AND "EFFICIENCY"

Judicial scrutiny of agreed damages provisions has received criticism from some academics using economic analysis. An example is Goetz & Scott, Liquidated Damages, Penalties and the Just Compensation Principle: Some Notes on an Enforcement Model and a Theory of Efficient Breach, 77 Colum.L.Rev. 554 (1977).

The authors make these points, among others:

> (1) One explanation for judicial limitations on the parties' contract-making power may be sought in the belief that an overly-compensatory damage clause signals some impairment of the process by which agreement was reached, such as fraud, duress, or mistake. But this explanation does not justify the general rule invalidating penalty clauses, for invalidation occurs even when the clause is shown to have resulted from a fairly-bargained exchange. Furthermore, modern contract law provides an arsenal of more particularized weapons for striking down agreements that do not result from fair bargaining. A blunderbuss rule invalidating all penalty clauses is not needed in order to deal effectively with defects in the agreement process.
>
> (2) Those who argue in support of "efficient breaches" (efficient in the sense that at least the breacher is better off and the justly-compensated innocent party is no worse off) fear that an *in terrorem* penalty clause would, if valid and enforceable, discourage efficient breaches. But there are countervailing arguments. One is that the efficient breach would not necessarily be precluded by recognizing the validity of a penalty clause. It would remain open to the parties to renegotiate, after the breach, the allocation of efficiency gains between breacher and non-breacher.
>
> (3) The postulated objective of the damage remedy, just compensation, is not necessarily achieved if the law's measurement rules do not recognize as provable, or compensable, all of the

losses—perhaps idiosyncratic or subjective values—that the promisee may contemplate or suffer. What a court sees as a penalty clause may instead be an effort to bargain for an amount that is in fact what is needed to put the injured party in the same position he or she would be in had the other performed.

Are these arguments persuasive? If penalty-type clauses generally seem associated with a breakdown in the bargaining process, or perhaps inattention at the time of contracting, is there something to be said for a flat rule rather than a fact-specific inquiry into the reasons for imbalance? Moreover, is it likely that most—or even many—liquidated damages clauses are intended to protect idiosyncratic or subjective values?

Before leaving liquidated damages and the question of allowing parties to set damages themselves, it is worth noting the direction one is led when approaching the question of contract remedies from an economic perspective. Return to Holmes's basic insight that a damages-based contracts regime essentially gives the person who makes a legally enforceable promise a choice between performing and paying a sum of money. For some modern law-and-economics scholars, it is but a short step to the conclusion that every contract includes an option in the technical sense. In lieu of performance, the promisor has an option to pay a fixed amount of money. Damages, seen in this light, are merely the price promisors pay to release themselves from the obligation to perform. So, the problem of determining the appropriate damage award is simply a matter of option pricing. What amount would two sophisticated parties agree upon if they were negotiating explicitly for this option? Indeed, we should imagine that when two parties negotiate at arm's length, one of the issues they should settle is the price the promisor must pay if he chooses not to perform. And if they do, why should we think that expectation damages—or any of the other measures we have explored—is a good prediction of the price of this option? Given all the variables that must be taken into account—mitigation, overreliance, imperfect information, costly renegotiation, imperfect factfinding after the fact—there may be little reason to think that the parties should fix on an option price that is equal to expectation damages. This is the view some scholars have advanced. Robert E. Scott & George Triantis, Embedded Options and the Case Against Compensation in Contract Law, 104 Colum. L. Rev. 1428 (2004).

The remedy for breach is, from this perspective, no different from any other term in a contract. It may be in the parties' mutual interest that the goods be sold with a warranty. So, too, it may be in their mutual interest that the promisor have the option of paying expectation damages in the event of breach. But the parties may be better off without a warranty. So, too, the parties may be better off if the price of nonperformance were something other than expectation damages. From this perspective, the problem of contract damages is simply a problem of establishing a sensible default rule. Alternatively, it may suggest that the law should take a different path—instead of providing for damages, the law might require breaching parties actually to perform. This issue is explored in the next section.

SECTION 6. ENFORCEMENT IN EQUITY

INTRODUCTORY NOTE

The preceding section opened up the question of agreed remedies, attempts by the parties themselves to regulate damage awards. In a grand case that suggests what is to come in this section, Manchester Dairy System v. Hayward, 82 N.H. 193, 132 A. 12 (1926), the parties' agreement included two provisions addressed to remedies in the event of breach.

Plaintiff Dairy System (the Ass'n) entered into a contract with Hayward by which he agreed to sell to the Ass'n, for three years, all the dairy products produced on his farm. The Ass'n agreed to pay a monthly base price and to distribute the balance of each year's net earnings among its members, including Hayward, according to the quantity and quality of dairy products furnished. The contract recited that it was one of a series of identical contracts made between the Ass'n and its members, that it would be impracticable and extremely difficult to determine damages from any breach, and therefore each member agreed to pay the Ass'n $5 per cow as liquidated damages for any breach through selling milk or dairy products to other buyers. The contract also provided that, in the event of breach or threatened breach by a member, the Ass'n "shall be entitled to an injunction to prevent breach or threatened breach thereof, or to a decree for specific performance hereof." It was provided also that the Ass'n could not replace by purchase in the open market any dairy products that members failed to deliver.

In the Association's action for specific performance against Hayward, the trial court found that he had never delivered any milk from his 12 cows. The evidence showed that "there was plenty of milk to be had in the open market in the territory covered by the Manchester Dairy System." The trial court concluded that the contract was binding on Hayward, but refused an injunction against selling to others since the court knew him to be "a man of honor" who would perform his duties once he understood them. The court added that even if an injunction were issued and Hayward persisted in violating it, the result would have to be either fine or imprisonment—punishments that would be "neither merited by, nor a reasonable remedy for, a breach of his duty to deliver to this plaintiff the milk of his twelve cows." The trial court therefore denied all equitable relief. On appeal, the Supreme Court reversed, on this reasoning:

> (1) The contract clause expressly providing for equitable relief was ineffective. "Jurisdiction over the subject matter of a controversy cannot be created or conferred by the agreement of the parties."
>
> (2) But equity can enforce a contract, even one relating to personal property, where the legal remedy is not adequate. This contract was one of a series which together constituted a single agreement binding all member-subscribers to the Ass'n and to each other. It was a condition of the multi-party compact that the Ass'n could not replace in the open market milk that any member failed to deliver. Each withdrawal by a member would cast a larger share

of the group's operating expenses on the remaining members. If one member could breach with impunity, so might others, and each withdrawal "would inevitably tend to promote further withdrawals and impair the ability of the Ass'n to secure new members."

(3) The provision for liquidated damages of $5 per cow did not make the legal remedy adequate, since, for the reasons noted, the harm done was more far-reaching and could not be measured. Nor did this clause show the parties' intent that defendant was to have an option either to perform or pay the $5. Strict performance by members was essential to the survival of the Ass'n and far more important to it than this small sum. Any doubt on this issue was removed by the clause calling for an injunction or specific performance in the event of breach.

(4) The trial court was right in denying affirmative specific performance. This would have been "a cumbersome and expensive process" and could have been accomplished "only by placing the defendant's milk-producing operations in charge of the officers of the court." But there is no such objection to the negative form of order, an injunction against selling to others, which amounts to indirect enforcement by relying on defendant's own interest to induce him to perform.

(5) It may be that enforcement of the decree would impose on the defendant some burden that would be out of proportion to the benefit accruing to the plaintiff. The case must therefore be returned to the trial court so that it might examine this question. But the hardship involved in fine and imprisonment, punishments imposed if Hayward persisted in his defiance of the court's injunctive order, would not be the kind of hardship that could be taken into account at all, since it would be due only to his own disobedience.

Manchester Dairy, it might be noted, was handed down by the same court that three years later authored Hawkins v. McGee.

Edge Group WAICCS LLC v. Sapir Group LLC

United States District Court, Southern District of New York, 2010.
705 F. Supp. 2d 304.

DOLINGER, UNITED STATES MAGISTRATE JUDGE. Plaintiff Edge Group WAICCS, LLC ("Edge Group") commenced this lawsuit to seek specific performance of a contract for the sale of an interest in a limited liability company. The anticipated transaction would have involved a payment of $20 million by defendant Sapir Group LLC ("Sapir") in exchange for a 50 percent interest in WAICCS Las Vegas 2 LLC, a limited liability company that was the sole member of another limited liability company, WAICCS Las Vegas 3 LLC. WAICCS 3 in turn holds a 20.4 percent undivided ownership interest in a parcel of undeveloped real estate in Las Vegas, Nevada. . . .

[On May 1, 2008, Sapir entered into a binding contract for the sale to Sapir of Edge Group's interest in WAICCS 2.] The closing was scheduled for May 30, 2008. Before the scheduled closing, plaintiff delivered to Sapir all required documents for the transaction to close. On May 29, 2008, however, Sapir notified Edge Group that it had decided not to go through with the closing and purchase. The decision by Sapir was not based on any failure of Edge Group to perform. Instead, defendant stated that it had decided to abandon the transaction because of the speculative nature of the project planned for development on the site.

Plaintiff commenced suit on June 4, 2008, seeking principally specific performance. It amended its complaint a few days later, and Sapir filed an answer, including several affirmative defenses, on September 16, 2008. The principal thrust of the answer is that, under the Amended Option Agreement, plaintiff's only remedy for the breach is payment of the escrow funds. . . .

Both sides seek summary judgment on the question of whether Edge Group should be awarded specific performance. That form of relief involves an exercise of the court's equitable powers. For Edge Group to justify its entitlement to such a remedy, it must first establish the existence of a contract with Sapir, Sapir's breach of that contract by non-performance, Edge Group's substantial performance of its obligations under the Option Agreement and its ability and willingness to undertake any additional steps required of it under the contract. In addition, Edge Group must demonstrate that the invocation of the court's powers in equity is justified by the absence of an adequate remedy at law.

There is no dispute in this case that a valid and binding contract providing an option to Sapir was entered into by way of the assignment of the original option from Credit Suisse to Sapir in conjunction with amendments to the Option Agreement. There is also no real dispute that, pursuant to the terms of that amended Agreement, defendant gave notice of its exercise of the option on May 1, 2008, within the contractual period for doing so, and that this step created a binding contract for the sale to Sapir of Edge Group's interest in WAICCS 2. The record also reflects that Edge Group fulfilled all of its pre-closing obligations under the contract, that Sapir communicated on May 29—one day before the scheduled closing—its refusal to go ahead with the purchase, and that that decision was not a consequence of any failure by Edge Group to perform or of any other form of misconduct by plaintiff.

In sum, there is no question that the parties entered into a valid contract for the sale of plaintiff's interest in WAICCS 2 and that defendant breached its contractual obligation to purchase that interest. The remaining question is whether, in these circumstances, it is appropriate for the court to order specific performance of that contract by Sapir because of the inability of legal damages to compensate plaintiff fully.

In assessing this question, we note that the guiding consideration is " 'the difficulty of proving damages with reasonable certainty.' " Van

Wagner Adver. Corp., 67 N.Y.2d at 193, 501 N.Y.S.2d at 632, 492 N.E.2d 756 (quoting Restatement (Second) of Contracts § 360[a] (1981)). Although case law refers, in appropriate circumstances, to the uniqueness of the product that was the subject of a breached contract in a sale context, that is ultimately not the test; rather, in all cases the court must address the practical question of whether the damages of the aggrieved party can be reliably determined:

> The point at which breach of a contract will be redressable by specific performance thus must lie not in any inherent physical uniqueness of the property but instead in the uncertainty of valuing it. "What matters, in measuring money damages, is the volume, refinement, and reliability of the available information about substitutes for the subject matter of the breached contract. When the relevant information is thin and unreliable, there is a substantial risk that an award of money damages will either exceed or fall short of the promisee's actual loss. Of course this risk can always be reduced—but only at great cost when reliable information is difficult to obtain. Conversely, when there is a great deal of consumer behavior generating abundant and highly dependable information about substitutes, the risk of error in measuring the promisee's loss may be reduced at much smaller cost. In asserting that the subject matter of a particular contract is unique and has no established market value, a court is really saying that it cannot obtain, at reasonable cost, enough information about substitutes to permit it to calculate an award of money damages without imposing an unacceptably high risk of undercompensation on the injured promisee."

Id. at 193, 501 N.Y.S. 2d at 632, 492 N.E. 2d 756 (quoting Anthony T. Kronman, "Specific Performance", 45 U. Chi. L.Rev. 351, 362 (1978)).

In applying this test, the trial court has broad discretion, although certain parameters have been recognized by the New York courts. Thus, real estate is deemed to be inherently unique, a notion that has led to a pattern of decisions granting purchasers specific performance of real-estate sale contracts. Similarly, the courts have typically held that the shares of closely held corporations are not readily appraised and hence that specific performance is properly granted on contracts for the sale of those shares. More generally, the courts look to the specific circumstances of the case to determine whether there is a sufficiently reliable means of measuring value for purposes of awarding contract damages. E.g., JMG Custom Homes, Inc. v. Ryan, 45 A.D.3d 1278, 1281, 844 N.Y.S.2d 817, 819–20 (4th Dep't 2007) (granting specific performance of an oral agreement to exchange two all-terrain vehicles and a snowmobile for a discount on the purchase price of a home because of the difficulty of calculating the value of the vehicles); Garber v. Siegel, 194 Misc. 966, 969, 87 N.Y.S.2d 597, 600 (Sup. Ct. Kings County 1948), modified on other grounds, 274 A.D. 1068, 1068, 86 N.Y.S.2d 456, 456 (2d Dep't 1949) (granting plaintiff specific performance of contract for sale of carbonated-beverage route and business where plaintiff helped develop business serving specific customers for many years and his loss of future profits could not readily be ascertained). See also Destiny USA Holdings, LLC, 69 A.D.3d at 221–22, 889 N.Y.S.2d at 801–02 (granting preliminary injunction requiring bank to fund draw requests on construction loan because of uncertainty in calculating damage to plaintiff's reputation and other harm stemming from inability to complete "groundbreaking" and "unprecedented" environmentally-friendly development project).

In this case, Sapir argues that measuring damages from its breach is not so inherently imprecise as to justify specific performance. It also argues that specific performance should be denied here based on two other equitable principles. It first cites plaintiff's obligation to mitigate its damages, and then asserts that specific performance should not be granted because it does not currently have the cash in hand to perform its end of the bargain, that is, to pay the $19 million owed for the purchase over and above the escrowed funds, an argument premised on the notion that specific performance will not be ordered if performance is impossible. *See Restatement (Second) of Contracts* § 357 cmt. C (1981). We address these arguments separately. . . .

In support of the contention that, as a matter of law, a legal remedy is adequate here, defendant notes that contract damages are normally measured by the difference between the value to the injured party of the performance that should have been provided by the breaching party and what the plaintiff was left with in the wake of the breach. Applying this principle, defendant contends that the difference between the $20 million purchase price and the value of Edge Group's interest in WAICCS 2 at the time of defendant's breach may be reliably determined. For this proposition, Sapir relies principally on the fact that an appraisal of the real estate parcel owned in common by WAICCS 3 and other parties was performed shortly after defendant's breach, and resulted in a valuation of $788 million. Defendant further asserts that this valuation should be binding on plaintiff because the appraisal was prepared on behalf of the property owners, including Edge Group, outside of the context of this litigation, and was later used to extend the payment schedule for a loan secured by the property. As further evidence of value, defendant also mentions, albeit without documentation, that Sapir itself paid approximately $21 million at about the same time for a share of a company that was a co-tenant of the Las Vegas property. Based on these facts, defendant asserts that the court can value the Edge Group's interest that Sapir failed to purchase for $20 million, and that in fact the value of that interest exceeded the purchase price, thus—unless the one million dollar deposit is considered liquidated damages—compelling the conclusion that plaintiff is entitled to no damages. We consider these arguments in turn.

The appraisal of the property owned in part by WAICCS 3—which Sapir cites to establish the value of Edge Group's interest in WAICCS

2—was undertaken in June 2008 at the request of Credit Suisse, not Edge Group, although that fact is not crucial for present purposes. More relevant, however, are certain details about both the context of the appraisal, the substance of the appraisal report, and the testimony of the person who prepared it.

The appraisal was of the Las Vegas parcel itself, not of the value of an interest in WAICCS 2, which was the asset to be sold under the Option Agreement. This distinction is important for several reasons.

Edge Group's ownership interest was in WAICCS 2, which in turn had an ownership interest in WAICCS 3, which in turn had an interest, in the form of an undivided tenancy-in-common with several other entities, in the undeveloped real property that was appraised. Moreover, the terms that governed the tenancy-in-common of the parcel sharply limited the ability of WAICCS 3—in which Edge Group held an interest through WAICCS 2—to sell its interest in the property. Thus, WAICCS 3 was precluded from selling a majority of its interest absent the unanimous consent of the other co-tenants in the Las Vegas parcel, and it could not sell even a minority of its interest to any broadly-defined competitor of those co-tenants. It is not surprising, then, that the sale of the Edge Group interest in WAICCS 2 was characterized by Credit Suisse as "very complicated to say the least."

The June 2008 appraisal of the parcel, cited by Sapir, did not consider the impact of these restrictions since it was looking only to the prospects for sale of the real estate rather than of the encumbered Edge Group interest in one of the two LLCs in the ownership chain. Necessarily, then, that appraisal would not reflect a valuation of the Edge Group's interest, much less an assessment of the viability of valuing that interest.

Apart from the general irrelevance of the June 2008 appraisal to the question of the adequacy of a legal remedy in this case, the substance of the appraisal report—viewed in light of the testimony of the appraiser—reflects that it has no probative weight even as an assessment of the value of the parcel at the time of defendant's breach, much less as an indicator that one could reliably value the LCC interest of plaintiff. The same appraiser had performed an appraisal of the property in January 2008 and offered the figure of $788 million. He then performed a comparable appraisal in June of that year and, in an identically-worded report, he arrived at the same figure. In his deposition testimony, however, he conceded that he had found no comparable sales during the relevant period and hence had simply utilized the prior number. Moreover, he conceded that he had had no pertinent data or information on which to base an appraisal, stating "we didn't have evidence to get to our conclusions."

The market conditions at that time only underscore the absence of a basis for the June 2008 appraisal. As all parties concede, the appraisal was made during the period of the recent financial and real-estate bubble collapse and accompanying major economic downturn, including a collapse in the market for commercial real estate on the Strip in Las Vegas. Indeed, as the appraiser testified, there was a major downturn in business during this period, including in the gaming industry, and there were no sales of comparable properties from late 2007 to April 2009. Indeed, it was apparently at least in part because of these conditions (1) that Edge was very anxious to sell its interest, (2) that Sapir was the only potential buyer that Credit Suisse could locate, (3) that Sapir decided at the last minute to repudiate its contractual obligation to purchase because the investment was too "speculative," and (4) that Alex Sapir testified that "[i]t wouldn't be a good deal to put any new money in this deal in the current environment."

Under all of these circumstances, . . . the appraiser could not be a competent expert on the valuation of the parcel itself as of June 2008, much less on the value of the Edge Group's interest in WAICCS 2. Necessarily, then, the appraiser's June 2008 appraisal of the parcel cannot be deemed at all probative as to the availability of a reasonably accurate valuation of the plaintiff's interest in WAICCS 2.

As for defendant's brief allusion to its asserted purchase of an interest in another entity, which purportedly had an interest in the parcel at issue, it offers no details or documentation, and relies solely on a passing reference by Alex Sapir. That brief and conclusory testimony is plainly not sufficient to establish that the value of plaintiff's interest in WAICCS 2 can be reliably determined.

Given that doubts about the adequacy of a damage remedy should be resolved in favor of awarding specific performance, Restatement (Second) Contracts § 359 cmt. a (1981), and in light of the fact that none of the methods that defendant has devised for calculating the value of Edge Group's interest in WAICCS 2 at the time of defendant's breach are reliable, we conclude that Edge Group is entitled to summary judgment on the inability to calculate, and therefore the inadequacy of, its legal damages. . . .

To the extent that defendant may be relying on two other arguments targeting the propriety of specific performance under traditional equitable principles, we review them briefly. First, Sapir has asserted in its answer that all relief should be denied because plaintiff failed adequately to mitigate its loss. Additionally, Sapir contends that it would be impossible for it to perform its obligations under the contract to purchase Edge Group's interest. We review these claims in turn.

Insofar as Sapir asserts that plaintiff failed to mitigate its damages, the argument fails first and foremost because mitigation is not required in order to justify specific performance. In addition, defendant cannot demonstrate, as a matter of law, that plaintiff failed to make reasonable attempts to mitigate. There is no dispute that Credit Suisse attempted to find a buyer on behalf of plaintiff, and could locate only Sapir, which in turn defaulted on its purchase contract, apparently as a result of market conditions. Moreover, as plaintiff points out, during the pendency of this lawsuit—filed only days after the default—it engaged in efforts to sell its interest to Sapir, albeit at a reduced price, and that effort apparently led to the scheduling of a closing, only to be frustrated when Sapir once again backed out at the last minute. In short, the evidentiary record is consistent with reasonable efforts by plaintiff to mitigate.

Additionally, Sapir argues that specific performance may not be awarded because it is incapable of performing. In support of that contention, it proffers a declaration by Alex Sapir, asserting in entirely conclusory terms and without the benefit of any documentation, that defendant currently—or at least when Alex Sapir executed his declaration—has only $4,000 in cash and cash equivalents on hand and is more than $250,000,000 in debt. This skeletal assertion is plainly inadequate to demonstrate as a matter of law that defendant cannot perform even if ordered by a court to do so.

Both sides concur that impossibility may bar specific performance, but they differ on the precise scope of this rule. Plaintiff asserts that the test is whether the defendant was capable of performing at the time of the breach, not later on, and in support of this contention it notes that otherwise a breaching party may manipulate the outcome by deliberately divesting itself of the capacity to perform after its breach. Applying this standard, Edge Group asserts that Sapir was plainly capable of performing at the time of the breach, for which proposition it cites the deposition testimony of Alex Sapir that Sapir had the $20 million dollar purchase price available on the closing date. It also cites testimony to the effect that Alex Sapir and his company had available to them essentially limitless financing from Alex's father, Tamir Sapir, who was to provide the funds to purchase Edge Group's interest on the original closing date. It further offers facts from which one could draw the inference that defendant's finances have been deliberately manipulated to permit it to claim financial incapacity to pay for the option that it contracted to purchase less than two years ago.

Defendant does not meaningfully dispute that it had the capacity at the time of the breach to pay for Edge Group's interest in WAICCS 2. Indeed, Alex Sapir admitted at his deposition that it could have done so, saying that "[a]t the time we decided we had better uses for our funds" and that it could have closed had it wanted to do so. As noted, it even represents that it purchased an interest in another entity for more than $21 million only days before the cancellation of the closing with the Edge Group. In its opposition papers it asserts, however, that it has since lost the ability to perform—although it does not even attempt to document this assertion—and it presses the notion that this incapacity precludes equitable relief for the plaintiff.

We conclude that specific performance may be precluded by impossibility of performance either at the time of breach or at the time that court relief is sought. The courts have long recognized that impossibility (or even impracticability) of performance at the time that performance was due may excuse enforcement of a contract if the impossibility was brought about by *force majeure,* or circumstances that were not caused by the party. In such a case, the court will read into the contract a clause excusing performance if an essential element to the contract ceases to be available prior to the time at which performance is due absent the fault of either party. In those circumstances, the aggrieved party cannot establish the existence of an enforceable contract at the time that performance was due, and therefore the remedy of specific performance will not be available to it.

It is equally the case, however, that if a party cannot perform at the time of the application for specific performance, that fact will preclude the grant of specific performance. See Restatement (Second) of Contracts § 357 cmt. c (1981) ("[A] court will not order a performance that is impossible.") As the New York Court of Appeals has made plain, a court should not order specific performance, or other equitable relief, unless the defendant is capable of complying: "The court will not make what may prove to be a futile order." S.E.S. Importers., Inc. v. Pappalardo, 464, 442 N.Y.S.2d 453, 458, 425 N.E.2d 841 (1981).

As we have observed, there is no question on the current record that defendant was able to perform as of May 30, 2008. As for whether it is now unable to do so, its bare proffer to that effect plainly does not justify a determination, as a matter of law, that specific performance is unwarranted. Indeed, defendant's financial status is likely to be a fairly complex matter to unearth, and it makes no effort whatsoever to justify its bare contention other than by allusion to cash or equivalents on hand and the amount of its debt, and the conclusory assertion by Mr. Sapir that the company cannot perform. Moreover, and most strikingly, Mr. Sapir's representation is seemingly in direct conflict with testimony that he gave at his deposition less than two months prior to his execution of his July 30, 2009 supplemental declaration; at that deposition, he testified that Sapir could still close the sale if it wanted to do so. In short, the record does not remotely justify . . . relief for defendant on this aspect of plaintiff's case based on impossibility or impracticability.

There remains for consideration whether plaintiff has itself adequately justified, as a matter of law, the appropriateness of equitable relief. For the reasons that we have noted, the record reflects that a remedy at law, in the form of damages, is not likely to be adequate because of the undisputed circumstances that render any attempt to value Edge Group's interest at the time of defendant's breach mere speculation. That interest was in an unlisted limited-liability company for which there was no apparent market at the time. Moreover, it appears that valuation of plaintiff's interest was in any event likely to be highly chancy since the company was restricted in its ability to sell its interest in the LLC, and the ability to value that interest was further clouded by the facts (1) that the

LLC had an interest only in another LLC (also apparently not publicly or actively traded), (2) that that LLC's value was contingent on the valuation of the undeveloped Las Vegas parcel in which it had a tenancy-in-common with a number of other entities and for which there was no apparent market during the relevant time, and (3) that that LLC was significantly restricted in its ability to transfer its interest in the tenancy-in-common to another entity. In short, specific performance appears amply justified provided that Sapir is capable of complying with such an order or that any incapacity to do so is attributable to its own deliberate actions designed to frustrate relief in this case.

Defendant's showing on impossibility of performance is at best thin to evanescent. Moreover, insofar as it relies solely on the declaration of Alex Sapir, it runs into the well-established rule in this circuit that a party may not evade summary judgment by proffering an affidavit (or declaration) that directly contradicts the affiant's prior deposition testimony. On its face Mr. Sapir's declaration appears to do precisely that. The only possible way to avoid that conclusion would be if defendant could demonstrate that between the time of Mr. Sapir's deposition on June 4, 2009 and the date of the execution of his supplemental declaration on July 30, 2009 some new event occurred that so altered Sapir's financial position as to fundamentally undermine its conceded ability in June 2009 to pay $20 million to acquire Edge Group's interest in WAICCS 2.

Because that question is not answered on the current record, we are prepared to conduct a brief evidentiary hearing on that narrow issue in the event that Sapir can offer competent evidence in support of the notion that its financial status materially changed between June 4 and July 30, 2009 so as preclude its ability to perform its obligations under the Option Agreement as amended. Absent Sapir's ability to make such a showing—and subject to our ruling below regarding the purported preclusive effect of the escrow provision of the Option Agreement—we conclude that Edge Group has established the appropriateness of the equitable remedy of specific performance for Sapir's breach. . . .

Curtice Bros. Co. v. Catts

72 N.J.E.Q. 831, 66 A. 935 (1907)

Complainant, operator of a canning plant, sued for specific performance of a contract wherein defendant, a farmer, had agreed to sell his entire tomato crop from specified land. Vice-Chancellor Leaming rejected defendant's claim that the court was without power to grant equitable relief, saying: "The fundamental principles which guide a court of equity . . . are essentially the same whether the contracts relate to realty or to personalty. [Because] damages for the breach of contract for the sale of personalty are, in most cases, easily ascertainable and recoverable at law, courts of equity . . . withhold equitable relief. Touching contracts for the sale of land, the reverse is the case.

But no inherent difference between real estate and personal property controls the exercise of the jurisdiction. Where no adequate remedy at law exists, specific performance of a contract touching the sale of personal property will be decreed with the same freedom as in the case of a contract for the sale of land. . . .

"Complainant's factory has a capacity of about one million cans of tomatoes. The season for packing lasts about six weeks. The preparations made for this six weeks of active work must be carried out in all features to enable the business to succeed. These preparations are primarily based upon the capacity of the plant. . . . With this known capacity and an estimated average yield of tomatoes per acre the acreage of land necessary to supply the plant is calculated. To that end, the contract now in question was made, with other like contracts, covering a sufficient acreage to insure the essential pack. . . . [A] refusal of the parties who contract to supply a given acreage to comply with their contracts leaves the factory helpless, except to whatever extent an uncertain market may perchance supply the deficiency. The condition which arises from the breach of the contracts is not merely a question of the factory being compelled to pay a higher price for the product. Losses sustained in that manner could, with some degree of accuracy, be estimated. The condition which occasions the irreparable injury by reason of the breaches of the contracts is the inability to procure at any price at the time needed and of the quality needed the necessary tomatoes to insure the successful operation of the plant. . . . [T]he very existence of contracts [of this nature] proclaims their necessity to the economic management of the factory. This aspect of the situation bears no resemblance to that of an ordinary contract for the sale of merchandise in the course of an ordinary business. [This] business and its needs are extraordinary. . . . The breach of the contract by one planter differs but in degree from a breach by all.

"The objection that to specifically perform the contract personal services are required will not divest the court of its powers to preserve the benefits of the contract. Defendant may be restrained from selling the crop to others, and, if necessary, a receiver can be appointed to harvest the crop. A decree may be devised pursuant to the prayer of the bill."

Reed Foundation Inc. v. Franklin D. Roosevelt Four Freedoms Park LLC

Supreme Court, Appellate Division, New York, 2013.
108 A.D.3d 1, 964 N.Y.S.2d 152.

ACOSTA, J. Can aesthetic considerations trump a carefully considered and crafted contractual provision dictating the specific location of an inscription on a work of art? We hold that they cannot.

This case revolves around the Franklin D. Roosevelt Four Freedoms Park (the Park), which commemorates FDR's famous "Four Freedoms" speech. The Park is located on four acres of land at the southern tip of

Roosevelt Island. It was designed in the 1970s by the distinguished architect, the late Louis I. Kahn. For over 30 years, efforts to develop the Park had been unsuccessful. Interest in the park was renewed in 2005 when Reed and Jane Gregory Rubin, the current officers of petitioner The Reed Foundation (the Foundation), funded an exhibit about the history of the long dormant project entitled "Coming to Light."

At the Rubins' urging, the Franklin & Eleanor Roosevelt Institute formed the Franklin D. Roosevelt Four Freedoms Park, LLC (the LLC) and undertook to raise the funds necessary to complete the Park. In March 2010, the Foundation contracted to give the LLC a $2.5 million grant. In exchange for the grant, the LLC contractually agreed to carving Recognition Text (i.e., text recognizing the Rubin's and the Foundation's grant) at a specific location near a bust [of FDR] which was to be housed in the park. The Foundation was among the very first donors to make a grant in connection with this project, at a time when there remained considerable doubt as to whether the LLC could raise the funds necessary to complete the project. The Foundation's grant enabled the LLC to qualify for essential public funding from New York State and New York City, after which the LLC was able to raise the necessary funds to complete the Park. It was only after the necessary funds were raised and the Park essentially completed that the LLC reneged on its obligation to engrave the recognition text at the specified location, citing aesthetic concerns.

The Foundation's grant is governed by a series of interrelated agreements, including a Grant Agreement, entered into by the Foundation, the LLC and The Franklin & Eleanor Roosevelt Institute, which is the sole member of the LLC, and a Recognition Agreement, executed by the Foundation and the LLC.

The agreements detail the LLC's obligation to engrave specific text recognizing the Foundation and its founders (the Threshold Recognition Text) on a 12-foot by 12-foot granite wall, which is part of a structure in the Park called the "Threshold" (or the Niche) that houses a bronze bust of FDR. It was to read, "IN HONOR OF VERA D. RUBIN AND SAMUEL RUBIN. THE REED FOUNDATION." As depicted in the photographs, the placement of the Threshold Recognition Text was to be low to the ground, in small font less than two inches high along the bottom of a solid 12 foot by 12 foot granite wall on the west-facing side of the Threshold. On June 21, 2012, the Foundation consented to a request by the LLC that the lettering for the Threshold Recognition Text be changed from black to a muted gray.

The Grant Agreement provides that the Foundation's grant will fund construction of the Park, including "the carving of, and/or other display of, the Threshold Recognition Text." Under the Grant Agreement, the LLC agreed to "construct the Recognition in accordance with the terms, conditions and specifications set forth in the Recognition Agreement." The Grant Agreement, in Section 7, "Termination/Survival," gives the Foundation alone the right in its sole discretion, to terminate the Grant

Agreement by written notice of termination to the Institute and the LLC, (1) "if any aspect of the Project materially changes or it becomes impracticable to comply with requirements of Sections 1 and 2 of the Recognition Agreement" or (2) "a Default (as defined in the Recognition Agreement) occurs."

The Recognition Agreement sets forth the "terms, conditions and specifications for the construction, placement and design of the Recognition and the use of [the Foundation's funds] with respect to the [Park]" and specifies the precise location and wording of the "Threshold Recognition Text," as well as requirements for the carving and maintenance of the inscription.

Section 6 of the Recognition Agreement defines "default" to mean, among other things, "if any aspect of construction of the . . . Park materially changes or it becomes impracticable to comply with requirements of Sections 1–4 of this Recognition Agreement." Importantly, under this section, the LLC also agreed that the Foundation would be entitled to specific performance in the event of the LLC's breach.

By July 2012, the LLC had completed the inscription of an excerpt from the Four Freedoms speech on the south-facing side of the Threshold but had not yet commenced the engraving of the Threshold Recognition Text. Instead of completing the Threshold Recognition Text, the LLC began pressuring the Foundation to consent to relocate the Foundation's Recognition Text to an area called the "Grand Staircase" at the opposite end of the Park, where other donors' names were going to be engraved. The Foundation declined, and insisted that the LLC honor the Recognition Agreement.

On October 2, 2012, just over two weeks before the Park's scheduled dedication, the LLC advised the Foundation that it was refusing to perform because "[o]ur architects and consultants have told us" that including the Recognition Text on the Threshold is not the "best aesthetic." The Foundation seeks specific performance. The LLC offered to return the Foundation's money.

The Foundation commenced this proceeding, seeking a declaration that the LLC breached its contractual obligations, and an order directing specific performance of the agreements. In opposition to the petition, and notwithstanding the terms of the agreements, the LLC now argued, in an affidavit by its chairman, that carving the Recognition Text where the Foundation insisted was totally inconsistent with the objective of the Foundation's own gift, and that this was a case that "cries out for equitable relief, not tipping on the side of a selfish private interest, but on the side of the public in a lasting historical monument." The LLC also submitted an affidavit of Jack Reynolds, director of the Yale University Art Gallery, who maintained that to inscribe the Recognition Text "within the heart of Louis Kahn's public architectural masterwork is akin to signing a donor's name within the frame of great painting, something . . . that no donor would ever insist on . . . doing to a great Picasso or Van Gogh canvas upon donating such to a museum." In addition, the LLC submitted an affidavit of the stone carver who carved the Sculpture Niche who agreed that the proposed inscription would be inappropriate and not in keeping with Kahn's design and his artistic intention, and with an affidavit by Nathaniel Kahn, the architect's son who stated that placing the Recognition Text on the sculpture niche would damage his father's design, the "aesthetic purity of the space, and the purpose of the Park."

Aesthetic considerations extraneous to a contract cannot trump its terms. We thus find that the LLC breached its contractual obligations to the Foundation. We find further that the motion court properly ordered specific performance by directing the engraving of the Recognition Text in accordance with the Recognition Agreement. In the Recognition Agreement, the LLC expressly agreed

> "that the Foundation's remedies at law for a failure to perform, breach or threatened breach of Section 1 ["Threshold Recognition Text"] and 2 ["agreements, Representations and Warranties"] of this Recognition Agreement would be inadequate and the Foundation would suffer irreparable damages as a result of such failure to perform, breach or threatened breach. In recognition of this fact, the LLC agrees that, in the event of the LLC's failure to perform, breach or threatened breach, in addition to any remedies at law, the Foundation, without posting any bond, shall be entitled to seek equitable relief in the form of specific performance."

The LLC's failure to perform would deprive the Foundation of recognition of its substantial contribution to the Park in an inscription placed in a unique location that has special significance to the Foundation. . . .

The LLC does not contend that it is unable to complete the agreed engraving. Rather, it has chosen not to do so because its "advisors" believe, on aesthetic grounds, that there should be no such engraving on the Threshold. Nor do the Termination provisions in the Grant Agreement support the LLC's view, since they address situations in which, for example, the niche is not constructed.

The time for the LLC to have voiced its aesthetic concerns was at the time the Recognition Agreement was negotiated, not after it had "accepted and spent the Foundation's money," See Allegheny Coll. v. National Chautauqua County Bank of Jamestown, 246 N.Y. 369, 379, 159 N.E. 173 (1927). As the Court of Appeals explained in *Allegheny*, "the [donor] does not say: I hand you $1,000, and you may make up your mind later . . . whether you will undertake to commemorate my name. What she says is in effect is this: "I hand you $1,000, and if you are unwilling to commemorate me, the time to speak is now,"

Furthermore, while the LLC cites a public interest in protecting the aesthetics of the Park, the public interest in enforcing donor recognition agreements outweighs the shifting aesthetic concerns regarding the LLC.

(Indeed, the failure "to protect the interest of donors" risks the result that "donors may become more hesitant to contribute at all." [Smithers v. St. Luke's-Roosevelt Hosp. Ctr., 281 A.D.2d 127, 140, 723 N.Y.S.2d 426 (2001).] Moreover, "a donor's desire to perpetuate his name as a benefactor of a particular charitable institution and humankind is not a selfish one. These desires are deeply ingrained in human nature and are effective motivating forces in donations of this character." Id.

COMMENT: THE HISTORY OF EQUITY

The division between "law" and "equity" is a peculiarity of the Anglo-American legal order. There has never existed in any other developed system of law the strange phenomenon of two separate sets of courts, administered by different judges and giving different types of remedies, on grounds that were radically different. Yet this was the state of affairs in Anglo-American law for about 500 years. Both in England and the United States attempts began more than a century ago, through legislation, to combine the two competing systems of law and equity. But the 500 years of history that came before still leave an enduring mark on our legal system.

The explanation for the basic division between law and equity can be stated briefly—English law was built and perfected much too soon. This would have been no misfortune at all if the early lawyers and judges had not then proceeded to enclose themselves in their system, refusing to admit new forms of writs, new grounds of action or defense, and new conceptions of morality and policy. The freezing of doctrine and, behind that, the freezing of minds, were never complete, for slow growth and change continued within the common law system. But the freeze was already quite deep by the year 1300. Thereafter, when gross injustices or inadequacies in the legal system were revealed, there was no place to turn but to the King. One might wonder why appeal was not made to the legislature. The Parliament, it is true, had emerged as a somewhat representative assembly, with a share of legislative power, but its members did not conceive it to be their task to grind out correctives to rules of private law. Furthermore, the Parliament came to be dominated by lawyers, who had a stake in the established order and who, it seems, believed that rules of law should not be casually tinkered with. The Parliament did legislate occasionally, but through most of this formative period it stood as a center of resistance to change, not as a source of innovation.

As protest developed and the grievances of suitors multiplied, it was natural that the Chancellor should be the main repository of complaints. The Chancellor was the chief officer of state, equivalent to a modern Prime Minister, as well as the head of the chief secretariat of the Crown and custodian of the King's Great Seal. In the Chancellor's name were issued the ordinary, standard writs through which common law actions were started. It was simply good administration to turn over to the Chancellor's staff the devising of ways for dealing with new problems. In this period the Chancellors were churchmen—bishops at least—and this fact must have influenced their innovations, whether they drew on canon law, reflected religious ideas, or merely acted as educated citizens unencumbered by the technical limitations of the common law. We must stress that the Chancellor was a very high magistrate, with a large responsibility for the administration of royal justice. At this stage in European history, and not only in England, kings had a personal and inescapable duty to render justice to their subjects. This duty could be assigned to courts but the delegation could not wholly discharge the King's responsibility. It was as hard then as it is now to determine precisely what is "justice," but the King's high officials had to seek an answer.

The reforms and innovations accomplished by the English Chancellors had far-reaching consequences throughout private law, including the law of contract. As we shall see in Chapter 2, until the end of the middle ages the common law remedies for enforcing promises were extremely limited. The action of *debt* carried most of the workload. It could be used whenever a promised exchange had been completed on one side so that an obligation on the other side to pay a "sum certain" in money had arisen. If a promise was made in an instrument under seal, the action of covenant was available. But for an array of informal promises, there simply was no common law action to provide a remedy. It seems clear, though the evidence is indirect, that by the year 1400 the Chancery had begun to enforce informal promises. Perhaps the Chancellors were influenced, as common lawyers quite surely were not, by theories of canon law that urged the sanctity of promises and condemned breaches as violations of faith reposed. Recurring and predictable interventions by the Chancellors must have put pressure on the common law judges to extend their remedies, as they eventually did through development of the action of assumpsit, a subject that we have discussed before, supra pp. 142–147, and to which we shall return at the start of the next chapter.

The methods of enforcement developed by the Chancellors differed markedly from the money judgment that became virtually the exclusive sanction of the common law. Specific remedies ordering the defendant to do or not do a particular act were not unusual in the earliest stages of development of the common law, but most of them rapidly became obsolete. There are some survivals of course—e.g., replevin to enable an owner to recover goods and ejectment to recover possession of land that another holds illegally. The so-called "extraordinary remedies" (mandamus, prohibition, quo warranto, habeas corpus, and certiorari) also continue to be used to control inferior courts, public officials, or state-created agencies like corporations. But in the main-stream development of the common law, it was the judgment for money damages that became the standard remedy. If the judgment debtor did not pay voluntarily, the debtor's assets were subject to seizure and sale by a court officer. If no assets could be found, a common law court would do nothing more. In earlier times, the judgment defendant could be imprisoned for nonpayment, but this severe compulsion was eliminated when nineteenth century reforms abolished imprisonment for debt.

The approach of the Chancellors was different from the beginning. The core idea inspiring the Chancellor's enforcement proceedings was contempt, which in its earlier forms meant disobedience or subversion of duly-constituted authority. The primitive idea of contempt was quite undifferentiated. Contempt could consist of armed entry into the King's palace, infringement of a protection given by the King to a particular person, or a refusal to appear before the King or his council. There could even be contempt of a feudal lord or of a manorial or borough court. From this same central source also stemmed contempt of a legislative assembly, which includes the refusal of a witness to testify in a legislative inquiry. There could also be contempt of a common law court. Both common law and equity judges can punish as contempt any conduct that seriously interferes with the orderly exercise of judicial functions—disturbances in the court room, refusal of witnesses to testify, bribery of jurors, misconduct or corruption on the part of officers of the court, insulting comment by lawyers, and even published statements that undermine public confidence in the courts.

The special feature of the Chancellors' remedies in enforcing contracts was that punishment for contempt was used for simple disobedience of a judicial order. The order could be affirmative (to execute and deliver a deed of land) or negative (for Catts to deliver his tomatoes to no one but Curtice Bros.), or both. In the framing of orders, the Chancellor claimed and exercised a wide discretion, a discretion suitable for an official who spoke in such a special sense on behalf of the King himself. The primary sanction for contempt of the Chancellor was, from the outset, personal arrest. The duration of the arrest, the terms for release from arrest, and any supplementary sanctions were all at the Chancellor's discretion. On the whole, modern legislation has done little to control or limit this discretion.

Within the last century, American courts have attempted to refine and differentiate further within the limits of their inherited powers. Primary for this purpose is the distinction between civil and criminal contempt, a distinction that existed vaguely for a long time but is now being drawn more sharply. *Civil contempt* usually is described as a proceeding whose sole (or primary) aim is to give a remedy to the party in whose interest the equity decree was originally issued. If the sanction used is imprisonment, the contemnor is to be jailed only to enforce compliance; if the contemnor obeys, release must follow (stated in extreme form: "the keys to prison are in the defendant's own pocket"). If a money fine is assessed against the contemnor, as it clearly may be, the fine is then to be measured by the injury caused through breach of the decree, and it is to be paid, as damages, to the opposite party, for whose protection the decree was issued. Similarly, if other coercive measures are used, such as seizure of the contemnor's assets through so-called "sequestration," the purpose of such measures in civil contempt is the enforcement of compliance, so that the pressure must end when compliance ensues. On the other hand, the purpose of *criminal contempt* is primarily to punish in order to vindicate the authority of the court and to "preserve the dignity of the law." Criminal contempt is a kind of crime, but a special crime since it is an offense against the particular court and only that court can punish the guilty party. For that matter, it is clear in civil contempt also that the court whose decree has been violated is the only court that can entertain contempt proceedings. If a money fine rather than imprisonment is used in criminal contempt, a wide discretion is reserved to the court, subject only to review for abuse of discretion. The fine assessed is payable, not to the injured litigant, but to county, state, or federal government.

The "adequacy-of-legal-remedies" test comes from this history. The work done by the Chancellors was always understood as interstitial. Their self-restraint came from inertia and tradition. The Chancellors never sought to develop a complete system that might displace the common law; they were to supplement the common law and ameliorate its harshness. The correctives of equity courts were intended for those cases for which the common law did not adequately provide. Then who was to judge what was "adequate"? From the beginning, and always, the Chancellor.

There was a brief episode in the early 1600s when lawyers, led by Sir Edward Coke, seem to have aimed to set up controls that would, in some degree, have transferred to common law judges the power to decide when equitable relief was justified. The writ of habeas corpus, which was later to become the Great Writ for the defense of individual freedom against government repression, had at that time a highly indeterminate role. There were some strong indications that common law judges sought to use habeas corpus to cut back the Chancellors' power to imprison for contempt (and thereby to review indirectly the grounds for decision in equity cases). Another line of attack was suggested by the writ of prohibition that was issued in 1616 by the King's Bench, in Bromage v. Genning, 1 Rolle 368, with Sir Edward Coke presiding. It was addressed not to the Court of Chancery itself, but to a lesser court of equity sitting in Wales, and directed it *not* to decree specific performance of a promise by an owner of land to lease the land to another. The reason given by the King's Bench for this intervention seems at this distance somewhat contrived—that an order for specific performance would "subvert" the promisor's choice either to perform or pay damages. If this line had been pursued, it would have meant that in 1907 in New Jersey (whose law and equity were still separately administered), a judge sitting on the "law" (i.e., the jury) docket could have issued a prohibition to Vice Chancellor Leaming in Curtice Bros. v. Catts, forbidding him, under the threat of going to jail himself, from issuing or enforcing the injunction that he had decided to give to Curtice Bros. As a result of other acts of aggression against the Chancery, Coke was removed from judicial office shortly thereafter. This was a stunning event at the time and made a lasting impression. It seems most unlikely that Coke or the other common law judges intended to eliminate equitable remedies altogether, for they had become indispensable to the working of English society, as they clearly are in our own. But after the defeat of Coke, it was finally and forever established that the adequacy test and the other self-denying ordinances that restrict equitable relief would be administered by the judges who were sitting "in equity," as components of the decision whether the equitable relief requested of them should be given and, if so, in what form.

During the nineteenth century, in this country and in England, there were strong movements aiming at basic reforms and modernization of court organization and procedure. The program that became most widely known (and adopted in over 30 states) was the Field Code of Civil Procedure. Many ideas advanced by the Field Code were included in other reform programs, some of them equally comprehensive. Since the middle of the last century, the Federal Rules of Civil Procedure have provided a model for further reforms through state legislation or judicial rule-making. One common feature of these reform programs is the organization of a unified court system, with the same judges sitting on both law and equity cases. Separate dockets are maintained only because in actions that were historically brought "at law" jury trial must be made available, this being a requirement of the Seventh Amendment of the United States Constitution for the federal courts and a requirement of some state constitutions as well. There are now only a few states in which separate law and equity courts are maintained. In a couple of these states, the importance of the separation is considerably reduced by introducing jury trial as the standard means for finding disputed facts in equity cases. So almost everywhere the historical distinctions have become much blurred. It remains to be seen whether they have disappeared altogether.

Mainly for historical reasons, therefore, the remedial system of Anglo-American law starts with the money judgment as the standard remedy for breach of contract. Specific relief is reserved for situations in which the aggrieved party can show that a money-judgment remedy would be "inadequate" for some particular reason. Some very different solutions developed in Europe are described in Dawson, Specific Performance in France and Germany, 57 Mich.L.Rev. 495 (1959). On the question whether specific performance is granted in this country for reasons other than "inadequacy," a most useful discussion can be found in Laycock, The Death of the Irreparable Injury Rule, 103 Harv.L.Rev. 687 (1990).

Before leaving this sketch of history, we should recall an additional dimension of equity practice that was relevant to the problems facing the buyer in Curtice Bros. v. Catts. If court dockets were as crowded in 1907 as they are today, it may seem surprising that Curtice Bros. could have expected an equity suit to succeed in getting timely delivery of vine-ripened tomatoes suitable for canning. The decision to pursue that remedy may be made understandable by recalling a standard feature of equity practice, the power of trial judges to issue orders in advance of a full trial on the merits. We saw this power exercised in the Indiana phase of the litigation involving Dempsey (see Comment, supra p. 54).

Restatement of Contracts, Second

§ 360. Factors Affecting Adequacy of Damages

In determining whether the remedy in damages would be adequate [to protect the expectation interest of the injured party], the following circumstances are significant:

(a) the difficulty of proving damages with reasonable certainty,

(b) the difficulty of procuring a suitable substitute performance by means of money awarded as damages, and

(c) the likelihood that an award of damages could not be collected.

[The UCC's provision on a buyer's right to specific performance, § 2–716(1), states: "Specific performance may be decreed where the goods are unique or in other proper circumstances." It is generally understood that this section preserves the historical "adequacy" test of equity jurisdiction. Will the factors entering into a decision as to the adequacy of damages under UCC 2–716(1) be much different from those enumerated in Rest.2d § 360?]

Paloukos v. Intermountain Chevrolet Co.

99 Idaho 740, 588 P.2d 939 (1978)

Paloukos paid a $120 deposit and signed a form agreeing to purchase from intermountain a 1974 Chevrolet pickup truck for $3,650. It was understood that the pickup was to be ordered from the manufacturer. Intermountain returned the deposit five months later, informing Paloukos by letter that the dealership would be unable to deliver the vehicle "because of a product shortage." *Held*, dismissal below of a claim for specific performance was proper. Where goods "are unique or in other proper circumstances," UCC 2–716(1) makes specific performance available to a purchaser. "Although the UCC may have liberalized some of the old common law rules, see [§ 2–716, Comment 1], specific performance nevertheless remains an extraordinary remedy generally available only where other remedies are in some way inadequate." Paloukos alleged no facts suggesting anything unique about the pickup or indicating why damages would not be adequate relief. Market value was readily ascertainable. Moreover, Paloukos does not allege that Intermountain has in its possession a conforming pickup it could sell to him. "[T]he courts will not order the impossible, such as ordering the seller to sell to the buyer that which the seller does not have." [Another court found § 2–716's "other proper circumstances" for granting specific performance, reasoning that a particular auto's "mileage, condition, ownership and appearance"—in this case, a limited edition 1977 Corvette "Indy Pace car," of which only 6,000 were manufactured—can make it "difficult, if not impossible, to obtain its replication without considerable expense, delay and inconvenience." Sedmak v. Charlie's Chevrolet, Inc., 622 S.W.2d 694 (Mo.Ct.App. 1981).]

NOTE: SPECIFIC PERFORMANCE AND OUTPUT CONTRACTS

As concerns goods, the typical specific performance situation today probably involves a long-term output or requirements contract. While a buyer's inability to cover is evidence of UCC 2–716's "other proper circumstances," ability to cover does not itself foreclose equitable relief. Take, for example, Eastern Rolling Mill v. Michlovitz, 157 Md. 51, 145 A. 378 (1929). Plaintiffs, wholesalers at Harrisburg, Pa., bought and sold iron and steel scrap. In October 1927, they contracted to buy from Eastern, a manufacturer of sheet steel in Baltimore, all the scrap steel that would accumulate during the next five years as a by-product of Eastern's milling operations. The price to be paid was variable. For deliveries made during each quarter, the price was to be $3 a ton less than the price quoted at the beginning of that quarter by the Iron Age, a trade publication, as the market price in the Philadelphia market for scrap of the type Eastern produced. For nine months, deliveries were made and paid for, but in the summer of 1928 Eastern repudiated the contract, which by its terms was to run until September 30, 1932. Specific performance, sued for by the plaintiffs, was held properly granted, on this reasoning: There will be no difficulties in enforcing equity's decree, since the subject matter is the actual scrap made and accumulated at a specific plant. But the quantity of scrap defendant will produce in its operations is uncertain; if the plant suffers an interruption or closes down, there will be none. How could a jury determine the contract price, derived from a variable market price, during the years yet to come? Any estimate of damages would be "speculative," not compensatory. To remit plaintiffs to an action at law would be to force them "to sell their profits at a conjectural price." A court will do that, "substitute damages by guess" for a contractual performance, only when "there's no equity stirring."

COMMENT: THE VENDEE'S EQUITY ACTION

When a duty to transfer an interest in land is in question, the buyer (the vendee) enjoys the special treatment the law of specific performance accords contracts for the sale of land.

The case of Gartrell v. Stafford, 12 Neb. 545, 11 N.W. 732 (1882), is representative of the standard analysis and outcome. The vendor, a resident of California, agreed in writing to sell land in Nebraska to plaintiff, who lived in the Nebraska County in which the land was situated. When the vendor refused to convey, plaintiff, in Nebraska, sued for and was awarded specific performance of the contract. On appeal, the court summarily rejected the vendor's arguments for a reversal:

> The first objection made by the appellant is, that an action of this kind can only be brought where the defendant resides or may be summoned. But this objection is not well taken. An action to enforce specific performance of a contract for the conveyance of real estate is of two-fold character, viz: *in rem* and *in personam*. In the one case the decree of the court operates directly upon the land. In the other, where the court has jurisdiction of the parties, it may compel them to perform, although the land may be situated outside the state. . . . There is no doubt that an action may be brought against a non-resident in the county where the land in controversy is situated.
>
> The second objection . . . is that the plaintiff has an adequate remedy at law in an action for damages. The rule contended for by the appellant undoubtedly applies to contracts for the sale of personal property, the reason being that damages in such cases are readily calculated on the market price of property such as wheat,

> corn, wool, etc., . . . and thus afford as complete a remedy to the purchaser as the delivery of the property. Adderley v. Dixon, 1 Sim. & Stu., 607. But the rule is a qualified one and is limited to cases where compensation in damages furnishes a complete and satisfactory remedy. . . . The jurisdiction of courts of equity to decree specific performance of contracts for the sale of real estate is not limited, as in cases respecting chattels, to special circumstances, but is universally maintained, the reason being that a purchaser of a particular piece of land may reasonably be supposed to have considered the locality, soil, easements, or accommodations of the land, generally, which may give a peculiar or special value to the land to him, that could not be replaced by other land of the same value, but not having the same local conveniences or accommodations. [Story's Eq., § 746.] An action for damages would not, therefore, afford adequate relief.

1. Adequacy of Legal Remedy

Does the judge writing in Gartrell v. Stafford convince you that damages cannot be an adequate remedy for land-contract vendees? Suppose, for example, that the subject of the sale is Lot 101 in Broadmoor Subdivision and that the entire subdivision is flat and treeless and has not been built on at all, so that if some vandal ran off with the lot-number stakes no one but a surveyor could come within a hundred yards of locating Lot 101? Would it be harder to measure damages in such a case than, for instance, in the sale of a 2003 Ford SUV with the seller refusing to perform?

One can find many judicial opinions (e.g., Curtice Bros. v. Catts, p. 209) saying that there is "no inherent difference" between contracts for the sale of land and contracts for the sale of goods, and that they are simply governed by different presumptions—of inadequacy of damages in sales of land, of adequacy in the sale of anything else. In land contracts the presumption of inability to value land is, most of the time, conclusive. It is a working rule, about as firm as any working rule we have, that the vendee can have specific performance of such a contract if *adequacy of the legal remedy* is the only objection. There are perhaps 15 other objections that may prevent specific performance, but you will find that if an interest in land is to be transferred through the contract the inadequacy of the legal remedy is presupposed.

Anyone asserting legal propositions in such sweeping terms must be ready to retreat here and there, where the line is over-extended. We, too, have learned this. So what about the case where the vendee has contracted to sell the land in question to a third party and has no purpose other than to turn the land into money? If the vendee has made a resale contract at a higher price, is not a money judgment for the difference satisfaction in full? At least one court has reached this conclusion and therefore denied specific performance (Hazelton v. Miller, 25 App.D.C. 337 (1905)); another has held that equity should refuse its aid to "such bare-faced gambling," since one of the curses of the country is the "speculative craze" that drives people into the search for "easy money" (Schmid v. Whitten, 114 S.C. 245, 103 S.E. 553 (1920)). This issue was confronted more directly in Loveless v. Diehl, 235 Ark. 805, 364 S.W.2d 317 (1962). There the vendees had an option, granted as one of the terms of a lease, to buy land for $21,000. They exercised the option at a time when they had already contracted to sell the land to another for $22,000. The vendees admitted that they could not pay for the land themselves, and could buy it only if the resale contract went through as planned. The first reaction of the Supreme Court, "exercising the sound discretion" of a court of equity, was that the vendees should be awarded only the $1,000 difference, since this would put them precisely where they aimed to be. But on rehearing the court confessed, almost with embarrassment, that it had erred: in land contracts "*it is as much a matter of course for a court of equity to decree its specific performance as for a court of law*" to give damages (the court repeated that it was *a matter of course* three times, each time with italics). Whether the vendees "kept it, sold it, or gave it away was no concern of the sellers." It should be noted, however, that there was one other reason why the court became so aroused—the vendees had invested $5,000 in improvements while occupying as lessees, and these would accrue to the vendors if specific performance were denied, but if it were granted the vendees could get at least $1,000 back. You will run across this issue—the effect of vendee's resale—later in this book. In general, it can be said that the position taken in Hazelton v. Miller does not appear to have many adherents. See, e.g., Miller v. LeSea Broadcasting, Inc., 87 F.3d 224 (7th Cir. 1996); Justus v. Clelland, 133 Ariz. 381, 651 P.2d 1206 (Ct.App. 1982). Apart from the ordinary practice regarding land contracts, the fact that a vendee who has made a contract to resell the property would itself be in breach unless specific performance could be obtained, is, in most places, an added consideration favoring that remedy. Texaco, Inc. v. Creel, 310 N.C. 695, 314 S.E.2d 506 (1984).

As one other small qualification, we should note that decisions in Idaho have limited land vendees to the damage remedy unless they can show that the land is needed for some "particular, unique purpose." Watkins v. Paul, 95 Idaho 499, 511 P.2d 781 (1973); Wood v. Simonson, 108 Idaho 699, 701 P.2d 319 (Ct.App. 1985). We are not aware that these decisions have made any impression anywhere else.

At a later point, we shall encounter the vendor's suit for specific performance. One question will be whether a vendor's equity action also depends on a finding of an inadequate legal remedy (as Idaho, with consistency, says it does, Suchan v. Rutherford, 90 Idaho 288, 410 P.2d 434 (1966); Perron v. Hale, 108 Idaho 578, 701 P.2d 198 (1985)), or whether other doctrines enter in. We shall see that the reason most commonly given for allowing the vendor specific performance of a land contract is "mutuality" and not inadequacy. But, as we shall also see, equity's special conception of mutuality may involve the vendor in other and related difficulties.

2. *In Rem* and *In Personam*

The phrases *in rem* and *in personam* carry a great load of procedural technicalities, exploration of which can wait till a much later stage. But the problem is evident. The land involved in *Gartrell* was in Nebraska; the owner-vendor was in California and apparently intended to stay there. The process of a state court is effective only within the boundaries of the state, and even if suit had been brought in a federal court the plaintiff could not have secured a writ that could be served or would generate sanctions against a nonresident defendant. It is not merely a question of the ineffectiveness of process. It is quite fundamental to our thinking about the powers of courts that personal service of process is necessary within the territorial limits in which the court operates, if a judgment or decree is to impose a personal liability of any kind on a litigant. There are important exceptions to this statement, but they will have to be examined in other courses.

In traditional practice, an equity decree giving specific performance of a promise to convey land was enforced primarily by imprisonment or threat of imprisonment of the promisor, to compel execution of a deed. The process in the older equity cases was *in personam* in the highest degree—against the body of the defendant. What then is the court to do about Stafford, basking in the sunshine of California?

The explanations are to be found in two types of statutes that have enlarged the traditional powers of equity courts. Both types were in force in Nebraska at the time of Gartrell v. Stafford. The first contributed the so-called "self-executing decree." If a litigant has been ordered by a court to execute a conveyance or release, such statutes provide that the decree itself will operate as a conveyance or release if the person to whom the order was directed has not complied within the time limit set. Some statutes provide as alternative machinery that the county sheriff (or a deputy) will execute a deed. In that case, the sheriff would obviously serve as a purely ministerial officer, whose authority would be derived from the court order, not from the disobedient litigant. It is usual for such statutes to add that the decree (or sheriff's deed), if it involves an interest in land, can be recorded as a conveyance in the local title registry, and to confer on the court power to issue a "writ of possession" and put the prevailing litigant in possession of the asset involved.

Statutes providing for self-executing decrees are very common. Many of these statutes, by explicit statement or by the inclusiveness of statutory language, also authorize decrees for the transfer of title to identified personal property. Rule 70 of the Federal Rules of Civil Procedure now has a similar provision applying to the decrees of federal courts.

The opinion in Gartrell v. Stafford suggested another sense in which a specific performance action could be *in rem*—that it could be brought in the county where the land in controversy was located, against a nonresident defendant. The implication was clear that a court sitting in that county could operate "directly on the land," even though there had not been and could not be any personal service of process within the state on the absent party. The power to act in this way was the product of another type of legislation that was already very common by the late 1800s and was in force at the time in Nebraska. The power is most often employed in litigation over interests in land, though some statutes include other kinds of property. Instead of personal service of process, the statutes authorize "service by publication" (sometimes called "substituted service"). This consists of publication of a specified number of notices for a specified number of weeks in a local newspaper, with a further requirement that a copy of the notice be sent by registered mail to the last known address of the absent owner. The thought behind such legislation is that the asset in question, situated within the governmental area over which the court's power extends, can be brought under the "control" of the court by a symbolic act such as posting a notice on the premises. If the provisions for mailed as well as locally-published notices are fully satisfied, it is clear that there can be no objections on due process or other constitutional grounds. Whether land contracts in which vendees seek a transfer of the vendor's legal title are included in such legislation will obviously depend on statutory language. They usually are included.

As Gartrell v. Stafford also indicated, the power of a court at the situs of the land to act *in rem* did not in any way diminish the historic power to act *in personam* against a land-contract vendor on whom personal service of process had in fact been made. The classic forms of coercion—imprisonment and money fine—could then be used to compel the vendor to execute a deed, even of land in another state. An example is Bell v. Wadley, 206 Ark. 569, 177 S.W.2d 403 (1944), where it was held that an Arkansas court had acted within its powers in ordering conveyance of land in Missouri. Then what if the defendant in the action skips off beyond the reach of the court that issued the decree? Should the decree be recognized as *res judicata*, decisive of the issues, by a court that sits at the situs of the land? Suppose in the case just mentioned that the plaintiff in the Arkansas action simply took a certified copy of the decree to Missouri, showed it to the court in the county where the land was situated, and asked for judicial confirmation of his or her right to the land. It has not yet been held that the Missouri court in such a case would be bound by the federal constitution to give "full faith and credit" to the Arkansas decree, but on essentially these facts it was held as early as Burnley v. Stevenson, 24 Ohio St. 474 (1873), that the court at the situs should and would do so. R. Weintraub, Commentary on The Conflict of Laws 421–427 (3d ed. 1986), discusses the subject.

3. Equitable Ownership and the Trust Analogy

There is another dimension of the vendee's equity action. In early times, it was quite easy for Chancellors working in a separate court to effect a transfer of ideas—to infer from the equitable remedy, granted so routinely, that equitable rights had been created and that the vendee was "equitable owner" of the land described in the contract. This could only occur, of course, where the contract was still "executory," where the vendor had merely promised to convey legal title by deed and the object of the equity suit was to compel performance of the promise. In any case, this manner of speaking ("equitable owner") appears often in our law and it has a number of important consequences. Suppose, to take one example, that after agreeing to convey to A, the vendor wrongfully conveys the same land to B. Instead of suing for damages, the vendee A would have an option to sue the vendor in equity, joining as defendant the grantee B. If B, now invested with the legal title, had given "value" without notice, either actual or imputed, of A's contract, the action against B would fail. As a bona fide purchaser of the legal title for value, B would be protected as against A's prior "equity." But if B had either knowledge or reason to know of A's contract, or if B gave or promised no "value," then A would probably succeed and B would be ordered by court decree to reconvey to A.

One way to explain this result is to say that the first vendee, A, became "equitable" owner from the inception of the contract with the vendor. Quite obviously, this is nothing more than a shorthand way of expressing the predisposition of an equity court to order specific performance. But this phrasing at once suggests another familiar situation in which legal and "equitable" ownership of the same asset are conceived to co-exist. The analogy invoked is of course the express *trust*, which is usually created by the owner of some asset (land, goods, stocks, etc.), who transfers legal title to the asset to a trustee with directions to hold, administer, or dispose of the asset for the benefit of another (a minor child, a relative or friend, a church or other "charitable" organization, or perhaps even the transferor). At least by the fifteenth century, the Chancellors had begun to enforce such directions that the transferor (usually called the "settlor") had imposed, and to prevent the transferee-trustee from appropriating the asset entrusted. The Chancellors continued in later centuries to enforce such restrictions and protect the interests of the beneficiary (usually called the *cestui que trust*, degenerate French for "he who trusts"). The ease with which the legal title of the trustee was thus subjected to the controls of equity courts led before long to a manner of speaking—that, though the trustee might be legal owner, the beneficiary was the "equitable owner," to the extent and in the ways that the original transfer from settlor to trustee had directed. You can see that the trust provides at least an analogy to contracts for the sale of land, which, as we have seen, equity courts also enforce with regularity.

It was this manner of thinking which led, in cases like the example given above (the vendor wrongfully conveys to B land previously contracted to A), to a further extension of land-contract remedies. Some courts came to allow the vendee to sue the defaulting vendor in equity and recover, not the land itself, but, if the vendee so elected, the money proceeds of the vendor's wrongful resale. E.g., Timko v. Useful Homes Corp., 114 N.J.Eq. 433, 168 A. 824 (1933). This was explained by labelling the vendor a "trustee" of the land, accountable like any other trustee for profits made through misappropriation of trust assets ("wrongful conduct," said the *Timko* court of the breach in selling the vendee's lots). Again, the word "trust" in this context was understood by all to express no more than the regularity with which specific performance is given the parties to land contracts. In fact, the remedy awarded here—a money judgment in equity, measured by the proceeds realized from the resale—might well be thought of as a sort of substituted specific performance. Of course, a similar claim brought at law, in an action framed as one for damages measured by the gains of the defaulter, would likely encounter the doctrine applied in *Acme Mills*.

It is a different question whether it is useful to describe the vendee, from the inception of the land contract, as a trustee of the purchase money. If one were to look at the executory land contract from this angle of vision and to equate it with a trust, what element would usually be missing?

Fitzpatrick v. Michael

Court of Appeals of Maryland, 1939.
177 Md. 248, 9 A.2d 639.

[Plaintiff, a nurse then 52, was employed by defendant Michael in the summer of 1936 to give nursing care to defendant's wife; plaintiff cared for the wife until the wife's death in February 1937. At that time, plaintiff informed defendant of her intention of leaving, but defendant, who was then 76, asked plaintiff to stay on for a few days. She did so, and defendant then told her that he wanted company, someone to manage his house, drive his car, and care for him when he was ill. Defendant stated that if plaintiff would remain with him for the rest of his life and provide such company and services, defendant would pay her $8 a week, would provide a home and board for her in his house in Aberdeen, and would at his death leave her by will a life estate in the house, the life use of its furnishings, and full title to his automobiles. Plaintiff "accepted the offer" and continued to serve until April 6, 1939, managing defendant's home and garden, driving him to and from his office and on long trips, and nursing him during periods of illness. Defendant expressed to neighbors during this period his complete satisfaction with plaintiff's services, and in three successive wills executed by him the promised life estate in home and furnishings and the gift of the cars were all included. Then suddenly all was changed, plaintiff's explanation being that distant relatives had "poisoned his mind" against her. On April 4, 1939, defendant left his house and did not return. On April 6, defendant tried to force plaintiff to leave the house by cutting off the electricity, water, heat and telephone, and food supplies, and, when that blockade proved ineffective, he had plaintiff arrested for trespass. While she was under arrest defendant locked up the house so that plaintiff could not enter it, though she had property of her own inside.]

OFFUTT, J. . . . Following her removal from Michael's home, Miss Fitzpatrick on May 9th of this year filed the bill of complaint in this case, [asking] that the respondent Michael be required to specifically perform his contract with her, and that a receiver be appointed to take charge of "all the estate, both real and personal, of the respondent, to collect all money, rents, etc., and to pay this complainant the weekly sum of eight dollars ($8.00) per week as long as the respondent lives, and to provide her in the respondent's Aberdeen residence a home with board and lodging so long as the respondent lives, upon the complainant looking after the respondent's home, flowers, driving his automobile, and nursing and caring for the respondent in compliance with her said agreement, with the said respondent."

The defendant demurred to the bill for a general want of equity, the demurrer was sustained and the bill dismissed, and from that decree the plaintiff appealed.

There can be no possible doubt that upon those facts the plaintiff should be entitled to some relief against the defendant, but the question . . . is whether the remedy is equity.

A contract to make a will is not invalid because of its subject matter (69 A.L.R. 18), for, since one may bargain, sell, give away, or otherwise surrender every right and property interest which he has, there can be no sound reason why he cannot also validly agree to dispose of it by will. . . . Nor, since Michael may not have lived for a year after it was made, can it be said that, apart from any question of part performance, that the contract is invalid because it was not embodied in a writing signed by the party to be charged, as required by clause 5 of the fourth section of the Statute of Frauds[,] . . . because there was a possibility that it might be performed within a year. . . . But, as it relates to an interest in land, it is within clause 4 of the section[,] . . . and unenforceable unless the bar of the statute is removed. Fry on Spec.Perf., § 561 et seq. That may be done by sufficient proof that the plaintiff has performed it in part, and is willing and able to continue to do those things which she undertook to do. . . . The doctrine of part performance,[8] however, is peculiar to equity, and may not be invoked in courts of law[,] . . . so that, unless the facts present a case of equitable jurisdiction, the appellant has no remedy on the contract either at law or in equity. 69 A.L.R. 20.

But no ground of equitable jurisdiction can be found in the facts stated, unless it be that she has no adequate remedy at law. But even though there is no adequate remedy at law, equity will not, ordinarily, specifically enforce a contract for personal service, for these reasons, one, that the mischief likely to result from the enforced continuance of the relationship incident to the service when it has become personally obnoxious to one of the parties is so great that the best interests of society require that the remedy be refused (Fry on Spec.Perf. 5th Ed., secs. 110, 112), for, as stated by Fry, "The relation established by the contract of hiring and service is of so personal and confidential a character that it is evident that such contracts cannot be specifically enforced by the court against an unwilling party with any hope of ultimate and real success. . . ." The other reason is, that courts have not the means nor the ability to enforce such decrees. Pomeroy, Spec.Perf., secs. 22, 310.

Nevertheless there is a class of cases in which, although the contract is not actionable under the Statute of Frauds, it has been performed by the rendition of services the value of which cannot be estimated in terms of money, and in such cases, when it appears that a monetary award will not place the parties in statu quo, or adequately compensate the complaining party, equity may grant relief in the nature of a specific performance of the contract. . . . Executory contracts, are not, however, within the scope of that principle, which can only be invoked where the employment has been terminated by the expiration of the term of employment,

---

8 [The "part performance" doctrine in equity is examined in Chapter 2, infra p. 287.—Eds.]

by the death of one of the parties, or in some other manner inconsistent with the possibility of future or continuing service under the contract. For, during the term of employment, where it is for an indefinite period, when both parties are living and specific performance would mean compelling one party to accept and the other to render services, the reasons for the refusal of courts of equity to decree specific performance of such contracts apply, and that relief will be refused even though there be no adequate remedy at law, for it would result in a species of peonage on the part of the servant, or an enforced association with an obnoxious employee on the part of the master, which would be intolerable. . . .

The limitation which the rule imposes upon equitable jurisdiction at times results in the denial of any adequate remedy to one who has been injured by the breach of such a contract, and courts have striven to discover some alternate remedy which, in cases of unusual and extreme hardship, would afford to the promisee some measure of relief. So in England, where such contracts contained [express] negative covenants, while the courts at first, in cases where specific performance of the affirmative covenants could not be enforced, also refused to enforce the negative covenants, later, beginning with Lumley v. Wagner, 1 DeG.M. & G. 604, their power to enforce negative covenants was recognized, although that might indirectly result in compelling the specific performance of the affirmative covenants. . . . There is a distinction between cases in which the contract provides merely for employment and compensation, in which a refusal to serve or to pay is the negation of a promise to pay or to serve, and cases where the services involve and imply some rare and unusual quality in the promisor which, if given to a competitor of the promisee might cause him a loss by the diversion of custom in addition to what he might suffer from the loss of custom which the services of the promisor might attract, and that consideration apparently underlies the decisions in many of the cases enforcing negative covenants. There are, however, cases in which the doctrine of the enforcement of implied negative covenants has been carried far beyond the present state of law in England, and beyond what seems to be the weight of the best considered authority here, but, taking the law as we find it, it may safely be said that equity will not enforce a negative covenant, express or implied, in a contract which it cannot specifically enforce, unless a breach of the negative covenant will cause a loss to the promisee distinct from that resulting from the mere failure of the promisor to carry out his affirmative promise. Applying that principle to contracts for personal services, the sounder rule is that equity will not enforce negatively a contract which it could not enforce affirmatively, nor will it enjoin the breach of a negative covenant, express or implied, unless the breach will cause a loss to the promisee independent of the loss caused by the mere failure of the promisor to keep and perform his affirmative covenants. . . .

Applying those principles to the facts of this case, the conclusion that the plaintiff is not entitled to any relief in equity seems inevitable. The contract was essentially one for the rendition of personal services. They were varied, it is true, but they required no extraordinary or unusual skill, experience, or capacity. Under the employment, the appellant acted as nurse, chauffeur, companion, gardener, and housekeeper, and, while it may be difficult to appraise in monetary terms the value of services so varied, nevertheless they involved no more than [things customarily done] as a part of the ordinary routine of life. The reasons for the general rule that equity will not specifically enforce contracts for personal service apply with plenary force to the facts conceded here. Assuming that appellee broke the contract, that the breach was whimsical, arbitrary, and unjust, and induced by the intrigue of greedy relatives, nevertheless its enforcement would compel him to accept the personal services of an employee against his wish and his will. The court can no more compel him to accept her services under such conditions, than it could compel her to render them if he demanded them and she were unwilling to give them. It follows that the decree must be affirmed.

NOTE

The agreement fell within the land clause of the statute of frauds because Fitzpatrick was promised a life estate in defendant's residence. The court's reasons for concluding that it did not come within the "not-to-be-performed-within-one-year" clause represent the standard interpretation of that clause, as is explained in the Appendix.

Recall also that Fitzpatrick asked the court to appoint a "receiver" to take charge of defendant's residence, collect and pay plaintiff her wages, and ensure her occupancy. The appointment of a receiver is one of the administrative devices available to a court exercising equity powers. This possibility was suggested in Curtice Bros. v. Catts (p. 209). Rule 70 of the Federal Rules of Civil Procedure provides for this as well as other enforcement measures:

> If a judgment directs a party to execute a conveyance of land or to deliver deeds or other documents or to perform any other specific act and the party fails to comply within the time specified, the court may direct the act to be done at the cost of the disobedient party by some other person appointed by the court and the act when so done has like effect as if done by the party. On application of the party entitled to performance, the clerk shall issue a writ of attachment or sequestration against the property of the disobedient party to compel obedience to the judgment. The court may also in proper cases adjudge the party in contempt. If real or personal property is within the district, the court in lieu of directing a conveyance thereof may enter a judgment divesting the title of any party and vesting it in others and such judgment has the effect of a conveyance executed in due form of law. When any order or judgment is for the delivery of possession, the party in whose favor it is entered is entitled to a writ of execution or assistance upon application to the clerk.

Receivers can be used for a variety of purposes. Since it is generally understood that the principal justification for a receiver is to secure property in dispute from waste or loss, the device is often seen where there are allegations of mismanagement or fraud. Courts usually do not appoint receivers in order to grant ultimate relief; rather, appointments are viewed as a measure ancillary to the enforcement of some recognized equitable right—e.g., the collection of rents during a lengthy proceeding to foreclose a mortgage on the rental property, as in Hartford Fed. Sav. & Loan Ass'n v. Tucker, 196 Conn. 172, 491 A.2d 1084 (1985). A common use of the equity receivership formerly was in the rehabilitation of business enterprises that had experienced financial difficulties. Today, reorganizations are handled under Chapter 11 of the Bankruptcy Code, which is itself a linear descendant of the equity receivership and which still bears many of its distinctive features. The aim of the receivership (as with the modern statutory proceeding) usually was not, as in traditional bankruptcy, a prompt liquidation with sale of assets and payment of the proceeds to creditors. The aim was rather to administer the assets, often over years, to scale down or extend fixed money obligations, and generally to restore an ailing enterprise to health.

An example of successful use of a receiver in the enforcement of a private contract is Madden v. Rosseter, 114 Misc. 416, 187 N.Y.S. 462 and 117 Misc. 244, 192 N.Y.S. 113 (1921), where plaintiff, a resident of New York, and defendant, a resident of California, owned a thoroughbred stallion jointly. Their agreement provided that defendant was to have possession of the stallion in California in 1919 and 1920 and plaintiff was to have the horse in Kentucky during 1921 and 1922. Plaintiff secured personal service of process on defendant in an action for specific performance in New York state, and persuaded the court to appoint a receiver with power to go to California, retrieve the horse, and deliver it to plaintiff in Kentucky. The receiver carried out the order "with tact and diplomacy," without litigation, and was allowed $5,000 for his services, to be paid by defendant.

Lumley v. Wagner

Lord Chancellor's Court, 1852.
1 DeG, M. & G. 604, 42 Eng. Rep. 687.

[Benjamin Lumley, who ran the opera company at Her Majesty's Theatre, engaged Johanna Wagner to sing for the season exclusively for him. Frederick Gye, who ran the rival opera company at Covent Garden, persuaded Wagner to break her contract with Lumley and to sing for him instead. Lumley then tried to prevent Wagner from singing with his competitor.]

LORD ST. LEONARDS, L.C. The question which I have to decide . . . arises out of a very simple contract, the effect of which is, that the defendant Johanna Wagner should sing at Her Majesty's Theatre for a certain number of nights, and that she should not sing elsewhere (for that is the true construction) during that period. . . . [T]he points taken by the defendants' counsel . . . in effect come to this, namely, that a court of equity ought not to grant an injunction except in cases connected with specific performance, or where the injunction being to compel a party to forbear from committing an act (and not to perform an act), that injunction will complete the whole of the agreement remaining unexecuted. . . .

The present is a mixed case, consisting not of two correlative acts to be done, one by the plaintiff and the other by the defendants, which state of facts may have and in some cases has introduced a very important difference, but of an act to be done by Johanna Wagner alone, to which is superadded a negative stipulation on her part to abstain from the commission of any act which will break in upon her affirmative covenant—the one being ancillary to, and concurrent and operating together with the other. The agreement to sing for the plaintiff during three months at his theatre, and during that time not to sing for anybody else, is not a correlative contract. It is, in effect, one contract, and though beyond all doubt this court could not interfere to enforce the specific performance of the whole of this contract, yet in all sound construction and according to the true spirit of the agreement, the engagement to perform for three months at one theatre must necessarily exclude the right to perform at the same time at another theatre. It was clearly intended that Johanna Wagner was to exert her vocal abilities to the utmost to aid the theatre to which she agreed to attach herself. I am of opinion that if she had attempted, even in the absence of any negative stipulation, to perform at another theatre, she would have broken the spirit and true meaning of the contract as much as she would now do with reference to the contract into which she has actually entered.

Wherever this court has not proper jurisdiction to enforce specific performance, it operates to bind men's consciences, as far as they can be bound, to a true and literal performance of their agreements, and it will not suffer them to depart from their contracts at their pleasure, leaving the party with whom they have contracted to the mere chance of any damages which a jury may give. The exercise of this jurisdiction has, I believe, had a wholesome tendency towards the maintenance of that good faith which exists in this country to a much greater degree perhaps than in any other, and, although the jurisdiction is not to be extended, yet a judge would desert his duty who did not act up to what his predecessors have handed down as the rule for his guidance in the administration of such an equity.

It was objected that the operation of the injunction in the present case was mischievous, excluding the defendant Johanna Wagner from performing at any other theatre while this court had no power to compel her to perform at Her Majesty's Theatre. It is true that I have not the means of compelling her to sing, but she has no cause of complaint if I compel her to abstain from the commission of an act which she has bound herself not to do, and thus possibly cause her to fulfil her engagement. The jurisdiction which I now exercise is wholly within the power of the court, and, being of opinion that it is a proper case for interfering, I shall leave nothing unsatisfied by the judgment I pronounce. The effect, too, of the injunction, in restraining Johanna Wagner from singing elsewhere may, in the event of an action being brought against her by the plaintiff, prevent any such amount of vindictive damages being given against her as a jury might probably be inclined to give if she had carried her talents and exercised them at the rival theatre. The injunction may also, as I have said, tend to the fulfilment of her engagement, though, in continuing the injunction, I disclaim doing indirectly what I cannot do directly. . . .

Pingley v. Brunson

272 S.C. 421, 252 S.E.2d 560 (1979)

Brunson, an auto mechanic by trade, was also a part-time organ player for various businesses in and around Mullins, S.C. In late 1977, he entered into a contract to play the organ for Pingley's restaurant, three nights a week for $50 per night, for a period of three years. The contract stated that Pingley was to purchase musical instruments costing $4,262.96 for Brunson's use at the restaurant, and that the monthly payments for the instruments were to be made by deductions from Brunson's paychecks. The instruments were to be Brunson's when paid for, but any breach by Brunson would result in a forfeiture of his claim to the instruments. Brunson began playing for Pingley the night of December 6, performed on nine evenings thereafter, and then refused to perform further. Pingley sued for and was awarded both specific performance and an order enjoining Brunson from playing musical instruments for any other establishment during times in conflict with the Pingley contract. *Held*, reversed. Equity courts will not ordinarily decree specific performance in this type of case, particularly where, as here, personal services are to be performed on a continuous basis over a period of time. There is an exception "where the performer possesses unique and exceptional skill or ability in his area of expertise." Even though Pingley's witnesses asserted Brunson's "exceptional talent as a major attraction to an area establishment," the evidence revealed that "five other organists of comparable ability were available for hire in the Mullins area." Thus the substantial equivalent of the subject matter of this contract is readily obtainable by means of a money payment. So "we cannot conclude . . . that appellant's musical talent is of such a unique quality as to warrant an award of specific performance." The lower court's injunctive relief was also erroneous. The contract did not contain an express covenant not to compete or perform elsewhere. Absent an express negative covenant, a court as a rule does not enjoin an employee's furnishing of services to another during the term of a breached contract.

QUESTION

Suppose that Pingley, upon receiving the news of his defeat in South Carolina's high court, then brought a suit joining as defendants each restaurant in Mullins that had, in the interim, employed Brunson as an organist.

Pingley asked for an injunction preventing these restaurants from making use of Brunson's services. How should such a suit come out?

NOTE: ENFORCING NONCOMPETE PLEDGES

Assume Pingley's contract with Brunson had included this provision: "For a period of one year following Brunson's termination of employment under this agreement, whatever the basis or cause of the termination, voluntary or involuntary, Brunson agrees not to play any musical instrument in public, for compensation paid by any person, within a radius of 50 miles of Mullins, S.C." A leading decision, ABC v. Wolf, 52 N.Y.2d 394, 438 N.Y.S.2d 482, 420 N.E.2d 363 (1981), describes the law's general approach to an employee's promise to refrain from postemployment competition:

> After a personal service contract terminates, the availability of equitable relief against the former employee diminishes appreciably. Since the period of service has expired, it is impossible to decree affirmative or negative specific performance. Only if the employee has expressly agreed not to compete with the employer following the term of the contract, or is threatening to disclose trade secrets or commit another tortious act, is injunctive relief generally available at the behest of the employer. . . . Even where there is an express anticompetitive covenant, however, it will be rigorously examined and specifically enforced only if it satisfies certain established requirements. . . . Indeed, a court normally will not decree specific enforcement of an employee's anticompetitive covenant unless necessary to protect the trade secrets, customer lists or good will of the employer's business, or perhaps when the employer is exposed to specific harm because of the unique nature of the employee's services (see, e.g., . . . 6A Corbin, Contracts, § 1394). And, an otherwise valid covenant will not be enforced if it is unreasonable in time, space or scope or would operate in a harsh or oppressive manner. . . . There is, in short, general judicial disfavor of anticompetitive covenants contained in employment contracts. . . .
>
> Underlying the strict approach to enforcement of these covenants is the notion that, once the term of an employment agreement has expired, the general public policy favoring robust and uninhibited competition should not give way merely because a particular employer wishes to insulate himself from competition. . . . [Thus, the] rules governing enforcement of anticompetitive covenants and the availability of equitable relief after termination of employment are designed to foster [the legitimate] interests of the employer without impairing the employee's ability to earn a living or the general competitive mold of society.

Much of the material considered earlier in this chapter dealt with "enforcement difficulties" in a larger sense, that is, obstacles to recovery for losses actually incurred, through limitations imposed for reasons of fairness or practicability—e.g., mitigation, foreseeability, certainty. In this section, enforcement problems have centered mainly on when an "inadequate" damage remedy leads to relief in equity. An inevitable part of this landscape—recall, for example, *Manchester Dairy* and *Curtice Bros.*—is the practical problem of the ways and means of compelling compliance with an equity decree. When will difficulties anticipated in ordering specific enforcement result in the decision to withhold such a remedy?

The answer usually given is that specific performance will be refused when the decree will require extensive and unduly burdensome court supervision. So, for example, construction contracts, involving a large element of labor or services, traditionally have been viewed as instances where the burden of supervision calls for caution in the exercise of discretionary powers. E.g., Northern Delaware Indus. Dev. Corp. v. E.W. Bliss Co., 245 A.2d 431 (Del.Ch. 1968) ("a court of equity should not order specific performance of any building contract in a situation where it would be impractical to carry out such an order"). The *Ammerman* and *Grayson-Robinson* cases, immediately below, should be read against this general landscape.

City Stores Co. v. Ammerman

266 F. Supp. 766 (D. D.C. 1967)

Defendants owned land at Tyson's Corner, Fairfax County, Virginia, on which they hoped to construct a large shopping center. This would require rezoning by the Board of County Supervisors. Defendants earlier had applied to the Board for rezoning; a similar application was already pending from a rival group of developers, who planned a shopping center at a nearby site. The county planning commission, in a report to the Board, had recommended against the rezoning of defendants' site at Tyson's Corner. Plaintiff, owner of Lansburgh's Department Store in Washington, D.C., had been negotiating for a lease at the rival site. He was then asked by defendants to lend support for defendants' application, by expressing to the Board a preference for the Tyson's Corner site and a willingness to become a major tenant there, if the site were rezoned and developed. Defendants in writing assured plaintiff that if it supported their application plaintiff would be given an "opportunity" to become one of defendants' major tenants, "with rental and terms at least equal to that of any other major department store in the center." Plaintiff wrote the letter as requested, defendants' application for rezoning was granted, and defendants made leases to both the Woodward & Lothrop and the Hecht department stores, whose main stores also were located in Washington, D.C. When defendants then refused to lease to plaintiff a site in the center, plaintiff sued for specific performance. *Held*, defendants had given plaintiff an option with only two conditions—approval of the necessary rezoning and execution by defendants of leases to other major tenants which "could provide the essential terms of a lease to be offered to plaintiff." Both conditions have occurred and plaintiff has exercised the option so as to produce a valid contract. Plaintiff can have specific performance.

An order can be fashioned by examining the other leases. "Even though none of the stores in the center will be identical in design, it is apparent from defendants' own leases that complete equality of material terms governing occupancy, including amount of space and cost per square foot, and substantially equal terms on less material aspects of the lease, is within the customary contemplation of parties entering into shopping center agreements of the type at issue in this case." The lessors' own income was tied to the success of their lessees so that it will be to the lessors' advantage to ensure that one tenant be given "no distinct competitive advantage over another." All of the stores were to be subject to the overall design requirements of the center. Defendants were obligated, and will be ordered, to construct a building; there is no insuperable objection to this, especially since it is to be built on defendants' own land, so that plaintiff could not hire another contractor to build it at defendants' expense. If the parties should not be able in good faith to reach agreement on details, the court will appoint a special master to help them settle their differences, unless the parties prefer voluntarily to refer them to arbitration.

The essential criterion for a court of equity in deciding whether to enforce such contracts is the relative inadequacy of legal remedies. Here, even if it were possible, as it was not, to measure damages for breach of a contract to lease a store in a shopping center for a long period of years, money damages could not compensate plaintiff for the "almost incalculable future advantages that might accrue to it as a result of extending its operations into the suburbs."

[The decision was affirmed in a per curiam opinion, 394 F.2d 950 (D.C.Cir. 1968). The reviewing court emphasized that "damages could hardly compensate for the loss of the sought for opportunity to raise Lansburgh's image and economic position in the Metropolitan Washington area by its anticipated expansion into the suburbs." It also asserted that relief ordering building construction should not be withheld "unless the difficulties of supervision by the court outweigh the importance of enforcement to the plaintiff."]

Grayson-Robinson Stores v. Iris Constr. Corp.

8 N.Y.2d 133, 202 N.Y.S.2d 303, 168 N.E.2d 377 (1960)

Iris, owner of a tract of vacant land in Levittown, in 1955 agreed in writing with Grayson to erect on the tract a building, part of a shopping center, to be rented to Grayson as a retail department store for a term of 25 years. Possession was to be delivered to Grayson on or before September 1, 1957. The agreement called for arbitration of any disputes that might arise and incorporated the rules of the American Arbitration Association, which, among other things, empowered an arbitrator to award any just or equitable relief "including specific performance." After a public groundbreaking ceremony had been held and excavation for the shopping center had been commenced, Iris informed Grayson that it could not go further with the project because of difficulties in borrowing needed funds, unless Grayson agreed to an increase in rent. Grayson refused to pay more. Pursuant to the parties' contract, the dispute was submitted to a panel of arbitrators, who rejected the excuse offered by Iris that it could not borrow the money it needed. The arbitrators entered an award ordering Iris to "proceed forthwith with the improvements of the leased premises in accordance with the terms of said lease." The New York arbitration statute then in force provided that a written agreement to submit to arbitration any controversy thereafter arising "confers jurisdiction on the courts of the state to enforce it and to enter judgment on an award." The statute also directed that "the court shall not consider whether the claim with respect to which the arbitration is sought is tenable, or otherwise pass upon the merits of the dispute." By a 4-to-3 vote, the New York Court of Appeals affirmed a lower court order that defendant build the building, though as the dissent pointed out, the building would cost $5,000,000 and defendant had applied unsuccessfully to 27 lending institutions to secure the loan needed to undertake it. [In the end, the building was not completed, a court-appointed referee awarded plaintiff $3,287,483.10 for rental value lost as a result, and the case was settled by the parties for $550,000 to be paid by the defendant.]

COMMENT: ARBITRATION

The readiness of the New York court in *Grayson-Robinson* to carry out the mandate of the arbitrators, in an enterprise so extensive but also so unlikely to succeed, reflects a considerable reversal of early common law attitudes. Today, a preference for arbitration over ordinary judicial procedures has shown itself in a vast expansion in the use of arbitration clauses in many kinds of commercial transactions. Large segments of both the legal and the commercial worlds are now familiar with the uses and advantages of arbitration, and the reasons commonly given in support of the arbitral method of dispute settlement include much more than the claim that arbitration helps to relieve congestion in the courts. The emancipation of arbitrators from rules of judicial procedure can open a wider range of inquiry and at the same time speed decision. The parties can create their own forum and choose for it persons with specialized backgrounds and expertise. Experienced, professional arbitrators (organized into subject-matter panels by private organizations like the American Arbitration Association) frequently are familiar with the practices and expectations that have developed around transactions of the type involved in the dispute. Consequently, arbitrators may be able to find solutions that are more acceptable to the parties themselves.

The status of arbitration at common law was a strange hybrid. The agreement to submit to arbitration was not specifically enforceable; indeed, it was revocable by either party at any time prior to rendition of the arbitration award. This view was first expressed by Sir Edward Coke, who declared in a dictum in 1609 that any agreement to submit a dispute to arbitration was "of its own nature revocable." Vynior's Case, 8 Coke Rep. 81b (1609). The doctrine of "inherent revocability" was later put on the broad ground that a delegation of judicial powers to lay persons "ousted the courts of jurisdiction" and was therefore against public policy and void.[9] Accordingly, either party could repudiate the agreement, revoke the authority conferred (by contract) on an arbitrator, and bring a court action on the disputed claim. But the agreement to submit to arbitration was not in a strict sense illegal, nor was it wholly without legal effects. A damage remedy for breach of the promise to arbitrate was theoretically available.[10] More important, if an arbitrator was actually appointed and proceeded to render an award, the award was enforceable both at law and in equity. If it ordered payment of a sum of money, the successful claimant could sue on the award in an action of debt. If it established a duty to convey an interest in land, the one subject to the duty could be sued—again, on the award—for damages, or, since land was involved, specific performance.

Arbitration agreements are enforceable today principally because of legislation reversing common law attitudes. Most states have adopted arbitration statutes that provide for irrevocability of an arbitration agreement and for streamlined procedures for judicial enforcement.[11] The salient feature of the more advanced statutes is the prescription that written agreements to arbitrate any dispute, existing or prospective, are "valid, enforceable and irrevocable."[12] A party aggrieved by the other's refusal to honor a promise to arbitrate may simply move a court to compel arbitration. If suit is filed on a claim allegedly covered by an arbitration agreement, the defendant may similarly move the court to stay the action pending arbitration. For the enforcement of awards, the modern acts make available summary procedures to review and to ensure prompt implementation of the results of arbitration. The first major step was to eliminate the need to start an entirely new action. Now an arbitrator's award can be filed with the local trial court, and, under simplified procedures, it becomes a judgment enforceable directly by the

---

[9] The decisions are collected in 135 A.L.R. 79 (1941). 6A A. Corbin, Contracts § 1433, contains a critical evaluation of the notion of "ouster of jurisdiction."

[10] The damage remedy was usually inadequate because of the view at common law that only nominal damages are recoverable for breach or repudiation of the promise to arbitrate. See, e.g., Rubewa Products Co. v. Watson's Quality Turkey Products, Inc., 242 A.2d 609 (D.C.App. 1968).

[11] Modern arbitration legislation first appeared in the New York Arbitration Act of 1920 (now N.Y.Civ.Prac.Law §§ 7501–7514 (McKinney 1998)), which served as a model for other states and the federal government. The United States Arbitration Act (or Federal Arbitration Act, commonly referred to as the "FAA") followed in 1925, providing for arbitration solely in contracts involving maritime transactions and those evidencing transactions in interstate or foreign commerce. Act of Feb. 12, 1925, ch. 213, 43 Stat. 883–886, as amended, 9 U.S.C.A. §§ 1–14 (West 1999). As early as 1924, the Commissioners on Uniform State Laws drafted a model act; their efforts culminated in the Uniform Arbitration Act of 1955 (UAA). Uniform Arbitration Act (7 U.L.A. §§ 1–25). A large number of states have enacted the UAA in its entirety or with minor changes; others have departed from the model, although incorporating the essential elements of a modern arbitration statute. See M. Domke, Commercial Arbitration §§ 7:1–7:9 (3d ed. 2006). In 2000, the Uniform Law Commissioners adopted major revisions to the UAA, resulting in the revised Uniform Arbitration Act (RUAA). The preemptive effect of the FAA, the federal counterpart to the UAA, on state arbitration law is currently a most active question.

[12] A "modern" arbitration act is said to qualify for that designation by containing the following provisions: (1) irrevocability of agreements to arbitrate future disputes; (2) judicial power to compel a party to arbitrate at the request of the other; (3) judicial power to stay, pending arbitration, a court action instituted in violation of an arbitration agreement; (4) court authority to appoint arbitrators and fill vacancies when the parties fail to do so; (5) restrictions on judicial power to review awards of arbitrators; and (6) specification of the grounds for attack of awards, such as fraud or "evident mistake." Domke, § 7:1.

court's own processes. Above all else, arbitration statutes attempt to limit judicial involvement by restricting the issues a court may fairly consider.

The role given courts to uphold arbitration reflects the considerable respect for freedom of contract that arbitration statutes embody. The system is created, administered, and controlled through the parties' agreement. Though arbitration acts establish limited requirements for an effective agreement, such as the formality of a writing, they do not initiate or create an obligation to arbitrate. Nor do they delineate substantive law or attempt in any way to regulate business transactions. The statutory scheme presumes the existence of an agreement created by mutual assent, and it does not purport to displace the usual tests of contract formation and enforceability. A court order compelling arbitration is not a determination of substantive rights under the contract; it merely shifts the dispute to the agreed forum.

Yet when an arbitration award comes before a court for enforcement (and limited review), there is always present an important question of policy—to what extent should private parties be allowed by contract to transfer judicial functions to persons who may be wholly untrained in law and ready to disregard well-established rules? That legislatures have gone some distance in answering that question in favor of private autonomy is indicated by the following provision of the New York arbitration statute (McKinney's New York CPLR, § 7501):

> A written agreement to submit any controversy thereafter arising or any existing controversy to arbitration is enforceable without regard to the justiciable character of the controversy and confers jurisdiction on the courts of the state to enforce it and to enter judgment on an award. In determining any matter arising under this article, the court shall not consider whether the claim with respect to which arbitration is sought is tenable, or otherwise pass upon the merits of the dispute.

Does this mandated deference to arbitration extend also to remedies? In cases like *Grayson-Robinson*, for example, if the claim for specific enforcement had been presented initially to a court, it seems likely that problems of supervision would have led to a denial of relief. Yet the Commercial Arbitration Rules of the American Arbitration Association expressly provide that an arbitrator may grant any remedy or relief deemed "just and equitable and within the scope of the [parties'] agreement, including, but not limited to, specific performance of a contract." Should a court have to ignore its doubts because an arbitrator chosen by the parties has awarded specific relief? Does freedom of contract *require* the court to implement whatever remedy the arbitrator has ordered?

In a case decided the year before *Grayson-Robinson*, the New York Court of Appeals upheld an arbitration award that directed the "reinstatement" to his former position of a corporate manager of production and engineering. The arbitrators had found that the manager had been improperly discharged under an eleven-year contract that still had six years to run. Staklinski v. Pyramid Electric Co., 6 N.Y.2d 159, 188 N.Y.S.2d 541, 160

N.E.2d 78 (1959). Again, three judges dissented. They asked the question whether, if the employee had breached the agreement and an arbitrator had awarded specific performance, the employer could secure a court order forcing the employee to work for the corporation. Another question could be whether a court will enforce an arbitrator's award which specifically enforces a restrictive noncompetition covenant, even to the extent of enjoining an individual from engaging in like employment for a period of many years in the future. The New York Court of Appeals said "yes" in Matter of Sprinzen and Nomberg, 46 N.Y.2d 623, 415 N.Y.S.2d 974, 389 N.E.2d 456 (1979), deferring to the arbitrator's resolution of the issues of the restriction's reasonableness and necessity: "While there may be some doubt whether we would have enforced the restrictive covenant now before us had this dispute been adjudicated in the courts, such consideration is irrelevant to the disposition of this case, for courts will not second-guess the factual findings or the legal conclusions of the arbitrator."

Still a third question could be whether a court will enforce an arbitration award of punitive damages. As we shall see in many other cases involving arbitration, much turns on the preemptive effect of the Federal Arbitration Act. See Mastrobuono v. Shearson Lehman Hutton, Inc., 514 U.S. 52 (1995). A useful discussion can be found in Ware, Punitive Damages in Arbitration, 63 Ford.L.Rev. 529 (1994).

CHAPTER 2

THE DOMAIN OF LEGALLY ENFORCEABLE PROMISES

SECTION 1. INTRODUCTION

We are morally and ethically obliged to keep our promises, but it does not follow that promises should be legally enforceable on that account alone. Legal enforceability raises the stakes considerably. Holding a promise legally enforceable empowers one private citizen to call upon the state to use force (if necessary) against another. It is not something to be done lightly, especially when the judge must try to reconstruct the promise from evidence that is often conflicting and incomplete.

In this chapter, we focus upon the way in which common law courts have met the challenge of deciding when promises we are morally obliged to keep are also ones the state can force us to keep. We share intuitions about the cases at the extremes. The written promise of a giant corporation to sell goods to another giant corporation should be legally enforceable. A casual promise one friend makes to another in a social setting—perhaps about meeting for lunch or dinner—should not be. It would be surprising if any modern legal regime provided otherwise. But those trained in the law must learn exactly what mechanism a particular legal system uses to draw the line.

Under the Anglo-American law of contracts, whether a promise is legally enforceable turns in the first instance on whether there was a bargained-for exchange. For the cases at the extremes, this sorting mechanism works well. Social promises are not, by and large, bargained-for exchanges, while virtually all transactions in the marketplace are. In the next section of this chapter, we explore exactly how this principle works in operation by focusing on unusual cases, such as promises made in a family setting that may or may not constitute a bargained-for exchange. We then go on in subsequent sections to see how an alternative ground for enforcing promises—that of promissory estoppel—took hold during the last century.

To provide the necessary background, this introduction first explores alternative ways of distinguishing enforceable promises from those that are not and then sets out the historical path that led to where we are today, a place where courts refuse to enforce some promises, even when seriously made.

One way for a legal system to demarcate legally enforceable promises is to require a legal form, a particular ritual, that must be followed. German law, dating from the year 1900, provides a good example. It provides that promises of gift are void unless notarized. Another clause of the German Civil Code (BGB, art. 516(1)) defines a gift as a transfer by which "one person out of his property enriches another," if both parties "are agreed that the [transfer] is to occur without recompense." The latter feature of the definition—that both parties must have agreed on the absence of any recompense—was no doubt designed to separate the gift from other transactions, notably those including an element of agreed exchange.

Notarization in European countries is very different from what it is in the United States. The European notary is not one who merely certifies, by signing and affixing a seal, that statements in a writing are made under oath. The notary in Europe is a licensed public official, trained in law, who is required to keep full records of the documents that are sworn to by private parties. It is the notary's duty to ensure that these documents are fully understood, to interrogate their makers if necessary, and to inform signers of the legal consequences of their acts.

The drafting commission that prepared the German Code first reviewed the long experience with strict requirements for making valid gifts, both gifts by present transfer and by promises performable in the future. The commission's own conclusion was that requirements of form would be needed only for promises of gift. They were needed, the commission said, "to prevent overhasty promises of gift to exclude the doubt that often arises whether a serious promise had been made or only an expression of an intent to give in the future, and also to prevent, so far as possible, evasion of the requirements of form for testaments and gifts *causa mortis* [i.e., with death impending] and to eliminate disputes over gifts alleged to have been made by persons already dead. A mere requirement of a writing is not enough. Notarization must be required in view of the broad grounds for formalizing such transactions that transcend the interests of the parties involved. The evidence is preserved if the donor makes his promise before a court or notary. It is not necessary that acceptance by the donee be expressed in this form. It can be entirely informal, even his silence can be enough."

Formal rules indeed offer distinct advantages, as Professor Lon Fuller noted long ago in one of the most important law review articles ever written. Even today, his article bears careful study, especially the passage that follows.

Fuller, Consideration and Form

41 Colum. L. Rev. 799, 800–801 (1941)

"[I]t is said that enforcement is denied gratuitous promises because such promises are often made impulsively and without proper deliberation. . . . [T]he objection relates, not to the content and effect of the promise, but to the manner in which it is made. Objections of this sort, which touch the form rather than the content of the agreement, will be removed if the making of the promise is attended by some formality or ceremony, as by being under seal. On the other hand, it has been said that the enforcement of gratuitous promises is not an object of sufficient importance to our social and economic order to justify the expenditure of the time and energy necessary to accomplish it. Here the objection is one of 'substance' since it touches the significance of the promise made and not merely the circumstances surrounding the making of it.

"The task . . . is that of disentangling the 'formal' and 'substantive' elements in the doctrine of consideration. [We examine first] in general terms the formal . . . bases of contract liability. . . .

"The Evidentiary Function—The most obvious function of a legal formality is, to use Austin's words, that of providing 'evidence of the existence and purport of the contract, in case of controversy.' The need for evidentiary security may be satisfied in a variety of ways: by requiring a writing, or attestation, or the certification of a notary. It may even be satisfied, to some extent, by such a device as the Roman *stipulatio*, which compelled an oral spelling out of the promise in a manner sufficiently ceremonious to impress its terms on participants and possible bystanders.

"The Cautionary Function—A formality may also perform a cautionary or deterrent function by acting as a check against inconsiderate action. The seal in its original form fulfilled this purpose remarkably well. The affixing and impressing of a wax wafer—symbol in the popular mind of legalism and weightiness—was an excellent device for inducing the circumspective frame of mind appropriate in one pledging his future. To a less extent any requirement of a writing, of course, serves the same purpose, as do requirements of attestation, notarization, etc. . . .

"The Channeling Function—Though most discussions of the purposes served by formalities go no further than the analysis just presented, this analysis stops short of recognizing one of the most important functions of form. That a legal formality may perform a function not yet described can be shown by the seal. The seal not only insures a satisfactory memorial of the promise and induces deliberation in the making of it. It serves also to mark or signalize the enforceable promise; it furnished a simple and external test of enforceability. . . .

"If we look at the matter purely from the standpoint of the convenience of the judge, there is nothing to distinguish the forms used in legal transactions from the 'formal' element which to some degree permeates all legal thinking. Even in the field of criminal law 'judicial diagnosis' is 'facilitated' by formal definitions, presumptions, and artificial constructions of fact. The thing which characterizes the law of contracts and conveyances is that in this field forms are deliberately used, and are intended to be so used, by the parties whose acts are to be judged by the law. To the business man who wishes to make his own or another's promise binding, the seal was at common law available as a device for the accomplishment of his objective. In this aspect form offers a legal framework into which the party may fit his actions, or, to change the figure, it offers channels for the legally effective expression of intention. It is with this aspect of form in mind that I have described the third function of legal formalities as 'the channeling function.' "

COMMENT: FORMALISM AND THE SEAL

Long before developments in the sixteenth and seventeenth centuries brought a search for the criteria of enforceable promises, formality had played an important role in identifying the relatively few promises that were enforced. We can only speculate as to how well modern justifications for the use of formalities may have been understood by the early lawyers. It suffices to say that when the making of the promise was attended by solemn, ceremonial acts, enforcement by official agencies seemed justified. Indeed, at these early times it was probably normal to think of enforceability and formality as two sides of the same coin.

By the late Middle Ages, English law had developed the seal, a highly serviceable, all-purpose formality. It was used to authenticate transfers of ownership, especially transfers of interests in land by way of "deed," and also to make promises enforceable. For breach of a promise under seal the action of covenant, leading to a judgment for damages, became a standard common law remedy. Indeed, until about 1500 it was almost the only remedy available for breach of promise. There was, it is true, the still more ancient action of debt, which we saw in Chapter 1 (pp. 142–147). But debt's utility was limited, since it could be used only to recover a sum of money already due and fixed in amount. It was not until later—the sixteenth century—that common law courts developed a generalized damage remedy for breach of contract, special assumpsit, which gave damages for breach of a variety of informal promises that did not fit debt's pattern of the half-completed exchange. Until then, and indeed for a long time thereafter, especially in transactions that had been carefully planned because the interests at stake were important, the contract under seal was the prototype for consensual transactions.

Viewed in light of Professor Fuller's description of the functions that legal formalities can perform, the seal in its heyday deserved a high rating. The requirements were strict. In the early seventeenth century, according to the testimony of a well-known judge-reporter, Sir Edward Coke, in order to have a valid seal it was necessary that heated wax, impressed with a mark, be actually affixed to the document that was to be authenticated. As to the mark itself there was some leeway. Persons of importance would no doubt use their family seals embellished with mottos, but the impression could be made with a signet ring, a finger, or, according to one early report, the bite of a foretooth. Heating the seal and placing an imprint on the document would be quite likely to arrest the participants' attention. Signature or a mark by the person making the transfer or promise was also required. And there was one more step, delivery—a physical surrender of the document to the grantee or promisee or an authorized representative. A ceremony with all these elements was surely calculated—deliberately calculated, it seems, by those who conceived it—to produce persuasive evidence, to make a sharp impression on the participants, and to provide visible signs of authenticity.

If the prescribed formalities were followed, nothing more was needed to make a promise "under seal" enforceable. The requirement of consideration, which we will soon encounter, was invented as a control over informal (unsealed) promises long after promises under seal had come to be regularly enforced. Some modern decisions have mentioned a "presumption" of consideration that the seal produces, but in states where the seal still has its common law effects the presumption is conclusive (in other words, consideration is not needed). One question to keep in mind is whether persons who are fully competent should have power to bind themselves by promise merely because they seriously intend to do so. One way to confer this power is to provide a ceremonial—a stereotyped formality—such as the signing, sealing, and delivery of a written document. In more than half our states this is no longer possible.

In its classical development during the fifteenth and sixteenth centuries, common law doctrine made the sealed promise not only enforceable but almost invulnerable to attack. The person whose signature and seal appeared on a document could no doubt show that both were placed there through forgery. If a party did in fact sign and seal, it could also be shown that the very nature of the document itself had been misrepresented to the signer at the time of execution ("fraud in the factum"). But no other kind of fraud or mistake could be shown in a common law action (e.g., "fraud in the inducement," as where the buyer complained that a diseased horse had been fraudulently described as healthy by the seller). Nor could a promisor show that the other party's performance promised in return had not been received, or that the promisor had in fact fully performed but had neglected to secure a sealed cancellation or release of the obligation, or that the agreement evidenced by the sealed document had been superseded by a subsequent informal agreement of the parties.

These attitudes of common law courts were less than half the story, since the Chancellor adopted very different attitudes. Indeed, relief against misuse or abuse of sealed instruments had become, by the sixteenth century at least, a major activity of the Chancery. Fraud or mistake in the making of sealed contracts, payment without securing cancellation or release, and subsequent modification by informal agreement became standard grounds for intervention by the Chancellors. The correctives they introduced served to bring the sealed instrument back within the framework of a rational scheme of contract law. Some of these correctives were so obviously needed that they were gradually absorbed within the common law system. It has been true for a long time, for example, that payment can be pleaded by the obligor as a defense when sued at law on a sealed instrument. In many states, this is also true of fraud or mistake in the formation of the transaction. In other states, a legacy remains in the form of a distinction making the defenses of fraud, mistake, or breach by the opposite party "equitable" issues that must be decided by a judge rather than a jury. There were other problems that took longer to solve, such as the invulnerability of sealed promises to modification or revision by mutual agreement (the older law required an instrument of "equal dignity") and the limitation of the right to sue to the parties to the covenant (thus barring suit by beneficiaries and undisclosed principals). Difficulties of this kind were not inherent or inevitable features of formalized legal transactions. They reflected the technicality and rigidity that the common law showed in many other areas as well.

In order to preserve a legal formality a price must be paid. The history of the seal makes it plain that the opinion-makers in Anglo-American law did not consider the advantages gained to be worth the price. That history can be summarized briefly: gradual erosion of the requirements of form drained off the solemnity of the occasion and thereby destroyed the usefulness of the seal. The erosion occurred in several ways. Dilution of the requirement of delivery can illustrate the mental processes at work. It has been clear for a long time that the mere physical surrender of a document is meaningless by itself—the parties' purpose may be merely to permit another person to inspect it. The essential factor is the intent of the transferor to endow the document, by that act, with legal consequences. So a delivery to some third person or various kinds of "symbolic" delivery should do just as well, and restrictions or qualifications desired by the transferor (e.g., postponing all legal effect until some future event should occur) should be enforced. If, then, it was intent, not acts, that counted, why insist on the ancient formalities; was it really necessary to heat up wax and stick it on a piece of paper? Why not use another piece of paper on which a mark of some kind had already been made and stick it on with adhesive? Or why was it not enough for the signer merely to recite in the document that it was deemed to be under seal?

As printed forms came into wider circulation, it became common practice simply to print after the space provided for signature the word "seal" or the letters "L.S." Even signers who remembered some Latin would have no particular reason to know that L.S. is short-hand for the Latin phrase *locus sigilli,* meaning "place of the seal." These various dilutions of the ancient formality clearly were inspired by impatience with what seemed to be purely external trivia. Accepting these various substitutes could seem fully justified by the result—enlarging the power of promisors to bind themselves if they used the right words or did the right acts. The irony was that the words and acts used lost meaning, especially as they became standard features of widely-used printed forms. It is no wonder that the impulse grew stronger to cut off this path to promissory obligation and destroy the power altogether.

The attitudes that inspired modern legislation were expressed by the New York Law Revision Commission in 1941, in recommending a statute that deprived the seal of all legal effect (Report, pp. 359–360):

> The seal has degenerated into a L.S. or other scrawl which, in modern practice, is frequently a printed L.S. upon a printed form. To the average man it conveys no meaning, and frequently the parties to instruments upon which it appears have no idea of its legal effects. Moreover, under the present law, the character of an instrument which bears the magic letters, but which contains no recital of sealing, is left uncertain as to whether it is sealed, depending upon parol evidence of intent to be later adduced. . . . It would seem, therefore, that if a method of making promises binding without consideration is desirable, some method should be devised which more clearly than the seal brings to the attention of the promisor what he is doing, and which fixes the character of the instrument as of the time of its execution. . . .

> Concerning the broader question whether, and to what extent, a person should be able to bind himself by a promise without consideration, the Commission doubts the wisdom of any device that is applicable to all kinds of promises under all circumstances. Certainly the seal is not the best device, assuming that some such device is desirable.

Today, more than half of the American states have legislation, cast in general terms, depriving the seal of all legal effect (i.e., abolishing any distinction between sealed and unsealed contracts).[1] To these should be added another handful of states where the seal is not "abolished" but made merely "presumptive evidence" of consideration.[2] And for transactions in goods, the Uniform Commercial Code, adopted in all states except Louisiana, uses somewhat elliptical language (§ 2–203) but the effect seems clear enough—in a written contract for the sale of goods the "affixing" of a seal adds nothing. There are, however, still some states in which the use of a seal (perhaps only the word "seal" or the letters "L.S.") in a consensual transaction other than a sale of goods will have some legal consequences. The most important consequence, of course, is that consideration or some equivalent reason for enforcement does not need to be established. Quite often, also, a much longer period for the start of a court action after breach has occurred (a "statute of limitations") is provided for sealed instruments. There may be other procedural consequences, such as law-equity distinctions in fact-finding on certain issues, as we have suggested above. A state-by-state analysis of the seal's modern status is provided in 1 S. Williston, Contracts § 2:17.

A few additional pieces of history will bring the story of formality to the present day. For a brief interval in the 1700s, English law hesitated on the brink of making a mere writing a sufficient form, at least in commercial disputes between merchants. These efforts, led by Lord Mansfield, were emphatically rejected by the House of Lords in 1778, when it was made clear—if there had been any doubt—that the requirement of consideration was to apply to written as well as oral contracts.

Much later there appeared in this country a type of statute, usually one brief sentence in length, which provided that a "written instrument is presumptive evidence of consideration." Presently, in roughly 15 states, the incorporation of an agreement in a written instrument is declared by statute to "import" or give "presumptive evidence" of consideration.[3]

A different solution—indeed, in practical effect a substitute for the seal—was proposed in 1925 by the Commissioners on Uniform State Laws. That group's proposals for uniform legislation have been widely adopted by state legislatures over the years, including the Commissioner's joint effort with the American Law Institute in drafting and sponsoring the Uniform Commercial Code. The Uniform Written Obligations Act, which the Commissioners proposed in the 1920s, and whose adoption was urged by Professor

---

[1] E.g., Cal.Civ. Code §§ 1614, 1629 (West); Iowa Code Ann. §§ 537A.1–537A.3 (West).

[2] E.g., N.J.Stat.Ann. § 2A:82–3 (West).

[3] This type of provision appears in, e.g., California (West's Civ.Code § 1614); Iowa (West's Code Ann. §§ 537A.2, 537A.3); Kansas (Stat. §§ 16–107, 16–108); New Mexico (Stat.Ann. § 38–7–2); Tennessee (Code Ann. § 47–50–103).

Williston and other distinguished academics in the decades that followed, provides that a written release or promise, signed by the releasor or promisor, shall not be invalid for lack of consideration if the writing contains "an additional statement, in any form of language, that the signer intends to be legally bound." But this recommended statute did not receive as warm a reception as was the case with the Commissioners' other proposals. The Uniform Act was adopted in only two states; it is now in force only in Pennsylvania.

Congregation Kadimah Toras-Moshe v. DeLeo

Supreme Judicial Court of Massachusetts, 1989.
405 Mass. 365, 540 N.E.2d 691.

LIACOS, C.J. Congregation Kadimah Toras-Moshe (Congregation), an Orthodox Jewish synagogue, commenced this action [to] compel the administrator of an estate to fulfil the oral promise of the decedent to give the Congregation $25,000. The Superior Court . . . rendered summary judgment for the estate and dismissed the Congregation's complaint. [We now affirm.]

The facts are not contested. The decedent suffered a prolonged illness, throughout which he was visited by the Congregation's spiritual leader, Rabbi Abraham Halbfinger. During four or five of these visits, and in the presence of witnesses, the decedent made an oral promise to give the Congregation $25,000. The Congregation planned to use the $25,000 to transform a storage room in the synagogue into a library named after the decedent. The oral promise was never reduced to writing. The decedent died intestate in September, 1985. He had no children, but was survived by his wife.

The Congregation asserts that the decedent's oral promise is an enforceable contract under our case law, because the promise is allegedly supported either by consideration and bargain, or by reliance. . . . We disagree.

The [trial] judge determined that "[t]his was an oral gratuitous pledge, with no indication as to how the money should be used, or what [the Congregation] was required to do if anything in return for this promise." There was no legal benefit to the promisor nor detriment to the promisee, and thus no consideration. See Marine Contractors Co. v. Hurley, 365 Mass. 280, 310 N.E.2d 915 (1974); Gishen v. Dura Corp., 362 Mass. 177, 285 N.E.2d 117 (1972) (moral obligation is not legal obligation). Furthermore, there is no evidence in the record that the Congregation's plans to name a library after the decedent induced him to make or to renew his promise. Contrast Allegheny College v. National Chautauqua County Bank, 246 N.Y. 369, 159 N.E. 173 (1927) (subscriber's promise became binding when charity implicitly promised to commemorate subscriber).

As to the lack of reliance, the judge stated that the Congregation's "allocation of $25,000 in its budget[,] for the purpose of renovating a storage room, is insufficient to find reliance or an enforceable obligation." We agree. The inclusion of the promised $25,000 in the budget, by itself, merely reduced to writing the Congregation's expectation that it would have additional funds. A hope or expectation, even though well founded, is not equivalent to either legal detriment or reliance. . . .

The Congregation cites several of our cases in which charitable subscriptions were enforced. These cases are distinguishable because they involved written, as distinguished from oral, promises and also involved substantial consideration or reliance. See, e.g., Trustees of Amherst Academy v. Cowls, 6 Pick. 427, 434 (1828) (subscribers to written agreement could not withdraw "after the execution or during the progress of the work which they themselves set in motion"). . . . [We have] refused to enforce a promise in favor of a charity where there was no showing of any consideration or reliance. . . .

[W]e are of the opinion that in this case there is no injustice in declining to enforce the decedent's promise. . . . The promise to the Congregation is entirely unsupported by consideration or reliance.[4] Furthermore, it is an oral promise sought to be enforced against an estate. To enforce such a promise would be against public policy.[5]

Judgment affirmed.

NOTE: LEGAL FORMALITIES AND TRANSFERS OF PROPERTY

It is useful to remember that our legal system requires formalities for certain purposes. To make a will in most places in this country, a testator must perform the ceremonial of signing in the presence of witnesses, who must then sign in the testator's presence and in the presence of each other (if witnessing is dispensed with, other forms are usually prescribed). To accomplish a transfer of chattels or choses in action by gift, "delivery" is needed. To pass title to real estate, either by gift—e.g., the *Fischer* case, just ahead—or by bargain, a deed must ordinarily be signed and delivered. And, as we have seen, for promises falling within the statute of frauds enforceability depends on a writing signed by the "party to be charged."

In *DeLeo*, it appears the decedent was serious about his promise, for he repeated it on four or five occasions, with witnesses present. Of course, the decedent might have demonstrated his seriousness of purpose by writing a check for $25,000 and handing it to the congregation's representative.

---

4 We need not decide whether we would enforce an oral promise where there was a showing of consideration or reliance.

5 The defendant argues that, if the decedent was aware of impending death, yet made no gift during life, then the promise is in the nature of a promise to make a will, which is unenforceable, by virtue of the Statute of Frauds. See G.L. c. 259, §§ 5, 5A (1986 ed.). Under the view we take, we need not consider this argument.

Should a court in a case like *DeLeo* take into account the promisor's failure to make a completed gift?

The transaction in the *DeLeo* case—a promise of a gift made to a charitable, religious, or other nonprofit organization—will surface again in the materials ahead. Our concern then will be the court's indication that a showing of reliance might alter the outcome in such cases. For the moment, the *DeLeo* decision is noteworthy because the court chose not to rule on the question whether an "oral promise" of this nature would be enforceable even though supported by consideration or reliance. Had the promise been in writing, and consideration or reliance shown, it seems liability would not have been in doubt. What is the basis for dividing the field of gratuitous promises in the manner the court suggests? Note also the court's statement that enforcement of this promise against this defendant would be "against public policy."

Pitts v. McGraw-Edison Co.

329 F.2d 412 (6th Cir. 1964)

Plaintiff was a manufacturer's representative until his retirement from the business on July 1, 1955. For 25 years prior to that date, he sold defendant's products on a commission basis in an assigned territory working wholly independently of defendant and managing his own business, and employees, as he saw fit. Plaintiff had no contract of employment with defendant; their relationship was terminable at will by either at any time; defendant's sole obligation to plaintiff was to compensate him for sales made in the assigned territory; plaintiff was free to handle competitor's products, which he did for a time. Nevertheless, for five years after the parties' relationship ended by mutual agreement in 1955, defendant continued to pay plaintiff a 1% commission on all its sales in plaintiff's previous territory. When these payments were stopped in 1960, plaintiff sued alleging breach of a "retirement contract." Plaintiff sought to show that negotiations leading to his retirement were in substance "an offer [by defendant] that if he would retire as a manufacturer's representative on July 1, 1955, and turn over to his successor representative all of his customer account records[,] [defendant] would pay him monthly thereafter a 1% overwrite commission on [its] sales within the territory." Defendant countered that there could be no "retirement" of one who was never its employee and free to do as he pleased about employment; that it had simply terminated a business relationship it was authorized to end; that it had made no offer nor undertaken any contractual obligation to plaintiff respecting payments; and that even if its dealings with plaintiff could be construed as a retirement contract, any such contract lacked consideration. The trial court dismissed the complaint. On appeal, *held*, affirmed. Even assuming a promise of retirement benefits can be found, there remains the question of what "passed from plaintiff" to make the promise enforceable. Plaintiff says that although he made no express promise, the turning over of his valuable customer records, at defendant's request, constitutes consideration. But the findings below do not support this claim, for nothing defendant said at the time, orally or in writing, required plaintiff "to do anything whatsoever" or "circumscribed his actions in any manner." Plaintiff himself testified that, at and after his retirement, he did things for defendant he was not required to do. Hence the five-year payments to plaintiff were without consideration, "the result of voluntary action [by] defendant, [and] mere gratuities terminable at will."

In re Bayshore Yacht & Tennis Club Condo. Ass'n, Inc.

336 Bankr. 866 (Bankr. S.D. Fla. 2006)

In 1981, Coletta purchased three penthouse units in Bayshore Condominium (the debtor), which units were located on the eleventh floor of the building. At the time of purchase, as Coletta knew, elevator service within the building ceased at the tenth floor. Upon purchasing the units, Coletta attempted to convince Bayshore to provide elevator access to the eleventh floor. According to Coletta, on numerous occasions Bayshore's representatives committed to providing elevator access to the eleventh floor at no expense to Coletta. However, no action was ever taken on this alleged commitment, purportedly because Bayshore lacked sufficient funds. Coletta eventually sued Bayshore, alleging a contract to extend the elevator at Bayshore's expense. Bayshore maintained that it never promised to pay for any elevator extension. A bankruptcy court rejected Coletta's claim, saying, " 'A mere gratuitous promise of a future gift, lacking consideration, is unenforceable.' . . . Even assuming arguendo that the Debtor and its representatives did orally promise to provide elevator access to the eleventh floor at the Debtor's expense and Coletta subsequently accepted such a promise, Coletta cannot point to any consideration that he provided to induce a promise obligating Bayshore to pay for an alteration Coletta would otherwise have to pay for himself, nor is there any evidence that he detrimentally relied on such a promise. . . . Simply, the record reflects that Coletta asked, the Debtor allegedly promised and nothing happened over a span of twenty years. . . ."

SECTION 2. THE BARGAINED-FOR EXCHANGE

INTRODUCTORY COMMENT

In the nineteenth century, courts relied largely on the idea of "consideration" to distinguish the promises that were legally enforceable from those that were not. While theories of consideration were not spun out until that time, they all have roots in a much more distant past. We must speak again of the old forms of action, and in particular of special assumpsit. The history of consideration is tied in with special assumpsit in two quite different ways. First, and most obviously, there was no very great problem in defining the limits of promissory liability until the 1500s, when special assumpsit was made over into a generalized damage remedy for breach of informal promises. Second, the earliest origins of special assumpsit left an impression on lawyers' minds and may have helped to shape the ultimate doctrine of consideration.

With the action of covenant restricted to the enforcement of promises under seal, the early common law had only one form of action that could be used widely to enforce informal (unsealed) promises. This was the action of *debt*. Debt would lie to enforce any kind of a duty to pay a "sum certain" in money; the duty could arise from statute, custom, or promise. But if the promise was not under seal, there was a requirement that hardened into a rule—there must be a *quid pro quo* received by the promisor. In the standard cases where debt was used, the meaning of this term was plain enough. The plaintiff would have loaned money to the defendant and would be suing to enforce an express but unsealed promise of repayment; or goods would have been delivered or services rendered in reliance on an express promise of a money price. Situations of this type were appealing for a number of reasons, and the English common law, like early Roman law, responded by giving a remedy that was essentially contractual. But no general theory of contract was needed to justify enforcement of the unperformed promise in this type of case. There was the plain fact that the defendant had bargained for and actually received a gain, whose retention without payment would be unjust. The payment of money, the transfer of goods, or the rendition of services could not ordinarily be expected to occur without compensation. The performance actually rendered would, therefore, perform an evidentiary function; it would also confirm the plaintiff's contention that a promise of payment had in fact been made. Cases of this type have been aptly described as cases of "half-completed exchange" (Fuller, Consideration and Form, 41 Colum. L. Rev. 799, 815 (1941)). They were indeed exchanges, the product of agreement, but the dominant fact was that the exchange had been carried out only on one side.

The context from which the special assumpsit remedy gradually emerged was quite different. Trespass on the case was modeled on and derived from the writ of trespass, omitting the allegation of "force and arms." By the fifteenth century, trespass on the case was expanding steadily in various directions and was well on its way toward being, as it later became, the generalized tort remedy of the common law. To say that trespass on the case was a tort remedy in the fifteenth century describes the law in a distinctly contemporary way: lawyers of that century were only vaguely aware of such classifications. Yet aware of them they surely were, for they clung tenaciously to the idea that the defendant's "misfeasance" was the test for the availability of the special form of trespass on the case that came to be called special assumpsit. Typical of the thinking about the small cluster of cases that defined the line of growth is a comparatively early statement (the year was 1436) by Newton, a common lawyer who was soon to become Chief Justice:

> I fully agree that it is the law that if a carpenter promises me to make a house good and strong in a certain form and he makes me a house that is weak and bad and in another form, I will have an action of trespass on my case. So if a smith promises me to shoe my horse well and properly and he shoes him and drives in a nail, I shall have a good action. Also if a leech undertakes to cure me of my illnesses and he gives me medicines but does not cure me I shall

> have an action on my case. . . . And the cause is in all these cases that there is an undertaking and . . . the plaintiffs have suffered a wrong. (Year Book, 14 Henry VI, no. 58).

As a group, these illustrative cases were thought to share a common pattern: a loss was incurred by virtue of affirmative action taken in a manner not conforming to duty. Thus, a promisee who had relied on the representations implicit in a promisor's "undertaking," suffering harm as a result, was viewed as the victim of a "wrong"—in effect, a tort—for which an expanded assumpsit provided a remedy.

Where the informal promise was made but performance was not begun at all, the issue of enforceability was raised more sharply. During the fifteenth century, the transition period, the Year Book lawyers debated at length the distinction between "misfeasance" (cases of the type described above) and "nonfeasance" (a total failure to perform). Between these concepts lay a great white line, gray though it might be on the fringes. The common lawyers did not cross the line until the early 1500s, and even then, it seems, only with great reluctance, and perhaps mainly in order to compete with Chancery's expanding remedies. The cases involved disputes in which wrongs were committed and losses caused in relations that had originated in an agreement. The agreement or promise had the important function of defining the level of duty owed.

When it was agreed in the early part of the sixteenth century that trespass on the case (assumpsit) could provide a remedy where the promisor did not act at all, as well as where a promisor acted affirmatively but not in accordance with duty, some new and harder questions loomed up. The expanded remedy of assumpsit did not have a built-in limitation like the requirement of *quid pro quo* in debt. Should every informal promise now be enforceable? No limiting principle had yet been formulated in English law, and thus there was no good English term available to express the vague sensation that it was necessary to fix a cut-off point somewhere for obligation derived from promises.

The common lawyers had a very small vocabulary with which to describe the elements needed to make a promise enforceable. They had a few phrases that had been used for other purposes and that no doubt helped to precipitate thought in new directions. "Consideration" was, at the outset, the most pallid and least meaningful of these phrases, and only one of the words that began to appear to reflect this notion. Sometimes "consideration" was made synonymous with the *causa* that continental lawyers believed would clothe naked promises and make them respectable; at other times, the term was used interchangeably with the familiar *quid pro quo* of debt; at still other times the term was used reflexively and in effect became part of a "whereas" clause, as in pleadings or other documents that recited "in consideration that A" had paid money or done some other act, "B promised," etc. In short, the term "consideration," on its first appearance, merely expressed (obscurely, to be sure) the feeling that there should be some sufficient reason, ground, or motive that would justify enforcement of a promise.

After the Statute of Uses in 1535, common law judges began to enforce contracts for the sale of land that before could be enforced only in Chancery. They continued to use "bargain and sale," the familiar phrase the Chancellor had used in such cases. But the common law judges were bent on expanding the range of promissory transactions they would enforce. The main directions in which these expansions would go were fixed not by any theory ordained at the outset, but by the reasons urged by lawyers and pleaders for court intervention. More and more it became standard to allege that the promise had been given "for" some asset or act that the pleader proceeded to specify, and if this kind of connection was not shown, the action was likely to fail. As time went on, the something "for" which the promise was made was described increasingly as "the consideration," though the word carried a load of vaguer meanings, suggesting other motives for promising that might or might not be good enough. Over time, most of these vaguer meanings were stripped away and "consideration" was made over from an amorphous word drawn from common speech into a technical requirement for contract formation.

As the sixteenth century progressed, it became clear that common law courts had created the means for enforcing, and were prepared to enforce, a great variety of exchange transactions. In the transactions that were enforced there was one recurring element: each party had in fact desired some act or abstention of the other in return for which something would be given.

It must be stressed again that the thinking of lawyers around the year 1600 was centered on procedure and the forms of action. The practical question at the time was: "When will assumpsit lie?" A lawyer who would answer the question would surely have to take account of the assimilation of debt and assumpsit that was accomplished by Slade's Case in 1602 (recall the discussion of the Common Counts and Restitution, supra pp. 142–147).

Any generalization concerning the outer limits of contract liability, in the sixteenth century and later, had to include the two quite different core situations or cases: the "half-completed exchange" of debt (with its allegations that the promise in question had been given "for" some asset or performance) and the loss-through-fault situations of early assumpsit. Roughly corresponding to these two elements are *benefit to the promisor* and *detriment to the promisee,* either of which will suffice as consideration according to conventional statements of the modern doctrine. But the correspondence is only rough. In particular, the concept of detriment was rapidly generalized (and attenuated) so as to include much more than visible and measurable losses, caused by incompetent carpenters and blacksmiths. The common lawyers were practical people who thought in terms of particular cases. They were dimly aware that not every benefit or detriment would do, but it was not until much later—the nineteenth century—that another limiting principle, that of exchange through bargain, emerged as the core of consideration doctrine.

While courts would not necessarily inquire into the nature of the bargain or the fairness of the exchange, this conception of consideration required that there in fact be a bargain. A transaction that merely mimics the form of a bargained-for exchange is, under this view, suspect. In this sense, the doctrine of consideration is different from a legal formality such as a seal, where the ritual itself is all that matters.

Oliver Wendell Holmes (The Common Law 293–94 (1881)) offered his own formulation of this idea of consideration consisting of a bargained-for exchange:

> [I]t is the essence of a consideration that, by the terms of the agreement, it is given and accepted as the motive or inducement of the promise. Conversely, the promise must be made and accepted as the conventional motive or inducement for furnishing the consideration. The root of the whole matter is the relation of reciprocal conventional inducement, each for the other, between consideration and promise.

The question we pursue in this chapter concerns the extent to which it makes sense to enforce only those promises that are part of a bargained-for exchange. We look at how courts went about identifying the presence or absence of consideration and how, over the course of the twentieth century, they supplemented the idea of bargained-for consideration with an additional idea—that promises seriously made should be enforced if they were reasonably relied upon, at least to the extent of that reliance.

The next case focuses explicitly on the idea of the bargained-for exchange as the identifier of an enforceable promise, and thus on that unique feature of the common law of contracts, the doctrine of consideration.

Hamer v. Sidway

Court of Appeals of New York, 1891.
124 N.Y. 538, 27 N.E. 256.

Appeal from order of the General Term of the Supreme Court[,] made July 1, 1890, which reversed a judgment in favor of plaintiff entered upon a decision of the court on trial at Special Term and granted a new trial.

The plaintiff presented a claim [on an alleged contract] to the executor of William E. Story, Sr., for $5,000 and interest from the 6th day of February, 1875. She acquired it through several mesne assignments from William E. Story, 2d. The claim being rejected by the executor, this action was brought. It appears that William E. Story, Sr., was the uncle of William E. Story, 2d; that at the celebration of the golden wedding of Samuel Story and wife, father and mother of William E. Story, Sr., on the 20th day of March, 1869, in the presence of the family and invited guests, he promised his nephew that if he would refrain from drinking, using tobacco, swearing, and playing cards or billiards for money until he became twenty-one years of age he would pay him a sum of $5,000. The nephew assented thereto and fully performed the conditions inducing the promise. When the nephew arrived at the age of twenty-one years and on the 31st day of January, 1875, he wrote to his uncle informing him that he had performed his part of the agreement and had thereby become entitled to the sum of $5,000. The uncle received the letter and a few days later on the sixth of February, [1875,] he wrote and mailed to his nephew the following letter:

"W.E. Story, Jr.:

"Dear Nephew—Your letter of the 31st ult. came to hand all right, saying that you had lived up to the promise made to me several years ago. I have no doubt but you have, for which you shall have five thousand dollars as I promised you. I had the money in the bank the day you was 21 years old that I intend for you, and you shall have the money certain. Now, Willie, I do not intend to interfere with this money in any way till I think you are capable of taking care of it and the sooner that time comes the better it will please me. I would hate very much to have you start out in some adventure that you thought all right and lose this money in one year. The first five thousand dollars that I got together cost me a heap of hard work. You would hardly believe me when I tell you that to obtain this I shoved a jackplane many a day, butchered three or four years, then came to this city, and after three months' perseverence I obtained a situation in a grocery store. I opened this store early, closed late, slept in the fourth story of the building in a room 30 by 40 feet and not a human being in the building but myself. All this I done to live as cheap as I could to save something. I don't want you to take up with this kind of fare. I was here in the cholera season '49 and '52 and the deaths averaged 80 to 125 daily and plenty of smallpox. I wanted to go home, but Mr. Fisk, the gentleman I was working for, told me if I left then, after it got healthy he probably would not want me. I stayed. All the money I have saved I know just how I got it. It did not come to me in any mysterious way, and the reason I speak of this is that money got in this way stops longer with a fellow that gets it with hard knocks than it does when he finds it. Willie, you are 21 and you have many a thing to learn yet. This money you have earned much easier than I did besides acquiring good habits at the same time and you are quite welcome to the money; hope you will make good use of it. I was ten long years getting this together after I was your age. Now, hoping this will be satisfactory, I stop. . . .

Truly Yours,
"W.E. Story.

"P.S.—You can consider this money on interest."

The nephew received the letter and thereafter consented that the money should remain with his uncle in accordance with the terms and conditions of the letter. The uncle died on the 29th day of January, 1887, without having paid over to his nephew any portion of the said $5,000 and interest.

PARKER, J. The question . . . at the foundation of plaintiff's asserted right of recovery [is] whether by virtue of a contract defendant's testator William E. Story became indebted to his nephew William E. Story, 2d, on his twenty-first birthday in the sum of five thousand dollars. The trial court found as a fact that "on the 20th day of March, 1869, . . . William E. Story agreed to and with William E. Story, 2d, that if he would refrain from drinking liquor, using tobacco, swearing, and playing cards or billiards for money until he should become 21 years of age then he, the said William E. Story, would at that time pay him, the said William E. Story, 2d, the sum of $5,000 for such refraining, to which the said William E. Story, 2d, agreed," and that he "in all things fully performed his part of said agreement."

The defendant contends that the contract was without consideration to support it, and, therefore, invalid. He asserts that the promisee by refraining from the use of liquor and tobacco was not harmed but benefited; that that which he did was best for him to do independently of his uncle's promise, and insists that it follows that unless the promisor was benefited, the contract was without consideration. A contention, which if well founded, would seem to leave open for controversy in many cases whether that which the promisee did or omitted to do was, in fact, of such benefit to him as to leave no consideration to support the enforcement of the promisor's agreement. Such a rule could not be tolerated, and is without foundation in the law. The Exchequer Chamber, in 1875, defined consideration as follows: "A valuable consideration in the sense of the law may consist either in some right, interest, profit or benefit accruing to the one party, or some forbearance, detriment, loss or responsibility given, suffered or undertaken by the other." Courts "will not ask whether the thing which forms the consideration does in fact benefit the promisee or a third party, or is of any substantial value to anyone. It is enough that something is promised, done, forborne or suffered by the party to whom the promise is made as consideration for the promise made to him." (Anson's Prin. of Con. 63.)

"In general a waiver of any legal right at the request of another party is a sufficient consideration for a promise." (Parsons on Contracts, 444.) "Any damage, or suspension, or forbearance of a right will be sufficient to sustain a promise." (Kent, vol. 2, 465, 12th ed.)

Pollock, in his work on contracts, page 166, after citing the definition given by the Exchequer Chamber already quoted, says: "The second branch of this judicial description is really the most important one. Consideration means not so much that one party is profiting as that the other abandons some legal right in the present or limits his legal freedom of action in the future as an inducement for the promise of the first."

Now, applying this rule to the facts before us, the promisee used tobacco, occasionally drank liquor, and he had a legal right to do so. That right he abandoned for a period of years upon the strength of the promise of the testator that for such forbearance he would give him $5,000. We need not speculate on the effort which may have been required to give up the use of those stimulants. It is sufficient that he restricted his lawful freedom of action within certain prescribed limits upon the faith of his uncle's agreement, and now having fully performed the conditions imposed, it is of no moment whether such performance actually proved a benefit to the promisor, and the court will not inquire into it, but were it a proper subject of inquiry, we see nothing in this record that would permit a determination that the uncle was not benefited in a legal sense. . . .

We must now consider the effect of the letter, and the nephew's assent thereto. Were the relations of the parties thereafter that of debtor and creditor simply, or that of trustee and [beneficiary]? If the former, then this action is not maintainable, because barred by lapse of time. If the latter, the result must be otherwise. No particular expressions are necessary to create a trust. Any language clearly showing the settler's intention is sufficient if the property and disposition of it are definitely stated.

A person in the legal possession of money or property acknowledging a trust with the assent of the [beneficiary], becomes from that time a trustee if the acknowledgment be founded on a valuable consideration. His antecedent relation to the subject, whatever it may have been, no longer controls. If before a declaration of trust a party be a mere debtor, a subsequent agreement recognizing the fund as already in his hands and stipulating for its investment on the creditor's account will have the effect to create a trust. . . .

The order appealed from should be reversed and the judgment of the Special Term affirmed, with costs payable out of the estate.

NOTE

Louise Hamer, the nominal plaintiff in the case, was Willie's mother-in-law. The assignment to her was gratuitous and was done at the same time that others on Willie's side of the family consolidated all the rights they had against the uncle's estate to her. At the time he died, the uncle had two nieces of a deceased brother living with him. They seem the most likely beneficiaries of the estate. For a review of the trial record and suggestions about the dynamics underlying the case, see Baird, Reconstructing Contracts: *Hamer v. Sidway*, in Contracts Stories 265–303 (2007).

Earle v. Angell

157 Mass. 294, 32 N.E. 164 (1892)

Mary Dewitt said to her nephew, the plaintiff, that if he would agree to attend her funeral in the event that he outlived her, then Mary would give him $500 and pay his traveling expenses. Plaintiff testified that he made the promise as requested, and that after her death he attended Aunt Mary's funeral. Mary left a paper in a sealed envelope, reading as follows: "$500.00. Oxford, August 14th, 1883. If Benjamin A. Earle should come to my funeral, I order my executor to pay him the sum of five hundred dollars. Mary Dewitt." *Held*, plaintiff can recover from Mary's executor. The jury was warranted in finding a promise given for a promise. The case in its other aspects, said Holmes, J., is unexceptional. It is settled that "a contract to pay money after one's own death is valid." There is no legal difficulty with a contract "to pay a person $500, conditioned upon his attending the promisor's funeral, and in consideration of his promise to do so."

Whitten v. Greeley-Shaw

520 A.2d 1307 (Me. 1987)

The parties had engaged in an intermittent extra-marital relationship for a number of years. Defendant, complaining that plaintiff had not kept his promises in the past, then asked for "something in writing." Plaintiff allegedly replied, "[y]ou figure out what you want and I will sign it." Defendant thereupon drew up a one-page, typewritten document (entitled "agreement") which plaintiff signed without objection. The agreement required plaintiff to perform various "conditions made by [defendant]," including payment to her of $500 monthly, reimbursement of specified expenses, visits and phone calls at stated intervals, trips together, and gifts of jewelry (one trip and one piece of jewelry per year). No "condition" was explicitly imposed on defendant, though the agreement did provide that "[u]nder no circumstances will there be any calls made to my homes or offices without prior permission from me." Also, at some point in their relationship, plaintiff loaned defendant $64,000 to purchase a home, taking from her a mortgage on the property to secure a promissory note. When defendant defaulted on the note, plaintiff brought a foreclosure action in which defendant filed a counterclaim based on the parties' written agreement. The trial court denied defendant's counterclaim, ordering foreclosure of the mortgage. *Held*, judgment below affirmed; the agreement plaintiff signed is legally unenforceable. Defendant's promise not to call plaintiff without his permission could serve as consideration for plaintiff's return promises, since it is a promise "to forbear from engaging in an activity that she had the legal right to engage in." But such a promise must be "sought after" by plaintiff and "motivated by" his request that defendant not disturb him. There is no evidence whatsoever of this. The only clause in the agreement operating in plaintiff's favor was put there by defendant, not plaintiff, and only because, defendant testified, "she felt the plaintiff should get something in exchange for his promises." Clearly, the clause was neither "bargained for" by plaintiff nor "given in exchange for" his promises. It cannot constitute the consideration necessary to bind plaintiff to a contract.

NOTE: BARGAINED-FOR CONSIDERATION AS A FORMAL RULE

Suppose it had been shown in Earle v. Angell that Mary's nephew would have attended her funeral regardless of the promise of $500—e.g., that he had never missed a relative's funeral and that, on many occasions, he had said privately that he would be sure to get to Mary's funeral. Does the rationale of Hamer v. Sidway reach such a case?

It was noted earlier that donative promises made in social or family settings figure "prominently in the discussion of consideration." In fact, decisions on the doctrine of consideration have involved a wide assortment of conduct, ranging from the mere act of opening an envelope to "bringing about a miracle" (winning a lottery, allegedly by virtue of a bargained-for appeal, through prayer, to a specified saint). See, e.g., Harris v. Time, Inc., 191 Cal. App. 3d 449, 237 Cal. Rptr. 584 (1987); Pando v. Fernandez, 127 Misc. 2d 224, 485 N.Y.S.2d 162 (Sup. Ct. 1984). If consideration is found in unusual circumstances (that is, social or noncommercial settings), courts typically explain that the concepts "benefit" and "detriment" have "technical meanings" in contract law, and that "legal detriment" is to be distinguished from "detriment in fact." For example, a modern court has said that "a promise to give up smoking may be a benefit to the promisee's health, but [it] is also a legal detriment and sufficient consideration to support a contract." Davies v. Martel Lab. Servs., Inc., 189 Ill. App. 3d 694, 545 N.E.2d 475 (1989). You might think about why it is that consideration tests continue to be phrased in technical formulas (e.g., "real value in the eye of the law") which reveal little about the classes of transactions that are enforceable. Consider also whether it is appropriate to think of consideration, at least in one aspect, as little more than a formality which must be complied with as a condition of enforcing a promise in court. For example, if Aunt Mary's promise of $500 is enforceable even though the nephew would have agreed to attend her funeral without any pay at all, it seems not easy to say that the doctrine of consideration is a "substantive" rather than formal requirement of general contract law.

As you work through this chapter it may be useful to keep in mind the great variety of human activities that can be brought within the tests of consideration, tests which, as the pliability of the term "detriment" indicates, make possible the enforcement of a great many promises. Is every promise complying with the test deserving of enforcement? Look again at the court's analysis in Whitten v. Greeley-Shaw. Is there something in the case the court is not talking about?

Marmer v. Kaufman

Massachusetts Superior Court, 2009.
2009 WL 2002945, affirmed, 922 N.E.2d 862.

FEELEY, ASSOCIATE JUSTICE. . . . From approximately 1976 to 2000, Paul [Marmer] worked as a pharmacist at a family owned retail pharmacy. The pharmacy's stock was owned equally by Paul and his father Henry Marmer ("Henry"). As Henry aged, and the pharmacy became more reliant on technology, Paul assumed more responsibilities in operating the pharmacy. In recognition of Paul's additional responsibilities and duties in operating the pharmacy, Henry provided Paul certificates of deposit ("certificates") issued by a local bank. The certificates were issued in the name of Henry, as trustee for Paul. Upon the maturity of each certificate, rather than cashing out the certificate, the certificate automatically renewed.

In December 2002, Henry executed a Durable Power of Attorney in favor of June, his daughter and Paul's sister. Henry also provided June with the proceeds of numerous bank accounts and other assets in an attempt to become eligible for Medicaid assistance. Sometime after December 2002, June, acting under the durable power of attorney provided her by Henry, cashed in the certificates that had been issued for Paul's benefit. After learning of June's actions, Paul sued her in the Essex Probate and Family Court seeking to recover the amounts due him under the certificates. Paul's claim was dismissed, and the court's decision was affirmed by the Appeals Court.

On November 11, 2006, June died. June was survived by her three children, Richard, David, and April (collectively, the "children"). As a result of June's death, the family—the children and Paul—attempted to reconcile past family differences. This reconciliation included trying to deal with June's cashing of the certificates, as well as her actions to reduce Henry's wealth by placing his assets in her name in an attempt to make him Medicaid eligible for nursing home services. Richard, as the administrator of June's estate, repeatedly spoke with Paul regarding June's estate. At one point, Richard acknowledged that June may have improperly taken Paul's certificates, as well as other property that would have passed to Paul upon Henry's death, and even stated "we (the children) want to give you back what she (June) took from you (Paul)."

Shortly after June's death (November 2006) and until approximately August 2007, the children and Paul discussed entering into an agreement regarding the distribution of June's assets to settle their disputes. A proposed agreement which was never signed included terms requiring Richard, as the administrator of June's estate, to: (1) pay Paul $136,000 (plus what appears to be accrued interest) as reimbursement for the certificates; (2) give Paul one-half of June's assets; and (3) pay for Henry's nursing home care until Henry qualified for Medicaid. No agreement was ever signed reflecting the above mentioned terms, or any other terms. In his deposition testimony, Paul stated that he was not required to do anything in exchange for being repaid the amount owed on the certificates. Paul also stated that he owed neither Richard nor anyone else any obligation in return for one-half of June's assets. On November 9, 2007, Paul filed the present action seeking to enforce the oral agreements he claims he entered into with Richard. . . .

Richard seeks summary judgment arguing that even if his oral statements to Paul about making up for June's conduct—by repaying the $136,000 from the certificates and allowing Paul to receive one-half of June's assets—formed a contract, the contract is unenforceable and is invalid as it was not supported by consideration. Paul contends that the contract was supported by consideration, in the form of family unity and/or the substantial estate tax savings enjoyed by June's estate as a result of the agreement.

Even assuming Richard felt that Paul was entitled to the monetary value of the certificates' and half of June's assets because June wrongfully converted Paul's certificates and Henry's assets, that feeling, in and of itself, is not sufficient to establish contractual consideration. Additionally, any thawing of the family relations that Richard and the children hoped would result from the agreement constitutes neither a legal detriment to Paul, nor a legal benefit to Richard. Therefore, Paul's argument that improved family unity was sufficient to establish consideration in return for the value of the certificates and one-half of June's assets must fail. Essentially, Richard's statements are gratuitous promises that cannot be enforced for want of consideration.

Paul's argument that the substantial Massachusetts estate tax savings June's estate would enjoy constitutes consideration, and therefore makes the contract enforceable, is not persuasive. Richard's reason for his promises to Paul was simply to repay Paul what June had taken from him, it was not to improve the tax position of June's estate. The possible reduction in the estate's tax liabilities, if such was the case, was merely a side benefit that would attach to June's estate if money was given to Paul. Any tax benefit experienced by June's estate was not sought by Richard as his reason for entering into the agreement; Richard's desire for entering into the agreement was based on his desire to make amends for June's actions. Richard did not seek the tax benefit in exchange for his promise to Paul, and therefore any tax benefit experienced by June's estate does not constitute consideration.

Moreover, any benefit to June's estate in the form of tax savings, was not a benefit conferred on Richard by Paul. Clearly, Paul did not give Richard any possible estate tax benefit in exchange for Richard's promise to pay him money from June's estate. The same argument made by Paul herein, could have been made in the *DeLeo* case, where the promissor would have earned a tax deduction if his oral promise to contribute money to the congregation had been complied with. The Supreme Judicial Court in *DeLeo* found the gratuitous promise to donate money unenforceable for lack of consideration, despite an obvious tax benefit to the promissor derived from donating money to a religious organization. Here, any gratuitous promise to give money to Paul, despite any possible estate tax benefit, similarly fails for lack of consideration.

Since Richard received no benefit (and certainly none from Paul) in exchange for his promise to reimburse Paul $136,000 for the certificates and give Paul one-half of June's assets, and because Paul suffered no legal detriment in exchange for Richard's promises, any oral promises by Richard are unenforceable for lack of consideration. . . .

Restatement of Contracts, Second

§ 71. Requirement of Exchange; Types of Exchange

(1) To constitute consideration, a performance or a return promise must be bargained for.

(2) A performance or return promise is bargained for if it is sought by the promisor in exchange for his promise and is given by the promisee in exchange for that promise.

(3) The performance may consist of

(a) an act other than a promise, or

(b) a forbearance, or

(c) the creation, modification, or destruction of a legal relation.

(4) The performance or return promise may be given to the promisor or to some other person. It may be given by the promisee or by some other person.

§ 81. Consideration as Motive or Inducing Cause

(1) The fact that what is bargained for does not of itself induce the making of a promise does not prevent it from being consideration for the promise.

(2) The fact that a promise does not of itself induce a performance or return promise does not prevent the performance or return promise from being consideration for the promise.

[Rest.2d § 81 is intended to make explicit a limitation on § 71's "bargained for" test of consideration. A comment to § 81 observes that a promisor—even the typical commercial bargainer—may have more than one motive in negotiating an exchange, adding: "Unless both parties know that the purported consideration is mere pretense, it is immaterial that the promisor's desire for the consideration is incidental to other objectives and even that the other party knows this to be the case."]

Fischer v. Union Trust Co.

Supreme Court of Michigan, 1904.
138 Mich. 612, 101 N.W. 852.

[Bertha Fischer presented a claim against the estate of William Fischer, Sr., deceased, for damages for an alleged breach of a covenant in a deed. The claim was allowed by the commissioners, and the Union Trust Co., administrator, appealed to the circuit court. There was judgment for claimant on a verdict directed by the court, and defendant brings error. Reversed.]

On December 21, 1895, William Fischer, Sr., conveyed by warranty deed certain property in the city of Detroit to the claimant, Bertha Fischer, his daughter, who had been incompetent for a number of years, and so remains, and is at present at the retreat for the insane at Dearborn. The deed was a warranty deed, in the usual form, with a covenant against all incumbrances, excepting two mortgages, which the grantor "agrees to pay when the same become due." The land described in the deed comprised the homestead where the father and daughter lived, and the adjoining lot, with the house thereon. Mr. Fischer, after signing and acknowledging it, handed it to claimant, saying, "Here is a deed of the Jefferson and Larned street property." He said it was a "nice Christmas present." She took it and read it. One of her brothers gave her a dollar, which she gave to her father, who took it. She then handed the deed to her brother Alexander, and asked him to take care of it. He put it in his safe, and did not record it until June 30, 1902, about a year after the grantor's death, and 6½ years after its date. The reason given by the son for not recording is that there were unpaid taxes, in consequence of which, under the statute, it could not be recorded.

After the delivery of the deed, both grantor and grantee continued to live together on part of the property so conveyed. Mr. Fischer continued until his death to manage and control it, and to receive the rents therefrom, just as he had done before the giving of the deed. During that time he took care of his daughter the same as before. At the time of the execution of the deed, the grantor was considered by his sons to be worth about $50,000. He had no debts except the two mortgages, one of $3,000 and the other of $5,000. If he was then worth that amount, the larger part of it was in some way disposed of in his lifetime. The $3,000 mortgage was foreclosed for nonpayment, and satisfied out of part of the property conveyed. The claim at bar is based upon this appropriation of her property to pay the mortgage.

GRANT, J. The facts and circumstances of the delivery of the deed are not in dispute. Counsel differ only in the conclusion to be drawn from them. We think that the conceded facts show a delivery. After the deed was signed and acknowledged, the grantor made manual delivery of it to the grantee. She took it and handed it to her brother, evidently to be kept by him for her. The grantor reserved no control over it, and retained no right to withdraw or cancel it. He never attempted to. Under those circumstances the delivery was complete.

The meritorious question in the case is: Was the claimant in position to enforce the executory contract in the deed against her father while living, and to enforce it against his estate now that he is dead, or to recover damages at law for nonperformance? To say that the one dollar was the real, or such valuable consideration as would of itself sustain a deed of land worth several thousand dollars, is not in accord with reason or common sense. The passing of the dollar by the brother to his sister, and by her to her father, was treated rather as a joke than as any actual consideration. The real and only consideration for the deed and the agreement, therein contained, to pay the mortgages, was the grantor's love and affection for his unfortunate daughter, and his parental desire to provide for her support after he was dead. The consideration was meritorious, but is not sufficient to compel the performance of a purely executory contract. The deed was a gift, and the gift was consummated by its execution and delivery. The title to the land, subject to the mortgages, passed as against all except the grantor's creditors. The gift was expressly made subject to the mortgages, and coupled with it was a promise to pay them. This promise has no additional force because it is contained in the deed. It has no other or greater force than would a promise by him to pay mortgages upon her own land, or to pay her $8,000 in money, or his promise to her evidenced by a promissory note for a like amount, and given for the same purpose and the same consideration. . . .

If Mr. Fischer had voluntarily paid the mortgages, he would then simply have carried out his nonenforceable contract and have completed his gift, as, perhaps, he then intended to do. For some reason, perhaps a good one, he chose not to pay them. A void promise is no more effective than no promise, and the void promise in the deed had no more effect than if it had been omitted therefrom. If it is void for one purpose, it is void for all, and cannot be made available, either directly or indirectly. Only performance of the promise can be of any avail to the claimant.

A gift of personalty can be consummated only by an unconditional delivery of the thing. A gift of realty can be consummated only by the execution and delivery of a deed. If either is incumbered, the donor gives only what he had to give. He cannot give the interest of a third party in the property. However clear may be the intention of the donor to pay the incumbrances and thus give the entire property, he can accomplish this only by actually paying them. Neither his promise without a valuable consideration, nor his intention as evidenced by such promise, is of any avail to the donee. . . .

Judgment is reversed, and new trial ordered.

COMMENT: "NOMINAL" AND "MERITORIOUS" CONSIDERATION

The one dollar handed from brother to Bertha to father is a recurring episode in the case law. It raises the problem of "nominal" consideration, a problem which for a long time was associated with a famous statement in English legal history—"when a thing is to be done by the plaintiff, be it never so small, this is a sufficient consideration to ground an action." Sturlyn v. Albany, 1 Cro. Eliz. 67, 78 Eng. Rep. 327 (1587). Talk of nominal consideration led naturally to a somewhat more general idea, the "peppercorn theory of consideration."

An illustration attached to Restatement, Second § 79 reads as follows: "In consideration of one cent received, A promises to pay $600 in three yearly installments of $200 each. The one cent is merely nominal, and is not consideration for A's promise." This illustration is intended to make the point that a "nominal" consideration, in the situation described, does not satisfy conventional tests. Why not?

Consider Schnell v. Nell, 17 Ind. 29 (1861), which provided the inspiration for the Restatement's illustration. In an elaborate document replete with "whereas" clauses (and signed, under "seal," by all parties), Zacharias Schnell promised to pay three persons $200 each in three annual installments. These three persons had been given legacies of $200 each by the will of Zacharias' deceased wife, Theresa, but her will was ineffective because all of the property she owned was held jointly with her husband and passed to him at her death. These facts were recited in the document, and the promise of Zacharias was stated to be given "in consideration of all this, and the love and respect he bears to his wife." The document also acknowledged that Zacharias had received one cent from the promisees, who, it was recited, had agreed to pay that sum "in consideration of" Zacharias' promise. In an action by the promisees to collect the money promised, Zacharias was held to have a complete defense. Though the Indiana court was clear that inadequacy of consideration ordinarily will not vitiate a contract, this was not true where the exchange is of unequal sums of money (things of "fixed," not "indeterminate," value). Moreover, a promise to pay $600 for one cent "is an unconscionable contract, void, at first blush, upon its face, if it be regarded as an earnest one." This is so because "the one cent is, plainly, in this case, merely nominal, and intended to be so." Nor would Zacharias' belief that he must carry out his wife's intentions—a "moral consideration" at best—support a promise; similarly, his wife's services in the past, and the love he bore her, were but "past considerations," insufficient to make him liable on a promise.

To be sure, at the time Zacharias Schnell signed the impressive document he had no doubt employed a lawyer to create, he was a person bent on giving a binding promise. He had gone to some considerable trouble in arranging his formal commitment. The court's words—"merely nominal, and intended to be so"—go far to explain his inability to accomplish what he most certainly had intended to accomplish.

We will see more of nominal consideration. It would be a mistake to conclude either that the problem has disappeared or that the law no longer makes provision for an effective nominal consideration. For the time being, however, you should ask whether courts are distinguishing between actual bargains, regardless of whether they seem lopsided, and interactions that merely mimic the form of a bargain.

Justice Grant's reference to "meritorious consideration" in Fischer v. Union Trust Co. refers to a doctrine that emerged in the courts of equity. As to promises without consideration, equity courts have often expressed their adherence to common law requirements by repeating the familiar slogan that "equity will not aid a volunteer," meaning by "volunteer" a promisee in a simple promise of gift. There were, however, exceptions to the refusal of relief to the volunteer. A court of equity may be induced to act if a donor has attempted to carry out the gift but the actions taken are in some way incomplete or defective, and the donor has died in ignorance of this. An example would be a gift of land executed by the delivery of a deed which describes the subject of the gift incorrectly, perhaps by including too little land or by describing the wrong tract. The donor, if still living, normally could secure judicial reformation of the incorrect deed; often, the mistake could be corrected merely by the donor's making of a new deed. Where the donee is a near relative, "a natural object of bounty," and there are no competing claims of greater moral force, the intended donee will usually be allowed reformation—despite the status of a "volunteer." The consideration is deemed "meritorious." A critical fact in these cases is that the donor has died believing the transfer to be fully effective. If the donor were still alive, and resisting correction of a defective or incomplete document of gift, it is extremely unlikely that a reformation action by the donee would succeed.

Sharon v. Sharon

68 Cal. 29, 8 P. 614 (1885)

The plaintiff brought an action to enforce the defendant's written promise reading as follows: "Palace Hotel, San Francisco, Nov. 7, 1880. I hereby agree to pay Miss S. A. Hill two hundred and fifty dollars for each and every month of the year A.D. 1883. Wm. Sharon." Defendant's answer admitted the execution and delivery of the document and his non-payment of three of the monthly installments and alleged "that to induce plaintiff to desist from making unwelcome visits and annoying and disturbing him in his rooms, and on the consideration that she would cease to disturb and annoy him, or make any demands upon him" he executed the document in question. Defendant's answer contained also the statement that defendant "denies that there was ever any consideration for the note" sued on. *Held*, in this condition of the pleadings, judgment must be ordered for plaintiff for the un-paid installments.

Military College Co. v. Brooks

107 N.J. L. 28, 147 A. 488 (1929)

A military school brought an action on a $927 promissory note executed by defendant to cover his son's tuition and equipment for the year 1926–1927. Defendant claimed that his son was wrongfully dismissed in the middle of the first semester, and that he gave his note to cover the year's tuition and equipment because "at the time I had financial difficulties and [the note was given] rather than have a lawsuit which I thought would greatly injure my credit." In holding that the trial court was correct in ordering summary judgment for plaintiff on the note, the Supreme Court said: "Defendant does not seem to deny that the contract was for the full school year. If his son was rightfully dismissed, it is at least arguable that the full year's fee would be nevertheless payable. Defendant claimed the dismissal was wrongful, and plaintiff that it was rightful; and this raised a legitimate dispute of fact and perhaps of law also as to defendant's liability. In this situation defendant being so situated financially that a lawsuit, whatever its result, would in his judgment be disastrous to him, elected to buy his peace for the time being by giving the first note, which postponed any such suit until the maturity of that note, not to mention that by a renewal or renewals it was further postponed until February 18th, 1928, or nearly a year. This, under our decisions, was adequate consideration to support the note."

Restatement of Contracts, Second

§ 74. Settlement of Claims

(1) Forbearance to assert or the surrender of a claim or defense which proves to be invalid is not consideration unless

(a) the claim or defense is in fact doubtful because of uncertainty as to the facts or the law, or

(b) the forbearing or surrendering party believes that the claim or defense may be fairly determined to be valid.

(2) The execution of a written instrument surrendering a claim or defense by one who is under no duty to execute it is consideration if the execution of the written instrument is bargained for even though he is not asserting the claim or defense and believes that no valid claim or defense exists.

Illustrations:

1. A, a shipowner, has a legal duty to provide maintenance and care for B, a seaman. B honestly but unreasonably claims that adequate care is not available in a free public hospital and that he is entitled to treatment by a private physician. B's forbearance to press this claim is consideration for A's promise to be responsible for the consequences of any improper treatment in the public hospital.

2. A, knowing that he has no legal basis for complaint, frequently complains to B, his father, that B has made more gifts to B's other children than to A. B promises that if A will cease complaining, B will forgive a debt owed by A to B. A's forbearance to assert his claim of discrimination is not consideration for B's promise.

QUESTIONS

(1) The first Restatement of Contracts § 76(b) required "an honest and reasonable belief" in the "possible validity" of an invalid claim or defense in order for forbearance or surrender of the claim or defense to operate as consideration. Why do you suppose Restatement, Second § 74(1) drops that test and substitutes the different formulation?

(2) In a case adopting Restatement, Second § 74(1) as "the better reasoned approach," Dyer v. National By-Products, Inc., 380 N.W.2d 732 (Iowa 1986), the court assumed the invalidity of the forborne claim in issue and stated: "The requirement that the forbearing party assert the claim in good faith sufficiently protects the policy of the law that favors the settlement of controversies. . . . [However,] the issue of the validity of [the] claim should not be entirely overlooked. . . . [Such evidence] is relevant to show a lack of

honest belief in the validity of the claim asserted or forborne." Did the Iowa court read § 74(1) correctly?

(3) Is there any reason why standard consideration doctrine (e.g., Duncan v. Black) should stand in the way of the result called for by § 74(2)? Incidentally, the essential idea of § 74(2) is not a recent innovation; it was embraced by a number of our courts in the nineteenth century, including the United States Supreme Court, in Sykes v. Chadwick, 85 U.S. (18 Wall.) 141 (1873).

SECTION 3. PROMISES GROUNDED IN THE PAST

INTRODUCTORY COMMENT

The history of English law reveals two early groupings of cases in which a transaction was linked to a later, enforceable promise. One is indeed familiar at this point—the development whereby the action of assumpsit, through the off-shoot writ of indebitatus assumpsit, was made available as a general alternative to the action of debt. See Chapter 1, pp. 142–147. Here, expansion of assumpsit was accomplished by giving effect to the new promise of a debtor to pay a debt earlier incurred, the later promise being enforceable solely because of the support extended by the old debt. After Slade's Case in 1602, which eliminated the necessity of proving the subsequent promise, the significance of the past transaction was diminished by the procedural ease with which a creditor could use assumpsit on a simple contract claim. Nevertheless, despite the lessened importance of the pleading fiction, the proposition that a precedent debt is "consideration" (that is to say, a reason for enforcement) for a subsequent promise to pay the debt was carried forward in Anglo-American law. Corbin is clear about the situation today: "A past debt, still existing and enforceable, is a sufficient basis for the enforcement of a new promise by the debtor to pay it. This is true, whether the past debt is contractual or quasi-contractual in character." 1A A. Corbin, Contracts § 211.

A second line of cases associated with the notion of an operative "past" consideration is traceable to assumpsit actions in the early seventeenth century. Even with the expansion of assumpsit accomplished by Slade's Case, that action was still grounded on an express promise—the promise giving rise to the antecedent debt. Until the period 1610–1620, there was great reluctance to "imply" promises from conduct, as we so readily do today, or from requests that did not include express promises of payment. It was then recognized that if services were performed at the recipient's request, but without express promise of payment, the past act rendered at request was sufficient reason to enforce a later promise of payment. E.g., Lampleigh v. Brathwaite, 80 Eng. Rep. 255, Hob. 105 (K.B. 1616). Under this analysis, of course, the previous request and the subsequent promise may well assume the form of a single transaction; hence many of these problems eventually came to be handled by the theory of implied contract. Still, here was another situation in which promises could be enforced because of acts done in the past.

Another episode from history, dating from the late 1770s, should be mentioned. Lord Mansfield, a high Tory in politics, was in legal matters a notable reformer. You will learn later of his contributions to Commercial Law, particularly the assimilation of the "custom of merchants" into the common law. As to the doctrine of consideration, among Mansfield's efforts to dismantle the conventional requirement (one was an attempt to reduce it to a mere requirement of evidence) was a series of decisions identifying consideration with "moral obligation" or duty resting on "conscience." (A brief sketch of the story can be found in T. Plucknett, A Concise History of the Common Law 653–656 (5th ed. 1956).) Even though Mansfield's doctrines equating consideration with moral obligation were repudiated in England in the mid 1800s, the notions of "moral duty" and "conscientious obligation" continued to circulate in American decisions.

In fact, "moral obligation" is commonly invoked to explain three special situations in Anglo-American law: the promise to pay an obligation on which the statutory period of limitations has run; the bankrupt debtor's promise to pay a discharged debt; and the promise to pay a contract obligation incurred while a minor. Mills v. Wyman introduces these standard "exceptions" to the bargain test of consideration.

Mills v. Wyman

Supreme Judicial Court of Massachusetts, 1825.
20 Mass. (3 Pick.) 207.

. . . [A]ssumpsit brought to recover a compensation for the board, nursing, etc. of Levi Wyman, son of the defendant, from the 5th to the 20th of February, 1821. The plaintiff then lived at Hartford, in Connecticut; the defendant at Shrewsbury, in this state. Levi Wyman, at the time when the services were rendered, was about 25 years of age, and had long ceased to be a member of his father's family. He was on his return from a voyage at sea, and being suddenly taken sick at Hartford, and being poor and in distress, was relieved by the plaintiff in the manner and to the extent above stated. On the 24th of February, after all the expenses had been incurred, the defendant wrote a letter to the plaintiff, promising to pay him such expenses. There was no consideration for this promise, except what grew out of the relation which subsisted between Levi Wyman and the defendant, and Howe, J., before whom the case was tried [in] Common Pleas, thinking this not sufficient to support the action, directed a nonsuit. To this direction the plaintiff filed exceptions.

PARKER, C.J. General rules of law established for the protection and security of honest and fair-minded men, who may inconsiderately make promises without any equivalent, will sometimes screen men of a different character from engagements which they are bound *in foro conscientiae* to perform. This is a defect inherent in all human systems of legislation. The rule that a mere verbal promise, without any consideration, cannot be enforced by action, is universal in its application, and cannot be departed from to suit particular cases in which a refusal to perform such a promise may be disgraceful.

The promise declared on in this case appears to have been made without any legal consideration. The kindness and services towards the sick son of the defendant were not bestowed at his request. The son was in no respect under the care of the defendant. He was twenty-five years old, and had long left his father's family. On his return from a foreign country, he fell sick among strangers, and the plaintiff acted the part of the good Samaritan, giving him shelter and comfort until he died. The defendant, his father, on being informed of this event, influenced by a transient feeling of gratitude, promised in writing to pay the plaintiff for the expenses he had incurred. But he has determined to break this promise, and is willing to have his case appear on record as a strong example of particular injustice sometimes necessarily resulting from the operation of general rules.

It is said a moral obligation is a sufficient consideration to support an express promise; and some authorities lay down the rule thus broadly; but upon examination of the cases we are satisfied that the universality of the rule cannot be supported, and that there must have been some pre-existing obligation, which has become inoperative by positive law, to form a basis for an effective promise. The cases of debts barred by the Statute of Limitations, of debts incurred by infants, of debts of bankrupts, are generally put for illustration of the rule. Express promises founded on such pre-existing equitable obligations may be enforced; there is a good consideration for them; they merely remove an impediment created by law to the recovery of debts honestly due, but which public policy protects the debtors from being compelled to pay. In all these cases there was originally a *quid pro quo*, and according to the principles of natural justice the party receiving ought to pay; but the legislature has said he shall not be coerced; then comes the promise to pay the debt that is barred, the promise of the man to pay the debt of the infant, of the discharged bankrupt to restore to his creditor what by the law he had lost. In all these cases there is a moral obligation founded upon an antecedent valuable consideration. These promises, therefore, have a sound legal basis. They are not promises to pay something for nothing; not naked pacts, but the voluntary revival or creation of obligations which before existed in natural law, but which had been dispensed with, not for the benefit of the party obliged solely, but principally for the public convenience. If moral obligation, in its fullest sense, is a good substratum for an express promise, it is not easy to perceive why it is not equally good to support an implied promise. What a man ought to do, generally he ought to be made to do whether he promise or refuse. But the law of society has left most of such obligations to the interior forum, as the tribunal of conscience has been aptly called. Is there not a moral obligation upon every son who has become affluent by means of the education and advantages bestowed upon him by his father, to relieve that father from pecuniary embarrassment, to promote his comfort and happiness, and even to share with him his riches, if thereby he will be made happy? And yet such a son may, with impunity, leave such a father in any degree of penury above that which will expose the community in which he dwells, to the danger of being obliged to preserve him from absolute want. Is not a wealthy father under strong moral obligation to advance the interest of an obedient, well disposed son, to furnish him with the means of acquiring and maintaining a becoming rank in life, to rescue him from the horrors of debt incurred by misfortune? Yet the law will uphold him in any degree of parsimony, short of that which would reduce his son to the necessity of seeking public charity.

Without doubt there are great interests of society which justify withholding the coercive arm of the law from these duties of imperfect obligation, as they are called; imperfect, not because they are less binding upon the conscience than those which are called perfect, but because the wisdom of the social law does not impose sanctions upon them.

A deliberate promise in writing, made freely and without any mistake, one which may lead the party to whom it is made into contracts and expenses, cannot be broken without a violation of moral duty. But if there was nothing paid or promised for it, the law, perhaps wisely, leaves the execution of it to the conscience of him who makes it. It is only when the party making the promise gains something, or he to whom it is made loses something, that the law gives the promise validity. And in the case of the promise of the adult to pay the debt of the infant, of the debtor discharged by the statute of limitations or bankruptcy, the principle is preserved by looking back to the origin of that transaction, where an equivalent is to be found. . . .

For the foregoing reasons we are all of opinion that the nonsuit directed by the Court of Common Pleas was right, and that judgment be entered thereon for costs for the defendant.

QUESTION

Could Mills, showing that his services were reasonably worth $50, recover that sum from Levi Wyman's estate? The trial record tells us that Mills was an innkeeper. Watson, In the Tribunal of Conscience: *Mills v. Wyman* Reconsidered, 71 Tulane L. Rev. 1749, 1759 (1997). Does this change your view of the case?

COMMENT: PROMISES TO PAY BARRED OBLIGATIONS

New promises to perform obligations barred by the statute of limitations have long been subjected to special treatment. This was due in part to some accidents of history. A comprehensive statute of limitations was not adopted in England until 1623, when theories as to the grounds for, and limits on, contract liability were still relatively undeveloped. For more than one hundred years thereafter, the notion still circulated freely that "moral obligation" could suffice as a reason for enforcing promises (as we have said, that view lasted in England until the middle of the nineteenth century). Furthermore, it was not at all unnatural that the courts should minimize the effect of a not very ancient statute and regard it as precluding affirmative enforcement, but to not cut off the "honest debt" that survived. It followed that the protection given the obligor by the statute could be "waived" through a new promise, if the obligor chose.

When bankruptcy proceedings were more fully developed, so that they went beyond the liquidation of the bankrupt's assets to grant a discharge of existing obligations, the analogy was close enough to warrant transferring the same modes of thought to a new promise made after bankruptcy discharge. Indeed, it may have been still easier to think that an "honest debt" survived where the legal immunity was due merely to the fact that the debtor had become over-extended, was unable to perform, and needed a fresh start.

It also became well established that new promises can lift the protections from contract obligations that are accorded to minors. Until the twenty-first birthday arrives (or, pursuant to modern legislation in many states, the eighteenth), the young person is legally an "infant." All transfers or promises made during infancy can be disaffirmed (i.e., liability defeated), unless the securing of "necessaries" was involved. However, when the minor reaches the age of majority these "voidable" promises can be affirmed, in which event the promise acquires full legal effect. Making a new promise is one way to affirm. There is no particular harm in lumping minors' promises with obligations made unenforceable by a limitation statute or by bankruptcy discharge. But it is worth noting that infancy is only one of numerous grounds for making transactions voidable—fraud, duress, mental incompetency, even basic mistake can produce the same result. The explanation usually given in such cases is not that affirmance constitutes a "new promise." Rather, it is said that the disadvantaged party has exercised a choice to affirm rather than to rescind a voidable transaction, and this seems more descriptive of minors' promises also.

As to the prototype—the obligation barred by the statute of limitations—it should be stressed that our courts have not been as free in their treatment of statutes of limitation as they have been with statutes of frauds. Courts often assert that time limits on the bringing of actions serve desirable purposes, such as achieving finality for transactions long treated as closed and eliminating "stale" claims after evidence has been lost and memories have faded. Thus, a clause inserted at the inception of a contract, by which a party agreed not to plead the statute of limitations in the event of breach, would probably be held void everywhere. On the other hand, after default has occurred or is in prospect, a promise by the particular obligor not to plead the statute would quite surely be enforceable if there was bargain consideration meeting the usual tests. A firm assurance of this kind, even without a "bargain," would often justify a creditor in delaying suit and preclude a plea of the statute by the one who gave the assurance.

The vigilance of creditors may be relaxed as a result of conduct falling short of an express promise of the kind just described. Suppose a debt is in default on which the debtor, without comment, makes a part payment—e.g., by mailing a check. Suppose also that the applicable statute of limitations sets a time limit of six years for the start of suit. Should the six years be counted from the original date when the default occurred or from the date of the last payment? A literal reading might point to the date of default, for this is when a "cause of action" accrued. But this would mean that the creditor would be compelled to sue within the six-year limit even though the debtor had continued to make delayed payments, strung out perhaps over several years. This would be hard on the "honest" though delinquent debtor, but it would be even harder on the lenient creditor who may have been led to believe that the debt would be paid without the trouble of a lawsuit. Certainly the creditor should not be penalized for practicing leniency. Accordingly, it has long been agreed that not only delayed part payment of a contract debt but, in any kind of contract obligation, a new promise to perform (or an acknowledgment of liability) made after default and before the statutory period has expired will start the statute running all over again. (All of this can be found in Restatement, Second § 82.) A doctrine framed in these broad terms must be explained, at least in part, by the effect of part performance or a new promise in inducing creditors not to act and to trust that their indulgence would not leave them worse off. An unusually candid statement of this rationale appears in Graves v. Sawyer, 588 S.W.2d 542 (Tenn. 1979).

It seems worth repeating that extension of periods of limitations in the circumstances just discussed—part payment, acknowledgment, or new promise before the statutory period has expired—need not take the form of a new agreement. Unilateral action by the debtor is enough. Nor is it necessary to demonstrate the requirements for some version of estoppel.

The court in Mills v. Wyman had in mind a situation that was quite different, one in which the statutory bar had already fallen. Assume that a new promise was then made by the obligor to perform some or all of the barred obligation, though nothing new was received by the obligor in exchange for the promise. It has long been true that such promises are fully valid and take on what might be called a life of their own. Any conditions or limitations that they express ("I'll pay the whole debt when I sell my barn"; "I owed you $750 but I'll only pay $500") will be given full effect. E.g., Mun Seek Pai v. First Hawaiian Bank, 57 Haw. 429, 558 P.2d 479 (1977) (new promise to pay when "more or less financially able to" enforced upon finding condition of ability fulfilled). And the statutory period of limitation will start running on the new promise from the date it was made. This can hardly be explained as "waiver" of a waivable defense. As an explanation, waiver becomes still less convincing where the obligor makes no new promise at all but merely "acknowledges" the obligation or makes a part payment on the barred debt without saying or writing a word. If the statute of limitations created the bar, either acknowledgment or part payment will revive the debt. But with debts barred by discharge in bankruptcy, the courts were more demanding and only a new *express* promise would suffice; a promise implied from part payment or acknowledgment would not do. This insistence on the formality of an express promise is usually attributed to a belief that today the statutory discharge in bankruptcy reflects a more compelling public policy than is the case with a statute of limitations. See Restatement, Second § 83, comment a.

As one would expect, there has been much litigation over the sufficiency of acknowledgments, especially as concerns limitation periods or bars. Snyder v. Baltimore Trust Co., 532 A.2d 624 (Del. Super. Ct. 1986), is representative of the approach commonly taken. There must be a "clear, distinct and unequivocal" acknowledgment of the debt; a "vague or loose" admission will not do (e.g., "I'm going to look out for you"; "[t]he farm is big enough to pay you").

In explaining the revival of obligations rendered unenforceable by law, some courts speak of "past consideration." Of course, such phrasing hardly disguises the absence of present exchange which modern theories have made a crucial element in tests of consideration. More often courts invoke "moral obligation," as in Jones v. Jones, 242 F. Supp. 979, 982 (S.D.N.Y. 1965) ("there must be a new contract, consideration for which is the moral obligation to pay the original debt"). Corbin, too, spoke of the "moral obligation" to pay the barred debt—something wholly unaffected by the law's bar of limitations—as amounting to an operative past consideration for any new promise. 1A A. Corbin, Contracts § 214. Other explanations typically given are that the statute of limitations merely raises a rebuttable presumption of payment, that it only bars the remedy and does not destroy the right, or, as already noted, that the new promise or acknowledgment creates no new legal duty but merely "waives" a defense. Whatever its choice of language, a court usually will take care to make clear that it is invoking a very special kind of moral duty, a ghostly survival from the parties' past relations, and that these past relations continue to set limits on the obligor's power to make a binding promise.

Suppose, for example, a money debt of $1,000 that had been barred by time-limitation. The sheltered debtor, perhaps filled with remorse, then makes a new promise to pay $1,500. The legal effect is clear: the promise would be valid up to the amount of the barred debt; as to the $500 excess it would be void, for lack of consideration. But no, we must quickly take some of that statement back—some of the $500 might be viewed as payment of accrued interest. It may seem somewhat incongruous to think of interest running on an uncollectible debt, but with practice one can become accustomed even to this. Or suppose that the creditor, after the bar had fallen, assigned the original claim to a third party and the debtor then made a new promise. To whom is the money due? The answer is, to the assignee, for "something of the original vitality of the debt continues to exist" and the claim, though all remedies to enforce it were barred at the time, was assignable. Stanek v. White, 172 Minn. 390, 215 N.W. 784 (1927). A good discussion of the various legal effects of unenforceable debts (plus a collection of the cases) can be found in Webster v. Kowal, 394 Mass. 443, 476 N.E.2d 205 (1985).

The effect of new promise, acknowledgment, or part payment on obligations barred by the statute of limitations is so well known and widely accepted that statutes in all but a half-dozen or so of our states regulate such conduct by requiring a writing signed by the debtor for the promise or acknowledgment (but not the part payment) to have any legal effect. Modern federal bankruptcy law sharply limits the enforceability of a bankrupt's promises to repay discharged debts. This extensive body of regulation, which includes requirements for bankruptcy-court approval of reaffirmation agreements and a grant of power to the debtor to rescind such agreements in specific circumstances, appears in 11 U.S.C. § 524(c), (d). See, e.g., Lumby v. Lumby, 116 Wis. 2d 347, 341 N.W.2d 725 (App. 1983) (letter reaffirming discharged debt invalid since not in compliance with § 524's specified standards).

Webb v. McGowin

Court of Appeals of Alabama, 1935.
27 Ala. App. 82, 168 So. 196.

Action by Joe Webb against N. Floyd McGowin and Joseph F. McGowin, as executors of the estate of J. Greeley McGowin, deceased. From a judgment of nonsuit, plaintiff appeals.

BRICKEN, P.J. . . . The complaint [in assumpsit] as originally filed was amended. The demurrers to the complaint as amended were sustained, and because of this adverse ruling by the court the plaintiff took a nonsuit, and the assignment of errors on this appeal are predicated upon said action or ruling of the court.

A fair statement of the case presenting the questions for decision is set out in appellant's brief, which we adopt.

"On the 3d day of August, 1925, appellant while in the employ of the W.T. Smith Lumber Co., a corporation, and acting within the scope of his employment, was engaged in clearing the upper floor of Mill No. 2 of the company. While so engaged he was in the act of dropping a [75-pound] pine block from the upper floor of the mill to the ground below; this being the usual and ordinary way of clearing the floor, and it being the duty of the plaintiff in the course of his employment to so drop it. . . .

"As appellant was in the act of dropping the block to the ground below, he was on the edge of the upper floor of the mill. As he started to turn the block loose so that it would drop to the ground, he saw J. Greeley McGowin, testator of the defendants, on the ground below and directly under where the block would have fallen. . . . Had he turned it loose it would have struck McGowin with such force as to have caused him serious bodily harm or death. . . . The only safe and reasonable way to prevent this was for appellant to hold to the block and divert its direction [by] falling with it to the ground below. Appellant did this, and by holding to the block and falling with it[,] he diverted the course of its fall in such way that McGowin was not injured. In thus preventing the injuries to McGowin, appellant himself received serious bodily injuries, resulting in his right leg being broken, the heel of his right foot torn off and his right arm broken. He was badly crippled for life and rendered unable to do physical or mental labor.

"On September 1, 1925, in consideration of appellant having prevented him from sustaining death or serious bodily harm and in consideration of the injuries appellant had received, McGowin agreed with him to care for and maintain him for the remainder of appellant's life at the rate of $15 every two weeks from the time he sustained his injuries to and during the remainder of appellant's life; it being agreed that McGowin would pay this sum to appellant for his maintenance. Under the agreement McGowin paid or caused to be paid to appellant the sum so agreed on up until McGowin's death on January 1, 1934. After his death the payments were continued to and including January 27, 1934, at which time they were discontinued. Thereupon plaintiff brought suit to recover the unpaid installments accruing [after January 27, 1934,] up to the time of the bringing of the suit.

"The material averments of the different counts of the original complaint and the amended complaint are predicated upon the foregoing statement of facts." . . .

1. The [complaint shows] that appellant saved McGowin from death or grievous bodily harm. This was a material benefit to him of infinitely more value than any financial aid he could have received. Receiving this benefit, McGowin became morally bound to compensate appellant for the services rendered. Recognizing his moral obligation, he expressly agreed to pay appellant as alleged in the complaint and complied with this agreement up to the time of his death; a period of more than 8 years.

Had McGowin been accidentally poisoned and a physician, without his knowledge or request, had administered an antidote, thus saving his life, a subsequent promise by McGowin to pay the physician would have been valid. Likewise, McGowin's agreement . . . to compensate appellant for saving him from death or grievous bodily injury is valid and enforceable.

Where the promisee cares for, improves, and preserves the property of the promisor, though done without his request, it is sufficient consideration for the promisor's subsequent agreement to pay for the service, because of the material benefit received. . . .

In Boothe v. Fitzpatrick, 36 Vt. 681, the court held that a promise by defendant to pay for the past keeping of a bull which had escaped from defendant's premises and been cared for by plaintiff was valid, although there was no previous request, because the subsequent promise obviated that objection; it being equivalent to a previous request. On the same principle, had the promisee saved the promisor's life or his body from grievous harm, his subsequent promise to pay for the services rendered would have been valid. Such service would have been far more material than caring for his bull. Any holding that saving a man from death or grievous bodily harm is not a material benefit sufficient to uphold a subsequent promise to pay for the service, necessarily rests on the assumption that saving life and preservation of the body from harm have only a sentimental value. The converse of this is true. Life and preservation of the body have material, pecuniary values, measurable in dollars and cents. Because of this, physicians practice their profession charging for services rendered in saving life and curing the body of its ills, and surgeons perform operations. The same is true as to the law of negligence, authorizing the assessment of damages in personal injury cases based upon the extent of the injuries, earnings, and life expectancies of those injured.

In the business of life insurance, the value of a man's life is measured in dollars and cents according to his expectancy, the soundness of his body, and his ability to pay premiums. The same is true as to health and accident insurance.

It follows that if . . . appellant saved J. Greeley McGowin from death or grievous bodily harm, and McGowin subsequently agreed to pay him for the service rendered, it became a valid and enforceable contract.

2. It is well settled that a moral obligation is a sufficient consideration to support a subsequent promise to pay where the promisor has received a material benefit, although there was no original duty or liability resting on the promisor. . . .

The case at bar is clearly distinguishable from [cases] where the consideration is a mere moral obligation or conscientious duty unconnected with receipt by [the] promisor of benefits of a material or pecuniary nature. . . . Here the promisor received a material benefit constituting a valid consideration for his promise.

3. Some authorities hold that, for a moral obligation to support a subsequent promise to pay, there must have existed a prior legal or equitable obligation, which for some reason had become unenforceable, but for which the promisor was still morally bound. This rule, however, is subject to qualification in those cases where the promisor having received a material benefit from the promisee, is morally bound to compensate him for the services rendered and in consideration of this obligation promises to pay. In such cases the subsequent promise to pay is an affirmance or ratification of the services rendered carrying with it the presumption that a previous request for the service was made. . . .

4. . . . [I]n in saving McGowin from death or grievous bodily harm, appellant was crippled for life. This was part of the consideration of the contract declared on. McGowin was benefited. Appellant was injured. Benefit to the promisor or injury to the promisee is a sufficient legal consideration for the promisor's agreement to pay. . . .

5. Under [the complaint] the services rendered by appellant were not gratuitous. The agreement of McGowin to pay and the acceptance of payment by appellant conclusively shows the contrary.

6. The contract declared on was not void under the statute of frauds (Code 1923, § 8034). The demurrer on that ground was not well taken. . . .

From what has been said . . . the court below erred [in] sustaining the demurrer, and for this error the case is reversed and remanded.

SAMFORD, J. (concurring). The questions involved in this case are not free from doubt, and perhaps the strict letter of the rule, as stated by judges, though not always in accord, would bar a recovery by plaintiff, but following the principle announced by Chief Justice Marshall in Hoffman v. Porter, 2 Brock. 156, 159, where he says, "I do not think that law ought to be separated from justice, where it is at most doubtful," I concur in the conclusions reached by the court.

[On petition to the Supreme Court of Alabama, certiorari was denied, Justice Foster writing for the Supreme Court. 232 Ala. 374, 168 So. 199 (1936).]

FOSTER, J. We do not in all cases in which we deny a petition for certiorari to the Court of Appeals approve the reasoning and principles declared in the opinion, even though no opinion is rendered by us. It does not always seem to be important that they be discussed, and we exercise a discretion in that respect. But when the opinion of the Court of Appeals asserts important principles or their application to new situations, and it may be uncertain whether this court agrees with it in all respects, we think it advisable to be specific in that respect when the certiorari is denied. We think such a situation here exists. . . .

The opinion of the Court of Appeals . . . recognizes and applies the distinction between a supposed moral obligation of the promisor, based upon some refined sense of ethical duty, without material benefit to him, and one in which such a benefit did in fact occur. We agree with that court that if the benefit be material and substantial, and was to the person of the promisor rather than to his estate, it is within the class of material benefits which he has the privilege of recognizing and compensating either by an executed payment or an executory promise to pay. . . . The reason is emphasized when the compensation is not only for the benefits which the promisor received, but also for the injuries either to the property or person of the promisee by reason of the service rendered.

Writ denied.

Harrington v. Taylor

225 N.C. 690, 36 S.E.2d 227 (1945)

Defendant had assaulted his wife, who took refuge in plaintiff's house. The next day defendant gained access to the house and resumed the attack;

his wife grabbed an ax, knocked defendant down, and was about to split his head open when plaintiff intervened, catching on her hand the blow intended for defendant. Defendant's life was thereby saved, but plaintiff's hand was badly mutilated. Subsequently, defendant promised "to pay the plaintiff her damages." After paying only a small sum, defendant failed to pay anything more. *Held*, on demurrer, these facts fail to allege a cause of action. "[H]owever much the defendant should be impelled by common gratitude to alleviate the plaintiff's misfortune, a humanitarian act of this kind, voluntarily performed, is not such consideration as would entitle her to recover at law."

Restatement of Restitution

§ 112. General Rule

Illustrations: . . .

2. In the belief that with some assistance A will become a valuable citizen, B makes a gift to A of $1000. Upon receiving the money, A immediately begins to squander it, destroying all of B's expectations. B is not entitled to restitution, even of the unspent portion.

3. During A's absence and in the belief that A will be willing to pay for the work, B improves A's land, which is worth and is offered for sale at $5000, to such an extent that upon A's return he sells the land for $8000. B is not entitled to restitution from A.

Comment:

b. *Exceptional situations.* Under some conditions, it is desirable to encourage persons to interfere with the affairs of others. . . . [A] person or his belongings may be in such jeopardy that a stranger is privileged to intervene and to recover for his salvage services. . . . [These are] the types of situations in which the unasked-for conferring of benefit has been regarded as unofficious. Other similar situations may arise in which the desirability of permitting restitution is equally great and, if so, restitution should be granted in accordance with the principle that compensation for benefits conferred is denied only to officious intermeddlers or to persons who do not desire or who manifest no desire to have compensation for their services.

[The second branch of the "principle" stated—the actor's intention to charge where intervention is justified—is elaborated in the Restitution Restatement's § 114, comment c: "[A] person who acts entirely from motives of humanity is not entitled to restitution. The fact that the person acting is in the business of supplying the things or is acting in the course of his profession, is evidence of an intent to charge. On the other hand, a non-professional person who gives a comparatively small amount of service normally would be considered as having no intent to charge for the services, in the absence of evidence of such intent."]

NOTE: RESTITUTION ABSENT THE LATER PROMISE

Would Webb have recovered anything if McGowin had made no subsequent promise of compensation? Would the rescuer of the bull (Boothe v. Fitzpatrick, discussed in the *Webb* case) have recovered anything if the owner had not promised to pay for the bull's care and keep?

The *Webb* court likened the case before it to one in which an "accidentally poisoned" McGowin is saved by an unrequested physician, and a grateful McGowin then promises payment for the services rendered. Can this be right, given that doctors are typically allowed to recover even without such a promise? See Cotnam v. Wisdom, 83 Ark. 601, 104 S.W. 164 (1907). But the physician's case does not depend on a later promise. What does this suggest about how we should think about *Webb*? Consider a modern discussion of benefits conferred in the absence of bargain, Goldstick v. ICM Realty, 788 F.2d 456 (7th Cir. 1986), where Judge Posner wrote in part:

> A person who confers benefits gratuitously—officiously—obtains no legal claim for compensation. If [plaintiff, a lawyer seeking payment of a legal fee for tax work,] had appeared at a meeting of [defendant's] shareholders and serenaded them with his violin, and the shareholders had listened raptly, still [plaintiff] would have no claim of restitution against [the defendant company] for benefits conferred; he would have had to negotiate a contract with [defendant] in advance. . . . [Also, if plaintiff had a contract with another party,] plaintiff cannot bring [defendant] in through the back door by pointing out that [his] contractual performance conferred benefits on [defendant]. To illustrate, if you do work pursuant to a contract with X, you don't expect that Y, a nonparty, will pay you if X defaults, merely because Y was benefitted by your work; and expectation of payment is an essential element of a claim for restitution. For the doctrine of restitution does not make altruism a paying proposition. As its synonym "contract implied in law" brings out, it allows damages to be recovered in settings where (unlike our example of the unsolicited serenade) the parties would have agreed that there was a contractual obligation had the point occurred to them.

Henderson, Promises Grounded in the Past: The Idea of Unjust Enrichment and the Law of Contracts

57 Va. L. Rev. 1115, 1157–1161 (1971)

"[T]he law of consideration developed and prospered for the very reason that it was thought to be well-suited to the task of marking off and excluding sterile transactions. Thus, it would be difficult to overstate the extent to which the informal gratuitous promise has been a subject of central concern [in discussions] of the various rules of consideration. . . . At times, the disposition not to inquire into the adequacy of consideration, which provides doctrinal legitimacy for enforcement of the mixed gift, encourages the notion that close distinctions between bargain and gift are not of great weight. Yet the factor of motive has always been recognized as critical to bargain theory, and it has generally received sensitive and evenhanded treatment in the decisions. . . .

"Why, then, has the common law been reluctant to explore motivations for the purpose of distinguishing the promise to pay for benefit earlier received from the simple promise of a gift? The [answer] surely cannot be that these promises are indistinguishable. Once undertakings based clearly on gratitude or sentiment are isolated—as the case law of bargain theory has long done and as [§ 86] of the second Restatement envisions—a promise to do something in return for benefit already in hand is most persuasively explained on the basis of motivations of reciprocity, not benevolence. . . . [P]romises prompted by enrichment already taken can fairly be associated with the idea of exchange that forms the essential support for the whole of bargain contract. So long as the promisee acted originally with an expectation of compensation, or even where it is not clearly established that a gift-making motivation controlled [the] conferring of benefit, the net effect of a promise of a return is to conclude a kind of exchange. There is no intelligible reason to require the trailing promise to stand apart from the chain of events which sponsored it. . . . [E]ven assuming that such transactions cannot be fitted within expanded notions of bargain, at the very least they ought to be legally operative for the limited purpose of negating the assumption of gift which stands as an obstacle on the general question of liability.

". . . [I]t is settled beyond recall that unjust enrichment, viewed independently or as reinforcement of bargain, itself constitutes a substantive ground for the enforcement of promises. [Moreover,] the impressiveness of the [benefit] ground is enhanced when the enrichment factor is coupled with a promissory confession that it has created in the recipient a sense of moral obligation. . . .

"Perhaps the most obvious conclusion to be drawn from a study of the [benefit cases] is that concern about ill-considered promise making is largely misplaced. Given the usual sequence in which events unfold—i.e., a performance on one side, resulting in an often identifiable gain in the hands of the other party, followed by the other's promissory response—the transaction itself involves natural safeguards equivalent to those of form or present exchange. The time lag between performance and promise affords an opportunity for deliberation and the exercise of caution, as well as an evaluation of 'price,' not present in most conventional bargains. Still, promises to return benefit are traditionally not enforced in spite of the strong likelihood that they were seriously intended when made. To the extent that the decisions accept the natural guaranties of the benefit cases, they do so implicitly and usually only in connection with recoveries placed on the material benefit rule of moral obligation."

Restatement of Contracts, Second

§ 86. Promise for Benefit Received

(1) A promise made in recognition of a benefit previously received by the promisor from the promisee is binding to the extent necessary to prevent injustice.

(2) A promise is not binding under Subsection (1)

(a) if the promisee conferred the benefit as a gift or for other reasons the promisor has not been unjustly enriched; or

(b) to the extent that its value is disproportionate to the benefit.

Comment:

a. "Past consideration"; "moral obligation." Enforcement of promises to pay for benefit received has sometimes been said to rest on "past consideration" or on the "moral obligation" of the promisor, and there are statutes in such terms in a few states. Those terms are not used here: "past consideration" is inconsistent with the [conventional] meaning of consideration, and there seems to be no consensus as to what constitutes a "moral obligation." The mere fact of promise has been thought to create a moral obligation, but it is clear that not all promises are enforced. Nor are moral obligations based solely on gratitude or sentiment sufficient of themselves to support a subsequent promise. . . .

i. Partial enforcement. . . . [W]here a benefit received is a liquidated sum of money, a promise is not enforceable under this [s]ection beyond the amount of the benefit. Where the value of the benefit is uncertain, a promise to pay the value is binding and a promise to pay a liquidated sum may serve to fix the amount due if in all the circumstances it is not disproportionate to the benefit. See [Webb v. McGowin]. A promise which is excessive may sometimes be enforced to the extent of the value of the benefit, and the remedy may be thought of as quasi-contractual rather than contractual. In other cases a promise of disproportionate value may tend to show unfair pressure or other conduct by the promisee such that justice does not require any enforcement of the promise.

NOTE: PAST CONSIDERATION AND THE RESTATEMENT

When § 86 was before the annual meeting of the American Law Institute in 1965, Reporter Robert Braucher introduced this new category of binding promise with the comment that the accustomed ways of classifying and talking about the decisions giving effect to past consideration or moral obligation were a "rather unsatisfactory way to leave these cases." He proceeded to explain (42 A.L.I. Proc. 273–274):

> Actually, when you go through the cases in which this problem has been raised, it seemed to us that you discover that there is a principle, and so we have tried to capture the principle, although I think it is more of a principle than it is a rule.

> If you look at [§ 86], it bristles with nonspecific concepts; in particular, the qualification that the promise is binding to the extent necessary to prevent injustice would be entirely at large if we did not add subsection (2) which refers to the concept of unjust enrichment.
>
> [I think] the principle takes on meaning, and I think there is not a division here between a majority view and a minority view. . . . What you have, really, is a line of distinction between essentially gratuitous transactions and cases which are on the borderline of quasi-contracts, where promise removes difficulty. . . . If you look through the cases, the cases are a wide variety of miscellany, but we think there is a principle.

The cases digested below (*Edson*, *Muir*, and *Schoenkerman's Estate*) are part of the "miscellany" referred to by Reporter Braucher. Do they yield the "principle" of which he spoke? Despite the appearance of § 86, one continues to see promises for benefit received discussed in the consideration-based language of "material benefit" and "moral obligation." See, e.g., Worner Agency, Inc. v. Doyle, 133 Ill. App. 3d 850, 479 N.E.2d 468 (1985) (receipt of " 'beneficial' or 'meritorious' consideration [imposes] a moral obligation yielding an implied consideration" for a subsequent promise by the person benefitted). The conventional explanation of the moral obligation cases in terms of restitution—the approach of § 86 and most commentators—is challenged in Steve Thel & Edward Yorio, The Promissory Basis of Past Consideration, 78 Va. L. Rev. 1045 (1992).

Edson v. Poppe

24 S.D. 466, 124 N.W. 441 (1910)

Plaintiff, at the request of a tenant in possession of land owned by defendant, drilled a 250-foot well on the property and installed casing. Plaintiff alleged that the value of the labor and material expended was $250, that the well added to the value of the land and later occupants have regularly used it, and that after the well had been completed defendant promised to pay plaintiff the reasonable value of the work and materials. Plaintiff recovered a jury verdict below. Defendant appealed, claiming only past consideration was alleged. *Held*, judgment for plaintiff affirmed. "The allegation . . . here is that the digging and casing of the well in question inured directly to the defendant's benefit and that, after he had seen and examined the same, he expressly promised and agreed to pay plaintiff the reasonable value thereof." The circumstances did not indicate that plaintiff's drilling was "gratuitous" or "an act of voluntary courtesy to the defendant." The subsequent promise was therefore supported by sufficient consideration.

Muir v. Kane

55 Wash. 131, 104 P. 153 (1909)

Defendants employed plaintiff, a real estate broker, to find a purchaser for their home. The arrangement was oral, and by a state statute of frauds any agreement authorizing a broker to secure a buyer or seller of real estate was "void" unless in writing. Plaintiff secured a buyer, and a written contract of sale was prepared and signed by both the buyer and defendants. One clause of the contract contained a promise by defendants to pay plaintiffs $200 "for services rendered." *Held*, plaintiff can recover this sum. The contract clause did not comply with the statute, since it was not the written authority to the broker that the statute required. Furthermore, plaintiff's service had already been rendered when the contract of sale was signed. Nevertheless, though declared by the statute to be "void," there was no moral turpitude in the prior oral agreement. Defendants had a moral obligation to pay for the service that was fully as strong as that continuing after a statute of limitations has barred a once-enforceable debt.

In re Schoenkerman's Estate

236 Wis. 311, 294 N.W. 810 (1940)

Schoenkerman's wife died in 1928. There were two children of the marriage, a daughter then 17 and a son 13. Schoenkerman asked his wife's mother and sister, who lived in Chicago, to move to Milwaukee, live in his home to take care of the children, and to manage the household for them all. They did so, living in and managing his home until shortly before his death in 1939. A year earlier, in May 1938, Schoenkerman had executed two notes, promising $500 to his mother-in-law and $1,500 to his sister-in-law, on which they sued after his death. *Held*, the decedent was manifestly under a moral obligation to pay the claimants for their 10 years of service to him. Defendant, executor of Schoenkerman's estate, was right in contending that household services rendered and received by persons living together as a family are presumed to be gratuitous and that an express contract to pay would have had to be proved to overcome this presumption. But defendant was wrong in contending that there must have been at one time a legally enforceable obligation. In giving the notes, Schoenkerman plainly acknowledged a moral obligation that "afforded more than ample consideration." But the claim of the sister-in-law for the full value of her services, which she asserted to be $4,610, was correctly disallowed as to the excess over the $1,500 promised.

SECTION 4. RELIANCE ON A PROMISE

Seavey v. Drake

Supreme Court of New Hampshire, 1882.
62 N.H. 393.

Bill in Equity, for specific performance of a parol agreement of land. At the hearing the plaintiff offered to prove that he was the only child of Shadrach Seavey, the defendants' testate, who died in 1880. In January, 1860, the testator, owning a tract of land, and wishing to assist the plaintiff, went upon the land with him and gave him a portion of it, which the plaintiff then accepted and took possession of. The plaintiff had a [promissory] note against his father upon which there was due about $200, which he then or subsequently gave up to him. Subsequently his father gave him an additional strip of land adjoining the other tract. Ever since the gifts, the plaintiff has occupied and still occupies the land, and has paid all taxes upon it. He has expended $3,000 in the erection of a dwelling-house, barn, and stable, and in other improvements upon the premises. Some of the lumber for the house was given him by his father, who helped him do some of the labor upon the house.

The defendants moved to dismiss because no cause for equitable relief was stated, and because the parol contract, which is sought to be enforced, was without consideration, and is executory. The bill alleges a gift of the land to the plaintiff and a promise to give him a deed of it. The defendants also demurred, and answered denying the material allegations of the bill.

If the bill can be sustained on proof of these facts, or if not on these facts, but would be with the additional proof of a consideration for the promise, there is to be a further hearing, the plaintiff having leave to amend his bill. If on proof of these facts, either with or without proof of consideration, the bill cannot be sustained, it is to be dismissed.

SMITH, J. The bill alleges a promise by the defendants' testator to give the plaintiff a deed. The plaintiff offered to prove that the deceased gave him the land, and that he thereupon entered into possession and made valuable improvements. We assume that the plaintiff in his offer [of proofs] meant that he was induced by the gift of the land to enter into possession and make large expenditures in permanent improvements upon it. The evidence offered is admissible. Specific performance of a parol contract to convey land is decreed in favor of the vendee who has performed his part of the contract, when a failure or refusal to convey would operate as a fraud upon him. Johnson v. Bell, 58 N.H. 395. . . . The statute of frauds (G.L., c. 220, s. 14) provides that "No action shall be maintained upon a contract for the sale of land, unless the agreement upon which it is brought, or some memorandum thereof, is in writing, and signed by the party to be charged, or by some person by him thereto authorized in writing." Equity, however, lends its aid, when there has been part performance, to remove the bar of the statute, upon the ground that it is a fraud for the vendor to insist upon the absence of a written instrument, when he has permitted the contract to be partly executed.

It is not material . . . whether the promissory note given up by the plaintiff was or was not intended as payment or part payment for the land, for equity protects a parol gift of land equally with a parol agreement to sell it, if accompanied by possession, and the donee has made valuable improvements upon the property induced by the promise to give it. . . . There is no important distinction in this respect between a promise to give and a promise to sell. The expenditure in money or labor in the improvement of the land induced by the donor's promise to give the land to the party making the expenditure, constitutes, in equity, a consideration for the promise and the promise will be enforced. Crosbie v. M'Doual, 13 Ves. 148; Freeman v. Freeman, 43 N.Y. 34, 39. . . . Case discharged.

COMMENT: PART PERFORMANCE OF LAND CONTRACTS

There is much authority granting specific performance in equity after the kind of "part performance" that occurred in Seavey v. Drake. The land-contract clause in the statute of frauds quoted in *Seavey* is in substance the standard phrasing. There is of course no exception in the statutory language for the kind of "fraud" that involved no more than a refusal by the executor to perform the oral promise made by the father in his lifetime. It may be that this disregard of exact language began because of an original understanding that the statute of frauds did not apply to actions in equity. An early draft of the statute indicated this. But the language of the English statute of 1677, as finally adopted, drew no such distinction. Nor do most American versions, save for a small number that expressly authorize equitable relief after part performance of the kind discussed here (e.g., New York's Gen. Oblig. Law, § 5–703(4) states that "[n]othing contained in this section abridges the powers of courts of equity to compel the specific performance of agreements in cases of part performance").

The standard situation in which the part-performance doctrine displaces the statute of frauds does not involve a promise to convey land by way of gift, as in Seavey v. Drake, but an oral contract to sell land for money—an exchange in which the vendor has failed to sign a sufficient memorandum. In this context, the doctrine is certainly misdescribed. The most obvious and direct "part performance" of an ordinary land contract will be part payment of the purchase price, but it is agreed everywhere that mere payment of the price, in full or in part, will not make specific performance available. Jasmin v. Alberico, 135 Vt. 287, 376 A.2d 32 (1977), tells why: "[T]he reliance [must] be something beyond injury adequately compensable in money." If the vendee-promisee can be made whole by ordering restitution, there is no need for equity's intervention to protect the reliance of the performing party. Entry into possession by the promisee, with the promisor-owner's acquiescence, is the critical element. A substantial group of states has held that this is enough. In other states, entry into possession plus payment of some part of the price will suffice. Probably in most states possession plus permanent improvements will do. However, some states, like Massachusetts, have tied the whole doctrine explicitly into the reliance factor and require a showing that the oral purchaser has become committed in such a way that "irreparable" (meaning "unjust and unconscientious") injury will occur unless specific performance is given. Andrews v. Charon, 289 Mass. 1, 193 N.E. 737 (1935). Finally, at the other end of the spectrum are a few states which have firmly rejected "part performance" as a justification for specific performance of oral land contracts, though this has led to some peculiar results on the damage remedy side. 2 A. Corbin, Contracts § 443, tells the story in these states.

No elaborate effort is usually made to justify the part-performance route around the statute, but some clues to the reasons do appear. Occupancy by the vendee over an extended stretch of time, with no sign of protest from the vendor, does suggest that some fairly firm oral assurances have been given. When "improvements"—substantial repairs or new construction—are added, there emerges a course of conduct that gives direct and visual confirmation to the occupant's claim that entry was under a contract of sale. The vendor-owner can be called on to give some other explanation, if there is one—e.g., that there was an oral lease or other arrangement. Thus, conduct provides a kind of *evidence* that can be said to take the place of a signed memorandum, the evidence called for by the statute.

It is true that the "evidentiary" test tends to be strict. The plaintiff's actions, it is commonly said, must be "unequivocally referable"—even "exclusively referable"—to the alleged oral agreement; in some places, a higher standard of proof (e.g., "clear and convincing") is also added. Accordingly, if the conduct urged as "part performance" is readily explainable on other grounds (or not sufficiently substantial), or the underlying agreement alleged to have induced the conduct is not sufficiently demonstrated, the escape from the statute is lost. It must be remembered that part performance is both an equity doctrine and an "exception" to a formal requirement of general contract law. Hence the search for "what equity requires," especially at the pleading stage, is usually thorough, perhaps even grudging. E.g., Messner Vetere Berger v. Aegis Group, 93 N.Y.2d 229, 689 N.Y.S.2d 674, 711 N.E.2d 953 (1999).

The argument that appears in Seavey v. Drake and in many cases enforcing oral land contracts, that denial of specific performance because of the statute of frauds would itself produce "fraud," appears on first view to be little more than verbalism. Still, there are problems that this phrasing most inadequately defines, especially in the common case where the occupier has made "improvements" or incurred other expenses. Can these outlays be reimbursed if the occupier cannot have the land? If the occupier paid money or contributed work and labor that the vendor bargained for as part of the orally-agreed exchange, no difficulty would arise. It is agreed everywhere that the statute of frauds is no obstacle to quasi-contract restitution of performances rendered as part of the agreed exchange by a party not in default under an oral contract within the statute. But improvements, taxes, or other charges paid, and other expenditures that were not "requested" by the owner-vendor, are another story. Where such outlays are made by the vendee's own choice and fall outside the range of the oral agreement, there is real doubt whether any recovery can be allowed at all, even though the value of the real estate may have been permanently enhanced. See, e.g., Breen v. Phelps, 186 Conn. 86, 439 A.2d 1066 (1982) ("It is not evident from the complaint that restitution would be available [or] would provide an adequate remedy [for plaintiff's outlays of $6,300 for] labor and materials toward the repair and renovation of the premises"). You will see at once that the problem becomes one of reimbursing reliance losses. Can a *damage* remedy be given to reimburse for reliance losses where the breach, if any, is of an unenforceable contract? The case of Boone v. Coe (p. 128) has something to contribute on this.

In general, in the equity decisions on part performance as a ground for specific performance, there is a constant shuttling back and forth between the *evidence* that an oral contract was made, supplied by the conduct of the parties, and the *reliance* element that would make a refusal of specific performance a "fraud" on the vendee. Sometimes one of these elements seems to be uppermost in a court's mind, sometimes the other, and the facts of individual cases are exceedingly diverse. Also, as was true in *Seavey*, the equity cases giving specific performance after "part performance" tend not to devote much attention to the consideration defense (if one is raised). The primary issue—i.e., the most difficult—is thought to be the need to satisfy or circumvent the statutory writing requirement. Yet these equity cases can be added to the list of situations in which the reliance interest is protected (again, under a misdescribed doctrine), even though important requirements of contract formation and enforceability have not been met.

There has been some spillover of the *Seavey* doctrine to related situations. For example, there is respectable authority approving specific performance after "part performance" of oral contracts that are not performable within one year (2 A. Corbin, Contracts § 459). Then there is another category that might be described as "full performance," though that phrase is not always used. (It was used in Estate of Gorton, 167 Vt. 357, 706 A.2d 947 (1997): "[F]ull performance by one party in reliance on the agreement may support equitable enforcement where the parties cannot be returned to their former position.") Suppose, for example, an oral contract for the sale of land for money. If there were no more than this—no action taken by either party—neither vendor nor vendee could enforce the contract, in equity or at law, against the opposite party who pleaded the statute. But what if the vendor then proceeded to convey the legal title, thus rendering *in full* the performance promised? It plainly would be unjust for the vendee to keep the land without paying for it. One alternative would be to cancel the deed and order a reconveyance if the vendee refused to pay. But the deed itself would be persuasive evidence of a seriously-intended transaction, which had been so far performed that there was nothing left to do except pay money. The usual conclusion would be that by the vendor's conveyance the contract was "taken out" of the statute, and the vendee's promise to pay, though proved only by oral evidence, could be enforced, even at law. See also Nichols v. Nichols, 139 Vt. 273, 427 A.2d 374 (1981) (oral agreement to leave family farm to son if he farmed it, paid off bills, and cared for mother until her death specifically enforced where son fully performed agreement). Even with contracts that are "not to be performed within one year," decisions tend toward the same result and allow enforcement of the unperformed oral promise by the party who has fully performed. Mason v. Anderson, 146 Vt. 242, 499 A.2d 783 (1985), and Glass v. Minnesota Protective Life Ins. Co., 314 N.W.2d 393 (Iowa 1982), are representative examples. Cases on full performance by one party are collected in Willamette Quarries, Inc. v. Wodtli, 308 Or. 406, 781 P.2d 1196 (1989).

One of the haunting questions raised by the part-performance cases was whether there were compelling reasons, logical or historical, why judges sitting on law dockets should be impervious to proof of reliance on oral promises. They clearly were supposed to be under the traditional conception of "part performance." The avenue it opened was to equity only; a damage action would not lie on the same oral contract that the very same judge, if the case had been brought on the nonjury docket, would cheerfully enforce.

The first question, of course, was why the presence of a jury should make that much difference. Arguments began to be heard in 1677, when the statute of frauds was passed, that no effective means existed for controlling juries, and that the restrictive rules of evidence (such as the disqualification of the parties as witnesses) made perjury harder to detect. Furthermore, contract law itself was still relatively primitive, especially in its lack of restraints on damage recoveries (no requirements of foreseeability, mitigation, certainty, etc.). To some critics, the statute seemed more and more an anachronism. At the least, it seemed plausible to assert that the policies supporting the statute were not clear enough—or strong enough—to preclude redress for substantial reliance losses where the remedy of restitution was inadequate and damages alone could give indemnity.

The traditional view was not so easily dislodged, however, as a 1941 Washington case suggests.

Owners of an apartment building agreed orally to give Tenant a three-year written lease of an apartment then occupied by another tenant. Owners "understood" that Tenant would buy the occupant's furniture. Tenant did so, paying down $2,437.25 and obligating himself for an additional $2,600. Tenant entered into possession at once and paid rent for the next three months, but when he tendered the rent for the fourth month, he was informed by Owners that the building had been purchased by one Stone, who proceeded to evict him. Tenant defaulted on his contract to buy the furniture, forfeiting the payments already made. Tenant then sued for this loss (also for $58 spent in improving the apartment), and the jury rendered a verdict of $2,655.25 in his favor. Judgment on this verdict was reversed. It was improper to submit to the jury the question whether the conduct of the parties was "part performance," for that was an equitable issue for the judge and "in the very nature of things a judge cannot delegate his chancery powers to a jury under any imaginable circumstances." Equitable estoppel, as its name indicates, applied only in equity. Goodwin v. Gillingham, 10 Wash.2d 656, 117 P.2d 959 (1941).

There will be more ahead on the workings of the reliance principle as concerns a damage remedy for breach of an oral agreement deemed to fall within the statute of frauds.

Kirksey v. Kirksey

Supreme Court of Alabama, 1845.
8 Ala. 131.

Assumpsit by the defendant, against the plaintiff in error. The question is presented [upon] a case agreed, which shows the following facts:

The plaintiff was the wife of defendant's brother, but had for some time been a widow, and had several children. In 1840, the plaintiff resided on public land, under a contract of lease, she had held over, and was comfortably settled, and would have attempted to secure the land she lived on. The defendant resided in Talladega county, some sixty, or seventy miles off. On the 10th of October, 1840, he wrote to her the following letter:

"Dear sister Antillico—Much to my mortification, I heard, that brother Henry was dead, and one of his children. I know that your situation is one of grief, and difficulty. You had a bad chance before, but a great deal worse now. I should like to come and see you, but cannot with convenience at present. . . . I do not know whether you have a preference on the place you live on, or not. If you had, I would advise you to obtain your preference, and sell the land and quit the country, as I understand it is very unhealthy, and I know society is very bad. If you will come down and see me, I will let you have a place to raise your family, and I have more open land than I can tend; and on the account of your situation, and that of your family, I feel like I want you and the children to do well."

Within a month or two [of] receipt of this letter, the plaintiff abandoned her possession, without disposing of it, and removed with her family, to the residence of the defendant, who put her in comfortable houses, and gave her land to cultivate for two years, at the end of which time he notified her to remove, and put her in a house, not comfortable, in the woods, which he afterwards required her to leave.

A verdict being found for the plaintiff, for two hundred dollars, the above facts were agreed, and if they will sustain the action, the judgment is to be affirmed, otherwise it is to be reversed.

ORMOND, J. The inclination of my mind is, that the loss and inconvenience, which the plaintiff sustained in breaking up, and moving to the defendant's a distance of sixty miles, is a sufficient consideration to support the promise, to furnish her with a house, and land to cultivate, until she could raise her family. My brothers, however, think that the promise on the part of the defendant, was a mere gratuity, and that an action will not lie for its breach. The judgment of the Court below must therefore be reversed, pursuant to the agreement of the parties.

Ricketts v. Scothorn

Supreme Court of Nebraska, 1898.
57 Neb. 51, 77 N.W. 365.

SULLIVAN, J. . . . [T]he plaintiff, Katie Scothorn, recovered judgment against the defendant, Andrew D. Ricketts, as executor of the last will and testament of John C. Ricketts, deceased. The action was based upon [this] promissory note[:] "May the first, 1891. I promise to pay to Katie Scothorn on demand, $2,000, to be at 6 per cent. per annum. J. C. Ricketts." In the petition the plaintiff alleges that the consideration for the execution of the note was that she should surrender her employment as bookkeeper for Mayer Bros., and cease to work for a living. She also alleges that the note was given to induce her to abandon her occupation, and that, relying on it, and on the annual interest, as a means of support, she gave up the employment in which she was then engaged. These allegations of the petition are denied by the administrator. The material facts are undisputed. . . . John C. Ricketts, the maker of the note, was the grandfather of the plaintiff. Early in May—presumably on the day the note bears date—he called on her at the store where she was working. What transpired between them is thus described by Mr. Flodene, one of the plaintiff's witnesses: "A. Well, the old gentleman came in there one morning about nine o'clock, . . . and he unbuttoned his vest, and took out a piece of paper in the shape of a note; . . . and he says to Miss Scothorn, 'I have fixed out something that you have not got to work any more.' He says, none of my grandchildren work, and you don't have to. Q. Where was she? A. She took the piece of paper and kissed him, and kissed the old gentleman, and commenced to cry." It seems Miss Scothorn immediately notified her employer of her intention to quit work, and that she did soon after abandon her occupation. The mother of the plaintiff . . . testified that she had a conversation with her father, Mr. Ricketts, shortly after the note was executed, in which he informed her that he had given the note to the plaintiff to enable her to quit work; that none of his grandchildren worked, and he did not think she ought to. For something more than a year the plaintiff was without an occupation, but in September, 1892, with the consent of her grandfather, and by his assistance, she secured a position as bookkeeper. . . . On June 8, 1894, Mr. Ricketts died. He had paid one year's interest on the note, and a short time before his death expressed regret that he had not been able to pay the balance. In the summer or fall of 1892 he stated to his daughter, Mrs. Scothorn, that if he could sell his farm in Ohio he would pay the note out of the proceeds. He at no time repudiated the obligation.

We quite agree with counsel for the defendant that upon this evidence there was nothing to submit to the jury, and that a verdict should have been directed peremptorily for one of the parties. The testimony of Flodene and Mrs. Scothorn, taken together, conclusively establishes the fact that the note was not given in consideration of the plaintiff pursuing, or agreeing to pursue, any particular line of conduct. There was no promise on the part of the plaintiff to do, or refrain from doing, anything. Her right to the money promised in the note was not made to depend upon an abandonment of her employment with Mayer Bros., and future abstention from like service. Mr. Ricketts made no condition, requirement, or request. He exacted no quid pro quo. He gave the note as a gratuity, and looked for nothing in return. So far as the evidence discloses, it was his purpose to place the plaintiff in a position of independence, where she could work or remain idle, as she might choose. The abandonment of Miss Scothorn of her position as bookkeeper was altogether voluntary. It was not an act done in fulfillment of any contract obligation assumed when she accepted the note. The instrument in suit, being given without any valuable consideration, was nothing more than a promise to make a gift in the future of the sum of money therein named. Ordinarily, such promises are not enforceable, even when put in the form of a promissory note. But it has often been held that an action on a note given to a church, college, or other like institution, upon the faith of which money has been expended or obligations incurred, could not be successfully defended on the ground of a want of consideration. In this class of cases [involving promises to charities] the note in suit is nearly always spoken of as a gift or donation, but the decision is generally put on the ground that the expenditure of money or assumption of liability by the donee on the faith of the promise constitutes a valuable and sufficient consideration. It seems to us that the true reason is the preclusion of the defendant, under the doctrine of estoppel, to deny the consideration. . . .

. . . [I]s there an equitable estoppel which ought to preclude the defendant from alleging that the note in controversy is lacking in one of the essential elements of a valid contract? We think there is. An estoppel in pais is defined to be "a right arising from acts, admissions, or conduct which have induced a change of position in accordance with the real or apparent intention of the party against whom they are alleged." [A]s shown by the record before us, the plaintiff was a working girl, holding a position in which she earned a salary of $10 per week. Her grandfather, desiring to put her in a position of independence, gave her the note, accompanying it with the remark that his other grandchildren did not work, and that she would not be obliged to work any longer. In effect, he suggested that she might abandon her employment, and rely in the future upon the bounty which he promised. He doubtless desired that she should give up her occupation, but, whether he did or not, it is entirely certain that he contemplated such action on her part as a reasonable and probable consequence of his gift. Having intentionally influenced the plaintiff to alter her position for the worse on the faith of the note being paid when due, it would be grossly inequitable to permit the maker, or his executor, to resist payment on the ground that the promise was given without consideration. The petition charges the elements of an equitable estoppel, and the evidence conclusively establishes them. . . . The judgment is right, and is affirmed.

QUESTIONS

(1) It seems that Katie Scothorn's grandfather, like Willie Story's uncle, wanted something, perhaps some action. Are you satisfied that there was no bargain here?

(2) The court asserts that Katie Scothorn "alter[ed] her position for the worse." What do you understand the court to mean by its phrase "for the worse"? In a similar case, a grandfather's written promise of $17,000, given to enable a granddaughter to purchase a house available for that sum, was followed by the granddaughter's payment of $2,000 from her own savings for an extended "option contract" on the property. A Colorado court also applied "the equitable doctrine of estoppel," citing Ricketts v. Scothorn for the proposition that "a gift of the donor's own note may be sustained if the donee, in reliance on the note, has expended money or incurred liabilities which will, by legal necessity, cause loss or injury to the donee if the note is not paid." In re Estate of Bucci, 488 P.2d 216, 219 (Colo. Ct. App. 1971).

Prescott v. Jones

69 N.H. 305, 41 A. 352 (1898)

Defendant insurance agents had insured plaintiff's buildings for a year ending February 1. On January 23, they wrote plaintiff that they would renew the policy for another year on the same terms, "unless notified to the contrary." Plaintiff made no reply and defendants failed to renew the insurance. The buildings were destroyed by fire on March 1. Plaintiff brought suit alleging that he had understood the January 23 letter to be an agreement to insure, and that he relied on it, believing that a reply was unnecessary. A demurrer to plaintiff's complaint was entered below. *Held*, demurrer sustained. Defendants made an offer to insure, but there was no acceptance by plaintiff. An acceptance requires words or other overt action. As plaintiff neither paid the premium nor communicated a promise to do so, there was no acceptance and no contract. "Nor is there any estoppel against the defendants on the ground that the plaintiff relied upon their letter. . . . The letter was a representation only of a present intention or purpose on their part. 'It was not a statement of a fact or state of things actually existing, or past and executed, on which a party might reasonably rely as fixed and certain, and by which he might properly be guided in his conduct. . . . The intent of a party, however positive or fixed, concerning his future action, is necessarily uncertain as to its fulfillment, and must depend on contingencies, and be subject to be changed and modified by subsequent events and circumstances. . . . [The doctrine of estoppel] does not apply to such a representation. The reason on which the doctrine rests is that it would operate as a fraud if a party was allowed to aver and prove a fact to be contrary to that which he had previously stated to another for the purpose of inducing him to act and alter his condition. . . . But the reason wholly fails when the representation relates only to a present intention or purpose of a party, because, being in its nature uncertain, and liable to change, it could not properly form a basis or inducement upon which a party could reasonably adopt any fixed permanent course of action.' . . . To sum it up in a few words, the case presented is, in its legal aspects, one of a party seeking to reap where he had not sown, and to gather where he had not scattered." [This case, you will note, was decided the same year that the Nebraska court was delivering Ricketts v. Scothorn.]

NOTE: THE LIMITS OF EQUITABLE ESTOPPEL

It was noted earlier that equitable estoppel or estoppel in pais normally operates on representations of fact (see Note accompanying the *Acme Mills* case, supra p. 31). When equitable estoppel is applied, how would you describe the mechanics or "theory" of the doctrine? Courts commonly say that it "ordinarily is used defensively," to "prevent the assertion of an otherwise unequivocal right." E.g., Chrysler Credit Corp. v. Bert Cote's L/A Auto Sales, 707 A.2d 1311 (Me. 1998). The court in Prescott v. Jones was faithful to history in distinguishing promises of future action from factual representations about the past or present, and in limiting equitable estoppel to the latter. We shall see more of that distinction in the materials ahead. It is not too early to begin to think about how a "statement of fact" differs from a "statement of intention," and why such a distinction should matter.

Allegheny College v. National Chautauqua County Bank

Court of Appeals of New York, 1927.
246 N.Y. 369, 159 N.E. 173.

CARDOZO, C.J. The plaintiff, Allegheny College, is an institution of liberal learning at Meadville, Pennsylvania. In June 1921, a "drive" was in progress to secure for it an additional endowment of $1,250,000. An appeal to contribute to this fund was made to Mary Yates Johnston of Jamestown, New York. In response thereto, she signed and delivered . . . the following writing:

"Estate Pledge,
"Allegheny College Second Century Endowment
"Jamestown, N.Y., June 15, 1921.

"In consideration of my interest in Christian Education, and in consideration of others subscribing, I hereby subscribe and will pay to the order [of] Allegheny College . . . the sum of Five Thousand Dollars; $5,000.

"This obligation shall become due thirty days after my death, and I hereby instruct my Executor, or Administrator, to pay the same out of my estate. This pledge shall bear interest at the rate of . . . per cent per annum, payable annually, from . . . till paid. The proceeds of this obligation shall be added to the Endowment of said Institution, or expended in accordance with instructions on reverse side of this pledge.

(	"Name	Mary Yates Johnston,
(	"Address	306 East 6th Street.
(		"Jamestown, N.Y.
(	"Dayton E. McClain	Witness
(	"T.R. Courtis	Witness"

On the reverse side of the writing is the following indorsement: "In loving memory this gift shall be known as the Mary Yates Johnston Memorial Fund, the proceeds from which shall be used to educate students preparing for the Ministry. . . . This pledge shall be valid only on the condition that the provisions of my Will, now extant, shall be first met. Mary Yates Johnston."

The subscription was not payable by its terms until thirty days after the death of the promisor. The sum of $1,000 was paid, however, upon account in December, 1923, while the promisor was alive. The college set the money aside to be held as a scholarship fund for the benefit of students preparing for the ministry. Later, in July, 1924, the promisor gave notice to the college that she repudiated the promise. Upon the expiration of thirty days following her death, this action was brought against the executor of her will to recover the unpaid balance.

The law of charitable subscriptions has been a prolific source of controversy in this State and elsewhere. We have held that a promise of that order is unenforceable like any other if made without consideration. . . . On the other hand, though professing to apply to such subscriptions the general law of contract, we have found consideration present where the general law of contract, at least as then declared, would have said that it was absent. . . .

A classic form of statement identifies consideration with detriment to the promisee sustained by virtue of the promise. Hamer v. Sidway, 124 N.Y. 538, 27 N.E. 256. . . . So compendious a formula is little more than a half truth. There is need of many a supplementary gloss before the outline can be so filled in as to depict the classic doctrine. "The promise and the consideration must purport to be the motive each for the other, in whole or at least in part. It is not enough that the promise induces the detriment or that the detriment induces the promise if the other half is wanting," Wisconsin & Mich. Ry. Co. v. Powers, 191 U.S. 379, 386. . . . If A promises B to make him a gift, consideration may be lacking, though B has renounced other opportunities for betterment in the faith that the promise will be kept.

BENJAMIN N. CARDOZO
1870–1938

The half truths of one generation tend at times to perpetuate themselves in the law as the whole truths of another, when constant repetition brings it about that qualifications, taken once for granted, are disregarded or forgotten. The doctrine of consideration has not escaped the common lot. As far back as 1881, Judge Holmes in his lectures on the Common Law (p. 292), separated the detriment which is merely a consequence of the promise from the detriment, which is in truth the motive or inducement, and yet added that the courts "have gone far in obliterating this distinction." The tendency toward effacement has not lessened with the years. On the contrary, there has grown up of recent days a doctrine that a substitute for consideration or an exception to its ordinary requirements can be found in what is styled "a promissory estoppel" (Williston, Contracts, §§ 139, 116). Whether the exception has made its way in this State to such an extent as to permit us to say that the general law of consideration has been modified accordingly, we do not now attempt to say. Cases such as Siegel v. Spear & Co., 234 N.Y. 479, 138 N.E. 414, and DeCicco v. Schweizer, 221 N.Y. 431, 117 N.E. 807, may be signposts on the road. Certain, at least, it is that we have adopted the doctrine of promissory estoppel as the equivalent of consideration in connection with our law of charitable subscriptions. So long as those decisions stand, the question is not merely whether the enforcement of a charitable subscription can be squared with the doctrine of consideration in all its ancient rigor. The question may also be whether it can be squared with the doctrine of consideration as qualified by the doctrine of promissory estoppel.

We have said that the cases in this State have recognized this exception, if exception it is thought to be. Thus, in Barnes v. Perine, 12 N.Y. 18, the subscription was made without request, express or implied, that the church do anything on the faith of it. Later, the church did incur expense to the knowledge of the promisor, and in the reasonable belief that the promise would be kept. We held the promise binding, though consideration there was none except upon the theory of a promissory estoppel. . . . So in Roberts v. Cobb, 103 N.Y. 600, 9 N.E. 500, and Keuka College v. Ray, 167 N.Y. 96, 60 N.E. 325, the bounds of consideration as fixed by the old doctrine were subjected to a like expansion. Very likely, conceptions of public policy have shaped, more or less subconsciously, the rulings thus made. Judges have been affected by the thought that "defences of that character" are "breaches of faith toward the public, and especially toward those engaged in the same enterprise, and an unwarrantable disappointment of the reasonable expectations of those interested." W.F. Allen, J., in Barnes v. Perine, supra, [at] 24. . . . The result speaks for itself irrespective of the motive. Decisions which have stood so long, and which are supported by so many considerations of public policy and reason, will not be overruled to save the symmetry of a concept which itself came into our law, not so much from any reasoned conviction of its justice, as from historical accidents of practice and procedure (8 Holdsworth, History of English Law, 7 et seq.). The concept survives as one of the distinctive features of our legal system. We have no thought to suggest that it is obsolete or on the way to be abandoned. As in the case of other concepts, however, the pressure of exceptions has led to irregularities of form.

It is in this background of precedent that we are to view the problem now before us. The background helps to an understanding of the implications inherent in subscription and acceptance. This is so though we may find in the end that without recourse to the innovation of promissory estoppel the transaction can be fitted within the mould of consideration as established by tradition.

The promisor wished to have a memorial to perpetuate her name. She imposed a condition that the "gift" should "be known as the Mary Yates Johnston Memorial Fund." The moment that the college accepted $1,000 as a payment on account, there was an assumption of a duty to do whatever acts were customary or reasonably necessary to maintain the memorial fairly and justly in the spirit of its creation. The college could not accept the money, and hold itself free thereafter from personal responsibility to give effect to the condition. . . . More is involved in the receipt of such a fund than a mere acceptance of money to be held to a corporate use. . . . The purpose of the founder would be unfairly thwarted or at least inadequately served if the college failed to communicate to the world . . . the title of the memorial. By implication it undertook, when it accepted a portion of the "gift," that in its circulars of information and in other customary ways, when making announcement of this scholarship, it would couple with the announcement the name of the donor. The donor was not at liberty to gain the benefit of such an undertaking upon the payment of a part and disappoint the expectation that there would be payment of the residue. If the college had stated after receiving $1,000 upon account of the subscription that it would apply the money to the prescribed use, but that in its circulars of information and when responding to prospective applicants it would deal with the fund as an anonymous donation, there is little doubt that the subscriber would have been at liberty to treat this statement as the repudiation of a duty impliedly assumed, a repudiation justifying a refusal to make payments in the future. Obligation in such circumstances is correlative and mutual. A case much in point is New Jersey Hospital v. Wright, 95 N.J.L. 462, 113 A. 144, where a subscription for the maintenance of a bed in a hospital was held to be enforceable by virtue of an implied promise by the hospital that the bed should be maintained in the name of the subscriber. . . . A parallel situation might arise upon the endowment of a chair or a fellowship in a university by the aid of annual payments with the condition that it should commemorate the name of the founder or that of a member of his family. The university would fail to live up to the fair meaning of its promise if it were to publish in its circulars of information and elsewhere the existence of a chair or a fellowship in the prescribed subject, and omit the benefactor's name. A duty to act in ways beneficial to the promisor and beyond the application of the fund to the mere uses of the trust would be cast upon the promisee by the acceptance of the money. We do not need to measure the extent either of benefit to the promisor or of detriment to the promisee implicit in this duty. "If a person chooses to make an extravagant promise for an inadequate consideration it is his own affair" (8 Holdsworth, History of English Law, p. 17). It was long ago said that "when a thing is to be done by the plaintiff, be it never so small, this is a sufficient consideration to ground an action" [Sturlyn v. Albany, 1587, Cro.Eliz. 67]. The longing for posthumous remembrance is an emotion not so weak as to justify us in saying that its gratification is a negligible good.

We think the duty assumed by the plaintiff to perpetuate the name of the founder of the memorial is sufficient in itself to give validity to the subscription within the rules that define consideration for a promise of that order. When the promisee subjected itself to such a duty at the implied request of the promisor, the result was the creation of a bilateral agreement. Williston, Contracts, §§ 60–a, 68, 90, 370. . . . There was a promise on the one side and on the other a return promise, made, it is true, by implication, but expressing an obligation that had been exacted as a condition of the payment. A bilateral agreement may exist though one of the mutual promises be a promise "implied in fact," an inference from conduct as opposed to an inference from words. . . . We think the fair inference to be drawn from the acceptance of a payment on account of the subscription is a promise by the college to do what may be necessary on its part to make the scholarship effective. . . . Moreover, the time to affix her name to the memorial will not arrive until the entire fund has been collected. The college may thus thwart the purpose of the payment on account if at liberty to reject a tender of the residue. It is no answer to say that a duty would then arise to make restitution of the money. If such a duty may be imposed, the only reason for its existence must be that there is then a failure of "consideration." To say that there is a failure of consideration is to concede that a consideration has been promised since otherwise it could not fail. No doubt there are times and situations in which limitations laid upon a promisee in connection with the use of what is paid by a subscriber lack the quality of a consideration, and are to be classed merely as conditions (Williston, Contracts, § 112; Page, Contracts, § 523). "It is often difficult to determine whether words of condition in a promise indicate a request for consideration or state a mere condition in a gratuitous promise. An aid, though not a conclusive test in determining which construction of the promise is more reasonable is an inquiry whether the happening of the condition will be a benefit to the promisor. If so, it is a fair inference that the happening was requested as a consideration" (Williston, supra, § 112).[4] Such must be the meaning of this transaction unless we are prepared to hold that the college may keep the payment on account, and thereafter nullify the scholarship which is to preserve the memory of the subscriber. The fair implication to be gathered from the whole transaction is assent to the condition and the assumption of a duty to go forward with performance. . . . The subscriber does not say: I hand you $1,000, and you may make up your mind later, after my death, whether you will undertake to commemorate my name. What she says in effect is this: I hand you $1,000, and if you are unwilling to commemorate me, the time to speak is now.

The conclusion thus reached makes it needless to consider whether, aside from the feature of a memorial, a promissory estoppel may result from the assumption of a duty to apply the fund, so far as already paid, to special purposes not mandatory under the provisions of the college

[4] [Professor Williston preceded the quoted passage with an illustration that became quite famous in legal education. The illustration, known as the "tramp case," is as follows: "If a benevolent man says to a tramp: 'If you go around the corner to the clothing shop there, you may purchase an overcoat on my credit,' no reasonable person would understand that the short walk was requested as the consideration for the promise, but that in the event of the tramp going to the shop the promisor would make him a gift. Yet the walk to the shop is in its nature capable of being consideration. It is a legal detriment to the tramp to make the walk, and the only reason why the walk is not consideration is because on a reasonable construction it must be held that the walk was not requested as the price of the promise, but was merely a condition of a gratuitous promise."—Eds.]

charter (the support and education of students preparing for the ministry), an assumption induced by the belief that other payments sufficient in amount to make the scholarship effective would be added to the fund thereafter upon the death of the subscriber. . . .

The judgment of the Appellate Division and that of the Trial Term should be reversed, and judgment ordered for the plaintiff as prayed for in the complaint, with costs in all courts.

KELLOGG, J. (dissenting). The Chief Judge finds in the expression "In loving memory this gift shall be known as the Mary Yates Johnston Memorial Fund" an offer . . . to contract with Allegheny College. The expression makes no such appeal to me. Allegheny College was not requested to perform any act through which the sum offered might bear the title by which the offeror states that it shall be known. The sum offered was termed a "gift" by the offeror. . . . I can see no reason why we should strain ourselves to make it, not a gift, but a trade. . . . To me the words used merely expressed an expectation or wish on the part of the donor and failed to exact the return of an adequate consideration. But if an offer indeed was present, then clearly it was an offer to enter into a unilateral contract. The offeror was to be bound provided the offeree performed such acts as might be necessary to make the gift offered become known under the proposed name. This is evidently the thought of the Chief Judge, for he says: "She imposed a condition that the 'gift' should be known as the Mary Yates Johnston Memorial Fund." In other words, she proposed to exchange her offer of a donation in return for acts to be performed. Even so there was never any acceptance of the offer and, therefore, no contract, for the acts requested have never been performed. The gift has never been made known as demanded. Indeed, the requested acts, under the very terms of the assumed offer, could never have been performed at a time to convert the offer into a promise. This is so for the reason that the donation was not to take effect until after the death of the donor, and by her death her offer was withdrawn. (Williston on Contracts, § 62.) Clearly, although a promise of the college to make the gift known, as requested, may be implied, that promise was not the acceptance of an offer which gave rise to a contract. The donor stipulated for acts, not promises. "In order to make a bargain it is necessary that the acceptor shall give in return for the offer or the promise exactly the consideration which the offeror requests. If an act is requested, that very act and no other must be given. If a promise is requested, that promise must be made absolutely and unqualifiedly." (Williston on Contracts, § 73). "It does not follow that an offer becomes a promise because it is accepted; it may be, and frequently is, conditional, and then it does not become a promise until the conditions are satisfied; and in case of offers for a consideration, the performance of the consideration is always deemed a condition." (Langdell, Summary of the Law of Contracts, § 4.) It seems clear to me that there was here no offer, no acceptance of an offer, and no contract. Neither do I agree with the Chief Judge that this court "found consideration present where the general law of contract at least as then declared, would have said that it was absent" in the cases of Barnes v. Perine, 12 N.Y. 18 [and] Keuka College v. Ray, 167 N.Y. 96. In the Keuka College case an offer to contract, in consideration of the performance of certain acts by the offeree, was converted into a promise by the actual performance of those acts. This form of contract has been known to the law from time immemorial (Langdell, § 46) and for at least a century longer than the other type, a bilateral contract. (Williston, § 13.) It may be that the basis of the decision in Barnes v. Perine was the same as in the Keuka College case. . . . However, even if the basis of the decisions be a so-called "promissory estoppel," nevertheless they initiated no new doctrine. A so-called "promissory estoppel," although not so termed, was held sufficient by Lord Mansfield and his fellow judges as far back as the year 1765. Pillans v. Van Mierop, 3 Burr. 1663. Such a doctrine may be an anomaly; it is not a novelty. Therefore, I can see no ground for the suggestion that the ancient rule which makes consideration necessary to the formation of every contract is in danger of effacement through any decisions of this court. To me that is a cause for gratulation rather than regret. However, the discussion may be beside the mark, for I do not understand that the holding about to be made in this case is other than a holding that consideration was given to convert the offer into a promise. With that result I cannot agree and, accordingly, must dissent.

POUND, CRANE, LEHMAN and O'BRIEN, JJ., concur with CARDOZO, C.J.; KELLOGG, J., dissents in opinion, in which ANDREWS, J., concurs.

Konefsky, How to Read, or at Least Not Misread, Cardozo in the *Allegheny College* Case

36 Buffalo L. Rev. 645, 683–687 (1988)

"Exactly what was the problem Cardozo faced in this case? Litigation is easiest when strong facts mesh with firm law, but a good lawyer can make do with either strong facts or firm law. At first blush, Cardozo had neither. . . . [I]f anything was clear about classical contract law, it was that donative promises were unenforceable. . . .

"[Hamer v. Sidway] was hardly a secure precedent around which a great edifice had been erected. Indeed, it was more of a lighthouse than a castle. And promissory estoppel was hardly developed beyond the most classic of charitable subscription cases. With facts as weak as in *Allegheny College*, it would have been difficult for most judges to move the doctrine along in the direction that Cardozo wished. Normally, strong facts drag the doctrine with them. Yet, here again Cardozo's craft shows how much can be done with just a few raw materials, for he manages to push forward simultaneously on both doctrinal fronts. Simply by using *Hamer*, drawing a few inferences about the nature of reasonable conduct, and turning a piece of Holmes's objective theory on its head to create liability rather than limit it, Cardozo was able both to reinforce *Hamer* as a precedent and suggest a new and at the same time familiar way of thinking about what might be consideration. . . .

"By positioning, if only in dictum, promissory estoppel not as an exception to consideration doctrine, but squarely within it, Cardozo opened the possibility (though never realized by him or his court) that in the next case promissory estoppel could be found in a commercial circumstance. Bargain theory was used to make all doctrinal moves appear as mainstream as possible. To make such gains, in a two-front war with such poor troops on such unpromising terrain, bordered on the inspired.

"What are we left with at the end of this opinion? . . . [W]hatever consideration is, it is, at the least, an expansive, flexible and adaptable doctrine. . . . [A]s evidence of that insight, the concept of promissory estoppel is introduced, not as an exception to consideration doctrine, but as a continuation of the process of enlarging it. In other words, promissory estoppel is used informatively, as an historical lesson, and instrumentally, as a means to expand consideration."

Siegel v. Spear & Co.

234 N.Y. 479, 138 N.E. 414 (1923)

Decided four years before *Allegheny College*, this case was one of the "signposts on the road" identified by Judge Cardozo. Siegel had purchased furniture from Spear & Co., giving a mortgage to secure payment of the price and a promise not to remove the furniture from his New York apartment until it was paid for. Desiring to leave the city for the summer months, Siegel visited Spear's credit officer, McGrath, to discuss storing the furniture. McGrath agreed to "keep it for him free of charge." Siegel alleged that these arrangements included a promise by McGrath to insure the furniture for Siegel's benefit, made in this way: "At that time he said, 'You had better transfer your insurance policy over to our warehouse.' I said 'I haven't any insurance. I never thought of taking it out. . . .' But I said: 'Before the furniture comes down I will have my insurance man, who insures my life, have the furniture insured and transferred over to your place.' He said, 'That won't be necessary to get that from him; I will do it for you; it will be a good deal cheaper; I handle lots of insurance; when you get the next bill—you can send a check for that with the next installment.'" Siegel delivered the furniture to Spear in May. A month later it was destroyed by fire. No insurance had been purchased. Siegel sued Spear for his loss, recovered judgment below, and preserved his victory in the Court of Appeals against the claim that McGrath's promise lacked consideration. That court (including Cardozo) proceeded in this way:

"[T]here was in the nature of the case a consideration. . . . It is, of course, a fact that the defendant undertook to store the plaintiff's property without any compensation. The fact that it had a chattel mortgage [on the property] did not affect its relationship as a bailee without pay. Under these circumstances it was not liable for the destruction of the goods by fire unless due to its gross neglect. . . . There is no such element in this case.

"But if in connection with taking the goods McGrath also voluntarily undertook to procure insurance for the plaintiff's benefit, the promise was part of the whole transaction and was linked up with the gratuitous bailment. The bailee . . . was then under as much of an obligation to procure insurance as he was to take care of the goods.

"When McGrath stated that he would insure the furniture it was still in the plaintiff's possession. It was after his statements and promises that the plaintiff sent the furniture to the storehouse. The defendant or McGrath entered upon the execution of the trust. It is in this particular that this case differs from Thorne v. Deas (4 Johns. 84, 99) so much relied upon by the defendant. In that case A and B were joint owners of a vessel. A voluntarily undertook to get the vessel insured but neglected to do so. The vessel having been lost at sea it was held that no action would lie against A for the nonperformance of his promise, although B had relied upon that promise to his loss. It was said that there was no consideration for the promise. In that case there was the mere naked promise of A that he would insure the vessel. B parted with nothing to A. He gave up possession of none of his property to A, nor of any interest in his vessel. The case would have been decided differently, no doubt, if he had. As Chancellor Kent said in referring to the earlier cases: 'There was no dispute or doubt, but that an action upon the case lay for a misfeasance, in the breach of a trust undertaken voluntarily.' . . .

"Where one had gratuitously undertaken to carry the money of a bailor to a certain place and deliver it to another and after receiving the money the bailee gave it to a neighbor who undertook to make delivery and lost it, it was held that the bailee had violated his trust in handling the money, that he was guilty of gross negligence in not fulfilling the terms of the bailment. . . .

"From this aspect of the case we think there was a consideration for the agreement to insure. This renders it unnecessary to determine whether the plaintiff in refraining from insuring through his own agent at the suggestion of McGrath surrendered any right which would furnish a consideration for McGrath's promise.

"I find that Thorne v. Deas (supra) has been seldom cited upon this question of consideration and whether or not we would feel bound to follow it today must be left open until the question comes properly before us."

NOTE: THE EMERGENCE OF PROMISSORY ESTOPPEL

A decade after *Siegel*, a lower New York court, faced with another gratuitous promise respecting insurance (a promise to file an insured's proofs of loss in a timely manner), sought to reconcile the relevant New York precedents. It concluded: "The Court of Appeals having, in [*Siegel*], declined to overrule Thorne v. Deas, and having, in [*Allegheny College*], extended the doctrine of promissory estoppel only to the law relating to charitable subscriptions, we think we should go no further." Thorne v. Deas was therefore held controlling where defendant was at most guilty of nonfeasance. Comfort v. McCorkle, 149 Misc. 826, 268 N.Y.S. 192 (N.Y. Sup. Ct. 1933). It should be noted that, during this period, courts elsewhere were applying promissory estoppel (and § 90 of the first Restatement), not the misfeasance-nonfeasance test, when gratuitous promises to insure were found to have induced serious reliance. E.g., Lusk-Harbison-Jones, Inc. v. Universal Credit Co., 164 Miss. 693, 145 So. 623 (1933).

I. & I. Holding Corp. v. Gainsburg

276 N.Y. 427,12 N.E.2d 532 (1938)

Defendant Gainsburg signed a pledge to pay $5,000 in four annual installments to the Beth Israel Hospital Ass'n, "to aid and assist the . . . Ass'n in its humanitarian work and in consideration of others contributing to the same purposes." Beth Israel assigned its rights to plaintiff, who sued on the pledge alleging that "the said Beth Israel Hospital Ass'n proceeded in its humanitarian work, obtained other like subscriptions, expended large sums of money and incurred large liabilities." *Held*, the complaint stated a cause of action. Under these allegations, evidence could be admitted to prove that the subscription agreement was an offer of a unilateral contract binding when acted on. An invitation or request to perform the services need not be expressed, it can be implied. It is true that court decisions sustaining subscriptions for charitable purposes are subject to criticism "from a legalistic standpoint," but they have been enforced for a long time. It is not necessary to base the decision on promissory estoppel. It is enough that a request or invitation to the promisee to go on with its work can be implied.

LEHMAN, J., dissented, urging that there must be allegation and proof that the promise constituted a request which induced the promisee to promise or perform some act that it would not have promised or performed except for the inducement. "[Plaintiff] must prove that [it] changed its position . . . because of the promise, or—if we accept the doctrine of promissory estoppel—as a consequence of the promise. . . . Mere continuance of its charitable work as it might have done even if no promise had been made does not constitute consideration for the promise or give rise to a promissory estoppel."

Restatement of Contracts, Second

§ 90. Promise Reasonably Inducing Action or Forbearance

(1) A promise which the promisor should reasonably expect to induce action or forbearance on the part of the promisee or a third person and which does induce such action or forbearance is binding if injustice can be avoided only by enforcement of the promise. The remedy granted for breach may be limited as justice requires.

(2) A charitable subscription or a marriage settlement is binding under Subsection (1) without proof that the promise induced action or forbearance.

Salsbury v. Northwestern Bell Tel. Co.

221 N.W.2d 609 (Iowa 1974)

Defendant by letter promised to contribute $15,000 to a newly-formed college. The college failed after a brief period of operation, and defendant did not pay its pledge. Iowa's highest court held the promise enforceable without proof of detrimental reliance, reasoning that a requirement of evidence of reliance might result in the enforcement of fewer charitable promises. After criticizing cases that enforce charitable subscriptions "only on a fictional finding of consideration," the court rested on this ground: "Restatement of Contracts, Second, includes a new subparagraph, § 90(2), [providing that] 'A charitable subscription or a marriage settlement is binding . . . without proof that the promise induced action or forbearance.' We believe public policy supports this view. . . . It is true some fund raising campaigns are not conducted on a plan which calls for subscriptions to be binding. In such cases we do not hesitate to hold them not binding. . . . However, where a subscription is unequivocal the pledgor should be made to keep his word."

NOTE: PROMISSORY ESTOPPEL, CHARITABLE GIFTS, AND RELIANCE

In Congregation Kadimah Toras-Moshe v. DeLeo, supra p. 248, the court required consideration or reliance for enforcement of gift promises to charities. Moreover, in portions of the opinion not reproduced earlier, the *DeLeo* court (1) rejected plaintiff's claim that the Massachusetts decisions on charitable subscriptions "require[ ] so little consideration or reliance that, in practice, none is required," and (2) bypassed plaintiff's invitation to adopt Rest.2d § 90(2), concluding that this provision, when read in the light of its official comment and the language of § 90(1), means that consideration or reliance are not "absolute requirements" but remain "relevant considerations." The court then proceeded to find "no injustice" in refusing to enforce the decedent's promise of $25,000, finding it "entirely unsupported" by either consideration or reliance. 405 Mass. at 368, 540 N.E.2d at 693–694. The promise in *DeLeo* was oral, not in writing. Look back at the opinion to see what, if anything, the court might have done differently had consideration or reliance been shown.

The few courts that have explicitly addressed the *Salsbury* decision seem to have rejected it. E.g., Arrowsmith v. Mercantile-Safe Deposit & Trust Co., 313 Md. 334, 545 A.2d 674 (1988) ("the legislative process is more finely and continuously attuned for the societal fact-finding and evaluating required for resolution of this exclusively public policy-based argument"). Nevertheless, it is commonly believed that charitable subscriptions are enforced in this country, and that courts that have enforced such promises on the basis of promissory estoppel have done so despite the absence of significant reliance.

Stewart v. Cendant Mobility Services Corp.

Supreme Court of Connecticut, 2003.
837 A.2d 736.

PALMER, J. This appeal arises out of an action brought by the plaintiff, Elizabeth M. Stewart, against the defendant, Cendant Mobility Services Corporation (Cendant), her former employer, for damages resulting from Cendant's allegedly wrongful termination of her employment. Following a trial, a jury returned a verdict in part for the plaintiff, finding in her favor on her claims of promissory estoppel and . . . and awarding her $850,000 on those claims. The trial court rendered judgment in accordance with the jury verdict from which Cendant appeals. . . .

The jury reasonably could have found the following facts. The plaintiff and her husband were employed by Cendant, which provides relocation services to domestic and international corporations and their employees. Among other things, Cendant assists its corporate clients in finding new homes for their relocating employees and in selling those employees' old homes. The plaintiff worked in the sales division and was considered one of the top producers in the relocation services industry. The plaintiff's husband was an executive in the operations division at Cendant.

In April 1998, Cendant underwent a major corporate reorganization. Soon thereafter, Cendant terminated the plaintiff's husband from employment. At the time of her husband's termination, the plaintiff held the position of vice president of sales.

Because the plaintiff believed that her husband was likely to seek employment with one of Cendant's competitors in the relocation services field, she spoke with James Simon, Cendant's executive vice president of sales and the plaintiff's immediate supervisor, about the matter shortly after her husband's termination. The plaintiff explained to Simon that she was concerned about how her employment with Cendant might be affected if her husband ultimately accepted a position with a competitor. Simon told the plaintiff that she should not be concerned and that her husband's reemployment in the relocation services business would have no bearing on her employment with Cendant. Simon further represented to the plaintiff that Kevin Kelleher, Cendant's president and chief executive officer, also wished to assure the plaintiff that she had no reason to be concerned about her continued status as a highly valued employee in the event that her husband were to become associated with a competitor. On the basis of Simon's assurances, the plaintiff continued in her position with Cendant and did not pursue other employment opportunities.

On or about March 5, 1999, Cendant learned that the plaintiff's husband was performing consulting services for a competing firm. Upon obtaining this information, Cendant reduced the plaintiff's duties and limited her interaction with clients. Cendant also requested that the plaintiff verbally agree to the provisions of a document drafted by Cendant that purported to delineate her obligations to Cendant in relation to her husband's work on behalf of any competitor of Cendant. On June 11, 1999, Cendant allegedly terminated the plaintiff's employment when she declined to agree to the provisions of that document.

Thereafter, the plaintiff commenced this action against Cendant. In count one of her complaint, the plaintiff alleged that her conversation with Simon gave rise to an oral contract of employment and that her discharge by Cendant constituted a breach of that contract. In count two, the plaintiff claimed that her discharge violated an implied covenant of good faith and fair dealing. In count three, which is predicated on a theory of promissory estoppel, the plaintiff alleged that she had relied to her detriment on Simon's promise that her employment with Cendant would not be affected adversely by her husband's probable future employment with a competitor. . . .

Following a trial, the jury returned a verdict in favor of Cendant with respect to the plaintiff's claims of breach of contract and breach of an implied covenant of good faith and fair dealing. The jury returned a verdict in favor of the plaintiff with respect to her claims of promissory estoppel and . . . awarded her $850,000. Cendant filed motions to set aside the verdict and for judgment notwithstanding the verdict on the promissory estoppel and negligent misrepresentation claims, contending that the evidence was insufficient to support the jury's verdict in favor of the plaintiff on those claims. The trial court denied Cendant's postverdict motions and rendered judgment in accordance with the jury's verdict, from which Cendant appealed.

On appeal, Cendant challenges the trial court's denial of its motions to set aside the verdict and for judgment notwithstanding the verdict. Cendant renews its contention that the evidence was insufficient to support the jury's verdict with respect to the plaintiff's promissory estoppel claim. Cendant's contention is essentially twofold. First, Cendant claims that its purported promise to the plaintiff lacked the requisite clarity and definiteness necessary to establish promissory estoppel. Second, Cendant claims that the plaintiff failed to present evidence sufficient to establish that she had relied to her detriment on any such promise. We reject both of these claims and, therefore, affirm the judgment of the trial court inasmuch as the jury award of $850,000 is sustainable on the basis of the plaintiff's promissory estoppel claim. . . .

Cendant first contends that the jury reasonably could not have found that Simon's representations to the plaintiff were sufficiently clear and definite to constitute a promise for purposes of a claim of promissory estoppel. We disagree.

The following additional evidence and procedural history are necessary to our resolution of this issue. On direct examination, the plaintiff testified that, after her husband was fired, she became concerned that his termination and likely reemployment in the relocation services industry adversely would affect her employment with Cendant. The plaintiff testified that she "specifically asked [Simon] what would happen [to her] if [her husband competed] in the industry." According to the plaintiff, Simon replied that "he had absolutely no concerns about [her husband] entering the marketplace." The plaintiff also testified that Simon told her that "he had tremendous respect for both [the plaintiff] and [the plaintiff's husband and] that [they] had a lot of integrity." The plaintiff testified further that Simon told her that "[h]e had trust and faith in [her] and in [the plaintiff's husband] and he knew that [they] would be able to keep [their] lives separate and [that] he had absolutely no concerns about [her husband] entering the marketplace." According to the plaintiff, Simon "said that he would talk to [Kelleher] on her behalf . . . [and] assured [her] that this was not going to be a problem and that [she] was a highly valued employee and there was nothing to worry about."

The plaintiff further explained that Simon thereafter reported to her that "he had spoken to [Kelleher] about [her] concerns and that [Kelleher] wanted [Simon] to assure [her] that [she] was very highly valued, that [she] was an integral part of the company, [that] he had tremendous respect for [her] integrity and [that] there were no problems whatsoever with [the plaintiff] continuing the job in the event [that her husband] competed." On cross-examination, the plaintiff acknowledged that when she and Simon spoke, they were discussing a hypothetical future occurrence because she was not certain whether her husband would join another relocation services company. The plaintiff further testified on cross-examination that she did not believe that she was negotiating an employment contract when she spoke with Simon.

At the conclusion of the court's instructions to the jury, the jury was provided with a special verdict form containing interrogatories relating to each of the plaintiff's claims. With respect to the plaintiff's breach of contract claim, the jury was asked, inter alia, whether it found that Cendant had "made a definite offer sufficient to form a contractual agreement with the plaintiff. . . ." The jury answered no. With respect to the plaintiff's promissory estoppel claim, the jury was asked, inter alia, whether it found that Cendant had "made a clear, definite promise to [the plaintiff] . . . upon which it should have expected she would rely. . . ." The jury responded in the affirmative.

The following legal principles govern our analysis of Cendant's claim. "Under the law of contract, a promise is generally not enforceable unless it is supported by consideration. . . . This court has recognized, however, the development of liability in contract for action induced by reliance upon a promise, despite the absence of common-law consideration normally required to bind a promisor. . . . Section 90 of the *Restatement [(Second) of Contracts]* states that under the doctrine of promissory estoppel [a] promise which the promisor should reasonably expect to induce action or forbearance on the part of the promisee or a third person and which does induce such action or forbearance is binding if injustice can be avoided only by enforcement of the promise. [1 Restatement (Second), Contracts § 90, p. 242 (1981).] A fundamental element of promissory estoppel, therefore, is the existence of a clear and definite promise which a promisor could reasonably have expected to induce reliance. Thus, a promisor is not liable to a promisee who has relied on a promise if, judged by an objective standard, he had no reason to expect any reliance at all." D'Ulisse-Cupo v. Board of Directors of Notre Dame High School, 202 Conn. 206, 213, 520 A.2d 217 (1987).

Although the promise must be clear and definite, it need not be the equivalent of an offer to enter into a contract because "[t]he prerequisite for . . . application [of the doctrine of promissory estoppel] is a *promise* and not a bargain and *not* an *offer*." (Emphasis added.) 3 A. Corbin, Contracts (Rev. Ed. 1996) § 8.9, p. 29; This, of course, is consistent with the principle that, although "[a]n offer is nearly always a promise"; 1 E. Farnsworth, Contracts (2d Ed. 1998) § 3.3, p. 188; all promises are not offers. See 1 Restatement (Second), supra, at § 24, comment (b), p. 72 ("[w]hether or not a proposal is a promise, it is not an offer unless it specifies a promise or performance by the offeree as the price or consideration to be given by him").

Additionally, the promise must reflect a present intent to commit as distinguished from a mere statement of intent to contract in the future. "[A] mere expression of intention, hope, desire, or opinion, which shows no real commitment, cannot be expected to induce reliance"; 3 A. Corbin, Contracts, supra, at § 8.9, pp. 29–30; and, therefore, is not sufficiently promissory. The requirements of clarity and definiteness are the determinative factors in deciding whether the statements are indeed expressions of commitment as opposed to expressions of intention, hope, desire or opinion. Finally, whether a representation rises to the level of a promise is generally a question of fact, to be determined in light of the circumstances under which the representation was made.

Applying the foregoing principles, we conclude that there was sufficient evidence to support the jury's finding that Simon's representations to the plaintiff were sufficiently clear and definite to constitute a promise that her employment with Cendant would not be affected adversely if her husband subsequently secured employment with a competing relocation services firm. The plaintiff testified that: (1) she had approached Simon because she was concerned that her husband's employment with a competitor would have a negative effect on her employment with Cendant; (2) she expressed that concern in plain terms to Simon; and (3) Simon responded in equally unambiguous terms, in his own capacity and on behalf of Kelleher, that the plaintiff had no need to worry because her husband's future employment with a competitor would pose "no problems whatsoever" for her. On the basis of this testimony, the jury reasonably could have found that Simon's representations to the plaintiff constituted a clear and definite promise that her position with Cendant would not be affected adversely if her husband were to secure employment with a competing firm.

Relying primarily on our decision in *D'Ulisse-Cupo,* Cendant contends that, under our law of promissory estoppel, all promises in the employer-employee context, to be actionable, must contain the standard material terms of a contract of employment and clearly reflect an intent by the promisor to undertake conventional contractual liability. In other words, Cendant contends that any such promise must contain all of the elements of an offer to enter into a contract. We conclude that our holding in *D'Ulisse-Cupo* is not so broad.

In *D'Ulisse-Cupo,* the plaintiff, Maria D'Ulisse-Cupo, brought an action against the board of directors (board) and principal of Notre Dame High School (school) in West Haven. The board declined to offer D'Ulisse-Cupo a new contract after her prior contract to teach at the school had expired. D'Ulisse-Cupo alleged that authorized representatives of the board had made certain representations to her prior to the expiration of her teaching contract that suggested that she would be offered a new contract. D'Ulisse-Cupo alleged further that she relied on those representations to her detriment.

We concluded that the "representations [did] not invoke a cause of action for promissory estoppel because they [were] neither sufficiently promissory nor sufficiently definite to support contractual liability." We explained that the "representations manifested no present intention on the part of the [board] to undertake immediate contractual obligations to [D'Ulisse-Cupo]"; and that "none of the representations contained any of the material terms that would be essential to an employment contract, such as terms regarding the duration and conditions of [D'Ulisse-Cupo's] employment . . . and her salary and fringe benefits." Finally, we concluded that, "[a]t most, the [board] made representations to [D'Ulisse-Cupo] concerning the expectation of a future contract, but . . . stopped short of making [D'Ulisse-Cupo] a definite promise of employment on which she could reasonably have relied."

Although we acknowledge that certain language in *D'Ulisse-Cupo* might suggest that, for purposes of a claim of promissory estoppel, the promise upon which the promisee relies must be no less specific and definite than an offer to enter into a contract, we reject Cendant's claim urging that interpretation. Our observations in *D'Ulisse-Cupo* that the representations did not contain the material terms of a new employment contract and otherwise did not reflect an intent by the board to undertake immediate contractual liability were necessary to our determination of whether, in circumstances involving an alleged promise to rehire a employee under contract, the representations constituted a promise to commit or mere expressions of a future intent to enter into a contract. In other words, because D'Ulisse-Cupo alleged that she had been promised a contract of employment, our consideration of whether the contract terms were part of that purported promise and whether the representations reflected an intention to bind the board to a future contract was central to our resolution of D'Ulisse-Cupo's claim that those representations were sufficiently clear and definite such that her reliance on them was reasonable. Thus, when *D'Ulisse-Cupo* is viewed in the context of the particular claim addressed in that case, it is apparent that the language upon which Cendant relies is properly understood as explaining why the representations regarding a future employment contract were insufficiently promissory and definite to be actionable, and not properly understood as indicating that, for purposes of the doctrine of promissory estoppel, any promise relating to employment must be the equivalent of an offer to enter into a contract.

Finally, the present case is readily distinguishable from *D'Ulisse-Cupo*. Although Simon's representations related to the plaintiff's employment, they were far more limited in scope than the representations at issue in *D'Ulisse-Cupo*. Simon promised the plaintiff only that her employment would not be affected adversely by her husband's future employment with a competitor of Cendant. The plaintiff otherwise remained an at-will employee subject to termination at Cendant's sole discretion. Consequently, the issue of whether Simon's representations were sufficiently clear and definite to constitute a promise upon which the plaintiff reasonably could have relied is significantly narrower than the issue that was presented in *D'Ulisse-Cupo,* namely, whether the representations of the representatives of the school board constituted a promise of an entirely new employment contract even when those representations did not contain terms and conditions that necessarily comprise any such contractual arrangement. . . .

The defendant next claims that the evidence was insufficient to establish that the plaintiff detrimentally relied on Simon's representations. We also reject this claim.

The following additional facts are necessary to our disposition of this claim. As we previously have noted, the plaintiff testified on direct examination that she had approached Simon because she wanted to know whether, in light of her husband's likely future employment with a competing relocation services firm, she should stay at Cendant or seek other opportunities within the industry. After Simon assured her that she would suffer no adverse consequences in the event that her husband were to accept employment with a competitor, the plaintiff decided to remain at Cendant and "did not pursue other employment opportunities. . . ." The plaintiff testified during cross-examination, however, that, if Simon had told her that her husband's employment with another relocation services firm would pose a problem, she was not sure "what [she] would have done." The plaintiff also testified that when Simon made his representations to her, she was not investigating other employment opportunities. Additionally, the plaintiff acknowledged that she was an at-will employee and, therefore, subject to discharge at any time.

The plaintiff also adduced evidence that she was one of a relatively small number of highly talented salespeople in the relocation services industry. Indeed, Kelleher testified that the plaintiff would be regarded as a "valued asset" both within Cendant and in the industry on the basis of her productivity. Simon testified that such salespeople have no difficulty finding employment in the relocation services field. According to Simon, salespeople with the plaintiff's credentials "can walk in virtually anywhere" and receive a job offer.

In addition, offers to top performers in the relocation services industry typically include a signing bonus equivalent to some or all of the value of the employee's "pipeline," the industry term for the estimated total commissions due a salesperson, at a specific point in time, on the basis of consummated sales for which the company has not yet been paid in full. Because salespeople do not receive pipeline commissions if they leave a company to join a competitor before the company is paid by the client, signing bonuses are used as a recruitment tool by relocation service companies to induce salespeople employed by other companies to forgo their pipeline commissions and join the recruiting company. Although there are numerous salespeople who, like the plaintiff, do not receive accrued but uncollected commissions, those salespeople, in contrast to salespeople who are recruited by a competitor, are not sufficiently marketable to command a signing bonus. Finally, evidence adduced at trial established that the approximate value of the plaintiff's pipeline when she allegedly was terminated was $812,700, a sum that she never was paid.

To succeed on a claim of promissory estoppel, the party seeking to invoke the doctrine must have relied on the other party's promise. That reliance, of course, may take the form of action or forbearance. Nevertheless, the asserted reliance, regardless of its form, must result in a detrimental change in the plaintiff's position. Thus, "[t]o 'rely,' in the law of promissory estoppel, is not merely to do something in response to the inducement offered by the promise. There must be a cost to the promisee of doing it." Cosgrove v. Bartolotta, 150 F.3d 729, 733 (7th Cir. 1998).

Moreover, "[i]f the claimed reliance consists of the promisee's forbearance rather than an affirmative action, proof that this forbearance was induced by the promise requires a showing that the promisee *could have* acted." (Emphasis added.) 1 E. Farnsworth, supra, at § 2.19, p. 164. Implicit in this principle is the requirement of proof that the plaintiff actually *would have acted* in the absence of the promise.

In the present case, the plaintiff claimed that she relied on Simon's representations by forgoing other employment opportunities that would have resulted in a signing bonus approximately equivalent to her pipeline. Cendant contends that the plaintiff failed to adduce sufficient evidence to establish that she: (1) could have obtained such other employment; (2) would have sought employment elsewhere if Simon had told her that her position at Cendant would be affected adversely if her husband accepted a position with a competing firm; and (3) was not harmed by continuing as an employee of Cendant even if she did so in reliance on Simon's representations. We disagree with each of these contentions.

First, with respect to Cendant's claim that the evidence was inadequate to establish that the plaintiff could have secured a sales position with another relocation services firm, Simon testified that talented salespeople in the relocation services industry—and it was undisputed that the plaintiff was such a salesperson—frequently obtained such positions. Although, as Cendant notes, the plaintiff, herself, testified that she was unaware that any of those positions were available at the time she would have been seeking such a position, the jury nevertheless reasonably could have found, on the basis of Simon's testimony, that the plaintiff likely could have secured such a position if she had sought to do so.

With respect to the issue of whether the plaintiff *would* have departed Cendant if she had not received Simon's assurances, the plaintiff testified that she approached Simon about her husband's likely future employment with a competitor because she needed to decide whether to stay with Cendant or to look for a position elsewhere. The plaintiff also indicated that she elected to stay at Cendant rather than to seek other employment because of Simon's representations that her position at Cendant would not be affected negatively in the event that her husband secured employment with a competing firm. Although the plaintiff also testified that she was unsure what she would have done if Simon had not made those assurances, it was within the province of the jury to resolve any possible inconsistencies in the plaintiff's testimony in a manner favorable to the plaintiff. Thus, the jury reasonably could have found that the plaintiff would have left Cendant if Simon had not assured her as he did.

Finally, Cendant contends that the plaintiff suffered no harm by opting not to seek employment elsewhere after she had spoken with Simon about her husband's likely future employment with a competitor. We disagree. In remaining at Cendant, the plaintiff not only abandoned any opportunity to secure a position with another relocation services company, she also forwent a signing bonus that the jury reasonably could have found approximated the value of her pipeline. Accordingly, we conclude that the evidence was sufficient to warrant the jury's finding that the plaintiff reasonably relied on Simon's representations to her financial detriment.

The judgment is affirmed. . . .

COMMENT: PROMISSORY ESTOPPEL DAMAGES

Consider whether the theory underlying promissory estoppel naturally leads to the award of expectation damages. Comment d to § 90 of the Restatement, Second, offers the following:

> A promise binding under this section is a contract, and full-scale enforcement by normal remedies is often appropriate. But the same factors which bear on whether any relief should be granted also bear on the character and extent of the remedy. . . . Unless there is unjust enrichment of the promisor, damages should not put the promisee in a better position than performance of the promise would have put him. In the case of a promise to make a gift it would rarely be proper to award consequential damages which would place a greater burden on the promisor than performance would have imposed.

The case of Osborn v. Commanche Cattle Indus., 545 P.2d 827 (Okla. Ct. App. 1975), involved a three-year contract for services, terminable by either party "at any time by giving 30 days advance notice." In a suit on the contract for lost profits, not in promissory estoppel, the court said:

> [The expectation] interest is given legal protection to achieve the paramount objective of putting the promisee injured by the breach in the position in which he would have been had the contract been performed. . . . But [the promisee] may not recover more than the amount he might have gained by full performance. We think that the only legally protectible expectation interest in the party to a contract terminable by either party upon notice is the prospect of profit over the length of the notice period. Since his assurance of performance never extends beyond the length of the notice period, neither does his prospect of net gain. And allowing him under such circumstances to recover the profit he purportedly could have gained over the maximum life of the contract would be contrary to the whole purpose of permitting recovery of lost profits. Accordingly, [plaintiff was entitled only] to an instruction permitting recovery of lost profits for the length of the notice period—or thirty days from [defendant's] breach.

One question, surely, is whether standard contract notions, such as the differences between, and the respective limitations on, expectation and reliance damages, should be taken into account in measuring relief under promissory estoppel. That doctrine, classified traditionally as contractual, provides nonetheless an alternative basis to consideration for the enforcement of a promise. And, as noted, the promissory estoppel claim is undeniably "equitable" in nature, whatever the relief sought (it could be solely an injunction) or the context in which it appears in any particular case.

In 1926, during the extensive discussion by the American Law Institute of the original § 90 of the Restatement of Contracts, there was much attention paid to a hypothetical case put by Professor Williston, the Reporter of the Restatement: Johnny says to his uncle, "I want to buy a Buick car"; Uncle says, "Well, I will give you $1000." The question was asked by Mr. Frederick Coudert whether, if Johnny then proceeded to buy a car for $500, Uncle would be liable for $1,000.

> *Mr. Williston:* If Johnny had done what he was expected to do, or is acting within the limits of his uncle's expectation, I think the uncle would be liable for $1000; but not otherwise.
>
> *Mr. Coudert:* In other words, substantial justice would require that uncle should be penalized in the sum of $500.
>
> *Mr. Williston:* Why do you say "penalized"? . . .
>
> *Mr. Coudert:* Because substantial justice there would require, it seems to me, that Johnny get his money for his car, but should he get his car and $500 more? I don't see. . . .
>
> Mr. Williston: Either the promise is binding or it is not. If the promise is binding it has to be enforced as it is made. As I said to Mr. Coudert, I could leave this whole thing to the subject of quasi contracts so that the promisee under the circumstances shall never recover on the promise but he shall recover such an amount as will fairly compensate him for any injury incurred; but it seems to me you have to take one leg or the other. You have either to say the promise is binding or you have to go on the theory of restoring the status quo. 4 A.L.I.Proc. 98–99, 103–104 (App. 1926).

These comments should be read against the further statement of Professor Williston, the Reporter (4 A.L.I. Proc. 91 (App. 1926)):

> The qualification is necessary, if injustice can be avoided only by enforcement of the promise. . . . In some cases, in many cases perhaps, it will be possible for the promisee, if he is induced to do some act or pay some money, to recover back what he has given or the value of what he has done. If the court can get out of the difficulty by restoring the status quo, there is no necessity of enforcing the promise, but if detriment has been incurred by the promisee of a definite and substantial character and the status quo cannot be restored, then the proposition is that the court should enforce the promise.

We shall see more of the issue of the appropriate measure of damages for reliance-based liabilities. At this stage, it is clear that there exists an abundance of remedial theories for invoking the factor of detrimental reliance in contract settings. Promissory estoppel, a contract doctrine, seems to be very much like—and to overlap with; indeed, descend from—equitable estoppel, a doctrine derived from tort. The distinguishing feature of equitable estoppel is a misrepresentation, factual and material (again, equitable estoppel is said not to create an "independent" cause of action, but to raise an "affirmative defense"). Yet, if the element of carelessness by the speaker is added, an action in tort for negligent misrepresentation will lie, and if the misrepresentation is intentional ("scienter") or made recklessly, an expanded tort of fraud covers much of the same territory. (W. Keeton, et al., Prosser & Keeton on the Law of Torts 725–770 (5th ed. 1984), contains a helpful sketch of these tort doctrines.) It is, it seems, not at all difficult to portray a single transaction as a breach of some type of contract and as a tort (to say nothing of unjust enrichment and restitution).

A question still debated is whether promissory estoppel, which § 90 defines as a contract (a "promise" is "binding" in stated circumstances), is to be treated as a tort doctrine for purposes of damages. If it is (and a fair number of courts have said as much), it seems only natural to limit any recovery to actual losses suffered in reliance—i.e., restore the injured party to the position it would have occupied had the promise not been made. The permissive language of the Restatement, Second revision of § 90 ("may be limited") quite clearly introduces into the damages decision a large dose of trial-court discretion. In exercising discretion, is it a good idea to separate gift promises from promises made in bargain settings?

A number of cases are examined in Becker, Promissory Estoppel Damages, 16 Hofstra L. Rev. 131 (1987), where the author concludes that, under promissory estoppel, expectation damages are generally available in both donative and commercial settings, and that, in most cases, the measure of relief (full enforcement or reliance loss) can be understood on the basis of traditional contract principles. The thesis that expectancy is in fact the routine measure of relief under § 90—because judges actually enforce promises rather than protect reliance in such cases—is argued in Edward Yorio & Steve Thel, The Promissory Basis of Section 90, 101 Yale L.J. 111 (1991). See also Daniel A. Farber & John A. Matheson, Beyond Promissory Estoppel: Contract Law and the "Invisible Handshake," 52 U. Chi. L. Rev. 903 (1985) (study of § 90 cases over decade 1975–1985, reporting only one-sixth of courts addressing extent of relief limited recovery to reliance damages). In a word, despite § 90's specially-written grant of power to award relief "as justice requires," courts remain divided on the recovery of expectation damages on a claim for promissory estoppel—especially, it seems, when the claim is for lost-profits damages. E.g., Creative Demos, Inc. v. Wal-Mart Stores, Inc., 142 F.3d 367, 369 (7th Cir. 1998) (declaring that "in most states" promissory estoppel does not support a claim for profits lost). Part of the difficulty in determining whether § 90 brings its own measure of damages comes from the familiar phenomenon that we explored in Chapter 1—that expectation damages and reliance damages are often proxies for one another and that often the best way to measure one is to use the other.

NOTE: RELIANCE ON CONTRACT ADJUSTMENTS

Many promissory estoppel cases arise after a contractual relationship typically has been established, and the rendering of performance has begun. One of the parties then promises to modify or eliminate a term of the contract, or, perhaps, to discharge the contract altogether. The rub is that the promise is unsupported by consideration, for, as we shall see, it is hornbook law that modifications of a valid agreement, to be enforceable, must be supported by consideration or a common-law substitute.

The case of Fried v. Fisher, 328 Pa. 497, 196 A. 39 (1938), provides an example. In late 1932, Fried entered into a four-year lease of a building to Fisher and Brill, partners in a florist business. About a year into the lease, Fisher decided to dissolve his partnership with Brill and get out of the florist business, in order to open a restaurant in another city. This was acceptable to Brill, who agreed to take over the lease. Fisher sought out Fried on two occasions, each time telling Fried of his plans and making clear his desire to be released from all obligation under the lease. Fried replied that he "was perfectly satisfied if they [Brill and his son] assumed the balance of the lease, . . . just forget about it," and that "I am satisfied to have Mr. Brill assume the lease, and if it is going to help you any to get started in business, I release you." Thereupon Fisher dissolved the partnership with Brill and opened a restaurant, and Brill continued the florist business on the leased premises. Brill defaulted about a year and a half later, and Fried commenced suit against both Fisher and Brill to enforce the lease. A jury verdict for Fisher was affirmed on appeal, the court holding that Fried's promise to release Fisher was fully enforceable and a complete defense. The court said:

> It is beyond the pale of argument that a promise by a creditor to release one of the partners of a debtor firm from liability for an obligation is, in the absence of qualifying facts, legally unenforceable for want of consideration. . . . The necessity of consideration to support a contract . . . still remains firmly entrenched as one of the fundamental principles of the common law. See opinion by Cardozo, C.J., in Allegheny College v. National Chautauqua County Bank, 246 N.Y. 369, 159 N.E. 173. But just as the law has consistently upheld the doctrine that, under given circumstances, a person may be estopped by his conduct, his statements, or even his silence, if another has thereby been induced to act to his detriment, so from the earliest times there was recognized the principle that an estoppel might similarly arise from the making of a promise, even though without consideration, if it was intended that the promise be relied upon and in fact it was relied upon, and a refusal to enforce it would be virtually to sanction the perpetration of fraud or result in other injustice. . . . In recent years there has been adopted the phrase "promissory estoppel," [which by its language] indicat[es] that the basis of the doctrine is not so much one of contract, with a substitute for consideration, as an application of the general principle of estoppel to certain situations. . . .
>
> Illustrative cases abound in the reports. . . . Its most frequent application has been to cases in which a person announces his intention of abandoning an existing right, and thereby leads another, relying thereon, to some action or forbearance. Such cases have sometimes been referred to as well-recognized exceptions to the general proposition that, in order to give rise to an estoppel, a representation must relate to an existing fact and not be merely an expression of opinion or a promise of future performance. . . .
>
> The facts in the present case constitute a situation to which [promissory estoppel] peculiarly applies, because they involve the announcement by plaintiff of the intended abandonment of his right to enforce Fisher's liability for the rent, knowing that such announcement would be relied upon by him to the extent of his em-

> barking upon a new business venture. All the safeguarding features thrown around the doctrine of promissory estoppel to prevent its too loose application—that the promise be one likely to induce action, that such action be of a definite and substantial character, that the circumstances be such that injustice can be avoided only by the enforcement of the promise—are here present. Plaintiff contends that it was not shown that Fisher suffered a loss in the restaurant business, but he did substantially change his position by entering into that business upon the faith of plaintiff's promise, and when, at the trial of the case, Fisher was questioned by his counsel on this point for the purpose of proving the consequences of his reliance upon plaintiff's promise, counsel for plaintiff objected, and his objections were—in our opinion improperly—sustained by the court. Having succeeded in ruling out this testimony, plaintiff cannot now contend that proof of the facts thus barred was vital to Fisher's defense.

In the passages last quoted, the court indicated that it would have been proper to receive evidence "for the purpose of proving the consequences of [Fisher's] reliance." If Fried had introduced evidence that Fisher's restaurant was an outstanding success, likely to make Fisher wealthy, should the promise to release Fisher have been enforced? More precisely, if detrimental reliance is an essential element of promissory estoppel, what happens when reliance does not work to the actor's detriment but is in fact beneficial?

In light of the multiple theories at work in the preceding materials (i.e., the different ways of defining the reliance principle), it seems only natural to ask whether Fried v. Fisher might have been decided on another ground. Was promissory estoppel the only doctrine available to the court? Consider the *Mahban* digest below, which also involves contract adjustments or modifications.

Mahban v. MGM Grand Hotels, Inc.

100 Nev. 593, 691 P.2d 421 (1984)

Defendant leased space in its hotel to plaintiff, who operated a retail shop in the hotel's "arcade" area. The lease contained a clause permitting either party to terminate if "the leased premises are damaged or destroyed to such an extent that they cannot be put into tenantable condition by Lessor within 180 days after such damage or destruction." On November 21, a fire damaged the hotel; either party could have invoked the destruction-of-premises provision. About ten weeks later, on January 30, plaintiff received from defendant's arcade manager a letter which read in part:

> I would like to let you know additionally, that sometime late in February, our target date to re-open should be finalized. I hope to be able to notify you at that time when you will be able to begin remodeling within the arcade area. All plans for reconstruction must be submitted for approval, in advance of any work beginning, to me at my office.

Plaintiff says he relied on this letter by ordering merchandise for restocking his shop. Then, on March 17, plaintiff received a second letter from defendant, notifying of defendant's termination of the lease pursuant to the destruction-of-premises clause. Plaintiff sued for damages for breach, urging that defendant had lost the contractual power to terminate. The trial court awarded defendant summary judgment, concluding that plaintiff "could not have reasonably relied on the [January 30th letter because it] contained no misrepresentation as to whether defendant intended to waive its contractual rights." *Held*, summary judgment was inappropriate. It appears the trial court relied solely on "waiver," which is "the intentional relinquishment of a known right," but plaintiff also asserts equitable estoppel. In some situations, "there is a potential" for both theories to afford relief; "[r]ights may themselves be waived by a lessor, or he may by his conduct become estopped to assert them." Here, defendant's letter "allows an inference of an intent . . . not to exercise its termination right." Further, the letter instructs plaintiff concerning reconstruction plans. "[Construction plans] are generally acquired only at a substantial expense to one who obtains them. Although the record is unclear as to whether plaintiff actually invested in plans, the letter can be read to have encouraged acts or evidenced intent inconsistent with termination of the lease." Accordingly, there are material questions of fact on both waiver and estoppel issues. Defendant's contention that equitable estoppel "is a defense, not a cause of action for money damages," is of no avail. "[T]he underlying action [here] sought damages for breach of the lease agreement. . . . [E]quitable estoppel has been raised as a bar to defendant's assertion of its [contract] right to terminate. . . . As applied here, estoppel is, therefore, essentially a defense to a defense, rather than a claim for relief." [The court's opinion makes no mention of promissory estoppel.]

NOTE: DEMARCATING THE DOMAIN OF PROMISSORY ESTOPPEL

The principle that only promises that are part of a bargained-for exchange are legally enforceable seems at first to be straightforward: Was there a bargain or not? Willie is entitled to $5,000 from his uncle's estate because he had struck a bargain. There was a quid pro quo. Bertha could not recover from her father's estate because there was never an actual bargain, just an interaction that mimicked the form of a bargain. As cases such as *Allegheny College* illustrate, however, the doctrine is malleable. The difference between a bargain and a promise subject to a condition is often elusive. There might be a vanishingly small difference between a promise to give a nephew money provided he behaves and a promise to give money to the nephew in exchange for his good behavior.

The boundaries of promissory estoppel, however, may prove as elusive. The court must first assess whether reliance on the promise was reasonable. Something an uncle casually promises his nephew in ordinary conversation is quite different from a promise announced at a formal celebration before assembled friends and family. Much turns on exactly what was said and under what circumstances.

The uncertainties do not stop there, however. Someone might make a statement about her future intentions, and it might foreseeably lead someone else to act upon it. But the statement may be only a truthful statement about the person's intentions, not an affirmative undertaking to engage in a particular act. The uncle may truthfully tell his nephew that he anticipates giving him $5,000 when he turns twenty-one. The uncle might also foresee that the nephew will rely on this statement, and it may be reasonable for the nephew to do so. But this does not mean that the uncle has made a promise. In the next two cases, Richard Posner, in many ways the heir to Oliver Wendell Holmes Jr., wrestles with the problem of identifying, quite apart from reliance, whether there was a promise sufficient to trigger liability for promissory estoppel.

Garwood Packaging, Inc. v. Allen & Co., Inc.

United States Court of Appeals, Seventh Circuit, 2004.
378 F.3d 698.

POSNER, CIRCUIT JUDGE. This is a diversity suit, governed by Indiana law, in which substantial damages are sought on the basis of promissory estoppel. The suit pits Garwood Packaging, Inc., which created a packaging system designed to increase the shelf life of fresh meat, and its two principals, Garwood and McNamara, against Allen & Company (an investment company) and a vice-president of Allen named Martin. We shall refer to the plaintiffs collectively as "GPI" and the defendants collectively as "Allen." . . .

GPI had flopped in marketing its food-packaging system and by 1993 had run up debts of $3 million and was broke. It engaged Martin to help find investors. After an initial search turned up nothing, Martin told GPI that Allen (Martin's employer, remember) would consider investing $2 million of its own money in GPI if another investor could be found who would make a comparable investment. The presence of the other investor would reduce the risk to Allen not only by augmenting GPI's assets but also by validating Allen's judgment that GPI might be salvageable, because it would show that someone else was also willing to bet a substantial sum of money on GPI's salvation. To further reduce its risk Allen decided to off-load half its projected $2 million investment on other investors.

Martin located a company named Hobart Corporation that was prepared to manufacture $2 million worth of GPI packaging machines in return for equity in the company. Negotiations with Hobart proved arduous, however. There were two sticking points: the amount of equity that Hobart would receive and the obtaining of releases from GPI's creditors. Hobart may have been concerned that unless the creditors released GPI the company would fail and Hobart wouldn't be able to sell the packaging systems that it manufactured. Or it may have feared that the creditors would assert liens in the systems. All that is clear is that Hobart insisted on releases. They were also important to the other investors whom Allen wanted to bring into the deal, the ones who would contribute half of Allen's offered $2 million.

Martin told Garwood and McNamara (GPI's principals) that he would see that the deal went through "come hell or high water." Eventually, however, Allen decided not to invest, the deal collapsed, and GPI was forced to declare bankruptcy. The reason for Allen's change of heart was that the investors who it thought had agreed to put up half of "Allen's" $2 million had gotten cold feet. When Allen withdrew from the deal, no contract had been signed and no agreement had been reached on how much stock either Allen or Hobart would receive in exchange for their contributions to GPI. Nor had releases been obtained from the creditors.

GPI's principal claim on appeal, and the only one we need to discuss (the others fall with it), is that Martin's unequivocal promise to see the deal through to completion bound Allen by the doctrine of promissory estoppel, which makes a promise that induces reasonable reliance legally enforceable. . . .

[R]easonable reliance is seen as nearly as good a reason for thinking there really was a promise as bargained-for reliance is. In many such cases, it is true, no promise was intended, or intended to be legally enforceable; in those cases the application of the doctrine penalizes the defendant for inducing the plaintiff to incur costs of reliance. The penalty is withheld if the reliance was unreasonable; for then the plaintiff's wound was self-inflicted—he should have known better than to rely.

A relevant though puzzling difference between breach of contract and promissory estoppel as grounds for legal relief is that while the promise relied on to trigger an estoppel must be definite in the sense of being clearly a promise and not just a statement of intentions, its terms need not be as clear as a contractual promise would have to be in order to be enforceable. . . .

But . . . the vaguer the alleged promise the less likely it is to be found to *be* a promise. And if it is *really* vague, the promisee would be imprudent to rely on it—he wouldn't know whether reliance was worthwhile. The broader principle, which the requirement that the promise be definite and at least minimally clear instantiates, is that the promisee's reliance must be reasonable; if it is not, then not only is he the gratuitous author of his own disappointment, but probably there wasn't really a promise, or at least a promise intended or likely to induce reliance. The "promise" would have been in the nature of a hope or possibly a prediction rather than a commitment to do something within the "promisor's" power to do ("I promise it will rain tomorrow"); and the "promisee" would, if sensible, understand this. He would rely or not as he chose but he would know that he would have to bear the cost of any disappointment.

We note, returning to the facts of this case, that there was costly reliance by GPI, which forewent other opportunities for salvation, and by Garwood and McNamara, who moved from Indiana to Ohio to be near Hobart's plant where they expected their food-packaging system to be manufactured, and who forgave their personal loans to GPI and incurred other costs as well. The reliance was on statements by Martin, of which "come hell or high water" was the high water mark but is by no means an isolated example. If GPI's evidence is credited, as it must be in the procedural posture of the case, Martin repeatedly confirmed to GPI that the deal would go through, that Allen's commitment to invest $2 million was unconditional, that the funding would be forthcoming, and so on; and these statements induced the plaintiffs to incur costs they would otherwise not have done.

But were these real promises, and likely to be understood as such? Those are two different questions. A person may say something that he intends as merely a prediction, or as a signal of his hopes or intentions, but that is reasonably understood as a promise, and if so, as we know (this is the penal or deterrent function of promissory estoppel), he is bound. But what is a reasonable, and indeed actual, understanding will often depend on the knowledge that the promisee brings to the table. McNamara, with whom Martin primarily dealt, is a former investment banker, not a rube. He knew that in putting together a deal to salvage a failing company there is many a slip 'twixt cup and lips. Unless blinded by optimism or desperation he *had* to know that Martin could not mean *literally* that the deal would go through "come hell or high water," since if Satan or a tsunami obliterated Ohio that would kill the deal. Even if Allen had dug into its pockets for the full $2 million after the investors who it had hoped would put up half the amount defected, the deal might well not have gone through because of Hobart's demands and because of the creditors. GPI acknowledges that the Internal Revenue Service, one of its largest creditors, wouldn't give a release until paid in full. Some of GPI's other creditors also intended to fight rather than to accept a pittance in exchange for a release. Nothing is more common than for a deal to rescue a failing company to fall apart because all the creditors' consent to the deal cannot be obtained—that is one of the reasons for bankruptcy law. Again these were things of which McNamara was perfectly aware.

The problem, thus, is not that Martin's promises were indefinite, which they were not if GPI's evidence is credited, but that they could not have been reasonably understood by the persons to whom they were addressed (mainly McNamara, the financial partner in GPI) to *be* promises rather than expressions of optimism and determination. To move to Ohio, to forgive personal loans, to forgo other searches for possible investors, and so forth were in the nature of gambles on the part of GPI and its principals. They may have been reasonable gambles, in the sense that the prospects for a successful salvage operation were good enough that taking immediate, even if irrevocable, steps to facilitate and take advantage of the expected happy outcome was prudent. But we often reasonably rely on things that are not promises. A farmer plants his crops in the spring in reasonable reliance that spring will be followed by summer rather than by winter. There can be reasonable reliance on statements as well as on the regularities of nature, but if the statements are not reasonably understood as legally enforceable promises there can be no action for promissory estoppel.

Suppose McNamara thought that there was a 50 percent chance that the deal would go through and believed that reliance on that prospect would cost him $100,000, but also believed that by relying he could expect either to increase the likelihood that the deal would go through or to make more money if it did by being able to start production sooner and that in either event the expected benefit of reliance would exceed $100,000. Then his reliance would be reasonable even if not induced by enforceable promises. The numbers are arbitrary but the example apt. GPI and its principals relied, and may have relied reasonably, but they didn't rely on Martin's "promises" because those were not promises reasonably understood as such by so financially sophisticated a businessman as McNarama. So we see now that the essence of the doctrine of promissory estoppel is not that the plaintiff have reasonably relied on the defendant's promise, but that he have reasonably relied on its *being* a promise in the sense of a legal commitment, and not a mere prediction or aspiration or bit of puffery.

One last point. Ordinarily the question whether a plaintiff reasonably understood a statement to be a promise is a question of fact and so cannot be resolved in summary judgment proceedings. But if it is clear that the question can be answered in only one way, there is no occasion to submit the question to a jury. This, we believe, is such a case.

ATA Airlines, Inc. v. Federal Express Corp.

United States Court of Appeals, Seventh Circuit, 2012.
665 F.3d 882.

POSNER, CIRCUIT JUDGE. . . . In the event of a national emergency, the Department of Defense can use commercial aircraft drawn from what's called the "Civil Reserve Air Fleet" to augment the Department's own airlift capabilities. Composed of aircraft owned by commercial air carriers but committed voluntarily to the Department for use during emergencies, the Fleet is divided into separate "teams" of airlines, each with a "team leader." The teams pledge portions of their fleets for use by the Department during an emergency; the leader assembles the team and submits the team's bid to participate in the Civil Reserve Air Fleet.

The team members are not compensated directly for their commitment, but are compensated indirectly because in exchange for a team member's commitment the Department awards the member "mobilization value points" in proportion to the scale of the commitment. The more points a member has, the more non-emergency air transportation for the Department the member can bid on. The points are transferrable within teams. Smaller carriers value providing non-emergency service to the Department (for which of course they are compensated) more than the bigger ones (such as FedEx) do. So they want the larger carriers' points and are willing to pay for them, and as a result end up doing most of the non-emergency flying. The team leader—invariably a large carrier that therefore has a large number of mobilization value points because of its commitment to provide copious emergency service if needed—transfers points to the members of its team in exchange for a commission on their non-emergency military flights. The commission rate is the price term in the contractual arrangements between the team leader and each of the team's smaller carriers. (This case concerns the contractual relations among the members of one team rather than the contracts between the teams and the Department.)

FedEx is the leader of one of the teams, which before the alleged breach of contract included ATA and Omni Air International—small passenger and charter airlines that split between them the team's allotment of non-emergency military passenger service (as distinct from cargo service). The FedEx team's annual revenues from the provision of non-emergency services to the Department amount to about $600 million.

Relations among members of FedEx's team are defined in three separate contracts, each with a one-year term. One contract fixes both the allocation of military business among the team members and the commission rate for the team leader. This contract is negotiated separately between the leader and each team member (so actually it's more than one contract, but we can ignore that detail). A second contract identifies the team members and the aircraft they will commit to the military if the team's bid is accepted. A third defines the liability and insurance obligations of the team members. There are additional provisions in these contracts, but we can disregard them. We'll call the three contracts as a group the "tripartite contract."

The tripartite contract has as we said only a one-year term. (The year is the federal fiscal year, which runs from October 1 of the previous calendar year to September 30, so that the 2002 fiscal year, for example, began in October 2001. All our year references are to fiscal years.) But it was the team's practice to enter into a separate three-year agreement concerning the distribution of business among the team's members. Implementation of the agreement depended on the Defense Department's accepting the team's bid; otherwise there would be no business to divide among the team's members. And if the Department decided it wanted more or less service from the team than had been bid, this might affect the division of business, since a particular team member might have insufficient capacity to provide its allotted share of service if the service requirement increased, or alternatively might be badly hurt by a reduction in that requirement if its share were unchanged—there might for example be limited demand for or profit in a participant's nonmilitary business. The agreement also assumed that the parties would all end up on the FedEx team, though there was no contractual stipulation to that effect.

With so many contingencies, especially ones dependent on decisions entirely within the power and rights of each party, the agreement was a planning document rather than an enforceable contract. . . .

ATA's suit is based on one of these three-year "contracts," signed in 2006, in which ATA and (maybe) Omni agreed with FedEx that during the following three years (2007 through 2009) the team's passenger business would be divided equally between those two carriers. The "contract" is in the form of a letter from FedEx to them that reads as follows:

> The letter will serve as the agreement for the distribution between ATA and Omni of both fixed and expansion for both wide and narrow body passenger business in the AMC Long Range International Contract for FY07–FY09.
>
> It is agreed that the distribution for the above passenger segments will be fifty-fifty (50%–50%) respectively for both wide and narrow body and for both fixed and expansion.
>
> Please indicate your concurrence by signing as indicated below and returning to the undersigned.
>
> We look forward to a continued successful relationship over this period. . . .

The tripartite contracts for 2007 and 2008 incorporated the fifty/fifty division—but with a change in the 2008 contract: ATA's allotment was reduced by ten flights per month to enable them to be allotted instead to Northwest Airlines, a much bigger carrier, which wanted to start flying for the Civil Reserve Air Fleet. Northwest was already a participant in the FedEx team, but like FedEx (though without FedEx's responsibilities as team leader) had heretofore been a guarantor of emergency service to the military and thus a seller of points to the smaller airlines; 2008 would be the first time it would be a flying member of the team.

The change turned out to be pregnant with menace for ATA. For later that year FedEx decided to drop ATA from the team and, beginning in 2009, give the mobilization value points that would have gone to ATA to Delta, which had acquired Northwest shortly after the signing of the 2008 tripartite contract. FedEx's decision to replace ATA in 2009 caused ATA to withdraw from the team prematurely, in the middle of 2008 (we're not sure why). The withdrawal precipitated it into bankruptcy because it had very little nonmilitary business to fall back on.

ATA's breach of contract claim should never have been permitted to go to trial. Courts interpret and enforce contracts; they don't make contracts. . . .

[T]he letter agreement was not an enforceable contract. But it did contain a promise to divide the military passenger service to be provided by FedEx's team equally between ATA and Omni. The doctrine of promissory estoppel makes a promise enforceable even though it is not supported by consideration or otherwise enforceable under conventional principles of contract law, provided that the promisee reasonably incurred a cost in reliance on the promisor's fulfilling the promise and that the promisor should reasonably have anticipated that the promisee would rely in that way and might therefore be hurt if the promisor reneged.

One function of the doctrine of promissory estoppel . . . is to allow reasonable reliance to be substituted for consideration. The underlying idea is that a reasonable promisee wouldn't incur an unrecoverable cost in reliance on the promise's being fulfilled unless there really had been a promise, and so reasonable reliance is as good a basis for inferring the existence of a promise as consideration is. In this case, however, there is no question that there was a promise—the promise to share business fifty/fifty between ATA and Omni is in writing, in the letter agreement. The question is whether the promise was (or could reasonably have been understood to be) intended to induce, and could reasonably induce, reliance to the tune of $28 million.

If someone tells you "I promise you X, but don't hold me to it," the promisor is making clear that he is not inviting reliance and the promisee cannot, by ignoring the warning and relying on the promise to his detriment, make the promise enforceable. Such a "promise" may create an expectation but does not create a commitment, and so the promisee relies at his risk. Risk taking is ubiquitous in business and is perfectly reasonable because the expected benefits of a risky undertaking will often exceed the expected costs. It may have been reasonable for ATA to reckon that it had a good enough chance of getting half the passenger business of the FedEx team in the 2007–2009 period to justify its going ahead and acquiring the aircraft it would need to provide the service because its existing fleet was inadequate; it is the $28 million in allegedly unrecoverable expenses relating to that acquisition that ATA seeks to recoup by invoking promissory estoppel. But ATA could not reasonably have believed that FedEx intended to *commit* itself to split the passenger business equally between ATA and Omni during that period when so much was left to be agreed upon, and so FedEx cannot have been expected to anticipate that ATA would rely on the promise. ATA's lawyer acknowledged at the oral argument that his client may have been "imprudent" in failing to recognize the possibility that Northwest would want more of the team's business; and Northwest was (and Delta, which swallowed

Northwest, even more so, is) to ATA as the Dreamliner is to the DC-3. Acting on a hope is not reasonable reliance. . .

NOTE: CONTRACT FORMALITIES AND PROMISSORY ESTOPPEL

Traditional contract law had a number of formal rules, perhaps most notably a requirement that some types of contracts be written in order to be legally enforceable. Legislation stretching back more than three centuries requires that the party "sought to charged" must have signed a "memorandum" of the parties' agreement for certain classes of agreements to be enforceable. The original English Statute of Frauds, which provided the model for American legislation, became effective in 1677. The original English statute contained no general statement of purpose, but the introductory clause stated: "For prevention of many fraudulent practices, which are commonly endeavored to be upheld by perjury or subornation of perjury, be it enacted . . ." It has long been understood that the statute was enacted out of a distrust of the ability of juries to determine the truth of conflicting testimony about the making of a contract.

The common law action of assumpsit had opened the King's courts to the enforcement of oral promises. And since juries at the time decided cases on their own personal knowledge of the facts, not evidence submitted by others, it is not at all surprising that the statute's introductory clause should speak of "perjury or the subornation of perjury." The jury's discretion was therefore to be limited—at least in the transactions specified—by a requirement of "some memorandum . . . in writing, and signed by the party to be charged." Included among the transactions in the Statute of Frauds that need a writing are promises for the sale of real property and promises that are not to be performed within a year. The writing does not need to be a full-blown contract. A signed writing that evidences the existence of the contract and its essential terms suffices.

The Statute of Frauds serves in the first instance an evidentiary function. To be sure, insisting on a writing has conspicuous costs. Some bargains that were in fact struck will not be enforced. But one must offset this cost against the benefit of ensuring that it is easy for a jury to determine the underlying facts. It is much easy to know whether someone made a promise if it was put into writing.

The Statute of Frauds serves an additional, salutary purpose as well. The Statute of Frauds may improve the environment in which negotiations take place. In ordinary commercial dealings, the parties enter into negotiations before reaching a bargain. There may be several points at which one party or the other could, in the absence of a Statute of Frauds, insist that a deal of some kind had been reached even when (at least in the view of the other party) none had been. The possibility of one party later asserting that there was such a deal may lead the other to be less forthcoming during negotiations. The Statute of Frauds creates an environment in which parties involved in large transactions, such as those involving multi-year commitments or the sale of real property, know that they will be able to walk away from negotiations without the other insisting that there was a deal—as long as they have not signed anything. This makes them more willing to begin to negotiate in the first place.

Whatever the merits of formal rules such as the Statute of Frauds, they are in tension with the spirit of promissory estoppel. Once promises seriously made and reasonably relied upon became legally enforceable, courts had to confront the question of what would happen to the formal rules. Promissory estoppel focuses on the undertakings of each of the parties. If promissory estoppel works in the case of any promise that is reasonably relied on, it is not obvious how any place is left for formal legal rules. As the cases that follow suggest, courts have repeatedly faced the challenge of reconciling formal rules of contract with promissory estoppel.

DK Arena, Inc. v. EB Acquisitions I, LLC

Supreme Court of Florida, 2013.
112 So. 3d 85.

QUINCE, J. . . . In 2004, the fronton property [a sporting arena used for playing jai alai] belonged to petitioner DK Arena, Inc., a Delaware corporation wholly owned by celebrity boxing promoter, Don King. King originally acquired the property in 1999 with the intent of converting it into a boxing arena. When that use was found to be infeasible, the property was made available for sale. The property included a Tri-Rail station operated through a lease to the South Florida Regional Transit Authority. John Markey, CEO of EB Developers, a now-defunct development firm, was made aware of the property's availability during a meeting with a member of the Transit Authority's board of directors. Markey determined that the site would be suitable for a mixed-use commercial and residential development that would incorporate the existing Tri-Rail station. Markey was introduced to King, who agreed to sell the property. Markey formed respondent, EB Acquisitions I, LLC, to facilitate the purchase.

On July 20, 2004, EB entered into a written contract with DK Arena in which EB agreed to purchase the fronton property for $23 million. The contract required EB to place an initial deposit of $1 million into an escrow account. The contract also called for a due diligence period of sixty days from the date of the contract's signing. During that time, EB was permitted to conduct any inspections of the property it deemed necessary. If EB gave notice of cancellation to DK Arena within the sixty-day due diligence period, the contract called for the return of EB's deposit. Failure to give notice of cancellation would be considered EB's "as is" acceptance of the property. Closing was to occur within thirty days of the expiration of the due diligence period, at which time EB was required to pay DK

Arena the remaining $22 million of the purchase price. The contract further provided that any modifications to the contract would "not be binding unless in writing, signed and delivered by the party to be bound."

On the same day the contract was signed, the parties also executed an addendum to the contract. The addendum clarified that EB was permitted to terminate the agreement at any time during the due diligence period and stated that if EB did not give notice of termination within the sixty-day period, the deposit would be released to DK Arena. In addition, paragraph fourteen of the addendum, titled "Land Use Application," required DK Arena and "and its principal, Mr. Don King," to participate in the process of seeking local government approval for EB's development project and to participate in the project's marketing and promotion. At trial, King said he understood this provision to mean that he was required to use his personal influence to lobby in support of approval for the project. Despite King's participation, the addendum stated: "This transaction does not create a joint venture or partnership relationship among the Parties."

Shortly after the contract and the addendum were executed, Markey proposed that the parties amend the agreement to make King a partner in EB's development project. The parties continued to negotiate the terms of this proposed joint venture while EB began to seek government approval for the project. On September 13, 2004, the parties executed a written amendment to the contract extending the due diligence period by fourteen days. Markey testified that over the course of several meetings the parties worked out the key terms of the partnership agreement, which Markey said King agreed to. In his own testimony, King disputed Markey's claim that he agreed to the joint venture, explaining that while he listened to Markey's proposal and passed it on to his lawyers for review, he never agreed to it.

On October 4, the day the extended due diligence period was to expire, King, Markey, and their respective attorneys met at King's office. The parties discussed the status of the development project and Markey expressed concern that the project would not be approved by the Mangonia Park municipal government. Markey was also concerned that the due diligence period would expire before the terms of the parties' joint venture agreement could be "memorialized." King's actions at this point were disputed at trial. According to Markey, King agreed to hold the due diligence period in indefinite "abeyance" until the joint venture agreement could be completed. By contrast, King asserted that while he agreed to an extension of the due diligence period, the extension was limited to one week and the deposit was to be due on October 11 unless EB cancelled the contract before that date. Regardless, it is undisputed that the parties failed to make any written memorandum of the alleged agreement.

The following evening, Markey and King attended a meeting of the Mangonia Park Town Council. Markey presented site plans and renderings of the project, and King described the benefits he believed the project would bring to the community. The council expressed concern that it had not been given enough notice to review the proposal and scheduled an informational meeting for October 26, which King stated he would attend. Following the October 4 meeting, King met several times with County Commissioner Addie Greene. King testified that he tried to obtain Greene's support for the project. Greene told King that MGM had approached her about building an entertainment facility on the property. She encouraged King to review MGM's proposal.

King subsequently failed to attend the October 26 town council meeting. . . .

King testified at trial that from his perspective, he believed the escrow payment was due on October 11. He said that once that date had passed and EB failed to release the deposit, he considered EB to be in breach of the contract. Thus, King believed that he was no longer obligated to attend the October 26 meeting. . . .

DK Arena filed suit alleging a single count of breach of contract and seeking the release of the $1 million escrow deposit. EB filed an answer and asserted several counterclaims, including breach of contract, breach of an oral joint venture agreement, and breach of fiduciary duty. . . .

In its final judgment, the trial court . . . determin[ed], as a question of fact, that the due diligence period was extended for an indefinite period of time at the parties' meeting on October 4. . . .

The [district court] acknowledged that under the Statute of Frauds, all contracts for the sale of land must be in writing. The district court reasoned, however, that in this case "EB changed its position in reliance upon the oral agreement to extend the due diligence period—it did not give notice . . . that it intended to terminate the contract." Because EB relied on the parties' agreement to extend the due diligence period, the district court held that DK Arena was estopped from arguing that the agreement was invalid under the Statute of Frauds. . . .

In this opinion, we review the district court's finding that the oral extension of the contractual due diligence period was enforceable, notwithstanding the Statute of Frauds, under the "doctrine of estoppel." . . .

[These facts raise the same] question that arose in [Tanenbaum v. Biscayne Osteopathic Hospital, Inc., 190 So. 2d 777 (Fla. 1966)]: whether the doctrine of promissory estoppel should be adopted as an exception to the Statute of Frauds. Generally stated, promissory estoppel is "[t]he principle that a promise made without consideration may nonetheless be enforced to prevent injustice if the promisor should have reasonably expected the promisee to rely on the promise and if the promisee did actually rely on the promise to his or her detriment." Black's Law Dictionary 631 (9th ed. 2009). As the definition indicates, promissory estoppel traditionally serves as an exception to the requirement of consideration in the formation of a contract. . . .

Some jurisdictions . . . have held that promissory estoppel may operate as an exception to the Statute of Frauds as well as to the requirement of consideration. Section 139(a)(1) of the Second Restatement, entitled, "Enforcement By Virtue of Action in Reliance," expressly adopts this view:

> A promise which the promisor should reasonably expect to induce action or forbearance on the part of the promisee or a third person and which does induce the action or forbearance is enforceable *notwithstanding the Statute of Frauds* if injustice can be avoided only by enforcement of the promise. (Emphasis added).

State courts have taken varying approaches to the Restatement's position. Some courts have agreed with the Second Restatement's view that promissory estoppel may be applied to enforce oral promises that would otherwise be unenforceable under the Statute of Frauds. . . .

Notwithstanding the views of courts in other jurisdictions, this Court early on expressed skepticism of arguments in favor of an estoppel exception. . . .

[I]n *Tanenbaum,* we unequivocally rejected a promissory estoppel exception to Florida's Statute of Frauds. The petitioner in that case was a Pennsylvania physician who entered into an oral employment agreement with a Miami hospital, whereby the hospital agreed to employ the petitioner as a radiologist for a minimum of five years. In reliance on this agreement, the petitioner quit his job and moved to Florida. Several months later, the hospital notified the petitioner that his employment would be discontinued. The petitioner filed suit, alleging that the hospital had breached the oral agreement.

The hospital defended against the suit on the grounds that the oral employment contract, as an agreement not to be performed within one year of its making, fell within the Statute of Frauds and was thus unenforceable. . . .

Ultimately, we declined to adopt a promissory estoppel exception to Florida's Statute of Frauds, stating . . .

> The petitioner had but to follow the provisions of the Statute of Frauds to secure his rights under the arrangement with the respondent instead of taking the position, rather tardily[,] that they did not apply to him. Thirty-three years have passed since the Restatement we have quoted was adopted and there have been about 15 intervening sessions of the legislature at which the contents of Sec. 90 of the Restatement could have been incorporated into the act yet we know of no such effort or accomplishment.

Id. Accordingly, we held that the parties' oral agreement was unenforceable . . . .

Based on the precedent described above, we conclude that the [district court] improperly applied the doctrine of promissory estoppel in upholding an oral modification to the contract between EB and DK Arena. . . .

This case, if any, illustrates the usefulness of a writing requirement. At trial, the facts surrounding the modification were heavily disputed. Much confusion could have been avoided had the parties simply placed their agreement in writing. Indeed, the parties did so on one prior occasion, executing a written amendment to the contract extending the due diligence period until October 4, 2004.

Under the Statute of Frauds, any modification to the contract was unenforceable unless memorialized in a written document signed by the parties or their authorized representatives. Absent an amendment that complied with the requirements of the Statute, the parties were bound by their written agreement. The due diligence period therefore expired on October 4, 2004. On that date, EB lost its right to terminate the contract of sale at will. . . .

Classic Cheesecake Co. v. JPMorgan Chase Bank

United States Court of Appeals, Seventh Circuit, 2008.
546 F.3d 839.

POSNER, CIRCUIT JUDGE. This appeal requires us to interpret a gloss that the Indiana courts have placed on their state's statute of frauds: an oral agreement that the statute of frauds would otherwise render unenforceable creates a binding contract if failing to enforce the agreement would produce an "unjust and unconscionable injury and loss." . . .

Classic Cheesecake, a bakery company, managed to interest several hotels and casinos in Las Vegas in buying its products. To serve these new customers Classic needed additional capital—capital to establish a distribution center in Las Vegas, to hire employees to staff it, and to buy additional equipment. On July 27, 2004, principals of Classic visited a local office of the defendant bank and made a pitch to a vice president named Dowling for a loan that would be partially guaranteed by the Small Business Administration and therefore would have to be approved by that agency. They emphasized to Dowling that time was of the essence.

Dowling asked them for tax returns, accounts receivable, and other documentation in support of the loan application, and having received the documents she orally assured Classic's principals (according to Classic) that the loan would be approved, provided that student loans of one of the principals were paid off—a condition on which the Small Business Administration insisted because the loans had been financed in part by the federal government and were in default. On September 17 Dowling told Classic that the loan was a "go," and three days later one of Classic's principals asked Dowling to request that letters from the student loan agencies confirming that the loans had been repaid be sent directly to Dowling "to speed up the confirmation process." So Classic knew that Dowling's saying the loan was "a go" did not mean that the loan had been approved. But it seemed likely that it would be.

Yet in an email to Dowling on August 19, Dowling's superior at the bank had told her "I am still declining this request [Classic's request for a loan] primarily based on the following issues/concerns"—and he mentioned excessive leverage, lack of an established earnings record, inadequate cash flow, undercapitalization, insufficient revenues, too much reliance on projections, and "serious delinquencies and derogatory public record of guarantor" (referring to the principal who had defaulted on her student loans). He added that he had discussed the matter with the SBA and "the same issues/concerns as identified above prevailed."

Although the email was a downer, it did not flatly turn down the loan request, and Dowling must have expected that it would be approved, perhaps with modifications, eventually—for what had she to gain from stringing Classic along if she knew the loan would *never* be approved? But she may have exaggerated her confidence in the loan's eventual approval to prevent Classic from shopping elsewhere, though the plaintiffs do not allege that.

Not only did Dowling not share the contents of the discouraging email with Classic, but she continued to make verbal assurances that the loan would be approved. The plaintiffs must have been shocked when on October 12 she told them that the loan had been turned down. (As reasons she gave the concerns that her superior had expressed in the August email.) Classic claims that it and the other plaintiffs (the company's principals plus an affiliate) lost more than $1 million because of the bank's breach of what Classic deems an oral promise to make the loan. It claims that the breach delayed it from seeking loans elsewhere for a critical two and a half months and that as a result of the delay it and the other plaintiffs incurred in the aggregate a loss of more than $1 million. We'll assume the loss consisted entirely of costs incurred in reliance on the loan's being approved, although some of it undoubtedly consisted of consequential damages that could not be recovered in a suit for breach of contract consistently with the doctrine of Hadley v. Baxendale, 9 Exch. 341, 156 Eng. Rep. 145 (1854). That is true of the tax penalties that the plaintiffs had to pay because the loss allegedly due to the delay in obtaining a loan drained them of the cash they needed to pay their taxes, and it is even truer of the emotional distress they claim to have suffered as a result of the delay and ensuing financial loss. . . .

[The plaintiffs ground their claim on promissory estoppel. And so, under Indiana law,] the question becomes whether the bank's conduct could have been found to inflict an "unjust and unconscionable injury and loss" and so trump the bank's defense based on the statute of frauds. To answer the question requires us to explore the provenance of a phrase at once vague (what does "unjust and unconscionable" mean?) and redundant (how does "injury" differ from "loss"?).

The statute of frauds has long been controversial. The Farnsworth treatise says that "it has been the subject of constant erosion." 2 E. Allan Farnsworth, *Farnsworth on Contracts* § 6.1, p. 107 (3d ed. 2004). The particular erosive process that culminates in the doctrine of "unjust and unconscionable injury and loss" began—where else?—in an opinion by Justice Traynor, Monarco v. Lo Greco, 35 Cal.2d 621, 220 P.2d 737 (1950), that allowed the statute of frauds to be circumvented by a claim of promissory estoppel. (Even before then, the statute of frauds could be circumvented by equitable estoppel, but that required a misrepresentation concerning the statute of frauds itself, as where one party assured the other that no writing was necessary, or promised not to plead the statute of frauds in the event of a lawsuit.) Importantly, however, Justice Traynor limited the use of promissory estoppel to defeat the statute of frauds: only if "either an unconscionable injury or unjust enrichment would result from refusal to enforce" an oral promise would a defense based on the statute of frauds be negated. 220 P.2d at 741.

The *Monarco* opinion, like so many of Justice Traynor's innovations, caught on. Eventually it was picked up—and expanded—by the Restatement (Second) of Contracts (1981), which in § 139(1) allows promissory estoppel to defeat the statute of frauds "if injustice can be avoided only by enforcement of the [oral] promise." This notably loose formulation has been influential too, but not in Indiana. "Indiana courts have declined to embrace § 139 [of the *Restatement*], but have recognized the possibility of relief for 'injustice' in limited circumstances, while defining it much more narrowly than in § 139." Coca-Cola Co. v. Babyback's Int'l, Inc., 841 N.E.2d 557, 569 (Ind. 2006).

Indiana's formula is as follows:

> In order to establish an estoppel to remove the case from the operation of the Statute of Frauds, the party must show [ ] that the other party's refusal to carry out the terms of the agreement has resulted not merely in a denial of the rights which the agreement was intended to confer, but the infliction of an unjust and unconscionable injury and loss.
>
> In other words, neither the benefit of the bargain itself, nor mere inconvenience, incidental expenses, etc. short of a reliance injury so substantial and independent as to constitute an unjust and unconscionable injury and loss are sufficient to remove the claim from the operation of the Statute of Frauds. Id.

The formula itself—"unjust and unconscionable injury and loss"—does not tell us much, and it has not been further elaborated by the Indiana courts. Comparison with Justice Traynor's formula—"either an unconscionable injury or unjust enrichment"—deepens the mystery. The Traynor formula suggests two grounds for getting around the statute of frauds: unjust gain to the promisor or "unconscionable" injury to the promisee. The former seems the solider ground but is omitted in the Indiana formulation unless the "unjust" in "unjust . . . injury" should be understood as shorthand for unjust enrichment—but that would imply, contrary to the second paragraph of the formulation in *Babyback's*, that the rule is inapplicable if there is no gain to the party pleading the statute of frauds. In both formulas, the word "unconscionable" is confusing rather than clarifying, since if it is meant to invoke the doctrine of unconscionability it would duplicate unjust enrichment in the Traynor formula and contradict the second paragraph in the Indiana formula.

We can at least set aside any issue of unjust enrichment in this case. The bank made no money in its dealings with Classic and gained no other advantage; all it gained was this lawsuit against it. And anyway, to invoke the doctrine of unconscionability Classic would have to show that it had been taken advantage of because of its obvious ignorance or desperate circumstances, and there is nothing like that here. The bank was not trying to drive a hard bargain with Classic—it insisted on no unreasonable terms. And though a small business, Classic is not a hapless consumer, poor tenant, or mom and pop grocery store. It wanted a bank loan not to stave off disaster but to finance an expansion of its business to take advantage of an exciting business opportunity. Insistence on the repayment of the student loans that one of its principals had defaulted on (yet was capable of repaying, as events showed) was hardly unconscionable and anyway came from the Small Business Administration rather than from the bank. All else aside, the doctrine of unconscionability is a defense to the enforcement of a contract, and the bank is not trying to enforce a contract; it denies there *was* a contract.

We can get some help from the case law. In *Monarco*, the *fons et origo* [the source and origin] of the doctrine that the Indiana courts call "unjust and unconscionable injury and loss," there was both a big loss and unjust enrichment. When the plaintiff reached eighteen and wanted to leave home and make his own way in the world, his mother and stepfather promised him that if he stayed and worked on the family farm they would leave almost all their property (which was in joint tenancy) to him. He stayed, and worked hard, receiving in exchange only room and board and spending money. The farm prospered. But when the stepfather died twenty years later, he left his half interest in the farm to his own grandson. The element of unjust enrichment lay in the fact that the plaintiff had worked the farm for slight compensation for twenty years (giving up among other things the opportunity to obtain an education beyond high school) in the expectation that he would be well compensated when either his mother or his stepfather died. The farm had done well, in part no doubt because of the plaintiff's undercompensated efforts—his "sweat equity." So the grandson was indeed unjustly enriched. The plaintiff's having the rug pulled out from under him after working for twenty years for slight remuneration faintly echoed Laban's fraud on his son-in-law Jacob [in *Genesis*, Chapter 29, of the Bible]. After promising the hand of his younger daughter, Rachel, to Jacob in marriage in return for seven years' service to him, Laban tricked Jacob—whose work had enriched Laban—into marrying Laban's elder daughter, Leah, instead. Jacob was compelled to serve Laban for another seven years in order to be permitted to marry Rachel. As in *Monarco*, there was both unjust enrichment of the oral promisor and heavy loss to the promisee—seven more years of unpaid labor.

Only two cases (one a federal district court diversity case governed by Indiana law) have allowed a claim based on the Indiana formula to survive a motion for summary judgment, though in neither case did the plaintiff ultimately prevail. . . .

In the diversity case, Madison Tool & Die, Inc. v. ZF Sachs Automotive of America, Inc., 2007 WL 2286130 (S. D. Ind. 2007), the defendant orally agreed to make the plaintiff its auto parts supplier. To induce the plaintiff to retool its facilities so that it could supply the parts, the defendant announced that it was not working with any other suppliers and would therefore need the plaintiff to begin production within 30 days. So the plaintiff went out and bought a special machine for $415,000 to produce the parts for the defendant. The plaintiff made test parts for the defendant with the new machine, but rather than ordering any parts the defendant assured the plaintiff for three years that it would begin ordering parts soon. Yet it never did, and at the end of the period declared that it would not be using the plaintiff as a supplier after all.

In the other case, Keating v. Burton, 545 N.E.2d 35 (Ind. App. 1989), the defendant orally agreed to hire the plaintiff as a full-time employee with an option to purchase forty-nine percent of the defendant's company after three years of employment. In reliance on the agreement the plaintiff went to work for the defendant and claimed to have shut down his own company, which had been growing. (The court eventually found that the plaintiff had not abandoned his business entirely. But for purposes of getting a fix on Indiana law, all that matters is the evidence that was before the court when it decided not to grant summary judgment to the defendant.) After the plaintiff had been working for the defendant's company for a year and a half, the defendant so limited the plaintiff's responsibilities that he quit.

These cases are not as dramatic as *Monarco* or *Genesis* [Chapter] 29 and do not involve (so far as appears) substantial gain to the (oral) promisor. But there is a family resemblance, which helps us to understand the scope and operation of the Indiana formula as elaborated in the second paragraph of the indented quotation from *Babyback's* and as paraphrased in Spring Hill Developers, Inc. v. Arthur, 879 N.E.2d 1095, 1103 (Ind. App. 2008), as follows: the "injury must be not only (1) independent from the benefit of the bargain and resulting incidental expenses and inconvenience, but also (2) so substantial as to constitute an unjust and unconscionable injury." The benefit of the bargain would be what the promisee hoped to gain from the promise, which in *Madison* would have been the profit from selling auto parts to the defendant and in *Keating* the forty-nine percent share of the defendant's company. The plaintiffs lost those expectancies of course, but they suffered other losses as well—the cost of the machine in *Madison* that the plaintiff would not have bought had it not been for the oral promise and in *Keating* the plaintiff's alleged loss of his company. And those losses were significant in relation to the plaintiffs' net worth, satisfying the second part of the Indiana formula.

But what these cases really show is the mercury-like slipperiness of the Indiana formula, as of the *Monarco* formula as well. The "benefit of the bargain" is contract-speak for the expected profit from performing a contract; the "independent" loss of which the *Spring Hill* opinion spoke is the reliance loss—the expenses a party incurs to perform the contract. The plaintiff in *Madison* incurred the expense of the machine in reliance on the defendant's promise, and likewise with the plaintiff's giving up his business in *Keating*. A promise plus a reliance loss is what you need for promissory estoppel, yet the Indiana Supreme Court refused in *Babyback's* to endorse a *general* exception to the statute of frauds for promissory estoppel. So the whole weight of the doctrine of "unjust and unconscionable injury and loss" falls on the gravity of the injury, and the decisive distinction between *Monarco*, *Madison*, and *Keating* (and for that matter Jacob's grievance) on the one hand and the present case on the other hand is simply the duration of the injury in those cases relative to this one: 20 years, 3 years, 1.5 years, and 7 years (Jacob's case), versus in our case at most 2.5 months but more likely 3.5 weeks—the time that elapsed between Dowling's telling Classic on September 17 that the deal was a "go" and on October 12 that the loan application had been rejected. The more protracted the period during which reliance costs are being incurred, the stronger the inference that the oral promise was as the plaintiff represents it to be; for had there been no promise the plaintiff's conduct—his immense reliance cost relative to his resources—would have been incomprehensible.

Remember that the objection to placing promissory estoppel outside the statute of frauds is that it is too easy for a plaintiff to incur reliance costs in order to bolster his claim of an oral promise. The objection is attenuated if the reliance is so extensive that it is unlikely that the plaintiff would have undertaken it (buying an expensive specialized machine or giving up a growing company) merely to bolster a false claim. He might of course have misunderstood the "promisor" or been gambling on getting a contract, but courts seem not to think those possibilities likely enough to warrant a sterner rule. The compromise that the courts strike between the value of protecting reasonable reliance and the policy that animates the statute of frauds is to require a party that wants to get around the statute of frauds to prove an *enhanced* promissory estoppel, and the enhancement consists of proving a kind or amount of reliance unlikely to have been incurred had the plaintiff not had a good-faith belief that he had been promised remuneration.

This seems to us a better understanding of the "unjust and unconscionable" rule than ascribing it to judicial indignation at dishonorable behavior by promisors. It is a strength rather than a weakness of contract law that it generally eschews a moral conception of transactions. Liability for breach of contract is strict, rather than based (as tort liability generally is) on fault; punitive damages are unavailable even for deliberate breaches (and again note the contrast with tort law); and specific performance is exceptional—and when the only remedy for a breach of contract is compensatory damages, a promisor has in effect an option to perform or pay damages rather than a duty to perform (the duty the civil law expresses by the phrase *pacta sunt servanda*). . . .

Even though the behavior of the defendants in *Monarco* and the other cases we have discussed may well shock the conscience, the outcomes of those cases are defensible on the practical ground of protecting reasonable reliance in situations (and this is key) in which the contention that the reliance was induced by an oral promise is credible. The formulas the cases use to describe these situations, however, are not illuminating. Holmes warned that "the law is full of phraseology drawn from morals, and by the mere force of language continually invites us to pass from one domain to the other without perceiving it, as we are sure to do unless we have the boundary constantly before our minds." O.W. Holmes, "The Path of the Law," 10 Harv. L.Rev. 457, 459–60 (1897). Ruminating on the meaning of "unjust" and "unconscionable" will not separate the cases we have discussed from this case; reflection on reliance will.

The duration of reliance in the present case was much shorter than in the other cases that we have discussed, and the reliance is more easily imagined as based on hope than on a promise. And not all of it could be considered *reasonable* reliance, which is the only kind that can support a claim of promissory estoppel and *a fortiori* an invocation of the enhanced promissory-estoppel doctrine of the Indiana cases. The only reasonable reliance that the plaintiffs placed on Dowling's assurances was to cure (for less than $20,000) a delinquency somewhat earlier than they would otherwise have been forced to do. For the plaintiffs to treat the bank loan as a certainty because they were told by the bank officer whom they were dealing with that it would be approved was unreasonable, especially if, as the plaintiffs' damages claim presupposes, the need for the loan was urgent. Rational businessmen know that there is many a slip 'twixt cup and lips, that a loan is not approved until it is approved, that if a bank's employee tells you your loan application will be approved that is not the same as telling you it has been approved, and that if one does not have a loan commitment in writing yet the need for the loan is urgent one had better be negotiating with other potential lenders at the same time. The level of reliance that could be thought to have been reasonable in this case was not comparable to that involved in the other cases. In the end, this case turns out to be a routine promissory estoppel case, and that is not enough in Indiana to defeat a defense of statute of frauds. . . .

Kolkman v. Roth

Supreme Court of Iowa, 2003.
656 N.W.2d 148.

CADY, JUSTICE . . . Corrine Roth inherited 800 acres of farmland located in Des Moines County from her father following his death in December 1995. At the time, Dean Kolkman farmed the land pursuant to an oral crop-share lease. The lease term was year-to-year, with profits shared on a fifty-fifty basis between Kolkman and Roth's father. Roth also worked for her father on the farm over the years until approximately two years prior to his death. She was primarily involved in her father's livestock operation. Kolkman was also involved in the livestock operation, especially during the two years prior to the time Roth inherited the farm. During these two years, Kolkman ran the cattle operation under an arrangement similar to the grain operation.

In the spring of 1996, Roth asked Kolkman if he would continue to farm the ground and raise the cattle as he did for her father. Roth and Kolkman agreed that Kolkman would continue in the farming operation. They also agreed Kolkman and his wife would reside in one of the houses on the farm rent-free. Unfortunately, this agreement, and any additional terms, was not reduced to writing.

Kolkman and his wife moved to the farm in June 1996, and Kolkman successfully operated the farm, without incident, until 1999. During this time, Kolkman raised cattle, cultivated and harvested crops, and improved and cared for the land by fixing buildings and removing debris and manure. The farm was generally run down at the time it was inherited by Roth, and Kolkman improved its condition by performing work not typically done by a tenant farmer.

In 1999 Roth sought to charge Kolkman rent for the farmhouse in which he was residing in the amount of $550 a month. Roth also proposed a written farm lease between them that would terminate in 2000. Kolkman refused to execute the written proposals, and Roth sought to terminate the tenancy.

Kolkman responded by filing an action against Roth for breach of contract. He claimed the 1996 oral agreement with Roth included a term permitting him to live in the house rent free and remain the tenant on a fifty-fifty basis until he "retired or couldn't work any more." Kolkman further claimed he relied on this promise in several ways, including selling his former residence and moving to the farm, purchasing various farm equipment, and improving the land by making repairs and removing debris.

Roth denied any term regarding the length of their lease, and sought summary judgment. She claimed the statute of frauds prevented Kolkman from establishing an oral contract between the parties. The district court denied summary judgment and the case proceeded to trial. At trial, the district court, after finding Kolkman established the elements of promissory estoppel, determined the statute of frauds did not bar oral evidence of a lease. The jury then found the parties entered into a contract, supported by consideration, based on the terms asserted by Kolkman. It found Roth breached this contract and awarded Kolkman damages of $154,429. . . .

Under our statute of frauds, evidence of certain types of contracts is inadmissible, unless it is "in writing and signed by the party" sought to be charged. Iowa Code § 622.32 (1999). One type of contract included within the statute is a contract creating or transferring an interest in real estate other than leases for a term less than one year. . . .

Like most other rules, exceptions have been created to the statute of frauds. Iowa Code § 622.33 creates one such exception for contracts that fall within the real estate category. This section removes such oral agreements from the domain of the statute under two circumstances. The first circumstance is where the vendor of a real estate contract has received "the purchase money, or any portion thereof, . . . or when the vendee, with the actual or implied consent of the vendor, has taken and held possession of the premises under and by virtue of the contract." This language codifies the ancient doctrine of part performance, and permits the statute of frauds to be avoided where a party has rendered the type of part performance described in the statute. The rationale for the part performance exception actually lies in the principles of estoppel and fraud. The part performance exception exists to prevent the type of fraud that would occur "if the defendant were permitted to escape performance of his or her part of the oral agreement after permitting the plaintiff to perform in reliance upon the agreement." 73 Am. Jur. 2d Statute of Frauds § 313, at 13. Accordingly, part performance is not a substitute for evidence of a written contract, but is grounded in the theory that the defendant is estopped to assert the statute of frauds as a defense.

The second circumstance that will remove an oral real estate contract from the statute of frauds is derived from the concluding language of section 622.33, which makes the statute inapplicable under "any other circumstance which, by the law heretofore in force, would have taken the case out of the statute of frauds." Iowa Code § 622.33. We have interpreted this language to mean that the doctrine of promissory estoppel is available to remove an oral real estate contract from the statute of frauds. . . .

Promissory estoppel developed as a doctrine in the law in response to the strict traditional requirements for the formation of a contract, especially the requirement that all enforceable contracts be supported by consideration. . . . Thus, the theory behind promissory estoppel was to make parties "liable for their promises despite [the] absence of" consideration required under contract law. Schoff v. Combined Insurance Co., 604 N.W.2d 43, 48 (Iowa 1999). For this reason, we have viewed the effect of promissory estoppel to imply a contract in law based on detrimental reliance. However, other principles of contract law can conflict with the doctrine of promissory estoppel, such as the requirement of a writing for some types of contracts under the statute of frauds. . . . Thus, promissory estoppel is not only a substitute for consideration, but is also recognized as an exception to the statute of frauds even in cases where the promise may be supported by consideration.

Roth acknowledges both exceptions to the statute of frauds, but argues they must not be expanded so far as to apply to leases claimed to be in excess of one year. Roth points out we have refused to apply the part performance exception to oral leases for a term of more than one year, and, as a compatible doctrine, should similarly restrict promissory estoppel under the same circumstances.

We recognize part performance and promissory estoppel to be compatible doctrines as exceptions to the statute of frauds. They are both based on reliance and exist to prevent fraud, and are compatible because they share common goals. However, under section 622.33, the part performance exception is defined in relationship to a contract for the sale or purchase of real estate, not leases. Thus, it describes one type of circumstance that justifies avoidance of the statute of frauds to prevent it from working the same type of fraud it was designed to prevent. The doctrine of promissory estoppel has the same goal, but accomplishes it in other ways. The two exceptions are compatible, yet can embrace distinct circumstances. . . .

Promissory estoppel is broader than part performance and ultimately utilizes special standards to determine whether injustice can be avoided by enforcing a promise otherwise unenforceable under the statute of frauds.

Despite the broad development of the promissory estoppel doctrine over the years, Roth argues we have previously restricted its use as an exception to the statute of frauds to oral leases in a case decided over a century ago. See Powell v. Crampton, 102 Iowa 364, 71 N.W. 579 (1897). Roth argues we are obligated to recognize this early restriction today, especially in light of the language of section 622.33 that limits the second exception to circumstances where "the law heretofore in force" permitted the statute of frauds to be avoided.

In *Powell,* a tenant sought specific performance of an oral lease claimed to be for a term of five years. We held that the statute of frauds prevented proof of the lease, and the exceptions to the statute asserted by the tenant did not apply. However, the tenant did not raise promissory estoppel as an exception and we did not address the question whether promissory estoppel could be used as an exception to the statute of frauds. Instead, the tenant asserted the case fell outside of the statute of frauds based on part performance and based on the landlord's own testimony establishing the oral lease. Based on these arguments, the tenant claimed the landlord was "estopped from denying an oral contract to lease." We determined the part performance exception under the statute did not apply to leases and that the landlord's testimony was insufficient to constitute an admission of all of the lease terms. Although we concluded estoppel was not established, the decision did not consider the specific claim of promissory estoppel. Instead, it simply recognized, as we have since, that the estoppel doctrine lies at the heart of the exceptions to the statute of frauds, and the effect of establishing an exception to the statute is to estop the other party from asserting the statute of frauds to render oral proof of a contract incompetent. Consequently, *Powell* is not inconsistent with our development of the doctrine of promissory estoppel as a circumstance to establish an exception under section 622.33. Moreover, we have never rejected promissory estoppel as an exception in cases involving leases in excess of one year.

Finally, Roth claims that such unbridled use of the promissory estoppel exception will essentially swallow the statute of frauds rule when applied to real estate leases because a tenant will always be able to claim the existence of an oral lease in excess of one year. Roth claims this result is incongruous to the purposes behind the statute of frauds and the specific statutory exclusion for leases with a term less than one year. She argues our legislature would not have excluded oral leases for a term less than one year from the category of real estate cases covered under the statute of frauds, and then establish an exception to avoid the statute of frauds for leases in excess of one year.

We recognize other courts have been cautious to use promissory estoppel to overcome the statute of frauds. The argument advanced by Roth that the promissory estoppel doctrine essentially engulfs the statute of frauds is also commonly used by courts in those states that have been slow to apply promissory estoppel as an exception to the statute of frauds. Nevertheless, we find the argument insufficient to alter what we find to be our longstanding use of promissory estoppel as an exception to the statute of frauds.

The doctrine of promissory estoppel does not eviscerate the statute of frauds, but only applies to circumvent the statute when necessary to prevent an injustice. It requires the party asserting it as a means to avoid the statute of frauds to prove:

> (1) a clear and definite promise; (2) the promise was made with the promissor's clear understanding that the promisee was seeking assurance upon which the promisee could rely and without which he would not act; (3) the promisee acted to his or her

> substantial detriment in reasonable reliance on the promise; and (4) injustice can be avoided only by enforcement of the promise.

Schoff, 604 N.W.2d at 49. We require strict proof of all the elements. This includes strict proof of a promise that justifies reliance by the promisee. It also requires strict proof that the reliance inflicted injustice that requires enforcement of the promise. Clearly, much more than mere nonperformance of a promise must be shown to obtain the benefits of promissory estoppel. Thus, the strict standards we follow in applying promissory estoppel as a means to avoid the statute of frauds ameliorate the concerns presented by Roth and prevent the statute of frauds from being used to create an unjust result. Additionally, we observe that the majority of courts take a similar approach in applying the doctrine of promissory estoppel to the statute of frauds.

We also observe those jurisdictions that limit the use of promissory estoppel often point out the anomaly created by utilizing promissory estoppel to remove an oral promise from the statute of frauds when the very promise relied upon under promissory estoppel is the same promise declared unenforceable under the statute of frauds. Yet, even these jurisdictions seem to acknowledge that compelling circumstances have been encountered to justify the occasional use of promissory estoppel to avoid the statute of frauds. Thus, it is not really the use of the doctrine of promissory estoppel that is objectionable, and properly limited, promissory estoppel does serve the needed function of preventing the same fraud sought to be avoided by the statute of frauds itself. There is simply no strong reason to restrict the doctrine itself from any particular type of a contract included in the statute of frauds, as long as the doctrine is carefully applied.

Lastly, we perceive no inconsistency between permitting the promissory estoppel exception to the statute of frauds to be used in cases involving leases in excess of one year under a statutory scheme such as ours that excludes leases less than one year from the domain of the statute of frauds. To the contrary, it would be inconsistent to include certain types of leases within the real estate category of cases covered by the statute of frauds, then refuse to apply a broad exception for real estate cases, established to prevent fraudulent use of the statute of frauds, to such leases. . . .

CHAPTER 3

WHEN (AND HOW) PROMISES BECOME ENFORCEABLE

SECTION 1. MUTUAL ASSENT

INTRODUCTORY NOTE

The aim of this chapter is to examine the rules, doctrines, and techniques employed by courts in determining whether agreement has been achieved to such an extent that legal consequences should follow. To be sure, the problem of "communication" permeates the law's search for binding commitment. Agreement may be manifested wholly or partly by words, written or spoken, by acts, or even by a failure to act. Yet a casual glance through any dictionary is a sufficient reminder of the risk that one person's intention will not be revealed fully or accurately to another. A meaning intended by one party may be understood quite differently by the other. Moreover, doubts about the existence of any moment of real agreement between the parties can arise from any number of steps, or turns, in a negotiation. We have seen enough already to know that the inquiry made by legal agencies, when enforcement of an alleged agreement is demanded, is conducted through a complex procedure with restrictive rules of evidence; it cannot be equated with a psychologist's probe in depth.

Nevertheless, contract obligation is voluntarily assumed, resting on the assent of each party to the proposed exchange. The lawyer who demands or resists judicial enforcement is required to think and talk about the sort of agreement that initiates a contract, and to use the analytical tools and working rules by which this minimum initiating-agreement is determined.

An additional aim of this chapter is to suggest the difficulties encountered when one attempts to define in general terms the elements of agreement. The difficulties arise in large part from the range of human experience to which legal doctrines must apply. Consider the types of transactions in the cases that follow. Consider also the fact that these various consensual arrangements are discussed by the courts with a common vocabulary, and they are perceived as presenting a common problem—has sufficient agreement been achieved to justify enforcement in court? Is it too much to expect that problems appearing in such diverse forms will have enough common elements that a general theory can be made to include them all?

Raffles v. Wichelhaus

Court of Exchequer, 1864.
2 Hurlstone & Coltman 906.

Declaration. For that it was agreed between the plaintiff and the defendants, to wit, at Liverpool, that the plaintiff should sell to the defendants, and the defendants buy of the plaintiff, certain goods, to wit, 125 bales of Surat cotton, guaranteed middling fair merchant's Dhollorah, to arrive ex "Peerless" from Bombay; and that the cotton should be taken from the quay, and that the defendants would pay the plaintiff for the same at a certain rate, to wit, at the rate of 17¼ d. per pound, within a certain time then agreed upon after the arrival of the said goods in England.—Averments: that the said goods did arrive by the said ship from Bombay in England, to wit, at Liverpool, and the plaintiff was then and there ready and willing and offered to deliver the said goods to the defendants, etc. Breach: that the defendants refused to accept the said goods or pay the plaintiff for them.

Plea. That the said ship mentioned in the said agreement was meant and intended by the defendants to be the ship called the "Peerless," which sailed from Bombay, to wit, in October; and that the plaintiff was not ready and willing and did not offer to deliver to the defendants any bales of cotton which arrived by the last-mentioned ship, but instead thereof was only ready and willing, and offered to deliver to the defendants 125 bales of Surat cotton which arrived by another and different ship, which was also called the "Peerless," and which sailed from Bombay, to wit, in December.

Demurrer, and joinder therein.

Milward, in support of the demurrer.—The contract was for the sale of a number of bales of cotton of a particular description, which the plaintiff was ready to deliver. It is immaterial by what ship the cotton was to arrive, so that it was a ship called the "Peerless." The words "to arrive ex 'Peerless,' " only mean that if the vessel is lost on the voyage, the contract is to be at an end. [Pollock, C.B.—It would be a question for the jury whether both parties meant the same ship called the "Peerless."] That would be so if the contract was for the sale of a ship called the "Peerless;" but it is for the sale of cotton on board a ship of that name. [Pollock, C.B.—The defendant only bought that cotton which was to arrive by a particular ship. It may as well be said, that if there is a contract for the purchase of certain goods in warehouse A, that is satisfied by the delivery of goods of the same description in warehouse B.] In that case there would be goods in both warehouses; here it does not appear that the plaintiff had any goods on board the other "Peerless." [Martin, B.—It is imposing on the defendant a contract different from that which he entered into. Pollock, C.B.—It is like a contract for the purchase of wine coming from a particular estate in France or Spain, where there are two estates of that name.] The defendant has no right to contradict by parol evidence a written contract good upon the face of it. He does not impute misrepresentation or fraud, but only says that he fancied the ship was a different one. Intention is of no avail, unless stated at the time of the contract. [Pollock, C.B.—One vessel sailed in October and the other in December.] The time of sailing is no part of the contract.

Mellish (Cohen with him), in support of the plea.—There is nothing on the face of the contract to shew that any particular ship called the "Peerless" was meant; but the moment it appears that two ships called the "Peerless" were about to sail from Bombay there is a latent ambiguity, and parol evidence may be given for the purpose of shewing that the defendant meant one "Peerless" and the plaintiff another. That being so, there was no consensus ad idem, and therefore no binding contract.—He was then stopped by the Court.

Per Curiam—There must be judgment for the defendants.

[It has been reported that there were at least eleven ships called "Peerless" sailing the seven seas in 1863, including the two British vessels in question in Raffles v. Wichelhaus, both registered at the port of Liverpool. It is possible that, by specifying the ship in the contract, parties were able to lock in a fixed supply of cotton at a later date, something that was arguably important when the price of cotton was volatile and supplies uncertain, as it was during the American Civil War. In other words, these contracts were an early version of futures contracts. For a discussion of these issues, see Simpson, Contracts for Cotton to Arrive: The Case of the Two Ships *Peerless*, 11 Cardozo L.Rev. 287, 295 (1989).]

QUESTIONS

(1) Is Chief Baron Pollock's two-warehouse example distinguishable from the case of the two wine estates? Which is more like the principal case?

(2) Would the result be different if both parties had known there were two ships named Peerless sailing regularly from Bombay?

(3) What if both parties had known that there were two ships named Peerless sailing regularly from Bombay and both had understood the contract to refer to the same ship, sailing in October?

Flower City Painting Contractors v. Gumina Constr. Co.

591 F.2d 162 (2d Cir. 1979)

During performance of a painting subcontract, Flower, the sub, insisted that it was required to paint only interior walls of individual units within the apartment project, not exteriors. This reading of the subcontract depended upon a finding that the building plans and specifications had not been incorporated into the subcontract by reference. When Flower held to its interpretation by demanding additional compensation before proceeding with any exterior work, Gumina, the general contractor, cancelled the subcontract and removed Flower from the job. Flower sued for damages. The trial court adopted Gumina's interpretation of the subcontract and dismissed the complaint on the ground that Flower's "asking for extra pay for work it was obligated to do under its contract" was the equivalent of a repudiation, justifying cancellation. On appeal, the court preferred to bypass the "thorny problem" of repudiation presented by these facts. *Held*, judgment of dismissal affirmed under the rule of the *Peerless* case; no contract ever came into existence for lack of a "meeting of the minds in the first instance." Given the ambiguity created by multiple contract documents, two different understandings of the subject matter embraced by the contract are both possible and plausible. Yet the ambiguity might be resolved (in favor of Gumina) by construing the contract as incorporating the customary practice of the construction industry in the Rochester area, that painting subcontracts are awarded on "an entire project basis." But proof of a trade usage is not enough to establish the meaning of a contract, for a party is bound by usage only if "he either knows or has reason to know of its existence and nature." The proofs make clear that Flower did not know of the usage; hence the issue is whether it "had reason to know" of it. Flower was "a neophyte . . . painting contractor. This was its first substantial subcontract on a construction job. It would be unrealistic to hold it strictly to a 'reason to know' standard." Accordingly, "we cannot say that either party acted so unreasonably as to justify construing the ambiguity [against it]. Each party . . . held a different and reasonable view of the undertaking, Flower on the basis of its literal reading of the word 'units' and Gumina because of its supposition concerning trade practice. . . . Though the setting is new, the problem is old."

NOTE

In Konic Int'l Corp. v. Spokane Comput. Servs., Inc., 109 Idaho 527, 708 P.2d 932 (Ct. App. 1985), the seller had responded to the buyer's inquiry as to the price of certain computer equipment by saying "fifty-six twenty." The seller had meant $5,620; the buyer thought the asking price was $56.20; the misunderstanding was discovered not long after the equipment had been installed. The court, finding the parties equally at fault and bypassing other legal doctrines, treated the case as governed by the *Peerless* rule.

The *Konic* decision is noted in Colfax Envelope Corp. v. Local No. 458–3M, Chicago Graphic Commc'ns Int'l Union, 20 F.3d 750 (7th Cir. 1994) (Posner, J.):

> The premise—that a "meeting of the minds" is required for a binding contract—obviously is strained. . . . Most contract disputes arise because the parties did not foresee and provide for some contingency that has now materialized—so there was no meeting of minds on the matter at issue—yet such disputes are treated as disputes over contractual meaning, not as grounds for rescinding the contract and thus putting the parties back where they were before they signed it. So a literal meeting of the minds is not required for an enforceable contract. . . . [A] contract ought to be terminable without liability and the parties thus allowed to go their own ways when there is "no sensible basis for choosing between conflicting understandings" of the contractual language, as the court said in

an American *Raffles*-like case, Oswald v. Allen, 417 F.2d 43, 45 (2d Cir. 1969). . . .

If neither party can be assigned the greater blame for the misunderstanding, there is no nonarbitrary basis for deciding which party's understanding to enforce, so the parties are allowed to abandon the contract without liability. . . . These are not cases in which one party's understanding is more reasonable than the other's. Compare Restatement, supra, § 20(2)(b). If rescission were permitted in *that* kind of case, the enforcement of every contract would be at the mercy of a jury, which might be persuaded that one of the parties had genuinely held an idiosyncratic idea of its meaning, so that there had been, in fact, no meeting of the minds. . . . Intersubjectivity is not the test of an enforceable contract.

The clearest cases for rescission on the ground that there was "no meeting of the minds" (or, better, that there was a "latent ambiguity" in the sense that neither party knew that the contract was ambiguous) are ones in which an offer is garbled in transmission, [if] "transmission" is broadly construed. . . . [C]onsider *Konic International Corp.*[,] [where] both were equally at fault, being careless in their utterance and interpretation, respectively, of an ambiguous oral formula. . . .

It is common for contracting parties to agree—that is, to *signify* agreement—to a term to which each party attaches a different meaning. It is just a gamble on a favorable interpretation by the authorized tribunal should a dispute arise. Parties often prefer to gamble in this way rather than to take the time to try to iron out all their possible disagreements, most of which may never have any consequence. . . . When parties agree to a patently ambiguous term, they submit to have any dispute over it resolved by interpretation. That is what courts are *for* in contract cases—to resolve interpretive questions founded on ambiguity. It is when parties agree to terms that reasonably appear to each of them to be unequivocal but are not, cases like that of the ship Peerless where the ambiguity is buried, that the possibility of rescission on grounds of mutual misunderstanding, or, the term we prefer, latent ambiguity, arises.

Dickey v. Hurd

33 F.2d 415 (1st Cir. 1929)

Dickey, resident of Georgia, wrote to Hurd in Massachusetts asking the price for which Hurd would sell land he owned in Georgia. On July 8, 1926, Hurd replied "$15 per acre cash," adding, "I will give you till July 18, 1926 including that day to accept this offer." In two letters, written July 12 and July 15, Dickey expressed great interest in Hurd's land, stating that he would give his "answer" within the time limit. On July 17, Dickey telegraphed an acceptance and promised to send a down payment in a few days.

The telegram reached Hurd the same day. Hurd contended that the acceptance was ineffective because the offer called for the whole cash price to be paid by July 18. Bingham, J., said that the original offer was ambiguous, but Dickey's two letters indicated to Hurd that he believed only an "answer" was needed by July 18. When Hurd learned how Dickey interpreted the offer, it was Hurd's duty to inform him that the offer called for payment rather than a promise of payment. "It was not open to him to lie quietly by" until the time limit had expired, and then assert that full cash payment was required.

QUESTION

What if the plaintiff in Raffles v. Wichelhaus had known of the existence of both ships Peerless but defendant knew only the October Peerless?

Restatement of Contracts, Second

§ 20. Effect of Misunderstanding

(1) There is no manifestation of mutual assent to an exchange if the parties attach materially different meanings to their manifestations and

(a) neither party knows or has reason to know the meaning attached by the other; or

(b) each party knows or each party has reason to know the meaning attached by the other.

(2) The manifestations of the parties are operative in accordance with the meaning attached to them by one of the parties if

(a) that party does not know of any different meaning attached by the other, and the other knows the meaning attached by the first party; or

(b) that party has no reason to know of any different meaning attached by the other, and the other has reason to know the meaning attached by the first party.

NOTE

When Reporter Robert Braucher presented § 20 to the annual meeting of the American Law Institute in 1964, he explained that it was a "new construction" of the problem of the *Peerless* case—a problem he described as "general to the whole concept of mutual assent." Reporter Braucher added (41 A.L.I. Proc. 319–320 (1965)):

> I tried to straighten it out and get it into a form where I could understand it. . . . In my thinking about [mutual assent], this [§ 20] is a fairly fundamental proposition, and I refer back to it continually because it doesn't just deal with things that go to the heart of

> the transaction; . . . it also goes to understanding all kinds of incidental terms in a contract. The standard of interpretation may depend upon what one party understood and the other party knew he understood. I am anticipating here [the principles for determining rights and duties under a contract, where formation is not an issue], but it seemed to me you had to, in order to define mutual assent.

The *Peerless* decision has generated a considerable literature. See, e.g., Simpson, Contracts for Cotton to Arrive: The Case of the Two Ships *Peerless*, 11 Cardozo L. Rev. 287 (1989); Birmingham, Holmes on "Peerless": *Raffles v. Wichelhaus* and the Objective Theory of Contract, 47 U. Pitt. L. Rev. 183 (1985); G. Gilmore, The Death of Contract 35–44 (1974).

Some of the first readers of *Raffles* understood it to stand for the proposition that a contract came into being only if there were a subjective meeting of the minds. Oliver Wendell Holmes rejected this view. He believed that *Raffles* was consistent with an objective approach to determining the intent of the parties to enter into a contract. For him, the case turned on the accepted convention for proper names. Each of us is entitled to rely on the link that we make between a name and the person or object we associate with it. I can talk about someone I know by name and expect you to know to whom I am referring. If you are not sure, you need to ask. In this case, Raffles and Wichelhaus were objectively speaking of two different ships, as each was entitled to use "Peerless" to refer to the only ship each knew by that name. The same convention does not apply to ordinary nouns. I cannot use the word "pepper" when I mean "salt," and then later argue that there was never a meeting of the minds. If a merchant enters into a contract for "pepper," while genuinely thinking "salt," she will still be bound to deliver pepper. The words she actually spoke, as defined in the relevant lexicon, bind her regardless of what she was thinking. People communicate through a common language, and commerce depends upon the use of this common language. Merchants need to be able to take what they say to each other at face value. When you say "salt," I am entitled to hold you responsible for salt, regardless of what you subjectively intended.

Holmes's objectivist account of *Raffles* may not be the only or even the best reading of the case, but it has taken hold in large part because it comports so well with how lawyers and judges approach such problems. Indeed, as the noted legal historian Brian Simpson pointed out, it was a practicing lawyer who introduced *Raffles* to the canon, and his account of the case is, in large measure, an objective one. Judah P. Benjamin was a prominent leader of the Confederacy who reinvented himself as an English barrister after he was forced into exile. His treatise on sales has the first discussion of *Raffles*. He summarized the principle in this fashion:

> If *A* and *B* contract for the sale of the cargo per ship Peerless, and there be two ships of that name, and *A* mean one ship and *B* intend the other ship, there is no contract. But if there be but one ship Peerless, and *A* sell the cargo of that ship to *B*, the latter would not be permitted to excuse himself on the ground that he had in his mind the ship Peeress, and intended to contract for a cargo by this

> last-named ship. Men can only bargain by mutual communication, and if *A*'s proposal were unmistakable, as if it were made in writing, and *B*'s answer an unequivocal and unconditional acceptance, *B* would be bound, however clearly he might afterwards make it appear that he was thinking of a different vessel. For the rule of law is general, that whatever a man's real intention may be, if he manifests an intention to another party, so as to induce that other party to act upon it, he will be estopped from denying that the intention as manifested was his real intention.

See Judah P. Benjamin, A Treatise on the Law of Sale of Personal Property; Reference to the American Decisions and to the French Code and Civil Law 347–48 (J. Perkins ed., first American ed. 1875).

Learned Hand captured the objective approach to mutual assent in a vivid metaphor some years later:

> A contract has, strictly speaking, nothing to do with the personal, or individual, intent of the parties. A contract is an obligation attached by the mere force of law to certain acts of the parties, usually words, which ordinarily accompany and represent a known intent. If, however, it were proved by twenty bishops that either party, when he used the words, intended something else than the usual meaning which the law imposes upon them, he would still be held. . . .

Hotchkiss v. Nat'l City Bank of New York, 200 F. 287, 293 (S.D.N.Y. 1911). Everyone from Judah P. Benjamin to Holmes to Learned Hand can agree with the idea that parties to contracts adopt the formalities inherently associated with language. "Men can only bargain by mutual communication." If there is one ship Peerless and the contract unambiguously calls for cotton on the ship "Peerless," you cannot get off the hook by proving that you had the ship "Peeress" in mind when you entered into the deal. Everyone is both an objectivist and a formalist to at least this extent.

From the perspective of the practicing lawyer, however, the difference between a subjective and objective approach to the creation of the legally enforceable obligation may not in fact prove large. Even were a subjective test to apply, parties would still have to introduce evidence that persuades a jury of their subjective intent. Twenty bishops are likely to be available to testify as to my subjective intentions only when these intentions were objectively manifest. Similarly, if an objective test controlled, my subjective intent provides indirect evidence. Ordinarily, someone who subjectively intends to sell salt will appear objectively to want to sell salt. My subjective intention to sell salt (evidenced perhaps by telling my friends about the deal) is probative of my objective conduct (what I actually told you). See Kabil Devs. Corp. v. Mignot, 279 Or. 151, 566 P.2d 505 (Or. 1977).

A commitment to an objective approach does have consequences, however. When an objective benchmark is used to assess meaning, cases like *Raffles* tend to appear only in the rare cases when each party is entitled to use her own lexicon (such as when each refers to a proper noun). Parties are usually held to speak the same language. In these cases, when disputes arise, everyone agrees that there is a contract. The dispute is over the meaning of the agreement. Both parties agree that a single objective test determines what each said, but they disagree about what this test is. We shall return to this issue when we confront the problem of interpreting contracts in Chapter 4.

Embry v. Hargadine-McKittrick Dry Goods Co.

Court of Appeals, Missouri, 1907.
127 Mo.App. 383, 105 S.W. 777.

GOODE, J. . . . The appellant was an employee of the respondent company under a written contract to expire December 15, 1903, at a salary of $2,000 per annum. His duties were to attend to the sample department[,] of which he was given complete charge. It was his business to select samples for the traveling salesmen of the company, which is a wholesale dry goods concern, to use in selling goods to retail merchants. Appellant contends that on December 23, 1903, he was re-engaged by respondent, through its president, Thos. H. McKittrick, for another year at the same compensation and for the same duties stipulated in his previous written contract. On March 1, 1904, he was discharged, having been notified in February that, on account of the necessity of retrenching expenses, his services and that of some other employees would no longer be required. The respondent contends that its president never re-employed appellant after the termination of his written contract, and hence that it had a right to discharge him when it chose. The point with which we are concerned requires an epitome of the testimony of appellant and the counter testimony of McKittrick, [in] reference to the alleged re-employment. Appellant testified: That several times prior to the termination of his written contract on December 15, he had endeavored to get an understanding with McKittrick for another year, but had been put off from time to time. That on December 23d, eight days after the expiration of said contract, he called on McKittrick, in the latter's office, and said to him that as appellant's written employment had lapsed eight days before, and as there were only a few days between then and the 1st of January in which to seek employment with other firms, if respondent wished to retain his services longer he must have a contract for another year, or he would quit respondent's service then and there. That he had been put off twice before and wanted an understanding or contract at once so that he could go ahead without worry. That McKittrick asked him how he was getting along in his department, and appellant said he was very busy, as they were in the height of the season getting men out—had about 110 salesmen on the line and others in preparation. That McKittrick then said: "Go ahead, you're all right. Get your men out, and don't let that worry you." That appellant took McKittrick at his word and worked until February 15th without any question in his mind. It was on February 15th that he was notified his services would be discontinued on March 1st.

McKittrick denied this conversation as related by appellant, and said that, when accosted by the latter on December 23d, he (McKittrick) was working on his books in order to get out a report for a stockholders' meeting, and, when appellant said if he did not get a contract he would leave, that he (McKittrick) said: "Mr. Embry, I am just getting ready for the stockholders' meeting tomorrow. I have no time to take it up now. I have told you before I would not take it up until I had these matters out of the way. You will have to see me at a later time. I said: 'Go back upstairs and get your men out on the road.' I may have asked him one or two other questions relative to the department, I don't remember. The whole conversation did not take more than a minute."

Embry also swore that, when he was notified he would be discharged, he complained to McKittrick about it, as being a violation of their contract, and McKittrick said it was due to the action of the board of directors, and not to any personal action of his, and that others would suffer by what the board had done as well as Embry. Appellant requested an instruction to the jury setting out, in substance, the conversation between him and McKittrick according to his version, and declaring that those facts, if found to be true, constituted a contract between the parties that defendant would pay plaintiff the sum of $2,000 for another year, provided the jury believed from the evidence that plaintiff commenced said work believing he was to have $2,000 for the year's work. This instruction was refused, but the court gave another embodying in substance appellant's version of the conversation, and declaring it made a contract "if you (the jury) find both parties thereby intended and did contract with each other for plaintiff's employment for one year from and including December 23, at a salary of $2,000 per annum." Embry swore that, on several occasions when he spoke to McKittrick about employment for the ensuing year, he asked for a renewal of his former contract, and that on December 23d, the date of the alleged renewal, he went into Mr. McKittrick's office and told him his contract had expired, and he wanted to renew it for a year, having always worked under year contracts. Neither the refused instruction nor the one given by the court embodied facts quite as strong as appellant's testimony, because neither referred to appellant's alleged statement to McKittrick that unless he was re-employed he would stop work for respondent then and there.

It is assigned for error that the court required the jury, in order to return a verdict for appellant, not only to find the conversation occurred as appellant swore, but that both parties intended by such conversation to contract with each other for plaintiff's employment for the year from December, 1903. . . . [T]o put the question more precisely: Did what was said constitute a contract of re-employment on the previous terms irrespective of the intention or purpose of McKittrick?

Judicial opinion and elementary treatises abound in statements of the rule that to constitute a contract there must be a meeting of the minds of the parties, and both must agree to the same thing in the same sense. Generally speaking, this may be true; but it is not literally or universally true. That is to say, the inner intention of parties to a conversation subsequently alleged to create a contract cannot either make a contract of what transpired, or prevent one from arising, if the words used were sufficient to constitute a contract. In so far as their intention is an influential element, it is only such intention as the words or acts of the parties indicate. . . . In 9 Cyc. 245, we find the following text: "The law imputes to a person an intention corresponding to the reasonable meaning of his words and acts. It judges his intention by his outward expressions and excludes all questions in regard to his unexpressed intention. If his words or acts, judged by a reasonable standard, manifest an intention to agree in regard to the matter in question, that agreement is established, and it is immaterial what may be the real, but unexpressed, state of his mind on the subject." . . . In view of those authorities, we hold that, though McKittrick may not have intended to employ Embry by what transpired between them according to the latter's testimony, yet if what McKittrick said would have been taken by a reasonable man to be an employment, and Embry so understood it, it constituted a valid contract of employment for the ensuing year.

The next question is whether or not the language used was of that character, namely, was such that Embry, as a reasonable man, might consider he was re-employed for the ensuing year on the previous terms, and act accordingly. We do not say that in every instance it would be for the court to pronounce on this question, because, peradventure, instances might arise in which there would be such an ambiguity in the language relied on to show an assent by the obligor to the proposal of the obligee that it would be for the jury to say whether a reasonable mind would take it to signify acceptance of the proposal. . . . The general rule is that it is for the court to construe the effect of writings relied on to make a contract, and also the effect of unambiguous oral words. . . . However, if the words are in dispute, the question of whether they were used or not is for the jury. . . .

With these rules of law in mind, let us recur to the conversation of December 23d between Embry and McKittrick as related by the former. Embry was demanding a renewal of his contract, saying he had been put off from time to time, and that he had only a few days before the end of the year in which to seek employment from other houses, and that he would quit then and there unless he was reemployed. McKittrick inquired how he was getting along with the department, and Embry said they, i.e., the employés of the department, were very busy getting out salesmen. Whereupon McKittrick said: "Go ahead, you are all right. Get your men out, and do not let that worry you." We think no reasonable man would construe that answer to Embry's demand that he be employed for another year, otherwise than as an assent to the demand, and that Embry had the right to rely on it as an assent. The natural inference is, though we do not find it testified to, that Embry was at work getting samples ready for the salesmen to use during the ensuing season. Now, when he was complaining of the worry and mental distress he was under because of his uncertainty about the future, and his urgent need, either of an immediate contract with respondent, or a refusal by it to make one, leaving him free to seek employment elsewhere, McKittrick must have answered as he did for the purpose of assuring appellant that any apprehension was needless, as appellant's services would be retained by the respondent. The answer was unambiguous, and we rule that if the conversation was according to appellant's version, and he understood he was employed, it constituted in law a valid contract of re-employment, and the court erred in making the formation of a contract depend on a finding that both parties intended to make one. It was only necessary that Embry, as a reasonable man, had a right to and did so understand. . . .

The judgment is reversed, and the cause remanded.

New York Trust Co. v. Island Oil & Transport Corp.

34 F.2d 655 (2d Cir. 1929)

Island Oil, in order to circumvent restrictions on its owning and exploiting oil-bearing lands within 50 kilometers of the Mexican coast, organized several Mexican subsidiary corporations to appear as owners and operators. Island Oil held virtually all of the stock in the subsidiaries and in fact operated the oil fields; no significant role was played by the Mexican officers of the subsidiaries. Nevertheless, in compliance with Mexican law, accounts were kept that showed substantial sales of oil from the subsidiaries to Island Oil and balances due. Island Oil mortgaged its stock in the subsidiaries, and these shares were later sold in a foreclosure. In an equity receivership of Island Oil, a proceeding similar in purpose to a bankruptcy reorganization, the new owners of one of the subsidiaries filed a claim against the receiver of Island Oil for the balances. *Held*, decree dismissing the claim affirmed. The apparent sales of oil and the substantial balances due were shams. Judge Learned Hand, speaking for the Court:

"However, the form of utterance chosen is never final; it is always possible to show that the parties did not intend to perform what they said they would, as, for example, that the transaction was a joke. . . . It is quite true that contracts depend upon the meaning which the law imputes to the utterances, not upon what the parties actually intended; but, in ascertaining what meaning to impute, the circumstances in which the words are used are always relevant and usually indispensable. The standard is what a normally constituted person would have understood them to mean, when used in their actual setting. In the case at bar it is abundantly clear that no such person, making the records here in question in such a background, would have supposed that they represented actual sales of oil; that is, commercial transactions. They were made for quite other purposes, formally to conform with, and, if one chooses, to evade, the [law]. They were a sham, which nobody did, and nobody advised could, understand as intended to be more. . . .

"The question then becomes whether legal obligations shall be attached to utterances which would otherwise not create them, because they were part of a plan to deceive third persons. We are to distinguish between such a situation and one in which the person deceived has acted in reliance upon the truth of the utterances, and bases his rights upon them, for here we are only concerned with the existence of obligations between parties equally implicated. We cannot see why their common fault should so change the relations between them. Indeed, if we were asked to intervene between them, and give relief based upon the sham transaction, we might refuse; 'in pari delicto potior est conditio possidentis.' Here we must raise an obligation where none would otherwise exist, because by hypothesis both were concerned in a fraud upon a third. As compensation, this would be fruitless; as punishment, it would be capricious; as law, it would create an obligation ex turpi causa."

[Judge Hand, writing seven years later, said: "[W]hatever the formal documentary evidence, it is no objection that [the parties' understanding that a purported contract was not to bind them] contradicts the writing; a writing is conclusive only so far as the parties intend it to be the authoritative memorial of the transaction. Whatever the presumptions, their actual understanding may always be shown except so far as expressly or implicitly they have agreed that the writing alone shall control." In re H. Hicks & Son, 82 F.2d 277, 279 (2d Cir. 1936).]

Robbins v. Lynch

836 F.2d 330, 332 (7th Cir. 1988)

"References in cases to the importance of 'intent to be bound' are misleading if taken literally. As so frequently in law, 'intent' is a conclusion rather than a fact. A signatory to a contract is bound by its ordinary meaning even if he gave it an idiosyncratic one; private intent counts only if it is conveyed to the other party and shared. You can't escape contractual obligation by signing with your fingers crossed behind your back. . . . The parties are free to sign hortatory as well as binding documents; 'intent' is important in the sense that if the parties agree on a hortatory instrument the court may not convert it into a different kind. This sense of 'intent' denotes agreement between the parties and is not a license to allow undisclosed intent to dominate. Even statutes, widely said to follow the 'intent of the legislature,' draw meaning only from the visible indicators such as their structure, the nature of the problem at hand, and public statements (as in committee reports). Private intent is irrelevant."

SECTION 2. OFFER AND ACCEPTANCE

Bridge City Family Medical Clinic, P.C. v. Kent & Johnson, LLP

Court of Appeals of Oregon, 2014.
270 Or. App. 115, 346 P.3d 658.

GARRETT, J. . . . This appeal presents an issue of contract formation. Defendants represented plaintiff in an arbitration. Dissatisfied with the result, plaintiff contacted defendants' malpractice insurer, the Professional Liability Fund (PLF), regarding possible claims against defendants. Bunker, plaintiff's president, and Schafer, the adjuster on behalf of the PLF, exchanged several emails discussing a settlement. When plaintiff later brought this action, defendants moved for summary judgment, arguing that a binding settlement agreement had been reached. The trial court agreed, granted defendants' motion, and entered a judgment of dismissal. We affirm.

The issue on appeal turns entirely on the interpretation of correspondence that began on August 15, 2012, when Bunker first emailed Schafer. Bunker sent Schafer an email stating that she believed she was "entitled to something" as a result of how defendants had represented plaintiff during an arbitration. Her email included this text:

> I would like to discuss with you the option of a settlement. If there is a relatively reasonable but comparatively small amount of money that we could agree on to settle this matter I believe it would be mutually beneficial.

In a letter to Bunker dated August 20, 2012, Schafer wrote, "If you are interested in trying to resolve the claim for 'a comparatively small amount of money,' then I suggest you make a specific proposal that the PLF might consider."

On August 21, Bunker emailed back, "This is in response to your letter I received today. I am willing to settle this and move on for $40,000."

In a letter dated August 23, Schafer wrote the following:

> This will respond to your August 21, 2012 email proposing a settlement of $40,000.
>
> The PLF, on behalf of Kent & Johnson, will pay Bridge City Family Medical Clinic, P.C., the total sum of $10,000 in return for Bridge City's and your release of [defendants]. In addition, Kent & Johnson offer to release Bridge City and you from claims for reimbursement of $5,506.25 paid by Kent & Johnson to Judicial Dispute Resolution, LLC on Bridge City's behalf after Bridge City failed to pay that bill. For your information, enclosed is a copy of Judicial Dispute Resolution's July 13, 2011

invoice and Chris Kent's October 13, 2011 letter to you. If settlement on these terms is acceptable, I will prepare the necessary Mutual Release.

I want to remind you that the PLF is [defendants'] professional liability carrier. Our interests are adverse to yours and to those of Bridge City. I encourage you and Bridge City to obtain your own independent legal advice before you agree to any settlement or sign any settlement documents.

On August 27, Bunker sent Schafer a short email stating, "This will respond to your letter dated August 23, 2012 proposing a settlement of $10,000. I am willing to meet you in the middle and settle this matter immediately for $20,000."

Schafer responded to Bunker with a letter dated August 28:

This will respond to your August 27, 2012 email to me proposing a settlement of $20,000.

The PLF, on behalf of Kent & Johnson, will pay Bridge City Family Medical Clinic, PC the total sum of $13,500 in return for Bridge City's and your release of [defendants]. In addition, Kent & Johnson continue to offer to release Bridge City and you from claims for reimbursement of the $5,506.25 paid by Kent & Johnson to Judicial Dispute Resolution, LLC.

If these terms are acceptable, please confirm and I will draft an appropriate settlement document.

On August 29, Bunker emailed her response to Schafer, rejecting the $13,500 offer:

This is in response to your letter I received today dated 8/28/12. Your first counter offer of $10,000 was 25% of what I originally asked you for in my first letter. You point out that Mr. Kent and Ms. Johnson have offered to release me from the $5506.25; however they have already dismissed that claim against me as was noted in a letter to me in October of 2011. In response to your offer of $10,000, I again moved 50% to the middle at $20,000, in response you offered to move again about 25% to $13,500. By settling this claim now, nearly a year before the statute of limitations expires, I will be walking away from a claim that potentially may settle in my favor for hundreds of thousands of dollars. As such, I continue to remain torn as to the best course of action. Please meet me close to the $20,000 mark. I am willing to settle for $19,000.

Schafer replied to Bunker in a letter dated August 30, increasing PLF's offer to $15,000:

This will respond to your August 29, 2012 email to me proposing a settlement of $19,000.

> The PLF will pay $15,000 to settle this claim. All of the other terms are the same as my letter to you of August 28, 2012.
>
> If this is acceptable, I will prepare the Mutual Release for your review.

In a September 6 reply email, Bunker rejected the latest offer and stuck to the $19,000 number:

> This is in response to your most recent letter dated August 30, 2012 proposing a settlement for $15,000.
>
> I am still of the mind that I deserve to be compensated fully . . . . I originally asked for $40,000, which is a mere pittance comparatively. I continue to be willing to settle this for $19,000.

The correspondence continued with a September 7 letter from Schafer to Bunker:

> I am in receipt of your September 6, 2012 email renewing your offer to settle the claim against Kent & Johnson for $19,000.
>
> The PLF and Kent & Johnson accept your offer. Enclosed are duplicate originals of the Mutual Release I have prepared for your review and signature, if it is acceptable. Kent & Johnson have already approved it.
>
> If the Mutual Release is acceptable, please have it signed by Bridge City Family Medical Clinic, PC and you in the presence of a Notary Public and send one of the originals back to me. I have sent duplicate originals to Kent & Johnson for their signature and return to me and I will provide one to you once the document is fully executed.
>
> I have obtained a check in the amount of $19,000, payable to Bridge City Family Medical Clinic, P.C. We will hold that check until we receive a complete set of signed documents from you and Kent & Johnson. Once we have all the documents signed, we will transmit the settlement check to you. The Mutual Release will not be effective until all the parties have signed it. Signatures in counterpart are authorized in the Mutual Release. . . .
>
> I encourage you to consult with independent counsel of your choice, at your expense, regarding the terms of this Mutual Release. You are under no pressure to sign anything until you have had that opportunity. Whether you consult with outside counsel is up to you, but I want to be sure you have the opportunity if you choose to do so.

On September 24, having received no answer to his September 7 letter, Schafer wrote Bunker another letter reminding her that he was waiting for her response. On October 9, still having heard nothing, Schafer wrote the following letter:

> The purpose of this letter is to follow-up on my letter to you of September 24, 2012.
>
> You made a settlement offer on September 6, 2012, which was accepted by my letter to you of September 7, 2012. The PLF is ready to perform our settlement, and in fact, I have a settlement check in my file in the amount of $19,000, payable to Bridge City Family Medical Clinic, PC. I will send that check to you once the settlement documents are fully executed and in my possession.
>
> I look forward to receipt from you of the Mutual Release, executed by you and Bridge City Medical Clinic, PC. If there are any specific concerns you have with respect to the terms in the Mutual Release, please let me know. I would like to complete performance of our settlement.

Three weeks later, on October 30, 2012, plaintiff's attorney sent Schafer a letter stating that plaintiff "asked me to review the proposed settlement agreement as well as her files. She has decided not to settle on the terms set forth in your recent correspondence or, at this time settle."

On November 1, Schafer sent a letter to plaintiff's attorney stating, among other things, that plaintiff

> made a proposal, and we accepted it. Notwithstanding her unwillingness to sign the Mutual Release I sent to her, there is a settlement. If you and she want to discuss modification of the wording of the Mutual Release, I am amendable to those discussions, but this claim was settled, and the PLF and Kent & Johnson are ready, willing, and able to fully perform as agreed. The essential terms of the deal were agreed upon, and the settlement is enforceable.

Plaintiff subsequently brought this case against defendants, alleging professional malpractice. Defendants moved for summary judgment on the ground that the claim had been settled as a result of the communications between Bunker and Schafer. Defendants also served a request for admission that asked plaintiff to "[a]dmit that as a result of Exhibits A through N [the correspondence between Bunker and Schafer], the claim of plaintiff against defendants was agreed to be settled for a payment of $19,000 by the PLF and the mutual release of claims between defendants and against plaintiff." . . .

Even when it has not been reduced to a formal writing, a valid contract can be created "by [an] offer and its unqualified acceptance." Williams v. Burdick, 63 Or. 41, 49, 125 P. 844, 126 P. 603 (1912). To determine whether the parties intended to enter into a binding agreement, Oregon courts "examine the objective manifestations of intent, as evidenced by the parties' communications and acts." [Real Estate Loan Fund v. Hevner, 76 Or. App. 349, 354, 709 P.2d 727 (1985).] Those manifestations of intent must show that there has been a "meeting of the minds" as to the contract's terms and that no material terms remain for future negotiation. Phillips v. Johnson, 266 Or. 544, 555, 514 P.2d 1337 (1973). Thus, the offer to form a contract "must be certain so that upon an unqualified acceptance the nature and extent of the obligations of each party are fixed and may be determined with reasonable certainty." Klimek v. Perisich, 231 Or. 71, 78–79, 371 P.2d 956 (1962). Likewise,

> the acceptance must coincide with and be in the same terms as the offer, and . . . if a new provision is suggested the answer is a mere counter-offer, and, until that has been assented to by the one making the offer, there is no meeting of the minds and hence no contract.

Small v. Paulson, 187 Or. 76, 85, 209 P.2d 779 (1949).

Plaintiff argues that Bunker never made a clear, unequivocal offer capable of acceptance; rather, she merely expressed a "willingness" to settle. Plaintiff further argues that, even if there was an offer by plaintiff, Schafer's purported acceptance introduced a new term—the mutual release—that plaintiff never accepted. Plaintiff contends that, as a result, there was never a meeting of the minds between the parties on the material terms of an agreement. Defendants' view of the case is that plaintiff's *initial* communication on August 15 expressed a "willingness" to settle, Schafer's August 20 response invited plaintiff to make a specific offer, and the subsequent six communications were, in fact, a negotiation comprising offers and counteroffers. Defendants argue that the mutual release became a material term that plaintiff tacitly accepted by failing to object when Schafer repeatedly included it.

Defendants have the better argument. Bunker's first email indicated only a desire to "discuss with [Schafer] the option of a settlement." Schafer then asked Bunker to make a proposal. After that, the nature of the communications changed. Bunker promptly responded with the statement that she was "willing to settle this and move on for $40,000." A reasonable person in Schafer's position would have interpreted that statement as an offer to settle the dispute in exchange for a payment of $40,000.

Schafer responded with a counteroffer on August 23 that included two material terms: a payment of $10,000 and the execution of a mutual release. Schafer's letter was couched unmistakably in the form of an offer of settlement. Bunker's August 27 response said, "I am willing to meet you in the middle and settle this matter immediately for $20,000." As with her previous email, Bunker communicated not merely a willingness in principle to settle the dispute, but an unconditional offer to settle immediately for a specific amount. The same can be said of Schafer's August 28 letter (another unmistakable offer that moved the dollar figure to $13,500 and reiterated the need for a mutual release) and Bunker's August 29 reply (which proposed $19,000, again without condition). Schafer's August 30 counteroffer proposed $15,000 and expressly incorporated the other terms set forth in his August 28 letter. On September

6, Bunker declined to come down any further, replying, "I continue to be willing to settle this for $19,000." On September 7, Schafer accepted.

Plaintiff's attempt to characterize Bunker's series of communications as no more than a "statement of intention" is unpersuasive. Bunker initially indicated only her desire to pursue a settlement. No response to that email could have resulted in a binding contract. After being asked by Schafer to make a "specific proposal," however, that is precisely what Bunker did. Her statements that she would settle "immediately" for $40,000, $20,000, and then $19,000 were specific offers. The wording and tone of Bunker's emails indicate that she understood the exchange to be a negotiation toward an actual settlement, not a mere discussion. Moreover, although Schafer's communications encouraged Bunker to seek independent legal advice, Bunker's responses never made her offers contingent on review by an attorney (or on any other occurrence).

It is true that Bunker never expressly manifested her assent to the mutual release. But her express assent was not required in order for the mutual release to become a term of the contract, if Schafer would have reasonably understood Bunker to have accepted it. See Kitzke v. Turnidge, 209 Or. 563, 573, 307 P.2d 522 (1957) (" 'Though assent must be manifested in order to be legally effective, it need not be expressed in words. . . . Even where words are used, a contract includes not only what the parties said, but also what is necessarily to be implied from what they said.' ") (quoting Samuel Williston, 11 *Williston on Contracts* § 22A (3d ed. 1957)).

Under these circumstances, Schafer would have understood Bunker to have accepted the mutual release. In every one of his communications, Schafer made it clear that a mutual release would be included. In her responses, Bunker expressed no disagreement or concern regarding a mutual release. It is also significant that, in her August 29 email, Bunker said, "You point out that Mr. Kent and Ms. Johnson have offered to release me from the $5506.25; however they have already dismissed that claim against me as was noted in a letter to me in October of 2011." That statement demonstrates both that Bunker appreciated that a mutual release was to be included (she had not failed to notice or understand) and that she did not view it as a particularly noteworthy feature of a settlement. As Bunker continued to negotiate only the dollar term of the settlement and made no objection to the mutual release, a reasonable person on the other side of the negotiation would have understood that Bunker had assented to the inclusion of that term. Thus, in Bunker's final email on September 6, when she reiterated the $19,000 figure, the mutual release had become a term of the offers and counteroffers.

Plaintiff also argues that the exchange of correspondence failed to achieve a binding contract because Schafer's letter of September 7 said that the mutual release "will not be effective until all the parties have signed it." Plaintiff's argument conflates two distinct ideas. Parties can agree that a contract will not be binding unless and until it is reduced to writing. That is not what happened here. By the terms of Schafer's correspondence, the *release* was not to become effective until signed. The *contract* between the parties was achieved when they reached an accord on the dollar amount and *the fact that a release would be executed.* Thus, the signing of the release was a condition precedent to the performance of the contract, not to the formation of the contract.

Morrison v. Thoelke

District Court of Appeal of Florida, 1963.
155 So. 2d 889.

ALLEN, ACTING CHIEF JUDGE. Appellants, defendants and counter-plaintiffs in the lower court, appeal a summary final decree for appellees, plaintiffs and counter-defendants below. The appellees, owners of certain realty, sued to quiet title, specifically requesting that appellants be enjoined from making any claim under a recorded contract for the sale of the subject realty. [A]ppellants counterclaimed, seeking specific performance of the same contract and conveyance of the subject property to them. . . .

A number of undisputed facts were established[:] that appellees are the owners of the property, located in Orange County; that on November 26, 1957, appellants, as purchasers, executed a contract for the sale and purchase of the property and mailed the contract to appellees who were in Texas; that on November 27, appellees executed the contract and placed it in the mails addressed to appellants' attorney in Florida[;] [and] that after mailing said contract, but prior to its receipt in Florida, appellees called appellants' attorney and cancelled and repudiated the execution and contract. Nonetheless, appellants, upon receipt of the contract caused the same to be recorded. . . .

The basis of [the lower court's] decision [for appellees] was[:] . . . "[T]he contract executed by the parties hereto . . . [was] cancelled and repudiated by Plaintiffs prior to its receipt by Defendants . . . and [thus] there was no legal contract binding on the parties."

. . . [W]e are confronted with a question apparently of first impression in this jurisdiction[,] whether a contract is complete and binding when a letter of acceptance is mailed, thus barring repudiation prior to delivery to the offeror, or when the letter of acceptance is received, thus permitting repudiation prior to receipt. . . .

The appellant, in arguing that the lower court erred in giving effect to the repudiation of the mailed acceptance, contends that this case is controlled by the general rule that insofar as the mail is an acceptable medium of communication, a contract is complete and binding upon posting of the letter of acceptance. . . . Appellees, on the other hand, argue that the right to recall mail makes the Post Office Department the agent of the sender, and that such right coupled with communication of a renunciation prior to receipt of the acceptance voids the acceptance. In short, appellees argue that acceptance is complete only upon receipt of the mailed acceptance. . . .

[The court quoted at length from Williston on Contracts and other authority.]

A second leading treatise[,] Corbin, Contracts §§ 78, 80 (1950 Supp. 1961), also [discusses] the "rule" urged by appellants. Corbin writes: "Where the parties are negotiating at a distance from each other, the most common method of making an offer is by sending it by mail; and more often than not the offeror has specified no particular mode of acceptance. In such a case, it is now the prevailing rule that the offeree has power to accept and close the contract by mailing a letter of acceptance, properly stamped and addressed, within a reasonable time. The contract is regarded as made at the time and place that the letter of acceptance is put into the possession of the post office department."

Like the editor of Williston, Corbin negates the effect of the offeree's power to recall his letter:

"The postal regulations have for a long period made it possible for the sender of a letter to intercept it and prevent its delivery to the addressee. This has caused some doubt . . . as to whether an acceptance can ever be operative upon the mere mailing of the letter. . . .

"It is believed that no such doubt should exist. . . . [T]he fact that a letter can be lawfully intercepted by the sender should not prevent the acceptance from being operative on mailing. If the offer was made under such circumstances that the offeror should know that the offeree might reasonably regard this as a proper method of closing the deal, and the offeree does so regard it, and makes use of it, the contract is consummated even though the letter of acceptance is intercepted and not delivered."

Significantly, Corbin distinguishes cases involving bank drafts or bills of exchange from cases involving bilateral contracts[:] "It should be borne in mind that whenever the receipt of the letter is necessary to produce some legal effect, the interception, and resulting nondelivery of the letter will prevent that effect. For almost all purposes, other than the acceptance of an offer, the mere mailing of a letter is not enough to attain the purpose. Unless it is clearly otherwise agreed, the mailing of a letter is not a sufficient notice to quit a tenancy, it is not actual payment of money that is inclosed, it does not transfer title to a check or other document. . . ."

A [case] cited by appellee, Dick v. United States, 82 F.Supp. 326, 113 Ct.Cl. 94 (1949), involved mistaken acceptance of an offer evidenced by a government purchase order. The appellant, after mailing his acceptance wired a repudiation of the acceptance. The repudiation was received prior to the acceptance. Although remanding the cause for proofs, the court inferred that the fact of a mailed acceptance did not, as a matter of law, bar subsequent repudiation. . . . [T]he court, over a vigorous dissent, concluded that the Post Office was the sender's [offeree's] agent and that "delivery" was incomplete so long as the acceptance had not been received.

The same court, in Rhode Island Tool Co. v. United States, 128 F.Supp. 417, 130 Ct.Cl. 698 (1955), extended the principle that a contract was made only upon receipt of the acceptance to permit revocation of an offer after an acceptance [mistakingly stating too low a price] had been posted but prior to its receipt. Again predicating its decision on the postal regulations, the court concluded [that] "the [Post Office] becomes, in effect, the agency of the sender until actual delivery." . . .

The rule that a contract is complete upon deposit of the acceptance in the mails, [hereinbefore referred to as "deposited acceptance rule"] had its origin . . . in Adams v. Lindsell, 1 Barn. & Ald. 681, 106 Eng.Rep. 250 (K.B. 1818). In that case, the defendants had sent an offer to plaintiffs on September 2nd, indicating that they expected an answer "in course of post." The offer was misdirected and was not received and accepted until the 5th, the acceptance being mailed that day and received by defendant-offerors on the 9th. However, the defendants, who had expected to receive the acceptance on or before the 7th, sold the goods offered on the 8th of September. It was conceded that the delay had been occasioned by the fault of the defendants in initially misdirecting the offer.

Defendants contended that no contract had been made until receipt of the offer on the 9th. ". . . They relied on Payne v. Cave, 3 T.R. 148, and more particularly on Cooke v. Oxley, [ibid., 653]. In that case Oxley, who had proposed to sell goods to Cooke, and given him a certain time at his request, to determine whether he would buy them or not, was held not liable to the performance of the contract, even though Cooke, within the specified time, had determined to buy them, and given Oxley notice to that effect. So here the defendants who have proposed by letter to sell this wool, are not to be held liable, even though it be now admitted that the answer did come back in due course of post. Till the plaintiffs' answer was actually received there could be no binding contract between the parties; and before then the defendants had retracted their offer by selling the wool to other persons.

"But the court said that if that were so, no contract could ever be completed by the post. For if the defendants were not bound by their offer when accepted by the plaintiffs till the answer was received, then the plaintiffs ought not to be bound till after they had received the notification that the defendants had received their answer and assented to it. And so it might go on ad infinitum. The defendants must be considered in law as making, during every instant of the time their letter was traveling, the same identical offer to the plaintiffs, and then the contract is completed by the acceptance of it by the latter. Then as to the delay in notifying the acceptance, that arises entirely from the mistake of the defendants, and it therefore must be taken as against them that the plaintiffs' answer was received in course of post."

Examination of [Adams v. Lindsell] reveals three distinct factors deserving consideration. The first and most significant is the court's obvious concern with the necessity of drawing a line, with establishing some point at which a contract is deemed complete and their equally obvious concern with the thought that if communication of each party's assent were necessary, the negotiations would be interminable. A second factor, again a practical one, was the court's apparent desire to limit but not overrule the decision in Cooke v. Oxley, 3 T.R. 653 [1790], that an offer was revocable at any time prior to acceptance. In application to contracts negotiated by mail, this latter rule would permit revocation even after unqualified assent unless the assent was deemed effective upon posting. Finally, having chosen a point at which negotiations would terminate and having effectively circumvented the inequities of Cooke v. Oxley, the court, apparently constrained to offer some theoretical justification for its decision, designated a mailed offer as "continuing" and found a meeting of the minds upon the instant of posting assent. Significantly, the factor of the offeree's loss of control of his acceptance is not mentioned. . . .

[I]t would seem clear that in attempting to provide additional justification for the "deposited acceptance" rule, the courts, in fact, served only to confuse and weaken the essential validity of the rule. Thus, the observation that the offeror having chosen to utilize the mails should bear the risk of delay occasioned thereby was extended by subsequent cases to a point wherein the validity of the contract was made to turn on a theory of communication to an agent. . . . [T]his fictitious agency theory cannot withstand criticism. 1 Corbin, Contracts, § 78 (1950). . . .

Similarly, the "loss of control" theory, having its origin in the observation that under general contract principles an acceptance is manifest only when the offeree loses the power to suppress the manifestation, has, by a process of extension, come to be urged as a factor of primary legal significance. Yet . . . the "loss of control" was not deemed controlling in the earliest cases. Nor is the general principle that a manifestation of assent must be beyond the party's control to be effective any more sacred than the general rule that assent in contract must be communicated. Yet the latter is obviously qualified in the "deposited acceptance" rule and in many instances of unilateral contract. Why then should the "loss of control" principle not also be—or have been—qualified? . . .

The justification for the "deposited acceptance" rule proceeds from the uncontested premise of Adams v. Lindsell that there must be, both in practical and conceptual terms, a point in time when a contract is complete. In the formation of contracts inter praesentes this point is readily reached upon expressions of assent instantaneously communicated. In the formation of contracts inter absentes by post, however, delay in communication prevents concurrent knowledge of assents and some point must be chosen as legally significant. The problem raised by the impossibility of concurrent knowledge of manifest assent is discussed [in] Corbin, Contracts § 78 (1950).

> A better explanation of the existing rule seems to be that the mailing of a letter has long been a customary and expected way of accepting the offer. It is ordinary business usage. More than this, however, is needed to explain why the letter is operative on mailing rather than on receipt. . . . Even though it is business usage to send an offer by mail, it creates no power of acceptance until it is received. Indeed, most notices sent by mail are not operative unless actually received.
>
> The additional reasons for holding that a different rule applies to an acceptance and that it is operative on mailing may be suggested as follows: When an offer is by mail and the acceptance also is by mail, the contract must date either from the mailing of the acceptance or from its receipt. In either case, one of the parties will be bound by the contract without being actually aware of that fact. If we hold the offeror bound on the mailing of the acceptance, he may change his position in ignorance of the acceptance. . . . Therefore this rule is going to cause loss and inconvenience to the offeror in some cases. But if we adopt the alternative rule that the letter of acceptance is not operative until receipt, it is the offeree who is subjected to the danger of loss and inconvenience. He can not know that his letter has been received and that he is bound by contract until a new communication is received by him. His letter of acceptance may never have been received and so no letter of notification is sent to him; or it may have been received, and the letter of notification may be delayed or entirely lost in the mails. One of the parties must carry the risk of loss and inconvenience. We need a definite and uniform rule as to this. . . . The business community could no doubt adjust itself to either rule; but the rule throwing the risk on the offeror has the merit of closing the deal more quickly and enabling performance more promptly. It must be remembered that in the vast majority of cases the acceptance is neither lost nor delayed. . . . Also it is the offeror who has invited the acceptance.

. . . As Corbin indicated, there must be a choice made, and such choice may, by the nature of things, seem unjust in some cases. Weighing the arguments with reference not to specific cases but toward a rule of general application and recognizing the general and traditional acceptance of the rule as well as the modern changes in effective long-distance communication, it would seem that the balance tips, whether heavily or near imperceptibly, to continued adherence to the "Rule in Adams

v. Lindsell." This rule [is], in our view, in accord with the practical considerations and essential concepts of contract law. See Llewellyn, Our Case Law of Contracts; Offer and Acceptance II, 48 Yale L.J. 779, 795 (1939). . . . [T]raditional rules and concepts should not be abandoned save on compelling ground. . . . [W]e are constrained [to] hold that an acceptance is effective upon mailing and not upon receipt. . . .

[Here,] an unqualified offer was accepted and the acceptance made manifest. Later, the offerees sought to repudiate their initial assent. Had there been a delay in their determination to repudiate permitting the letter to be delivered to appellant, no question as to the invalidity of the repudiation would have been entertained. As it were, the repudiation antedated receipt of the letter. However, adopting the view that the acceptance was effective when the letter of acceptance was deposited in the mails, the repudiation was equally invalid and cannot alone, support the summary decree for appellees.

The summary decree is reversed and the cause remanded for further proceedings.

NOTE: REPLIES FROM A DISTANCE

Had plaintiffs not repudiated by a telephone call, but actually recaptured their acceptance letter from the post office, the result no doubt would have been the same. See, e.g., Soldau v. Organon, Inc., 860 F.2d 355 (9th Cir. 1988) (offeree's return to post office and persuading employee to open mailbox and retrieve acceptance is "of no legal consequence"). Observe also that the "mailbox rule" of Adams v. Lindsell means that a revocation of an offer is ineffective if received after an acceptance has been properly dispatched. A well-known English case explains why this should be so: "[B]oth legal principles and practical convenience require that a person who has accepted an offer not known . . . to have been revoked shall be in a position safely to act upon the footing" that a binding contract has been formed. Byrne & Co. v. Leon Van Tien Hoven & Co., 5 C.P.D. 344 (1880).

It seems clear that one original purpose of the mailbox rule was to protect offerees against uncommunicated revocations by offerors. But it was not long before the purpose was defined in somewhat broader terms, that of providing the offeree a firmer base for the decision whether to accept and, perhaps, for other action. What then should be done if the letter of acceptance, properly addressed and stamped, is deposited in the mail (or other appropriate medium of communication) and is thereafter abnormally delayed or lost altogether? Commencing as early as 1854 (Vassar v. Camp, 11 N.Y. 441), a series of decisions, still small in number, has extended the rule to such cases of loss or delay in transit. The Restatement (Second) § 63, comment b, approves this extension "in the interest of simplicity and clarity," though it concedes that the justification for the mailbox rule in these cases is less clear than in situations where there has been an attempt to revoke the offer. In applying the effective-upon-dispatch rule, acceptance by telegram is governed by the same tests as acceptance by mail.

Should the reasoning applied to an acceptance be carried over to a rejection of an offer that is lost or delayed in transit? The case of Egger v. Nesbit, 122 Mo. 667, 27 S.W. 385 (1894), involved not a rejection but a purported acceptance that imposed a new term and thus was a counteroffer, which was then lost in the mails and never delivered. The court held that an unconditional acceptance sent 10 days later was ineffective, since the offer had already been terminated. But the Restatement (Second) § 40 gives effect to an acceptance that arrives first, ahead of an intervening outright rejection. Section 40 states:

> Rejection or counter-offer by mail or telegram does not terminate the power of acceptance until received by the offeror, but limits the power so that a letter or telegram of acceptance started after the sending of an otherwise effective rejection or counter-offer is only a counter-offer unless the acceptance is received by the offeror before he receives the rejection or counter-offer.

Would a court that accepts the mailbox rule, including its extension to cases of loss or delay, commit the grave fault of inconsistency if it gave effect to an overtaking rejection which arrived ahead of an intervening acceptance? Is the refusal of the court to do this in Morrison v. Thoelke made necessary by the need to give offerees a dependable basis for the decision whether to accept? On what basis would such a refusal be justified?

At least one scholar has found the treatment of contracts by correspondence—"an oddity of liability"—to be instructive on our system of contract in general. Sharp, Reflections on Contract, 33 U. Chi. L. Rev. 211, 212–215 (1966). Cases and writings on the dispatch rule are collected in Soldau v. Organon, Inc., supra, and Mansfield v. Smith, 88 Wis. 2d 575, 277 N.W.2d 740 (1979). One point to note is that parties who have contracted to permit notice or other action by mail—that is, action not related to contract formation—may be found to have built into their bargain the principle of the common-law mailbox rule. E.g., Schikore v. BankAmerica Supp. Ret. Plan, 269 F.3d 956 (9th Cir. 2001) (ERISA plan administrator acted arbitrarily in refusing to apply common law's effective-on-dispatch principle to participant's benefit-election form mailed in accordance with plan procedures); University Emergency Med. Found. v. Rapier Inv., Ltd., 197 F.3d 18 (1st Cir. 1999) (common law default rule that notice is effective only on receipt, not mailing, is displaced by "time-honored mailbox rule" when parties contract to permit notice by mail).

Modern technology, including notably the widespread use of e-mail, suggests that an acceptance should be held effective when received, not when transmitted—i.e., the rules that apply when parties are in each other's presence should govern. See Electronic Messaging Services Task Force, The Commercial Use of Electronic Data Interchange—A Report and Model Trading Partner Agreement, 45 Bus. Law. 1645, 1665–1669 (1990). It is also the position indicated by the Restatement (Second) of Contracts § 64 when the parties are not in each other's presence and acceptance is by a "medium of substantially instantaneous two-way communication" (that is, principles applicable where the parties are in the presence of each other govern). There are presently few decisions raising the dispatch-or-receipt question as concerns transmissions other than letter or telegram. The Uniform Computer Information Transfer Act (UCITA), drafted in 1999 and adopted by only a few states, has attracted much criticism—e.g., that it is too complex and difficult to understand, particularly its unfamiliar terms—and various proposals for amendment. That model act, in § 215(a), states that "[r]eceipt of an electronic message is effective when received even if no individual is aware of its receipt."

Trinity Homes, LLC v. Fang

63 Va. Cir. 409, 2003 WL 22699791 (Va. Cir. Ct. 2003)

Stewart alleged that he placed the Agreement in his facsimile machine, dialed the number for Nicholson, pushed the button to start the facsimile and then went on an errand. The facsimile machine utilized by Stewart was not a modern version and did not provide any verification that a facsimile was being transmitted and/or that such facsimile was received. There are no phone records relative to the alleged transmission of the facsimile transmission by Stewart. Shortly after the time Stewart alleged he forwarded the facsimile to Nicholson, he received a phone call from Nicholson indicating that Defendants did not wish to sell the property nor enter into a contract with Complainants for that purpose. Transmitting a fax is not a two-way communication within the meaning of Restatement (Second) § 64 and is instead like mailing an acceptance under the Mailbox Rule, where an offer is accepted when it is deposited in the mail. The court concluded that the Mailbox Rule was applicable and thus the issue was one of fact—whether or not the facsimile transmission was actually forwarded or transmitted by Stewart to Nicholson. The burden was on Stewart to prove by preponderance of the evidence that the fax transmission was actually made and accomplished, and the court found the burden not met.

Restatement of Contracts, Second

§ 63. Time When Acceptance Takes Effect

Unless the offer provides otherwise,

(a) an acceptance made in a manner and by a medium invited by an offer is operative and completes the manifestation of mutual assent as soon as put out of the offeree's possession, without regard to whether it ever reaches the offeror; but

(b) an acceptance under an option contract is not operative until received by the offeror.

Comment: . . .

f. Option contracts. An option contract provides a dependable basis for decision whether to exercise the option; and removes the primary reason for the rule of Subsection (a). Moreover, there is no objection to speculation at the expense of a party who has irrevocably assumed that risk. Option contracts are commonly subject to a definite time limit, and the usual understanding is that the notification that the option has been exercised must be received by the offeror before that time. Whether or not there is such a time limit, in the absence of a contrary provision in the option contract, the offeree takes the risk of loss or delay in the transmission of the acceptance and remains free to revoke the acceptance until it arrives. Similarly, if there is such a mistake on the part of the offeror as justifies the rescission of his unilateral obligation, the right to rescind is not lost merely because a letter of acceptance is posted.

COMMENT: THE EUROPEAN APPROACH

The problems of contract formation in contracts by correspondence have been much discussed in other countries. Numerous solutions have been suggested and several have been tried. Nowhere outside Anglo-American law, however, has there been any strong and consistent support for the Adams v. Lindsell solution, making acceptance effective on dispatch.

The starting point in European discussions has been the proposition that communications should be effective only when received. The courts have thought it entirely appropriate that an offeror should be unaffected by acts of acceptance, such as a mailed letter, of which the offeror has no knowledge. After all, the offeree could retract the acceptance by a telegram that overtook an accepting letter and arrived first; therefore, the offeror should have a similar opportunity to repent. It seems worth noting that this parity rationale might lead to another solution, that of making both acceptance and revocation effective on dispatch. This is the result provided for by statute in a few states in this country.

In any case, the European notion that communications can have no effect until received leaves unanswered the question of how to protect the offeree during the interval required for transmission of the acceptance.

Insofar as the rule of Adams v. Lindsell is deemed to be a device for limiting the offeror's power of revocation, it raises the question whether one should not go further and hold the offeror to the time limits that the offer itself has defined. Consider, for example, the arguments of the first drafting commission that prepared the German Civil Code (Motives, I, pp. 165–166, 1888):

> It is necessary for commerce that the offeror be bound. If any offer is made the offeree must be able to rely on a contract being formed if he on his side notifies the offeror of his acceptance within the time limit. The offeree needs an assured point of departure for

> the decision he is about to make; he must under some circumstances take immediately the measures that will be necessary if the contract is entered into; he will reject and ignore other offers relating to the subject of the contract and will himself make offers in relation to it. . . . Because of the possible injury, willingness in general to enter into contract negotiations would be reduced and commerce would be burdened and hampered. The binding of the offeror also corresponds to his own intention as reasonably interpreted. This is clearest in cases where the offeror has set a definite time for the acceptance. Such a time limit, according to the conceptions of everyday life, has the meaning not only that the duration of the offer is limited but that the offeror for the time stated binds his own hands. . . . But if it is recognized that he is bound in the case of the express time limit, then it is not apparent why the same should not be true where the time limit is implied. An implied time limit is to be assumed in every offer. For an offer is made for the purpose of inducing acceptance by the offeree; the offeror must therefore intend that the offeree be allowed the time necessary for acceptance. . . . It has been suggested that the injury to which the offeree is exposed through revocation might be prevented by using various legal theories imposing on the revoking offeror a duty to compensate the offeree for what he would have had if the prospect of making the contract had not been presented to him. [But] such a duty to pay damages does not serve the needs of commerce. Commerce requires a smooth and rapid movement of transactions, whereas a recourse to damages, in ordinary experience, leads to lawsuits of a complex kind and uncertain outcome, and would cripple commerce.
>
> It cannot be doubted that some factors militate against binding the offeror. In particular there is the objection, not without weight, that the offeree is placed in a position to use to his own advantage changes in economic conditions that have occurred between the making of the offer and the receipt of his acceptance. He can, as is said, speculate at the expense of the offeror during this interval. But this danger for the offeror is not too great. He can always protect himself by expressly providing that the offer is not binding. If he does not consider such a provision desirable, he can at least reduce the danger by demanding immediate acceptance by the most rapid means of communication available to the offeree.

For such reasons as these, legislation in Europe—and in numerous other systems that have copied from Europe—has attacked the problem by providing that offers are irrevocable unless a power of revocation is expressly reserved. Nussbaum, Comparative Aspects of the Anglo-American Offer-And-Acceptance Doctrine, 36 Colum. L. Rev. 920 (1936), discusses this loophole left to the offeror. The civil-law result is thought to be precluded in Anglo-American law, in the absence of statute, by the requirement of consideration. But, as noted earlier, in order to bring the requirement of consideration into the picture it was necessary to make the further assumption that offers were a species under the genus of promise, so that an offer could be made irrevocable only by finding a binding promise, express or inferred, not to revoke the offer. The question, of course, is whether this transfer of ideas was necessary.

Moulton v. Kershaw

Supreme Court of Wisconsin, 1884.
59 Wis. 316, 18 N.W. 172.

[On September 19, 1882, defendants, salt dealers in Milwaukee, wrote to plaintiff, a dealer in La Crosse known by defendants to buy salt in large quantities, as follows: "Dear Sir: In consequence of a rupture in the salt trade, we are authorized to offer Michigan fine salt, in full car-load lots of 80 to 95 bbls., delivered at your city, at 85c. per bbl., to be shipped per C. & N.W. R.R. Co. only. At this price it is a bargain, as the price in general remains unchanged. Shall be pleased to receive your order." Plaintiff received the letter on September 20 and the same day wired defendants in reply: "Your letter of yesterday received and noted. You may ship me two thousand (2,000) barrels Michigan fine salt, as offered in your letter. Answer." This wire also was received on the 20th. The following day, the 21st, defendants notified plaintiff of their withdrawal of the September 19 letter. Upon defendants' refusal of a demand for delivery of 2,000 barrels, plaintiff sued to recover $800 damages. Defendants' demurrer to the complaint was overruled below, and defendants appealed.]

TAYLOR, J. The only question presented is whether the appellants' letter, and the telegram sent by the respondent in reply thereto, constitute a contract for the sale of 2,000 barrels of Michigan fine salt. . . . We are very clear that no contract was perfected by the order telegraphed by the respondent in answer to appellants' letter. . . .

[Respondent] claims that the letter [is] an offer to sell to the respondent, on the terms mentioned, any reasonable quantity of Michigan fine salt that he might see fit to order, not less than one car-load. . . . [A]ppellants claim that the letter is not an offer to sell any specific quantity of salt, but simply a letter such as a business man would send out to customers or those with whom he desired to trade, soliciting their patronage. To give the letter . . . the construction claimed for it [by] respondent, would introduce such an element of uncertainty into the contract as would necessarily render its enforcement a matter of difficulty, and in every case the jury trying the case would be called upon to determine whether the quantity ordered was such as the appellants might reasonably expect from the party. This question would necessarily involve an inquiry into the nature and extent of the business of the person to whom the letter was addressed, as well as to the extent of the business of the appellants. . . . And this question would not in any way depend upon the language used in the written contract, but upon proofs to be made outside of the writings. . . . If the letter of the appellants is an offer to sell salt to the respondent on the terms stated, then it must be held to be an offer to sell any quantity at the option of the respondent not less than one carload. The difficulty and injustice of construing the letter into such an offer is so apparent that the learned counsel for the respondent do not insist upon it, and consequently insist that it ought to be construed as an offer to sell such quantity as the appellants, from their knowledge of the business of the respondent might reasonably expect him to order.

Rather than introduce such an element of uncertainty into the contract, we deem it much more reasonable to construe the letter as a simple notice to those dealing in salt that the appellants were in a condition to supply that article for the prices named, and requested the person to whom it was addressed to deal with them. . . .

We do not wish to be understood as holding that a party may not be bound by an offer to sell personal property, where the amount or quantity is left to be fixed by the person to whom the offer is made, when the offer is accepted and the amount or quantity fixed before the offer is withdrawn. We simply hold that the letter [here] was not such an offer. If the letter had said to the respondent we will sell you all the Michigan fine salt you will order, at the price and on the terms named, then it is undoubtedly the law that the appellants would have been bound to deliver any reasonable amount the respondent might have ordered, possibly any amount, or make good their default in damages. The case [of Keller v. Ybarru, 3 Cal. 147,] was an offer of this kind with an additional limitation. The defendant in that case had a crop of growing grapes, and he offered to pick from the vines and deliver to the plaintiff, at defendant's vineyard, so many grapes then growing in said vineyard as the plaintiff should wish to take during the present year at ten cents per pound on delivery. The plaintiff, within the time and before the offer was withdrawn, notified the defendant that he wished to take 1,900 pounds of his grapes on the terms stated. The court held there was a contract to deliver the 1,900 pounds. In this case the fixing of the quantity was left to the person to whom the offer was made, but the amount which the defendant offered, beyond which he could not be bound, was also fixed by the amount of grapes he might have in his vineyard in that year. The case is quite different in its facts from the case at bar.

. . . [We] place our opinion upon the language of the letter of the appellants, and hold that it cannot be fairly construed into an offer. . . . The language is not such as a business man would use in making an offer to sell to an individual a definite amount of property. The word "sell" is not used. . . . They do not say, we offer to sell to you. They use general language proper to be addressed generally to those who were interested in the salt trade. It is clearly in the nature of an advertisement or business circular, to attract the attention of those interested in that business to the fact that good bargains in salt could be had by applying to them. . . . [T]he demurrer should have been sustained.

QUESTION

What if the seller's September 19 letter had been preceded by a wire from the buyer to the seller on September 17, saying: "Please advise us the best price you can make us on our order of 2,000 barrels of Michigan fine salt, either delivered here or your place, as you prefer"?

Sharp, Promissory Liability (pt. 1)

7 U.Chi.L.Rev. 1, 3–4 (1939)

"It is the offer which may start the trouble. A salt buyer receives a communication from a salt seller addressed to him personally, reading 'we are authorized to offer' salt at a specified price in unspecified quantities. There is a reference to 'rupture in the salt trade.' The buyer orders two thousand barrels, an amount the seller might reasonably anticipate. It has been held that there is no offer and so no contract. . . .

"After negotiations about the sale of land, in which uncertainties about the vendor's wife's willingness to release her dower interest have appeared, and $50,000 has been mentioned by the vendor, the purchaser writes the vendor 'will you and your wife accept $49,000?' The vendor replies, 'I will not sell for less than $56,000.' The purchaser wires 'I will accept.' It has been held that there is no offer and hence no contract.

"What is it that a sensible businessman is looking for in such a series of communications? We say an offer as distinguished from a mere statement of intention or invitation to deal, and we find that when we examine the matter further, we begin to talk naturally about promises. The offer which may be significant in these situations is also a promise."

Nguyen v. Barnes & Noble, Inc.

United States District Court, Central District California, 2015.
2015 WL 12766130.

STATON, U.S. DISTRICT JUDGE. . . . The First Amended Complaint alleges the following facts:

On August 21, 2011, Plaintiff Kevin Khoa Nguyen saw an internet advertisement for "16 GB HP TouchPad Tablets" being sold for $101.95 on Defendant Barnes & Noble, Inc.'s website, barnesandnoble.com. This tablet ordinarily retailed for $399, but after HP announced it was discontinuing production of the tablets, retailers including Barnes & Noble offered steep promotional discounts on them aimed at "liquidating the product, advertising the promoting business, and exposing customers to storefronts in hopes that they would purchase other goods as well."

Barnes & Noble offered the tablets on its website for $101.95 beginning on August 20, 2011, and "[f]or the next several hours or days . . . continued to accept payments from thousands of customers who were flocking to [its] site in order to purchase these advertised Tablets from a reputable source." Nguyen alleges, however, that Barnes & Noble actually sold out of the tablets "in a matter of minutes, yet . . . continued to represent that it had available units for sale."

Nguyen ordered two of the tablets from Barnes & Noble during the relevant period, submitting his credit card information, email address and shipping address in the process. He then received the following email from Barnes & Noble:

> Dear Kevin Nguyen,
>
> Your order is much appreciated.
>
> As soon as your order is scheduled to ship or ready to download, we'll let you know with a second email. So be on the lookout for it.
>
> Visit us again soon at BN.com. There's always something new at the world's largest bookstore. We've got thousands of new titles every week, the largest selection of eBooks, and inspiring choices at B&N Kids.
>
> Checking Your Order Is Easy Just click http://www.bn.com/orderstatus to log in and you'll be taken right to your order status page.
>
> Need to make changes? That's easy too. Just click http://www.bn.com/orderstatus and log in. We know you are excited to receive your order, so we ship quickly. If the status says "Cannot be removed" it is in process to ship to you.
>
> You've read this far into the email, which makes you a true reader. Thanks again for shopping with us. Come back and visit anytime at http://www.bn.com.
>
> —Barnes & Noble

Nguyen also received a Confirmation Order Form . . . .

Nguyen alleges that after placing his online order, Barnes & Noble placed a "hold" on his credit card for the purchase amount. As a result, he believed the purchase was "solidified and complete."

Fifteen hours after Nguyen purchased the tablets, however, Barnes & Noble sent the following email notifying Nguyen it was cancelling the transaction:

> Dear Valued Customer,
>
> We are writing to you regarding your recent Barnes & Noble order for "HP TouchPad Tablet with 16GB Memory".

> Due to unexpected customer demand for this item, our inventory was depleted prior to your order being processed so we are unable to fulfill this item as requested. Consequently, we have canceled your order and you will not be billed for this amount.
>
> You may see an authorization on your credit or debit card for the order, but please be assured you will not be charged. The authorization will be released in accordance with your bank's policies.
>
> We sincerely regret any inconvenience that this may have caused.
>
> Sincerely,
Barnes & Noble
Customer Service

Nguyen alleges that because he believed the purchase was complete and Barnes & Noble allowed fifteen hours to elapse before cancelling the order, he was "unable to obtain an HP Tablet during the liquidation period for the discounted price." He alleges that had he "known that Barnes & Noble would not honor the purchase he had made, he would have taken steps to purchase his TouchPads from another source during the fire-sale period." Instead, he had to purchase "substitute tablet technology," incurring "considerable expense" in doing so. Nguyen alleges thousands of consumers are in the same position because Barnes & Noble continued to sell the tablets on its website after its inventory was exhausted.

On April 17, 2012, Nguyen filed a Complaint against Barnes & Noble based on the above allegations . . . .

Barnes & Noble first moves to dismiss Nguyen's claim for breach of contract. It argues this claim fails because (1) the display of tablets for purchase on its website did not constitute an "offer" Nguyen could accept by placing his order, and (2) Nguyen's order constituted an offer that Barnes & Noble could accept only by shipping the tablet or promptly promising to ship the tablet, which it did not do. . . .

Barnes & Noble first argues its display of tablets for purchase on its website did not constitute an "offer" Nguyen could accept by placing his order.

In support of this proposition, Barnes & Noble cites numerous cases for the well-established rule that advertisements are ordinarily considered invitations to deal rather than offers in themselves.

Nguyen argues, however, that this case falls under the equally well-established exception to that rule holding that an advertisement will constitute an offer where it is so "clear, definite, and explicit" that it leaves "nothing open for negotiation." Trell v. Am. Ass'n for Advancement of Sci., 310 Fed.Appx. 447, 448 (2d Cir. 2009). For instance, in *Lefkowitz*, the defendant retailer's newspaper advertisement read as follows:

> Saturday 9 A.M. 2 Brand New Pastel Mink 3-Skin Scarfs Selling for $89.50. Out they go Saturday. Each . . . $1.00. 1 Black Lapin Stole Beautiful, worth $139.50 . . . $1.00. First Come First Served

Lefkowitz v. Great Minneapolis Surplus Store, Inc., 86 N.W. 2d 689, 690 (Minn. 1957). The plaintiff was the first customer to appear at that time seeking the black lapin coat, but the store refused to sell it to him. The Court found the advertisement was an offer because it was "clear, definite, and explicit, and left nothing open for negotiation." Id. at 691. Thus, the plaintiff validly accepted the offer by appearing at the store at the specified time and tendering the coat's purchase price.

The case at bar is closely analogous to *Lefkowitz*. Barnes & Noble's display of "HP TouchPad Tablet with 16GB Memory" for "$101.95 Online Price" was clear and definite as to the item in question and price at which it was to be sold. Moreover, Barnes & Noble's exhortation to visitors to "BUY THIS ITEM / Add to Bag" and then "check out" of the store clearly specified how website customers including Nguyen could accept the offer. Because this display was "clear, definite, and explicit" as to all essential terms—namely, the item to be sold, the price, and the manner of acceptance—it "left nothing open for negotiation" and therefore constituted an offer Nguyen could accept.

Barnes & Noble argues this result does not attain because there was still something left open for negotiation here. Specifically, Barnes & Noble suggests that a "reasonable consumer would understand based on the product listing and order process that he still had to identify himself, select a delivery method, and propose a payment method, and that only then would Barnes & Noble acknowledge the order and payment method and then further have to schedule shipping and ship the product." This argument proves too much; *Lefkowitz*, for instance, does not suggest that the parties had agreed on a precise method of payment. It was enough that the plaintiff "appear[ed] at the seller's place of business" at the appointed time and "offered the stated purchase price of the article." Nguyen, by clicking "BUY THIS ITEM / Add to Bag" and then checking out of Barnes & Noble's online store, did the same. The presence of certain ancillary terms still to be determined does not defeat the formation of a contract where the parties agree in all material respects.

Nor do the other cases cited by Barnes & Noble compel a contrary result. In many, the purported offers contained clear words of limitation putting the putative offeree on notice that acceptance would not necessarily consummate the transaction. Here, by contrast, Nguyen does not allege the existence of any such words of limitation. Rather, Barnes & Noble's invitation to "BUY THIS ITEM/Add to Bag" and then "check out" conveyed the opposite message—that the transaction would be consummated immediately.

Notably, none of the authorities cited by Barnes & Noble account for the context in which this transaction occurred—an online store. The advertisement-as-an-invitation-to-deal rule is explained in part by courts' reluctance to hold merchants to paper advertisements printed days or weeks before a sale occurs. This concern is irrelevant in the online marketplace, where a seller can be expected to track inventory and may instantly alter or delete a product listing.

In any case, the formation of a contract is determined by the parties' objective manifestations of intent. For the reasons noted above, the Court finds Barnes & Noble's online display of the tablets constituted an offer Nguyen could—and did—accept by placing his order. . . .

The parties alternatively debate whether Nguyen's order constituted an offer that Barnes & Noble accepted by promptly promising to ship the tablets to Nguyen. Although we have concluded that Barnes & Noble made the offer, we address this alternative argument as well.

Barnes & Noble asserts that shoppers on its website make "offers" when they purchase items, that Barnes & Noble accepts those offers only by shipping the product or by promptly promising to ship the product, and that, in this instance, it did neither. Here, as there is no allegation that Barnes & Noble ever shipped the product, only the promise to ship is at issue. Barnes & Noble argues that neither of its two emails to Nguyen promise shipment, but merely "acknowledge [Nguyen's] offer," and thus are not "couched in the 'vocabulary of acceptance.' " Barnes & Noble cites *Echo v. Whitson* for this proposition. 121 F.3d 1099, 1103 (7th Cir. 1997). That case is factually distinguishable, however. There, the defendant sent a letter in response to the plaintiff's purchase order "recapping [plaintiff's] 1993 Spring Booking of Units and Accessories" and stating that "[i]t is extremely important to verify that the information on these reports matches your records" because "mistakes and omissions can sometimes occur" when entering the orders into the computer. The Seventh Circuit held the letter's language revealed a "clarification purpose rather than any commitment to provide the [requested] goods."

The language in Barnes & Noble's emails to Nguyen is not so narrow. The Confirmation Order Form email informed Nguyen that the tablets "will ship as available" and that his credit card "will be charged when [the] order ships." This definitive language, which is notably lacking in qualification—it states that the tablets "will" ship "*as* available," not "*if* available"—reveals no "clarification purpose" or intent to verify Nguyen's order before proceeding further. . . .

Petterson v. Pattberg

Court of Appeals of New York, 1928.
248 N.Y. 86, 161 N.E. 428.

KELLOGG, J. . . . John Petterson, of whose last will and testament the plaintiff is executrix, was the owner of a parcel of real estate in Brooklyn, known as 5301 Sixth Avenue. The defendant was the owner of a bond executed by Petterson, which was secured by a third mortgage upon the parcel. On April 4th, 1924, there remained unpaid upon the principal the sum of $5,450. This amount was payable in installments of $250 on April 25th, 1924, and upon a like monthly date every three months thereafter. Thus the bond and mortgage had more than five years to run before the entire sum became due. Under date of the 4th of April, 1924, the defendant wrote Petterson as follows: "I hereby agree to accept cash for the mortgage which I hold against premises 5301 6th Ave., Brooklyn, N.Y. It is understood and agreed as a consideration I will allow you $780 providing said mortgage is paid on or before May 31, 1924, and the regular quarterly payment due April 25, 1924, is paid when due." On April 25, Petterson paid the defendant the installment of principal due on that date. Subsequently, on a day in the latter part of May, Petterson presented himself at the defendant's home, and knocked at the door. The defendant demanded the name of his caller. Petterson replied: "It is Mr. Petterson. I have come to pay off the mortgage." The defendant answered that he had sold the mortgage. Petterson stated that he would like to talk with the defendant, so the defendant partly opened the door. Thereupon Petterson exhibited the cash and said he was ready to pay off the mortgage according to the agreement. The defendant refused to take the money. Prior to this conversation Petterson had made a contract to sell the land to a third person free and clear of the mortgage to the defendant. Meanwhile, also, the defendant had sold the bond and mortgage to a third party. It, therefore, became necessary for Petterson to pay to such person the full amount of the bond and mortgage. It is claimed that he thereby sustained a loss of $780, the sum which the defendant agreed to allow upon the bond and mortgage if payment in full of principal, less that sum, was made on or before May 31st. The plaintiff has had a recovery for the sum thus claimed, with interest.

Clearly the defendant's letter proposed to Petterson the making of a unilateral contract, . . . a promise in exchange for the performance of an act. The thing conditionally promised by the defendant was the reduction of the mortgage debt. The act requested to be done, in consideration of the offered promise, was payment in full of the reduced principal of the debt prior to the due date thereof. "If an act is requested, that very act and no other must be given." (Williston on Contracts, § 73.) . . . It is elementary that any offer to enter into a unilateral contract may be withdrawn before the act requested to be done has been performed. (Williston on Contracts, § 60); . . . A bidder at a sheriff's sale may revoke his bid at any time before the property is struck down to him. . . . The offer of a reward in consideration of an act to be performed is revocable before the very act requested has been done. Shuey v. United States, 92 U.S. 73. . . .

An interesting question arises when, as here, the offeree approaches the offeror with the intention of proffering performance and, before actual tender is made, the offer is withdrawn. Of such a case Williston says: "The offeror may see the approach of the offeree and know that an acceptance is contemplated. If the offeror can say 'I revoke' before the offeree accepts, however brief the interval of time between the two acts, there is no escape from the conclusion that the offer is terminated." (Williston on Contracts, § 60–b.) In this instance Petterson, standing at the door of the defendant's house, stated to the defendant that he had come to pay off the mortgage. Before a tender of the necessary moneys had been made the defendant informed Petterson that he had sold the mortgage. That was a definite notice to Petterson that the defendant could not perform his offered promise and that a tender to the defendant, who was no longer the creditor, would be ineffective to satisfy the debt. "An offer to sell property may be withdrawn before acceptance without any formal notice to the person to whom the offer is made. It is sufficient if that person has actual knowledge that the person who made the offer has done some act inconsistent with the continuance of the offer, such as selling the property to a third person." Dickinson v. Dodds, 2 Ch.Div. 463. . . . Thus, it clearly appears that the defendant's offer was withdrawn before its acceptance had been tendered. It is unnecessary to determine, therefore, what the legal situation might have been had tender been made before withdrawal. It is the individual view of the writer that the same result would follow. This would be so, for the act requested to be performed was the completed act of payment, a thing incapable of performance unless assented to by the person to be paid. (Williston on Contracts, § 60–b.) Clearly an offering party has the right to name the precise act performance of which would convert his offer into a binding promise. Whatever the act may be until it is performed the offer must be revocable. However, the supposed case is not before us for decision. We think that in this particular instance the offer of the defendant was withdrawn before it became a binding promise, and, therefore, that no contract was ever made. . . .

The judgment of the Appellate Division and that of the Trial Term should be reversed and the complaint dismissed, with costs in all courts.

LEHMAN, J. (dissenting). The defendant's letter to Petterson constituted a promise on his part to accept payment at a discount of the mortgage he held, provided the mortgage is paid on or before May 31st, 1924. Doubtless by the terms of the promise itself, the defendant made payment of the mortgage by the plaintiff, before the stipulated time, a condition precedent to performance by the defendant of his promise to accept payment at a discount. If the condition precedent has not been performed, it is because the defendant made performance impossible by refusing to accept payment. . . . "It is a principle of fundamental justice that if a promisor is himself the cause of the failure of performance either of an obligation due him or of a condition upon which his own liability depends, he cannot take advantage of the failure." (Williston on Contracts, § 677.) The question in this case is . . . whether at the time the defendant refused the offer of payment, he had assumed any binding obligation, even though subject to condition.

The promise made by the defendant lacked consideration at the time it was made. Nevertheless the promise was not made as a gift or mere gratuity to the plaintiff. It was made for the purpose of obtaining from the [plaintiff] something which the [defendant] desired. It constituted an offer which was to become binding whenever the plaintiff should give . . . exactly the consideration which the defendant requested.

Here the defendant requested no counter promise from the plaintiff[,] [but] some act to be performed by the plaintiff. Until the act requested was performed, the defendant might undoubtedly revoke his offer. Our problem is to determine . . . what act the defendant requested as consideration for his promise.

The defendant undoubtedly made his offer as an inducement to the plaintiff to "pay" the mortgage before it was due. Therefore, it is said that "the act requested to be performed was the completed act of payment, a thing incapable of performance unless assented to by the person to be paid." In unmistakable terms the defendant agreed to accept payment, yet we are told that the defendant intended, and the plaintiff should have understood, that the act requested by the defendant, as consideration for his promise to accept payment, included performance by the defendant himself of the very promise for which the act was to be consideration. . . . So construed, the defendant's promise or offer, though intended to induce action by the plaintiff, is but a snare and delusion. The plaintiff could not reasonably suppose that the defendant was asking him to procure the performance by the defendant of the very act which the defendant promised to do, yet we are told that even after the plaintiff had done all else which the defendant requested, the defendant's promise was still not binding because the defendant chose not to perform.

I cannot believe that a result so extraordinary could have been intended when the defendant wrote the letter. "The thought behind the phrase proclaims itself misread when the outcome of the reading is injustice or absurdity." See Cardozo, Ch.J., in Surace v. Danna, 248 N.Y. 18, 161 N.E. 315. If the defendant intended to induce payment by the plaintiff and yet reserve the right to refuse payment when offered he should have used a phrase better calculated to express his meaning than the words: "I agree to accept." A promise to accept payment, by its very terms, must necessarily become binding, if at all, not later than when a present offer to pay is made.

I recognize that in this case only an offer of payment, and not a formal tender of payment, was made before the defendant withdrew his offer to accept payment. Even the plaintiff's part in the act of payment was then not technically complete. Even so, under a fair construction of the words of the letter I think the plaintiff had done the act which the defendant requested as consideration for his promise. The plaintiff offered to pay with present intention and ability to make that payment. A formal tender is seldom made in business transactions, except to lay the foundation for subsequent assertion in a court of justice of rights which spring from a refusal of the tender. If the defendant acted in good faith in making his offer to accept payment, he could not well have intended to draw a distinction in the act requested of the plaintiff in return, between an offer which unless refused would ripen into completed payment, and a formal tender. Certainly the defendant could not have expected or intended that the plaintiff would make a formal tender of payment without first stating that he had come to make payment. We should not read into the language of the defendant's offer a meaning which would prevent enforcement of the defendant's promise after it had been accepted by the plaintiff in the very way which the defendant must have intended it should be accepted, if he acted in good faith.

The judgment should be affirmed.

CARDOZO, C.J., POUND, CRANE and O'BRIEN, JJ., concur with KELLOGG, J.; LEHMAN, J., dissents in opinion, in which ANDREWS, J., concurs.

NOTE

The record in the case indicates that when Petterson called at Pattberg's home to pay off the mortgage, he took with him his spouse and a real estate broker who had assisted in Petterson's sale of the property to the third party. The broker testified that he was asked to go as a notary "to acknowledge Mr. Pattberg's signature" on a satisfaction of the mortgage. In order to record a discharge, it was necessary to have either such a notarized acknowledgement or the testimony of a subscribing witness (N.Y.—McKinney's Real Property Law, §§ 291, 304, 321). At trial, Pattberg tried to testify that he had mailed a letter to Petterson on May 3, revoking the offer of April 4, but this testimony was excluded by the trial court under the New York dead man's statute. (Petterson had died before the trial.) A jury having been waived, the trial judge gave judgment for the plaintiff. Do these circumstances give support for the majority's conclusion?

There is further information concerning Petterson v. Pattberg. In 1937, on the recommendation of the state's Law Revision Commission, New York enacted § 15–503 of the General Obligations Law. That statute, titled "Offer of Accord Followed by Tender," now reads as follows:

> (1) An offer in writing, signed by the offeror or by his agent, to accept a performance therein designated in satisfaction or discharge in whole or in part of any claim, cause of action, contract, obligation, or lease, or any mortgage or other security interest in personal or real property, followed by tender of such performance by the offeree or by his agent before revocation of the offer, shall

not be denied effect as a defense or as a basis of an action or counterclaim by reason of the fact that such tender was not accepted by the offeror or by his agent. . . .

You might consider whether § 15–503 alters the outcome of the *Petterson* decision.

Wormser, The True Conception of Unilateral Contracts

26 Yale L.J. 136–139 (1916)

Suppose A says to B, "I will give you $100 if you walk across the Brooklyn Bridge," and B walks—is there a contract? It is clear that A is not asking B for B's promise to walk across the Brooklyn Bridge. What A wants from B is the act of walking across the bridge. When B has walked across the bridge there is a contract, and A is then bound to pay B $100. At that moment there arises a unilateral contract. . . .

When an act is thus wanted in return for a promise, a unilateral contract is created when the act is done. It is clear that only one party is bound. B is not bound to walk across the Brooklyn Bridge, but A is bound to pay B $100 if B does so. Thus, in unilateral contracts, on one side we find merely an act, on the other side a promise. . . . [I]n bilateral contracts, A barters away his volition in return for another promise. . . . [B]oth parties, A and B, are bound from the moment that their promises are exchanged. . . .

Let us suppose that B starts to walk across the Brooklyn Bridge and has gone about one-half of the way across. At that moment A overtakes B and says to him, "I withdraw my offer." Has B then any rights against A? Again, let us suppose that after A has said "I withdraw by offer," B continues to walk across the Brooklyn Bridge and completes the act of crossing. Under these circumstances, has B any rights against A?

In the first of the cases just suggested, A withdrew his offer before B had walked across the bridge. What A wanted from B, what A asked for, was the act of walking across the bridge. Until that was done, B had not given to A what A had requested. The acceptance by B of A's offer could be nothing but the act of B's part of crossing the bridge. It is elementary that an offeror may withdraw his offer until it has been accepted. It follows logically that A is perfectly within his rights in withdrawing his offer before B has accepted it by walking across the bridge—the act contemplated by the offeror and the offeree as the acceptance of the offer. . . .

The objection is made, however, that it is very "hard" upon B that he should have walked half-way across the Brooklyn Bridge and should get no compensation. This suggestion, invariably advanced, might be dismissed with the remark that "hard" cases should not make bad law. . . . If B is not bound to continue to cross the bridge, if B is will-free, why should not A also be will-free? Suppose that after B has crossed half the bridge he gets tired and tells A that he refuses to continue crossing. B, concededly, would be perfectly within his rights in so speaking and acting. A would have no cause of action against B for damages. If B has a locus poenitentiae, so has A. They each have, and should have, the opportunity to reconsider and withdraw. . . .

To the writer's mind, the doctrine of unilateral contract is thus as just and equitable as it is logical. . . .

Suppose, reverting to the second case, that B completes the act of crossing the bridge after A has told him that the offer is withdrawn. Here too, B has no rights against A, since B had not accepted the offer until after A had duly communicated to B its revocation. An offer cannot be accepted after it has been revoked. B is laboring under an unrelievable error of law in proceeding to accept an offer which . . . had ceased to exist.

COMMENT: THE UNILATERAL CONTRACT

The unilateral contract came first in English law: "If you will shoe my horse, I will pay you two shillings." Later, the main center of attention for lawyers shifted to the bilateral contract, initiated by an exchange of promises. The theory of the unilateral contract, as we find it expounded by Professor Wormser, cannot claim the hallmark of antiquity, however; it was the creation of academic minds and law school classrooms in the latter part of the nineteenth century.

If one accepts Professor Wormser's premises, his argument may appear unassailable. The starting point is the proposition already encountered: every offer is revocable until accepted, in the absence of consideration or perhaps a seal. If the offer can be construed as calling for a promise and the promise is duly given, a contract is made and the hazards attendant upon the offeror's power to revoke an unaccepted offer are ended. But if the offer calls for an act, those hazards remain until the act, exactly as requested, is completed. Thus, simply stated, the theory may not seem particularly objectionable if the word "act" comprehends only conduct of the utmost simplicity, completed in a moment, such as handing over a lost wallet which the finder has just picked up from the street. We would rarely feel that real injustice was done if the offeror effectively revoked the offer just before this act was done, thereby depriving the finder of a reward.

Once the theory of the unilateral contract was formulated, however, it showed a tendency to reach out for a wide range of cases in which the conduct regarded as the acceptance required long or expensive preparation, or was in truth a series of acts extending over an appreciable period of time. Why was a theory which does no appreciable harm where the acceptance is a simple, unified act extended to situations where it would seem to compel results so obviously contrary to common sense and elementary decency? A part of the explanation may be found in a peculiar insensitivity of the legal mind, beguiled by the symmetry of a system, to the fact that all acts are not alike, that they vary in complexity, difficulty, and expense. Further explanation may be found, as Professor Llewellyn has argued (Our Case Law of Contract: Offer and Acceptance, 48 Yale L.J. 1, 779 (1938, 1939)), in a shift to the unilateral contract of requirements and assumptions built up around the bilateral contract, whose essence is present exchange of assurances—present agreement. When the offeror asks for present assurance of future action, the offeror may well be the "master of the offer," invested with a power to revoke until that assurance is given. Still, when the offeror has requested extended, difficult, or expensive action, but no commitment by the offeree in advance of the action, must it follow that the offeror is wholly free of responsibility unless and until the performance sought is received—exactly and completely?

Professor Wormser subsequently returned to the unilateral contract, saying: "Since that time I have repented, so that now, clad in sackcloth, I state frankly that my point of view has changed. I agree, at this time, with the rule set forth in the Restatement of Contracts of the American Law Institute, sec. 45." 3 J. Legal Educ. 146 (1950).

Restatement of Contracts, Second

§ 45. Option Contract Created by Part Performance or Tender

(1) Where an offer invites an offeree to accept by rendering a performance and does not invite a promissory acceptance, an option contract is created when the offeree tenders or begins the invited performance or tenders a beginning of it.

(2) The offeror's duty of performance under any option contract so created is conditional on completion or tender of the invited performance in accordance with the terms of the offer.

Comment: . . .

f. Preparations for performance. What is begun or tendered must be part of the actual performance invited in order to preclude revocation under this Section. Beginning preparations, though they may be essential to carrying out the contract or to accepting the offer, is not enough. Preparations to perform may, however, constitute justifiable reliance sufficient to make the offeror's promise binding under § 87(2). In many cases what is invited depends on what is a reasonable mode of acceptance. . . .

Illustration:

9. A makes a written promise to pay $5000 to B, a hospital, "to aid B in its humanitarian work." Relying upon this and other like promises, B proceeds in its humanitarian work, expending large sums of money and incurring large liabilities. Performance by B has begun, and A's offer is irrevocable.

NOTE

The Second Restatement preserves the theory and the effects, though not the language, of the first § 45. The obligation created by part performance is now called an "option contract," not a unilateral contract. This revision of terms follows the restaters' overall decision not to use the words "unilateral contract" in the Restatement, Second, but to speak descriptively of the different types of contracts which in common usage have been classified as unilateral. As might have been expected, this dropping of the term "unilateral contract" does not appear to have attracted followers in the courts or in the literature of contract law. Nor has it altered the fundamentals of the traditional unilateral contract; under a bargain for performance, the waiving of formal acceptance simply merges the essential elements of performance (consideration) and acceptance.

Carlill v. Carbolic Smoke Ball Co.

Court of Appeal, 1892.
[1893] 1 Q. B. 256.

The defendants, who were the proprietors and vendors of a medical preparation called "The Carbolic Smoke Ball," inserted in the Pall Mall Gazette of November 13, 1891, and in other newspapers, the following advertisement:

> £100 reward will be paid by the Carbolic Smoke Ball Company to any person who contracts the increasing epidemic influenza, colds, or any disease caused by taking cold, after having used the ball three times daily for two weeks according to the printed directions supplied with each ball. £1000 is deposited with the Alliance Bank, Regent Street, shewing our sincerity in the matter.
>
> During the last epidemic of influenza many thousand carbolic smoke balls were sold as preventives against this disease, and in no ascertained case was the disease contracted by those using the carbolic smoke ball.
>
> One carbolic smoke ball will last a family several months, making it the cheapest remedy in the world at the price, 10s., post free. The ball can be refilled at a cost of 5s. Address, Carbolic Smoke Ball Company, 27, Princes Street, Hanover Square, London.

The plaintiff, a lady, on the faith of this advertisement, bought one of the balls at a chemist's, and used it as directed, three times a day, from November 20, 1891, to January 17, 1892, when she was attacked by influenza. Hawkins, J., held that she was entitled to recover the £100. The defendants appealed. . . .

LINDLEY, L.J. . . . We must first consider whether this was intended to be a promise at all, or whether it was a mere puff which meant nothing. Was it a mere puff? My answer to that question is "No," and I base my answer upon this passage: "£1000 is deposited with the Alliance Bank, shewing our sincerity in the matter." Now, for what was that money deposited or that statement made except to negative the suggestion that this was a mere puff and meant nothing at all? The deposit is called in aid by the advertiser as proof of his sincerity in the matter—that is, the sincerity of his promise to pay this £100 in the event which he has specified. [T]here is the promise, as plain as words can make it.

Then it is contended that it is not binding. [First,] it is said that it is not made with anybody in particular. Now that point is common to the words of this advertisement and to the words of all other advertisements offering rewards. They are offers to anybody who performs the conditions named in the advertisement, and anybody who does perform the condition accepts the offer. In point of law this advertisement is an offer to pay £100 to anybody who will perform these conditions, and the performance of the conditions is the acceptance of the offer. . . .

But then it is said, "Supposing that the performance of the conditions is an acceptance of the offer, that acceptance ought to have been notified." Unquestionably, as a general proposition, when an offer is made, it is necessary in order to make a binding contract, not only that it should be accepted, but that the acceptance should be notified. But is that so in cases of this kind? I apprehend that they are an exception to that rule, or, if not an exception, they are open to the observation that the notification of the acceptance need not precede the performance. This offer is a continuing offer. It was never revoked, and if notice of acceptance is required—which I doubt very much, . . . the person who makes the offer gets the notice of acceptance contemporaneously with his notice of the performance of the condition. If he gets notice of the acceptance before his offer is revoked, that in principle is all you want. I, however, think that the true view, in a case of this kind, is that the person who makes the offer shews by his language and from the nature of the transaction that he does not expect and does not require notice of the acceptance apart from notice of the performance.

We, therefore, find here all the elements which are necessary to form a binding contract enforceable in point of law. . . . [T]he true construction of this advertisement is that £100 will be paid to anybody who uses this smoke ball three times daily for two weeks according to the printed directions, and who gets the influenza or cold or other diseases caused by taking cold within a reasonable time after so using it; and if that is the true construction, it is enough for the plaintiff.

I come now to the last point which I think requires attention—that is, the consideration. It has been argued that this is nudum pactum—that there is no consideration. We must apply to that argument the usual legal tests. Let us see whether there is no advantage to the defendants. It is said that the use of the ball is no advantage to them, and that what benefits them is the sale; and the case is put that a lot of these balls might be stolen, and that it would be no advantage to the defendants if the thief or other people used them. The answer to that, I think, is as follows. It is quite obvious that in the view of the advertisers a use by the public of their remedy, if they can only get the public to have confidence enough to use it, will react and produce a sale which is directly beneficial to them.

Therefore, the advertisers get out of the use an advantage which is enough to constitute a consideration.

But there is another view. Does not the person who acts upon this advertisement and accepts the offer put himself to some inconvenience at the request of the defendants? Is it nothing to use this ball three times daily for two weeks according to the directions at the request of the advertiser? Is that to go for nothing? It appears to me that there is a distinct inconvenience, not to say a detriment, to any person who so uses the smoke ball. I am of opinion, therefore, that there is ample consideration for the promise. . . .

It appears to me, therefore, that the defendants must perform their promise, and, if they have been so unwary as to expose themselves to a great many actions, so much the worse for them.

BOWEN, L.J. I am of the same opinion. We were asked to say that this document was a contract too vague to be enforced. . . . It seems to me that in order to arrive at a right conclusion we must read this advertisement in its plain meaning, as the public would understand it. It was intended to be issued to the public and to be read by the public. How would an ordinary person reading this document construe it? It was intended unquestionably to have some effect, and I think the effect which it was intended to have, was to make people use the smoke ball, because the suggestions and allegations which it contains are directed immediately to the use of the smoke ball as distinct from the purchase of it. It did not follow that the smoke ball was to be purchased from the defendants directly, or even from agents of theirs directly. The intention was that the circulation of the smoke ball should be promoted, and that the use of it should be increased. . . .

Then it was said that there was no notification of the acceptance of the contract. One cannot doubt that, as an ordinary rule of law, an acceptance of an offer made ought to be notified to the person who makes the offer, in order that the two minds may come together. Unless this is done . . . there is not that consensus which is necessary according to the English law—I say nothing about the laws of other countries—to make a contract. But there is this clear gloss to be made upon that doctrine, that as notification of acceptance is required for the benefit of the person who makes the offer, the person who makes the offer may dispense with notice to himself if he thinks it desirable to do so, and I suppose there can be no doubt that where a person in an offer made by him to another person, expressly or impliedly intimates a particular mode of acceptance as sufficient to make the bargain binding, it is only necessary for the other person to whom such offer is made to follow the indicated method of acceptance; and if the person making the offer, expressly or impliedly intimates in his offer that it will be sufficient to act on the proposal without communicating acceptance of it to himself, performance of the condition is a sufficient acceptance without notification. . . .

Now, if that is the law, how are we to find out whether the person who makes the offer does intimate that notification of acceptance will not be necessary in order to constitute a binding bargain? In many cases you look to the offer itself. [Y]ou extract from the character of the transaction that notification is not required, and in the advertisement cases it seems to me to follow as an inference to be drawn from the transaction itself that a person is not to notify his acceptance of the offer before he performs the condition, but that if he performs the condition notification is dispensed with. . . . If I advertise to the world that my dog is lost, and that anybody who brings the dog to a particular place will be paid some money, are all the police or other persons whose business it is to find lost dogs to be expected to sit down and write me a note saying that they have accepted my proposal? Why, of course, they at once look after the dog, and as soon as they find the dog they have performed the condition. The essence of the transaction is that the dog should be found. . . . It follows from the nature of the thing that the performance of the condition is sufficient acceptance without the notification of it, and a person who makes an offer in an advertisement of that kind makes an offer which must be read by the light of that common sense reflection. He does, therefore, in his offer impliedly indicate that he does not require notification of the acceptance of the offer. . . .

Appeal dismissed.

[For a description of the smoke ball, and the manufacturer's directions for its use, see Simpson, Quackery and Contract Law: The Case of the Carbolic Smoke Ball, 14 J.Leg.Stud. 345, 348–352 (1985). The defendant responded to the decision with another advertisement, which is reproduced above. Notice the fine print.]

Cobaugh v. Klick-Lewis, Inc.

Superior Court of Pennsylvania, 1989.
385 Pa. Super. 587, 561 A.2d 1248.

WIEAND, J. On May 17, 1987, Amos Cobaugh was playing in the East End Open Golf Tournament on the Fairview Golf Course in Cornwall, Lebanon County. When he arrived at the ninth tee he found a new Chevrolet Beretta, together with signs which proclaimed: "HOLE-IN-ONE Wins this 1988 Chevrolet Beretta GT Courtesy of KLICK-LEWIS Buick Chevy Pontiac $49.00 OVER FACTORY INVOICE in Palmyra." Cobaugh aced the ninth hole and attempted to claim his prize. Klick-Lewis refused to deliver the car. It had offered the car as a prize for a charity golf tournament sponsored by the Hershey-Palmyra Sertoma Club two days earlier, on May 15, 1987, and had neglected to remove the car and posted signs prior to Cobaugh's hole-in-one. After Cobaugh sued to compel delivery of the car, the parties entered a stipulation regarding the facts and then moved for summary judgment. The trial court granted Cobaugh's motion, and Klick-Lewis appealed. . . .

An offer is a manifestation of willingness to enter into a bargain, so made as to justify another person in understanding that his assent to that bargain is invited and will conclude it. [Rest.2d] of Contracts § 24. . . . Consistent with traditional principles of contract law pertaining to unilateral contracts, it has generally been held that "[t]he promoter of [a prize-winning] contest, by making public the conditions and rules of the contest, makes an offer, and if before the offer is withdrawn another person acts upon it, the promoter is bound to perform his promise." Annot., 87 A.L.R.2d 649, 661. The only acceptance of the offer that is necessary is the performance of the act requested to win the prize. . . .

Appellant argues that it did nothing more than propose a contingent gift and that a proposal to make a gift is without consideration and unenforceable. . . . We cannot accept this argument. Here, the offer specified the performance which was the price or consideration to be given. By its signs, Klick-Lewis offered to award the car as a prize to anyone who made a hole-in-one at the ninth hole. A person reading the signs would reasonably understand that he or she could accept the offer and win the car by performing the feat of shooting a hole-in-one. There was thus an offer which was accepted when appellee shot a hole-in-one. Accord: Champagne Chrysler-Plymouth, Inc. v. Giles, 388 So.2d 1343 (Fla.Dist.Ct.App. 1980) (bowling contest). . . .

The contract does not fail for lack of consideration. The requirement of consideration as an essential element of a contract is nothing more than a requirement that there be a bargained for exchange. . . . Consideration confers a benefit upon the promisor or causes a detriment to the promisee. . . . By making an offer to award one of its cars as a prize for shooting a hole-in-one at the ninth hole of the Fairview Golf Course, Klick-Lewis benefited from the publicity typically generated by such promotional advertising. In order to win the car, Cobaugh was required to perform an act which he was under no legal duty to perform. The car was to be given in exchange for the feat of making a hole-in-one. This was adequate consideration to support the contract. See, e.g.: Las Vegas Hacienda, Inc. v. Gibson, 77 Nev. 25, 359 P.2d 85 (1961) (paying fifty cents and shooting hole-in-one was consideration for prize). . . .[1]

There is no basis for believing that Cobaugh was aware that the Chevrolet automobile had been intended as a prize only for an earlier tournament. The posted signs did not reveal such an intent by Klick-Lewis, and the stipulated facts do not suggest that appellee had knowledge greater than that acquired by reading the posted signs. Therefore, we also reject appellant's final argument that the contract to award the prize to appellee was voidable because of mutual mistake. . . .

In Champagne Chrysler-Plymouth, Inc. v. Giles, supra, a mistake similar to that made in the instant case had been made. There, a car dealer had advertised that it would give away a new car to any bowler who rolled a perfect "300" game during a televised show. The dealer's intent was that the offer would continue only during the television show which the dealer sponsored and on which its ads were displayed. However, the dealer also distributed flyers containing its offer and posted signs advertising the offer at the bowling alley. He neglected to remove from the alley the signs offering a car to anyone bowling a "300" game, and approximately one month later, while the signs were still posted, plaintiff appeared on a different episode of the television show and bowled a perfect game. The dealer refused to award the car. A Florida

---

[1] The issue of an illegal contract . . . was not raised by appellant in the trial court or on appeal. . . .

Even if, as the dissent contends, this Court may act sua sponte to refuse enforcement of an illegal contract, it should not do so unless the illegality is clear. It is not clear in this case that to offer an automobile as a prize for a hole-in-one during a charity golf tournament was to introduce illegal gambling to the tournament. Courts of other jurisdictions have found similar offers legal and enforceable. See: Las Vegas Hacienda, Inc. v. Gibson, supra (contest to award prize to golfer who, having paid fee, scored a hole-in-one was not gambling and, therefore, created valid and enforceable contract). . . .

Finally, there was no evidence in this case that an element of chance was the dominant factor in shooting the hole-in-one. See: Commonwealth v. Laniewski, 173 Pa.Super. 245, 98 A.2d 215 (1953) (chance must be dominant factor). Even if this Court could legitimately consider the "facts" which the dissent introduces from a popular magazine, those statistics demonstrate that a professional golfer is generally twice as likely to shoot a hole-in-one as an amateur golfer. Under these circumstances, it cannot be said that skill is "almost an irrelevant factor." See: Las Vegas Hacienda, Inc. v. Gibson, supra, 77 Nev. at 29–30, 359 P.2d at 87 (where expert testified that "a skilled player will get it (the ball) in the area where luck will take over more often than an unskilled player," there was sufficient evidence to sustain a finding that the shooting of a hole-in-one was a feat of skill).

court held that if plaintiff reasonably believed that the offer was still outstanding when he rolled his perfect game, he would be entitled to receive the car. . . .

It is the manifested intent of the offeror and not his subjective intent which determines the persons having the power to accept the offer. [Rest.2d] of Contracts § 29. In this case the offeror's manifested intent, as it appeared from signs posted at the ninth tee, was that a hole-in-one would win the car. The offer was not limited to any prior tournament. The mistake upon which appellant relies was made possible only because of its failure to (1) limit its offer to the Hershey-Palmyra Sertoma Club Tournament and/or (2) remove promptly the signs making the offer after the Sertoma Tournament had been completed. It seems clear, therefore, that the mistake in this case was [not mutual but] unilateral and was the product of the offeror's failure to exercise due care. Such a mistake does not permit appellant to avoid its contract.

Affirmed.

POPOVICH, J. (dissenting). . . . [G]olf—as demonstrated by the vast majority of its practitioners who never have and never will score a round at par—is a sport requiring precise skills.

Making a hole-in-one, however, is such a fortuitous event that skill is almost an irrelevant factor. Because of that fact (an element of chance), combined with the payment of an entry fee to the East End Golf Tournament (consideration) and the automobile prize (reward), my view is that the necessary elements of gambling are present thus rendering the contract *sub judice* unenforceable as violating the Commonwealth's policy against gambling.[1] . . . I raise this issue *sua sponte* since we have no jurisdiction to enforce a contract in violation of public policy. . . .

By couching this transaction in terms of a unilateral contract, the majority seems to opine that scoring a hole-in-one is an act of skill which a golfer can choose to undertake. The truth is quite the opposite. . . . So few in fact [ever experience the thrill of a hole-in-one] that "aceing" a hole is truly an act of "luck" not skill. Consider the following statistics: In 1988, approximately 21.7 million golfers played 434 million rounds of golf with only 34,469 holes-in-one being reported to the United States Golf Association. *Golf Digest*, using figures amassed since 1952, estimates that a golfer of average ability playing a par-3 hole of average difficulty has a mere 1 in 20,000 chance of aceing the hole. While the chances increase [to 1 in 10,000] for a professional golfer, the possibility of a hole-in-one, even for the world's best players, is still remote. . . . [E]ven at 10,000 to 1, the professional's chances of aceing a hole are more akin to an act of God than a demonstration of skill. Clearly, the possibility of a

---

1 Under Pennsylvania law, the three elements of gambling are consideration, a reward and an element of chance. Commonwealth v. Weisman, 331 Pa.Super. 31, 479 A.2d 1063 (1984). . . . Illegal lotteries, gambling and bookmaking are strictly prohibited as delineated in 18 Pa.C.S.A. §§ 5512 (lotteries), 5513 (gaming devices, gambling) and 5514 (pool selling, bookmaking).

hole-in-one is sufficiently remote to qualify as the necessary gambling requirement of an element of chance.

Since all of the elements of gambling are present, . . . I would find that an unenforceable contract was created. While I recognize that there are a variety of socially acceptable forms of gambling indulged in by the public for the most charitable of purposes and the worthiest of causes, they are nonetheless illicit under Pennsylvania law. Dollar raffle tickets for the benefit of a hospital or a Little League Baseball Ass'n are bought and sold innocuously and routinely, and, yet, raffles constitute unsanctioned gambling. Only recently, under strict control, has bingo, a popular and social form of gambling, been legalized. 10 Pa.C.S.A. § 301 et seq. See also 4 Pa.C.S.A. § 325.101 et seq. (horse racing); 72 Pa.C.S.A. § 3761–1 et seq. (state lottery). Millions of citizens spend billions of dollars each year on sports betting in office pools or with the local bookmaker. However, only in one state, Nevada, is it legal so to do.

Thus, when such a rare case as this comes into court, it may be difficult to re-assert a public policy which everyday is violated by common experience. . . . Nevertheless, we cannot usurp the role of the legislature or turn our heads away from the fundamental substance of this transaction: it is a contract, a contract covering the context of gambling. Hence, it is unenforceable no matter how much condoned or indulged.

NOTE: UNKNOWN OFFERS OF REWARDS

Suppose Cobaugh, intent on his game, had failed to notice either the Beretta or the signs at the ninth tee. Knowledge of an offer typically becomes an issue in situations where, as in Cobaugh v. Klick-Lewis, the offeror bargains for a performance, not a return promise, but unlike that case, the performance is rendered in total ignorance of the offer. The common illustration is an advertised reward for specified action (e.g., the giving of information leading to the arrest and conviction of the person guilty of a certain crime), and an informant provides the information before learning that the offer has been made. In one such case, Glover v. Jewish War Veterans of United States, Post No. 58, 68 A.2d 233 (D.C. Mun. Ct. App. 1949), the court reviewed the authorities and concluded:

> While there is some conflict in the decided cases on the subject of rewards, most of such conflict has to do with rewards offered by governmental officers and agencies. So far as rewards offered by private individuals and organizations are concerned, there is little conflict on the rule that questions regarding such rewards are to be based upon the law of contracts.
>
> Since it is clear that the question is one of contract law, it follows that, at least so far as private rewards are concerned, there can be no contract unless the claimant when giving the desired information knew of the offer of the reward and acted with the inten-

> tion of accepting such offer; otherwise the claimant gives the information not in the expectation of receiving a reward but rather out of a sense of public duty or other motive unconnected with the reward. "In the nature of the case," according to Professor Williston, "it is impossible for an offeree actually to assent to an offer unless he knows of its existence."

Observe that *Glover* requires that an offeree know of the reward offer and "act with the intention of accepting" it. What do you understand the quoted phrase to mean? Does it rest on an "assent" principle? A "bargain" principle? Recall that an act can be consideration for another's promise even though it is only "partially" induced or motivated by the promise.

COMMENT: "MASTER OF THE OFFER"

There is a long tradition of speaking of the offeror as "the master of the offer." The phrase simply recognizes that an offeror has the power to determine not only the substance of the exchange and the identity of the offeree (that is, the person or persons in whom a power of acceptance is created), but such "procedural" matters as the time, place, and form or mode of acceptance. Thus, as Cobaugh v. Klick-Lewis illustrates, an offeror may waive formal acceptance (a communicated promise); it is enough that the offeree performs as specified in the offer. Our concern here is whether the offering party, by specifying requirements or limitations, has fixed a course for entry into a contract.

The case of Caldwell v. Cline, 109 W. Va. 553, 156 S.E. 55 (1930), provides a well-known example. On January 29, Cline dated and addressed a letter to Caldwell, proposing to exchange land on specified terms. The letter said "will give you eight days in which" to accept or reject. Caldwell received the letter on February 2; six days later, on February 8, Caldwell wired Cline: "Land deal is made. Prepare deed to me." This telegram reached Cline on February 9. Upon Cline's refusal to proceed with the deal, Caldwell brought a bill in equity for specific performance. The trial court, believing that Caldwell's acceptance was untimely, dismissed the suit on demurrer.

On appeal, Caldwell's allegations were held sufficient to withstand a demurrer. Cline was wrong in urging that the eight-day limitation ran from January 29, the date of the letter, for "when a person uses the post to make an offer, the offer is not made when it is posted but when it is received." It followed that Cline's words had no "legal existence" until his letter was received by Caldwell on February 2, and thus the acceptance reaching Cline on the 9th was timely. Moreover, the "eight-days" language "is, without more, conclusive of the offeror's intention" to date the time limit from the moment the letter was put in Caldwell's hands.

Suppose Cline's letter of the 29th had been delayed in the mails and had not reached Caldwell until March 2. Could Caldwell have made a contract by accepting on March 10?

Suppose Amos Cobaugh had hit the hole-in-one on June 15 (with the car and the sign still on the ninth tee), a full month after the charity golf tournament in which Klick-Lewis had put up the Beretta GT as a prize. At what point does Cobaugh no longer have a power of acceptance?

That issue was present in the further example provided by Textron, Inc. v. Froelich, 223 Pa. Super. 506, 302 A.2d 426 (1973). During a telephone conversation with a broker of steel products, seller offered the broker two different lots of steel rods at stated prices. The conversation ended with the broker saying that he thought he wanted the rods, but that he also wanted time to check with his customers before accepting the offer. Nothing was said about a time limit on the offer. Some five weeks later, the broker called back and agreed to buy one lot of the rods at the offered price; two days thereafter, the broker telephoned again to purchase the other lot, also on the terms previously discussed. The seller replied to both phone calls by saying, "Fine, thank you."

The rods were not delivered, and a lawsuit resulted in which the broker was nonsuited on his claim of breach of contract. The trial judge, relying on the often-repeated proposition that "an oral offer ordinarily terminates with the end of the conversation," concluded that no contract was formed by virtue of lapse of the offer. A reviewing court disagreed, stating the rule to be that if no time for expiration of a power of acceptance is specified in the offer, the power terminates at the end of a reasonable time. " 'What is a reasonable time is a question of fact, depending on the nature of the contract proposed, the usages of business and other circumstances of the case which the offeree . . . either knows or has a reason to know.' . . . There may be times when a judge could find as a matter of law that an oral offer made in the course of a conversation terminates with [the conversation]. If there is any doubt as to what is a reasonable interpretation, the decision should be left to the jury. [Here,] it is possible that a jury could have found that the oral offer continued beyond the end of the conversation. We need not, however, decide this appeal on that issue." As the sentence last quoted indicates, the court ultimately rested its reversal and remand for trial on an alternative ground. What might that ground have been?

Pine River State Bank v. Mettille

333 N.W.2d 622 (Minn. 1983)

Confronting the question whether an employer's power to discharge an at-will employee had been limited by disciplinary procedures contained in a personnel handbook, the court said: "If the handbook language constitutes an offer, and the offer has been communicated by dissemination of the handbook to the employee, the next question is whether there has been an acceptance of the offer and consideration furnished. . . . [W]here an at-will employee retains employment with knowledge of new or changed conditions, the new or changed conditions may become a contractual obligation. In this manner, an original employment contract may be modified or replaced by a subsequent unilateral contract. The employee's retention of employment constitutes acceptance. . . . [B]y continuing to stay on the job, although free to leave, the employee supplies the necessary consideration. . . . An employer's offer of a unilateral contract may very well appear in a personnel handbook as the employer's response to the practical problem of transaction costs. . . . [A]n employer, such as the bank here, may prefer not to write a separate contract with each individual employee. . . . [W]e do not think that applying the unilateral contract doctrine to personnel handbooks unduly circumscribes the employer's discretion. . . . [Nor do we believe that] handbook provisions relating to job security require special treatment [or] are an exception to the general rule just discussed."

NOTE: ALTERING THE TERMS OF AT-WILL EMPLOYMENT

The unilateral contract has been used in disputes growing out of at-will employment, as a basis for affording employees both job security and economic benefits. This is, of course, but one dimension of the general erosion of the doctrine of at-will employment currently taking place. Still, it seems that the personnel handbook has spurred something of a rebirth of the unilateral contract. (Examples of the unilateral contract expanding liabilities and redefining relationships in other areas, some nontraditional, are examined in Pettit, Modern Unilateral Contracts, 63 B.U. L. Rev. 551 (1983).) One matter to watch in the employment context is the test of "bargain" that is to be applied. Some courts have openly approved departures from traditional "bargain theory" in the employee-handbook cases. See, e.g., Anderson v. Douglas & Lomason Co., 540 N.W.2d 277 (Iowa 1995) (employee suing to enforce promise in handbook need not show knowledge of promise, else those who read handbook would be treated differently from those who did not).

The *Pine River State Bank* analysis, which conceptualizes at-will employment as a unilateral contract that is accepted by the employee's continuing to work, is seen often in the employment cases. It was central to the decision in Torosyan v. Boehringer Ingelheim Pharm., Inc., 234 Conn. 1, 662 A.2d 89 (1995), where the court sustained a finding of an "implied contract" providing that an at-will employee could be terminated only "for cause." The court, in a remarkably elaborate exposition of the usual theory, made these points, among others: (1) All employer-employee relationships not governed by express contracts necessarily involve some type of "implied contract"—there is "a bargain of some kind." (2) The typical implied contract of employment includes terms specifying wages, working hours, job responsibilities and the like; because it is for an indefinite term—does not limit the terminability of employment—the default rule is employment at will. But a term so supplied, like any other contract term, can be modified by the parties' agreement. (3) The contents of any particular implied contract of employment are to be determined by examining the factual circumstances of the parties' relationship "in light of legal rules governing unilateral contracts." (4) In order to find an implied contract incorporating specific representations orally made by the employer or contained in provisions in an employee manual, the trier of fact must find that the representations or issuance of a manual or handbook to the employee was an "offer"—i.e., a promise that, if the employee worked for the company, his or her employment would thereafter be governed by the oral or written statements. If an offer is found, it is then necessary to find the employee's "acceptance" of the offer. (5) Subsequent oral representations or the issuance of subsequent handbooks must be evaluated by the same criteria—an offer to modify preexisting employment terms and acceptance of the proposed modifications, resulting in the "substitution of a new implied contract for the old." (6) When an employer issues a manual that confers greater rights than an employee previously had, the employee's continued work ordinarily demonstrates acceptance of the offer of new rights. This is a logical conclusion because the employer's likely motive for increasing job security is to encourage continued employment. (7) Conversely, when an employer issues a manual that "substantially interferes with an employee's legitimate expectations about the terms of employment," the employee's continued work after notice of those terms cannot be taken as conclusive evidence of consent to the terms. Continued work is admissible evidence of consent to the new contract, but cannot itself mandate a finding of consent. This must be so else an employee with a termination-for-cause contract would have no way to insist on its contractual rights; the only choices would be to resign or continue working, either of which would result in the loss of the very right at issue.

The principle that promises made in an employee handbook may be binding on an employer is no doubt accepted by most courts. Yet there are disagreements both as to the theory of liability and the circumstances justifying a finding of handbook-based obligation. For example, suppose the handbook, in conspicuous terms, reserves to the employer the right to modify unilaterally the handbook's terms. Should it follow that any offer made in issuing the handbook is illusory? Any reliance by an employee unreasonable?

There is also the question whether a disclaimer, included originally or added later, is a complete defense to a suit based on an employee handbook, whether the claim is for breach of contract or of promissory estoppel. Presumably, any promisor is free by clear and forthright disclaimer to deny legally binding effect to the promise. The fighting issue, of course, is whether, by virtue of packaging and presentation, the disclaimer's meaning or intended effect is put in doubt. Since employment at will is the norm in this country (at least the *legal* norm), should it be enough that a handbook states that it is "not a contract" or "gives no legal rights"? It seems at least some courts require that the handbook state in addition that the employee can be terminated at the will of the employer. E.g., Russell v. Board of Cty. Comm'rs, 952 P.2d 492 (Okla. 1997).

NOTE: THE OFFER AS "OPTION CONTRACT" REVISITED

An offeror most certainly has at hand the means for regulating the formation of a contract. The offeree alone may possess the power to close the contract, but that power is taken subject to any specifications laid down by the creator of the power. Not even compliance with the offeror's requirements suffices to ensure that the power of acceptance will be intact when the offeree gets around to using it. The offeror, it will be remembered, retains the power to revoke a simple offer until the very moment of acceptance—even without an explicit reservation of authority to do so. One need only recall Petterson v. Pattberg, where a highly respected court declared—albeit in dictum—that an offer could be revoked even after acceptance had been tendered.

But what if the offeror includes a statement (indeed, a promise) that the offer will remain available for a stated period? An opportunity to answer this question was presented in 1876 by the landmark case of Dickinson v. Dodds (Court of Appeal, Chancery Division), 2 Ch.D. 463. On Wednesday, June 10, 1874, defendant Dodds delivered to Dickinson a written offer to sell a parcel of land, with buildings, on specified terms. The offer provided that it would "be left over until" 9:00 a.m. on Friday, June 12. On Thursday, however, Dodds signed a contract to sell the property to one Allan. On the same day, Dickinson was informed by a person named Berry that Dodds had been "offering or agreeing" to sell to Allan. On Thursday evening, Dickinson left a written acceptance with Dodds' mother-in-law, with whom Dodds was then staying, but she failed to give it to him. On Friday morning about seven o'clock, first Berry, acting as Dickinson's agent, and then Dickinson himself, found Dodds at the local railway station and handed him duplicates of the acceptance. In each instance, Dodds replied that the acceptance was too late as he had sold the property. On defendant's appeal, a decree for specific performance was reversed. The court held that Dickinson's power to accept the offer had ended when, on Thursday, he received Berry's report that Dodds had sold the property to Allan. Dickinson then knew that Dodds "was no longer minded to sell the property to him as plainly and clearly as if Dodds had told him in so many words 'I withdraw the offer.' "

Nor did Dodds' assurance ("this offer to be left over until Friday") alter the result, because "[t]hat [language] shows it was only an offer. There was no consideration given for the undertaking or promise. . . . [It] being a mere *nudum pactum* was not binding, and . . . any moment before a complete acceptance by Dickinson of the offer, Dodds was as free as Dickinson himself."

The English court's first point laid the foundation for the principle of indirect communication of a revocation. Though still valid, this principle usually has been restricted to facts reasonably close to those of Dickinson v. Dodds. The following is a conventional formulation of the principle: "Where an offer is for the sale of an interest in land or in other things, if the offeror, after making the offer, sells or contracts to sell the interest to another person, and the offeree acquires reliable information of that fact, before he has exercised his power of creating a contract by acceptance of the offer, the offer is revoked." Berryman v. Kmoch, 221 Kan. 304, 310, 559 P.2d 790, 795 (1977). Why should the rule be so circumscribed? Why should it not extend to any offer and to any reliable information about what the offeror has been up to since making the original offer?

The second point of interest in the Dickinson v. Dodds analysis was that even the offeror's specification of a life span for the offer did not prevent its termination. There are at least two lines of explanation for this clearly remarkable proposition. One is rooted in the extreme subjectivism that occupied the minds of judges and contract theorists well toward the end of the nineteenth century. Consider Christopher Columbus Langdell's statement in 1880: "An offer is merely one of the elements of a contract; and it is indispensable to the making of a contract that the wills of the contracting parties do, in legal contemplation, concur at the moment of making it. An offer, therefore, which the party making it has no power to revoke, is a legal impossibility." (Law of Contracts § 78 (2d ed. 1880)). You will recognize, of course, that even when Langdell wrote, English law had already loosened, if not broken, the grip of subjectivism. Dickinson v. Dodds itself is proof of that, for there was no suggestion that Dodds' sale to Allan would itself have been enough to terminate Dickinson's power of acceptance before he learned of the sale.

Another possible explanation can be found in the power of legal classifications. Recall that the document Dodds gave Dickinson was called an offer, but the court immediately put it in the broad category of "undertaking or promise." This classification seemed naturally to lead to a search for those factors recognized as identifiers of the enforceable promise. Unable to find any, the court was impelled to conclude that Dodds was free to back away from his "undertaking or promise" before Dickinson's acceptance. Would it not have been entirely rational to say simply that an offer is not a promise, it is an offer? Such a classification might have invoked the basic premise of an offeror's control, with the result that an offer would be effective and immune to revocation to the extent defined in the offer itself. This is the approach adopted in German law and by some modern statutes in this country.

The principal result of these dual influences—subjectivism and the dictates of an unnecessary classification—was a need for devices to "reinforce" the power of acceptance so as to keep the subject of the offer off the market during the period the offeror has given the offeree for deliberation. What followed is a familiar story, most notably the carrying over to offers of principles generalized in the Second Restatement.

Restatement of Contracts, Second

§ 87. Option Contract

(1) An offer is binding as an option contract if it

(a) is in writing and signed by the offeror, recites a purported consideration for the making of the offer, and proposes an exchange on fair terms within a reasonable time; or

(b) is made irrevocable by statute.

NOTE: MAKING OFFERS IRREVOCABLE

Section 87(1) of the Restatement, Second provides an alternative avenue to enforcement when traditional consideration is lacking. Observe that

§ 87(1) does not require that the "purported consideration" for an offer actually be delivered. The ALI Reporter responsible for the drafting of the section has said that it provides for "nominal consideration." Braucher, Freedom of Contract and the Second Restatement, 78 Yale L.J. 598, 605 (1969). What is it in § 87(1) that gives effect to "nominal consideration?" See, e.g., Knott v. Racicot, 442 Mass. 314, 812 N.E.2d 1207 (2004), where the Massachusetts high court added to its holding (that the giving of consideration was required for sealed option contracts) the further statement that "[w]e henceforth adopt the Restatement (Second) Contracts § 87(1)." At least one court (only one, it appears) has rejected § 87(1) outright, characterizing it as a "minority position." Lewis v. Fletcher, 101 Idaho 530, 617 P.2d 834 (1980). As to false recitals of consideration for an option, it is fair to say that the cases preceding the Second Restatement's § 87(1) were in fact divided. No such division is to be found, however, when consideration, whether or not nominal, is in fact given. Courts, free to examine the parties' entire dealings in search of consideration for an option, often find a promise, even one dependent on parol evidence. E.g., Matter of Estate of Jorstad, 447 N.W.2d 283 (N.D. 1989) (son's oral promise to stay and work parents' farm, made on eve of execution of writing giving son option to purchase farm, constitutes consideration for option).

Statutes providing for irrevocable offers not limited to the purchase or sale of goods were already in place in a number of states by the middle of the last century. UCC 2–205 also includes a provision for firm offers when they are in writing. Again, the common pattern was to substitute for consideration the giving of a signed writing which, by its terms, stated assurances of irrevocability. For example, a "firm offer" statute was enacted in New York in 1941; it remains relatively unchanged today, as § 5–1109 of the General Obligations Law:

> Written Irrevocable Offer. Except as otherwise provided in [UCC] 2–205 with respect to an offer by a merchant to buy or sell goods, when an offer to enter into a contract is made in a writing signed by the offeror, . . . which states that the offer is irrevocable during a period set forth or until a time fixed, the offer shall not be revocable during such period or until such time because of the absence of consideration for the assurance of irrevocability. When such a writing states that the offer is irrevocable but does not state any period or time of irrevocability, it shall be construed to state that the offer is irrevocable for a reasonable time.

There are other examples of statutory firm offers, including legislation barring a bidder for government work from withdrawing a bid after the appropriate officials have opened the bids.

SECTION 3. LIABILITY ARISING FROM PRELIMINARY NEGOTIATIONS

James Baird Co. v. Gimbel Bros.

United States Court of Appeals, Second Circuit, 1933.
64 F.2d 344.

L. HAND, CIRCUIT JUDGE. The plaintiff sued the defendant for breach of a contract to deliver linoleum under a contract of sale; the defendant denied the making of the contract; the parties tried the case to the judge under a written stipulation and he directed judgment for the defendant. The facts . . . were as follows: The defendant, a New York merchant knew that the Dep't of Highways in Pennsylvania had asked for bids for the construction of a public building. It sent an employee to the office of a contractor in Philadelphia, who had possession of the specifications, and the employee there computed the amount of the linoleum which would be required on the job, underestimating the total yardage by about one-half the proper amount. In ignorance of this mistake, on December twenty-fourth the defendant sent to some twenty or thirty contractors, likely to bid on the job, an offer to supply all the linoleum required by the specifications at two different lump sums, depending upon the quality used. These offers concluded[:] "If successful in being awarded this contract, it will be absolutely guaranteed, . . . [and] we are offering these prices for reasonable" (sic), "prompt acceptance after the general contract has been awarded." The plaintiff, a contractor in Washington, got one of these on the twenty-eighth, and on the same day the defendant learned its mistake and telegraphed all the contractors to whom it had sent the offer, that it withdrew it and would substitute a new one at about double the amount of the old. This withdrawal reached the plaintiff at Washington on the afternoon of the same day [the twenty-eighth], but not until after it had put in a bid at Harrisburg at a lump sum, based as to linoleum upon the prices quoted by the defendant. The public authorities accepted the plaintiff's bid on December thirtieth, the defendant having meanwhile written a letter of confirmation of its withdrawal, received on the thirty-first. The plaintiff formally accepted [defendant's] offer on January second, and, as the defendant persisted in declining to recognize the existence of a contract, sued it for damages on a breach.

Unless there are circumstances to take it out of the ordinary doctrine, since the offer was withdrawn before it was accepted, the acceptance was too late. Restatement of Contracts, § 35. To meet this, the plaintiff argues as follows: It was a reasonable implication from the defendant's offer that it should be irrevocable in case the plaintiff acted upon it, that is to say, used the prices quoted in making its bid, thus putting itself in a position from which it could not withdraw without great loss. While it might have withdrawn its bid after receiving the revocation, the time had passed to submit another, and as the item of linoleum was a very trifling part of the cost of the whole building, it would have been an unreasonable hardship to expect it to lose the contract on that account, and probably forfeit its deposit. While it is true that the plaintiff might in advance have secured a contract conditional upon the success of its bid, this was not what the defendant suggested. It understood that the contractors would use its offer in their bids, and would thus in fact commit themselves to supplying the linoleum at the proposed prices. The inevitable implication from all this was that when the contractors acted upon it, they accepted the offer and promised to pay for the linoleum, in case their bid were accepted.

LEARNED HAND
1872–1961

It was of course possible for the parties to make such a contract, and the question is merely as to what they meant; that is, what is to be imputed to the words they used. Whatever plausibility there is in the argument, is in the fact that the defendant must have known the predicament in which the contractors would be put if it withdrew its offer after the bids went in. However, it seems entirely clear that the contractors did not suppose that they accepted the offer merely by putting in their bids. If, for example, the successful one had repudiated the contract with the public authorities after it had been awarded to him, certainly the defendant could not have sued him for a breach. If he had become bankrupt, the defendant could not prove against his estate. It seems plain therefore that there was no contract between them. And if there be any doubt as to this, the language of the offer sets it at rest. The phrase, "if successful in being awarded this contract," is scarcely met by the mere use of the prices in the bids. Surely such a use was not an "award" of the contract to the defendant. Again, the phrase, "we are offering these prices for . . . prompt acceptance after the general contract has been awarded," looks to the usual communication of an acceptance, and precludes the idea that the use of the offer in the bidding shall be the equivalent. It may indeed be argued that this last language contemplated no more than an early notice that the offer had been accepted, the actual acceptance being the bid, but that would wrench its natural meaning too far, especially in the light of the preceding phrase. The contractors had a ready escape from their difficulty by insisting upon a contract before they used the figures; and in commercial transactions it does not in the end promote justice to seek strained interpretations in aid of those who do not protect themselves.

But the plaintiff says that even though no bilateral contract was made, the defendant should be held under the doctrine of "promissory estoppel." This is to be chiefly found in those cases where persons subscribe to a venture, usually charitable, and are held to their promises after it has been completed. It has been applied much more broadly, however, and has now been generalized in § 90, of the Restatement of Contracts. We may arguendo accept it as it there reads, for it does not apply to the case at bar. Offers are ordinarily made in exchange for a consideration, either a counter-promise or some other act which the promisor wishes to secure. In such cases they propose bargains; they presuppose that each promise or performance is an inducement to the other. . . . But a man may make a promise without expecting an equivalent; a donative promise, conditional or absolute. The common law provided for such by sealed instruments, and it is unfortunate that these are no longer generally available. The doctrine of "promissory estoppel" is to avoid the harsh results of allowing the promisor in such a case to repudiate, when the promisee has acted in reliance upon the promise. Siegel v. Spear & Co., 234 N.Y. 479, 138 N.E. 414. Cf. Allegheny College v. National Bank, 246 N.Y. 369, 159 N.E. 173. But an offer for an exchange is not meant to become a promise until a consideration has been received, either a counter-promise or whatever else is stipulated. To extend it would be to hold the offeror regardless of the stipulated condition of his offer. In the case at bar the defendant offered to deliver the linoleum in exchange for the plaintiff's acceptance, not for its bid, which was a matter of indifference to it. That offer could become a promise to deliver only when the equivalent was received; that is, when the plaintiff promised to take and pay for it. There is no room in such a situation for the doctrine of "promissory estoppel."

Nor can the offer be regarded as of an option, giving the plaintiff the right seasonably to accept the linoleum at the quoted prices if its bid was accepted, but not binding it to take and pay, if it could get a better bargain elsewhere. There is not the least reason to suppose that the defendant meant to subject itself to such a one-sided obligation. True, if so construed, the doctrine of "promissory estoppel" might apply, the plaintiff having acted in reliance upon it, though, so far as we have found, the decisions are otherwise. Ganss v. Guffey Petroleum Co., 125 App.Div. 760, 110 N.Y.S. 176; Comstock v. North, 88 Miss. 754, 41 So. 374. As to that, however, we need not declare ourselves.

Judgment affirmed.

Drennan v. Star Paving Co.

Supreme Court of California, 1958.
51 Cal. 2d 409, 333 P.2d 757.

TRAYNOR, J. Defendant appeals from a judgment for plaintiff in an action to recover damages caused by defendant's refusal to perform certain paving work according to a bid it submitted to plaintiff.

On July 28, 1955, plaintiff, a licensed general contractor, was preparing a bid on the "Monte Vista School Job" in the Lancaster school district. Bids had to be submitted before 8:00 p.m. Plaintiff testified that it was customary in that area for general contractors to receive the bids of subcontractors by telephone on the day set for bidding and to rely on them in computing their own bids. Thus on that day plaintiff's secretary, Mrs. Johnson, received by telephone between fifty and seventy-five subcontractors' bids for various parts of the school job. As each bid came in, she wrote it on a special form, which she brought into plaintiff's office. He then posted it on a master cost sheet setting forth the names and bids of all subcontractors. His own bid had to include the names of subcontractors who were to perform one-half of one per cent or more of the construction work, and he had also to provide a bidder's bond of ten per cent of his total bid of $317,385 as a guarantee that he would enter the contract if awarded the work.

Late in the afternoon, Mrs. Johnson had a telephone conversation with Kenneth Hoon, an estimator for defendant. He gave his name and telephone number and stated that he was bidding for defendant for the paving work at the Monte Vista School according to plans and specifications and that his bid was $7,131.60. At Mrs. Johnson's request he repeated his bid. Plaintiff listened to the bid over an extension telephone in his office and posted it on the master sheet after receiving the bid form from Mrs. Johnson. Defendant's was the lowest bid for the paving. Plaintiff computed his own bid accordingly and submitted it with the name of defendant as the subcontractor for the paving. When the bids were opened on July 28th, plaintiff's proved to be the lowest, and he was awarded the contract.

Moulin Archives, San Francisco

ROGER J. TRAYNOR
1900–1983

On his way to Los Angeles the next morning plaintiff stopped at defendant's office. The first person he met was defendant's construction engineer, Mr. Oppenheimer. Plaintiff testified: "I introduced myself and he immediately told me that they had made a mistake in their bid to me the night before, they couldn't do it for the price they had bid, and I told him I would expect him to carry through with their original bid because I had used it in compiling my bid and the job was being awarded them. And I would have to go and do the job according to my bid and I would expect them to do the same."

Defendant refused to do the paving work for less than $15,000. Plaintiff testified that he "got figures from other people" and after trying for several months to get as low a bid as possible engaged L & H Paving Co. to do the work for $10,948.60.

The trial court found on substantial evidence that defendant made a definite offer to do the paving on the Monte Vista job according to the plans and specifications for $7,131.60, and that plaintiff relied on defendant's bid in computing his own bid for the school job and naming defendant therein as the subcontractor for the paving work. Accordingly, it entered judgment for plaintiff in the amount of $3,817.00 (the difference between defendant's bid and the cost of the paving to plaintiff) plus costs.

Defendant contends that there was no enforceable contract between the parties [since] it made a revocable offer and revoked it before plaintiff communicated his acceptance to defendant.

There is no evidence that defendant offered to make its bid irrevocable in exchange for plaintiff's use of its figures in computing his bid. Nor is there evidence that would warrant interpreting plaintiff's use of defendant's bid as the acceptance thereof, binding plaintiff, on condition he received the main contract, to award the subcontract to defendant. In sum, there was neither an option supported by consideration nor a bilateral contract binding on both parties.

Plaintiff contends, however, that he relied to his detriment on defendant's offer and that defendant must therefore answer in damages for its refusal to perform. . . . Did plaintiff's reliance make defendant's offer irrevocable?

Section 90 of the Restatement of Contracts states: "A promise which the promisor should reasonably expect to induce action or forbearance of a definite and substantial character on the part of the promisee and which does induce such action or forbearance is binding if injustice can be avoided only by enforcement of the promise." This rule applies in this state. . . .

Defendant's offer constituted a promise to perform on such conditions as were stated expressly or by implication therein or annexed thereto by operation of law. (See 1 Williston, Contracts [3rd ed.], [§§ 24A, 61].) Defendant had reason to expect that if its bid proved the lowest it would be used by plaintiff. It induced "action . . . of a definite and substantial character on the part of the promisee."

Had defendant's bid expressly stated or clearly implied that it was revocable at any time before acceptance we would treat it accordingly. It was silent on revocation, however, and we must therefore determine whether there are conditions to the right of revocation imposed by law or reasonably inferable in fact. In the analogous problem of an offer for a unilateral contract, the theory is now obsolete that the offer is revocable at any time before complete performance. Thus § 45 of the Restatement provides: "If an offer for a unilateral contract is made, and part of the consideration requested in the offer is given or tendered by the offeree in response thereto, the offeror is bound by a contract, the duty of immediate performance of which is conditional on the full consideration being given or tendered within the time stated in the offer, or, if no time is stated therein, within a reasonable time." In explanation, comment *b* states that the "main offer includes as a subsidiary promise, necessarily implied, that if part of the requested performance is given, the offeror will not revoke his offer, and that if tender is made it will be accepted. Part performance or tender may thus furnish consideration for the subsidiary promise. Moreover, merely acting in justifiable reliance on an offer may in some cases serve as sufficient reason for making a promise binding (see § 90)."

Whether implied in fact or law, the subsidiary promise serves to preclude the injustice that would result if the offer could be revoked after the offeree had acted in detrimental reliance thereon. Reasonable reliance resulting in a foreseeable prejudicial change in position affords a compelling basis also for implying a subsidiary promise not to revoke an offer for a bilateral contract.

The absence of consideration is not fatal to the enforcement of such a promise. It is true that in the case of unilateral contracts the Restatement finds consideration for the implied subsidiary promise in the part performance of the bargained for exchange, but its reference to § 90 makes clear that consideration for such a promise is not always necessary. The very purpose of § 90 is to make a promise binding even though there was no consideration "in the sense of something that is bargained for and given in exchange." (1 Corbin, Contracts 634 et seq.) Reasonable reliance serves to hold the offeror in lieu of the consideration ordinarily required to make the offer binding. In a case involving similar facts the Supreme Court of South Dakota stated that "we believe that reason and justice demand that the doctrine [of § 90] be applied to the present facts. . . . [T]he defendants in executing the agreement [which was not supported by consideration] made a promise which they should have reasonably expected would induce the plaintiff to submit a bid based thereon to the Government, that such promise did induce this action, and that injustice can be avoided only by enforcement of the promise." Northwestern Eng'g Co. v. Ellerman, 69 S.D. 397, 408, 10 N.W.2d 879, 884; . . . cf. James Baird Co. v. Gimbel Bros., 2 Cir., 64 F.2d 344.

When plaintiff used defendant's offer in computing his own bid, he bound himself to perform in reliance on defendant's terms. Though defendant did not bargain for this use of its bid neither did defendant make it idly, indifferent to whether it would be used or not. On the contrary, it is reasonable to suppose that defendant submitted its bid to obtain the subcontract. It was bound to realize the substantial possibility that its bid would be the lowest, and that it would be included by plaintiff in his bid. It was to its own interest that the contractor be awarded the general contract; the lower the subcontract bid, the lower the general contractor's bid was likely to be and the greater its chance of acceptance and hence the greater defendant's chance of getting the paving subcontract. Defendant had reason not only to expect plaintiff to rely on its bid but to want him to. Clearly defendant had a stake in plaintiff's reliance on its bid. Given this interest and the fact that plaintiff is bound by his own bid, it is only fair that plaintiff should have at least an opportunity to accept defendant's bid after the general contract has been awarded to him.

It bears noting that a general contractor is not free to delay acceptance after he has been awarded the general contract in the hope of getting a better price. Nor can he reopen bargaining with the subcontractor and at the same time claim a continuing right to accept the original offer. See, R.J. Daum Constr. Co. v. Child, Utah, 247 P.2d 817. [Here,] plaintiff promptly informed defendant that plaintiff was being awarded the job and that the subcontract was being awarded to defendant.

Defendant contends, however, that its bid was the result of mistake and that it was therefore entitled to revoke it. . . . Plaintiff, however, had no reason to know that defendant had made a mistake in submitting its bid, since there was usually a variance of 160 percent between the highest and lowest bids for paving in the desert around Lancaster. He committed himself to performing the main contract in reliance on defendant's figures. Under these circumstances defendant's mistake, far from relieving it of its obligation, constitutes an additional reason for enforcing it, for it misled plaintiff as to the cost of doing the paving. Even had it been clearly understood that defendant's offer was revocable until accepted, it would not necessarily follow that defendant had no duty to exercise reasonable care in preparing its bid. It presented its bid with knowledge of the substantial possibility that it would be used by plaintiff; it could foresee the harm that would ensue from an erroneous underestimate of the cost. Moreover, it was motivated by its own business interest. Whether or not these considerations alone would justify recovery for negligence had the case been tried on that theory (see Biakanja v. Irving, 49 Cal.2d 647, 320 P.2d 16), they are persuasive that defendant's mistake should not defeat recovery under the rule of § 90. . . . As between the subcontractor who made the bid and the general contractor who reasonably relied on it, the loss resulting from the mistake should fall on the party who caused it. . . .

The judgment is affirmed.

Restatement of Contracts, Second

§ 87. Option Contract

(2) An offer which the offeror should reasonably expect to induce action or forbearance of a substantial character on the part of the offeree before acceptance and which does induce such action or forbearance is binding as an option contract to the extent necessary to avoid injustice.

Goodman v. Dicker

United States Court of Appeals, District of Columbia Circuit, 1948.
169 F.2d 684.

PROCTOR, J. This appeal is from a judgment of the District Court in a suit by appellees for breach of contract.

Appellants are local distributors for Emerson Radio & Phonograph Corp. in the District of Columbia. Appellees, with the knowledge and encouragement of appellants, applied for a "dealer franchise" to sell Emerson's products. The trial court found that appellants by their representations and conduct induced appellees to incur expenses in preparing to do business under the franchise, including employment of salesmen and solicitation of orders for radios. Among other things, appellants represented that the application had been accepted; that the franchise would be granted, and that appellees would receive an initial delivery of thirty to forty radios. Yet, no radios were delivered, and notice was finally given that the franchise would not be granted.

The case was tried without a jury. The court held that a contract had not been proven but that appellants were estopped from denying the same by reason of their statements and conduct upon which appellees relied to their detriment. Judgment was entered for $1500, covering cash outlays of $1150 and loss of $350, anticipated profits on sale of thirty radios.

The main contention of appellants is that no liability would have arisen under the dealer franchise had it been granted because, as understood by appellees, it would have been terminable at will and would have imposed no duty upon the manufacturer to sell or appellees to buy any fixed number of radios. From this it is argued that the franchise agreement would not have been enforceable (except as to acts performed thereunder) and cancellation by the manufacturer would have created no liability for expenses incurred by the dealer in preparing to do business.

Further, it is argued that as the dealer franchise would have been unenforceable for failure of the manufacturer to supply radios appellants would not be liable to fulfill their assurance that radios would be supplied.

We think these contentions miss the real point of this case. We are not concerned directly with the terms of the franchise. We are dealing with a promise by appellants that a franchise would be granted and radios supplied, on the faith of which appellees with the knowledge and encouragement of appellants incurred expenses in making preparations to do business. Under these circumstances we think that appellants cannot now advance any defense inconsistent with their assurance that the franchise would be granted. Justice and fair dealing require that one who acts to his detriment on the faith of conduct of the kind revealed here should be protected by estopping the party who has brought about the situation from alleging anything in opposition to the natural consequences of his own course of conduct. Dair v. United States, 1872, 16 Wall. 1, 4. In Dickerson v. Colgrove, 100 U.S. 578, 580, the Supreme Court, in speaking of equitable estoppel, said: ". . . The vital principle is that he who by his language or conduct leads another to do what he would not otherwise have done, shall not subject such person to loss or injury by disappointing the expectations upon which he acted. . . . This remedy is always so applied as to promote the ends of justice." . . .

In our opinion the trial court was correct in holding defendants liable for moneys which appellees expended in preparing to do business under the promised dealer franchise. These items aggregated $1150. We think, though, the court erred in adding the item of $350 for loss of profits on radios promised under an initial order. The true measure of damage is the loss sustained by expenditures made in reliance upon the assurance of a dealer franchise. As thus modified, the judgment is [a]ffirmed.

American Nat'l Bank v. A.G. Sommerville, Inc.

191 Cal. 364, 216 P. 376 (1923)

Sommerville Co. sold two automobiles to Tomlinson for $3,900 each. Tomlinson signed two contracts, each of which described one of the automobiles and recited that Tomlinson "hereby acknowledges receipt of said property." Each contract also provided that if Sommerville, the seller, assigned to a third party the right to the money promised, Tomlinson "shall be precluded from in any manner attacking the validity of this contract on the ground of fraud, duress, mistake, want of consideration, or failure of consideration, or upon any other ground, and all moneys payable under this contract . . . shall be paid to such assignee or holder without recoupment, setoff or counterclaim of any sort whatsoever." Sommerville promptly assigned its rights under the two contracts to an investment company, which in turn assigned to plaintiff Bank. When plaintiff sued to collect the unpaid balances on the contracts, Tomlinson pleaded that he had never received either of the two automobiles and that neither of them was or ever had been in existence. At trial, Tomlinson tried to testify that he had not received the automobiles, but the court ruled his testimony inadmissible by reason of the quoted provisions of the two contracts. On Tomlinson's appeal, the California Supreme Court stated that the recitals in the contract could not of their own force preclude him from showing either that there was no consideration or that the consideration promised him had not been given; and this was equally true as to an assignee of Sommerville. The court then said that Tomlinson could be precluded through estoppel *in pais* from showing the falsity of a statement of fact on which another had relied. The statements in the contracts were made for the purpose of being acted on. If they were acted on by plaintiff, an estoppel *in pais* would arise, but plaintiff must prove this and the case should be remanded for a determination of this issue of fact.

D'Ulisse-Cupo v. Board of Dirs. of Notre Dame High Sch.

202 Conn. 206, 520 A.2d 217, 221–223 (1987)

A school board did not rehire a teacher despite representations that she would be given a new contract. The teacher sued for damages, resting on a contract claim of promissory estoppel and a tort claim of negligent misrepresentation. The reviewing court said: "We agree [that the representations plaintiff alleges] do not invoke a cause of action for promissory estoppel because they are neither sufficiently promissory nor sufficiently definite to support contractual liability. . . . We disagree [that the representations are] insufficient to sustain a cause of action for negligent misrepresentation. . . . [E]ven an innocent misrepresentation of fact 'may be actionable if the declarant has the means of knowing, ought to know, or has the duty of knowing the truth.' . . . The governing principles are set forth [in] § 552 of the Rest.2d of Torts: 'One who, in the course of his business, profession or employment . . . supplies false information for the guidance of others in their business transactions, is subject to liability for pecuniary loss caused to them by their justifiable reliance upon the information, if he fails to exercise reasonable care or competence in obtaining or communicating the information.' [D]efendants argue that if they cannot be held liable in contract for their representations based on promissory estoppel, they likewise cannot be held liable in tort for negligent misrepresentation. For purposes of a cause of action for negligent misrepresentation, however, the plaintiff need not prove that the representations made by the defendants were promissory. It is sufficient to allege that the representations contained false information [and that] defendants did not exercise reasonable care in communicating with plaintiff about her prospects for reemployment." [Observe that plaintiff made no claim that defendants' representations were knowingly deceptive, that is, fraudulent. Observe also that the court is clear on the point that the "contractual" remedy of promissory estoppel is wholly independent of a tort remedy for negligent misrepresentation.]

QUESTION

There is reason to think that liability in *Goodman* could have been based on the tort of negligent misrepresentation. Does that possibility lend support to, or undercut, the court's decision to rest on "estoppel"?

Hoffman v. Red Owl Stores, Inc.

Supreme Court of Wisconsin, 1965.
26 Wis. 2d 683, 133 N.W.2d 267.

[Hoffman and his spouse, the plaintiffs, owned and operated a bakery in Wautoma. In 1959, Hoffman began discussions with representatives of Red Owl, which owned and operated a number of grocery supermarkets and franchised "agency stores" owned by others, about opening a Red Owl store. Hoffman mentioned that he had only $18,000 capital; he was "repeatedly assured" by Red Owl representatives that that amount would be sufficient to set him up in a Red Owl agency store. Relying on Red Owl's assurances, in 1961 Hoffman bought the fixtures and inventory of a small grocery store in Wautoma and leased the building in which it was operated, in order to gain experience in the grocery business. After the Hoffmans had run the store profitably for three months, Hoffman, on Red Owl's advice, sold the fixtures and inventory in June 1961, receiving Red Owl's assurance that he would be set up in business in another location by fall. Red Owl selected a site for a new store in Chilton and, on Red Owl's suggestion, Hoffman obtained an option on the site, paying down $1,000 of the $6,000 purchase price. With continuing assurances from Red Owl that "everything is ready to go" and that he should get his capital together, the Hoffmans sold their bakery building. They rented a house in Chilton, paid one month's rent, and, pending the opening of the Chilton store, moved to Neenah where defendant had suggested that Hoffman might gain valuable experience by working in a Red Owl store.

Although the Hoffmans' capital was understood from the beginning to be limited to $18,000, Red Owl raised the required amount to $24,100 after the Hoffmans had sold their grocery store and made the down payment on the Chilton lot. In November 1961, the required sum was increased to $26,100. In February 1962, Red Owl presented another proposal that Hoffman interpreted to require of him a total of $34,000, of which $13,000 was to come from his father-in-law as a gift. Hoffman thereupon told Red Owl he could not go along with this proposal and this "terminated the negotiations between the parties." The Hoffmans sued to recover damages.]

The case was submitted to the jury on a special verdict with the first two questions answered by the court. This verdict, as returned by the jury, was as follows:

"Question No. 1: Did the Red Owl Stores, Inc. and Joseph Hoffman on or about mid-May of 1961 initiate negotiations looking to the establishment of Joseph Hoffman as a franchise operator of a Red Owl Store in Chilton? Answer: Yes. (Answered by the Court.)

"Question No. 2: Did the parties mutually agree on all of the details of the proposal so as to reach a final agreement thereon? Answer: No. (Answered by the Court.)

"Question No. 3: Did the Red Owl Stores, Inc., in the course of said negotiations, make representations to Joseph Hoffman that if he fulfilled certain conditions that they would establish him as a franchise operator of a Red Owl Store in Chilton? Answer: Yes.

"Question No. 4: If you have answered Question No. 3 'Yes,' then answer this question: Did Joseph Hoffman rely on said representations and was he induced to act thereon? Answer: Yes.

"Question No. 5: If you have answered Question No. 4 'Yes,' then answer this question: Ought Joseph Hoffman, in the exercise of ordinary care, to have relied on said representations? Answer: Yes.

"Question No. 6: If you have answered Question No. 3 'Yes,' then answer this question: Did Joseph Hoffman fulfill all the conditions he was required to fulfill by the terms of the negotiations between the parties up to January 26, 1962? Answer: Yes.

"Question No. 7: What sum of money will reasonably compensate the plaintiffs for such damages as they sustained by reason of:

"(a) The sale of the Wautoma store fixtures and inventory?

"Answer: $16,735.00.

"(b) The sale of the bakery building?

"Answer: $2,000.00.

"(c) Taking up the option on the Chilton lot?

"Answer: $1,000.00.

"(d) Expenses of moving his family to Neenah?

"Answer: $140.00.

"(e) House rental in Chilton?

"Answer: $125.00."

Plaintiffs moved for judgment on the verdict while defendants moved to change the answers to Questions 3, 4, 5, and 6 from "Yes" to "No," and in the alternative for relief from the answers to the subdivisions of Question 7 or a new trial. On March 31, 1964, the circuit court entered the following order:

"IT IS ORDERED in accordance with said decision on motions after verdict hereby incorporated herein by reference:

"1. That the answer of the jury to Question No. 7(a) be and the same is hereby vacated and set aside and that a new trial be had on the sole issue of the damages for loss, if any, on the sale of the Wautoma store, fixtures and inventory.

"2. That all other portions of the verdict of the jury be and hereby are approved and confirmed and all after-verdict motions of the parties inconsistent with this order are hereby denied."

Defendants have appealed from this order and plaintiffs have cross-appealed from paragraph 1, thereof.

CURRIE, C.J. The [appeals] present these questions: (1) Whether [we] should recognize causes of action grounded on promissory estoppel as exemplified by [Restatement] § 90? (2) Do the facts in this case make out a cause of action for promissory estoppel? (3) Are the jury's findings with respect to damages sustained by the evidence?

. . . Since 1933, the closest approach this court has made to adopting the rule of [§ 90] occurred in the recent case of Lazarus v. American Motors Corp. (1963), 21 Wis.2d 76, 123 N.W.2d 548, wherein the court stated: "We recognize that upon different facts it would be possible for a seller of steel to have altered his position so as to effectuate the equitable considerations inherent in § 90."

While it was not necessary [in *Lazarus*] to adopt the promissory estoppel rule of the Restatement, we are squarely faced [here] with that issue. Not only did the trial court frame the special verdict on the theory of [§] 90, . . . but no other possible theory has been presented [which] would permit plaintiffs to recover. Of other remedies considered, that of an action for fraud and deceit seemed to be the most comparable. An action at law for fraud, however, cannot be predicated on unfulfilled promises unless the promisor possessed the present intent not to perform. Suskey v. Davidoff (1958), 2 Wis.2d 503, 87 N.W.2d 306. . . . Here, there is no evidence that would support a finding that Lukowitz [Red Owl's agent] made any of the promises, upon which plaintiffs' complaint is predicated, in bad faith with any present intent that they would not be fulfilled by Red Owl. . . .

Because we deem the [§ 90] doctrine of promissory estoppel . . . [to supply] a needed tool which courts may employ in a proper case to prevent injustice, we endorse and adopt it. The record here discloses a number of promises and assurances given to Hoffman by Lukowitz in behalf of Red Owl upon which plaintiffs relied and acted upon to their detriment.

Foremost were the promises that for the sum of $18,000 Red Owl would establish Hoffman in a store. After Hoffman had sold his grocery store and paid the $1,000 on the Chilton lot, the $18,000 figure was changed to $24,100. Then in November, 1961, Hoffman was assured that if the $24,100 figure were increased by $2,000 the deal would go through. Hoffman was induced to sell his grocery store fixtures and inventory in

June, 1961, on the promise that he would be in his new store by fall. In November, plaintiffs sold their bakery building on the urging of defendants and on the assurance that this was the last step necessary to have the deal with Red Owl go through.

. . . [T]here was ample evidence to sustain the answers of the jury to the questions of the verdict with respect to the promissory representations made by Red Owl, Hoffman's reliance thereon in the exercise of ordinary care, and his fulfillment of the conditions required of him by the terms of the negotiations had with Red Owl.

There remains . . . the question of law raised by defendants that agreement was never reached on essential factors necessary to establish a contract between Hoffman and Red Owl. Among these were the size, cost, design, and layout of the store building; and the terms of the lease with respect to rent, maintenance, renewal, and purchase options. This poses the question of whether the promise necessary to sustain a cause of action for promissory estoppel must embrace all essential details of a proposed transaction[,] so as to be the equivalent of an offer that would result in a binding contract between the parties if the promisee were to accept the same.

Originally the doctrine of promissory estoppel was invoked as a substitute for consideration rendering a gratuitous promise enforceable as a contract. . . . [T]he acts of reliance by the promisee to his detriment provided a substitute for consideration. If promissory estoppel were to be limited to only those situations where the promise giving rise to the cause of action must be so definite with respect to all details that a contract would result were the promise supported by consideration, then the defendants' instant promises to Hoffman would not meet this test. However, § 90 . . . does not impose the requirement that the promise giving rise to the cause of action must be so comprehensive in scope as to meet the requirements of an offer that would ripen into a contract if accepted by the promisee. Rather the conditions imposed are:

> (1) Was the promise one which the promisor should reasonably expect to induce action or forbearance of a definite and substantial character on the part of the promisee?
>
> (2) Did the promise induce such action or forbearance?
>
> (3) Can injustice be avoided only by enforcement of the promise?

We deem it would be a mistake to regard an action grounded on promissory estoppel as the equivalent of a breach of contract action. . . . [I]t is desirable that fluidity in the application of the concept be maintained. While the first two of the above listed three requirements of promissory estoppel present issues of fact which ordinarily will be resolved by a jury, the third requirement, that the remedy can only be invoked where necessary to avoid injustice, is one that involves a policy decision by the court. Such a policy decision necessarily embraces an element of discretion.

We conclude that injustice would result here if plaintiffs were not granted some relief. . . .

Defendants attack all the items of damages awarded by the jury.

The bakery building at Wautoma was sold at defendants' instigation in order that Hoffman might have the net proceeds available as part of the cash capital he was to invest in the Chilton store venture. . . . [I]t was sold at a loss of $2,000. Defendants contend that half of this loss was sustained by Mrs. Hoffman because title stood in joint tenancy. They point out that no dealings took place between her and defendants. . . . Ordinarily only the promisee and not third persons are entitled to enforce the remedy of promissory estoppel against the promisor. However, if the promisor actually foresees, or has reason to foresee, action by a third person in reliance on the promise, it may be quite unjust to refuse to perform the promise. 1A Corbin, Contracts, [§] 200. Here not only did defendants foresee that it would be necessary for Mrs. Hoffman to sell her joint interest in the bakery building, but defendants actually requested that this be done. We approve the jury's award of $2,000 damages for the loss incurred by both plaintiffs in this sale.

Defendants attack on two grounds the $1,000 awarded because of Hoffman's payment of that amount on the purchase price of the Chilton lot. The first is that this $1,000 had already been lost at the time the final negotiations with Red Owl fell through in January, 1962, because the remaining $5,000 of purchase price had been due on October 15, 1961. The record does not disclose that the lot owner had foreclosed Hoffman's interest in the lot for failure to pay this $5,000. The $1,000 was not paid for the option, but had been paid as part of the purchase price at the time Hoffman elected to exercise the option. This gave him an equity in the lot which could not be legally foreclosed without affording Hoffman an opportunity to pay the balance. The second ground of attack is that the lot may have had a fair market value of $6,000, and Hoffman should have paid the remaining $5,000 of purchase price. [But] it would be unreasonable to require Hoffman to have invested an additional $5,000 in order to protect the $1,000 he had paid. Therefore, we find no merit to defendants' attack upon this item of damages.

We also determine it was reasonable for Hoffman to have paid $125 for one month's rent of a home in Chilton after defendants assured him everything would be set when plaintiff sold the bakery building. This was a proper item of damage.

Plaintiffs never moved to Chilton because defendants suggested that Hoffman get some experience by working in a Red Owl store in the Fox River Valley. Plaintiffs, therefore, moved to Neenah instead of Chilton. After moving, Hoffman worked at night in an Appleton bakery but held himself available for work in a Red Owl store. The $140 moving expense would not have been incurred if plaintiffs had not sold their bakery building in Wautoma in reliance upon defendants' promises. We consider the $140 moving expense to be a proper item of damage.

We turn now to the damage item with respect to which the trial court granted a new trial, i.e., that arising from the sale of the Wautoma grocery store fixtures and inventory for which the jury awarded $16,735. The trial court ruled that Hoffman could not recover for any loss of future profits for the summer months following the sale on June 6, 1961, but that damages would be limited to the difference between the sales price received and the fair market value of the assets sold, giving consideration to any goodwill attaching thereto by reason of the transfer of a going business. There is no direct evidence presented as to what this fair market value was on June 6, 1961. The evidence did disclose that Hoffman paid $9,000 for the inventory, added $1,500 to it and sold it for $10,000 or a loss of $500. His 1961 federal income tax return showed that the grocery equipment had been purchased for $7,000 and sold for $7,955.96. Plaintiffs introduced evidence of the buyer that during the first eleven weeks of operation of the grocery store his gross sales were $44,000 and his profit was $6,000 or roughly 15 percent. On cross-examination he admitted that this was gross and not net profit. Plaintiffs contend that in a breach of contract action damages may include loss of profits. However, this is not a breach of contract action.

The only relevancy of evidence relating to profits would be with respect to proving the element of goodwill in establishing the fair market value of the grocery inventory and fixtures sold. Therefore, evidence of profits would be admissible to afford a foundation for expert opinion as to fair market value.

Where damages are awarded in promissory estoppel instead of specifically enforcing the promisor's promise, they should be only such as in the opinion of the court are necessary to prevent injustice. Mechanical or rule of thumb approaches to the damage problem should be avoided. . . . "The wrong is not primarily in depriving the plaintiff of the promised reward but in causing the plaintiff to change position to his detriment. It would follow that the damages should not exceed the loss caused by the change of position, which would never be more in amount, but might be less, than the promised reward." Seavey, Reliance on Gratuitous Promises or Other Conduct, 64 Harv.L.Rev. (1951), 913, 926. . . .

At the time Hoffman bought the equipment and inventory of the small grocery store at Wautoma he did so in order to gain experience in the grocery store business. At that time discussion had already been had with Red Owl representatives that Wautoma might be too small for a Red Owl operation and that a larger city might be more desirable. Thus Hoffman made this purchase more or less as a temporary experiment. Justice does not require that the damages awarded him, because of selling these assets at the behest of defendants, should exceed any actual loss sustained measured by the difference between the sales price and the fair market value.

Since the evidence does not sustain the large award of damages arising from the sale of the Wautoma grocery business, the trial court properly ordered a new trial on this issue. Order affirmed.

NOTE: PRELIMINARY NEGOTIATIONS AND AGREEMENTS TO AGREE

Hoffman involves an extended interaction between parties who never entered into a formal contract with one another. Scholars continue to use the facts as set out in the record in *Hoffman* as a vehicle to analyze the circumstances under which the conduct of parties during negotiations should give rise to legal liability. For contrasting approaches, compare Whitford & Macaulay, *Hoffman v. Red Owl Stores*: The Rest of the Story, 61 Hastings L.J. 801 (2010), with Scott, *Hoffman v. Red Owl Stores* and the Limits of Legal Method, 61 Hastings L.J. 859 (2010).

It is possible, however, to take the view that looking at precontractual negotiations through the lens of promissory estoppel is a mistake. Alan Schwartz and Robert E. Scott describe the legal landscape in the following way:

> For at least fifty years, a particular pattern of commercial behavior has engendered considerable litigation and substantial scholarly commentary. Two commercial parties agree to attempt a transaction and agree also on the nature of their respective contributions, but neither the transaction nor what the parties are to do is precisely described, and neither may be written down. The parties do not agree and, indeed, may never have attempted to agree on important terms such as the price. After the parties agree upon what they can, and before uncertainty is resolved, one or both of them make a sunk-cost investment. This pattern of commercial behavior suggests that the parties have made a "preliminary agreement" that will have one of two legally significant outcomes: If the transaction turns out to be profitable after uncertainty is resolved, the parties will make their agreement more concrete and then conduct the transaction. But if the transaction turns out to be unprofitable, the parties will abandon the project. Disputes sometimes arise under these preliminary agreements after one or both of the parties have invested. One party may then abandon the project even though the other party protests the first party's exit. In particular, the disappointed party believes that he is entitled to compensation either for his expectation or for his investment cost while the other party believes that she is entitled to exit without liability. A court must then decide whether to protect the promisee's expectation interest, or to protect his reliance interest by reimbursing his sunk cost, or to award him nothing.

> Legal scholars and practicing lawyers have poorly understood these types of cases. This is partly because the legal doctrines invoked in preliminary agreement cases are also used to support unrelated claims of precontractual liability. As a consequence, the governing criteria when reliance on a preliminary agreement is an issue have been obscured. The first task, therefore, is to characterize more precisely the commercial patterns and the associated legal rules that control precontractual liability.
>
> Parties have made a "fully binding contract" when they have agreed on all material terms and memorialized their agreement in a final written document. If the parties have not yet reached a fully binding contract, their negotiations will fall into one of three categories. First, the parties have engaged in "preliminary negotiations" when they have discussed a deal but have not agreed to one. In this event, the disappointed party can recover nothing. Second, the parties have agreed on all material terms and intend to memorialize this agreement in a formal document. In the interval between agreement and memorialization, the promisor has had a change of heart. Courts treat this type of agreement as a fully binding contract when the evidence supports a finding that the parties did not intend the formalization of their agreement to be essential. As is usual with binding contracts, courts protect the promisee's expectation interest. Third, the parties have made a preliminary agreement as defined above when they have agreed on certain terms but left other terms open, so that the best inference from their negotiations is that they have made a binding preliminary commitment to pursue a profitable transaction. Here, the emerging legal rule requires parties to such preliminary agreements to bargain in good faith over open terms. Should the promisor—the party who prefers to exit—fail to bargain in good faith, she will be liable for the promisee's reliance expenditures. The parties are not required to agree to a deal, however, because their preliminary agreement does not commit them to pursue an unprofitable project.

Schwartz & Scott, Precontractual Liability and Preliminary Agreements, 120 Harv. L. Rev. 661, 662–65 (2007).

In the cases that follow, consider whether the Schwartz and Scott excerpt captures the dynamic of what courts are doing, especially with respect to the calculation of damages.

Main Street Baseball, LLC. v. Binghamton Mets Baseball Club, Inc.

United States District Court, Northern District New York, 2015.
103 F. Supp. 3d 244.

HURD, DISTRICT JUDGE. . . . [Plaintiff] Main Street Baseball is a Florida limited liability company. David Heller ("Heller") is Main Street

Baseball's principal and president. Heller manages and co-owns several minor league teams including the Wilmington Blue Rocks, a Single-A team that plays in Wilmington, Delaware. [Plaintiff] Minker is an investor and co-owns the Wilmington Blue Rocks with Heller. Heller and Minker sought to upgrade their team in Wilmington from a Single-A to a Double-A team; they aimed to purchase a Double-A team and move it to Wilmington, while selling the Wilmington Blue Rocks to a buyer who would relocate that team.

[Defendant] Binghamton Mets Baseball Club owns the BMets. The BMets play in the twelve-team Eastern League of Minor League Baseball and are the Double-A affiliate of the New York Mets. Michael Urda ("Urda") is president of the BMets. [Defendant] Beacon Sports is an investment banking firm for the professional sports industry; they brokered the BMets transaction that is at issue here. Richard Billings ("Billings") is principal of Beacon Sports.

In May 2014, Heller and Minker began discussions with Billings regarding their desire to purchase the BMets, and signed a confidentiality agreement to obtain relevant information regarding the team. Heller and Minker were introduced to Urda in August 2014, and by December 2014, they had reached an agreement with Urda and Billings regarding the sale of the BMets. As is customary in the industry, a Letter of Intent ("LOI") was to be drafted by attorneys to memorialize the terms. The LOI was executed on January 5, 2015. The nine-page LOI contained, among other terms, a sixty-day "no shopping" period during which defendants could not negotiate with other buyers. The LOI provided for the negotiation of, and ultimate execution, of an Asset Purchase Agreement ("APA").

Urda requested Heller and Minker put $100,000 into escrow within two days of executing the LOI. While Heller and Minker were prepared to do so, plaintiffs claim it took Billings more than two weeks to finalize the escrow agreement because Urda repeatedly changed who the agent would be. Plaintiffs eventually put the money into escrow on January 23, 2015. In the meantime, plaintiffs' attorney drafted the APA.

In early February 2015, Heller and Urda exchanged drafts of the APA at Urda's suggestion to save on legal fees. On February 14, Urda advised that his attorney would review the APA on February 18. In the meantime, Urda made changes to the APA which plaintiffs accepted. On February 25, fifty-one days into the sixty-day no shopping period, Urda forwarded his lawyer's comments. According to plaintiffs, Urda made many new demands but remained ready to execute the APA. Plaintiffs contend defendants' proposed changes altered the material terms of the LOI, in direct contravention of the LOI. One such change related to the parties' indemnification obligations, which plaintiffs claim the LOI provided for without reference to a deductible or cap. Defendants contend that a deductible and cap were to be negotiated before the APA was finalized, but that plaintiffs refused to negotiate these terms. On February

28, Urda advised Heller that he would be traveling out-of-state starting March 19 and that he wanted the APA to be finalized before that date.

Between February 28 and March 11, 2015, emails were exchanged between the parties and their attorneys. According to Main Street Baseball and Minker, Binghamton Mets Baseball Club and Beacon Sports refused to finalize the APA consistent with the LOI, as required by the LOI. Despite this, Urda never indicated the deal was off. On March 11, defendants' attorney emailed plaintiffs' attorney and advised that defendants remain interested in selling but that the sixty-day no shopping period had expired (as of March 5) and they would simultaneously consider other offers. On March 13, defendants' attorney emailed plaintiffs' attorney and advised that defendants were ceasing negotiations with plaintiffs. Heller and Minker allege that on March 19, they heard that the BMets had already entered into a LOI with another buyer.

Plaintiffs argue the LOI was a binding contract for the purchase of the team. Binghamton Mets Baseball Club and Beacon Sports contend the LOI is not binding, and expired at the end of the sixty-day period. The LOI states it is intended to pursue the proposed acquisition of the team. While the LOI was executed on January 5, 2015, plaintiffs did not send a first draft of the APA to defendants until February 4. Defendants contend they were ready and willing to execute the February 25 draft which included changes by their attorney. Instead, plaintiffs objected to that draft, would not agree to the proposed changes, including a deductible or cap on indemnification, and failed to provide proposed changes back to defendants.

Pursuant to the LOI, usual customary representations and warranties were still to be negotiated in the APA. Defendants claim these terms included indemnities, while plaintiffs contend the LOI fully provided for all indemnities. In addition to Heller and Minker's alleged unwillingness to negotiate defendants' proposed changes, Heller and Minker themselves made new demands for the APA, such as adding an arbitration provision and the award of prevailing party attorneys' fees which defendants did not agree to, and which were not a part of the LOI.

Binghamton Mets Baseball Club and Beacon Sports contend that the parties could not agree on these and many other issues, so they advised Main Street Baseball and Minker on March 11, 2015 that the exclusivity period had ended. Also on March 11, Urda spoke with Joseph McEacharn, president of the Eastern League of Professional Baseball Clubs, Inc. who was aware of the LOI between the parties. Urda advised McEacharn that the exclusivity period with plaintiffs had ended and they were unable to reach an agreement. McEacharn advised that he knew of another interested buyer who would contact Urda shortly. That buyer did so, and defendants executed a LOI with the new potential buyer on March 13. . . .

By their motion, Main Street Baseball and Minker seek to preliminarily enjoin Binghamton Mets Baseball Club and Beacon Sports from discussing, negotiating, or agreeing with any other party concerning the sale of the BMets baseball team for six months. They contend the parties could take expedited discovery during the next six months, followed by a hearing on the merits of plaintiffs' claims. Defendants urge that the temporary restraining order in place should be vacated and the preliminary injunction denied, but if granted, plaintiffs should be required to post a bond for $8.5 million, the purchase price of the team. . . .

Main Street Baseball and Minker argue they are likely to succeed on the merits of their breach of contract claim, or at a minimum, there is a serious question going to the merits and a balance of hardships tips in their favor. Binghamton Mets Baseball Club and Beacon Sports challenge plaintiffs' likelihood of success on the merits on two grounds. First, defendants argue the LOI was not a binding contract. Second, defendants argue that even if the LOI was binding in some way, they did not breach any contractual obligations.

To establish a breach of contract claim under New York law, a plaintiff must plausibly allege "(1) the existence of a contract between itself and that defendant; (2) performance of the plaintiff's obligations under the contract; (3) breach of the contract by that defendant; and (4) damages to the plaintiff caused by that defendant's breach." Diesel Props S.r.l. v. Greystone Bus. Credit II LLC, 631 F.3d 42, 52 (2d Cir. 2011). The parties agree as to these familiar elements, but dispute the existence of a binding contract. Accordingly, the breach of contract claim first depends on whether the LOI was a binding contract. . . .

By its plain terms, the LOI contemplates the preparation and execution of additional documentation, namely, an APA. The LOI therefore belongs to a class of agreements known as "preliminary agreements which . . . provide for the execution of more formal agreements." Adjustrite Sys., Inc. v. GAB Bus. Servs., Inc., 145 F.3d 543, 547 (2d Cir. 1998). "[W]here the parties contemplate further negotiations and the execution of a formal instrument," a preliminary agreement ordinarily "does not create a binding contract." Brown v. Cara, 420 F.3d 148, 153 (2d Cir. 2005). "In some circumstances, however, preliminary agreements can create binding obligations." Id. The questions then, are: (1) whether the LOI created binding obligations; and (2) if so, whether those obligations included a commitment by defendants to sell the team to plaintiffs, or merely an obligation to negotiate in good faith. At the preliminary injunction stage, plaintiffs carry the burden to demonstrate that they are likely to succeed on the merits of their breach of contract claim, or that there is a serious question going to the merits and a balance of hardships tips in their favor.

The Second Circuit classifies binding preliminary commitments into one of two categories. Agreements within the first category are Type I preliminary agreements—"fully binding preliminary agreement[s], which [are] created when the parties agree on all the points that require negotiation (including whether to be bound) but agree to memorialize their agreement in a more formal document." Agreements of this type render the parties "fully bound to carry out the terms of the agreement even if the formal instrument is never executed." Adjustrite, 145 F.3d at 548.

Agreements within the second category are Type II preliminary agreements—"binding preliminary commitment[s]" that are "binding only to a certain degree" because "the parties agree on certain major terms, but leave other terms open for further negotiation." *Id.* Type II agreements "do[ ] not commit the parties to their ultimate contractual objective." Adjustrite, 145 F.3d at 548. Rather, they bind the parties "to the obligation to negotiate the open issues in good faith in an attempt to reach the . . . objective within the agreed framework." *Id.* If the parties "fail to reach such a final agreement after making a good faith effort to do so, there is no further obligation." *Id.*

The LOI bound defendants to sell and plaintiffs to purchase the BMets if it constituted a Type I agreement, but not if it constituted a Type II agreement or was, in the alternative, not binding in any respect. The LOI merely bound the parties to negotiate in good faith if it constituted a Type II agreement. Plaintiffs argue the LOI is a Type I agreement, binding the parties to the sale, or at a minimum, a Type II agreement which defendants breached. Defendants contend the LOI is not a Type I nor Type II agreement, and even if interpreted as a Type II agreement, plaintiffs have not plausibly alleged a breach of contract. . . .

The first and most important factor [in determining whether the agreement is a Type I or Type II preliminary agreement] is whether the language of the agreement "discloses an intention by the parties to be bound to the ultimate objective." Brown, 420 F.3d at 154. The relevant inquiry is whether the agreement expressly states that the parties will not be bound in the absence of a further, definitive written instrument. *Id.* There does not appear to be such a reservation here. The LOI is nine pages long and clearly sets forth the parameters of the transaction. It begins: "[t]his letter outlines the terms of our mutual and *fully binding* intention (the "Letter of Intent") to pursue the proposed acquisition of the Binghamton Mets baseball club." (emphasis added). It explicitly states that it "shall constitute a legally binding commitment of the Parties to execute and deliver the Asset Purchase Agreement . . . and fulfill such other obligations and satisfy such other conditions related thereto to facilitate Purchaser receiving all necessary Baseball Approvals to close the contemplated transaction herein." The LOI further notes that after executing the APA, "Seller would sell, convey, transfer, assign, and deliver to Purchaser, and Purchaser would purchase, acquire and assume, in exchange for the Purchase Price set forth in Section 3, all of Seller's assets, properties and rights." . . .

Where, as here, an agreement uses language that is committal, and specifies each party's performance in detail, it is indicative of a Type I agreement.

Moreover, the LOI specified in detail what would become of the deal if the parties were unable to execute an APA by the end of the sixty-day period. Also in support of finding the LOI constitutes a Type I agreement is the LOI's drafting history, which courts are both permitted and required to consider. According to plaintiffs, the parties negotiated the terms of the sale for four months (August to December 2014), and after shaking hands on December 8, 2014, they spent the next two and a half weeks exchanging multiple drafts of the LOI. According to plaintiffs, Urda stressed that he wanted the LOI to be binding, to which Heller and Minker agreed.

At the same time, however, other language in the LOI supports the conclusion that the LOI is at most a Type II agreement. Although "not necessarily controlling," labels "such as 'letter of intent' or 'commitment letter' " may "be helpful indicators of the parties' intentions." Teachers Ins. & Annuity Ass'n of Am. v. Tribune Co., 670 F. Supp. 491, 497 (S.D.N.Y. 1987). Defendants point to the opening sentence of the LOI, which as described above, states that "[t]his letter *outlines* the terms of our mutual and fully binding intention . . . *to pursue* the *proposed* acquisition." LOI, at 2 (emphasis added). Similarly, in Brown, 420 F.3d at 154, the subject memorandum of understanding purported to "outline the terms under which [the parties] will *work together* to develop, build, market, and manage a new real estate venture." *Id.* (emphasis in original). The Second Circuit found that language to be "decidedly non-committal" and concluded that the agreement was not a Type I agreement. *Id.*

Further, the assertion that the LOI "shall constitute a legally binding commitment" is prefaced by the phrase "[n]otwithstanding anything to the contrary contained in this Letter of Intent." The phrase "[n]otwithstanding" or similar, could suggest it overrides any binding obligations the LOI otherwise purports to impose. Moreover, the "legally binding commitment" described above applies "except as set forth in Sections 5, 6, 8, 9, 10, 12 and 13 [of the LOI]." Notably, Section 12 clarifies that "the Parties agree to use their reasonable best efforts to negotiate, execute and deliver, prior to the expiration of the No-Shopping Period [Section 9], a mutually agreeable Asset Purchase Agreement. . . ." The express language of the LOI sets an end to the parties' negotiation of the final agreement, the APA. Thus it could be concluded that any obligations to sell and purchase the team terminated at the expiration of the sixty-day no shopping period. Finally, the LOI expressly contemplated the future drafting and execution of the APA, in which "[t]he obligations of the Parties shall be spelled out in greater specificity." These provisions suggest an intent by the parties not to be bound by the "ultimate objective."

These provisions and the competing interpretations lead to the conclusion that there are, at a minimum, serious questions as to whether the language of the agreement weighs more strongly in favor of plaintiffs or defendants. . . .

The second factor [in determining whether the agreement is a Type I or Type II preliminary agreement] is satisfied either where both parties undertake performance, or where one party begins performance with the knowledge or approval of the other party. At defendants' request, plaintiffs made their first payment—the $100,000 First Security Deposit into escrow—toward purchase of the team. While defendants point out that the LOI contemplated at least one, and possibly two additional security deposits, this does not negate plaintiffs' partial performance. This favor weighs in favor of a finding that the LOI was possibly a Type I agreement, or at a minimum, a Type II agreement. . . .

[With regard to the third factor,] [t]he existence of open terms "is always a factor tending against the conclusion that the parties have reached a binding agreement," Tribune, 670 F. Supp. at 499, and there is a " 'strong presumption against finding binding obligation[s]' " in an agreement that " 'include[s] open terms . . . and expressly anticipate[s] future preparation and execution of contract documents,' " Arcadian Phosphates, Inc. v. Arcadian Corp., 884 F.2d 69, 73 (2d Cir. 1989). "At the same time, the parties' intent is ultimately controlling: if the parties intended to be bound despite the presence of open terms, courts should not frustrate their achieving that objective or disappoint legitimately bargained contract expectations, provided that the agreement is not so fragmentary as to be incapable of sustaining binding legal obligation." Vacold, 545 F.3d at 128. As the Second Circuit further elaborated in [Vacold LLC v. Cerami, 545 F.3d 114, 128 (2d Cir. 2008)]:

> If a preliminary agreement contains "no issues outstanding that were perceived by the parties as requiring negotiation, their agreement should be seen as a[ ] Type I binding obligation," [Shann v. Dunk, 84 F.3d 73, 82 (2d Cir. 1996)], notwithstanding that the parties may intend to memorialize their understanding in more formal documents. But if, in contrast, the parties enter into a preliminary agreement perceiving that open issues remain to be worked out and intending simply to bind themselves to good-faith efforts at further negotiation, then the preliminary agreement, if an agreement at all, is a type II obligation.

It appears the parties fully agreed to all the material terms of the transaction in the lengthy LOI. They agreed to the total purchase price of $8.5 million and the timing of payment of the purchase price including the payment of multiple security deposits. They agreed to maintenance of contracts and business relationships, assignment of the stadium lease, and retention of employees. Plaintiffs contend the parties also agreed to assumption of liabilities, retained obligations and indemnification, and risk of loss, and the only terms that needed to be "fleshed out" in a formal agreement were "representations and warranties customary for a transaction of this nature."

In contrast, Binghamton Mets Baseball Club and Beacon Sports point out that the LOI expressly contemplated further negotiations by the parties and the LOI refutes Main Street Baseball and Minker's contention that only minor issues remained to be added to the APA. Section 12 provides:

> The Parties agree to use their reasonable best efforts to negotiate, execute and deliver, prior to the expiration of the No-Shopping Period, a mutually agreeable [APA] containing provisions consistent herewith and such other terms and provisions as are normally included in asset purchase agreements . . . including, without limitation, usual and customary representations and warranties, disclosures, and indemnities.

Specifically, defendants argue the issue of indemnification was left open, and that while Section 4 provides for indemnification, it does not indicate any cap or deductible. Instead, Section 12 provides for the later negotiation of indemnities. Defendants also point out the new terms which plaintiffs themselves attempted to negotiate during the sixty-day period, including a guarantee of no loss during the 2015 season, an arbitration and prevailing party fees provision, and responsibility for the collection of accounts receivable. Defendants argue that these provisions, not in the LOI, establish that plaintiffs also believed there to be open terms left to negotiate following the execution of the LOI.

These provisions and the competing interpretations lead to a finding that there is, at a minimum, a serious question as to the merits of plaintiffs' claims. . . .

[The court concludes that the plaintiffs meet the other elements necessary to entitle them to a preliminary injunction preventing a sale of the club until a resolution of the merits.]

SIGA Techs., Inc. v. PharmAthene, Inc.

Supreme Court of Delaware, 2013.
67 A.3d 330.

STEELE, CHIEF JUSTICE. . . . Plaintiff-Appellee PharmAthene, Inc., and Defendant-Appellant SIGA Technologies, Inc., are both Delaware corporations engaged in biodefense research and development. In 2004, SIGA acquired an antiviral drug for the treatment of smallpox, ST-246. At that time, the drug's viability, potential uses, safety, and efficacy were all unknown, but the drug had enormous potential.

By late 2005, SIGA had experienced difficulty developing the drug and was running out of money. NASDAQ threatened to delist SIGA's shares and SIGA's largest shareholder, MacAndrews & Forbes (MAF), was unwilling to invest additional money. SIGA estimated it needed approximately $16 million to complete the development process.

As a result of SIGA's difficulties, SIGA's management began discussing a possible collaboration with PharmAthene. Thomas Konatich,

SIGA's Chief Financial Officer, contacted Eric Richman, PharmAthene's Vice President of Business Development and Strategies. Richman desired a merger between the two companies, but SIGA resisted because of its past experience with PharmAthene. According to Richman's contemporaneous notes, SIGA insisted on framing a license agreement before discussing a merger because of that past experience and because SIGA needed an immediate cash infusion to stabilize its financial situation. By the end of 2005, both SIGA's and PharmAthene's conservative estimates valued ST-246 at approximately $1 billion.

In late 2005 and early 2006, Konatich and Richman outlined the terms of a license agreement. Konatich kept Donald Drapkin, Chairman of SIGA's Board of Directors and MAF's Vice Chairman, well informed about the negotiations. Konatich and Richman also assembled negotiation teams on behalf of their companies. On January 3, 2006, Richman sent Konatich and Dr. Dennis Hruby, SIGA's Chief Scientific Officer, a proposed term sheet based on his discussions with SIGA about a license agreement for ST-246. On January 4, Hruby replied: "Thanks for the prompt response. We are most interested in trying to make this a mutually agreeable term sheet and moving on to the next step."

Konatich and Richman continued to exchange draft term sheets. Much of the negotiation focused on upfront cash payments and funding guarantees. On January 16, Richman sent Konatich a revised term sheet that provided for a total deal size of $16 million, an increased upfront payment of $6 million, and significant cash milestone payments. When Konatich forwarded this term sheet to Drapkin, he recommended that Drapkin speak directly to Richman to present SIGA's Board of Directors' position on PharmAthene's proposal.

On January 17, the Vice Chancellor [the judge at the trial level] found that Drapkin and Richman discussed the term sheet during a telephone call and Drapkin requested that Richman make two changes. Richman testified that Drapkin told him that if the changes were acceptable to PharmAthene, then "[w]e have got a deal on the term sheet, and it's ready to present to your board for approval." At a January 18 PharmAthene board meeting, Richman presented the January 16 term sheet and explained Drapkin's proposed changes. Jeffrey Baumel, PharmAthene's outside counsel, drafted the minutes for that board meeting. The term sheet was not signed, however, and the minutes do not state that the board approved the term sheet. . . .

On January 18, 2006, the PharmAthene board decided that it preferred a merger with SIGA instead of a license agreement, so representatives of PharmAthene and SIGA met to begin merger discussions on January 23 at MAF's office in New York City. Because of SIGA's precarious financial position, SIGA asked PharmAthene to provide bridge financing so that SIGA could continue developing ST-246 while merger negotiations proceeded. Richman and two other PharmAthene representatives testified that PharmAthene agreed to consider raising funds for a bridge loan on the condition that PharmAthene would obtain at least a license for ST-246 if merger negotiations fell through.

On February 10, 2006, David Wright, PharmAthene's Chief Financial Officer, sent Drapkin a draft merger term sheet that included the following provision regarding a license agreement:

> SIGA and PharmAthene will negotiate the terms of a definitive License Agreement in accordance with the terms set forth in the Term Sheet . . . attached on Schedule 1 hereto. The License Agreement will be executed simultaneously with the Definitive [Merger] Agreement and will become effective only upon the termination of the Definitive [Merger] Agreement.

Drapkin testified that he thought PharmAthene was confused and had no interest in a license agreement. But, the Vice Chancellor found Drapkin undermined that testimony when he admitted "that he understood that PharmAthene wanted to negotiate two documents at once when he received the draft merger term sheet with the license agreement attached."

On February 22, 2006, the parties once again met at MAF's office. Drapkin and another SIGA board member attended. Baumel reiterated PharmAthene's desire to execute simultaneously a merger agreement and a license agreement (in case the merger did not close). Relying on testimony from Baumel, Richman, and Wright, the Vice Chancellor found that Drapkin told PharmAthene he was not going to pay lawyers to draft a formal license agreement and suggested PharmAthene just attach the [two-page license agreement term sheet ("LATS")] to the merger agreement. Relying on Baumel's testimony, the Vice Chancellor found that Drapkin told PharmAthene that "this approach would be as good as a license agreement and would guarantee PharmAthene, at a minimum, a license if negotiations for a merger fell through."

The PharmAthene board reviewed a final merger term sheet on March 1, 2006. That term sheet specifically referred to the LATS and included a copy of the LATS as an exhibit. Again relying on testimony from Baumel, Richman, and Wright, the Vice Chancellor found that during a March 6 meeting, "Drapkin reiterated that 'in any case, if the merger doesn't close, [PharmAthene] will get [its] license.' " On March 10, the parties signed a merger letter of intent and attached the merger term sheet and the LATS.

On March 20, 2006, SIGA and PharmAthene entered into a Bridge Loan Agreement in which PharmAthene loaned SIGA $3 million for expenses relating to the merger, developing ST-246, and overhead. The Bridge Loan Agreement designates New York law as its governing law. It also specifically contemplates that the parties might not ultimately agree on either a merger or a license agreement. Bridge Loan Agreement

Section 2.3 obligates the parties to negotiate in good faith a license agreement in accordance with the terms of the LATS if the merger is terminated . . . .

With the Bridge Loan Agreement signed, PharmAthene provided SIGA with financial and administrative support while the parties redevoted attention to their proposed merger terms. On June 8, 2006, PharmAthene and SIGA signed the Merger Agreement, which selects Delaware law as its choice of law. Merger Agreement Section 12.3 is substantively identical to Bridge Loan Agreement Section 2.3 and provides that if the merger is terminated, the parties agree to negotiate in good faith a definitive license agreement in accordance with the LATS's terms. Section 13.3 stipulates that each of the parties must use their "best efforts to take such actions as may be necessary or reasonably requested by the other parties hereto to carry out and consummate the transactions contemplated by this Agreement." Section 12.4 provides that those provisions, among others, survive the Merger Agreement's termination. The Merger Agreement had a dropdead date of September 30, 2006.

The Vice Chancellor found that SIGA's key representatives understood that PharmAthene and SIGA were likely to enter into a lasting relationship, either by a merger or a license agreement. Several comments by SIGA representatives indicate that SIGA began experiencing seller's remorse after SIGA received a $5.4-million-dollar grant from the National Institutes of Health. As the parties continued preparing for the merger, SIGA achieved several milestones. For example, SIGA's Audit Committee approved an agreement with a clinical trial organization to perform the first human trial of ST-246. In September 2006, the National Institutes of Health awarded SIGA $16.5 million to develop the drug. After receiving this grant, SIGA representatives expressed remorse over having agreed to the merger.

As the Merger Agreement's September 30 drop-dead date approached, the SEC still had not approved SIGA's draft proxy statement. PharmAthene asked SIGA to extend the drop-dead date. On October 4, SIGA's Board of Directors met and decided to terminate the Merger Agreement. Shortly after terminating the Merger Agreement, SIGA publicly announced it had received the $16.5 million NIH grant and that ST-246 provided 100% protection against smallpox in a primate trial. After that announcement, SIGA sold two million shares of its stock at $4.54 per share, more than three times SIGA's 2005 share price. . . .

On November 21, 2006, SIGA sent PharmAthene a 102-page Draft LLC Agreement. The Vice Chancellor contrasted the LATS to the Draft LLC Agreement thusly:

> [T]he Draft LLC Agreement included the following economic changes: (1) the upfront payment from PharmAthene to SIGA increased from $6 million to $100 million; (2) the milestone payments to SIGA increased from $10 million to $235 million; (3) the royalty percentages owed to SIGA increased from 8%, 10%,

> and 12% depending on the amount of sales to 18%, 22%, 25%, and 28%; and (4) SIGA would receive 50% of any remaining profit whereas the LATS provided for profit sharing only from U.S. government sales having a margin of 20% or more. In addition, several noneconomic terms were revised to favor SIGA heavily and to undermine PharmAthene's control of ST-246. These provisions included: (1) SIGA's right to resolve disputes unilaterally; (2) SIGA's ability to block any distribution to PharmAthene; (3) PharmAthene's obligation to fund fully the LLC's costs, despite having to split profits 50/50; and (4) SIGA's right to terminate the LLC under certain conditions, with PharmAthene having no right to cure and with all rights to the product reverting to SIGA. . . .

The express contractual language in the Bridge Loan and Merger Agreements obligated the parties to "negotiate in good faith with the intention of executing a definitive License Agreement in accordance with the terms set forth in the" LATS. The question becomes whether the language "in accordance with the terms set forth" means that the parties had a duty, as the Vice Chancellor found, "to negotiate toward a license agreement with economic terms substantially similar to the terms of the LATS" (or at least not inconsistent with the LATS's terms) or whether the parties intended the LATS merely as a "jumping off point."

Although the LATS itself is not signed and contains a footer on each page stating "Non Binding Terms," the record supports the Vice Chancellor's factual conclusion that "incorporation of the LATS into the Bridge Loan and Merger Agreements reflects an intent on the part of both parties to negotiate toward a license agreement with economic terms substantially similar to the terms of the LATS if the merger was not consummated." The Vice Chancellor recognized that while "the economic terms [SIGA] proposed in the Draft LLC Agreement may not have 'directly contradict[ed]' the LATS . . ., they differed dramatically from the LATS in favor of SIGA" to the extent that they "virtually disregarded the economic terms of the LATS other than using them as a skeletal framework for the *types* of payments that would be made without giving any meaningful weight to the dollar amounts or percentages [SIGA] had negotiated earlier."

SIGA notes that requiring parties to propose terms "substantially similar" to those in a term sheet introduces some uncertainty and litigation risk into negotiations. Because a trial judge must find both that a party's proposed terms are substantially dissimilar and that the party proposed those terms in bad faith, we think SIGA overstates the litigation risk. Under Delaware law, "bad faith is not simply bad judgment or negligence, but rather it implies the conscious doing of a wrong because of dishonest purpose or moral obliquity; it is different from the negative idea of negligence in that it contemplates a state of mind affirmatively operating with furtive design or ill will." Not only did SIGA's negotiating position differ substantially from the LATS's terms, but also the Vice Chancellor also correctly concluded that SIGA took that position in bad faith.

The record supports the Vice Chancellor's finding that "SIGA disregarded [the LATS's] terms and attempted to negotiate a definitive license agreement that contained economic and other terms drastically different and significantly more favorable to SIGA than those in the LATS." . . . Evidence that "SIGA began experiencing 'seller's remorse' during the merger negotiations for having given up control of what was looking more and more like a multi-billion dollar drug" bolsters the Vice Chancellor's finding that SIGA failed to negotiate in good faith for a definitive license agreement in accordance with the terms of the LATS. Therefore, we affirm the Vice Chancellor's conclusion that SIGA acted in bad faith when negotiating the license agreement in breach of its contractual obligations under both the Merger Agreement and the Bridge Loan Agreement. . . .

We reverse the Vice Chancellor's conclusion that SIGA was liable on the basis of promissory estoppel. . . .

The Vice Chancellor based his finding of liability arising from promissory estoppel on "SIGA's promise to afford [PharmAthene] a good faith opportunity to obtain control of ST-246, and not solely in exchange for interest on a secured loan." Promissory estoppel does not apply, however, where a fully integrated, enforceable contract governs the promise at issue. The promise to negotiate in good faith for a definitive license agreement in accordance with the LATS's terms is expressly included in both the Bridge Loan and Merger Agreements. Therefore, a claim based on promissory estoppel cannot lie and a Vice Chancellor must look to the contract as the source of a remedy on the breach of an obligation to negotiate in good faith. . . .

We now turn to the question of what is the proper contractual remedy for breach of an agreement to negotiate in good faith where the court finds as fact that the parties, had they negotiated in good faith, would have reached an agreement.

Our decision in [Titan Investment Fund II, LP v. Freedom Mortg. Corp., 58 A.3d 984 (Del. 2012),] leaves open the question of whether expectation damages are available where the trial judge makes a factual finding that the parties would have reached agreement but for the defendant's breach. In fashioning his remedy, the Vice Chancellor noted the lack of consensus. We now hold that where the parties have a Type II preliminary agreement to negotiate in good faith, and the trial judge makes a factual finding, supported by the record, that the parties would have reached an agreement but for the defendant's bad faith negotiations, the plaintiff is entitled to recover contract expectation damages.

In this case, the Vice Chancellor made two key factual findings, supported by the record: (1) "the parties memorialized the basic terms of a transaction in . . . the LATS, and expressly agreed in the Bridge Loan and Merger Agreements that they would negotiate in good faith a final transaction in accordance with those terms" and (2) "but for SIGA's bad faith negotiations, the parties would have consummated a license agreement." The Vice Chancellor's factual conclusions support a finding that SIGA and PharmAthene entered into a Type II preliminary agreement and that neither party could in good faith propose terms inconsistent with that agreement. Because we had not previously addressed whether Delaware recognizes Type II preliminary agreements and permits a plaintiff to recover expectation damages, and because it is unclear to what extent the Vice Chancellor based his damages award upon a promissory estoppel holding rather than upon a contractual theory of liability predicated on a Type II preliminary agreement, we reverse the Vice Chancellor's damages award and remand the case for reconsideration of the damages award consistent with this opinion. . .

SECTION 4. CONTRACTS WITHOUT BARGAINING

Livingstone v. Evans

Supreme Court of Alberta, 1925.
[1925] 4 D.L.R. 769.

WALSH, J. The defendant, T.J. Evans, through his agent, wrote to the plaintiff offering to sell the land in question for $1800 on terms. On the day that he received this offer the plaintiff wired this agent as follows:—"Send lowest cash price. Will give $1600 cash. Wire." The agent replied to this by telegram as follows "Cannot reduce price." Immediately upon the receipt of this telegram the plaintiff wrote accepting the offer. [In the interim, defendant had entered into a contract to sell the land to one Williams, who was joined as a defendant in the present action.] It is admitted by the defendants that this offer and the plaintiff's acceptance of it constitute a contract for the sale of this land to the plaintiff[,] unless the intervening telegrams above set out put an end to his offer so that the plaintiff could not thereafter bind him to it by his acceptance of it.

. . . [W]hen an offer has been rejected it is thereby ended and it cannot be afterwards accepted without the consent of him who made it. The simple question . . . before me is whether the plaintiff's counter-offer was in law a rejection of the defendants' offer which freed them from it. [Hyde v. Wrench (1840), 3 Beav. 334, 49 E.R. 132,] is the authority for the contention that it was. The defendant offered to sell for 1000. The plaintiff met that with an offer to pay 950 and (to quote from the judgment)—"he thereby rejected the offer previously made by the Defendant. . . . [I]t was not competent for him to revive the proposal of the Defendant, by tendering an acceptance of it."

Stevenson v. McLean (1880), 5 Q.B.D. 346, . . . is easily distinguishable from Hyde v. Wrench. . . . Lush, J., who decided it[,] held that the letter there relied upon as constituting a rejection of the offer was not a new proposal "but a mere inquiry, which should have been answered and not treated as a rejection" but the Judge said that if it had contained an offer it would have likened the case to Hyde v. Wrench.

Hyde v. Wrench has stood without question for 85 years. . . . [The case] has firmly established . . . that the making of a counter-offer is a rejection of the original offer.

The plaintiff's telegram was undoubtedly a counter-offer. True, it contained an inquiry as well but that clearly was one which called for an answer only if the counter-offer was rejected. In substance it said: "I will give you $1600 cash. If you won't take that wire your lowest cash price." In my opinion it put an end to the defendants' liability under their offer unless it was revived by the telegram in reply to it.

The real difficulty in the case . . . arises out of the defendants' telegram "cannot reduce price." If this was simply a rejection of the plaintiff's counter-offer it amounts to nothing. If, however, it was a renewal of the original offer it gave the plaintiff the right to bind the defendants to it by his subsequent acceptance of it.

With some doubt I think that it was a renewal of the original offer or at any rate an intimation to the plaintiff that he was still willing to treat on the basis of it. It was, of course, a reply to the counter-offer and to the inquiry in the plaintiff's telegram. But it was more than that. The price referred to in it was unquestionably that mentioned in his letter. His statement that he could not reduce that price strikes me as having but one meaning, namely, that he was still standing by it and, therefore, still open to accept it. . . .

I am, therefore, of the opinion that there was a binding contract for sale of this land to the plaintiff of which he is entitled to specific performance. . . . [Defendant's] subsequent agreement to sell the land to the defendant Williams [is] of no avail as against the plaintiff's contract. . . .

QUESTIONS

(1) Suppose plaintiff's wire reply to defendant's original offer had read: "Your price of $1,800 seems high to me though the terms are o.k. Is your figure firm, or might you talk about $1,600 on the same terms?" Suppose further that defendant wired back: "I accept the deal at $1,600." Contract?

(2) Suppose plaintiff had drawn a line through the $1,800 figure in defendant's original letter, decreased the price to $1,600 (initialing the price change), signed the letter at the bottom, and mailed it back to defendant, who looked at the document but did nothing further. Not hearing from defendant for a week, plaintiff then wrote: "I accept your offer to sell for $1,800." Contract?

COMMENT: THE "DEVIANT ACCEPTANCE" AT COMMON LAW

One of the striking features of the common law governing the formation of a contract is the "deviant acceptance" rule. The introduction of "new" or "variant" terms means that the offer is dead and the process of contract formation must start over again. The rule, however, is alleviated somewhat by a number of qualifying doctrines. For example, immaterial variances between offer and acceptance are usually disregarded. Further, if the offeree's acceptance attempts only to make explicit terms that were already implicit in the offer, or the offeree merely "suggests" a new term without insisting on its inclusion, or the offeree appends an expression of lack of enthusiasm, perhaps even outright dissatisfaction (the so-called "grumbling acceptance"), the acceptance usually is effective. See, e.g., Massachusetts Hous. Fin. Agency v. Whitney House Assoc., 37 Mass. App. Ct. 238, 638 N.E.2d 1378 (1994); Panhandle Eastern Pipe Line Co. v. Smith, 637 P.2d 1020 (Wyo. 1981); Curtis Land & Loan Co. v. Interior Land Co., 137 Wis. 341, 118 N.W. 853 (1908). And it may make a difference whether a party invokes the deviant-acceptance rule "defensively" (e.g., original offeror seeks to avoid offeree's more onerous demand) or "offensively" (e.g., offeree seeks to escape contract formation on basis of its own additional demand). Hollywood Fantasy Corp. v. Gabor, 151 F.3d 203 (5th Cir. 1998) (noting reluctance to use offeree's modification as basis for finding no contract when, as here, offeror agrees that those modifications became part of contract).

The fighting issue in the deviant-acceptance cases is of course one of interpretation—whether the offeree's purported acceptance is absolute (with, perhaps, a mere inquiry attached) or conditional. To give an example, in Ardente v. Horan, 117 R.I. 254, 366 A.2d 162 (1976), the vendor's attorney prepared and forwarded to the vendee a written contract of purchase and sale (an offer, said the court). The vendee's attorney returned three things: (1) the contract properly signed by the vendee; (2) a $20,000 deposit required by the contract; and (3) an accompanying letter which read in part: "My clients are concerned that the following items remain with the real estate:" a) dining room set and tapestry wall covering in dining room; b) fireplace fixtures throughout; c) the sun parlor furniture. I would appreciate your confirming that these items are a part of the transaction, as they would be difficult to replace. Was the acceptance "absolute" or "conditional"? The court said that "an acceptance may be valid despite conditional language if the acceptance is clearly independent of the condition." Does this statement make the decision easier? In the end, the court was of the view that the attorney's letter was "not consistent with an absolute acceptance accompanied by a request for a gratuitous benefit." The purported acceptance was therefore a rejection of the vendor's offer, and no contract resulted.

When the answering communication is held to be qualified (conditional), and thus deviant, the analysis typically resumes with an inquiry as to whether the response found to operate as a rejection can also serve as a counteroffer which the original offeror (now an offeree) can in turn accept. If it can, again there must be conformity between the acceptance and the counteroffer, the penalty for nonconformity being that the slate is cleaned to await a resumption of bargaining activity.

The overall impression given by this analysis is that the bargaining process itself is neat and orderly, a series of steps that follow in logical progression—like the stately course of common law pleadings in the golden age of Chitty. The actual process of agreement-making often will not be so orderly, however, for haste and sloppiness, and disregard for lawyerly niceties, commonly attend commercial dealing. Moreover, the widespread use of business forms both produces much transaction-untidiness and, as we shall see, creates loopholes for escape under the traditional analysis. But the difficulty is more serious than this. With transactions that are fairly complex, the process of reaching agreement is likely to be an elaborate one of suggesting, demanding, conceding on some issues but resisting on others, searching out middle grounds, and adopting strategies for eventual compromise. Some discussions may be conducted in face-to-face meetings or by telephone, the balance of negotiations by mail or by exchange of written drafts. If agreement is reached ultimately, it may be next to impossible to identify the offeror, the offer (meaning a definitive proposal on the block for acceptance), or the acceptance. In short, the process of reaching agreement often will not conform to the ideal of orderly progression that conventional analysis assumes, and this non-conformity becomes more likely as the contemplated transaction becomes more complex and the process of negotiation more costly and time-consuming. The impact of contemporary technology on common law doctrines, such as the now pervasive use of email, must also be taken into account.

In the last half of the twentieth century, orthodox common-law analysis of contract formation has undergone significant rethinking and renovation. The general direction is by § 2–204 of the Uniform Commercial Code, which authorizes formation of a contract for the sale of goods in any manner sufficient to show agreement and declares unnecessary an actual identification of the offeror, the offeree, and the moment of making the contract. The Restatement, Second takes a similar path in § 22. One consequence is that, today, there is a greater tolerance of incomplete agreements. And, as we shall see just ahead, the UCC tolerates even contradiction in offer and acceptance, thereby restricting greatly the deviant-acceptance rule of the common law. But it would be a mistake to believe that the courts have discarded the traditional views entirely, or that they are likely to do so any time soon. It remains important for lawyers to understand the theoretical underpinnings and limitations of common law doctrine.

There is need to mention one final aspect of the deviant acceptance rule at common law. Events that ordinarily terminate a power of acceptance, including a deviant acceptance, do not have that effect when the offer that created the power is a binding option. See, e.g., Humble Oil & Refining Co. v. Westside Investment Corp., 428 S.W.2d 92 (Tex. 1968) (offeree's counteroffer during option period does not terminate the power of acceptance). Is it difficult to explain why the option contract has such special durability?

PROBLEM

V writes P offering to sell V's farm for $100,000, payment to be $10,000 down and the balance in equal annual installments. The letter adds: "I'm sure you will ultimately decide this is a bargain, so I will hold my offer open for 30 days even if you reject it in the meantime." P promptly replies: "I will give you $88,000 cash for your farm." Not hearing anything from V for a week, P then writes: "I accept your original terms for $100,000 deal." Has a contract been formed?

NOTE: CONTRACT FORMATION THROUGH EXCHANGE OF PRINTED FORMS

The case that follows provides one of the numerous examples we will encounter of the exchange of printed forms as a method of contract formation. One need not observe modern commercial practice for very long before concluding that merchants—"professionals" says the UCC—do not negotiate the details of every transaction. They prefer instead to exchange forms containing the standard terms on which they conduct business. Attorneys representing each side of recurrent transactions, such as sales and purchases of goods, will have prepared their own forms. Consequently, the chances are pretty good that differences will exist between the seller's "acknowledgment" or "sales order" and the buyer's "purchase order." Such differences—e.g., a limitation of seller's liability for defective quality, an agreement to submit to arbitration all claims arising out of the contract, reservations of power to cancel or to suspend performance on the happening of stated contingencies, etc.—may seem relatively unimportant at the moment the deal is concluded. But they can cause trouble later. When that happens and disputes cannot be resolved, it is safe to predict that one party will then try to impose a term from its form on the other.

At the formation stage, each party may attempt through standardized language to get the other's assent to its own form. Typically this is done by a term requesting that the form be signed and returned, or by a provision declaring that failure to object within a specified time shall constitute assent. In most cases, however, the purchaser's order will be acknowledged by the seller's own form, or vice-versa, with neither party expressly assenting to the other's form and with no effort made to reconcile conflicting terms. Whatever the mechanics of the particular exchange of forms, appropriately dubbed "the battle of the forms," it is obvious that this process of achieving assent differs greatly from that presupposed by orthodox formation doctrine. Instead of discussion and settlement of important details by negotiation, with all (or most) of the terms reflecting the considered judgment of both parties, attention is fixed on only a few key elements. The rest is left to standardized language.

At a later time we shall be interested in whether a party to a contract uses its bargaining position to take advantage of someone else. For present purposes, however, we assume that the bargaining process is not defective in any significant respect and the parties find themselves at the start on a more-or-less level playing field.

In recent decades, discussions of contract formation through exchange of printed forms have focused on the Uniform Commercial Code rules governing sales transactions, most notably § 2–207. The chief innovation of UCC 2–207 was its abandonment of the very principle of a formal rule of offer and acceptance. In place of a formal rule, the section substitutes a general standard under which the court is to look to the gist of the parties' communications to determine if they have formed a contract. In so doing, the court is to overlook any express terms in those communications that do not fairly reflect the parties' agreement.

Much has been written about § 2–207. Helpful guidance on Code methodology is provided in Brown, Restoring Peace in the Battle of the Forms: A Framework for Making Uniform Commercial Code Section 2–207 Work, 69 N.C. L. Rev. 893 (1991), and von Mehren, The "Battle of the Forms": A Comparative View, 38 Am. J. Comp. L. 265 (1990).

Richardson v. Union Carbide Indus. Gases, Inc.

Superior Court of New Jersey, Appellate Division, 2002.
347 N.J. Super. 524, 790 A.2d 962.

BRAITHWAITE, J. . . . Prior to 1988, Hoeganaes [a co-defendant with Union Carbide] operated furnace 2S, which was used for annealing iron powders. In 1988, Hoeganaes undertook the conversion of furnace 2S to a distalloy furnace. Part of the conversion process required the purchase of a powder transporter system or a "dense phase system" to transport iron powder to the input end of the furnace. Hoeganaes purchased the system from Rage [another do-defendant] after inquiring from two other possible sellers.

On or about September 26, 1988, Rage proposal number 3313 for a transporter system for iron powder and a transfer system for steel powder was submitted [to] Hoeganaes. Hoeganaes issued purchase order No. 21584 to Rage for that equipment. The transporter system for iron powder, referred to in the Rage proposal as System I, was installed on furnace 2S.

Subsequently, Rage submitted two more proposals to Hoeganaes. Number 3353 was for target boxes and Number 3375 was for control logic panels. Hoeganaes issued purchase order Number 23952 in response to these two proposals. By May 1989, the conversion of furnace 2S was completed.

The proposals issued by Rage were typed in a letter format addressing the items desired by Hoeganaes. At the base of each page of each proposal, the following language in capital letters was typed: "ANY PURCHASE ORDER ISSUED AS A RESULT OF THIS QUOTE IS MADE

EXPRESSLY SUBJECT TO THE TERMS AND CONDITIONS ATTACHED HERETO IN LIEU OF ANY CONFLICTING TERMS PROPOSED BY PURCHASER." The terms and conditions attached to Rage's proposals were standard terms that were sent with every proposal and appeared in standard boilerplate format. The terms and conditions were not discussed during Rage's meetings with Hoeganaes.

At the top of the [Rage] terms and conditions was a Limitation of Acceptance which stated:

> LIMITATION OF ACCEPTANCE. This sale (including all services) is limited to and expressly made conditional on Purchaser's assent to these Terms and Conditions as well as all other provisions contained in any other document to which these Terms and Conditions are attached. Purchaser agrees: (a) These Terms and Conditions . . . shall be deemed to supercede and take precedence over all prior writings, representations or agreements regarding this sale; (b) These Terms and Conditions . . . shall represent our complete agreement; (c) Any inconsistent, conflicting or additional terms or conditions proposed by Purchaser in any order, acceptance or other document or form shall be void and without effect unless Seller shall specifically and expressly accept same in writing; (d) No modification of these Terms and Conditions . . . will be affected by Seller's shipment of goods/equipment or the provision of services following receipt of Purchaser's order, acceptance or other document or form containing terms which are inconsistent, conflicting or in addition to these Terms and Conditions . . .; and (e) Any acceptance of goods/equipment or services, or payment constitutes an acceptance by Purchaser of these Terms and Conditions . . .

The Rage terms and conditions also had an indemnity clause, which stated:

> INDEMNITY. Purchaser shall indemnify and hold Seller harmless against and in respect of any loss, claim or damage (including costs of suit and attorneys' fees) or other expense incident to or in connection with: the goods/equipment; the furnishing of design, installation (including site preparation) or other services; processing or use by any person of any goods/equipment or system (including personal injury to the employees of Seller and Purchaser); or Purchaser's violation of any provision of these Terms and Conditions or the provisions of any document to which these Terms and Conditions are attached unless such loss, claim or damage is due solely and directly to the negligence or willful misconduct of Seller.

At the bottom of the purchase orders issued by Hoeganaes the following language in bold face type appeared: "THIS ORDER IS ALSO SUBJECT TO THE TERMS AND CONDITIONS ON THE REVERSE

SIDE OF THIS PAGE[.]" The reverse side of the purchase orders included the following section at the top of the boilerplate terms and conditions section:

> 1. Compliance with Terms and Conditions of Order—The terms and conditions set forth below, along with the provisions set forth on the front page hereof, constitute the entire contract of purchase and sale between Buyer and Seller. Any provisions in the Seller's acceptance, acknowledgment or other response to this Order which are different from or in addition to any of the terms and conditions and other provisions of this Order are hereby objected to by Buyer and such different or additional provisions shall not become a part of Buyer's contract of purchase and sale.

Furthermore, the reverse side also contained the following indemnity clause and a clause stating that the purchase order constituted the entire agreement:

> 14. Indemnification—Seller agrees to indemnify and hold harmless and protect Buyer, its affiliated and subsidiary companies, successors, assigns, customers and users of its products from and against all losses, damages, liabilities, claims, demands (including attorneys fees'), and suits at law or equity that arise out of, or are alleged to have arisen out of, directly or indirectly, any act of omission or commission, negligent or otherwise, of Seller, its sub-contractors, their employees, workmen, servants or agents, or otherwise out of the performance or attempted performance by Seller of this purchase order.
>
> 16. This purchase order contains the entire agreement between the parties and the provisions hereof or rights hereunder may be modified or waived only in writing by Buyer's authorized officials. All matters in connection herewith shall be determined under the laws of New Jersey.

Thus, both Rage and Hoeganaes exchanged documents, pertinent here, with conflicting indemnity clauses. Other than as expressed in the boilerplate language, neither side objected to the language in the documents and the contract was performed.

Plaintiff Jeffrey Richardson was an employee of Hoeganaes when he was injured by the explosion of furnace 2S on May 13, 1992. On September 15, 1994, plaintiff filed suit against numerous defendants including Hoeganaes and Rage. Plaintiff alleged that Rage "did design, manufacture, maintain, assemble, inspect, test, sell and/or distribute the systems and facilities design and/or its component parts" for the furnace which caused his injuries. Plaintiff alleged breaches of the Products Liability Act, N.J.S.A. 2A:58–1 to –11, implied and express warranties and negligence. In its answer, Rage cross-claimed against Hoeganaes seeking contractual indemnification. Hoeganaes, in its answer to the cross-claim, denied any right to indemnification arising out of the contract. . . .

The relevant statutory provision is 2–207, which provides as follows:

Additional Terms in Acceptance or Confirmation.

> (1) A definite and seasonable expression of acceptance or a written confirmation which is sent within a reasonable time operates as an acceptance even though it states terms additional to or different from those offered or agreed upon, unless acceptance is expressly made conditional on assent to the additional or different terms.
>
> (2) The additional terms are to be construed as proposals for addition to the contract. Between merchants such terms become part of the contract unless:
>
> > (a) the offer expressly limits acceptance to the terms of the offer;
> >
> > (b) they materially alter it; or
> >
> > (c) notification of objection to them has already been given or is given within a reasonable time after notice of them is received.
>
> (3) Conduct by both parties which recognizes the existence of a contract is sufficient to establish a contract for sale although the writings of the parties do not otherwise establish a contract. In such case the terms of the particular contract consist of those terms on which the writings of the parties agree, together with any supplementary terms incorporated under any other provisions of this Act.

. . . We note that 2–207 addresses "additional terms in acceptance" and also uses the language "different" terms [in 2–207(1)]. In 2–207(2), however, where the standard to determine whether additional terms become part of the parties' contract, the word "different" is not employed.

Section 2–207 is silent on the question of whether "additional or different terms" mean the same thing. There is seemingly no agreement on that question. Northrop v. Litronic Indus., 29 F.3d 1173, 1175 (7th Cir. 1994). It is unclear whether the reference to "different" terms in the acceptance, 2–207(1), means that the drafters intended "different" to be treated like "additional" terms under 2–207(2).

Comment three of 2–207 suggests that both additional and different terms are governed by 2–207(2). However, comment six of 2–207 advances the proposition that conflicting terms in exchanged writing must be assumed to be mutually objected to by each party with the result of a mutual "knock-out" of the conflicting terms.

Scholars differ on this subject. One commentator supports the view that the drafting history of the provision indicates that the word "different" was intentionally deleted from the final draft of 2–207(2) so that different terms would not be treated under that subsection. . . . Others, however, believe that different equates to additional and assert that the drafting history indicates that the omission of "or different" from 2–207(2) was a drafting error. . . .

There are, however, three recognized approaches by the courts to the issue of conflicting terms in contracts under circumstances such as here. . . . The majority view is that the conflicting terms fall out and, if necessary, are replaced by suitable UCC gap-filler provisions. . . .

The minority view is that the offeror's terms control because the offeree's different terms cannot be saved by 2–207(2), because that section applies only to additional terms. . . .

The third view assimilates "different" to "additional" so that the terms of the offer prevail over the different terms in the acceptance only if the latter are materially different. This is the least adopted approach. . . .

We conclude that the majority approach, the "knock-out" rule, is preferable and should be adopted in New Jersey. We reach this conclusion because the other approaches are inequitable and unjust and run counter to the policy behind 2–207, which addresses a concern that existed at common law.

At common law, there could be no meeting of the minds and thus no contract, unless there was agreement on all the terms of the contract. This was the "mirror-image" rule, which Article 2 of the UCC jettisoned by recognizing the existence of a contract even though certain terms remain in conflict or are unresolved. This change was meant to facilitate the completion of large-scale business transactions and practically is a necessity, in light of the way the American economy functions today. . . .

Section 2–207 was enacted to reform the common law mirror-image rule and reject the last-shot doctrine which accorded undue advantage to the mere order in which forms were sent. . . . Our adoption of the "knock-out" rule advances the goal of reformation of the common law mirror-image rule.

The motion judge recognized that each party created its own forms with its own terms that conflicted, yet still proceeded to transact business without objection. The judge noted:

> The truth is, and this really is the truth, what's happening is some little person some place writing these little—trying to plan it out, trying to conflict these things out, but the business people are out there delivering and taking money. And if the people really want to really get into all of this, then they should have taken their stuff away and they should have said, ooh, you know, we—you know, this is real here and, sorry, I'm not going

to be able to take your check and, sorry, you're not going to be able to keep the stuff, but they're not doing that. They're just playing a little game with forms.

In granting the motion for summary judgment, the judge implicitly adopted the "knock-out" rule. An approach other than the knock-out rule for conflicting terms would result in Rage, or any offeror, always prevailing on its terms solely because it sent the first form. That is not a desirable result, particularly when the parties have not negotiated for the challenged clause.

Now we address Rage's [assertion] that the motion judge erred in analyzing the matter under 2–207(3) rather than 2–207(2). We are satisfied that under either analysis the result is the same and, therefore, summary judgment was properly granted to Hoeganaes.

Section 2–207(2) sets forth the standard to determine if additional terms of an acceptance become part of the contract. . . .

Applying this section here leads inescapably to the conclusion that Rage's indemnity clause did not become part of the contract. Although Rage's offer specifically limited acceptance to the terms of its offer, Hoeganaes' acceptance materially altered Rage's offer with respect to the issue of indemnification. Additionally, Hoeganaes' acceptance objected to any terms or conditions of the Rage offer that were different from or in addition to any of the terms of its own acceptance.

Moreover, comment six to 2–207, which expresses the "knock-out" rule that we addressed earlier in this opinion, supports the conclusion that Rage's indemnity clause did not become part of the contract. Thus, 2–207(2) offers no support for Rage's position.

Applying 2–207(3) leads to the same result. Here, the contested provision addressed indemnity and only became relevant after plaintiff was injured, some three years after the conversion of the furnace was completed. Pursuant to 2–207(3), the conduct of the parties recognizes the existence of a contract and the "terms of the particular contract consist of those terms on which the writings of the parties *agree*, together with any supplementary terms incorporated under any other provisions of this Act." (Emphasis added). Because the parties' writings disagree on indemnity, that term did not become part of the contract.

Affirmed.

NOTE: THE QUALIFIED OR CONDITIONAL ACCEPTANCE TODAY

The *Richardson* court shows how alternative paths through § 2–207 leave the parties where they would have been had they signed a contract that omitted any mention of the disputed term. Whatever the path taken, this outcome is found in many cases decided under § 2–207. See Baird & Weisberg, Rules, Standards, and the Battle of the Forms: A Reassessment of § 2–

207, 68 Va. L. Rev. 1217 (1982). Courts end up treating the battle of the forms in the same way that they would treat an exchange of forms in which certain elements of the contract are left unaddressed by the parties. In doing this, they act in a way that parallels the Code's general solution to incompleteness problems, contained in § 2–204(3). If § 2–204(3) applies, the court will supply the missing terms by referring to certain "off-the-rack" terms of the Code, which themselves are generally open-ended standards rather than rules, or by referring to the custom and usage of the parties or their trade. Thus, under § 2–204(3), the incompleteness of the exchanged forms is no bar to finding a bargain.

UCC 2–207 applies only to contracts involving the sale of goods. The shadow it casts on other types of contracts may not be large. The first Restatement of Contracts was firmly committed to the requirement of a matching or "mirror-image" acceptance, § 60 providing: "A reply to an offer, though purporting to accept it, which adds qualifications or requires performance of conditions, is not an acceptance but is a counter-offer." The revised version, Restatement, Second § 59, appears to reflect a somewhat different view: "A reply to an offer which purports to accept it but is conditional on the offeror's assent to terms additional to or different from those offered is not an acceptance but is a counter-offer." The official comment to the revised § 59 states that a "qualified or conditional acceptance proposes an exchange different from that proposed by the original offeror. . . . [It] is a counter-offer and ordinarily terminates the power of acceptance of the original offeree." If the adjective "qualified" in this sentence embraces the same substance as the term "adds qualifications" in the original § 60, the revision would not seem to point to any departure from the matching-acceptance rule. The new official comment immediately adds, however, that "a definite and seasonable expression of acceptance is operative despite the statement of additional or different terms if the acceptance is not made to depend on assent to the additional or different terms."

The second Restatement clearly illustrates the effect of the Sales Article of the UCC on the general law of contracts in the second half of the last century. Equally clear is the quasi-legislative impact the drafters of the second Restatement were seeking. Though originally conceived as a systematic "restatement" of established common law rules, with innovation or choice among rules deemed limited to situations in which case authority was lacking or sharply divided, the Restatement, Second appears to have adopted a more activist, reforming posture. The rewritten Restatement § 59 clearly reflects the influence of the UCC's § 2–207. Even now, however, it is unclear whether the courts, in applying acceptance doctrines, have carried that influence over to nongoods cases. See, e.g., Logan Ranch v. Farm Credit Bank of Omaha, 238 Neb. 814, 472 N.W.2d 704 (1991); Okemo Mountain, Inc. v. Okemo Trailside Condos., Inc., 139 Vt. 433, 431 A.2d 457 (1981); Grossman v. McLeish Ranch, 291 N.W.2d 427 (N.D. 1980).

Outside of contracts involving the sale of goods controlled by the Uniform Commercial Code, courts continue to insist that the two parties be in sync before a contract is formed. In *Bridge City Family Medical Clinic, P.C. v. Kent & Johnson, LLP,* a court was willing to find acceptance of an offer even though terms of the release had yet to be worked out, but the court there insisted that the terms were not material. Where parties ask for materially different terms, courts, outside of cases governed by the UCC, find that no contract is formed. Representative is Miller v. Flegenheimer, 161 A.3d 524, 532 (Vt. 2016), a case in which the sale of a business was negotiated through an exchange of emails:

> Buyer later argued that his response was not a counter-offer by stating that he would give in on all the terms in his draft that differ from the terms in seller's e-mail. However, intent to be bound is an objective test to be determined at the time of agreement. Further, regarding counteroffers in Vermont:
>
> > It has long been the law in Vermont and elsewhere that an acceptance of an offer, to be good, must in every respect meet and correspond with the offer. An acceptance on terms varying from those proposed is, in effect, a counter proposal, and is not binding until it is itself accepted.
>
> Okemo Mountain, Inc. v. Okemo Trailside Condos., Inc., 139 Vt. 433, 435, 431 A.2d 457, 459 (1981). Therefore, the court erred in finding that buyer's response to seller's offer was an acceptance with additional proposals, and we conclude that buyer's response was a counteroffer.

ProCD, Inc. v. Zeidenberg

United States Court of Appeals, Seventh Circuit, 1996.
86 F.3d 1447.

EASTERBROOK, CIRCUIT JUDGE. Must buyers of computer software obey the terms of shrinkwrap licenses? The district court held not, [concluding that] they are not contracts because the licenses are inside the box rather than printed on the outside. . . . [W]e disagree. . . . Shrinkwrap licenses are enforceable unless their terms are objectionable on grounds applicable to contracts in general (for example, if they are unconscionable). . . . Because no one argues that the terms of the license at issue here are troublesome, we remand with instructions to enter judgment for the plaintiff.

ProCD, the plaintiff, has compiled information from more than 3,000 telephone directories into a computer database. We may assume that this database cannot be copyrighted. . . . ProCD sells a version of the database, called SelectPhone, on CD-ROM discs. (CD-ROM means "compact disc—read only memory." The "shrinkwrap license" gets its name from the fact that retail software packages are covered in plastic or cellophane "shrinkwrap," and some vendors, though not ProCD, have written licenses that become effective as soon as the customer tears the wrapping from the package. Vendors prefer "end user license," but we use the more common term.) . . . Customers [use] the data with the aid of an application program that ProCD has written. This program, which is copyrighted, searches the database in response to users' criteria (such as "find all people named Tatum in Tennessee, plus all firms with 'Door Systems' in the corporate name"). The resulting lists . . . can be read and manipulated by other software, such as word processing programs.

The database in SelectPhone cost more than $10 million to compile and is expensive to keep current. It is much more valuable to some users than to others. The combination of names, addresses, and SIC codes enables manufacturers to compile lists of potential customers. Manufacturers and retailers pay high prices to specialized information intermediaries for such mailing lists; ProCD offers a potentially cheaper alternative. People with nothing to sell could use the database as a substitute for calling long distance information, or as a way to look up old friends who have moved to unknown towns, or just as an electronic substitute for the local phone book. ProCD decided to engage in price discrimination, selling its database to the general public for personal use at a low price (approximately $150 for the set of five discs) while selling information to the trade for a higher price. It has adopted some intermediate strategies too: access to the SelectPhone database is available via the America Online service for the price America Online charges to its clients (approximately $3 per hour), but this service has been tailored to be useful only to the general public. . . .

To make price discrimination work, however, the seller must be able to control arbitrage. An air carrier sells tickets for less to vacationers than to business travelers, using advance purchase and Saturday-night-stay requirements to distinguish the categories. A producer of movies segments the market by time, releasing first to theaters, then to pay-per-view services, next to the videotape and laserdisc market, and finally to cable and commercial tv. Vendors of computer software have a harder task. Anyone can walk into a retail store and buy a box. Customers do not wear tags saying "commercial user" or "consumer user." Anyway, even a commercial-user-detector at the door would not work, because a consumer could buy the software and resell to a commercial user. That arbitrage would break down the price discrimination and drive up the minimum price at which ProCD would sell to anyone.

Instead of tinkering with the product and letting users sort themselves—for example, furnishing current data at a high price that would be attractive only to commercial customers, and two-year-old data at a low price—ProCD turned to the institution of contract. Every box containing its consumer product declares that the software comes with restrictions stated in an enclosed license. This license, which is encoded on the CD-ROM disks as well as printed in the manual, and which appears on a user's screen every time the software runs, limits use of the application program and listings to noncommercial purposes.

Matthew Zeidenberg bought a consumer package of SelectPhone in 1994 from a retail outlet in Madison, Wisconsin, but decided to ignore the license. He formed Silken Mountain Web Services, Inc., to resell the information in the SelectPhone database. The corporation makes the database available on the Internet to anyone willing to pay its price—which, needless to say, is less than ProCD charges its commercial customers. . . . ProCD filed this suit seeking an injunction against further dissemination that exceeds the rights specified in the licenses (identical in each of the three packages Zeidenberg purchased). The district court held the licenses ineffectual because their terms do not appear on the outside of the packages. The court added that . . . a purchaser does not agree to—and cannot be bound by—terms that were secret at the time of purchase. 908 F.Supp. at 654.

Following the district court, we treat the licenses as ordinary contracts accompanying the sale of products, and therefore as governed by the common law of contracts and the [UCC]. Whether there are legal differences between "contracts" and "licenses" (which may matter under the copyright doctrine of first sale) is a subject for another day. . . . Zeidenberg [urges,] and the district court held, that placing the package of software on the shelf is an "offer," which the customer "accepts" by paying the asking price and leaving the store with the goods. Peeters v. State, 154 Wis. 111, 142 N.W. 181 (1913). In Wisconsin, as elsewhere, a contract includes only the terms on which the parties have agreed. . . . So far, so good—but one of the terms to which Zeidenberg agreed by purchasing the software is that the transaction was subject to a license. Zeidenberg's position therefore must be that the printed terms on the outside of a box are the parties' contract—except for printed terms that refer to or incorporate other terms. But why would Wisconsin fetter the parties' choice in this way? Vendors can put the entire terms of a contract on the outside of a box only by using microscopic type, removing other information that buyers might find more useful (such as what the software does, and on which computers it works), or both. The "Read Me" file included with most software, describing system requirements and potential incompatibilities, may be equivalent to ten pages of type; warranties and license restrictions take still more space. Notice on the outside, terms on the inside, and a right to return the software for a refund if the terms are unacceptable (a right that the license expressly extends), may be a means of doing business valuable to buyers and sellers alike. [See] Restatement (2d) of Contracts § 211 comment a (1981) ("Standardization of agreements serves many of the same functions as standardization of goods and services. . . .").

Transactions in which the exchange of money precedes the communication of detailed terms are common. Consider the purchase of insurance. The buyer goes to an agent, who explains the essentials (amount of coverage, number of years) and remits the premium to the home office, which sends back a policy. On the district judge's understanding, the terms of the policy are irrelevant because the insured paid before receiving them. Yet the device of payment, often with a "binder" (so that the insurance takes effect immediately even though the home office reserves the right to withdraw coverage later), in advance of the policy, serves buyers' interests by accelerating effectiveness and reducing transactions costs. Or consider the purchase of an airline ticket. The traveler calls the carrier or an agent, is quoted a price, reserves a seat, pays, and gets a ticket, in that order. The ticket contains elaborate terms, which the traveler can reject by canceling the reservation. To use the ticket is to accept the terms, even terms that in retrospect are disadvantageous. See Carnival Cruise Lines, Inc. v. Shute, 499 U.S. 585 (1991). . . . Just so with a ticket to a concert. The back of the ticket states that the patron promises not to record the concert; to attend is to agree. A theater that detects a violation will confiscate the tape and escort the violator to the exit. One *could* arrange things so that every concertgoer signs this promise before forking over the money, but that cumbersome way of doing things not only would lengthen queues and raise prices but also would scotch the sale of tickets by phone or electronic data service.

Consumer goods work the same way. Someone who wants to buy a radio set visits a store, pays, and walks out with a box. Inside the box is a leaflet containing some terms, the most important of which usually is the warranty, read for the first time in the comfort of home. By Zeidenberg's lights, the warranty in the box is irrelevant; every consumer gets the standard warranty implied by the UCC in the event the contract is silent; yet so far as we are aware no state disregards warranties furnished with consumer products. Drugs come with a list of ingredients on the outside and an elaborate package insert on the inside. The package insert describes drug interactions, contraindications, and other vital information—but, if Zeidenberg is right, the purchaser need not read the package insert, because it is not part of the contract.

Next consider the software industry itself. Only a minority of sales take place over the counter, where there are boxes to peruse. A customer may place an order by phone in response to a line item in a catalog or a review in a magazine. Much software is ordered over the Internet by purchasers who have never seen a box. Increasingly software arrives by wire. There is no box; there is only a stream of electrons, a collection of information that includes data, an application program, instructions, many limitations ("MegaPixel 3. 14159 cannot be used with BytePusher 2.718"), and the terms of sale. The user purchases a serial number, which activates the software's features. On Zeidenberg's arguments, these unboxed sales are unfettered by terms—so the seller has made a broad warranty and must pay consequential damages for any shortfalls in performance, two "promises" that if taken seriously would drive prices through the ceiling or return transactions to the horse-and-buggy age.

According to the district court, the UCC does not countenance the sequence of money now, terms later. . . . One of the court's reasons—that by proposing as part of the draft Article 2B a new UCC 2–2203 that would explicitly validate standard-form user licenses, the American Law Institute and the National Conference of Commissioners on Uniform Laws have conceded the invalidity of shrinkwrap licenses under current law, see 908 F.Supp. at 655–56—depends on a faulty inference. To propose a change in a law's *text* is not necessarily to propose a change in the law's *effect*. New words may be designed to fortify the current rule with a more precise text that curtails uncertainty. To judge by the flux of law review articles discussing shrinkwrap licenses, uncertainty is much in need of reduction—although businesses seem to feel less uncertainty than do scholars, for only three cases (other than ours) touch on the subject and none directly addresses it. . . .

What then does the current version of the UCC have to say? We think that the place to start is § 2–204(1). . . . A vendor, as master of the offer may invite acceptance by conduct, and may propose limitations on the kind of conduct that constitutes acceptance. A buyer may accept by performing the acts the vendor proposes to treat as acceptance. And that is what happened. ProCD proposed a contract that a buyer would accept by *using* the software after having an opportunity to read the license at leisure. This Zeidenberg did. He had no choice, because the software splashed the license on the screen and would not let him proceed without indicating acceptance. So although the district judge was right to say that a contract can be, and often is, formed simply by paying the price and walking out of the store, the UCC permits contracts to be formed in other ways. ProCD proposed such a different way, and without protest Zeidenberg agreed. Ours is not a case in which a consumer opens a package to find an insert saying "you owe us an extra $10,000" and the seller files suit to collect. Any buyer finding such a demand can prevent formation of the contract by returning the package, as can any consumer who concludes that the terms of the license make the software worth less than the purchase price. . . .

Section 2–606, which defines "acceptance of goods," reinforces this understanding. A buyer accepts goods under § 2–606(1)(b) when, after an opportunity to inspect, he fails to make an effective rejection under § 2–602(1). ProCD extended an opportunity to reject if a buyer should find the license terms unsatisfactory; Zeidenberg inspected the package, tried out the software, learned of the license, and did not reject the goods. We refer to § 2–606 only to show that the opportunity to return goods can be important; acceptance of an offer differs from acceptance of goods after delivery, see Gillen v. Atalanta Systems, Inc., 997 F.2d 280, 284 n. 1 (7th Cir. 1993); but the UCC consistently permits the parties to structure their relations so that the buyer has a chance to make a final decision after a detailed review.

Some portions of the UCC impose additional requirements on the way parties agree on terms. A disclaimer of the implied warranty of merchantability must be "conspicuous." UCC 2–316(2), incorporating UCC

1–201(10). Promises to make firm offers, or to negate oral modifications, must be "separately signed." UCC §§ 2–205, 2–209(2). These special provisos reinforce the impression that, so far as the UCC is concerned, other terms may be as inconspicuous as the forum-selection clause on the back of the cruise ship ticket in *Carnival Lines.* Zeidenberg has not located any Wisconsin case—for that matter, any case in any state—holding that under the UCC the ordinary terms found in shrinkwrap licenses require any special prominence, or otherwise are to be undercut rather than enforced. In the end, the terms of the license are conceptually identical to the contents of the package. . . . [S]o, we believe, Wisconsin would not let the buyer pick and choose among terms. Terms of use are no less a part of "the product" than are the size of the database and the speed with which the software compiles listings. Competition among vendors, not judicial revision of a package's contents, is how consumers are protected in a market economy. . . .

Reversed and remanded.

Hill v. Gateway 2000, Inc.

105 F.3d 1147 (7th Cir. 1997)

Judge Easterbrook revisited contract-formation issues raised in *ProCD,* and wrote: "A customer picks up the phone, orders a computer, and gives a credit card number. Presently a box arrives, containing the computer and a list of terms, said to govern unless the customer returns the computer within 30 days. Are these terms effective as the parties' contract, or is the contract term-free because the order-taker did not read any terms over the phone and elicit the customer's assent?

"One of the terms in the box containing a Gateway 2000 system was an arbitration clause. Rich and Enza Hill, the customers, kept the computer more than 30 days before complaining about its components and performance. They filed suit in federal court. . . . Gateway asked the district court to enforce the arbitration clause; the judge refused, [finding no valid agreement to arbitrate].

"The Hills say that the arbitration clause did not stand out; they concede noticing the statement of terms but deny reading it closely enough to discover the agreement to arbitrate, and they ask us to conclude that they therefore may go to court. Yet an agreement to arbitrate must be enforced 'save upon such grounds as exist at law or in equity for the revocation of any contract.' 9 U.S.C. § 2. . . . A contract need not be read to be effective. . . . Terms inside Gateway's box stand or fall together. If they constitute the parties' contract because the Hills had an opportunity to return the computer after reading them, then all must be enforced.

"*ProCD* holds that terms inside a box of software bind consumers who use the software after an opportunity to read the terms and to reject them by returning the product. Likewise, Carnival Cruise Lines, Inc. v. Shute, 499 U.S. 585 (1991), enforces a forum-selection clause that was included among three pages of terms attached to a cruise ship ticket. *ProCD* and *Carnival Cruise Lines* exemplify the many commercial transactions in which people pay for products with terms to follow. . . . Gateway shipped computers with the same sort of accept-or-return offer *ProCD* made to users of its software. . . .

"Plaintiffs ask us to limit *ProCD* to software, but where's the sense in that? *ProCD* is about the law of contract, not the law of software. Payment preceding the revelation of full terms is common for [many] endeavors. Practical considerations support allowing vendors to enclose the full legal terms with their products. Cashiers cannot be expected to read legal documents to customers before ringing up sales. If the staff at the other end of the phone for direct-sales operations such as Gateway's had to read the four-page statement of terms before taking the buyer's credit card number, the droning voice would anesthetize rather than enlighten many potential buyers. Others would hang up in a rage over the waste of their time. And oral recitation would not avoid customers' assertions (whether true or feigned) that the clerk did not read term X to them, or that they did not remember or understand it. Writing provides benefits for both sides of commercial transactions. Customers as a group are better off when vendors skip costly and ineffectual steps such as telephonic recitation, and use instead a simple approve-or-return device. Competent adults are bound by such documents, read or unread. . . .

"For their second sally, the Hills contend that ProCD should be limited to executory contracts (to licenses in particular), and therefore does not apply because both parties' performance of this contract was complete when the box arrived at their home. This is legally and factually wrong: legally because the question at hand concerns the *formation* of the contract rather than its *performance*, and factually because both contracts were incompletely performed. *ProCD* did not depend on the fact that the seller characterized the transaction as a license rather than as a contract; we treated it as a contract for the sale of goods and reserved the question whether for other purposes a 'license' characterization might be preferable. 86 F.3d at 1450. All debates about characterization to one side, the transaction in *ProCD* was no more executory than the one here: Zeidenberg paid for the software and walked out of the store with a box under his arm, so if arrival of the box with the product ends the time for revelation of contractual terms, then the time ended in *ProCD* before Zeidenberg opened the box. But of course ProCD had not completed performance with delivery of the box, and neither had Gateway. One element of the transaction was the warranty, which obliges sellers to fix defects in their products. The Hills have invoked Gateway's warranty and are not satisfied with its response, so they are not well positioned to say that Gateway's obligations were fulfilled when the motor carrier unloaded the box. What is more, both ProCD and Gateway promised to help customers to use their products. Long-term service and information obligations are common in the computer business, on both hardware and software sides. Gateway offers 'lifetime service' and has a round-the-clock telephone hotline to fulfil this promise. . . . The document in Gateway's box includes promises of future performance that some consumers value highly; these promises bind Gateway just as the arbitration clause binds the Hills. . . .

"At oral argument the Hills propounded still another distinction: the box containing ProCD's software displayed a notice that additional terms were within, while the box containing Gateway's computer did not. The difference is functional, not legal. Consumers browsing the aisles of a store can look at the box, and if they are unwilling to deal with the prospect of additional terms can leave the box alone, avoiding the transactions costs of returning the package after reviewing its contents. Gateway's box, by contrast, is just a shipping carton; it is not on display anywhere. Its function is to protect the product during transit, and the information on its sides is for the use of handlers ('Fragile!' 'This side Up!') rather than would-be purchasers.

"Perhaps the Hills would have had a better argument if they were first alerted to the bundling of hardware and legal-ware after opening the box and wanted to return the computer in order to avoid disagreeable terms, but were dissuaded by the expense of shipping. What the remedy would be in such a case—could it exceed the shipping charges?—is an interesting question, but one that need not detain us because the Hills knew before they ordered the computer that the carton would include *some* important terms, and they did not seek to discover these in advance. Gateway's ads state that their products come with limited warranties and lifetime support. How limited was the warranty—30 days, with service contingent on shipping the computer back, or five years, with free onsite service? What sort of support was offered? Shoppers have three principal ways to discover these things. First, they can ask the vendor to send a copy before deciding whether to buy. The Magnuson-Moss Warranty Act requires firms to distribute their warranty terms on request, 15 U.S.C. § 2302(b)(1)(A); the Hills do not contend that Gateway would have refused to enclose the remaining terms too. Concealment would be bad for business, scaring some customers away and leading to excess returns from others. Second, shoppers can consult public sources (computer magazines, the Web sites of vendors) that may contain this information. Third, they may inspect the documents after the product's delivery. Like Zeidenberg, the Hills took the third option. By keeping the computer beyond 30 days, the Hills accepted Gateway's offer, including the arbitration clause. . . . [They must] submit their dispute arbitration."

Klocek v. Gateway, Inc.

104 F. Supp. 2d 1332 (D. Kan. 2000)

A computer purchaser sued Gateway, whose practice was to include a copy of its "Standard Terms" in the box containing the computer cables and instruction manuals. Gateway, invoking the arbitration clause in its Standard Terms, urged the court to follow *Hill* and *ProCD*. The court declined, on this reasoning: The Seventh Circuit provided no explanation for its conclusion that "the vendor is the master of the offer." Indeed, in typical consumer transactions, the purchaser is the offeror, and the vendor is the offeree. While it is possible for the vendor to be the offeror, Gateway provided no factual evidence which would support such a finding in this case. It can therefore be assumed for purposes of the motion to dismiss that plaintiff offered to purchase the computer (either in person or through catalog order) and that Gateway accepted plaintiff's offer (either by completing the sales transaction in person or by agreeing to ship and/or shipping the computer to plaintiff).

Under § 2–207, the Standard Terms constitute either an expression of acceptance or written confirmation. As an expression of acceptance, the Standard Terms would constitute a counteroffer only if Gateway expressly made its acceptance conditional on plaintiff's assent to the additional or different terms. Gateway provided no evidence that at the time of the sales transaction it had informed plaintiff that the transaction was conditioned on plaintiff's acceptance of the Standard Terms. Moreover, the mere fact that Gateway shipped the goods with the terms attached did not communicate to plaintiff any unwillingness to proceed without plaintiff's agreement to the Standard Terms.

Because plaintiff was not a merchant, additional or different terms contained in the Standard Terms did not become part of the parties' agreement unless plaintiff expressly agreed to them. Gateway's argument that plaintiff demonstrated acceptance of the arbitration provision by keeping the computer more than five days after the date of delivery must fail. Gateway stated only that it enclosed the Standard Terms inside the computer box for plaintiff to read afterwards. It provided no evidence that it had informed plaintiff of the five-day review-and-return period as a condition of the sales transaction, or that the parties contemplated additional terms to the agreement. The act of keeping the computer past five days was not itself sufficient to demonstrate that plaintiff expressly agreed to the Standard Terms. Nor was there evidence sufficient to support a finding under Kansas or Missouri law that plaintiff agreed to the arbitration provision. Gateway's motion to dismiss must therefore be overruled.

NOTE

A number of courts have accepted Judge Easterbrook's analysis, but as *Klocek* suggests, other courts and a number of commentators have rejected it, sometimes harshly. Richard Epstein examines both the Seventh Circuit opinion and the District Court opinion it reversed in *ProCD v. Zeidenberg*: Do Doctrine and Function Mix?, in Contract Stories 94 (2007). These two opinions capture the contours of a debate that has gone on ever since. Epstein praises both, and observes, "The two contrasting opinions reflect a profound difference in the role economic analysis plays in influencing the legal analysis. That difference is encapsulated in the distinction between doctrine versus function: Judge Crabb is the faithful doctrinalist and Judge Easterbrook the ardent functionalist." Id. at 95. Does this explain the difference in the approaches or is it more likely something else is at work?

Specht v. Netscape Commc'ns Corp.

United States Court of Appeals for the Second Circuit, 2002.
306 F.3d 17.

SOTOMAYOR, CIRCUIT JUDGE. [W]e are asked to determine whether plaintiffs-appellees ("plaintiffs"), by acting upon defendants' invitation to download free software made available on defendants' webpage, agreed to be bound by the software's license terms (which included the arbitration clause at issue), even though plaintiffs could not have learned of the existence of those terms unless, prior to executing the download, they had scrolled down the webpage to a screen located below the download button. We agree with the district court that a reasonably prudent Internet user in circumstances such as these would not have known or learned of the existence of the license terms before responding to defendants' invitation to download the free software, and that defendants therefore did not provide reasonable notice of the license terms. In consequence, plaintiffs' bare act of downloading the software did not unambiguously manifest assent to the arbitration provision contained in the license terms. . . .

In three related putative class actions, plaintiffs alleged that, unknown to them, their use of SmartDownload transmitted to defendants private information about plaintiffs' downloading of files from the Internet, thereby effecting an electronic surveillance of their online activities in violation of two federal statutes, the Electronic Communications Privacy Act and the Computer Fraud and Abuse Act.

Specifically, plaintiffs alleged that when they first used Netscape's Communicator—a software program that permits Internet browsing—the program created and stored on each of their computer hard drives a small text file known as a "cookie" that functioned "as a kind of electronic identification tag for future communications" between their computers and Netscape. Plaintiffs further alleged that when they installed SmartDownload—a separate software "plug-in" that served to enhance Communicator's browsing capabilities—SmartDownload created and stored on their computer hard drives another string of characters, known as a "Key," which similarly functioned as an identification tag in future communications with Netscape. According to the complaints in this case, each time a computer user employed Communicator to download a file from the Internet, SmartDownload "assume[d] from Communicator the task of downloading" the file and transmitted to Netscape the address of the file being downloaded together with the cookie created by Communicator and the Key created by SmartDownload. These processes, plaintiffs claim, constituted unlawful "eavesdropping" on users of Netscape's software products as well as on Internet websites from which users employing SmartDownload downloaded files.

In the time period relevant to this litigation, Netscape offered on its website various software programs, including Communicator and SmartDownload, which visitors to the site were invited to obtain free of charge. It is undisputed that five of the six named plaintiffs—Michael

Fagan, John Gibson, Mark Gruber, Sean Kelly, and Sherry Weindorf—downloaded Communicator from the Netscape website. These plaintiffs acknowledge that when they proceeded to initiate installation of Communicator, they were automatically shown a scrollable text of that program's license agreement and were not permitted to complete the installation until they had clicked on a "Yes" button to indicate that they accepted all the license terms. If a user attempted to install Communicator without clicking "Yes," the installation would be aborted. All five named user plaintiffs expressly agreed to Communicator's license terms by clicking "Yes." The Communicator license agreement that these plaintiffs saw made no mention of SmartDownload or other plug-in programs, and stated that "[t]hese terms apply to Netscape Communicator and Netscape Navigator" and that "all disputes relating to this Agreement (excepting any dispute relating to intellectual property rights)" are subject to "binding arbitration in Santa Clara County, California."

Although Communicator could be obtained independently of SmartDownload, all the named user plaintiffs, except Fagan, downloaded and installed Communicator in connection with downloading SmartDownload. Each of these plaintiffs allegedly arrived at a Netscape webpage captioned "SmartDownload Communicator" that urged them to "Download With Confidence Using SmartDownload!" At or near the bottom of the screen facing plaintiffs was the prompt "Start Download" and a tinted button labeled "Download." By clicking on the button, plaintiffs initiated the download of SmartDownload. Once that process was complete, SmartDownload, as its first plug-in task, permitted plaintiffs to proceed with downloading and installing Communicator, an operation that was accompanied by the clickwrap display of Communicator's license terms described above.

The signal difference between downloading Communicator and downloading SmartDownload was that no clickwrap presentation accompanied the latter operation. Instead, once plaintiffs Gibson, Gruber, Kelly, and Weindorf had clicked on the "Download" button located at or near the bottom of their screen, and the downloading of SmartDownload was complete, these plaintiffs encountered no further information about the plug-in program or the existence of license terms governing its use. The sole reference to SmartDownload's license terms on the "SmartDownload Communicator" webpage was located in text that would have become visible to plaintiffs only if they had scrolled down to the next screen.

Had plaintiffs scrolled down instead of acting on defendants' invitation to click on the "Download" button, they would have encountered the following invitation: "Please review and agree to the terms of the *Netscape SmartDownload software license agreement* before downloading and using the software." Plaintiffs Gibson, Gruber, Kelly, and Weindorf averred in their affidavits that they never saw this reference to the SmartDownload license agreement when they clicked on the "Download" button. They also testified during depositions that they saw no reference to license terms when they clicked to download SmartDownload, although under questioning by defendants' counsel, some plaintiffs added that they could not "remember" or be "sure" whether the screen shots of the SmartDownload page attached to their affidavits reflected precisely what they had seen on their computer screens when they downloaded SmartDownload.

In sum, plaintiffs Gibson, Gruber, Kelly, and Weindorf allege that the process of obtaining SmartDownload contrasted sharply with that of obtaining Communicator. Having selected SmartDownload, they were required neither to express unambiguous assent to that program's license agreement nor even to view the license terms or become aware of their existence before proceeding with the invited download of the free plug-in program. Moreover, once these plaintiffs had initiated the download, the existence of SmartDownload's license terms was not mentioned while the software was running or at any later point in plaintiffs' experience of the product.

Even for a user who, unlike plaintiffs, did happen to scroll down past the download button, SmartDownload's license terms would not have been immediately displayed in the manner of Communicator's click-wrapped terms. Instead, if such a user had seen the notice of SmartDownload's terms and then clicked on the underlined invitation to review and agree to the terms, a hypertext link would have taken the user to a separate webpage entitled "License & Support Agreements." The first paragraph on this page read, in pertinent part:

> The use of each Netscape software product is governed by a license agreement. You must read and agree to the license agreement terms BEFORE acquiring a product. Please click on the appropriate link below to review the current license agreement for the product of interest to you before acquisition. For products available for download, you must read and agree to the license agreement terms BEFORE you install the software. If you do not agree to the license terms, do not download, install or use the software.

Below this paragraph appeared a list of license agreements, the first of which was "*License Agreement for Netscape Navigator and Netscape Communicator Product Family* (Netscape Navigator, Netscape Communicator and Netscape SmartDownload)." If the user clicked on that link, he or she would be taken to yet another webpage that contained the full text of a license agreement that was identical in every respect to the Communicator license agreement except that it stated that its "terms apply to Netscape Communicator, Netscape Navigator, and Netscape SmartDownload." The license agreement granted the user a nonexclusive license to use and reproduce the software, subject to certain terms:

> BY CLICKING THE ACCEPTANCE BUTTON OR INSTALLING OR USING NETSCAPE COMMUNICATOR,

> NETSCAPE NAVIGATOR, OR NETSCAPE SMART-DOWNLOAD SOFTWARE (THE "PRODUCT"), THE INDIVIDUAL OR ENTITY LICENSING THE PRODUCT ("LICENSEE") IS CONSENTING TO BE BOUND BY AND IS BECOMING A PARTY TO THIS AGREEMENT. IF LICENSEE DOES NOT AGREE TO ALL OF THE TERMS OF THIS AGREEMENT, THE BUTTON INDICATING NON-ACCEPTANCE MUST BE SELECTED, AND LICENSEE MUST NOT INSTALL OR USE THE SOFTWARE.

Among the license terms was a provision requiring virtually all disputes relating to the agreement to be submitted to arbitration:

> Unless otherwise agreed in writing, all disputes relating to this Agreement (excepting any dispute relating to intellectual property rights) shall be subject to final and binding arbitration in Santa Clara County, California, under the auspices of JAMS/EndDispute, with the losing party paying all costs of arbitration.

. . . Mutual manifestation of assent, whether by written or spoken word or by conduct, is the touchstone of contract. Although an onlooker observing the disputed transactions in this case would have seen each of the user plaintiffs click on the SmartDownload "Download" button, a consumer's clicking on a download button does not communicate assent to contractual terms if the offer did not make clear to the consumer that clicking on the download button would signify assent to those terms. California's common law is clear that "an offeree, regardless of apparent manifestation of his consent, is not bound by inconspicuous contractual provisions of which he is unaware, contained in a document whose contractual nature is not obvious." [Windsor Mills, Inc. v. Collins & Aikman Corp., 25 Cal. App. 3d 987, 992, 101 Cal. Rptr. 347, 351 (1972).]

Arbitration agreements are no exception to the requirement of manifestation of assent. . . . Clarity and conspicuousness of arbitration terms are important in securing informed assent. "If a party wishes to bind in writing another to an agreement to arbitrate future disputes, such purpose should be accomplished in a way that each party to the arrangement will fully and clearly comprehend that the agreement to arbitrate exists and binds the parties thereto." Commercial Factors Corp. v. Kurtzman Bros., 131 Cal. App. 2d 133, 134–35, 280 P.2d 146, 147–48 (1955). Thus, California contract law measures assent by an objective standard that takes into account both what the offeree said, wrote, or did and the transactional context in which the offeree verbalized or acted. . . .

Defendants argue that plaintiffs must be held to a standard of reasonable prudence and that, because notice of the existence of SmartDownload license terms was on the next scrollable screen, plaintiffs were on "inquiry notice" of those terms. We disagree with the proposition that a reasonably prudent offeree in plaintiffs' position would necessarily have known or learned of the existence of the SmartDownload license agreement prior to acting, so that plaintiffs may be held to have assented to that agreement with constructive notice of its terms. It is true that "[a] party cannot avoid the terms of a contract on the ground that he or she failed to read it before signing." Marin Storage & Trucking, Inc. v. Benco Contracting and Engineering, Inc., 89 Cal. App. 4th 1042, 1049, 107 Cal. Rptr. 2d 645, 651 (2001). But courts are quick to add: "An exception to this general rule exists when the writing does not appear to be a contract and the terms are not called to the attention of the recipient. In such a case, no contract is formed with respect to the undisclosed term." *Id.*

Most of the cases cited by defendants in support of their inquiry-notice argument are drawn from the world of paper contracting.

[R]eceipt of a physical document containing contract terms or notice thereof is frequently deemed, in the world of paper transactions, a sufficient circumstance to place the offeree on inquiry notice of those terms. "Every person who has actual notice of circumstances sufficient to put a prudent man upon inquiry as to a particular fact, has constructive notice of the fact itself in all cases in which, by prosecuting such inquiry, he might have learned such fact." Cal. Civ. Code § 19. These principles apply equally to the emergent world of online product delivery, pop-up screens, hyperlinked pages, clickwrap licensing, scrollable documents, and urgent admonitions to "Download Now!". What plaintiffs saw when they were being invited by defendants to download this fast, free plug-in called SmartDownload was a screen containing praise for the product and, at the very bottom of the screen, a "Download" button. Defendants argue that under the principles set forth in the cases cited above, a "fair and prudent person using ordinary care" would have been on inquiry notice of SmartDownload's license terms.

We are not persuaded that a reasonably prudent offeree in these circumstances would have known of the existence of license terms. Plaintiffs were responding to an offer that did not carry an immediately visible notice of the existence of license terms or require unambiguous manifestation of assent to those terms. Thus, plaintiffs' "apparent manifestation of . . . consent" was to terms "contained in a document whose contractual nature [was] not obvious." Windsor Mills, 25 Cal. App. 3d at 992, 101 Cal. Rptr. At 351. Moreover, the fact that, given the position of the scroll bar on their computer screens, plaintiffs may have been aware that an unexplored portion of the Netscape webpage remained below the download button does not mean that they reasonably should have concluded that this portion contained a notice of license terms. In their deposition testimony, plaintiffs variously stated that they used the scroll bar "[o]nly if there is something that I feel I need to see that is on—that is off the page," or that the elevated position of the scroll bar suggested the presence of "mere[ ] formalities, standard lower banner links" or "that the page is bigger than what I can see." Plaintiffs testified, and defendants did not refute, that plaintiffs were in fact unaware that defendants intended to attach license terms to the use of SmartDownload.

We conclude that in circumstances such as these, where consumers are urged to download free software at the immediate click of a button, a reference to the existence of license terms on a submerged screen is not sufficient to place consumers on inquiry or constructive notice of those terms. The SmartDownload webpage screen was "printed in such a manner that it tended to conceal the fact that it was an express acceptance of [Netscape's] rules and regulations." [Larrus v. First Nat. Bank of San Mateo County, 122 Cal. App. 2d 884, 889, 266 P.2d 143, 147 (1954).] Internet users may have, as defendants put it, "as much time as they need[ ]" to scroll through multiple screens on a webpage, but there is no reason to assume that viewers will scroll down to subsequent screens simply because screens are there. When products are "free" and users are invited to download them in the absence of reasonably conspicuous notice that they are about to bind themselves to contract terms, the transactional circumstances cannot be fully analogized to those in the paper world of arm's-length bargaining. . . .

Defendants cite certain well-known cases involving shrinkwrap licensing and related commercial practices in support of their contention that plaintiffs became bound by the SmartDownload license terms by virtue of inquiry notice. For example, in Hill v. Gateway 2000, Inc., 105 F.3d 1147 (7th Cir. 1997), the Seventh Circuit held that where a purchaser had ordered a computer over the telephone, received the order in a shipped box containing the computer along with printed contract terms, and did not return the computer within the thirty days required by the terms, the purchaser was bound by the contract. In *ProCD, Inc. v. Zeidenberg,* the same court held that where an individual purchased software in a box containing license terms which were displayed on the computer screen every time the user executed the software program, the user had sufficient opportunity to review the terms and to return the software, and so was contractually bound after retaining the product.

These cases do not help defendants. To the extent that they hold that the purchaser of a computer or tangible software is contractually bound after failing to object to printed license terms provided with the product, *Hill* and *Brower* do not differ markedly from the cases involving traditional paper contracting discussed in the previous section. Insofar as the purchaser in *ProCD* was confronted with conspicuous, mandatory license terms every time he ran the software on his computer, that case actually undermines defendants' contention that downloading in the absence of conspicuous terms is an act that binds plaintiffs to those terms. . . .

After reviewing the California common law and other relevant legal authority, we conclude that under the circumstances here, plaintiffs' downloading of SmartDownload did not constitute acceptance of defendants' license terms. Reasonably conspicuous notice of the existence of contract terms and unambiguous manifestation of assent to those terms by consumers are essential if electronic bargaining is to have integrity and credibility. We hold that a reasonably prudent offeree in plaintiffs' position would not have known or learned, prior to acting on the invitation to download, of the reference to SmartDownload's license terms hidden below the "Download" button on the next screen. We affirm the district court's conclusion that the user plaintiffs, including Fagan, are not bound by the arbitration clause contained in those terms. . . .

Nguyen v. Barnes & Noble Inc.

United States Court of Appeals, Ninth Circuit, 2014.
763 F.3d 1171.

NOONAN, CIRCUIT JUDGE. . . . The underlying facts are not in dispute. Barnes & Noble is a national bookseller that owns and operates hundreds of bookstores as well as the website <www.barnesandnoble.com>. In August 2011, Barnes & Noble, along with other retailers across the country, liquidated its inventory of discontinued Hewlett-Packard Touchpads ("Touchpads"), an unsuccessful competitor to Apple's iPad, by advertising a "fire sale" of Touchpads at a heavily discounted price. Acting quickly on the nationwide liquidation of Touchpads, Nguyen purchased two units on Barnes & Noble's website on August 21, 2011, and received an email confirming the transaction. The following day, Nguyen received another email informing him that his order had been cancelled due to unexpectedly high demand. Nguyen alleges that, as a result of "Barnes & Noble's representations, as well as the delay in informing him it would not honor the sale," he was "unable to obtain an HP Tablet during the liquidation period for the discounted price," and was "forced to rely on substitute tablet technology, which he subsequently purchased . . . [at] considerable expense." . . .

In April 2012, Nguyen filed this lawsuit in California Superior Court on behalf of himself and a putative class of consumers whose Touchpad orders had been cancelled, alleging that Barnes & Noble had engaged in deceptive business practices and false advertising in violation of both California and New York law. Barnes & Noble removed the action to federal court and moved to compel arbitration under the Federal Arbitration Act ("FAA"), arguing that Nguyen was bound by the arbitration agreement in the website's Terms of Use.

The website's Terms of Use are available via a "Terms of Use" hyperlink located in the bottom left-hand corner of every page on the Barnes & Noble website, which appears alongside other hyperlinks labeled "NOOK Store Terms," "Copyright," and "Privacy Policy." These hyperlinks also appear underlined and set in green typeface in the lower lefthand corner of every page in the online checkout process.

Nguyen neither clicked on the "Terms of Use" hyperlink nor actually read the Terms of Use. Had he clicked on the hyperlink, he would have been taken to a page containing the full text of Barnes & Noble's Terms of Use, which state, in relevant part: "By visiting any area in the Barnes & Noble.com Site, creating an account, [or] making a purchase via the Barnes & Noble.com Site . . . a User is deemed to have accepted the Terms of Use." Nguyen also would have come across an arbitration provision . . . .

Nguyen contends that he cannot be bound to the arbitration provision because he neither had notice of nor assented to the website's Terms of Use. Barnes & Noble, for its part, asserts that the placement of the "Terms of Use" hyperlink on its website put Nguyen on constructive notice of the arbitration agreement. Barnes & Noble contends that this notice, combined with Nguyen's subsequent use of the website, was enough to bind him to the Terms of Use. The district court disagreed, and Barnes & Noble now appeals. . . .

The FAA requires federal district courts to stay judicial proceedings and compel arbitration of claims covered by a written and enforceable arbitration agreement. The FAA limits the district court's role to determining whether a valid arbitration agreement exists, and whether the agreement encompasses the disputes at issue. The parties do not quarrel that Barnes & Noble's arbitration agreement, should it be found enforceable, encompasses Nguyen's claims. The only issue is whether a valid arbitration agreement exists. . . .

"While new commerce on the Internet has exposed courts to many new situations, it has not fundamentally changed the principles of contract." Register.com, Inc. v. Verio, Inc., 356 F.3d 393, 403 (2d Cir. 2004). One such principle is the requirement that "[m]utual manifestation of assent, whether by written or spoken word or by conduct, is the touchstone of contract." Specht v. Netscape Commc'ns Corp., 306 F.3d 17, 29 (2d Cir. 2002) (applying California law).

Contracts formed on the Internet come primarily in two flavors: "clickwrap" (or "click-through") agreements, in which website users are required to click on an "I agree" box after being presented with a list of terms and conditions of use; and "browsewrap" agreements, where a website's terms and conditions of use are generally posted on the website via a hyperlink at the bottom of the screen. Barnes & Noble's Terms of Use fall in the latter category.

"Unlike a clickwrap agreement, a browsewrap agreement does not require the user to manifest assent to the terms and conditions expressly . . . [a] party instead gives his assent simply by using the website." Hines v. Overstock.com, Inc., 668 F.Supp.2d 362, 366–67 (E.D.N.Y. 2009). Indeed, "in a pure-form browsewrap agreement, the website will contain a notice that—by merely using the services of, obtaining information from, or initiating applications within the website—the user is agreeing to and is bound by the site's terms of service." Fteja v. Facebook, Inc., 841 F.Supp.2d 829, 837 (S.D.N.Y. 2012). Thus, "by visiting the website—something that the user has already done—the user agrees to the Terms of Use not listed on the site itself but available only by clicking a hyperlink." *Id.* "The defining feature of browsewrap agreements is that the user can continue to use the website or its services without visiting the page hosting the browsewrap agreement or even knowing that such a webpage exists." Be In, Inc. v. Google Inc., 2013 WL 5568706, at *6 (N.D. Cal. 2013). "Because no affirmative action is required by the website user to agree to the terms of a contract other than his or her use of the website, the determination of the validity of the browsewrap contract depends on whether the user has actual or constructive knowledge of a website's terms and conditions." Van Tassell v. United Mktg. Grp., LLC, 795 F. Supp. 2d 770, 790 (N.D. Ill. 2011).

Were there any evidence in the record that Nguyen had actual notice of the Terms of Use or was required to affirmatively acknowledge the Terms of Use before completing his online purchase, the outcome of this case might be different. Indeed, courts have consistently enforced browsewrap agreements where the user had actual notice of the agreement. Courts have also been more willing to find the requisite notice for constructive assent where the browsewrap agreement resembles a clickwrap agreement—that is, where the user is required to affirmatively acknowledge the agreement before proceeding with use of the website.

But where, as here, there is no evidence that the website user had actual knowledge of the agreement, the validity of the browsewrap agreement turns on whether the website puts a reasonably prudent user on inquiry notice of the terms of the contract. Whether a user has inquiry notice of a browsewrap agreement, in turn, depends on the design and content of the website and the agreement's webpage. Where the link to a website's terms of use is buried at the bottom of the page or tucked away in obscure corners of the website where users are unlikely to see it, courts have refused to enforce the browsewrap agreement. On the other hand, where the website contains an explicit textual notice that continued use will act as a manifestation of the user's intent to be bound, courts have been more amenable to enforcing browsewrap agreements. In short, the conspicuousness and placement of the "Terms of Use" hyperlink, other notices given to users of the terms of use, and the website's general design all contribute to whether a reasonably prudent user would have inquiry notice of a browsewrap agreement.

Barnes & Noble argues that the placement of the "Terms of Use" hyperlink in the bottom left-hand corner of every page on the Barnes & Noble website, and its close proximity to the buttons a user must click on to complete an online purchase, is enough to place a reasonably prudent user on constructive notice. It is true that the location of the hyperlink on Barnes & Noble's website distinguishes this case from *Specht,* the leading authority on the enforceability of browsewrap terms under New York law. There, the Second Circuit refused to enforce an arbitration provision in a website's licensing terms where the hyperlink to the terms was located at the bottom of the page, hidden below the "Download" button that users had to click to initiate the software download. Then-Second Circuit Judge Sotomayor, writing for the panel, held that "a reference to the existence of license terms on a submerged screen is not sufficient to place consumers on inquiry or constructive notice of those terms." 306 F.3d at 32. By contrast, here the "Terms of Use" link appears either directly below the relevant button a user must click on to proceed in the checkout process or just a few inches away. On some pages, the content of the webpage is compact enough that a user can view the link without scrolling. On the remaining pages, the hyperlink is close enough to the "Proceed with Checkout" button that a user would have to bring the link within his field of vision in order to complete his order.

But the proximity or conspicuousness of the hyperlink alone is not enough to give rise to constructive notice, and Barnes & Noble directs us to no case law that supports this proposition. The most analogous case the court was able to locate is *PDC Labs., Inc. v. Hach Co.,* [2009 WL 2605270 (C.D. Ill. 2009)], an unpublished district court order cited by neither party. There, the "Terms [and Conditions of Sale] were hyperlinked on three separate pages of the online . . . order process in underlined, blue, contrasting text." *Id.* at *3. The court held that "[t]his contrasting text is sufficient to be considered conspicuous," thereby placing a reasonable user on notice that the terms applied. *Id.* It also observed, however, that the terms' conspicuousness was reinforced by the language of the final checkout screen, which read, " 'STEP 4 of 4: *Review terms,* add any comments, and submit order,' " and was followed by a hyperlink to the Terms. *Id.* (emphasis added).

As in *PDC,* the checkout screens here contained "Terms of Use" hyperlinks in underlined, color-contrasting text. But *PDC* is dissimilar in that the final screen on that website contained the phrase "Review terms." This admonition makes *PDC* distinguishable, despite the court's explanation that the blue contrasting hyperlinks were sufficiently conspicuous on their own. That the *PDC* decision couched its holding in terms of procedural unconscionability rather than contract formation further distinguishes it from our case.

In light of the lack of controlling authority on point, and in keeping with courts' traditional reluctance to enforce browsewrap agreements against individual consumers, we therefore hold that where a website makes its terms of use available via a conspicuous hyperlink on every page of the website but otherwise provides no notice to users nor prompts them to take any affirmative action to demonstrate assent, even close proximity of the hyperlink to relevant buttons users must click on—without more—is insufficient to give rise to constructive notice. While failure to read a contract before agreeing to its terms does not relieve a party of its obligations under the contract, the onus must be on website owners to put users on notice of the terms to which they wish to bind consumers.

Given the breadth of the range of technological savvy of online purchasers, consumers cannot be expected to ferret out hyperlinks to terms and conditions to which they have no reason to suspect they will be bound.

Barnes & Noble's argument that Nguyen's familiarity with other websites governed by similar browsewrap terms, including his personal website <www.kevinkhoa.com>, gives rise to an inference of constructive notice is also of no moment. Whether Nguyen has experience with the browsewrap agreements found on other websites such as Facebook, LinkedIn, MySpace, or Twitter, has no bearing on whether he had constructive notice of Barnes & Noble's Terms of Use. There is nothing in the record to suggest that those browsewrap terms are enforceable by or against Nguyen, much less why they should give rise to constructive notice of Barnes & Noble's browsewrap terms. . . .

We hold that Nguyen had insufficient notice of Barnes & Noble's Terms of Use, and thus did not enter into an agreement with Barnes & Noble to arbitrate his claims.

Meyer v. Uber Technologies, Inc.

United States Court of Appeals, Second Circuit, 2017.
868 F.3d 66.

CHIN, CIRCUIT JUDGE. In 2014, . . . Spencer Meyer downloaded onto his smartphone a software application offered by . . . Uber Technologies, Inc. ("Uber"), a technology company that operates, among other things, a ride-hailing service. Meyer then registered for an Uber account with his smartphone. After using the application approximately ten times, Meyer brought this action on behalf of himself and other similarly situated Uber accountholders against Uber's co-founder and former Chief Executive Officer, defendant-appellant Travis Kalanick, alleging that the Uber application allows third-party drivers to illegally fix prices. The district court joined Uber as a defendant and denied motions by Kalanick and Uber to compel arbitration. In doing so, the district court concluded that Meyer did not have reasonably conspicuous notice of and did not unambiguously manifest assent to Uber's Terms of Service when he registered. The district court held that Meyer therefore was not bound by the mandatory arbitration provision contained in the Terms of Service. . . .

In support of its motion to compel arbitration, Uber submitted a declaration from Senior Software Engineer Vincent Mi, in which Mi represented that Uber maintained records of when and how its users registered for the service and that, from his review of those records, Mi was able to identify the dates and methods by which Meyer registered for a user account. Attached to the declaration were screenshots of the two screens that a user registering in October 2014 with an Android-operated smartphone would have seen during the registration process.

The first screen, at which the user arrives after downloading the application and clicking a button marked "Register," is labeled "Register" and includes fields for the user to enter his or her name, email address, phone number, and a password (the "Registration Screen"). The Registration Screen also offers the user the option to register via a Google+ or Facebook account. According to Uber's records, Meyer did not sign up using either Google+ or Facebook and would have had to enter manually his personal information.

After completing the information on the Registration Screen and clicking "Next," the user advances to a second screen labeled "Payment" (the "Payment Screen"), on which the user can enter credit card details or elect to make payments using PayPal or Google Wallet, third-party payment services. According to Uber's records, Meyer entered his credit card information to pay for rides. To complete the process, the prospective user must click the button marked "REGISTER" in the middle of the Payment Screen.

Below the input fields and buttons on the Payment Screen is black text advising users that "[b]y creating an Uber account, you agree to the TERMS OF SERVICE & PRIVACY POLICY." The capitalized phrase, which is bright blue and underlined, was a hyperlink that, when clicked, took the user to a third screen containing a button that, in turn, when clicked, would then display the current version of both Uber's Terms of Service and Privacy Policy. Meyer recalls entering his contact information and credit card details before registering, but does not recall seeing or following the hyperlink to the Terms and Conditions. He declares that he did not read the Terms and Conditions, including the arbitration provision.

When Meyer registered for an account, the Terms of Service contained [a] mandatory arbitration clause. . . .

The Terms of Service further provided that the American Arbitration Association ("AAA") would hear any dispute, and that the AAA Commercial Arbitration Rules would govern any arbitration proceeding. . . .

We consider first whether there is a valid agreement to arbitrate between Meyer and Uber and then whether defendants have waived their right to enforce any such agreement to compel arbitration. . . .

Where there is no evidence that the offeree had actual notice of the terms of the agreement, the offeree will still be bound by the agreement if a reasonably prudent user would be on inquiry notice of the terms. Whether a reasonably prudent user would be on inquiry notice turns on the "[c]larity and conspicuousness of arbitration terms," [Specht v. Netscape Commc'ns Corp., 306 F.3d 17, 30 (2d Cir. 2002)]; in the context of web-based contracts, as discussed further below, clarity and conspicuousness are a function of the design and content of the relevant interface.

Thus, only if the undisputed facts establish that there is "[r]easonably conspicuous notice of the existence of contract terms and unambiguous manifestation of assent to those terms" will we find that a contract has been formed. *See Specht,* 306 F.3d at 35. . . .

"While new commerce on the Internet has exposed courts to many new situations, it has not fundamentally changed the principles of contract." Register.com, Inc. v. Verio, Inc., 356 F.3d 393, 403 (2d Cir. 2004). "Courts around the country have recognized that [an] electronic 'click' can suffice to signify the acceptance of a contract," and that "[t]here is nothing automatically offensive about such agreements, as long as the layout and language of the site give the user reasonable notice that a click will manifest assent to an agreement." Sgouros v. TransUnion Corp., 817 F.3d 1029, 1033–34 (7th Cir. 2016).

With these principles in mind, one way in which we have previously distinguished web-based contracts is the manner in which the user manifests assent—namely, "clickwrap" (or "click-through") agreements, which require users to click an "I agree" box after being presented with a list of terms and conditions of use, or "browsewrap" agreements, which generally post terms and conditions on a website via a hyperlink at the bottom of the screen. Courts routinely uphold clickwrap agreements for the principal reason that the user has affirmatively assented to the terms of agreement by clicking "I agree." Browsewrap agreements, on the other hand, do not require the user to expressly assent. . . .

Of course, there are infinite ways to design a website or smartphone application, and not all interfaces fit neatly into the clickwrap or browsewrap categories. Some online agreements require the user to scroll through the terms before the user can indicate his or her assent by clicking "I agree." Other agreements notify the user of the existence of the website's terms of use and, instead of providing an "I agree" button, advise the user that he or she is agreeing to the terms of service when registering or signing up.

In the interface at issue in this case, a putative user is not required to assent explicitly to the contract terms; instead, the user must click a button marked "Register," underneath which the screen states "By creating an Uber account, you agree to the TERMS OF SERVICE & PRIVACY POLICY," with hyperlinks to the Terms of Service and Privacy Policy. . . .

Insofar as it turns on the reasonableness of notice, the enforceability of a web-based agreement is clearly a fact-intensive inquiry. Nonetheless, on a motion to compel arbitration, we may determine that an agreement to arbitrate exists where the notice of the arbitration provision was reasonably conspicuous and manifestation of assent unambiguous as a matter of law. . . .

Meyer attests that he was not on actual notice of the hyperlink to the Terms of Service or the arbitration provision itself, and defendants do not point to evidence from which a jury could infer otherwise. Accordingly, we must consider whether Meyer was on inquiry notice of the arbitration provision by virtue of the hyperlink to the Terms of Service on the Payment Screen and, thus, manifested his assent to the agreement by clicking "Register." . . .

In considering the question of reasonable conspicuousness, precedent and basic principles of contract law instruct that we consider the perspective of a reasonably prudent smartphone user. "[M]odern cell phones . . . are now such a pervasive and insistent part of daily life that the proverbial visitor from Mars might conclude they were an important feature of human anatomy." Riley v. California, ___ U.S. ___, 134 S.Ct. 2473, 2484 (2014). As of 2015, nearly two-thirds of American adults owned a smartphone, a figure that has almost doubled since 2011. Consumers use their smartphones for, among other things, following the news, shopping, social networking, online banking, researching health conditions, and taking classes. In a 2015 study, approximately 89 percent of smartphone users surveyed reported using the internet on their smartphones over the course of the week-long study period. A purchaser of a new smartphone has his or her choice of features, including operating systems, storage capacity, and screen size.

Smartphone users engage in these activities through mobile applications, or "apps," like the Uber App. To begin using an app, the consumers need to locate and download the app, often from an application store. Many apps then require potential users to sign up for an account to access the app's services. Accordingly, when considering the perspective of a reasonable smartphone user, we need not presume that the user has never before encountered an app or entered into a contract using a smartphone. Moreover, a reasonably prudent smartphone user knows that text that is highlighted in blue and underlined is hyperlinked to another webpage where additional information will be found.

Turning to the interface at issue in this case, we conclude that the design of the screen and language used render the notice provided reasonable as a matter of California law. The Payment Screen is uncluttered, with only fields for the user to enter his or her credit card details, buttons to register for a user account or to connect the user's pre-existing PayPal account or Google Wallet to the Uber account, and the warning that "By creating an Uber account, you agree to the TERMS OF SERVICE & PRIVACY POLICY." The text, including the hyperlinks to the Terms and Conditions and Privacy Policy, appears directly below the buttons for registration. The entire screen is visible at once, and the user does not need to scroll beyond what is immediately visible to find notice of the Terms of Service. Although the sentence is in a small font, the dark print contrasts with the bright white background, and the hyperlinks are in blue and underlined. This presentation differs sharply from the screen we considered in *Nicosia*, which contained, among other things, summaries of the user's purchase and delivery information, "between fifteen and twenty-five links," "text . . . in at least four font sizes and six colors," and several buttons and advertisements. [Nicosia v. Amazon.com, Inc., 834 F.3d 220, 236–37 (2d Cir. 2016).] Furthermore, the notice of the terms and conditions in *Nicosia* was "not directly adjacent" to the button intended to manifest assent to the terms, unlike the text and button at issue here.

In addition to being spatially coupled with the mechanism for manifesting assent—*i.e.*, the register button—the notice is temporally coupled. As we observed in [Schnabel v. Trilegiant Corp., 697 F.3d 110, 1127 (2d Cir. 2012)]:

> inasmuch as consumers are regularly and frequently confronted with non-negotiable contract terms, particularly when entering into transactions using the Internet, the presentation of these terms at a place and time that the consumer will associate with the initial purchase or enrollment, or the use of, the goods or services from which the recipient benefits at least indicates to the consumer that he or she is taking such goods or employing such services subject to additional terms and conditions that may one day affect him or her.

Here, notice of the Terms of Service is provided simultaneously to enrollment, thereby connecting the contractual terms to the services to which they apply. We think that a reasonably prudent smartphone user would understand that the terms were connected to the creation of a user account.

That the Terms of Service were available only by hyperlink does not preclude a determination of reasonable notice. Moreover, the language "[b]y creating an Uber account, you agree" is a clear prompt directing users to read the Terms and Conditions and signaling that their acceptance of the benefit of registration would be subject to contractual terms. As long as the hyperlinked text was itself reasonably conspicuous—and we conclude that it was—a reasonably prudent smartphone user would have constructive notice of the terms. While it may be the case that many users will not bother reading the additional terms, that is the choice the user makes; the user is still on inquiry notice.

Finally, we disagree with the district court's determination that the location of the arbitration clause within the Terms and Conditions was itself a "barrier to reasonable notice." In *Sgouros*, the Seventh Circuit determined that the defendant's website actively misled users by "explicitly stating that a click on the button constituted assent for TransUnion to obtain access to the purchaser's personal information," without saying anything about "contractual terms," and without any indication that "the same click constituted acceptance of the Service Agreement." 817 F.3d at 1035–36. The website did not contain a hyperlink to the relevant agreement; instead, it had a scroll box that contained the entirety of the agreement, only the first three lines of which were visible without scrolling, and it had no prompt for the reader to scroll for additional terms. Here, there is nothing misleading. Although the contract terms are lengthy and must be reached by a hyperlink, the instructions are clear and reasonably conspicuous. Once a user clicks through to the Terms of Service, the section heading ("Dispute Resolution") and the sentence waiving the user's right to a jury trial on relevant claims are both bolded.

Accordingly, we conclude that the Uber App provided reasonably conspicuous notice of the Terms of Service as a matter of California law and turn to the question of whether Meyer unambiguously manifested his assent to those terms. . . .

Although Meyer's assent to arbitration was not express, we are convinced that it was unambiguous in light of the objectively reasonable notice of the terms, as discussed in detail above. As we described above, there is ample evidence that a reasonable user would be on inquiry notice of the terms, and the spatial and temporal coupling of the terms with the registration button "indicate[d] to the consumer that he or she is . . . employing such services subject to additional terms and conditions that may one day affect him or her." Schnabel, 697 F.3d at 127. A reasonable user would know that by clicking the registration button, he was agreeing to the terms and conditions accessible via the hyperlink, whether he clicked on the hyperlink or not.

The fact that clicking the register button had two functions—creation of a user account and assent to the Terms of Service—does not render Meyer's assent ambiguous. The registration process allowed Meyer to review the Terms of Service prior to registration, unlike web platforms that provide notice of contract terms only after the user manifested his or her assent. Furthermore, the text on the Payment Screen not only included a hyperlink to the Terms of Service, but expressly warned the user that by creating an Uber account, the user was agreeing to be bound by the linked terms. Although the warning text used the term "creat[e]" instead of "register," as the button was marked, the physical proximity of the notice to the register button and the placement of the language in the registration flow make clear to the user that the linked terms pertain to the action the user is about to take.

The transactional context of the parties' dealings reinforces our conclusion. Meyer located and downloaded the Uber App, signed up for an account, and entered his credit card information with the intention of entering into a forward-looking relationship with Uber. The registration process clearly contemplated some sort of continuing relationship between the putative user and Uber, one that would require some terms and conditions, and the Payment Screen provided clear notice that there were terms that governed that relationship.

Accordingly, we conclude on the undisputed facts of this case that Meyer unambiguously manifested his assent to Uber's Terms of Service as a matter of California law. . . .

NOTE: CLICKWRAP LICENSES AND THE REASONABLY PRUDENT CONSUMER

In reflecting on the question of the enforceability of clauses set out on web pages that require multiple clicks to access, consider how much the law should take into account the behavior of the typical consumer. *Specht* puts forward tests suggesting that the test of consent should turn on whether terms were "reasonably conspicuous." This approach implies that the "reasonably prudent" consumer pays at least some attention to such terms. Everyday experience suggests that is not the case. Few of us bother to read any terms that can be accessed only by scrolling down or clicking a hyperlink. To the extent that the legal rule finds the various terms binding because the typical reader will be aware of them, it is completely out of touch.

Some have suggested that the failure of most to read is not itself troubling. They reason that, as long as a large enough informed minority reads the terms, sellers need to provide attractive ones in order not to lose customers. Hence, sellers will offer terms to which typical consumers would agree if they had read them. See, e.g., Alan Schwartz & Louis Wilde, Intervening in Markets on the Basis of Imperfect Information: A Legal and Economic Analysis, 127 U. Pa. L. Rev. 630 (1979). The relevant test therefore should not be whether the typical consumer reads the terms, but rather whether a large enough minority do. Recent empirical work, however, calls into doubt even this line of thought. A study that tracked the Internet browsing behavior of over forty thousand households found that only one or two out of every thousand retail software shoppers chooses to access the license agreement, and those few that do spend too little time, on average, to have read more than a small portion of the license text. See Bakos, Marotta-Wurgler & Trossen, Does Anyone Read the Fine Print? Consumer Attention to Standard Form Contracts, 43 J. Legal Stud. 1 (2014). If not even an informed minority is reading the contract terms, what is the basis for enforcing them? We shall return to this question in Chapter 6, when we examine standardized fine print terms and the doctrine of unconscionability.

The facts of *ProCD* and *Netscape* raise an additional issue. By the time cases work their way through the legal system, the underlying contracting environment may change significantly. These remain the leading cases, even though shrinkwrap licenses no longer exist and the Netscape browser has long disappeared from the scene. The way consumers acquire new software has completely changed. App stores did not exist at the time either case was decided. How applicable is the reasoning of these cases to a world that has already changed and continues to change?

NOTE: CONDUCT AS ASSENT

The assent required for the formation of a contract can be inferred from many things. A failure to object, viewed against a given background, may be enough. At the same time, it is necessary to recall a maxim underlying the rules of contract formation mentioned earlier in this book: "The offeror is master of the offer." The power to specify an acceptable exchange, in form and in content, surely includes the power to designate the response that will constitute a valid acceptance. Yet, as we have seen, the offeror's power to set the bargain's terms often will be exercised only in part, not in full, perhaps even not at all. So it is not in the least unusual to find commercial dealings lacking formal structure or documentation. If an express contract is established, it will of course bar claims of implied undertakings on matters within its scope—unless the express contract has itself been modified by the parties' conduct.

The main event, as concerns activity lacking explicit bargaining, is just ahead. But first it is necessary to take a brief look at two issues lurking in the implied-contract cases. One is the effect of failing to reply to an offer (so-called "silence as acceptance"). The other concerns the limits, if any, on an offerer's power to bring about a contract by declaring that another's failure to reply or act constitutes acceptance. The governing principles are assembled in Restatement, Second § 69, which is reproduced below. In examining the classifications made by the section, it is a good idea to keep in mind some concepts traditionally associated with "implied contract" (indeed, with contract in general): restitution, reliance, estoppel, request, and bargain.

Restatement of Contracts, Second

§ 69. Acceptance by Silence or Exercise of Dominion

(1) Where an offeree fails to reply to an offer, his silence and inaction operate as an acceptance in the following cases only:

(a) Where an offeree takes the benefit of offered services with reasonable opportunity to reject them and reason to know that they were offered with the expectation of compensation.

(b) Where the offeror has stated or given the offeree reason to understand that assent may be manifested by silence or inaction, and the offeree in remaining silent and inactive intends to accept the offer.

(c) Where because of previous dealings or otherwise, it is reasonable that the offeree should notify the offeror if he does not intend to accept.

(2) An offeree who does any act inconsistent with the offeror's ownership of offered property is bound in accordance with the offered terms unless they are manifestly unreasonable. But if the act is wrongful as against the offeror it is an acceptance only if ratified by him.

Hobbs v. Massasoit Whip Co.

Supreme Judicial Court of Massachusetts, 1893.
158 Mass. 194, 33 N.E. 495.

HOLMES, J. This is an action for the price of eel skins sent by the plaintiff to the defendant, and kept by the defendant some months, until they were destroyed. It must be taken that the plaintiff received no notice that the defendant declined to accept the skins. The case comes before us on exceptions to an instruction to the jury, that, whether there was any prior contract or not, if skins are sent to the defendant, and it sees fit, whether it has agreed to take them or not, to lie back, and to say nothing, having reason to suppose that the man who has sent them believes that it is taking them, since it says nothing about it, then, if it fails to notify, the jury would be warranted in finding for the plaintiff.

Standing alone, and unexplained, this proposition might seem to imply that one stranger may impose a duty upon another, and make him a purchaser, in spite of himself, by sending goods to him, unless he will take the trouble, and be at the expense, of notifying the sender that he will not buy. The case was argued for the defendant on that interpretation. But, in view of the evidence, we do not understand that to have been the meaning of the judge, and we do not think that the jury can have understood that to have been his meaning. The plaintiff was not a stranger to the defendant, even if there was no contract between them. He had sent eel skins in the same way four or five times before, and they had been accepted and paid for. On the defendant's testimony, it is fair to assume that, if it had admitted the eel skins to be over twenty-two inches in length, and fit for its business, as the plaintiff testified, and the jury found that they were, it would have accepted them; that this was understood by the plaintiff; and, indeed, that there was a standing offer to him for such skins. In such a condition of things, the plaintiff was warranted in sending the defendant skins conforming to the requirements, and even if the offer was not such that the contract was made as soon as skins corresponding to its terms were sent, sending them did impose on the defendant a duty to act about them; and silence on its part, coupled with a retention of the skins for an unreasonable time, might be found by the jury to warrant the plaintiff in assuming that they were accepted, and thus to amount to an acceptance.... Taylor v. Dexter Engine Co., 146 Mass. 613, 16 N.E. 462. The proposition stands on the general principle that conduct which imports acceptance or assent is acceptance or assent in the view of the law, whatever may have been the actual state of mind of the party,—a principle sometimes lost sight of in the cases. O'Donnell v. Clinton, 145 Mass. 461, 14 N.E. 747.

Exceptions overruled.

COMMENT: THE PRIVILEGE OF SILENCE

Courts typically say that "silence will not constitute acceptance of an offer in the absence of a duty to speak." If such assertions are to be believed, it is essential to determine the kinds of circumstances in which such a "duty" will be found.

One formulation intended to accommodate the duty-to-speak cases can be found in § 69(1)(c) of the Restatement, Second. An illustration of the legal effects of "previous dealings or otherwise" is provided by Ammons v. Wilson & Co., 176 Miss. 645, 170 So. 227 (1936), a case much like Hobbs v. Massasoit Whip Co. Plaintiff, a wholesale grocer, was visited on August 23 and 24 by defendant's sales representative, to whom plaintiff gave a large order for shortening. In early September, plaintiff inquired when shipment would be made; on September 4, defendant gave notice that the order had been rejected. During the preceding eight months, a number of orders submitted by plaintiff through the same salesperson had been accepted and shipped by defendant not more than one week from the time they were given. The court held that it was for the jury to say whether defendant's delay and silence for 12 days implied an acceptance of plaintiff's order. The court made no mention of a "duty to speak." Rather, in the language of the Restatement (First) of Contracts § 72(1)(c) (now § 69 in the Restatement, Second), it applied the test of whether "the offeree has given the offeror reason to understand that the silence or inaction is intended by the offeree as a manifestation of assent." The legal concept of a duty to speak was thus replaced by a standard of "reasonable understanding," applied by the jury in the light of the full context in which the parties dealt. Is this what Justice Holmes had in mind in *Hobbs*, when he spoke of conduct "warrant[ing] the plaintiff in assuming" an acceptance had occurred?

Does a similar standard of reasonable understanding explain the fate of "additional" terms under § 2–207(2) of the Uniform Commercial Code? You will recall that "between merchants," additional, nonmaterial terms in an accepting form become part of the contract unless timely notice of objection is given. The Official Comment to the section reasons that if there is a failure to respond to such proposals, "it is both fair and commercially sound to assume that their inclusion has been assented to." Given the *Hobbs* analysis and result, as well as the principle stated in § 69(1)(c), it should be clear that even though an offeree's new term is a "material alteration" under UCC 2–207(2), prior dealings between the parties may provide a basis for concluding that the offeree was reasonable in inferring assent to the term from the offeror's failure to object to it. See, e.g., Union Carbide Corp. v. Oscar Mayer Foods Corp., 947 F.2d 1333 (7th Cir. 1991).

As for the first category of silence-is-acceptance cases sketched by Restatement § 69 ("the offeree takes the benefit of offered services"), a classic example is the unobjecting owner of the cows in Collins v. Lewis (p. 480). Again, it is not enough that the actor expected to be paid; it must be shown that the party to be charged in some manner "assented." A further example is provided by Moore v. Kuehn, 602 S.W.2d 713 (Mo. Ct. App. 1980), where defendant had asked plaintiff for a list of repairs needed to restore a building.

After plaintiff provided such a list, with prices, defendant told plaintiff to proceed with one item on the list. Plaintiff did not stop after completing that work, but continued on with the other items, completing the entire list. Defendant was at all times aware of plaintiff's activities but said nothing. As you no doubt have guessed, defendant's silence in circumstances where he might easily have applied the brakes to plaintiff resulted in a contract to pay for the benefits received at the listed prices.

In applying the principle stated in § 69(1)(a), the fighting issue often will be whether the offeree had the requisite "reason to know." That was the situation in McGurn v. Bell Microproducts, Inc., 284 F.3d 86 (1st Cir. 2002), where Bell mailed McGurn a signed offer of employment stating that if he was terminated within the first twelve months of employment, he would be given a severance package worth $120,000. In signing and returning the offer letter, McGurn crossed out the word "twelve" and replaced it with "twenty-four," initialing his alteration but otherwise not calling it to Bell's attention. Bell's Human Resources department received the returned letter, filing it without examining its contents. Bell terminated McGurn thirteen months later and refused to pay him the severance package, claiming that the twelve-month period stipulated in the offer letter had passed, and that McGurn's alteration was a counteroffer which Bell had never accepted. A federal district court thought otherwise, granting summary judgment to McGurn for the reason that "a presumably sophisticated employer who receives a signed letter of engagement from a prospective employee and fails to read the letter, does so at its peril." A divided reviewing court was unable to agree that Bell's silence, as a matter of law, constituted acceptance of McGurn's counteroffer and remanded the case for a trial addressing whether the modification "should have been noticed" (i.e., whether, under the circumstances, Bell should be expected to re-read the returned offer).

The applicant for insurance is usually characterized as an offeror. What if the risk that the applicant sought to cover materializes before the insurance company has taken any action on the application? An insurance company surely is entitled to a reasonable opportunity to assess the information in the application and to determine what it wants to do. Unless the insurer, by its mode of doing business, has departed from the usual practice and has itself made the offer, or has entered into a contract of "temporary insurance" (e.g., Smith v. Westland Life Ins. Co., 15 Cal. 3d 111, 123 Cal. Rptr. 649, 539 P.2d 433 (1975)), or, through language in the application itself, has contracted to act in a timely manner, there is no basis for holding that it has underwritten the risk from the time the person wanting insurance has submitted an application.

But what if the insurance company takes no action promptly, remaining wholly silent for a lengthy period after receiving the application? A number of courts have found in the insurer's silence an "implied" acceptance and have grounded liability in the insurance contract, especially where an unreasonable delay is coupled with retention of an initial premium paid at the time of the application. E.g., St. Paul Fire & Marine Ins. Co. v. Ingall, 228 Mich. App. 101, 577 N.W.2d 188 (1998); Mardirosian v. Lincoln Nat'l Life Ins. Co., 739 F.2d 474 (9th Cir. 1984) (silence respecting efforts to reinstate lapsed policy amounts to "waiver" of right to refuse reinstatement); Dibble v. Security of Am. Life Ins. Co., 404 Pa. Super. 205, 590 A.2d 352 (1991). Other courts have accorded the applicant protection on a tort basis. The usual rationale is that the insurer, acting under a franchise from and under the regulation of the state, is under a duty to provide insurance to all qualified applicants and, to this end, the insurer is under a duty to act with reasonable promptness in processing the application and notifying the applicant of the action taken. See, e.g., Kukuska v. Home Mut. Hail-Tornado Ins. Co., 204 Wis. 166, 235 N.W. 403 (1931). The measure of recovery appears to be the same whether a contract or tort theory is used. The cases are collected in Hill v. Chubb Life American Ins. Co., 182 Ariz. 158, 894 P.2d 701 (1995) ("courts and commentators have struggled with whether liability for delay in processing an insurance application sounds in tort or in contract").

The cases on implied contracts through silence are collected and discussed in Grosse, Silence as Acceptance, 9 S.U. L. Rev. 81 (1982).

Austin v. Burge

156 Mo. App. 286, 137 S.W. 618 (1911)

Defendant's father-in-law paid for a two-year subscription to plaintiff's newspaper, directing that it be sent to defendant. After the subscription had run out, plaintiff continued to send the paper for several years. Twice defendant paid bills submitted by plaintiff for the subscription price, each time directing that the paper be stopped. Plaintiff still sent the paper and defendant regularly took it home from the post office and read it. On plaintiff's suit for the subscription price, judgment for defendant reversed. "The law in respect to contractual indebtedness for a newspaper is not different from that relating to other things that have not been made the subject of an express agreement. Thus one may not have ordered supplies for his table, or other household necessities, yet if he continue to receive and use them, under circumstances where he had no right to suppose they were a gratuity, he will be held to have agreed by implication, to pay their value."

NOTE: UNSOLICITED MERCHANDISE

Senders of unsolicited goods have aroused a legislative response. Congress and nearly all state legislatures have enacted "unsolicited goods" statutes, the most common provisions of which authorize the recipient to treat unordered merchandise as a gift. An example at the state level is provided by the Michigan Unlawful Trade Practices Act (Mich. Comp. Laws Ann. § 445.131), which provides: "The receipt of any such unsolicited goods shall be deemed for all purposes an unconditional gift to the recipient[ ] [who] may refuse to accept delivery of the goods, is not bound to return them to the sender, and may use or dispose of them in any manner he sees fit without any obligation [to] the sender."

The federal act, a provision of the Postal Reorganization Act of 1970, Pub.L. No. 91–375, 84 Stat. 749, appears in 39 U.S.C. § 3009. It provides:

> (a) Except for (1) free samples clearly and conspicuously marked as such, and (2) merchandise mailed by a charitable organization soliciting contributions, the mailing of unordered merchandise or of communications prohibited by subsection (c) of this section constitutes an unfair method of competition and an unfair trade practice. . . .
>
> (b) Any merchandise mailed in violation of subsection (a) of this section, or within the exceptions contained therein, may be treated as a gift by the recipient, who shall have the right to retain, use, discard, or dispose of it in any manner he sees fit without any obligation whatsoever to the sender. . . .
>
> (c) No mailer of any merchandise mailed in violation of subsection (a) of this section, or within the exceptions contained therein, shall mail to any recipient of such merchandise a bill for such merchandise or any dunning communications.

This statute presumably alters the Restatement's "exercise-of-dominion" provision, § 69(2), as would similar state legislation. So-called "negative-option" plans, typically used by book clubs, are distinguishable in that the consumer subscribes in advance (a contract). Such plans are regulated by a rule of the Federal Trade Commission (16 C.F.R. § 425.1).

Martin v. Little, Brown & Co.

Superior Court of Pennsylvania, 1981.
304 Pa. Super. 424, 450 A.2d 984.

WIEAND, J. This appeal was taken from an order sustaining preliminary objections in the nature of a demurrer to appellant's pro se complaint in assumpsit. The trial court held that a contract had not been made and that there could be no recovery on quantum meruit where appellant had volunteered information which enabled appellee, a publisher of books, to effect a recovery against a third person for copyright infringement. We agree and, accordingly, affirm.

. . . [O]n September 28, 1976, the appellant, James L. Martin, directed a letter to Bantam Books in which he advised the addressee that portions of a paperback publication entitled "How to Buy Stocks" had been plagiarized by the authors of a later book entitled "Planning Your Financial Future." Appellant's letter offered to provide a copy of the book, in which appellant had highlighted the plagiarized passages, with marginal references to the pages and paragraphs of the book from which the passages had been copied. By letter dated October 21, 1976 and signed by Robin Paris, Editorial Assistant, the appellee, Little, Brown & Co., invited appellant to send his copy of "Planning Your Financial Future." This was done, and appellee acknowledged receipt thereof in writing.

Thereafter, appellant made inquiries about appellee's investigation but received no response. Appellant was persistent, however, and upon learning that appellee . . . was pursuing a claim of copyright infringement, he demanded compensation for his services. Appellee denied that it had contracted with appellant or was otherwise obligated to compensate appellant for his work or for his calling the infringement to the publisher's attention. Nevertheless, appellee offered an honorarium in the form of a check for two hundred dollars, which appellant retained but did not cash. Instead, he filed suit to recover one-third of the recovery effected by appellee.

These facts and all reasonable inferences therefrom have been admitted by appellee's demurrer. . . . [W]e are guided by the rule that a demurrer may be sustained only in clear cases, and all doubts must be resolved in favor of the sufficiency of the complaint. . . .

The facts alleged . . . are insufficient to establish a contractual relationship between appellant and appellee. Appellant's initial letter did not expressly or by implication suggest a desire to negotiate. Neither did appellee's letter of October 21, 1976, which invited appellant to send his copy of the offending publication, constitute an offer to enter a unilateral contract [an exchange of appellant's performance for appellee's promise]. It was no more than a response to an initial letter by appellant in which he notified appellee of a copyright infringement and expressed a willingness to forward a copy of the infringing work in which he had highlighted copied portions and cited pages of appellee's work which had been copied. Appellant's letter did not suggest that he intended to be paid, and appellee's response did not contain an offer to pay appellant if he forwarded his copy of the infringing work. In brief, payment to appellant was not discussed in any of the correspondence which preceded the forwarding of appellant's work to appellee.

"A contract, implied in fact, is an actual contract which arises where the parties agree upon the obligations to be incurred, but their intention, instead of being expressed in words, is inferred from their acts in the light of the surrounding circumstances." [In re Home Protection Bldg. & Loan Ass'n, 143 Pa.Super. 96, 17 A.2d 755 (1941).] An implied contract is an agreement which legitimately can be inferred from the intention of the parties as evidenced by the circumstances and "the ordinary course of dealing and the common understanding of men." Hertzog v. Hertzog, 29 Pa. 465 (1857). "Generally, there is an implication of a promise to pay for valuable services rendered with the knowledge and approval of the recipient, in the absence of a showing to the contrary. A promise to pay the reasonable value of the service is implied where one performs for another, with the other's knowledge, a useful service of a character that is usually charged for, and the latter expresses no dissent or avails himself of the service. A promise to pay for services can, however, only be implied when they are rendered in such circumstances as authorized the party performing to entertain a reasonable expectation of their payment by the party benefited. The service or other benefit must not be given as a gratuity or without expectation of payment, and the person benefited must do something from which his promise to pay may be fairly inferred." Home Protection Bldg. & Loan Ass'n, supra. . . . When a person requests another to perform services, it is ordinarily inferred that he intends to pay for them, unless the circumstances indicate otherwise. Restatement Restitution § 107(2) (1937).[1] However, where the circumstances evidence that one's work effort has been voluntarily given to another, an intention to pay therefor cannot be inferred. [Here,] the facts alleged . . . disclose a submission of information from appellant to appellee without any discussion pertaining to appellee's payment therefor. Clearly, there was no basis upon which to infer the existence of a unilateral contract.

Similarly, there is no factual premise to support a finding that appellee is entitled to recover in quasi-contract for the information supplied by appellant. Where one person has been unjustly enriched at the expense of another he or she must make restitution to the other. DeGasperi v. Valicenti, 198 Pa.Super. 455, 181 A.2d 862 (1962). However, unjust enrichment is the key to an action for restitution. . . . The vehicle for achieving restitution is a quasi-contract, or contract implied in law. "Unlike true contracts, quasi-contracts are not based on the apparent intention of the parties to undertake the performances in question, nor are they promises. They are obligations created by law for reasons of justice." Schott v. Westinghouse Elec. Corp., 436 Pa. 279, 290, 259 A.2d 443, 449 (1969). . . . "Quasi-contracts may be found in the absence of any expression of assent by the party to be charged and may indeed be found in spite of the party's contrary intention." [Schott v. Westinghouse], at 290–91, 259 A.2d at 449. To sustain a claim of unjust enrichment, it must be shown by the facts pleaded that a person wrongly secured or passively received a benefit that it would be unconscionable to retain. . . .

As a general rule, volunteers have no right to restitution. Reiver v. Safeguard Precision Prods., 240 Pa.Super. 572, 361 A.2d 371 (1976). . . . Appellant was a volunteer. It was he who made the unsolicited suggestion that he would be willing to submit to appellee his copy of "Planning Your Financial Future" with notations to show which portions had been purloined from "How to Buy Stocks." His offer to do so was not conditioned upon payment of any kind. He did not suggest, either expressly or by implication, that he expected to be paid for this information or for time spent in reducing the same to writing. Thus, . . . he was purely a volunteer and cannot properly be reimbursed for unjust enrichment.[2]

---

1 [Section 107(2) provides: "In the absence of circumstances indicating otherwise, it is inferred that a person who requests another to perform services for him or to transfer property to him thereby bargains to pay therefor."—Eds.]

2 The parties have not briefed and our decision makes it unnecessary that we consider the damages which appellant would otherwise be entitled to recover. It is clear, however, that such damages are measured by the reasonable value of services rendered and not by a percentage of the recovery achieved by appellee as a result of the copyright infringement first observed by appellant. . . .

Finally, appellant's complaint contains a count in trespass for intentional infliction of mental distress.[2] The basis of this claim is an alleged statement by appellee's counsel that if appellant instituted suit, a counterclaim would be filed for abuse of process.

The Restatement (Second) of Torts § 46, provides: "One who by extreme and outrageous conduct intentionally or recklessly causes severe emotional distress to another is subject to liability for such emotional distress." Under this rule, "[l]iability has been found only where the conduct has been *so outrageous in character, and so extreme in degree, as to go beyond all possible bounds of decency, and to be regarded as atrocious, and utterly intolerable in a civilized community*. Generally, the case is one in which the recitation of the facts to an average member of the community would arouse his resentment against the actor, and lead him to exclaim, 'Outrageous.'" Jones v. Nissenbaum, Rudolph & Seidner, 244 Pa.Super. 377, 383, 368 A.2d 770, 773 (1976). . . .

The mere threat of a legal counterclaim, even if entirely lacking in merit, will not generally satisfy the strict standard required to make out a case of outrageous conduct. The adversary nature of litigation invariably involves a turbulent contest of wills. Appellant, a law student who threatened to avail himself of the judicial process to assert a claim, cannot properly complain when his adversary threatens to file a counterclaim. This did not give rise to an action for the emotional distress, if any, which appellant suffered when he learned that a new dimension would be added to the litigation. The claim was properly dismissed.

Collins v. Lewis

111 Conn. 299, 149 A. 668 (1930)

Plaintiff, a deputy sheriff, attached and took away cows found in the possession of one Kinne. Plaintiff later learned that the cows belonged to defendant and that Kinne held them under a conditional-sale contract. A few days later, plaintiff returned the cows to Kinne's farm but Kinne refused to take them. Subsequently, plaintiff offered to return the cows to defendant but was told that defendant had no place for them at that time. Plaintiff's attorney then informed defendant that the cows were being kept for him and that he would be held for the cost of their keep. After being boarded by plaintiff for thirty-eight days, the cows were sold by defendant and taken away by the new purchaser. The court said: "It is to be noted that during this period he [defendant] knew from the letter which had been sent to him by counsel for the plaintiff, that the plaintiff was holding the cows for him with the expectation of being paid for their care and keep. By selling the cows and taking possession of them, he thus appropriated the benefit of the thirty-eight days' care and keep which had been bestowed upon them by the plaintiff. It was

---

[2] [Recall the discussion of this tort in the Note accompanying Valentine v. General American Credit, supra p. 114.—Eds.]

under these established facts that the trial court held there was an implied contract created by law, that the defendant would pay the plaintiff."

"A true implied contract can only exist where there is no express one. It is one which is inferred from the conduct of the parties though not expressed in words. Such a contract arises where a plaintiff, without being requested to do so, renders services under circumstances indicating that he expects to be paid therefor, and the defendant, knowing such circumstances, avails himself of the benefit of those services. In such a case, the law implies from the circumstances, a promise by the defendant to pay the plaintiff what those services are reasonably worth. . . . 'One may . . . be required to compensate another for the benefits conferred by the other's labor and services, either accepted by or necessarily accruing to the beneficiary, when, having reasonable ground to believe that the labor is being done or service performed in the expectation of compensation, he stands silently by and permits the labor or service to continue.' Chesebro v. Lockwood, 88 Conn. 219, 224, 91 A. 188. Upon this record as it stands, therefore, we sustain the conclusion of the trial court that there was an implied contract, that this defendant would pay the reasonable cost of the care and keep of these cows."

Seaview Ass'n of Fire Island, N.Y., Inc. v. Williams

69 N.Y.2d 987, 517 N.Y.S.2d 709, 510 N.E.2d 793 (1987)

Plaintiff, a homeowners' association, owned and maintained the streets, walkways, and beaches of Seaview, an unincorporated community of some 330 homes used largely for summer recreation. Plaintiff provided many community services, including recreational facilities. Each Seaview property owner was assessed a share of plaintiff's annual operating expenses; the assessment policy was generally known in the community (the forms of notice included posted signs). Defendants, year-round residents active in the real estate business, owned seven houses in Seaview (their first purchase was in 1963), but refused to pay any assessments, contending that nonmembers of the association and nonusers of the recreational facilities cannot be charged. In plaintiff's suit to recover assessments against defendants for an eight-year period, the trial court, finding an "implied contract" to pay assessments, awarded judgment for plaintiff. *Held*, there is ample evidence to support the trial court's findings. Defendants had "actual or constructive knowledge" of the nature of the community and plaintiff's activities for the benefit of residents. Their purchases impliedly accepted "the conditions accompanying ownership of property" in Seaview. "The resulting implied-in-fact contract includes the obligation to pay a proportionate share of the full cost of maintaining [plaintiff's] facilities and services, not merely the reasonable value of those actually used by any particular resident."

Martin v. Campanaro

156 F.2d 127 (2d Cir. 1946)

"The claimants are entitled to recover on a quantum meruit basis. But 'quantum meruit' is ambiguous; it may mean (1) that there is a contract 'implied in fact' to pay the reasonable value of the services, or (2) that, to prevent unjust enrichment, the claimant can recover on a quasi-contract (an 'as if' contract) for that reasonable value. . . . The confusion involved in the use of the old phrase 'implied contracts' to label both those 'implied in fact' and 'implied in law' (now called 'quasi-contracts') has not been entirely obliterated. Nor is it easy to eradicate. Thus it is said that a quasi-contract is 'imposed by law . . . irrespective of, and sometimes in violation of, . . . intention' and therefore not a 'true' contract, while a 'true' contract, (including a contract 'implied in fact') arises from 'intent.' Williston, sec. 3; Woodward, The Law of Quasi Contracts (1913), sec. 4."

[As noted (the Comment on the Common Counts, p. 142), the phrase "quantum meruit" can be (and is) used to describe liabilities resting in either contract or quasi-contract. Some courts have attempted to limit it to contract implied-in-fact, in order to distinguish the action for "unjust enrichment" applicable when contract principles are unavailable. E.g., Paffhausen v. Balano, 708 A.2d 269 (Me. 1998). Nevertheless, the phrase probably is used most often to mean quasi-contract, something different from a contract implied in fact, which depends on the parties' intentions. One court's statement is fairly representative of this usage: "The whole point of quantum meruit recovery is to compensate plaintiffs who have provided a benefit to defendants but who do *not* have a contract—express or implied—with those defendants." In re De Laurentiis Entertainment Group Inc., 963 F.2d 1269 (9th Cir. 1992).]

QUESTIONS

(1) What do you suppose would have happened in Collins v. Lewis if the defendant had not sold the cows and kept the money proceeds, but had refused altogether to have anything more to do with the cows?

(2) Suppose the defendant in Collins v. Lewis, when told by plaintiff's attorney that he would be held for the expenses of keeping the cows, had replied that he would pay plaintiff nothing. Suppose also that 38 days later defendant recovered the cows through judicial proceedings (e.g., a replevin action) and sold them to a third party. Is defendant liable for plaintiff's expenses?

(3) Both Martin v. Little, Brown & Co. and Collins v. Lewis limit any recovery to the reasonable value of services rendered. If the plaintiff establishes a restitution claim in such cases, why shouldn't the measure of recovery be the defendant's net gain?

SECTION 5. LIMITED AND INDEFINITE PROMISES

INTRODUCTORY COMMENT

A number of the cases to this point have involved promises given in exchange for acts (or abstentions from action) or promises that induced reliance, again in the form of acts or abstentions. Attention has not been called, as it now must be, to the special problems that may arise where nothing more than an exchange of promises has occurred—the so-called "bilateral contract." Applying the tests of consideration, is it enough that each party has made a promise to the other? Does the form or content of the promise make a difference?

It is worth noting again that problems with a bilateral contract could not arise so long as the action of debt was the common law's chosen instrument for the enforcement of informal promises. Consider, for example, an agreement made in the year 1450 and involving an exchange of oral promises—150 bushels of wheat for £10. On the original exchange of promises, no obligation in debt arose; that action would lie only if the wheat had been actually delivered, or at least a "property" in the wheat transferred to the buyer. One or the other was essential to provide the quid pro quo on which the obligation in debt depended. In modern terminology, though the transaction may have begun as bilateral, it would have to become "unilateral" through performance on one side if the action of debt was to lie. Even after 1500, when special assumpsit began to expand as a remedy on promises, the great bulk of the cases involved plaintiffs who had already performed.

When actions on executory, bilateral transactions began to appear, they encountered no difficulty from the evolving doctrine of consideration. As early as 1555 (Pecke v. Redman, 2 Dyer 113a), the enforceability of an exchange of promises was taken for granted without discussion. In the sixteenth century, when lawyers began to search for some limits to liabilities arising from promises, the status of bilateral contracts seemed simple enough. When doubts were raised, for example, in Strangborough v. Warner, 4 Leon. 3 (1589), they were laid to rest with the flat statement that "a promise against a promise will maintain an action on the case."

It was in the nineteenth century effort to systematize and rationalize the doctrine of consideration that this simple affirmation came to seem inadequate, and new difficulties were manufactured. With attention focused on the concept of "detriment," which already had become the principal analytical tool, the question was asked: Where is the detriment in making a promise that enables it to serve as the consideration for a counter-promise? The answer first suggested was that the detriment lay in the promisor's legal obligation created by the promise. Critics pointed out that this response rested on circular reasoning. Legal obligation would result only if A's promise would be enforced by a court, and that would happen only if there were a consideration for it. One must therefore look at B's promise, and if it will provide consideration only if it in turn is legally enforceable, we are called upon to assume the very conclusion we set out to establish. Some participants in the debate argued that the way to get off this merry-go-round was to find the required detriment in A's mere act of promising. This, too, proved too much, for if A supplied consideration by merely mouthing words of promise, it would seem to be neither necessary nor proper to inquire into the content of A's apparent assurances or their legal consequences. Moreover, while it is possible to find that a party bargained wholly and exclusively for the other's statement of certain words, this is not the ordinary meaning or purpose of transactions in which "promises" are exchanged. Corbin observed long ago that the proposer of a bargain seeks both words of promise and the actual performance promised. 1 A. Corbin, Contracts § 142.

We need not pursue further the course of these nineteenth century debates on which so much ingenuity was expended. It is sufficient to point out that while they were taking place it was generally assumed that bilateral contracts—promise for promise—were here to stay, and that most of them were enforceable. We should add a small caveat, however. If for some reason a performance would not provide consideration if actually rendered, the same reason would presumably have the same effect if the performance were postponed and made the subject of a promise. If, for example, the legal-duty rule applied and the act to be performed consisted of nothing more than performance of some already-existing duty, the fact that it was promised would not help. The converse is equally true. It is a working rule, more than 99 percent reliable, that a promise is consideration if the performance promised, either act or forbearance, or both, would be consideration if it alone were bargained for.

Even with this limitation, however, the bilateral contract presents a cluster of problems that makes it inadequate merely to repeat the simple affirmation of 1589—"a promise against a promise" can be enough to create a contract. These problems arise because of the desire of at least one of the promisors to retain some measure of flexibility in confronting an uncertain and changing world. How much freedom may a promisor retain without impairing the basis for binding the other party? Consider the problems presented by the two digested cases that follow.

Davis v. General Foods Corp.

21 F. Supp. 445 (S.D.N.Y. 1937)

Plaintiff wrote defendant saying that she had an idea and recipe for a new food product. Defendant wrote back, acknowledging receipt of plaintiff's letter and adding: "We shall be glad to examine your idea, but only with the understanding that the use to be made of it by us, and the compensation, if any, to be paid therefor, are matters resting solely in our discretion." After disclosing her recipe plaintiff sued in contract and quantum meruit, alleging that defendant had used her recipe in its business but had refused to compensate her. *Held*, defense motion for judgment on the pleadings granted. Defendant's letter cannot give rise to a binding agreement. " 'One of the commonest kind of promises too indefinite for legal enforcement is where the promisor retains an unlimited right to decide later the nature or extent of his performance. This unlimited choice . . . makes [the promise] merely illusory.' " Nor can there be recovery in quantum meruit. It is true that the law will presume a promise to pay reasonable value where a party has acted in reliance on an alleged contract, the terms of which are too indefinite for enforcement. But "where the form or character of the promise leads to the conclusion that the plaintiff did not rely upon it as a contractual obligation but trusted the fairness and liberality of the defendant, there is not only no contract but no misreliance upon a supposed contract, and consequently no legal obligation whatever."

Nat Nal Serv. Stations v. Wolf

304 N.Y. 332, 107 N.E.2d 473 (1952)

Plaintiff, operator of a service station, sued defendant wholesalers to recover a discount on over 900,000 gallons of gasoline purchases. The complaint alleged an oral agreement that "so long as plaintiff purchased [its gas requirements] through defendants and [they] accepted the same," defendants would pay plaintiff a discount on each gallon purchased. According to plaintiff, the promise of a discount was made when "the defendants desired to increase the volume of their orders for gasoline [with Socony and Standard Oil, their suppliers], and hence came to me with the proposition that if I would give my orders for gasoline through them, thereby increasing their volume, they would pay to me an amount equal to the discount received by them from the oil companies upon whatever orders I gave to them, and if they accepted my orders. I did give the defendants orders which they accepted and then transmitted in their name to the oil companies, under which they received a discount of at least one cent a gallon." The Appellate Division, reversing Special Term, granted defendants' motion for summary judgment and dismissed the complaint, on the ground that the agreement could not, by its terms, "be performed within one year from the making thereof." On further appeal, *held*, reversed; there is nothing in the terms of the oral agreement to bring it within the statute of frauds. Conway, J., explained:

"The agreement alleged here was clearly one at will and for no definite or specific time and thus by its terms did not of necessity extend beyond one year from the time of its making. . . . [N]either party obligated itself to do anything. Unless and until plaintiff had offered to place an order for gasoline and the defendants had accepted such offer and filled the order, only then did there come into existence a legal obligation, viz., the obligation of defendants to pay the agreed discount. . . . The plaintiff could have purchased the same gasoline through someone other than defendants. On the other hand if the plaintiff placed an order the defendant was under no obligation to accept it. Neither party was obligated to deal with the other. Each time the plaintiff offered to buy gasoline from defendants and the defendants accepted the offer and sold gasoline, there was concluded a separate contract and there became due from defendants the discount specified, but neither party was ever obligated to enter into another such contract. . . . [D]efendants were free at any and all times to discontinue payment of a discount either by refusing to accept an order or by notification to plaintiff that thenceforth no discounts would be paid. Plaintiff was at all times free to place all its orders for gasoline elsewhere or to notify defendants that no further orders would be offered to them for acceptance. We are confronted with an alleged contract by the terms of which neither party was bound to do anything at any time."

PROBLEMS

Clauses making the contract terminable by one or both parties on short notice are common. For example, in Laclede Gas Co. v. Amoco Oil Co., 522 F.2d 33 (8th Cir. 1975), the court, finding that a power to cancel given only the buyer did not render the buyer's side of the contract illusory, said: "There is no necessity that for each stipulation in a contract binding one party there must be a corresponding stipulation binding the other. . . . [A] cancellation clause will invalidate a contract only if its exercise is *unrestricted*."

(1) Suppose a contract for the sale of 500 wool sweaters to be delivered by Seller in installments of 100 a month, with a provision for payment by Buyer for each installment at the rate of $30 a sweater, within 60 days after delivery. Would the contract be enforceable by either party if it contained any one of the following clauses:

> (A) "Seller reserves the right to cancel this contract immediately in the event of any default in payment by Buyer";
>
> (B) "Seller reserves the right to cancel this contract on 10 days' notice";
>
> (C) "Seller reserves the right to cancel this contract on the giving of notice"?

(2) Suppose further that Seller had signed the contract but Buyer had not. Then Buyer repudiated after taking delivery of the first 100 sweaters shipped by Seller. Suppose also that the contract included this clause: "Seller reserves the right to cancel this agreement at any time without notice." Could Seller recover damages for Buyer's refusal to take the full 500 sweaters? Recover the agreed price for the 100 sweaters Buyer accepted? Consult UCC 2–201; 2–607(1).

COMMENT: MUTUALITY OF OBLIGATION

The business of promoting contract "mutuality" came into our case law not much more than a century ago. To have consideration, it was said, "both parties must be bound or neither will be." There is, to be sure, an apparent evenhandedness in such a maxim. Talk of a requirement of "mutuality"—of some degree of balance in obligations—is encountered frequently enough in the cases, even today, that we must pause to consider its general reliability.

Suppose a contract that is defective for some reason, such as fraud perpetrated by one party. A promises to sell B a car, B promises to pay A the agreed price, but during negotiations A misrepresents the year, mileage, and condition of the car. If B's reliance on the misrepresentations is justified ("reasonable" in the circumstances), quite clearly B will have an election to rescind the transaction when the fraud is discovered. Does this mean that

B's promise is so lacking in binding effect that B cannot enforce A's promise? B may decide after all to "affirm" the transaction and take the car with an allowance in damages for its defective condition. A moment's reflection will indicate how undesirable it is to allow A to escape liability by setting up his own fraud. The same sort of problem would arise if A used duress—let us say, pointed a gun at B to make B sign. Or suppose that B is mentally incapable or an infant. Insane persons and infants can avoid liability on their promises, which are usually described as "voidable." Professor Williston argued (1 S. Williston, Contracts § 105) that the promise of an infant or insane person means no more than "I promise to perform if I choose"; that such a promise if expressed in words would be illusory; and that any doctrine finding consideration in such a promise "must be regarded as an exception to the general principles of consideration." But if one is concerned less with preserving the symmetry of legal doctrine than with examining the purposes that doctrine must serve, the problem takes on a different aspect. There is indeed an apparent injustice in binding the adult or the mentally-competent party, while escape is left open for the infant or the mentally incapacitated. On the other hand, the power of avoidance given to the infant or the mentally ill is intended as protection against disadvantageous agreements. Is this larger purpose served by holding such persons incapable of making advantageous agreements in bilateral form, i.e., through an exchange of promises? Or, phrased another way, the question is whether infants, the insane, or other seriously handicapped persons must be required always to perform first in order to be able to enforce promises made to them by other people. It is not altogether surprising to find that so far as consideration doctrines in law actions are concerned, the answer is "no."

A similar problem arises with the statute of frauds, which usually requires a memorandum signed by "the party to be charged" where the promise in question comes within the statutory classes. What if one party has signed, but the other has not? Again, there is the inequality noted above; the signer is bound even though that party would have no means of compelling performance of any return promise by the other party had the latter breached. In effect, the nonsigner is given a kind of unintended option. Before condemning this result, however, one should ask whether it is necessary, or wise, to go beyond the statutory provision, which requires safeguards only for "the party to be charged." The conclusion generally is that we should not, that an oral promise rendered unenforceable by the statute of frauds is still a promise and that it provides consideration for a written counterpromise.

The Restatement of Contracts, Second § 78 deals with these miscellaneous situations inclusively, as follows: "The fact that a rule of law renders a promise voidable or unenforceable does not prevent it from being consideration."

This principle, coupled with the examples already given, leaves little doubt that the maxim that "both must be bound or neither will be," in the broad sweep of its language, will not stand scrutiny. But what should be the law's approach where the avenue of escape is provided not by a rule of law but by the terms of the promise itself? Are there special problems of fairness in contracts framed as bilateral? Is there some recognized principle compelling the conclusion that a promise of limited commitment, one that reserves to the promisor an option or alternative in some form, is fatally defective and cannot render a return promise enforceable? If there is, the question then must be whether it is an independent principle of general contract law, an offshoot or byproduct of consideration doctrine, or possibly something else.

Our present concern is "mutuality of obligation." The use of mutuality as a factor influencing the grant or refusal of specific performance in equity ("mutuality of remedy") has some distinctive features and will come up later.

Wood v. Lucy, Lady Duff-Gordon

Court of Appeals of New York, 1917.
222 N.Y. 88, 118 N.E. 214.

CARDOZO, J. The defendant styles herself "a creator of fashions." Her favor helps a sale. Manufacturers of dresses, millinery and like articles are glad to pay for a certificate of her approval. The things which she designs, fabrics, parasols and what not, have a new value in the public mind when issued in her name. She employed the plaintiff to help her to turn this vogue into money. He was to have the exclusive right, subject always to her approval, to place her indorsements on the designs of others. He was also to have the exclusive right to place her own designs on sale, or to license others to market them. In return, she was to have one-half of "all profits and revenues" derived from any contracts he might make. The exclusive right was to last at least one year from April 1, 1915, and thereafter from year to year unless terminated by notice of ninety days. The plaintiff says that he kept the contract on his part, and that the defendant broke it. She placed her indorsement on fabrics, dresses and millinery without his knowledge, and withheld the profits. He sues her for the damages and the case comes here on demurrer.

The agreement of employment is signed by both parties. It has a wealth of recitals. The defendant insists, however, that it lacks the elements of a contract. She says that the plaintiff does not bind himself to anything. It is true that he does not promise in so many words that he will use reasonable efforts to place the defendant's indorsements and market her designs. We think, however, that such a promise is fairly to be implied. The law has outgrown its primitive stage of formalism when the precise word was the sovereign talisman, and every slip was fatal. It takes a broader view today. A promise may be lacking, and yet the whole writing may be "instinct with an obligation," imperfectly expressed, Scott, J., in McCall Co. v. Wright, 133 App.Div. 62, 117 N.Y.S. 775. . . . If that is so, there is a contract.

Good Housekeeping Magazine

LADY DUFF-GORDON
Of the English nobility who employs psychology
in designing clothes for women

The implication of a promise here finds support in many circumstances. The defendant gave an *exclusive* privilege. She was to have no right for at least a year to place her own indorsements or market her own designs except through the agency of the plaintiff. The acceptance of the exclusive agency was an assumption of its duties. . . . We are not to suppose that one party was to be placed at the mercy of the other. Hearn v. Stevens & Bro., 111 App.Div. 101, 97 N.Y.S. 566. . . . Many other terms of the agreement point the same way. We are told at the outset by way of recital that "the said Otis F. Wood possesses a business organization adapted to the placing of such indorsements as the said Lucy, Lady Duff-Gordon has approved." The implication is that the plaintiff's business organization will be used for the purpose for which it is adapted. But the terms of the defendant's compensation are even more significant. Her sole compensation for the grant of an exclusive agency is to be one-half of all the profits resulting from the plaintiff's efforts. Unless he gave his efforts, she could never get anything. Without an implied promise, the transaction cannot have such business "efficacy as both parties must have intended that at all events it should have." Bowen, L.J., in The Moorcock, 14 P.D. 64, 68. But the contract does not stop there. The plaintiff goes on to promise that he will account monthly for all moneys received by him, and that he will take out all such patents and copyrights and trademarks as may in his judgment be necessary to protect the rights and articles affected by the agreement. It is true, of course, as the Appellate Division has said, that if he was under no duty to try to market designs or to place certificates of indorsement, his promise to account for profits or take out copyrights would be valueless. But in determining the intention of the parties, the promise *has* a value. It helps to enforce the conclusion that the plaintiff *had* some duties. His promise to pay the defendant one-half of the profits and revenues resulting from the exclusive agency and to render accounts monthly, was a promise to use reasonable efforts to bring profits and revenues into existence. For this conclusion, the authorities are ample. . . .

The judgment of the Appellate Division should be reversed, and the order of the Special Term affirmed. . . . [The vote in the Court of Appeals was 4 to 3.]

NOTE

The source of Cardozo's gap-filling implication seems clear enough. Even though Lady Duff-Gordon sold endorsements and not goods, if the case arose today presumably UCC 2–306(2) would not hinder the interpretive move Cardozo made.

It is reported that Lucy brought Wood's lawsuit upon herself by arranging with Sears, Roebuck and Co. to sell her dresses through its catalogues. This move was apparently heralded as a stunning marketing tactic for the times, placing Lucy at the forefront of commercial practice. A trade journal commented that the announcement of the agreement with Sears threw "a bomb into the camp of rival mail-order houses." Pratt, American Contract Law at the Turn of the Century, 39 S. Car. L. Rev. 415, 439 (1988).

But the suit brought by Wood was not Lady Duff-Gordon's only encounter with the legal system. In April 1919, a judgment of $1,500 was entered against her in a suit brought by Muriel Ridley, a dancer, for breach of contract. Although Lady Duff-Gordon had asserted that she was unable to pay the $1,500 judgment, it is reported that her lawyer quickly sent Ridley a check in full payment when the contents of Duff-Gordon's Park Avenue (New York) apartment were attached. The whole affair apparently turned Lady Duff-Gordon sour on America, for, when asked by the judge in these proceedings whether she had purchased any Liberty Bonds, she replied: "Why should I buy any? This country means nothing to me. I have had nothing but trouble over here. It is an awful country." N.Y.Times, April 13, 1919, at 22, col. 2.

It seems Lady Duff-Gordon's troubles continued. Her exclusive dress firm, Lucile Ltd., with boutiques in New York, Chicago, London, and Paris, subsequently went into bankruptcy proceedings; she was accused by some of contributing to the failure of the company by her "unjustifiable extravagance." N.Y.Times, April 19, 1923, at 23, col. 3. Although Lady Duff-Gordon was highly regarded as a dress designer (she is said to have coined the term "chic"), her fame was not without its costs—including injury to her standing in the English nobility. Because of her business activities, her name was stricken from the list of persons admitted at Court. N.Y.Times, April 22, 1935, at 17, col. 1.

Lady Duff-Gordon's most notorious court appearance by far came earlier, as a result of the 1912 trip with her husband, Sir Cosmo, on the ill-fated liner Titanic. The couple escaped death, but not the taint of scandal. As the story unfolded in a British Court of Inquiry, the Duff-Gordons had managed to escape in a lifeboat that was less than one-third filled with survivors. It was alleged that Sir Cosmo, afraid that the boat would be swamped, had dissuaded the crew of the lifeboat from turning back to pick up more people. (There was evidence that, after the tragedy, Sir Cosmo had sent to each crew member a gift of £5.) His actions attracted further attention when it was revealed that two witnesses testifying at the inquiry had been "coached" on their testimony by an attorney sent on behalf of the Duff-Gordons. Perhaps that is why Lady Duff-Gordon was described as leaving the inquiry's witness box "white to the lips." N.Y.Times, May 21, 1912, at 4, col. 3.

Harold Spencer of the New York Daily News was among those who showed compassion for Sir Cosmo. Spencer asked in his column: "Who shall throw the first stone? Who shall say how he would have acted if faced with the sudden and unexpected figure of death on that cold, dark Atlantic?" (quoted in the N.Y.Times, May 18, 1912, at 4, col. 1). Something close to that view prevailed in the end, for the British court exonerated the Duff-Gordons of all charges of improper conduct.

Lady Duff-Gordon died in 1935, at the age of 72.

Sun Printing & Publishing Ass'n v. Remington Paper & Power Co., Inc.

Court of Appeals of New York, 1923.
235 N.Y. 338, 139 N.E. 470.

CARDOZO, J. Plaintiff agreed to buy and defendant to sell 1,000 tons of paper per month during the months of September, 1919, to December,

1920, inclusive, 16,000 tons in all. Sizes and quality were adequately described. Payment was to be made on the 20th of each month for all paper shipped the previous month. The price for shipments in September, 1919, was to be $3.73¾ per 100 pounds, and for shipments in October, November, and December, 1919, $4 per 100 pounds. "For the balance of the period of this agreement the price of the paper and length of terms for which such price shall apply shall be agreed upon by and between the parties hereto fifteen days prior to the expiration of each period for which the price and length of term thereof have been previously agreed upon, said price in no event to be higher than the contract price for news print charged by the Canadian Export Paper Co. to the large consumers, the seller to receive the benefit of any differentials in freight rates."

Between September, 1919, and December of that year, inclusive, shipments were made and paid for as required by the contract. The time then arrived when there was to be an agreement upon a new price and upon the term of its duration. The defendant in advance of that time gave notice that the contract was imperfect, and disclaimed for the future an obligation to deliver. Upon this the plaintiff took the ground that the price was to be ascertained by resort to an established standard. It made demand that during each month of 1920 the defendant deliver 1,000 tons of paper at the contract price for news print charged by the Canadian Export Paper Co. to the large consumers, the defendant to receive the benefit of any differentials in freight rates. The demand was renewed month by month till the expiration of the year. This action has been brought to recover the ensuing damage.

Seller and buyer left two subjects to be settled in the middle of December and at unstated intervals thereafter. One was the price to be paid. The other was the length of time during which such price was to govern. Agreement as to the one was insufficient without agreement as to the other. If price and nothing more had been left open for adjustment, there might be force in the contention that the buyer would be viewed, in the light of later provisions, as the holder of an option. This would mean that, in default of an agreement for a lower price, the plaintiff would have the privilege of calling for delivery in accordance with a price established as a maximum. The price to be agreed upon might be less, but could not be more, than "the contract price for news print charged by the Canadian Export Paper Co. to the large consumers." The difficulty is, however, that ascertainment of this price does not dispense with the necessity for agreement in respect of the term during which the price is to apply. Agreement upon a maximum payable this month or today is not the same as an agreement that it shall continue to be payable next month or tomorrow. Seller and buyer understood that the price to be fixed in December for a term to be agreed upon would not be more than the price then charged by the Canadian Export Paper Co. to the large consumers. They did not understand that, if during the term so established the price charged by the Canadian Export Paper Co. was changed, the price payable to the seller would fluctuate accordingly. This was conceded by plaintiff's counsel on the argument before us. The seller was to receive no more during the running of the prescribed term, though the Canadian Maximum was raised. The buyer was to pay no less during that term, though the maximum was lowered. In the brief, the standard was to be applied at the beginning of the successive terms, but once applied was to be maintained until the term should have expired. While the term was unknown, the contract was inchoate.

The argument is made that there was no need of an agreement as to time unless the price to be paid was lower than the maximum. We find no evidence of this intention in the language of the contract. The result would then be that the defendant would never know where it stood. The plaintiff was under no duty to accept the Canadian standard. It does not assert that it was. What it asserts is that the contract amounted to the concession of an option. Without an agreement as to time, however, there would be not one option, but a dozen. The Canadian price today might be less than the Canadian price tomorrow. Election by the buyer to proceed with performance at the price prevailing in one month would not bind it to proceed at the price prevailing in another. Successive options to be exercised every month would thus be read into the contract. Nothing in the wording discloses the intention of the seller to place itself to that extent at the mercy of the buyer. Even if, however, we were to interpolate the restriction that the option, if exercised at all, must be exercised only once, and for the entire quantity permitted, the difficulty would not be ended. Market prices in 1920 happened to rise. The importance of the time element becomes apparent when we ask ourselves what the seller's position would be if they had happened to fall. Without an agreement as to time, the maximum would be lowered from one shipment to another with every reduction of the standard. With such an agreement, on the other hand, there would be stability and certainty. The parties attempted to guard against the contingency of failing to come together as to price. They did not guard against the contingency of failing to come together as to time. Very likely they thought the latter contingency so remote that it could safely be disregarded. In any event, whether through design or through inadvertence, they left the gap unfilled. The result was nothing more than "an agreement to agree." Defendant [had the right to insist that, to be legally enforceable,] there was need of something more. The right is not affected by our appraisal of the motive.

We are told that the defendant was under a duty, in default of an agreement, to accept a term that would be reasonable in view of the nature of the transaction and the practice of the business. To hold it to such a standard is to make the contract over. The defendant reserved the privilege of doing its business in its own way, and did not undertake to conform to the practice and beliefs of others. We are told again that there was a duty, in default of other agreement, to act as if the successive terms were to expire every month. The contract says they are to expire at such intervals as the agreement may prescribe. There is need, it is true, of no high degree of ingenuity to show how the parties, with little change of language, could have framed a form of contract to which obligation would attach. The difficulty is that they framed another. We are not at liberty to revise while professing to construe.

We do not ignore the allegation of the complaint that the contract price charged by the Canadian Export Paper Co. to the large consumers "constituted a definite and well-defined standard of price that was readily ascertainable." The suggestion is made by members of the court that the price so charged may have been known to be one established for the year, so that fluctuation would be impossible. If that was its character, the complaint should so allege. The writing signed by the parties calls for an agreement as to time. The complaint concedes that no such agreement has been made. The result, prima facie, is the failure of the contract. In that situation the pleader has the burden of setting forth the extrinsic circumstances, if there are any, that make agreement unimportant. There is significance, moreover, in the attitude of counsel. No point is made in brief or in argument that the Canadian price, when once established, is constant through the year. On the contrary, there is at least a tacit assumption that it varies with the market. The buyer acted on the same assumption when it renewed the demand from month to month, making tender of performance at the prices then prevailing. If we misconceive the course of dealing, the plaintiff by amendment of its pleading can correct our misconception. The complaint as it comes before us leaves no escape from the conclusion that agreement in respect of time is as essential to a completed contract as agreement in respect of price. The agreement was not reached, and the defendant is not bound.

The question is not here whether the defendant would have failed in the fulfillment of its duty by an arbitrary refusal to reach any agreement as to time after notice from the plaintiff that it might make division of the terms in any way it pleased. No such notice was given, so far as the complaint discloses. The action is not based upon a refusal to treat with the defendant and attempt to arrive at an agreement. Whether any such theory of liability would be tenable we need not now inquire. Even if the plaintiff might have stood upon the defendant's denial of obligation as amounting to such a refusal, it did not elect to do so. Instead, it gave its own construction to the contract, fixed for itself the length of the successive terms, and thereby coupled its demand with a condition which there was no duty to accept. We find no allegation of readiness, and offer to proceed on any other basis. The condition being untenable, the failure to comply with it cannot give a cause of action. . . .

CRANE, J. (dissenting). I cannot take the view of this contract that has been adopted by the majority. . . .

Surely these parties must have had in mind that some binding agreement was made for the sale and delivery of 16,000 tons rolls of paper, and that the instrument contained all the elements necessary to make a binding contract. . . . If this be so, the court should spell out a binding contract, if it be possible. I not only think it possible, but think the paper itself clearly states a contract recognized under all the rules at law. It is said that the one essential element of price is lacking; that the provision above quoted is an agreement to agree to a price, and that the defendant had the privilege of agreeing or not, as it pleased; that, if it failed to agree to a price, there was no standard by which to measure the amount the plaintiff would have to pay. The contract does state, however, just this very thing. Fifteen days before the 1st of January, 1920, the parties were to agree upon the price of the paper to be delivered thereafter, and the length of the period for which such price should apply. However, the price to be fixed was not "to be higher than the contract price for news print charged by the Canadian Export Paper Co. to large consumers." Here, surely, was something definite. The 15th day of December arrived. The defendant refused to deliver. At that time there was a price for news print charged by the Canadian Export Paper Co. If the plaintiff offered to pay this price, which was the highest price the defendant could demand, the defendant was bound to deliver. This seems to be very clear.

But, while all agree that the price on the 15th day of December could be fixed, the further objection is made that the period during which that price should continue was not agreed upon. There are many answers to this.

We have reason to believe that the parties supposed they were making a binding contract; that they had fixed the terms by which one was required to take and the other to deliver; that the Canadian Export Paper Co. price was to be the highest that could be charged in any event. These things being so, the court should be very reluctant to permit a defendant to avoid its contract.

On the 15th of the fourth month, the time when the price was to be fixed for subsequent deliveries, there was a price charged by the Canadian Export Paper Co. to large consumers. As the defendant failed to agree upon a price, made no attempt to agree upon a price, and deliberately broke its contract, it could readily be held to deliver the rest of the paper, 1,000 rolls a month, at this Canadian price. There is nothing in the complaint which indicates that this is a fluctuating price, or that the price of paper as it was on December 15th was not the same for the remaining 12 months. Or we can deal with this contract month by month. The deliveries were to be made 1,000 tons per month. On December 15th 1,000 tons could have been demanded. The price charged by the Canadian Export Paper Co. on the 15th of each month on and after December 15, 1919, would be the price for the 1,000-ton delivery for that month. Or, again, the word as used in the miscellaneous provision quoted is not "price," but "contract price"—"in no event to be higher than the contract price." Contract implies a term or period, and, if the evidence should show that the Canadian contract price was for a certain period of weeks or months, then this period could be applied to the contract in question. Failing any other alternative, the law should do here what it has done in so many other cases—apply the rule of reason and compel parties to contract in the light of fair dealing. It could hold this defendant to deliver its paper as it agreed to do, and take for a price the Canadian Export Paper Co. contract price for a period which is reasonable under all the circumstances and conditions as applied in the paper trade.

To let this defendant escape from its formal obligations when any one of these rulings as applied to this contract would give a practical and just result is to give the sanction of law to a deliberate breach. . . .

HISCOCK, C. J., and POUND, MCLAUGHLIN, and ANDREWS, JJ., concur with CARDOZO, J. CRANE, J., reads dissenting opinion with which HOGAN, J., concurs.

Restatement of Contracts, Second

§ 33. Certainty

(1) Even though a manifestation of intention is intended to be understood as an offer, it cannot be accepted so as to form a contract unless the terms of the contract are reasonably certain.

(2) The terms of a contract are reasonably certain if they provide a basis for determining the existence of a breach and for giving an appropriate remedy.

(3) The fact that one or more terms of a proposed bargain are left open or uncertain may show that a manifestation of intention is not intended to be understood as an offer or as an acceptance.

Comment: . . .

b. Certainty in basis for remedy. The rule stated in Subsection (2) reflects the fundamental policy that contracts should be made by the parties, not by the courts, and hence that remedies for breach of contract must have a basis in the agreement of the parties. Where the parties have intended to make a contract and there is a reasonably certain basis for granting a remedy, the same policy supports the granting of the remedy. . . . See [UCC] § 2–204(3) and Comment. Thus the degree of certainty required may be affected by the dispute which arises and by the remedy sought. Courts decide the disputes before them, not other hypothetical disputes which might have arisen. . . .

Illustrations:

1. A agrees to sell and B to buy goods for $2,000, $1,000 in cash and the "balance on installment terms over a period of two years," with a provision for liquidated damages. If it is found that both parties manifested an intent to conclude a binding agreement, the indefiniteness of the quoted language does not prevent the award of the liquidated damages.

2. A agrees to sell and B to buy a specific tract of land for $10,000, $4,000 in cash and $6,000 on mortgage. A agrees to obtain the mortgage loan for B or, if unable to do so, to lend B the amount, but the terms of loan are not stated, although both parties manifest an intent to conclude a binding agreement. The contract is too indefinite to support a decree of specific performance against B, but B may obtain such a decree if he offers to pay the full price in cash. . . .

e. Indefinite price. Where the parties manifest an intention not to be bound unless the amount of money to be paid by one of them is fixed or agreed and it is not fixed or agreed there is no contract. [UCC] § 2–305(4). Where they intend to conclude a contract for the sale of goods, however, and the price is not settled, the price is a reasonable price at the time of delivery [in the circumstances stated in UCC 2–305(1)]. . . . Similar principles apply to contracts for the rendition of service. . . .

Illustrations:

7. A promises to sell and B to buy goods "at cost plus a nice profit." The quoted words strongly indicate that the parties have not yet concluded a bargain.

8. A promises to do a specified piece of work and B promises to pay a price to be thereafter mutually agreed. The provision for future agreement as to price strongly indicates that the parties do not intend to be bound. If they manifest an intent to be bound, the price is a reasonable price at the time for doing the work.

Micro Capital Investors, Inc. v. Broyhill Furniture Industries, Inc.

Court of Appeals of North Carolina, 2012.
728 S.E.2d 376.

ELMORE, JUDGE. . . . This case revolves around a furniture manufacturing plant and warehouse in Lenoir. The plant, known as the Harper Plant, occupies approximately 333,677 square feet. The warehouse, known as the Harper Warehouse, shares a wall with the Harper Plant but is much smaller, occupying approximately 80,000 square feet. In addition to a wall, the Plant and Warehouse share a heating system, which is at the center of this dispute. Two wood-burning boilers generated heat for both the Plant and the Warehouse using wood waste, a byproduct of the furniture manufacturing process. The boilers are located in the Plant and send steam to pipes and radiators in the Warehouse. They also provide the steam energy needed to operate the equipment used to manufacture furniture in the Plant.

In 2005, The Woodsmiths Company (Woodsmiths) sought to buy the Harper Plant from defendant after a hurricane destroyed its primary manufacturing facility in Florida. However, Woodsmiths could not obtain financing for the purchase, so it arranged for another company, The

Whittier Group, Inc. (Whittier), to purchase the plant and manufacturing equipment and then lease them to Woodsmiths. Whittier and defendant agreed on the terms of purchase and executed an Agreement of Sale (Agreement) on 31 October 2005; however, the deal fell through because the parties could not agree on how to split the cost of heating the Plant and the Warehouse, which would remain occupied by defendant and was not part of the transaction.

The parties continued to negotiate, and Woodsmiths brought in a second investor, plaintiff, at Whittier's insistence. On 8 November 2005, plaintiff, defendant, and Whittier executed an Amendment to Agreement of Sale (Amendment), which amended the Agreement to provide that Whittier would purchase the Plant's machinery and equipment and plaintiff would purchase the Plant's real property. The Amendment replaced the "Purchase Price" section of the Agreement with new language, which eliminated a financing provision and required the full purchase price to be paid by check at the closing. The Amendment also included these provisions:

> 3. *Continuing Effect.* Except as expressly modified by the terms and provisions of this Amendment, each and every term and provision of the Agreement is unchanged and shall continue in full force and effect. . . .
>
> 6. *Terms.* Except as otherwise set forth herein, all capitalized terms utilized in this Amendment shall have the meaning ascribed to those same terms in the Agreement.

After the Amendment was executed and the sale completed, plaintiff entered into a lease with Woodsmiths for the use of the Plant. Under the lease, Woodsmiths agreed to pay for all utilities, including heat. Woodsmiths also entered into a lease with Whittier for the use of the Plant equipment. Although the lease agreement itself is not in the appellate record, paid invoices show that Woodsmiths paid Whittier $40,000 per month for use of the equipment. Defendant continued to occupy the Warehouse.

The Agreement included a number of exhibits and schedules, including Exhibit D, the post-closing schedule. According to section 2 of the Agreement, "Machinery and Equipment Sold and Purchased," Exhibit D dictated that defendant remove the machinery and equipment listed in Exhibit C "prior to Closing or after Closing according to" the post-closing schedule, which was attached and incorporated by reference. Exhibit D included the following two sections, which address the heating system:

> 9. Seller shall assist Buyer in determining the best course of action to heat the Premises over the winter. Should Buyer and Seller agree that converting one or both boilers to natural gas capable is most advantageous, Seller shall assist Buyer in retrofitting a natural gas fired burner to one or both boilers in the Premises. If another solution is selected, Seller will assist Buyer

> in purchasing and installing such a solution. Notwithstanding anything contained herein to the contrary, Seller shall not be obligated to pay any part of the expense incurred to purchase, install, retrofit or modify any equipment or facilities under this paragraph.
>
> 10. The Leased Warehouse does not contain its own heating system and will need to be serviced by whatever heating system is decided upon for the Premises. Buyer shall supply sufficient heat from the heating system in the Premises to adequately heat the Leased Warehouse from the date of Closing to the date Seller no longer continues to rent the Leased Warehouse. Buyer may charge Seller for one-fourth (1/4th) of the total heating bill for the Premises and the Leased Warehouse, subject to adjustment in the event either party's operations require more heat than currently anticipated. Buyer agrees to sign such further documents as Seller requires at Closing to evidence the agreement in this paragraph.

Despite the language in section 10 of Exhibit D (Section 10), defendant was not charged for heating the Warehouse until 25 February 2009, when Woodsmiths sent a letter to defendant seeking $384,342 to compensate Woodsmiths for one quarter of the heating expenses generated during the previous four winters (a total of $1,537,369). The letter, written by Michael Munoz, included the following relevant language:

> In November 2005 I purchased from Broyhill Furniture Industries Inc. the Harper plant located at 418 NW Prospect St., Lenoir, NC. As part of that purchase, my company was required to provide heat to the co-located warehouse for the duration of Broyhill's lease of that facility. I have been providing heat over the last 4 seasons per Exhibit D, Section 10. Section 10 allows me to charge Broyhill 25% of my heating costs. I have never invoiced Broyhill for these costs and I wish to do so now.

Defendant paid $50,000 in response to this demand and offered to pay additional funds for heat when it received proof that heat was actually supplied to the Warehouse. On 31 October 2009, Munoz sent a second letter to defendant with an updated cost breakdown showing that defendant's share of Woodsmiths's heating expense was now $459,968. Defendant refused to pay because it was never provided with sufficient documentation to support Woodsmiths's contention that heat was supplied to the Warehouse or the costs associated with generating that heat.

Plaintiff then brought this lawsuit on 30 December 2009, suing defendant for breach of contract. Plaintiff's claim hinges on Section 10, which it claims requires defendant to "be responsible" for one quarter of the "total heating bill" for the Plant and Warehouse. In its complaint, plaintiff alleged that it had supplied heat to the Warehouse since November 2005 and had invoiced defendant for $474,302, although it did not include that invoice with the complaint or within the appellate record.

On 29 November 2010, defendant moved for summary judgment, arguing that the agreement was unenforceable because the term "total heating bill" was ambiguous and the parties had never reached an agreement about what elements would properly comprise the "total heating bill." . . .

Plaintiff argues that defendant's obligation under Section 10 is enforceable, while defendant counters that Section 10 is not enforceable because the term "total heating bill" is too indefinite, demonstrating that there was no meeting of the minds as to that essential term. We agree with defendant.

> There is no contract unless the parties assent to the same thing in the same sense. A contract is the agreement of two minds—the coming together of two minds on a thing done or to be done. A contract, express or implied, executed or executory, results from the concurrence of minds of two or more persons, and its legal consequences are not dependent upon the impressions or understandings of one alone of the parties to it. It is not what either thinks, but what both agree.

Williams v. Jones, 322 N.C. 42, 49, 366 S.E.2d 433, 438 (1988). "[I]n order to constitute a valid and enforceable contract there must be an agreement of the parties upon the essential terms of the contract, definite within themselves or capable of being made definite." Brawley v. Brawley, 87 N.C.App. 545, 549, 361 S.E.2d 759, 762 (1987). "[A] contract will not be held unenforceable because of uncertainty if the intent of the parties can be determined from the language used, construed with reference to the circumstances surrounding the making of the contract, and its terms reduced to a reasonable certainty." Id.

Under other circumstances, the term "total heating bill" might be definite, but under these circumstances, it was not. Because of the unusual heating system—wood-burning boilers that run on wood waste, a byproduct of the manufacturing process that takes place within the Plant, which also power the manufacturing equipment—there was no "heating bill" from a third party like the power company. Instead, Woodsmiths generated invoices that were broken down into the following components: direct consumable expense, utilities, boiler dust machinery rents/leases, labor, and fire and boiler insurance. A former Broyhill employee stated that he was surprised by these charges and, in his view, "the only charges that should be on a heating bill for the property would be fuel, boiler operator wages, and a nominal fee for utilities." It is clear from the record that, before the Amendment was executed, the parties discussed at length how the properties were heated and whether plaintiff should install a different heating system, given the general decline in furniture manufacturing and thus an associated decline in the availability of wood waste. However, from both Munoz's testimony and the affidavits submitted by defendant's employees, the parties never agreed what components would constitute a "total heating bill" and, thus, the term was too indefinite to be enforceable. Accordingly, we affirm the order of the superior court granting defendant's motion for summary judgment. . . .

Plaintiff next argues that the trial court abused its discretion by denying its motion to amend its complaint. We disagree. . . .

The substance of the . . . amendment was to add a claim for *quantum meruit,* a claim that could have been argued in the alternative in the original complaint or in the first amended complaint based on the information known to plaintiff at the time. At the motion hearing, the only explanation offered by plaintiff for the delay was that the motion was a response to defendant's summary judgment motion; plaintiff wanted to present an alternative theory of recovery "in case summary judgment was granted in favor of the defendant." However, plaintiff could have argued *quantum meruit* in the alternative before defendant moved for summary judgment, and plaintiff did not offer any explanation for its failure to do so. Accordingly, we cannot conclude that the trial court abused its discretion by denying the motion.

ERVIN, JUDGE, concurring in part and dissenting in part. . . . As I read the relevant contractual language, the parties clearly agreed that Plaintiff was obligated to provide adequate heat to the warehouse from the facilities that provided heat to the entire premises and that Defendant would pay one quarter of the "total heating bill" in return for the provision of that service. I also conclude that the expression "total heating bill," when read in light of the fact that there was no third party supply of heat to the premises, clearly makes reference to the cost incurred in providing the needed heat. At an absolute minimum, this understanding of the parties' contract is a reasonable construction of the relevant contractual language which the jury should be allowed to consider in the course of deciding this case. [T]he agreement between the parties can reasonably be construed to mean that the price to be paid for the heat supplied to the warehouse would be one-fourth of the cost incurred in connection with the provision of heat to the entire premises. As a result, the ultimate question before the Court is whether a provision requiring Defendant to pay one-fourth of the cost of providing heat to the premises is so vague as to be unenforceable. I do not believe that it is.

The "cost" of providing a particular service is, in essence, "an amount that has to be paid or spent to buy or obtain something." *New Oxford English Dictionary* 392 (3d ed. 2010). For that reason, I believe that the relevant contractual language requires Defendant to pay one-fourth of the amount that Plaintiff had to spend in order to provide heat to the premises in return for the provision of heat to the warehouse. Although the exact cost of heating the premises is not set out in the agreement, I believe that the cost of providing that service can, in fact, be calculated, with the cost incurred in heating the premises being nothing more than a question of fact that should be resolved by the trier of fact following the presentation of the parties' evidence. As a result, I do not believe that the price term at issue here is so vague as to be unenforceable and disagree with the Court's conclusion to the contrary.

The other arguments advanced in support of the result reached by the Court do not strike me as persuasive. The fact that the parties may not have discussed the specific components of the required cost determination in detail at the time that they executed the contract and now disagree over how the relevant cost should be calculated does not, in my view, suffice to show that the price term at issue here is so vague as to be unenforceable given that the applicable standard is a relatively clear one and given that the relevant amount can be calculated using the applicable standard. Similarly, the fact that the parties appear to have contemplated a possible change in the manner in which the premises were to be heated does not mean that there was no "total heating bill" associated with the operation of whatever facilities were actually used to provide needed heat. Furthermore, the fact that "Buyer agrees to sign such further documents as Seller requires at Closing to evidence the agreement in this paragraph" does not establish that the price term is unenforceable given that the standard set out in the contract is, in my view, sufficiently clear and given that there is no evidence that Defendant ever requested that additional documents be executed at or before the time that the underlying transaction closed. Although Defendant contends that the relevant contractual language is nothing more than an unenforceable agreement to agree, the language in question clearly requires Plaintiff to provide adequate heat to Defendant and requires Defendant to pay one quarter of the cost of heating the premises in return for the provision of that service. The fact that the parties agreed to make an "adjustment in the event either party's operations require more heat than currently anticipated" does not strike me as relevant given the absence of any indication that either party ever requested that an adjustment of the type contemplated by this language be made. In addition, the fact that heat was provided to the premises using a system that served a number of different purposes, while perhaps adding an additional layer of complexity to the cost calculation, does not suffice to render the relevant price term unenforceable given the finder of fact's ability to make appropriate cost allocations. Finally, the fact that Plaintiff's calculation of the cost of providing heat to the premises has "evolved" and includes, at least in my opinion, certain costs that are not encompassed within the price term set out in the contract does not render the price term unenforceable given the parties' ability to present evidence concerning what is and is not a proper component of the cost of providing heat and the ability of the trier of fact to determine what is and is not a proper component of the cost of heating the premises. Thus, none of the arguments advanced in support of the result reached by the Court strike me as persuasive. . . .

NOTE: INDEFINITENESS AND PROMISSORY ESTOPPEL

The doctrine of "indefiniteness" may be linked to the other core ideas of classical contract doctrine. Requiring definiteness gives every legally enforceable promise a yes/no, on/off character. Recall the facts of *Embry*. If you believe conduct is insufficient to form a contract, then the boss is free to fire the worker several months after their conversation, even if the worker has given up the chance to move elsewhere. But if you think there is a contract, the boss is liable the second after the conversation takes place to the full extent of expectation damages, regardless of whether the worker has relied in any way.

Someone sympathetic to the idea of promissory estoppel might take a different view of indefiniteness. The liability of one person to another should not turn sharply on a single, discontinuous moment. There should not be a single moment at which something someone said shifted from being utterly unenforceable to being enforceable to the full value of the promise. It makes far more sense to hold people to their words to the extent that others reasonably rely on them. The question of liability should not turn on whether the promise was sufficiently definite. We should assess the conduct of the parties and establish relative culpability as we do with other sorts of injury. The more definite the promise, the more one can reasonably rely on it, but the definitiveness of the promise is not itself a touchstone. Consider this line of thought in reading the next case.

Blinn v. Beatrice Community Hosp. and Health Center, Inc.

Supreme Court of Nebraska, 2006.
270 Neb. 809, 708 N.W.2d 235.

GERRARD, J. . . . Robert Blinn . . . was fired by his employer, Beatrice Community Hospital and Health Center, Inc. (Beatrice). Blinn sued Beatrice for breach of contract and promissory estoppel. . . .

Blinn testified that in June 2002, he had received a job offer from a Kansas hospital. The Kansas job would have been at a larger hospital and would have offered more responsibility and income potential than Blinn's job of executive director, medical staff development, at Beatrice. It was Blinn's understanding that the Kansas offer was for a position that Blinn could keep until he retired. Blinn was 67 years old at the time he received the offer. Blinn then went to the Beatrice administrator, Larry Emerson, seeking assurances about the permanency of Blinn's position with Beatrice, and drafted a resignation letter he intended to submit to Beatrice unless he received full assurances that Beatrice wanted him to stay. Blinn said:

> Well, I went in and asked him if I could visit, and I shut the door in his office and handed him this letter, and he read it, and he told me that he did not want me to leave. He assured me that I was doing a good job, and most importantly, he said, "Bob, we've got at least five more years of work to do." And I left his office feeling fully assured and fully confident that he had no negatives, 'cause I gave him total opportunity here to tell me.
>
> I left his office feeling he wanted me there, that he wanted me to stay there and that I should stay there and that we had plenty of work to do and that I could get the job done.

Blinn also asked for Emerson's permission to talk to the chairman of Beatrice's board of directors to seek similar assurances. Blinn testified that the chairman of the board said: "We want you to stay," and I said, "Well, it's really important to me, because whether I stay here or whether I go to [the Kansas hospital], I want it to be the last job I ever have," and [the chairman] assured me he wanted me to stay there and I could stay there until I retired.

However, Blinn was asked to resign by Beatrice in January 2003, and his employment with Beatrice was terminated in February. . . .

We turn first to Blinn's breach of contract claim, which rests on Blinn's contention that the representations made to him by his superiors were sufficient to modify his status as an at-will employee. When employment is not for a definite term and there are no contractual, statutory, or constitutional restrictions upon the right of discharge, an employer may lawfully discharge an employee whenever and for whatever cause it chooses. Oral representations may, standing alone, constitute a promise sufficient to create contractual terms which can modify the at-will status of an employee. However, the burden of proving the existence of an employment contract and all the facts essential to the cause of action is upon the person who asserts the contract.

The question is whether the assurances allegedly given to Blinn were sufficiently definite in form to constitute an offer of a unilateral contract. The language which forms the basis of an alleged employment contract, whether oral or written, must constitute an offer definite in form which is communicated to the employee, and the offer must be accepted and consideration furnished for its enforceability. Under those circumstances, the employee's retention of employment constitutes acceptance of the offer of a unilateral contract because by continuing to stay on the job although free to leave, the employee supplies the necessary consideration for the job.

The question under such circumstances is whether the employer manifests a clear intent to make a promise as an offer of employment other than employment at will, and to be bound by it, so as to justify an employee in understanding that a commitment has been made. Whether a proposal is meant to be an offer for a unilateral contract is determined by the outward manifestations of the parties, not by their subjective intentions. There must be a meeting of the minds or a binding mutual understanding between the parties to the contract.

Here, even viewed in the light most favorable to Blinn, the assurances offered to him were not sufficiently definite in form to constitute an offer of a unilateral contract. The statement that "we've got at least five more years of work to do" is not a clear offer of definite employment and does not manifest an intent to create a unilateral contract. . . .

An employee's subjective understanding of job security is insufficient to establish an implied contract of employment to that effect, and the record here does not establish sufficient evidence to conclude that any employee of Beatrice intended to offer a contract of employment on terms other than employment at will.

For that reason, the Court of Appeals erred in concluding that there was a genuine issue of material fact with respect to Blinn's breach of contract claim. . . .

Recovery on a theory of promissory estoppel is based upon the principle that injustice can be avoided only by enforcement of a promise. Under the doctrine of promissory estoppel, a promise which the promisor should reasonably expect to induce action or forbearance is binding if injustice can be avoided only by enforcement of the promise.

Under Nebraska law, the doctrine of promissory estoppel does not require that the promise giving rise to the cause of action must meet the requirements of an offer that would ripen into a contract if accepted by the promisee. Simply stated, there is no requirement of "definiteness" in an action based upon promissory estoppel. Instead of requiring reasonable definiteness, promissory estoppel requires only that reliance be reasonable and foreseeable.

Here, we agree with the determination made by the Court of Appeals that there is a genuine issue of material fact with respect to Blinn's promissory estoppel claim. While the statements allegedly made by Blinn's superiors were insufficiently definite to offer a contract of employment on terms other than employment at will, there is a genuine issue of material fact as to whether Blinn was promised terms of employment that could reasonably have been expected to induce Blinn to forgo the job opportunity in Kansas of which he had informed Beatrice. Under the circumstances, when considering the lesser requirement that Nebraska law imposes on a promise that forms the basis of a promissory estoppel cause of action, we conclude that the district court erred in not finding a genuine issue of material fact. . . .

Under the *Restatement* view, a "promise" for purposes of promissory estoppel must meet the same requirements as a "promise" for purposes of contract formation. Generally speaking, under the *Restatement*, when a promise is made, but a contract is not formed because of a lack of consideration, reasonable reliance by the promisee can still render the promisor liable for breach of the promise. In short, analysis of the promise is the same as that for a contract, except that the promisee's reliance on the promise replaces the missing consideration.

But in Nebraska, we have rejected that view. As noted earlier, we have held that there is no requirement of "definiteness" in an action based upon promissory estoppel. Rosnick v. Dinsmore, 235 Neb. 738, 457 N.W.2d 793 (1990). In *Rosnick*, we departed from the Restatement view that a promise for estoppel purposes requires the same definiteness as a promise for contract purposes. In Whorley v. First Westside Bank, 240 Neb. 975, 485 N.W.2d 578 (1992), we expressly considered the Restatement view, cited conflicting authority, and reaffirmed our holding in *Rosnick.* Contrary to the Restatement view, the law in Nebraska is that a promissory estoppel action may be based on an alleged promise that is insufficiently definite to form a contract, but upon which the promisee's reliance is reasonable and foreseeable. The difference between contract and promissory estoppel, then, is that a contract requires that the promisor intend to make a binding promise—a binding mutual understanding or "meeting of the minds"—while promissory estoppel requires only that the promisee's reliance on the promise be reasonable and foreseeable, even if the promisor did not intend to be bound. A promisor need not intend a promise to be binding in order to foresee that a promisee may reasonably rely on it.

. . . Because promissory estoppel does not require definiteness, an employer need not intend to contractually modify an employee's at-will employment in order for an employee to reasonably and foreseeably believe that his or her terms of employment have been changed and, therefore, act in reliance on that belief. Here, there is insufficient evidence to conclude that Beatrice intended to offer Blinn a unilateral contract. But there is sufficient evidence, if believed by the trier of fact, to conclude that Blinn reasonably and foreseeably relied on Beatrice's assurances of a fixed term of employment, and Beatrice breached that promise. There is a genuine issue of material fact to be decided. . . .

PART TWO

IDENTIFYING THE SUBSTANTIVE OBLIGATIONS OF THE PARTIES

INTRODUCTORY NOTE: THE LAW'S ROLE IN CREATING THE BARGAINING ENVIRONMENT AND FILLING THE GAPS

The first part of this book explored the origins and development of the three core principles of contract law identified at the end of the nineteenth century: (1) that those who fail to keep a legally enforceable promise are liable to pay expectation damages; (2) that only promises that are part of a bargained-for exchange are legally enforceable; and (3) that legally enforceable promises come into being at a particular moment in time, that moment at which, from an objective point of view, one party accepts the offer of the other. In this Part, we turn to the problem of establishing the terms of the bargain that the parties strike.

When parties bargain, they must understand the ground rules that the law puts in place. There are things each party can and cannot take for granted. As we shall see, parties do not have to disclose information that is equally accessible to both parties. A party cannot hold the other liable for omitting relevant information unless she obtains an affirmative representation that none is being withheld. But the bargaining environment is not one in which anything goes. Both parties have a duty to act in good faith. They must both be honest in fact and observe reasonable commercial standards of fair dealing. These background rules are the focus of the first section of Chapter 4.

The second section of Chapter 4 focuses on how courts go about understanding the undertakings of each of the parties. As we saw at the end of Chapter 3, courts will not make a contract when the parties have failed to do so. But many agreements that are sufficiently definite to be enforceable still have gaps that need to be filled. Judges must resort to a number of tools to identify the bargain that parties have reached. Even in the case of a large transaction in which parties hire sophisticated lawyers, ambiguities can never be eliminated entirely.

Although not formally embedded in the law, there are three heuristics that courts often use to flesh out enforceable bargains. Depending on the context, one or more of them may prove useful. The first of these is a resort to custom and usage of trade. Other things being equal, it is reasonable to suppose that parties to a particular contract agreed to do business in the same way that reputable merchants in the same trade usually conduct their affairs. When a merchant agrees to sell shoes, it is reasonable to think she undertakes to provide shoes that pass without objection in the trade under the contract description. See UCC 2–314.

The second heuristic, commonly associated with Oliver Wendell Holmes, is one that we saw in *Globe Refining* in Chapter 1. See p. 97 supra. To discover the unspoken terms of the contract, the judge asks what bargain the parties would have reached if they had thought about it. As Justice Holmes put it:

> The extent of liability . . . should be worked out on terms which it fairly may be presumed he would have assented to if they had been presented to his mind.

It is implausible, for instance, to think that someone who promises to transport a package for a small sum would agree to pay enormous damages for a delay for which she is not at fault. She is simply not being paid enough to bear such a risk.

The third heuristic, which is a variation on the second, is commonly associated with Richard Posner. To identify the bargain, one starts with the idea that commercial parties want to maximize the benefits of trade. They will therefore allocate risks to the party best able to bear them. So, if it is much easier for factory to have a back-up generator than it is for the power company to ensure that service will never go down, then the power company is liable only for the losses that would have arisen if there were such a back-up generator. The risk for damages that arise from not having a generator fall on the factory.

Each of these gap-filling heuristics has conspicuous weaknesses. Customs may be hard to pin down. Moreover, there may be differences between what parties do in ordinary circumstances and what they would commit to doing in unusual ones. Stores, for instance, might ordinarily accept returns, but this does not mean that it makes sense to bind storeowners to do so under all circumstances.

Holmes's heuristic requires imagining a world in which bargaining is possible. Such a world is necessarily different from our own. It may be so different that asking what parties would do may not tell us what makes sense for parties in our world. Moreover, trying to envision the nature of a world in which parties have bargained explicitly over terms is often an unworkable task . A judge who is told to discover the implicit bargain might ends up imposing terms based on nothing more than her own unfettered intuitions.

The third heuristic has similar pitfalls. Weighing costs and benefits often fails to take into account the other important aspects of the situation. The calculus of weighing costs and benefits may give the judge a false illusion of objectivity and precision. Those who invoke these tools without reflection may paper over difficulties that would appear if the problem were examined with situation sense and attention to nuance.

Notwithstanding these weaknesses, judges in one way or another often rely on these heuristics (sometimes explicitly; often not) to fill in gaps in the parties' bargain. Depending on the circumstances, one may prove more useful than the other.

The third section of Chapter 4 explores formal rules that go beyond merely trying to identify what the parties promised. They impose limits on the bargain, quite apart from what the parties intended. These rules, like any formal rules, are artificial. When formal rules are applied, some bargains that parties actually struck are not enforced. For example, the parol evidence rule provides that, when the parties create a writing and the writing itself says that it reflects the entire agreement of the parties, a court will not look beyond the writing itself. It will ignore evidence that parties in fact reached some other bargain. It will enforce the written bargain, even if there is compelling evidence that the actual agreement included different terms.

As applied to any particular case, formal rules are necessarily unsatisfactory. They force the factfinder to put on blinders. But formal rules can, at least in theory, offer benefits to contracting parties as a general matter. Lon Fuller identified some of them in the seminal article *Consideration and Form*, see p. 242 supra in Chapter 2. In particular, rules can serve certain types of functions.

A rule can serve an *evidentiary* function. If one announces a rule that requires the factfinder to look to a written document, if one exists, and give it special weight, parties will put in more effort when creating them. A more carefully written document will, in turn, make the factfinding process more accurate. When courts take writings seriously, parties will as well.

Formal rules can also serve a *channeling* function. Parties will find it easier to understand their rights and obligations when they know that their written contract definitively establishes them. This is particularly important in cases between corporate actors in deals that last a long time. The people who perform the contract may come on the scene long after those who drafted it have left. It is easier for parties to understand their own obligations as well as those of others if they can rely on what the written agreement says. They do not need to track down people who left the company long before to know what it is they are supposed to do and what they can demand from their contracting opposite.

Finally, formal rules can, although it seems counter-intuitive, serve a *shaping* function by altering the environment in which parties bargain with each other in a way that, in theory at least, provides benefits. When parties know that they are bound only to what is written, they can approach their negotiations differently. They are free to float trial balloons without fearing that a suggestion that once was put forward will later be found to be part of the bargain even though the negotiations ultimately took a different path. Whether formal rules can in fact bring such benefits in practice as well as in theory is the focus of the third section of Chapter 4.

The final parts of the chapter focus on sorting out the rights between the parties when circumstances prove to be radically different from what either thought at the time of their original bargain. Both parties, perhaps, thought that the statue was centuries old—then it is found to be fake. Alternatively, both may think something—a chair, a desk—to be an ordinary piece of furniture and it turns out to be a rare antique. On a larger scale, conditions might change unexpectedly. The theater at which the performance was supposed to take place burns down; extreme weather disrupts normal operations. Contract law must have a way to resolve disputes when the parties find themselves in circumstances so at odds with their original understanding that the deal they struck may no longer make sense.

The second and last chapter of this Part—Chapter 5—focuses on conditions. In addition to identifying the promises parties make to one another, courts must also identify the conditions under which parties are obliged to keep their promises and those that release their obligation. For example, each party's obligation to perform might depend on the other party performing as well. Performance by one party may be a condition to performance by the other. Such a condition gives the innocent party an additional option in the face of breach. The innocent party can always hold someone who breaks a promise responsible for the breach, but she might instead (or in addition) prefer to walk away from the deal entirely. Rather than accept a defective performance with a price adjustment that reflects expectation damages, she might want to reject it entirely.

CHAPTER 4

IDENTIFYING THE BARGAIN

SECTION 1. TERMS OF ENGAGEMENT

INTRODUCTORY NOTE

Contract law creates an environment in which bargaining takes place. But this bargaining is not entirely free-wheeling. Background rules are needed with respect to every agreement. At a minimum, virtually every legal system insists that merchants do not lie to one other. But this still leaves much unclear. The case that follows, decided by the Supreme Court in the wake of the War of 1812, puts in place one of the most basic background rules.

Laidlaw v. Organ

Supreme Court of the United States, 1817.
15 U.S. 178.

[Plaintiff Organ] filed his petition . . . in the court below, stating, that on the 18th day of February, 1815, he purchased of [defendant Laidlaw] 111 hogsheads of tobacco, as appeared by the copy of a bill of parcels annexed, and that the same were delivered to him by the said Laidlaw & Co., and that he was in the lawful and quiet possession of the said tobacco, when, on the 20th day of the said month, the said Laidlaw & Co., by force, and of their own wrong, took possession of the same, and unlawfully withheld the same from the petitioner, notwithstanding he was at all times, and still was, ready to do and perform all things on his part stipulated to be done and performed in relation to said purchase, and had actually tendered to the said Laidlaw & Co. bills of exchange for the amount of the purchase money, agreeably to the said contract. . . . Wherefore the petition prayed that the said Laidlaw & Co. might be cited to appear and answer to his plaint, and that judgment might be rendered against them for his damages, [etc.] . . .

[T]he cause was tried by a jury, who returned the following verdict, to wit: "The jury find for [the buyer Organ], for the tobacco named in the petition, without damages, payable as per contract." Whereupon the court rendered judgment "that [Organ] recover of [Laidlaw] the said 111 hogsheads of tobacco . . . and ordered, that the marshal deliver the said tobacco to [Organ], and that he have execution for his costs aforesaid, upon [Organ's] depositing in this court his bills of exchange for the amount of the purchase money. . . ."

[Laidlaw] filed the following bill of exceptions, to wit: . . . [O]n the night of the 18th of February, 1815, Messrs. Livingston, White, and Shepherd brought from the British fleet the news that a treaty of peace had been signed at Ghent by the American and British commissioners, contained in a letter from Lord Bathurst to the Lord Mayor of London, published in the British newspapers, and that Mr. White caused the same to be made public in a handbill on Sunday morning, 8 o'clock, the 19th of February, 1815, and that the brother of Mr. Shepherd, one of these gentlemen, and who was interested in one-third of the profits of the purchase set forth in [Organ's] petition, had, on Sunday morning, the 19th of February, 1815, communicated said news to [Organ]; that [Organ], on receiving said news, called on Francis Girault, (with whom he had been bargaining for the tobacco mentioned in the petition, the evening previous,) said Francis Girault being one of the said house of trade of Peter Laidlaw & Co., soon after sunrise on the morning of Sunday, the 19th of February, 1815, before he had heard said news. Said Girault asked if there was any news which was calculated to enhance the price or value of the article about to be purchased; and that the said purchase was then and there made, and the bill of parcels annexed to the plaintiff's petition delivered to [Organ] between 8 and 9 o'clock in the morning of that day; and that in consequence of said news the value of said article had risen from 30 to 50 per cent. There being no evidence that [Organ] had asserted or suggested any thing to the said Girault, calculated to impose upon him with respect to said news, and to induce him to think or believe that it did not exist; and it appearing that the said Girault, when applied to, on the next day, Monday, the 20th of February, 1815, on behalf of [Organ], for an invoice of said tobacco, did not then object to the said sale, but promised to deliver the invoice to [Organ] in the course of the forenoon of that day; the court charged the jury to find for [Organ]. . . .

MARSHALL, C.J. The question in this case is, whether the intelligence of extrinsic circumstances, which might influence the price of the commodity, and which was exclusively within the knowledge of the vendee, ought to have been communicated by him to the vendor? The court is of opinion that he was not bound to communicate it. It would be difficult to circumscribe the contrary doctrine within proper limits, where the means of intelligence are equally accessible to both parties. But at the same time, each party must take care not to say or do any thing tending to impose upon the other. The court thinks that the absolute instruction of the judge was erroneous, and that the question, whether any imposition was practised by the vendee upon the vendor ought to have been submitted to the jury. For these reasons the judgment must be reversed. . . .

NOTE: NONDISCLOSURE AND CONCEALMENT

When Chief Justice Marshall says that those in Organ's position must take care not "to impose upon the other," he is using the word "impose" as it was used in the eighteenth and early nineteenth century. At that time, "impose" meant to cheat or otherwise deceive through representations that were false. Chief Justice Marshall is holding that, even though Organ had no affirmative duty to disclose, there needs to be a jury trial to determine whether Organ's conduct was deceptive. The jury needs to decide whether Organ's reaction when asked whether he had news that would affect the price was, in the words of Laidlaw's lawyer, "equivalent to a false answer, and as much calculated to deceive as the communication of the most fabulous intelligence."

In finding that Organ could profit from his knowledge of the peace treaty, Chief Justice Marshall observes that the news about the end of the war was "equally accessible" to both parties. Courts commonly find such accessibility decisive in nondisclosure cases, but determining what information is equally accessible to both parties is not always straightforward. Indeed, *Laidlaw* itself illustrates this point. Organ learned that the war was over before anyone else, not through extra diligence on his part, but rather through inside knowledge. The brother of his business partner was the aide-de-camp to the commander of naval defenses in New Orleans, and he had been among those whom Andrew Jackson sent to the British to negotiate the exchange of prisoners and the return of escaped slaves. While there, he learned that a treaty had been signed and that the war was over. The brother conveyed this information to Organ, who then tried to trade on this information. Far from acquiring "equally accessible" information through careful diligence, Organ acquired knowledge of the war's end through his own private channel with a government official. This aspect of the case is set out in Joshua Kaye, Disclosure, Information, The Law of Contracts, and the Mistaken Use of *Laidlaw v. Organ*, 79 Miss. L.J. 577 (2010).

We must also confront the issue that required a remand in *Organ*. Even after we settle upon how much needs to be disclosed in any context, we still need a way to understand what counts as a misrepresentation. What constitutes "fraud" in any context turns on what is said and what is left unsaid. Misrepresentations include not only outright lying, but also behavior and actions that are misleading. In some environments, an answer that is technically completely accurate may nevertheless constitute a misrepresentation. Consider the apocryphal advertising slogan promoting tuna in the face of strong demand for salmon, "Guaranteed not to turn pink in the can." This is a misrepresentation to the extent it would lead a reasonable person to believe that salmon turns pink only after it is canned.

Johnson v. Healy

Supreme Court of Connecticut, 1978.
176 Conn. 97, 405 A.2d 54.

PETERS, J. This case arises out of the sale of a new one-family house by its builder, the defendant John J. Healy, to the plaintiff, Ronald K. Johnson. The plaintiff bought the house, located in Naugatuck, in 1965, for $17,000. Between 1968 and 1971, the house settled in such a way as to cause major displacements in various foundation walls, and substantial damage to the sewer lines. In 1971, the plaintiff instituted this law suit alleging misrepresentation and negligence on the part of the defendant builder-vendor. The court below found for the plaintiff on the claims of misrepresentation, for the defendant on the claims of negligence, and assessed damages. Both parties have appealed. . . .

The claims of misrepresentation are based on [facts] amply supported by the evidence below. As part of the negotiations leading to the contract of sale of the house, the plaintiff inquired about the quality of its construction. The defendant replied that the house was made of the best material, that he had built it, and that there was nothing wrong with it. These representations were relied upon by the plaintiff. . . . The damage which the house sustained because of its uneven settlement was due to improper fill which had been placed on the lot beneath the building at some time before the defendant bought the lot, as a building lot, in 1963. On the basis of these findings, the trial court concluded that the defendant had made an express warranty coextensive with the doctrine of implied warranty of workmanship and habitability in cases involving the sale of new homes by a builder. . . .

The defendant assigns as error the trial court's conclusion that defendant bore responsibility for a condition of which he had no knowledge, actual or constructive. The trial court found that defendant's representations, although innocent, amounted to an express warranty of workmanlike construction and fitness for habitation. Since those representations reasonably induced reliance in the purchase of the house, the defendant was held liable despite the absence of written warranties concerning the fitness or condition of the home in the contract of sale or the deed of conveyance.

The scope of liability for innocent misrepresentation has varied with time and with context, in American law generally and in this court. Traditionally, no cause of action lay in contract for damages for innocent misrepresentation; if the plaintiff could establish reliance on a material innocent misstatement, he could sue for rescission, and avoid the contract, but he could not get affirmative relief. . . . In tort, the basis of responsibility, although at first undifferentiated, was narrowed, at the end of the nineteenth century, to intentional misconduct, and only gradually expanded, in this century, to permit recovery in damages for negligent misstatements. Prosser, Torts (4th Ed. 1971) § 107. At the same time, liability in warranty, that curious hybrid of tort and contract law, became firmly established. . . . In contracts for the sale of tangible chattels, express warranty encompasses material representations which are false, without regard to the state of mind or the due care of the person making the representation. For breach of express warranty, the injured plaintiff has always been entitled to choose between rescission and damages. Although the description of warranty liability has undergone clarification in the [UCC], which supersedes the Uniform Sales Act, these basic remedial principles remain unaffected. At the same time, liability in tort, even for misrepresentations which are innocent, has come to be the emergent rule for transactions that involve a commercial exchange. See Restatement (Second), Torts § 524A (1958); Prosser, Torts (4th Ed. 1971) § 107.

In Connecticut law, strict liability for innocent misrepresentation in the sale of goods is well established. As long ago as Bartholomew v. Bushnell, 20 Conn. 271 (1850), this court held that "[i]f a man sell a horse to another, and expressly warrant him to be sound, the contract is broken, if the horse prove otherwise. The purchaser, in such case, relies *upon the contract*; and it is immaterial to him, whether the vendor did, or did not, know of the unsoundness of the horse. In either case, he is entitled to recover all the damages, which he has sustained." For similar reasons, strict liability for innocent misrepresentation was imposed in a construction contract in E. & F. Constr. Co. v. Stamford, 114 Conn. 250, 158 A. 551 (1932). In *Stamford*, the defendant's erroneous description of subsurface conditions materially affected the plaintiff's excavation costs. This court held the misrepresentation to be actionable, even though there was no allegation of fraud or bad faith, because it was false and misleading, "in analogy to the right of a vendee to elect to retain goods which are not as warranted, and to recover damages for the breach of warranty." Id., 258, 158 A. 553. *Stamford* quotes [from] 3 Williston, Contracts § 1512 (1920): " 'If a man makes a statement in regard to a matter upon which his hearer may reasonably suppose he has the means of information, . . . and the statement is made as part of a business transaction, or to induce action from which the speaker expects to gain an advantage, he should be held liable for the consequences of reliance upon his misstatement.' " Id., 259, 158 A. 554. *Bartholomew* and *Stamford* together make it clear that liability for innocent misrepresentation is not a novelty in this state, that such liability is based on principles of warranty, and that such warranty law is not confined to contracts for the sale of goods.

Extension of warranty liability for innocent misrepresentation to a builder-vendor who sells a new home is, as a matter of policy, consistent with the developing law of vendor and purchaser generally. In the not too distant past, it is true, *caveat emptor* dominated the law of real estate. . . . In this state, however, *caveat emptor* has not been allowed to stand in the way of imposition of liability for negligent misrepresentations. See Warman v. Delaney, 148 Conn. 469, 172 A.2d 188 (1961). . . . Furthermore, Scribner v. O'Brien, Inc., 169 Conn. 389, 363 A.2d 160 (1975), recognized the propriety of claims for negligence, express warranty, and, in dictum, implied warranty, and thus effectively and explicitly ended the role of *caveat emptor* in sales of new homes by builder-vendors.

[Here], as the trial court concluded, liability for innocent misrepresentation is entirely appropriate. Although the defendant vendor had built no houses other than this one, this information was not disclosed to the buyer until the sale had been concluded; the defendant had been otherwise engaged in the real estate business for about thirty years. Although indefinite, the defendant's statement that there was "nothing wrong" with the house could reasonably have been heard by the plaintiff as an assertion that the defendant had sufficient factual information to justify his general opinion about the quality of the house. In context, this statement of opinion could reasonably have induced reliance. . . .

The claims for negligence in construction depend upon a showing by plaintiff that defendant knew, or should have known, that the subsurface conditions of the building were substandard, and thus required special plans for the footings and the foundation of the house that he was building. The trial court found that defendant had no actual knowledge of the soil defects, a finding which plaintiff does not directly attack. The issue therefore is the defendant's constructive notice of the lot's instability despite its apparent content of standard bank run gravel. It is significant that the building inspector, who approved the construction plans, was found to have had no notice. At the time of this building project, test borings to determine soil suitability were not customary for residential construction. Although there was testimony which might have supported a different finding, the trial court was not bound to accept as persuasive even testimony that was not directly contradicted. . . . Its conclusion of absence of notice is amply supported by other evidence and must therefore stand. Without notice, the claims for negligence are unsustainable. . . .

The assessment of damages in the trial court was an award in the amount of $5000 for breach of warranties and not for negligence. The plaintiff attacks this award as inadequate, since it does not measure damages by the cost of repairs. The defendant attacks the award as excessive because it does not measure the difference between the value of the property as warranted and as sold.

The plaintiff's claim for damages was twofold: $882.50 for sewer repairs occasioned by the settling of the foundation which damaged the sewer line, and $27,150 as an estimate, procured in 1971, for the cost of constructing a new foundation. The court specifically found that the cost of replacing the foundation would in all likelihood exceed the value of the house, originally purchased for $17,000.

Apart from the sewer repair costs, plaintiff incurred, from 1965 to 1970, additional expenditures of $5112 in connection with the house. These expenses were largely, but not exclusively, incurred in making repairs. The trial court concluded that, since a substantial part of the $5112 was for repairs attributable to the faulty settlement of the house, he would allocate to damages an amount which, when added to the $882.50 sewer costs, would produce a total recovery of $5000. The court noted that, in late 1971, when plaintiff first complained to defendant about problems with the house, defendant offered to repurchase the property for the purchase price of $17,000 and the expense of repairs then represented by plaintiff to approximate $5000.

The general rule for measurement of damages upon breach of warranty is to award the prevailing party such compensation as will place him in the same position as he would have enjoyed had the property been as warranted. This is the general rule of contract law, and was discussed extensively, and applied to the sale of a new residential house, in Levesque v. D & M Builders, Inc., 170 Conn. 177, 365 A.2d 1216 (1976). *Levesque* involved a buyer who wanted to relocate a house misplaced on a building lot. This court refused to permit relocation costs of $10,800 to be awarded for breach of contract and warranty, when the original contract price had been $22,600. *Levesque* adopts a rule that limits damages to the diminished value of the building whenever the cost of repairs is dramatically larger than is the difference in value. Although the costs of repair may more precisely place the injured party in the same physical position as full performance, policy dictates limitation to diminution of value to avoid unreasonable economic waste. It is clear that *Levesque* forbids recovery of the costs of a new foundation in the case before us, since the price discrepancy between reconstruction cost and contract price is even larger than it was in *Levesque*. Moreover, *Levesque* involved a defendant whose default could hardly be characterized as innocent. Contract restraints are particularly appropriate when damages are awarded, as in this case, for misrepresentations which, though actionable, are totally innocent. See Hill, "Damages for Innocent Misrepresentation," 73 Colum. L. Rev. 679 (1973), and Hill, "Breach of Contract as a Tort," 74 Colum. L. Rev. 40 (1974). The trial court was therefore correct in refusing to measure damages by the $27,150 estimated to be required to replace the foundation.

The proper test for damages was the difference in value between the property had it been as represented and the property as it actually was. This standard is notoriously more difficult to apply than to state. Reasonable costs of repair may therefore sometimes furnish a reasonable approximation of diminished value. Richard v. A. Waldman & Sons, Inc., 155 Conn. 343, 232 A.2d 307 (1967). . . . Reliance expenses often serve as a surrogate for damages otherwise inaccessible to proof. See the classic articles, Fuller & Perdue, "The Reliance Interest in Contract Damages: 1," 46 Yale L.J. 52 (1936–1937), and Fuller & Perdue, "The Reliance Interest in Contract Damages: 2," 46 Yale L.J. 373 (1936–1937). The trial court's reference to the $5112 expended by plaintiff with regard to the house would have been an acceptable resource for the inquiry into diminution of value, if only the $5112 list had accurately distinguished between expenses for repairs and expenses for improvements. To the extent that reliance expenses are probative of losses incurred because of breach, they must be expenses demonstrably incident to breach. The tender of a particular sum by the defendant in negotiation of an aborted settlement is no more dispositive than is the plaintiff's unwillingness to agree to a rescission and to insist, as he had a right to do, on affirmative relief in damages.

Under these circumstances, the court's award of damages was in error, the judgment is set aside, and the case is remanded with direction to render judgment for the plaintiff to recover such damages as he may prove on a new trial limited to the issue of damages.

QUESTION

Suppose defendant knew of the "improper fill" but made no representations of any kind respecting the house or subsurface conditions and plaintiff asked no questions. Would defendant have a duty to disclose the soil defects?

Eytan v. Bach

374 A.2d 879 (D.C. App. 1977)

The purchasers of three paintings brought an action to recover the price of $157.50 paid to defendant, a retailer of antiques and second-hand furniture. The three paintings—the purchasers learned subsequently—were not original productions of unknown nineteenth-century artists, but were recent reproductions that had been placed in old frames (we are not told by whom). Plaintiffs had "inspected and touched" several paintings displayed in defendant's Georgetown shop, ultimately selecting the three in question, "because the brittleness of the material, cracks in the paint, discoloration, grease stains on the back, and punctures in the frame . . . led them to believe these particular items were old." It was conceded that defendant had made no express representation, either that the paintings were "originals or ancient." At trial, defendant insisted that the paintings, even though reproductions, were worth "considerably more" than plaintiffs had paid; he said that he had cut his prices in order to make the sale. The trial judge summarily dismissed the complaint upon finding "no controverted issues of material fact." Based on a "general knowledge of the economics of the locality," the average price paid for each of the paintings—approximately $50—was "a sufficiently small amount to put any purchaser on notice that he was not buying a legitimate antique original work of art." Plaintiffs appealed, urging that "because [they] had, in the course of their inspection, displayed such interest in indicia of age, it became the legal duty of the dealer to disclose the true facts before the sale was completed."

On appeal, the dismissal was affirmed. "[I]n certain circumstances, concealment of a 'material fact is as fraudulent as a positive direct misrepresentation.' " But this issue is not raised by the record here. "What the [lower] court [held] was that a purchaser who bought artificially aged copies of primitive paintings for the low unit prices upon which he and the dealer ultimately agreed, could not credibly assign as fraud the fact that the articles purchased turned out not to be vastly more valuable. . . . [T]he customer not having inquired as to whether the canvases were originals[,] we perceive no duty upon the part of the vendor to inform him of the obvious. If a customer went into a jewelry store and bought for $50 an item which looked like a diamond pendant set with pearls, it would plainly not be incumbent upon the sales clerk to warn the customer that what he had selected was a piece of costume jewelry with synthetic gems."

NOTE: CLASSIFYING MISREPRESENTATION

It is commonly understood that the tort of misrepresentation takes three forms—intentional ("deceit" at common law), negligent, and innocent. In Johnson v. Healy, the focus was on innocent misrepresentation, a representation made in blameless ignorance of its falsity. (Some courts speak of "equitable fraud," to make clear that proof that a statement was knowingly false is not required.) Nevertheless, the court's opinion included this statement: "In tort, the basis of responsibility, although at first undifferentiated, was narrowed, at the end of the nineteenth century, to intentional misconduct, and only gradually expanded, in this century, to permit recovery in damages for negligent misstatements." Considerable history underlies that statement. The main point is that there occurred a major relaxation of the element of scienter ("evil mind," intent to defraud) which was central to the common law action of deceit. For example, the absence of honest belief which is involved when a statement is made in complete ignorance of its truth or falsity (at the least, a "reckless" statement, because made with no concern about truth or falsity), was treated in many courts as equivalent to actual knowledge of falsity. Also, courts came to find fraud in a statement made as of one's own knowledge when that knowledge did not exist; such a representor was deemed to misstate the state of his knowledge as to the fact misrepresented. The element of the speaker's knowledge of the falsity was therefore allowed to substitute for the element of intent to defraud.

The result was that it became possible to award damages in what was called a deceit action where the representor's fault consisted essentially of negligence (perhaps even innocent ignorance of falsity). Emphasis on negligence or on mere falsity removed the need to show specific intent to defraud. The term "fraud" therefore could be used to describe both intentional and negligent misrepresentation, even though liability for the latter is understood to exist alongside and independently of the traditional liability in deceit. The problem of classification that developed in the first half of the twentieth century was not helped by the murkiness of language found in the decisions. The court in Florenzano v. Olson, 387 N.W.2d 168 (Minn. 1986), sought to sort out at least the major outlines of the problem:

> Because fraud, in its broadest form, can be understood to encompass actions that result from both deceit and negligence, the line between the two theories of culpability can sometimes disappear. . . . [A]n actionable misrepresentation requires proof either that the misrepresenter acted dishonestly or in bad faith, i.e., with fraudulent intent, or, alternatively, that the misrepresenter was negligent. . . . Fraud is distinguished from negligence by the element of scienter required. Fraud is an intentional tort and scienter is an essential element. . . . We have stated that a representation is

> made with fraudulent intent when it is known to be false or, in the alternative, when it is asserted as of the representer's own knowledge when he or she does not in fact know whether it is true or false. . . . This formula can be ambiguous. . . . The language of [the] cases, if read out of context, could blur the meaning of the term "fraudulent intent" such that it is indistinguishable from the failure to use reasonable care required to prove liability in negligence. . . .
>
> A misrepresentation is made negligently when the misrepresenter has not discovered or communicated certain information that the ordinary person in his or her position would have discovered or communicated. Proof of the subjective state of the misrepresenter's mind, whether by direct evidence or by inference, is not needed to prove negligence. [This] is proved by measuring one's conduct against an objective standard of reasonable care or competence. In [this state], one making representations is held to this duty of care only when supplying information, either for the guidance of others in the course of a transaction in which one has a pecuniary interest, or in the course of one's business, profession, or employment. [We thus] adopt the [Rest.2d Torts § 552] definition of negligent misrepresentation.

As the reference to § 552 of the Rest.2d of Torts indicates, liability for negligent misrepresentation is usually more restricted—narrower in scope—than that for fraudulent misrepresentation. Also, in many courts, a plaintiff's proofs of negligent misrepresentation are measured by the usual standard applied in civil actions (a preponderance of the evidence), not the heightened standard of proof ("clear and convincing") typically found in fraud actions.

Universal Health Services, Inc. v. United States

Supreme Court of the United States, 2017.
136 S.Ct. 1989.

THOMAS, JUSTICE. [Yarushka Rivera, a teenage beneficiary of Massachusetts' Medicaid program, received counseling services for several years at Arbour Counseling Services, a satellite mental health facility owned and operated by a subsidiary of petitioner Universal Health Services, Inc. She had an adverse reaction to a medication that a purported doctor at Arbour prescribed after diagnosing her with bipolar disorder. Her condition worsened, and she eventually died of a seizure. Respondents, her mother and stepfather, later discovered that few Arbour employees were actually licensed to provide mental health counseling or authorized to prescribe medications or offer counseling services without supervision.

Respondents filed a *qui tam* suit, alleging that Universal Health had violated the False Claims Act (FCA). That Act imposes significant penalties on anyone who "knowingly presents . . . a false or fraudulent claim for payment or approval" to the Federal Government, 31 U.S.C. § 3729(a)(1)(A). Respondents sought to hold Universal Health liable under what is commonly referred to as an "implied false certification theory of liability," which treats a payment request as a claimant's implied certification of compliance with relevant statutes, regulations, or contract requirements that are material conditions of payment and treats a failure to disclose a violation as a misrepresentation that renders the claim "false or fraudulent." Specifically, respondents alleged, Universal Health (acting through Arbour) defrauded the Medicaid program by submitting reimbursement claims that made representations about the specific services provided by specific types of professionals, but that failed to disclose serious violations of Massachusetts Medicaid regulations pertaining to staff qualifications and licensing requirements for these services. Universal Health thus allegedly defrauded the program because Universal Health knowingly misrepresented its compliance with mental health facility requirements that are so central to the provision of mental health counseling that the Medicaid program would have refused to pay these claims had it known of these violations.

Because the FCA did not have its own definition of "fraud," the Court turned to the common law. By submitting claims for payment using payment codes corresponding to specific counseling services, Universal Health represented that it had provided specific types of treatment. And Arbour staff allegedly made further representations by using National Provider Identification numbers corresponding to specific job titles. By conveying this information without disclosing Arbour's many violations of basic staff and licensing requirements for mental health facilities, Universal Health's claims constituted misrepresentations. "Because common-law fraud has long encompassed certain misrepresentations by omission, 'false or fraudulent claims' include more than just claims containing express falsehoods."]

. . . . The claims in this case do more than merely demand payment. They fall squarely within the rule that half-truths—representations that state the truth only so far as it goes, while omitting critical qualifying information—can be actionable misrepresentations. A classic example of an actionable half-truth in contract law is the seller who reveals that there may be two new roads near a property he is selling, but fails to disclose that a third potential road might bisect the property. See Junius Constr. Co. v. Cohen, 257 N.Y. 393, 400, 178 N.E. 672, 674 (1931) (Cardozo, J.). "The enumeration of two streets, described as unopened but projected, was a tacit representation that the land to be conveyed was subject to no others, and certainly subject to no others materially affecting the value of the purchase." Likewise, an applicant for an adjunct position at a local college makes an actionable misrepresentation when his resume lists prior jobs and then retirement, but fails to disclose that his "retirement" was a prison stint for perpetrating a $12 million bank fraud.

So too here. . . . [T]hese representations were clearly misleading in context. Anyone informed that a social worker at a Massachusetts mental health clinic provided a teenage patient with individual counseling services would probably—but wrongly—conclude that the clinic had complied with core Massachusetts Medicaid requirements . . . . By using payment and other codes that conveyed this information without disclosing Arbour's many violations of basic staff and licensing requirements for mental health facilities, Universal Health's claims constituted misrepresentations.

Los Angeles Unified School District v. Great American Insurance Co.

Supreme Court of California, 2010.
234 P.3d 490.

WERDEGAR, JUSTICE. We have long recognized that "[a] contractor of public works who, acting reasonably, is misled by incorrect plans and specifications issued by the public authorities as the basis for bids and who, as a result, submits a bid which is lower than he would have otherwise made may recover in a contract action for extra work or expenses necessitated by the conditions being other than as represented." Souza & McCue Constr. Co. v. Superior Court, 370 P.2d 338 (Cal. 1962). In this case we decide whether a contractor may also recover when the plans and specifications are correct, but the public authority failed to disclose information in its possession that materially affected the cost of performance. The question has divided the Courts of Appeal. . . .

We hold a contractor need not prove an affirmative fraudulent intent to conceal. Rather—with the qualifications stated below—a public entity may be required to provide extra compensation if it knew, but failed to disclose, material facts that would affect the contractor's bid or performance. Because public entities do not insure contractors against their own negligence, relief for nondisclosure is appropriate only when (1) the contractor submitted its bid or undertook to perform without material information that affected performance costs; (2) the public entity was in possession of the information and was aware the contractor had no knowledge of, nor any reason to obtain, such information; (3) any contract specifications or other information furnished by the public entity to the contractor misled the contractor or did not put it on notice to inquire; and (4) the public entity failed to provide the relevant information. . . .

In 1996, the Los Angeles Unified School District (District) entered into a contract with Lewis Jorge Construction Management, Inc. (Lewis Jorge) to construct an elementary school for approximately $10.1 million according to plans and specifications developed by the District. In 1999, the District terminated the contract, declaring Lewis Jorge to be in material breach and default. The District then sought proposals from other contractors, including Hayward Construction Company (Hayward), to correct defects in Lewis Jorge's work and complete the project. The District provided prospective bidders with copies of the original plans and specifications and also with 108 pages of what the parties characterize as a "current correction list" or sometimes as "pre-punch lists," cataloging work by the previous contractor that the District's inspectors and subinspectors found to be defective, incomplete or missing.

Although the pre-punch lists appear to refer only to defects visible by simple inspection, they include language indicating the District also intended to make the contractor awarded the job responsible for unlisted defects in existing work. A list provided by the District's chief inspector accordingly recited: "Corrections or comments made in regard to the pre-punch list during this review do not relieve the Contractor from compliance with the requirements of the drawings and specifications. This review is only for General Conformance with the design concept of this project and general compliance with the information given in the Contract Documents. . . . "

After receiving the plans, specifications and pre-punch lists, and conducting a site inspection, Hayward submitted a proposal to do the work on a time and materials basis, stating a "guaranteed maximum price" of $4.5 million. The District accepted Hayward's bid, and in June 1999 the parties entered into a contract to complete the project. The written agreement recites that Hayward agreed to "correct deficiencies in the work performed by the former contractor, without limitation, as noted on the current correction list issued by the District." It also recites that the maximum amount payable by the District for the cost of the work plus Hayward's fee would not exceed $4.5 million. And, "[a]s to any warranties in the Contract Documents, including those as to defective workmanship and materials, the Contractor assumes responsibility for his own work, materials, equipment and services and the work, materials, equipment and services done by subcontractors and supplied by material men and suppliers working under such subcontractors, including patent (evident) defective work done by the former contractor that the Contractor is required to correct to complete the Project." Great American Insurance Company (Great American) issued a performance bond for $4.5 million, guaranteeing Hayward's performance of the contract.

Shortly after beginning work, Hayward informed the District it had significantly underestimated the cost of the remedial work, explaining that the existing work had nonconformities and deficiencies that had not been noted on the pre-punch lists and could not have been detected by simple observation. For example, the pre-punch lists called for repairing and cleaning portions of the exterior stucco, but Hayward reported that upon removing some of the plaster surfacing, it discovered it could make acceptable repairs only by removing and replacing the entire exterior surface plus portions of an underlying material. The pre-punch lists also called for fixing tiles at a few locations, but Hayward reported that after removing selected tiles for repair, it determined the entire installation of tile was unacceptable. In the end, Hayward sought extra compensation in the amount of $2,847,592 for work necessitated by what it characterized as latent defects.

The District disputed that Hayward was entitled to any sum above the $4.5 million guaranteed maximum, but paid Hayward an extra $1 million under an express reservation of rights to take action to recover the additional compensation. It then instituted this action against Hayward and Great American. Hayward cross-complained, asserting it was entitled to the additional compensation because it had been required to perform work that had not been specified in the contract and the prepunch lists, that the District had breached the contract by misrepresenting and concealing material facts and conditions, and that the District had breached an express or implied warranty that the plans and specifications it provided were complete and accurately depicted the work required to complete the project. In support of these theories, Hayward alleged the District had failed to disclose the full nature and extent of the defects in the existing construction, and had failed to disclose information that would have put Hayward on notice that some of its assumptions about the scope of the work required were faulty. For example, Hayward asserted the District had failed to disclose a consultant's report that would have alerted Hayward to the defects in the stucco work and further asserted that the District was aware Hayward's intended method for curing stucco discoloration would not be effective. . . .

The plans and specifications furnished by the District to Hayward were developed in connection with the original construction project awarded to the previous contractor, and Hayward does not suggest that its difficulties were in any way affected by some misrepresentation or omission in them. Hayward contends, rather, the District breached the implied warranty by failing to impart information in its possession that would have put Hayward on notice of latent defects in the work done by the previous contractor. We have not had occasion to resolve a case brought solely on a theory of nondisclosure. We have, however, recognized there are instances when a public entity's nondisclosure may provide grounds for relief. . . .

The *Restatement Second of Contracts* is in accord that nondisclosure may be actionable, explaining: "A person's nondisclosure of a fact known to him is equivalent to an assertion that the fact does not exist in the following cases only: (a) where he knows that disclosure of the fact is necessary to prevent some previous assertion from being a misrepresentation or from being fraudulent or material; (b) where he knows that disclosure of the fact would correct a mistake of the other party as to a basic assumption on which that party is making the contract and if nondisclosure of the fact amounts to a failure to act in good faith and in accordance with reasonable standards of fair dealing; (c) where he knows that disclosure of the fact would correct a mistake of the other party as to the contents or effect of a writing, evidencing or embodying an agreement in whole or in part; (d) where the other person is entitled to know the fact because of a relation of trust and confidence between them." Rest.2d Contracts, § 161. . . .

The District argues that to allow recovery without a showing of fraudulent intent would force public entities to act as insurers for contractors, encourage underbidding, and relieve bidding contractors from the necessity of conducting their own investigations into the conditions of performance. The argument fails to acknowledge the limitations on liability inherent in the superior knowledge doctrine and also recognized by California law.

The point is illustrated by our opinion in *Wunderlich v. State of California*, 65 Cal. 2d 777 [(1967)]. The state there had reported the results of tests conducted at a particular site for the presence of sand and gravel that might be used in a construction project. The contractor assumed from the state's report that the site would produce all the sand and gravel needed for the project; when that assumption proved incorrect, the contractor sued for damages. We found in favor of the state, thus impliedly concluding the state had no obligation to obtain and report information that would enable the contractor to accurately estimate its costs. Liability turned on whether the reports the state had furnished were misleading. We held: "[T]he question is whether, under the circumstances of the indefinite nature of the statements and the existence of exculpatory provisions, the bidder could *justifiably* rely on the statements. It does not appear that plaintiffs could have done so, and the state is not responsible for the subjective interpretation placed upon the information by bidders." Id. at 786. . . .

Thus, existing law holds that public entities have no obligation to investigate the costs of performance independent from the obligation to provide prospective bidders with correct plans and specifications. A public entity is not responsible for erroneous assumptions drawn by a contractor from accurate information provided by the public entity or for unsupported assumptions drawn from the public entity's silence, nor does it have any duty to disclose information that is reasonably available or that the contractor knew or had a realistic opportunity to discover. . . .

In sum, established law provides public entities substantial protection against careless bidding practices by contractors and forecloses the possibility that a public entity will be held liable when a contractor's own lack of diligence prevented it from fully appreciating the costs of performance. This being so, protection against careless bidding practices does not require that we allow contractors damaged by a public entity's misleading nondisclosure to recover only on a showing the public entity harbored a fraudulent intent. . . .

The District asserts that allowing actions for nondisclosure will lead to burdensome practices and costly litigation by compelling public entities to disclose every scrap of information that might relate to a project and encouraging contractors to comb through the entity's files for material that might be used to support an actionable nondisclosure. The danger, we think, is overstated. [S]ignificant restrictions already exist on the ability of contractors to recover from public entities on theories of tort or quantum meruit. And in actions for breach of contract, contractors can recover neither for extra work that would have been bid had they exercised due diligence nor for work occasioned by unanticipated conditions either unknown to the public entity or which the public entity had no reason to believe the contractor would not itself discover. Nondisclosure is actionable, moreover, only if the information at issue materially affects the cost of performance, reducing the possibility that a public entity soliciting bids on a project might easily overlook it. Given these limitations on recovery, as between a truly blameless contractor and the nondisclosing public entity that received the benefit of the contractor's work, requiring the public entity to pay for that benefit is hardly unjust. . . .

[W]e hold that a contractor on a public works contract may be entitled to relief for a public entity's nondisclosure in the following limited circumstances: (1) the contractor submitted its bid or undertook to perform without material information that affected performance costs; (2) the public entity was in possession of the information and was aware the contractor had no knowledge of, nor any reason to obtain, such information; (3) any contract specifications or other information furnished by the public entity to the contractor misled the contractor or did not put it on notice to inquire; and (4) the public entity failed to provide the relevant information. The circumstances affecting recovery may include, but are not limited to, positive warranties or disclaimers made by either party, the information provided by the plans and specifications and related documents, the difficulty of detecting the condition in question, any time constraints the public entity imposed on proposed bidders, and any unwarranted assumptions made by the contractor. The public entity may not be held liable for failing to disclose information a reasonable contractor in like circumstances would or should have discovered on its own, but may be found liable when the totality of the circumstances is such that the public entity knows, or has reason to know, a responsible contractor acting diligently would be unlikely to discover the condition that materially increased the cost of performance. . . .

NOTE: DISCLOSURE DUTIES

Cases often arise in which someone says something that, while true on its own terms, is misleading in light of what has come before. In the words of the Restatement of Torts, one is required to disclose "matters known to him that he knows to be necessary to prevent his partial or ambiguous statement of the facts from being misleading." Restatement (Second) of Torts § 551. One is also required to disclose "subsequently acquired information that he knows will make untrue or misleading a previous representation that when made was true or believed to be so."

Much turns on whether the parties have equal access to the information. Say I have a storeroom by the ocean that I have converted to an amusement center containing a number of different concessions, with pinball machines and other devices that might or might not be legal. I sell my amusement center to you, knowing that the police plan to raid the establishment and close down many parts of it. Dyke v. Zaiser, 182 P.2d 344 (Cal. App. 1947). Or, I own a rubbish collection business and sell it to you, knowing that there is a strong possibility that the city will let a contract for the rubbish collection and render the business superfluous. Jappe v. Mandt, 278 P.2d 940 (Cal. App. 1955). Courts have not decided these cases uniformly, but the difficulties they raise in identifying what counts as a misrepresentation complicate the blackletter doctrine of *Laidlaw* considerably. See Kim Lane Scheppelle, Legal Secrets: Equality and Efficiency in the Common Law 269–98 (1988).

A most illuminating effort to sort out the pieces of the problem is made in Wonnell, The Structure of a General Theory of Nondisclosure, 41 Case W. Res. L.Rev. 329 (1991). Consider the guidance provided by the passages taken from the following opinions:

(a) Matthews v. Kincaid, 746 P.2d 470 (Alaska 1987): The Restatement (Second) Torts [§ 551(2)] suggests that a duty to disclose [arises in situations involving] facts that are concealed or unlikely to be discovered because of the special relationship between the parties, the course of their dealings, or the nature of the fact itself. A duty to disclose is rarely imposed where the parties deal at arm's length and where the information is the type which the buyer would be expected to discover by ordinary inspection and inquiry. . . . [Here,] the lack of off-street parking [for the four-plex] is an obvious fact which the ordinary purchaser [of the apartment building] would be expected to discover, before she bought the property.

(b) Federal Dep. Ins. Corp. v. W.R. Grace & Co., 877 F.2d 614 (7th Cir. 1989): An omission can of course be actionable as a fraud. . . . But not every failure by a seller (or borrower, or employee, etc.) to disclose information to the buyer (or lender, or employer, etc.) that would cause the latter to reassess the deal is actionable. A general duty of disclosure would turn every bargaining relationship into a fiduciary one. . . . [But the seller] must disclose that the house he is trying to sell is infested with termites. . . . [The distinction] is illustrated [by a case] where the failure to disclose an assessor's valuation was held not to be actionable, since the valuation was a matter of public record and therefore ascertainable by the buyer at reasonable cost. . . . [But if] you go to a bank for a loan on your house, and the bank tentatively agrees to make it, and on the day before the loan papers are to be signed the house is destroyed by a flood and you don't disclose the fact at the signing, then we suppose . . . that you are guilty of fraud even if you made no representation that the house was still in existence.

(c) Hill v. Jones, 151 Ariz. 81, 725 P.2d 1115 (Ct. App. 1986): Suffice it to say that [caveat emptor's] vitality has waned during the latter half of the twentieth century. . . . The modern view is that a vendor has an affirmative duty to disclose material facts where: 1. Disclosure is necessary to prevent a previous assertion from being a misrepresentation or from being fraudulent or material; 2. Disclosure would correct a mistake of the other party as to a basic assumption on which that party is making the contract and if nondisclosure amounts to a failure to act in good faith and in accordance with reasonable standards of fair dealing; 3. Disclosure would correct a mistake of the other party as to the contents or effect of a writing . . .; 4. The other person is entitled to know the fact because of a relationship of trust and confidence between them. [Rest.2d Contracts § 161; see Rest.2d Torts § 551.] . . . The doctrine imposing a duty to disclose is akin to [rules] pertaining to relief [for] mistake. Although the law of contracts supports the finality of transactions, over the years courts have recognized that under [certain] circumstances it is unjust to strictly enforce the policy favoring finality. Thus, e.g., even a unilateral mistake . . . may justify rescission. There is also a judicial policy promoting honesty and fair dealing in business relationships. This policy is expressed in the law of fraudulent and negligent misrepresentations. Where a misrepresentation is fraudulent or where a negligent misrepresentation is one of material fact, the policy of finality rightly gives way to the policy of promoting honest dealings. . . . Thus, nondisclosure may be equated with . . . fraud and misrepresentation. . . . [This is especially so where] nondisclosure of material facts affect[s] the value of property, [and the facts] are not reasonably capable of being known to the buyer.

Again, various statutes dealing with "deceptive" and "unfair" trade practices—many limited to specified consumer transactions, some applying to commercial parties as well—may encompass the full range of the misrepresentation cases, including nondisclosure. A useful discussion of the statutory approach can be found in Shell, Substituting Ethical Standards for Common Law Rules in Commercial Cases: An Emerging Statutory Trend, 82 Nw. L. Rev. 1198 (1988). As concerns residential real estate, a number of states have enacted statutes governing disclosures in the transfer of such property. See, e.g., Amyot v. Luchini, 932 P.2d 244 (Alaska 1997) (statute requiring "good faith" disclosure of house's defects bars purchaser's theory of innocent misrepresentation respecting matters covered in mandatory disclosure form).

As the next case illustrates, when one party is a fiduciary to another, duties may not stop with a duty to disclose. Even without knowledge, a fiduciary might not be able to profit at the expense of the person to whom duties are owed.

Jackson v. Seymour

Supreme Court of Appeals of Virginia, 1952.
193 Va. 735, 71 S.E.2d 181.

EGGLESTON, J. In May, 1950, Lucy S. Jackson filed her bill of complaint [seeking] rescission of a deed dated February 18, 1947, and recorded the next day, whereby she had conveyed to her brother, Benjamin J. Seymour, a tract of thirty-one acres of land. . . . [S]he alleged that she had been induced by her brother to convey the land to him for the sum of $275, through his representations to her that it was "of no value except for a pasture" and that [$275] was "a good price therefor;" that relying upon the representations of her brother, in whom she reposed complete confidence with respect to his management of her property and business affairs, and being unfamiliar with the land and unaware that there was merchantable timber growing thereon she had conveyed it to him at that price; that about two and one-half years later she discovered for the first time that . . . there was on the land considerable merchantable timber, of the stumpage value of from $3,200 to $5,000, and that subsequent to his acquisition of the land her brother had cut and sold the timber at a price unknown to her, but with considerable profit to himself.

She further alleged that the statements and representations made to her by her brother, through which she had been induced to sell him the land, were "false and were fraudulently made;" that she had offered to restore to him the [$275] he had paid for the property, with interest, upon the condition that he would rescind the transaction, and that he had rejected this offer. The prayer of the bill was that the deed be canceled and that the defendant be required to account to her for all moneys which he may have realized from the sale of the timber taken from the land. . . .

In his answer the defendant . . . denied that he had made any representations to her that [$275] was the fair value of the land or that it "had no value except for a pasture." He alleged that he had purchased the property from her at her urgent request and for her accommodation, and that, at the time he had no knowledge "of the existence of merchantable timber upon said land." [He] further denied all charges of fraud or misrepresentations[,] [but] admitted that since he had acquired the property he had cut and marketed from this and an adjoining tract of land 148,055 feet of timber, from which he had realized the sum of $2,353.42. He denied the plaintiff's right to have the deed rescinded or to have an accounting by him. . . . Inasmuch as the trial court's findings of fact are binding on us the evidence will be summarized from the viewpoint most favorable to the defendant.

Since 1931 Mrs. Jackson had been the owner of a farm of 166 acres in Brunswick county which adjoined lands owned by her brother. . . . After the death of her husband (the date of which is not shown) Mrs. Jackson sought and obtained the assistance of her brother, who is a successful farmer and business man, in renting the farm for her. He rented the tillable portions of the farm, collected the rents, and made settlements with her which she never questioned. . . . [T]hey were devoted to each other and she had, as she says, "the utmost confidence in him."

In 1946 Tazewell Wilkins approached Seymour about the purchase of a tract of Seymour's land containing 30.46 acres for a pasture. He also wanted to buy the adjoining tract of 31 acres, which was a part of the land owned by Mrs. Jackson. Seymour told Wilkins that while he was willing to take $275 for his (Seymour's) land, he did not own the 31-acre tract and suggested that Wilkins see Mrs. Jackson about buying it. While Seymour also conveyed this information to Mrs. Jackson the record discloses no negotiations between Wilkins and Mrs. Jackson for the purchase of her land.

In February, 1947, Mrs. Jackson approached her brother, saying that she was in need of funds and was anxious to sell the 31-acre tract in which Wilkins had shown interest. Seymour did not want to buy the property, but because of his sister's need for money he agreed to purchase it at $275, which was the price which had been mentioned in his negotiations with Wilkins. The brother was then unaware that there was valuable timber on the land and contemplated using it for a pasture. Seymour gave his sister a check for $275 and she signed a receipt therefor. On the next day Mrs. Jackson executed and delivered a deed conveying the property to her brother. The deed was prepared by a local attorney at Seymour's request and expense.

A short while after Seymour had acquired the property it came to his attention that some trees had been cut from the tract. Upon investigation he discovered for the first time that there was valuable timber on the land. The evidence does not disclose the exact quantity and value of this timber. It shows that in 1948 Seymour cut from the land which he had purchased from his sister and from adjoining lands owned by him, 148,055 feet of lumber and that the greater portion of this came from the Jackson tract. This timber had a stumpage value of approximately $20 per 1,000 feet.

The land in controversy is located in an isolated section and it is undisputed that Mrs. Jackson had never been on it and knew nothing of its character. While Seymour had hunted in the vicinity and been within sight of the property he had never actually been on the land. To use his own words, "I was positive that it was just naked land" and worth $8 or $9 an acre. Thus, neither vendor nor vendee knew that there was valuable timber growing on the land. On cross-examination Seymour admitted that the presence of timber on the land "was not within the contemplation" of him and his sister at the time the sale was consummated. He testified that if he had known of this timber he would not have bought the property from her for $275. . . .

Upon the conclusion of the evidence the lower court dictated from the bench an opinion holding that the plaintiff's allegations of *actual* fraud had not been sustained by the evidence... It took under advisement whether under the allegations of the bill the plaintiff was entitled to relief on the ground of *constructive* fraud because of the "confidential relationship" of the parties and the "gross inadequacy in price."

While the court had the matter under consideration the plaintiff tendered an amendment to her bill which in substance charged that she was unfamiliar with the character of the land, was unaware that there was any merchantable timber on it, that she had sold it "under an honest and material mistake of fact with reference to the subject matter of the contract," and that to permit the deed to stand "would operate as a fraud" upon her rights. There was no allegation that the vendee . . . was likewise mistaken as to the existence of timber on the land at the time the sale was consummated. Thus the amendment fell short of alleging a mutual mistake. . . .

About sixty days after the amendment had been tendered the lower court rejected it on the ground that it had been "tendered too late. . . ." It further held that since the plaintiff had grounded her case on actual fraud, and since [she] had failed to sustain that charge or make out a case within the scope of the bill, she was not entitled to the relief prayed for. . . . [T]he plaintiff has appealed.

Under our view of the case it is unnecessary that we deal with the [rejection of] the amendment to the bill. We are of opinion that . . . the plaintiff is entitled to equitable relief on the ground of constructive fraud, and that such relief is within the scope of the allegations of the original bill of complaint.

. . . [S]hortly after the defendant had acquired this tract of land[,] he cut and marketed therefrom timber valued at approximately ten times what he had paid for the property. A mere statement of the matter shows the gross and shocking inadequacy of the price paid.

This is not the ordinary case in which the parties dealt at arm's length and the shrewd trader was entitled to the fruits of his bargain. The parties were brother and sister. He was a successful business man and she a widow in need of money and forced by circumstances . . . to sell a part of the lands which she had inherited. Because of their friendly and intimate relations she entrusted to him and he assumed the management and renting of a portion of this very land. . . . [Moreover,] neither of the parties knew of the timber on the land and we have from the defendant's own lips the admission that as it turned out "afterwards" he had paid a grossly inadequate price for the property and that he would not have bought it from her for the small amount paid if he had then known of the true situation. . . .

The controlling principles were thus stated in Planters Nat. Bank v. Heflin Co., 166 Va. 166, 184 S.E. 216: "Mere failure of consideration or want of consideration will not ordinarily invalidate an executed contract. The owner of the historic estate of 'Blackacre' can give it away, and he can sell it for a peppercorn. Courts, though they have long arms, cannot relieve one of the consequences of a contract merely because it was unwise. . . . [B]ut where inadequacy of price is such as to shock their conscience equity is alert to seize upon the slightest circumstance indicative of fraud, either actual or constructive." . . .

Clearly, the inadequacy of consideration here meets that definition. In addition to the gross inadequacy of consideration we have the confidential relation of the parties, the pecuniary distress of the vendor, and the mutual mistake of the parties as to the subject matter of the contract. . . . [T]o permit the transaction to stand would result in constructive fraud upon the rights of the plaintiff. Hence, she is entitled to relief in equity. . . . While the bill alleges actual fraud, it also contains allegations of these constituent elements of constructive fraud: The confidential relation of the parties; the reliance by the plaintiff upon the advice and judgment of the defendant in her business affairs; the gross inadequacy of the price paid; her offer to restore the purchase price and rescind the transaction, and his rejection of the offer.

In Moore v. Gregory, 146 Va. 504, 131 S.E. 692, we [said]: " 'Constructive fraud is a breach of legal or equitable duty which, irrespective of the moral guilt of the fraud feasor, the law declares fraudulent because of its tendency to deceive others, to violate public or private confidence, or to injure public interests. Neither actual dishonesty of purpose nor intent to deceive is an essential element of constructive fraud. . . .' Constructive fraud may be inferred from the intrinsic nature and subject of the bargain itself." 146 Va., at 523, 527,131 S.E., at 697–698.

. . . [T]he lower court should have entered a decree granting the plaintiff's prayer for a rescission of the conveyance and restoring the parties to the *status quo* in so far as practicable. By way of incidental relief the plaintiff is entitled to recover of the defendant the fair stumpage value of the timber removed by the latter from the land, with interest from the date of such removal, and the fair rental value of the property during the time the defendant was in possession. The defendant is entitled to a return of the purchase price paid by him, with interest from the date that the plaintiff offered to rescind the transaction, and taxes paid by him on the land since the date of the conveyance, with interest.

The decree appealed from is reversed and the cause remanded for further proceedings in conformity with the views here expressed.

COMMENT: FIDUCIARY DUTIES

The doctrines expressed in Jackson v. Seymour owe much of their currency in this country to Justice Story, who, in 1842, wrote (1 Equity Jurisprudence 256–258 (3d ed.)):

> Mere inadequacy of price, or any other inequality in the bargain, is not, however, to be understood as constituting, per se, a

> ground to avoid a bargain in Equity. For Courts of Equity, as well as Courts of Law, act upon the ground, that every person who is not, from his peculiar condition or circumstances, under disability, is entitled to dispose of his property in such manner ... as he chooses; and whether his bargains are wise and discreet, or profitable or unprofitable, or otherwise, are considerations, not for Courts of Justice, but for the party himself to deliberate upon....
>
> Still, however, there may be such an unconscionableness or inadequacy in a bargain, as to demonstrate some gross imposition or undue influence; and in such cases Courts of Equity ought to interfere upon the satisfactory ground of fraud. But then such unconscionableness or such inadequacy should be made out, as would (to use an expressive phrase) shock the conscience and amount in itself to conclusive and decisive evidence of fraud. And where there are other ingredients in the case of a suspicious nature, or peculiar relations between the parties, gross inadequacy of price must necessarily furnish the most vehement presumption of fraud.

One large and important area for the application of these ideas, in particular constructive fraud ("constructive" because based on the inadequacy of the consideration), is the group of relationships usually described as "confidential" and "fiduciary." Both are terms of broad reach, and their outer limits are ill-defined. A "fiduciary" relationship is one whose successful functioning requires a high degree of candor and reliability between the participants. As one court has said, "[a] fiduciary, unlike an ordinary contract promisor, undertakes to treat the affairs of the promisee as if they were the promisor's own affairs." Olympia Hotels Corp. v. Johnson Wax Dev. Corp., 908 F.2d 1363 (7th Cir. 1990). Illustrations are the relations of trustee and beneficiary of an express trust, principal and agent, attorney and client, business partners, guardian and minor ward, even directors of a corporation and its stockholders. In addition to categories of relations, fiduciary duties are sometimes imposed on an ad hoc basis. The key is again one person's ascendancy over another, achieved through the placing of trust and confidence on one side and the assumption of a position of influence on the other. The standards of disclosure and disinterestedness are not the same in all fiduciary relationships, and often the requirements are one-sided in the sense that higher standards are imposed on one participant than on the other.

A "confidential" relationship, on the other hand, is not so much the product of a legal status as it is the result of unusual trust or confidence reposed in fact (e.g., Von Hake v. Thomas, infra p. 804, which speaks of one party exercising "extraordinary influence over the other"). Blood relationship or marriage will be the most common examples, though the list of "confidential relations" extends far beyond those sources. Intimate personal friendship between such persons as physician and patient, minister and parishioner, or next-door neighbors is commonly enough. All that is required is proof that in fact the parties did not deal on equal terms, that there was a high degree of confidence reposed in the honesty and good faith of the other party. Then, too, the categories of "confidential" and "fiduciary" relationship are not mutually exclusive; both presumably exist, for example, when an attorney undertakes representation of a client. The mere willingness to enter into a "fiduciary" relationship often will be a mark of confidence reposed, sufficient for the relationship to be "confidential" as well.

In neither type of relationship is bargaining between the participants wholly excluded. The principal requirement is one of full disclosure of all of the elements that have a bearing on the transaction or the terms of the bargain made. This means, however, that any transfer or exchange between the parties, either by way of gift or bargain, will be examined closely to be sure that there was full disclosure and no unfair advantage taken. The technique chiefly used is framed as a procedural handicap: the party in whom trust or confidence is reposed, and who seems to have profited, is forced to assume the burden of showing that the transaction was in every way fair and beyond suspicion. This burden is often difficult to carry; for many courts, the starting premise will be that the transaction is "prima facie voidable." If the burden is not sustained, the transaction will be set aside or its enforcement denied. Though these high standards originated primarily in equity, there is no reason today why they would not be applied at law where a legal remedy is appropriate, by way of either defense or affirmative action aiming at rescission.

NOTE: WAIVER OF DISCLOSURE DUTIES

Situations can arise in which parties try to waive whatever disclosure duties they have. For example, a duty may arise with the sale of distressed debt. Notwithstanding *Laidlaw*, when it comes to buying and selling financial instruments, failure to disclose material nonpublic information can trigger liability. The U.S. Supreme Court suggested that such a duty to disclose exists in face-to-face transactions in Strong v. Repide, 213 U.S. 419 (1909). Interpretations of the securities laws, in particular Rule 10b–5, may also impose such duties under at least some circumstances. If both parties want to escape from such obligations, they need to change the bargaining environment. On the face of it, this might not seem possible. Deceptive practices are the epitome of bad faith, and the duty to act in good faith is a duty that cannot be waived. Nevertheless, parties may be able to put themselves in the same position as they would be if they could waive such disclosure obligations.

Reliance is an essential element of any action based on deception. You cannot sue me for deception if you know that my statements to you were not true. A reasonable person does not rely on statements she knows to be untrue. Because you do not rely, the misstatement does not damage you. Hence, to bring an action based on deception, you must show both that I lied and that you reasonably relied on the lie. The requirement of reliance in any action based on failure to disclose therefore provides a path for parties to put themselves in the same position they would be in if waiver were possible: they must endeavor to disable themselves from later claiming reliance on what the other party did or did not tell them.

Investors in distressed debt commonly seek to restructure their bargaining environment in this fashion through an exchange of letters in which each first acknowledges that the other might be in possession of material nonpublic information, and then affirms that she is not relying in any way on the failure of her contracting opposite to disclose it. These "Big Boy" letters, as they are called, may keep either party from bringing an action against the other later on. If a party signs a document in which she states that she is not relying either on any information provided by the other party or any information that the other party has but failed to disclose, she will later find it hard to assert that she did in fact rely. In the absence of reliance, any action based on deceptive conduct cannot succeed. See Eshmoili, Big Boy Letters: Trading on Inside Information, 94 Cornell L. Rev. 133 (2008).

The practice of signing Big Boy letters would not persist if they were used solely to allow one party to take advantage of the other party. If parties who asked for such letters were trying only to trade on the basis of private information, the act of demanding a Big Boy letter would itself reveal that the demanding party was in possession of it. These letters are more likely written because both parties think they are better off with greater transactional certainty, even though it is at the cost of less protection for nondisclosure.

The potential for abuse here is manifest. See Korobkin, The *Borat* Problem in Negotiation: Fraud, Assent, and the Behavioral Law and Economics of Standard Form Contracts, 101 Cal. L. Rev. 51 (2013). For example, a filmmaker intent upon making fools of ordinary people might put on a thick, Slavic accent and claim, falsely, that he is a journalist doing a documentary (which will be called "Cultural Learnings of America for Make Benefit Glorious Nation of Kazakhstan") for distribution exclusively in his home country. He then hands his unsuspecting subjects a release that gives him permission to use any film he shoots and show it anywhere. The release also includes a clause to the effect that the subjects are not relying on any representations he made to them before they signed.

The signers of the release later discover they are without a legal remedy when it turns out that he is not from Kazakhstan at all, but is instead a British comedian who specializes in revealing the racism, homophobia, and gullibility of ordinary people. Even though they have been deliberately defrauded, the victims of such a movie producer have no ability to recover if a court takes the document they signed at face value—even when the film ultimately grosses more than $260 million and makes them look ridiculous. See Psenicska v. Twentieth Century Fox Film Corp., 2008 WL 4185752 (S.D.N.Y. 2008).

The effect of statements in a document in which a party recites that she is not relying on disclosures or nondisclosures by the other is the question the courts face in the following two cases.

Rissman v. Rissman

United States Court of Appeals, Seventh Circuit, 2000.
213 F.3d 381.

EASTERBROOK, CIRCUIT JUDGE. Gerald Rissman formed Tiger Electronics to make toys and games. In 1979 Gerald gave his sons Arnold, Randall, and Samuel large blocks of stock in the firm: Gerald kept 400 shares and gave Randall 400, Arnold 100, and Samuel 100. In 1986 both Gerald and Samuel withdrew from the venture. Tiger bought Gerald's stock, and Arnold bought Samuel's, leaving Randall with two-thirds of the shares and Arnold with the rest. Randall managed the business while Arnold served as a salesman. Arnold did not elect himself to the board of directors, though Tiger employed cumulative voting, which would have enabled him to do so. When the brothers had a falling out, Arnold sold his shares to Randall for $17 million. Thirteen months later, Tiger sold its assets (including its name and trademarks) for $335 million to Hasbro, another toy maker, and was renamed Lion Holdings. Arnold contends in this suit under the federal securities laws (with state-law claims under the supplemental jurisdiction) that he would not have sold for as little as $17 million, and perhaps would not have sold at all, had Randall not deceived him into thinking that Randall would never take Tiger public or sell it to a third party. Arnold says that these statements convinced him that his stock would remain illiquid and not pay dividends, so he sold for whatever Randall was willing to pay. Arnold now wants the extra $95 million he would have received had he retained his stock until the sale to Hasbro.

Because the district judge granted summary judgment to the defendants, we must assume that Randall told Arnold that he was determined to keep Tiger a family firm. Likewise we must assume that Randall secretly planned to sell after acquiring Arnold's shares. But we need *not* assume that Arnold relied on Randall's statements (equivalently, that the statements were material to and caused Arnold's decision), and without reliance Arnold has no claim under § 10(b) or Rule 10b–5. Arnold asked Randall to put in writing, as part of the agreement, a representation that Randall would never sell Tiger. Randall refused to make such a representation. Instead he warranted (accurately) that he was not aware of any offers to purchase Tiger and was not engaged in negotiations for its sale. The parties also agreed that if Tiger were sold before Arnold had received all installments of the purchase price, then payment of the principal and interest would be accelerated. Having sought broader assurances, and having been refused, Arnold could not persuade a reasonable trier of fact that he relied on Randall's oral statements. Having signed an agreement providing for acceleration as a consequence of sale, Arnold is in no position to contend that he relied on the impossibility of sale.

Indeed, Arnold represented as part of the transaction that he had *not* relied on any prior oral statement:

> The parties further declare that they have not relied upon any representation of any party hereby released [Randall] or of their attorneys [Glick], agents, or other representatives concerning the nature or extent of their respective injuries or damages.

That is pretty clear, but to foreclose quibbling Arnold made these warranties to Randall:

> (a) no promise or inducement for this Agreement has been made to him except as set forth herein; (b) this Agreement is executed by [Arnold] freely and voluntarily, and without reliance upon any statement or representation by Purchaser, the Company, any of the Affiliates or O.R. Rissman or any of their attorneys or agents except as set forth herein; (c) he has read and fully understands this Agreement and the meaning of its provisions; (d) he is legally competent to enter into this Agreement and to accept full responsibility therefor; and (e) he has been advised to consult with counsel before entering into this Agreement and has had the opportunity to do so.

Arnold does not contend that any representation in the stock purchase agreement is untrue or misleading; his entire case rests on Randall's oral statements. Yet Arnold assured Randall that he had not relied on these statements. Securities law does not permit a party to a stock transaction to disavow such representations—to say, in effect, "I lied when I told you I wasn't relying on your prior statements" and then to seek damages for their contents. Stock transactions would be impossibly uncertain if federal law precluded parties from agreeing to rely on the written word alone. "Without such a principle, sellers would have no protection against plausible liars and gullible jurors." Carr v. CIGNA Securities, Inc., 95 F.3d 544, 547 (7th Cir. 1996).

Two courts of appeals have held that non-reliance clauses in written stock-purchase agreements preclude any possibility of damages under the federal securities laws for prior oral statements. Jackvony v. RIHT Financial Corp., 873 F.2d 411 (1st Cir. 1989) (Breyer, J.); One-O-One Enterprises, Inc. v. Caruso, 848 F.2d 1283 (D.C. Cir. 1988) (R.B. Ginsburg, J.). Several of this circuit's opinions intimate agreement with these decisions, though we have yet to encounter a situation squarely covered by them. *Jackvony* and *One-O-One* fit Arnold's claim like a glove, and we now follow those cases by holding that a written anti-reliance clause precludes any claim of deceit by prior representations. The principle is functionally the same as a doctrine long accepted in this circuit: that a person who has received written disclosure of the truth may not claim to rely on contrary oral falsehoods. A non-reliance clause is not identical to a truthful disclosure, but it has a similar function: it ensures that both the transaction and any subsequent litigation proceed on the basis of the parties' writings, which are less subject to the vagaries of memory and the risks of fabrication.

Memory plays tricks. Acting in the best of faith, people may "remember" things that never occurred but now serve their interests. Or they may remember events with a change of emphasis or nuance that makes a substantial difference to meaning. Express or implied qualifications may be lost in the folds of time. A statement such as "I won't sell at current prices" may be recalled years later as "I won't sell." Prudent people protect themselves against the limitations of memory (and the temptation to shade the truth) by limiting their dealings to those memorialized in writing, and promoting the primacy of the written word is a principal function of the federal securities laws.

Failure to enforce agreements such as the one between Arnold and Randall could not make sellers of securities better off in the long run. Faced with an unavoidable risk of claims based on oral statements, persons transacting in securities would reduce the price they pay, setting aside the difference as a reserve for risk. If, as Arnold says, Randall was willing to pay $17 million and not a penny more, then a legal rule entitling Arnold to an extra $95 million if Tiger should be sold in the future would have scotched the deal (the option value of the deferred payment exceeds 1¢), leaving Arnold with no cash and the full risk of the venture. Arnold can't have both $17 million with certainty and a continuing right to one-third of any premium Randall negotiates for the firm, while bearing no risk of loss from the fickle toy business; that would make him better off than if he had held his shares throughout.

Negotiation could have avoided this litigation. Instead of taking the maximum Randall was willing to pay unconditionally, Arnold could have sought a lower guaranteed payment (say, $10 million) plus a kicker if Tiger were sold or taken public. Because random events (or Randall's efforts) would dominate Tiger's prosperity over the long run, the kicker would fall with time. Perhaps Arnold could have asked for 25% of any proceeds on a sale within a year, diminishing 1% every other month after that (so that Randall would keep all proceeds of a sale more than 62 months after the transaction with Arnold). Many variations on this formula were possible; all would have put Randall to the test, for if he *really* planned not to sell, the approach would have been attractive to him because it reduced his total payment. Likewise it would have been attractive to Arnold if he believed that Randall wanted to sell as soon as he could receive more than two-thirds of the gains. Yet Arnold never proposed a payment formula that would share the risk (and rewards) between the brothers, and the one he proposes after the fact in this litigation—$17 million with certainty and a perpetual right to one-third of any later premium—is just about the only formula that could not conceivably have been the outcome of bargaining.

Arnold calls the no-reliance clauses "boilerplate," and they were; transactions lawyers have language of this sort stored up for reuse. But the fact that language has been used before does not make it less binding when used again. Phrases become boilerplate when many parties find that the language serves their ends. That's a reason to enforce the promises, not to disregard them. People negotiate about the presence of boilerplate clauses. The sort of no-reliance clauses that appeared in the Rissmans' agreement were missing from other transactions .... Still other transactions ... include "strict reliance" clauses, entitling one party to rely on every representation ever made by the other. Arnold could have negotiated for the elimination of the no-reliance clauses, or the inclusion of a strict-reliance clause, but in exchange he would have had to accept a price lower than $17 million. Judges need not speculate about the reason a clause appears or is omitted, however; what matters when litigation breaks out is what the parties actually signed.

Contractual language serves its functions only if enforced consistently. This is one of the advantages of boilerplate, which usually has a record of predictable interpretation and application. If as Arnold says the extent of his reliance is a jury question even after he warranted his non-reliance, then the clause has been nullified, and people in Arnold's position will be worse off tomorrow for reasons we have explained....

ROVNER, CIRCUIT JUDGE, concurring.

I join in the majority opinion, and agree that under the facts of this case, the non-reliance clause precludes damages for the prior oral statements. I write separately only to explain further the basis for, and scope of, that holding. As the majority opinion notes, our holding follows that of the courts of appeals in Jackvony v. RIHT Financial Corp., 873 F.2d 411 (1st Cir. 1989) (Breyer, J.) and One-O-One Enterprises, Inc. v. Caruso, 848 F.2d 1283 (D.C. Cir. 1988) (R.B. Ginsburg, J.). The reasoning in those cases, as well as other cases in this court, reveals that all circumstances surrounding the transaction are relevant in determining whether reliance on prior oral statements can be deemed reasonable. Thus, although it may be determinative in many—and perhaps most—cases, the existence of a non-reliance clause will not automatically preclude damages for prior oral statements.

In *Jackvony*, the First Circuit set forth eight factors that are relevant in determining whether an investor's reliance on prior statements was reasonable: (1) the sophistication and expertise of the plaintiff in financial and securities matters; (2) the existence of long standing business or personal relationships; (3) access to the relevant information; (4) the existence of a fiduciary relationship; (5) concealment of the fraud; (6) the opportunity to detect the fraud; (7) whether the plaintiff initiated the stock transaction or sought to expedite the transaction; and (8) the generality or specificity of the misrepresentations. The court then held that the reliance on the prior statements in *Jackvony* was unreasonable because the prior statements were vague, Jackvony was a sophisticated investor, the written proxy statement instructed Jackvony not to rely on any other statements, Jackvony seemed anxious to expedite the transaction, and Jackvony helped draft the written acquisition documents. Thus, the *Jackvony* court did not hold that a non-reliance statement precludes a fraud claim in all cases, but noted that it is a factor that may defeat a claim of reliance.

Similarly, the D.C. Circuit in *One-O-One*, in holding that an integration clause rendered reliance on prior representations unreasonable, set forth the context in which that written agreement was reached. Specifically, the court noted that the parties reached the written agreement after eight months of vigorous negotiations involving many offers, promises and representations, and that the integration clause was included to avoid misunderstandings as to what was agreed upon in the course of those extensive negotiations. The court also rejected the plaintiffs' claim of fraud in the inducement based on the circumstances present in that particular case, holding that "[w]e have here the case of 'a party with the capacity and opportunity to read a written contract, who [has] execute[d] it, not under any emergency, and whose signature was not obtained by trick or artifice;' such a party, if the parol evidence rule is to retain vitality, 'cannot later claim fraud in the inducement.' " Id. at 1287. . .

Thus, both *Jackvony* and *One-O-One* recognize that courts must consider all of the surrounding circumstances in determining whether reliance on a prior oral settlement is reasonable, and that the existence of a non-reliance clause is but one factor, albeit a fairly convincing one in many cases. This is also consistent with our decision in *Carr v. CIGNA Securities, Inc.*, 95 F.3d 544, 547 (7th Cir. 1996), which held that "[i]f a literate, competent adult is given a document that in readable and comprehensible prose says *X* . . . and the person who hands it to him tells him, orally, not *X* . . . our literate competent adult cannot maintain an action for fraud against the issuer of the document." In discussing disclaimers in the context of a fiduciary relationship, *Carr* noted that a written disclaimer may not provide a safe harbor in every case, because "[n]ot all principals of fiduciaries are competent adults; not all disclaimers are clear; and the relationship involved may involve such a degree of trust invited by and reasonably reposed in the fiduciary as to dispel any duty of self-protection by the principal." Id. at 548. The reasonableness of the reliance thus depends on an analysis of the surrounding circumstances. Just as it would be unreasonable to expect a person to pore through a 427-page document looking for "nuggets of intelligible warnings," a person may not claim reasonable reliance when a written disclaimer is apparent in an eight-page document.

This is nothing new. The issue of reasonable reliance has always depended upon an analysis of all relevant circumstances. I write separately merely to avoid the inevitable quotes in future briefs characterizing our holding as an automatic rule precluding any damages for fraud based on prior oral statements when a non-reliance clause is included in a written agreement. The world is not that simple, and our holding today cannot be interpreted so simplistically. On the facts in this case, involving extensive negotiations aided by counsel and with numerous rejections of efforts to include the oral representations in the written agreement, the non-reliance clause rendered any reliance on the prior statements unreasonable.

Cirillo v. Slomin's Inc.

Supreme Court, Nassau County, New York, 2003.
768 N.Y.S.2d 759.

WINSLOW, JUSTICE. . . . This is an action for fraud, negligence and breach of warranty in connection with the installation and operation of an alarm system by Slomin's Inc. ("Slomin's") in the home of plaintiffs Vincenzo and Concetta Cirillo. The Slomin's system purchased by plaintiffs provided for central station monitoring, which contemplated the transmission of a signal from the alarm system via the telephone lines in the event of a break-in. . . . Plaintiffs allege that, in purchasing the alarm system and entering into the Contracts, they relied on the following representations made by Slomin's agent Howard S. Goldberg ("Goldberg") and/or contained in the written promotional materials provided to plaintiffs prior to the execution of the Contracts:

- That plaintiffs were purchasing a "top of the line" alarm system, guaranteed to keep their home safe from intruders.
- That the said alarm system was "hooked" into a central monitoring station operated and maintained by defendant and that, in the event of intrusion, the alarm system would "go off" automatically.
- That response time, in the event of an emergency, would be less than five minutes.
- That the system was fail safe in that, if the phone wires in the junction box were cut, the alarm would automatically "trip," alerting the central monitoring station and the police would respond within minutes.
- That, to Goldberg's "knowledge," in the three years immediately preceding the installation of the said alarm system at Plaintiffs' home, there had not been any successful burglaries of homes that had a similar system installed by Defendant.
- That the defendant, its employees, agents and servants, were experts in the installation, maintenance and operation of central station alarm systems, and that they were the "best" on Long Island, if not in the State of New York, in the installation, maintenance and operation of such stations.

On January 6, 2002, the plaintiffs' home was burglarized, at which time the home telephone lines were cut. Plaintiffs maintain that either the alarm system failed to transmit a signal or defendant's central monitoring agents failed to appreciate it. In either event, plaintiffs assert, the police were not notified until plaintiffs returned home and called them from a neighbor's telephone. Plaintiffs allege that they sustained substantial loss as a result of the burglary and the failure of Slomin's to timely notify the police.

Plaintiffs commenced this action in April 2002, asserting claims of fraud, negligence and breach of warranty. Defendant now moves to dismiss . . . on the ground that all causes of action are barred by the express terms of the Contracts. In particular, defendant refers to the merger clauses, disclaimers of representations and warranties, exculpatory clauses and limitation of liability or liquidated damages clauses contained [in] the Contracts. . . .

Courts generally refrain from disturbing arms-length transactions, and where the language of a contract is unambiguous, it is generally enforced according to its terms. The Contracts at issue here articulate an unambiguous intent to negate or limit Slomin's liability in almost every circumstance, and, on their face, present a defense to plaintiff's claims. However, New York courts have long recognized certain circumstances, including but not limited to fraud, in which even the most flawlessly drafted contract provisions may be subject to judicial scrutiny, and even avoided, in the interest of justice or sound public policy. The question is whether such circumstances exist here. . . .

The Courts shall first consider whether plaintiffs have a claim for fraud, and the legal effect upon such claim of the contractual provisions purporting to bar liability. To establish a *prima facie* case of fraud, the plaintiff must show that: (1) the defendant made a material representation of fact that was false; (2) the defendant knew that the representation was false and made it with intent to deceive (scienter); (3) the plaintiff justifiably relied upon defendant's misrepresentation; and (4) the plaintiff suffered some loss or harm as a result of such reliance. . . .

Here, plaintiffs' fraud claim is based upon the alleged representation by Goldberg that the system would transmit an alarm signal to the central monitoring station even if the telephone lines were cut. For purposes of this motion to dismiss, the Court must assume that Goldberg did, in fact, make such representation. Given that Slomin's moving papers concede that the system was *not* designed to work in such circumstances, Goldberg's alleged representation must have been false at the time it was made. Although plaintiff does not claim that Goldberg knew it was false, plaintiff need not speculate as to the extent of Goldberg's knowledge, as such facts are peculiarly within defendant's knowledge at this stage of the proceedings. Further, knowledge of falsity is not indispensable, if fraud also includes reckless misstatement and "the pretense of knowledge when knowledge there is none." Ultramares Corp. v. Touche,

255 N.Y. 170, 174 N.E. 441 [(1931)] (Cardozo, Ch. J.). As plaintiff is entitled to the benefit of every favorable inference for purposes of this motion, it can be inferred from the context of the alleged statement that Goldberg intended to induce plaintiffs to purchase the Slomin's alarm system and monitoring service, and that Goldberg, at minimum, assumed a pretense of knowledge in trying to conclude the sale. The Court concludes that the facts alleged in the complaint are sufficient to put defendants on notice of the misconduct complained of, and thus are sufficient to withstand dismissal . . . .

The Court turns to the Contract provisions that purport to bar liability. Each Contract contains a provision substantially as follows:

> Full Agreement; Severability. This agreement constitutes the full understanding of the parties and there are no oral Agreements, understandings or representations between the parties. This Agreement may not be amended or modified except in writing signed by both parties. Should any provision of this Agreement be deemed void, the remaining parts shall not be affected.

Defendant argues that this merger clause, together with the parol evidence rule . . . bar any claim based upon alleged oral representations. However, the parol evidence rule and such general merger clauses exclude extrinsic evidence to contradict or vary the terms of a written instrument in the context of a suit to *enforce* an oral representation. Both are "ineffectual to exclude evidence of fraudulent representations" in an action to rescind a contract or to recover loss sustained as a result of fraudulent inducement. Sabo v. Delman, 3 N.Y.2d 155, 164 N.Y.S.2d 714, 143 N.E.2d 906.

Defendant further argues that the Contracts contain specific disclaimers that do not fall within the rule articulated in *Sabo v. Delman* and that, consequently, defeat plaintiffs' claim. The *Sabo* rule, that fraud in the inducement vitiates a contract, is subject to exception. If a "plaintiff has, in the plainest language announced and stipulated that it is not relying on any representations as to the very matter as to which it now claims it was defrauded[, s]uch a specific disclaimer destroys the allegations in plaintiff's complaint that the agreement was executed in reliance upon these contrary representations." Danann Realty Corp. v. Harris, 5 N.Y.2d 317, 320, 184 N.Y.S.2d 599, 157 N.E.2d 597 [(1959)]. The specific disclaimer clause will be given effect particularly where it limits the authority of the agent to make extrinsic representations, and thus puts the plaintiff on notice that the agent's statements may not be relied upon.

In the case at bar, all of the Contracts provide: "The salesman has no authority to change any terms or make representations other than contained in this Agreement, and the buyer represents that none have been made to or relied upon by the Buyer." Section 8 of the Service Plan provides, in relevant part: "Customer acknowledges that . . . Slomin's has made no representations . . . and that customer has not relied upon any representations . . ." Section 7 of the Monitoring Agreement states, in relevant part: "Subscriber acknowledges that . . . Slomin's has made no representations or warranties and that subscriber has not relied upon any representations . . ."

However, these disclaimer clauses appear are [sic] no more than a reiteration of the general disclaimer contained in the merger clause, with the possible exception of the denial of the salesman's authority. The clauses disclaim reliance upon any oral representation, and do not identify any particular subject matter, let alone the very matter as to which plaintiffs claim they were defrauded. In *Danann* the disclaimer clause enumerated specific matters (e.g., the physical condition, rents, leases, expenses, operation or any other matter related to the subject premises) as to which the purchaser disclaimed reliance and certified that he had made independent investigation. The alleged oral misrepresentations concerned one of these very matters (the operating expenses and profits).

More troubling is the language contained in Section 7 of the Service Plan and substantially reiterated on the back of the Installment Agreement: "Slomin's makes no representation or warranty that the alarm system or that services supplied by Slomin's may not be circumvented, compromised or defeated or that the alarm system or services will in all cases provide the protection for which they were intended." This disclaimer is specific as to its subject matter, and Goldberg's representation to the effect that the system would not be compromised by cutting the telephone wires falls within its scope.

Nonetheless, the rule in *Danann* should not be rigidly or automatically applied with respect to any of the disclaimers cited above. . . .

A consumer's reliance upon the representations of the seller's sales agent may be justifiable, especially with respect to technical matters (such as the capabilities of an alarm system), presumably within the agent's expertise, which are incapable of independent verification by the consumer. This is true, even in the presence of a boilerplate clause in the sales contract denying the agent's authority to speak. Upon whom or what else is the consumer supposed to rely? The merchant presumably trains and presents its salespersons to consumers for purposes of providing them with information about the company's product or service. Such merchant cannot be permitted to escape all responsibility for the information provided simply by including a disclaimer of authority in a form contract. It cannot cloak its agents with authority on the one hand, and then deny it on the other.

This case provokes the following questions: Is the consumer's claim, innately, any less reliable than the purported disclaimer of reliance? The consumer must sign the contract if he wants to obtain the product or service, and ordinarily must adopt it wholesale, without opportunity to negotiate as to particular provisions. Can the consumer really be said to "represent" a state of facts (i.e., that no oral representations were made to him), by virtue of his acquiescent signature? What if such state of facts is rendered untrue by the acts of the merchant's sales agent? In such circumstances, the consumer's claim that he relied upon the sales agent's oral representations is no more inherently unreliable than the compulsory boilerplate disclaimer. To reflexively disallow parol evidence on the basis of such disclaimer, is to reward the ingenuity of draftsmen at the expense of sound public policy, and to invite sales agents, armed with impenetrable contracts, to lie to their customers. Here, the danger of fraudulent claims is outweighed by the danger of unrestrained fraud against the consumer.

In the limited context of such consumer sales transactions, a better rule is to examine the plaintiff's claims on a case-by-case basis to determine their reliability. If the allegations state with particularity the oral representations relied upon, together with contextual facts, in sufficient detail to permit the court to gauge their inherent credibility, then the plaintiff should be permitted to go forward with his proof, notwithstanding the existence of a specific disclaimer in the contract form. The plaintiffs here have satisfied that test. Note that, in its motion papers, Slomin's never denies that Goldberg actually made the statements attributed to him. Thus, not only are plaintiffs' allegations credible, but they are also unrefuted. In these circumstances, to dismiss the action on the basis of the disclaimer clause would require the Court to ignore reality in favor of a contractual myth. The Court finds that the disclaimers of reliance contained in the Contracts do not shield Slomin's from liability and do not prevent plaintiff from proving fraud in the inducement. . . .

SECTION 2. INTERPRETING THE PROMISE

INTRODUCTORY NOTE

An observer of contract has provided this sketch (Charny, Hypothetical Bargains: The Normative Structure of Contract Interpretation, 89 Mich. L. Rev. 1815, 1819–1820 (1991)):

> The law must supply a set of background conditions to interpretation and enforcement of contracts—commonly referred to as "default rules." Without default rules, no contract could have legal effect. This is the case for two reasons. Most fundamentally, no text can completely specify its own means of interpretation. A contractual statement that purported to be such a complete specification would itself have to be interpreted by some set of rules of interpretation. If the text purported to supply those rules, then those rules would have to be interpreted, and so on, ad infinitum. Thus, the default rules must, at a minimum, contain a set of rules about how the language of contract is to be interpreted.
>
> Second, . . . an important set of practical constraints limits the completeness of contracts. In almost all transactions, it would be

extremely costly to draft a contract that purported explicitly to address the obligations of the parties for all conceivable future contingencies. As a practical matter, then, most contracts are quite incomplete. The law supplies these missing terms. For example, the doctrines of mistake and impracticability add terms to address low-probability contingencies; so do doctrines that impose general duties, such as the duty of good faith. Correlatively, once the parties know that the law will supply the term, they take that into account when calculating the benefits of drafting an express term.

An examination of the flow of contract litigation passing daily through our courts indicates that relatively few cases involve serious controversy over principle or doctrine. Rather, it seems that the great majority of cases involve disputes over either (a) the facts (what happened, what the parties said and did) or (b) the proper meaning to be ascribed to the facts.

Our concern at the moment is with the second type of dispute—the giving of meaning to words and other conduct. The need to interpret words and actions, as we have seen, is not limited to situations where the parties have stated their agreement in writing. Still, interpreting written agreements raises problems that merit special consideration. If a court concludes that the writing incorporates the parties' entire agreement, or even their understanding on some parts of the transaction, the parol evidence rule operates to exclude proof of additional, divergent terms. But a fighting issue may remain: Can the words and conduct of the parties leading to the formalization of the agreement be used to elucidate the terms of the writing? Can testimony about intentions alter, or substitute for, contractual language? The policies underlying the parol evidence rule—a desire for certainty and predictability, coupled with an interest in reducing litigation and some unease about juries—would seem to signal caution in allowing contracting parties to testify as to what they in fact meant their words to mean, particularly when the testimony is contrary to the apparent meaning of the words in the contract. At the same time, it seems unrealistic to assume that the parties' meaning in using key terms will always—or even most of the time—be unquestionably clear from the face of the writing. And even if a contractual term is clear, other terms in the contract—perhaps even circumstances outside the contract—may alter its apparent meaning or show that a literal interpretation yields a dubious result.

Even if a court admits proof of surrounding circumstances and all other indications of the intended meaning of words, ambiguities and apparent inconsistencies may remain. Resort may then be had to certain rules of thumb devised by the courts and perhaps grounded in common experience. For example, where words of general import conflict with more specific language, the latter will likely govern. Again, where certain specifics falling into a general class are expressly mentioned and no language of broader inclusion is used, the proper inference may be that other specifics in the same class are to be excluded. No effort will be made here to catalog these ancillary rules of interpretation (sometimes called "canons of construction"), but you should be alert for them as they appear from time to time in the cases. It suffices to observe that their utility is limited. It has been said that they tend to "hunt in pairs," that is, a rule of interpretation pointing toward one meaning may be counterbalanced by another rule of equal respectability, leading to quite a different meaning. For example, the rule favoring specific over general language may, if invoked by an insurance company in a dispute over the meaning of language in the policy, be countered by the "rule" that ambiguity should be resolved against the party responsible for drafting the document. Thus, the "canons" of interpretation become little more than tools of advocacy. Rarely will they be decisive.

There is a further general point, by way of orientation. Since interpretation of a contract depends always on context, it is a "cultural" undertaking. One must bring to the task certain background baggage, as Judge Posner explained in Beanstalk Group, Inc. v. AM General Corp., 283 F.3d 856, 859–862 (7th Cir. 2002):

> [The plaintiff] is correct that written contracts are usually enforced in accordance with the ordinary meaning of the language used in them and without recourse to evidence, beyond the contract itself, as to what the parties meant. This presumption simplifies the litigation of contract disputes. . . . It is a strong presumption, motivated by an understandable distrust in the accuracy of litigation to reconstruct contracting parties' intentions, but it is rebuttable—here by two principles of contract interpretation that are closely related in the setting of this suit. The first is that a contract will not be interpreted literally if doing so would produce absurd results, in the sense of results that the parties, presumed to be rational persons pursuing rational ends, are very unlikely to have agreed to seek. . . .
>
> This is an interpretive principle, not a species of paternalism. "The letters between plaintiff and defendant were from one merchant to another. They are to be read as businessmen would read them, and only as a last resort are to be thrown out altogether as meaningless futilities. . . . If literalness is sheer absurdity, we are to seek some other meaning whereby reason will be instilled and absurdity avoided." Outlet Embroidery Co. v. Derwent Mills, 254 N.Y. 179, 172 N.E. 462, 463 (1930) (Cardozo, C.J.). "There is a long tradition [of] reading contracts sensibly; contracts—certainly business contracts of the kind involved here—are not parlor games but the means of getting the world's work done. . . . True, parties can contract for preposterous terms. If contract language is crystal clear or there is independent extrinsic evidence that something silly was actually intended, a party may be held to its bargain, absent some specialized defense." Rhode Island Charities Trust v. Engelhard Corp., 267 F.3d 3, 7 (1st Cir. 2001). . . . The second principle is that a contract must be interpreted as a whole. . . . Sentences are not isolated units of meaning, but take meaning from other sentences in the same document.
>
> The second principle thus is linguistic; the first reflects the fact that interpretation is a cultural as well as a linguistic undertaking. To interpret a contract or other document, it is not enough to have

> a command of the grammar, syntax, and vocabulary of the language in which the document is written. One must know something about the practical as well as the purely verbal context of the language to be interpreted. In the case of a commercial contract, one must have a general acquaintance with commercial practices. This doesn't mean that judges should have an M.B.A. or have practiced corporate or commercial law, but merely that they be alert citizens of a market-oriented society so that they can recognize absurdity in a business context. A blinkered literalism, a closing of one's eyes to the obvious, can produce nonsensical results. . . .
>
> The cultural background that a judge brings to the decision of a contract case includes as we said a general knowledge of how the world operates, including the commercial world, and this knowledge, precisely because it is general rather than being knowledge of the specific facts of the case ("adjudicative facts"), can show that the literal interpretation of a particular contractual term would be unsound, in which event no evidence need be taken.

The concept of "ambiguity" provides our starting point. Courts commonly say that a written contract that is "clear on its face" may not be altered by testimony about what a party intended the contractual language to mean. That is to say, where the language of the contract is clear and unambiguous, it is to be given effect according to its terms. But may a court—guided initially, and primarily, by the actual words of the contract—nonetheless consider extrinsic evidence for the very purpose of determining whether those words are ambiguous? To what extent must any ambiguity emanate from within, rather than without, the written agreement?

Judges should resist relying on their own intuitions about what words mean. What seems obvious at first often becomes less so on closer investigation. In the bankruptcy of Caesars Entertainment, hundreds of millions of dollars turned on the meaning the word "and." It might seem that "and" is a word whose meaning is unambiguous, but things are not so simple.

The dispute involved the meaning of a particular clause in a contract in which Caesars' parent company guaranteed one of its loans. The question was whether the guarantee was still in effect or whether it had terminated. The contract contained the following language:

> The Parent Guarantee shall terminate . . . upon:
>
> > the Issuer ceasing to be a Wholly Owned Subsidiary of Harrah's Entertainment;
> >
> > the Issuer's transfer of all or substantially all of its assets to, or merger with [a third party]; and
> >
> > . . . the Issuer's obligations under this Indenture are discharged in accordance with the terms of this Indenture. . .

There was a decent argument that one of conditions was met, but it was clear that not all three of them had been satisfied. The threshold interpretive question was therefore whether the guarantee terminated when *any* of these conditions was met or only when all three were. Hence, answering the question of whether all three conditions needed to be met was the threshold issue. This turned on the way in which "and" is used to link the subsections together. Is the word "and" just before the third clause being used conjunctively or disjunctively? The lender put the question in a way that it thought answered itself: Did the word "and" in this context mean "and" or did it mean "or"? It took the former view.

It might seem that the lender's position is ironclad. After all, "and" does not mean "or." Timothy Grinsell has suggested the matter is not so simple. In the first instance, the meaning of any word turns on the practice of native speakers. Therefore one must ask whether native speakers can use the word "and" disjunctively. He suggests that they can. Consider the following three sentences and ask whether a native speaker might utter them, and, if so, what they mean:

- If you're too successful at roulette and blackjack, the pit boss will keep an eye on you.
- If the stove and the heater break, the handyman will come.
- If you're hunting for deer, bears, and rabbits, you will need a license.

Do some native speakers talk this way? And if they do, what do they mean? Will the pit boss will keep an eye only if you are successful at both games or will you get her attention if you are too successful at either one? Will the handyman come only when the stove and the heater both fail? Is a license needed only for those who are hunting all three animals? These examples illustrate that there are some conditions under which "and" can be used disjunctively. In other words, "and" can mean "or." Whether it was used in this fashion in the Caesars loan document is not clear, but it is not as simple as it might first seem.

The ambiguity that exists here even for the word "and" suggests we must guard against using untutored intuition. Consider the following case in which a court confronts entirely ordinary language.

Hegel v. The First Liberty Insurance Corp.

United States Court of Appeals, Eleventh Circuit, 2015.
778 F.3d 1214.

GILMAN, CIRCUIT JUDGE. . . . The Hegels had a homeowner's insurance policy with First Liberty for their Spring Hills, Florida residence, effective October 5, 2010. This policy insured against "Sinkhole Loss" as an exception to the policy's exclusion for damage caused by earth movement. Under the policy, "Sinkhole Loss means *structural damage to the building,* including the foundation, caused by sinkhole activity." (Emphasis added.) The policy, however, did not define the term "structural damage." . . .

The Hegels allege that, on March 1, 2011, they "discovered damage to their home, including, but not limited to, progressive physical damage to the walls and floors of the residence." They subsequently submitted a claim for their damages to First Liberty under their homeowner's policy.

First Liberty retained Structural Engineering and Inspections, Inc. (SEI) to investigate the claim in September 2011. SEI concluded in a report that the Hegels' residence "*DOES NOT MEET* the criteria for *Structural Damage* as defined by Florida Statutes § 627.706 [2011]." (Emphases in original.) The SEI report noted some cracking and other issues, but determined that nothing rose to the level of "structural damage" as defined in the 2011 version of the statute. In addition, SEI listed several possible causes for the observed damage that were unrelated to sinkholes, including differential settlements and ordinary concrete shrinkage. First Liberty accordingly denied the Hegels' claim in October 2011, stating that their residence "ha[d] not sustained structural damage to the building or foundation" and that the damage was "related to normal concrete shrinkage, differential settlement, and improper embedment of [the] foundation."

In November 2011, the Hegels requested a neutral evaluation by a public adjuster. Kevin Scott, the neutral evaluator engaged for the claim, issued a report in July 2012. He noted that if the sinkhole claim was made under a policy with an effective date before May 17, 2011, then the 2011 definition of "structural damage" set forth in Florida Statutes § 627.706 would not apply. His report concluded that the damage to the Hegels' residence was "the result of a combination of factors, including sinkhole activity," but that "the observed distresses to the house can primarily be attributed to minor differential settlement of the structure and normal shrinkage/drying characteristics of the masonry materials." Ultimately, Scott recommended subsurface grouting, at an estimated cost of $105,075, to remediate the sinkhole activity. He did not, however, apply any particular definition of "structural damage" to his evaluation, finding only that "[t]here was physical damage that resulted from settlement."

The Hegels subsequently hired Central Florida Testing Laboratories, Inc. (CFTL) to review the findings and recommendations of SEI and the neutral evaluator, and to conduct additional testing. CFTL, in a report issued in March 2013, found damage consisting of "widespread, minor cracking to both the exterior and interior of the home." Like the neutral evaluator, CFTL determined that sinkhole activity was a contributing cause of the damage. To fully remediate the effects of the sinkhole activity, the report recommended shallow chemical grouting in addition to the deep compaction grouting program proposed by the neutral evaluator, and estimated the total cost at $145,775. The Hegels next retained Champion Foundation Repair to prepare a bid based on CFTL's recommended remediation plan, with the bid coming in at $141,180. Finally, the Hegels retained Triad Consulting Group (Triad) to estimate the cost of repairing cosmetic damages. Triad's bid totaled $20,743.17. . . .

Both the Hegels and First Liberty contend that the term "structural damage" is unambiguous and should be given its "plain meaning," but the parties disagree on what that meaning is. Even the district judges in the Middle District of Florida, in interpreting the same term in similar insurance policies under Florida law, have reached opposite conclusions.

This court has held that "differing interpretations of the same provision is evidence of ambiguity, particularly when a term is not explicitly defined or clarified by the policy." Dahl-Eimers v. Mut. of Omaha Life Ins. Co., 986 F.2d 1379, 1382 (11th Cir. 1993). On the other hand, the lack of a definition in a policy "does not necessarily render the term ambiguous and in need of interpretation by the courts." State Farm Fire & Cas. Co. v. CTC Dev. Corp., 720 So.2d 1072, 1076 (Fla. 1998). And the directive to interpret insurance policies liberally in favor of the insured applies "[o]nly when a genuine inconsistency, uncertainty, or ambiguity in meaning remains after resort to the ordinary rules of construction." Excelsior Ins. Co. v. Pomona Park Bar & Package Store, 369 So.2d 938, 942 (Fla. 1979).

Here, no genuine ambiguity exists because construing "structural damage" to mean simply any "damage to the structure" in the context of the insurance policy is facially unreasonable. Defining "structural damage" as such merely begs the question of what is "structural" or "structure," and what does either mean within the phrase "structural damage to the building"? Terms and phrases cannot be viewed in isolation; "courts must construe an insurance contract in its entirety, striving to give every provision meaning and effect." Dahl-Eimers, 986 F.2d at 1381 (citing Excelsior Ins. Co. v. Pomona Park Bar & Package Store, 369 So.2d 938, 941 (Fla. 1979)).

The district court awarded the Hegels damages for all subsurface and cosmetic repairs based on the parties' stipulation that there was "physical damage to Plaintiffs' home." Because "structural damage" is necessary for the Hegels to recover under the policy, the court must have equated "physical damage to Plaintiffs' home" with "structural damage to the building." Equating the two, however, essentially defines "structural damage" as "physical damage"—an untenable result. Such a construction would render the word "structural" meaningless because all property damage is physical, thereby violating a foundational rule of contract construction that every word be given effect. Indeed, at oral argument, counsel for the Hegels was unable to identify what type of damage to the property would not be "structural" under their preferred definition.

The key problem here is one of confusion between the words "structural" and "structure." In construing insurance-policy terms, Florida courts "commonly adopt the plain meaning of words contained in legal and non-legal dictionaries." Brill v. Indianapolis Life Ins. Co., 784 F.2d 1511, 1513 (11th Cir. 1986). "Structural" is an adjective, defined in the *Oxford English Dictionary* as "[f]orming a necessary part of the structure of a building or other construction, as distinct from its decoration or fittings." *Structural,* adj., Oxford English Dictionary, http://www.oed.com/view/Entry/191887 (June 2014) (last visited Feb. 26, 2015). The noun "structure," on the other hand, is simply a synonym for a building. *See Structure,* n., Oxford English Dictionary, http://www.oed.com/view/Entry/191895 (June 2014) (last visited Feb. 26, 2015) (defining "structure" as "[a] building, an edifice").

Based on these definitions, "damage to the structure" would encompass any physical damage to a building, even if only cosmetic, whereas "structural damage" would exclude damage to a building's "decoration or fittings." Any structural damage would necessarily encompass damage to the building, but the opposite is not necessarily true; i.e., many types of lesser damage to a building would not be structural damage. To equate "structural damage" with any "damage to the structure," as the district court did, is thus untenable.

Even the Hegels in their appellate brief appear to retreat from the district court's definition, arguing instead that the "damage must be to the structure itself as determined by professional engineers." But this definition is no better than the district court's definition because it fails to account for how professional engineers assess "structural damage." Kevin Scott, the neutral evaluator and a professional engineer, defined the term as follows: "It's damage which impedes the structural components from supporting the loads that they are intended to support. That is my engineering opinion of structural damage." Scott's definition is essentially the same as the only published district-court decision to squarely decide the plain meaning of the term. See Gonzalez v. Liberty Mut. Fire Ins. Co., 981 F.Supp.2d 1219, 1231 (M.D.Fla. 2013) (interpreting "structural damage" to mean "damage that impairs the structural integrity of the building"). We agree with the excellent analysis in *Gonzalez* and therefore construe the phrase "structural damage to the building" to mean "damage that impairs the structural integrity of the building." . . .

Stephen Mouritsen has argued that the problem in *Hegel* is much harder than the court suggests. See Mouritsen, Contract Interpretation with Corpus Linguistics, 94 Wash. L. Rev. ___ (forthcoming 2019). Dictionaries capture only incompletely the different ways in words are commonly used. For this reason, Mouritsen warns, one should be cautious about relying on them to establish the plain meaning of a contract. It is easy, he points out, to find many uses of the phrase "structural damage" in ordinary texts such as newspapers that do not involve damage to a structure that "impairs structural integrity":

> "The building, which was built in 1872, one year after the Great Chicago Fire, suffered structural damage to the exterior, but business continued as usual . . . ."

"The . . . car plowed into a building across the street from the old downtown Sanford Courthouse mid-morning, causing minor structural damage to its exterior."

"The district, facing 'serious structural damage' at the façade at Ernie Davis [Middle School], is putting up netting in case bricks fall."

Frigaliment Importing Co. v. B.N.S. International Sales Corp.

United States District Court, Southern District of New York, 1960.
190 F. Supp. 116.

FRIENDLY, J. The issue is, what is chicken? Plaintiff says "chicken" means a young chicken, suitable for broiling and frying. Defendant says "chicken" means any bird of that genus that meets contract specifications on weight and quality, including what it calls "stewing chicken" and plaintiff pejoratively terms "fowl." Dictionaries give both meanings, as well as some others not relevant here. To support its, plaintiff sends a number of volleys over the net; defendant essays to return them and adds a few serves of its own. Assuming that both parties were acting in good faith, the case nicely illustrates Holmes' remark "that the making of a contract depends not on the agreement of two minds in one intention, but on the agreement of two sets of external signs—not on the parties' having meant the same thing but on their having said the same thing." The Path of the Law, in Collected Legal Papers, p. 178. I have concluded that plaintiff has not sustained its burden of persuasion that the contract used "chicken" in the narrower sense.

The action is for breach of the warranty that goods sold shall correspond to the description. Two contracts are in suit. In the first, dated May 2, 1957, defendant, a New York sales corporation, confirmed the sale to plaintiff, a Swiss corporation, of

> US Fresh Frozen Chicken, Grade A, Government Inspected, Eviscerated 2½–3 lbs. and 1½–2 lbs. each all chicken individually wrapped in cryovac, packed in secured fiber cartons or wooden boxes, suitable for export
>
> 75,000 lbs. 2½–3 lbs. .... @$33.00
>
> 25,000 lbs. 1½–2 lbs. .... @$36.50
>
> per 100 lbs. FAS New York
>
> scheduled May 10, 1957 pursuant to instructions from Penson & Co., New York.

The second contract, also dated May 2, 1957, was identical save that only 50,000 lbs. of the heavier "chicken" were called for, the price of the smaller birds was $37 per 100 lbs., and shipment was scheduled for May

30. The initial shipment under the first contract was short but the balance was shipped on May 17. When the initial shipment arrived in Switzerland, plaintiff found, on May 28, that the 2½–3 lbs. birds were not young chicken suitable for broiling and frying but stewing chicken or "fowl"; indeed, many of the cartons and bags plainly so indicated. Protests ensued. Nevertheless, shipment under the second contract was made on May 29, the 2½–3 lbs. birds again being stewing chicken. Defendant stopped the transportation of these at Rotterdam. . . .

Since the word "chicken" standing alone is ambiguous, I turn first to see whether the contract itself offers any aid to its interpretation. Plaintiff says the 1½–2 lbs. birds necessarily had to be young chicken since the older birds do not come in that size, hence the 2½–3 lbs. birds must likewise be young. This is unpersuasive—a contract for "apples" of two different sizes could be filled with different kinds of apples even though only one species came in both sizes. Defendant notes that the contract called not simply for chicken but for "US Fresh Frozen Chicken, Grade A, Government Inspected." It says the contract thereby incorporated by reference the Department of Agriculture's regulations, which favor its interpretation; I shall return to this after reviewing plaintiff's other contentions.

The first hinges on an exchange of cablegrams which preceded execution of the formal contracts. The negotiations leading up to the contracts were conducted in New York between defendant's secretary, Ernest R. Bauer, and a Mr. Stovicek, who was in New York for the Czechoslovak government at the World Trade Fair. A few days after meeting Bauer at the fair, Stovicek telephoned and inquired whether defendant would be interested in exporting poultry to Switzerland. Bauer then met with Stovicek, who showed him a cable from plaintiff dated April 26, 1957, announcing that they "are buyer" of 25,000 lbs. of chicken 2½–3 lbs. weight, Cryovac packed, grade A Government inspected, at a price up to 33¢ per pound, for shipment on May 10, to be confirmed by the following morning, and were interested in further offerings. After testing the market for price, Bauer accepted, and Stovicek sent a confirmation that evening. Plaintiff stresses that, although these and subsequent cables between plaintiff and defendant, which laid the basis for the additional quantities under the first and for all of the second contract, were predominantly in German, they used the English word "chicken"; it claims this was done because it understood "chicken" meant young chicken whereas the German word, "Huhn," included both "Brathuhn" (broilers) and "Suppenhuhn" (stewing chicken), and that defendant, whose officers were thoroughly conversant with German, should have realized this. Whatever force this argument might otherwise have is largely drained away by Bauer's testimony that he asked Stovicek what kind of chickens were wanted, received the answer "any kind of chickens," and then, in German, asked whether the cable meant "Huhn" and received an affirmative response. . . .

Plaintiff's next contention is that there was a definite trade usage that "chicken" meant "young chicken." Defendant showed that it was only beginning in the poultry trade in 1957, thereby bringing itself within the principle that "when one of the parties is not a member of the trade or other circle, his acceptance of the standard must be made to appear" by proving either that he had actual knowledge of the usage or that the usage is "so generally known in the community that his actual individual knowledge of it may be inferred." 9 Wigmore, Evidence (3d ed. § 1940) 2464. Here there was no proof of actual knowledge of the alleged usage; indeed, it is quite plain that defendant's belief was to the contrary. In order to meet the alternative requirement, the law of New York demands a showing that "the usage is of so long continuance, so well established, so notorious, so universal and so reasonable in itself, as that the presumption is violent that the parties contracted with reference to it, and made it a part of their agreement." Walls v. Bailey, 1872, 49 N.Y. 464, 472–473.

Plaintiff endeavored to establish such a usage by the testimony of three witnesses and certain other evidence. Strasser, resident buyer in New York for a large chain of Swiss cooperatives, testified that "on chicken I would definitely understand a broiler." However, the force of this testimony was considerably weakened by the fact that in his own transactions the witness, a careful businessman, protected himself by using "broiler" when that was what he wanted and "fowl" when he wished older birds. . . . [A] witness' consistent failure to rely on the alleged usage deprives his opinion testimony of much of its effect. Niesielowski, an officer of one of the companies that had furnished the stewing chicken to defendant, testified that "chicken" meant "the male species of the poultry industry. That could be a broiler, a fryer or a roaster," but not a stewing chicken; however, he also testified that upon receiving defendant's inquiry for "chickens," he asked whether the desire was for "fowl or frying chickens" and, in fact, supplied fowl, although taking the precaution of asking defendant, a day or two after plaintiff's acceptance of the contracts in suit, to change its confirmation of its order from "chickens," as defendant had originally prepared it, to "stewing chickens." Dates, an employee of Urner-Barry Company, which publishes a daily market report on the poultry trade, gave it as his view that the trade meaning of "chicken" was "broilers and fryers." In addition to this opinion testimony, plaintiff relied on the fact that the Urner-Barry service, the Journal of Commerce, and Weinberg Bros. & Co. of Chicago, a large supplier of poultry, published quotations in a manner which, in one way or another, distinguish between "chicken," comprising broilers, fryers and certain other categories, and "fowl," which, Bauer acknowledged, included stewing chickens. This material would be impressive if there were nothing to the contrary. However, there was, as will now be seen.

Defendant's witness Weininger, who operates a chicken eviscerating plant in New Jersey, testified "Chicken is everything except a goose, a duck, and a turkey. Everything is a chicken, but then you have to say, you have to specify which category you want or that you are talking about." Its witness Fox said that in the trade "chicken" would encompass all the various classifications. Sadina, who conducts a food inspection service, testified that he would consider any bird coming within the classes of "chicken" in the Department of Agriculture's regulations to be a chicken. The specifications approved by the General Services Administration include fowl as well as broilers and fryers under the classification "chickens." Statistics of the Institute of American Poultry Industries use the phrases "Young chickens" and "Mature chickens," under the general heading "Total chickens," and the Department of Agriculture's daily and weekly price reports avoid use of the word "chicken" without specification. . . .

Defendant makes a further argument based on the impossibility of its obtaining broilers and fryers at the 33¢ price offered by plaintiff for the 2½–3 lbs. birds. There is no substantial dispute that, in late April, 1957, the price for 2½–3 lbs. broilers was between 35 and 37¢ per pound, and that when defendant entered into the contracts, it was well aware of this and intended to fill them by supplying fowl in these weights. It claims that plaintiff must likewise have known the market since plaintiff had reserved shipping space on April 23, three days before plaintiff's cable to Stovicek, or, at least, that Stovicek was chargeable with such knowledge. It is scarcely an answer to say, as plaintiff does in its brief, that the 33¢ price offered by the 2½–3 lbs. "chickens" was closer to the prevailing 35¢ price for broilers than to the 30¢ at which defendant procured fowl. Plaintiff must have expected defendant to make some profit—certainly it could not have expected defendant deliberately to incur a loss. . . .

When all the evidence is reviewed, it is clear that defendant believed it could comply with the contracts by delivering stewing chicken in the 2½–3 lbs. size. Defendant's subjective intent would not be significant if this did not coincide with an objective meaning of "chicken." Here it did coincide with one of the dictionary meanings, with the definition in the Department of Agriculture Regulations to which the contract made at least oblique reference, with at least some usage in the trade, with the realities of the market, and with what plaintiff's spokesman had said. Plaintiff asserts it to be equally plain that plaintiff's own subjective intent was to obtain broilers and fryers; the only evidence against this is the material as to market prices and this may not have been sufficiently brought home. In any event it is unnecessary to determine that issue. For plaintiff has the burden of showing that "chicken" was used in the narrower rather than in the broader sense, and this it has not sustained.

This opinion constitutes the Court's findings of fact and conclusions of law. Judgment shall be entered dismissing the complaint with costs.

NOTE

Courts are charged with understanding the language, customs, and practices of the parties to a contract. We should be cautious, however, about thinking that courts can readily identify a common language of the trade. Lisa Bernstein has done the foundational work here. See, e.g., Lisa Bernstein, Merchant Law in a Merchant Court: Rethinking the Code's Search for Immanent Business Norms, 144 U. Pa. L. Rev. 1765 (1996). Trade usage may not be clear. It may not be constant across time and place. See Emily Kadens, The Myth of the Customary Law Merchant, 90 Tex. L. Rev. 1153 (2012). And even if it were both clear and constant, a court may not be able to access it. There are also deeper problems. It is often a mistake to infer legal obligations from the customs and practices of merchants. Merchants may adopt regular practices that are never intended to generate a legal obligation. Hotels commonly allow guests to check in early when rooms are available, but does this mean that they are *legally obligated* to check guests in early if rooms are available? Another problem arises when we try to extract legal rules from the norms that exist within a merchant community. These norms arise from regular transactions within a single culture when things are going well. Lawsuits arise only when things have fallen apart. The norms from ordinary times may not be apt. Even if they were, lawsuits frequently involve amateurs or outsiders or people from different commercial cultures. We cannot rely on usage of trade unless we know which usage we are supposed to choose.

Commercial practice arises in a particular context that is often hard for outsiders to divine. A historian in the distant future who knew nothing about the 1960s except a series of amendments to the rules of a country club would see the introduction of all sorts of rules requiring members to wear ties and jackets. She might infer that people's dress became increasingly formal and fastidious during this period. This historian, however, would be making a mistake because she did not understand the context. Such rules were not required at the club until the late 1960s because before then everyone wore a tie and jacket as a matter of course. Rules became necessary only because dress was becoming increasingly casual. The relevant commercial practice in any case is something we have to construct from fragmentary bits of evidence. While most think that courts ought to try to understand the language and the customary practices of merchants in interpreting contracts, these indicia may give us less guidance than we think.

Posner, The Law and Economics of Contract Interpretation

83 Tex. L. Rev. 1581, 1603–1605 (2005)

If a contract is not clear on its face, but instead is vague or ambiguous, the judge will have to go outside the contract to decide what it means. But he can go outside it without getting entangled in the sort of factual disagreements that require a trial to untangle—in other words, without taking evidence. He can for example use common sense, which 'is as much a part of contract interpretation as is the dictionary or the arsenal of canons.' . . .

Suppose the litigants present rival interpretations of their contract to the judge, and it is apparent, without the need for a trial to resolve a factual disagreement, that one of these interpretations would make the contract extremely one-sided. That would be a reason—call it common sense or, if some explicit economic reasoning is employed, the promotion of efficiency—for the judge to choose the other interpretation. '[S]ince most though of course not all contracts involve the exchange of things of commensurate value, an interpretation that makes a contract grossly one-sided is suspect.' 'People usually don't pay a price for a good or service that is wildly in excess of its market value, or sell a good or service . . . for a price hugely less than its market value. . . .' More broadly, 'An interpretation which sacrifices a major interest of one of the parties while furthering only a marginal interest of the other should be rejected in favor of an interpretation which sacrifices marginal interests of both parties in order to protect their major concerns.'

A closely related principle is that if it is apparent, again without having to conduct a trial to resolve factual disagreements, that one of the rival interpretations proposed does not make commercial sense, the interpretation will be rejected because it probably does not jibe with what the parties understood when they signed the contract. '[A] contract will not be interpreted literally if doing so would produce absurd results, in the sense of results that the parties, presumed to be rational persons pursuing rational ends, are very unlikely to have agreed to seek.' And even if an interpretation makes sense, it will be rejected if the rival interpretation is markedly more sensible. 'Agreements, especially commercial arrangements, are designed to make sense. If one reading produces a plausible result for which parties might be expected to bargain, that reading has a strong presumption in its favor as against another reading producing an unlikely result (e.g., windfall gains, conditions that cannot be satisfied, dubious incentives).'

[Many interpretative methods]—trying to determine the parties' actual intentions, trying to determine their hypothetical intentions, trying to figure out the efficient resolution of their dispute, and trying to confine interpretation to the words of the contract rather than dumping the interpretive issue in the lap of a jury—tend to merge in practice. It would be one thing to impose the efficient solution in the teeth of the parties' agreement. That would be not only paternalistic but also reckless, because it would be rare that a judge or jury had a better sense of what would be an efficient transaction than the parties themselves had. But often, when the parties' intentions are not readily inferable from the written contract, the best, the most cost-efficient, way to resolve their dispute is not to take testimony and conduct a trial; it is to use commercial or economic common sense to figure out how, in all likelihood, the parties would have provided for the contingency that has arisen had they foreseen it. . . .

Weber Manufacturing Technologies, Inc. v. Plasan Carbon Composites, Inc.

United States District Court, Eastern District Michigan, 2016.
2016 WL 4073545.

ROSEN, UNITED STATES DISTRICT JUDGE. . . . Plasan contends that website statements made by Weber constitute express warranties. Specifically, Defendant intends to offer statements made by Weber that it delivers only "World Class Tooling" for automotive suppliers and others, and that it had specialized automotive tooling expertise such that it would deliver:

- "Excellence in Class 'A' body panels for hoods, deck lids, fenders, doors and quarter panels."
- "Tooling solutions for pickup truck boxes, fan shrouds, grille opening panels, rear end panels, lift gate panels, engine covers, oil pan covers and valve covers."
- "Full range of tooling for Automotive applications, both Interior & Exterior."
- "Tooling designed and built for either prototype or production runs."
- "Weber Manufacturing Technologies Inc. is committed to producing high quality tools that meet or exceed all customer requirements. Using dedicated project management from the early stages of conceptual tool design to the final delivery of the completed mold, we provide total customer satisfaction through every stage of the project."
- "We are committed to achieving total customer satisfaction in all aspects of our business and hold ourselves to the highest standards for superior quality, well-designed and constructed products, state of the art technology, on-time delivery, and world-class value."
- "Certified dimensional accuracy is critical on all of our projects. Every tool we supply is fully inspected, using one of our in-house CMM machines. All critical mold features are checked to customer supplied CAD part data. Comprehensive inspection reports are provided to satisfy a wide variety of customer specifications."

Having reviewed and examined these statements and the screen shots of Weber's website pages on which they appear, the Court agrees with Weber that most of these statements are nothing more than "trade puffing" which courts have precluded as irrelevant and/or unduly prejudicial. While the Court acknowledges that courts have held that catalog descriptions or advertisements may create an express warranty, the statements involved in those cases were far more specific than the statements set forth above upon which Plasan relies.

Conversely, courts have held that generalized expressions of opinion and praise of a party's own products do not create an express warranty; rather they constitute nothing more than trade puffing.

As evidence that the trade puffing nature of most of these statements did not induce Plasan to enter into the specific contractual relationship at issue, the parties had a lengthy pre-existing business relationship prior to their embarking on the specific production relationship presented here. Plasan was well familiar with Weber's capabilities, and it strains credulity that Plasan relied upon such generalized claims of quality on a website as a basis for entering into this particularly highly technical, cutting-edge production contract.

Having said this, there is one less generalized statement upon which Plasan claims to rely which may be sufficiently specific to pass muster here. i.e., the statement [about dimensional accuracy being critical]. . . .

Assuming Plasan is able to lay a foundational nexus between having read this statement, its relevance to this particular contract, and relying upon it in deciding to enter into the instant contractual relationship with Weber, this statement would be admissible. The remaining more general statements of opinion and praise for Weber's products appearing on Weber's website will not be allowed as evidence of any express warranties.

NOTE: THE DUTY OF GOOD FAITH AND FAIR DEALING

In addition to interpreting the words that parties include in their agreements, courts must also at times confront what parties leave unsaid. Among other things, common law courts read every contract as if each party promised to act in good faith during the course of the contractual relationship.

Restatement of Contracts, Second

§ 205. Duty of Good Faith and Fair Dealing

Every contract imposes upon each party a duty of good faith and fair dealing in its performance and its enforcement.

Comment:

a. *Meanings of "Good Faith."* . . . The phrase "good faith" is used in a variety of contexts, and its meaning varies somewhat with the context. [Here the phrase] emphasizes faithfulness to an agreed common purpose and consistency with the justified expectations of the other party; it excludes a variety of types of conduct characterized as involving "bad faith" because they violate community standards of decency, fairness, or reasonableness. The appropriate remedy for a breach of the duty of good faith varies with the circumstances. . . .

d. Good Faith Performance. . . . [T]he obligation [of good faith in performance] goes further than [subterfuges and evasions]: bad faith may be overt or may consist of inaction, and fair dealing may require more than honesty. . . . [T]he following types [of bad faith] are among those which have been recognized in judicial decisions: evasion of the spirit of the bargain, lack of diligence and slacking off, willful rendering of imperfect performance, abuse of a power to specify terms, and interference with or failure to cooperate in the other party's performance.

[When this section was before the annual meeting of the ALI in 1970, Robert Braucher, the Reporter, said: "I don't think you can find a case in the whole history of the common law in which a court says that good faith is not required in the performance of a contract or in enforcement of a contract. Now, the trouble with this section, of course, is that it's very general, very abstract. . . . Anyway, the principle is to be found in judicial opinions. I haven't invented it." 47 A.L.I. Proc.489–491 (1970).]

As Justice Braucher observed, it is hard to imagine anyone who would want to give her contracting opposite the ability to act in bad faith. But, as the following two cases show, it is not always easy to identify the contours of such a duty.

Market Street Associates Ltd. Partnership v. Frey

United States Court of Appeals, Seventh Circuit, 1991.
941 F.2d 588.

POSNER, CIRCUIT JUDGE. . . . In 1968, J.C. Penney Co., the retail chain, entered into a sale and leaseback arrangement with General Electric Pension Trust in order to finance Penney's growth. Under the arrangement Penney sold properties to the pension trust which the trust then leased back to Penney for a term of 25 years. Paragraph 34 of the lease entitles the lessee to "request Lessor [the pension trust] to finance the costs and expenses of construction of additional Improvements upon the Premises," provided the amount of the costs and expenses is at least $250,000. Upon receiving the request, the pension trust "agrees to give reasonable consideration to providing the financing of such additional Improvements and Lessor and Lessee shall negotiate in good faith concerning the construction of such Improvements and the financing by Lessor of such costs and expenses." Paragraph 34 goes on to provide that, should the negotiations fail, the lessee shall be entitled to repurchase the property at a price roughly equal to the price at which Penney sold it to the pension trust in the first place, plus 6 percent a year for each year since the original purchase. So if the average annual appreciation in the property exceeded 6 percent, a breakdown in negotiations over the financing of improvements would entitle Penney to buy back the property for less than its market value (assuming it had sold the property to the pension trust in the first place at its then market value).

One of these leases was for a shopping center in Milwaukee. In 1987 Penney assigned this lease to Market Street Associates, which the following year received an inquiry from a drugstore chain that wanted to open a store in the shopping center, provided (as is customary) that Market Street Associates built the store for it. Whether Market Street Associates was pessimistic about obtaining financing from the pension trust, still the lessor of the shopping center, or for other reasons, it initially sought financing for the project from other sources. But they were unwilling to lend the necessary funds without a mortgage on the shopping center, which Market Street Associates could not give because it was not the owner but only the lessee. It decided therefore to try to buy the property back from the pension trust. Market Street Associates' general partner, Orenstein, tried to call David Erb of the pension trust, who was responsible for the property in question. Erb did not return his calls, so Orenstein wrote him, expressing an interest in buying the property and asking him to "review your file on this matter and call me so that we can discuss it further." At first, Erb did not reply. Eventually Orenstein did reach Erb, who promised to review the file and get back to him. A few days later an associate of Erb called Orenstein and indicated an interest in selling the property for $3 million, which Orenstein considered much too high.

That was in June of 1988. On July 28, Market Street Associates wrote a letter to the pension trust formally requesting funding for $2 million in improvements to the shopping center. The letter made no reference to paragraph 34 of the lease; indeed, it did not mention the lease. The letter asked Erb to call Orenstein to discuss the matter. Erb, in what was becoming a habit of unresponsiveness, did not call. On August 16, Orenstein sent a second letter—certified mail, return receipt requested—again requesting financing and this time referring to the lease, though not expressly to paragraph 34. The heart of the letter is the following two sentences: "The purpose of this letter is to ask again that you advise us immediately if you are willing to provide the financing pursuant to the lease. If you are willing, we propose to enter into negotiation to amend the ground lease appropriately." The very next day, Market Street Associates received from Erb a letter, dated August 10, turning down the original request for financing on the ground that it did not "meet our current investment criteria": the pension trust was not interested in making loans for less than $7 million. On August 22, Orenstein replied to Erb by letter, noting that his letter of August 10 and Erb's letter of August 16 had evidently crossed in the mails, expressing disappointment at the turn-down, and stating that Market Street Associates would seek financing elsewhere. That was the last contact between the parties until September 27, when Orenstein sent Erb a letter stating that Market Street

Associates was exercising the option granted it by paragraph 34 to purchase the property upon the terms specified in that paragraph in the event that negotiations over financing broke down.

The pension trust refused to sell, and this suit to compel specific performance followed. Apparently the price computed by the formula in paragraph 34 is only $1 million. The market value must be higher, or Market Street Associates wouldn't be trying to coerce conveyance at the paragraph 34 price; whether it is as high as $3 million, however, the record does not reveal.

The district judge granted summary judgment for the pension trust on two grounds that he believed to be separate although closely related. The first was that, by failing in its correspondence with the pension trust to mention paragraph 34 of the lease, Market Street Associates had prevented the negotiations over financing that are a condition precedent to the lessee's exercise of the purchase option from taking place. Second, this same failure violated the duty of good faith, which the common law of Wisconsin, as of other states, reads into every contract. In support of both grounds the judge emphasized a statement by Orenstein in his deposition that it had occurred to him that Erb mightn't know about paragraph 34, though this was unlikely (Orenstein testified) because Erb or someone else at the pension trust would probably check the file and discover the paragraph and realize that if the trust refused to negotiate over the request for financing, Market Street Associates, as Penney's assignee, would be entitled to walk off with the property for (perhaps) a song. The judge inferred that Market Street Associates didn't want financing from the pension trust—that it just wanted an opportunity to buy the property at a bargain price and hoped that the pension trust wouldn't realize the implications of turning down the request for financing. Market Street Associates should, the judge opined, have advised the pension trust that it was requesting financing pursuant to paragraph 34, so that the trust would understand the penalty for refusing to negotiate.

We begin our analysis by setting to one side two extreme contentions by the parties. The pension trust argues that the option to purchase created by paragraph 34 cannot be exercised until negotiations over financing break down; there were no negotiations; therefore they did not break down; therefore Market Street Associates had no right to exercise the option. This argument misreads the contract. Although the option to purchase is indeed contingent, paragraph 34 requires the pension trust, upon demand by the lessee for the financing of improvements worth at least $250,000, "to give reasonable consideration to providing the financing." The lessor who fails to give reasonable consideration and thereby prevents the negotiations from taking place is breaking the contract; and a contracting party cannot be allowed to use his own breach to gain an advantage by impairing the rights that the contract confers on the other party. Often, it is true, if one party breaks the contract, the other can walk away from it without liability, can in other words exercise self-help.

But he is not required to follow that course. He can stand on his contract rights.

But what exactly are those rights in this case? The contract entitles the lessee to reasonable consideration of its request for financing, and only if negotiations over the request fail is the lessee entitled to purchase the property at the price computed in accordance with paragraph 34. It might seem therefore that the proper legal remedy for a lessor's breach that consists of failure to give the lessee's request for financing reasonable consideration would not be an order that the lessor sell the property to the lessee at the paragraph 34 price, but an order that the lessor bargain with the lessee in good faith. But we do not understand the pension trust to be arguing that Market Street Associates is seeking the wrong remedy. We understand it to be arguing that Market Street Associates has no possible remedy. That is an untenable position.

Market Street Associates argues, with equal unreason as it seems to us, that it could not have broken the contract because paragraph 34 contains no express requirement that in requesting financing the lessee mention the lease or paragraph 34 or otherwise alert the lessor to the consequences of his failing to give reasonable consideration to granting the request. There is indeed no such requirement (all that the contract requires is a demand). But no one says there is. The pension trust's argument, which the district judge bought, is that either as a matter of simple contract interpretation or under the compulsion of the doctrine of good faith, a provision requiring Market Street Associates to remind the pension trust of paragraph 34 should be read into the lease.

It seems to us that these are one ground rather than two. A court has to have a reason to interpolate a clause into a contract. The only reason that has been suggested here is that it is necessary to prevent Market Street Associates from reaping a reward for what the pension trust believes to have been Market Street's bad faith. So we must consider the meaning of the contract duty of "good faith." The Wisconsin cases are cryptic as to its meaning though emphatic about its existence, so we must cast our net wider. We do so mindful of Learned Hand's warning, that "such words as 'fraud,' 'good faith,' 'whim,' 'caprice,' 'arbitrary action,' and 'legal fraud' . . . obscure the issue." Thompson-Starrett Co. v. La Belle Iron Works, 17 F.2d 536, 541 (2d Cir. 1927). Indeed they do. The particular confusion to which the vaguely moralistic overtones of "good faith" give rise is the belief that every contract establishes a fiduciary relationship. A fiduciary is required to treat his principal as if the principal were he, and therefore he may not take advantage of the principal's incapacity, ignorance, inexperience, or even naïveté. If Market Street Associates were the fiduciary of General Electric Pension Trust, then (we may assume) it could not take advantage of Mr. Erb's apparent ignorance of paragraph 34, however exasperating Erb's failure to return Orenstein's phone calls was and however negligent Erb or his associates were in failing to read the lease before turning down Orenstein's request for financing.

But it is unlikely that Wisconsin wishes, in the name of good faith, to make every contract signatory his brother's keeper, especially when the brother is the immense and sophisticated General Electric Pension Trust, whose lofty indifference to small (≤ $7 million) transactions is the signifier of its grandeur. In fact the law contemplates that people frequently will take advantage of the ignorance of those with whom they contract, without thereby incurring liability. The duty of honesty, of good faith even expansively conceived, is not a duty of candor. You can make a binding contract to purchase something you know your seller undervalues. Laidlaw v. Organ, 15 U.S. (2 Wheat.) 178, 181 n. 2, 4 L.Ed. 214 (1817). That of course is a question about formation, not performance, and the particular duty of good faith under examination here relates to the latter rather than to the former. But even after you have signed a contract, you are not obliged to become an altruist toward the other party and relax the terms if he gets into trouble in performing his side of the bargain. Otherwise mere difficulty of performance would excuse a contracting party—which it does not.

But it is one thing to say that you can exploit your superior knowledge of the market—for if you cannot, you will not be able to recoup the investment you made in obtaining that knowledge—or that you are not required to spend money bailing out a contract partner who has gotten into trouble. It is another thing to say that you can take deliberate advantage of an oversight by your contract partner concerning his rights under the contract. Such taking advantage is not the exploitation of superior knowledge or the avoidance of unbargained-for expense; it is sharp dealing. Like theft, it has no social product, and also like theft it induces costly defensive expenditures, in the form of overelaborate disclaimers or investigations into the trustworthiness of a prospective contract partner, just as the prospect of theft induces expenditures on locks.

The form of sharp dealing that we are discussing might or might not be actionable as fraud or deceit. That is a question of tort law and there the rule is that if the information is readily available to both parties the failure of one to disclose it to the other, even if done in the knowledge that the other party is acting on mistaken premises, is not actionable. [Citing cases, including Guyer v. Cities Service Oil Co., 440 F. Supp. 630 (E.D. Wis. 1977).] All of these cases, however, with the debatable exception of *Guyer*, involve failure to disclose something in the negotiations leading up to the signing of the contract, rather than failure to disclose after the contract has been signed. (*Guyer* involved failure to disclose during the negotiations leading up to a renewal of the contract.) The distinction is important, as we explained in Maksym v. Loesch, 937 F.2d 1237, 1242 (7th Cir. 1991). Before the contract is signed, the parties confront each other with a natural wariness. Neither expects the other to be particularly forthcoming, and therefore there is no deception when one is not. Afterwards the situation is different. The parties are now in a cooperative relationship the costs of which will be considerably reduced by a measure of trust. So each lowers his guard a bit, and now silence is more apt to be deceptive.

Moreover, this is a contract case rather than a tort case, and conduct that might not rise to the level of fraud may nonetheless violate the duty of good faith in dealing with one's contractual partners and thereby give rise to a remedy under contract law. This duty is, as it were, halfway between a fiduciary duty (the duty of *utmost* good faith) and the duty merely to refrain from active fraud. Despite its moralistic overtones it is no more the injection of moral principles into contract law than the fiduciary concept itself is. It would be quixotic as well as presumptuous for judges to undertake through contract law to raise the ethical standards of the nation's business people. The concept of the duty of good faith like the concept of fiduciary duty is a stab at approximating the terms the parties would have negotiated had they foreseen the circumstances that have given rise to their dispute. The parties want to minimize the costs of performance. To the extent that a doctrine of good faith designed to do this by reducing defensive expenditures is a reasonable measure to this end, interpolating it into the contract advances the parties' joint goal.

It is true that an essential function of contracts is to allocate risk, and would be defeated if courts treated the materializing of a bargained-over, allocated risk as a misfortune the burden of which is required to be shared between the parties (as it might be within a family, for example) rather than borne entirely by the party to whom the risk had been allocated by mutual agreement. But contracts do not just allocate risk. They also (or some of them) set in motion a cooperative enterprise, which may to some extent place one party at the other's mercy. "The parties to a contract are embarked on a cooperative venture, and a minimum of cooperativeness in the event unforeseen problems arise at the performance stage is required even if not an explicit duty of the contract." AMPAT/Midwest, Inc. v. Illinois Tool Works Inc., 896 F.2d 1035, 1041 (7th Cir. 1990). The office of the doctrine of good faith is to forbid the kinds of opportunistic behavior that a mutually dependent, cooperative relationship might enable in the absence of rule. . . . The contractual duty of good faith is thus not some newfangled bit of welfare-state paternalism or the sediment of an altruistic strain in contract law, and we are therefore not surprised to find the essentials of the modern doctrine well established in nineteenth century cases, a few examples being Bush v. Marshall, 47 U.S. (6 How.) 284, 291, 12 L.Ed. 440 (1848); Chicago, Rock Island & Pac. R.R. v. Howard, 74 U.S. (7 Wall.) 392, 413, 19 L.Ed. 117 (1868); Marsh v. Masterson, 101 N.Y. 401, 410–11, 5 N.E. 59, 63 (1886), and Uhrig v. Williamsburg City Fire Ins. Co., 101 N.Y. 362, 4 N.E. 745 (1886). . . .

We could of course do without the term "good faith," and maybe even without the doctrine. We could, as just suggested, speak instead of implied conditions necessitated by the unpredictability of the future at the time the contract was made. Suppose a party has promised work to the promisee's "satisfaction." As Learned Hand explained, "he may refuse to look at the work, or to exercise any real judgment on it, in which case he has prevented performance and excused the condition." Thompson-Starrett Co. v. La Belle Iron Works, supra, 17 F.2d at 541. That is, it was an implicit condition that the promisee examine the work to the extent necessary to determine whether it was satisfactory; otherwise the performing party would have been placing himself at the complete mercy of the promisee. The parties didn't write this condition into the contract either because they thought such behavior unlikely or failed to foresee it altogether. In just the same way—to switch to another familiar example of the operation of the duty of good faith—parties to a requirements contract surely do not intend that if the price of the product covered by the contract rises, the buyer shall be free to increase his "requirements" so that he can take advantage of the rise in the market price over the contract price to resell the product on the open market at a guaranteed profit. If they fail to insert an express condition to this effect, the court will read it in, confident that the parties would have inserted the condition if they had known what the future held. Of similar character is the implied condition that an exclusive dealer will use his best efforts to promote the supplier's goods, since otherwise the exclusive feature of the dealership contract would place the supplier at the dealer's mercy. Wood v. Duff-Gordon, 222 N.Y. 88, 118 N.E. 214 (1917) (Cardozo, J.).

But whether we say that a contract shall be deemed to contain such implied conditions as are necessary to make sense of the contract, or that a contract obligates the parties to cooperate in its performance in "good faith" to the extent necessary to carry out the purposes of the contract, comes to much the same thing. They are different ways of formulating the overriding purpose of contract law, which is to give the parties what they would have stipulated for expressly if at the time of making the contract they had had complete knowledge of the future and the costs of negotiating and adding provisions to the contract had been zero.

. . . The dispositive question in the present case is simply whether Market Street Associates tried to trick the pension trust and succeeded in doing so. If it did, this would be the type of opportunistic behavior in an ongoing contractual relationship that would violate the duty of good faith performance however the duty is formulated. There is much common sense in Judge Reynolds' conclusion that Market Street Associates did just that. The situation as he saw it was as follows. Market Street Associates didn't want financing from the pension trust (initially it had looked elsewhere, remember), and when it learned it couldn't get the financing without owning the property, it decided to try to buy the property. But the pension trust set a stiff price, so Orenstein decided to trick the pension trust into selling at the bargain price fixed in paragraph 34 by requesting financing and hoping that the pension trust would turn the request down without noticing the paragraph. His preliminary dealings with the pension trust made this hope a realistic one by revealing a sluggish and hidebound bureaucracy unlikely to have retained in its brontosaurus's memory, or to be able at short notice to retrieve, the details of a small lease made twenty years earlier. So by requesting financing without mentioning the lease Market Street Associates might well precipitate a refusal before the pension trust woke up to paragraph 34. It is true that Orenstein's second letter requested financing "pursuant to the lease." But when the next day he received a reply to his first letter indicating that the pension trust was indeed oblivious to paragraph 34, his response was to send a lulling letter designed to convince the pension trust that the matter was closed and could be forgotten. The stage was set for his thunderbolt: the notification the next month that Market Street Associates was taking up the option in paragraph 34. Only then did the pension trust look up the lease and discover that it had been had.

The only problem with this recital is that it construes the facts as favorably to the pension trust as the record will permit, and that of course is not the right standard for summary judgment. The facts must be construed as favorably to the nonmoving party, to Market Street Associates, as the record permits. . . . When that is done, a different picture emerges. On Market Street Associates' construal of the record, $3 million was a grossly excessive price for the property, and while $1 million might be a bargain it would not confer so great a windfall as to warrant an inference that if the pension trust had known about paragraph 34 it never would have turned down Market Street Associates' request for financing cold. And in fact the pension trust may have known about paragraph 34, and either it didn't care or it believed that unless the request mentioned that paragraph the pension trust would incur no liability by turning it down. Market Street Associates may have assumed and have been entitled to assume that in reviewing a request for financing from one of its lessees the pension trust would take the time to read the lease to see whether it bore on the request. Market Street Associates did not desire financing from the pension trust initially—that is undeniable—yet when it discovered that it could not get financing elsewhere unless it had the title to the property it may have realized that it would have to negotiate with the pension trust over financing before it could hope to buy the property at the price specified in the lease.

On this interpretation of the facts there was no bad faith on the part of Market Street Associates. It acted honestly, reasonably, without ulterior motive, in the face of circumstances as they actually and reasonably appeared to it. The fault was the pension trust's incredible inattention, which misled Market Street Associates into believing that the pension trust had no interest in financing the improvements regardless of the purchase option. We do not usually excuse contracting parties from failing to read and understand the contents of their contract; and in the end what this case comes down to—or so at least it can be strongly argued—is that an immensely sophisticated enterprise simply failed to read the contract. On the other hand, such enterprises make mistakes just like the rest of us, and deliberately to take advantage of your contracting partner's mistake during the performance stage (for we are not talking about taking advantage of superior knowledge at the formation stage) is a breach of good faith. To be able to correct your contract partner's mistake at zero cost to yourself, and decide not to do so, is a species of opportunistic behavior that the parties would have expressly forbidden in the contract had they foreseen it. The immensely long term of the lease amplified the possibility of errors but did not license either party to take advantage of them.

The district judge jumped the gun in choosing between these alternative characterizations. The essential issue bearing on Market Street Associates' good faith was Orenstein's state of mind, a type of inquiry that ordinarily cannot be concluded on summary judgment, and could not be here. If Orenstein believed that Erb knew or would surely find out about paragraph 34, it was not dishonest or opportunistic to fail to flag that paragraph, or even to fail to mention the lease, in his correspondence and (rare) conversations with Erb, especially given the uninterest in dealing with Market Street Associates that Erb fairly radiated. To decide what Orenstein believed, a trial is necessary. As for the pension trust's intimation that a bench trial (for remember that this is an equity case, since the only relief sought by the plaintiff is specific performance) will add no illumination beyond what the summary judgment proceeding has done, this overlooks the fact that at trial the judge will for the first time have a chance to see the witnesses whose depositions he has read, to hear their testimony elaborated, and to assess their believability.

The judgment is reversed and the case is remanded for further proceedings consistent with this opinion.

NOTE

Professor Todd Rakoff offers the following critique of Judge Posner's opinion (Good Faith in Contract Performance: Market Street Associates Ltd. Partnership v. Frey, 120 Harv. L. Rev. 1187 (2007)):

> *Market Street Associates* offers what seems to me an excellent examination of the doctrine of good faith. But as to its treatment of the work still needed to reach a decision, I am more doubtful. Judge Posner cited a lot of cases, both from his own circuit and from common law "greats" like Cardozo, Hand, and Friendly. But he did not rely on any prior opinion as a precedent to be directly applied to the facts before him. Nor did he use the cases to build an analytical series covering the remaining middle ground. Rather, he offered us

a general approach (which the cases were taken to illustrate) and a specific outcome. . . .

The connection between this general method and [his] specific conclusion seems unclear. Judge Posner's own explanation of why "tried to trick" was the "dispositive" standard was that "this would be the type of opportunistic behavior in an ongoing contractual relationship that would violate the duty of good faith performance however the duty is formulated." But the trial judge did not deny that intentional trickery would be bad faith; what he claimed was that the duty went further, requiring the lessee (regardless of motive) to remind the lessor of paragraph 34 as a precondition to later claiming rights under it. To justify the Seventh Circuit's reversal, it is not enough to allow that the duty of good faith goes as far as Judge Posner specified; one has to show that it goes no further. More is needed.

The only textual support for [Posner's narrow formulation of the duty of good faith] is the statement he made at one point that "[i]t would be quixotic as well as presumptuous for judges to undertake through contract law to raise the ethical standards of the nation's business people." Admittedly, that statement is ambiguous. It might be read simply to say that judges should try to give the parties what they (and not the judges) would have wanted. But it might also be read as evincing a fear that if judges (perhaps especially trial judges) are not restrained, they will not be very good at creating implied terms; even if appellate courts tell them to aim only to give the parties what they would have wanted, judges' natural tendency will be to state a higher standard. Or, to put the matter more particularly, perhaps Judge Posner favored the reading of the obligation of good faith nearest to intentional tort—the outlaw-tricky-behavior reading—because he thought it would yield the best results overall when implemented by the courts.

The point is not simply that Judge Posner may have generalized, that he might have been concerned with the proper scope of good faith in the run of cases and not just in the particular instance he faced. The claim that business people do not expect from each other actions that facilitate each other's required performances, and only expect their partners not to be "tricky," is not always wrong, but in the view recognized by many prior cases it is wrong often enough that we ought not ground a doctrine on it.

Rather, the point is that Judge Posner's statement might rest on the proposition that policing really smelly behavior is the most that judges can reliably and usefully do—on an assessment, that is, of judicial capabilities rather than of actual commercial practice. That claim, in turn, might come from a belief that, all things considered, trial judges are usually better at understanding interpersonal human relations than they are at decoding the workings of commercial relationships, so that their creation of implied terms in the latter situations will be unreliable. Or it might come from a belief that it is better to set the default rule of good faith at a minimal level in order to put pressure on commercial parties to specify their expectations up front, rather than to have them rely on the judges after the fact, because even if the judges are competent, the parties are more competent. Or it might come from both of these beliefs. These claims would support the result in *Market Street Associates*, although whether Judge Posner, or the panel, thought about them must remain a matter of speculation. . . .

Security Plans, Inc. v. CUNA Mutual Insurance Society

United States Court of Appeals, Second Circuit, 2014.
769 F.3d 807.

SACK, CIRCUIT JUDGE. . . . Security Plans, Inc., formerly known as Creditor Services, Inc., is a corporation based in Mendon, New York, which until 2002 specialized in the sale of credit-related insurance products, primarily to credit unions. Security Plans' primary products were credit life and credit disability insurance, which promise to pay the outstanding balance on a loan in the event the borrower dies or becomes disabled. In 2002, Security Plans agreed to sell substantially all of its assets to CUNA Mutual Insurance Society, a company incorporated in Iowa, with its principal office in Madison, Wisconsin. The parties set in motion a plan to transfer Security Plans' insurance clients (its "book of business") to CUNA Mutual. The merger was completed on January 2, 2003. . . .

An Asset Purchase Agreement, dated May 31, 2002, set forth the terms of this merger. CUNA Mutual agreed to pay $3 million immediately plus an additional performance-based payment to be made three years after the merger was concluded for Security Plans' property and book of business. The deferred-payment component of this compensation package is commonly referred to as an "earnout." Under this contract, the maximum possible earnout was $2.2 million.

CUNA Mutual also executed three-year employment agreements with each of the three Security Plans shareholders, in which the shareholders agreed to assist in transitioning the book of business. Each former Security Plans client would have to decide individually whether to accept CUNA Mutual as its new insurer, and the earnout was therefore designed to encourage the shareholders to convert as many clients as possible.

The basic formula for calculating the earnout is not in dispute. The performance of Security Plans' book of business would be calculated annually for three years after closing, and then another three years of performance would be projected based on the data from the third year. Two variables would largely determine the size of the earnout: a weighted average of total written premiums brought in by the acquired business, and a weighted average of the business's combined loss ratios. These two amounts would be used to calculate a preliminary total earnout, which would then be reduced by service fees and other reimbursements paid to credit unions. This reduced figure would represent the final payment.

The Asset Purchase Agreement also provided:

> [Security Plans] acknowledges that [CUNA Mutual] is under no obligation to operate its business after Closing in a manner focused on maximizing the Earn-Out . . . and may operate the business in accordance with its best business judgment.

This dispute concerns two factors that affected the calculation of the earnout. First, Security Plans contends, CUNA Mutual used incorrect figures to calculate loss ratios for these accounts, thereby leading to a lower earnout than that to which Security Plans was entitled. Second, Security Plans argues, CUNA Mutual imposed an excessive deduction relating to service fees paid to credit unions. . . .

Insurers are required by accounting rules and by statute to carry claim reserves, which are kept in anticipation of future liabilities. Claim reserves are, for accounting purposes, considered to be a component of incurred claims. Increases in incurred claims ordinarily will, all other things being equal, increase a company's loss ratio. Higher loss ratios would reduce Security Plans' earnout.

The parties agree that the loss ratios recorded for Security Plans' book of business for 2003 through 2005—the relevant reporting period for the earnout—were "atypically high." Their unusually high loss ratios were largely attributable to the fact that, during the same period, CUNA Mutual was carrying abnormally high claim reserves on all of its business, including the Security Plans policies. CUNA Mutual began to release claim reserves in 2006 to compensate for the problem, but it did not correct the reserves concerning Security Plans' book of business in time to affect the earnout.

The reason for the magnitude of the claim reserves is not entirely clear. CUNA Mutual has asserted that, although the reserve levels were later revised downward, their size during the 2003 to 2005 time period resulted from "the exercise of business judgment by CUNA Mutual's actuaries." The plaintiff disputes that, characterizing the reserve levels as a systemic, company-wide error, which CUNA Mutual sought to correct in 2006 by releasing what ultimately amounted to millions of dollars in excess reserves. In other words, the plaintiff suggests that rather than deliberately keeping high claim reserves as a strategic or actuarial decision, CUNA Mutual failed to correct aberrations that distorted the performance data until 2006. . . .

The plaintiff . . . contends that the defendant's handling of the claim reserves and the resultant earnout calculation violated the implied covenant of good faith and fair dealing. New York law implies such a covenant in all contracts. Pursuant to this principle, "neither party shall do anything which will have the effect of destroying or injuring the right of the other party to receive the fruits of the contract." Moran v. Erk, 11 N.Y.3d 452, 456, 872 N.Y.S.2d 696, 901 N.E.2d 187, 190 (2008). A breach of the covenant is considered a breach of the underlying contract.

The implied covenant does not "undermine a party's 'general right to act on its own interests in a way that may incidentally lessen' " the other party's expected benefit. M/A-COM Sec. Corp. v. Galesi, 904 F.2d 134, 136 (2d Cir. 1990). The covenant will be breached only in a narrow range of cases. A plaintiff must show substantially more than evidence that the defendant's actions were negligent or inept. The plaintiff must instead demonstrate something more, such as that the defendant "act[ed] arbitrarily or irrationally in exercising [the] discretion" afforded to it under the contract. [Dalton v. Educ. Testing Serv., 87 N.Y.2d 384, 389, 639 N.Y.S.2d 977, 663 N.E.2d 289, 291 (1995).]

The plaintiff alleges two violations of the implied covenant of good faith and fair dealing. Only one of them, we think, has merit based on the record at summary judgment. First, the plaintiff argues, the defendant acted irrationally or arbitrarily in setting (or failing to correct) the excessive claim reserves, thus causing the higher loss ratios and the lower earnout calculation of which the plaintiff complains. We agree with the district court that this aspect of the claim cannot withstand the defendant's motion for summary judgment inasmuch as the record contains nothing to suggest anything more than negligence in CUNA Mutual's handling of the claim reserves. Negligence in operating a business, as we have explained, is insufficient to support a claim under the implied covenant. We therefore focus, as the plaintiff does in its briefs, on its second argument: that CUNA Mutual acted arbitrarily when it refused to provide a revised earnout calculation in light of an alleged system-wide error concerning claim reserves.

The implied covenant's prohibition on arbitrary or irrational exercises of discretion may apply to this second claim. The Asset Purchase Agreement expressly confers on the defendant broad discretion to "operate the business in accordance with its best business judgment." And the contract places on the defendant the responsibility for calculating the earnout, thereby conferring a limited discretion in selecting the values—such as loss ratios and written premium—that enter into the calculation in the first place. This latter form of limited discretion is indeed the subject of the plaintiff's claim in this case, and the plaintiff may therefore argue that the defendant acted arbitrarily or irrationally in handling the earnout calculation.

Furthermore, the provision in the Asset Purchase Agreement entitling CUNA Mutual to exercise its "best business judgment" in the operation of the merged business, does not displace *Dalton*'s requirement that discretion be exercised in a non-arbitrary manner. While New York courts generally will not disturb actions taken pursuant to a party's business judgment, the New York Court of Appeals has explained in a related context that arbitrary decision-making is incompatible with the exercise of legitimate business judgment. Therefore, a provision entitling the defendant to act in its best business judgment does not alter the scope of our inquiry, which is already limited to arbitrary or irrational exercises of discretion.

The record on appeal, moreover, presents sufficient evidence to create a triable issue of fact as to the defendant's handling of the earnout calculation. The parties understood that the earnout would be based on the "performance" of Security Plans' former book of business. Although Security Plans' business appeared to perform poorly during the relevant period, it was understood by CUNA Mutual managers that a system-wide problem with excessive claim reserves had distorted the performance data. This realization led several of the managers to consider the relevant loss ratio numbers with suspicion, thinking they were too high and thus not entirely accurate. These managers apparently took initial steps to recalculate the earnout using more accurate figures that would have benefited the plaintiff, but appeared to abandon that effort before any revised calculation was completed and supplied.

Making all inferences in the plaintiff's favor, a rational trier of fact could properly conclude that it was arbitrary for the defendant to refuse to revise the earnout calculation in order to correct for the suspect numbers. On this record, a trier of fact could, but would not necessarily be required to, conclude that: (i) the initial decision that set high claim reserves for the earnout period was made by mistake, and not as a result of actuarial judgment; (ii) this mistake caused Security Plans' performance data to be distorted in ways that negatively affected the earnout; (iii) this mistake was noticed in time to revise the earnout calculation accordingly, and such revision was possible; (iv) the mistake was acknowledged by all parties concerned; and (v) CUNA Mutual, for no valid business reason, decided not to adjust the earnout calculation. In making this second decision not to revise the calculation, CUNA Mutual was exercising its contractually conferred authority as the party charged with calculating the earnout, but a trier of fact could find it exercised this discretion arbitrarily.

In other words, this is not a case in which the plaintiff alleges only that that the defendant's mismanagement or ineptitude in running the business post-merger damaged its ultimate payment. Although nothing in the record indicates that the initial decision to set abnormally high claim reserves was anything more serious than negligence, the plaintiff also has presented evidence suggesting that CUNA's managers recognized their error and understood that the numbers used to calculate the earnout calculation were faulty insofar as they did not reflect the business's performance. Despite this awareness, CUNA Mutual declined to provide the plaintiff with a revised calculation, and their reasons for doing so are unclear from the record developed at the time of the motion for summary judgment. A trier of fact could conclude that the decision was arbitrary.

On remand, the plaintiff's claim based on the implied covenant will depend, in large measure, on the defendant's reasons for not revising the calculation. If CUNA Mutual can convince the trier of fact that it had a genuine and colorable business justification for its decision, then its actions will not have been arbitrary, and thus will not have violated the implied covenant. For example, CUNA Mutual manager Rich Fischer testified that he did, in fact, conduct a revised calculation with more appropriate numbers, but that any earnout was nonetheless wiped out by other contractually permitted deductions. This testimony might provide one possible convincing explanation for CUNA Mutual's behavior. But because the defendant has not produced any documentary evidence of a revised calculation, this justification hinges largely on the credibility of Fischer's testimony. Credibility determinations are inappropriate at the summary judgment stage. This testimony is therefore not conclusive on appeal.

Alternatively, further proceedings may challenge the premise that CUNA Mutual's high claim reserves from 2003 to 2005 were kept as a result of a company-wide error. We have relied, in this opinion, on evidence in the summary judgment record that treats the high claim reserves as erroneous and the resulting loss ratios as suspicious and unreliable. If the high reserves were kept as a result of a consciously risk-averse business strategy, as the defendant appears to suggest, then the numbers used to calculate the earnout may seem less dubious, and the decision to use them in the calculation may not have been arbitrary.

We are required on this appeal to accept all factual inferences in the plaintiff's favor, and we therefore express no view on the ultimate consequences of adopting these alternative characterizations of the facts. We raise these issues only to illustrate the possibility that the defendant's earnout calculation may, after further proceedings, be characterized as a non-arbitrary exercise of business judgment. Of course, it may not be. . . .

SECTION 3. THE EFFECTS OF ADOPTING A WRITING

INTRODUCTORY NOTE

A writing is essential to the full enforceability of some types of agreements. The most familiar are the classes of agreements included in the statute of frauds. For them, a note or memorandum is needed. In other situations, statutes expand the writing requirement by making it necessary to put the "contract" itself in writing—for example, agreements to submit disputes to arbitration and, in many states, such "consumer" transactions as home-improvement and automotive-repair contracts. Still, it remains true that many important bargains are entirely exempt from any form of writing requirement. There are, of course, good reasons for putting agreements in written form. A document provides guidance during performance, and evidence of the scope of obligation should disputes arise; it also signals, through the act of signing, the moment when contractual relations begin. But when the agreement is reduced to writing, the parties may also encounter a number of problems (and legal doctrines) peculiarly associated with written undertakings.

One group of problems is dealt with under the rubric of the "parol evidence rule," which purports to restrict the use of evidence of negotiating history to vary the terms of a written agreement intended to be the final expression of the parties' deal. But it is not easy to state a single, authoritative "parol evidence rule," largely because it is not "a rule" at all but a whole body of more or less discrete doctrines, about which are clustered overlapping and connected rules and concepts (e.g., "extrinsic evidence," "plain meaning," "four corners").

Mitchill v. Lath

Court of Appeals of New York, 1928.
247 N.Y. 377, 160 N.E. 646.

ANDREWS, J. In the fall of 1923 the Laths owned a farm. This they wished to sell. Across the road, on land belonging to Lieutenant-Governor Lunn, they had an ice house which they might remove. Mrs. Mitchill looked over the land with a view to its purchase. She found the ice house objectionable. Thereupon "the defendants orally promised and agreed, for and in consideration of the purchase of their farm by the plaintiff, to remove the said ice house in the spring of 1924." Relying upon this promise, she made a written contract to buy the property for $8,400. . . . Later receiving a deed, she entered into possession and has spent considerable sums in improving the property for use as a summer residence. The defendants have not fulfilled their promise as to the ice house and do not intend to do so. We are not dealing, however, with their moral delinquencies. The question before us is whether their oral agreement may be enforced in a court of equity.

This requires a discussion of the parol evidence rule—a rule of law which defines the limits of the contract to be construed. . . . It is more than a rule of evidence and oral testimony even if admitted will not control the written contract, unless admitted without objection. Brady v. Nally, 151 N.Y. 258, 45 N.E. 547. It applies, however, to attempts to modify such a contract by parol. It does not affect a parol collateral contract distinct from and independent of the written agreement. It is, at times, troublesome to draw the line. Williston, in his work on Contracts (§ 637) points out the difficulty. "Two entirely distinct contracts," he says, "each for a separate consideration may be made at the same time and will be distinct legally. Where, however, one agreement is entered into wholly or partly in consideration of the simultaneous agreement to enter into another, the transactions are necessarily bound together. . . . Then if one of the agreements is oral and the other is written, the problem arises whether the bond is sufficiently close to prevent proof of the oral agreement." That is the situation here. It is claimed that the defendants are called upon to do more than is required by their written contract in connection with the sale as to which it deals.

The principle may be clear, but it can be given effect by no mechanical rule. As so often happens, it is a matter of degree, for as Professor Williston also says where a contract contains several promises on each side it is not difficult to put any one of them in the form of a collateral agreement. If this were enough written contracts might always be modified by parol. Not form, but substance, is the test.

In applying this test the policy of our courts is to be considered. We have believed that the purpose behind the rule was a wise one not easily to be abandoned. Notwithstanding injustice here and there, on the whole it works for good. . . . New York has been less open to arguments that would modify this particular rule, than some jurisdictions elsewhere. Thus in Eighmie v. Taylor, 98 N.Y. 288, it was held that a parol warranty might not be shown although no warranties were contained in the writing.

Under our decisions before such an oral agreement as the present is received to vary the written contract at least three conditions must exist, (1) the agreement must in form be a collateral one; (2) it must not contradict express or implied provisions of the written contract; (3) it must be one that parties would not ordinarily be expected to embody in the writing; or put in another way, an inspection of the written contract, read in the light of surrounding circumstances must not indicate that the writing appears "to contain the engagement of the parties, and to define the object and measure the extent of such engagement." Or again, it must not be so clearly connected with the principal transaction as to be part and parcel of it.

THE ICE HOUSE

The respondent does not satisfy the third of these requirements. It may be, not the second. We have a written contract for the purchase and sale of land. The buyer is to pay $8,400 in the way described. She is also to pay her portion of any rents, interest on mortgages, insurance premiums and water meter charges. She may have a survey made of the premises. On their part the sellers are to give a full covenant deed of the premises as described[;] . . . they sell the personal property on the farm and represent they own it; they agree that all amounts paid them on the contract and the expense of examining the title shall be a lien on the property; they assume the risk of loss or damage by fire until the deed is delivered; and they agree to pay the broker his commissions. Are they to do more? Or is such a claim inconsistent with these precise provisions? It could not be shown that the plaintiff was to pay $500 additional. Is it also implied that the defendants are not to do anything unexpressed in the writing?

That we need not decide. At least, however, an inspection of this contract shows a full and complete agreement, setting forth in detail the obligations of each party. On reading it one would conclude that the reciprocal obligations of the parties were fully detailed. Nor would his opinion alter if he knew the surrounding circumstances. The presence of the ice house, even the knowledge that Mrs. Mitchill thought it objectionable would not lead to the belief that a separate agreement existed with regard to it. Were such an agreement made it would seem most natural that the inquirer should find it in the contract. Collateral in form it is found to be, but it is closely related to the subject dealt with in the written agreement—so closely that we hold it may not be proved.

Where the line between the competent and the incompetent is narrow the citation of authorities is of slight use. Each represents the judgment of the court on the precise facts before it. How closely bound to the contract is the supposed collateral agreement is the decisive factor in each case. . . .

[T]he judgment of the Appellate Division and that of the Special Term should be reversed and the complaint dismissed, with costs in all courts.

LEHMAN, J. (dissenting). I accept the general rule as formulated by Judge Andrews. I differ with him only as to its application to the facts shown in the record. . . . I concede at the outset that parol evidence to show additional conditions and terms of the conveyance would be inadmissible. There is a conclusive presumption that the parties intended to integrate in that written contract every agreement relating to the nature or extent of the property to be conveyed, the contents of the deed to be delivered, the consideration to be paid as a condition precedent to the delivery of the deeds, and indeed all the rights of the parties in connection with the land. The conveyance of that land was the subject-matter of the written contract and the contract completely covers that subject.

The parol agreement which the court below found the parties had made was collateral to, yet connected with, the agreement of purchase and sale. It has been found that the defendants induced the plaintiff to agree to purchase the land by a promise to remove an ice house from land not covered by the agreement of purchase and sale. No independent consideration passed to the defendants for the parol promise. To that extent the written contract and the alleged oral contract are bound together. . . .

Judge Andrews has formulated a standard to measure the closeness of the bond. Three conditions, at least, must exist before an oral agreement may be proven to increase the obligation imposed by the written agreement. I think we agree that the first condition that the agreement "must in form be a collateral one" is met by the evidence. I concede that this condition is met in most cases. . . . The difficulty here, as in most cases, arises in connection with the two other conditions.

The second condition is that the "parol agreement must not contradict express or implied provisions of the written contract." Judge Andrews voices doubt whether this condition is satisfied. The written contract has been carried out. . . . By the oral agreement the plaintiff seeks to hold the defendants to other obligations to be performed by them thereafter upon land which was not conveyed to the plaintiff. The assertion of such further obligation is not inconsistent with the written contract unless the written contract contains a provision, express or implied, that the defendants are not to do anything not expressed in the writing. Concededly there is no such express provision in the contract, and such a provision may be implied, if at all, only if the asserted additional obligation is "so clearly connected with the principal transactions as to be part and parcel of it," and is not "one that the parties would not ordinarily be expected to embody in the writing." . . . In this case, therefore, the problem reduces itself to the one question whether or not the oral agreement meets the third condition.

THE MITCHILL RESIDENCE

I have conceded that upon inspection the contract is complete. . . . That engagement was on the one side to convey land; on the other to pay the price. The plaintiff asserts further agreement based on the same consideration to be performed by the defendants after the conveyance was complete, and directly affecting only other land. It is true, as Judge Andrews points out, that "the presence of the ice house, even the knowledge that Mrs. Mitchill thought it objectionable, would not lead to the belief that a separate agreement existed with regard to it;" but the question we must decide is whether or not, assuming an agreement was made for the removal of an unsightly ice house from one parcel of land as an inducement for the purchase of another parcel, the parties would ordinarily or naturally be expected to embody the agreement for the removal of the ice house from one parcel in the written agreement to convey the other parcel. Exclusion of proof of the oral agreement on the ground that it varies the contract embodied in the writing may be based only upon a finding or presumption that the written contract was intended to cover the oral negotiations for the removal of the ice house which lead up to the contract of purchase and sale. To determine what the writing was intended to cover "the document alone will not suffice. What it was intended to cover cannot be known till we know what there was to cover. The question being whether certain subjects of negotiation were intended to be covered, we must compare the writing and the negotiations before we can determine whether they were in fact covered." (Wigmore on Evidence [2d ed.], § 2430.)

The subject-matter of the written contract was the conveyance of land. The contract was so complete on its face that the conclusion is inevitable that the parties intended to embody in the writing all the negotiations covering at least the conveyance. The promise by the defendants to remove the ice house from other land was not connected with their obligation to convey, except that one agreement would not have been made unless the other was also made. The plaintiff's assertion of a parol agreement by the defendants to remove the ice house was completely established by the great weight of evidence. It must prevail unless that agreement was part of the agreement to convey and the entire agreement was embodied in the writing.

The fact that in this case the parol agreement is established by the overwhelming weight of evidence is, of course, not a factor which may be considered in determining the competency or legal effect of the evidence. Hardship in the particular case would not justify the court in disregarding or emasculating the general rule. It merely accentuates the outlines of our problem. The assumption that the parol agreement was made is no longer obscured by any doubts. The problem then is clearly whether the parties are presumed to have intended to render that parol agreement legally ineffective and non-existent by failure to embody it in the writing. Though we are driven to say that nothing in the written contract which fixed the terms and conditions of the stipulated conveyance suggests the existence of any further parol agreement, an inspection of the contract, though it is complete on its face in regard to the subject of the conveyance, does not, I think, show that it was intended to embody negotiations or agreements, if any, in regard to a matter so loosely bound to the conveyance as the removal of an ice house from land not conveyed.

The rule of integration undoubtedly frequently prevents the assertion of fraudulent claims. Parties who take the precaution of embodying their oral agreements in a writing should be protected against the assertion that other terms of the same agreement were not integrated in the writing. The limits of the integration are determined by the writing, read in the light of the surrounding circumstances. A written contract, however complete, yet covers only a limited field. I do not think that in the written contract for the conveyance of land here under consideration we can find an intention to cover a field so broad as to include prior agreements, if any such were made, to do other acts on other property after the stipulated conveyance was made. . . .

CARDOZO, C.J., POUND, KELLOGG and O'BRIEN, JJ., concur with ANDREWS, J.; LEHMAN, J., dissents in opinion in which CRANE, J., concurs.

NOTE: BELIEVABILITY AND "NATURALNESS"

Plaintiff had sued for specific performance. On December 20, 1926, the trial court issued a decree ordering defendants to remove the ice house by December 25, or, alternatively, pay plaintiff $8,000 in damages. Among the findings on which the decree was based were the following (Record, p. 9):

> In the fall of 1923, the defendants orally promised and agreed, for and in consideration of the purchase of their farm by the plaintiff, to remove the said ice house by the spring of 1924. That the plaintiff relied upon the said promise and agreement of the defendants and was induced by the representations made, to and did purchase the farm by deed of conveyance delivered December 19, 1923.
>
> That thereafter the plaintiff took immediate possession of the premises and made extensive repairs and improvements to the house and grounds, costing over $23,000, during the course of some of which the defendants were employed. . . . That the presence of the ice house and the operation of the ice business therein, injuriously affects the value of plaintiff's property and decreases the value in about the sum of $8,000.

Judge Lehman, hearing the appeal in *Mitchill*, made note of these findings. Yet his dissent included this statement: "The fact that in this case the parol agreement is established by the overwhelming weight of evidence is, of course, not a factor which may be considered in determining the competency or legal effect of the evidence." Should this statement be accepted as sound judicial practice in applying the parol evidence rule? The trial judge presumably makes the application, that is, the first cut respecting the admissibility of extrinsic evidence. Is it likely to matter whether the judge, after considering all the parties' evidence, believes that the alleged oral agreement was: (a) most surely made; (b) probably made; (c) probably not made; or (d) most surely not made (a whopper of an untruth)?

Consider also whether Judge Lehman's assertion is connected in any way to the third "condition" or test of admissibility announced by Judge Andrews—i.e., was the oral agreement one the parties "would not ordinarily be expected to embody in the writing"? This test represents standard Restatement (First) doctrine; § 240(1)(b) states that an oral agreement is not superseded by a later writing if it is not inconsistent with the writing and is "such an agreement as might naturally be made as a separate agreement by parties situated as were the parties to the written contract." Corbin has written of this provision (3 A. Corbin, Contracts § 584):

> [It] requires the court to determine what would be "natural" and what would not. The party offering the parol evidence always asserts . . . that [the parties] in fact made the "oral agreement." Should he not always be allowed to show that what they in fact did was "natural"? Even if it was not "natural," the evidence is offered to prove that the parties in fact made the oral agreement and that they did not execute the writing as a complete "integration." The parol evidence rule purports only to exclude evidence in case there is an "integration" that the evidence is offered to contradict or vary.

> The proof of a provision that is merely "additional" neither contradicts nor varies the writing. . . . Whether or not it was "natural" for the parties to do as they did bears only on the credibility of the evidence offered. This form of language makes the admissibility of an added but not inconsistent term practically discretionary with the court.

NOTE: THE PAROL EVIDENCE RULE AND THE STATUTE OF FRAUDS

The parol evidence rule and the statute of frauds are two formal doctrines of contract law involving written documents. The relationship between the two can be sketched out in general terms.

(1) The statute of frauds makes certain kinds of contracts unenforceable unless evidenced by a signed memorandum (in sales of goods, part payment or "acceptance and receipt" will suffice). Thus, a writing is required only in the sense that the lack of a writing is a defense to enforcement of a contract. The statute is not a basis for challenging the existence of a contract, for it establishes no requirements for the making of a contract. The parol evidence rule, on the other hand, does not require a writing at all, except in the sense that it can apply only where there is a written document adopted by the parties as the "integration" of their agreement.

(2) The statute of frauds can be satisfied by writings that were never effective, or intended to be, as an "integration" of the agreement. The signed memorandum can consist of a series of letters, a single letter addressed to a third person, a will, a written and signed offer that is later orally accepted, or a memorandum prepared and signed some time after the date of the oral agreement. The memorandum need only be signed by "the party to be charged," and it can be supplied at any time prior to the action brought upon the contract (in some states prior to trial), and this can be done without the knowledge or consent of the other party.

(3) The statute of frauds requires that a memorandum be signed by "the party to be charged," but the parol evidence rule can operate on a document signed by either party; indeed, there is no reason for requiring signature by either, provided the written statement was adopted by agreement of the parties as the expression of the contract.

(4) The statute of frauds is based on a distrust of oral evidence and for this reason requires written evidence. The parol evidence rule, on the other hand, is grossly misnamed; to the extent that it operates, it excludes both written and oral evidence from sources extraneous to the integrated statement.

(5) The parol evidence rule does not prevent a subsequent modification or adjustment by oral agreement. It should be noted, however, that

a later oral agreement may itself fall under one of the clauses of the statute of frauds (e.g., if an interest in land is involved, or if not performable within one year.)

Estate of Stanley Kauffmann v. Rochester Institute of Technology

United States District Court, W.D.N.Y., 2018.
2018 WL 3731445.

SIRAGUSA, J. . . . Plaintiff Stanley Kauffmann ("Kauffmann") was an author of numerous movie reviews primarily for THE NEW REPUBLIC, "an independent journal of opinion promoting novel solutions to the challenges of our time," and founded in 1914, with its principal office in New York City.

At issue in this case is the republication of 141 of those reviews in a book authored by third-party defendant Robert J. Cardullo ("Cardullo") and published by an entity belonging to [the Rochester Institute of Technology ("RIT")]. The book is entitled *The Millennial Critic: Stanley Kauffmann on Film: 1999–2009.* The Estate of Stanley Kauffmann ("the Estate") claims that forty-four of those reviews violated Kauffmann's copyright in them. RIT claims that Kauffmann did not own the copyright to those works in Cardullo's book, since he and THE NEW REPUBLIC agreed in 2004 that all the reviews Kauffman wrote for the journal were a "work made for hire" as defined in the Copyright Act of 1976. . . .

Although the complaint does not state when the articles were published by THE NEW REPUBLIC, RIT states in its memorandum of law that the 2004 letter signed by Kauffmann and his editor at the paper, "although dated after the articles at issue were first published by THE NEW REPUBLIC in 1999, demonstrates that the parties intended, even prior to creation of the articles, that they were 'works made for hire.' " . . .

The facts are mostly undisputed; however, the inferences to be drawn from them are highly disputed. The Estate's claim of infringement, and RIT's defense, rely principally on the letter revealed in discovery that was sent by Leon Wieseltier, Literary Editor of THE NEW REPUBLIC to Stanley Kauffman, dated March 22, 2004. Because of the letter's central importance to the resolution of the motion and cross motion for summary judgment, the Court will quote it in its entirety:

March 22, 2004

Stanley Kauffmann
Penthouse C
10 West 15th Street
New York, NY 10011

Dear Stanley,

Like many publishing companies, The New Republic is working to expand into the web and related technologies, and in so doing, afford you maximum exposure. We've had a wonderful relationship with you over the years and see this expansion as a great opportunity to further promote you and your talents for our mutual benefit. Recent Supreme Court decisions have made it necessary that we explicitly confirm the terms under which you write for The New Republic.

Thus, in the interest of responsibly managing our business, we are making efforts to memorialize in writing all of our agreements with our writers, including freelance contributors. Our agreement with you has always been an oral understanding, and among other things we do want to ensure that we are not violating your rights in any way. To that end, we'd like to confirm with you our understanding, of our past relationship with you, as well as our relationship with you and your contributions to The New Republic going forward.

We have always understood that you have been writing articles for The New Republic as a freelance contributor. We have also always understood in doing business with you that, in light of our regular monthly compensation arrangement with you, all articles you have written for The New Republic have been "works made for hire," as that term is defined under the US Copyright laws. We'd like to confirm with you that the above understanding of our business relationship with you is correct, but also that the above understanding will remain in effect as to any future articles you write for The New Republic, unless and until we and you both agree otherwise in writing.

Please acknowledge your agreement with us about this by so indicating with your signature below.

Many thanks,	Date: March 24, 2004
Sincerely,	Agreed: ✓
/s/ Leon Wieseltier	Author Signature: /s/ Stanley Kauffmann
Leon Wieseltier	
Literary Editor	

The parties agree that the letter on its face is a contract and that Kauffmann signed the agreement in the space provided.

RIT relies heavily on the letter to establish that Kauffmann's reviews written for THE NEW REPUBLIC were works for hire. . . . RIT therefore argues that as works made for hire, the articles published by it in Cardullo's book do not infringe any copyright owned by Kauffmann, or the Estate.

The Estate attacks the letter agreement on a number of fronts: the fact that agreement encompassed works authorized by Kaufmann over a forty-six year period; the fact that THE NEW REPUBLIC gave to Kauffmann the copyrights for works published under the 1909 Copyright Act; an affidavit from the letter's author stating he did not understand the phrase "works made for hire"; an affidavit from a close friend of Kauffmann's stating, *inter alia*, that Kauffmann believed he owned the copyright to all his writings; evidence that Kauffmann licensed his writings that had been published in THE NEW REPUBLIC to others; and arguments that Kauffmann, at age 88 at the time of the letter, with a sick wife, trusted his editor, Leon Wieseltier, and would have signed anything requested, even without understanding the ramifications. Significantly, at oral argument, both sides agreed that the letter was on its face a contract and that New York law controlled.

However, neither side ever addressed what the Court would characterize as the "elephant in the room," the parol evidence rule. The 2004 letter agreement purports to memorialize in writing a preexisting oral contract, evidently dating back to when Kauffmann started writing for THE NEW REPUBLIC in 1958. On its face, it is unambiguous. Both parties agree that since he started writing for the journal, "all articles [he has] written for The New Republic have been 'works made for hire," as that term is defined under the US Copyright laws." By signing the letter, and checking the line "agreed," Kauffmann assented to that understanding. Therefore, on its face, the letter contains all the terms necessary for a contract: offer, acceptance, consideration, mutual assent, and an intent to be bound.

Viewing the Letter as a contract, and having found that its terms are unambiguous, the Estate's submission of extrinsic evidence regarding the Letter is admissible only if it is permitted under the parol evidence rule. That rule is well established under New York law:

> [A]bsent fraud or mutual mistake, where the parties have reduced their agreement to an integrated writing, the parol evidence rule operates to exclude evidence of all prior or contemporaneous negotiations between the parties offered to contradict or modify the terms of their writing.

Marine Midland Bank-S. v. Thurlow, 53 N.Y.2d 381, 389 (1981). In a case relied upon by both parties, the district court addressed a situation where the terms of the agreement (proved only by an endorsement on a payment check) were not always clear. In that case, the district court held that "there should be evidence of the oral agreement which the one-line written statement memorializes." Playboy Enterprises, Inc. v. Dumas, 831 F. Supp. 295, 308 (S.D.N.Y.), opinion modified on reargument, 840 F. Supp. 256 (S.D.N.Y. 1993), and aff'd in part, rev'd in part, 53 F.3d 549 (2d Cir. 1995). No such problem is present here. The 2004 letter sets out the agreement clearly and, unlike the *Playboy* case, uses the term of art in the Copyright Act: "work[s] made for hire." . . .

End Line Investors Ltd. v. Wells Fargo Bank, N.A.

United States District Court, Southern District of New York, 2018.
2018 WL 3231649.

GARDEPHE, UNITED STATES DISTRICT JUDGE. . . . In the spring of 2013, Jaffe & Asher [the Firm] entered into discussions with Wells Fargo about performing Wells Fargo's consumer debt collection work in New York and New Jersey. Jaffe & Asher's main contact at Wells Fargo for these discussions was Jo-Karen Whitlock, a Wells Fargo Client Services Manager.

At that time, Jaffe & Asher maintained only a small office in New Jersey that did not meet Wells Fargo's audit standards. In discussions with the Firm, Whitlock represented that Wells Fargo would immediately begin placing New York consumer debt collection accounts with the Firm, that there were about 2,000 existing New Jersey Wells Fargo consumer debt collection accounts placed with other law firms, and that if the Firm opened a New Jersey office that met Wells Fargo's audit standards, the Bank would place all of these New Jersey collection accounts as well as all future New Jersey collection accounts with the Firm (the "Oral Agreement"). Relying on these representations, the Firm leased office space in New Jersey and incurred other expenses in bringing that office into compliance with Wells Fargo's audit requirements.

On May 23, 2013, Wells Fargo informed the Firm that it was prepared to begin placing New York and New Jersey consumer debt collection accounts with the Firm, and that the Firm's work on these matters would begin shortly after it signed a Legal Services Agreement—a Wells Fargo standard form retainer agreement. The Firm signed the retainer agreement that same day, and Wells Fargo then began placing collection accounts with the Firm. Wells Fargo did not place all of its existing New Jersey consumer debt collection accounts with the Firm, however, nor did it place all future New Jersey collection accounts with the Firm.

Plaintiff End Line Investors, Ltd. is the assignee of the Firm's claims against Wells Fargo . . .

The Legal Services Agreement (the "Written Agreement") is a twenty-one page, single-spaced document that sets forth in great detail the terms and conditions under which the Firm will provide legal services to Wells Fargo.

The Written Agreement entered into by the Bank and the Firm recites that "Wells Fargo wishes to retain [the] Firm to perform the services stated herein." The "Services" to be performed by the Firm are defined to "include reducing debts owed to Wells Fargo to judgment and executing on those judgments, in accordance with state, local and federal laws and Wells Fargo Policies and Procedures." In the Written Agreement, the Firm takes on a host of responsibilities concerning the Bank, including obligations to safeguard its confidential information and "customer/consumer information"; comply with all applicable laws and regulations; maintain all necessary licenses; avoid conflicts of interest; maintain malpractice insurance; indemnify the Bank from all losses resulting from the Firm's gross negligence or willful misconduct; and maintain records on all accounts and files provided by the Bank. The Bank likewise takes on certain obligations with respect to the Firm, including the obligation to pay the Firm's attorneys' fees.

Attachments to the Written Agreement set forth detailed cost structures and invoice procedures, and impose certain obligations on the Firm once the Bank refers a consumer account to the Firm for collection. For example, "[w]ithin two (2) business days of receipt of a Placement [of a consumer collection matter], [the] Firm [is obligated to] acknowledge receipt of or reject the Placement." Nowhere in the Written Agreement or its attachments does Wells Fargo take on an obligation to place any portion of its New York and New Jersey collection work with the Firm, however.

The Written Agreement provides that it may be terminated by either the Bank or the Firm on ten-days' written notice. In the event of termination, the parties agree that "Wells Fargo shall have full power and authority to take possession of [its] Files, assume any and all information and documentation that Wells Fargo selects, and prosecute the Services to Completion." Jaffe & Asher agrees to provide to the Bank, within ten days of termination, an updated report concerning all accounts being handled by the Firm; all funds held on behalf of the Bank and all files being handled by the Firm; and all bills for each customer account and all outstanding invoices. For its part, the Bank agrees to pay the Firm "the amount due and owing for Services accrued to the Termination Date within sixty days." . . .

Finally, the Written Agreement contains the following integration clause:

> This Agreement embodies the entire understanding and agreement between the Parties with respect to its subject matter and supersedes any and all prior agreements, arrangements and understandings, whether oral or written, with respect to its subject matter.

. . . In New York, "[a] completely integrated contract precludes extrinsic proof to add to or vary its terms." Primex Int'l Corp. v. Wal-Mart Stores, 89 N.Y.2d 594, 600 (1997). The rationale for this rule is that the presence of an integration clause establishes "the parties' intent that the [a]greement [in question] is to be considered a completely integrated writing."

Here, the Written Agreement is "complete on its face," see Manolis v. Brecher, 2014 WL 642849 (S.D.N.Y. 2014), and "extrinsic proof to add to or vary [the] terms [of the Written Agreement]" may not be considered. Primex, 89 N.Y.2d at 600.

Any party seeking to overcome the "strong presumption of exclusion" resulting from an integration clause faces a high bar. See Lee v. Joseph E. Seagram & Sons, Inc., 552 F.2d 447, 452 (2d Cir. 1977). As the New York Court of Appeals said with respect to a lease that contained an integration clause, "if the lease before us—complete on its face and drafted designedly and explicitly to prevent reliance upon any promise or agreement not included—could be varied and undermined by parol evidence, few written instruments would be safe or secure." Fogelson v. Rackfay Const. Co., 300 N.Y. 334, 340 (1950). Accordingly, unless the Oral Agreement constitutes a "collateral agreement"—as discussed below—the integration clause bars consideration of parol evidence concerning the relationship between the Bank and the Firm.

An integration clause in a written agreement will not bar consideration of parol evidence concerning an agreement that is collateral to the written agreement. "[P]arol evidence is admissible if the alleged agreement is collateral, that is, one which is separate, independent and complete . . . although relating to the same object." Miller v. Hekiman Labs., Inc., 257 F. Supp. 2d 506, 513 (N.D.N.Y. 2003). Three conditions must be met for evidence of a collateral contract to be admitted: "(1) [t]he agreement must in form be a collateral one; (2) it must not contradict express or implied provisions of the written contract; (3) it must be one that parties would not ordinarily be expected to embody in the writing." Mitchill v. Lath, 247 N.Y. 377, 381 (1928).

Here, the alleged Oral Agreement is collateral in form and was allegedly entered into before the Written Agreement was signed. Accordingly, the first condition is satisfied.

The second condition—whether the alleged collateral agreement contradicts an express or implied term of a written contract—is not satisfied. In purporting to place obligations on the Bank to use the Firm for the Bank's collection work, the Oral Agreement contradicts an express provision of the Written Agreement: the integration provision. The integration provision states that "[t]his Agreement embodies the entire understanding and agreement between the Parties with respect to its subject matter." In purporting to place additional obligations on the Bank in connection with its relationship with the Firm, the alleged Oral Agreement contradicts the Written Agreement.

The alleged promises making up the Oral Agreement fall squarely within the "subject matter" of the Written Agreement. As discussed above, the Written Agreement sets forth the terms and conditions governing the relationship between the Firm and Wells Fargo, and addresses in detail the parties' obligations to each other. Nowhere among these obligations is there any requirement for Wells Fargo to place a certain amount of collection work with the Firm.

The third condition—that the alleged collateral agreement is not "one that parties would . . . ordinarily be expected to embody in the writing"—is likewise not satisfied. To the contrary, one would expect that an agreement obligating the Bank to send all of its consumer collection work to the Firm would be addressed in the Written Agreement, which sets forth the terms and conditions governing the Bank's relationship with the Firm. Given that the Bank and the Firm are highly sophisticated parties, the absence of any language in the Written Agreement imposing an obligation on the Bank to use the Firm for its collection work constitutes compelling evidence that there was no such agreement. In any event, one would expect that any such agreement or understanding would be embodied in the Written Agreement.

Because the second and third conditions for consideration of a purported collateral agreement are not met here, evidence of the alleged Oral Agreement may not be considered. . . .

The Court concludes that the alleged Oral Agreement is not collateral to the Written Agreement. Accordingly, parol evidence regarding the alleged Oral Agreement is not admissible to vary the terms of the Written Agreement, and Plaintiff's breach of contract claim premised on the alleged Oral Agreement will be dismissed. . . .

Under New York law, a claim for promissory estoppel requires "(1) a promise that is sufficiently clear and unambiguous; (2) reasonable reliance on the promise by a party; and (3) injury caused by the reliance." Condor Funding, LLC v. 176 Broadway Owners Corp., 147 A.D.3d 409, 411 (1st Dep't 2017).

Integration clauses are generally fatal to promissory estoppel claims premised on parol evidence. In Fariello v. Checkmate Holdings, LLC, [82 A.D.3d 437, 438, 918 N.Y.S.2d 408 (1st Dep't 2011)], for example, the First Department ruled that plaintiff's "promissory estoppel cause of action was properly dismissed, since it was barred by the retainer agreement[,] which explicitly set forth that the agreement contained the entire understanding of the parties." Similarly, in Capricorn Inv'rs III, L.P. v. Collbrands Intern., Inc., 66 A.D.3d 409, 410 (1st Dep't 2009), the First Department ruled that plaintiff's "promissory estoppel claim was properly dismissed because it was flatly contradicted by the parties' written agreement[,] which covered the same subject matter and expressly superseded all other prior agreements and understandings, written and oral." See also Sec. Plans, Inc. v. CUNA Mut. Ins. Soc., 769 F.3d 807, 816 (2d Cir. 2014) (applying New York law and holding that "a party may not maintain a promissory estoppel claim where the promises on which the claim is based are expressly contradicted by a later written agreement covering the same subject matter"); Tobin v. The Rector, 2017 WL 5466705, at *3 (S.D.N.Y. 2017) ("[T]he parties' valid written agreement precludes recovery under the cause[ ] of action sounding in promissory estoppel which arises out of the same subject matter."). Here, the Written Agreement covers the same subject matter as the Oral Agreement and contains an integration clause. As a result, Plaintiff's promissory estoppel claim fails. . . .

"Under New York law, the elements for a negligent misrepresentation claim are that (1) the defendant had a duty, as a result of a special relationship, to give correct information; (2) the defendant made a false representation that he or she should have known was incorrect; (3) the information supplied in the representation was known by the defendant to be desired by the plaintiff for a serious purpose; (4) the plaintiff intended to rely and act upon it; and (5) the plaintiff reasonably relied on it to his or her detriment." Hydro Inv'rs, Inc. v. Trafalgar Power Inc., 227 F.3d 8, 20 (2d Cir. 2000). Further, "the alleged misrepresentation must be factual in nature and not promissory or relating to future events." Id.

Plaintiff's negligent misrepresentation claim fails for multiple reasons. As an initial matter, the alleged misrepresentation relates to future conduct: that Wells Fargo "would place all of its existing and future New Jersey Accounts with [Jaffe & Asher] in volume if the Firm opened up a dedicated New Jersey office that met Wells Fargo's audit standards." This statement is a promise about future conduct, and thus cannot be the basis for a negligent misrepresentation claim. In Yellow Cab SLS Jet Management v. Schwartz, 2014 WL 2111688, at *1 (S.D.N.Y. 2014), for example, plaintiff claimed that it had signed a non-disclosure agreement based on defendant's promise that it would be the exclusive manufacturer and distributer of another company's vending machines. Judge Rakoff held that defendant's alleged representation was "a promise of a future working relationship, which is not actionable as negligent misrepresentation." Id. Similarly here, Wells Fargo allegedly promised that it would send all of its New Jersey collection work to the Firm if it upgraded its New Jersey office to meet certain Bank audit requirements. The Bank's alleged promise about future conduct is not a factual statement that can support a negligent misrepresentation claim.

Moreover, Plaintiff has not pled facts demonstrating that the Bank owed a special duty to the Firm as the result of a "special relationship" between Jaffe & Asher and the Bank. Under New York law, a plaintiff alleging a "special relationship" for purposes of a negligent misrepresentation claim must demonstrate that (1) "the person making the representation held or appeared to hold unique or special expertise"; (2) that "a special relationship of trust or confidence existed between the parties"; or (3) that "the speaker was aware of the use to which the information would be put and supplied it for that purpose." LBBW Luxemburg S.A. v. Wells Fargo Sec. LLC, 10 F. Supp. 3d 504, 525–26 (S.D.N.Y. 2014) (quoting Kimmell v. Schaefer, 89 N.Y.2d 257, 264 (1996)). As the New York Court of Appeals has stressed,

> liability for negligent misrepresentation has been imposed only on those persons who possess unique or specialized expertise, or who are in a special position of confidence and trust with the injured party such that reliance on the negligent misrepresentation is justified. Professionals, such as lawyers and engineers, by virtue of their training and expertise, may have special relationships of confidence and trust with their clients, and in certain situations we have imposed liability for negligent misrepresentation when they have failed to speak with care. Kimmell, 89 N.Y.2d at 263.

Here, the retainer agreement created an attorney-client relationship between the Bank and the Firm—a relationship that permitted the Bank to repose a special measure of trust and confidence in the Firm. However, this "special relationship" runs in favor of Wells Fargo, not the Firm. Plaintiff has cited no law suggesting that it may use against the Bank the fact that it owes a fiduciary duty to the Bank as a result of the attorney-client relationship. . . .

Accordingly, Plaintiff's negligent misrepresentation claim will be dismissed. . . .

The Complaint also alleges a claim for breach of the implied covenant of good faith and fair dealing premised on the Written Agreement. . . . However, the covenant "cannot be construed so broadly as effectively to nullify other express terms of a contract, or to create independent contractual rights." Fesseha v. TD Waterhouse Inv'r Servs., Inc., 305 A.D.2d 268, 268 (1st Dep't 2003).

Plaintiff alleges that "[a]t the time of the execution of the [Written] Agreement, both parties understood that Wells Fargo would be placing all of its existing and future New Jersey Accounts with the Firm if the Firm opened up a dedicated New Jersey office that met Wells Fargo's audit standards." The Written Agreement reflects no such understanding and imposes no such obligation on the Bank, however. In attempting to shoehorn such a requirement into the Written Agreement through an implied covenant claim, the Firm is endeavoring to "create [an] independent contractual right[ ]" that does not exist in the Written Agreement. As the cases cited above demonstrate, the implied covenant cannot be used for this purpose. Accordingly, Plaintiff's good faith and fair dealing claim will be dismissed. . . .

NOTE: ALTERNATIVE APPROACHES TO THE PAROL EVIDENCE RULE

As the last two cases illustrated, courts applying New York law today apply the parol evidence rule in a way that is completely consistent with the spirit of *Mitchill v. Lath*. Courts in other jurisdictions, however, have shown a greater willingness to look beyond the written documents of the parties and are considerably more reluctant to exclude evidence when doing so would turn a blind eye to the parties' agreement in fact.

Hatley v. Stafford

Supreme Court of Oregon, 1978.
284 Or. 523, 588 P.2d 603.

HOWELL, J. Plaintiff, lessee, filed this action for trespass against defendants, lessors. The property involved is a 52-acre farm in Lane County. The defendants contended they were entitled under the lease agreement to terminate the lease and recover possession. The following is the entire written agreement of the parties[:]

"Oct. 16, 1974

"Stafford Farm agrees to rent to Mike Hatley, Rt. 1 Box 83, Halsey, Ore. approximately 52 acres till Sept. 1st 1975 for the purpose of growing wheat with the follow[ing] condition:—Stafford Farm shall have the right to buy out Mr. Mike Hatley at a figure of his cost per acre but not to exceed $70 per acre. This buy out is for the express purpose of developing a Mobile Home Park.

"Terms shall be $1800 paid on or before Jan. 20th 1975 balance due Sept. 20, 1975. The Rent figure shall be $50 per acre.

"Stafford Farm
"By /s/ Robert R. Stafford Mgr.
/s/ Mike Hatley"

Plaintiff Hatley alleged that between June 8 and June 11, 1975, defendants trespassed on the property by taking possession of the farm and cutting the immature wheat crop. The defendants [answered] that they exercised their right to terminate the lease in order to build a mobile home park and that they offered to pay plaintiff his cost per acre but not to exceed $70 per acre. Plaintiff demanded $400 per acre, the fair market value of the wheat crop. [Plaintiff's reply] alleged that the written agreement was not the entire integrated agreement of the parties, and that the parties orally agreed the buy out provision of the lease would apply only for a period of 30 to 60 days after the execution of the lease.

The trial court allowed plaintiff to introduce evidence concerning the alleged oral agreement. . . . The jury returned a verdict for plaintiff. . . . The only error asserted on [defendants'] appeal is that the trial court erred in allowing admission of the parol evidence relating to the time limit on the buy out agreement.

The parol evidence rule[1] applies only to those aspects of a bargain that the parties intend to memorialize in the writing. . . . The fact that a writing exists does not bring the rule into play if the parties do not intend the writing to embody their final agreement. . . . Neither does the rule apply when the parties intended the writing to contain only part of their agreement. . . .

[The] plaintiff sought to show that the written lease was a "partial integration," i.e., that the written contract included some, but not all, of the terms of the actual agreement. Defendants contend that such a showing could be made only if the oral agreement was "not inconsistent" with the writing and was "an agreement as might naturally be made as a separate agreement." . . . Plaintiff argues that these limitations apply only after it has been demonstrated that the writing is a complete integration, that whether a writing was intended to be a complete integration is a question of fact, and that the jury may consider any relevant evidence in deciding this question of fact. Both parties find support for their positions in past opinions by this court. . . .

The inconsistency in our prior decisions reflects a long-standing disagreement among courts and commentators generally as to the applicability of the parol evidence rule. . . . The rule apparently was an outgrowth of the law governing contracts under seal. Because the King's word was indisputable, the King's seal on a document made the document uncontestable. 9 J. Wigmore, Evidence 83, § 2426 (3d ed. 1940). The status of writings was further enhanced by the enactment of the Statute of Wills and the Statute of Frauds, both of which made certain transactions legally unenforceable unless they were in writing. This theory was gradually applied to contracts generally, until finally the writing came to be regarded as the agreement itself, rather than merely as evidence of the agreement. Id. at 91.

Modernly, the parol evidence rule has often been justified on grounds of commercial certainty. If parol evidence were allowed to be offered in contradiction of writings, it has been feared that the likelihood of perjury would increase. . . . It is also believed that the rule is needed to ensure that juries will not decide cases on the "equities," the theory being that

---

[1] ORS § 41.740 states, in pertinent part:

"When the terms of an agreement have been reduced to writing by the parties, it is to be considered as containing all those terms, and therefore there can be, between the parties and their representatives or successors in interest, no evidence of the terms of the agreement, other than the contents of the writing. . . ."

Concededly, a literal reading of this statute would exclude any parol evidence of the terms of an agreement once that agreement had been reduced to writing. . . . This court, however, has never read the statute in such a manner, but instead has treated the statute as a codification of the common law parol evidence rule. . . . Although [our] decisions may be inconsistent with a literal reading of the statute, which has been in effect since 1862, they can be justified under the general rule that statutes codifying the common law are to be construed in a manner consistent with the common law. . . .

the economic underdog will most often be the party seeking to vary the terms of the writing by parol evidence. . . . On the other hand, it has been observed that in a modern society where much of business is transacted over the telephone, contracts that are partly oral and partly written have become increasingly common. . . . Moreover, in an era of adhesion contracts and unequal bargaining power, the extent to which many writings actually embody the agreement of the parties is debatable. . . . Finally, it is doubtful that the rule discourages perjury, since the rule can be avoided by fabricating an oral agreement subsequent to the execution of the writing. . . .

The rule does, however, serve an important function. If the parties *in fact* have assented to the writing as the embodiment of their entire agreement, each should be able to rely on the terms of the writing as conclusive evidence of what they have agreed to. . . .

The difficulty arises when one of the parties asserts . . . that the writing does not contain all the terms of the actual agreement. Because the parol evidence rule applies only to complete and final integrations, and because the existence of an integration depends on the intent of the parties, it has been argued that any relevant evidence of the parties' intent should be admissible and that the actual intent of the parties should be a factual question for the jury. As we observed in De Vore v. Weyerhaeuser Co., [265 Or. 388, 508 P.2d 220 (1973), cert. denied, 415 U.S. 913 (1974)], however, a rule allowing the jury to consider any relevant evidence in deciding whether the writing was intended to be a complete integration "without any limitations, would emasculate, if not 'repeal,' the parol evidence rule, which is a rule adopted by statute in Oregon. . . ." 265 Or. at 401. Consequently, we have recognized the criteria of § 240 of the [first] Restatement of Contracts as imposing limitations on the admissibility of evidence in cases involving the partial integration doctrine. We believe these limitations remain appropriate, despite our occasional statements to the contrary.

On the other hand, the Restatement criteria are not to be applied mechanically or formalistically. . . . [T]he purpose of the parol evidence rule is to give special effect to writings only in those cases where the parties intended the writing to be a final and complete statement of their agreement. . . .

. . . [M]ention should be made of the functions of court and jury in cases involving the parol evidence rule. Both plaintiff and defendants appear to have assumed that the jury decides whether or not the parties intended their writing to be a final and complete integration. Such is not the law. As McCormick notes, "The question [of whether the parties intended their writing to be a complete integration] is one for the court, for it relates to the admission or rejection of evidence." [McCormick, Handbook of the Law of Evidence 437, § 215 (1954).] In deciding that the parties did not intend the writing to be an integration, however, the court does not decide that the alleged oral terms actually were agreed upon.

That determination is left to the jury. The court's decision is one of admissibility, not probity.[2]

[Here,] the trial court decided that the [parties'] written agreement was not a complete integration of their actual agreement, and permitted plaintiff to introduce evidence that the buy out provision in the written lease was subject to an oral time limitation. No contention is made that the oral agreement was supported by separate consideration, so the trial court's ruling can be upheld only if the agreement: (1) was "not inconsistent" with the written lease and (2) was "such an agreement as might naturally be made as a separate agreement *by parties situated as were parties to the written contract*." DeVore v. Weyerhaeuser Co., supra, . . . (emphasis added).

Defendant argues that the oral time limitation is "clearly inconsistent" with the terms of the written lease, reasoning that a buy out provision with no time limitation in a lease for a fixed term must be read to run for the entire term of the lease. We do not define the term "inconsistent" so broadly. To be "inconsistent" within the meaning of the partial integration doctrine, the oral term must contradict an *express provision* in the writing. As the court observed in Hunt Foods & Indus. v. Doliner, 26 App.Div.2d 41, 270 N.Y.S.2d 937 (1966): "In a sense any oral provision which would prevent the ripening of the obligations of a writing is inconsistent with the writing. But that obviously is not the sense in which the word is used. . . . To be inconsistent the term must contradict or negate *a term of the writing*. A term or condition which has a lesser effect is provable." 270 N.Y.S.2d at 940 (emphasis added). . . .

In [this] case, nothing is contained in the writing with respect to the duration of the buy out provision. Therefore, the oral time limitation is "not inconsistent" with the terms of the writing.

Defendants argue that even if the oral term is not inconsistent with the terms of the writing, the parol evidence should have been excluded because the oral term "naturally" would have been included in the writing. We disagree.

In determining whether or not an oral term is one that "naturally" would have been included in the writing, the trial court is not limited to a consideration of the face of the document. "[T]he surrounding circumstances, as well as the written contract, may be considered." Blehm v. Ringering, 260 Or. 46, 50, 488 P.2d 798 (1971). When considering the surrounding circumstances, the trial court should be aware of the fact

---

[2] Wigmore explains the procedure thusly: ". . . There is a preliminary question for the judge to decide as to the intent of the parties, and upon this he hears evidence on both sides; his decision here, *pro* or *con*, concerns merely this question preliminary to the ruling of law. If he decides that the transaction was covered by the writing, he does not decide that the excluded negotiations did not take place, but merely that *if* they did take place they are nevertheless legally immaterial. If he decides that the transaction was not intended to be covered by the writing, he does not decide that the negotiations did take place, but merely that *if* they did, they are legally effective, and he then leaves to the jury the determination of fact whether they did take place." 9 J. Wigmore, Evidence 98 § 2430 (3d ed. 1940).

that parties with business experience are more likely to reduce their entire agreement to writing than parties without such experience[,] . . . and that this is especially true when the parties are represented by counsel on both sides. . . . The relative bargaining strength of the parties also should be considered, since a transaction not negotiated at arm's length may result in a writing that omits essential terms. . . . And, of course, the apparent completeness and detail of the writing itself may lead the court to conclude the parties intended the writing to be a complete integration. . . .

This is not to say, however, that the trial court should readily admit parol evidence whenever one of the parties claims a writing does not include all the terms of an agreement. The court should presume that the writing was intended to be a complete integration, at least when the writing is complete on its face, and should admit evidence of consistent additional terms only if there is substantial evidence that the parties did not intend the writing to embody the entire agreement. . . .

[T]here are a number of facts [here] that could have led the trial court to conclude that it was natural for the parties, "situated as were parties to the written contract," to have omitted the time limitation on the buy out provision from the written lease. First, this was not a sophisticated business transaction in which the parties could be expected to include all the terms of their agreement in the writing. . . . The lease was a handwritten document that hardly shows the kind of careful preparation that accompanies a formal integration. . . . Moreover, the agreement was concluded by the parties themselves, without counsel to advise them of the consequences of the writing. This case is therefore analogous to the leading case of Masterson v. Sine, 68 Cal.2d 222, 65 Cal.Rptr. 545, 436 P.2d 561 (1968), where the court, per Chief Justice Traynor, stated: "There is nothing in the record to indicate that the parties to this family transaction, through experience in land transactions or otherwise, had any warning of the disadvantages of failing to put the whole agreement in the deed. This case is one, therefore, in which it can be said that a collateral agreement such as that alleged 'might naturally be made as a separate agreement.' " 65 Cal.Rptr. at 549, 436 P.2d at 565.

Finally, the trial court was entitled to consider the fact that a literal reading of the written contract would have led to an unreasonable result. Plaintiff was contending the wheat crop he had planted would be worth $400 per acre at harvest. The written agreement, standing alone, would have allowed the defendants to exercise the buy out provision the day before harvest and pay plaintiff $70 per acre for wheat worth $400 per acre. While the mere fact that a contract is one-sided does not by itself justify a conclusion that the writing does not embody the entire agreement of the parties, the trial court may consider that fact in deciding whether the parties intended additional provisions to be included in the agreement. . . .

For these reasons, we hold that there was sufficient evidence to justify the trial court's decision to admit the parol evidence. . . . [T]he question of whether the parties actually agreed to the time limitation was properly left to the jury.

[One judge dissented, arguing that the majority had rewritten the statute on parol evidence, rendering it "meaningless."]

NOTE: APPLYING THE PAROL EVIDENCE RULE

The *Hatley* court identified a "number of facts" which it thought supported a conclusion that the parties' omission of the oral agreement from the writing was "natural" in the circumstances. In Lee v. Joseph E. Seagram & Sons, Inc., 552 F.2d 447 (2d Cir. 1977), a federal court applying New York law on the integration question covered similar ground, with the same outcome. It said in part: "[I]ntegration is most easily inferred in the case of real estate contracts for the sale of land [citing Mitchill v. Lath] or leases. . . . In more complex situations, in which customary business practice may be more varied, an oral agreement can be treated as separate and independent of the written agreement even though the written contract contains a strong integration clause." The case involved a written agreement for the sale of business assets; the seller was permitted to introduce proofs of an oral agreement by the purchaser to relocate persons associated with the seller in a business in a different city. Since the written agreement dealt only with the sale of assets, the oral agreement did not "vary or contradict" the writing.

Masterson v. Sine, the case deemed "analogous" by the *Hatley* majority, involved a brother's conveyance of a ranch to a sister and her husband, the deed reserving to the grantors (Masterson and his wife) an option to repurchase the property on stated terms. Later, the grantor-brother was adjudged bankrupt, and the trustee in bankruptcy sued to enforce the option on behalf of creditors. The Masterson family resisted the suit by offering extrinsic evidence that the parties had wanted the ranch kept in the family and that the option was therefore understood to be "personal" to the grantors and not assignable or otherwise available to third persons. The California court (5 to 2), reversing the trial judge, found it "natural" for the parties to have kept their agreement of nontransferability separate from the deed. In addition to the passage quoted in *Hatley*, Chief Justice Traynor said: "The option clause in the deed . . . does not explicitly provide that it contains the complete agreement, and the deed is silent on the question of assignability. Moreover, the difficulty of accommodating the formalized structure of a deed to the insertion of collateral agreements makes it less likely that all the terms of such an agreement were included."

Note also *Hatley*'s test of an "inconsistent" term, a test derived from the often-cited *Hunt Foods* decision. The materials that follow will reveal differing views on the appropriate definition of "contradiction" or "inconsistency" when the task is to determine whether a writing is or is not an integrated agreement, completely or only partially. It may be helpful to look at illustration 2 accompanying Rest.2d § 213 (see below). Is the problem of oral-written conflict presented there like, or unlike, that posed by *Hatley*?

The excerpts from the Restatement, Second reproduced below summarize the established rules for addressing whether a contract is a complete or partial integration. A point worth noting is the role of a "merger" or "integration" clause, a term of the writing which itself excludes agreements not found in the writing. Courts have divided over the weight to be given such clauses, some holding them conclusive as to the parties' intention respecting integration, others deeming a merger provision to be a factor only, perhaps at best presumptive evidence of an intention to completely integrate. Observe what the restaters, in the comment on Restatement 2d § 216 (p. 600), have to say on the matter. Might "context"—say, unequal bargaining power between the parties, or concerns about public policy—contribute to the law's uncertain state concerning the effect to be given a merger clause?

Restatement of Contracts, Second

§ 209. Integrated Agreements

(1) An integrated agreement is a writing or writings constituting a final expression of one or more terms of an agreement.

(2) Whether there is an integrated agreement is to be determined by the court as a question preliminary to determination of a question of interpretation or to application of the parol evidence rule.

(3) Where the parties reduce an agreement to a writing which in view of its completeness and specificity reasonably appears to be a complete agreement, it is taken to be an integrated agreement unless it is established by other evidence that the writing did not constitute a final expression.

§ 213. Effect of Integrated Agreement on Prior Agreements (Parol Evidence Rule)

(1) A binding integrated agreement discharges prior agreements to the extent that it is inconsistent with them.

(2) A binding completely integrated agreement discharges prior agreements to the extent that they are within its scope. . . .

Comment: . . .

b. Inconsistent terms. Whether a binding agreement is completely integrated or partially integrated, it supersedes inconsistent terms of prior agreements. To apply this rule, the court must make preliminary determinations that there is an integrated agreement and that it is inconsistent with the terms in question. See § 209. Those determinations are made in accordance with all relevant evidence, and require interpretation both of the integrated agreement and of the prior agreement. . . . [T]he integrated agreement must be given a meaning to which its language is reasonably susceptible when read in the light of all the circumstances.

Illustrations: . . .

2. A orally agrees to sell a city lot to B. The city is installing a sidewalk in front of the lot, and A orally agrees to pay the cost to be assessed by the city in an amount not exceeding $45. B then retains a lawyer to draw up a written agreement, and A and B execute it, A without reading it. The agreement provides that A will pay all costs of the installation of the sidewalk, but does not mention any dollar limit. If the written agreement is a binding integrated agreement, any agreement for a $45 limit is discharged.

§ 214. Evidence of Prior or Contemporaneous Agreements and Negotiations

Agreements and negotiations prior to or contemporaneous with the adoption of a writing are admissible in evidence to establish

(a) that the writing is or is not an integrated agreement;

(b) that the integrated agreement, if any, is completely or partially integrated;

(c) the meaning of the writing, whether or not integrated;

(d) illegality, fraud, duress, mistake, lack of consideration, or other invalidating cause;

(e) ground for granting or denying rescission, reformation, specific performance, or other remedy.

§ 216. Consistent Additional Terms

(1) Evidence of a consistent additional term is admissible to supplement an integrated agreement unless the court finds that the agreement was completely integrated.

(2) An agreement is not completely integrated if the writing omits a consistent additional agreed term which is

(a) agreed to for separate consideration, or

(b) such a term as in the circumstances might naturally be omitted from the writing.

Comment: . . .

b. *Consistency*. . . . The determination whether an alleged additional term is consistent or inconsistent with the integrated agreement requires interpretation of the writing in the light of all the circumstances, including the evidence of the additional term. For this purpose, the meaning of the writing includes not only the terms explicitly stated but also those fairly implied as part of the bargain of the parties in fact. It does not include a term supplied by a rule of law designed to fill gaps where the parties have not agreed otherwise, unless it can be inferred that the parties contracted with reference to the rule of law. . . .

e. Written term excluding oral terms ("merger" clause). Written agreements often contain clauses stating that there are no representations, promises or agreements between the parties except those found in the writing. Such a clause . . . if agreed to is likely to conclude the issue whether the agreement is completely integrated. Consistent additional terms may then be excluded even though their omission would have been natural in the absence of such a clause. But such a clause does not control the question whether the writing was assented to as an integrated agreement. . . .

Interform Co. v. Mitchell

575 F.2d 1270, 1275–1277 (9th Cir. 1978)

The court observed that: "One view is to treat the writing as having a unique and quite compelling force. . . . The writing becomes the focus of attention and the judge by assuming the function of a reasonable person determines whether the writing did supersede all previous undertakings and, if so, its meaning to a reasonable person situated as [were the parties to the writing.] Williston §§ 616–17. An integrated writing clear in meaning to the reasonable person constitutes the contract between the parties. In this manner the judge can fix the legal relations of the parties without aid of a jury and provide a measure of security to written agreements. . . .

"Another, and opposing view, imparts to the writing no unique or compelling force. A writing is integrated when the parties intend it to be and it means what they intended it to mean. Corbin on Contracts § 581 at 442, § 582 at 448–57, § 583 at 485 (1960). . . . In theory, therefore, integration may be lacking even if the additional terms ordinarily and naturally would have been included in the writing and an integrated writing can have a meaning to which a reasonably intelligent person, situated as described above, could not subscribe. Corbin § 544 at 145–46. Again, in theory, this view accords the jury, when the trial employs one, a potentially larger role in the process of fixing contractual relations and provides somewhat less security to written agreements. . . .

"It is unlikely that any jurisdiction will inflexibly adopt one approach to the exclusion of the other; each is likely to influence the conduct of judges and the disposition of cases. However, it must be acknowledged that the influence of Corbin's way is stronger now, . . . than when he and Williston grappled during the drafting of the American Law Institute's first Restatement of Contracts. . . .

"Moreover, [the UCC 2–202] reflects Corbin's influence. It precludes contradiction of 'confirmatory memoranda' by prior or contemporaneous oral agreements when the writing was '*intended* by the parties as a final expression of their agreement' and permits the introduction of consistent additional terms 'unless the court finds the writing to have been *intended* also as a complete and exclusive statement of the terms of the agreement.' (Italics added). The focus plainly is on the intention of the parties, not the integration practices of reasonable persons acting normally and naturally."

Hoffman v. Chapman

Court of Appeals of Maryland, 1943.
182 Md. 208, 34 A.2d 438.

DELAPLAINE, J. This appeal was brought by Joseph Hoffman and wife from a decree . . . reforming their deed for a house and lot in a suburban real estate development at Kensington.

On August 18, 1941, William Chapman and wife, of Gaithersburg, through a real estate agent, agreed to sell to appellants part of Lot 4 in the section known as Homewood on Edgewood Road, the size to be 96 by 150 feet. The purchase price of this part, improved by a bungalow, was $3,600. Before the parcel was surveyed, appellants were given immediate possession. After the survey was made, the real estate agent sent the plat to the Suburban Title Corp. with instructions to examine the title and arrange for settlement. On October 20, 1941, when appellants made final payment in the office of the title company, they clearly understood that they were receiving only a part of Lot 4 containing one dwelling; but the deed actually conveyed the entire lot, which was improved by other dwelling property. When the mistake was discovered some time afterwards, they [appellants] were requested to deed back the unsold part, but they refused to reconvey. The grantors thereupon entered suit in equity to reform the deed on the ground of mistake.

It is a settled principle that a court of equity will reform a written instrument to make it conform to the real intention of the parties, when the evidence is so clear, strong and convincing as to leave no reasonable doubt that a mutual mistake was made in the instrument contrary to their agreement. Gaver v. Gaver, 119 Md. 634, 87 A. 396. . . . It is a general rule of the common law that parol evidence is inadmissible to vary or contradict the terms of a written instrument. . . . But equity refuses to enforce this rule whenever it is alleged that fraud, accident or mistake occurred in the making of the instrument, and will admit parol evidence to reform the instrument, even though it is within the Statute of Frauds. . . . "A court of equity would be of little value," Justice Story said, "if it could suppress only positive frauds, and leave mutual mistakes, innocently made, to work intolerable mischiefs contrary to the intention of parties. It would be to allow an act, originating in innocence, to operate ultimately as a fraud by enabling the party, who receives the benefit of the mistake, to resist the claims of justice under the shelter of a rule framed to promote it. . . . We must, therefore, treat the cases in which equity affords relief, and allows parol evidence to vary and reform written contracts and instruments upon the ground of accident and mistake, as properly forming, like cases of fraud, exceptions to the general rule which excludes parol evidence. . . ." 1 Story, Equity Jurisprudence, 12th Ed., Secs. 155, 156.

It was urged by appellants that there was no meeting of the minds as to the exact location of the parcel sold, and therefore the contract of sale is void. [We] cannot agree. . . . If an agreement is so vague and indefinite that the court finds it impossible to gather from it the full intention of the parties, it must be held void, for the court cannot make an agreement for the parties. De Bearn v. De Bearn, 126 Md. 629, 95 A. 476. Yet the law does not favor, but leans against, the annulment of contracts on the ground of uncertainty. If the intent of the parties can be ascertained from the express terms of the contract or by fair implication, the contract should be sustained. . . . Of course, if the parties to a contract of sale did not understand each other as to the identity of the property, they cannot invoke the aid of equity, for in such a case there was no meeting of the minds. Page v. Higgins, 150 Mass. 27, 22 N.E. 63. However, where there is no mistake as to the identity of the property, but merely an incorrect description, whether in conveying too much property or too little, or referring to property entirely different from that intended to be conveyed, the court will correct the description, except as against *bona fide* purchasers for value without notice. Stoneham Five Cents Savings Bank v. Johnson, 295 Mass. 390, 3 N.E.2d 730. . . .

Equity reforms an instrument . . . simply to enforce the actual agreement of the parties to prevent an injustice which would ensue if this were not done. Chief Justice Alvey warned: "The court will never, by assuming to rectify an instrument, add to it a term or provision which had not been agreed upon. . . ." Stiles v. Willis, 66 Md. 552, 556, 8 A. 353, 354. . . .

Appellants insisted that the mistake in the deed was not due to their fault, but to culpable negligence of the grantors and their agents, and that no relief can be granted because the mistake was unilateral. It is axiomatic that equity aids the vigilant, and will not grant relief to a litigant who has failed to exercise reasonable diligence. In Boyle v. Rider, 136 Md. 286, 110 A. 524, it was stated that people cannot sign papers carelessly and then expect a court to excuse them from their negligence, especially when their action has misled others. But mere inadvertence, or negligence not amounting to a violation of a positive legal duty, does not bar a complainant from relief, especially if the defendant has not been prejudiced thereby. . . . Hence, it is not necessary for the complainant in a suit for a reformation to prove that he exercised diligence to ascertain what the instrument contained at the time he signed it. The term "mistake" conveys the idea of fault, and the mere fact that a mistake was made in the phraseology of an instrument does not establish such negligence as to preclude the right of reformation; for if it did, a court of equity could never grant relief in such a case. . . .

The general rule is accepted in Maryland that a mistake of law in the making of an agreement is not a ground for reformation, and where a mistake, either of law or of fact, is unilateral, equity will not afford relief except by rescinding the agreement on the ground of fraud, duress or other inequitable conduct. . . . The mistake in this case was not unilateral. Here the draftsman of the deed was acting as the agent of the parties. His mistake in the description of the real estate became the mistake of all the parties. . . . Where a deed is intended to carry into execution a written or oral agreement, but fails to express the manifest intention of the parties on account of a mistake of the draftsman, whether from carelessness, forgetfulness or lack of skill, equity will rectify the mistake to make the deed express the real intentions of the parties. . . .

As it is beyond doubt that a mutual mistake was made in the description of [this] property[,] the decree reforming the deed will be affirmed.

NOTE

As *Hoffman* illustrates, a written contract may not reflect the actual agreement of the parties because of mistake. Discrepancy between the written and the actual agreement might also be explained by the parties' intentional acts; they may deliberately omit an agreed term from the writing or insert a sham term, e.g., New York Trust Co. v. Island Oil & Transport Co., supra p. 356. *Hoffman* applies standard equity doctrine to protect the actual agreement in a mistake setting, without hindrance from the parol evidence rule. But where the writing says what the parties intended it to say, even though their agreement was different, reformation to insert omitted terms has been denied by most decisions. Do you see why?

Hoffman v. Chapman indicates clearly enough that the remedy of reformation awarded was conceived to be "equitable," and that the parol evidence rule would have prevented any contradiction or correction of the deed at law. This is the traditional view. As was to be expected, modern procedural reforms raised some new questions. Particularly in a case already in equity for independent reasons, if the facts alleged and proved justify reformation it should be enough that there is a general prayer for relief, as there usually will be. Furthermore, modern notions of fact-pleading would seem to authorize whatever remedy the facts make appropriate, whether the litigant asked for it or not. This much at least would probably be agreed in all the states.

The major question, however, is whether the issue of mistake in expression in a written document (better called "mistake in integration") should be turned over for decision to a jury. Under the older system, the issue of reformation, being equitable, was decided by a judge. The judge could let a jury hear the evidence and render a verdict, but the verdict would be merely advisory and the judge could disregard it altogether. We have the impression that advisory verdicts were and are rarely used in actions for reformation brought, in the usual way, in equity. It has become quite deeply ingrained on courts and lawyers that the issue of reformation, where grounds exist, should be settled by a judge, not a jury.

Illinois National Insurance Co. v. Wyndham Worldwide Operations, Inc.

United States Court of Appeals, Third Circuit, 2011.
653 F.3d 225.

FISHER, CIRCUIT JUDGE. . . . Illinois National issues insurance products and services. Jet Aviation offers aircraft maintenance, completions and refurbishment, engineering, and fixed base operations, along with aircraft management, charter services, aircraft sales and personnel services. Wyndham is a recognized service leader in the hospitality industry.

Illinois National provided insurance coverage to Jet Aviation and to some of Jet Aviation's clients, so long as Jet Aviation managed the client's aircraft and aircraft usage. Jet Aviation managed an aircraft owned by Wyndham and provided insurance for that aircraft pursuant to the terms of a series of Aircraft Management Services Agreements.

In 2001, Wyndham's predecessor, Cendant Operations, Inc., and Jet Aviation entered into the first of these Aircraft Management Services Agreements. Among other things, the agreements obligated Jet Aviation to provide domestic flight planning and scheduling, flight crew staffing, and management of scheduled and unscheduled maintenance for Wyndham's aircraft. If Wyndham's aircraft was not available when needed, Jet Aviation could arrange for an aircraft for Wyndham's use from another source. Pursuant to the Aircraft Management Services Agreements, Jet Aviation agreed to procure insurance for Wyndham's aircraft while it was managed by Jet Aviation. The agreement also stated that it would provide Wyndham with insurance coverage when Wyndham used non-owned aircraft at the direction of Jet Aviation.

For successive one-year periods beginning in 2004, and through the 2008 policy year, a series of aircraft fleet management insurance policies were purchased by Jet Aviation and issued by Illinois National. Each was negotiated by Illinois National and Jet Aviation, directly and through their agents. The policies contained endorsements that provided coverage for Jet Aviation's clients. These clients were identified on the endorsements as "Insured Owners" and also as "Named Insured." The 2004–2007 Policies contain the following Managed Aircraft Endorsement . . .

> 5) The insurance afforded by this policy for the interest of the "Insured Owner" described in Item 1 of this endorsement or Jet Aviation Business Jets, Inc. (as fully described in Item 1 of the Declarations Page) is extended to other Aircraft insured under this policy but excluding any Non-Owned Aircraft unless such Non-Owned Aircraft is operated by or used at the direction of Jet Aviation Business Jets, Inc. . . .

In the negotiations leading up to the 2008 policy, Jet Aviation proposed new language for the endorsement. The revised endorsement, which was integrated into the 2008 policy, replaced "Jet Aviation" with "Named Insured." It provided . . .

> 5) The insurance afforded by this policy for the interest of the "Insured Owner" described in Item 1. of this endorsement or Named Insured (as fully described in Item 1 of the Declarations Page) is extended to other Aircraft insured under this policy but excluding any Non-Owned Aircraft unless such Non-Owned Aircraft is operated by or used at the direction of the Named Insured. . . .

Jet Aviation and Illinois National claim that the drafting change was designed to make it more clear that entities affiliated with Jet Aviation were covered. Both contracting parties have stated that they believed that it did not expand coverage to entities that were unaffiliated with Jet Aviation, such as Wyndham. However, the modification, as written, appears to provide third parties with coverage when using non-owned aircraft without Jet Aviation's involvement.

Despite being drafted to seemingly provide expanded coverage, Wyndham's premium declined from $61,250 for the 2007 policy to $45,367 for the 2008 policy. Wyndham did not know about the change made to the endorsement for 2008 and continued to obtain non-owned aircraft liability coverage through a policy issued by StarNet Insurance Company ("StarNet").

It is undisputed that neither Wyndham nor its brokers was involved in the negotiations or drafting of the revised provisions of the endorsement. It was negotiated between Illinois National and Jet Aviation.

In August 2008, Jason Ketcheson, a Wyndham employee, rented a Cessna 172 from Aviation Adventures to travel to a work-related meeting in Oregon. Jet Aviation had no involvement in this transaction. Ketcheson crashed into a house in Gearhart, Oregon, killing five people. As a result, various claimants have sued Wyndham for damages. The crash may have triggered coverage under the language of the 2008 policy. . . .

Illinois National filed suit against Wyndham seeking a declaratory judgment that the 2008 policy did not cover claims arising out of the August 2008 Cessna crash. It argued that the District Court should find that the 2008 policy, as written, did not provide coverage to Wyndham, or alternatively, that if the contract as written would provide coverage, the District Court should exercise its equitable power of reformation because there had been mutual mistake in the drafting of the contract between Illinois National and Jet Aviation. Wyndham filed a counterclaim seeking coverage under the 2008 policy for the August 2008 Cessna crash, filing a motion to dismiss Illinois National's claim and a motion for summary judgment. Both sides filed statements of material facts not in dispute; additionally, Illinois National filed a supplemental statement of disputed material facts and requested more discovery. . . .

[I]n New Jersey, even an unambiguous contract may be reformed when there was mutual mistake and the written contract does not match what the parties intended. A mutual mistake is "1. A mistake in which each party misunderstands the other's intent. . . . [or] 2. A mistake that is shared and relied on by both parties to a contract." Black's Law Dictionary 1023 (8th ed. 2004).

Mutual mistake is evaluated by determining the understanding of the parties at the time the contract was formed. A party seeking reformation for mutual mistake must show that both parties labored under the same misapprehension as to a particular and essential fact. The understanding of persons who were not contracting parties at the time of consummation of a contract is irrelevant.

"The power of a court of equity to reform deeds and other writings for the correction of mistakes stands among its most ancient and useful powers." Cummins v. Bulgin, 37 N.J.Eq. 476, 476 (1883). That power is not limited to the original parties to the contract, but extends to all those standing in privity with them.

The District Court held that "because Wyndham did not participate in the negotiation and drafting of the 2008 policy, there can be no mutual mistake." We believe this is an errant interpretation of New Jersey law. Reformation on the basis of mutual mistake can be granted even when it is to the disadvantage of a third party.

Turning to the facts, Illinois National and Jet Aviation were the only parties that negotiated and drafted the 2008 policy. As Wyndham admits, it "had [no] involvement with . . . [the] revision to the Endorsement. [The contracting parties] never communicated with Wyndham to discuss the revision or request input. . . . [And,] Wyndham never had an opportunity to form an understanding of what [the contracting parties] intended when [they] inserted 'Named Insured.'" Jet Aviation and Illinois National agree that their intent, at the time the contract was drafted, was to limit coverage for non-owned aircraft to aircraft used by or at the direction of Jet Aviation.

Under these circumstances, the District Court erred by not analyzing the contract under the principles of mutual mistake set forth under New Jersey law. On remand, the District Court should evaluate Illinois National's and Jet Aviation's intent as well as Wyndham's arguments that reformation may be inequitable due to negligence and because the remedy is sought after an accident. . . .

NYGAARD, CIRCUIT JUDGE, dissenting.

The majority's exclusive focus upon mutual mistake, and the intent of Illinois National and Jet Aviation is, I respectfully submit, misplaced. There is no mutual mistake here, only negligence and ignorance—neither of which is a legitimate basis for an equitable reformation of the contract. The insurer made changes to its policy, and negligently sold the altered policy to the insured, who was ignorant of the changes. Although Jet Aviation facilitated the procurement of Wyndham's aircraft insurance coverage with Illinois National, this fact does not eliminate the general contractual obligations of the insurer to the insured. As written, the Endorsement—expressing the aircraft insurance coverage purchased by Wyndham—extended the indemnification of Jet Aviation's policy with Illinois National to insure the non-owned aircraft of the "Named Insured." The Endorsement explicitly references Wyndham as a "Named Insured." The insurer indemnified the insured on these terms and these words are binding.

As we have previously stated, New Jersey law insists that insurance policies are to be interpreted according to their "plain, ordinary meaning." Colliers Lanard & Axilbund v. Lloyds of London, 458 F.3d 231, 236 (3d Cir. 2006). The plain meaning of a contract can be overridden only in rare, exceptional circumstances. Moreover, while I do not read any patent or latent ambiguity here, in such instances policies generally "should be construed to sustain coverage." President v. Jenkins, 180 N.J. 550, 853 A.2d 247, 254 (2004). There is simply no support in state law for the conclusion that the insurer's failure to read the plain language of its own policy before issuing it to the insured justifies supplanting these well-accepted tenets of contract and insurance law with considerations of equity to reform the contract. This is particularly so where, as here, the insurer seeks reformation post-loss. Judge Brown analyzed these issues thoroughly and reasonably. For these reasons, I respectfully dissent.

SECTION 4. FORMAL LEGAL RULES AND CONTRACT INTERPRETATION

Pacific Gas & Elec. Co. v. G.W. Thomas Drayage & Rigging Co.

Supreme Court of California, 1968.
69 Cal. 2d 33, 69 Cal. Rptr. 561, 442 P.2d 641.

TRAYNOR, C.J. Defendant appeals from a judgment for plaintiff in an action for damages for injury to property under an indemnity clause of a contract.

In 1960 defendant entered into a contract with plaintiff to furnish the labor and equipment necessary to remove and replace the upper metal cover of plaintiff's steam turbine. Defendant agreed to perform the work "at [its] own risk and expense" and to "indemnify" plaintiff "against all loss, damage, expense and liability resulting from . . . injury to property, arising out of or in any way connected with the performance of this contract." Defendant also agreed to procure not less than $50,000 insurance to cover liability for injury to property. Plaintiff was to be an additional named insured, but the policy was to contain a cross-liability clause extending the coverage to plaintiff's property.

During the work the cover fell and injured the exposed rotor of the turbine. Plaintiff brought this action to recover $25,144.51, the amount it subsequently spent on repairs. During the trial it dismissed a count based on negligence and thereafter secured judgment on the theory that the indemnity provision covered injury to all property regardless of ownership.

Defendant offered to prove by admissions of plaintiff's agents, by defendant's conduct under similar contracts entered into with plaintiff, and by other proof that in the indemnity clause the parties meant to cover injury to property of third parties only and not to plaintiff's property. Although the trial court observed that the language used was "the classic language for a third party indemnity provision" and that "one could very easily conclude that . . . its whole intendment is to indemnify third parties," it nevertheless held that the "plain language" of the agreement also required defendant to indemnify plaintiff for injuries to plaintiff's property. Having determined that the contract had a plain meaning, the court refused to admit any extrinsic evidence that would contradict its interpretation.

When a court interprets a contract on this basis, it determines the meaning of the instrument in accordance with the "extrinsic evidence of the judge's own linguistic education and experience." (3 Corbin on Contracts (1960 ed.) [§ 579].) The exclusion of testimony that might contradict the linguistic background of the judge reflects a judicial belief in the possibility of perfect verbal expression. (9 Wigmore on Evidence (3d ed. 1940) § 2461.) This belief is a remnant of a primitive faith in the inherent potency and inherent meaning of words.

The test of admissibility of extrinsic evidence to explain the meaning of a written instrument is not whether it appears to the court to be plain and unambiguous on its face, but whether the offered evidence is relevant to prove a meaning to which the language of the instrument is reasonably susceptible. . . .

A rule that would limit the determination of the meaning of a written instrument to its four-corners merely because it seems to the court to be clear and unambiguous, would either deny the relevance of the intention of the parties or presuppose a degree of verbal precision and stability our language has not attained.

Some courts have expressed the opinion that contractual obligations are created by the mere use of certain words, whether or not there was any intention to incur such obligations. Under this view, contractual obligations flow, not from the intention of the parties but from the fact that they used certain magic words. Evidence of the parties' intention therefore becomes irrelevant.

In this state, however, the intention of the parties as expressed in the contract is the source of contractual rights and duties. A court must ascertain and give effect to this intention by determining what the parties meant by the words they used. Accordingly, the exclusion of relevant, extrinsic evidence to explain the meaning of a written instrument could be justified only if it were feasible to determine the meaning the parties gave to the words from the instrument alone.

If words had absolute and constant referents, it might be possible to discover contractual intention in the words themselves and in the manner in which they were arranged. Words, however, do not have absolute and constant referents. "A word is a symbol of thought but has no arbitrary and fixed meaning like a symbol of algebra or chemistry." [Pearson v. State Social Welfare Board, 54 Cal. 2d 184, 195 (1960.] The meaning of particular words or groups of words varies with the "verbal context and surrounding circumstances and purposes in view of the linguistic education and experience of their users and their hearers or readers (not excluding judges).... A word has no meaning apart from these factors; much less does it have an objective meaning, one true meaning." (Corbin, The Interpretation of Words and the Parol Evidence Rule (1965) 50 Cornell L.Q. 161, 187.) Accordingly, the meaning of a writing "can only be found by interpretation in the light of all the circumstances that reveal the sense in which the writer used the words. The exclusion of parol evidence regarding such circumstances merely because the words do not appear ambiguous to the reader can easily lead to the attribution to a written instrument of a meaning that was never intended." . . .

Although extrinsic evidence is not admissible to add to, detract from, or vary the terms of a written contract, these terms must first be determined before it can be decided whether or not extrinsic evidence is being offered for a prohibited purpose. The fact that the terms of an instrument appear clear to a judge does not preclude the possibility that the parties chose the language of the instrument to express different terms. That possibility is not limited to contracts whose terms have acquired a particular meaning by trade usage,[6] but exists whenever the parties' understanding of the words used may have differed from the judge's understanding.

Accordingly, rational interpretation requires at least a preliminary consideration of all credible evidence offered to prove the intention of the parties.[7] (Civ.Code, § 1647; Code Civ.Proc. § 1860; see also 9 Wigmore on

---

[6] Extrinsic evidence of trade usage or custom has been admitted to show that the term "United Kingdom" in a motion picture distribution contract included Ireland (Ermolieff v. R.K.O. Radio Pictures (1942) 19 Cal.2d 543, 122 P.2d 3); that the word "ton" in a lease meant a long ton or 2,240 pounds and not the statutory ton of 2,000 pounds (Higgins v. Cal. Petroleum, etc., Co. (1898) 120 Cal. 629, 52 P. 1080); that the word "stubble" in a lease included not only stumps left in the ground but everything "left on the ground after the harvest time" (Callahan v. Stanley (1881) 57 Cal. 476). . . .

[7] When objection is made to any particular item of evidence offered to prove the intention of the parties, the trial court may not yet be in a position to determine whether in the light of all of the offered evidence, the item objected to will turn out to be admissible as tending to prove a meaning of which the language of the instrument is reasonably susceptible or inadmissible as tending to prove a meaning of which the language is not reasonably susceptible. In such case

Evidence, § 2470.) Such evidence includes testimony as to the "circumstances surrounding the making of the agreement . . . including the object, nature and subject matter of the writing" so that the court can "place itself in the same situation in which the parties found themselves at the time of contracting." . . . If the court decides, after considering this evidence, that the language of a contract, in the light of all the circumstances, is "fairly susceptible of either one of the two interpretations contended for," . . . extrinsic evidence relevant to prove either of such meanings is admissible.[8] In the present case the court erroneously refused to consider extrinsic evidence offered to show that the indemnity clause in the contract was not intended to cover injuries to plaintiff's property. Although that evidence was not necessary to show that the indemnity clause was reasonably susceptible of the meaning contended for by defendant, it was nevertheless relevant and admissible on that issue. Moreover, since that clause was reasonably susceptible of that meaning, the offered evidence was also admissible to prove that the clause had that meaning and did not cover injuries to plaintiff's property.[9] Accordingly, the judgment must be reversed. . . .

---

the court may admit the evidence conditionally by either reserving its ruling on the objection or by admitting the evidence subject to a motion to strike. (See Evid.Code, § 403.)

[8] Extrinsic evidence has often been admitted in such cases on the stated ground that the contract was ambiguous. . . . This statement of the rule is harmless if it is kept in mind that the ambiguity may be exposed by extrinsic evidence that reveals more than one possible meaning.

[9] The court's exclusion of extrinsic evidence in this case would be error even under a rule that excluded such evidence when the instrument appeared to the court to be clear and unambiguous on its face. The controversy centers on the meaning of the word "indemnify" and the phrase "all loss, damage, expense and liability." The trial court's recognition of the language as typical of a third party indemnity clause and the double sense in which the word "indemnify" is used in statutes and defined in dictionaries demonstrate the existence of an ambiguity. [Quoting statutes and dictionaries.]

Plaintiff's assertion that the use of the word "all" to modify "loss, damage, expense and liability" dictates an all inclusive interpretation is not persuasive. If the word "indemnify" encompasses only third-party claims, the word "all" simply refers to all such claims. The use of the words "loss," "damage," and "expense" in addition to the word "liability" is likewise inconclusive. These words do not imply an agreement to reimburse for injury to an indemnitee's property since they are commonly inserted in third-party indemnity clauses, to enable an indemnitee who settles a claim to recover from his indemnitor without proving his liability. (Carpenter Paper Co. v. Kellogg (1952) 114 Cal.App.2d 640, 251 P.2d 40. Civ.Code, § 2778, provides: "1. Upon an indemnity against liability . . . the person indemnified is entitled to recover upon becoming liable; 2. Upon an indemnity against claims, or demands, or damages, or costs . . . the person indemnified is not entitled to recover without payment thereof; . . .")

The provision that defendant perform the work "at his own risk and expense" and the provisions relating to insurance are equally inconclusive. By agreeing to work at its own risk defendant may have released plaintiff from liability for any injuries to defendant's property arising out of the contract's performance, but this provision did not necessarily make defendant an insurer against injuries to plaintiff's property. Defendant's agreement to procure liability insurance to cover damages to plaintiff's property does not indicate whether the insurance was to cover all injuries or only injuries caused by defendant's negligence.

Columbia Nitrogen Corp. v. Royster Co.

451 F.2d 3 (4th Cir. 1971)

Royster manufactured and marketed mixed fertilizers, the principal components of which were nitrogen, phosphate and potash. Columbia was primarily a producer of nitrogen, although it manufactured some mixed fertilizer. For several years Royster had been a major purchaser of Columbia's products, but Columbia had never been a significant customer of Royster. In the fall of 1966, Royster constructed a facility which enabled it to produce more phosphate than it needed in its own operations. After extensive negotiations, the companies executed a contract for Royster's sale of a minimum of 31,000 tons of phosphate each year for three years to Columbia, with an option to extend the term. The contract stated the price per ton, subject to an escalation clause dependent on production costs. Phosphate prices soon plunged precipitously. Unable to resell the phosphate at a competitive price, Columbia ordered only part of the scheduled tonnage. At Columbia's request, Royster lowered its price for diammonium phosphate on shipments for three months in 1967, but specified that subsequent shipments would be at the original contract price. Even with this concession, Royster's price was still substantially above the market. As a result, Columbia ordered less than a tenth of the phosphate Royster was to ship in the first contract year. When pressed by Royster, Columbia offered to take the phosphate at the current market price and resell it without brokerage fee. Royster, however, insisted on the contract price. When Columbia refused delivery, Royster sold the unaccepted phosphate for Columbia's account at a price substantially below the contract price. It then sued Columbia for breach.

Columbia defended by offering the testimony of witnesses with long experience in the trade that because of uncertain crop and weather conditions, farming practices, and government agricultural programs, express price and quantity terms in contracts for materials in the mixed-fertilizer industry are mere projections to be adjusted according to market forces. Columbia also offered proof of its business dealings with Royster over the six-year period preceding the phosphate contract. Columbia claimed these proofs evidenced a pattern of repeated and substantial deviation from the stated amount or price. This experience, Columbia wanted to argue to the factfinder, formed the basis of an understanding on which it depended in conducting negotiations with Royster.

Held, Columbia's proffered evidence was improperly excluded. A finding of ambiguity is not necessary for the admission of extrinsic evidence of the usage of the trade or the parties' course of dealing. UCC 2–202 expressly allows evidence of course of dealing or usage of trade to explain or supplement terms intended by the parties as a final expression of their agreement; "the test of admissibility is not whether the contract appears on its face to be complete in every detail, but whether the proffered evidence of course of dealing and trade usage reasonably can be construed as consistent with the express terms of the agreement." Columbia may therefore present evidence that there was "a practice of mutual adjustments so prevalent in the industry and in prior dealings between the parties that it formed a part of the agreement governing this transaction."

Robert Indus. v. Spence

362 Mass. 751, 291 N.E.2d 407 (1973)

"[T]here was no error in the admission of evidence of the facts and circumstances of the transaction, including the situation and relations of the parties, for the purpose of applying the terms of the written contract to the subject matter and removing and explaining any uncertainty or ambiguity which arose from such application. Stoops v. Smith, 100 Mass. 63, 66. A [contract] is to be read in the light of the circumstances of its execution, which may enable the court to see that its words are really ambiguous. . . . When the written agreement, as applied to the subject matter, is in any respect uncertain or equivocal in meaning, all the circumstances of the parties leading to its execution may be shown for the purpose of elucidating, but not of contradicting or changing its terms. . . . Expressions in our cases to the effect that evidence of circumstances can be admitted only after an ambiguity has been found on the face of the written instrument have reference to evidence offered to contradict the written terms. . . . After interpretation has called to its help all those facts which make up the setting in which the words are used, however, the words themselves remain the most important evidence of intention[.]" [Is this court saying that a trial judge may properly hear evidence in aid of interpretation even before deciding whether the written agreement is ambiguous?]

[The authorities indicating "a retreat from the four-corners standard," in favor of a contextual inquiry into ambiguity (the position taken in the Restatement, Second § 212), are collected in C.R. Anthony Co. v. Loretto Mall Partners, 112 N.M. 504, 817 P.2d 238 (1991). Courts employing a "context" approach typically caution that extrinsic evidence is admitted only "for the purpose of aiding in the interpretation of what is in the instrument, and not for the purpose of showing intention independent of the instrument." Berg v. Hudesman, 115 Wash. 2d 657, 801 P.2d 222 (1990). Judge Keeting's discussion of procedures for resolving disputes over meaning, in Donoghue v. IBC USA (Publications), Inc., 70 F.3d 206, 214–216 (1st Cir. 1995), captures the essence of the ambiguity problem.]

Federal Dep. Ins. Corp. v. W.R. Grace & Co.

877 F.2d 614 (7th Cir. 1989)

"Most of the modern cases in the 'four corners' line stand for the unexceptionable proposition that 'language in a contract is not rendered ambiguous simply because the parties do not agree upon its meaning.' . . . The fact that parties to a contract disagree about its meaning does not show that it is ambiguous, for if it did, then putting contracts into writing would provide parties with little or no protection. . . . [T]he words of the contract are not lightly to be ignored. The nature of the offer of proof to show an ambiguity is therefore critical. Although a self-serving statement [that] a party did not understand the contract to mean what it says (or appears to say) will not suffice, an offer to show that anyone who understood the context of the contract would realize it couldn't mean what an untutored reader would suppose it meant will."

Restatement of Contracts, Second

§ 212. Interpretation of Integrated Agreement

(2) A question of interpretation of an integrated agreement is to be determined by the trier of fact if it depends on the credibility of extrinsic evidence or on a choice among reasonable inferences to be drawn from extrinsic evidence. Otherwise a question of interpretation of an integrated agreement is to be determined as a question of law.

Comment: . . .

d. *"Question of law."* Analytically, what meaning is attached to a word or other symbol by one or more people is a question of fact. But general usage as to the meaning of words . . . is commonly a proper subject for judicial notice without the aid of evidence extrinsic to the writing. Historically, moreover, . . . questions of interpretation of written documents have been treated as questions of law in the sense that they are decided by the trial judge rather than by the jury. Likewise, since an appellate court is commonly in as good a position to decide such questions as the trial judge, they have been treated as questions of law for purposes of appellate review. Such treatment has the effect of limiting the power of the trier of fact to exercise a dispensing power in the guise of a finding of fact, and thus contributes to the stability and predictability of contractual relations. In cases of standardized contracts like insurance policies, it also provides a method of assuring that like cases will be decided alike.

NOTE: FORMAL RULES AND THE RESOLUTION OF AMBIGUITY

It is possible for formal rules to reduce uncertainty and miscommunication in the first instance. We might want a rule that induces the party with information to disclose it. When a contract has two possible meanings and one party is aware of the ambiguity and the other is not, the rule might provide that it is the party who knows of the ambiguity that must resolve the ambiguity, or else be held to the single meaning ascribed to the contract by the other side. The purpose of such a rule is not to try to capture a meeting of minds, but rather to induce parties to be forthcoming when they bargain with one another. The next case provides an example of such an approach.

United Rentals, Inc. v. RAM Holdings, Inc.

Court of Chancery of Delaware, 2007.
937 A.2d 810.

CHANDLER, Chancellor. In classical mythology, it took a demigod to subdue Cerberus, the beastly three-headed dog that guarded the gates of the underworld. In his twelfth and final labor, Heracles journeyed to Hades to battle, tame, and capture the monstrous creature. In this case, plaintiff United Rentals, Inc. journeyed to Delaware to conquer a more modern obstacle that, rather than guards the gates to the afterlife, stands in the way of the consummation of a merger. Nevertheless, like the three heads of the mythological Cerberus, the private equity firm of the same name presents three substantial challenges to plaintiff's case: (1) the language of the Merger Agreement, (2) evidence of the negotiations between the parties, and (3) a doctrine of contract interpretation known as the forthright negotiator principle. In this tale the three heads prove too much to overcome.

First, the language of the Merger Agreement presents a direct conflict between two provisions on remedies, rendering the Agreement ambiguous and defeating plaintiff's motion for summary judgment. Second, the extrinsic evidence of the negotiation process, though ultimately not conclusive, is too muddled to find that plaintiff's interpretation of the Agreement represents the common understanding of the parties. Third, under the forthright negotiator principle, the subjective understanding of one party to a contract may bind the other party when the other party knows or has reason to know of that understanding. Because the evidence in this case shows that defendants understood this Agreement to preclude the remedy of specific performance and that plaintiff knew or should have known of this understanding, I conclude that plaintiff has failed to meet its burden and find in favor of defendants. . . .

On November 19, 2007, plaintiff United Rentals, Inc. ("URI" or the "Company") filed its complaint in this action. Thereafter, on November 29, 2007, URI moved for summary judgment. In its motion for summary judgment, URI sought an order from this Court specifically enforcing the terms of the July 22, 2007 "Agreement and Plan of Merger" (the "Merger Agreement" or the "Agreement") among URI and defendants RAM Holdings, Inc. ("RAM Holdings") and RAM Acquisition Corp. ("RAM Acquisition" and, together with RAM Holdings, "RAM" or the "RAM Entities").[4]
. . .

URI is a Delaware corporation with its principal place of business in Greenwich, Connecticut. Founded in 1997, it is a publicly traded company listed on the New York Stock Exchange. URI is the largest equip-

---

[4] Both because RAM is controlled by Cerberus, as defined below, and because the witnesses' testimony often does not distinguish among these Cerberus-controlled entities, I will sometimes refer to defendants as "Cerberus," though Cerberus is *not* a party to this action; only RAM Holdings and RAM Acquisition are defendants in this case.

ment rental company in the world based on revenue, earning $3.64 billion in 2006. The Company consists of an integrated network of over 690 rental locations in forty-eight states, ten Canadian provinces, and one location in Mexico. The Company serves construction and industrial customers, utilities, municipalities, homeowners and others. . . .

Throughout the course of negotiation of the Merger Agreement, URI contends that it communicated to RAM's principal attorney contract negotiator, Peter Ehrenberg of Lowenstein Sandler PC ("Lowenstein"), that URI wanted to restrict RAM's ability to breach the Merger Agreement and unilaterally refuse to close the transaction. URI further maintains that URI's counsel, Eric Swedenburg of Simpson Thacher & Bartlett LP ("Simpson"), made clear to Ehrenberg that it was very important to URI that there be "deal certainty" so that RAM could not simply refuse to close if debt financing was available.

On the other side of the negotiation table, the RAM entities argue that Ehrenberg consistently communicated that Cerberus had a $100 million walkaway right and that URI knowingly relinquished its right to specific performance under the Merger Agreement. . . .

URI argues that the plain and unambiguous language of the merger agreement allows for specific performance as a remedy for the RAM Entities' breach. Section 9.10 expressly invests URI with a right to seek specific performance to enforce the Merger Agreement and to obtain an order enjoining RAM to (i) make reasonable best efforts to obtain financing and satisfy the Merger Agreement's closing conditions, and (ii) consummate the transactions when financing is available and has not been drawn down by RAM as a result of its breach of the Merger Agreement.

Section 9.10, however, explicitly states that it is "subject in all respects to Section 8.2(e) hereof, which Section shall govern the rights and obligations of the parties . . . under the circumstances provided therein." Section 8.2(e) describes the $100 million Parent Termination Fee payable to URI as the "sole and exclusive" remedy against RAM under the Agreement when there has been a termination of the Merger Agreement by URI. Further, section 8.2(e) provides that

> In no event, whether or not this Agreement has been terminated pursuant to any provision hereof, shall [RAM or Cerberus Partners] . . . be subject to any liability in excess of the Parent Termination Fee for any or all losses or damages relating to or arising out of this Agreement or the transactions contemplated by this Agreement, . . . and in no event shall the Company seek equitable relief or seek to recover any money damages in excess of such amount from [RAM or Cerberus Partners]. . . .

Relying heavily on the canon of construction that requires harmonization of seemingly conflicting contract provisions, URI contends that specific performance under section 9.10 remains a viable remedy despite the language of section 8.2(e). URI offers two chief reasons in support of this position. First, section 8.2(e)'s $100 million Parent Termination Fee operates as the "sole and exclusive" remedy only if one of the parties terminates the agreement. Termination is a defined term in the Agreement, however, and it is not equivalent to a breach. URI contends (and RAM does not dispute) that neither party has terminated the agreement pursuant to section 8. Thus, the Termination Fee is not necessarily the "sole and exclusive remedy" in this case. Second, URI submits that the outright prohibition of equitable remedies in the last sentence of section 8.2(e) is limited to equitable remedies that involve monetary compensation like restitution or rescission. The sentence commands that "in no event shall [URI] seek equitable relief or seek to recover any money damages in excess of [the $100 million Termination Fee] from [RAM or Cerberus]." URI argues that the prepositional phrase ("in excess of the" termination fee) modifies *both* "equitable relief" and "money damages." This reading is required, URI says, because otherwise this sentence would render section 9.10 "mere surplusage" devoid of any meaning in violation of longstanding principles of contractual interpretation. Moreover, URI points to the final sentence of section 8.2(a) as proof that the Agreement contemplates a right to specific performance: "The parties acknowledge and agree that, subject to Section 8.2(e), nothing in this Section 8.2 shall be deemed to affect their right to specific performance under Section 9.10." According to URI, section 8.2(a) shows that the parties were aware of the "specific performance" remedy and could have expressly eliminated it. The Merger Agreement does not do so; instead, it explicitly provides that both specific performance and injunctive relief are available remedies.

The RAM Entities counter that URI's interpretation is unreasonable. First, they argue, it is URI's position that would render portions of the Agreement "mere surplusage." If the operation of section 8.2(e) were in fact limited, as URI asserts, to circumstances in which the Merger Agreement had been properly terminated by either party, there would be no need to include a sentence in section 9.10 subjecting the specific performance provisions of section 9.10 to section 8.2(e) because specific performance, by law, would be unavailable in those circumstances; one cannot specifically perform an agreement that has been terminated. Thus, section 8.2(e) must have applicability outside the context of termination. Second, the RAM Entities argue that is unreasonable to limit the phrase "equitable relief" to those equitable remedies that include monetary damages.

Reading the Agreement as a whole and with the aid of the fundamental canons of contract construction, I conclude that URI's interpretation is reasonable. The parties explicitly agreed in section 9.10 that "irreparable damage would occur in the event that any of the provisions of this Agreement were not performed in accordance with their specific terms or were otherwise breached." They further agreed that "the Company shall be entitled to see an injunction or injunctions . . . to enforce compliance." Given this clarion language supporting the existence and availability of specific performance, it is reasonable to read the limitations of section 8.2(e) in the manner URI has championed. RAM's arguments to the contrary are ultimately unpersuasive. Neither party has terminated the Agreement pursuant to the termination provisions of section 8.1, and the context of the final sentence of section 8.2(e) allows one to reasonably conclude that "equitable relief" in that sentence means only equitable relief involving monetary damages. URI's interpretation thus represents a reasonable harmonization of apparently conflicting provisions. . . .

Though defendants fail to demonstrate that plaintiff's interpretation of the Merger Agreement is unreasonable as a matter of law, defendants do succeed in offering a reasonable alternative interpretation. In opposing URI's motion for summary judgment, defendants deny that the provisions of the Merger Agreement conflict so as to require harmonization. The relationship between sections 9.10 and 8.2(e), as set forth in section 9.10 is, defendants contend, clear: section 9.10 is "subject to" section 8.2(e). Section 8.2(e) then provides that "in no event shall [URI] seek equitable relief or seek to recover any money damages in excess of such amount [*i.e.,* the $100 million termination fee] from [RAM or Cerberus]." RAM argues that section 8.2(e) operates to prohibit URI from seeking any form of equitable relief (including specific performance) under all circumstances, relegating URI's relief to only the $100 million termination fee. [D]efendants contend that Delaware law specifically permits the parties to establish supremacy and subservience between provisions such that, where the terms of one provision are expressly stated to be "subject to" the terms of a second provision, the terms of the second provision will control, even if the terms of the second provision conflict with or nullify the first provision. Additionally, RAM argues, unlike plaintiff's interpretation, RAM's interpretation utilizes only the plain meaning of "equitable relief." As described above, plaintiff, in proposing a reconciliation of the section 8.2(e) limitation on equitable relief with the right of specific performance in section 9.10, urges this Court to read the words "equitable relief" and "money damages" as modified by the phrase "in excess of" the termination fee. Defendants' interpretation of this portion of the provision is, however, at least as reasonable as (if not more than) that of plaintiff. The phrase "in excess of" appears, grammatically, to modify only "money damages."

Plaintiff argues that if RAM had wanted to eliminate URI's rights to specific performance in all circumstances, it could have simply stricken out clause (b) of section 9.10. Though the Court has no doubt that this simple (and seemingly obvious) drafting approach would have been superior, on a motion for summary judgment, I cannot look beyond the text of the agreement to inquire into the motivations of the parties or to consider ways in which a particular end may have been more efficiently achieved and more clearly articulated. An interpretation of the Agreement that relies on the parties' addition of hierarchical phrases, instead of the deletion of particular language altogether, is not unreasonable as a matter of law.

Having considered all of plaintiff's arguments, I must conclude that plaintiff has not shown that defendants' interpretation is unreasonable as a matter of law. The contracting parties here chose terms, such as "subject to," that impose a hierarchy among provisions. Defendants' interpretation of those terms and the provisions they affect is not, I conclude, unreasonable. . . .

It is probably unlikely that a single, *unambiguous* agreement can simultaneously affirm and deny the availability of a specific performance remedy. If there is such an unambiguous contract, it is certainly not the contract at issue in this case. Both URI and RAM have proffered reasonable readings of the Merger Agreement, and because "provisions in controversy are fairly susceptible of different interpretations or may have two or more different meanings, there is ambiguity." Thus, plaintiff's and defendants' arguments suffer the same flaw, which is fatal at this stage: each party is unable to demonstrate that its proposed interpretation of the Merger Agreement is the *only* interpretation of the Agreement that is reasonable as a matter of law. In such a case, summary judgment is inappropriate because the court is presented with a genuine issue of material fact: what was the intent of the parties? Therefore, I must consider extrinsic evidence to ascertain the meaning of the Merger Agreement. . . .

The Court heard testimony from seven witnesses over a two-day trial in order to resolve the factual issue of what was the common understanding of the parties with respect to remedies in the Merger Agreement. The Merger Agreement, of course, is a contract, and the Court's goal when interpreting a contract "is to ascertain the shared intention of the parties." . . .

Having determined that the contract is ambiguous on account of its conflicting provisions, the Court permitted the parties to introduce extrinsic evidence of the negotiation process. Such extrinsic evidence may include "overt statements and acts of the parties, the business context, prior dealings between the parties, [and] business custom and usage in the industry." This evidence may lead to "a single 'correct' or single 'objectively reasonable' meaning." Restated, the extrinsic evidence may render an ambiguous contract clear so that an "objectively reasonable party in the position of either bargainer would have understood the nature of the contractual rights and duties to be." In such a case, the Court would enforce the objectively reasonable interpretation that emerges.

The Court must emphasize here that the introduction of extrinsic, parol evidence does not alter or deviate from Delaware's adherence to the objective theory of contracts. As I recently explained to counsel in this case, the private, subjective feelings of the negotiators are irrelevant and unhelpful to the Court's consideration of a contract's meaning, because the meaning of a properly formed contract must be shared or common. That is not to say, however, that a party's subjective understanding is never instructive. On the contrary, in cases where an examination of the extrinsic evidence does not lead to an obvious, objectively reasonable conclusion, the Court may apply the forthright negotiator principle.[120] Under this principle, the Court considers the evidence of what one party *subjectively* "believed the obligation to be, coupled with evidence that the other party knew or should have known of such belief."[121] In other words, the forthright negotiator principle provides that, in cases where the extrinsic evidence does not lead to a single, commonly held understanding of a contract's meaning, a court may consider the subjective understanding of one party that has been objectively manifested and is known or should be known by the other party. It is with these fundamental legal principles in mind that I consider the factual record developed at trial. . . .

The evidence presented at trial conveyed a deeply flawed negotiation in which both sides failed to clearly and consistently communicate their client's positions. First, I find that the extrinsic evidence is not clear enough to conclude that there is a single, shared understanding with respect to the availability of specific performance under the Merger Agreement. Second, I employ the forthright negotiator principle to make two additional findings. With respect to URI, I find that even if the Company believed the Agreement preserved a right to specific performance, its attorney Eric Swedenburg categorically failed to communicate that understanding to the defendants during the latter part of the negotiations. Finally, with respect to RAM, although it could have easily avoided this entire dispute by striking section 9.10(b) from the Agreement, I find that its attorney did communicate to URI his understanding that the Agreement precluded any specific performance rights. Consequently, I conclude that URI has failed to meet its burden and determine that the Merger Agreement does not allow a specific performance remedy. . . .

The parties began their negotiations very far apart. URI circulated a draft that included numerous provisions favorable to their side, including several mechanisms by which URI could specifically enforce the merger against Cerberus. RAM responded with a "heavy-handed" mark-up. Early conversations led to no agreement, and URI simply ignored many of the proposed changes that RAM initially made. Although RAM ultimately succeeded in striking many of the provisions entitling URI to specific performance, and although RAM did modify section 8.2(e) to try to limit the availability of equitable relief, section 9.10 in the final agreement continued to speak of the Company's right to specific performance. Testimony revealed that communications between the parties routinely skirted the issue of equitable relief and only addressed it tangentially or implicitly. The defendants put forth some evidence suggesting that by

---

[120] Comrie v. Enterasys Networks, Inc., 837 A.2d 1, 13 (Del. Ch. 2003).

[121] U.S. West, Inc. v. Time Warner, Inc., C.A. No. 14555, 1996 WL 307445 (Del. Ch. June 6, 1996).

mid to late July Swedenburg had agreed to give up specific performance, but it was not conclusive. Mr. Seitz, URI's attorney, deftly questioned RAM's chief negotiator Ehrenberg about the clarity and wisdom of his curious editing of section 9.10, a provision Ehrenberg also contends he nullified, but this did not uncover "a single 'correct' or single 'objectively reasonable' meaning'" for the Agreement. Indeed, because "a review of the extrinsic evidence does not lead the Court to an 'obvious' conclusion," I must apply the forthright negotiator principle to determine the proper interpretation of this contract. . . .

Based on the evidence presented at trial, I find that the defendants understood the agreement to eliminate any right to specific performance and that URI either knew or should have known of defendants' understanding. Cerberus seems to have come to this transaction halfheartedly and unenthusiastic about committing. It took issue with a great deal of the initial draft agreement URI circulated and failed to submit a bid by the proposed deadline. The defendants offered a go-shop period with a lower break fee to allow URI to shop itself to other bidders without the fear of paying a huge termination fee. Moreover, Cerberus lowered its bid significantly. Cerberus was not acting like an eager buyer and was not willing to do this deal on the terms initially proposed by URI.

Testimony from two of Cerberus's leaders, CEO Stephen Feinberg and managing director Steven Mayer, demonstrated that the firm believed it had the ability to walk away from this agreement relatively unscathed. Indeed, Feinberg, though evidently unsure of what "specific performance" means, did think "very clearly that to the extent we didn't complete the merger, that our—our liability and our—what we'd have to come up with was a hundred million and that we could not be forced to close the deal." Mayer, who participated more directly in the negotiations and who reviewed the Merger Agreement both in drafts and in final form, testified that he "believe[s] there was an explicit understanding that Cerberus could choose not to close the transaction for any reason or no reason at all and pay a maximum amount of a hundred million dollars." In addition to the Cerberus executives, lawyers for Cerberus testified to and produced contemporaneous notes corroborating their subjective understanding that the $100 million termination fee was the "sole and exclusive" recourse available to URI in the event of a failure to close.

I also find that defendants communicated this understanding to URI in such a way that URI either knew or should have known of their understanding. Initially, Cerberus conveyed its position by means of the drafts and mark-ups it sent to Swedenburg. For example, on June 18, 2007, Ehrenberg sent Simpson his initial mark-ups to the draft circulated by URI. In that mark-up, Ehrenberg wrote, "OUR CLIENT WILL NOT AGREE TO A GUARANTEE." Ehrenberg also removed a provision from section 6.10 "that would have required the buyer to take enforcement actions against the lenders and other persons providing the financing." Finally, Ehrenberg struck portions of section 9.10(b) that would have allowed URI to specifically enforce the Equity Commitment Letter and the Guarantee and to specifically enforce the consummation of the transaction. While discussing these, Swedenburg told Ehrenberg that he would likely not incorporate many of the changes, would send it back, and would expect Cerberus's next mark-up to be "less voluminous."

Nevertheless, Ehrenberg persisted. In a conversation that occurred sometime between June 25 and July 10, Ehrenberg and Swedenburg discussed the extent of the defendants' potential liability. During this conversation, Swedenburg indicated "that it was important for his client to assure that . . . Cerberus and the RAM entities showed up at the closing." Ehrenberg "explained to Mr. Swedenburg that that was a significant problem." At a July 10 meeting of the attorneys, it was decided that the issue of liability needed to be decided by the principals, but that Cerberus would be willing to enter a limited guarantee agreement.

The next important meeting occurred on July 12, 2007. There, via telephone, Mayer represented to the URI team that "Cerberus would not proceed with the negotiations or with the deal unless there was an arrangement where, if the Cerberus parties, to include RAM, failed to close, the obligation would be to pay a fee." Both Ehrenberg and Mayer testified that the URI team agreed to this point on the twelfth.

After this meeting, Ehrenberg and his team returned to the Merger Agreement and made several important revisions. The draft they produced was circulated early in the morning on July 15, 2007 along with new versions of the Equity Commitment Letter and the Limited Guarantee. I find several edits significant in these documents:

1. the Equity Commitment Letter expressly disclaims any third-party beneficiaries and exceptions to allow for suit against the Cerberus entities were removed;

2. the "no recourse" provisions of the Limited Guarantee were expanded to make them farther reaching;

3. section 9.10 was edited to remove references to the Equity Commitment Letter and the final sentence was added to make the provision subservient to section 8.2(e);

4. section 8.2(e) was substantially rewritten to include a limitation on liability and to provide explicitly that "in no event shall the Company seek equitable relief. . . ."

Although . . . these edits do not provide a perfectly clear expression of RAM's position that the agreement bars specific performance, they are substantial enough that they should have at least put Swedenburg and URI on notice that RAM had a different understanding than URI did. Subsequent communications between the parties go substantively beyond this, and unquestionably convey RAM's position.

Swedenburg made very few changes to this draft. He struck the provision about the Company's ability to "seek equitable relief," but he ultimately did not stand by this revision. When Ehrenberg received Swedenburg's edits, he circulated an agenda for a meeting to discuss the Merger Agreement. On that agenda, Ehrenberg listed "limitation of liability in 8.2(e)" as a topic for discussion, and by this he "intended to address the deletion of the words equity relief." At that meeting, Mr. Swedenburg spent his time lobbying for a higher break-up fee, one that would be "painful," because the potential reputational harm Cerberus would suffer from walking away would not be enough to deter them from doing so. Perhaps more importantly, the RAM attorneys also explained to Swedenburg the importance of the words "equitable relief" that Swedenburg had stricken from the Merger Agreement: "it was important for us that the language that he struck be restored to reflect the agreement that the only remedy available to United Rentals, if Cerberus didn't proceed with the closing, was the break-up fee-reverse break-up fee." Testimony indicated that Swedenburg put up no fight on this issue. He tersely replied, "I get it."

I find this testimony to be credible and I find that it is supported by certain of defendants' exhibits and by Swedenburg's testimony. First, the agenda that Ehrenberg circulated specifically references section 8.2(e). Second, Holt's notes from the July 19 meeting support the proposition that this conversation happened and that Swedenburg assented. Third, Swedenburg essentially capitulated on this point during cross examination. Conceding that he quickly assented to the reinsertion of the language he had removed from section 8.2(e), Swedenburg then testified that he knew "equitable relief included specific performance," that this was "probably why [he] did strike it," admitted that Ehrenberg conveyed how important that provision was to Cerberus, and then concluded by suggesting he knew it would have been a good idea to inquire further about why this provision was so important to Cerberus, but that he failed to so inquire because it "was at the end of an agenda, there was [sic] more negotiations to go, et cetera, et cetera." I find it frankly incredible that Swedenburg could have recognized the import of the language he was striking and that Cerberus considered that language key but manifestly failed to make any further inquiry. Swedenburg, the original architect of this transaction, testified that one lynchpin of his "construct" was the seller's ability to force the sale to close. By the end of this July 19 meeting, Swedenburg either knew or should have known that Cerberus's understanding of the Agreement was fundamentally inconsistent with that construct.

If Swedenburg's faltering on July 19 were not enough to put URI on notice of Cerberus's understanding, the July 21 telephone conversation between the UBS representatives (McNeal and Kochman) and Mayer surely was. On that call, Mayer mentioned something about Cerberus's ability to walk away from the deal. Kochman responded forcefully, declaring that his client, URI, would never agree to this deal if it were merely an option. Mayer reassured him that Cerberus was committed to the deal, but never conceded that the contract amounted to anything other than an option. McNeal and Kochman reported this conversation to Horowitz, and Brad Jacobs, then-CEO/Chairman of URI. Horowitz, who evidently cannot remember much of this deal, failed to raise this issue with Swedenburg, the chief negotiator, or with Ehrenberg. On July 22, the very next day, the Agreement was executed. At that time, I conclude that URI had ample reason to know that Cerberus understood the Agreement to bar the remedy of specific performance. . . .

Although some in the media have discussed this case in the context of Material Adverse Change ("MAC") clauses, the dispute between URI and Cerberus is a good, old-fashioned contract case prompted by buyer's remorse. As with many contract disputes, hindsight affords the Court a perspective from which it is clear that this case could have been avoided: if Cerberus had simply deleted section 9.10(b), the contract would not be ambiguous, and URI would not have filed this suit. The law of contracts, however, does not require parties to choose optimally clear language; in fact, parties often riddle their agreements with a certain amount of ambiguity in order to reach a compromise. Although the language in this Merger Agreement remains ambiguous, the understanding of the parties does not. . . .

One may plausibly upbraid Cerberus for walking away from this deal, for favoring their lenders over their targets, or for suboptimal contract editing, but one cannot reasonably criticize the firm for a failure to represent its understanding of the limitations on remedies provided by this Merger Agreement. From the beginning of the process, Cerberus and its attorneys have aggressively negotiated this contract, and along the way they have communicated their intentions and understandings to URI. Despite the Herculean efforts of its litigation counsel at trial, URI could not overcome the apparent lack of communication of *its* intentions and understandings to defendants. Even if URI's deal attorneys did not affirmatively and explicitly agree to the limitation on specific performance as several witnesses allege they did on multiple occasions, no testimony at trial rebutted the inference that I must reasonably draw from the evidence: by July 22, 2007, URI knew or should have known what Cerberus's understanding of the Merger Agreement was, and if URI disagreed with that understanding, it had an affirmative duty to clarify its position in the face of an ambiguous contract with glaringly conflicting provisions. Because it has failed to meet its burden of demonstrating that the common understanding of the parties permitted specific performance of the Merger Agreement, URI's petition for specific performance is denied. . . .

SECTION 5. MISTAKE

INTRODUCTORY NOTE

During the course of the contractual relationship, there are several different kinds of "mistakes" that both parties can make. One type of mistake arises when each of the parties has a different understanding about the bargain that was struck. To use an example discussed earlier, p. 346, a written contract provides for the sale of cotton shipped on board the Peerless. One party reasonably believes that the contract refers to the ship of that name that sailed from Bombay in October and the other reasonably believes that the contract refers to another ship also called Peerless that sailed in December. This sort of mistake requires us to ask whether there was ever an objective meeting of the minds in the first instance.

Another sort of mistake arises when both parties agree on the terms of the contract, but the written document they create provides for something else. This sort of mistake gives rise to the question of whether the court should exercise its power to "reform" the agreement and hold the parties to the deal that they in fact struck.

In this section, we focus on a third sort of mistake. Both parties are in sync with each other, but they are both fundamentally mistaken about the same thing. In the case that follows, both parties believed that a cow was barren, when it was in fact pregnant. The question that arises is whether, when both parties make a mistake about something so fundamental to the bargain that they struck, it still makes sense to enforce it.

Sherwood v. Walker

Supreme Court of Michigan, 1887.
66 Mich. 568, 33 N.W. 919.

MORSE, J. Replevin for a cow. Suit commenced in justice's court. Judgment for plaintiff. Appealed to circuit court of Wayne county, and verdict and judgment for plaintiff. . . . The defendants bring error. . . .

The main controversy depends upon the construction of a contract for the sale of the cow. The plaintiff claims that the title passed, and bases his action upon such claim. The defendants contend that the contract was executory, and by its terms no title to the animal was acquired by plaintiff.

The defendants reside at Detroit, but are in business at Walkerville, Ontario, and have a farm at Greenfield, in Wayne County, upon which were some blooded cattle supposed to be barren as breeders. The Walkers are importers and breeders of polled Angus cattle.

The plaintiff [Sherwood] is a banker living at Plymouth, in Wayne County. He called upon the defendants at Walkerville for the purchase of some of their stock, but found none there that suited him. Meeting one of the defendants afterwards, he was informed that they had a few head upon their Greenfield farm. He was asked to go out and look at them, with the statement at the time that they were probably barren, and would not breed. May 5, 1886, plaintiff went out to Greenfield and saw the cattle. A few days thereafter, he called upon one of the defendants with the view of purchasing a cow, known as "Rose 2d of Aberlone." After considerable talk, it was agreed that defendants would telephone Sherwood at his home in Plymouth in reference to the price. The second morning after this talk he was called up by telephone, and the terms of the sale were finally agreed upon. He was to pay five and one-half cents per pound, live weight, fifty pounds shrinkage. He was asked how he intended to take the cow home, and replied that he might ship her from King's cattle-yard. He requested defendants to confirm the sale in writing, which they did by sending him the following letter [dated May 15, 1886]: "T.C. SHERWOOD, *Dear Sir*: We confirm sale to you of the cow Rose 2d of Aberlone, lot 56 of our catalogue, at five and a half cents per pound, less fifty pounds shrink. We inclose herewith order on Mr. Graham for the cow. You might leave check with him, or mail to us here, as you prefer. Yours truly, HIRAM WALKER & SONS."

The order upon Graham inclosed in the letter read as follows: "May 15, 1886. *George Graham*: You will please deliver at King's cattle-yard to Mr. T.C. Sherwood, Plymouth, the cow Rose 2d of Aberlone, lot 56 of our catalogue. Send halter with cow, and have her weighed. Yours truly, HIRAM WALKER & SONS."

On [May 21] the plaintiff went to defendants' farm at Greenfield, and presented the order and letter to Graham, who informed him that the defendants had instructed him not to deliver the cow. Soon after, the plaintiff tendered [$80] to Hiram Walker[,] demand[ing] the cow. Walker refused to take the money or deliver the cow. The plaintiff then instituted this suit. After he had secured possession of the cow under the writ of replevin, the plaintiff caused her to be weighed by the constable who served the writ. . . . She weighed 1,420 pounds. . . .

The defendants [at trial] introduced evidence tending to show that at the time of the alleged sale it was believed by both the plaintiff and themselves that the cow was barren and would not breed; that she cost $850, and if not barren would be worth from $750 to $1,000; that after the date of the letter, and the order to Graham, the defendants were informed by said Graham that in his judgment the cow was with calf, and therefore they instructed him not to deliver her to plaintiff, and on the twentieth of May, 1886, telegraphed to the plaintiff what Graham thought about the cow being with calf, and that consequently they could not sell her. The cow had a calf in the month of October following. . . .

HIRAM WALKER
1816–1898

It appears from the record that both parties supposed this cow was barren and would not breed, and she was sold by the pound for an insignificant sum as compared with her real value if a breeder. She was evidently sold and purchased on the relation of her value for beef, unless the plaintiff had learned of her true condition, and concealed such knowledge from the defendants. . . . The circuit judge ruled that [the sale could not be avoided], and it made no difference whether she was barren or not. I am of the opinion that the court erred in this. . . . [I]t must be considered as well settled that a party who has given an apparent consent to a contract of sale may refuse to execute it, or he may avoid it after it has been completed, if the assent was founded, or the contract made, upon the mistake of a material fact,—such as the subject-matter of the sale, the price, or some collateral fact materially inducing the agreement; and this can be done when the mistake is mutual. . . .

If there is a difference or misapprehension as to the substance of the thing bargained for, if the thing actually delivered or received is different in substance from the thing bargained for and intended to be sold, then there is no contract; but if it be only a difference in some quality or accident, even though the mistake may have been the actuating motive to the purchaser or seller, or both of them, yet the contract remains binding. . . .

It seems to me, however, that [here] the mistake or misapprehension of the parties went to the whole substance of the agreement ["the root of the matter"]. If the cow was a breeder, she was worth at least $750; if barren, she was worth not over $80. The parties would not have made the contract of sale except upon the understanding and belief that she was incapable of breeding, and of no use as a cow. It is true she is now the identical animal that they thought her to be when the contract was made; there is no mistake as to the identity of the creature. Yet the mistake was not of the mere quality of the animal, but went to the very nature of the thing. A barren cow is substantially a different creature than a breeding one. There is as much difference between them for all purposes of use as there is between an ox and a cow that is capable of breeding and giving milk. If the mutual mistake had simply related to the fact whether she was with calf or not for one season, then it might have been a good sale; but the mistake affected the character of the animal for all time, and for her present and ultimate use. She was not in fact the animal, or the kind of animal, the defendants intended to sell or the plaintiff to buy. She was not a barren cow, and, if this fact had been known, there would have been no contract. The mistake affected the substance of the whole consideration, and it must be considered that there was no contract to sell or sale of the cow as she actually was. . . .

The court should have instructed the jury that if they found that the cow was sold, or contracted to be sold, upon the understanding of both parties that she was barren, and useless for the purpose of breeding, and that in fact she was not barren, but capable of breeding, then the defendants had a right to rescind . . . and the verdict should be in their favor.

The judgment of the court below must be reversed, and a new trial granted. . . .

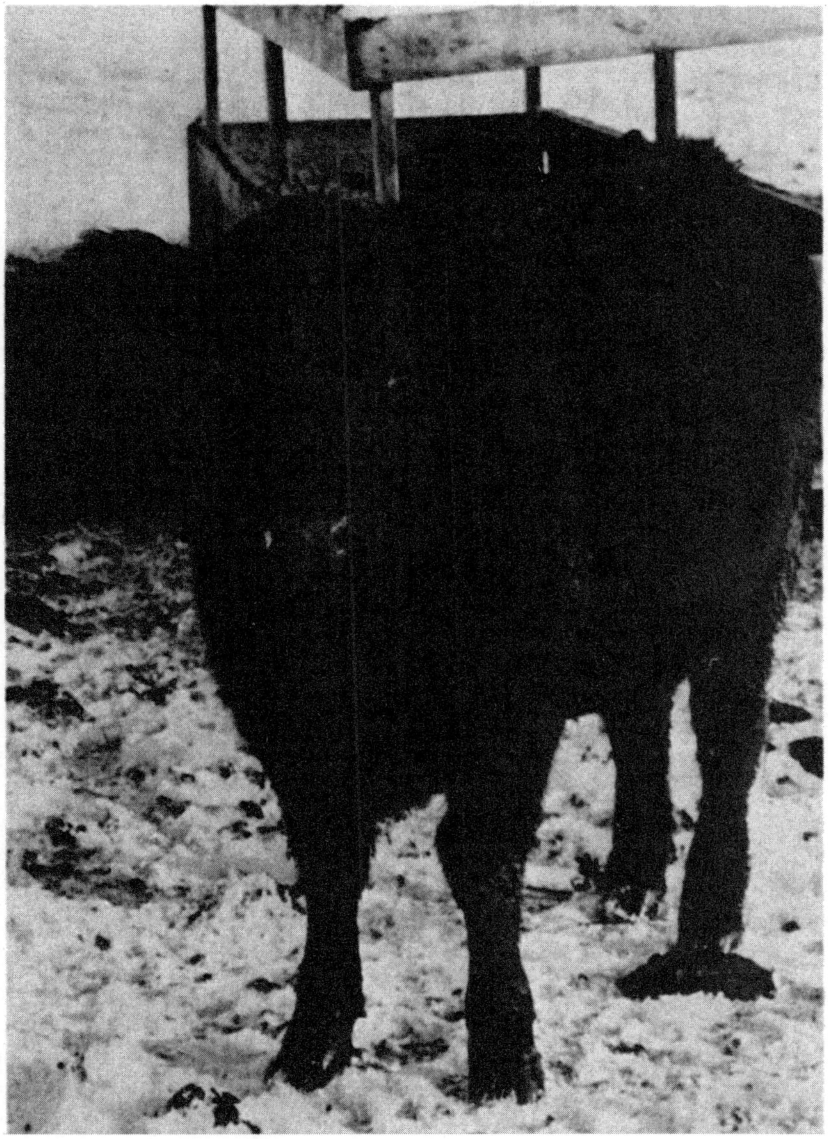

BLACK ANGUS IN PENSIVE MOOD

SHERWOOD, J. (dissenting). . . . [T]he record shows that the plaintiff is a banker and farmer as well, carrying on a farm, and raising the best breeds of stock, and lived in Plymouth, in the county of Wayne, 23 miles from Detroit; that the defendants lived in Detroit, and were also dealers in stock of the higher grades; that they had a farm at Walkerville, in Canada, and also one in Greenfield in said county of Wayne, and upon these farms the defendants kept their stock. The Greenfield farm was about 15 miles from the plaintiff's. In the spring of 1886 the plaintiff, learning that the defendants had some "polled Angus cattle" for sale, was desirous of purchasing some of that breed, and meeting the defendants, or some of them, at Walkerville, inquired about them, and was informed that they had none at Walkerville, "but had a few head left on their farm in Greenfield, and asked the plaintiff to go and see them, stating that in all probability they were sterile and would not breed." In accordance with said request, the plaintiff, on the fifth day of May, went out and looked at the defendants' cattle at Greenfield, and found one called "Rose, Second," which he wished to purchase, and the terms were finally agreed upon at five and a half cents per pound. . . . The sale was in writing, and the defendants gave an order to the plaintiff directing the man in charge of the Greenfield farm to deliver the cow to plaintiff. This was done on the fifteenth of May. On the twenty-first of May plaintiff went to get his cow, and the defendants refused to let him have her; claiming at the time that the man in charge at the farm thought the cow was with calf, and, if such was the case, they would not sell her for the price agreed upon. The record further shows that the defendants, when they sold the cow, believed the cow was not with calf, and barren; that from what the plaintiff had been told by defendants (for it does not appear he had any other knowledge or facts from which he could form an opinion) he believed the cow was farrow, but still thought she could be made to breed. The foregoing shows the entire interview and treaty between the parties as to the sterility and qualities of the cow sold to the plaintiff. The cow had a calf in the month of October. There is no question but that the defendants sold the cow representing her of the breed and quality they believed the cow to be, and that the purchaser so understood it. And the buyer purchased her believing her to be of the breed represented by the sellers, and possessing all the qualities stated, and even more. He believed she would breed. There is no pretense that the plaintiff bought the cow for beef, and there is nothing in the record indicating that he would have bought her at all only that he thought she might be made to breed. Under the foregoing facts,—and these are all that are contained in the record material to the contract,—it is held that because it turned out that the plaintiff was more correct in his judgment as to one quality of the cow than the defendants, and a quality, too, which could not by any possibility be positively known at the time by either party to exist, the contract may be annulled by the defendants at their pleasure. I know of no law, and have not been referred to any, which will justify any such holding. . . .

In this case neither party knew the actual quality and condition of this cow at the time of the sale. The defendants say, or rather said to the plaintiff, "they had a few head left on their farm in Greenfield, and asked plaintiff to go and see them, stating to plaintiff that in all probability they were sterile and would not breed." Plaintiff did go as requested, and found there three cows, including the one purchased, with a bull. The cow had been exposed, but neither knew she was with calf or whether she would breed. The defendants thought she would not, but the plaintiff says that he thought she could be made to breed, but believed she was not with calf. The defendants sold the cow for what they believed her to be, and the plaintiff bought her as he believed she was. . . . I know of no authority by which this Court can alter the contract thus made by these parties in writing. . . .

. . . There was no mistake of any such material fact by either of the parties. . . . There was no difference between the parties, nor misapprehension, as to the substance of the thing bargained for, which was a cow supposed to be barren by one party, and believed not to be by the other. As to the quality of the animal, subsequently developed, both parties were equally ignorant, and as to this each party took his chances. If this were not the law, there would be no safety in purchasing this kind of stock. . . . [I]f either party had superior knowledge as to the qualities of this animal to the other, certainly the defendants had such advantage.

I understand the law to be well settled that "there is no breach of any implied confidence that one party will not profit by his superior knowledge as to facts and circumstances" equally within the knowledge of both, because neither party reposes in any such confidence unless it be specially tendered or required, and that a general sale does not imply warranty of any quality, or the absence of any; and if the seller represents to the purchaser what he himself believes as to the qualities of an animal, and the purchaser buys relying upon his own judgment as to such qualities, there is no warranty in the case, and neither has a cause of action against the other if he finds himself to have been mistaken in judgment. . . . The judgment should be affirmed.

Jerome M. Eisenberg, Inc. v. Hall

Supreme Court, Appellate Division, 2017.
48 N.Y.S. 3d 71.

ACOSTA, PRESIDING JUSTICE, MAZZARELLI, ANDRIAS, FEINMAN, WEBBER, JJ. . . . Jerome M. Eisenberg buys and sells antiquities. He is a principal of plaintiff Jerome M. Eisenberg, Inc. (Eisenberg, Inc.), and a Qualified Appraiser of the Appraisers Association of America. He is a self-proclaimed expert in classical antiquities with a doctorate in Roman, Egyptian, and Near Eastern Art.

Defendants Maurice E. Hall, Jr. (Hall), Michael Hall Collections, Inc., and Michael Hall Fine Arts, Inc. are art dealers that mainly deal in sixteenth to nineteenth century European art. Hall was a principal and sole shareholder of both Hall entities. Hall asserts that his expertise is in Renaissance art and that he is merely an "amateur collector" of classical antiquities. Eisenberg also stated that he did not believe Hall to be an expert in classical antiquities.

This appeal deals with plaintiff securing from defendants a bust and a statue that they believed to be ancient but were later revealed to be modern forgeries.

In February 2009, Eisenberg visited Hall's townhouse, out of which Hall operated his business, and secured a marble head or bust of Faustina II, purported to be ancient Roman . . . . Some months later plaintiff sold the Faustina Bust to the Mougins Museum of Classical Art in France. In or about September 2011, the Mougins Museum informed plaintiff that the Faustina Bust was a fake in that it was modern and not ancient. The museum sent plaintiff a report by Professor R.R.R. Smith of Oxford University and Susan Walker, a curator at the British Museum, who opined that the bust was likely modern.

In April 2011, plaintiff obtained from defendants [a bronze warrior statue purported to be Etruscan or Roman era (the Etruscan Warrior)]. Plaintiff subsequently sent photographs of the statue to Dr. Michael Padgett at Princeton University, who opined that the piece had some stylistic inconsistencies. Plaintiff then submitted the statue to Oliver Bobin of the Centre d'Innovation et de Recherche pour l'Analyse et le Marquage for metallographic analysis. Bobin determined that the Etruscan Warrior was actually from the nineteenth or twentieth century and therefore was not ancient.

Plaintiff alleges that due to the "mutual mistake" of the parties regarding whether the items were ancient, it is entitled to summary judgment.

We agree with the motion court's decision that plaintiff is not entitled to summary judgment on its breach of contract claim pursuant to the doctrine of mutual mistake. Although the record reflects that both plaintiff and defendants mistakenly assumed at the time of the transactions that the items at issue were ancient, issues of fact exist as to whether plaintiff bore the risk of that mistake due to its "[c]onscious ignorance" of the items' authenticity. P.K. Dev. v. Elvem Dev. Corp., 226 A.D.2d 200, 201, 640 N.Y.S.2d 558 (1st Dept. 1996).

"Generally, a contract entered into under a mutual mistake of fact is voidable and subject to rescission" because it "does not represent the 'meeting of the minds' of the parties" Matter of Gould v. Board of Educ. of Sewanhaka Cent. High School Dist., 81 N.Y.2d 446, 453, 599 N.Y.S.2d 787, 616 N.E.2d 142 (1993). In order to justify rescission, "[t]he mutual mistake must exist at the time the contract is entered into and must be substantial." Id.

The doctrine of mutual mistake "may not be invoked by a party to avoid the consequences of its own negligence." P.K. Dev. v. Elvem Dev. Corp., 226 A.D.2d at 201, 640 N.Y.S.2d 558. Where a party "in the exercise of ordinary care, should have known or could easily have ascertained" the relevant fact—here, whether the items were ancient—that party is deemed to have been "[c]onscious[ly] ignoran[t]" and barred from seeking rescission or other damages. This is true "[e]ven where a party must go beyond its own efforts in order to ascertain relevant facts (such as obtaining experts' reports)," [226 A.D.2d at 201–02, 640 N.Y.S.2d 558.]

The conscious ignorance exception applies only where a party is aware that his knowledge is limited but decides to contract anyway "in the hope that the facts accord with his wishes," thus assuming "[t]he risk of the existence of the doubtful fact . . . as one of the elements of the bargain," [Backus v. MacLaury, 278 App. Div. 504, 507, 106 N.Y.S.2d 401 (4th Dept. 1951).]

We agree with the dissent that both plaintiff and defendants shared the mistaken belief that the Faustina Bust and the Etruscan Warrior were "ancient." Where we diverge is that we find that the record at this time does not support a finding that Eisenberg did not consciously ignore his uncertainty as to a crucial fact.

Questions exist as to whether Eisenberg genuinely believed the bust and statue to be ancient, or was aware that they might not be ancient but decided to assume this risk. Plaintiff presented evidence that Eisenberg is an expert on classical antiquities and a qualified appraiser who generally relies on his own expertise in evaluating works unless he is unsure of a piece's authenticity. He could thus have reasonably accepted that the items were ancient "based on [a] rational assessment of the source and style of work," [Richard L. Feigen & Co. v. Weil, 1992 N.Y. Misc. LEXIS 711, *15 (Sup. Ct., N.Y. County 1992).] Moreover, as to the Etruscan Warrior, Hall admittedly informed Eisenberg that he believed it to be from the private collection of renowned art collector J. Pierpont Morgan as signified by a painted red number. Eisenberg could have rationally relied on Morgan's reputation in addition to his own observations.

However, plaintiff also admits in its complaint that several other items purchased from defendants later turned out to be inauthentic. This suggests that plaintiff should have been on notice that the items might not be ancient—at least by the time of the later Etruscan Warrior purchase.

The circumstances surrounding the transactions, including the visits to Hall's townhouse and bedroom, with little or no discussion of the provenance of the pieces, as well as plaintiff's admission that several other items purchased from defendants turned out to be inauthentic, cast plaintiff's professed certainty as to the authenticity of the items into doubt and could support a finding that plaintiff was on notice that the items might not be ancient.

All concur except Andrias, J. who dissents in a memorandum as follows:

ANDRIAS, J. (dissenting). It is undisputed that both plaintiff and defendants shared the mistaken belief that the sculptures at issue were "ancient," and that the purchase prices were based on that assumption. Nevertheless, the majority affirms the denial of plaintiff's motion for summary judgment on its cause of action for breach of contract on the ground that "issues of fact exist as to whether plaintiff bore the risk of that mistake due to its '[c]onscious ignorance' of the items' authenticity."

Because I believe that the requisite "meeting of the minds" is absent and that there is no evidence that plaintiff consciously ignored its "uncertain[ty] as to a crucial fact," Richard L. Feigen & Co. v. Weil, 1992 N.Y. Misc. LEXIS 711, *12 (Sup.Ct., N.Y. County 1992), I respectfully dissent.

Defendants, art dealers specializing in sixteenth to nineteenth century European art, sold a marble bust of Faustina II (the Faustina Bust), thought to be ancient Roman, and a bronze warrior statue (the Etruscan Warrior), thought to be ancient Etruscan or Roman, to plaintiff, a buyer and seller of antiquities. Plaintiff's principal, Jerome M. Eisenberg, and defendant Maurice E. Hall, who negotiated the sales, both believed that the statues were authentic. However, Eisenberg, a Qualified Appraiser of the Appraisers Association of America and a self-proclaimed expert in classical antiquities with a doctorate in Roman, Egyptian, and Near Eastern Art, relied on his own expertise in purchasing the works, which were later revealed to be modern forgeries. . . .

The record establishes that defendants presented the Faustina Bust and Etruscan Warrior to plaintiff as ancient items. As the majority concedes, Eisenberg could have reasonably accepted that the items were ancient based on his own expertise and a "rational assessment of the source and style of work." *Feigen,* 1992 N.Y. Misc. LEXIS 711, *15. Moreover, as to the Etruscan Warrior, Hall admittedly informed Eisenberg that he believed it to be from the private collection of renowned art collector J. Pierpont Morgan. As the majority acknowledges, "Eisenberg could have rationally relied on Morgan's reputation in addition to his own observations." While Hall and Eisenberg disagreed whether that statue was Etruscan or Roman, the dispositive fact is that they both believed it to be ancient, and that there was a rational basis for that belief.

There is no evidence demonstrating that Eisenberg did not genuinely believe that the items were ancient or that he was "uncertain as to a crucial fact" regarding their authenticity following his inspections. *Feigen,* 1992 N.Y. Misc. Lexis 711, *12. That plaintiff purchased several items in the past that were later determined to be fakes does not establish conscious disregard of any facts pointing to the inauthenticity of the sculptures at issue. Plaintiff's money was refunded in each of those cases and the particular circumstances of those transactions and the discovery of the fakes is unclear. Moreover, given that those transactions were rescinded and did not result in a financial loss, they should not form the basis of imposing a heightened duty of inquiry on plaintiff.

Whether Hall affirmatively offered the items for sale or made any affirmative representations is of no consequence. Plaintiff does not premise its breach of contract claim on the breach of a contractual warranty. Rather, the claim is based on the premise that there was no meeting of the minds because the parties were mutually mistaken about a material fact. The basis of the bargain and the statues' value lay in the items being ancient, which proved to be untrue.

Even if Eisenberg is the more credentialed expert in classical antiquities among the two, Hall is an established dealer in fine arts who sold those items. In any event, "there is no authority for the proposition . . . that in a contract between an expert and non-expert, rescission based on mutual mistake is unavailable to the expert." *Feigen,* 1992 Misc. LEXIS 711, *13. In *Feigen,* the seller of a drawing that both parties assumed to be a Matisse, but which turned out to be a forgery, argued that the buyer, an art dealer, acted with conscious ignorance because it failed to authenticate the drawing before purchasing it. Justice Moskowitz, then sitting as a trial judge, held that the conscious ignorance exception to the mutual mistake doctrine did not apply because "both parties, far from assuming any risk, mistakenly assumed the facts underlying the transaction." In so ruling, Justice Moskowitz rejected the defendant's argument that the plaintiff had a duty to authenticate the drawing because it had more expertise, stating that the plaintiff "was not asked to nor did it have any substantive or legal obligation to go beyond a 'cursory inquiry' as to its authenticity." Id. at *15. . . .

Following *Feigen,* in Uptown Gallery, Inc. v. Doniger, 1993 N.Y. Misc. LEXIS 661, *3–4 (Sup.Ct., N.Y. County 1993), the court rejected the defendant's conscious ignorance claim, stating that "[t]his is not a case where the parties were uncertain as to a crucial fact, consciously ignored it and despite this uncertainty contracted. To the contrary, both parties entered into the contract based on the assumption that the painting being purchased was an authentic Bernard Buffet." The court rejected the defendant's argument that it would be more reasonable under the circumstances to place the risk of loss on the buyer, stating "[t]here is no reason why defendant should be entitled to a windfall based on its sale of a painting which was not what either party believed it to be. The painting was clearly not worth the contract price and there is no basis for allowing defendant to receive much more for the painting than what it is worth." This rationale is equally applicable to the facts in this case. . . .

Accordingly, I would grant plaintiff summary judgment rescinding the sales.

QUESTIONS

The American Law Institute, through various Restatements, has offered the following illustrations (among others) of the rules and principles applicable to mistake:

> (1) A contracts to sell and B to buy a tract of land, the value of which has depended mainly on the timber on it. Both A and B believe that the timber is still there, but in fact it has been destroyed by fire. The contract is voidable by B. [Restatement (Second) of Contracts § 152 comment b, illustration 1 (1981).]

(2) A contracts to sell and B to buy a tract of land. A and B both believe that A has good title, but neither has made a title search. The contract provides that A will convey only such title as he has, and A makes no representation with respect to title. In fact, A's title is defective. The contract is not voidable by B. . . . [(Second) of Contracts § 154 comment b, illustration 1 (1981).]

(3) Twelve-year-old Collector examines a baseball card offered for sale by Dealer. A price label on the item reads "1200." Collector asks the sales clerk to confirm the price of the card; the clerk, a temporary employee alone in the shop, surmises that it must be $12.00. Collector pays $12.00 and takes the card. Collector is aware that the market price of this card is approximately $1200 and that Dealer is presumably offering it for sale at this price. The transaction between the parties did not result in a valid sale. Dealer is entitled to recover the card on tender of $12.00. [Restatement (Third) of Restitution Tentative Draft No. 3 § 34 comment e, illustration 23 (2004).]

(4) A enters a second-hand bookstore where, among books offered for sale at one dollar each, he discovers a rare book having, as A knows, a market value of not less than $50. He hands this [book] to the proprietor with one dollar. The proprietor, reading the name of the book and the price tag, keeps the dollar and hands the book to A. The book dealer is not entitled to restitution. . . . [Restatement of Restitution § 12 comment c, illustration 9 (1937).]

Which of these illustrations is most nearly like Sherwood v. Walker as seen by the majority? As seen by the dissenter?

NOTE: STILL MORE ON *SHERWOOD V. WALKER*

1. The Replevin Remedy

Had there been no issue of mistake in the cow case, would Sherwood have been granted the remedy he sought—replevin? Apparently so, as there was evidence to sustain a finding by the jury that the parties had intended "title" to Rose to pass to Sherwood before delivery was to occur. Today, the buyer's remedy of replevin no longer depends upon this common-law idea of passage of "title" or "property." Section 2–716(3) of the UCC provides in part: "The buyer has a right of replevin for goods identified to the contract if after reasonable effort he is unable to effect cover for such goods or the circumstances reasonably indicate that such effort will be unavailing[.]" With mutual mistake removed from the case, how would Sherwood have fared under this statute?

2. Reformulating *Sherwood*

In Lenawee County Bd. of Health v. Messerly, 417 Mich. 17, 331 N.W.2d 203 (1982), decided nearly a full century after Sherwood v. Walker, the Supreme Court of Michigan condemned the distinction between mistakes "running to value" and those "touching the substance of the consideration," declaring that the distinction was "inexact and confusing" and served "only as an impediment to a clear and helpful analysis" of the mistake cases. The case involved a seller and a purchaser who had believed that the small, three-unit apartment building that was the subject of the sale could be used to generate rental income. Problems with the building's septic system were discovered a week after the transaction was closed. These sewage problems led local health authorities to condemn the property and enjoin habitation of the premises. The ensuing litigation established that the septic system could not be remedied within the confines of the 600-square-foot parcel. Nor was it feasible to pump and haul the sewage. The property, for which the purchaser had paid $25,500, was therefore valueless (worse yet, it had a negative value).

Was this a mistake merely as to quality or value, and thus not "material" but only "collateral" to the agreement? The court, indicating that *Sherwood* should be "limited to [its] facts," stated its new approach this way:

> [W]e think the better-reasoned approach is a case-by-case analysis whereby rescission is indicated when the mistaken belief relates to a basic assumption of the parties upon which the contract is made, and which materially affects the agreed performance of the parties. . . . Restatement, Contracts, 2d § 152. Rescission is not available, however, to relieve a party who has assumed the risk of loss in connection with the mistake.

Is this test much different from the analysis employed in Sherwood v. Walker? The *Lenawee County* court apparently thought it was announcing a different test, for it indicated that the result in *Sherwood* "might have been different" had the court engaged in the sort of risk-of-loss analysis that the Michigan court was now embracing. Look again at the opinions in Sherwood v. Walker. Was there no inquiry into which of the parties should assume the risk of loss? How does one answer the question of "essences" or "roots" without making some judgment about the customary allocation of risks between sellers and buyers? Again, a court must "gap-fill" by drawing an inference as to risk allocation. That ordinarily is done by asking what the parties were contemplating (in one court's words, whether "the post-contract discovery comes out of left field") and whether one was more at fault than the other.

It is necessary to add that the ultimate result in *Lenawee County* was placed on a ground not available in *Sherwood*. Despite the court's conclusions that the parties' beliefs as to the suitability of the premises constituted a "[mutual] mistake as to a basic assumption," and that the agreed exchange had been "materially affect[ed]," rescission was nevertheless denied because the contract itself allocated to the purchaser the risk of habitability, in the form of a clause which read:

> Purchaser has examined this property and agrees to accept same in its present condition. There are no other or additional written or oral understandings.

This clause, the court said, is a "persuasive indication" that the parties wished to assign to the purchaser all risks as to the condition of the property.

Unless the "as is" clause applied to unknown defects, it would have no meaning. But such a clause would not preclude a purchaser from alleging fraud or misrepresentation as a basis for rescission.

Kull, Mistake, Frustration, and the Windfall Principle of Contract Remedies

43 Hastings L.J. 1, 2, 5–6 (1991)

"A substantial body of case law supports an important but unacknowledged rule of contract doctrine: that the proper legal response to certain problems resulting from contracts that are 'incomplete' or 'not fully specified' is to leave the parties alone. Such a rule stands in sharp contrast to the usual prescription of modern commentary, which recommends that 'gaps' in contracts be 'filled' by judicial intervention to serve a variety of social ends. . . . [T]he characteristic and traditional response of our legal system to cases of mistaken and frustrated contracts is neither to relieve the disadvantaged party nor to assign the loss to the superior risk bearer, but to leave things alone. The party who has balked at performing will not be forced to proceed, but the completed exchange will not be recalled. Walker will not be forced to deliver to Sherwood a breeding cow sold for the price of beef; but neither will [the seller] be allowed to recover the yellow diamond, already delivered, unwittingly sold to the buyer for the price of a topaz. . . .

"The principle of inertia that frequently seems to guide the remedies for mistake and frustration . . . is neither arbitrary nor illogical. Disparities between anticipation and realization in contractual exchange, the risk of which has not been allocated by the parties, are in the nature of 'windfalls' (including those, carrying adverse consequences, that might more properly be described as 'casualties'). The law will not act to enforce such windfalls—to compel an exchange on terms that were not bargained for—because its objective is limited to giving effect to the parties' agreement. But if the parties have not allocated the risk of a particular windfall or casualty to one of them, neither have they allocated it to the other. There is thus no basis in their bargain on which to justify a court's intervention to shift windfall benefits and burdens in either direction. . . . [E]xcluding for the moment considerations of fairness, it will ordinarily be a matter of indifference [to society] whether the windfall cost or benefit, once realized, falls to A or B. Reallocation after the event thus invokes significant administrative costs while achieving no social advantage. The judicial disposition to let windfalls lie—to answer the claim of mistake or frustration by confirming the status-quo—[therefore raises the question] whether the traditional rule [the 'windfall principle'] may not serve ['gap-filling'] ends with equal or greater efficiency."

Lakshmi Grocery & Gas, Inc. v GRJH, Inc.

Supreme Court, Appellate Division, Third Department, 2016.
138 A.D.3d 1290, 30 N.Y.S.3d 743.

GARRY, JUSTICE. . . . Plaintiff is a corporation owned by third-party defendants, Ravinder Sharma and Yosho Lakshmi. In the summer of 2010, Sharma contacted James Metz, an officer of defendant with whom Sharma had previously had successful business dealings, to inquire about commercial opportunities in New York. Metz responded that a gas station and convenience store owned by defendant was available for lease. After discussions with Metz and defendant's president, Alicia Metz, plaintiff agreed to take over the store and made certain payments to defendant. Third-party defendants signed a combined lease and contractor agreement but, almost immediately after taking control of the store, discovered records indicating that the store's sales were lower than plaintiff had been led to believe. After attempting unsuccessfully to modify the contract terms, third-party defendants vacated the store and requested a refund of their initial payments, which defendant refused to pay.

Plaintiff brought the instant action for rescission of the contract based upon fraudulent inducement. Defendant joined issue and commenced a third-party breach of contract action against third-party defendants. During the subsequent bench trial, plaintiff moved to conform the pleadings to the proof and pursue rescission based upon an additional theory of mutual mistake. Supreme Court granted the motion, found that a mutual mistake had occurred, awarded damages to plaintiff, rescinded the contract and dismissed the third-party action. Defendant appeals. . . .

Plaintiff's complaint alleged that defendant acted intentionally in misrepresenting the store's sales as being greater than they actually were. At trial, Sharma testified that before he signed the contractor agreement, he repeatedly asked for the store's inside sales figures—that is, sales of such items as groceries, coffee and cigarettes, which he testified are a critical factor in a convenience store's profitability. Early in September 2010, Alicia Metz responded with an email stating that the store's sales for August 2010 totaled approximately $22,000. Several days after taking over the store, however, Sharma discovered sales records revealing that the true figure for August 2010 was approximately $15,500, an amount that he testified was too low to permit the successful operation of the store. He stated that he would not have signed the contract if he had known the correct sales figures. Alicia Metz testified that the figures she provided to Sharma actually represented the store's inside sales for August 2009 and were provided as "representative sales" because the complete figures for August 2010 were not yet available. She stated that she "mismarked" the figures as representing August 2010 sales, acting in error and good faith. . . .

[The trial court] did not err in rescinding the contract on the basis of mutual mistake. A contract may be rescinded when it is shown by clear and convincing proof that a mutual mistake existed when the contract was executed that was so substantial that there was no "true meeting of the parties' minds" Carney v Carozza, 16 AD3d 867, 868–869 (2005). Here, the testimony that defendant's president acted erroneously in sending incorrect sales figures to Sharma, as well as Sharma's testimony that the true figures were not discovered until after the contract was signed and were too low to permit successful operation of the business, constituted clear and convincing proof that a substantial mutual mistake occurred such that there was no meeting of the minds as to the basis for the store's profitability.

As for defendant's claim that plaintiff was negligent in failing to obtain more complete sales records before signing the contract, negligence may bar rescission when a party fails to take advantage of "easily accessible" means of ascertaining the truth. Da Silva v Musso, 53 NY2d 543, 551 (1981). Here, in addition to Sharma's testimony that he asked repeatedly for the August 2010 sales records before receiving what proved to be erroneous information, he also testified that he asked to inspect the store's books but was not permitted to do so. Sharma stated that he was told that he could visit the store while posing as a customer, but could not speak to employees or inspect sales records. Alicia Metz and James Metz both denied that Sharma had asked to inspect the store's records, but Alicia Metz admitted that defendant had a policy of prohibiting prospective contractors from speaking with employees to avoid warning them of the potential transfer. Sharma testified that he trusted James Metz based upon their longstanding business relationship and relied upon his assurances that the store was profitable. [The] Supreme Court credited Sharma's testimony that a level of trust existed between them and found that plaintiff's exercise of due diligence, although minimal, was reasonable. . . . Given plaintiff's lack of ready access to the store records and the longstanding trusting relationship between Sharma and James Metz, we find no negligence sufficient to bar rescission. Accordingly, Supreme Court properly dismissed defendant's third-party action.

PETERS, P.J., ROSE and DEVINE, JJ., concur. Ordered that the judgment is affirmed, without costs.

Gartner v. Eikill

319 N.W.2d 397 (Minn. 1982)

"[A]ll parties assumed the property conveyed to be property that could be developed. The mistake, as in *Sherwood*, was not of *monetary* value of the land, but 'went to the very nature' of the property. In *Sherwood*, neither party had any way of discovering whether the cow was in fact barren. [These sellers] argue that [the purchaser] could have gone to City Hall and inquired about the zoning and that because he did not do so, he is not entitled to rescind the transaction. The failure of a party to investigate, however, will not always preclude rescission. . . . Here, [the purchaser] does not appear to have been negligent at all. He inquired [of sellers' realtor] regarding the zoning of the property and was assured that it was zoned M-1 and was suitable for commercial use. . . . [A]lthough he had purchased real estate on several previous occasions, he had never before found it necessary to go to City Hall to determine whether additional zoning restrictions existed. He had no reason to suspect that any such restriction prohibited the development of [this] property. His reliance on [sellers'] agent's statements was reasonable; we do not believe that he had any duty to inquire further. . . . [The sellers] thought that they were selling property suitable for commercial use; [the purchaser] thought he was buying property suitable for commercial use. . . . [A] mutual mistake of fact occurred that entitled [the purchaser] to a rescission of the conveyance."

Elsinore Union Elementary School Dist. v. Kastorff

Supreme Court of California, 1960.
54 Cal. 2d 380, 6 Cal. Rptr. 1, 353 P.2d 713.

SCHAUER, J. Defendants, a building contractor and his surety, appeal from an adverse judgment in this action by plaintiff school district to recover damages allegedly resulting when defendant Kastorff, the contractor, refused to execute a building contract pursuant to his previously submitted bid to make certain additions to plaintiff's school buildings. . . . [B]ecause of an honest clerical error in the bid and defendant's subsequent prompt rescission he was not obliged to execute the contract[;] the judgment should therefore be reversed.

Pursuant to plaintiff's call for bids, defendant Kastorff secured a copy of the [construction] plans and specifications and proceeded to prepare a bid to be submitted by the deadline of 8 p.m., August 12, 1952, at Elsinore, California. Kastorff testified that in preparing his bid he employed worksheets upon which he entered bids of various subcontractors for such portions of the work as they were to do, and that to reach the final total of his own bid for the work he carried into the right-hand column of the worksheets the amounts of the respective sub bids which he intended to accept and then added those amounts to the cost of the work which he would do himself[;] that there is "a custom among subs [to] delay giving . . . their bids until the very last moment"; that the first sub bid for plumbing was in the amount of $9,285 and he had received it "the afternoon of the bid-opening," but later that afternoon when "the time was drawing close for me to get my bids together and get over to Elsinore" (from his home in San Juan Capistrano) he received a $6,500 bid for the plumbing. Erroneously thinking he had entered the $9,285 plumbing bid in his total column and had included that sum in his total bid and realizing that the second plumbing bid was nearly $3,000 less than the first, Kastorff then deducted $3,000 from the total amount of his bid and entered the resulting total of $89,994 on the bid form as his bid for the school construction. Thus the total included no allowance whatsoever for the plumbing work.

Kastorff then proceeded to Elsinore and deposited his bid with plaintiff. When the bids were opened shortly after 8 p.m. that evening, it was discovered that of the five bids submitted that of Kastorff was some $11,306 less than the next lowest bid. The school superintendent and board members present thereupon asked Kastorff whether he was sure his figures were correct, Kastorff stepped out into the hall to check with the person who had assisted in doing the clerical work on the bid, and a few minutes later returned and stated that the figures were correct. He testified that he did not have his worksheets or other papers with him to check against at the time. The board thereupon, on August 12, voted to award Kastorff the contract. . . .

[The next morning, August 13, Kastorff checked his worksheets with the School District's architect, who supported Kastorff's claim that he had failed to carry over the plumbing figure of $9,285 so that it was not included in the "total" column in arriving at the bid of $89,994. On August 13, the architect informed the school superintendent of the mistake by telephone; on August 14, Kastorff wrote the school board to describe his error, asking in both instances to be released from his bid. On August 15, the board voted at a special meeting not to release him; on August 28, it notified him in writing that he had been awarded the contract. When a written contract was sent to Kastorff, he returned it and again asked to be released. Plaintiff then let the contract to the next lowest bidder, in the amount of $102,900. Plaintiff sued to recover from Kastorff the $12,906 difference between this figure and Kastorff's $89,994 bid, and to recover $4,999.60 from the surety on the bond posted by Kastorff.

The trial court found that Kastorff's worksheet showed he had not carried over from the left-hand column the figure for the plumbing subcontractor's bid, but found no evidence that the right-hand column had been used in calculating the total bid. The trial court also found that the School District did not know of Kastorff's withdrawal of his bid when it requested him to sign the contract; hence, the court concluded that it would not be inequitable or unjust to require Kastorff to perform at a price of $89,994, since this was the price that he intended to bid. The trial court gave judgment for plaintiff in the amounts sued for.]

In reliance upon M.F. Kemper Constr. Co. v. City of Los Angeles (1951), 37 Cal.2d 696, 235 P.2d 7, and Lemoge Elec. v. County of San Mateo (1956), 46 Cal.2d 659, 297 P.2d 638, defendants urged that where, as [here], a contractor makes a clerical error in computing a bid on a public work he is entitled to rescind.

In the *Kemper* case one item on a worksheet in the amount of $301,769 was inadvertently omitted by the contractor from the final tabulation sheet and was overlooked in computing the total amount of a bid. . . . The error was caused by the fact that the men preparing the bid were exhausted after working long hours under pressure. When the bids were opened it was found that plaintiff's bid was $780,305, and the next lowest bid was $1,049,592. Plaintiff discovered its error several hours later and immediately notified defendant's board of public works of its mistake in omitting one item [from] its bid. Two days later it explained its mistake to the board and withdrew its bid. A few days later it submitted to the board evidence which showed the unintentional omission of the $301,769 item. The board nevertheless passed a resolution accepting plaintiff's erroneous bid of $780,305, and plaintiff refused to enter into a written contract at that figure. The board then awarded the contract to the next lowest bidder, the city demanded forfeiture of plaintiff's bid bond, and plaintiff [sued] to cancel its bid and obtain discharge of the bond. The trial court found that the bid had been submitted as the result of an excusable and honest mistake of a material and fundamental character, that plaintiff company had not been negligent in preparing the proposal, that it had acted promptly to notify the board of the mistake and to rescind the bid, and that the board had accepted the bid with knowledge of the error. The court further found and concluded that it would be unconscionable to require the company to perform for the amount of the bid, that no intervening rights had accrued, and that the city had suffered no damage or prejudice. . . . [T]his court affirmed. . . .

[The Supreme Court in *Kemper* had pointed out that, by statute, a bid filed with the governmental agency on a publicly-financed project, when opened and declared, acquired "the status of an irrevocable option, a contract right of which the city could not be deprived without its consent unless the requirements for rescission were satisfied." Nevertheless, as the court emphasized, the city had actual notice of the error before it attempted to accept the bid. The omission of $301,769, when the next lowest bid was $1,049,592, was clearly a material mistake. Any carelessness of the bidder did not rise to the level of "neglect of legal duty," and the city would lose nothing except "the benefit of an inequitable bargain."]

In the *Lemoge* case, supra, the facts were similar to *Kemper*, except that plaintiff Lemoge did not attempt to rescind but instead, after discovering and informing defendant of inadvertent clerical error in the bid, entered into a formal contract with defendant on the terms specified in the erroneous bid, performed the required work, and then sued for reformation. . . . Although this court affirmed the trial court's determination that plaintiff was not, under the circumstances, entitled to have the contract reformed, we also reaffirmed [a contractor's] right to rescind [in such situations].

[In *Lemoge*, the plaintiff had submitted a bid of $172,421; the next lowest bid was $197,500. A clerk on plaintiff's staff had listed the cost of certain materials as $104.52 when the correct figure was $10,452; with sales tax and other markups, the total bid was understated by $11,744.39. The complaint seeking reformation was dismissed on demurrer, without leave to amend, even though the complaint had alleged that defendant knew the amount of the mistake and its cause before it accepted plaintiff's bid. The court said that the defendant never agreed to pay more than $172,421, the amount of plaintiff's bid, and that the purpose of reformation is to make the writing express the agreed intent of the parties.]

The rules stated [in] *Kemper* and *Lemoge* would appear to entitle defendant to relief here, were it not for the findings of the trial court adverse to defendant. However, certain of such findings are clearly not supported by the evidence and others are immaterial to the point at issue. The finding that it is not true that the right-hand column of figures on the bid sheet was totaled for the purpose of arriving at the total bid, and that it cannot be ascertained from the evidence for what purpose either the bid sheets or the right-hand column total thereon were used in arriving at the total bid, is without evidentiary support in the face of the worksheets which were introduced in evidence and of the uncontradicted testimony not alone of defendant Kastorff, but also of plaintiff's own architect and witness Rendon, explaining the purpose of the worksheets and the nature of the error which had been made. [These sheets] plainly show the entry of the sums of $9,285 and of $6,500 in the left-hand columns as the two plumbing sub bids which were received by defendant, and the omission from the right-hand totals column of any sum whatever for plumbing.

The same is true of the finding that although "on or about August 15" plaintiff received Kastorff's letter of August 14 explaining the error in his bid, it was not true that plaintiff knew at any time that the bid was intended to be other than as submitted. Again, it was shown by the testimony of plaintiff's architect, its school superintendent, and one of its board members, all produced as plaintiff's witnesses, that the board was informed of the error and despite such information voted at its meeting of August 15 not to grant defendant's request to withdraw his bid.

Further, we are persuaded that the trial court's view, as expressed in the finding set forth in the margin,[3] that "Kastorff had ample time and opportunity after receiving his last subcontractor's bid" to complete and check his final bid, does not convict Kastorff of that "neglect of legal duty" which would preclude his being relieved from the inadvertent clerical error of omitting from his bid the cost of the plumbing. (See Civ.Code, § 1577; *Kemper*, supra.) Neither should he be denied relief from an unfair, inequitable, and unintended bargain simply because, in response to inquiry from the board when his bid was discovered to be much the lowest submitted, he informed the board, after checking with his clerical assistant, that the bid was correct. He did not have his worksheets present to

[3] Other findings are that Kastorff "in the company of his wife and another couple left San Juan Capistrano for Elsinore . . . at 6:00 P.M. on August 12, 1952, a distance of 34 miles. . . . Kastorff had ample time and opportunity after receiving his last subcontractor's bid to extend the figures on his bid sheet from one column to the other, to check and recheck his bid sheet figures and to take his papers to Elsinore and to check them there prior to close of receipt of bids at 8:00 P.M."

inspect at that time, he did thereafter inspect them at what would appear to have been the earliest practicable moment, and thereupon promptly notified plaintiff and rescinded his bid. [Further,] Kastorff's bid agreement, as provided by plaintiff's own bid form, was to execute a formal written contract only after receiving written notification of acceptance of his bid, and such notice was not given to him until some two weeks following his rescission.

If the situations of the parties were reversed and plaintiff and Kastorff had even executed a formal written contract (by contrast with the preliminary bid offer and acceptance) calling for a fixed sum payment to Kastorff large enough to include a reasonable charge for plumbing but inadvertently through the *district's* clerical error omitting a mutually-intended provision requiring Kastorff to furnish and install plumbing, we have no doubt but that the district would demand and expect reformation or rescission. [Here,] the district expected Kastorff to furnish and install plumbing; surely it must also have understood that he intended to, and that his bid did, include a charge for such plumbing. The omission of any such charge was as unexpected by the board as it was unintended by Kastorff. Under the circumstances the "bargain" for which the board presses (which action we, of course, assume to be impelled by advice of counsel and a strict concept of official duty) appears too sharp for law and equity to sustain.

Plaintiff suggests that in any event the amount of the plumbing bid omitted from the total was immaterial. The bid as submitted was in the sum of $89,994, and whether the sum for the omitted plumbing was $6,500 or $9,285 (the two sub bids), the omission of such a sum is plainly material to the total. In *Lemoge*, . . . the error which it was declared would have entitled plaintiff to rescind was the listing of the cost of certain materials as $104.52, rather than $10,452, in a total bid of $172,421. Thus the percentage of error here was larger than in *Lemoge*, and was plainly material.

The judgment is reversed.

S.T.S. Transport Serv., Inc. v. Volvo White Truck Corp.

766 F.2d 1089 (7th Cir. 1985)

Judge Cudahy writing: "[T]he cases have also avoided contracts—though more reluctantly—where only one party is mistaken as to the facts. In the typical case of this sort, a seller or contractor will miscalculate in adding up a list of items. . . . It is true that [if] the mistake result[s] from a miscalculation as to the economic climate, to undo the contract would fly in the face of the very reason for having contracts in the first place. . . . But that problem is solved by excluding miscalculations of judgment. . . . The mistake in this case relates to the price, which must be conceded to be material. The mistake must also have occurred in spite of the exercise of reasonable care. Although reasonable care is as difficult to be precise about in this sort of case as it is elsewhere, there are some fairly clear groupings of mistake cases that can serve as guideposts. Most helpful is the knowledge that courts will generally grant relief for errors which are 'clerical or mathematical.'

"The reason for the special treatment for such errors, of course, is that they are difficult to prevent, and that no useful social purpose is served by enforcing the mistaken term. No incentives exist to make such mistakes; all the existing incentives work, in fact, in the opposite direction. There is every reason for a contractor to use ordinary care. . . . Naturally there are cases of extreme negligence to which this presumption [of rescission rather than enforcement] should not apply; and there is an exception of sorts where the contract has been relied upon[,] [for reliance, in this context,] is no different from the question whether the parties can be put into the position they were in at the time the contract was signed. . . . Although it would be wrong to suppose that 'merely' mathematical or clerical errors are easily distinguished from other errors such as those of judgment[,] the distinction is clear enough for ordinary purposes. A merely mathematical or clerical error occurs when some term is either one-tenth or ten times as large as it should be; when a term is added in the wrong column; when it is added rather than subtracted; when it is overlooked."

COMMENT: UNILATERAL MISTAKE

1. The Grounds for Rescission

When only one of the contracting parties was mistaken, we have a case of unilateral rather than mutual mistake. Unilateral mistake, we are told (recall Cobaugh v. Klick-Lewis, p. 392), is generally not a ground for rescinding a contract—or reforming one, says California's *Lemoge* decision. But exceptions have appeared, as *Elsinore* suggests. Not surprisingly, the "exceptional" case awarding relief usually has involved a party who knew of and, saying nothing, claimed the benefit of, another's mistake. This, of course, is but another way of recasting basic objective theory—that is to say, the recipient of an incorrectly worded or transmitted offer may not always make a contract by accepting it. For example, long ago the California court indicated that a seller's price quotation, erroneously transcribed and delivered by a telegraph company, could contractually bind the seller to the incorrect price—provided the buyer had no reason to suspect that a mistake had been made. Germain Fruit Co. v. Western Union Telegraph, 137 Cal. 598, 70 P. 658 (1902). To be sure, if a party reasonably and detrimentally relied on the mistaken expression of the party seeking rescission, cases such as Drennan v. Star Paving Co. tell why the exceptions are inapplicable.

In any event, a question raised by *Elsinore* is the content, and the scope, of the defense of unilateral mistake.

The California court returned to such matters in Donovan v. RRL Corp., 26 Cal.4th 261, 109 Cal.Rptr.2d 807, 27 P.3d 702 (2001), where, because of typographical and proofreading errors by a local newspaper, defendant auto dealer's advertisement of a 1995 Jaguar XJ6 erroneously listed the price at

$25,995, not the intended $37,995. Plaintiff read the advertisement, examined and test drove the vehicle, and said to defendant's salesperson: "Okay. We will take it at your price of $25,995." When there was no reply, plaintiff produced the ad; the salesperson immediately said, "That's a mistake." Defendant's sales manager was summoned and, confirming the mistake and refusing to sell at the advertised price, the manager apologized and offered to reimburse plaintiff for his fuel, time, and effort expended in traveling to the dealership. The manager, when pressed by plaintiff for a selling price, offered to let him take it for $37,016. Plaintiff, insisting on a deal at the advertised price, then brought a lawsuit for breach of contract.

The trial court, finding that plaintiff had no reason to suspect the mistake, nevertheless entered judgment for defendant, holding that the advertisement was not a valid offer because defendant's "unilateral mistake of fact" vitiated contractual intent. An intermediate court of appeal rejected that view, finding that any defects in contract formation were cured by a California statute making it unlawful for an auto dealer to refuse to sell a motor vehicle at the advertised price (i.e., the statute "tips the scale in favor of construing" the ad as an offer that, in the circumstances, reasonably invited plaintiff's acceptance by the act of tendering the advertised price.) On further appeal, the California Supreme Court agreed that a contract was made by plaintiff's tender of the advertised price. Nonetheless, defendant had a complete defense of rescission for unilateral mistake, on this reasoning:

> The court of appeal erred in crediting plaintiff's contention that unilateral mistake affords grounds for rescission only where the other party is—or should have been—aware of the mistake. *Kemper* and *Elsinore* establish that relief for mistake is not so limited, but is authorized where "enforcement of the contract would be unconscionable." This additional ground is now recognized generally in Rest.2d Contracts, § 153, which is based in part on *Elsinore*. Here, there was a material mistake regarding a basic assumption upon which defendant contracted. Even assuming defendant's failure to review the work of the newspaper's advertising staff constituted negligence, such an omission does not amount to "neglect of a legal duty" sufficient to preclude equitable relief for mistake. Moreover, enforcing the contract with the mistaken price would give defendant $12,000 less than the intended price, an error of 32 percent. That defendant subsequently sold the car for $38,399 is proof of its actual market value. And since defendant had paid $35,000 for the vehicle and incurred additional costs in preparing it for sale, a forced sale at the advertised price would result in defendant losing more than $9,000 of its original investment. Plaintiff, in contrast, would obtain a $12,000 "windfall," simply for coming to the dealership and stating a willingness to pay the advertised price. As in *Elsinore*, a party who is promptly informed of the other's discovery of an honest mistake that results in an "unfair, one-sided" contract should not be permitted to demand enforce-

ment. That decision, where there was no procedural unconscionability (indeed, the mistaken contractor was afforded an opportunity to verify accuracy of price before acceptance), settles the point that "overly harsh results" are alone enough to warrant rescission for unilateral mistake.

2. Information and Mistake

Cases like *Elsinore* suggest that there are circumstances in which a mistake can be inferred from the price stated in the offer. In fact, relief is routinely given in the mistaken-bid cases if the bidder-offeror's error reasonably should have been known by the offeree before acceptance. By one count, in 109 of 187 construction-bidding cases of all types decided between 1969 and 1977, the mistaken bidder was awarded some form of relief. Jones, The Law of Mistaken Bids, 48 Cinn. L. Rev. 43 (1979).

The refusal to permit the offeree with superior information to enjoy the advantage of the mistaken bid stands in contrast to the results in the standard cases where there is an imbalance in the parties' information and the less-informed party may have been greatly disadvantaged by that imbalance. In some situations, of course, as where a fiduciary or confidential relation gives rise to a duty to disclose, the knowledgeable party is required to share information—"required" in the sense of putting at risk the right to enforce the agreement if disclosure is not made. But if the parties stand in an arm's-length relationship, courts have been reluctant to impose a duty of disclosure that would erase the knowledgeable party's advantage. Can this attitude be reconciled with the courts' routine refusal to permit an offeree to "snap up" an offer which the offeree has reason to know is based on incomplete or erroneous information?

One answer from an economic perspective has been offered by Kronman, Mistake, Disclosure, Information, and the Law of Contracts, 7 J. Legal Stud. 1 (1978). According to the author, the risk of mistake represents a cost to both society and the contracting parties, because a mistake entails a misallocation, or waste, of resources. Since information prevents mistakes, a court concerned with economic efficiency should assign the risk of mistake—where the parties themselves have not done so—to the better (lower-cost) information-gatherer, thereby promoting the discovery of information at the least cost (and reducing the transaction costs of contracting). Thus, where the mistake in a bid is known or reasonably should have been known to the offeree, the risk should be assigned to that party. At that stage, the offeree can more cheaply rectify the error. To explain the apparent conflict between the mistaken-bidder cases and the cases sanctioning nondisclosure, Kronman distinguishes "casually acquired" information from that which is "deliberately acquired." Information which has been deliberately acquired through research or by expertise necessarily involves a discovery cost to its possessor, which must be offset by some benefit if the search or development is to be worthwhile. A rule of nondisclosure therefore promotes efficiency by encouraging the deliberate search for socially-useful information. On the other hand, casually-acquired information—for example, knowledge of a mistaken bid gathered by reviewing a group of bids—is discovered by happenstance and is, therefore, cost-free. Denying its possessors the benefits of such chanced-upon information, Kronman argues, will have no effect on the amount of information generated because there are no expenses which must be compensated.

Kronman recognizes, however, that high administration costs prohibit a case-by-case scrutiny to determine whether specific information has been acquired deliberately or casually. An alternative approach, he suggests, would be for the courts to adopt blanket rules for categories of cases, with the categories determined on the basis of whether a type of information (e.g., information about defects in goods or realty offered for sale) is, in general, more likely to be generated by chance or by deliberate search. "The greater the likelihood that such information will be deliberately produced rather than casually discovered, the more plausible the assumption becomes that a blanket rule permitting nondisclosure will have benefits that outweigh its costs."

Is it clear that the mistaken-bid cases can be explained in the manner Professor Kronman suggests? If it is recognized that there are difficulties in applying the deliberate-casual distinction to offerees of construction bids, what is one to think about the soundness of the distinction in other situations?

NOTE: THE WARRANTY ALTERNATIVE

A claim of rescission for mistake does not necessarily depend on statements passing between contracting parties (yes, what is said in the contract, or in negotiations, is relevant on whether the party seeking relief bears the risk of mistake). Nonetheless, the mistake cases, commonly arising from sales of things, most often property, also commonly involve affirmative statements by the seller of the thing. Such statements may be challenged as deliberate or careless misrepresentations amounting to fraud or some similar tort. Or a seller's representations may be interpreted as a warranty of performance. The point is that the legal landscape changes with misstatements of fact in the picture. To see how the UCC handles warranties in the sale of goods, turn again to § 2–313 on "express" warranties. Then look once more at the "implied" warranties of merchantability and fitness defined in §§ 2–314 and 2–315. Attempts to disclaim warranty liability are regulated by § 2–316, and § 2–714(2) deals with relief for breach of warranty. A much-litigated question is whether a seller's statement is interpretable as a warranty of performance (it may be puffing, mere opinion). Another is whether the law will read into a contract an off-the-rack warranty. Consider the two cases that come next.

Tribe v. Peterson

Supreme Court of Wyoming, 1998.
964 P.2d 1238.

TAYLOR, J. Appellant, Steve Tribe, purchased his first horse, Moccasin Badger, from appellees, [the] Petersons. Asserting that the sellers had expressly guaranteed that the horse would never buck, Tribe brought suit against the Petersons for breach of warranty when Moccasin Badger unceremoniously ejected [him] from the saddle, shattering his left wrist. After the district court denied Tribe's motion for summary judgment on the issue of express warranty, the subsequent trial resulted in the jury's rejection of [his] claims and a "no buck" verdict. [He] then moved for judgment as a matter of law, or in the alternative, a new trial. Both motions were denied. Finding that the jury acted reasonably, we affirm. . . .

The known history of Moccasin Badger (Badger) begins with his purchase in August 1994 by Larry Painter, a rancher who had bought and sold horses "[a]ll [his] life." When Painter bought and owned Badger, the horse was "plumb gentle. . . ." Mr. Painter brought Badger to his Uncle Oliver's in Rapid City, South Dakota in January 1995, describing him at that time: "Well, he was real gentle. And as far as we was concerned anybody could ride him that had any experience at all riding." Oliver Painter was not called as a witness at trial, but the parties read into the record the stipulation [that] "if he did testify, he would [say] that Moccasin Badger was calm and gentle while he was around him[,] [and he] did not have any experiences where he bucked."

In February 1995, Oliver Painter advertised the sale of Badger, and the Petersons responded. After Mrs. Peterson rode Badger and found him to be very calm and gentle, and a second visit revealed the same disposition, they purchased him for $2,200. During the first month the Petersons owned Badger, they rode him "two to three times a week." "[N]eeding a little money," the Petersons decided to sell Badger at the "Leo Perino sale," which attracts buyers from all over the world.

To ensure that Badger was sound and ready for sale, the Petersons twice brought Badger to Dr. Margie Jones, a board certified horse veterinarian from Sturgis, South Dakota, and Mr. Peterson trained Badger every day for a month prior to the sale. Dr. Jones testified that she found Badger to be "sound," and after performing an extensive physical examination and riding Badger, she concluded that Badger "was gentle and kind and he did what I asked him to."

The Leo Perino sale was held in Newcastle, Wyoming on June 3, 1995. Tribe and his wife attended the sale, accompanied by Steve Stoddard. The Tribes had moved to Wyoming in 1993 after selling Mr. Tribe's car dealership in northern California and purchasing a 12,000 acre ranch near Colony. The Tribes leased all but 400 acres to Stoddard, who they asked to assist them in recommending a place to purchase a horse which would be gentle enough for very inexperienced riders. Stoddard recommended the Leo Perino sale. . . .

Badger's description in the sale brochure represented him as a "quiet . . . and extra gentle gelding easy to catch, haul and shoe," and "overly kind which makes him a definite kids prospect. . . ." Stoddard initially noticed Badger while Mr. Peterson was roping with [the horse] in the arena. Stoddard spoke with Mr. Peterson, [who] told him that Badger "was five years old and that he was really gentle." Later, Stoddard approached the Petersons to get a better look at Badger, at which time Stoddard and Mrs. Tribe rode Badger. Stoddard found the horse to be "very gentle and very well-broke to ride." According to Stoddard, he asked Mr. Peterson if the horse "had any buck in him" to which Peterson responded, "No." Peterson told Stoddard that the horse had never bucked with him or any of its previous owners. The testimony conflicts, however, as to whether Mr. Peterson "guaranteed" the horse would never buck in the future. Stoddard stated he got a "guarantee" from both Petersons, while the Petersons denied they made such a guarantee, insisting it would be impossible to guarantee that any horse would not buck in the future.

Nonetheless, Tribe purchased Badger on his belief that he had been guaranteed that this horse would never buck. Upon returning to the ranch, Mrs. Tribe rode Badger without incident. The third time [she] rode Badger, however, she was thrown. Ten days later, after riding Badger, Mrs. Tribe asked Mr. Tribe if he wanted to ride. When he said he did, she resaddled the horse[,] Tribe got on [and] almost immediately was thrown to the ground, shattering his wrist. Some time later, Tribe contacted the Petersons to inform them of the injury, tape recording one conversation with Mr. Peterson. . . .

Tribe contends that, as a matter of law, the written description in the sale brochure and verbal representations of the Petersons created an express warranty that Badger was a calm and gentle horse which would never buck. "An express warranty is created by any affirmation of fact made by the seller to the buyer which relates to the goods and becomes a part of the basis of the bargain." Garriffa v. Taylor, 675 P.2d 1284, 1286 (Wyo. 1984), see also Wyo. Stat. [UCC] § 34.1–2–313(a)(ii) (1997) ("Any description of the goods which is made part of the basis of the bargain creates an express warranty that the goods shall conform to the description [.]"). "In order for an express warranty to exist, there must be some positive and unequivocal statement concerning the thing sold which is relied on by the buyer and which is understood to be an assertion concerning the items sold and not an opinion." *Garriffa*, 675 P.2d at 1286. A representation which expresses the seller's opinion, belief, judgment or estimate does not constitute an express warranty. . . . [W]hether there was an affirmation of fact which amounted to an express warranty [depends on a] consideration of all the circumstances surrounding a sale and should be made by the trier of fact.

The verdict form at trial asked only: "Are defendants liable to the plaintiff for damages for breach of an express warranty?" We therefore do not know if the jury determined there was no express warranty or whether a warranty was given but not breached. Either way, the jury's conclusion could reasonably be reached on the evidence presented at trial.

We begin by examining the description of Badger in the sales brochure. Tribe insists that this description guaranteed a gentle horse, and that the fact that he and his wife were thrown establishes that Badger was not gentle or calm. The testimony of all the witnesses, however, reveals that Badger was calm and gentle with everyone but the Tribes. . . .

Moreover, Mrs. Tribe telephoned Mrs. Peterson within four or five days after the sale to say: "I want you to know I'm really getting along well with Badger. I just love him. Do you have anymore like him that we could buy?" Finally, evidence was presented which established that the disposition of a horse may be affected by the rider, the equipment, the type of feed, or a new environment. Mr. Perino affirmed that "even gentle horses" may buck. Clearly, there was evidence to support a finding that the description of Badger in the brochure was the Peterson's well-founded opinion regarding Badger's disposition. Further, even if the brochure constituted an express warranty that Badger was calm and gentle, the evidence supports the conclusion that the warranty was not breached.

We next examine Tribe's contention that he was given a guarantee that Badger would never buck. . . . It appears a "no buck" warranty is a hard sell to a Wyoming jury. Obviously, the record supports the jury's conclusion that representations regarding Badger's past behavior were true, and no express warranty was given as to Badger's future behavior.

Tribe's claim to judgment as a matter of law on the theory of negligent misrepresentation is equally without merit. There is overwhelming evidence that the information provided by the Petersons did not misrepresent Badger's disposition. . . . We also note that Tribe's reliance on his alleged naivete is contradicted by the fact that Stoddard, who accompanied Tribe and advised him in the purchase of the horse, was "knowledgeable about horses." It is undisputed that all discussions allegedly relating to a "guarantee" were with Stoddard, not Tribe. . . .

The jury reached a patently reasonable verdict, and therefore we affirm. . . .

SECTION 6. CHANGED CIRCUMSTANCES JUSTIFYING NONPERFORMANCE

INTRODUCTORY NOTE

When parties write contracts, they cannot consider every remote contingency. Some unanticipated events can change underlying circumstances so much that the sensible course is to call off the entire transaction. A painter promises to paint someone's portrait, but dies before completing it. One person promises to sell her car, but through no fault of her own, the car is destroyed before delivery and before the buyer has paid anything. Actual performance in both cases has become impossible. If performance is not excused, one party will necessarily be in breach and be liable for expectation damages. Should the artist (or, more precisely, her estate) or the car owner be held in breach or does it make more sense to call the entire deal off?

There are good reasons to think that the parties would agree to release the other from liability in such cases if they thought about it. When someone dies or the goods are destroyed, expectation damages are not apt to be high. The person who wanted the portrait can find another painter. The person who agreed to buy the car can find another seller. Moreover, even if there were damages, insisting on damages will do little or nothing to make their performance more likely. The breach does not arise because of some general change in market conditions that make the contract a bad deal for the breacher. The painter hardly wants to die, and the owner of the car bears the loss from the destruction of the car. (The buyer loses only to the extent that she bought at below-market price. Even if it were a very good deal, this amount is still likely to be much smaller than the value of the car.) The legal rule that holds the painter and the car owner liable would give little added incentive to either take additional precautions. By assumption, they were not at fault for the inability to perform the promise.

Moreover, these are circumstances in which any expectation damages need to be tempered by the other party's obligation to minimize the loss that follows in the wake of the breach. In these situations, the greatest danger might be that the innocent party will fail to invest enough time and energy in finding another portrait painter or another car. Even with an obligation to mitigate damages, the ability to get expectation damages might take away from the innocent party the incentive to minimize the costs from the unexpected event. Ensuring such incentives are in place looms large in the classic excuse case. See Victor Goldberg, Framing Contract Law: An Economic Perspective 333–47 (2006).

There is another reason, one based on observed contracting behavior, to think that it makes sense to have a background rule that calls off contractual obligations when circumstances change. When sophisticated parties bargain at arm's length, they often include in their contracts what is called a force majeur clause. Such a clause calls off contractual obligations in the event of specified events, such as floods, fires, or "Acts of God." These clauses can be quite elaborate, but they work the same way as a background rule that excuses parties when performance proves impossible. Such a widespread practice among experienced parties may reflect a sensible allocation of risks. If it does, it makes sense to provide it as a default rule when parties do not have the time or the money to bargain over the matter explicitly.

In addition to cases in which the promisor's performance is literally impossible, there are also situations in which performance remains possible, but circumstances have changed so fundamentally that it no longer makes sense. This problem of "frustration" raise similar issues. The two cases that gave the doctrines their initial shape follow, and they are succeeded by cases that set out the modern contours.

The hardest problems arise when the unexpected event arises after one or both parties have partially performed. Finding that circumstances have changed and that the contract is called off still leaves open the question of how to sort out the rights of the parties. Neither party is at fault, but someone will have to bear the loss. Courts in this country and in England have struggled to find a sensible path, and the law remains unsettled. These issues are explored in the second half of this section.

Taylor v. Caldwell

King's Bench, 1863.
3 Best & S. 826.

BLACKBURN, J. . . . [P]laintiff and defendants had, on the 27th May, 1861, entered into a contract by which the defendants agreed to let the plaintiffs have the use of The Surrey Gardens and Music Hall on four days then to come, viz., the 17th June, 15th July, 5th August and 19th August, for the purpose of giving a series of four grand concerts, and day and night fetes at the Gardens and Hall on those days respectively; and the plaintiffs agreed to take the Gardens and Hall on those days, and pay £100 for each day.

The parties inaccurately call this a "letting," and the money to be paid a "rent;" but the whole agreement is such as to shew that the defendants were to retain the possession of the Hall and Gardens so that there was to be no demise of them, and that the contract was merely to give the plaintiffs the use of them on those days. Nothing however . . . depends on this. The agreement then proceeds to set out various stipulations between the parties as to what each was to supply for these concerts and entertainments, and as to the manner in which they should be carried on. The effect of the whole is to shew that the existence of the Music Hall in the Surrey Gardens in a state fit for a concert was essential for the fulfilment of the contract. . . .

After the making of the agreement, and before the first day on which a concert was to be given, the Hall was destroyed by fire. This destruction . . . was without the fault of either party, and was so complete that in consequence the concerts could not be given as intended. And the question we have to decide is whether . . . the loss which the plaintiffs have sustained is to fall upon the defendants. The parties when framing their agreement evidently had not present to their minds the possibility of such a disaster, and have made no express stipulation with reference to it, so that the answer to the question must depend upon the general rules of law applicable to such a contract.

There seems no doubt that where there is a positive contract to do a thing, not in itself unlawful, the contractor must perform it or pay damages for not doing it, although in consequence of unforeseen accidents, the performance of his contract has become unexpectedly burthensome or even impossible. The law is so laid down in 1 Roll.Abr. 450 [and the] case of Hall v. Wright, E.B. & E. 746. But this rule is only applicable when the contract is positive and absolute, and not subject to any condition either express or implied; and there are authorities which . . . establish the principle that where, from the nature of the contract, it appears that the parties must from the beginning have known that it could not be fulfilled unless when the time for the fulfillment of the contract arrived some particular specified thing continued to exist, so that, when entering into the contract, they must have contemplated such continuing existence as the foundation of what was to be done; there, in the absence of any express or implied warranty that the thing shall exist, the contract is not to be construed as a positive contract, but as subject to an implied condition that the parties shall be excused in case, before breach, performance becomes impossible from the perishing of the thing without default of the contractor.

. . . [T]his implication tends to further the great object of making the legal construction such as to fulfil the intention of those who entered into the contract. For in the course of affairs men in making such contracts in general would, if it were brought to their minds, say that there should be such a condition. . . .

There is a class of contracts in which a person binds himself to do something which requires to be performed by him in person; and such promises, e.g. promises to marry, or promises to serve for a certain time, are never in practice qualified by an express exception of the death of the party; and therefore in such cases the contract is in terms broken if the promisor dies before fulfillment. Yet it was very early determined that, if the performance is personal, the executors are not liable; Hyde v. The Dean of Windsor, Cro.Eliz. 552, 553. See 2 Wms.Exors. 1560, 5th ed., where a very apt illustration is given. "Thus," says the learned author, "if an author undertakes to compose a work, and dies before completing it, his executors are discharged from this contract: for the undertaking is merely personal in its nature, and, by the intervention of the contractor's death, has become impossible to be performed." . . . In Hall v. Wright, E.B. & E. 746, 749, Crompton J., puts another case. "Where a contract depends upon personal skill, and the act of God renders it impossible, as, for instance, in the case of a painter employed to paint a picture who is struck blind, it may be that the performance might be excused."

It seems that in those cases the only ground on which the parties or their executors, can be excused from the consequences of the breach of the contract is, that from the nature of the contract there is an implied condition of the continued existence of the life of the contractor, and perhaps in the case of the painter of his eyesight. In the instances just given, the person, the continued existence of whose life is necessary to the fulfilment of the contract, is himself the contractor, but that does not seem in itself to be necessary to the application of the principle. . . . In the ordinary form of an apprentice deed the apprentice binds himself in unqualified terms to "serve until the full end and term of seven years to be fully complete and ended," during which term it is covenanted that the apprentice his master "faithfully shall serve," and the father of the apprentice in equally unqualified terms binds himself for the performance by the apprentice of all and every covenant on his part. (See the form, 2 Chitty on Pleading, 370, 7th ed. by Greening.) It is undeniable that if the apprentice dies within the seven years, the covenant of the father that he shall perform his covenant to serve for seven years is not fulfilled, yet surely it cannot be that an action would lie against the father? Yet the only reason why it would not is that he is excused because of the apprentice's death.

These are instances where the implied condition is of the life of a human being, but there are others in which the same implication is made as to the continued existence of a thing. For example, where a contract of sale is made[,] transferring presently the property in specific chattels, which are to be delivered by the vendor at a future day; there, if the chattels, without the fault of the vendor, perish in the interval, the purchaser must pay the price and the vendor is excused from performing his contract to deliver, which has thus become impossible.

[This rule] is established by the case of Rugg v. Minett, 11 East, 210, where the article that perished before delivery was turpentine, and it was decided that the vendor was bound to refund the price of all those lots in which the property had not passed; but was entitled to retain without deduction the price of those lots in which the property had passed, though they were not delivered, and though in the conditions of sale, which are set out in the report, there was no express qualification of the promise to deliver on payment. It seems in that case rather to have been taken for granted than decided that the destruction of the thing sold before delivery excused the vendor from fulfilling his contract to deliver on payment. . . .

It may, we think, be safely asserted to be now English law, that in all contracts of loan of chattels or bailments if the performance of the promise of the borrower or bailee to return the things lent or bailed, becomes impossible because it has perished, this impossibility (if not arising from the fault of the borrower or bailee from some risk which he has taken upon himself) excuses the borrower or bailee from the performance of his promise to redeliver the chattel.

The great case of Coggs v. Bernard, 1 Smith's L.C. 171, 5th ed.; 2 L.Raym. 909, is now the leading case on the law of bailments, and Lord Holt, in that case, referred so much to the Civil law that it might perhaps be thought that this principle was there derived direct from the civilians, and was not generally applicable in English law except in the case of bailments; [but] the same law had been already adopted by the English law as early as The Book of Assises. The principle seems to us to be that, in contracts in which the performance depends on the continued existence of a given person or thing, a condition is implied that the impossibility of performance arising from the perishing of the person or thing shall excuse the performance.

In none of these cases is the promise in words other than positive, nor is there any express stipulation that the destruction of the person or thing shall excuse the performance; but that excuse is by law implied, because from the nature of the contract it is apparent that the parties contracted on the basis of the continued existence of the particular person or chattel. . . . [L]ooking at the whole contract [here], we find that the parties contracted on the basis of the continued existence of the Music Hall at the time when the concerts were to be given. . . . [T]herefore, the Hall having ceased to exist, without fault of either party, both parties are excused, the plaintiffs from taking the gardens and paying the money, the defendants from performing their promise to give the use of the Hall and Gardens and other things. Consequently the rule must be absolute to enter the verdict for the defendants.

QUESTION

Is there conflict between Blackburn's statement that the "parties when framing their agreement evidently had not present to their minds the possibility of such a disaster" and the later assertion that "they must have contemplated such continuing existence [of the music hall] as the foundation of what was to be done"?

Krell v. Henry

Court of Appeal, 1903.
[1903] 2 K.B. 740.

Appeal from a decision of Darling, J. The plaintiff, Paul Krell, sued the defendant, C.S. Henry for £50, being the balance of a sum of £75, for which the defendant had agreed to hire a flat at 56A, Pall Mall on the days of June 26 and 27, for the purpose of viewing the processions to be held in connection with the coronation of His Majesty [Edward VII]. The defendant denied his liability, and counterclaimed for the return of the sum of £25, which had been paid as a deposit, on the ground that, the processions not having taken place owing to the serious illness of the King, there had been a total failure of consideration for the contract. . . .

The facts [were undisputed]. The plaintiff on leaving the country in March, 1902, left instructions with his solicitor to let his suite of chambers at 56A, Pall Mall on such terms and for such period (not exceeding six months) as he thought proper. On June 17, 1902, the defendant noticed an announcement in the windows of the plaintiff's flat to the effect that windows to view the coronation processions were to be let. The defendant interviewed the housekeeper on the subject, when it was pointed out to him what a good view of the processions could be obtained from the premises, and he eventually agreed with the housekeeper to take the suite for the two days in question for a sum of £75.

On June 20, the defendant wrote the following letter to the plaintiff's solicitor: "I am in receipt of yours of the 18th instant, inclosing form of agreement for the suite of chambers on the third floor at 56A, Pall Mall, which I have agreed to take for the two days the 26th and 27th instant, for the sum of £75. For reasons given you I cannot enter into the agreement, but as arranged over the telephone I inclose herewith cheque for £25, as deposit, and will thank you to confirm to me that I shall have the entire use of these rooms during the days (not the nights) of the 26th and 27th instant. You may rely that every care will be taken of the premises and their contents. On the 24th inst. I will pay the balance, viz., £50, to complete the £75 agreed upon."

On the same day the defendant received the following reply from the plaintiff's solicitor: "I am in receipt of your letter of today's date inclosing cheque for £25 deposit on your agreeing to take Mr. Krell's chambers on the third floor at 56A, Pall Mall for the two days, the 26th and 27th June, and I confirm the agreement that you are to have the entire use of these rooms during the days (but not the nights), the balance, £50, to be paid to me on Tuesday next the 24th instant."

The processions not having taken place [on] June 26 and 27, the defendant declined to pay the balance of £50. . . . Hence the present action. Darling J., held, upon the authority of Taylor v. Caldwell, 3 B. & S. 826, and The Moorcock, (1889) 14 P.D. 64, that there was an implied condition in the contract that the procession should take place, and gave judgment for the defendant on the claim and counter-claim. The plaintiff appealed.

VAUGHAN WILLIAMS, L.J. The real question [here] is the extent of the application in English law of the principle of the Roman law which has been adopted and acted on in many English decisions, and notably in the case of Taylor v. Caldwell, 3 B. & S. 826. That case at least makes it clear that "where, from the nature of the contract, it appears that the parties must from the beginning have known that it could not be fulfilled unless . . . some particular specified thing continued to exist, so that when entering into the contract they must have contemplated such continued existence as the foundation of what was to be done; there, [absent] any express or implied warranty that the thing shall exist, the contract is not to be considered a positive contract, but as subject to an implied condition that the parties shall be excused in case, before breach, performance becomes impossible from the perishing of the thing without default of the contractor." Thus far it is clear that the principle of the Roman law has been introduced into the English law. . . .

I do not think that [the principle] is limited to cases in which the event causing the impossibility of performance is the destruction or nonexistence of some thing which is the subject-matter of the contract or of some condition or state of things expressly specified as a condition of it. I think that you first have to ascertain, not necessarily from the terms of the contract, but, if required, from necessary inferences, drawn from surrounding circumstances[,] what is the substance of the contract, and then to ask the question whether that substantial contract needs for its foundation the assumption of the existence of a particular state of things. If it does, this will limit the operation of the general words, and [if] the contract becomes impossible of performance by reason of the nonexistence of the state of things assumed by both contracting parties as the foundation of the contract, there will be no breach of the contract thus limited.

Now what are the facts of the present case? The contract is contained in [the] two letters of June 20. . . . These letters do not mention the coronation, but speak merely of the taking of Mr. Krell's chambers, or, rather, of the use of them. . . . [T]he plaintiff [had] exhibited on his premises, third floor, 56A, Pall Mall, an announcement to the effect that windows to view the Royal coronation procession were to be let, and [defendant] was induced by that announcement to apply to the housekeeper on the premises, who said that the owner was willing to let the suite of rooms for the purpose of seeing the Royal procession for both days, but not nights, of June 26 and 27. . . . [T]he use of the rooms was . . . for the purpose of seeing the Royal procession. It was not a demise of the rooms, or even an agreement to let and take the rooms. It is a license to use rooms for a particular purpose and none other. [And] the taking place of those processions on the days proclaimed along the proclaimed route, which passed 56A, Pall Mall, was regarded by both contracting parties as the foundation of the contract; and I think that it cannot reasonably be supposed to have been in the contemplation of the contracting parties, when the contract was made, that the coronation would not be held on the proclaimed days, or the processions not take place on those days along the proclaimed route. . . .

It was suggested in the course of the argument that if the occurrence, on the proclaimed days, of the coronation and the procession in this case were the foundation of the contract, and if the general words are thereby limited or qualified, so that in the event of the nonoccurrence of the coronation and procession along the proclaimed route they would discharge both parties from further performance of the contract, it would follow that if a cabman was engaged to take some one to Epsom on Derby Day at a suitable enhanced price for such a journey, say £10, both parties to the contract would be discharged in the contingency of the race at Epsom for some reason becoming impossible; but I do not think this follows, for I do not think that in the cab case the happening of the race would be the foundation of the contract. No doubt the purpose of the engager would be to go to see the Derby, and the price would be proportionately high; but the cab had no special qualifications for the purpose which led to the selection of the cab for this particular occasion. Any other cab would have done as well. Moreover, under the cab contract, the hirer, even if the race went off, could have said, "Drive me to Epsom; I will pay you the agreed sum; you have nothing to do with the purpose for which I hired the cab," and if the cabman refused he would have been guilty of a breach of contract, there being nothing to qualify his promise to drive the hirer to Epsom on a particular day. Whereas in the case of the coronation, there is not merely the purpose of the hirer to see the coronation procession, but it is the coronation procession and the relative position of the rooms which is the basis of the contract as much for the lessor as the hirer; and I think that if the King, before the coronation day and after the contract, had died, the hirer could not have insisted on having the rooms on the days named. It could not in the cab case be reasonably said that seeing the Derby race was the foundation of the contract. . . . Whereas in the present case, where the rooms were offered and taken, by reason of their peculiar suitability from the position of the rooms for a view of the coronation procession, surely the view of the coronation procession was the foundation of the contract, which is a very different thing from the purpose of the man who engaged the cab—namely, to see the race—being held to be the foundation of the contract. Each case must be judged by its own circumstances. In each case one must ask oneself first, what, having regard to all the circumstances, was the foundation of the contract? Secondly, was the performance of the contract prevented? Thirdly, was the event which prevented the performance of the contract of such a character that it cannot reasonably be said to have been in the contemplation of the parties at the date of the contract? If all these questions are answered in the affirmative (as I think they should be in this case), both parties are discharged from further performance of the contract. . . . [T]he coronation procession was the foundation of this contract, and the non-happening of it prevented the performance of the contract. . . . The test seems to be whether the event which causes the impossibility was or might have been anticipated and guarded against. It seems difficult to say, in a case where both parties anticipate the happening of an event, which anticipation is the foundation of the contract, that either party must be taken to have anticipated, and ought to have guarded against, the event which prevented the performance of the contract. . . .

[Here,] where we have to ask ourselves whether the object of the contract was frustrated by the non-happening of the coronation procession[,] parol evidence is admissible to shew that the subject of the contract was rooms to view the coronation procession. . . . When once this is established, I see no difficulty whatever in the case. It is not essential to the application of the principle of Taylor v. Caldwell that the direct subject of the contract should perish or fail to be in existence at the date of performance of the contract. It is sufficient if a state of things or condition expressed in the contract and essential to its performance perishes or fails to be in existence at that time. . . . This disposes of the plaintiff's claim for £50 unpaid balance of the price agreed. . . . The defendant at one time set up a cross-claim for the return of the £25 he paid at the date of the contract. As that claim is now withdrawn it is unnecessary to say anything about it. I have only to add that the facts of this case do not bring it within the principle laid down in Stubbs v. Holywell Ry. Co., L.R., 2 Ex. 311, that in the case of contracts falling directly within the rule of Taylor v. Caldwell the subsequent impossibility does not affect rights already acquired, because the defendant had the whole of June 24 to pay the balance, and the public announcement that the coronation and processions would not take place on the proclaimed days was made early on the morning of the 24th, and no cause of action could accrue till the end of that day. . . .

Appeal dismissed.

The Isle of Mull

278 F. 131 (4th Cir. 1921)

On May 19, 1913, the Isles Steamship Co., a British corporation, chartered the steamship Isle of Mull to plaintiff Gans Steamship Line, a New York corporation. The charter contract provided for a term of "about five years" and a rental of £1,370 a month. The ship began service under the charter on January 7, 1914. On June 10, 1915, the ship was requisitioned by the British Admiralty, which assumed control two days later and retained control for more than the five-year period of the charter contract. The British government fixed as compensation to the owner £2,361 and 15 shillings a month, i.e., £991 and 15 shillings a month more than the rental specified in plaintiff's charter contract. Plaintiff then sued for damages measured by the difference between the market value of the use of the ship, alleged to be £5,110 a month, and the rent plaintiff had agreed to pay. The trial court held that the charter contract had not been frustrated and that plaintiff was entitled to the difference between the contract rate and the greater price paid by the British government. On appeal, this decree was reversed and plaintiff's suit dismissed. The legal authority of the British government to requisition the vessel could not be questioned in American courts. At the time the ship was requisitioned it was impossible to forecast the duration of the war, but the enormous resources mobilized on both sides and the urgent need of Britain to employ its full sea power made it unlikely that the Isle of Mull would be released before the end of the five-year period of the charter. Plaintiff argued that defendant owner would be unjustly enriched by retaining the excess paid by the British government. But defendant argued for a definite rule discharging both parties at once, permitting them promptly to readjust their affairs, and operating independently of the gains or losses of either party. This was the view adopted by the English courts where, as here, the frustration was or probably would be total. Under this view, if compensation paid for the requisitioned asset exceeded the contract rate, this was the owner's gain, just as inadequate compensation would be the owner's loss. The court, adopting, in effect, the English rule, concluded that the contract was wholly discharged and defendant was not required to account for the profit it had received.

The Opera Company of Boston, Inc. v. The Wolf Trap Foundation for the Performing Arts

United States Court of Appeals, Fourth Circuit, 1987.
817 F.2d 1094.

RUSSELL, CIRCUIT JUDGE. . . . The Opera Company of Boston, Inc. [is] an operatic organization recognized both nationally and internationally. The defendant The Wolf Trap Foundation for the Performing Arts is an organization for the advancement of the performing arts headquartered at Vienna, Virginia, and as such sponsors at the Filene Center in the Wolf Trap Park operatic performances and similar artistic programs. The Filene Center is located in the Wolf Trap National Park and is a part of the various facilities maintained and controlled by the National Park Service. It consists of a main stage tower, an auditorium and an open lawn. The main stage tower contains the stage, dressing rooms and space for the scenery and electrical effects. In front of the tower is a covered auditorium seating approximately 3,500 people. Beyond this is the uncovered lawn providing seating for an additional 3,000 people. The Park provides parking space. This parking area is separated from the Center itself. A number of pathways leading from the parking area to the Filene Center are available. The distance of the parking area from the Center varies from approximately 300 to 700 yards. Ordinarily, when there are any night performances at the Center, the roads in the park, the parking area and the pathways to the Center are lighted for the guidance of patrons at performances at the Center.

This suit between the parties arises under a contract between the plaintiff The Opera Company of Boston, Inc. (Opera Company) and the defendant The Wolf Trap Foundation for the Performing Arts (Wolf Trap) by which the Opera Company for its part agreed to give four "fully staged orchestrally accompanied [operatic] performances to the normally recognized standards" of the Opera Company on the nights of June 12, 13, 14 and 15, 1980 at the Filene Center. For this the Opera Company was to be paid by Wolf Trap $272,000 payable under a schedule providing for payment of $20,000 at the signing of the contract and a further $40,000 on April 1, 1980, with the balance payable in four equal installments before the rise of the curtain on each performance. Wolf Trap, in turn, for its part under the contract was obliged to make the above payments and also to furnish the place of performance including an undertaking "to provide lighting equipment as shall be specified by the Opera Company of Boston's lighting designer."

Both parties to the contract performed apparently all their obligations under the contract through the operatic performance on June 14. These performances had been fully sold as well as had the remaining performance on June 15. During this final day, the weather was described as hot and humid, with rain throughout the day. Sometime between 6:00 and 6:30 p.m. a severe thunderstorm arose causing an electrical power outage. As a result all electrical service in the Park, in its roadways, parking area, pathways and auditorium were out. Conferences were had among representatives of the Park Service and that of Wolf Trap. The public utility advised that it would be at least after eleven o'clock before any service by it could be resumed in the Park and that it was likely power might not be available before morning. Various alternatives for supplying power were considered but none was regarded as relieving the situation. Already some 3,000 people were in the Park for the performance; 3,500 more were expected before 8:00 p.m. when the performance was to begin. The Park Service recommended the immediate cancellation of the performance and advised Wolf Trap if the performance were not cancelled, it disclaimed any responsibility for the safety of the people who were to attend as well as those who were to perform. It was the Park Service's view that a prompt cancellation was necessary to enable the parties to leave the park safely and to prevent others from coming. Wolf Trap agreed and the performance was cancelled. While some of these discussions were being carried on a representative of the Opera Company was present but she took no part in the decision to cancel, though she voiced no objection. Since the performance was cancelled, Wolf Trap failed to make the final payment under the contract to the Opera Company. Five years after the cancellation, the Opera Company filed this suit to recover the balance due under the contract. Wolf Trap defended on the ground that performance by it of its obligation under the contract was excused under the doctrine of impossibility of performance. The basis for this defense was that the final performance by the Opera Company for which payment was claimed had been cancelled because a performance was impracticable as a result of the power outage. . . .

The doctrine of impossibility of performance as an excuse or defense for a breach of contract was for long smothered under a declared commitment to the principle of sanctity of contracts. This rationale for constrained application of the doctrine was expressed by the United States Supreme Court in Dermott v. Jones (2 Wall.), 69 U.S. 1, 8, (1864):

> The principle which controlled the decision of the cases referred to rests upon a solid foundation of reason and justice. It regards

> the sanctity of contracts. It requires parties to do what they have agreed to do. If unexpected impediments lie in the way, and a loss must ensue, it leaves the loss where the contract places it. If the parties have made no provision for a dispensation, the rule of law gives none. It does not allow a contract fairly made to be annulled, and it does not permit to be interpolated what the parties themselves have not stipulated.

The growth of commercial activity in the nineteenth century, however, made this rigidity of the doctrine of impossibility both "economically and socially unworkable," see Cook v. Deltona Corp., 753 F.2d 1552, 1558 (11th Cir. 1985), and in Taylor v. Caldwell, 3 B. & S. 826, 122 Eng. Rep. 309, 324, 6 R.C. 603 (1863), the English courts recognized these changed conditions and, relying largely on civil law precedents, relaxed the constraints on the doctrine by the principle of sanctity of contracts as followed by the English courts since *Paradine v. Jayne,* Alleyn, 27, 23d Charles II (1670). It based such relaxation on the theory of an implied condition arising without express condition in the contract itself. . . .

[T]he fullest statement of the modern doctrine of impossibility or impracticability is that of Judge Wright, speaking for the Court, in Transatlantic Financing Corporation v. United States, 363 F.2d 312, 315 (D.C. Cir. 1966):

> The doctrine of impossibility of performance has gradually been freed from the earlier fictional and unrealistic strictures of such tests as the "implied term" and the parties' "contemplation." . . . The doctrine ultimately represents the ever-shifting line, drawn by courts hopefully responsive to commercial practices and mores, at which the community's interest in having contracts enforced according to their terms is outweighed by the commercial senselessness of requiring performance. When the issue is raised, the court is asked to construct a condition of performance based on the changed circumstances, a process which involves at least three reasonably definable steps.

In line with these cases, we accept as the correct statement of the modern and prevailing doctrine of impossibility of performance as a defense to a breach of contract to be essentially as equitable in character "based [to quote Williston] on the unfairness or unreasonableness of giving [the contract] the absolute force which its words clearly state" and to be applied under the circumstances so well stated in *Transatlantic.*

Manifestly the first fact to be established in making out this modern defense of impossibility or impracticability of performance is the existence of an "occurrence of an event, the non-occurrence of which was a basic assumption on which the contract was made." And, in determining the existence of such occurrence, it is necessary to have in mind the Restatement's definition of an "occurrence" in this context as that which, because of the "destruction, or such deterioration" of a "specific thing necessary for the performance" of the contract "makes performance impracticable." The occurrence, as *Transatlantic* puts it, must be unexpected but it does not necessarily have to have been unforeseeable. A requirement of absolute non-foreseeability as a condition to the application of the doctrine would be so logically inconsistent that in effect it would nullify the doctrine. This was recognized by Judge Clark in L.N. Jackson & Co. v. Royal Norwegian Government, 177 F.2d 694, 699 (2d Cir. 1949), where he said that to require an absolute absence of foreseeability would, if accepted,

> practically destroy the doctrine of supervening impossibility, notwithstanding its present wide and apparently growing popularity. Certainly the death of a promisor, the burning of a ship, the requisitioning of a merchant marine on the outbreak of a war could, and perhaps should, be foreseen. In fact, the more common expression of the rule appears to be in terms which tend to state the burden the other way, e.g., that "the duty of the promisor is discharged, unless a contrary intention has been manifested" or "in the absence of circumstances showing either a contrary intention or contributing fault on the part of the person subject to the duty." . . .

[A]s Williston has said, practically any occurrence can be foreseen but whether the foreseeability is sufficient to render unacceptable the defense of impossibility is "one of degree" of the foreseeability and whether the non-occurrence of the event was sufficiently unlikely or unreasonable to constitute a reason for refusing to apply the doctrine. And that is the rule which we think accords with modern reasoning of the doctrine as an equitable doctrine and is the one we approve.

The second fact to be determined in the proposed application of the doctrine is that the frustration of performance was substantial. To satisfy this requirement "[t]he frustration must be so severe that it is not fairly to be regarded as within the risks [the obligor] assumed under the contract." Comment a, § 265 of Restatement (Second) of Contracts. And, finally, the defendant asserting the defense must establish that performance was impossible as that term has been defined in the refinements of the doctrine.

In summary, then, a party relying on the defense of impossibility of performance must establish (1) the unexpected occurrence of an intervening act, (2) such occurrence was of such a character that its non-occurrence was a basic assumption of the agreement of the parties, and (3) that occurrence made performance impracticable. When all those facts are established the defense is made out. . . .

Applying the law as above stated to the facts of this case, we conclude, as did the district judge, that the existence of electric power was necessary for the satisfactory performance by the Opera Company on the night of June 15. While he seems to conclude that public safety was the main consideration on which the cancellation was based, he found that the power outage was the reason assigned for cancellation, and in that connection he found it to be questionable that "a generator could [have been] set up to provide additional light for the theater itself (when power from the utility company became unavailable) and still provide adequate light for the people who had to move backstage." Such findings meet the requirement of Restatement (Second) on Contracts § 263 for an event, the "non-occurrence of which was a basic assumption on which the contract was made" and accordingly satisfies the definition of an impracticability which will relieve the obligor of his duty to perform as declared in § 265 of such Restatement (which we have accepted as the proper present statement of the doctrine of impossibility of performance as a defense to a breach of contract suit). Moreover, the facts as found make out impracticability of performance under the phraseology of the doctrine of impossibility in the Virginia case of [Housing Authority, Etc. v. East Tenn. L. & P. Co., 183 Va. 64, 31 S.E.2d 273 (1944)]. The district judge, however, refused to sustain the defense because he held that if the contingency that occurred was one that could have been foreseen reliance on the doctrine of impossibility as a defense to a breach of contract suit is absolutely barred. As we have said, this is not the modern rule and he found that the power outage was foreseeable. In this the district judge erred. Foreseeability, as we have said, is at best but one fact to be considered in resolving first how likely the occurrence of the event in question was and, second whether its occurrence, based on past experience, was of such reasonable likelihood that the obligor should not merely foresee the risk but, because of the degree of its likelihood, the obligor should have guarded against it or provided for non-liability against the risk. This is a question to be resolved by the trial judge after a careful scrutiny of all the facts in the case. The trial judge in this case made no such findings. The cause must be remanded for such findings. In connection with that remand, the parties may be permitted to offer additional evidence on the matters in issue. . . .

The judgment herein must, therefore, be vacated and the action remanded to the district court to make findings, based on a statement of reasons, whether the possible foreseeability of the power failure in this case was of that degree of reasonable likelihood as to make improper the assertion by Wolf Trap of the defense of impossibility of performance. . . .

Chase Precast Corp. v. John J. Paonessa Co.

Supreme Judicial Court of Massachusetts, 1991.
409 Mass. 371, 566 N.E.2d 603.

LYNCH, J. . . . The claim of the plaintiff, Chase Precast Corp. (Chase), arises from the cancellation of its contracts with [defendant] Paonessa to supply median barriers in a highway reconstruction project of the Commonwealth. Chase brought an action to recover its anticipated profit on the amount of median barriers called for by its supply contracts with Paonessa but not produced. Paonessa brought a cross action against the Commonwealth for indemnification in the event it should be held liable to Chase. After a jury-waived trial, [the] judge ruled for Paonessa on the basis of impossibility of performance.[2] Chase and Paonessa cross appealed. The Appeals Court affirmed, noting that the doctrine of frustration of purpose more accurately described the basis of the trial judge's decision than the doctrine of impossibility. We agree [and] we now affirm.

. . . In 1982, the Commonwealth, through the Department of Public Works (department), entered into two contracts with Paonessa for resurfacing and improvements to two stretches of Route 128. Part of each contract called for replacing a grass median strip between the north and southbound lanes with concrete surfacing and precast concrete median barriers. Paonessa entered into two contracts with Chase under which Chase was to supply, in the aggregate, 25,800 linear feet of concrete median barriers according to the [department's] specifications for highway construction. . . .

The highway reconstruction began in the spring of 1983. By late May, the department was receiving protests from angry residents who objected to use of the concrete median barriers and removal of the grass median strip. Paonessa and Chase became aware of the protest around June 1. On June 6, a group of 100 citizens filed [a suit] to stop installation of the concrete median barriers and other aspects of the work. On June 7, anticipating modification by the department, Paonessa notified Chase by letter to stop producing concrete barriers for the projects. Chase did so upon receipt of the letter the following day. On June 17, the department and the citizens' group entered into a settlement which provided, in part, that no additional concrete median barriers would be installed. On June 23, the department deleted the permanent concrete median barriers item from its contracts with Paonessa.

Before stopping production on June 8, Chase had produced approximately one-half of the median barriers called for by its contracts with Paonessa, and had delivered most of them to the construction sites. Paonessa paid Chase for all that it had produced, at the contract price. Chase suffered no out-of-pocket expense as a result of cancellation of the remaining portion of barriers.

This court has long recognized and applied the doctrine of impossibility. . . . See, e.g., Boston Plate & Window Glass Co. v. John Bowen Co., 335 Mass. 697, 141 N.E.2d 715 (1957). . . . On the other hand, although we have referred to the doctrine of frustration of purpose[,] we have never clearly defined it. See Mishara Constr. Co. v. Transit-Mixed Concrete Corp., 365 Mass. 122, 310 N.E.2d 363 (1974). . . . Other jurisdictions have explained the doctrine as follows: when an event neither anticipated nor

---

[2] The judge also ruled that the Department of Public Works had the right to cancel the order for median barriers under its general contracts with Paonessa, particularly under subsection 4.06 of those contracts. See note 3, infra.

caused by either party, the risk of which was not allocated by the contract, destroys the object or purpose of the contract, thus destroying the value of performance, the parties are excused from further performance. [See] Lloyd v. Murphy, 25 Cal.2d 48, 153 P.2d 47 (1944).

In *Mishara Constr. Co.*, we called frustration of purpose a "companion rule" to the doctrine of impossibility.[3] . . . [A] definition of frustration of purpose is found in the Restatement (Second) of Contracts § 265 (1981):

> Where, after a contract is made, a party's principal purpose is substantially frustrated without his fault by the occurrence of an event the non-occurrence of which was a basic assumption on which the contract was made, his remaining duties to render performance are discharged, unless the language or the circumstances indicate the contrary.

This definition is nearly identical to the defense of "commercial impracticability," found in the [UCC], G.L. c. 106, § 2–615, which this court, in *Mishara*[,] held to be consistent with the common law of contracts regarding impossibility of performance. . . .

Paonessa bore no responsibility for the department's elimination of the median barriers from the projects. Therefore, whether it can rely on the defense of frustration turns on whether elimination of the barriers was a risk allocated by the contracts to Paonessa. *Mishara*, 365 Mass. at 129, articulates the relevant test:

> The question is, given the commercial circumstances in which the parties dealt: Was the contingency which developed one which the parties could reasonably be thought to have foreseen as a real possibility which could affect performance? Was it one of that variety of risks which the parties were tacitly assigning to the promisor by their failure to provide for it explicitly? If it was, performance will be required. If it could not be so considered, performance is excused.

. . . Paonessa's contracts with the department contained a standard provision allowing the department to eliminate items or portions of work found unnecessary.[6] The purchase order agreements between Chase and

---

[3] Clearly frustration of purpose is a more accurate label for the defense argued in this case[,] since "[p]erformance was not literally impossible. Nothing prevented Paonessa from honoring its contract to purchase the remaining sections of median barrier, whether or not the [department] would approve their use in the road construction." 28 Mass.App.Ct. 639, 644 n. 5, 554 N.E.2d 868 (1990).

[6] The contracts contained the following provision:

"4.06 Increased or Decreased Contract Quantities.

"When the accepted quantities of work vary from the quantities in the bid schedule, the Contractor shall accept as payment in full, so far as contract items are concerned, payment at the original contract unit prices for the accepted quantities of work done.

"The Engineer may order omitted from the work any items or portions of work found unnecessary to the improvement and such omission shall not operate as a waiver of any condition of the Contract nor invalidate any of the provisions thereof, nor shall the Contractor have any claim for anticipated profit.

Paonessa[,] [which were prepared by Chase,] do not contain a similar provision. This difference in the contracts does not mandate the conclusion that Paonessa assumed the risk of reduction in the quantity of the barriers. It is implicit in the judge's findings that Chase knew the barriers were for department projects [and] that Chase was aware of the department's power to decrease quantities of contract items. . . . Chase had been a supplier of median barriers to the department in the past. The provision giving the department the power to eliminate items or portions thereof was standard in its contracts. . . . The judge found that Chase had furnished materials under and was familiar with the so-called "Unit Price Philosophy" in the construction industry, whereby contract items are paid for at the contract unit price for the quantity of work actually accepted. Finally, the judge's finding that "[a]ll parties were well aware that lost profits were not an element of damage in either of the public works projects in issue" further supports the conclusion that Chase was aware of the department's power to decrease quantities, since the term prohibiting claims for anticipated profit is part of the same sentence in the standard provision as that allowing the engineer to eliminate items or portions of work.

In *Mishara*, we held that, although labor disputes in general cannot be considered extraordinary, whether the parties in a particular case intended performance to be carried out, even in the face of a labor difficulty, depends on the facts known to the parties at the time of contracting with respect to the history of and prospects for labor difficulties. [Here,] even if the parties were aware generally of the department's power to eliminate contract items, the judge could reasonably have concluded that they did not contemplate the cancellation for a major portion of the project of such a widely used item as concrete median barriers, and did not allocate the risk of such cancellation.[7]

Our opinion in Chicopee Concrete Serv. v. Hart Eng'g Co., 398 Mass. 476, 498 N.E.2d 121 (1986), does not lead to a different conclusion. Although we held there that a provision of a prime contract requiring city approval of subcontractors was not incorporated by reference into the subcontract, we nevertheless stated that, if the record had supported the conclusion that the subcontractor knew, or at least had notice of, the approval clause, the result might have been different. Id. at 478–479, 498 N.E.2d 121.[8] . . . Judgment affirmed.

"No allowance will be made for any increased expenses, loss of expected reimbursement therefor or from any other cause."

[7] The judge did not explicitly find that cancellation of the barriers was not contemplated and that the risk of their elimination was not allocated by the contracts. However, the judge's decision imports every finding essential to sustain it if there is evidence to support it. . . .

[8] This court held in John Soley & Sons v. Jones, 208 Mass. 561, 95 N.E. 94 (1911), that, where by its terms the prime contract could be cancelled if the defendant was not making sufficient progress on the work, and the plaintiff knew of the article of cancellation, nevertheless, even if it was mutually understood that the defendant did not intend to perform unless the prime contract remained in force, the defendant was not relieved from performance on the ground of impossibility where it failed to provide for the risk of cancellation in its contract with

---

World of Boxing LLC v. King

United States District Court, S.D.N.Y., 2014.
56 F. Supp. 3d 507.

SCHEINDLIN, DISTRICT JUDGE. . . . Plaintiffs Vladimir Hrunov and Andrey Ryabinskiy are Russian boxing promoters who do business as World of Boxing ("WOB"). Defendant Don King ("King") is an American boxing promoter who does business as Don King Productions. On January 28, 2014, King and WOB entered into an Agreement In Principle ("Agreement"), in which King promised to produce Guillermo Jones ("Jones") for a bout against Denis Lebedev ("Lebedev") on April 25, 2014. The day the bout was supposed to take place, Jones tested positive for furosemide, an illicit, performance-enhancing diuretic. The positive drug test precluded Jones from competing, and the bout was called off. . . .

King likens his plight to that of a singing troupe manager who signed a contract with a theater owner, promising that the troupe would play for two weeks, only to have the lead singer fall ill on the eve of the first show. When the theater owner sued for breach, the New York Court of Appeals excused the manager's non-performance on the grounds that "[c]ontracts for personal services"—contracts that require action by a specific person—"are subject to [the] implied condition[ ] that . . . if [the person] dies, or without fault on the part of the covenantor becomes disabled, the obligation to perform is extinguished." [Spalding v. Rosa, 71 N.Y. 40, 44 (1877).] Likewise here, argues King: by ingesting furosemide, Jones "disabled" himself from participating in a WBA-sponsored bout, thereby "extinguishing" King's obligation to perform.

New York law is very clear, however, that an impossibility defense is only available if the frustration of performance was "produced by an unanticipated event that could not have been foreseen or guarded against in the contract." [Kel Kim, Corp. v. Central Mkts., Inc., 70 N.Y.2d 900, 902, 524 N.Y.S.2d 384, 519 N.E.2d 295 (1987).] In this case, two key facts compel the conclusion that Jones's ingestion of furosemide was not "unanticipated"—i.e., that King should have foreseen the possibility of Jones testing positive and guarded against it in the contract. *First,* Jones had a history of doping. The result of the first Cruiserweight Title match between Jones and Lebedev—in May 2013—had to be vacated because

---

the plaintiff. To the extent that holding is contrary to our decision in this case, we decline to follow it, and refer to our adoption in *Mishara*, 365 Mass. at 130, 310 N.E.2d 363, of the following statement: "Rather than mechanically apply any fixed rule of law, where the parties themselves have not allocated responsibility, justice is better served by appraising all of the circumstances, the part the various parties played, and thereon determining liability," quoting [Badhwar v. Colorado Fuel & Iron Corp., 138 F.Supp. 595, 607 (S.D.N.Y. 1955), aff'd, 245 F.2d 903 (2d Cir. 1957)]. See West Los Angeles Inst. v. Mayer, 366 F.2d 220 (9th Cir. 1966), cert. denied, 385 U.S. 1010 (1967) ("foreseeability of the frustrating event is not alone enough to bar rescission if it appears that the parties did not intend the promisor to assume the risk of its occurrence").

Jones tested positive for furosemide after the fact. *Second,* the Agreement provided for mandatory pre-bout drug testing, as required by the 2013 WBA Resolution.

King tries to turn these facts around. Noting how "stunned" and "shocked" he was to learn of the positive drug test on April 25, 2014, King reports that "it defie[d] belief, that Jones, aware that he would be subjected to pre-bout drug testing due to his previous positive result, *would again test positive* for the same banned substance." Put otherwise, King "believed that the mandatory drug testing provision . . . would preclude another potential positive drug test, because [Jones] knew that [he] would be subject to random [ ] testing." Therefore, in King's view, he should not be punished for failing to foresee such a "plainly remote and unlikely event."

While King's dismay is understandable—it *is* stunning that Jones was foolish enough to test positive for the same drug twice—his argument misconstrues the term "unanticipated event." King casts the question in terms of probability: an event is "unanticipated," in his view, if it is unlikely to occur. What the case law has in mind, however, are not improbable events, but events that fall outside the sphere of what a reasonable person would plan for. Even assuming that King is right about the likelihood of a second positive test, it strains credibility to call the event "unanticipated."

King's own testimony proves the point. By way of explaining why the Agreement was silent about what to do in the event of a second positive test, King admits that he thought the "mandatory drug testing provision" would "preclude" Jones from ingesting furosemide. No doubt he did. From this testimony, however, no one could reasonably conclude that King had not anticipated the possibility of a second positive test. Rather, the inescapable conclusion is that King *had* anticipated such a possibility—and having anticipated it, he believed the threat of a mandatory drug test would ward it off. That King's belief turned out to be mistaken is no basis for relieving him of his contract obligations.

In essence, King argues that he should not be held liable because Jones's decision to take furosemide was outside of King's control: short of "imprison[ing] Jones," there was no way for him to perform. But this argument ignores what *was* in King's control: the decision not to bargain for more protective contract terms.

After all, WOB could *also* invoke the "imprisonment" logic—in support of the opposite view. If I were to rule that Jones's ingestion of furosemide effectively dissolved the Agreement, and that King's failure to perform was therefore excused, WOB might reasonably object that *it* had no way—short of imprisoning Jones—to avoid the economic loss of that outcome. Ultimately, the reality is that Jones's poor decision-making was costly to both parties. The question is which party—King or WOB—should have to shoulder those costs. The law makes it clear that the answer is King. As the party who promised to secure Jones's participation,

King "assumed the risk" of foreseeable events that might frustrate his ability to make good on that promise. Because the risk of a second positive test was foreseeable—so foreseeable, in fact, that the Agreement set out a mandatory testing provision to lessen its likelihood—King's breach cannot be excused. . . .

Hemlock Semiconductor Operations, LLC v. SolarWorld Industries Sachsen GmbH

United States Court of Appeals, Sixth Circuit, 2017.
867 F.3d 692.

GILMAN, CIRCUIT JUDGE. Hemlock Semiconductor Operations, LLC (Hemlock) and SolarWorld Industries Sachsen GmbH (Sachsen) are both involved in manufacturing components of solar-power products. They entered into a series of long-term supply agreements (LTAs), by which Hemlock in Michigan would supply Sachsen in Germany with set quantities of polycrystalline silicon (polysilicon) at fixed prices between the years 2006 and 2019. . . .

Two provisions of the LTAs are particularly relevant to the present case. First, a "take-or-pay" provision required that Sachsen purchase a specified quantity of polysilicon each year at a fixed price. The take-or-pay provision obligated Sachsen to pay this yearly amount even if it declined to take delivery of the polysilicon. Second, in the event that Sachsen failed to pay the specified amount for a given year, Hemlock had the right to terminate the LTAs. Sachsen would then owe Hemlock the full remaining balance of the LTA price, including amounts due for future years. We will refer to this second provision as "the liquidated-damages provision."

After entering into the LTAs, Hemlock began a massive expansion of its manufacturing facilities in the United States at a cost of over $4 billion. The LTAs acknowledged the planned expansion several times. Sachsen was required to make significant advance payments to Hemlock under the LTAs, which were then credited against the purchase price of the polysilicon. Although the LTAs do not explicitly describe the reason for the advance payments, Sachsen acknowledges that the purpose of the payments was to help fund Hemlock's expansion.

For the first few years of the LTAs' existence, Sachsen obtained polysilicon from Hemlock at a price far below the then-current market value. This began to change in 2009, however, when the Chinese government started subsidizing its national production of polysilicon. The result was that the market price of polysilicon eventually dropped below the LTA price.

In response, Hemlock and Sachsen negotiated a temporary adjustment to the LTA price in 2011. After that agreement expired the following year, the parties attempted to negotiate further amendments but were unable to reach an agreement. . . .

In March 2013, Hemlock sent Sachsen a "Shortfall Notice" that set forth the quantities of polysilicon that Sachsen had failed to purchase under the LTAs in 2012 and that demanded payment pursuant to the take-or-pay provision. Sachsen responded by insisting that it "did not fall short of any purchase obligations," that the parties had permanently amended the LTAs, and that Hemlock had waived the ability to enforce the LTAs. Two days later, Hemlock sued, seeking the full amount due under the liquidated-damages provision. . . .

Sachsen . . . argues that the district court erred in concluding that the doctrines of commercial impracticability and frustration of purpose do not excuse Sachsen's breach of contract. The theory underlying both defenses is that the Chinese government (1) illegally subsidized its national production of polysilicon and dumped massive quantities of the product onto the market, causing the price of polysilicon to fall; and (2) committed acts of "criminal industrial espionage" against Sachsen's U.S.-based sister company, SWIA. As a result of these illegal actions, Sachsen argues, the price of polysilicon plummeted, rendering Sachsen's performance impracticable and frustrating the purpose of entering into the LTAs.

We will assume without deciding that the alleged illegal actions by the Chinese government actually occurred. Hemlock does not in fact dispute Sachsen's evidence that these actions were deemed illegal by both U.S. and E.U. authorities. Rather, Hemlock argues that the district court properly rejected Sachsen's affirmative defenses because the drop in the price of polysilicon, regardless of cause, was simply a change in market conditions that does not excuse contract performance. . . .

Sachsen asserts the affirmative defenses of commercial impracticability and impossibility. Both parties and the district court discuss these defenses interchangeably. We will therefore refer to these defenses collectively as "commercial impracticability."

Under Michigan law, a party charged with breaching a contract can assert as an affirmative defense that its performance was rendered impracticable. Capital One Bank v. Ponte, 2013 WL 6692511, at *10 (Mich. Ct. App. 2013). Performance need not be impossible, but "there must be a showing of impracticability because of extreme and unreasonable difficulty, expense, injury or loss involved." Roberts v. Farmers Ins. Exch., 737 N.W.2d 332, 342 (Mich. App. 2007). The impracticability defense applies only if "an unanticipated circumstance has made performance of the promise vitally different from what should reasonably have been within the contemplation of both parties when they entered into the contract." Capital One Bank, 2013 WL 6692511, at *10. In other words, the defense is viable only if an unforeseen event occurs and "the non-occurrence of that event [was] . . . a basic assumption on which both parties made the contract." Karl Wendt Farm Equip. Co. v. Int'l Harvester Co., 931 F.2d 1112, 1117 (6th Cir. 1991).

The expectation that current market conditions will continue for the life of the contract is not such a basic assumption, so shifts in market prices ordinarily do not constitute impracticability. Likewise, the simple fact that a contract has become unprofitable for one of the parties is generally insufficient to establish impracticability. This is especially true when the parties have entered into a contract for the sale of goods at fixed prices because such contracts are made for the very purpose of establishing a stable price despite a fluctuating market. Chainworks, Inc. v. Webco Indus., Inc., 2006 WL 461251, at *10 (W.D. Mich. Feb. 24, 2006).

Even relatively drastic changes in the market have been held insufficient to trigger the impracticability defense. In Karl Wendt Farm Equipment Co. v. International Harvester Co., 931 F.2d 1112, 1117 (6th Cir. 1991), for example, this court concluded that the Michigan Supreme Court would not apply the impracticability defense when International Harvester (IH) "experienced a dramatic downturn in the farm equipment market," decided to go out of business, and breached a dealership agreement by unilaterally terminating it. The court rejected IH's argument that impracticability excused its contractual duties under circumstances where IH was losing over two million dollars per day. Although the market shift was drastic, it did not alter the parties' basic assumptions underlying the contract. The court also noted that applying the doctrine of impracticability would contravene the parties' intentions regarding assumption of the risk. Because the contract provided for termination procedures in the event that certain conditions occurred, the court concluded that IH had to bear the risk of financial loss until those procedures were completed; excusing IH's performance would therefore have unfairly burdened the plaintiff dealer.

Similarly, a district court applying Michigan law concluded that a defendant could not assert an impracticability defense based on the economic downturn of 2008. See Flathead-Michigan I, LLC v. Penninsula Dev., LLC, 2011 WL 940048, at *3–4 (E.D. Mich. 2011). The fact that the 2008 market collapse and the ensuing recession were unusually disastrous economic shifts did not excuse the defendant's performance, the court reasoned, because "[t]he state of the market is one of the things on which the parties are gambling when the contract . . . is made." Id. at *4.

Sachsen, however, argues that the impracticability defense should apply because the illegal actions of the Chinese government caused an out-of-the-ordinary drop in the market price for polysilicon. According to Sachsen, the fact that a third party's illegal actions allegedly caused this market shift differentiates the present case from *Karl Wendt* and other cases finding that changes in market conditions are not a basis for the impracticability defense.

The district court disagreed, reasoning that the allegedly illegal actions of the Chinese government were irrelevant because they had "simply caused a market shift in pricing, making it unprofitable for [Sachsen] to perform as promised." In so ruling, the court incorporated its reasoning from the court's decision in Hemlock's case against another company, Kyocera, under a nearly identical LTA. See Hemlock Semiconductor Corp. v. Kyocera Corp., 2016 WL 67596, at *4 (E.D. Mich. 2016). Because Sachsen's argument "amount[ed] only to claims of 'economic unprofitableness,'" the court concluded that the impracticability defense did not apply for the reasons stated in *Karl Wendt*. See id. at *4.

We find the district court's reasoning persuasive. Our research has not revealed any caselaw from either this court or the Michigan courts supporting the proposition that a third party's illegal actions can render the performance of a contract impracticable. Hemlock and Sachsen presumably would not have specifically foreseen the allegedly illegal actions of the Chinese government when the parties entered into the LTAs. But the possibility that the market price for polysilicon could skyrocket or plummet for a myriad of reasons would have been well within their contemplation. The fact that the LTAs provided a fixed price for polysilicon suggests that the parties anticipated that the market price could change and that they wanted to establish a stable price that would operate independently of the market. Allowing Sachsen to escape its obligation to pay that price simply because the purported illegal actions contributed to the price drop would be unfair to Hemlock.

Applying the impracticability defense here could also open up a flood of similar arguments based on allegedly illegal actions of third parties. In the context of global market fluctuations, which can be affected by the actions of many businesses from different countries, defendants in breach-of-contract cases could easily claim that a violation of the law by a third-party actor contributed to a market shift. Allowing parties to litigate the causes of market shifts would swallow the general rule that a contract's unprofitability does not warrant application of the impracticality defense.

We also note that Sachsen could have protected itself against a large drop in the market price of polysilicon during the fourteen-year term of the LTAs by requiring a renegotiation if the market price dropped a certain percentage or dollar amount below the contract price. But no such condition was included in the LTAs despite the sophistication of both the parties and their lawyers. Sachsen thus knowingly assumed the unfiltered risk of a drop in price for a high-tech product during a long-term, fixed-price contract. . . .

Sachsen makes the related argument that the Chinese government's illegal actions frustrated Sachsen's purpose in entering into the LTAs. Frustration of purpose and impracticability are "overlapping defenses." Flathead-Michigan I, 2011 WL 940048, at *4. Both defenses require proof that an unforeseen event altered "a basic assumption on which the contract was made." Liggett Rest. Grp., Inc. v. City of Pontiac, 260 Mich.App. 127, 676 N.W.2d 633, 637 (2003). The frustration-of-purpose defense also requires that the unforeseen event thwart the parties' purpose in making the contract to such a degree that "one party's performance [becomes] virtually worthless to the other." Id. Like the impracticability defense, the frustration-of-purpose defense generally cannot be based on an argument that the continuation of existing market conditions was a "basic assumption" on which the contract was made. Karl Wendt Farm Equip. Co. v. Int'l Harvester Co., 931 F.2d 1112, 1119–20 (6th Cir. 1991). And courts usually will not assume that "mutual profitability" was the primary purpose of a contract.

The frustration-of-purpose defense is inapplicable to the present case for the same reasons that the impracticability defense is inapplicable. Sachsen points to no evidence that the "primary purpose" of the LTAs was anything other than what the district court found it to be—"for Hemlock to provide [Sachsen] with a stable supply of polysilicon at a predictable price." The court incorporated its reasoning from the court's earlier decision in *Kyocera*. Sachsen's frustration-of-purpose argument essentially amounts to a claim that "mutual profitability" was the purpose of the LTAs. But this argument is unconvincing in light of the fact that the LTAs establish a fixed price under which either party could suffer depending on the relationship of the market price to the LTA price. . . .

Sachsen also relies on Chang v. Pacificorp, 212 Or.App. 14, 157 P.3d 243 (2007), an Oregon Court of Appeals decision concluding that the defendant had established a genuine issue of material fact on its impracticability and frustration-of-purpose defenses. In *Chang*, the defendant asserted these defenses based on a third party's illegal manipulation of the Dow COB index, an index of market prices for electricity in the relevant geographic area. Id. at 246. The contract at issue in *Chang* relied on the index in setting prices.

Hemlock convincingly points out that *Chang* is distinguishable because (1) the parties' very purpose in adopting the contract provision in that case was to use the index to allocate risks, and (2) that purpose was frustrated when the index ceased to accurately reflect the true market price for electricity in the relevant geographic area. Here, the contract price was fixed specifically to avoid market fluctuations, just the opposite of the pricing mechanism in *Chang*. We thus agree that *Chang* is readily distinguishable. In sum, the district court did not err in rejecting Sachsen's impracticability and frustration-of-purpose defenses. . . .

COMMENT: RELIEF FOLLOWING DISCHARGE

In Krell v. Henry, as the court pointed out, defendant had abandoned his counterclaim for restitution of the £25 sent in with his letter of June 20.

The court therefore did not have to face the question whether money already paid on the contract must be restored. Also, since the £50 sued for by the plaintiff was not due until the end of the day on which the illness of the king was announced, June 24, the court did not have to face another question—what if the £50 was already due (say on June 22) and unpaid, so that plaintiff's right to that sum was "already acquired"?

Both of these questions were raised the next year in Chandler v. Webster, [1904] 1 K.B. 493, where the Court of Appeal held on very similar facts that (1) money paid down before the king's illness was announced could not be recovered, and (2) money due before the frustrating event must be paid by the hirer of the unused room. The court put it that "the law leaves the parties where they were, and relieves them both from further performance of the contract." It would have been more accurate to say that the parties were to be left at the point where they *contracted* to be at the moment when the unexpected event occurred. The court admitted that this result was "to some extent an arbitrary one," but justified it by saying: "Time has elapsed and the position of both parties may have been more or less altered, and it is impossible to adjust or ascertain the rights of both parties with exactitude." This solution is counterintuitive. The parties were left suspended at the point where they had planned to be when the unforeseen event occurred, despite the conclusion already reached by the court that their contractual plan had been so shattered that the contract could not be enforced.

This solution—suspension in midair, leaving in place obligations already matured—has been rejected by almost all American courts, and was rejected in England in the *Fibrosa* case in 1943 (Fibrosa Spolka Akcyjna v. Fairbairn L.C.B., Ltd., [1943] A.C. 32). But the *Fibrosa* case brought to the surface the problem that evidently made the judge in Chandler v. Webster so uneasy—what if one of the parties, before the supervening event, had made expenditures in preparing to perform? For example, what if the owner of the hired space in Krell v. Henry had erected stands for the onlookers in conformity with the terms of the hiring agreement and these stands were useless for any other purpose? In the *Fibrosa* case, an English manufacturer had agreed to manufacture, deliver, and install, in Poland, textile machinery ordered by Fibrosa, a Polish company. Delivery and installation of the machinery became impossible after the German invasion of Poland and Britain's declaration of war. Of the contract price of £4800, Fibrosa had paid £1000. When Fibrosa demanded return of the £1000, the seller refused to return it on the ground that "considerable work had been done on the machines." Fibrosa's action for restitution ultimately succeeded in the House of Lords; the full £1000 was recovered without any deduction for the seller's loss in work done on this special order. The common law, the judges concluded, "does not attempt to apportion a prepaid sum in such circumstances" and any remedy would have to come from the legislature.

Parliament did respond with the Law Reform (Frustrated Contracts) Act, 1943 (6 & 7 Geo. VI, c. 40). The effect of this statute is to allow restitution of money paid, and of the value of any "benefit" conferred through part performance of a frustrated contract, but, if the court "considers it just to do so," it may allow deduction of expenses incurred by the receiver of the benefit if these expenses were incurred before the supervening event and were "in, or for the purpose of, the performance of the contract." Thus, a compromise was struck. The following opinion tries to apply it.

Gamerco SA v. ICM/Fair Warning (Agency) Limited

High Court, Queen's Bench Division, 1995.
[1995] E.M.L.R. 263.

GARLAND, J. The plaintiffs, a Spanish corporation, are pop concert promoters. The second defendants, Missouri Storm Incorporated, are the corporate persona of the group Guns 'n' Roses. The group proposed to tour Europe from mid-May until early July of 1992. There would be some twenty-four open air concerts in twelve countries. The venues were for the most part sports stadia such as Wembley, the Olympic Stadium in Berlin and the Feijenoord Stadium in Rotterdam. The last three concerts were to be in Lisbon, Madrid and another venue in Spain, preferably Barcelona. The agency which undertook the organisation of the tour was the first defendant, ICM Fair Warning Agency Limited, the moving spirit of which was Mr. John Jackson. His task was to select promoters in the countries where the group was to perform and to negotiate contracts on its behalf. The plaintiff corporation was the chosen promoter in Spain. The director most actively involved was Guy Mercader, who gave evidence. Another director who gave evidence was Francisco Martinez. The plaintiffs' offices are in Barcelona, but they promote pop concerts throughout Spain. They make use of service companies locally: in this case Osbon SA, which is based in Madrid. The local service company would be responsible for obtaining necessary permits and supplying labour to prepare the venue.

The second defendants took with them on tour specialist contractors for sound, video, lighting, catering and transport together with members of their own staff. Apart from the six members of the group there were twenty 'band touring personnel' and seventy-six 'crew touring personnel,' of whom approximately thirty were either staff or self-employed under a corporate identity. The transport required was a Boeing 727 chartered from MGM Grand Air for fifty-three days, ten articulated trucks, two generator trucks, four twelve-berth sleeper coaches and one fourteen-berth, all hired with drivers for fifty-three days.

In the event, the tour consisted of twenty concerts in the twelve countries with a promoter in each country. So far as these proceedings are concerned, the plaintiffs were to promote a concert on 4 July in Madrid, guaranteeing the second defendants $1.1 million or 90% of the net door receipts, whichever was the greater. The plaintiffs were responsible for erecting the stage (through Belgian contractors, Stageco), the roof and generally preparing the venue. The group's previous engagement was in Lisbon on 2 July. The original itinerary had been 27 June: Turin; 28

June: Rome; 2 July: Lisbon. No concert was arranged in Rome, but on 1 July there was an additional concert in Seville.

These proceedings have arisen because the Madrid concert was to take place in the Vincente Calderon Stadium (the home of Atletico Madrid) but on 30 June engineers reported that the stadium was constructed with high alumina cement (HAC) and that it could not safely be used until further investigations had been carried out. On 1 July both the Madrid City Council and the appropriate arm of central government banned the use of the stadium. The permit to hold the event was revoked. The parties became aware of these events early on 2 July.

Attempts were made to find an alternative venue. The other large stadium, the Bernabeu (home of Real Madrid), was undergoing repairs. The Rockodromo had been closed for two years and was in no fit state to be used. The owners of the Jarama motor racing circuit would not allow it to be used; the police objected to the use of the racecourse; and other football grounds were too small to accommodate the holders of the 44,500 tickets that had been sold. On 3 July there were press releases and public announcements cancelling the concert. The plaintiffs had paid the second defendants $412,500 on account. There was a balance of $362,500—both sums net of tax. In fact the plaintiffs had arranged for the balance to be paid on 30 June, but due to an error by the bank this had not been effected by the time of the cancellation when the plaintiffs wanted their money back. There is an issue of fact whether on 3 July Mr. Goldstein of the second defendants had told Guy Mercader that the defendants would pay back the $412,500. Both parties had incurred expenses in preparation for the concert. . . .

The contract was to appear and actually to give a performance at the Vincente Calderon starting at 22.30 lasting 90 minutes. This could not be done, not because a permit was revoked but because the stadium had been found to be unsafe. In any event it was impossible for the defendants to perform their side of the bargain; they could not appear in the stadium any more than the plaintiffs could perform their obligations to erect the stage, the roof and generally to prepare the venue. . . .

The contract having been discharged by frustration, the plaintiffs were entitled to recover from the second defendants the advance payment of $412,500 (less the sum returned by the first defendants) by virtue of . . . the 1943 Act which is in the following terms:

> All sums paid or payable to any party in pursuance of a contract before the time when the parties were so discharged (in this Act referred to as 'the time of discharge') shall, in the case of sums so paid, be recoverable from him as money received by him for the use of the party by whom the sums were paid, and, in the case of sums so payable, cease to be payable. . . .
>
> Provided that, if the party to whom the sums were so paid or payable incurred expenses before the time of discharge in, or for

> the purpose of, the performance of the contract, the court may, if it considers it just so to do, having regard to all the circumstances of the case, allow him to retain or, as the case may be, recover the whole or any part of the sums so paid or payable, not being an amount in excess of the expenses so incurred. . . .
>
> In estimating, for the purposes of the foregoing provisions of this section, the amount of any expenses incurred by any parties to the contract, the court may, without prejudice to the generality of the said provisions, include such sum as appears to be reasonable in respect of overhead expenses and in respect of any work or services performed personally by the said party. . . .

. . . The defendants' claim for expenses was set out as a schedule to their defence and counterclaim. . . .

. . . Some of the salaries in Schedule 1 appear to relate to persons other than those included in the lists 'Band Touring Personnel' and 'Crew Touring Personnel' but may be admissible in a calculation of overheads . . . . 'Labour costs' includes three of the group but not Axl Rose, Slash and Duff McKagen, and includes the more exotic members of the retinue, the Witch Doctor and Masseuse. . . .

The 'per diem' is a cash payment of dollars per day to forty-seven of the total retinue. There was virtually no evidence at all of those payments.

These expenses had been calculated at two-sevenths of weekly rates on the basis that they were 'incurred' in respect of 4 and 5 July, as have the hotel bills under '*Accommodations*.'

'*Production'* refers to four contractors engaged for the whole tour, as were MGM Grand Air, Transam Trucking (who supplied the articulated trucks and generator trucks) and Wharfedale Coaches (who provided the sleeper coaches). The defendants have taken two fifty-thirds of the total cost, the tour lasting fifty-three days. The plaintiffs' argument is that the labour costs were not incurred specifically for the concert in Madrid but for the whole European tour. There was a performance in Lisbon on 2 July. Costs would have been incurred on 3 July. Mr. Oppenheim's evidence was that some staff would have been retained for the next tour, possibly on half pay, and some laid off. All wage slips produced are for the period 1 to 15 July which suggests that the staff concerned would have been paid, Madrid concert or no.

Very similar considerations apply to the Production and Travel costs. To what extent they can be said to have been incurred 'in or for the purpose of' the performance of this contract is a very open question on which I would have welcomed a great deal more assistance than the defendants were prepared to offer.

So far as '*Accommodations'* are concerned, the plaintiffs say that these cannot have been 'incurred' before 2 July as hotel costs are conventionally incurred from day to day. Clearly, with such a large retinue advance booking was essential, but no evidence was given that these costs were incurred as a result of reservations which could not be cancelled for 4 and 5 July, and they were general living expenses which would (like the labour costs) have been incurred in any event.

The plaintiffs' further submission is that the contract was, as a matter of law, discharged on 2 July. The defendants therefore have to demonstrate that any claimed expense was incurred before that date. They have not sought to address the point and have based their claims on expenses arising on 4 and 5 July. . . .

The best I can do is to accept that the defendants did incur some expenses, but the extent of them is wholly unproven except in relation to liability and cancellation insurances which, at the end of the day, were not seriously in contention. It is the case of doing the best I can, but on the evidence available to me I arrive at a figure of $50,000. . . .

It is self-evident that any rigid rule is liable to produce injustice. . . . I see no indication in the Act, the authorities, or the relevant literature that the court is obliged to incline either towards total retention or equal division. Its task is to do justice in a situation which the parties neither contemplated nor provided for, and to mitigate the possible harshness of allowing all loss to lie where it has fallen.

I have not found my task easy. As I have made clear, I would have welcomed assistance on the true measure of the defendants' loss and the proper treatment of overhead and non-specific expenditure. Because the defendants have plainly suffered some loss, I have made a robust assumption. In all the circumstances, and having particular regard to the plaintiffs' loss, I consider that justice is done by making no deduction under the proviso. . . .

I therefore allow the plaintiffs' claim for $412,500 without set-off and dismiss the counterclaim. The plaintiffs will be entitled to interest, and I ask if the declaration sought in the statement of claim is still sought in view of the finding that I have made.

Facto v. Pantagis

Superior Court of New Jersey, Appellate Division, 2007.
390 N.J. Super. 227, 915 A.2d 59.

SKILLMAN, P.J.A.D. This is a breach of contract action arising out of the cancellation of a wedding reception due to a power failure.

Plaintiffs contracted with defendant Snuffy Pantagis Ent., Inc., t/a Pantagis Renaissance, a banquet hall in Scotch Plains, for a wedding reception for 150 people, to be held between 6 p.m. and 11 p.m. on Saturday, August 3, 2002. The total contract price was $10,578, all of which was to be paid in advance. The contract contained a *force majeure* clause, which stated: "Snuffy's will be excused from performance under this contract if it is prevented from doing so by an act of God (e.g., flood, power failure, etc.), or other unforeseen events or circumstances."

Less than forty-five minutes after the reception began, there was a power failure in the area where the Pantagis Renaissance is located. At the time, plaintiffs were in an upstairs room with the bridal party, and their guests were downstairs being served alcoholic beverages and hors d'oeuvres. The power failure caused all the lights, except emergency lights, to go out and the air conditioning system to shut off. In addition, the band plaintiffs had hired for the reception refused to play without lights or the electricity required to operate their instruments, and the lack of lighting impeded the wedding photographer and videographer from taking pictures.

On the day of the reception, the temperature was in the upper 80s or low 90s and the humidity was high. As a result, plaintiffs and their guests became extremely uncomfortable within a short time after the power failure. According to plaintiffs, some of the guests resorted to pouring water over their heads to keep cool.

When it became evident that electricity would not be restored quickly, the manager of the Pantagis Renaissance offered to reschedule the reception. However, many of plaintiffs' guests had traveled a substantial distance to attend the wedding and would not have been able to return on another date. Therefore, plaintiffs declined the offer.

There was some dispute regarding the services provided after the power failure. Plaintiffs testified that the Pantagis Renaissance stopped serving alcoholic beverages around 7:30 p.m. and that the only food it served in addition to hors d'oeuvres was salad. However, the banquet hall's general manager testified that the facility continued to serve alcoholic beverages until after 9 p.m. and that it served plaintiffs and their guests salad and pasta and started to serve them dinner.

Shortly after 9 p.m., there was some kind of altercation between one of plaintiffs' guests and an employee of the Pantagis Renaissance. As a result, the banquet hall called the police, who arrived around 9:30 p.m. By this time, the batteries operating the emergency lights had begun to run out of power, and the only illumination was provided by candelabras on the tables. Therefore, the manager of the Pantagis Renaissance asked the police to evacuate the facility, which was then occupied not only by plaintiffs and their guests but also the attendees at four other wedding receptions.

Plaintiffs subsequently brought this breach of contract action seeking recovery of the $10,578 they prepaid for the wedding reception plus the $6,000 paid to the band, $3,810 paid to the wedding photographer and $3,242.09 paid to the videographer. Plaintiffs' complaint also asserted a negligence claim.

The case was tried in a half-day bench trial. The trial court concluded in a brief oral opinion that plaintiffs' breach of contract claim was barred by the *force majeure* clause of the contract because the power failure was an "unusual extraordinary unexpected circumstance" that could not be avoided by "reasonable human foresight." . . .

[T]he Pantagis Renaissance was "prevented from" substantial performance of the contract. The power failure began less than forty-five minutes after the start of the reception and continued until after it was scheduled to end. The lack of electricity prevented the band from playing, impeded the taking of pictures by the photographer and videographer and made it difficult for guests to see inside the banquet hall. Most significantly, the shutdown of the air conditioning system made it unbearably hot shortly after the power failure began. It is also undisputed that the power failure was an area-wide event that was beyond the Pantagis Renaissance's control. These are precisely the kind of circumstances under which the parties agreed, by inclusion of the *force majeure* clause, that the Pantagis Renaissance would be excused from performance. Therefore, the trial court correctly concluded that defendants did not breach the contract.

However, the court erred in concluding that because defendants did not breach the contract, plaintiffs are not entitled to recover the money they prepaid for the wedding reception. Where one party to a contract is excused from performance as a result of an unforeseen event that makes performance impracticable, the other party is also generally excused from performance. As explained in *Corbin:*

> A promisor should not be compelled to give something for nothing. The parties agreed upon an exchange of performances, and an exchange cannot now take place. Even if not stated in express terms, the promisor's duty is constructively conditional on the return performance by the promisee. Even though the nonperforming promissee is not in default because the impossibility doctrine discharges the duty, it cannot demand something for nothing from the other party. [14 Corbin on Contracts § 78.2 (Perillo rev. 2001).]

The same rule applies if a party to a contract is excused from performance by a *force majeure* clause that expressly sets forth certain categories of unforeseen events that will render performance impracticable. Therefore, the power failure that relieved the Pantagis Renaissance of the obligation to furnish plaintiffs with a wedding reception also relieved plaintiffs of the obligation to pay the contract price for the reception.

Nevertheless, since the Pantagis Renaissance partially performed the contract by starting the reception before the power failure, it is entitled, under principles of quantum meruit, to recover the value of the services it provided to plaintiffs. . . .Accordingly, the final judgment dismissing plaintiffs' complaint is reversed and the case is remanded to the trial court for further proceedings in conformity with this opinion.

Carroll v. Bowersock

Supreme Court of Kansas, 1917.
100 Kan. 270, 164 P. 143.

[Plaintiff agreed to construct a reinforced concrete floor in defendant's warehouse. After removing the old floor, plaintiff put in concrete footings, built wooden forms for concrete pillars to support the floor, and installed reinforcing rods in these column forms. The warehouse was then totally destroyed by fire, without the fault of either party. Plaintiff sued to recover for his performance prior to the fire, prevailing in the trial court. Defendant appealed.]

BURCH, J. . . . It is apparent that the [trial] court permitted recovery for substantially what the plaintiff had done by way of performance of the contract before the fire.

The contract was to place the floor in a specific warehouse. Destruction of the warehouse without fault of either party put an end to construction of a floor in that warehouse. No warehouse except the one destroyed having been contemplated or contracted about, the defendant could not be charged with delinquency for not building another. . . . If continued existence of the particular warehouse to which the contract related were not taken for granted by both parties, the plaintiff would be bound by his contract and could not recover at all, no concrete floor having been constructed.

It was not material that the defendant collected insurance on the warehouse, purchased before the contract was made. The insurance covered nothing but property of the defendant. He paid for the insurance and was entitled to it, just as the plaintiff would have been entitled to insurance on his property had he seen fit to insure. If any part of the plaintiff's labor and material was incorporated into the insured building, so that the insurance covered it as substance of the structure, the plaintiff can recover, if at all, not because of the insurance, but because of the incorporation.

If a contractor should engage to furnish all labor and material and build a house, and the house should burn before completion, the loss falls on him. If a contractor should engage to refloor two rooms of a house already in existence, and should complete one room before the house burned, he ought to be paid something. So far the authorities are in substantial agreement.

The principle upon which the contractor may recover in [the reflooring] case [is that] [p]erformance was prevented without fault of either party, and the true rule is that neither party can be charged with delinquency because the contract cannot be fulfilled.

The contractor cannot give and the owner cannot obtain that which they contracted about. . . . [T]he law must deal with the new situation of the parties created by the fire. The owner cannot be called on to reimburse the contractor merely because the contractor has been to expense in taking steps tending to performance. A contractor may have purchased special material to be used in repairing a house, and may have had much mill work done upon it. If the material remain in the mill and the house burn, there can be no recovery. If the milled material be delivered at the house ready for use, and the house burn, there can be no recovery. It takes something more to make the owner liable for what the contractor has done toward performance. The owner must be benefited. . . . The only basis on which the law can raise an obligation on the part of the owner is the consideration he has received by way of benefit, advantage, or value to him.

The question whether or not the owner has been benefited frequently presents difficulties. Sometimes the question is answered by the owner's own conduct, as when by taking possession, or by insuring as his own property, or by other act, he evinces a purpose to appropriate the contractor's material and labor. Sometimes the circumstances are such that the owner is precluded from rejecting the fruits of the contractor's efforts if he would, as when one room is finished under a contract to refloor two. In such cases it merely confuses the matter to bring in the terms "acceptance," "assent," and similar expressions indicative of the owner's attitude. If he should pay, it is not because assent or acceptance of benefit is "implied," or because he is "regarded as accepting benefit," but because of the fact that he has been benefited.

The test of benefit received has been variously stated. Sometimes it is said that benefit accrues whenever the contractor's material and labor, furnished and performed according to the contract, have become attached to the owner's realty. The facts of particular cases suggest different forms of expression. . . . [We are] inclined to approve the form adopted [in] Young v. Chicopee, 186 Mass. 518, 72 N.E. 63. . . . The action was one for labor and material furnished to repair a bridge destroyed by fire while the work was proceeding. The contract required at least half of the material to be "upon the job" before work commenced. The contractor complied with this condition, and distributed material "all along the bridge" and on the river bank. A portion of the material thus distributed but not wrought into the structure was destroyed by fire. Liability for work done upon and material wrought into the structure was not disputed, but the contractor sought to make good his entire loss. The [Massachusetts] court said: "[I]t would seem that the liability of the owner in a case like this should be measured by the amount of the contract work done which, at the time of the destruction of the structure, had become so far identified with it as that but for the destruction it would have inured to him as contemplated by the contract." 186 Mass. 546, 72 N.E. 64.

Applying the test stated[,] it is clear that the plaintiff should recover for the work done in cutting the old floor away from the wall and in removing such part of the old floor as was necessary. The warehouse was improved to that extent by labor, the benefit of which had inured to the defendant when the fire occurred. If the fire had not occurred, the undesirable floor would have been out of the way, precisely as the contract contemplated. Likewise, the contractor should recover for the completed concrete footings.

The contractor should not recover for material furnished or labor performed in the construction of either column or floor forms. They were temporary devices, employed to give form to the structure which was to be produced. They were not themselves wrought into the warehouse, were to be removed when the work was completed, and inured to nobody's benefit but that of the contractor. The contractor should not recover for either upright or floor rods, or for the labor of putting them in place. While the rods were wired together, they were not attached to the building and would not have been wrought into the structure until the concrete was poured. If the fire had not occurred the contractor could have removed the rods without dismembering or defacing the warehouse, and the defendant could not have held the rods as amalgamated into the fabric of his structure. There should be no recovery for superintendence and use of tools, except as regards that part of the work done which had become identified with the warehouse itself. Other items sued for should be allowed or disallowed by application of the principle indicated. . . .

The defendant says . . . that cutting away the old floor from the walls of the building and concrete footings for a floor which was never laid were of no value to him. The test is whether or not the work would have inured to his benefit as contemplated by the contract if the fire had not occurred. The cutting away of the old floor was done according to the contract, and the defendant had the benefit of that work as soon as it was finished. . . . [P]utting in the concrete footings was the next step in the construction. . . . Those footings would have inured to his benefit [if] the fire had not occurred. They became a part of his warehouse. . . . [H]e was benefited by them at the time of their incorporation into his structure. Test of a completed concrete floor was one of the things rendered impossible by the fire. . . .

The judgment of the district court is reversed, and the cause is remanded with direction to take such additional evidence as may be necessary and determine the rights of the parties according to the views which have been expressed.

JOHNSTON, C.J. (dissenting, joined by DAWSON, J.). I am of the opinion that the upright rods set up and tied together were a part of the building, and a recovery for them should be allowed.

Albre Marble and Tile Co., Inc. v. John Bowen Co.

Supreme Judicial Court of Massachusetts, 1959.
338 Mass. 394.

SPALDING, JUSTICE. The declaration in this action of contract contains four counts. The plaintiff in counts 1 and 2 seeks damages for the defendant's alleged breach of two subcontracts under which the plaintiff agreed to supply labor and materials to the defendant as general contractor of the Chronic Disease Hospital and Nurses' Home in Boston. In counts 3 and 4 the plaintiff seeks to recover the value of work and labor furnished by it to the defendant at the defendant's request. The defendant's substitute answer in defence to the first two counts states that the performance of the subcontracts became impossible when the defendant's general contract with the Commonwealth was declared invalid by this court in Gifford v. Commissioner of Public Health, 328 Mass. 608, 105 N.E.2d 476. The defendant's answer to counts 3 and 4 (based on quantum meruit) states that no payment could be demanded because the plaintiff did not possess an architect's certificate for the work done; and that in no event could the defendant be required to pay the plaintiff until it was itself paid by the Commonwealth, and it had received no such payments except those which had been made before the Gifford decision. . . .

The defendant in its affidavit maintains that the tile and marble work to be furnished by the plaintiff could not have been done until late in the construction process; that no tile or marble was actually installed in the building; and that the expenses incurred by the plaintiff prior to the time the general contract was declared invalid consisted solely of expenditures in preparation for performance. [T]he defendant maintains that where a building contract has been rendered impossible of performance a plaintiff may not recover for expenses incurred in preparation for performance, but may recover only for the labor and materials 'wrought into' the structure. Therefore, the defendant says, the plaintiff should take nothing here.

The plaintiff places its reliance upon a clause appearing in both contracts which provides in part: "It is agreed you [the plaintiff] will furnish and submit all necessary or required samples, shop drawings, tests, affidavits, etc., for approval, all as ordered or specified . . . ." The plaintiff in effect concedes that no labor or materials were actually wrought into the structure, but argues that the contract provision quoted above placed its preparatory efforts under the supervision of the defendant, and that this circumstance removes this case from the ambit of those decisions which apply the 'wrought-in' principle. . . .

The problem of allocating losses where a building contract has been rendered impossible of performance by a supervening act not chargeable to either party is a vexed one. In situations where the part performance of one party measurably exceeds that of the other the tendency has been to allow recovery for the fair value of work done in the actual performance of the contract and to deny recovery for expenditures made in reliance upon the contract or in preparing to perform. This principle has sometimes been expressed in terms of 'benefit' or 'lack of benefit.' In other words, recovery may be had only for those expenditures which, but for the supervening act, would have enured to the benefit of the defendant as contemplated by the contract. The 'wrought-in' principle applied in building contract cases is merely a variant of this principle. . . .

Although the matter of denial of reliance expenditures in impossibility situations seems to have been discussed but little in judicial opinions, it has, however, been the subject of critical comment by scholars. In England the recent frustrated contracts legislation provides that the court may grant recovery for expenditures in reliance on the contract or in preparation to perform it where it appears '*just to do so having regard to all the circumstances of the case*' (emphasis supplied). 6 & 7 George VI, c. 40.

We are of opinion that the plaintiff here may recover for those expenditures made pursuant to the specific request of the defendant as set forth in the contract clause quoted above. A combination of factors peculiar to this case justifies such a holding without laying down the broader principle that in every case recovery may be had for payments made or obligations reasonably incurred in preparation for performance of a contract where further performance is rendered impossible without fault by either party.

The factors which determine the holding here are these: First, this is not a case of mere impossibility by reason of a supervening act. The opinion of this court in M. Ahern Co. v. John Bowen Co. Inc., 334 Mass. 36, 133 N.E.2d 484, points out that the defendant's involvement in creating the impossibility was greater than that of its subcontractors. The facts regarding the defendant's conduct are set forth in that opinion and need not be restated. Although the defendant's conduct was not so culpable as to render it liable for breach of contract, nevertheless, it was a contributing factor to a loss sustained by the plaintiff which as between the plaintiff and the defendant the latter ought to bear to the extent herein permitted.

We attach significance to the clause in the contract, which was prepared by the defendant, specifically requesting the plaintiff to submit samples, shop drawings, tests, affidavits, etc., to the defendant. This is not a case in which all efforts in preparation for performance were solely within the discretion and control of the subcontractor. We are mindful that in Young v. Chicopee, 186 Mass. 518, 72 N.E. 63, recovery of the value of materials brought to the construction site at the specific request of the defendant therein was denied. But in that case the supervening act rendering further performance impossible was a fire not shown to have been caused by the fault of either party. We are not disposed to extend that holding to a situation in which the defendant's fault is greater than the plaintiff's.

Moreover, the acts requested here by their very nature could not be 'wrought into' the structure. In Angus v. Scully, 176 Mass. 357, 57 N.E. 674, recovery for the value of services rendered by house movers was allowed although the house was destroyed midway in the moving. The present case comes nearer to the rationale of the *Angus* case than to that of the *Young* case. . . .

CHAPTER 5

CONDITIONS AND THE INTERDEPENDENCE OF PROMISES

INTRODUCTORY NOTE

Conditions are a pervasive feature of contracts, and their basic features can be readily summarized. The Second Restatement of Contracts in § 224 defines a condition as "an event, not certain to occur, which must occur, unless its nonoccurence is excused, before performance under a contract becomes due." Conditions are often within the control of the parties, but they need not be. The law of contracts enforces such conditions according to their terms, but problems of interpretation inevitably arise. For example, consider a general contractor who promises to pay its subcontractor when it is paid. Is the effect of this language merely to provide an estimate of the time at which the subcontractor is going to be paid or does it condition the general contractor's obligation upon its own receipt of payment? In other words, when a general contractor uses this language is it effectively shifting the risk of nonpayment to the subcontractor?

The impossibility and frustration cases in the last chapter can be seen as about implicit conditions. Henry's obligation to pay for the apartment was implicitly conditioned on the coronation taking place as scheduled. In the case of implicit conditions, we need to flesh them out in the same fashion that we flesh out promises. We need to identify a set of conditions to serve as default rules.

Performance of the promise by each party is ordinarily itself a condition of the other's obligation to perform. As we shall see, at common law, each party's promise was first thought independent and stood on its own. Only in the late eighteenth century did the law change. It became established that, when one party fails to perform, the other party, in addition to being able to sue for damages, has the right to call off her own performance. She can refuse to perform, and she will have a defense against any action the other side might bring against her for her refusal to keep her own promise. The failure of the other party to satisfy a condition, in other words, gives the innocent party both a sword (the ability to bring a damage action) and a shield (a defense against any effort by the other party to sue for breach).

In the case of a one-shot sale of goods, the innocent party can insist on goods whose condition complies perfectly with the other party's contractual obligations. This is the "perfect tender rule." The rule, however, is not as demanding as it might first appear. The test is not whether the goods are perfect in some Platonic sense, but rather whether they correspond to the obligations under the contract. Corn can contain up to 4 percent foreign matter and still pass in the trade as No. 2 grade corn. Hence, a buyer of No. 2

grade corn has no right to refuse a delivery that is 3 percent dirt. There is still perfect tender, as even a shipment with this much dirt still complies with the contract description.

There is greater room for slack when the dispute is over something other than the condition of goods. As a general matter, in the absence of an agreement to the contrary, only a breach of a material promise (or, to say the same thing, a failure to perform substantially) gives the other a right to cease performance and walk away from her own obligations.

To begin our study of conditions, we focus upon the basic question of the interdependence of promises and conditions and examine how the law took its present shape.

SECTION 1. THE INTERDEPENDENCE OF PROMISES

Nichols v. Raynbred

Court of King's Bench, 1615.
Hobart, 88.

Nichols brought an assumpsit against Raynbred, declaring that in consideration that Nichols promised to deliver the defendant to his own use a cow, the defendant promised to deliver him 50 shillings: adjudged for the plaintiff in both courts, that the plaintiff need not aver the delivery of the cow, because it is promise for promise. Note here the promises must be at one instant, for else they will both be nuda pacta.

COMMENT: THE DEPENDENCY OF PROMISES

Nichols v. Raynbred illustrates early attitudes toward what is now described as "the dependency of mutual promises." Is this not a strange way to look at an agreement consisting of promises—by their terms, unqualified and unconditional—to exchange goods or services for a stated price? Again, some historical perspective is needed.

The problem of "dependency" had not been particularly troublesome before the time of this case. For those informal promises enforced through the action of debt, the requirement of *quid pro quo* meant that the performance for which the money was promised must have been already rendered—i.e., the plaintiff's half of the exchange would have had to be completed. When special assumpsit became available in the sixteenth century, the whole emphasis was on what we now call the unilateral contract, where the defendant-promisor who had not performed was again protected through having secured the other party's performance. In other words, the experience of the early common law (say, before 1600) was very heavily focused on the unilateral type of obligation, while the assumption here is that "dependency" is almost entirely a problem of bilateral contracts.

The issue of "dependency" could arise, of course, in connection with agreements under seal. It was entirely possible for two persons, in the same sealed instrument, to make "covenants" to each other, looking forward ultimately to an exchange of performances. The question then would be whether one covenantee could sue the other without having given or tendered performance. The answer provided by Chief Justice Fineux in a Year Book case in 1500 was this:

> If one covenant with me to serve me for a year, and I covenant with him to give him £20, if I do not say "for the same cause," he shall have an action for the £20, although he never serves me; otherwise, if I say he shall have £20 "for the same cause." So if I covenant with a man that I will marry his daughter, and he covenants with me to make an estate to me and his daughter, and to the heirs of our two bodies begotten; though I afterwards marry another woman, or his daughter marry another man; yet I shall have an action of covenant against him, to compel him to make this estate; but if the covenant be that he will make the estate to us "for the same cause," then he shall not make the estate until we are married.

The report concludes that "such was the opinion of the court," and Rede, J., said "it is so without doubt." Y.B. 15 Henry VII, fol. 10b, pl. 17 (1500). You will note that there is in this passage a notion of "dependency" in rudimentary form; the insertion of the small phrase "for the same cause" would suffice to tie the two performances together in each of the cases supposed. This is probably as far as one could expect construction to be carried by common lawyers at this stage.

Nichols v. Raynbred indicates that literalism was transferred from sealed instruments to informal promises enforced through assumpsit, during the early period when assumpsit was expanding. Indeed, there is much evidence to suggest that the same attitudes persisted and were even extended during the next 150 years. An illustration is the King's Bench decision in 1669, Pordage v. Cole, 1 Wms. Saunders 319, which became notorious for various reasons. In this case, a vendor of land sued the vendee at law, relying on an instrument under seal in which the vendee promised £775 for the lands in question, to be paid before a particular day which had passed by the time of the action. The vendor did not expressly promise to convey the lands; there was merely the statement that the vendee promised the vendor £775 "for all his lands," but with this phrase it would seem that even the requirements of Fineux, J., back in 1500, had been satisfied. The defendant demurred to the vendor's declaration, relying mainly on the ground that "the plaintiff in his declaration has not averred that he had conveyed the lands, or at least tendered a conveyance of them; for the defendant has no remedy to obtain the lands, and therefore the plaintiff ought to have conveyed them, or tendered a conveyance of them, before he brought his action for the money." But the demurrer was overruled. The court stated that the language of the instrument "amounted" to a promise by the vendor to convey the land and the defendant therefore had a remedy of covenant for damages if the vendor did not convey. The only qualification was the admission that "it might be otherwise" if no promise by the vendor to convey could be extracted from the language of the instrument.

There were in this period some expressions of dissatisfaction with results like that of Pordage v. Cole. The best known complaint is that of Willes, C.J., (reported in Willes, 496) who, in 1744, referred to his dislike of "those cases, though they are too many to be now overruled, where it is determined that the breach of one covenant, though plainly relative to the other, cannot be pleaded in bar to an action brought for the breach of the other, but the other party must be left to bring his action for the breach of the other; as where there are two covenants in a deed, the one for repairing and the other for finding timber for the reparations; this notion plainly tending to make two actions instead of one, and to a circuity of action and multiplying actions, both which the law so much abhors." Willes suggested that the defendant should at least be permitted to plead the plaintiff's failure to render the performance promised, though he (Willes) would not impose on the plaintiff the burden of pleading and proving performance affirmatively. Willes concluded, however, that "this has been so often determined otherwise, that it is too late now to alter the law in this respect." He evidently did not foresee the towering Scot, Lord Mansfield.

In the procedures criticized by Willes, is the only objection circuity and multiplication of actions? Doesn't the central problem look familiar, though we now see it through a different telescope? Recall, again, that the typical contract has a performing party and a paying party, and that, because each acts separately, the party who is required by the contract to perform first is in need of protection against a failure by the other.

Before leaving the pre-Mansfield history, we should note that Pordage v. Cole achieved immortality by a strange kind of transmigration. After Mansfield had done his work and retired from the bench, Serjeant Williams, a prominent lawyer and law reporter, sought to summarize the results of Mansfield's innovations through a statement of "rules" appended as a note to Pordage v. Cole. The publication did not occur until 1791, long after the whole structure of common law doctrine on which Pordage v. Cole (decided in 1669) rested had been undermined. The result was a confusing picture for later generations. Serjeant Williams' "rules" have been much quoted and we will see something of them. But first a look at Lord Mansfield and the decision which set in motion the modern machinery of the bilateral contract.

Kingston v. Preston

Court of King's Bench, 1773.
2 Doug. 689.

This was an action of debt, for nonperformance of covenants contained in certain articles of agreement between the plaintiff and the defendant.

The declaration stated [t]hat, by articles made the 24th of March 1770, the plaintiff, for the considerations thereinafter mentioned, covenanted, with the defendant, to serve him for one year and a quarter next ensuing, as a covenant-servant, in his trade of a silk-mercer at £200 a year, and in consideration of the premises, the defendant covenanted, that at the end of the year and a quarter, he would give up his business of a mercer to the plaintiff, and a nephew of the defendant, or some other person to be nominated by the defendant, and give up to them his stock in trade, at a fair valuation; and that, between the young traders, deeds of partnership should be executed for 14 years, and, from and immediately after the execution of the said deeds, the defendant would permit the said young traders to carry on the said business in the defendant's house.

Then the declaration stated a covenant by the plaintiff, that he would accept the business and stock in trade, at a fair valuation, with the defendant's nephew, or such other person, etc. and execute such deeds of partnership, and, further, that the plaintiff should, and would, at, and before the sealing and delivery of the deeds, cause and procure good and sufficient security to be given to the defendant, to be approved of by the defendant, for the payment of £250 monthly, to the defendant, in lieu of a moiety of the monthly produce of the stock in trade, until the value of the stock should be reduced to £4000.

Then the plaintiff averred, that he had performed, and been ready to perform, his covenants, and assigned for breach, on the part of the defendant, that he had refused to surrender and give up his business, at the end of the said year and a quarter.

The defendant pleaded, 1. That the plaintiff did not offer sufficient security; and, 2. That he did not give sufficient security for the payment of the £250 etc.

And the plaintiff demurred generally to both pleas.

On the part of the plaintiff, the case was argued by Mr. Buller, who contended, that the covenants were mutual and independent, and, therefore, a plea of the breach of one of the covenants to be performed by the plaintiff was no bar to an action for a breach by the defendant of one of which he had bound himself to perform, but that the defendant might have his remedy for the breach by the plaintiff, in a separate action. On the other side, Mr. Grose insisted, that the covenants were dependent in their nature, and, therefore, performance must be alleged: The security to be given for the money, was manifestly the chief object of the transaction, and it would be highly unreasonable to construe the agreement, so as to oblige the defendant to give up a beneficial business, and valuable stock in trade, and trust to the plaintiff's personal security, (who might, and indeed was admitted to be worth nothing,) for the performance of his part.

National Portrait Gallery, London

WILLIAM MURRAY, EARL OF MANSFIELD
1705–1793

In delivering the judgment of the court, Lord Mansfield expressed himself to the following effect:

There are three kinds of covenants: 1. Such as are called mutual and independent, where either party may recover damages from the other, for the injury he may have received by a breach of the covenants in his favour, and where it is no excuse for the defendant, to allege a breach of the covenants on the part of the plaintiff. 2. There are covenants which are conditions and dependent, in which the performance of one depends on the prior performance of another, and, therefore, till this prior condition is performed, the other party is not liable to an action on his covenant. 3. There is also a third sort of covenants, which are mutual conditions to be performed at the same time; and, in these, if one party was ready, and offered, to perform his part, and the other neglected, or refused to perform his, he who was ready, and offered, has fulfilled his engagement, and may maintain an action for the default of the other; though it is not certain that either is obliged to do the first act.

His Lordship then proceeded to say, that the dependence or independence of covenants was to be collected from the evident sense and meaning of the parties, and, that, however transposed they might be in the deed, their precedency must depend on the order of time in which the intent of the transaction requires their performance. That, in the case before the court, it would be the greatest injustice if the plaintiff should prevail: The essence of the agreement was, that the defendant should not trust to the personal security of the plaintiff, but, before he delivered up his stock and business, should have good security for the payment of the money. The giving such security, therefore, must necessarily be a condition precedent.

Judgment was accordingly given for the defendant, because the part to be performed by the plaintiff was clearly a condition precedent.

---

5 S. Williston, Contracts

§ 619 (3d ed. 1961)

"Since an express condition, like a condition implied in fact, depends for its validity on the manifested intention of the parties, it has the same sanctity as the promise itself. Though the court may regret the harshness of such a condition, as it may regret the harshness of a promise, it must, nevertheless, generally enforce the will of the parties unless to do so would violate public policy. Where, however, the law itself has ['constructively'] imposed the condition, in absence of or irrespective of the manifested intention of the parties, it can deal with its creation as it pleases, shaping the boundaries of the constructive condition in such a way as to do justice and avoid hardship."

Restatement of Contracts, Second

§ 234. Order of Performances

(1) Where all or part of the performances to be exchanged under an exchange of promises can be rendered simultaneously, they are to that extent due simultaneously, unless the language or the circumstances indicate the contrary.

Comment: . . .

b. When simultaneous performance possible under agreement. . . . Cases in which simultaneous performance is possible under the terms of the contract can be grouped into five categories: (1) where the same time is fixed for the performance of each party; (2) where a time is fixed for the performance of one of the parties and no time is fixed for the other; (3) where no time is fixed for the performance of either party; (4) where the same period is fixed within which each party is to perform; (5) where different periods are fixed within which each party is to perform. The requirement of simultaneous performance applies to the first four categories. . . .

§ 238. Effect on Other Party's Duties of a Failure to Offer Performance

Where all or part of the performances to be exchanged under an exchange of promises are due simultaneously, it is a condition of each party's duties to render such performance that the other party either render or, with manifested present ability to do so, offer performance of his part of the simultaneous exchange.

Addie v. Kjaer

United States Court of Appeals, Third Circuit, 2014.
737 F.3d 854.

ROTH, CIRCUIT JUDGE. . . . The Sellers own two properties in the Virgin Islands: Estate Great St. James, which is an island off the coast of St. Thomas, and Estate Nazareth, which is a launch point providing access to Estate Great St. James from St. Thomas. In 2004, Robert Addie, a Florida real estate investor, and Jorge Perez, a financial advisor to high-net-worth individuals, sought to purchase these properties. Perez persuaded Jason Taylor, his client and a former Miami Dolphins player to join the deal. . . .

In June 2004, Addie, Perez, and Taylor (collectively, the Buyers) entered into two land contracts (Contracts of Sale) and an Escrow Agreement to purchase Estate Great St. James and Estate Nazareth from the Sellers for $21 million and $2.5 million, respectively. Premier Title Company, Inc., served as the escrow agent and was party to the Escrow Agreement. Kevin D'Amour, the Sellers' attorney-in-fact, was the sole owner and principal of Premier. The Buyers assert that they were not aware of D'Amour's role at Premier when they entered into the Escrow Agreement.

The Contracts of Sale required the Buyers to submit an initial deposit of $1 million. Closing was to occur "at a mutually acceptable time of day within sixty (60) days of the execution of this Agreement." The contracts permitted the Buyers to extend the closing an additional thirty days by paying a $500,000 nonrefundable deposit. The duty of the Buyers under the contract was to pay the purchase price at closing, less the deposit. The duty of the Sellers was to deliver "Clear and Marketable" title and "[a]ssignments of all permits, submerged land leases and other licenses necessary for the existence and occupancy of the dock and other improvements on the Real Property, together with the required governmental consents thereto." The Contracts of Sale defined Clear and Marketable title as "such title as is acceptable to and insurable by Buyer's title insurance company on ALTA Form B Owner's Policy (or other reasonable form) free and clear of exceptions except licenses and easements, if any, for public utilities serving only the Real Property."

The Escrow Agreement required Premier to receive the Buyers' deposits and then to release the deposits to the Sellers. Premier agreed to release the first deposit to the Sellers within twenty-four hours after the Sellers delivered the escrow documents to the Buyers, as long as Premier received written notice from the Buyers that they were satisfied with the documents. . . .

Under the Contracts of Sale, the Buyers agreed to forfeit the deposits to the Sellers as liquidated damages in the event of the Buyers' default or failure or refusal to perform, through no fault of the Seller. The Sellers agreed to return the deposits in the event of the Sellers' default or failure or refusal to perform, through no fault of the Buyer. The Contracts of Sale required the non-defaulting party to send written notice of default, and the defaulting party would have ten days from the receipt of written notice to cure the default. . . .

On June 4, 2004, Addie, Perez, and the Sellers' attorney, Kevin D'Amour, met in Miami to sign the Contracts of Sale and the Escrow Agreement. Unable to attend the meeting, Taylor signed the Contracts of Sale and Escrow Agreement on June 15, 2004, and faxed them to D'Amour.

Taylor alone funded the initial $1 million deposit by sending three wire transfers to the escrow account between June 9 and June 11. During July, D'Amour, acting on behalf of Premier, made several deliveries of escrow documents to the Buyers. Included in the documents were the Coastal Zone permits for the use of the docks at Estate Nazareth and Estate Great St. James. The permits for both docks had already expired. Also among the documents, the commitment for title insurance contained a number of exceptions to the required coverage, including an exception for "any portion or portions of the [properties] subject to or contiguous with property subject to the Virgin Islands Open Shoreline Act" and an exception for a Right of Way Agreement for a road on Estate Nazareth.

D'Amour began to request that the Buyers authorize the release of the deposit to the Sellers. On August 3, Perez authorized release of the deposit in an email stating: "I have spoken to Hank Smock [local counsel to the Buyers], and he has advised me that we can go ahead and release the first deposit of $1,000,000." Based on this email, D'Amour, acting on behalf of Premier, released the deposit to the Sellers.

Taylor also unilaterally funded the second deposit of $500,000 to extend the closing date by sending three wire transfers to the escrow account between August 5 and August 19. On August 20, D'Amour emailed the Buyers asking them to "confirm by return email that the Escrow Agent [Premier] may release the [second deposit], subject to the terms of the Escrow Agreement." D'Amour did not receive written confirmation from the Buyers but nonetheless, acting on behalf of Premier, released the deposit to the Sellers.

In early September, the Sellers and the Buyers discussed extending the closing a second time. D'Amour informed the Buyers that the Sellers agreed to extend the closing date, stating:

> As a follow-up to my conversation with Jorge yesterday, my clients have consented to a one-week extension of time to close. The original closing date was September 4, 2004. Since this fell on a Saturday, the next business day was September 7, 2004. (see Section 4). The closing date is now September 14, 2004. Time is of the Essence. This extension shall not be deemed a waiver of any rights the sellers have under the Contract.

As of September 14, the Buyers had not paid the purchase price and the Sellers had not conveyed either updated assignments of permits or a Clear and Marketable title. On September 16, D'Amour sent the Buyers a notice of default, informing them that they had ten days to cure. On September 22 and 23, the Buyers demanded the immediate return of the escrow money, claiming that the Sellers were unable to deliver Clear and Marketable title. On September 24, D'Amour sent a request to the Buyers that they confirm their intentions to cure the default. The Buyers never responded. . . .

As the Restatement instructs, agreements concerning an exchange of promises require performance to be exchanged simultaneously whenever possible, unless the agreement indicates otherwise. This simultaneous exchange of performances creates concurrent conditions, under which performance by one party creates a condition precedent for performance by the other party.

Here, the Sellers were required to convey Clear and Marketable title and assignments of all permits, leases, and licenses necessary for the existence and occupancy of the docks in exchange for the Buyers' payment of the balance of the purchase price. . . .

The Sellers maintain that they offered performance by tendering escrow documents that demonstrated the Sellers' present ability to close because (1) the documents "complied with the essential terms of the contract" and (2) the "Buyers waived any defects in the documents." The Sellers also maintain that sending notices of default to Buyers beginning on September 16, 2004, constituted valid offers of performance.

In a contract with concurrent conditions, a party is not required to perform until the other party makes a valid offer to perform. If no party performs, neither party is in default, nor liable for breach. Thus, a claimant alleging breach of a contract that contains concurrent conditions must at least show that he or she offered to perform, and that the other party defaulted. The Restatement further instructs that a valid offer to perform "must be made with the manifested present ability to make it good, but the offeror need not go so far as actually to hold out that which he is to deliver." However, "[w]hen it is too late for either to make such an offer, both parties are discharged by the non-occurrence of a condition." [Restatement (Second) of Contracts § 238 cmt. a. (1981).]

The Sellers' delivery of escrow documents did not amount to a valid offer of performance. First, the escrow documents contained non-conforming documents, such as the expired dock permits and the exceptions to the commitment for title insurance. Moreover, this transaction involved two sets of contracts, in which the Sellers agreed to two separate deliveries. Under the Escrow Agreement, the Sellers agreed to deliver the escrow documents, while under the Contracts of Sale the Sellers agreed to deliver Clear and Marketable title and assignments "at a mutually acceptable time of day." The Clear and Marketable title and the assignments were never delivered. The Escrow Agreement provided that "[a]t the Closing (as such term is defined in the Contracts of Sale) the Escrow Agent shall deliver the Escrow Documents to the Buyer." However, as the District Court correctly stated, this provision does not "diminish the Sellers' involvement in the conveyance of the property." The common law, as it is generally understood and applied in the United States, supports the conclusion that the Seller must do more than deliver a deed into escrow to convey title. Therefore, despite Sellers' assertions that the documents "complied with the essential terms of the contract" and that the "Buyers waived any defects in the documents," Clear and Marketable title was not delivered.

Furthermore, the Sellers' notices of default to the Buyers beginning on September 16, 2004, did not amount to valid offers of performance. After September 15, neither party was required to perform. The District Court held that the last day to close was September 15. Therefore, the duties of the parties had already been discharged on September 16 because neither party performed. We therefore hold that the Sellers did not provide a valid offer of performance. . . .

[T]he contracts imposed concurrent conditions on the parties, which both parties failed to perform, resulting in the discharge of both parties['] duties under the contracts. For these reasons, we therefore affirm the holding of the District Court that no one could recover for breach of contract. . . .

Here, the law in the Virgin Islands is silent with regard to awarding restitution in cases involving valid contracts. Therefore, we look to the Restatement (Second) of Contracts for applicable law:

> A party whose duty of performance does not arise or is discharged as a result of impracticability of performance, frustration of purpose, nonoccurrence of a condition or disclaimer by a beneficiary is entitled to restitution for any benefit that he has

> conferred on the other party by way of part performance or reliance.

Restatement (Second) of Contracts § 377 (1981). For example, the Restatement illustrates: "*A* contracts to sell a tract of land to *B* for $100,000. After *B* has made a part payment of $20,000, *A* wrongfully refuses to transfer title. *B* can recover the $20,000 in restitution." *Id.* at § 373 illus. 1.

Here, the District Court erred by failing to apply this Restatement provision. In applying the Restatement (Second) of Contracts, it is clear that restitution is in order. Taylor provided a deposit of $1.5 million to the Sellers with the intent to purchase the two properties with Addie and Perez. However, all of the parties failed to perform within the timeframe specified in the contracts, and their respective duties were discharged. Thus, as the Restatement instructs, Taylor is entitled to restitution for the benefit of the deposit that he conferred to the Sellers.

We therefore hold that Taylor is entitled to restitution of the $1.5 million deposit from the Sellers.

NOTE: BREACH BY ANTICIPATORY REPUDIATION

A "repudiation" is said to occur when a party's statements or actions can fairly be interpreted to mean that the party will not or cannot perform its contractual obligations. Recall, for example, the notice to stop work given the contractor in Rockingham County v. Luten Bridge Co., p. 72. There is, of course, much litigation over the question whether particular words and/or actions constitute a repudiation of the contract. A particularly troublesome problem arises when, in mid-course, one party demands that the other do something not required by their agreement. If such a demand is accompanied by a statement that the demanding party will not perform its contractual duties unless the additional term is met, a finding of anticipatory breach is likely. E.g., Chamberlin v. Puckett Constr., 277 Mont. 198, 921 P.2d 1237 (1996). Again, the standard rule is that a breach occurs when it is reasonably certain that a party is not going to meet its obligations under the contract.

Another cluster of problems centers on the effects of a breach by repudiation, distinguished from a breach by simple nonperformance. A contract plaintiff's standing in court may rest wholly on the good fortune of a finding that the defaulter has also repudiated the contract. The principal effects of the so-called "anticipatory breach" are stated in Restatement, Second § 253:

> (1) Where an obligor repudiates a duty before he has committed a breach by non-performance and before he has received all of the agreed exchange for it, his repudiation alone gives rise to a claim for damages for total breach.

(2) Where performances are to be exchanged under an exchange of promises, one party's repudiation of a duty to render performance discharges the other's remaining duties to render performance.

A repudiation may, of course, have an additional consequence: it may excuse the nonoccurrence of a condition.

Many of the remedial problems associated with anticipatory repudiation are familiar at this point. It is now necessary to stress that the doctrine of anticipatory breach is applicable to bilateral contracts which contemplate some future performance by the nonbreaching party. A principal effect of the doctrine is to free that party (the nonrepudiator) of its obligations of future performance.

Price v. Van Lint

Supreme Court of New Mexico, 1941.
46 N.M. 58, 120 P.2d 611.

SADLER, J. . . . [T]he district court had before it for construction the following agreement in writing, signed by the plaintiff and by the defendant, for claimed breach of which the former sought damages, to-wit:

"Cimarron, N.M. 12–23–1939

"This agreement, entered into by V.J. Van Lint party of the first part and C.S. Price, party of the second part,

"First party agrees to deposit the sum of fifteen hundred on or before the first day of February, A.D. 1940 for which security said party of the second part agrees to give mortgage-deed and insurance for the full sum of fifteen hundred dollar*d*s and agr*r*es to use the above named amount for erecting a building on the land purchased from the Maxwell Land Grant Co. for which a warranty-deed will be executed and delivered. Party of the second part agrees to keep all taxes and insurance paid up to date on the above described property.

"Party of the second part Party of the first part

"(Sgd.) C.S. Price (Sgd.) V.J. Van Lint."

This inartificially drawn contract resulted from the joint efforts of the parties thereto, the plaintiff having contributed its phraseology in seemingly extemporaneous dictation to the defendant who furnished the mechanical skill of reducing it to form on the typewriter.

The parties [both] resided at Cimarron. . . . The defendant was local agent for Maxwell Land Grant Co. . . . but without authority to execute a deed on its behalf. The plaintiff, desiring to purchase a small tract of land near Cimarron and to construct a building thereon in which to conduct a business, negotiated with the defendant touching the matter. The contract in question resulted. [It] reflects the plaintiff's plan for financing both the purchase of the site and the construction of the building.

Anticipatory of the loan mentioned in the writing, the defendant advanced for the plaintiff's account the sum of $134, the agreed sale price of the tract being purchased as a site, repayable from the proceeds of the loan. This sum, along with a deed prepared by the defendant, in due course was dispatched to Amsterdam in the [Netherlands]. Likewise and in due course, said deed was returned from Amsterdam, apparently the residence of officials of the grantor with authority to act in this connection, and duly delivered to the plaintiff in the early part of March, 1940. Both parties were aware of the necessity of these steps being taken to consummate the purchase and that a considerable time would necessarily elapse before the deed could be delivered to the plaintiff.

In the meantime, the plaintiff seemed anxious to proceed with the construction of the proposed building. The defendant had left Cimarron in late December for a sojourn of more than two months at Corpus Christi, Texas. Apparently, meeting with disappointment in realizing funds from which to make the agreed loan, the defendant sought release from the contract. . . . This is shown by the correspondence passing between the parties. Indeed, the tenor of defendant's letters to him was such that the plaintiff very well might have elected to claim an anticipatory breach of the agreement. But he did not do so. On the contrary, he refused to release defendant from the contract and on January 16, 1940, caused his attorney to make telegraphic demand on defendant for performance, declaring: "Your contract has not been canceled and Price (the plaintiff) will hold you liable to any actual damages which may result to him by your failure to comply with agreement. . . . If money agreed to be loaned not here by February first you will be held liable for actual damages. . . ."

The trial court made the following additional findings: . . . "That the plaintiff has never tendered to the defendant any mortgage deed; that the defendant has never offered to or been willing to advance to the plaintiff the balance of the agreed loan prior to the receiving from the plaintiff of a valid mortgage deed on said premises; that the plaintiff has never repaid to the defendant the sum of $134.00 advanced to him by the defendant or any part thereof or any interest thereon." . . .

The court [also] found that the loan was to be for a period of two years; that the loan was to bear interest at the rate of 10% per annum; that the mortgage was to cover the land being purchased by the plaintiff from Maxwell Land Grant Co.; and that the "deposit" was to be made at First National Bank in Raton.

It further found that prior to his departure for Corpus Christi, the defendant informed Lorenzo Rosso[,] . . . doing business as Cimarron Mercantile Co., and R.E. Adams of Springer, New Mexico, doing business as R.E. Adams Lumber Co., of his agreement to make a loan of $1,500 to the plaintiff; that on January 9, 1940, the defendant [wrote] to said Lorenzo Rosso . . . stating that the contemplated loan to plaintiff was not going through due to unforeseen difficulties met with by the defendant; that a similar notice was given by defendant to R.E. Adams Lumber Co.; and "that some time thereafter both Cimarron Mercantile Co. and R.E. Adams Lumber Co. refused to extend any substantial further credit to the plaintiff."

It was also found that because of defendant's refusal to advance the amount of the loan to plaintiff on or before February 1, 1940, the plaintiff was compelled to suspend construction work on his building; that but for said refusal, the building would have been ready for use and occupancy by February 10, 1940, instead of April 27, 1940.

The trial court concluded: "That the written agreement . . . required the defendant to deposit the balance of the agreed loan on or before February 1, 1940, and that the amount so deposited should be immediately paid to the plaintiff, whether or not the plaintiff should at that time have received a deed to the real estate, and whether or not the plaintiff should at that time be the legal owner or the record owner of said real estate, and whether or not the plaintiff at that immediate time should be able to give a valid mortgage, and whether or not the real estate at that time should be free from liens and encumbrances; that the defendant, in refusing to deposit said balance for the plaintiff's immediate use on or before February 1, breached said agreement, and the defendant is liable to the plaintiff for the damages resulting therefrom."

Having thus concluded, the court rendered judgment in plaintiff's favor for $543.55 being the aggregate amount of plaintiff's damage[,] . . . after deducting therefrom $134 advanced by defendant to cover the purchase price of the real estate with accrued interest thereon.

. . . The [trial] court held in substance [that] the written agreement, interpreted in the light of the unchallenged findings, imposed upon the defendant the obligation to deposit to the plaintiff's credit in the bank named the amount of the loan, notwithstanding the fact that because of the delayed delivery of the deed, the plaintiff could not then deliver to the defendant the mortgage which was to furnish the security for the loan.

The correctness of the trial court's ruling on this question . . . involves the determination whether the plaintiff's promise to give a mortgage to secure the promised loan and the defendant's promise to make the loan are dependent or independent covenants of the contract. If the former, then the plaintiff's failure to allege performance denies him the right of recovery. If the latter, the defendant was under obligation to perform his covenant and look to his remedy for any breach of performance on the plaintiff's part. . . .

The rule of decision is not to construe promises as independent unless the nature of the contract or the surrounding circumstances compel a contrary inference. In other words, interpretation favors the conclusion of an agreed exchange of performance as the true intent of the parties unless such a construction does violence to the language employed in the light of known facts and circumstances. . . .

In Glaser v. Dannelley [23 N.M. 593, 170 P. 63], our holding [was]: "Where a contract contains mutual promises to pay money or perform some other act, and the time for performance for one party is to, or may, arrive before the time for performance by the other, the latter promise is an independent obligation, and nonperformance thereof merely raises a cause of action in the promisee, and does not defeat the right of the party making it to recover for a breach of the promise made to him."

This holding is but an application of the first portion of Rule 1 of the well known Sergeant Williams' Rules, annexed as a note to Pordage v. Cole, 1 Wm.Saund. 319"1" . . . While certain of Sergeant Williams' rules are the subject of critical comment[,] . . . we find nothing [critical] of that portion of Rule 1 approved by us in Glaser v. Dannelley. We think it is decisive of the question presented. When we apply it to [this] situation . . . we are compelled to hold with the trial court that the mutual covenants are independent of each other.

We are not unfamiliar with the rule that where the mutual covenants go to the entire consideration on both sides, they are considered mutual conditions and dependent unless there are clear indications to the contrary. 17 C.J.S., Contracts § 344. We seek, then, in the findings, something to support the trial court's conclusion that the covenants are independent. The contract in question was made on December 23, 1939. It obligated the defendant to deposit in First National Bank in Raton the amount of the loan on or before February 1, 1940. It obligated the plaintiff to give as security a mortgage on the land he was purchasing from Maxwell Land Grant Co. It was well known to both parties that the deed must go to . . . the Netherlands for execution by proper officers of the corporate grantor and that a considerable period would "necessarily elapse before said deed could be delivered to the plaintiff." While it may be said to have been within the contemplation of the parties that by expedient passage and return, a delivery could occur before the defendant was called upon to perform by depositing the loan in the bank agreed upon; nevertheless, and necessarily, the parties must have known that the day for performance by defendant might arrive before the plaintiff would be in a position to give the promised mortgage following delivery of his deed upon its return from abroad. This brings the case squarely within the test applied in Glaser v. Dannelley, supra.

It is the general rule that a breach of contract to loan money, standing alone, imposes no liability to damages. But this rule does not apply where there are extraordinary circumstances, as in this case, which result in injury. The defendant knew that the plaintiff was preparing to erect a building on the lot he had purchased, and to assist the plaintiff in securing material for the erection of such building, he notified certain material dealers that he had agreed to make the loan for the intended purpose. This caused the dealers to furnish to plaintiff a portion of the materials necessary for the erection of the building, which was commenced the 20th day of December, [1939]. Thereafter the defendant, knowing the reliance placed upon his agreement by plaintiff and the material dealers, notified the same dealers after considerable material had been furnished, that he would not make the loan. Thereupon, they not only refused to continue furnishing material but filed materialmen's liens against the property to secure that previously supplied. The result was that the plaintiff was unable to secure a substitute loan until the 12th day of April, 1940, by reason of which the building was not ready for occupancy until the 27th of April, two months and seventeen days after it would have been completed had the loan been made by defendant as provided in the contract.

These extraordinary circumstances resulted in injury to the plaintiff, and defendant is liable for the consequential damages. . . . "Damages for breach of a contract to lend money are measured by the cost of obtaining the use of money during the agreed period of credit, less interest at the rate provided in the contract, plus compensation for other unavoidable harm that the defendant had reason to foresee when the contract was made." Restatement of the Law, "Contracts" § 343. . . .

The item of $35 paid to Fred C. Stringfellow, attorney for Santa Fe Builders Supply Co. who made the substitute loan to plaintiff, was correctly allowed. This was for examination of the abstract of title and other papers, and for closing the loan. This is an ordinary and usual expense in connection with the loaning of money upon real property and must have been contemplated by the parties. . . .

The court found that the [plaintiff] was entitled to $298.75 damages, "being the net loss to the plaintiff in respect of the profits which the plaintiff would have received from the operation of his business in his new building during the period from February 10, 1940, to April 27, 1940." This was arrived at by the conclusion that the profits would amount to $5 a day for the time mentioned and that there should be deducted therefrom $31.25 which would be the saving of interest for the like period. The evidence upon which this finding was based was that of the plaintiff which was in substance that he intended to operate a night club in the building; that, prior thereto, he had operated a saloon in [Cimarron], and that based upon his knowledge of the saloon business, he estimated that the net profits would be not less than $5 per day.

There is no evidence from which the jury could determine for itself the amount of the lost profits (if any) plaintiff sustained during the two months and 17 days, except the conclusion of the plaintiff himself, that it was $5 a day. Undoubtedly, the plaintiff was entitled to recover his actual loss of profits by reason of the circumstances we have mentioned, if they were capable of legal ascertainment. . . . But we are of the opinion that there was no basis in the evidence for the conclusion of the witness (apparently testifying as an expert) that his profits for the time lost would have been $5 a day. It was purely a speculative estimate unsupported by any substantial testimony. But aside from the considerations stated from the fact that plaintiff was entering into a new business never opened up, any mere estimate as to profits is too remote and speculative to establish damages. . . .

We are of the opinion that item "H" in the sum of $62.50 for rental lost by the plaintiff during the period from February 10 to April 27 was proven by substantial testimony. It establishes a rental value of the restaurant portion of the building, thereafter rented at $25 a month.

The item allowed by the court of $173.40 for necessary travel expenses incurred by the plaintiff in attempting to secure another loan was proved by substantial evidence and correctly allowed by the court. . . .

We find that the trial court allowed the damages in the sum of $420.05 erroneously, in that there was no substantial evidence to support the several items aggregating that sum. That there was substantial evidence to support items of damage aggregating $270.90. If the appellee will enter a remittitur in this court in the sum of $420.05, the judgment will be affirmed for the balance and the costs of the appeal will be divided equally between the parties, failing which the judgment will be reversed and the cause remanded with instructions to the district court to grant a new trial, said costs to be charged to appellee. The appellant's counterclaim, properly allowed, is taken care of in the remittitur authorized.

QUESTIONS

(1) If the deed had arrived from Amsterdam on January 26, could plaintiff have insisted on payment of the $1,500 promised on February 1 without tendering a mortgage?

(2) What if the deed had arrived in early March, but plaintiff, instead of demanding the money promised on February 1, had remained entirely silent and had made no demand on defendant until March 15, after the deed had arrived?

Sharp, Promissory Liability (pt. 2)

7 U.Chi.L.Rev. 250, 269–272 (1940)

"As more complicated contracts, at various stages of performance, came before the courts, it became increasingly apparent that it is the absence of conditions which creates the troublesome problems of adjustment when one party to a bilateral contract has not performed, or is likely not to perform, part of his undertakings, and the other party relies on this circumstance, not simply for a cause of action but for an excuse for discontinuing performance on his part. Again, the extent of the risks which parties must be regarded as taking and the unfairness of contracts infected with serious lack of foresight, are the factors to be considered. . . .

"Two extreme and simple treatments of the effect of one party's default on the other's obligations are thinkable. Each might simply have a cross action against the other. . . . At the opposite extreme, every default might be treated as an excuse for the other party, and the defaulting party protected against unfairness resulting from his part performance, by quasi-contractual relief to prevent unjust enrichment or forfeiture or both. . . . Neither of these simple solutions has, of course, been adopted by the courts. After struggling . . . to discover some indication of the parties' expectations about the variety of contingencies which may occur in the course of performance, the courts recognized that they were dealing with a problem which could not be solved by interpretation. As in cases of mistake and impossibility, some attempt was made to distinguish between 'substantial' and other differences. The suggestion that such a word could be used to describe a systematic, metaphysical or scientific test, while comforting, is, of course, illusory. The word may be used to describe the results of a practical judgment; but the difficult necessity of making the practical judgment remains. . . .

"One reminder of the impossibility of solving these questions by resort either to interpretation or to such clear-cut rules as are suggested by the effect of a specified order of performance, appears in the cases dealing with the effect of default on a party who was to perform first. If a party has let the time for the first performance pass, and is then not in a position to perform himself when he calls for performance on the other side, it appears that some principle not dependent on interpretation requires that the other party be excused. This principle, on examination, seems closely related to the principles applicable to mistake and impossibility."

Conley v. Pitney Bowes

United States Court of Appeals, Eighth Circuit, 1994.
34 F.3d 714.

M. ARNOLD, CIRCUIT JUDGE. Conley initiated this action . . . against his employer Pitney Bowes after he had been denied continued disability benefits for a claim arising from injuries suffered in an automobile accident. The company removed the case to the [federal district court] because the suit related to benefits under the Employee Retirement Income Security Act, 29 U.S.C. § 1001 et seq. (ERISA). The district court granted the defendants's motion for summary judgment, 839 F.Supp. 1364, and this appeal followed. At issue is whether a claimant must exhaust administrative procedures when, contrary to the requirements of his plan, the letter denying his benefits does not inform him of appeal procedures.

ERISA does not explicitly require exhaustion of administrative or plan remedies. The doctrine is, in this context, a creature either of contract or judicial invention. We have required exhaustion in ERISA cases only when it was required by the particular plan involved. . . . The appellant concedes that the plan which is the subject of the suit before us does contain, in fact, such a requirement.

The language of the plan requiring exhaustion is complimented . . . by language that requires that any notice of denial of benefits be accompanied by explicit instructions informing the plan participant of the procedures for appeal. Section 7.8(a) of the plan document requires that the plan administrator provide to "any person whose claim for benefits has been denied . . . a written notification of the denial. The written notification shall include . . . an explanation of the claim appeal procedure." This plan language comports with the requirements of 29 C.F.R. § 2560.50:–1(f)(4), which dictates that the "[c]ontent of notice . . . to every claimant who is denied a claim for benefits . . . set[ ] forth . . . [a]ppropriate information as to the steps to be taken if the participant or beneficiary wishes to submit his or her claim for review."

The present case, therefore, may be distilled to one of contract. Two terms of an ERISA plan are the focus of this dispute, namely, an exhaustion clause and a clause requiring notice of appeal procedures. . . .

The terms that are at the center of this dispute are promises that were exchanged as part of a complex agreement. While pension and benefit plans are typically characterized as being unilateral contracts (agreements where an offer is accepted by a performance), the promises in the plan before us are more properly characterized as a bilateral contract (an agreement where promises of future performance are exchanged). See Corbin on Contracts § 21 (one vol. ed. 1962). . . .

One well established rule of contract construction is that "[i]n bilateral contracts for an agreed exchange of performances, . . . where one party's performance is to be rendered prior in time to that of the other, it is a constructive condition precedent to the latter's duty." Simpson, Handbook of the Law of Contracts § 152 (1965). See also Restatement (Second) of Contracts § 237 (1981) ("[I]t is a condition of each party's remaining duties to render performances to be exchanged under an exchange of promises that there be no material failure by the other party to render any such performance due at an earlier time.") . . . Such a "performance is as much a condition precedent to the other's duty as though expressly made so." Simpson, § 152; See also Loud v. Pomona Land & Water Co., 153 U.S. 564, 577 (1894) (agreement to convey land "*after* the making of the payment and full performance" rendered such payment and performance a condition precedent to the duty to convey. (emphasis in original)). . . .

Application of these principles to the case at hand is straightforward. Because appellees were obligated to inform appellant of the appeal procedure at the time they denied him benefits, appellees performance had necessarily to precede exhaustion by the plaintiff. A defense under the exhaustion clause, therefore, may not be asserted absent performance of the notice clause, since they are presumed to be the subject of promises made in exchange for each other.

The appellees maintain that failure to impose the exhaustion requirement would be contrary to the public policy behind such a requirement. We disagree. Exhaustion is a very important concept in our jurisprudence, with deep roots in the principles of federalism and comity. See e.g., Rose v. Lundy, 455 U.S. 509 (1982). . . . We believe, however, that the freedom of contract between autonomous parties is a more important principle than even the very important judicially-created doctrine of exhaustion. Furthermore, where exhaustion is a bargained-for term of a contract, freedom of contract is not necessarily inconsistent with the principles underlying exhaustion requirements.

Requiring plan administrators to provide notice of appeals procedure as required by contract and the Secretary's regulations is not inconsistent with the goals that exhaustion typically furthers. Indeed, such a requirement serves much the same purpose as the exhaustion clause, namely, to avert resort to federal litigation where an administrative procedure is available. In fact, inclusion of such a term serves to avoid not only frivolous suits, but mistakenly filed suits as well. To advance the purposes of the Act, the Secretary's regulations, the contract, and the principles underlying the exhaustion and notice terms, we must construe and enforce the whole contract, including the notice of appeals procedure requirement.

In their motion for summary judgment and their supporting memorandum, the defendants-appellees rely expressly and exclusively upon Conley's failure to exhaust the plan's procedures. They do not allege that Conley had actual knowledge of the plan's procedures, thereby making any breach of the plan's notice requirements immaterial. The district court appears to have felt that the plaintiff-appellant's possession of the summary plan description gave him constructive knowledge of the appeals procedures. The terms of the plan and the requirements of the regulation, however, confer upon a claimant a right to more than just a copy of the summary plan description. He had a contractual right to information on the appeals procedure included with his notice of denial of benefits. On summary judgment, the movant is not entitled to the benefit of a legal rule that the summary plan description gave claimant constructive knowledge of the appeals procedures.

. . . [T]he defendants-appellees further assert that Conley did not deny having actual knowledge of the plan's procedures. This argument, however, puts the cart before the horse. The defendants-appellees never alleged, either in their answer, their motion for summary judgment, or their memorandum in support of their motion, that Conley or his attorney had actual knowledge of the plan's appeals process. We do not think that Conley could be expected to deny something of which he had not been accused. . . .

For the foregoing reasons, we reverse the judgment of the district court, and remand for proceedings consistent with this opinion.

GIBSON, SENIOR CIRCUIT JUDGE, dissenting. . . . I would affirm the judgment of the district court for the reasons articulated in its decision.

Conley's testimony is very clear that after he received the letter denying benefits he turned it over to his lawyer. He felt that he should be getting a pension, disability or something, so retained the lawyer to look after his interests. He let the lawyer handle it and do the work. In addition to the letter, he gave a copy of the benefit plans book to the lawyer. The booklet set forth in clear detail the claim appeal procedure.

The court today elevates form over substance and ignores the factual situation before the district court and on which it ruled. This is not a case where an employee failed to file an application for review because he was not told of the procedures, but rather one where the employee relied on his lawyer, who dropped the ball.

Bell v. Elder

782 P.2d 545 (Utah Ct.App. 1989)

The Bells' contract to purchase undeveloped land for $25,000 required the Elders, sellers and defendants, to furnish culinary water to the property, for which the Bells, upon acquiring a building permit, were to pay a hook-up and installation fee. A lawsuit for rescission and restitution of the down payment, brought unsuccessfully by the Bells, followed the deal's collapse. The reviewing court said: "[A]lthough the contract contains a promise by the Elders to supply water, as well as a related promise by the Bells to obtain a building permit for the construction of a house to receive the water, no time is specified for performing either promise. . . . The situation at trial consisted of the Bells [asking] to rescind the contract on the grounds that the Elders had breached an obligation to actually furnish water to the property, and [the Elders] insisting that they would supply the required water when the Bells demanded it and performed their obligations. The question thus presented boils down to the order in which these parties must perform. . . . [Since the] contract is silent on the time or times for actually furnishing water and for obtaining a building permit[,] . . . the law implies a covenant and condition that the related obligations be performed concurrently. . . . [N]either party could claim a breach by the other until the party claiming the breach tendered performance of its concurrent obligation. . . . This case demonstrates that the rule requiring tender before claiming breach of a concurrent promise is not a mere formality or trap for the unwary. Here, the claimant's tender would demonstrate the continued practical vitality and purposefulness of the promise owed the claimant. Public policy and common sense oppose the waste of installing a culinary water line to serve land which, for all that appears, will remain unused. The rule requiring tender thus serves, among other purposes, to prevent a claimant from insisting upon a purposeless performance, or from avoiding his own obligations on pretext. Inasmuch as the [Bells'] failure to perform their own obligations precludes recovery on their claims, the judgment of dismissal is affirmed."

K & G Constr. Co. v. Harris

Court of Appeals of Maryland, 1960.
223 Md. 305, 164 A.2d 451.

[Plaintiff, owner and general contractor, entered into a contract with defendant subcontractor for the excavating and earth-moving work required in a housing project. The contract contained the following provisions: (1) defendant agreed to perform the work "in a workmanlike manner and in accordance with the best practices," without delay, as called for by plaintiff, it being agreed that "time was of the essence"; (2) plaintiff had the right to terminate the contract and employ a substitute to perform the work in the event of delay by defendant, and defendant agreed to indemnify plaintiff for any loss caused thereby, but nothing in this provision "shall be construed to deprive Contractor [plaintiff] of any rights or remedies it would otherwise have as to damage for delay"; (3) defendant was to submit to plaintiff by the 25th day of each month a requisition for work performed during the preceding month, and plaintiff agreed to pay 90 percent of each requisition by the 10th of the following month; (4) defendant agreed to carry liability insurance against property damage caused in the progress of the work, and plaintiff was not obligated to make payments under the contract until the insurance requirements were met.

Defendant performed work under the contract during July 1958, for which it submitted a requisition on July 25. This requisition would have entitled defendant to a progress payment on August 10. On August 9, however, defendant's bulldozer operator drove his machine too close to a house belonging to plaintiff, causing the collapse of a wall and other damage amounting to $3,400. Both defendant and its insurer denied liability for this damage. Because the damage was not repaired or paid for, plaintiff refused to make the progress payment due defendant on August 10. Defendant continued work until September 12, when it left the job because of plaintiff's refusal to pay the July and August requisitions, notifying plaintiff that it was willing to resume work but only on payment for work already done. Plaintiff continued to refuse to pay, asked defendant to complete the work, and, on defendant's refusal, had the remaining work done by another excavator at a cost increase of $450. It was stipulated that defendant had completed work for which it had not been paid in the amount of $1,484.50, and that if it had completed the remainder of the work under the contract it would have realized a profit on that portion amounting to $1,340.

Plaintiff sued for both the damages caused by the bulldozer, alleging negligence of the operator, and the additional $450 required to have the work completed by another contractor. Defendant counterclaimed for the value of work performed and for the lost profits on the remainder of the job. By agreement of the parties, plaintiff's claim for bulldozer damage was submitted to a jury, which found for plaintiff in the amount of $3,400. The judgment for this sum has been paid by defendant. Plaintiff's other claim and defendant's counterclaims were submitted to the court for determination without a jury. The trial court found for defendant on both counterclaims and plaintiff appealed.]

PRESCOTT, J. . . . Does a contractor, damaged by a subcontractor's failure to perform a portion of his work in a workmanlike manner, have a right, under the circumstances of this case, to withhold, in partial satisfaction of said damages, an installment payment, which, under the terms of the contract, was due the subcontractor, unless the negligent performance of his work excused its payment? . . .

It is immediately apparent that our decision turns upon the respective rights and liabilities of the parties under that portion of their contract whereby the subcontractor agreed to do the excavating and earth-moving work in "a workmanlike manner, and in accordance with the best practices," with time being of the essence of the contract, and the contractor agreed to make progress payments therefor on the 10th day of the months following the performance of the work by the subcontractor. The subcontractor contends, of course, that when the contractor failed to make the payment due on August 10, he breached his contract and thereby released him (the subcontractor) from any further obligation to perform. The contractor, on the other hand, argues that the failure of the subcontractor to perform his work in a workmanlike manner constituted a material breach of the contract, which justified his refusal to make the August 10 payment; and, as there was no breach on his part, the subcontractor had no right to cease performance on September 12, and his refusal to continue work on the project constituted another breach, which rendered him liable to the contractor for damages. . . . Did the contractor have a right, under the circumstances, to refuse to make the progress payment, due on August 10, 1958? . . .

While the courts assume, in deciding the relation of one or more promises in a contract to one or more counter-promises, that the promises are dependent rather than independent, the intention of the parties, as shown by the entire contract as construed in the light of the circumstances of the case, [is] the controlling factor. . . .

Considering the presumption that promises and counter-promises are dependent[,] . . . we have no hesitation in holding that the promise and counter-promise under consideration here were mutually dependent, that is to say, the parties intended performance by one to be conditioned on performance by the other; and the subcontractor's promise was, by the explicit wording of the contract, precedent to the promise of payment, monthly, by the contractor. . . . [I]t is the general rule that where a total price for work is fixed by a contract the work is not rendered divisible by progress payments. It would, indeed, present an unusual situation if we were to hold that a building contractor, who has obtained someone to do work for him and has agreed to pay each month for the work performed in the previous month, has to continue the monthly payments, irrespective of the degree of skill and care displayed in the performance of work, and his only recourse is by way of suit for ill-performance. If this were the law, it is conceivable, in fact, probable, that many contractors would become insolvent before they were able to complete their contracts. As was stated [in] Measures Bros. Ltd. v. Measures, 2 Ch. 248: "Covenants are to be construed as dependent or independent according to the intention of the parties and the good sense of the case."

We hold that when the subcontractor's employee negligently damaged the contractor's wall, this constituted a breach of the subcontractor's promise to perform his work in a "workmanlike manner, and in accordance with the best practices." . . . And there can be little doubt that the breach was material: the damage to the wall amounted to more than double the payment due on August 10. 3A Corbin, Contracts, § 708, says: "The failure of a contractor's [in our case, the subcontractor's] performance to constitute 'substantial' performance may justify the owner [in our case the contractor] in refusing to make a progress payment. . . . If the refusal to pay an installment is justified on the owner's [contractor's] part, the contractor [subcontractor] is not justified in abandoning work by reason of that refusal. His abandonment of the work will itself be a wrongful repudiation that goes to the essence, even if the defects in performance did not." . . . Professor Corbin, in § 954, states further: "The unexcused failure of a contractor to render a promised performance when it is due is always a breach of contract. . . . Such failure may be of such great importance as to constitute what has been called herein a 'total' breach. . . . For a failure of performance constituting such a 'total' breach, an action for remedies that are appropriate thereto is at once maintainable. Yet the injured party is not required to bring such action. He has the option of treating the non-performance as a 'partial' breach only." . . . In permitting the subcontractor to proceed with work on the project after August 9, the contractor, obviously, treated the breach by the subcontractor as a partial one. As the promises were mutually dependent and the subcontractor had made a material breach in his performance, this justified the contractor in refusing to make the August 10 payment; hence, as the contractor was not in default, the subcontractor again breached the contract when he, on September 12, discontinued work on the project, which rendered him liable (by the express terms of the contract) to the contractor for his increased cost in having the excavating done—a stipulated amount of $450. . . .

The appellees suggest [a minor point] that may be disposed of rather summarily. . . . [They] contend that the contractor had no right to refuse the August 10 payment, because the subcontractor had furnished the insurance against property damage, as called for in the contract. There is little, or no, merit in this suggestion. The subcontractor and his insurance company denied liability. The furnishing of the insurance by him did not constitute a license to perform his work in a careless, negligent, or unworkmanlike manner; and its acceptance by the contractor did not preclude his assertion of a claim for unworkmanlike performance directly against the subcontractor.

Judgment against the appellant reversed; and judgment entered in favor of the appellant against the appellees for $450, the appellees to pay the costs.

Stanley Gudyka Sales Co. v. Lacy Forest Products Co.

915 F.2d 273 (7th Cir. 1990)

Lacy, a dealer in wood products, contracted for the services of a similar dealer, Gudyka, who was to be compensated by an agreed split of the profits on sales Gudyka made. Their agreement provided for termination by either party for "just cause." Some months after entering into the agreement, Lacy terminated Gudyka on the ground that he had failed to promptly remit to Lacy $3,000 of commissions (Lacy's share) collected from a customer. At the time, Lacy owed Gudyka $46,000 in commissions from all other accounts (this sum was eventually paid). Gudyka filed suit against Lacy, alleging the termination was without "just cause" and therefore a breach of contract. *Held*, judgment for Gudyka affirmed. "The self-help remedy [afforded by the 'doctrine of conditions'] is only available where termination is in proportion to the 'need' for accountability from the breaching party, and where the breach is material rather than 'insignificant.' The district court determined that Lacy's use of the 'self-help remedy' of [termination] was not proportional to its need and that the amount Gudyka owed to Lacy, as compared with the amounts Lacy owed Gudyka, was an 'insignificant' breach. [Also,] the district court found that because Lacy knew how much Gudyka owed it, Lacy was obligated to give Gudyka notice and an opportunity to cure its breach. [If] Gudyka did not cure, Lacy still had the alternative self-help remedy of deducting (as it later did deduct) the [$3,000] from [Gudyka's monthly] commission check. Without having given notice and an opportunity to cure, the district court [properly found that the termination] was without 'just cause.' . . . The 'doctrine of conditions' is not a tool which will 'permit a party to . . . us[e] an insignificant breach as a pretext for avoiding his contractual obligations.' "

NOTE

K & G Constr. and *Gudyka Sales* pursue the ever-present distinction between total and partial breach. And *K & G* tells us something basic about the law of conditions that builds upon that gateway to self-protective measures: If the performing party stops performing, or performs badly, the paying party can stop paying. Yet *Gudyka* is a reminder that not every self-help response to breach on the other side is legitimate, for the law reads into the doctrine of conditions implicit limitations, even obligations (e.g., the familiar duty to give notice and an opportunity to cure a breach). Suppose, in *K & G*, there had been no bulldozer incident; rather, the general, short on cash, simply failed to make the August 10th payment due the sub for the preceding month's work. Suppose further that this breach continued for a period of time. The Restatement, Second § 237, in illustrations 1 and 2, tells of such a story:

> 1. A contracts to build a house for B for $50,000, progress payments to be made monthly in an amount equal to 85% of the price of the work performed during the preceding month, the balance to be paid on the architect's certificate of satisfactory completion of the house. Without justification B fails to make a $5,000 progress payment. A thereupon stops works on the house and a week goes by. A's failure to continue the work is not a breach and B has no claim against A. B's failure to make the progress payment . . . operates as the non-occurrence of a condition of A's remaining duties of performance. . . . If B offers to make the delayed payment and in all the circumstances it is not too late to cure the material breach, A's duties to continue the work are not discharged. A has a claim against B for damages for partial breach because of the delay.
>
> 2. The facts being otherwise as stated in Illustration 1, B fails to make the progress payment or to give any explanation or assurances for one month. If, in all the circumstances, it is now too late for B to cure his material failure of performance . . ., A's duties to continue the work are discharged. Because B's failure to make the progress payment was a breach, A also has a claim against B for total breach of contract.

K & G also includes the point that the injured party is free to treat the other's breach by nonperformance—even a "material" breach—as partial only. If that happens (the injured party, through its actions, continues to live with the contract, perhaps asking the defaulter to do so as well), is it appropriate to speak of such conduct as "waiver"? Waiver of what? A cause of action for damages? We shall see more of these questions ahead.

---

6 S. Williston, Contracts

§ 832 (3d ed. 1961)

"Where conditions are concurrent, the allegation of tender need not be of absolute tender. A tender conditional on contemporaneous performance by the defendant is sufficient and necessary. It has sometimes been said that in such a case readiness and willingness on the part of the plaintiff is a sufficient allegation; or even that this is not part of the plaintiff's case, but, though in suits for specific performance a different rule prevails in many jurisdictions, to maintain an action at law the plaintiff must not only be ready and willing but he must have manifested this before bringing his action, by some offer of performance to the defendant, for, otherwise, both parties might be ready and willing and each stay at home waiting for the other to come forward. While the situation is possible of each of two parties having a right to specific performance against the other, it is not possible that each shall have a right to damages for a total breach of the contract.

"It is one of the consequences of concurrent conditions that a situation may arise where no right of action ever arises against either party. Since a conditional tender is necessary to put either party in default, so long as both parties remain inactive, neither is liable and neither has acquired a right of action. Moreover, the possibility of putting either party in default will cease if the delay is too long." [Courts usually find that the tender requirement is satisfied by conduct amounting to the giving of notice of readiness to perform. Also, a demand for the other's performance of a concurrent act is understood to indicate readiness and an offer to perform.]

NOTE

Recall that in Bell v. Elder, p. 712, a vendee who had failed to tender lost a suit for restitution of the part of the price paid at closing (the report of the case does not tell us the amount paid down). In Cleary v. Folger, 84 Cal. 316, 24 P. 280 (1890), neither party had tendered performance, but the vendee, in an action for money had and received, was allowed to recover his down payment minus the vendor's damages resulting from the vendee's failure to perform. The court relied on an express "time-is-of-the-essence" clause and concluded that since the date for performance had passed, "the contract is at an end." If this was a proper conclusion (both parties were discharged from their contract obligations), how could the vendor be awarded "damages" by a deduction from the vendee's recovery?

In a similar vendor-vendee "stalemate" situation (neither had performed and both were denied contract damages), a court awarded the vendee restitution of earnest money deposits of some $15,000 (plus interest and cancellation of a note). An appellate court approved, on this reasoning: The vendee's complaint had asked for "such other and further relief [deemed] just and equitable" in the circumstances. In essence, what the trial court did amounted to "rescission," which is an "equitable remedy" requiring the fashioning of an "equitable solution." There is no abuse of discretion in crafting a solution that returns the parties to their precontract positions. Willener v. Sweeting, 107 Wash. 2d 388, 730 P.2d 45 (1986).

Corbin, Conditions in the Law of Contracts

28 Yale L.J. 739, 743, 745–746 (1919)

"The word 'condition' is used in the law of property as well as in the law of contract and it is used with some variation in meaning. . . . In its proper sense the word *'condition' means some operative fact subsequent to acceptance and prior to discharge*, a fact upon which the rights and duties of the parties depend. Such a fact may be an act of one of the two contracting parties, an act of a third party, or any other fact of our physical world. It may be a performance that has been promised or a fact as to which there is no promise.

". . . [A]ny operative fact may with some propriety be said to be a cause or condition of the legal relations that are consequent thereon. . . . An offer is a cause (or condition) of the power in the offeree. An acceptance is a cause (or condition) of contractual rights and duties. Nevertheless in contract law it is not common to speak of these facts as conditions. . . . . The term condition is more properly restricted to facts subsequent to acceptance and prior to discharge. . . .

"A promise is always made by the act or acts of one of the parties . . .; a fact can be made to operate as a condition only by the agreement of both parties or by the construction of the law. The purpose of a promise is the creation of a duty or a disability in the promisor; the purpose of constituting some fact as a condition is always the postponement of an instant duty (or other specified legal relation). The fulfilment of a promise discharges a duty; the occurrence of a condition creates a duty. The non-fulfilment of a promise is called a breach of contract, and creates in the other party a . . . right to damages; it is the failure to perform that which was required by a previous duty. The non-occurrence of a condition will prevent the existence of a duty in the other party; but it may not create any [duty to pay damages] at all, and it *will* not unless someone has promised that it shall occur. . . .

"It may be observed that both a promise and a condition are means that are used to bring about certain desired action by another person. For example, an insurance company desires the payment of premiums. One means of securing this desired object would be to obtain a promise by the insured to pay premiums; on failure to pay them an action would lie. In fact, however, insurance policies seldom contain such a promise; the payment of the premiums is secured in a more effective way than that. The insurance company makes its own duty to pay the amount of the policy expressly conditional upon the payment of premiums. Here is no express promise of the insured creating a duty to pay premiums, but there is an express condition precedent to his right to recover on the policy. Payment by the insured is obtained not by holding a lawsuit over him *in terrorem* but by hanging before him a purse of money to be reached only by climbing the ladder of premiums. Before bilateral contracts became enforceable this was the only contractual way for a promisor to secure his desired object."

Howard v. Federal Crop Ins. Corp.

United States Court of Appeals, Fourth Circuit, 1976.
540 F.2d 695.

WIDENER, CIRCUIT JUDGE. Plaintiff-appellants sued to recover for losses to their 1973 tobacco crop due to alleged rain damage. The crops were insured by defendant-appellee, Federal Crop Ins. Corp. (FCIC). Suits were brought in a state court in North Carolina and removed to the United States District Court. The three suits . . . were combined for disposition in the district court and for appeal. The district court granted summary judgment for the defendant and dismissed all three actions. We remand for further proceedings. Since we find for the plaintiffs as to the construction of the policy, we express no opinion on the procedural questions.

[FCIC], an agency of the United States, in 1973, issued three policies to the Howards, insuring their tobacco crops, to be grown on six farms, against weather damage and other hazards.

The Howards (plaintiffs) established production of tobacco on their acreage, and have alleged that their 1973 crop was extensively damaged by heavy rains, resulting in a gross loss to the three plaintiffs in excess of $35,000. The plaintiffs harvested and sold the depleted crop and timely filed notice and proof of loss with FCIC, but, prior to inspection by the adjuster for FCIC, the Howards had either plowed or disked under the tobacco fields in question to prepare the same for sowing a cover crop of rye to preserve the soil. When the FCIC adjuster later inspected the fields, he found the stalks had been largely obscured or obliterated by plowing or disking and denied the claims, apparently on the ground that the plaintiffs had violated a portion of the policy which provides that the stalks on any acreage with respect to which a loss is claimed shall not be destroyed until the corporation makes an inspection.

The holding of the district court is best capsuled in its own words: "The inquiry here is whether compliance by the insureds with this provision of the policy was a condition precedent to the recovery. The court concludes that it was and that the failure of the insureds to comply worked a forfeiture of benefits for the alleged loss."

There is no question but that apparently after notice of loss was given to defendant, but before inspection by the adjuster, plaintiffs plowed under the tobacco stalks and sowed some of the land with a cover crop, rye. The question is whether, under paragraph 5(f) of the tobacco endorsement to the policy of insurance, the act of plowing under the tobacco stalks forfeits the coverage of the policy. Paragraph 5 [is] entitled *Claims*. Pertinent to this case are subparagraphs 5(b) and 5(f), which are as follows:

> "5(b) *It shall be a condition precedent* to the payment of any loss that the insured establish the production of the insured crop on a unit and that such loss has been directly caused by one or more of the hazards insured against during the insurance period for the crop year for which the loss is claimed, and furnish any other information regarding the manner and extent of loss as may be required by the Corporation. (Emphasis added)."
>
> "5(f) The tobacco stalks on any acreage of tobacco of types 11a, 11b, 12, 13, or 14 with respect to which a loss is claimed *shall not be destroyed until the Corporation makes an inspection.* (Emphasis added)."

The arguments of both parties are predicated upon the same two assumptions. First, if subparagraph 5(f) creates a condition precedent, its violation caused a forfeiture of plaintiffs' coverage. Second, if subparagraph 5(f) creates an obligation (variously called a promise or covenant) upon plaintiffs not to plow under the tobacco stalks, defendant may recover from plaintiffs (either in an original action, or, in this case, by a counterclaim, or as a matter of defense) for whatever damage it sustained because of the elimination of the stalks. However, a violation of subparagraph 5(f) would not, under the second premise, standing alone, cause a forfeiture of the policy.

Generally accepted law provides us with guidelines here. There is a general legal policy opposed to forfeitures. . . . Insurance policies are generally construed most strongly against the insurer. . . . When it is doubtful whether words create a promise or a condition precedent, they will be construed as creating a promise. Harris & Harris Const. Co. v. Crain & Denbo, Inc., 256 N.C. 110, 123 S.E.2d 590 (1962). The provisions of a contract will not be construed as conditions precedent in the absence of language plainly requiring such construction. *Harris*, 123 S.E.2d at 596. . . .

Plaintiffs rely most strongly upon the fact that the term "condition precedent" is included in subparagraph 5(b) but not in subparagraph 5(f). It is true that whether a contract provision is construed as a condition or an obligation does not depend entirely upon whether the word "condition" is expressly used. . . . However, the persuasive force of plaintiffs' argument in this case is found in the use of the term "condition precedent" in subparagraph 5(b) but not in subparagraph 5(f). Thus, it is argued that the ancient maxim to be applied is that the expression of one thing is the exclusion of another.

The defendant places principal reliance upon the decision of this court in Fidelity-Phenix Fire Ins. Co. v. Pilot Freight Carriers, 193 F.2d 812 (4th Cir. 1952). Suit there was predicated upon a loss resulting from theft out of a truck covered by defendant's policy protecting plaintiff from such a loss. The insurance company defended upon the grounds that the plaintiff had left the truck unattended without the alarm system being on. The policy contained six paragraphs limiting coverage. Two of those imposed what was called a "condition precedent." They largely related to the installation of specified safety equipment. Several others, including paragraph 5, [began] with the phrase, "It is further warranted." In paragraph 5, the insured warranted that the alarm system would be on whenever the vehicle was left unattended. Paragraph 6 starts with the language: "The assured agrees, by acceptance of this policy, that the foregoing conditions precedent relate to matters material to the acceptance of the risk by the insurer." Plaintiff recovered in the district court, but [the] judgment was reversed because of a breach of warranty of paragraph 5, the truck had been left unattended with the alarm off. In that case, plaintiff relied upon the fact that the words "condition precedent" were used in some of the paragraphs but the word "warranted" was used in the paragraph in issue. In rejecting that contention, this court said that "warranty" and "condition precedent" are often used interchangeably to create a condition of the insured's promise, and "[m]anifestly the terms 'condition precedent' and 'warranty' were intended to have the same meaning and effect." 193 F.2d at 816.

Fidelity-Phenix thus does not support defendant's contention here. . . . Unlike the case at bar, each paragraph in *Fidelity-Phenix* contained either the term "condition precedent" or the term "warranted." We held that, in that situation, the two terms had the same effect in that they both involved forfeiture. That is well established law. . . . In the case at bar, the term "warranty" or "warranted" is in no way involved, either in terms or by way of like language, as it was in *Fidelity-Phenix.* The issue upon which this case turns, then, was not involved in Fidelity-*Phenix.* . . .

The Restatement of the Law of Contracts states:

> § 261. Interpretation of Doubtful Words as Promise or Condition
>
> Where it is doubtful whether words create a promise or an express condition, they are interpreted as creating a promise; but the same words may sometimes mean that one party promises a performance and that the other party's promise is conditional on that performance.

Two illustrations (one involving a promise, the other a condition) are used in the Restatement:

> 2. A, an insurance company, issues to B a policy of insurance containing promises by A that are in terms conditional on the happening of certain events. The policy contains this clause: "provided, in case differences shall arise touching any loss, *the matter shall be submitted to impartial arbitrators,* whose award shall be binding on the parties." This is a promise to arbitrate and does not make an award a condition precedent of the insurer's duty to pay.
>
> 3. A, an insurance company, issues to B an insurance policy in usual form containing this clause: "In the event of disagreement as to the amount of loss it shall be ascertained by two appraisers and an umpire. The loss shall *not be payable until 60 days after the award of the appraisers when such an appraisal is required.*" This provision is not merely a promise to arbitrate differences but makes an award a condition of the insurer's duty to pay in case of disagreement. (Emphasis added.)

We believe that subparagraph 5(f) in the policy here under consideration fits illustration 2 rather than illustration 3. Illustration 2 specifies something to be done, whereas subparagraph 5(f) specifies something not to be done. Unlike illustration 3, subparagraph 5(f) does not state any conditions under which the insurance shall "not be payable," or use any words of like import. We hold that the district court erroneously held, on the motion for summary judgment, that subparagraph 5(f) established a condition precedent to plaintiffs' recovery which forfeited the coverage.

From our holding that defendant's motion for summary judgment was improperly allowed, it does not follow the plaintiffs' motion for summary judgment should have been granted, for if subparagraph 5(f) be not construed as a condition precedent, there are other questions of fact to be determined. At this point, we merely hold that the district court erred in holding, on the motion for summary judgment, that subparagraph 5(f) constituted a condition precedent with resulting forfeiture.

The explanation defendant makes for including subparagraph 5(f) in the tobacco endorsement is that it is necessary that the stalks remain standing in order for the Corporation to evaluate the extent of loss and to determine whether loss resulted from some cause not covered by the policy. However, was subparagraph 5(f) inserted because without it the Corporation's opportunities for proof would be more difficult, or because they would be impossible? Plaintiffs point out that the Tobacco Endorsement, with subparagraph 5(f), was adopted in 1970, and crop insurance goes back long before that date. Nothing is shown as to the Corporation's prior 1970 practice of evaluating losses. Such a showing might have a bearing upon establishing defendant's intention in including 5(f). Plaintiffs state, and defendant does not deny, that another division of the Department of Agriculture, or the North Carolina Department, urged that tobacco stalks be cut as soon as possible after harvesting as a means of pest control. Such an explanation might refute the idea that plaintiffs plowed under the stalks for any fraudulent purpose. Could these conflicting directives affect the reasonableness of plaintiffs' interpretation of defendant's prohibition upon plowing under the stalks prior to adjustment?

We express no opinion on these questions. . . . Nothing we say here should preclude FCIC from asserting as a defense that the plowing or disking under of the stalks caused damage to FCIC if, for example, the amount of the loss was thereby made more difficult or impossible to ascertain whether the plowing or disking under was done with bad purpose or innocently. To repeat, our narrow holding is that merely plowing or disking under the stalks does not of itself operate to forfeit coverage under the policy.

The case is remanded for further proceedings not inconsistent with this opinion.

Merritt Hill Vineyards, Inc. v. Windy Heights Vineyard, Inc.

61 N.Y.2d 106, 472 N.Y.S.2d 592, 460 N.E.2d 1077 (1984)

At the closing of an agreement entered into six months earlier, plaintiff, the purchaser, learned that defendants, the sellers, had failed to secure two things provided for in the agreement—a title insurance policy and an FHA mortgage confirmation statement. Plaintiff thereupon refused to close and demanded return of its $15,000 deposit. When defendants did not return the deposit, plaintiff brought suit asserting two causes of action, one for return of the $15,000 deposit and one for $26,000 in damages alleged to have been suffered as a result of defendants' failure to perform. *Held*, summary judgment for return of plaintiff's deposit affirmed. "A condition [is] 'an event, not certain to occur, which must occur, unless its nonoccurrence is excused, before performance under a contract becomes due.' (Restatement, Contracts 2d § 224). Here, the contract requirements of a title insurance policy and mortgage confirmation . . . are contained in a section of the agreement entitled 'Conditions Precedent to Purchaser's Obligation to Close,' which provides that plaintiff's obligation to pay the purchase price and complete the purchase . . . is 'subject to' fulfillment of those requirements. No words of promise are employed. Defendants' agreement to sell the stock of the vineyard, not those conditions, was the promise by defendants for which plaintiff's promise to pay the purchase price was exchanged." But defendants' failure to fulfill these conditions entitles plaintiff only to a return of its deposit, not to a recovery of damages. "While a party's failure to fulfill a condition excuses performance by the other party whose performance is so conditioned, it is not, without an independent promise to perform the condition, a breach of contract subjecting the nonfulfilling party to liability for damages."

NOTE

In *Merritt Hill*, if there had been no section entitled "Conditions Precedent" and no "subject to" language, and the agreement simply stated that a title insurance policy and FHA mortgage statement "shall be furnished the purchaser on or before closing," should the court have found a promise? The issue, here and in general, is the degree of clarity required to override the law's presumption against conditions. Language alleged to create a condition is to be strictly interpreted; special scrutiny is the rule of thumb.

The opinion in Howard v. FCIC is not entirely clear about the court's basis for choosing between promise and condition, though the court does appear to be influenced by a term's specification of action or inaction ("something to be done" or "something not to be done") and by an explicit statement of consequences if the specified event does not occur. Another court has taken a different approach: "The test for distinguishing promises from conditions calls for inquiry as to whose words undertake the performance of the act. Are they the words of the person who is doing the act? If so, the words are interpreted, unless a contrary intent is plain, as a *promise* by that person to perform that act. If the words purport to be those of a party who is not doing the act, they are interpreted as limiting the promise of that party by making the performance of the act a condition." Mularz v. Greater Park City Co., 623 F.2d 139, 142–143 (10th Cir. 1980).

As you study the cases ahead, consider whether any single test is adequate to the task of distinguishing conditions from promises. Consider also Restatement, Second § 226, illustration 6, which purports to show the usual process of "interpretation" at work:

> A contracts to sell and B to buy a house for $50,000. The contract recites that financing is to take the form of "$30,000 mortgage

from X Bank" on stated terms and provides that B's duty is "conditional upon B's ability to arrange above described financing." B is unable to get the mortgage from X Bank but A offers to take a $30,000 purchase money mortgage on the stated terms and makes a conditional offer to deliver a deed. B refuses to perform. Although circumstances may show a contrary intention, the quoted language will ordinarily be interpreted so that the condition occurs only if B is able to get the mortgage from X Bank, and not if B is able to get a similar mortgage from A. Under this interpretation, B's refusal is not a breach.

SECTION 2. IMPLICIT LIMITS ON CONDITIONS

Cox v. SNAP, Inc.

United States Court of Appeals, Fourth Circuit, 2017.
859 F.3d 304.

DIANA GRIBBON MOTZ, CIRCUIT JUDGE. . . . In 2006, SNAP, a Virginia corporation, sought to expand its business in the field of federal procurement by contracting with Curtis Cox, a Maryland resident and the president of C² Technologies, an established government contracting firm. On January 12, 2006, the parties executed a memorandum of understanding in which Cox agreed "to promote and market [SNAP] in exchange for obtaining an equity stake" in the company. For purposes of this appeal, there is no dispute that the memorandum constitutes a binding contract.

Under the terms of this contract, Cox and C² Technologies agreed to provide various forms of assistance to SNAP. Among other things, they agreed to use their best efforts to help SNAP obtain specific contracts, to consider SNAP for any potential leads, and to provide SNAP with approximately $240,000 worth of marketing support and assistance.

In return, the contract provides that "[o]n January 12, 2006," the same day the parties executed the contract, SNAP "will issue a non-qualified stock option to Mr. Cox granting him the right to purchase 308 shares, representing five (5%) percent of the total authorized shares of stock of [SNAP]." The contract announces SNAP's intention to execute a stock split, under which Cox's options would increase proportionally. It gives SNAP the right to re-purchase Cox's options at any time after January 1, 2008 and gives Cox the right to require SNAP to repurchase his options—a "put option"—any time after January 1, 2011. The repurchase price is payable to Cox "over a five-year period with interest at the then current prime rate."

Cox attempted to exercise his put option on March 18, 2011 in a letter to SNAP President Navneet Gupta. The parties discussed but never came to a resolution regarding Cox's request. On October 6, 2015, Cox sent Gupta a second letter demanding that SNAP pay him the full value of his options. On October 9, 2015, Gupta replied that "[SNAP] owes you nothing."

A month later, in November 2015, Cox filed suit for breach of contract against SNAP in Virginia state court. . . .

Cox contended that the contract itself issued the options and therefore gave him the right to require SNAP to repurchase those options. Cox relied on three arguments. First, paragraph 1 of the contract required SNAP to issue the options on January 12, 2006—the very same day the parties executed the contract. Thus, Cox argued, even if this language were ambiguous, he should prevail in accordance with *contra proferentem*, the rule that courts should construe ambiguous contractual terms against the drafter (here SNAP) under certain circumstances. Second, Cox relied on the general presumption against construing a contract to create conditions precedent and argued that the parties never intended the "will issue" language to serve as a condition precedent to Cox's put option. Third, Cox argued that, under the prevention doctrine, SNAP waived any such condition precedent by refusing to issue the stock options. . . .

We turn first to liability. The parties dispute whether the contract itself conveyed stock options to Cox or merely obligated SNAP to issue those options at some point in the future.

If, as Cox maintains, the contract conveyed stock options to him, SNAP clearly breached the contract by refusing to repurchase them when Cox exercised his put option. For there is no dispute that Cox otherwise exercised his put option in accordance with the terms of the agreement, and SNAP has not preserved any defense for its refusal to repurchase Cox's options.

However, SNAP maintains that the contract did not convey stock options to Cox. Rather, according to SNAP, in the contract it merely *promised* to issue stock options to Cox, and the contract therefore made the issuance of stock options a condition precedent to SNAP's obligation to repurchase those options. SNAP contends that because it never issued those options, it never incurred the obligation to repurchase them from Cox. SNAP maintains that its refusal to issue the stock options was the only conceivable basis for Cox's lawsuit, and the limitations period for this claim expired well before November 2015, when Cox filed his initial complaint in state court. Thus, in SNAP's view, the statute of limitations bars Cox's only potentially meritorious claim.

SNAP has taken a self-defeating position. Even if issuing the stock options was a condition precedent to SNAP's obligation to repurchase, SNAP has excused that condition by breaching its promise to issue the options, and so the prevention doctrine dooms its case. Under the prevention doctrine, "if a promisor prevents or hinders fulfillment of a condition to his performance, the condition may be waived or excused." Moore Bros.

Co. v. Brown & Root, Inc., 207 F.3d 717, 725 (4th Cir. 2000). For the prevention doctrine to apply, Cox need only show that SNAP materially contributed to the non-occurrence of the condition. . . .

SNAP controlled whether the stock options issued, and, even under its own interpretation, it had a contractual obligation to issue those options. By refusing to do so, SNAP plainly forfeited its right to rely on their issuance as an unfulfilled condition precedent to its obligation to repurchase Cox's options. When a condition in a contract fails to occur solely because a party breached one of its other obligations in the very same contract, there is no doubt that the party caused the non-occurrence for the purposes of the prevention doctrine. . . .

According to SNAP, the prevention doctrine does not apply here because it only withheld the options after Cox first materially breached the contract. . . . SNAP has waived this first material breach defense by failing to advance it in seeking summary judgment. Moreover, even if SNAP had preserved the defense, it would offer no help. On SNAP's own reading, the contract required SNAP to issue the stock options to Cox on the same day the parties executed the contract. Thus, SNAP materially breached the contract by failing to issue those stock options, well before Cox could have plausibly breached his obligation to provide the promotion and marketing assistance he had promised.

SNAP also argues that the prevention doctrine applies only when a party affirmatively obstructs a condition from occurring, not when it merely refrains from bringing the condition about. This asserted limitation does not stand up to scrutiny. . . . Both the Supreme Court of Virginia and the Restatement have made clear that a promisor prevents or hinders the occurrence of a condition when it wrongfully refuses to cooperate, either by actively interfering with the occurrence of a condition or by withholding cooperation the promisor was obligated to give.

Accordingly, when a party materially contributes to the non-occurrence of a condition precedent by failing to bring that condition about, the condition is excused if the party's inaction is wrongful under the circumstances. Violation of a contractual duty is plainly wrongful for the purposes of the prevention doctrine. Here, even assuming SNAP's reading of the contract is correct, there is no doubt that SNAP had an obligation to bring about the condition it now tries to hide behind. Because it refused to do so with no justification or excuse, the prevention doctrine applies.

Thus, even if we read the contract as merely incorporating a promise to issue stock options, SNAP cannot avoid liability to Cox. . . .

Restatement of Contracts, Second

§ 227. Standards of Preference with Regard to Conditions

(1) In resolving doubts as to whether an event is made a condition of an obligor's duty, and as to the nature of such an event, an interpretation is preferred that will reduce the obligee's risk of forfeiture, unless the event is within the obligee's control or the circumstances indicate that he has assumed the risk.

Illustrations:

1. A, a general contractor, contracts with B, a sub-contractor, for the plumbing work on a construction project. B is to receive $100,000, "no part of which shall be due until five days after Owner shall have paid Contractor therefor." B does the plumbing work, but the owner becomes insolvent and fails to pay A. A is under a duty to pay B after a reasonable time.

2. A, a mining company, hires B, an engineer, to help reopen one of its mines for "$10,000 to be payable as soon as the mine is in successful operation." $10,000 is a reasonable compensation for B's service. B performs the required services, but the attempt to reopen the mine is unsuccessful and A abandons it. A is under a duty to pay B $10,000 after the passage of a reasonable time.

3. A, a mining company, contracts with B, the owner of an untested experimental patented process, to help reopen one of its mines for $5,000 paid in advance and an additional "$15,000 to be payable as soon as the mine is in successful operation." $10,000 is a reasonable compensation for B's services. B performs the required services, but because the process proves to be unsuccessful, A abandons the attempt to reopen the mine. A is under no duty to pay B any additional amount. . . .

NOTE

The result indicated in illustration 1 to Restatement, Second § 227 is widely understood to represent prevailing views on the type of "pay-when-paid" clause found there. Is that surprising? One court embraced this proposition: "If there is no express language to the contrary in the written document (and no extrinsic evidence), . . . where payment is stipulated to occur on an event, the occurrence of the event fixes only a time for payment; it is not . . . a substantive condition of the legal responsibility to pay." Schuler-Haas Elec. Co. v. Aetna Cas. & Sur. Co., 40 N.Y.2d 883, 389 N.Y.S.2d 348, 357 N.E.2d 1003 (1976). Under such a standard, what is one to conclude when the face of the subcontract explicitly makes payment from the owner to the general contractor a "condition precedent" to any payment to the subcontractor? Is this "express language to the contrary"?

Ewell v. Landing

199 Md. 68, 85 A.2d 475 (1952)

Landing loaned $550 in cash to Payne, who promised to repay this sum when he had "sold his timber." Payne died without repaying. In an action brought by Landing against Payne's executor, the evidence was inconclusive as to whether Payne's timber had been sold. Judgment for Landing was nevertheless affirmed. An obligation to pay money can clearly be made contingent on the occurrence of a future event. But here Payne's selling of the timber must have constituted merely a convenient time for payment. "[T]here can be no doubt that there was absolute liability, and that payment was merely postponed until timber could be sold." It could not have been the intention of the parties that if the timber were not sold plaintiff could recover nothing. As an earlier case had said: "Such a result would be a mockery of justice."

Amies v. Wesnofske

255 N.Y. 156, 174 N.E. 436 (1931)

Amies and Hines, real estate brokers, were hired under an oral agreement by the Wesnofskes as agents for the sale of the Wesnofskes' farm. It was agreed they would be paid $5,000, half on the signing of any contract of sale and half on "closing." Amies and Hines found vendees who, on December 9, 1925, signed a written contract to purchase the farm for $124,000, of which $10,000 was paid down and $30,000 was to be paid April 9, 1926. In April, the vendees found themselves unable to finance the purchase as they had intended. After postponement of closing until June 1, 1926, the vendees declined to proceed further and it was agreed between them and the Wesnofskes that the latter would keep the $10,000 paid and the contract obligations of both parties should cease. Amies and Hines thereafter brought an action for the balance of the agreed commission, $2,500, but a majority of the court denied recovery. The majority said that the words "when," "after," and "as soon as" are just as effective as "if" to create an express condition, with the result that when the event referred to by such a phrase does not occur no duty of performance arises. Active conduct of the conditional promisor, "preventing or hindering the fulfillment of the condition, eliminates it and makes the promise absolute," but from this it does not follow that a vendor of land promises the broker to procure the vendee's performance. "The broker, in placing reliance upon the self-interest of the vendor in procuring performance from the vendee, is ordinarily secure." Where, as here, the vendor is "passive and neutral" there is no prevention or hindrance that will excuse the condition.

Royal-Globe Ins. Co. v. Craven

Supreme Judicial Court of Massachusetts, 1992.
411 Mass. 629, 585 N.E.2d 315.

ABRAMS, J. At issue is the liability under an uninsured motorist policy of Royal-Globe Ins. Co. (Royal-Globe) to its insured, Theresa M. Craven (Craven), for personal injuries suffered by Craven in a hit and run accident. Royal-Globe sought a declaratory judgment that it was not liable to Craven because Craven's notice to Royal-Globe was not timely. . . . On cross-motions for summary judgment, the [trial] judge entered a summary judgment for Craven, denied Royal-Globe's motion for summary judgment, and ordered that the matter proceed to arbitration. Royal-Globe appealed. . . . We reverse and order that a judgment be entered declaring that Royal-Globe is not liable to Craven because Craven's notice to Royal-Globe was not timely. . . .

. . . In the early morning of September 19, 1979, Craven was injured in a hit and run automobile accident. [She says] an unidentified motor vehicle forced her automobile off the road and into a wall barrier. Craven was taken by ambulance to a hospital, where she was treated for a number of serious injuries. She remained in intensive care for several days and was released from the hospital twenty-three days after the accident.

Craven gave Royal-Globe formal notice of her claim on January 23, 1980. Royal-Globe denied her claim for recovery under her uninsured motorist policy on April 6, 1981.[2] On December 12, 1984, Craven filed a demand for arbitration of her uninsured motorist claim. On March 11, 1985, Royal-Globe filed [suit] seeking a declaration that it had no obligation to submit to arbitration as it was not liable under the policy.[3]

Royal-Globe asks us to reverse the summary judgment for Craven on the ground that Craven did not comply with her contractual obligation to give timely notice of her claim.[4] . . . The uninsured motorist policy in effect at the time of the accident requires notice to both the police and the insurer "[w]ithin [twenty-four] hours . . . if [the insured has] . . . been involved in a hit and run accident." The judge concluded, however, that Craven "was in the intensive care unit during the first twenty-four hours [after the accident]" and could not be expected to notify the police and her insurance company within twenty-four hours. . . . Craven therefore was excused from the twenty-four hour notice requirement. . . . There was no error in that determination.

---

[2] Royal-Globe paid Craven's claims under her Personal Injury Protection and Medical Payments policies and her claim for property damages.

[3] The arbitration has been stayed pending the outcome of this action.

[4] The standard Massachusetts automobile insurance policy in question instructs the insured what to do "[w]hen [t]here is an [a]ccident or [l]oss." The policy requires that the insured notify both the police and the insurance company within twenty-four hours if the insured has "been involved in a hit and run accident." The policy further requires that, in all events, the insurance company "must be notified *promptly* of the accident or loss" (emphasis added).

Royal-Globe [urges] that even if twenty-four hour notice was excused because of disability, the requirement should be reimposed once the disability is removed. Under this interpretation of the policy, disability tolls the running of the twenty-four hour period but does not dispense with it. The judge concluded that in the event that twenty-four hour notice is excused initially by disability, as was the case here, the policy requires prompt notice but not necessarily twenty-four hour notice. We agree. The language of the policy puts a time pressure on the insured to notify the company immediately after the disability is removed.

Royal-Globe contends that based on the undisputed facts in this record, Craven's notification, given more than four months after the accident and more than three months after her release from the hospital, was not prompt. We agree. Royal-Globe argues, and Craven does not dispute, that Craven was released from the hospital twenty-three days after the accident and that she stopped using medication one week after leaving the hospital. While at home, Craven was able to leave her home to visit doctors and dine out with her family[;] [she] also communicated with her office. Craven returned to work roughly three months after the accident; she did not give notice to Royal-Globe for another month. On this record, we cannot tell precisely when Craven's disability was removed, but it is clear that she did not notify Royal-Globe immediately thereafter.[6]

The burden of proving that she gave her notice promptly was on Craven. . . . Regardless of when her disability is determined to have disappeared, Craven's notice to Royal-Globe was not "performed readily or immediately[; nor was it] given without delay or hesitation." Webster's Third New Int'l Dictionary 1816 (1961). Giving "prompt" its fair meaning, Craven did not notify Royal-Globe promptly as a matter of law.[7]

Craven contends that Royal-Globe is estopped from raising her failure of notice as a basis to deny liability[,] [urging] that from the time she notified Royal-Globe of her claim, the company investigated the claim, communicated with her counsel about the status of the claim, and even informed her counsel of the possibility that liability might be denied because of a failure of proof—all without ever reserving the right to deny the claim based on late notice. The absence of such a reservation of rights,

[6] The judge reasoned that, where there is an ambiguous provision in an insurance policy, the court must construe it strictly against the insurer. There was, however, no ambiguity in the policy's use of the term "promptly." . . .

[7] We have said, albeit in dicta, that an insured "did not act with reasonable promptness" when it waited forty-six days after learning of a claim before notifying its insurer. Depot Cafe, Inc. v. Century Indem. Co., 321 Mass. 220, 225, 72 N.E.2d 533 (1947). Similarly, an injured plaintiff who did not notify his insurer of his claim on the policy for two months and six days did not act "with reasonable promptness" and thereby violated the policy's requirement of immediate notice. Wainer v. Weiner, 288 Mass. 250, 252, 192 N.E. 497 (1934). In construing analogous notice provisions, we have held that similar, and even shorter, delays in notifying insurers barred recovery. . . .

Craven argues, estops the company from denying liability because of her late notice.[8]

"In order to work an estoppel it must appear that one has been induced by the conduct of another to do something different from what otherwise would have been done and which has resulted to his harm. . . ." [DiMarzo v. Am. Mutual Insurance Co., 389 Mass. 85, 112, 449 N.E.2d 1189 (1983)]. . . . As we have previously noted, "where the denial of liability takes place after the expiration of the period for . . . [giving prompt notice], it cannot be said that the insured has been induced to forego steps to prevent a default under the policy, for the default has already occurred. Consequently, there is no basis for an estoppel." [Milton Ice Co. v. Travelers Indemnity Co., 320 Mass. 719, 722, 71 N.E.2d 232 (1947)]. . . .

Because Craven's notice was not prompt, and because Royal-Globe was not estopped from defending against liability on the basis of Craven's late notice, a judgment declaring that Royal-Globe is not liable to Craven because the notice was not timely should be entered. . . .

Semmes v. Hartford Ins. Co.

80 U.S. (13 Wall.) 158 (1871)

Plaintiff, a resident of Mississippi, brought suit on a policy of fire insurance issued by defendant, a Connecticut company. As recounted in the opinion, Plaintiff's loss occurred on January 5, 1860; suit was begun on October 31, 1866. Defendant relied on a provision of the policy to the effect that "no suit . . . should be sustainable in any court unless such suit should be commenced within the term of twelve months next after any loss or damage should occur." The lower court held the suit barred by this provision, notwithstanding plaintiff's contention that the Civil War had prevented commencement of the action within 12 months of the loss. That court reasoned that the 12-month provision was like a statute of limitation, and thus the running of the 12 months was suspended ("tolled") during the period of disability created by the war. Nevertheless, by tacking the time between the date of the loss and the commencement of the war to the time between the close of the war and the commencement of the action, the trial court concluded that plaintiff had waited more than the 12 months allowed by the contract.

Held, reversed and remanded for a new trial. "[T]he period of twelve months . . . does not open and expand itself so as to receive within it three or four years of legal disability . . . and then close together at each end of that period so as to complete itself, as though the war had never occurred. It is

---

[8] Craven also argues that Royal-Globe's payment of her personal injury protection, medical benefits, and collision benefits claims is inconsistent with its denial of benefits under the uninsured motorist policy. Royal-Globe replies, however, that these benefits are recoverable in a one-car accident. Timely notice of these claims is thus not as crucial to the insurance company. Generally in a one-car accident, fault is not an issue. Craven's argument would require litigation as to claims in which there is no controversy, if there are some claims in dispute. We decline to adopt such a rule.

true that, in regard to the limitation imposed by statute . . . the time may be so computed, but there the law imposes the limitation and the law imposes the disability. [It is] a necessary legal logic that the one period should be taken from the other. . . . Such is not the case as regards this contract. The defendant has made its own special and hard provision on that subject. . . . The condition is that no suit or action shall be sustainable unless commenced within the *time of twelve months next after the loss shall occur*, and in case such action shall be commenced after the expiration of twelve months *next after such* loss, the lapse of time shall be taken . . . as conclusive evidence against the validity of the claim. . . . [I]f the plaintiff shows any reason which in law rebuts the presumption, which, on the failure to sue within twelve months, is, by the contract, made conclusive against the validity of the claim, that presumption is not revived again by the contract. . . . There is nothing in the contract which does it. . . . Nor does the same evil consequence follow from removing absolutely the bar of the contract that would from removing absolutely the bar of the statute, for when the bar of the contract is removed there still remains the bar of the statute, and though the plaintiff may show by his disability to sue a sufficient answer to the twelve months provided by the contract, he must still bring his suit within the reasonable time fixed by the legislative authority, that is, by the statute of limitations.

"We have no doubt that the disability to sue imposed on the plaintiff by the war relieves him from the consequences of failing to bring suit within twelve months after the loss, because it rendered a compliance with that condition impossible and removes the presumption which that contract says shall be conclusive against the validity of the plaintiff's claim. That part of the contract, therefore, presents no bar to the plaintiff's right to recover."

NOTE

Semmes, like *Royal-Globe*, revisits excuse for "impracticability." Only now the inquiry is about the nonoccurrence of a condition, not the discharge of an underlying duty. Suppose the policy in *Semmes* had made it a condition of defendant's liability that premiums be paid annually, and that plaintiff, contending that the Civil War had rendered him unable to pay the premium for the year in which the loss occurred, nonetheless sued on the policy, tendering in court the overdue premium? New York Life Ins. Co. v. Statham, 93 U.S. (3 Otto) 24 (1876), was a consolidation of three actions brought on life insurance policies issued by defendant before 1860, insuring the lives of Mississippi residents who died after the outbreak of the Civil War. Payment of funds between North and South having been forbidden by both belligerents, premiums were not paid on the policies after the start of hostilities. Each policy contained the clause: "In case the said [insured] shall not pay the said premium on or before the several days hereinbefore mentioned for the payment thereof, then and in every such case the said company shall not be liable to the payment of the sum insured, or in any part thereof, and this policy shall cease and determine." The Court declared that the contract in each case was not merely a contract to insure for a single year, with a privilege of renewal from year to year by paying an annual premium, but that it was an "entire" contract for insurance for life, subject to discontinuance on nonpayment of the premiums stipulated. The Court nevertheless declared, without citing *Semmes*, that prompt payment of premiums was essential to the conduct of the insurance business and the calculation of insurance risks, and that nonpayment of premiums voided the policies. But since the nonpayment was caused by an act of government without fault of the insured, restitution should be awarded of the "equitable value" of the policies, measured by the premiums paid minus "the value of the assurance enjoyed by [the insured] whilst the policy was in existence." A similar conclusion was reached in Abell v. Penn Mut. Life Ins. Co., 18 W. Va. 400 (1881), though with a different method of measuring restitution, which aimed to prevent retention of any "profit" by the insurance company.

If you are familiar with Civil War history, the opinion in *Semmes* will seem strange, as it reports that the loss took place on January 5, 1860 and Mississippi did not secede from the Union until more than a year later (January 9, 1861), and Fort Sumter surrendered to Confederate forces later still (April 13, 1861). Nineteenth century reports of opinions, however, were at times unreliable, as this report illustrates. The record of the case makes clear that the fire was in fact on January 5, 1861, just a few days before Mississippi seceded. In assessing whether the filing of the claim was timely you should bear in mind that the Civil War came to an end in the first part of 1865 and the claim itself was not filed until late in 1866.

---

enXco Development Corp. v. Northern States Power Co.

United States Court of Appeals, Eighth Circuit, 2014.
758 F.3d 940.

SMITH, CIRCUIT JUDGE. . . . enXco develops renewable energy projects throughout the United States, especially solar and wind projects. NSP is an electric and gas company that provides energy to customers throughout Minnesota and the Dakotas.

enXco and NSP entered into two contracts in October 2008. The contracts involved a wind-energy-generation project in North Dakota known as the Merricourt Project ("Project"). The parties termed the first contract the Developed Wind Project Purchase and Sale Agreement (PSA). Under the PSA, enXco agreed to develop the Project site, which included obtaining the requisite permits. During this initial phase of the Project, enXco owned the Project's real estate and assets. Upon closing of the PSA, NSP would essentially purchase the Project's real estate and assets for $15 million.

The second, much larger contract was the Engineering, Procurement, and Construction Agreement (EPCA). Pursuant to the EPCA, NSP agreed to pay enXco over $350 million for engineering, procurement of infrastructure, construction, commissioning, start-up, and testing of the

Project. The parties agree that one of the principal benefits of this two-contract structure was that neither party had an obligation to proceed with the EPCA until the parties closed the PSA, which would not occur unless the Project developed according to their expectations.

The PSA included various conditions precedent that each party had to satisfy prior to the "Long-Stop Date" set for March 31, 2011. According to enXco, the Long-Stop Date was not a point of contention during contract negotiations. In fact, enXco selected the actual date without argument from NSP. enXco contends that "[t]he purpose of a long-stop date is to serve as a milestone against which to measure whether a project is 'buildable' . . . and such dates are regularly extended." In fact, in two of the parties' previous wind-farm projects, the parties agreed to modify their contracts to postpone the applicable long-stop date.

The PSA also provided that "[t]he obligation of [NSP] to consummate the transactions contemplated by this [PSA] shall be subject to fulfillment at or prior to the Closing of each of the following conditions." One condition precedent required enXco to obtain a Certificate of Site Compatibility (CSC). The CSC is a permit that the North Dakota Public Service Commission (NDPSC) issues that must be obtained before the parties could begin construction on the Project. The PSA also included a provision that stated "that in no event shall the Closing occur later than the Long-Stop Date." It also included the following termination clause:

> This Agreement may be terminated prior to the Closing: (i) by either [NSP], on the one side, or [enXco], on the other side, upon written notice to the other Party of such termination, in the event the Closing has not occurred or the conditions precedent to Closing in favor of the terminating Party have not been fulfilled or waived on or before the Long-Stop Date. . . .

It also provided that termination could occur without any liability accruing to the terminating party. Finally, the EPCA provided that the parties could terminate the EPCA should they fail to close the PSA.

enXco had approximately twenty-nine months after the execution of the contracts until the Long-Stop Date to obtain the CSC. Under North Dakota law, a party must submit a letter to the NDPSC, stating that it intends to construct an energy conversion facility. After an applicant like NSP submits this letter, it must wait one year before submitting its CSC application. enXco requested and received from the NDPSC a waiver of the one-year requirement in January 2009; thus, enXco could have submitted its application as early as January 2009.

A CSC application must demonstrate that the project would have a limited impact on endangered species. Unfortunately for enXco, the United States Fish and Wildlife Service (USFWS) warned enXco that the Project could have a deleterious effect on two species of birds because of the proposed physical locations of the wind turbines. Chris Sternhagen, enXco's Project Development Manager, testified that this problem delayed its submission of the CSC application. He would later testify, however, that the turbine layout actually "played very little impact as to the schedule."

In any event, almost two years expired before enXco submitted the CSC application in October 2010. Thus, enXco had less than six months to obtain the CSC by the Long-Stop Date. North Dakota law, however, allowed the NDPSC to consider the completed CSC application for up to six months after its receipt. Nonetheless, Sternhagen testified that a NDPSC staff member informed him that a decision would be reached in two-to-four months.

The NDPSC scheduled a statutorily mandated public hearing on the permit for December 21, 2010. Unfortunately, the hearing was postponed due to a snowstorm. The NDPSC conducted the hearing on February 10, 2011, but on March 17, 2011, the NDPSC discovered that the hearing occurred in the wrong county contrary to North Dakota law. As a result, a new hearing had to be scheduled, but North Dakota law also required a twenty-day public notice. Thus, the hearing was not rescheduled to occur until after the Long-Stop Date. enXco petitioned the NDPSC to waive the twenty-day notice requirement. In support of this petition, Sternhagen informed the NDPSC that, unless the NDPSC waived the twenty-day requirement, "NSP can terminate the [PSA] between the parties, effectively terminating this Project." At the resulting NDPSC meeting on the petition, enXco's counsel informed the NDPSC that "NSP would have the contractual ability to terminate April 1 and there's nothing that we can do as enXco to prevent that" if enXco did not obtain the CSC prior to the Long-Stop Date. The NDPSC denied the petition. On April 1, 2011, NSP terminated the PSA and thus the EPCA as well after the Long-Stop Date passed. enXco nonetheless obtained the CSC on June 8, 2011.

From execution of the contracts in October 2008 until their termination in April 2011, wind-energy-generation profit prospects declined such that NSP stood to lose significant amounts of money should it proceed with the Project. Apparently, the market for wind turbines dried up significantly during this time. As a result, NSP had the economic incentive to avoid the contract—a fact that enXco emphasizes. Because the particular wind turbines that enXco purchased were already outdated, enXco could not resell them on the secondary market. Therefore, enXco redeployed them for use in a different project in Texas.

enXco purchased the turbines for $216 million. Experts testified that the turbines' post-termination value was between $83.3 million and $123 million, minus the $10 million cost enXco incurred to relocate them. Thus, the turbines diminished in value between $93 million and $141 million. enXco's valuation expert determined that the value of the Project's assets like real estate and permits totaled $0 because of the lack of market for the Project and the $15 million cost in maintaining the assets.

However, enXco representatives testified that enXco still hoped the Project site would eventually be profitable.

enXco sued NSP on May 4, 2011, in response to a declaratory judgment action that NSP filed based on its termination of the contracts. The district court consolidated the cases, staying NSP's declaratory-judgment action pending the resolution of enXco's suit. enXco sued for declaratory relief and damages for breach of contract. The parties agreed, and the district court concluded, that Minnesota law applied to their contracts. . . .

enXco concedes that it failed to obtain the CSC prior to the Long-Stop Date. Furthermore, enXco does not dispute that in so doing it failed to satisfy a condition precedent rather than an ordinary contract term. enXco agrees that if we strictly construe the condition precedent, then NSP had the contractual right to terminate the contracts. However, enXco contends that we should excuse its failure to obtain the CSC by the Long-Stop Date based upon the legal doctrines of temporary impracticability and disproportionate forfeiture. . . .

enXco contends that the doctrine of temporary impracticability should excuse its failure to satisfy the condition precedent that it obtain the CSC by the Long-Stop Date. More specifically, enXco argues that it was impracticable for it to obtain the CSC by the Long-Stop Date because of delays from a snowstorm, a hearing location error, and state law notice requirements. enXco contends that "inclement weather and regulatory error," which delayed the NDPSC's processing of enXco's CSC application for five months, made it "impracticable to obtain the CSC." As a result of this alleged impracticability, enXco was excused from fulfilling the condition precedent, rendering NSP's termination of the PSA and EPCA a breach of contract. Additionally, enXco argues that Minnesota law recognizes the doctrine of temporary impracticability as applied to conditions precedent in a contract. Finally, enXco argues that Minnesota law allows plaintiffs to use the doctrine of temporary impracticability as a sword or offensive legal mechanism to pursue breach-of-contract claims in addition to defendants' use of the doctrine as a shield or defense against such actions. . . .

The Restatement also recognizes that impracticability may sometimes be only temporary:

> Impracticability of performance or frustration of purpose that is only temporary suspends the obligor's duty to perform while the impracticability or frustration exists but does not discharge his duty or prevent it from arising unless his performance after the cessation of the impracticability or frustration would be materially more burdensome than had there been no impracticability or frustration. Restatement (Second) of Contracts § 269.

The Restatement further provides for application of the doctrine of temporary impracticability to situations where a promisor violates a condition precedent, stating, "Impracticability excuses the non-occurrence of a condition if the occurrence of the condition is not a material part of the agreed exchange and forfeiture would otherwise result." Restatement (Second) of Contracts § 271.

Assuming, without deciding, that Minnesota courts would apply the doctrine of temporary impracticability to conditions precedent for use as a sword, we conclude that the doctrine has no application on these facts. enXco argues that the several delays in holding a proper public hearing produced temporary impracticability. However, enXco waited approximately two years before applying for the CSC. enXco could have applied as early as January 2009, yet it waited until October 2010. enXco submitted its application less than six months before the Long-Stop Date, and North Dakota law expressly authorizes the NDPSC to consider the application for up to six months. The PSA's time table contemplated and assumed that the NDPSC process could be lengthy and not entirely predictable.

The various sources of delay were all foreseeable and manageable in the time frame agreed to in the contracts. Although problems surfaced related to endangered birds, enXco likely could have pursued some type of accommodation with the USFWS or NDPSC in order to ensure a timely submission of its application. Or, it could have insisted on a later Long-Stop Date, especially since the actual date was not a point of contention between the parties. enXco could have also negotiated for a more flexible Long-Stop Date (e.g., "The Long-Stop Date shall be no earlier than one year after enXco submits its application for a CSC."). In sum, enXco, by exercise of appropriate diligence within the terms of the agreement, could likely have avoided the circumstances that caused it to fail a condition precedent. . . .

Here, the parties specifically contemplated what would occur in the event that the CSC was not obtained by the Long-Stop Date: NSP could terminate the contract. The PSA language regarding the satisfaction of conditions precedent and the termination clause expressly say so. The parties foresaw the risk of regulatory and weather delays and accounted for them. Although they could not foresee the specific circumstances that led to the non-occurrence of the condition, it is clear that the parties anticipated that the CSC might not be obtained in time. Furthermore, the doctrine of temporary impracticability does not apply when the government fails to issue a permit in a timely manner, especially where the parties recognized this possibility. Consequently, the district court correctly declined to apply the doctrine of temporary impracticability. . . .

enXco argues that it suffered a disproportionate forfeiture. enXco experienced an approximately $100 million diminution in value of its properties. On the other hand, NSP suffered no meaningful harm from enXco's tardy CSC. enXco further argues that Minnesota courts recognize that the doctrine of disproportionate forfeiture applies to the non-fulfillment of a condition precedent as well as for use as a sword rather than a shield. The district court determined that enXco did not suffer a disproportionate forfeiture because it retained title to all of the real estate and assets involved in the Project. enXco never transferred any of this property to NSP. . . .

Assuming, without deciding, that Minnesota courts would apply the doctrine of disproportionate forfeiture to the non-occurrence of conditions precedent and for use as a breach-of-contract sword, we conclude that enXco has not suffered a disproportionate forfeiture. We reach this conclusion despite the alleged materiality of the condition precedent at issue. The Restatement notes that a "forfeiture" "refer[s] to the denial of compensation that results when the obligee loses his right to the agreed exchange after he has relied substantially, as by preparation or performance on the expectation of that exchange." Restatement (Second) of Contracts § 229 cmt. b. The Restatement further states:

> In determining whether the forfeiture is "disproportionate," a court must weigh the extent of the forfeiture by the obligee against the importance to the obligor of the risk from which he sought to be protected and the degree to which that protection will be lost if the non-occurrence of the condition is excused to the extent required to prevent forfeiture.

Weighing these competing interests as the Restatement suggests can be difficult.

Nevertheless, we have recognized that forfeitures may be appropriate where they are "consonant with notions of fairness and justice under the law." Klipsch, Inc. v. WWR Tech., Inc., 127 F.3d 729, 737 (8th Cir. 1997). This court in *Klipsch* noted that forfeiture may be fair and just where able counsel represented sophisticated parties. Also, forfeitures are legitimate when the parties included an express termination clause in the contract. Additionally, no forfeiture occurs where the breaching party maintained ownership of the assets comprising the contract. . . .

Here, enXco parted with nothing. It still maintained possession and ownership of the Project assets and real estate. enXco transferred the Project's physical capital for use in other projects, and it hopes to employ the real property associated with the Project in the future. NSP did not obtain ownership of any property as a result of termination. NSP therefore did not receive something for little or nothing. Notably, both enXco and NSP are sophisticated parties who have developed similar projects in the past. They were both represented by counsel during contract negotiations, which took place over the course of several months. In conclusion, we leave the parties to their bargain and do not apply the doctrine of disproportionate forfeiture. . . .

COMMENT: WAIVER OF CONDITIONS

Waiver, like estoppel, is a general doctrine of American law. "Generality" means, of course, that a doctrine may take different forms as bases for application are varied. Courts and commentators commonly say that waiver and estoppel are "distinct but related doctrines," that is, despite distinguishable elements, they overlap in application and, at times, are discussed in words used interchangeably (e.g., a court may ask whether the proofs add up to "waiver by estoppel"). It might be said that the function of these doctrines was to terminate contract rights and discharge contract duties. They involve the elimination of express conditions to a promised performance, not the alteration of underlying rights or duties that is normally accomplished through an agreed modification of a promise. 3A A. Corbin, Contracts § 752.

It is another question whether a condition once eliminated by waiver or estoppel can be revived. One continues to find in the cases statements that "[a] waiver once made is irrevocable and cannot be revived." Tri-City Jewish Ctr. v. Blass Riddick Chilcote, 159 Ill. App. 3d 436, 512 N.E.2d 363 (1987), appeal denied, 118 Ill. 2d 552, 520 N.E.2d 393 (1988). What about a land contract with an express condition of installment payments on the first day of each month, and "waiver" by the vendor's acceptance of successive payments 10, 12, and 15 days late; can the vendor reinstate the condition by notice communicated well in advance of the next payment day? A similar question may arise as to insurance premiums accepted late, or accepted through an agent when direct payment to the home office is required. You may expect that many conditions can be revived within certain limits that are not always well defined.

There is need to add a word on the relevance of the consideration requirement in applying the contractual doctrine of waiver. Since consideration is used in our law only in connection with a bargain ("an agreement to exchange"), it was necessary to provide that some promises are binding without consideration. Promises found to constitute a "waiver" by virtue of an obligor's manifested intention to disregard an unfulfilled condition are so classified.

Joca-Roca Real Estate, LLC v. Brennan

United States Court of Appeals, First Circuit, 2014.
772 F.3d 945.

SELYA, CIRCUIT JUDGE. Federal law favors agreements to arbitrate. Thus, when contracting parties provide that disputes arising under a contract will be resolved by arbitration, federal courts ordinarily will honor that choice. But arbitration clauses are not set in cement: such clauses can be waived, either expressly or through conduct. The court below found such a conduct-based waiver and denied the plaintiff's motion to stay court proceedings in order to clear the way for arbitration. The plaintiff appeals. We affirm.

The stage is easily set. On September 18, 2005, plaintiff-appellant Joca-Roca Real Estate, LLC and defendant-appellee Robert T. Brennan, Jr., entered into an asset purchase agreement (the Agreement). The Agreement paved the way for the transfer of title to certain real property that served as the site of an intermodal vehicle dealership in South Lebanon, Maine. The Agreement contained a broad provision requiring submission of all disputes "concerning the validity, interpretation and enforcement" of the Agreement to an arbitrator for final and binding resolution.

The plaintiff came to believe that the defendant had misled it concerning certain attributes of the purchased property. Acting on this belief, the plaintiff sued the defendant in the United States District Court for the District of Maine on March 4, 2013. Invoking diversity jurisdiction, the plaintiff's complaint asserted claims for fraud and breach of contract arising out of the Agreement. Notably, the plaintiff commenced this civil action without making the slightest effort to pursue arbitration.

The defendant answered the complaint, raising as an affirmative defense (which it subsequently never pressed) the plaintiff's "fail[ure] to seek relief in the manner required under" the Agreement. A magistrate judge promptly entered a scheduling order closing discovery in August of 2013 and setting the case for trial in January of 2014. The parties began discovery and, at their joint behest, the magistrate judge granted several extensions of the discovery deadline. That deadline was eventually enlarged to December 16, 2013; the trial date was moved back to February 3, 2014; and the parties were directed to notify the court of their intent to file summary judgment motions by December 23, 2013.

During the course of pretrial proceedings, the parties conducted sixteen depositions, propounded and answered interrogatories, and produced and exchanged thousands of pages of documents. In the process, the magistrate judge held no fewer than four telephone conferences to resolve discovery disputes and scheduling conflicts.

On December 6, 2013, the plaintiff moved to stay proceedings pending arbitration. The motion offered no explanation for the plaintiff's cunctation in invoking the Agreement's arbitration provision. The defendant objected and notified the court of his intent to move for summary judgment. The magistrate judge then denied the motion to stay on the ground that the plaintiff had waived its arbitral rights. The plaintiff took a first-tier appeal of this ruling to the district judge, who summarily affirmed the denial of the stay. . . .

Generally speaking, what contracting parties take they can give away—and parties to a contract normally are free to waive the right to arbitration. Such a waiver may be either express or implied. This case deals only with implied waiver.

In considering whether a waiver can be implied, we start with the strong federal policy favoring arbitration agreements. Given the strength of this policy, "mere delay in seeking [arbitration] without some resultant prejudice" is insufficient to ground a finding of conduct-based waiver. Creative Solutions Grp., Inc. v. Pentzer Corp., 252 F.3d 28, 32 (1st Cir. 2001). The party advocating waiver has the burden of demonstrating prejudice. . . .

It is common ground that a party must invoke its right to arbitration in a timeous manner or else risk forfeiting that right. Here, the plaintiff commenced a civil action, vigorously prosecuted it, and then—after many months of active litigation—tried to switch horses midstream to pursue an arbitral remedy. To make matters worse, it made this abrupt about-face in the absence of any material change in circumstances.

Seen in this light, the plaintiff's belated resort to arbitration was anything but timely. The plaintiff chose to eschew an available arbitral forum and, instead, brought suit in the federal district court. The defendant then reminded the plaintiff of the availability of arbitration through an affirmative defense. The plaintiff turned a blind eye to this reminder and waited more than eight months before seeking a stay in order to pursue arbitration. By that time, the close of discovery was hard at hand, a summary judgment motion was in the offing, and trial was less than two months away. Undue delay is manifest.

Here, moreover, the delay is more troubling because the plaintiff never offered any explanation for it. When directly questioned about the plaintiff's lack of any explanation for its belated decision to abandon the courtroom in favor of an arbitral forum, appellate counsel was wholly uninformative. We are left to infer that the change in direction may well reflect the plaintiff's dissatisfaction with the way the court case was proceeding—and we do not condone the use of an arbitration clause as a parachute when judicial winds blow unfavorably. . . .

Some degree of prejudice ordinarily may be inferred from a protracted delay in the assertion of arbitral rights when that delay is accompanied by sufficient litigation activity. That inference makes good sense: during such a period of delay, the opposing party usually will incur cost, measured in both out-of-pocket expense and the value of time.

So it is here: the plaintiff's conduct evinced a clear intent to forgo arbitration and resolve the disputed matter through litigation. In response, the defendant undertook the discovery that he believed necessary to mount a defense. Over a period of more than eight months, the parties engaged actively in discovery; and the defendant incurred what must have been substantial costs associated with more than a dozen depositions, interrogatories, document production, and conferences with the magistrate judge and opposing counsel. With trial looming, an eleventh-hour stay in favor of arbitration would have forced the defendant into a new forum and, in the bargain, postponed resolution of the underlying controversy. That would cause the defendant further prejudice and nullify one of the primary benefits of arbitration: its use as a cost-effective and expedient alternative to litigation.

The plaintiff resists the conclusion that the defendant would be prejudiced by a stay. It insists that delay, by itself, cannot constitute the requisite prejudice. This overly broad argument fails to account for the myriad forms of prejudice that may result from a belated invocation of rights.

We agree that mere delay in asserting a right to arbitrate, without more, does not require a finding of waiver. Here, however, there is more: this is not a case in which no significant activity occurred during the period of delay. We evaluate whether any particular period of delay supports a finding of prejudice based largely on what did (or did not) take place during that period. . . .

According due weight to the chronology and circumstances recounted above, we think it is nose-on-the-face plain that the defendant demonstrated that granting a stay would cause him prejudice. We think it equally plain that the district court did not err in concluding that the plaintiff has, through its conduct, waived its right to demand arbitration. . . .

Parsons v. Halliburton Energy Services, Inc.

Supreme Court of Appeals of West Virginia, 2016.
237 W. Va. 138.

CHIEF JUSTICE, KETCHUM. . . . The plaintiff worked for the defendant from June until October 2013. On December 3, 2013, the plaintiff filed a complaint in the Circuit Court of Kanawha County alleging that the defendant did not timely pay him his final wages as required by the West Virginia Wage Payment and Collection Act ("the WPCA"). The plaintiff's complaint also sought to create a class action composed of other former employees of the defendant who were not timely paid their final wages.

On July 7, 2014, some seven months after the plaintiff filed his complaint, the defendant's first court filing was a motion seeking to compel the plaintiff to participate in arbitration. The plaintiff responded to the motion by arguing that the defendant had waived its contractual right to arbitration by failing to timely raise arbitration, and by acting inconsistently with its contractual right to arbitration in the previous seven months. The defendant never filed an answer to the plaintiff's complaint before moving to compel arbitration, yet the plaintiff contends the defendant still participated in the litigation.

As evidence of the defendant's participation, the plaintiff asserts that shortly after the complaint was filed, on December 16, 2013, counsel for the defendant exchanged e-mails with plaintiff's counsel asking for a forty-five-to-sixty day filing extension to plead in the lawsuit. Defense counsel stated the defendant was "in the process of tracking down whether and to what extent" other employees were not paid in accordance with the WPCA, and offered to produce information about other employees to "short-circuit" discovery and litigation. Plaintiff's counsel agreed to the delay by the defendant.

On April 21, 2014, defense counsel contacted plaintiff's counsel by e-mail and asked for additional time to plead. Defense counsel asked if he was "still okay with the responsive pleading deadline and, if we're close, can I ask that it be pushed out again?" In a subsequent phone conversation with plaintiff's counsel, defense counsel said he expected to respond to the plaintiff's needs within two to three weeks.

Some five months after the complaint was filed, on May 22, 2014, plaintiff's counsel wrote an e-mail to defense counsel. Plaintiff's counsel noted that defense counsel had not produced the promised information, and said the plaintiff was not providing "an open-ended extension for Halliburton to respond[.]" A new defense lawyer (within the same firm) promptly responded to the e-mail from plaintiff's counsel. The new defense lawyer stated the prior lawyer was no longer working on the case, and said she would need additional time to "get a handle on the status" of the case. Two new lawyers noted their appearances as counsel for the defendant in the last week of June 2014, and the defendant's first substantive filing in the court record—the motion to compel arbitration—was filed on July 7, 2014.

In an order dated November 14, 2014, the circuit court granted the defendant's motion, dismissed the plaintiff's complaint and compelled the parties to participate in arbitration. The circuit court determined that the defendant had not waived its rights under the arbitration provision. Although the defendant admitted to a seven-month delay before moving for arbitration, the circuit court found that the defendant had "not actively participated in this lawsuit." Moreover, the circuit court found the plaintiff was required, but had failed, to prove he was prejudiced by the defendant's actions or delay.

The plaintiff now appeals the circuit court's order dismissing his complaint and compelling him to arbitrate his claims against the defendant. . . .

The facts below are not disputed, and the parties agree that the plaintiff's claims fall within the scope of a clear and unambiguous arbitration agreement. Additionally, the plaintiff does not challenge the enforceability of the arbitration agreement under West Virginia's general contract law. The sole question on appeal is whether the defendant's actions, viewed under principles of state contract law, served to waive its contractual right to arbitration.

The plaintiff insists the defendant actively participated in the underlying litigation by volunteering to produce class-wide discovery and by repeatedly seeking extensions of time to file a responsive pleading. The plaintiff argues the defendant's actions were contrary to its contractual right to avoid the court system and demonstrated the defendant's intent to waive the protection afforded by the contractual arbitration provision.

The defendant counters that these actions did not rise to a level of "substantial participation" in the litigation process, and on balance are not of enough significance to demonstrate waiver. Furthermore, the defendant asserts the plaintiff was required to establish "actual prejudice" before a court could find waiver of a contract right, and asserts the plaintiff failed to meet this burden.

It is a well-established principle of contract law that contract rights can be waived. Under West Virginia contract law (and the contract law of most other states), the "waiver" of a contract right is "defined as the voluntary, intentional relinquishment of a known right." Hoffman v. Wheeling Sav. & Loan Ass'n, 133 W. Va. 694, 712, 57 S.E.2d 725, 735 (1950). . . .

Waiver of a contract right may be made by an express statement or agreement, or it may be implied from the conduct of the party who is alleged to have waived a right. . . . "Of course a waiver may be express or it may be inferred from actions or conduct, but all the attendant facts, taken together, must amount to an intentional relinquishment of a known right, in order that a waiver may exist." Blue v. Hazel-Atlas Glass Co., 106 W.Va. 642, 650, 147 S.E. 22, 25–26 (1929).

To rely upon the doctrine of waiver under the common law, a party is not required to show prejudice or detrimental reliance caused by the opposing party's waiver of a contract right. As Chief Justice Davis stated, "The doctrine of waiver focuses on the conduct of the party against whom waiver is sought, and requires that party to have intentionally relinquished a known right. There is no requirement of prejudice or detrimental reliance by the party asserting waiver." Potesta v. U.S. Fid. & Guar. Co., 202 W. Va. 308, 315–16, 504 S.E.2d 135, 142–43 (1998).

Waiver does not require proof of prejudice or detrimental reliance because "[w]aiver is within the control of the party who chooses to relinquish a condition [in the contract], quite apart from whether another party relies on relinquishment." 8 Catherine M.A. McCauliff, *Corbin on Contracts* § 40.1 (1999). "Waiver is essentially unilateral in its character; it results as a legal consequence from some act or conduct of the party against whom it operates; no act of the party in whose favor it is made is necessary to complete it." Equitable Life Assur. Soc'y of U.S. v. Ellis, 105 Tex. 526, 147 S.W. 1152, 1157 (1912). . . .

In summary, on the question of prejudice or detrimental reliance, the distinction between the common law doctrines of estoppel and waiver is simple: estoppel requires proof of prejudice or detrimental reliance; waiver does not. We therefore hold that the common-law doctrine of waiver focuses on the conduct of the party against whom waiver is sought, and requires that party to have intentionally relinquished a known right. A waiver may be express or may be inferred from actions or conduct, but all of the attendant facts, taken together, must amount to an intentional relinquishment of a known right. There is no requirement of prejudice or detrimental reliance by the party asserting waiver. . . .

We turn now to the instant case. The undisputed facts are that there is a written arbitration agreement that encompasses the dispute between the parties. While the burden was on the plaintiff to prove the defendant knew of its right to arbitrate, we presume the defendant at least constructively knew because it was both a signatory to the arbitration contract and asserted the arbitration contract in its first court filing. The plaintiff filed his complaint in December 2013, and the defendant's first filing in the circuit court was a motion to dismiss that clearly asserted the arbitration agreement.

There is nothing in the record to suggest the defendant expressly waived its right to arbitrate. The defendant also did not implicitly waive its contractual right to arbitration by answering or responding to the civil complaint without asserting its right.

The question then becomes whether the defendant implicitly waived the right to arbitrate, by acting inconsistently with the right between December 2013 and the filing of the motion to dismiss in July 2014. The delay alone is meaningless; it is the circumstances surrounding the defendant's acts and language that determine whether the defendant implicitly intended to waive the right to arbitrate. The record essentially shows that the defendant asked, three times, for additional time to respond to the plaintiff's complaint. The plaintiff acceded to these requests, even though he was under no obligation to do so. . . . The defendant made no formal, substantive response to any of the plaintiff's requests. On this record we cannot find any error in the circuit court's conclusion that the defendant acted consistently with the arbitration agreement, and did not participate in the plaintiff's lawsuit prior to July 2014. Viewing the totality of the circumstances, the defendant did not implicitly waive its right to arbitrate through its acts and language. . . .

NOTE: TIMELINESS AS AN EXPRESS CONDITION

If the parties to a contract wish to make timely performance a material element of their agreement, there is nothing to stop them. Timeliness, like other bargainable items, is mainly a matter of contract and not of law. The question whether a contract must be performed at the exact time specified usually takes the form of an inquiry into whether "time is of the essence." Many written agreements include a time-is-of-the-essence clause. The typical case involves a duty to pay money on a stated date—for example, a land-contract installment of $500 on or before June 15. Is the vendee's payment of $500 no later than June 15 an "express condition" of the vendor's duties under the contract? Whether performance at the specified time is of the essence is most certainly a question of the parties' intent, to be determined, as a matter of fact, from the language of the contract and the circumstances attending its negotiation. Because interpretation always has a context, Professor Corbin's warning about the hazards of boilerplate bears repeating: "It is not desirable to try to achieve [the conditioning of a duty upon a performance on or by a specified time] by merely putting into the contract the words 'time is of the essence of this contract.' " 3A A. Corbin, Contracts § 715.

If time is found to be "of the essence," courts usually say that performance on the designated date is "mandatory." One matter worth special attention is how (and by whom) the question of timely performance is raised—that is, the type of claim or defense brought to court. Another is that in many courts, perhaps most, contract provisions specifying dates for performance are more strictly enforced in actions at law than in suits for equitable relief. Still another is the course-of-performance conduct of the parties in relation to terms specifying dates or schedules for performance. It should be noted that the rule that time ordinarily is not of the essence in transactions involving real property applies to the occurrence of a contractual condition as well as to the performance of a contractual duty. Kakalik v. Bernardo, 184 Conn. 386, 439 A.2d 1016 (1981). In light of what we have seen, might the same be said of building or construction contracts?

Commercial Resource Group, LLC v. The J.M. Smucker Co.

United States Court of Appeals, Eighth Circuit, 2014.
753 F.3d 790.

KELLY, CIRCUIT JUDGE. . . . In March 2001, Smucker leased a commercial building in West Fargo, North Dakota, from CRG. The parties negotiated an amendment to the lease in 2005. The amendment provided that the lease would continue for an initial two-year term, and it gave Smucker an option to renew the lease for up to four additional one-year terms. After the initial term, the lease was set to renew automatically on July 1st of each year unless Smucker provided CRG written notice of its intent to terminate 180 days prior, i.e., by January 1st. The original lease specified the address to which the written notice should be sent ("original address"). On September 15, 2006, CRG's management company informed Smucker of CRG's change of address and notified Smucker that "all future rent payments and lease correspondence" should be sent to the new address ("2006 address"). Smucker received this notice and began sending rent payments to the new address. The lease was not modified to reflect the change of address.

In late 2009, Smucker decided to close down its West Fargo facility. On December 22, 2009, Smucker sent a notice of termination to CRG by way of Federal Express ("FedEx"); however, Smucker sent the notice to the original address instead of the 2006 address. On December 23, 2009, Smucker received an email from FedEx stating "FedEx attempted, but was unable to complete delivery [of the December 22, 2009, notice]."

FedEx "[r]ecommended" that Smucker "[c]ontact [FedEx] to provide correct delivery address and/or additional delivery information." Smucker took no action. FedEx sent a second email a week later, on December 30, 2009. The second email stated, "FedEx attempted, but was unable to complete delivery." This email instructed that "[n]o action is required" because "[t]he package is being returned to the shipper." Smucker took no additional action prior to the January 1st deadline for terminating the lease.

After the deadline passed, Smucker sent a second termination notice to CRG, this time to the 2006 address. The notice was dated January 4, 2010, and it arrived on January 5, 2010. This second notice stated Smucker wanted to terminate the lease. It also explained that Smucker had sent a timely termination notice to the original address, but that notice had been returned "as undeliverable." The parties disagree as to whether this second notice effectively terminated the lease.

The district court found that Smucker had substantially performed the contract and should not be held responsible for a "minor delay" that was the result of "an honest mistake in mailing." The court emphasized that Smucker "made a good faith attempt" and "acted promptly to correct [its mistake]." As such, the district court held that "[t]o punish Smucker in the form of hundreds of thousands of dollars . . . would be an unconscionable result . . . especially where time was not of the essence to the contract and where the untimely notice did not result in any demonstrable injury to CRG." Therefore, the district court granted Smucker summary judgment on the basis of substantial performance. . . .

The parties agree that the lease was to renew automatically unless Smucker provided written notice to CRG of its intent to terminate the lease by January 1, 2010. There is also no dispute that Smucker's notice failed to arrive by that date. Rather, at issue in this case is whether the district court erred by: (1) failing to treat the lease cancellation provision as an option to terminate; and (2) allowing Smucker equitable relief despite failure to strictly comply with the terms of the option. . . .

The district court treated the lease cancellation provision as a standard contract provision and found that: (1) Smucker had substantially performed its obligations under the lease; and (2) time was not of the essence to the lease. CRG claims the lease cancellation provision was an option to terminate the lease and as such required strict compliance, including strict compliance with the time provisions. . . .

Under North Dakota law, a lease is a contract between two parties, and "[t]he rules of contract construction are . . . applied to leases." Langer v. Bartholomay, 745 N.W.2d 649, 655 (N.D. 2008). As with other contracts, "[w]hether or not a [lease] requires performance at the exact time specified in the [lease] depends on whether or not time is of the essence." Langer, 745 N.W.2d at 657. "[U]nless the intent that time is of the essence is manifest from the face of the [lease], whether the parties intended time to be of the essence is a question of fact." *Id.* "Where time is not of the essence, [i.e., is non-material,] a reasonable delay in performance does not constitute a breach of contract." *Id.* Instead, under the doctrine of "substantial performance," a party is relieved of exact compliance with the terms of a lease if the breach of the lease terms is non-material. In this case, the district court held that time was not of the essence to the contract, and therefore Smucker's slight delay was not a material breach.

However, option contracts are treated differently than regular contracts. An option is an irrevocable offer by the offeror to perform. Matrix Props. Corp. v. TAG Invs., 609 N.W.2d 737, 742 (N.D. 2000). "Courts generally construe the attempt to exercise an option strictly and require exact compliance because the optionee is free to exercise the option if he chooses, but an optionor is bound to perform if the option is properly exercised." Langer, 745 N.W.2d at 657–58. "As a matter of law . . . time [is] of the essence" in exercising an option contract. Id. at 658. "[T]he optionee must perform the terms of the option within the specified time and upon the terms and conditions provided in the agreement." Id. at 657. North Dakota applies the same rules to an option in a lease as to an option to buy property, whether for an option to renew a lease or an option to terminate.

The lease in this case contained an option to terminate, not simply a lease cancellation provision. While the original lease provided an option to renew the lease for up to three years, the amendment to the lease made renewal automatic and termination optional. . . .

Through the provision for automatic extensions, CRG, the lessor, made an irrevocable offer to extend the lease and no longer had the ability to terminate the lease at the end of the current term—the lease would automatically renew based solely on the actions of the lessee, Smucker. The lease could only be cancelled by Smucker, and only if Smucker provided written notice to CRG by a specified date. As a result, after the amendment, Smucker held an option to terminate the lease.

As an option to terminate the lease, the cancellation provision must be "strictly construed" and "require[s] exact compliance." Langer, 745 N.W.2d at 658. Also, "as a matter of law . . . time [is] of the essence" to the option. *Id.* Given the significant differences between a standard lease cancellation provision and an option to terminate, we find the district court erred in failing to treat the cancellation provision in this case as an option to terminate. . . .

The Supreme Court of North Dakota has twice suggested the possibility that equitable relief may be available when a party fails to timely exercise an option. . . . Generally, "[a] court may invoke its equitable powers and an option may nevertheless be enforced even if the holder failed to exercise it within the specified time if: (1) the delay is slight[;] (2) the delay has not prejudiced the other party[;] and (3) a failure to grant relief would result in such hardship as to make literal enforcement of the option unconscionable." [Langer, 745 N.W.2d at 658.] The Supreme Court of North Dakota has also noted, however, that courts generally limit equitable relief to a very particular situation: "[e]quitable relief is generally granted in cases where a lessee has made valuable improvements to the property in expectation of renewing a lease, but the lessee's notice to renew is slightly past the deadline, and the relief is necessary to avoid the inequitable forfeiture or literal compliance is unconscionable." Id. at 658–59. . . .

Assuming without deciding that equitable relief is an available remedy in this case, we find there is no showing of unconscionability upon enforcement of the lease. . . .

Sahadi v. Continental Illinois Nat'l Bank & Trust Co. of Chicago

706 F.2d 193 (7th Cir. 1983)

"The Bank [urges] that no room for a 'materiality' analysis and its concomitant factual inquiry exists here because the payment of the interest on or before November 15 was an 'express condition' of the Bank's forbearance, and thus its terms were required to be exactly fulfilled. This [argument] suffers from its conclusory assumption of what it seeks to prove—that the payment of the interest on the precise named date rather than payment . . . in a reasonably prompt manner was of threshold importance to the completion of the contract. In short, asking whether a provision is a 'condition' is similar to stating the 'materiality' question: both seek to determine whether its performance was a *sine qua non* of the contract's fulfillment. And that determination may not be made through a mechanical process."

Schultz v. Los Angeles Dons, Inc.

107 Cal. App.2d 718, 238 P.2d 73 (1951)

A professional football player brought an action to recover the $7,500 balance of the $8,000 salary under a contract to play for the 1948 season. The contract permitted the Club to terminate the contract during the training season, on payment to the player of his expenses, but one clause stated: "If this contract is terminated by Club by reason of Player's failure to render his services hereunder due to disability resulting directly from injuries sustained in the performance of his services hereunder and written notice of such injury is given by the Player as provided in Regulation 6, Club agrees to pay Player" his full season's salary. Regulation 6 stated that "written notice of any injury sustained by Player in rendering services under his contract, stating the time, place, cause and nature of the injury shall be delivered to Club by Player within 10 days of the sustaining of the injury." During the training season in July 1948, plaintiff, after taking part in two vigorous scrimmages, developed pain in the back of his leg and numbness in his foot, both of which he reported at once, orally, to the head coach and the trainer. During the next few days, the trainer gave plaintiff treatments, with little success, and plaintiff was then examined, under the head coach's orders, by three orthopedic surgeons, who reported that it would be very dangerous for plaintiff to play any more football because of an injury to his back. The trainer made full written reports of plaintiff's injury to the insurance company from which the Club had purchased insurance. *Held*, the Club's termination of plaintiff's contract, by notice given in August, was not justified by plaintiff's failure to give written notice of his injury. "The apparent purpose of the required notice was to make certain that appellant was promptly and fully informed of any such injury so that it could take the necessary steps to have its trainer and doctors treat the injury and protect its investment in respondent [plaintiff]. It may also have had some relation to the insurance carried on respondent by appellant. The evidence clearly establishes that respondent promptly gave appellant, through its trainer and coach, all information in his possession in regard to the injury, and that appellant took full advantage of it by having respondent treated by its trainer and examined and treated by one of its doctors on July 19th and shortly thereafter by two others, and that these doctors made written reports to appellant of their findings. By so doing, appellant waived the requirement of written notice. In addition, the trainer sent the reports about the injury to the insurance company. Appellant was therefore as fully protected as if the required information had been given in writing. A written notice from respondent would have been an idle act." [Is this waiver, estoppel, or "interpretation"? Does it matter what it is called?]

NOTE: TIMELY NOTICE AND INSURANCE POLICIES

Courts are divided on whether an insurer defending on the basis of an insured's failure to give timely notice under the policy is required to show that it suffered actual prejudice. See Aetna Cas. & Sur. Co. v. Murphy, 206 Conn. 409, 538 A.2d 219 (Conn. 1988). Yet there is apparently broad agreement on one point: where a "notice-prejudice" rule in some form is applied to a contractual condition, it will likely be in the area of insurance. If a contract not involving insurance unmistakably establishes an express condition requiring the giving of written notice by a specified date, there is much authority holding that "substantial compliance" (say, the giving of oral notice) will not suffice. Some other basis for excusing the nonoccurrence of the condition must be found. One court has summarized its approach in the notice cases in this way: "Inasmuch as we are not dealing here with a situation where plaintiff stands to suffer forfeiture or undue hardship, we perceive no justification for engaging in a 'materiality-of-the-nonoccurrence' analysis. To do so would simply frustrate the clearly expressed intention of the parties. Freedom of contract prevails in an arm's length transaction between sophisticated parties[,] and in the absence of countervailing public policy concerns there is no reason to relieve them of the consequences of their bargain." Oppenheimer & Co. v. Oppenheim, Appel, Dixon & Co., 86 N.Y.2d 685, 636 N.Y.S.2d 734, 660 N.E.2d 415 (1995).

The Restatement, Second § 229, which focuses attention not on the time a contract is made but on ensuing events, is yet another instance of what courts "may" do in order to avoid forfeiture. Among the diverse examples provided by the restaters to show § 229's discretionary principle at work is the following (illustration 2):

> A, an ocean carrier, carries B's goods under a contract providing that it is a condition of A's liability for damage to cargo that "written notice of claim for loss or damage must be given within 10 days after removal of goods." B's cargo is damaged during carriage and A knows of this. On removal of the goods, B notes in writing on the delivery record that the cargo is damaged, and five days later informs A over the telephone of a claim for that damages and invites A to participate in an inspection within the ten day period. A inspects the goods within the period, but B does not given written notice of its claim until 25 days after removal of the goods. Since the purpose of requiring the condition of written notice is to alert the carrier and enable it to make a prompt investigation, and since this purpose had been served by the written notice of damage and the oral notice of claim, the court may excuse the non-occurrence of the condition to the extent required to allow to recovery by B.

SECTION 3. CONDITIONS OF "SATISFACTION"

Fursmidt v. Hotel Abbey Holding Corp.

Supreme Court of New York, Appellate Division, 1960.
10 A.D.2d 447, 200 N.Y.S.2d 256.

RABIN, J. The plaintiff and his father had been rendering valet and laundry services at the Hotel Abbey for a great many years[,] . . . [in] space in the hotel basement. On February 1, 1958, the plaintiff entered into an agreement in writing with the defendant, the owner of the hotel, which provided for the plaintiff to render such services for an additional three-year period for which the defendant was to receive compensation of $325 per month. This agreement provided in Paragraph "5" thereof as follows:

"It is distinctly understood and agreed that the services to be rendered by the second party [plaintiff] shall meet with the approval of the first party [defendant], who shall be the sole judge of the sufficiency and propriety of the services."

In September, 1958 the defendant informed the plaintiff that he was to discontinue his services as of October 1, 1958. The plaintiff thereafter removed from the premises. . . . Upon such discontinuance the valet and laundry service was resumed by a third party who paid to the defendant the sum of $250 per month as consideration for the concession.

The plaintiff claims that the defendant had no right to terminate the contract. . . . The defendant defends saying that the services did not meet with its approval and were unsatisfactory. It counterclaims for damages which it claims it sustained by reason of plaintiff's breach of the contract in failing to render adequate and proper service.

The defendant takes the position that it had a right to terminate the agreement if it genuinely and honestly felt that the services rendered were unsatisfactory to it and did not meet with its approval, urging that under the contract it was to be the sole judge of the "sufficiency and propriety of the services." Accordingly it urges that it was not for the court or a jury to pass upon the reasonableness of such conclusion if in fact it was a conclusion honestly arrived at by it.

The Trial Court disagreed holding that it was not enough that the defendant be dissatisfied, even though such dissatisfaction be not feigned, but implicit in law was a requirement that such dissatisfaction be reasonably grounded. Consequently, the Court in its charge gave to the jury for resolution not only the question of whether the defendant was in fact dissatisfied but also the question as to whether such dissatisfaction was reasonable. Under the Court's charge therefore even though the jury found the dissatisfaction to be genuine it would be obliged to find for the plaintiff if nonetheless it found that such dissatisfaction had no reasonable basis. In other words the court substituted the judgment of a reasonable man in place of the judgment of the defendant. . . .

Provisions in agreements calling for performance to the satisfaction of a party fall into two general categories. In contracts relating to operative fitness, utility or marketability the provision "is construed as a matter of law as imposing only the requisite of satisfying a reasonable man" (3 Williston, Contracts, § 675A [Rev.Ed.]). For example, such a construction has been given to "satisfaction" provisions where the performance called for was the installation of machinery, . . . and where repairs were to be made to a boiler (Duplex Safety Boiler Co. v. Garden, 101 N.Y. 387, 4 N.E. 749).

On the other hand a literal construction of the "satisfaction" provisions is made where the agreements provide for performance involving "fancy, taste, sensibility, or judgment" of the party for whose benefit it was made (10 N.Y.Jur., Contracts, § 302). Such a result obtains in cases calling for performance to one's satisfaction in the making of a garment, the giving of a course of instruction, the services of an orchestra, the making of recordings by a singer and the painting of a portrait (see cases cited in 2 Clark, N.Y. Law of Contracts, § 928).

The resolution of the issue here presented lies with the determination of whether the instant agreement is one relating to operative fitness, utility or marketability or one involving fancy, taste, sensibility or judgment. We find that it comes within the rules applicable to the latter class. . . .

In reaching this determination we recognize that the performance here called for does not lie at either extreme of the respective categories. However, it is by far closer to the category involving taste or judgment than the one where "satisfaction" is complied with by reasonable performance. Such a conclusion is inescapable when the agreement is examined in the light of its purpose.

This agreement provided that the defendant was to exercise strict control and direction of almost every aspect of the plaintiff's operation. The prices were to be fixed by the defendant; disputes with hotel guests were to be finally resolved by the defendant; the specific hours of service were to be established by the defendant "to conform to the convenience of its guests"; the plaintiff's employees had to be approved by the defendant as were their uniforms; and all the billing was to be done through the defendant as though it were rendering the services to the guests.

Thus, it appears that the primary and overriding objective of the defendant . . . was to ensure to its guests proper, efficient, courteous and reasonable valet and laundry facilities as an integral part of the overall personal services rendered by the hotel to the end that the good will of the guests be retained. It becomes clear therefore that the performance here called for is much removed from that involving mechanical fitness, utility or marketability. In such cases there is a "positive, objective standard" against which the performance may be measured. Wynkoop Hallenbeck Crawford Co. v. Western Union Tel. Co., 268 N.Y. 108, 196 N.E. 760. Contra in cases involving taste and judgment such standards of reasonableness cannot be established. In this case the defendant did not bargain for a particular type of pressing, stitching or laundering but rather for a relationship between the plaintiff's organization and the hotel's guests as would protect and enhance the good will so essential to the operation of the hotel business. No objective standards of reasonableness can be set up by which the effectiveness of the plaintiff's performance in achieving the effect sought can be measured. It is for that reason that in cases of this nature the honest judgment of the party rather than that of a jury is all that is required. . . .

It was therefore error for the Trial Court to give to the jury the question of the reasonableness of the defendant's asserted dissatisfaction. Sufficient that the jury be satisfied that it was a dissatisfaction honestly arrived at. While in determining the question as to the bona fides of the defendant's dissatisfaction, evidence as to the quality of the plaintiff's services may well be admissible as having probative value, the ultimate and only question to be decided by the jury . . . is whether the defendant's dissatisfaction was bona fide or feigned.

It may very well be that the charge of the court is correct for the purpose of determining whether the plaintiff breached the agreement so as to entitle the defendant to damages on its counterclaim as distinguished from its right to terminate the contract. Honest dissatisfaction on the part of the defendant, although entitling it to terminate will not, in and of itself, entitle it to recover damages on its counterclaim. Such determination will depend on the facts surrounding the manner of the plaintiff's performance in relation to what he was obliged to do under the agreement and accordingly we do not pass on that phase of the case at this time.

[Reversed on the law and a new trial ordered.]

Haymore v. Levinson

8 Utah 2d 66, 328 P.2d 307 (1958)

Plaintiff builder contracted to sell to defendants, for $36,000, a house that plaintiff had almost completed. The contract provided that $3,000 of the purchase price was to be held in escrow until "satisfactory completion" of a list of items attached to the contract. Defendants moved into the house while plaintiff continued construction. When plaintiff finished the work and requested release of the $3,000 from escrow, defendants refused, asserting that they were not satisfied with certain of the items. After discussion, plaintiff agreed to take care of another list of items which defendants insisted must be completed. When plaintiff and his workers appeared to do this work, however, defendants expressed dissatisfaction with the second list and demanded still further work, but plaintiff would not agree. Defendants then told plaintiff that, unless he agreed to do all the work they had requested and in the manner they required, he could do nothing. On plaintiff's refusal of this demand, he was ordered off the property. Plaintiff recovered judgment for $2,739, that is, the $3,000 escrow less $261 which the trial court found to be the "total value" of certain "minor deficiencies" in plaintiff's performance. *Held*, affirmed. Building contracts generally fall into a class where "taste, fancy or sensibility" is not of predominant importance; therefore, a condition of satisfaction involves an objective standard on such matters as "operative fitness, mechanical utility or structural completion. . . . [T]he party favored by such a provision has no arbitrary privilege of declining to acknowledge satisfaction and [such party] cannot withhold approval unless there is apparent some reasonable justification for doing so." The trial court correctly applied this standard.

Breslow v. Gotham Securities Corp.

77 Misc. 2d 721, 354 N.Y.S.2d 550 (N.Y. Civ. Ct. 1974)

"Where an attorney has fully performed the objectives of a contingent retainer agreement for his client, these tidings of comfort are ordinarily sufficient to warrant payment of the fee in full. In this case the client would press beyond mere comfort and would infuse the lawyer-client relationship with qualities of aesthetic joy. . . . Plaintiff, an experienced law firm in the securities field, was retained by defendant, an underwriter, to render customary legal services in connection with a SEC Regulation A public stock offering. The basic terms of the oral retainer are [undisputed]: if the offering were successfully completed, the underwriter was to receive a $20,000 expense allowance from the proceeds, and of this sum plaintiff was to be entitled to half, or the sum of $10,000. Defendant has paid the sum of $3,500 but resists payment of the balance of $6,500, and plaintiff now moves for summary judgment. Although the offering was fully sold, and defendant received the $20,000 expense allowance, the underwriter asserts . . . that plaintiff's services did not measure up to 'the quality of service rendered to defendant by previous attorneys' and that 'the services rendered did not meet such standards and plaintiff was so advised.'

"It may well be true that defendant had known some giant oaks (albeit anonymous at the present time) in the forest of the bar, and that they cast a long shadow in the underwriting business. So vague a standard, however, given its maximum effect, would amount to nothing more than a condition in the contract that performance be personally satisfactory. The ingredient of personal satisfaction in contractual arrangements, however, is subject to certain well-recognized limitations. . . . Clearly this case, [compared with *Fursmidt*,] falls into the [operative fitness or utility] category as a matter of law. [Defendant's] asserted lack of satisfaction cannot, in the face of conceded full performance, raise an issue of fact for trial, for 'that which the law shall say a contracting party ought in reason to be satisfied with, that the law will say he is satisfied with.' "

Morin Bldg. Prods. Co. v. Baystone Constr., Inc.

717 F.2d 413 (7th Cir. 1983)

"[M]ost cases conform to the position stated in § 228 of the Restatement (Second) of Contracts (1979): if 'it is practicable to determine whether a reasonable person in the position of the obligor would be satisfied, an interpretation is preferred under which the condition [that the obligor be satisfied with the obligee's performance] occurs if such a reasonable person in the position of the obligor would be satisfied.' We do not understand the majority position to be paternalistic. . . . The requirement of reasonableness is read into a contract not to protect the weaker party but to approximate what the parties would have expressly provided with respect to a contingency that they did not foresee, if they had foreseen it. Therefore the requirement is not read into every contract, because it is not always a reliable guide to the parties' intentions. In particular, the presumption that the performing party would not have wanted to put himself at the mercy of the paying party's whim is overcome when the nature of the performance contracted for is such that there are no objective standards to guide the court. It cannot be assumed in such a case that the parties would have wanted a court to second-guess the buyer's rejection. So 'the reasonable person standard is employed when the contract involves commercial quality, operative fitness, or mechanical utility which other knowledgeable persons can judge. . . . The standard of good faith is employed when the contract involves personal aesthetics or fancy.' "

SECTION 4. PROTECTING THE EXCHANGE ON BREACH

At the start of this casebook, cases such as *Groves*, *Peevyhouse*, and *Landis* raised the question of how damages should be calculated when the promisor breached and the cost of repairs greatly exceeded their market value. In this section, we face cases that arise out of similar facts, and raise several additional problems. The first problem arises when the promisor breaches and the promisee seeks to walk away from the contract. The issue is the right to terminate before performance is completed, not the amount of damages when promised performance is completed, but proves defective. This issue is the focus of the first case. In the other cases, the breaching party is the one seeking relief. The threshold question, again one that arises before damages are measured, is whether the breaching party has the right to recover in restitution. The next question is whether, as an alternative to recovering under a restitution theory, the breaching party can sue under the contract. Only if this question is answered in the affirmative do we return to the question of how to calculate contract damages. (Damages become relevant again as they must be deducted from the recovery of the breaching party.)

Strouth v. Pools by Murphy and Sons, Inc.

Appellate Court of Connecticut, 2003.
79 Conn. App. 55, 829 A.2d 102.

LAVERY, C.J. . . . The plaintiffs, owners of a residence in West Suffield, contacted the defendant in May, 1998, because they were interested in having a swimming pool installed in their yard. Ed Carter, the defendant's salesman at that time, visited the property and met with the plaintiffs on May 19, 1998. After viewing a color brochure depicting various shapes for pools and spas, the plaintiffs decided on a peanut shaped pool with a circular six-foot interior spa. They informed Carter of their choice. Carter drew a contract for the construction of a pool. The contract specified a "custom" shaped pool, forty feet long by twenty feet wide.

Dennis Murphy, the defendant's president, arrived at the property on July 16, 1998, to commence excavation. He showed Caroline Strouth a picture of the kidney shaped pool he planned to dig and laid out staking. She told Murphy that the picture he was showing her did not look like the pool she was expecting. Murphy assured her that the pool would look like she expected it to when completed. The excavation was in the shape of a kidney. After the excavation was complete, a crew arrived to install the steel frame (rebar). An electrician and plumber also did work at the property. The rebars outlined an almond-shaped spa, not a circular spa.

After receiving a bill from the defendant for additional excavation time incurred because the defendant hit ledge on the first day of excavation, Robert Strouth telephoned the defendant to complain about the extra cost. He spoke to Joseph Murphy, the father of Dennis Murphy and an employee of the defendant. After a short, acrimonious conversation, Joseph Murphy abruptly terminated the conversation. Robert Strouth did not have an opportunity to complain that the pool was not excavated in the shape for which he and his wife had contracted.

Four days later, Robert Strouth contacted the defendant and ordered it to discontinue all work at the property. Carter telephoned the plaintiffs several times to try to work out a completion of the pool. On September 20, 1998, the defendant sent a letter to the plaintiffs in which it offered to complete the pool at the property with a circular spa. There was never an offer to reconfigure the pool in a peanut shape. Substantial additional work would have been needed to complete the kidney shaped pool, which was not the pool for which the plaintiffs had contracted. The excavation remained, in a deteriorated condition, in the backyard.

In 1999, the plaintiffs brought the present action. As to the defendant, they claimed damages for breach of contract, unjust enrichment and unfair trade practices in violation of the Connecticut Unfair Trade Practices Act. The defendant filed a counterclaim, alleging breach of contract. The court rendered judgment for the plaintiffs on the breach of contract claim and awarded damages in the amount of $10,618.63. The court rendered judgment for the defendant on the plaintiffs' claims of unjust enrichment and unfair trade practices, and for the plaintiffs on the defendant's counterclaim.

In its memorandum of decision, the court determined that the word "custom," used in the contract to describe the shape of the pool, was ambiguous. It found that the plaintiffs believed they were contracting for a peanut shaped pool and that the defendant subsequently interpreted the contract as calling for a kidney shaped pool. Because "custom" could describe a kidney shaped pool or a peanut-shaped pool, the court determined that the ambiguity should be construed against the party who drew the contract, which was the defendant. The court concluded that "[t]he parties entered into a contract on May 19, 1998, for construction of a peanut shaped pool, forty feet long by twenty feet wide with an interior, circular six-foot spa." The court determined that the kidney shaped pool, begun by the defendant, was a substantial deviation from the pool for which the plaintiffs had contracted. It therefore held that the defendant's failure to build the pool in a peanut shape with a circular interior spa was a material breach of the parties' contract that justified the plaintiffs in terminating additional construction of the kidney-shaped pool. . . .

The defendant first claims that the court improperly determined that the construction of a kidney shaped pool constituted a material breach of the parties' contract. Specifically, the defendant argues that the construction of a kidney-shaped pool would have amounted to substantial performance of the parties' contract and, therefore, the plaintiffs breached the parties' contract when they ordered the defendants to discontinue all work at the property. We are not persuaded.

The issue here is whether the construction of a kidney-shaped pool, when the contract called for a peanut-shaped pool, constituted a material breach of the parties' contract so as to justify the plaintiffs in not performing their remaining duties under the contract. The defendant does not challenge the underlying facts found by the court. . . .

The court, in its memorandum of decision, did not specifically apply the standards of materiality enunciated in § 241 of the Restatement. The court did, however, find that the construction of a kidney-shaped pool would be a substantial deviation from the shape of the pool for which the plaintiffs contracted and that the plaintiffs "were not obliged to have a pool built in their backyard that did not conform to the pool for which they contracted." The court also found that although the defendant had offered to complete the pool with a circular spa, it never offered to reconfigure the pool to a peanut shape. Thus, it would appear that the court, essentially, focused on the criteria set forth in § 241(a) and (d) to reach its conclusion that the construction of a kidney shaped pool constituted a material breach of the parties' contract. Under the circumstances, we cannot say that the court's conclusion was clearly erroneous.

Although the defendant argues that the construction of a kidney-shaped pool would not deprive the plaintiffs of the benefit that they reasonably expected because the pool would still be fit for its intended use, we are not convinced that constructing a pool in the shape of a kidney, when the contract called for a pool in the shape of a peanut, would have constituted substantial performance. We therefore conclude that the court's determination that the defendant materially breached the parties' contract, thereby excusing the plaintiffs from any further performance due under the contract, was not clearly erroneous. . . .

The defendant's next claim is that the court improperly failed to award restitution. Specifically, the defendant claims that it is entitled to "restitution for its costs, labor and expenses in the amount of $5471, which included $2158 for the commission paid to Ed Carter . . . $1000 for the first day of excavation . . . $750 for the second day of excavation . . . $908 for installation of the steel rebar . . . and $505 for installation of plumbing. . . ." We decline to review that claim. . . .

Because the defendant did not raise the issue of restitution in its pleading and because it does not appear that the parties actually litigated that issue, the defendant's claim for restitution was not before the court properly. . . .

Plante v. Jacobs

Supreme Court of Wisconsin, 1960.
10 Wis. 2d 567, 103 N.W.2d 296.

Suit to establish a lien to recover the unpaid balance of the contract price plus extras of building a house for the defendants, [the] Jacobs, who in their answer allege no substantial performance and breach of the contract by the plaintiff and counterclaim for damages due to faulty workmanship and incomplete construction. . . . After a trial to the court, judgment was entered for the plaintiff in the amount of $4,152.90 plus interest and costs, from which the defendants appealed and the plaintiff petitioned for a review. . . .

The Jacobs, on or about January 6, 1956, entered into a written contract with the plaintiff to furnish the materials and construct a house upon their lot in Brookfield, . . . in accordance with plans and specifications, for the sum of $26,765. During the course of construction the plaintiff was paid $20,000. Disputes arose between the parties, the defendants refused to continue payment, and the plaintiff did not complete the house[,] [but] duly filed his lien.

The trial court found the contract was substantially performed and was modified in respect to lengthening the house two feet and the reasonable value of this extra was $960. The court disallowed extras amounting to $1,748.92 claimed by the plaintiff because they were not agreed upon in writing in accordance with the terms of the agreement. In respect to defective workmanship the court allowed the cost of repairing the following items: $1,550 for the patio wall; $100 for the patio floor; $300 for cracks in the ceiling of the living room and kitchen; and $20.15 credit balance for hardware. The court also found the defendants were not damaged by the misplacement of a wall between the kitchen and the living room, and the other items of defective workmanship and incompleteness were not proven. The amount of these credits allowed the defendants was deducted from the gross amount found owing the plaintiff, and the judgment was entered for the difference and made a lien on the premises. . . .

HALLOWS, J. The defendants argue the plaintiff cannot recover any amount because he has failed to substantially perform the contract. The plaintiff conceded he failed to furnish the kitchen cabinets, gutters and downspouts, sidewalk, closet clothes poles, and entrance seat amounting to $1,601.95. This amount was allowed to the defendants. The defendants claim some 20 other items of incomplete or faulty performance by the plaintiff and no substantial performance because the cost of completing the house in strict compliance with the plans and specifications would amount to 25 or 30 percent of the contract price. The defendants especially stress the misplacing of the wall between the living room and the kitchen, which narrowed the living room in excess of one foot. The cost of tearing down this wall and rebuilding it would be approximately $4,000. The record is not clear why and when this wall was misplaced, but the wall is completely built and the house decorated and the defendants are living therein. Real estate experts testified that the smaller width of the living room would not affect the market price of the house.

The defendants rely on Manitowoc Steam Boiler Works v. Manitowoc Glue Co., 1903, 120 Wis. 1, 97 N.W. 515, for the proposition there can be no recovery on the contract as distinguished from quantum meruit unless there is substantial performance. This is undoubtedly the correct rule at common law. . . . The question here is whether there has been substantial performance. The test of what amounts to substantial performance seems to be whether the performance meets the essential purpose of the contract. In the *Manitowoc* case the contract called for a boiler having a capacity of 150 percent of the existing boiler. The court held there was no substantial performance because the boiler furnished had a capacity of only 82 percent of the old boiler and only approximately one-half of the boiler capacity contemplated by the contract. In Houlahan v. Clark, 1901, 110 Wis. 43, 85 N.W. 676, the contract provided the plaintiff was to drive pilings in the lake and place a boat house thereon parallel and in line with a neighbor's dock. This was not done and the contractor so positioned the boat house that it was practically useless to the owner. Manthey v. Stock, 1907, 133 Wis. 107, 113 N.W. 443, involved a contract to paint a house and to do a good job, including the removal of the old paint where necessary. The plaintiff did not remove the old paint, and blistering and roughness of the new paint resulted. The court held that the plaintiff failed to show substantial performance. . . .

Substantial performance as applied to construction of a house does not mean that every detail must be in strict compliance with the specifications and the plans. Something less than perfection is the test . . . unless all details are made the essence of the contract. This was not done here. There may be situations in which features or details of construction of special or of great personal importance, which if not performed, would prevent a finding of substantial performance of the contract. In this case the plan was a stock floor plan. No detailed construction of the house was shown on the plan. There were no blueprints. The specifications were standard printed forms with some modifications and additions written in by the parties. Many of the problems that arose during the construction had to be solved on the basis of practical experience. No mathematical rule relating to the percentage of the price, of cost of completion or of completeness can be laid down to determine substantial performance of a building contract. Although the defendants received a house with which they are dissatisfied in many respects, the trial court was not in error in finding the contract was substantially performed.

The next question is what is the amount of recovery when the plaintiff has substantially, but incompletely, performed. For substantial performance the plaintiff should recover the contract price less the damages caused the defendant by the incomplete performance. Both parties agree. Venzke v. Magdanz, 1943, 243 Wis. 155, 9 N.W.2d 604, states the correct rule for damages due to faulty construction amounting to such incomplete performance, which is the difference between the value of the house as it stands with faulty and incomplete construction and the value of the house if it had been constructed in strict accordance with the plans and specifications. This is the diminished-value rule. The cost of replacement or repair is not the measure of such damage, but is an element to take into consideration in arriving at value under some circumstances. The cost of replacement or the cost to make whole the omissions may equal or be less than the difference in value in some cases and, likewise, the cost to rectify a defect may greatly exceed the added value to the structure as corrected. The defendants argue that under the *Venzke* rule their damages are $10,000. The plaintiff on review argues the defendants' damages are only $650. Both parties agree the trial court applied the wrong rule to the facts.

The trial court applied the cost-of-repair or replacement rule as to several items, relying on Stern v. Schlafer, 1943, 244 Wis. 183, 11 N.W.2d 640, 12 N.W.2d 678, wherein it was stated that when there are a number of small items of defect or omission which can be remedied without the reconstruction of a substantial part of the building or a great sacrifice of work or material already wrought in the building, the reasonable cost of correcting the defect should be allowed. However, [this] court [has] held [that] when the separation of defects would lead to confusion, the rule of diminished value could apply to all defects.

In this case no such confusion arises in separating the defects. The trial court disallowed certain claimed defects because they were not proven. This finding was not against the great weight and clear preponderance of the evidence and will not be disturbed on appeal. Of the remaining defects claimed by the defendants, the court allowed the cost of replacement or repair except as to the misplacement of the living-room wall. Whether a defect should fall under the cost-of-replacement rule or be considered under the diminished-value rule depends upon the nature and magnitude of the defect. This court has not allowed items of such magnitude under the cost-of-repair rule as the trial court did. Viewing the construction of the house as a whole and its cost we cannot say, however, that the trial court was in error in allowing the cost of repairing the plaster cracks in the ceilings, the cost of mud jacking and repairing the patio floor, and the cost of reconstructing the non-weight-bearing and nonstructural patio wall. Such reconstruction did not involve an unreasonable economic waste.

The item of misplacing the living room wall . . . was clearly under the diminished-value rule. There is no evidence that defendants requested or demanded the replacement of the wall in the place called for by the specifications during the course of construction. To tear down the wall now and rebuild it in its proper place would involve a substantial destruction of the work, if not all of it, which was put into the wall and would cause additional damage to other parts of the house and require replastering and redecorating the walls and ceilings of at least two rooms. Such economic waste is unreasonable and unjustified. The rule of diminished value contemplates the wall is not going to be moved. Expert witnesses for both parties, testifying as to the value of the house, agreed that the misplacement of the wall had no effect on the market price. The trial court properly found that the defendants suffered no legal damage, although the defendants' particular desire for specified room size was not satisfied. For a discussion of these rules of damages for defective or unfinished construction and their application see Restatement, 1 Contracts, § 346(1)(a) and illustrations. . . .

Judgment affirmed.

3A A. Corbin, Contracts

§ 702 (1960)

"When we use the term 'substantial performance of a promissory duty,' we always mean something less than full and exact performance of that duty. As so used, therefore, substantial performance is not a complete discharge of duty. It is not a defense in a suit against the building contractor for damages. Judgment will not be prevented from going against him in such a suit by his averring and proving that he performed almost in full, that his deviations have been small, that the owner can live comfortably in the house, or that the value to the owner is very nearly as great as it would have been had exact performance been rendered. . . . One who has rendered substantial performance, but less than full performance, and has already received the agreed price, has a defense in a suit by the owner for the restitution of that price. There has been no such 'failure of consideration' as to create a quasi-contractual duty of restitution. The reason is not merely the fact that the contractor is in possession or that 'possession is nine points' in the law. It is because the contractor had a right to the payment when it was made and could have maintained suit for it."

Jacob & Youngs v. Kent

Court of Appeals of New York, 1921.
230 N.Y. 239, 129 N.E. 889.

CARDOZO, J. The plaintiff built a country residence for the defendant at a cost of upwards of $77,000, and now sues to recover a balance of $3,483.46, remaining unpaid. The work of construction ceased in June, 1914, and the defendant then began to occupy the dwelling. There was no complaint of defective performance until March, 1915. One of the specifications for the plumbing work provides that "all wrought-iron pipe must be well galvanized, lap welded pipe of the grade known as 'standard pipe' of Reading manufacture."

The defendant learned in March, 1915, that some of the pipe, instead of being made in Reading, was the product of other factories. The plaintiff was accordingly directed by the architect to do the work anew. The plumbing was then encased within the walls except in a few places where it had to be exposed. Obedience to the order meant more than the substitution of other pipe. It meant the demolition at great expense of substantial parts of the completed structure. The plaintiff left the work untouched, and asked for a certificate that the final payment was due. Refusal of the certificate was followed by this suit.

The evidence sustains a finding that the omission of the prescribed brand of pipe was neither fraudulent nor willful. It was the result of the oversight and inattention of the plaintiff's subcontractor. Reading pipe is distinguished from Cohoes pipe and other brands only by the name of the manufacturer stamped upon it at intervals of between six and seven feet. Even the defendant's architect, though he inspected the pipe upon arrival, failed to notice the discrepancy. The plaintiff tried to show that the brands installed, though made by other manufacturers, were the same in quality, in appearance, in market value, and in cost as the brand stated in the contract—that they were, indeed, the same thing, though manufactured in another place. The evidence was excluded, and a verdict directed for the defendant. The Appellate Division reversed, and granted a new trial.

We think the evidence, if admitted, would have supplied some basis for the inference that the defect was insignificant in its relation to the project. The courts never say that one who makes a contract fills the measure of his duty by less than full performance. They do say, however, that an omission, both trivial and innocent, will sometimes be atoned for by allowance of the resulting damage, and will not always be the breach of a condition to be followed by a forfeiture. The distinction is akin to that between dependent and independent promises, or between promises and conditions. Some promises are so plainly independent that they can never by fair construction be conditions of one another. Others are so plainly dependent that they must always be conditions. Others, though dependent and thus conditions when there is departure in point of substance, will be viewed as independent and collateral when the departure is insignificant. Considerations partly of justice and partly of presumable intention are to tell us whether this or that promise shall be placed in one class or in another. The simple and the uniform will call for different remedies from the multifarious and the intricate. The margin of departure within the range of normal expectation upon a sale of common chattels will vary from the margin to be expected upon a contract for the construction of a mansion or a "skyscraper." There will be harshness sometimes and oppression in the implication of a condition when the thing upon which labor has been expended is incapable of surrender because united to the land, and equity and reason in the implication of a like condition when the subject-matter, if defective, is in shape to be returned.

From the conclusion that promises may not be treated as dependent to the extent of their uttermost minutiae without a sacrifice of justice, the progress is a short one to the conclusion that they may not be so treated without a perversion of intention. Intention not otherwise revealed may be presumed to hold in contemplation the reasonable and probable. If something else is in view, it must not be left to implication. There will be no assumption of a purpose to visit venial faults with oppressive retribution.

Those who think more of symmetry and logic in the development of legal rules than of practical adaptation to the attainment of a just result will be troubled by a classification where the lines of division are so wavering and blurred. Something, doubtless, may be said on the score of consistency and certainty in favor of a stricter standard. The courts have balanced such considerations against those of equity and fairness, and found the latter to be the weightier. The decisions in this state commit us to the liberal view, which is making its way, nowadays, in jurisdictions slow to welcome it. Where the line is to be drawn between the important and the trivial cannot be settled by a formula. "In the nature of the case precise boundaries are impossible." 2 Williston on Contracts, § 841. The same omission may take on one aspect or another according to its setting. Substitution of equivalents may not have the same significance in fields of art on the one side and in those of mere utility on the other. Nowhere will change be tolerated, however, if it is so dominant or pervasive as in any real or substantial measure to frustrate the purpose of the contract. There is no general license to install whatever, in the builder's judgment, may be regarded as "just as good." The question is one of degree, to be answered, if there is doubt, by the triers of the facts, and, if the inferences are certain, by the judges of the law. We must weigh the purpose to be served, the desire to be gratified, the excuse for deviation from the letter, the cruelty of enforced adherence. Then only can we tell whether literal fulfillment is to be implied by law as a condition. This is not to say that the parties are not free by apt and certain words to effectuate a purpose that performance of every term shall be a condition of recovery. That question is not here. This is merely to say that the law will be slow to impute the purpose, in the silence of the parties, where the significance of the default is grievously out of proportion to the oppression of the forfeiture. The willful transgressor must accept the penalty of his transgression. For him there is no occasion to mitigate the rigor of implied conditions. The transgressor whose default is unintentional and trivial may hope for mercy if he will offer atonement for his wrong.

In the circumstances of this case, we think the measure of the allowance is not the cost of replacement, which would be great, but the difference in value, which would be either nominal or nothing. . . . It is true that in most cases the cost of replacement is the measure. The owner is entitled to the money which will permit him to complete, unless the cost of completion is grossly and unfairly out of proportion to the good to be attained. When that is true, the measure is the difference in value. . . . The rule that gives a remedy in cases of substantial performance with compensation for defects of trivial or inappreciable importance has been developed by the courts as an instrument of justice. The measure of the allowance must be shaped to the same end.

The order should be affirmed, and judgment absolute directed in favor of the plaintiff upon the stipulation, with costs in all courts.

NOTE

The record in *Jacob & Youngs* indicates (R. 106) that the contract between the parties contained the following provision, which was not mentioned by the court:

> Any work furnished by the Contractor, the material or workmanship of which is defective or which is not fully in accordance with the drawings and specifications, in every respect, will be rejected and is to be immediately torn down, removed and remade or replaced in accordance with the drawings and specifications, whenever discovered.

Was Cardozo right in his assertion that the question of intention to make "performance of every term . . . a condition . . . is not here"? Suppose the contract had said: "Payment of Contractor by Owner shall be on condition that no pipe other than that of Reading manufacture has been used in the work"?

Reynolds v. Armstead

166 Colo. 372, 443 P.2d 990 (1968)

Plaintiff contracted to apply a brick veneer to defendant's house, expressly promising to use "new brick matching as closely as possible the color and appearance of [the] existing brickwork." Although plaintiff failed (for reasons not disclosed in the opinion) to use such brick, the trial court found the veneer was in all other respects of sound construction and entered judgment for plaintiff for the contract price of $535.25, less "damages" in the amount of $267.63 caused defendant by plaintiff's failure to perform fully. *Held*, affirmed. As a matter of law, plaintiff's breach, which damaged the appearance of the house to the extent of half the contract price of the veneer work, was "material." Thus, this failure substantially to perform deprived plaintiff of the right to recover under the "theory" of express contract. But plaintiff is entitled to the judgment entered on a "theory" of quantum meruit. [In assessing what this court did and said, it may be useful to recall and compare Britton v. Turner and Pinches v. Swedish Evangelical Lutheran Church, supra pp. 161–169.]

NOTE: RESTITUTION FOR THE "WILLFUL" DEFAULTER

The "willful" breach and the issue of restitution for defaulters are familiar subjects at this stage (see, e.g., Chapter 1, pp. 170–171). As Judge Cardozo indicated, things might be different for the willful defaulter, at least as concerns a recovery on the contract. There is need to add only a brief word on whether a party's own nonperformance precludes a restitution remedy.

In Glazer v. Schwartz, 276 Mass. 54, 176 N.E. 613 (1931), plaintiff sought recovery for labor and materials furnished under a contract to construct a house and garage for $14,700, of which $13,000 had been paid. Defendant counterclaimed for damages caused by plaintiff's failure to complete the work in accordance with the specifications. At trial, it was found that plaintiff had substantially performed the contract but that his failure to perform fully was "willful." It was also found that plaintiff had failed to supply materials worth $200 and that the value of the house as built was $500 less than it would have been if plaintiff had performed fully. The Supreme Judicial Court held that recovery on the contract itself required "complete performance." Recovery in quantum meruit, on the other hand, was said to be available in Massachusetts only if the owner obtains "substantially what was called for by the contract" *and* the failure to perform fully is not willful. Plaintiff, therefore, could recover nothing. As for defendant, not only was there no duty to pay the contract balance of $1,700, but defendant was entitled to "affirmative relief" in the form of damages of $200 for materials not supplied *plus* "the cost of making the structure conform . . . to the contract"—a figure which, on remand, might well turn out to be greater than the $500 already found to represent diminution in value of the premises.

It was surely predictable that the *Glazer* court's treatment of the willful defaulter would again come before the Massachusetts high court. One such occasion, some two decades later, was Ficara v. Belleau, 331 Mass. 80, 117 N.E.2d 287 (1954), where builders had agreed to install a heating and cooling system for $6,200, but "intentionally and willfully" abandoned performance after the owner had paid them $4,200. The owner reasonably paid another contractor $2,361 to finish the work and sued builders for this amount, relying on Glazer v. Schwartz. The lower court gave the owner judgment for only $361, which was affirmed on appeal. Insofar as *Glazer* indicated that the owner in this case could recover $2,361, the Massachusetts court refused to follow it, declaring that the owner was attempting, in effect, to collect exemplary damages and to obtain a $6,200 heating and cooling system for $4,200. The court said: "It is not the policy of our law to award damages which would put a plaintiff in a better position than if the defendant had carried out the contract. . . . The plaintiff is entitled to be made whole and no more. This is true in an action against a defendant for breach of contract, albeit a willful one, even though the same defendant in suing as a plaintiff on the same contract might be barred" by the rule denying both contract and quasi-contract remedies to the willful defaulter.

Massachusetts continues to adhere to the overall view that a contractor's failure to perform in full bars recovery on the contract, but that one who both substantially performs and makes a "good faith" effort to perform fully may recover in quantum meruit. Peabody, N.E., Inc. v. Town of Marshfield, 426 Mass. 436, 689 N.E.2d 774 (1998) (but denying recovery of overhead costs in determining defaulter's quantum meruit award, since such costs—expenses not chargeable to a particular contract or work—"do not directly confer any value or benefit" on defendant). It seems that a principal measure of good faith is the absence of intentional departures from the contract. See, e.g., J.A. Sullivan Corp. v. Commonwealth, 397 Mass. 789, 494 N.E.2d 374 (1986). But, of course, only a few states have fallen in line with Massachusetts on the question of remedies available to a defaulting provider of services. Further clues as to the general common law standing of the "willful" defaulter today are provided by the New York case described immediately below.

Hadden v. Consolidated Edison Co. of New York

34 N.Y.2d 88, 356 N.Y.S.2d 249, 312 N.E.2d 445 (1974)

This case presented the question whether an employee's pension could be revoked when, after the employee's retirement, the employer discovered facts which would have been grounds for discharge "for cause" (and thus a loss of an expected pension) had they been known during employment. The newly-discovered facts were that in the last year or two of his employment, Hadden, then a vice-president of Con Edison, had secretly accepted cash totaling $15,000 and other benefits from contractors doing business with Con Edison. Upon obtaining this information through transcripts of Hadden's testimony in criminal proceedings involving others, Con Edison promptly terminated Hadden's pension. He sued to compel resumption of his pension benefits, which amounted to nearly $4,000 a month. After holding that the termination was not authorized by any provision of the pension contract, the Court of Appeals turned to the question whether "Hadden's misconduct in the latter years of his employment [excuses] Con Edison from paying his pension benefits."

The court, through Rabin, J., said: "While there is no language in the Plan expressly conditioning pension payments upon the employee's performing honestly and loyally, there is little difficulty in regarding these qualifications as a constructive condition of Con Edison's duty [to] make pension payments. . . . If the party in default has substantially performed, the other party's performance is not excused. . . . This doctrine, familiar in construction contract situations, is not limited to that area, but applies to employment contracts as well. . . . Weighing the factors involved we find that Hadden's performance has been substantial. Con Edison has received the benefit of his 37 years of employment. . . . The value of Hadden's performance to Con Edison over the course of nearly four decades is not substantially impaired by his disloyalty in some of those later years. In so stating we do not condone his actions or disregard the fact that his breach was willful."

At this point, the court's opinion includes the following footnote: "In deciding controversies in the field of construction contracts, it has frequently been said that a 'willful' breach defeats a claim of substantial performance. (See, e.g., Jacob & Youngs v. Kent . . .). Our treating willfulness here as one of several factors to be considered in determining whether Hadden's performance is substantial does not compel a different result in those cases. Weighing willfulness as one of several relevant factors is also supported by authority. . . . Since employment contracts are divisible, the situation presented by an employee's breach in some, but not all, of the years of his employment relationship is somewhat analogous to the problem encountered in installment contracts where there has been a material breach with regard to one of the installments. . . . In the present case, while Hadden's willful misconduct may have been a material breach with regard to a specific term of his employment, it does not impair the value of his nearly four decades of work for the Company."

Hathaway v. Sabin

Supreme Court of Vermont, 1891.
63 Vt. 527, 22 A. 633.

MUNSON, J. . . . The contract required the defendant to furnish a hall [the Blanchard Opera House] for the concert, and to pay $75 after the entertainment. The plaintiff alleged readiness to perform on his part, and assigned as the breach the defendant's failure to furnish a hall. The court directed a verdict for the plaintiff for $75 and interest. The defendant insists that, inasmuch as the non-payment of the $75 was not assigned as the breach, and as there was no proof of any loss except in the non-payment of the $75, there was no proof of loss from any breach complained of, and that consequently there could be no recovery. We think it cannot be said that the proof of loss in the non-receipt of the $75 did not apply to the breach declared upon. The plaintiff was ready to give the concert, and on giving it would have been entitled to the $75, but he was prevented from giving it by the defendant's failure to furnish a hall. This failure was properly assigned as the breach from which the plaintiff suffered damage. The plaintiff does not sue for the compensation to which he would have been entitled if the contract had been carried out, but for the damages he has sustained in being compelled to leave the contract unperformed. The breach is not the non-payment of the unearned compensation, but the failure to perform the antecedent stipulation which would have enabled the plaintiff to earn it.

The defendant also contends that he was excused from opening and heating the hall by the apparent impossibility of the musicians' reaching the town. During the 36 hours preceding the evening appointed for the concert a snow-storm of unusual violence prevailed in Montpelier and vicinity, which early on the day of the concert rendered the streets of that village and the roads from the surrounding country practically impassable. The quartette by which the concert was to be given was in Barre,[1]

---

[1] [For those who may not know northern Vermont, Barre is located about five miles from Montpelier.—Eds.]

having gone there from Montpelier the evening before, and trains on the spur from Montpelier to Barre were suspended. Late in the afternoon, however, an irregular train went to Barre, and on this the musicians returned to Montpelier, arriving early in the evening, and going to the hall at the time appointed. It is claimed that the defendant's conduct must be tested by the situation as it was at the time when action on his part became necessary, and that he is saved from liability by the doctrine that, when one party ascertains that the other will not be able to perform what he has undertaken, the party ascertaining this is excused from performing the obligations resting upon him. It is doubtless true that, when one party has put it out of his power to perform, the other party can maintain an action without having tendered performance on his part. But a party who becomes involved in difficulties for which he is not responsible, if ultimately able to perform, is not to be deprived of the benefits of his contract because of an assumption by the other party that the difficulties would prove insurmountable. Here the defendant was mistaken in supposing that the plaintiff would not be able to perform, and we know of no rule which permits him to plead reasonable cause to believe so in excuse for the failure on his part. It is apparent, also, that the defendant's course was determined before the time when action on his part became necessary. It was not necessary to commence the heating of the hall until 4 o'clock in the afternoon, but about 10 o'clock in the forenoon the defendant telephoned the manager[2] that, owing to the condition of the streets in Montpelier, it would be impossible to have the entertainment that evening. It is evident from this that the defendant based his action upon his belief that there would be no audience, rather than upon the supposition that the musicians could not reach the place of entertainment. He did not wait until it was necessary to take action about the hall before deciding that there could be no concert. But, at the time when action on his part became necessary, there was nothing in the situation which could relieve him from liability. The contract contains no provision for his protection from such a misfortune, and the loss must fall on him.

The defendant also insists that upon being held liable he was entitled to have the damages assessed by the jury. We think, however, that the plaintiff was entitled to have this verdict directed. Having incurred all the expense necessary to enable him to give the concert, the plaintiff's damages were necessarily the amount to which he would have been entitled for giving it. It is not for the defendant to say that the damages were less than the amount he had agreed to pay, when the plaintiff had done and incurred everything on his part, and was prevented from earning the compensation agreed upon solely by the defendant's failure. The message sent the manager in the forenoon, even if treated as a sufficient notice to stop performance, did not require any different action as regards the damages. It afforded no ground for an application of the doctrine which

[2] [The record in this case indicates that "the manager" who received defendant's telephone call at 10 a.m. on the day of the concert was the plaintiff Hathaway, the musicians' representative.—Eds.]

forbids the making of expense after receiving notice of the repudiation of a contract; for the expense afterwards incurred by the musicians was only such as was required by the situation in which the notice found them. Neither did the case permit an application of the rule which requires a party who is stopped in the performance of a contract for service to do what he can to lessen the damages by seeking like employment elsewhere. Judgment affirmed.

Vermont Historical Society

BLANCHARD OPERA HOUSE

QUESTIONS

(1) Assume defendant had heated and otherwise readied the hall, and the musicians were in place at 8 p.m. But no audience appeared, and defendant, pointing to an "act of God," canceled the concert? Does defendant owe the musicians $75?

(2) Suppose defendant had employed an event staff and prepared the hall, a full audience appeared, but the musicians, despite extraordinary effort, remained stranded in Barre at 8 p.m. Are the musicians liable in damages to defendant? Can they collect the $75 by bringing a lawsuit?

NOTE: A ROADMAP FOR "INSECURITY"

In cases governed by the UCC, § 2–609—titled "Right to Adequate Assurances of Performance" and dating from the 1950s—confers yet another self-help remedy (there was no such right to demand assurances under the common law of most of our states). The methodology for "insecurity" the section prescribes has been hailed for its recognition of "the desirability of providing an opportunity for dialogue to establish whether the parties intend to repudiate or to fulfill their contractual obligations." Conference Ctr. v. TRC—The Research Corp. of New England, 189 Conn. 212, 455 A.2d 857 (1983). Hence it is not surprising that over the years UCC 2–609 came to be seen as a source of general law, and that, in Restatement, Second § 251, reproduced immediately below, its principle has been extended to all contracts. That extension beyond UCC boundaries has, in general, been characterized by courts as "sound," and in keeping with the "traditional common-law developmental method." C.L. Maddox, Inc. v. Coalfield Services, 51 F.3d 76 (7th Cir. 1995); Norcon Power Partners v. Niagara Mohawk Power Corp., 92 N.Y.2d 458, 682 N.Y.S.2d 664, 705 N.E.2d 656 (1998). Whether under § 2–609 or Rest.2d § 251, observe that the "assurances" privilege comes into play only when one party believes the other may break the contract when the other's performance comes due. Observe also that a party demanding assurances is calling for something not required by the parties' contract.

Restatement of Contracts, Second

§ 251. When a Failure to Give Assurance May be Treated as a Repudiation

(1) Where reasonable grounds arise to believe that the obligor will commit a breach by non-performance that would of itself give the obligee a claim for damages for total breach . . ., the obligee may demand adequate assurance of due performance and may, if reasonable, suspend any performance for which he has not already received the agreed exchange until he receives such assurance.

(2) The obligee may treat as a repudiation the obligor's failure to provide within a reasonable time such assurance of due performance as is adequate in the circumstances of the particular case.

Comment: . . .

b. *Relation to other rules.* An obligee who believes, for whatever reason, that the obligor will not or cannot perform without a breach, is always free to act on that belief. . . . If he can prove that his belief would have been confirmed, he is at least shielded from liability even if he has failed to give a performance that is due before that of the obligor or has, by making alternative arrangements, done an act that amounts to a repudiation. . . . If, however, the obligee's belief is incorrect, his own failure to perform or his making of alternate arrangements may subject him to a claim for damages for total breach. This [s]ection affords him an opportunity, in appropriate cases, [to] avoid the uncertainties that would otherwise inhere in acting on his belief.

§ 268. Effect on Other Party's Duties of a Prospective Failure Justified by Impracticability or Frustration

(1) A party's prospective failure of performance may, except as stated in Subsection (2), discharge the other party's duties or allow him to suspend performance under the rules stated in §§ 251(1) and 253(2)

even though the failure would be justified under the rules stated in this Chapter.

(2) The rule stated in Subsection (1) does not apply if the other party assumed the risk that he would have to perform in spite of such a failure.

Comment:

a. Relation to other rules. This Restatement adopts the principle "that a continuing sense of reliance and security that the promised performance will be forthcoming when due, is an important feature of the bargain." Comment 1 to Uniform Commercial Code § 2–609; see Comment a to § 251. If there is reason to expect that a party will not perform as promised, the other party has the protection afforded by the rules stated in §§ 250 and 253 if the first party has repudiated, and by the rule stated in § 251 if reasonable grounds for insecurity have arisen with respect to the first party's future performance. However, those sections apply only if such prospective non-performance would amount to a breach. This Section applies when the prospective non-performance would not be a breach because of the rules on impracticability of performance or frustration of purpose stated in this Chapter. Subsection (2) makes it clear that if the other party has assumed the risk that he will have to perform although he receives no return performance, his duties are not discharged. . . .

Illustration:

1. *A*, an impresario, contracts with *B*, a singer, for an engagement for three months beginning on January 1. On the preceding November 30, *B* contracts pneumonia, and states to *A* that he will be unable to sing before February 1. *A* employs another singer to fill *B*'s place. On January 1, *B*, having recovered, offers to perform but *A* refuses. Since *B*'s statement would have been a repudiation under the rule stated in § 250 but for the operation of the rules on impracticability of performance stated in §§ 261 and 262, *A*'s duty to employ *B* is discharged, and *A* is not liable to *B* for breach of contract.

c. Failure to give assurances. If reasonable grounds arise to believe that a party will not perform because of impracticability of his performance or frustration of his purpose, the other party cannot demand assurances and treat a failure to give them as a repudiation under the rule stated in § 251, because the prospective non-performance would not be a breach. It therefore gives him no claim for breach of contract. Nevertheless, under the rule stated in this Section, he may in a proper case suspend his own performance and treat a failure to give assurance as discharging any remaining duties that he has to render the agreed exchange.

Illustrations:

2. *A*, an impresario, contracts with *B*, a singer, for an engagement for three months beginning on January 1. On the preceding November 30, *B* contracts pneumonia, and *A* is advised by competent medical authority that *B* will not be able to sing before February 1. *A* reasonably demands assurances of due performance by B. B ignores the

demand, and A employs another singer to fill *B*'s place. On January 1, B, having recovered, offers to perform, but *A* refuses. Since *B*'s failure to furnish assurance of due performance would have been a repudiation under the rule stated in § 251 but for the operation of the rules on impracticability of performance stated in §§ 261 and 262, *A*'s duty to employ *B* is discharged, and *A* is not liable to *B* for breach of contract.

Printing Center of Texas, Inc. v. Supermind Pub. Co.

Court of Appeals of Texas, 1984.
669 S.W.2d 779.

CANNON, J. Appellee sued appellant for refund of a deposit made under a written contract to print 5000 books entitled "Supermind Supermemory." Appellee alleged that it rightfully rejected the books upon delivery under Tex.Bus. & Com.Code Ann. § 2.601 (Tex. UCC) and that it has a right to cancel the contract and recover the part of the purchase price paid under Tex.Bus. & Com.Code Ann. § 2.711 (Tex. UCC).... [In omitted passages, the court noted that the case may have been tried below "on the wrong legal theory." The parties proceeded on the assumption the Texas UCC governed. But the Code is limited to transactions involving the sale of goods, and, said the court, services are "the essence or dominant factor" of this contract for the printing of books. Hence common-law rejection rules, not UCC Article 2, would apply in this case. Nevertheless, appellant, in failing to assign error on the point, was found to have waived it on appeal, the court concluding: "We indulge in the doubtful assumption that [the UCC] governs the [parties'] contract to enable us to adequately consider appellant's points of error."]

Appellant contends in its second point of error that jury finding that the books failed to conform to the contract is so against the great weight and preponderance of the evidence as to be manifestly unjust. This finding is related to whether appellee had a right to reject the books under § 2.601, which states in part: "[I]f the goods or tender of delivery fail in any respect to conform to the contract, the buyer may (1) reject the whole...."

This provision has been called the perfect tender rule because it supposedly allows a buyer to reject whenever the goods are less than perfect. This statement is not quite accurate; under § 2.601 the tender must be perfect only in the sense that the proffered goods must conform to the contract in every respect. Conformity does not mean substantial performance; it means complete performance. The long standing doctrine of sales law that "there is no room in commercial contracts for the doctrine of substantial performance" is carried forward into § 2.601 of the Code.... Substantial compliance is not the legal equivalent of conformity with the contract under § 2.601.

In analyzing whether tendered goods are conforming, the contract of the parties must first be determined. "Conform" is defined in § 2.106(b), as "in accordance with the obligations under the contract." The contract of the parties includes more than the words used by the parties. It encompasses "the bargain of the parties in fact as found in their language or by implication from other circumstances including course of dealing or usage of trade or course of performance as provided in the Code." § 1.201(11) and § 1.201(3). Thus, the terms of a contract may be explained and supplemented through trade usage, but it may not be used to contradict an express term. The existence and scope of trade usage must be proved as facts. A buyer has a right to reject goods under § 2.601 if the goods fail to conform to either the express or implied terms of the contract.

Once the contract of the parties has been determined, the evidence must be reviewed to see if the right goods were tendered at the right time and place. If the evidence does establish nonconformity in some respect, the buyer is entitled to reject if he rejects in good faith. [Section] 1.203 provides that, "Every contract or duty within this Act imposes an obligation of good faith in its performance or enforcement." Since the rejection of goods is a matter of performance, the buyer is obligated to act in good faith when he rejects the goods. Where the buyer is a merchant, his standard of good faith rejection requires honesty in fact and observance of reasonable commercial standards of fair dealing in the trade. If the seller alleges that the buyer rejected in bad faith, the seller has the burden of proof on this issue. Evidence of circumstances which indicate that the buyer's motivation in rejecting the goods was to escape the bargain, rather than to avoid acceptance of a tender which in some respect impairs the value of the bargain to him, would support a finding of rejection in bad faith. Thus, evidence of rejection of the goods on account of a minor defect in a falling market would in some instances be sufficient to support a finding that the buyer acted in bad faith when he rejected the goods.

The written contract between the parties which is expressed in a bid proposal dated July 31, 1981 covers only essential terms such as quantity, trim size, and type of paper and cover. The type of paper specified in the contract was thirty pound white newsprint. Appellee's witness testified that he was shown a sample of the newsprint to be used and that the tendered books were not the same color as the sample. The witness stated the pages of the books were gray while the sample was white. This testimony is evidence of nonconformity because any sample which is made part of the basis of the bargain creates an express warranty that the whole of the goods shall conform to the sample. § 2.313(a)(3).

Other nonconformities which appellee alleges and offers proof of are off center cover art, crooked pages, wrinkled pages and inadequate perforation on a pull out page. The contract does not expressly address any of these matters. Although evidence of trade usage may have indicated that these conditions are contrary to the standards of commercial practice within the publishing industry, appellant failed to offer evidence of trade usage to supplement the contract. However, appellant knew that appellee wanted the books printed for sale to the public. In these circumstances, it is implied in the contract that the books be commercially acceptable and appealing to the public. Section 2.314 states that a warranty that the goods shall be merchantable is implied in a contract for their sale and that for goods to be merchantable, they must pass without objection in the trade and be fit for the ordinary purposes for which such goods are used. A jury could reasonably conclude that books with crooked and wrinkled pages, off center cover art, and inadequate perforation are not fit for sale to the public. We find sufficient evidence to support the jury's finding that the books did not conform to the contract.

Appellant contends that if nonconformities exist, they are minor and that appellee rejected the books in bad faith. Appellant has failed to carry its burden to prove that appellee rejected the books in bad faith. First, we do not agree with appellant's contention that the alleged nonconformities should be classified as minor. Second, there is no evidence which indicates that appellee's primary motivation in rejection of the books was to escape a bad bargain. We also note that appellant has waived its defense of rejection in bad faith by its failure to request an issue on this defense, because it has not conclusively established it under the evidence.

Appellant's second point of error is overruled. . . .

Prescott & Co. v. J.B. Powles & Co.

113 Wash. 177, 193 P. 680 (1920)

On January 12, 1918, buyer placed with seller, in Seattle, the following order: "Sold to J.B. Powles Co. How ship, Boat. When, March. 300 crates Australian onions, $94 per ton. Cost, freight & insurance Frisco. Acceptance Australia." The parties understood there was but one ship sailing monthly between the Australian port of shipment and San Francisco, and thus a March shipment would be by the S.S. Sonoma. The seller had ready the 300 crates called for, but was allowed to load only 240, the remainder of the Sonoma's space being taken at the last moment by the government of the United States, to ship wheat. The buyer refused to accept the 240 crates shipped. The seller thereupon resold these crates at less than the contract price and sued the buyer to recover the resulting loss, including the expenses of resale. Trial of the case resulted in a judgment against the buyer for the full amount claimed. *Held*, judgment reversed; seller's action dismissed. "[D]elivery of goods [must generally] be of the exact quantity ordered, otherwise the buyer may refuse to receive them. . . . Since the seller [was bound] to deliver the exact quantity ordered, may he be excused from making full delivery because our national government (rightfully as we must assume), as a war measure, commandeered the only available shipping space for its necessities? Much as [we] would like to so hold, the authorities lay down the contrary rule. Had [the seller] been sued for damages for failure to ship the full order, this act by the government might have afforded a defense, but having sued on the contract, it is essential to a recovery that a full performance be shown, and no excuse not provided for in the contract will justify a recovery where the performance is partial only, save only an act of the buyer rendering performance impossible or a waiver by it. . . ."

Ramirez v. Autosport

88 N.J. 277, 440 A.2d 1345 (1982)

Pollock, J., writing for the court: "In the nineteenth century, sellers were required to deliver goods that complied exactly with the sales agreement. See Filley v. Pope, 115 U.S. 213 (1885) (buyer not obliged to accept otherwise conforming scrap iron shipped to New Orleans from Leith, rather than Glasgow, Scotland, as required by contract). . . . That rule, known as the 'perfect tender' rule, remained part of the law of sales well into the twentieth century. By the 1920's, the doctrine was so entrenched in the law that Judge Learned Hand declared '[t]here is no room in commercial contracts for the doctrine of substantial performance.' Mitsubishi Goshi Kaisha v. J. Aron & Co., Inc., 16 F.2d 185, 186 (2d Cir. 1926). The harshness of the rule led courts to seek to ameliorate its effect and to bring the law of sales in closer harmony with the law of contracts, which allows rescission only for material breaches. . . . Nevertheless, a variation of the perfect tender rule appeared in the Uniform Sales Act. N.J.S.A. 46:30–75 (purchasers permitted to reject goods or rescind contracts for any breach of warranty); N.J.S.A. 46:30–18 to –21 (warranties extended to include all the seller's obligations to the goods). See Honnold, Buyer's Right of Rejection, A Study in the Impact of Codification Upon a Commercial Problem, 97 U.Pa.L.Rev. 457, 460 (1949). The chief objection to the continuation of the perfect tender rule was that buyers in a declining market would reject goods for minor nonconformities and force the loss on surprised sellers. . . . To the extent that a buyer [under § 2–601] can reject goods for any nonconformity, the UCC retains the perfect tender rule. . . . The Code, however, mitigates the harshness of the [rule] and balances the interests of buyer and seller."

[The "perfect tender" rule of § 2–601 is noted by Justice Pollock. It would be a good idea to look also at UCC 2–607(1) and (2), as well as the index of a buyer's Code remedies in general, provided in § 2–711. Note also that § 2–601, by its terms, excludes installment contracts falling within the scope of § 2–612. It would be a good idea to look closely at the three subdivisions of § 2–612. The first point to note is the broad definition of an "installment contract." Observe also the test of "materiality" stated in 2–612(2) and (3). Why should installment contracts involving goods be subject to a test of "substantial impairment" while a one-shot, unitary sales contract is governed by a rule of "perfect tender" (softened, of course, by § 2–508)?]

Beck & Pauli Lithographing Co. v. Colorado Milling & Elevator Co.

52 F. 700 (8th Cir. 1892)

Plaintiff was engaged in lithographing and printing at Milwaukee. In June 1889, defendant, a Colorado company engaged in milling, entered into a contract to purchase from plaintiff more than 300,000 copies of engraved letterhead paper, bills, envelopes, and cards, together with some advertising material. The contract provided that plaintiff would prepare designs of defendant's buildings, together with sketches of its trademarks, submit these designs to defendant for approval, execute engravings "in first class style," and furnish the engraved letterhead paper and other material "in the course of the year" 1889. Plaintiff's lithographing process involved the preparation of a sketch which was then transferred to stone, with a separate stone for each color used. The process required from two to three months; the most expensive part was the artists' work and the reproduction on stone. Sketches and proofs were submitted to and approved by defendant, the last proof being approved on November 16, 1889. In December 1889, plaintiff shipped the finished product by rail in five boxes, four of which did not arrive in Denver until the morning of January 1, 1890, and one of which did not arrive until January 4. Plaintiff tendered delivery of all five boxes before January 8, but defendant refused to receive or examine them, asserting that delivery was too late. In an action brought by plaintiff for the contract price, the trial court directed a verdict for defendant. On appeal, this ruling was overturned and the case remanded for further proceedings. The court said that stipulations as to the time of performance are not necessarily of the essence, unless express provisions of the contract or the nature of the subject matter indicates that the parties intended performance on time to be a condition precedent. In the ordinary contracts of merchants for the sale or manufacture of marketable commodities, time clauses should be strictly construed "on account of the frequent and rapid interchange and use of such commodities made necessary by the demands of commerce." But this was a contract for artistic skill and labor, to be bestowed on articles that would not be saleable to any other buyer. There was nothing to indicate that delivery a few days late would be harmful to defendant, but if there was injury, defendant's remedy was in damages for the delay. Its refusal to accept delivery was not justified by this trifling delay. [The Comment that follows considers the applicability of the UCC to facts like those in *Beck & Pauli*.]

COMMENT: "GOODS" AND "SERVICES"—THE SCOPE OF THE UCC SALES ARTICLE

Because a more demanding law of performance is commonly applied in sales of goods than in other types of transactions, many contractual disputes will present a troublesome problem of classification. If a contract provides only for a present or future transfer of goods from seller to buyer, no difficulty usually arises and the law of sales set out in Article 2 of the UCC can safely be assumed to govern disputes that may arise. Under the UCC, § 2–105, "goods" are defined as "all things . . . which are movable at the time of identification to the contract for sale." The first phase of any inquiry into the type of contract sued on therefore centers on the nature of particular items at the time of identification to the contract (are they movable and thus "goods" within the scope of the Code?).

An issue as to the applicability of sales law is likely to arise in three common types of transactions.

(a) The contract may provide for the transfer of ownership of goods, as well as incorporeal rights or realty. An example is an agreement to sell a going business—its inventory of movable goods, buildings and fixtures, and good will. If disputes arise, one obvious solution is to apply Article 2 to issues involving "goods" and to decide others under general contract law. This is the course taken by many decisions, e.g., Foster v. Colorado Radio Corp., 381 F.2d 222 (10th Cir. 1967), and Kazerouni v. De Satnick, 228 Cal. App. 3d 871, 279 Cal.Rptr. 74 (1991), though there is support for a test of "reasonable characterization of the transaction as a whole," that is, scrutiny of the assets to be sold to determine whether the bulk qualifies as "goods" under the Code's definition. Fink v. DeClassis, 745 F. Supp. 509 (N.D.Ill. 1990); Advent Systems Ltd. v. Unisys Corp., 925 F.2d 670 (3d Cir. 1991), quoting De Filippo v. Ford Motor Co., 516 F.2d 1313 (3d Cir. 1975), cert. denied, 423 U.S. 912 (1975) ("[t]o segregate 'goods' assets from 'non-goods' assets . . . would be to make the contract divisible and impossible of performance within the intention of the parties").

(b) The rendition of a service often involves the transfer of ownership of goods. *Beck & Pauli Lithographing*, supra, provides an example of a sale not only of goods but also of services (a "hybrid" transaction). When dealing with such cases, most courts have made the classification (and thus the applicable law) turn on what is found to be the "essence" of the contract, the "main objective" of the parties, or the "dominant aspect" of the transaction—i.e., which aspect of the transaction, the sale of goods or the sale of services, predominates. A popular statement of this general approach to "mixed" goods and service contracts can be found in Bonebrake v. Cox, 499 F.2d 951, 960 (8th Cir. 1974): "The [test] is not whether they are mixed, but, granting that they are mixed, whether their predominant factor, their thrust, their purpose, reasonably stated, is the rendition of service, with goods incidentally involved (e.g., contract with artist for painting) or is a transaction of sale, with labor incidentally involved (e.g., installation of a water heater in a bathroom)." Under this test, virtually every jurisdiction that has addressed the question whether a franchise or dealership agreement is predominantly for the sale of goods has concluded that it is. So, too, according to the weight of authority, is the sale of custom computer software. Conversely, agreements to provide specified materials and install a roof for a building (Quality Guaranteed Roofing v. Hoffmann-La Roche, 302 N.J. Super. 163, 694 A.2d 1077 (App.Div. 1997)), to supply and install a grain-storage system (Valley Farmers' Elevator v. Lindsay Bros. Co., 398 N.W.2d 553 (Minn. 1987)), to supply the structural steel and build a bridge (Schenectady Steel Co. v. Bruno Trimpoli General Constr. Co. Inc., 43 A.D.2d 234, 350 N.Y.S.2d 920 (1974), aff'd, 34 N.Y.2d 939, 359 N.Y.S.2d 560, 316 N.E.2d 875 (1974)), and to give a blood transfusion (Howell v. Spokane & Inland Empire Blood Bank, 114 Wash. 2d 42, 785 P.2d 815 (1990)), have been classified as service contracts to which sales law was not applicable.

If, however, the rendition of services is not central to a mixed contract ("not at the heart" of the contract), there is a general trend to view any transaction weighted towards goods as governed by the UCC. See, e.g., Judge Coffin's discussion in Cambridge Plating Co. v. Napco, Inc., 991 F.2d 21 (1st Cir. 1993). See also Micro Data Base Sys. v. Dharma Sys., 148 F.3d 649 (7th Cir. 1998) (where sale of goods predominates, but contract price includes a charge for labor in the manufacture of the goods, "we doubt it should even be called a 'hybrid' sale, for this would imply that every sale of goods is actually a hybrid sale, since labor is a service and labor is an input into the manufacture of every good"). Here, too, there is an occasional call for bypassing the "predominant factor" test in favor of severance of a mixed goods-services transaction. For example, in Stephenson v. Frazier, 399 N.E.2d 794 (Ind. App. Ct. 1980), the contract called for the sale of a modular home, the construction of a foundation for the home, and the installation of a septic system. The court held only the sale of the modular home ("movable goods") to be governed by the Code; those portions of the contract pertaining to services were left to common law principles. (For a different view in Indiana, and elsewhere, see Baker v. Compton, 455 N.E.2d 382 (Ind. App. 1983); In re Trailer & Plumbing Supplies, 133 N.H. 432, 578 A.2d 343 (1990).)

(c) Many persons and businesses elect not to purchase equipment but to lease instead. Should the rights and obligations of the parties depend on whether they are classified as seller-buyer or lessor-lessee? Since § 2–102 defines the applicability of Article 2 in terms of "transactions in goods," it is arguable that this term is more embracing than "contract of sale" and that an agreement for equipment-leasing falls within the technical reach of the Code. There is some authority to this effect, at least to the extent of bringing into play the implied warranty provisions of the Code. See Owens v. Patent Scaffolding Co., 77 Misc. 2d 992, 354 N.Y.S.2d 778 (1974), rev'd on other grounds, 50 A.D.2d 866, 376 N.Y.S.2d 948 (1975). Even if the transaction falls technically outside the scope of Article 2, however, sales-law results may be reached because of the view that many leases are closely analogous to, and not economically different from, a sale. Barco Auto Leasing Corp. v. PSI Cosmetics, Inc., 125 Misc. 2d 68, 478 N.Y.S.2d 505 (N.Y.Civ.Ct. 1984); Xerox Corp. v. Hawkes, 124 N.H. 610, 475 A.2d 7 (1984). The general subject of extension of Code provisions by analogy is examined in Note, Disengaging Sales Law From the Sale Construct: A Proposal to Extend the Scope of Article 2 of the UCC, 96 Harv. L. Rev. 470 (1982). Article 2A on the law of leases, added to the UCC in May 1987, is discussed in Note, Article 2A of the Uniform Commercial Code: An Unnecessary Perpetuation of the Lease-Sale Distinction, 54 Brooklyn L.Rev. 1357 (1989).

On the general issue of extending the UCC by analogy, there is considerable evidence that Code principles will govern breaches of duty to provide services. For example, assume that a court adhering to the "goods supplied" approach to mixed transactions concludes that a particular contract is predominantly for services. The court may nevertheless rule that exclusion from

Article 2 does not foreclose the application of Code policies. An example of this can be found in Semler v. Knowling, 325 N.W.2d 395 (Iowa 1982), where an implied warranty of fitness was found in a contract to supply and install sewer pipes and fittings. See also Midwest Dredging Co. v. McAninch Corp., 424 N.W.2d 216 (Iowa 1988), which collects cases extending relief for implied warranty in various nonconstruction contexts.

PART THREE

The Boundaries of Contract

CHAPTER 6

POLICING THE BARGAIN

INTRODUCTORY NOTE

The basic theme of this chapter, that courts "police" the bargains made by private parties, has been implicit in many of the decisions already encountered. Even though the law's formal requirements for enforceability of a contract have been met, a court may nonetheless intervene because of an abuse in bargaining or a defect in the substance of the bargain (say, violation of a positive rule of law). Yet there is a fundamental tension between the regulatory function and certain premises of our political-economic tradition—e.g., "freedom of contract," "private autonomy," "security of transactions." These concepts, of course, have their corollaries in judicial attitudes; judges, over many years, have said that it is the function of courts to enforce the parties' agreement, not to make a new agreement for them or shelter one party from obligations that have proved burdensome. To be sure, the traditional attitudes have not been superseded or abandoned; their influence remains pervasive. Nevertheless, it is a fact that a "policing" function emerged in the middle of the last century. The body of regulation examined in this chapter serves as a reminder that the law of contract enjoys no immunity from the large and puzzling issues of political, economic, and judicial philosophy.

SECTION 1. COMPETENCY AND OTHER LIMITS

Halbman v. Lemke

Supreme Court of Wisconsin, 1980.
99 Wis. 2d 241, 298 N.W.2d 562.

CALLOW, J. . . . On or about July 13, 1973, James Halbman, Jr., a minor, entered into an agreement with Michael Lemke whereby Lemke agreed to sell Halbman a 1968 Oldsmobile for the sum of $1,250. Lemke was the manager of L & M Standard Station in Greenfield, and Halbman was an employee at L & M. . . . Halbman paid Lemke $1,000 cash and took possession of the car. Arrangements were made for Halbman to pay $25 per week until the balance was paid, at which time title would be transferred. About five weeks after the purchase agreement, and after Halbman had paid a total of $1,100 of the purchase price, a connecting rod on the vehicle's engine broke. Lemke, while denying any obligation, offered to assist Halbman in installing a used engine in the vehicle if Halbman, at his expense, could secure one. Halbman declined the offer and in September took the vehicle to a garage where it was repaired at a cost of $637.40. Halbman did not pay the repair bill.

In October of 1973 Lemke endorsed the vehicle's title over to Halbman, although the full purchase price had not been paid by Halbman, in an effort to avoid any liability for the operation, maintenance, or use of the vehicle. On October 15, Halbman returned the title to Lemke by letter which disaffirmed the purchase contract and demanded the return of all money theretofore paid by Halbman. Lemke did not return the money. . . .

The repair bill remained unpaid, and the vehicle remained in the garage where the repairs had been made. In the spring of 1974, in satisfaction of a garageman's lien for the outstanding amount, the garage elected to remove the vehicle's engine and transmission and then towed the vehicle to the residence of James Halbman, Sr., the father of the plaintiff minor. Lemke was asked several times to remove the vehicle from the senior Halbman's home, but he declined to do so, claiming he was under no legal obligation to remove it. During the period when the vehicle was at the garage and then subsequently at the home of the plaintiff's father, it was subjected to vandalism, making it unsalvageable.

Halbman [sued for] return of the $1,100 he had paid toward the purchase [and] Lemke counterclaimed for $150, the amount still owing on the contract. . . . [T]he trial court granted judgment [to] Halbman, concluding that when a minor disaffirms a contract for the purchase of an item, he need only offer to return the property remaining in his hands without making restitution for any use or depreciation. . . . [T]he court also allowed interest to the plaintiff dating from the disaffirmance of the contract. . . . The appellate court affirmed. . . .

The sole issue [is] whether a minor, having disaffirmed a contract for the purchase of an item which is not a necessity and having tendered the property back to the vendor, must make restitution to the vendor for damage to the property prior to the disaffirmance. Lemke argues that he should be entitled to recover for the damage to the vehicle up to the time of disaffirmance, which he claims equals the amount of the repair bill.

Neither party challenges the absolute right of a minor to disaffirm a contract for the purchase of items which are not necessities. . . . [T]he doctrine of incapacity or the "infancy doctrine," is one of the oldest and most venerable of our common law traditions. . . . [I]ts purpose is the protection of minors from foolishly squandering their wealth through improvident contracts with crafty adults who would take advantage of them in the marketplace. . . . Thus[,] a contract of a minor for items which are not necessities is void or voidable at the minor's option. . . .

Once there has been a disaffirmance, however, [problems] arise regarding the rights and responsibilities of the parties relative to the disposition of the consideration exchanged on the contract. As a general rule a minor who disaffirms a contract is entitled to recover all consideration he has conferred incident to the transaction. . . . In return the minor is expected to restore as much of the consideration as, at the time of disaffirmance, remains in the minor's possession. . . . Restatement of Restitution, § 62, comment b (1937); Restatement (Second) of Contracts, [§ 14], comment c. . . . The minor's right to disaffirm is not contingent upon the return of the property, however, as disaffirmance is permitted even where such return cannot be made. Olson v. Veum, 197 Wis. 342, 222 N.W. 233 (1928) . . . . [But here we] have a situation where the property cannot be returned to the vendor in its entirety because it has been damaged and therefore diminished in value, and the vendor seeks to recover the depreciation. . . .

The law regarding . . . the consideration exchanged on a disaffirmed contract is characterized by confusion, inconsistency, and a general lack of uniformity as jurisdictions attempt to reach a fair application of the infancy doctrine in today's marketplace. [See] Navin, The Contracts of Minors Viewed from the Perspective of Fair Exchange, 50 N.C.L.Rev. 517 (1972); Note, Restitution in Minors' Contracts in California, 19 Hastings L.Rev. 1199 (1968) . . . . That both parties rely on this court's decision in Olson v. Veum, supra, is symptomatic of the problem.

In *Olson* a minor, with his brother, an adult, purchased farm implements and materials, paying by signing notes payable at a future date. Prior to the maturity of the first note, the brothers ceased their joint farming business, and the minor abandoned his interest in the material purchased by leaving it with his brother. The vendor initiated an action against the minor to recover on the note, and the minor (who had by then reached majority) disaffirmed. . . . [We held] that the contract of a minor for the purchase of items which are not necessities may be disaffirmed even when the minor cannot make restitution. Lemke calls our attention to the following language in that decision:

> [There is a] substantial distinction between a mere denial by an infant of contract liability where the other party is seeking to enforce it and those cases where he who was the minor not only disaffirms such contract but seeks the aid of the court to restore to him that with which he has parted at the making of the contract. In the one case he is using his infancy merely as a shield, in the other also as a sword. 197 Wis. at 344, 222 N.W. 233.

From this Lemke infers that when a minor, as a plaintiff, seeks to disaffirm a contract and recover his consideration, different rules should apply than if the minor is defending against an action on the contract by the other party. . . .

Additionally, Lemke [argues] that a disaffirming minor's obligation to make restitution turns upon his ability to do so[,] [and that the obligation is excused] only when restitution is not possible. Here Lemke holds Halbman's $1,100, and accordingly there is no question as to Halbman's ability to make restitution.

Halbman argues in response that, while the "sword-shield" dichotomy may apply where the minor has misrepresented his age to induce the contract, that did not occur here and he may avoid the contract without making restitution notwithstanding his ability to do so.

The principal problem is the use of the word "restitution" in *Olson*. A minor, as we have stated, is under an enforceable duty to return to the vendor, upon disaffirmance, as much of the consideration as remains in his possession. When the contract is disaffirmed, title to that part of the purchased property which is retained by the minor revests in the vendor; it no longer belongs to the minor. See, e.g., Restatement (Second) of Contracts, [§ 14], comment c. . . . The rationale for the rule is plain: a minor who disaffirms a purchase and recovers his purchase price should not also be permitted to profit by retaining the property purchased. The infancy doctrine is designed to protect the minor, sometimes at the expense of an innocent vendor, but it is not to be used to bilk merchants out of property as well as proceeds of the sale. Consequently, it is clear that, when the minor no longer possesses the property which was the subject matter of the contract, the rule requiring the return of property does not apply.[1] The minor will not be required to give up what he does not have. . . . *Olson* does no more than set forth the foregoing rationale[;] the word "restitution" as it is used in that opinion is limited to the return of the property to the vendor. . . .

Here Lemke seeks restitution of the value of the depreciation by virtue of the damage to the vehicle prior to disaffirmance. Such a recovery would require Halbman to return more than that remaining in his possession. It seeks compensatory value for that which he cannot return. Where there is misrepresentation by a minor or willful destruction of property, the vendor may be able to recover damages in tort. . . . But absent these factors, as [here], to require a disaffirming minor to make restitution for diminished value is, in effect, to bind the minor to a part of the obligation which by law he is privileged to avoid. . . . The cases upon which the petitioner relies for the proposition that a disaffirming minor must make restitution for loss and depreciation would at some point force the minor to bear the cost of the very improvidence from which the infancy doctrine is supposed to protect him; we cannot follow them.

---

1 Although we are not presented with the question here, we recognize there is considerable disagreement . . . on whether a minor who disposes of the property should be made to restore the vendor with something in its stead. The general rule appears to limit the minor's responsibility for restoration to specie only. . . . But see: Boyce v. Doyle, 113 N.J.Super. 240, 273 A.2d 408 (1971), adopting a "status quo" theory which requires the minor to restore the precontract status quo, even if it means returning proceeds or other value; Fisher v. Taylor Motor Co., 249 N.C. 617, 107 S.E.2d 94 (1959), requiring the minor to restore only the property remaining in the hands of the minor, " 'or account for so much of its value as may have been invested in other property which he has in hand or owns and controls.' " Finally, some attention is given to the "New Hampshire Rule" or benefits theory, which requires the disaffirming minor to pay for the contract to the extent he benefited from it. Hall v. Butterfield, 59 N.H. 354 (1879). . . .

. . . [M]odifications of the rules governing the capacity of infants to contract are best left to the legislature. Until such changes are forthcoming, however, we . . . believe [our] result is consistent with the purpose of the infancy doctrine.

The decision of the court of appeals is affirmed.

[Courts applying the *Halbman* rule often register doubts about "the wisdom of this approach," inviting legislative intervention. E.g., Swalberg v. Hannegan, 883 P.2d 931 (Utah Ct. App. 1994). Since, historically, the typical disaffirmance case has involved a minor's purchase of a car, is that surprising?]

Webster Street Partnership v. Sheridan

220 Neb. 9, 368 N.W.2d 439 (1985)

Two minors (ages 17 and 18), unable to pay the agreed rent, disaffirmed a lease for an apartment after only a short period of occupancy. They had paid the landlord a total of $500 in rent and a security deposit, which sum they demanded be returned. The landlord refused this demand and brought suit seeking an additional $630 for accrued rent and expenses. *Held*, judgment of $500 restitution for the minors. A disaffirming infant is liable only for the value of "necessaries" supplied under the contract. That term is flexible and varies with the facts of each case; it is not confined to things that are required for bare subsistence, but "depends on the social position and situation in life of the infant, as well as upon his own fortune and that of his parents." However, goods or other items of property are not necessaries if the infant has a parent or guardian who is willing and able to supply them. Here, neither minor "was in need of shelter but, rather, [both] had chosen to voluntarily leave home, with the understanding that they could return whenever they desired." One may "at first blush" believe that such a disaffirmance rule is unfair. "Yet, on further consideration, the wisdom of the rule is apparent. If, indeed, landlords may not contract with minors, except at their peril, they may refuse to do so. In that event, minors who voluntarily leave home but who are free to return will be compelled to return to their parents' home—a result which is desirable." Because the facts of this case make clear that the apartment was not a necessary, neither the minors nor their parents are liable, and the landlord's claim of emancipation is of no moment.

NOTE: LIMITS ON DISAFFIRMANCE

As *Halbman* and *Webster Street Partnership* indicate, at common law a minor who attempts to disaffirm a contract for "necessaries" does not escape liability. The explanation usually given rests on quasi-contractual principles. See, e.g., State of Ohio, University of Cincinnati Hosp. v. Cohen, 57 Ohio App. 3d 30, 566 N.E.2d 187 (1989) (benefit received from antecedent transaction involving necessaries results in an unjustly-retained enrichment for which the law implies a promise of "reasonable value"). For the doctrine of necessaries to apply, however, it must be shown that the minor entered into a contract—express or implied in fact—for the goods or services in question. Stated differently, a minor is not liable for necessaries furnished on someone else's credit. Why such a rule? If a minor has received but not contracted for necessaries, is anyone liable? One or both of the minor's parents? On what reasoning?

Incidentally, a minor's right to disaffirm survives for a "reasonable time" after reaching the age of majority (in most places in this country, and for most purposes, lowered from 21 to 18 beginning in the 1970s). A state legislature may of course alter an infant's common-law rights, as by a statute conferring upon infants, through a parent's consent binding the infant, the right to make enforceable agreements respecting certain matters. Litigation under such statutes is likely to involve child models, actors, or athletes. E.g., Shields v. Gross, 58 N.Y.2d 338, 448 N.E.2d 108 (1983).

The question of the validity of a contract signed by the minor's parent arose in Sharon v. City of Newton, 437 Mass. 99 (2002). There, the defendant, conceding that minors may ratify or disaffirm their own contracts on reaching majority, nevertheless prevailed on the theory that the parent could effectively waive the minor's claim for negligence against the city by signing the release in dispute. Among the plaintiff's arguments against finding a waiver was the argument that allowing the parent to do what the minor cannot do violates public policy. The Massachusetts high court thought otherwise:

> While the common-law rule has been narrowed somewhat by statute,[9] it remains our law that the contract of a minor is generally voidable when she reaches the age of majority. Merav unequivocally repudiated the release (to the extent it might be deemed a contract executed by her) by filing suit against the city. . . .
>
> The purpose of the policy permitting minors to void their contracts is "to afford protection to minors from their own improvidence and want of sound judgment." Frye v. Yasi, 327 Mass. 724, 728, 101 N.E.2d 128 (1951). This purpose comports with common sense and experience and is not defeated by permitting parents to exercise their own providence and sound judgment on behalf of their minor children. Parham v. J.R. 442 U.S. 584, 602 (1979) ("The law's concept of the family rests on a presumption that parents possess what a child lacks in maturity, experience, and capacity for judgment required for making life's difficult decisions."). . . . Moreover, our law presumes that fit parents act in furtherance of the welfare and best interests of their children . . . and with respect to

[9] See, e.g., G.L. c. 167E, § 10 (student under eighteen admitted to institution of higher learning has full legal capacity to act on her own behalf in contracts and other transactions regarding financing of education); G.L. c. 175 § 128 (certain contracts for life or endowment insurance may not be voided by minor over fifteen years of age); G.L. c. 175 § 113K (minor over sixteen permitted to contract for motor vehicle liability insurance); G.L. c. 112, § 12E (minor over twelve found to be drug dependent may consent to treatment for dependency); G.L. c. 112, § 12F (minor may consent to medical or dental treatment if she meets criteria outlined in statute).

> matters relating to their care, custody, and upbringing have a fundamental right to make those decisions for them. . . .
>
> Merav's father signed the release in his capacity as parent because he wanted his child to benefit from participating in cheerleading. . . . He made an important family decision cognizant of the risk of physical injury to his child and the financial risk to the family as a whole. In the circumstances of a voluntary, nonessential activity, we will not disturb this parental judgment. This comports with the fundamental liberty interest of parents in the rearing of their children, and is not inconsistent with the purpose behind our public policy permitting minors to void their contracts. . . .
>
> Our views with respect to the . . . enforceability of releases signed by parents on behalf of their children for [the] purposes [involved here] are also consistent with and further the public policy of encouraging athletic programs for the Commonwealth's youth. To hold that releases of [this] type are unenforceable would expose public schools, who offer many of the extracurricular sports opportunities available to children, to financial costs and risks that will inevitably lead to the reduction of those programs.

Should one be surprised to learn that courts in many places do not subscribe to the public policy views expressed in *Sharon*? For a roundup of this line of cases, see Cooper v. Aspen Skiing Co., 48 P.3d 1229 (Colo. 2002) ("Colorado's public policy [reflected in many special statutes] affords minors significant protections which preclude parents from releasing a minor's own prospective claim for negligence"; "in the tort context especially, a minor should be [protected from both his own improvidence as well as] from unwise decisions made on his behalf by parents who are routinely asked to release their child's claims for liability" and whose actions "may as a practical matter leave the minor in an unacceptably precarious position with no recourse, no parental support, and no method to support or care for himself").

NOTE: MENTAL COMPETENCE

For a considerable time, the view prevailed that mental incompetency of one of the parties made a contract entirely void. An emphatic and much-quoted statement to this effect was made by the United States Supreme Court in 1872 (Dexter v. Hall, 82 U.S. (15 Wall.) 9, 20), with a logic that, as framed, seems irresistible:

> The fundamental idea of a contract is that it requires the assent of two minds. But a lunatic, or a person non compos mentis, has nothing which the law recognizes as a mind, and it would seem, therefore, upon principle, that he cannot make a contract that will have any efficacy as such.

This consequence—total nullity—is still called for by statute in a few states. Elsewhere it has become standard to describe transactions entered into by persons shown to have been mentally incompetent at the time as merely "voidable." It thus becomes possible for the party suffering under such disability to enforce a transaction that has proved advantageous. At the same time, means are usually provided for protecting the interests of others who in dealing with the disabled person were unaware of the disability.

There may be special complications where a court previously has entered a formal decree declaring the individual in question to be incompetent. Surely the legal effect of such a decree should depend on its purpose. If its purpose is to appoint a guardian to care for and preserve the estate of the handicapped person, some statutes authorizing such proceedings have been read as prescribing that, until the adjudication has been reversed in a later proceeding, all of the incompetent's commercial transactions are void. The effect of such a reading is to establish incapacity as a "status." An argument supporting such a view is that otherwise the guardian's management and control of the incompetent's affairs may be nullified or, at the least, hampered. But mental or emotional disorder may be cured or remissions may occur, with no interested party having enough incentive to apply for termination of the guardianship by the court that decreed it. Several state courts have concluded that a guardianship order does not have this conclusive, status-creating effect and is only one of numerous admissible facts that may show a person's incompetence for the purpose of voiding a contract. Still less should a previous court order for involuntary commitment to a hospital for medical or custodial care have the effect of invalidating transactions by the hospitalized individual. The court order, or a diagnosis by a hospital's medical or psychiatric staff, would of course be admissible as evidence, but the need for hospital care and treatment can arise from such a diversity of causes that, on the difficult legal issue as to whether capacity to enter the particular transaction had been impaired, a record of hospitalization should have, and nowadays would have, very little weight. Of course, the timing of the hospitalization in relation to the transaction in question will count for something.

As for the substantive tests of mental incompetency, consider the approach of Faber v. Sweet Style Mfg. Corp., 40 Misc. 2d 212, 242 N.Y.S.2d 763 (N.Y. Supp. Ct. 1963). In that case, a rapidly-moving plaintiff, found to be in the depressed phase of a manic-depressive illness, entered into a contract to purchase land for a commercial venture. Despite the absence of a finding of the transaction's unfairness, the court declared the contract rescinded. Justice Meyer said:

> The standards by which competence to contract is measured were, apparently, developed without relation to the effects of particular mental diseases or disorders and prior to recognition of manic-depressive psychosis as a distinct form of mental illness. . . . Primarily they are concerned with capacity to understand: Aldrich v. Bailey, 132 N.Y. 85, 87–88, 30 N.E. 264—"so deprived of his mental faculties as to be wholly, absolutely, and completely unable to understand or comprehend the nature of the transaction;" Paine v. Aldrich, 133 N.Y. 544, 546, 30 N.E. 725—"such mental capacity at the time of the execution of the deed that he could collect in his mind without prompting all the elements of the transaction, and retain them for a sufficient length of time to perceive their obvious

relations to each other, and to form a rational judgment in regard to them;" Matter of Delinousha v. National Biscuit Co., 248 N.Y. 93, 95, 161 N.E. 431, 432—"A contract may be avoided only if a party is so affected as to be unable to see things in their true relations and to form correct conclusions in regard thereto." . . . If cognitive capacity is the sole criterion used, the manic must be held competent, [for] manic-depressive psychosis affects motivation rather than ability to understand.

The law does, however, recognize stages of incompetence other than total lack of understanding. Thus it will invalidate a transaction when a contracting party is suffering from delusions if there is "some such connection between the insane delusions and the making of the deed as will compel the inference that the insanity induced the grantor to perform an act the purport and effect of which he could not understand, and which he would not have performed if thoroughly sane." . . . Moreover, it holds that understanding of the physical nature and consequences of an act of suicide does not render the suicide voluntary within the meaning of a life insurance contract if the insured "acted under the control of an insane impulse caused by disease, and derangement of his intellect, which deprived him of the capacity of governing his own conduct in accordance with reason." Newton v. Mut. Benefit Life Ins. Co., 76 N.Y. 426, 429. . . . Finally, Paine v. Aldrich, supra, and the Delinousha case consider not only ability to understand but also capacity to form "a rational judgment" or "correct conclusions." Thus, capacity to understand is not, in fact, the sole criterion. Incompetence to contract also exists when a contract is entered into under the compulsion of a mental disease or disorder but for which the contract would not have been made.

The second restaters, in writing and explaining the Restatement section that follows, echo the approach of *Faber*.

Restatement of Contracts, Second

§ 15. Mental Illness or Defect

(1) A person incurs only voidable contractual duties by entering into a transaction if by reason of mental illness or defect

(a) he is unable to understand in a reasonable manner the nature and consequences of the transaction, or

(b) he is unable to act in a reasonable manner in relation to the transaction and the other party has reason to know of his condition.

(2) Where the contract is made on fair terms and the other party is without knowledge of the mental illness or defect, the power of avoidance under Subsection (1) terminates to the extent that the contract has been so performed in whole or in part or the circumstances have so changed

that avoidance would be unjust. In such a case a court may grant relief as justice requires.

Comment:

a. *Rationale.* A contract made by a person who is mentally incompetent requires the reconciliation of two conflicting policies: the protection of justifiable expectations and of the security of transactions, and the protection of persons unable to protect themselves against imposition. . . . [I]t has been asserted that mental incompetency has no effect on a contract unless other grounds of avoidance are present, such as fraud, undue influence, or gross inadequacy of consideration; it is now widely believed that such a rule gives inadequate protection to the incompetent and his family, particularly where the contract is entirely executory. . . .

d. *Operative effect of incompetency.* Where no guardian has been appointed, the effect on executory contracts of incompetency by reason of mental illness or defect is very much like that of infancy. Regardless of the other party's knowledge or good faith and regardless of the fairness of the terms, the incompetent person on regaining full capacity may affirm or disaffirm the contract, or the power to affirm or disaffirm may be exercised on his behalf by his guardian or after his death by his personal representative. . . .

e. *Effect of performance.* Where the contract has been performed in whole or in part, avoidance is permitted only on equitable terms. In the traditional action at law, the doing of equity by or on behalf of the incompetent was accomplished by a tender before suit, but in equity or under modern merged procedure it is provided for in the decree. Any benefits still retained by the incompetent must be restored or paid for, and restitution must be made for any necessaries furnished under the contract. . . . If the other party knew of the incompetency at the time of contracting, or if he took unfair advantage of the incompetent, consideration not received by the incompetent or dissipated without benefit to him need not be restored.

Ortelere v. Teachers' Retirement Bd.

25 N.Y.2d 196, 303 N.Y.S.2d 362, 250 N.E.2d 460 (1969)

Grace Ortelere, a 60-year-old teacher who had taught in the New York City schools since 1924, had a "nervous breakdown" in March 1964. In July of that year, a psychiatrist diagnosed her condition as a psychosis, involutional melancholia. Electroshock and tranquilizer treatments, given for six weeks, were discontinued when it was suspected that she had cerebral arteriosclerosis; this diagnosis was later confirmed. The psychiatrist continued to see her until March 1965, when she had a cerebral thrombosis which caused her death on April 7, 1965. Not quite two months earlier, on February 11, she had applied to the Teachers' Retirement Board for retirement, electing to have all her retirement benefits paid to her "without option." The effect of this election was to give her, for her life, the maximum payments permitted ($450 a month) and to leave no reserve after her death, from which payments could be made to her husband (she also had two children). Some ten years earlier she had filed with the Board an election to take smaller allowances in her own lifetime (at the rate of $375 a month), and thus leave a reserve for payments to her husband, with whom she had at the time of her death been "happily married for 38 years" (the court's characterization). The husband, an electrician, had given up his $222-a-week job in order to stay at home to care for his wife when she became severely depressed. The couple owned their home and had $8,000 in savings, but without the husband's income they would be almost entirely dependent on the income from the wife's retirement benefits.

The psychiatrist who had seen Grace Ortelere monthly from July 1964 until March 1965, described her condition as follows: "At no time since she was under my care was she ever mentally competent"; that "[m]entally she couldn't make a decision of any kind, actually, of any kind, small or large." He also described how involutional melancholia affects the judgment processes of those afflicted: "They can't think rationally, no matter what the situation is. They will even tell you, 'I used to be able to think of anything and make any decision. Now,' they say, 'even getting up, I don't know whether I should get up or whether I should stay in bed.' Or, 'I don't even know how to make a slice of toast any more.' Everything is impossible to decide, and everything is too great an effort to even think of doing. They just don't have the effort, actually, because their nervous breakdown drains them of all their physical energies."

In an action brought by Ortelere's husband (also executor) to set aside her application for retirement "without options," the trial court found that she had been mentally incompetent when she made the application and declared it "null and void and of no legal effect." The Appellate Division reversed by a divided vote, holding the proofs of mental incompetency insufficient. The Court of Appeals, 4 to 2, reversed the Appellate Division.

Judge Breitel spoke for the majority: "[The] traditional standards governing competency to contract were formulated when psychiatric knowledge was quite primitive. They fail to account for one who by reason of mental illness is unable to control his conduct even though his cognitive ability seems unimpaired. . . . Hence, because the cognitive rules are, for the most part, too restrictive and rest on a false factual basis they must be re-examined. Once it is understood that, accepting plaintiff's proof, Mrs. Ortelere was psychotic and because of that psychosis could have been incapable of making a voluntary selection of her retirement system benefits, there is an issue that a modern jurisprudence should not exclude, merely because her mind could pass a 'cognition' test based on nineteenth century psychology. . . ."

Judge Breitel then pointed out that the Retirement Board was or should have been aware of Grace Ortelere's condition, since it, or the Board of Education, knew that she was on leave of absence for medical reasons and had consulted the staff psychiatrist of the Board of Education, at the Board's request. Also, there were no significant changes of position by the Board other than some changes in its actuarial computations. The choice she made "while under psychiatric care, ill with cerebral arteriosclerosis, aged 60, and with a family in which she had always manifested concern, was so unwise and foolhardy that a factfinder might conclude that it was explainable only as a product of psychosis."

There was a vigorous dissent by Jasen, J., summarized as follows:

(1) The evidence established conclusively that Ortelere understood that she had selected the maximum payment during her lifetime.

(2) Her letter of inquiry sent to the Board three days before her election was made showed a mind "fully in command" of the salient features of the retirement system.

(3) Her retirement pay had become the family's only source of income, since both spouses had retired; so securing a $75 a month increase in income (from $375 to $450) was a necessity for them and a rational decision for her.

(4) The present state of knowledge does not enable psychiatry to give a fixed rule for each type of mental disorder. The legal rules determining mental capacity are general enough to encompass all types of incapacity, and they are phrased in such a manner that they can be understood and applied by juries of lay people. The generally accepted test—capacity to understand the nature and consequences of the transaction—represents a balance struck between the security of transactions and protection to the mentally handicapped. It is workable in practice and fair in result. To minimize injustices, "the line should be drawn as clearly as possible." Any benefit "to those who understand what they are doing, but are unable to exercise self-discipline, will be outweighed by frivolous claims which will burden our courts and undermine the security of contracts."

Sparrow v. Demonico

461 Mass. 322, 960 N.E.2d 296 (2012)

Sparrow filed a complaint alleging she was entitled to a one-half interest in the family home against her sister Susan. The parties and the attorneys who were representing them participated in mediation that resulted in a settlement. When Sparrow sought an order enforcing the agreement, alleging that the Demonicos reneged on their obligations under it, the Demonicos claimed that the agreement was unenforceable because Susan had, in their view, experienced a mental breakdown during the mediation and thus lacked the capacity to authorize settlement.

It has been long established that a contract is voidable by a person who, due to mental illness or defect, lacked the capacity to contract at the time of entering into the agreement. As Justice Holmes observed, it is a question of fact whether a person was competent to enter into a transaction—that is, whether the person suffered from "insanity" or "was of unsound mind, and incapable of understanding and deciding upon the terms of the contract." See Wright v. Wright, 139 Mass. 177, 182, 29 N.E. 380 (1885). Over time, however, the traditional test for contractual incapacity evolved to incorporate an increased understanding of the nature of mental illness in its various forms. Based on this understanding, courts in Massachusetts and elsewhere have adopted a second, alternative test for incapacity. There may be circumstances when, although a party claiming incapacity has some, or sufficient, understanding of the nature and consequences of the transaction, the contract would still be voidable where, by reason of mental illness or defect, the person is unable to act in a reasonable manner in relation to the transaction and the other party has reason to know of his condition. This modern test—also described as an "affective" or "volitional" test—recognizes that competence can be lost, not only through cognitive disorders, but through affective disorders that encompass motivation or exercise of will.

Under this modern, affective test, where a person has some understanding of a particular transaction which is affected by mental illness or defect, the controlling consideration is whether the transaction in its result is one which a reasonably competent person might have made. The evidence required to support a finding of incapacity to contract, whether considered under the traditional or modern standard, need not in all cases demonstrate that a party suffers from a mental illness or defect that is permanent, degenerative, progressive, or of significant duration. Although such incapacity has historically been established by evidence of a long-standing mental illness, nothing requires such evidence. The inquiry as to the capacity to contract focuses on a party's understanding or conduct only at the time of the disputed transaction.

The defendants contended that the evidence established Susan's incapacity without showing a permanent, degenerative, progressive, or long-standing mental illness. Susan's asserted mental impairment arose and was limited to the period of the mediation session. The defendants argued that this evidence was sufficient to support a conclusion of incapacity, despite the lack of medical evidence or expert testimony as to the nature of Susan's mental impairment and its effect on her decision-making ability.

The court concluded, however, that medical evidence is necessary to establish that a person lacked the capacity to contract due to the existence of a mental condition. There was lay evidence that Susan's speech was "slurr[ed]," that she was in a state of uncontrollable crying, and that she had experienced an inability to focus or "think rationally" throughout the day of the mediation. Susan testified also that she had recently discontinued taking the prescribed medication Zoloft. However, she presented no medical evidence regarding a diagnosis that would have required her to take the medication, or the effect, if any, that ceasing to take the medication would have had on her medical or mental condition. There was also no evidence that Susan's condition at the mediation was related to or caused by her discontinuing the medication. There was no expert or medical testimony to explain the effect of Susan's experiences or behavior on her ability to understand the agreement, to appreciate what was happening, or to comprehend the reasonableness of the settlement terms or the consequences to her of authorizing the settlement. Without such medical evidence, there was no basis to conclude that Susan lacked the capacity to contract. Under the modern test to establish Susan's incapacity, the evidence was insufficient. There was no evidence that the settlement agreement was unreasonable, or that a reasonably competent person would not have entered into it.

COMMENT: "UNDERSTANDING" THE TRANSACTION

The tests of mental incompetency originally formulated by the courts were expressed in ordinary language and did not purport to reproduce the findings of medical science, which for a long time could contribute little in any event. Cognition tests were central, but they were embellished with so many qualifying adjectives that one diligent reader of court opinions described the net result as "ambiguous, self-contradictory and practically meaningless." Green, Judicial Tests of Mental Incompetency, 6 Mo. L. Rev. 141 (1941). The tests showed little or no recognition of the enduring difficulties that advances in modern psychiatry have illuminated by disclosing both the variety of forms that mental defect and disorder can take and the vast differences among them. It is difficult indeed to adhere consistently to a single all-encompassing test when mental and emotional disturbances show as much diversity as in the small group of examples given here.

The workings of private litigation in struggling for answers to the question of sufficient understanding, and the wide range of inquiry required, are described in a valuable early study by Green, Proof of Mental Incompetency and the Unexpressed Major Premise, 53 Yale L.J. 271, 298–311 (1944). Of particular interest is the "inarticulate premise" Professor Green found implicit in most decisions: that transactions under scrutiny should be tested also by their own terms, the degree of "abnormality" they show. If they are gifts—many are—experience will supply a basis for judging whether the bounty to the particular recipient shows such eccentricity as to call for explanation. If the dealings purport to be an exchange transaction, do the terms, including the fairness of the exchange, show rational calculation, that is, a result which a reasonably competent person might have made?

Kelly v. Provident Life & Accident Insurance Co.

United States District Court, Southern District of California, 2010.
734 F. Supp. 2d 1085.

HAYES, DISTRICT JUDGE. . . . Defendant issued Plaintiff two own-occupation disability insurance policies in the early 1980s which provided a combined benefit of $5,500 per month. At the time he purchased the policies, Plaintiff sold insurance as a General Agent for General American Life Insurance Company. Pursuant to the disability policies, Plaintiff could claim total disability if he was unable "to perform the substantial and material duties of his occupation" and was "under the care and attendance of a Physician." In May of 1986, Plaintiff began seeing psychologist Russell Gold, Ph.D., who diagnosed Plaintiff with depression, dysthymic disorder, and schizoid personality disorder. Dr. Gold attributed Plaintiff's condition to stress from contentious divorce proceedings. Plaintiff filed a claim for complete disability in September of 1986. Defendant accepted the claim and began paying benefits. Plaintiff continued to see Dr. Gold for the thirteen-year period he received disability benefits from Defendant.

In addition to paying benefits of $5,500 per month, in 1986 and 1987, Defendant paid Plaintiff's business expenses, such as rent for his office, salaries of employees, utilities, and accounting services.

While Plaintiff was on disability benefits, various insurance companies terminated their relationship with Plaintiff as an agent. . . .

Over the course of Plaintiff's disability claim, Defendant investigated Plaintiff's medical condition and whether Plaintiff had returned to work on multiple occasions. . . .

During the investigation, Blochl contacted the San Diego District Attorney's Office, the United States' Attorney's Office, and the FBI to report insurance fraud. A deputy district attorney informed Blochl that "Mr. Kelly should be asked if he in fact has sold policies after his date of disability and whether or not he has an office. Very specific questions about sales, marketing, and prospecting should be asked" and warned Blochl that "the questions on the Insured's Supplementary Statement of Claim form were vague." Defendants never asked Plaintiff these questions. The deputy district attorney also "suggested that the Insured should be examined under oath by Provident attorneys regarding this claim. She indicated that very specific questions about the insured[']s alleged disability and possible insurance related activity should be explored." Defendant never conducted such an interview. In his deposition, Blochl testified that when he investigated Plaintiff and contacted various law enforcement agencies, he was unaware that Plaintiff had ever informed Defendant that he was continuing to provide some services to existing clients, that he was unaware that Plaintiff's attorney had provided Plaintiff's business records to Defendant in 1990, and that he was unaware that Plaintiff had informed Defendant that Plaintiff had initiated some new policies. Blochl testified in his deposition that this information would have affected his determination of whether fraud had been committed and that this information was the reason the FBI declined to pursue the case after a preliminary investigation.[5] . . .

On August 18, 1999, Defendant sent Plaintiff a letter notifying him that it was terminating his benefits, although it would provide him with benefits through August 16, 1999, which was the date it concluded Plaintiff was not disabled. The letter informed Plaintiff that he was required to pay his premiums in order to continue coverage under his policies. Plaintiff sent a series of letters to Defendant after the termination and Dr. Gold also wrote to Defendant on Plaintiff's behalf. In April of 2000, Defendant stated it was reviewing Plaintiff's submissions and would get back to him. However, Defendant never responded.

---

[5] Although Plaintiff was never charged criminally in connection with the alleged insurance fraud, he was convicted of tax evasion in 2004.

In November of 2000, Plaintiff was served with process in *Provident Life and Accident Insurance Co. v. Kelly,* the prior litigation before this Court. Defendant Provident, as a plaintiff in that suit, alleged claims for fraud, conspiracy to defraud, breach of the covenant of good faith and fair dealing, rescission, and restitution against Kelly. Defendant Provident also sued Kelly Insurance Services, Inc. and Wobegone Enterprises, Inc., alleging a cause of action for conspiracy to defraud.

Plaintiff attempted to retain his former attorney, Steinberg, to represent him and the companies [but] Steinberg told Plaintiff that he did not handle defense cases and advised Plaintiff to hire another attorney. Plaintiff attempted to hire an attorney, but could not afford the fees and could not find an attorney who would take his case on a contingency basis because he was a defendant. Plaintiff contacted Defendant, seeking a settlement, because Defendant had previously offered Plaintiff $330,000 to surrender the policies. Defendant's attorney, Gregory Scarlett, told Plaintiff that he would put the lawsuit on hold while he looked into a settlement.

On April 11, 2001, Plaintiff learned that a clerk's default had been entered against him and the companies and that Defendant was moving for default judgment. Plaintiff, proceeding *pro se,* wrote a letter to Judge Huff explaining that he had not responded to the lawsuit because of his conversation with Defendant's attorney. Plaintiff stated he believed the litigation was on hold. In the letter, Plaintiff also stated that he did not own either of the corporate defendants, rather his wife Anna did. At this time, Plaintiff was still under investigation by the FBI, which he found "tremendously upsetting. . . ." Plaintiff did not understand how he could be accused of fraud because "Provident never asked for any additional information" about his "limited work" after Steinberg sent Defendant his work records in 1990. Plaintiff states "I did not understand how I could lie about something I was never asked about."

Because Plaintiff was not an attorney, he could not file an answer or oppose default judgment on behalf of the corporate defendants, and Defendant obtained a default judgment. Although Plaintiff's wife, not Plaintiff, was the registered agent for service of process, she was never served. Plaintiff's wife states in a declaration that the default judgment

> put a tremendous financial strain on Richard and I. With Richard unable to work, I needed to make money to support us both. I counted on the income from my insurance sales, including the residual commissions flowing through Wobegone, in order to make ends meet. When Provident entered default against my company, it took away this source of income entirely.

After the default judgment, Plaintiff began drinking heavily. Plaintiff's wife states that his condition worsened after Defendant cut off Plaintiff's disability benefits and during the lawsuit and that at one point, she discovered he had been researching suicide. On July 2, 2001 and July 5, 2001, Plaintiff and Defendant's attorney attended an early neutral evaluation conference before the magistrate judge. Plaintiff settled his case with Defendant, giving up his claim for disability benefits in exchange for Defendant agreeing to dismiss the lawsuit and "giving up its judgment against Anna's company." The settlement agreement was signed by both parties on November 21, 2001. Plaintiff states he signed the settlement agreement "because I did not have the mental or emotional capacity to engage in the conflictual situation that Provident had created. I did not sign the agreement because it was what I wanted to do, but because I could not resist Provident's pressure."

Plaintiff submitted the declaration of Dr. Lynn Ponton, M.D., a Professor of Clinical Psychiatry at the University of California, San Francisco, who reviewed Plaintiff's medical records and the records of the three [independent medical examinations] with Defendant's selected doctors. Based on her review of the records, Dr. Ponton offers her opinion that Plaintiff suffers from Avoidant Personality Disorder with schizoid features. Dr. Ponton states "Avoidant Personality Disorder is often characterized by shifts in the level of avoidant behavior depending on the level of conflict associated with certain interpersonal relationships." Dr. Ponton states that Plaintiff's condition creates "undue susceptibility to [ ] pressure," such as the pressure that Defendant's investigations, the prior lawsuit, and the investigations of alleged insurance fraud by various law enforcement agencies would create. Under this pressure, given Plaintiff's diagnosis, "[h]is depression and social avoidance would have been at an all-time high" at the time of the settlement. . .

[Under] California Civil Code § 1575,

Undue influence consists:

> 1. In the use, by one in whom a confidence is reposed by another, or who holds a real or apparent authority over him, of such confidence or authority for the purpose of obtaining an unfair advantage over him;
>
> 2. In taking an unfair advantage of another's weakness of mind; or,
>
> 3. In taking a grossly oppressive and unfair advantage of another's necessities or distress.

A seminal California appellate case defined undue influence as follows:

> "[u]ndue influence . . . is a shorthand legal phrase used to describe persuasion which tends to be coercive in nature, persuasion which overcomes the will without convincing the judgment. The hallmarks of such persuasion is high pressure, a pressure which works on mental, moral, or emotional weakness to such an extent that it approaches the boundaries of coercion. In this sense, undue influence has been called overpersuasion."

[Odorizzi v. Bloomfield School Dist., 246 Cal. App. 2d 123, 130, 54 Cal. Rptr. 533 (1966).] If the party seeking to rescind a contract is a "person of subnormal capacities," even subjecting them to "ordinary force" may constitute undue influence.

Odorizzi lists seven factors which "generally accompany" overpersuasion:

> (1) discussion of the transaction at an unusual or inappropriate time, (2) consummation of the transaction in an unusual place, (3) insistent demand that the business be finished at once, (4) extreme emphasis on untoward consequences of delay, (5) the use of multiple persuaders by the dominant side against a single servient party, (6) absence of third-party advisers to the servient party, (7) statements that there is no time to consult financial advisers or attorneys. If a number of these elements are simultaneously present, the persuasion may be characterized as excessive.

[Id. at 133.] Although *Odorizzi* states these factors are generally present, the Ninth Circuit's previous ruling in this case states "[t]he *Odorizzi* list was not described as exhaustive. Some contracts might be formed through undue influence even if most or all of the *Odorizzi* factors are absent." In Keithley v. Civil Service Bd. of the City of Oakland, 11 Cal. App. 3d 443, 451, 89 Cal. Rptr. 809 (1970), a California Court of Appeals made the same point: "[i]ndeed, there are no fixed definitions or inflexible formulas. Rather, we are concerned with whether from the entire context it appears that one's will was overborne and he was induced to do or forbear to do an act which he would not do, or would do, if left to act freely." The same opinion notes "direct evidence of undue influence is rarely obtainable and, thus the court is normally relegated to determination by inference from the totality of facts and circumstances."

At least one California appellate decision addresses mental illness as a form of "weakness of the mind." See Smalley v. Baker, 262 Cal. App. 2d 824, 834, 69 Cal. Rptr. 521 (1968). In *Smalley*, the court held that a manic depressive man was competent to enter a contract, but that his mental illness was a "weakness of the mind" pursuant to California Civil Code § 1575(2) because his "judgment was affected." Id. at 836, 69 Cal.Rptr. 521. The court explained that "the lesser weakness of the mind [which does not render a party incompetent] referred to in section 1575 need not be long lasting or wholly incapacitating, but may consist of such factors as a lack of vigor due to age, physical condition, emotional anguish, or a combination of such factors." Id. at 835, 69 Cal.Rptr. 521. However, Smalley ultimately lost because there was "no claim or showing that Baker knew or was aware of Smalley's mental illness, or that he took advantage of such illness so as to bring Civil Code section 1575 into play." Id. at 836, 69 Cal.Rptr. 521.

Plaintiff's statements, Plaintiff's wife's statements, the records of a long period of psychological counseling . . . and the fact that Defendant paid Plaintiff disability benefits for thirteen years could lead a reasonable jury to conclude that Plaintiff was suffering from mental illness which amounts to "weakness of the mind" under California law. Although Defendant disputes Plaintiff's diagnosis, viewed in the light most favorable to Plaintiff, this evidence could lead a reasonable jury to conclude that Defendant knew that Plaintiff was unusually susceptible to pressure.

The Court must next examine whether there is evidence that could lead a reasonable jury to determine that Defendant took unfair advantage of Plaintiff's weakened state of mind. Although Defendant contends the Court should only consider the settlement negotiations, the Court finds that the appropriate inquiry is broader. The ultimate question is "whether from the *entire context* it appears that [Plaintiff's] will was overborne." *See* Keithley, 11 Cal.App.3d at 451, 89 Cal.Rptr. 809 (emphasis added). In this case, the "entire context" of the settlement agreement includes Defendant's investigation of Plaintiff's claim, Defendant's termination of Plaintiff's benefits, Defendant reporting that Plaintiff had committed insurance fraud to various law enforcement agencies, and Defendant suing Plaintiff. The Court must determine whether there is sufficient evidence in the record, viewed in the light most favorable to Plaintiff, that a jury could find that Defendant acted in bad faith in its investigation and subsequent termination of Plaintiff's benefits and by suing Plaintiff in order to take advantage of Plaintiff's weakened state of mind. This determination requires an examination of California law on own occupation disability insurance policies and bad faith termination.

Under California law, own occupation insurance policies define total disability not as " 'an absolute state of helplessness but means such disability as renders the insured unable to perform the substantial and material acts necessary to the prosecution of a business or occupation in the usual or customary way.' " Hangarter v. Provident Life and Accident Ins. Co., 373 F.3d 998, 1006 (9th Cir. 2004) (quoting Erreca v. Western States Life Ins. Co., 19 Cal.2d 388, 121 P.2d 689 (1942)). Regardless of the definition of "total disability" in an own occupation insurance policy, "California law *requires* courts to deviate from the explicit policy definition of 'total disability' in the occupational policy context." Hangarter, 373 F.3d at 1006.

Under California law, "[t]he fact that the insured may do some work or transact some business duties during the time for which he claims indemnity for total disability or even the fact that he may be physically able to do so is not conclusive evidence that his disability is not total, if reasonable care and prudence require that he desist." Id. at 1007. If an insured can perform the duties of his occupation intermittently, but cannot do so in a "continuous, normal" way, the insured is totally disabled under California law. An insured's income is irrelevant to the disability determination. "[T]he magnitude of [the insured's] enterprise and his income therefrom . . . have *no proper place* in the determination of whether [the insured] is totally disabled [because such insurance] *does not insure against loss of income.*" Id. at 1009.

In determining whether an insurer acted in bad faith by denying coverage, the fact-finder must determine whether the denial was reasonable. . . .

There is evidence in the record which, viewed in the light most favorable to Plaintiff, could lead a jury to conclude that, despite knowing that Plaintiff was mentally ill, Defendant terminated Plaintiff's coverage in bad faith after conducting a biased investigation, contacted law enforcement agencies to instigate an investigation of Plaintiff for the purposes of harassment and sued Plaintiff for the return of all benefits without a valid basis for doing so in order to take unfair advantage of Plaintiff's weakness of mind. Although Defendant points out that none of the *Odorizzi* factors are present, this is not dispositive, as the Ninth Circuit previously ruled. The *Odorizzi* list of factors is not exclusive, and under California law, all of the circumstances surrounding contract negotiations should be examined to determine whether a party to a contract engaged in "overpersuasion." Keithley, 11 Cal. App. 3d at 451, 89 Cal. Rptr. 809. If a jury determined that Defendant took these actions in bad faith in order to pressure Plaintiff to surrender his benefits via a settlement agreement, it could find that Defendant "took unfair advantage of [Plaintiff's] weakness of mind," allowing rescission of the settlement agreement for undue influence. Defendant's motion for summary judgment on Plaintiff's rescission claim is denied. . . .

Von Hake v. Thomas

705 P.2d 766 (Utah 1985)

"A confidential relationship [where one party, having gained the trust and confidence of another, exercises extraordinary influence over the other,] is a prerequisite to proving constructive fraud. . . . The law presumes that one ordinarily makes his or her own judgments, however imperfect, and acts on them; it does not readily assume that one's will has been overborne by another. Therefore, the law does not lightly recognize the existence of a confidential relationship. . . . [Here,] the evidence is insufficient to establish that [such] a relationship arose between Von Hake and Thomas. Although Von Hake was 82 years old and distressed over the imminent [foreclosure] sale of the ranch he had owned for forty years, and Thomas clearly induced Von Hake to believe that he was interested in 'saving' the ranch, those facts alone did not require Thomas to act as a fiduciary toward Von Hake. No evidence suggests that Von Hake so trusted Thomas that Thomas was able to substitute his will for Von Hake's. . . . The parties had no long-established relationship of trust[,] . . . nor was Thomas's relationship to Von Hake one that traditionally imposes a fiduciary duty, such as an attorney/client relationship. . . . And while Von Hake was elderly, there is no evidence that he was feeble or not in full possession of his faculties. Von Hake at all times was aware that he could and should consult his own attorney about the deal he was making, although admittedly [Thomas] talked him out of doing so. It is true that Thomas worked hard to ingratiate himself with Von Hake and to gain his confidence, but that is likely to be true of anyone who defrauds another. There is no evidence that at any time Von Hake relinquished control over his own decision making. Rather, these facts present something of a 'garden variety' fraud case, in which one party intentionally or recklessly misrepresents a presently existing material fact, thereby inducing another to reasonably rely and act upon that falsehood to the other's detriment."

NOTE

While it is possible to isolate a pure issue of legal capacity in the cases (think of *Ortelere*), impaired capacity more typically figures into the broader inquiries that are opened up by claims of undue influence and breach of confidential or fiduciary obligation, where the question is whether undue advantage has been taken of physical or emotional weakness, or dependency, or of trust and confidence reposed. Should an effort be made to distinguish the standards of competency applied in these two contexts?

Even when individuals are competent to contract, the state may declare some matters off limits. Gambling contracts, for example, are typically not enforceable, as are contracts involving activities that are illegal. The refusal to enforce the promise follows from the law's attitude towards the underlying activity. As the case coming next shows, however, the state sometimes removes matters from the domain of contract even when the activity itself is permitted.

In re Baby M

Supreme Court of New Jersey, 1988.
109 N.J. 396, 537 A.2d 1227.

WILENTZ, C.J. [We are] asked to determine the validity of a contract that purports to provide a new way of bringing children into a family. For a fee of $10,000, a woman agrees to be artificially inseminated with the semen of another woman's husband; she is to conceive a child, carry it to term, and after its birth surrender it to the natural father and his wife. The intent of the contract is that the child's natural mother will thereafter be forever separated from her child. The wife is to adopt the child, and she and the natural father are to be regarded as its parents for all purposes. The contract providing for this is called a "surrogacy contract," the natural mother inappropriately called the "surrogate mother." . . .

We find no offense to our present laws where a woman voluntarily and without payment agrees to act as a "surrogate" mother, provided that she is not subject to a binding agreement to surrender her child. Moreover, our holding today does not preclude the Legislature from altering the current statutory scheme, within constitutional limits, so as to permit surrogacy contracts. Under current law, however, the surrogacy agreement before us is illegal and invalid. . . .

In February 1985, William Stern and Mary Beth Whitehead entered into a surrogacy contract. It recited that Stern's wife, Elizabeth, was infertile, that they wanted a child, and that Mrs. Whitehead was willing to provide that child as the mother with Mr. Stern as the father.

The contract provided that through artificial insemination using Mr. Stern's sperm, Mrs. Whitehead would become pregnant, carry the child to term, bear it, deliver it to the Sterns, and thereafter do whatever was necessary to terminate her maternal rights so that Mrs. Stern could thereafter adopt the child. Mrs. Whitehead's husband, Richard,[1] was also a party to the contract; Mrs. Stern was not. Mr. Whitehead promised to do all acts necessary to rebut the presumption of paternity under the Parentage Act. Although Mrs. Stern was not a party to the surrogacy agreement, the contract gave her sole custody of the child in the event of Mr. Stern's death. Mrs. Stern's status as a nonparty to the surrogate parenting agreement presumably was to avoid the application of the baby-selling statute to this arrangement.

Mr. Stern, on his part, agreed to attempt the artificial insemination and to pay Mrs. Whitehead $10,000 after the child's birth, on its delivery to him. In a separate contract, Mr. Stern agreed to pay $7,500 to the Infertility Center of New York ("ICNY"). The Center's advertising campaigns solicit surrogate mothers and encourage infertile couples to consider surrogacy. ICNY arranged for the surrogacy contract by bringing the parties together, explaining the process to them, furnishing the contractual form, and providing legal counsel.

The history of the parties' involvement in this arrangement suggests their good faith. William and Elizabeth Stern were married in July 1974, having met at the University of Michigan, where both were Ph.D. candidates. Due to financial considerations and Mrs. Stern's pursuit of a medical degree and residency, they decided to defer starting a family until 1981. Before then, however, Mrs. Stern learned that she might have multiple sclerosis and that the disease in some cases renders pregnancy a serious health risk. Her anxiety appears to have exceeded the actual risk, which current medical authorities assess as minimal. Nonetheless that anxiety was evidently quite real, Mrs. Stern fearing that pregnancy might precipitate blindness, paraplegia, or other forms of debilitation. Based on the perceived risk, the Sterns decided to forego having their own children. The decision had special significance for Mr. Stern. Most

1 Subsequent to the trial court proceedings, Mr. and Mrs. Whitehead were divorced, and soon thereafter Mrs. Whitehead remarried. Nevertheless, in the course of this opinion we will make reference almost exclusively to the facts as they existed at the time of trial, the facts on which the decision we now review was reached. We note moreover that Mr. Whitehead remains a party to this dispute. For these reasons, we continue to refer to appellants as Mr. and Mrs. Whitehead.

of his family had been destroyed in the Holocaust. As the family's only survivor, he very much wanted to continue his bloodline.

Initially the Sterns considered adoption, but were discouraged by the substantial delay apparently involved and by the potential problem they saw arising from their age and their differing religious backgrounds. . . .

The paths of Mrs. Whitehead and the Sterns to surrogacy were similar. Both responded to advertising by ICNY. The Sterns' response, following their inquiries into adoption, was the result of their long-standing decision to have a child. Mrs. Whitehead's response apparently resulted from her sympathy with family members and others who could have no children (she stated that she wanted to give another couple the "gift of life"); she also wanted the $10,000 to help her family. . . .

Mrs. Whitehead had reached her decision concerning surrogacy before the Sterns, and had actually been involved as a potential surrogate mother with another couple. After numerous unsuccessful artificial inseminations, that effort was abandoned. Thereafter, the Sterns learned of the Infertility Center, the possibilities of surrogacy, and of Mary Beth Whitehead. The two couples met to discuss the surrogacy arrangement and decided to go forward. On February 6, 1985, Mr. Stern and Mr. and Mrs. Whitehead executed the surrogate parenting agreement. After several artificial inseminations over a period of months, Mrs. Whitehead became pregnant. The pregnancy was uneventful and on March 27, 1986, Baby M was born. . . .

Her birth certificate indicated her name to be Sara Elizabeth Whitehead and her father to be Richard Whitehead. In accordance with Mrs. Whitehead's request, the Sterns visited the hospital unobtrusively to see the newborn child.

Mrs. Whitehead realized, almost from the moment of birth, that she could not part with this child. She had felt a bond with it even during pregnancy. Some indication of the attachment was conveyed to the Sterns at the hospital when they told Mrs. Whitehead what they were going to name the baby. She apparently broke into tears and indicated that she did not know if she could give up the child. She talked about how the baby looked like her other daughter, and made it clear that she was experiencing great difficulty with the decision.

Nonetheless, Mrs. Whitehead was, for the moment, true to her word. Despite powerful inclinations to the contrary, she turned her child over to the Sterns on March 30 at the Whiteheads' home.

The Sterns were thrilled with their new child [who they named Melissa]. They had planned extensively for its arrival, far beyond the practical furnishing of a room for her. It was a time of joyful celebration—not just for them but for their friends as well. . . .

Later in the evening of March 30, Mrs. Whitehead became deeply disturbed, disconsolate, stricken with unbearable sadness. She had to have her child. She could not eat, sleep, or concentrate on anything other than her need for her baby. The next day she went to the Sterns' home and told them how much she was suffering.

The depth of Mrs. Whitehead's despair surprised and frightened the Sterns. She told them that she could not live without her baby, that she must have her, even if only for one week, that thereafter she would surrender her child. The Sterns, concerned that Mrs. Whitehead might indeed commit suicide, not wanting under any circumstances to risk that, and in any event believing that Mrs. Whitehead would keep her word, turned the child over to her. It was not until four months later, after a series of attempts to regain possession of the child, that Melissa was returned to the Sterns, having been forcibly removed from the home where she was then living with Mr. and Mrs. Whitehead, the home in Florida owned by Mary Beth Whitehead's parents.

The struggle over Baby M began when it became apparent that Mrs. Whitehead could not return the child to Mr. Stern. . . . Mr. Stern filed a complaint seeking enforcement of the surrogacy contract. He alleged, accurately, that Mrs. Whitehead had not only refused to comply with the surrogacy contract but had threatened to flee from New Jersey with the child in order to avoid even the possibility of his obtaining custody. The court papers asserted that if Mrs. Whitehead were to be given notice of the application for an order requiring her to relinquish custody, she would, prior to the hearing, leave the state with the baby. And that is precisely what she did. After the order was entered, *ex parte*, the process server, aided by the police, in the presence of the Sterns, entered Mrs. Whitehead's home to execute the order. Mr. Whitehead fled with the child, who had been handed to him through a window while those who came to enforce the order were thrown off balance by a dispute over the child's current name.

The Whiteheads immediately fled to Florida with Baby M. They stayed initially with Mrs. Whitehead's parents. . . . For the next three months, the Whiteheads and Melissa lived at roughly twenty different hotels, motels, and homes in order to avoid apprehension. From time to time Mrs. Whitehead would call Mr. Stern to discuss the matter; the conversations, recorded by Mr. Stern on advice of counsel, show an escalating dispute about rights, morality, and power, accompanied by threats of Mrs. Whitehead to kill herself, to kill the child, and falsely to accuse Mr. Stern of sexually molesting Mrs. Whitehead's other daughter.

Eventually the Sterns discovered where the Whiteheads were staying, commenced supplementary proceedings in Florida, and obtained an order requiring the Whiteheads to turn over the child. Police in Florida enforced the order, forcibly removing the child from her grandparents' home. She was soon thereafter brought to New Jersey and turned over to the Sterns. The prior order of the court, issued *ex parte*, awarding custody of the child to the Sterns *pendente lite*, was reaffirmed by the trial court after consideration of the certified representations of the parties (both represented by counsel) concerning the unusual sequence of events that had unfolded. Pending final judgment, Mrs. Whitehead was awarded limited visitation with Baby M.

The Sterns' complaint, in addition to seeking possession and ultimately custody of the child, sought enforcement of the surrogacy contract. Pursuant to the contract, it asked that the child be permanently placed in their custody, that Mrs. Whitehead's parental rights be terminated, and that Mrs. Stern be allowed to adopt the child, *i.e.*, that, for all purposes, Melissa become the Sterns' child.

The trial took thirty-two days over a period of more than two months. [T]he bulk of the testimony was devoted to determining the parenting arrangement most compatible with the child's best interests. [The trial court] held that the surrogacy contract was valid; ordered that Mrs. Whitehead's parental rights be terminated and that sole custody of the child be granted to Mr. Stern; and . . . immediately entered an order allowing the adoption of Melissa by Mrs. Stern, all in accordance with the surrogacy contract. Pending the outcome of the appeal, we granted a continuation of visitation to Mrs. Whitehead, although slightly more limited than the visitation allowed during the trial.

Although clearly expressing its view that the surrogacy contract was valid, the trial court devoted the major portion of its opinion to the question of the baby's best interests. The inconsistency is apparent. The surrogacy contract calls for the surrender of the child to the Sterns, permanent and sole custody in the Sterns, and termination of Mrs. Whitehead's parental rights, all without qualification, all regardless of any evaluation of the best interests of the child. As a matter of fact the contract recites (even before the child was conceived) that it is in the best interests of the child to be placed with Mr. Stern. In effect, the trial court awarded custody to Mr. Stern, the natural father, based on the same kind of evidence and analysis as might be expected had no surrogacy contract existed. Its rationalization, however, was that while the surrogacy contract was valid, specific performance would not be granted unless that remedy was in the best interests of the child. The factual issues confronted and decided by the trial court were the same as if Mr. Stern and Mrs. Whitehead had had the child out of wedlock, intended or unintended, and then disagreed about custody. The trial court's awareness of the irrelevance of the contract in the court's determination of custody is suggested by its remark that beyond the question of the child's best interests, "[a]ll other concerns raised by counsel constitute commentary."

On the question of best interests—and we agree, but for different reasons, that custody was the critical issue—the court's analysis of the testimony was perceptive, demonstrating both its understanding of the case and its considerable experience in these matters. We agree substantially with both its analysis and conclusions on the matter of custody.

The court's review and analysis of the surrogacy contract, however, is not at all in accord with ours. . . .

We have concluded that this surrogacy contract is invalid. Our conclusion has two bases: direct conflict with existing statutes and conflict with the public policies of this State, as expressed in its statutory and decisional law.

One of the surrogacy contract's basic purposes, to achieve the adoption of a child through private placement, though permitted in New Jersey "is very much disfavored." Its use of money for this purpose—and we have no doubt whatsoever that the money is being paid to obtain an adoption and not, as the Sterns argue, for the personal services of Mary Beth Whitehead—is illegal and perhaps criminal. In addition to the inducement of money, there is the coercion of contract: the natural mother's irrevocable agreement, prior to birth, even prior to conception, to surrender the child to the adoptive couple. Such an agreement is totally unenforceable in private placement adoption. Even where the adoption is through an approved agency, the formal agreement to surrender occurs only *after* birth . . ., and then, by regulation, only after the birth mother has been offered counseling. Integral to these invalid provisions of the surrogacy contract is the related agreement, equally invalid, on the part of the natural mother to cooperate with, and not to contest, proceedings to terminate her parental rights, as well as her contractual concession, in aid of the adoption, that the child's best interests would be served by awarding custody to the natural father and his wife—all of this before she has even conceived, and, in some cases, before she has the slightest idea of what the natural father and adoptive mother are like.

The foregoing provisions not only directly conflict with New Jersey statutes, but also offend long-established State policies. These critical terms, which are at the heart of the contract, are invalid and unenforceable; the conclusion therefore follows, without more, that the entire contract is unenforceable. . . .

Our law prohibits paying or accepting money in connection with any placement of a child for adoption. Violation is a high misdemeanor. Excepted are fees of an approved agency (which must be a non-profit entity) and certain expenses in connection with childbirth.

Considerable care was taken in this case to structure the surrogacy arrangement so as not to violate this prohibition[:] . . . the adopting parent, Mrs. Stern, was not a party to the surrogacy contract; the money paid to Mrs. Whitehead was stated to be for her services—not for the adoption; the sole purpose of the contract was stated as being that "of giving a child to William Stern, its natural and biological father"; the money was purported to be "compensation for services and expenses and in no way . . . a fee for termination of parental rights or a payment in exchange for consent to surrender a child for adoption"; the fee to the Infertility Center ($7,500) was stated to be for legal representation, advice, administrative work, and other "services." Nevertheless, it seems clear that the money was paid and accepted in connection with an adoption.

The Infertility Center's major role was first as a "finder" of the surrogate mother whose child was to be adopted, and second as the arranger of all proceedings that led to the adoption. Its role as adoption finder is demonstrated by the provision requiring Mr. Stern to pay another $7,500 if he uses Mary Beth Whitehead again as a surrogate, and by ICNY's agreement to "coordinate arrangements for the adoption of the child by the wife." The surrogacy agreement requires Mrs. Whitehead to surrender Baby M for the purposes of adoption. The agreement notes that Mr. *and Mrs.* Stern wanted to have a child, and provides that the child be "placed" with Mrs. Stern in the event Mr. Stern dies before the child is born. The payment of the $10,000 occurs only on surrender of custody of the child and "completion of the duties and obligations" of Mrs. Whitehead, including termination of her parental rights to facilitate adoption by Mrs. Stern. As for the contention that the Sterns are paying only for services and not for an adoption, we need note only that they would pay nothing in the event the child died before the fourth month of pregnancy, and only $1,000 if the child were stillborn, even though the "services" had been fully rendered. Additionally, one of Mrs. Whitehead's estimated costs, to be assumed by Mr. Stern, was an "Adoption Fee," presumably for Mrs. Whitehead's incidental costs in connection with the adoption.

Mr. Stern knew he was paying for the adoption of a child; Mrs. Whitehead knew she was accepting money so that a child might be adopted; the Infertility Center knew that it was being paid for assisting in the adoption of a child. The actions of all three worked to frustrate the goals of the statute. It strains credulity to claim that these arrangements, touted by those in the surrogacy business as an attractive alternative to the usual route leading to an adoption, really amount to something other than a private placement adoption for money.

The prohibition of our statute is strong. Violation constitutes a high misdemeanor, a third-degree crime, carrying a penalty of three to five years imprisonment. The evils inherent in baby-bartering are loathsome for a myriad of reasons. The child is sold without regard for whether the purchasers will be suitable parents. The natural mother does not receive the benefit of counseling and guidance to assist her in making a decision that may affect her for a lifetime. In fact, the monetary incentive to sell her child may, depending on her financial circumstances, make her decision less voluntary. Furthermore, the adoptive parents[5] may not be fully informed of the natural parents' medical history.

Baby-selling potentially results in the exploitation of all parties involved. Conversely, adoption statutes seek to further humanitarian goals, foremost among them the best interests of the child. The negative consequences of baby-buying are potentially present in the surrogacy

---

[5] Of course, here there are no "adoptive parents," but rather the natural father and his wife, the only adoptive parent. As noted, however, many of the dangers of using money in connection with adoption may exist in surrogacy situations.

context, especially the potential for placing and adopting a child without regard to the interest of the child or the natural mother.

The termination of Mrs. Whitehead's parental rights, called for by the surrogacy contract and actually ordered by the court fails to comply with the stringent requirements of New Jersey law. Our law, recognizing the finality of any termination of parental rights, provides for such termination only where there has been a voluntary surrender of a child to an approved agency or to the Division of Youth and Family Services ("DYFS"), accompanied by a formal document acknowledging termination of parental rights, or where there has been a showing of parental abandonment or unfitness. A termination may ordinarily take one of three forms: an action by an approved agency, an action by DYFS, or an action in connection with a private placement adoption. . . .

In this case a termination of parental rights was obtained not by proving the statutory prerequisites but by claiming the benefit of contractual provisions. [I]t is clear that a contractual agreement to abandon one's parental rights, or not to contest a termination action, will not be enforced in our courts. The Legislature would not have so carefully, so consistently, and so substantially restricted termination of parental rights if it had intended to allow termination to be achieved by one short sentence in a contract.

Since the termination was invalid, it follows, as noted above, that adoption of Melissa by Mrs. Stern could not properly be granted. . . .

It is clear that the Legislature so carefully circumscribed all aspects of a consent to surrender custody—its form and substance, its manner of execution, and the agency or agencies to which it may be made—in order to provide the basis for irrevocability. It seems most unlikely that the Legislature intended that a consent not complying with these requirements would also be irrevocable, especially where, as here, that consent falls radically short of compliance. . . .

Contractual surrender of parental rights is not provided for in our statutes as now written. Indeed, in the Parentage Act, there is a specific provision invalidating any agreement "between an alleged or presumed father and the mother of the child" to bar an action brought for the purpose of determining paternity "[r]egardless of [the contract's] terms." Even a settlement agreement concerning parentage reached in a judicially-mandated consent conference is not valid unless the proposed settlement is approved beforehand by the court. There is no doubt that a contractual provision purporting to constitute an irrevocable agreement to surrender custody of a child for adoption is invalid. . . .

The surrogacy contract's invalidity, resulting from its direct conflict with the above statutory provisions, is further underlined when its goals and means are measured against New Jersey's public policy. The contract's basic premise, that the natural parents can decide in advance of birth which one is to have custody of the child, bears no relationship to the settled law that the child's best interests shall determine custody. The fact that the trial court remedied that aspect of the contract through the "best interests" phase does not make the contractual provision any less offensive to the public policy of this State. . . .

The point is made that Mrs. Whitehead *agreed* to the surrogacy arrangement, supposedly fully understanding the consequences. Putting aside the issue of how compelling her need for money may have been, and how significant her understanding of the consequences, we suggest that her consent is irrelevant. There are, in a civilized society, some things that money cannot buy. In America, we decided long ago that merely because conduct purchased by money was "voluntary" did not mean that it was good or beyond regulation and prohibition. Employers can no longer buy labor at the lowest price they can bargain for, even though that labor is "voluntary," or buy women's labor for less money than paid to men for the same job, or purchase the agreement of children to perform oppressive labor, or purchase the agreement of workers to subject themselves to unsafe or unhealthful working conditions. There are, in short, values that society deems more important than granting to wealth whatever it can buy, be it labor, love, or life. Whether this principle recommends prohibition of surrogacy, which presumably sometimes results in great satisfaction to all of the parties, is not for us to say. We note here only that, under existing law, the fact that Mrs. Whitehead "agreed" to the arrangement is not dispositive. . . .

In sum, the harmful consequences of this surrogacy arrangement appear to us all too palpable. In New Jersey the surrogate mother's agreement to sell her child is void. Its irrevocability infects the entire contract, as does the money that purports to buy it. . . .

Having decided that the surrogacy contract is illegal and unenforceable, we now must decide the custody question without regard to the provisions of the surrogacy contract that would give Mr. Stern sole and permanent custody. (That does not mean that the existence of the contract and the circumstances under which it was entered may not be considered to the extent deemed relevant to the child's best interests.) With the surrogacy contract disposed of, the legal framework becomes a dispute between two couples over the custody of a child produced by the artificial insemination of one couple's wife by the other's husband. Under the Parentage Act the claims of the natural father and the natural mother are entitled to equal weight, *i.e.*, one is not preferred over the other solely because he or she is the father or the mother. The applicable rule given these circumstances is clear: the child's best interests determine custody. . . .

Based on all of this we have concluded, independent of the trial court's identical conclusion, that Melissa's best interests call for custody in the Sterns. . . .

. . . Our reversal of the trial court's order, however, requires delineation of Mrs. Whitehead's rights to visitation. It is apparent to us that this factually sensitive issue, which was never addressed below, should not be determined *de novo* by this Court. We therefore remand the visitation issue to the trial court. . . .

NOTE

Professor Carol Sanger has offered the following observations about the case (Sanger, In the Matter of Baby M, in Contract Stories 127, 157 (2007)):

> In removing surrogacy from the realm of permissible commercial activity in New Jersey, Justice Wilentz focused on what he saw as the pernicious role of the middleman. By taking money out of the equation, entrepreneurs would have to go elsewhere to extract surplus from trades like this, and that is certainly what happened. Surrogacy brokers decamped to jurisdictions where surrogacy was permitted or to those still in legal limbo, as New Jersey had been. But Baby M had revealed surrogacy's potential for heartbreak—or, as many contended, heartbreak's inevitability—and many state legislatures took note. Some banned commercial surrogacy outright; others were content to make surrogacy contracts legal but unenforceable. And in many jurisdictions, brokers have come in for special mention. Some states, such as Colorado, ban payment to the mothers but permit it to the broker. Others, such as the United Kingdom, permit payment to the mother but completely ban the broker. It is an offense in the United Kingdom to negotiate a commercial deal or even to advertise for a volunteer surrogate. Where surrogacy is legal, as in California, it appears to thrive. With this array of options, couples can now decide whether to follow the law of their own state or country, or to forum shop in the global market of reproductive tourism.

P.M. v. T.B.

Supreme Court of Iowa, 2018.
907 N.W.2d 522.

WATERMAN, JUSTICE. . . . In this appeal, we must decide a question of first impression: whether gestational surrogacy contracts are enforceable under Iowa law. The plaintiffs, the intended parents, are a married couple unable to conceive their own child. They signed a contract with the defendants, the surrogate mother and her husband, who, in exchange for future payments of up to $13,000 and medical expenses, agreed to have the surrogate mother impregnated with embryos fertilized with the plaintiff-father's sperm and the ova (eggs) of an anonymous donor. The defendants agreed to deliver the baby at birth to the intended parents. The surrogate mother became pregnant with twins, but after demanding additional payments, refused to honor the agreement. The babies were born prematurely, and one died. The intended parents sued to enforce the contract and gain custody of the surviving child. . . .

P.M. and C.M. were high school sweethearts but parted ways when P.M. joined the Navy upon graduation. After marrying and divorcing other spouses, they reconnected and married each other in 2013. They now live in Cedar Rapids. P.M. had two children from his first marriage, and C.M. had four children from hers. The Ms were nearing age fifty and wanted to have a child together. C.M. was no longer able to conceive, so the Ms placed an advertisement on Craigslist in 2015 seeking a woman willing to act as a surrogate mother.

T.B. and D.B. married each other in January 2009 and live in Muscatine. T.B. has four children from a prior marriage; D.B. has no children and had never been married. The Bs want to have children together. In 2010, T.B. had a tubal pregnancy which was life-threatening and incapable of leading to the birth of a viable child, so she surgically terminated the pregnancy. T.B. and D.B. continued to try to conceive without success. The Bs realized they would need the services of a reproductive endocrinologist in order to have a child. T.B. learned that the Bs' insurance would not cover infertility treatment or in vitro fertilization (IVF). They decided they needed to supplement D.B.'s income to pay for assisted reproduction procedures.

T.B. responded to the Ms' Craigslist advertisement. The four met for dinner in Coralville and got along well at first. They agreed that T.B. would gestate two embryos fertilized in vitro with P.M.'s sperm and the eggs of an anonymous donor. The Ms selected Midwest Fertility Clinic (Midwest) in Downers Grove, Illinois, to perform the IVF and embryo transfers. Midwest required a written contract between the parties, so the Ms hired a lawyer to draft the agreement. Its stated purpose was "to enable the Intended Father [P.M.] and the Intended Mother [C.M.] to have a child who is biologically related to one of them." In exchange for the gestational service, the Ms agreed to pay up to $13,000 for an IVF procedure for T.B. to enable her and D.B. to conceive their own child. This payment was conditioned upon T.B. surrendering custody of a live child upon birth.

> The Intended Parents [the Ms] agree that after the Gestational Carrier [T.B.] has delivered a live child pursuant to this contract for the Intended Parents, the Intended Parents will pay for an IVF (Invitro Fertilization) cycle for the Gestational Carrier and her husband up to the amount of $13,000.

The contract also provided that the Ms would pay T.B.'s pregnancy-related medical expenses. At T.B.'s request, an additional term was included stating that "[i]n the event the child is miscarried or stillborn during the pregnancy, the amount of $2,000 will be paid to the Gestational Carrier." The four adults signed the final "Gestational Carrier Agreement" (the Surrogacy Agreement) on January 5, 2016. . . .

On March 27, Midwest implanted two embryos into T.B.'s uterus. The embryos were the ova of an anonymous donor fertilized with P.M.'s sperm. On April 4, blood testing confirmed T.B.'s pregnancy. The parties' relationship soon began to break down over their disagreement as to payment of medical expenses. All four attended the first ultrasound, which D.B. videotaped. The Ms later objected to his videotaping and to T.B. posting information about the baby on social media.

Their relationship worsened after the women exchanged text messages on April 13. They were discussing whether T.B. could attend a doctor's appointment scheduled by the IVF coordinator when C.M. wrote, "Well we have to go next Thursday [because the coordinator] made the [appointment] and this is our journey not anyone else's. She said you have to end with [a doctor's] exam in Chicago and [a] couple more ultrasounds. . . ." T.B. replied, "I'm not going through this with you today. She just called me." C.M. replied, "We are in charge we hired you so just let us be parents and enjoy this ok!"

A second ultrasound confirmed that T.B. was carrying viable twins. T.B. shared that news with the Ms, but the relationship remained rocky. . . .

Twin babies were born thirteen weeks prematurely on August 31. T.B. did not tell the Ms about the birth. The babies were placed in the neonatal intensive care unit. One died eight days after birth. T.B. did not inform the Ms about the baby's illness or death. The Bs unilaterally arranged for the deceased baby's cremation.

On October 24, the Ms, still unaware of the birth, filed a petition for declaratory judgment and temporary and permanent injunction. On October 31, the Ms filed a motion for an emergency ex parte injunction, alleging their belief that the babies had been born. The same day, the district court entered an order granting a temporary injunction that ordered T.B. and D.B. to surrender custody of "Baby H" to the Ms. The order prohibited T.B. and D.B. from acting inconsistently with the terms of the Surrogacy Agreement. The Ms have had physical custody of Baby H since that date. . . .

We must decide whether the district court erred by enforcing the gestational surrogacy contract, terminating the presumptive parental rights of the surrogate mother and her husband, and placing permanent custody of Baby H with the biological father. We begin with an overview of the law governing gestational surrogacy arrangements. We next determine whether this gestational surrogacy contract is enforceable under Iowa law. We then address the respective legal rights of the parties. We conclude the district court correctly enforced the contract. . . .

"In general terms, surrogacy is the process by which a woman makes a choice to become pregnant and then carry to full term and deliver a baby who, she intends, will be raised by someone else." In re Paternity of F.T.R., 349 Wis.2d 84, 833 N.W.2d 634, 643 (2013) (quoting Thomas J. Walsh, *Wisconsin's Undeveloped Surrogacy Law*, 85 Wis. Lawyer. 16, 16 (March 2012) [hereinafter Walsh]). The woman who carries the child is the "surrogate mother." An "intended parent" is "an individual . . . who manifests the intent . . . to be legally bound as the parent of a child resulting from assisted or collaborative reproduction." Id. Surrogacies are categorized as "traditional" or "gestational."

> In a traditional surrogacy, the surrogate is the genetic mother of the child and is artificially inseminated with the sperm of the intended father or a sperm donor. In a gestational surrogacy, the surrogate is not genetically related to the child; instead, "sperm is taken from the father (or from a donor) and an egg is taken from the mother (or from a donor), fertilization happens outside the womb (called *in vitro fertilization*), and the fertilized embryos are then implanted into the surrogate mother's uterus."

Id. This case involves a gestational surrogacy because T.B. is not genetically related to the child. T.B. is the surrogate mother, while P.M. and C.M. are the intended parents.

The law regarding surrogacy agreements has evolved with advances in medically assisted reproductive science. . . .

In the minority of states with statutes specifically addressing surrogacy, the enactments generally impose greater restrictions on traditional surrogacies, and most of the statutes can be grouped into three categories:

> First, some states have legislatively prohibited all surrogacy contracts, declaring their terms unenforceable and, in some instances, imposing criminal penalties for those who attempt to enter into or assist in creating such a contract. A second category of states prohibit only certain types of surrogacy contracts—typically those involving a traditional surrogacy. Finally, states in the third category authorize both traditional and gestational surrogacy contracts, subject to regulation and specified limitations. In re Baby, 447 S.W.3d 807, 819–20 (Tenn. 2014). . . .

T.B. argues the Surrogacy Agreement is unenforceable under Iowa law as inconsistent with statutory provisions and public policy. We first examine whether this contract between consenting adults is "prohibited by statute, condemned by judicial decision, [or] contrary to the public morals." Dier v. Peters, 815 N.W.2d 1, 12 (Iowa 2012). We find no such statutory or judicial prohibition in our state. To the contrary, the Iowa legislature tacitly approved of surrogacy arrangements by exempting them from potential criminal liability for selling children. "Also, we need to consider the public policy implications of an opposite ruling." Id. Banning gestational surrogacy contracts would deprive infertile couples of perhaps the only way to raise their own biological children and would limit the contractual rights of willing surrogates. We join the better-reasoned cases from other jurisdictions rejecting arguments that gestational surrogacy contracts are void against public policy. . . .

We start with the presumption that under Iowa law a "contractual agreement is binding on the parties." Water Dev. Co. v. Lankford, 506 N.W.2d 763, 766 (Iowa 1993). "The power to invalidate a contract on public policy grounds must be used cautiously and exercised only in cases free from doubt." Thomas v. Progressive Cas. Ins., 749 N.W.2d 678, 687 (Iowa 2008). The party claiming the contract is contrary to public policy bears the burden of proof. Walker v. Gribble, 689 N.W.2d 104, 111 (Iowa 2004). We reiterate that "[t]o strike down a contract on public policy grounds, we must conclude that 'the preservation of the general public welfare outweighs the weighty societal interest in the freedom of contract." In re Marriage of Witten, 672 N.W.2d 768, 780 (Iowa 2003).

In *Witten*, we addressed the enforceability of a contract executed by a married couple, Trip and Tamera Witten, and the University of Nebraska Medical Center that stored their frozen embryos. Id. at 772–73. "Because Tamera was unable to conceive children naturally, they had eggs taken from Tamera artificially fertilized with Trip's sperm." Id. at 772. The couple later divorced, and the contract "did not explicitly deal with the possibility of divorce." Id. at 772–73. Tamera sought "custody" of the embryos to have them "implanted in her or a surrogate mother in an effort to bear a genetically linked child." Id. at 772. Trip argued the district court should enforce the contract, which required mutual consent of the parties for any use of the embryos. The district court ruled the contract controlled and enjoined both parties from using the embryos without the written approval of the other party. Tamera appealed, and we affirmed, holding that neither party could use the embryos without the contemporaneous consent of the other.

Our decision was consistent with the terms of the contract signed by the Wittens. But we stated a broader holding

> that agreements entered into at the time in vitro fertilization is commenced are enforceable and binding on the parties, "subject to the right of either party to change his or her mind about disposition up to the point of use or destruction of any stored embryo."

Id. at 782. We concluded that "judicial enforcement of an agreement between a couple regarding their future family and reproductive choices would be against the public policy of this state." Id. But we concluded the embryo dispositional agreement remains enforceable as between the donors and the medical facility.

We see important differences between an embryo disposition agreement signed by the egg and sperm donor during their marriage and the gestational surrogacy agreement at issue here. The former addresses disposition of the parties' own genetic material and assumed the marriage will continue. We noted the judicial reluctance to compel procreation of a biological son or daughter after one donor changed his mind. By contrast, the surrogate mother, T.B., is not the genetic or biological mother of Baby H. All parties sought the birth of Baby H. We conclude the public policy limitations in play in that case are inapposite. We turn to cases specifically adjudicating challenges to gestational surrogacy contracts. . . .

T.B. argues a surrogacy agreement violates public policy against the exploitation of women, and contends,

> Surrogacy agreements, if enforced embody deviant societal pressures, the object of which is to use the woman, and destroy her interests as a mother to satisfy the desires of third parties. Surrogacy exploits women by treating the mother as if she is not a whole woman. It assumes she can be used much like a breeding animal and act as though she is not, in fact, a mother.

Yet T.B. entered into the Surrogacy Agreement voluntarily. She had given birth to four children of her own before signing the Surrogacy Agreement and was no stranger to the effects of pregnancy. T.B. does not allege she signed the Surrogacy Agreement under economic duress or that its terms are unconscionable.

The California Supreme Court rejected a similar exploitation argument in [Johnson v. Calvert, 851 P.2d 776, 785 (Cal. 1993) (en banc)]:

> Although common sense suggests that women of lesser means serve as surrogate mothers more often than do wealthy women, there has been no proof that surrogacy contracts exploit poor women to any greater degree than economic necessity in general exploits them by inducing them to accept lower-paid or otherwise undesirable employment. We are likewise unpersuaded by the claim that surrogacy will foster the attitude that children are mere commodities; no evidence is offered to support it. . . .
>
> The argument that a woman cannot knowingly and intelligently agree to gestate and deliver a baby for intending parents carries overtones of the reasoning that for centuries prevented women from attaining equal economic rights and professional status under the law. To resurrect this view is both to foreclose a personal and economic choice on the part of the surrogate mother, and to deny intending parents what may be their only means of procreating a child of their own genetic stock. Certainly in the present case it cannot seriously be argued that Anna, a licensed vocational nurse who had done well in school and who had previously borne a child, lacked the intellectual wherewithal or life experience necessary to make an informed decision to enter into the surrogacy contract.

California courts continue to reject the view that surrogacy agreements unfairly exploit women. We reach the same conclusion.

T.B. alternatively argues the Surrogacy Agreement violates the state's public policy favoring families. . . . T.B. characterizes surrogacy agreements as deliberately destroying the surrogate mother-child relationship (a relationship, we note, that would not exist but for the Ms' contribution of their embryos in reliance on T.B.'s willingness to serve as a gestational carrier). We conclude that gestational surrogacy agreements *promote* families by enabling infertile couples to raise their own children and help bring new life into this world through willing surrogate mothers. . .

For these reasons, we hold the Surrogacy Agreement is enforceable under existing Iowa law. We emphasize that T.B.'s legal attack is on surrogacy agreements in general. We do not foreclose the possibility that a surrogacy agreement in a particular case could be subject to specific contract defenses, such as fraud, duress, or unconscionability. . . .

SECTION 2. DURESS AND COERCIVE RENEGOTIATION

Batsakis v. Demotsis

Court of Civil Appeals of Texas, 1949.
226 S.W.2d 673.

MCGILL, J. This is an appeal from a judgment of the [district court]. Appellant was plaintiff and appellee was defendant in the trial court. . . . Plaintiff sued defendant to recover $2,000 with interest at the rate of 8% per annum from April 2, 1942, alleged to be due on the following instrument, being a translation from the original, which is written in the Greek language:

"Peiraeus
April 2, 1942

"Mr. George Batsakis
Konstantinou Diadohou #7
Peiraeus

"Mr. Batsakis:

"I state by my present (letter) that I received today from you the amount of two thousand dollars ($2,000) of United States of America money, which I borrowed from you for the support of my family during these difficult days and because it is impossible for me to transfer dollars of my own from America.

"The above amount I accept with the expressed promise that I will return to you again in American dollars either at the end of the present war or even before in the event that you might be able to find a way to collect them (dollars) from my representative in America to whom I shall write and give him an order relative to this. You understand until the final execution (payment) to the above amount an eight per cent interest will be added and paid together with the principal. I thank you and I remain yours with respects.

"The recipient,
(Signed) Eugenia The. Demotsis."

Trial to the court . . . resulted in a judgment in favor of plaintiff for $750 principal, and interest at the rate of 8% per annum from April 2, 1942 to the date of judgment, totaling $1163.83, with interest thereon at the rate of 8% per annum until paid. Plaintiff [appeals].

The court sustained certain special exceptions of plaintiff to defendant's first amended original answer on which the case was tried, and struck therefrom paragraphs II, III and V. Defendant excepted to such action of the court, but has not cross-assigned error here. The answer, stripped of such paragraphs, consisted of a general denial contained in paragraph I thereof, and of paragraph IV, which is as follows:

"IV. That under the circumstances alleged in Paragraph II of this answer, the consideration upon which said written instrument sued upon by plaintiff herein is founded, is wanting and has failed to the extent of $1975, and defendant pleads specially under the verification hereinafter made the want and failure of consideration stated, and now tenders, as defendant has heretofore tendered to plaintiff, $25 as the value of the loan of money received by defendant from plaintiff, together with interest thereon.

"Further, in connection with this plea of want and failure of consideration defendant alleges that she at no time received from plaintiff himself or from anyone for plaintiff any money or thing of value other than, as hereinbefore alleged, the original loan of 500,000 drachmae. That at the time of the loan by plaintiff to defendant of said 500,000 drachmae the value of 500,000 drachmae [in] Greece in dollars of money of the United States of America, was $25, and also at said time the value of 500,000 drachmae of Greek money in the [United States] in dollars was $25. . . . The plea of want and failure of consideration is verified by defendant as follows."

The allegations in paragraph II which were stricken, referred to in paragraph IV, were that the instrument sued on was signed and delivered in Greece on or about April 2, 1942, at which time both plaintiff and defendant were residents of and residing in Greece, and

"[Defendant] avers that on or about April 2, 1942 she owned money and property and had credit in the United States of America, but was then and there in Greece in straitened financial circumstances due to the conditions produced by World War II and could not make use of her money and property and credit existing in the [United States]. That in the circumstances the plaintiff agreed to and did lend to defendant the sum of 500,000 drachmae, which at that time, on or about April 2, 1942, had the value of $25 in money of the [United States]. That the said plaintiff, knowing defendant's financial distress and desire to return to [America], exacted of her the written instrument plaintiff sues upon, which was a promise by her to pay to him the sum of $2,000 of United States of America money."

Plaintiff specially excepted to paragraph IV because the allegations thereof were insufficient to allege either want of consideration or failure of consideration, in that it affirmatively appears therefrom that defendant received what was agreed to be delivered to her, and that plaintiff breached no agreement. The court overruled this exception, and such action is assigned as error. Error is also assigned because of the court's failure to enter judgment for the whole unpaid balance of the principal of the instrument with interest as therein provided.

Defendant testified that she did receive 500,000 drachmas from plaintiff. It is not clear whether she received all the 500,000 drachmas or only a portion of them before she signed the instrument in question. Her testimony clearly shows that the understanding of the parties was that plaintiff would give her the 500,000 drachmas if she would sign the instrument. She testified:

> "Q. [W]ho suggested the figure of $2,000?
>
> "A. That was how he asked me from the beginning. He said he will give me five hundred thousand drachmas provided I signed that I would pay him $2,000 American money."

The transaction amounted to a sale by plaintiff of the 500,000 drachmas in consideration of the execution of the instrument sued on, by defendant. It is not contended that the drachmas had no value. Indeed, the judgment indicates that the trial court placed a value of $750 on them or on the other consideration which plaintiff gave defendant for the instrument if he believed plaintiff's testimony. Therefore the plea of want of consideration was unavailing. A plea of want of consideration amounts to a contention that the instrument never became a valid obligation in the first place. National Bank of Commerce v. Williams, 125 Tex. 619, 84 S.W.2d 691.

Mere inadequacy of consideration will not void a contract. 10 Tex.Jur., Contracts, Sec. 89, p. 150; Chastain v. Texas Christian Missionary Society, Tex.Civ.App., 78 S.W.2d 728.

Nor was the plea of failure of consideration availing. Defendant got exactly what she contracted for according to her own testimony. The court should have rendered judgment in favor of plaintiff against defendant for the principal sum of $2,000 evidenced by the instrument sued on, with interest as therein provided. We construe the provision relating to interest as providing for interest at the rate of 8% per annum. The judgment is reformed so as to award appellant a recovery against appellee of $2,000 with interest thereon at the rate of 8% per annum from April 2, 1942. Such judgment will bear interest at the rate of 8% per annum until paid on $2,000 thereof and on the balance interest at the rate of 6% per annum. As so reformed, the judgment is affirmed.

NOTE: GREECE IN 1942

The promise of Eugenia Demotsis was given not quite one year after the German armies had invaded Greece. The invasion occurred on April 6, 1941, and despite bitter resistance by the Greeks, soldiers and civilians, the main forces of the Greek armies surrendered to the Nazis on April 23, 1941. The devastation from the fighting itself was enormous, and continued after the surrender as a result of reprisals ordered by the Nazis for Greek resistance. Large numbers of country people fled to the cities, a very large portion to Athens and its adjoining port city, Peiraeus. The disruption that resulted for all forms of economic activity was magnified by a galloping inflation of the currency.

Greece before the war had long been deficient in agricultural products; only one-fifth of its land was arable. It was necessary even in normal times to import about half its food supplies, especially cereals. The German and Italian forces, during the occupation, confiscated large stocks of food. Imports were almost entirely cut off, on the West by an Allied blockade and to the North by continuing military operations. It was later estimated that in 1941 the average daily diet for all Greeks was about 900 calories per person, and until the end of the occupation (October 1944) the intake never rose above an average of 1,400 calories per person, well below normal requirements of 2,500 to 3,000. There is no way of knowing how many thousands died of malnutrition, most of them in the cities. Some estimates for the country as a whole ran into the hundreds of thousands. Finally, as accounts of this vast tragedy reached the outside world, the leading belligerents agreed to grant safe passage to shipments of food and medical supplies under the direction of Swiss and Swedish Red Cross officials. The shipments began to arrive in the last six months of 1942 and attained a substantial volume in 1943. (There is a brief account of these events in B. Sweet-Escott, Greece, A Political and Economic Survey, 1939–1953, 93–96 (1954).)

Zuckerman v. The Metropolitan Museum of Art

United States District Court, Southern District of New York, 2018.
307 F. Supp. 3d 304.

PRESKA, SENIOR UNITED STATES DISTRICT JUDGE. This is an action by Laurel Zuckerman, the Ancillary Administratrix of the estate of Alice Leffmann (the sole heir of Paul Friedrich Leffmann) (the "Leffmann estate"), to recover from New York's Metropolitan Museum of Art (the "Museum") a monumental work by Pablo Picasso entitled "The Actor," 1904–1905, oil on canvas, 77 1/4 x 45 3/8 in., signed lower right Picasso . . . .

In 1912, the Leffmanns purchased the Painting, which was one of their most valuable acquisitions. From 1912 until at least 1929, the Leffmanns presented the Painting at a variety of exhibitions in Germany, where they were identified as the owners of the Painting. The Painting was also featured in newspaper articles, magazines, and monographs.

During this time and until the start of the Nazi period, Paul and Alice, German Jews, lived in Cologne, Germany. They had sizeable assets, including Atlantic Gummiwerk, a rubber manufacturing company that was one of the leading concerns of its kind in Europe, which Paul co-owned with Herbert Steinberg; real estate investment properties in Cologne (Hohenzollernring 74 and Friesenwall 77); and their home located at Haydnstrasse 13, Koln-Lindenthal. The Leffmanns' home included a collection of Chinese and Japanese artifacts and other artworks, including the masterwork by Pablo Picasso that is the subject of this action.

Beginning in 1933, the world the Leffmanns knew in Germany began to change dramatically. Adolf Hitler came to power, and racist laws directed against Jews were quickly enacted and enforced, leading to the adoption of the Nuremberg Laws ("The Laws for the Protection of German Blood and German Honor") on September 15, 1935. The Nuremberg Laws deprived all German Jews, including Paul and Alice, of the rights and privileges of German citizenship, ended any normal life or existence for Jews in Germany, and relegated all Jews to a marginalized existence. . . .

On September 16, 1935, the Leffmanns were forced to sell their home to an Aryan German corporation, Rheinsiche Braunkohlensyndikats GmbH Köln. On December 19, 1935, Leffmann and his Jewish partner, Herbert Steinberg, were forced to transfer ownership of Atlantic Gummiwerk to Aloys Weyers (their non-Jewish minority business partner). On July 27, 1936, the Leffmanns were forced to sell all of their real estate investments to Feuerversicherungsgessellschaft Rheinland AG, another Aryan German corporation. In return, the Leffmanns had no choice but to accept only nominal compensation. Indeed, these were not real sales at all but essentially thefts by Nazi designees of substantially everything the Leffmanns ever owned. Some time prior to their departure from Germany, Paul and Alice had arranged for The Actor to be held in Switzerland by a non-Jewish German acquaintance, Professor Heribert Reiners. Reiners kept The Actor in his family home in Fribourg, where it remained for its entire stay in Switzerland. For this reason only, The Actor was saved from Nazi confiscation.

Paul and Alice, like so many other German Jews, found themselves faced with the threat of growing violence, the risk of imprisonment, and possibly deportation and death. Thus, to avoid the loss of the property they had left—and potentially their lives—they began planning their flight from Germany, liquidating their remaining assets in Germany to enable them to survive and escape. The Leffmanns fled Germany in the spring of 1937. By that time, the Nazi regime had already put in place its ever-tightening network of taxes, charges, and foreign exchange regulations designed to arrogate Jewish-owned assets to itself. Emigrants were only able to leave with a tiny fraction of their assets. Consequently, upon their escape from the Reich, the Leffmanns had been dispossessed of most of what they once owned. . . .

The Leffmanns would have preferred neutral Switzerland to Italy, as Italian Fascists were already in power and close relations with Nazi Germany had begun to develop. However, a long-term stay in Switzerland would have been virtually impossible. Italy, as opposed to Switzerland, was one of the few European countries still allowing the immigration of German Jews. So that is where the Leffmanns went, hoping that Italy's significant Jewish population would provide a safe haven from the Nazi onslaught. . . .

In April 1937 the Leffmanns crossed the border into Italy, going first to Milan and then to Florence, where their newly acquired house and factory were located. . . .

As the situation grew increasingly desperate for Jews living in Italy, it became clear that it would only be a matter of time before the Fascist regime's treatment of Jews would mimic that of Hitler's Nazis. Paul and Alice had to make plans to leave, and this would require money. . . .

In April 1938, in the face of the growing Nazi persecution spreading across Europe and into Italy, Paul escalated his efforts to liquidate The Actor. In September 1936, after they had been forced by the Nazis to part with nearly everything they owned, the Leffmanns had rejected an offer to sell The Actor from the notorious art dealer, C.M. de Hauke of Jacques Seligmann & Co. (whom the U.S. State Department later identified as a trafficker in Nazi-looted art). Nearly two years later, on April 12, 1938, the Leffmanns, in an even more desperate state, reached out to de Hauke asking him if he would be interested in purchasing the Painting. . . .

For the Leffmanns, the time to flee Italy was quickly approaching, so they continued to try to sell the Painting through de Hauke. Trying to raise as much cash as possible for the flight, the Leffmanns responded to a letter from de Hauke, telling him that they had already rejected an offer obtained through another Paris dealer, Käte Perls, for U.S. $12,000 (net of commission). It is clear from the letter that the Leffmanns were desperately trying to improve their leverage to maximize the amount of hard currency they could raise.

Violence was increasing, and the persecution of Jews was on the rise. Foreign Jews in Italy risked arrest and had reason to fear possible deportation and death. The Leffmanns were in fear of their liberty and their lives. Just days after telling de Hauke that they had rejected Mrs. Perls' low offer, in late June 1938, the Leffmanns sold the Painting at the very price they told Perls and de Hauke they would not consider. They finally accepted Kate Perls' offer of U.S. $13,200 (U.S. $12,000 after a standard ten percent selling commission), who was acting on behalf of her ex-husband, Hugo Perls, also an art dealer, and art dealer Paul Rosenberg, with whom Perls was buying the Painting.

On July 26, 1938, Frank Perls, Kate's son (who was also a dealer) wrote to automobile titan Walter P. Chrysler Jr., asking if he would be interested in purchasing The Actor. Having just acquired a Picasso masterpiece from a German Jew on the run from Nazi Germany living in Fascist Italy for a low price that reflected the seller's desperate circumstances and the extraordinary prevailing conditions, Frank Perls misrepresented to Chrysler that the Painting was purchased by Mrs. Perls from "an Italian collector." . . .

The Leffmanns temporarily resided in Bern, Switzerland, but, unable to stay, prepared to flee yet again, this time to Brazil. In addition to bribes that were typically required to obtain necessary documentation, Brazil would only provide visas for Jews who could transfer more than 400 contos (USD $20,000) to the Banco do Brasil. On May 7, 1941, the Leffmanns, still on the run, immigrated to Rio de Janeiro, Brazil, where they lived for the next six years. But even in Brazil, they could not escape the effects of the ongoing war. All German residents living there, including the Leffmanns, were forced to pay a levy imposed by the Brazilian government of 20,000 Swiss Francs ("SF") (or about U.S. $4,641).

Given the various payments required by Switzerland, as well as those that the Leffmanns would need to enter Brazil, the Leffmanns depended on the $12,000 (or approximately SF 52,440 in 1938) they received from the sale of The Actor, as it constituted the majority of the Leffmanns' available resources in June 1938. Had the Leffmanns not fled for Brazil when they did, they likely would have suffered a much more tragic fate at the hands of the Nazi regime and its allies.

The Leffmanns were not able to return to Europe until after the War had ended. In 1947, they settled in Zurich, Switzerland. Paul Leffmann died on May 4, 1956 in Zurich, Switzerland at the age of 86. He left his entire estate to his wife, Alice Brandenstein Leffmann. Alice Leffmann died on June 25, 1966 in Zurich, Switzerland at the age of 88. She left her entire estate to 12 heirs (all relatives or friends).

The immediate history of the Painting after Perls and Rosenberg purchased it in June of 1938 is unclear, but it is known that after the purchase, art dealer Paul Rosenberg loaned the Painting to the Museum of Modern Art ("MoMA") in New York in 1939. In the paperwork documenting the loan, Rosenberg requested that MoMA insure the Painting for $18,000 (a difference of $6,000, or a 50 percent increase over what had been paid to the Leffmanns less than a year earlier). Sometime prior to October 28, 1940, the Painting was consigned for sale by Rosenberg to the well-known M. Knoedler & Co. Gallery in New York, New York. On November 14, 1941, M. Knoedler & Co. sold the Painting to Thelma Chrysler Foy ("Foy") for $22,500 (a difference of U.S. $9,300, or a 70 percent increase from the price paid to the Leffmanns). Thelma Chrysler Foy donated the Painting to the Museum in 1952, where it remains today. The Museum accepted this donation. . . .

Under New York law, "to void a contract on the ground of economic duress," Plaintiff must plead and show that the 1938 transaction "was procured by means of (1) a wrongful threat that (2) precluded the exercise of its free will." Interpharm, Inc. v. Wells Fargo Bank, Nat. Ass'n, 655 F.3d 136, 142 (2d Cir. 2011).

In characterizing a "wrongful threat," New York "law demands threatening conduct that is wrongful, i.e., outside a party's legal rights." Interpharm, 655 F.3d at 142. "Critically," under New York law, the defendant must have caused the duress. See Mandavia v. Columbia Univ., 912 F.Supp.2d 119, 127–28 (S.D.N.Y. 2012), aff'd, 556 Fed.Appx. 56 (2d Cir. 2014) (quoting [Kramer v. Vendome Grp. LLC, 2012 WL 4841310, at *6 (S.D.N.Y. 2012)] (stating that "to prove duress, a plaintiff must demonstrate that the difficult circumstances" or wrongful threat "she faces are a result of the *defendant's* actions . . . to constitute duress, a *defendant's* actions must have amounted to threats that preclude[d] the exercise of [a plaintiff's] free will").

Moreover, courts have noted that "an element of economic duress is . . . present when many contracts are formed." VKK Corp. v. Nat'l Football League, 244 F.3d 114, 123 (2d Cir. 2001). For that reason, a party seeking to void a contract on the basis of economic duress bears a heavy burden.

Here, first, Plaintiff is unable to plead "a wrongful threat" by the Defendant Museum or the counterparties to the 1938 transaction. Specifically, Plaintiff does not plead that Kate Perls, Hugo Perls or Paul Rosenberg, respectively the negotiator and purchasers on the other side of the Leffmann transaction, or the Museum used "wrongful" or "threatening conduct . . . outside [their] legal rights" in effectuating the 1938 sale. Rather, Plaintiff states that "but for the Nazi and Fascist persecution to which [the Leffmanns] had been . . . subjected," they "would not have disposed of this seminal work at that time." Effectively, Plaintiff claims that the "circumstances in Fascist Italy," not the counterparties to the 1938 transaction or the Museum, forced the Leffmanns to sell the Painting under duress. However, the 1938 transaction occurred between private individuals, not at the command of the Fascist or Nazi governments. As in *Bakalar*, "there is no . . . evidence that the Nazis ever possessed the [Painting], and therefore . . . this Court cannot infer duress based on Nazi seizure." Bakalar v. Vavra, 819 F.Supp.2d 293, 300 (S.D.N.Y. 2011), aff'd, 500 Fed.Appx. 6 (2d Cir. 2012). Thus, although the Leffmanns felt economic pressure during the undeniably horrific circumstances of the Nazi and Fascist regimes, that pressure, when not caused by the counterparties to the transaction (or the Defendant) where the duress is alleged, is insufficient to prove duress with respect to the transaction.

Second, Plaintiff fails to plead that the Leffmanns entered into the 1938 transaction by force that "preclude[ed] the exercise of [their] free will." Orix Credit All., Inc. v. Bell Realty, Inc., 1995 WL 505891, at *4 (S.D.N.Y. 1995). Rather, Paul Leffmann exercised his free will in "explor[ing] the possibility of selling his masterpiece, The Actor, with dealers in Paris." The Leffmanns took nearly two years from the time they received an initial offer to sell the Painting in September, 1936, until they negotiated for its sale in June, 1938. In the interim, the Painting was in Switzerland for safekeeping.

Additionally, the Leffmanns negotiated with several parties prior to the 1938 transaction, rejected offers from other dealers, and attempted to "improve [their] leverage to maximize" the sale price before ultimately accepting an offer from Perls and Rosenberg, the proceeds of which the Leffmanns retained and used in later years. Each transaction occurred between private individuals, not at the behest of Nazi or Fascist officials. Accordingly, these allegations are fatal to a claim of duress as Plaintiff is unable to show "a wrongful threat by the *other party* which precluded the exercise of [Paul's] free will in making the contract at issue." Mfrs. Hanover Tr. Co. v. Jayhawk Assocs., 766 F. Supp. 124, 128 (S.D.N.Y. 1991).

Third, Plaintiff fails to plead facts demonstrating that the Leffmanns had "no other alternative" than to engage in the 1938 transaction. Kramer v. Vendome Grp. LLC, 2012 WL 4841310, at *6 (S.D.N.Y. 2012). Plaintiff's assertion that the Leffmanns were "forced by the circumstances in Fascist Italy to sell [the Painting] under duress in 1938" conflates the Leffmanns' need "to raise as much cash as possible" with the Leffmanns having "no other alternative." The fact that the Leffmanns spent several years looking to sell the Painting, rejected other offers, and had additional assets including properties in Italy that they sold to an Italian businessman in 1937, suggests that they had other financial alternatives. . . .

Embola v. Tuppela

127 Wash. 285, 220 P. 789 (1923)

Tuppela prospected for gold in Alaska, acquired a gold mine worth $500,000, but was then adjudged insane and committed to an asylum in Oregon. On his release after four years' confinement, Tuppela learned that his Alaska mine had been sold by his guardian. He searched but found no one willing to advance him funds for use in recovering the property. Then, destitute and without work, Tuppela encountered the plaintiff, a "close friend" of 30 years, who gave him shelter and money for support. Tuppela later said to plaintiff: "You have already let me have $270. If you will give me $50 more so I can go to Alaska and get my property back, I will pay you ten thousand dollars when I win my property." Plaintiff at once gave him $50, Tuppela went to Alaska and, after litigation lasting three years, won back his gold mine. Remembering his agreement, Tuppela asked "his trustee" (apparently, in the interim, Tuppela had again become incompetent) to pay plaintiff $10,000. The trustee refused, claiming that the contract was "unconscionable," not supported by adequate consideration, and in violation of usury laws. Plaintiff sued the trustee, recovering judgment for the $10,000 Tuppela had promised. Affirming, the Supreme Court agreed that all objections to the contract must fail. Tuppela's mind was "sound" when he gave his promise, and he considered the exchange "fair and to his advantage." It was unlikely he would ever recover his property, as an attorney had told him. "The risk of losing the money advanced was as great [as it would be] under a grubstake contract." A contingency that may never occur makes a transaction such as this "an investment and not a loan"; usury is not a concern. The uncertain event conditioning Tuppela's promise also "supports the finding that the consideration was not inadequate."

COMMENT: "ADEQUACY" OF CONSIDERATION

In Chapter 2, we encountered talk of "nominal" consideration in connection with purported bargains that in fact involved a great disparity in values. There is perhaps no more accepted proposition in Anglo-American contract law than the one requiring but a single line of space in Batsakis v. Demotsis: "Mere inadequacy of consideration will not void a contract." The same can be said of the corollary principle, that "ordinarily the courts will not inquire into the adequacy of consideration."

The failure of the early common law to review the "adequacy" of consideration is quite understandable. We have seen that developments in the sixteenth and seventeenth centuries were mainly procedural, and thus technical, in nature (should assumpsit be extended to particular types of informal promises?). Because the emphasis was on the harm suffered by the promisee, it was inevitable that attention was drawn to the question whether enforcement was called for. The emerging test of consideration, cabined by the assumpsit remedy, was not seen as an occasion for raising challenges to unequal bargains. The Chancellor, of course, was available to entertain claims of hardship, claims for revision or cancellation of obligations that, for any number of reasons, had become onerous (see Chapter 1, supra pp. 214–218). Later, in the eighteenth and nineteenth centuries, the reluctance of courts to take up "adequacy" directly was put on other grounds. The Arkansas case of Buckner v. McIlroy, 31 Ark. 631 (1877), provides an example:

> While it is true a right of action does not arise on a mere naked promise, yet, if there be any legal consideration for the promise, the court will not inquire into its adequacy,—"The law having no means of deciding upon this matter, and it being considered unwise to interfere with the facility of contracting, and the free exercise of the judgment and will of the parties, by not allowing them to be the judges of the benefits to be derived from their bargains, provided there be no incompetency to contract, and the agreement violate no rule of law. It is, indeed, necessary that the consideration be of some value, but it is sufficient if it be of slight value only. [E.g.,] the compromise or abandonment of a doubtful right is a sufficient consideration for a contract, even when it turns out that the point given up was in truth against the promisee." 1 Chitty on Contracts (11 Ed.) 29.

Modern views of the social gains realized through private exchange transactions remain rooted in these nineteenth century ideas about economic individualism and enlightened self-interest. You will note that the Restatement, Second § 71 (supra p. 263) uses only the term "consideration," dropping all reference to the *Buckner* court's talk of "sufficient consideration." One puzzle over the years has been the historical distinction between "sufficiency" of consideration and "adequacy" of consideration; the former was said to be required while an inquiry into the latter was deemed inappropriate.

Still, a brief word of caution is necessary. One should not conclude that the broad prohibition against review of "adequacy" has meant that the fairness of an exchange is not a legal concern. In fact, there exists a vast body of doctrine and special rules—both judicially-declared and legislative in origin, much of it developed in equity—which courts invoke regularly in passing on the fairness of bargains, including the problem of equivalence. We shall see once again in this chapter that refusing enforcement of a contract is by no means an uncommon event. All we have observed to this point is that the requirement of consideration, standing alone, is not a front-line insurer of fair exchanges. It is another question whether, as one court has asserted, the inadequacy of consideration is "more properly construed as a factor relevant in the application of other rules." Oh v. Wilson, 112 Nev. 38, 910 P.2d 276 (1996).

NOTE: ECONOMIC DURESS AND CHANGED CIRCUMSTANCES

Because legal remedies are necessarily imperfect, one party can find itself in a position to exact modifications from the other once both have spent time and money performing. One party can demand that the other accept less than what she is owed or face the prospect of lengthy and uncertain litigation. Courts are reluctant to enforce modifications made under such conditions. At the same time, circumstances can change, and it might be that a modification of the contract might will be in everyone's interest. The challenge courts face is distinguishing between renegotiations that are coercive and those that are mutually beneficial. In the cases that follow, courts sometimes accept the idea that, to be enforceable, a modification, like the underlying promise itself, must be supported by consideration. In the cases that follow, consider whether such a test does an effective job of separating the modifications that should be enforced from those that should not be.

Alaska Packers' Ass'n v. Domenico

United States Court of Appeals, Ninth Circuit, 1902.
117 F. 99.

ROSS, CIRCUIT JUDGE. The libel in this case was based upon a contract alleged to have been entered into between the libelants and the appellant corporation on the 22d day of May, 1900, at Pyramid Harbor, Alaska, by which it is claimed the appellant promised to pay each of the libelants, among other things, the sum of $100 for services rendered and to be rendered. . . .

The evidence shows that on March 26, 1900, [in] San Francisco, the libelants entered into a written contract with the appellant, whereby they agreed to go from San Francisco to Pyramid Harbor, Alaska, and return, on board such vessel as might be designated by the appellant, and to work for the appellant during the fishing season of 1900, at Pyramid Harbor, as sailors and fishermen, agreeing to do "regular ship's duty, both up and down, discharging and loading; and to do any other work whatsoever when requested to do so by the captain or agent of the Alaska Packers' Ass'n." By the terms of this agreement, the appellant was to pay each of the libelants $50 for the season, and two cents for each red salmon in the catching of which he took part.

On the 15th day of April, 1900, 21 of the libelants signed shipping articles by which they shipped as seamen on the Two Brothers, a vessel chartered by the appellant for the voyage between San Francisco and Pyramid Harbor, and also bound themselves to perform the same work for the appellant provided for by the previous contract of March 26th; the appellant agreeing to pay them therefor the sum of $60 for the season, and two cents each for each red salmon in the catching of which they should respectively take part. Under these contracts, the libelants sailed on board the Two Brothers for Pyramid Harbor, where the appellant had about $150,000 invested in a salmon cannery. The libelants arrived there early in April of the year mentioned, and began to unload the vessel and fit up the cannery. A few days thereafter, to wit, May 19th, they stopped work in a body, and demanded of the company's superintendent there in charge $100 for services in operating the vessel to and from Pyramid Harbor, instead of the sums stipulated for in and by the contracts; stating that unless they were paid this additional wage they would stop work entirely, and return to San Francisco. The evidence showed, and the court below found, that it was impossible for the appellant to get other men to take the places of the libelants, the place being remote, the season short and just opening; so that, after endeavoring for several days without success to induce the libelants to proceed with their work in accordance with their contracts, the company's superintendent, on the 22d day of May, so far yielded to their demands as to instruct his clerk to copy the contracts executed in San Francisco, substituting, for the $50 and $60 payments, respectively, of those contracts, the sum of $100, which document, so prepared, was signed by the libelants before a shipping commissioner whom they had requested to be brought from Northeast Point; the superintendent, however, testifying that he at the time told the libelants that he was without authority to enter into any such contract, or to in any way alter the contracts made between them and the company in San Francisco. Upon the return of the libelants to San Francisco at the close of the fishing season, they demanded pay in accordance with the terms of the alleged contract of May 22d, when the company denied its validity, and refused to pay other than as provided for by the contracts of March 26th and April 5th, respectively. . . .

. . . [T]he libelants undertook to show [at trial] that the fishing nets provided by the respondent were defective, and that it was on that account that they demanded increased wages. On that point, the evidence was substantially conflicting, and the finding of the court was against the libelants. . . . The evidence being sharply conflicting in respect to these facts, the conclusions of the court, who heard and saw the witnesses, will not be disturbed. . . .

The real questions [here are] questions of law, and [it] will be necessary to consider but one of those. Assuming that the appellant's superintendent at Pyramid Harbor was authorized to make the alleged contract of May 22d, . . . was it supported by a sufficient consideration? . . . [T]he libelants agreed in writing, for certain stated compensation, to render their services to the appellant in remote waters . . .; and, after having entered upon the discharge of their contract, and at a time when it was impossible for the appellant to secure other men in their places, the libelants, without any valid cause, absolutely refused to continue the services they were under contract to perform unless the appellant would consent to pay them more money. Consent to such a demand, under such circumstances, if given, was, in our opinion, without a consideration, for the reason that it was based solely upon the libelants' agreement to render the exact services, and none other, that they were already under contract to render. . . . [T]hey willfully and arbitrarily broke that obligation. As a matter of course, they were liable to the appellant in damages, and it is quite probable, as suggested by the court below[,] that they may have been unable to respond in damages. But we are unable to agree with the conclusions there drawn, from these facts, in these words:

"Under such circumstances, it would be strange, indeed, if the law would not permit the defendant to waive the damages caused by the libelants' breach, and enter into the contract sued upon,—a contract mutually beneficial to all the parties thereto, in that it gave to the libelants reasonable compensation for their labor, and enabled the defendant to employ to advantage the large capital it had invested in its canning and fishing plant."

Certainly, it cannot be justly held [that] there was any voluntary waiver on the part of the appellant of the breach of the original contract. The company itself knew nothing of such breach until the expedition returned to San Francisco, and the testimony is uncontradicted that its superintendent at Pyramid Harbor . . . distinctly informed the libelants that he had no power to alter the original or to make a new contract; and it would, of course, follow that, if he had no power to change the original, he would have no authority to waive any rights thereunder. The circumstances of the present case bring it, we think, directly within the sound and just observations [made in] [King v. Duluth, M & N Railway Co., 61 Minn. 482, 63 N.W. 1105]:

"No astute reasoning can change the plain fact that the party who refuses to perform, and thereby coerces a promise from the other party to the contract to pay him an increased compensation for doing that which he is legally bound to do, takes an unjustifiable advantage of the necessities of the other party. Surely it would be a travesty on justice to hold that the party so making the promise for extra pay was estopped from asserting that the promise was without consideration. A party cannot lay the foundation of an estoppel by his own wrong, where the promise is simply a repetition of a subsisting legal promise. . . ."

[The court then referred to Lingenfelder v. Wainwright Brewing Co., 103 Mo. 578, 15 S.W. 844 (1891), where an architect, Jungenfeld, was employed by Wainwright to draw plans for a refrigerator plant. Jungenfeld was also president of the Empire Refrigerator Co., manufacturer of refrigerating equipment, and "was largely interested therein." Over Jungenfeld's protest, Wainwright awarded a contract for refrigerating equipment to a competitor of Jungenfeld's company. Jungenfeld then took away his plans and refused to perform further. Wainwright "was in great haste to have its brewery completed for divers reasons," and to secure a new architect and new plans would take much time. Wainwright thereupon agreed to pay Jungenfeld five percent of the price of the refrigerating equipment it had purchased from the competitor if Jungenfeld would continue his work as supervising architect. The court in the principal case proceeded to quote from the opinion of the Missouri court, which refused to allow recovery of the five percent promised to Jungenfeld:]

"It is urged upon us by respondents that this was a new contract. New in what? Jungenfeld was bound by his contract to design and supervise this building. Under the new promise, he was not to do anything more or anything different. What benefit was to accrue to Wainwright? He was to receive the same service from Jungenfeld under the new, that Jungenfeld was bound to tender under the original, contract. What loss, trouble, or inconvenience could result to Jungenfeld that he had not already assumed? No amount of metaphysical reasoning can change the plain fact that Jungenfeld took advantage of Wainwright's necessities, and extorted the promise of five per cent on the refrigerator plant as the condition of his complying with his contract already entered into. . . . To permit plaintiff to recover under such circumstances would be to offer a premium upon bad faith, and invite men to violate their most sacred contracts that they may profit by their own wrong. That a promise to pay a man for doing that which he is already under contract to do is without consideration is conceded by respondents. . . . But it is 'carrying coals to Newcastle' to add authorities on a proposition so universally accepted, and so inherently just and right in itself. . . . [R]espondents do not controvert the general proposition. Their contention is, and the circuit court agreed that, when Jungenfeld declined to go further on his contract, the defendant then had the right to sue for damages, and not having elected to sue Jungenfeld, but having acceded to his demand for the additional compensation, defendant cannot now be heard to say his promise is without consideration. While it is true Jungenfeld became liable in damages for the obvious breach of his contract, we do not think it follows that defendant is estopped from showing its promise was made without consideration. . . . [W]hen a party merely does what he has already obligated himself to do, he cannot demand an additional compensation therefor; and although, by taking advantage of the necessities of his adversary, he obtains a promise for more, the law will regard it as nudum pactum, and will not lend its process to aid in the wrong." . . .

It results from the views above expressed that the judgment must be reversed, and the cause remanded, with directions to the court below to enter judgment for the respondent, with costs. It is so ordered.

NOTE

In Selmer Co. v. Blakeslee-Midwest Co., 704 F.2d 924, 927 (7th Cir. 1983), Judge Posner analyzed *Alaska Packers* and observed, "Although the technical ground of decision was the absence of fresh consideration for the modified agreement, it seems apparent . . . that the court's underlying concern was that the modified agreement had been procured by duress in the form of the threat to break the original contract." In his view, the vice at which the law should aim are attempts "to exploit the contract promisee's lack of an adequate legal remedy."

Austin Instrument, Inc. v. Loral Corp.

Court of Appeals of New York, 1971.
29 N.Y.2d 124, 324 N.Y.S.2d 22, 272 N.E.2d 533.

FULD, C.J. The defendant, Loral Corp., seeks to recover payment for goods delivered under a contract which it had with the plaintiff Austin Instrument, on the ground that the evidence establishes, as a matter of law, that it was forced to agree to an increase in price on the items in question under circumstances amounting to economic duress.

In July of 1965, Loral was awarded a $6,000,000 contract by the Navy for the production of radar sets. The contract contained a schedule of deliveries, a liquidated damages clause applying to late deliveries and a cancellation clause in case of default by Loral. The latter thereupon solicited bids for some 40 precision gear components needed to produce the radar sets, and awarded Austin a subcontract to supply 23 such parts[;] [Austin] commenced delivery in early 1966.

In May 1966, Loral was awarded a second Navy contract for the production of more radar sets and again went about soliciting bids. Austin bid on all 40 gear components but, on July 15, a [Loral] representative informed Austin's president, Krauss, that his company would be awarded the subcontract only for those items on which it was low bidder. The Austin officer refused to accept an order for less than all 40 of the gear parts and on the next day he told Loral that Austin would cease deliveries of the parts due under the existing subcontract unless Loral consented to substantial increases in the prices provided for by that agreement—both retroactively for parts already delivered and prospectively on those not yet shipped—and placed with Austin the order for all 40 parts needed under Loral's second Navy contract. Shortly thereafter, Austin did, indeed, stop delivery. After contacting 10 manufacturers of precision gears and finding none who could produce the parts in time to meet its commitments to the Navy,[1] Loral acceded to Austins demands; in a letter dated July 22, Loral wrote to Austin that "We have feverishly surveyed other sources of supply and find that because of the prevailing military exigencies, were they to start from scratch as would have to be the case, they could not even remotely begin to deliver on time to meet the delivery requirements established by the Government. . . . Accordingly, we are left with no choice or alternative but to meet your conditions."

Loral thereupon consented to the price increases insisted upon by Austin under the first subcontract and the latter was awarded a second subcontract making it the supplier of all 40 gear parts for Loral's second contract with the Navy. Although Austin was granted until September to resume deliveries, Loral did, in fact, receive parts in August and was able to produce the radar sets in time to meet its commitments to the Navy on both contracts. After Austin's last delivery under the second subcontract in July, 1967, Loral notified it of its intention to seek recovery of the price increases.

On September 15, 1967, Austin instituted this action against Loral to recover an amount in excess of $17,750 which was still due on the second subcontract. On the same day, Loral commenced an action against Austin claiming damages of some $22,250—the aggregate of the price increases under the first subcontract—on the ground of economic duress. [Loral made no claim on the second subcontract.] The two actions were consolidated and, following a trial, Austin was awarded the sum it requested and Loral's complaint against Austin was dismissed on the ground that it was not shown that "it could not have obtained the items in question from other sources in time to meet its commitment to the Navy under the first contract." A closely divided Appellate Division affirmed (35 A.D.2d 387, 316 N.Y.S.2d 528, 532) . . . .

The applicable law is clear. . . . A contract is voidable on the ground of duress when it is established that the party making the claim was forced to agree to it by means of a wrongful threat precluding the exercise of his free will. . . . The existence of economic duress or business compulsion is demonstrated by proof that "immediate possession of needful

[1] The best reply Loral received was from a vendor who stated he could commence deliveries some time in October.

goods is threatened" [or,] more particularly, in cases such as the one before us, by proof that one party to a contract has threatened to breach the agreement by withholding goods unless the other party agrees to some further demand. However, a mere threat by one party to breach the contract by not delivering the required items, though wrongful, does not in itself constitute economic duress. It must also appear that the threatened party could not obtain the goods from another source of supply and that the ordinary remedy of an action for breach of contract would not be adequate.

We find without any support in the record the conclusion reached by the courts below that Loral failed to establish that it was the victim of economic duress. On the contrary, the evidence makes out a classic case, as a matter of law, of such duress.

It is manifest that Austin's threat—to stop deliveries unless the prices were increased—deprived Loral of its free will. . . . Loral's relationship with the Government is most significant. . . . [I]ts contract called for staggered monthly deliveries of the radar assets, with clauses calling for liquidated damages and possible cancellation on default. Because of its production schedule, Loral was, in July, 1966, concerned with meeting its delivery requirements in September, October and November, and it was for the sets to be delivered in those months that the withheld gears were needed. Loral had to plan ahead, and the substantial liquidated damages for which it would be liable, plus the threat of default, were genuine possibilities. Moreover, Loral did a substantial portion of its business with the Government, and it feared that a failure to deliver as agreed upon would jeopardize its chances for future contracts. . . . It was perfectly reasonable for Loral, or any other party similarly placed, to consider itself in an emergency, duress situation.

. . . [T]he parts necessary for production of the radar sets to be delivered in September were delivered to Loral on September 1, and the parts needed for the October schedule were delivered in late August and early September. Even so, Loral had to "work [around] the clock" to meet its commitments. Considering that the best offer Loral received from the other vendors it contacted was commencement of delivery sometime in October, which, as the record shows, would have made it late in its deliveries to the Navy in both September and October, Loral's claim that it had no choice but to accede to Austin's demands is conclusively demonstrated.

We find unconvincing Austin's contention that Loral, in order to meet its burden, should have contacted the Government and asked for an extension of its delivery dates so as to enable it to purchase the parts from another vendor. Aside from the consideration that Loral was anxious to perform well in the Government's eyes, it could not be sure when it would obtain enough parts from a substitute vendor to meet its commitments. The only promise which it received from the companies it contacted was for *commencement* of deliveries, not full supply, and, with vendor delay common in this field, it would have been nearly impossible to know the length of the extension it should request. It must be remembered that Loral was producing a needed item of military hardware. Moreover, there is authority for Loral's position that nonperformance by a subcontractor is not an excuse for default in the main contract. (See, e.g., McBride & Wachtel, Government Contracts, § 35.10, [11].) . . .

Loral also had the burden of demonstrating that it could not obtain the parts elsewhere within a reasonable time, and there can be no doubt that it met this burden. The 10 manufacturers whom Loral contacted comprised its entire list of "approved vendors" for precision gears, and none was able to commence delivery soon enough. As Loral was producing a highly sophisticated item of military machinery requiring parts made to the strictest engineering standards, it would be unreasonable to hold that Loral should have gone to other vendors, with whom it was either unfamiliar or dissatisfied, to procure the needed parts. . . .

It is hardly necessary to add that Loral's normal legal remedy of accepting Austin's breach of the contract and then suing for damages would have been inadequate under the circumstances, as Loral would still have had to obtain the gears elsewhere with all the concomitant consequences mentioned above. In other words, Loral actually had no choice, when the prices were raised by Austin, except to take the gears at the "coerced" prices and then sue to get the excess back.

Austin's final argument is that Loral, even if it did enter into the contract under duress, lost any rights it had to a refund of money by waiting until July, 1967, long after the termination date of the contract, to disaffirm it. It is true that one who would recover moneys allegedly paid under duress must act promptly to make his claim known. . . . In this case, Loral delayed making its demand for a refund until three days after Austin's last delivery on the second subcontract. Loral's reason—for waiting until that time—is that it feared another stoppage of deliveries which would again put it in an untenable situation. Considering Austin's conduct in the past, this was perfectly reasonable. . . .

In sum, the record before us demonstrates that Loral agreed to the price increases in consequence of the economic duress employed by Austin. Accordingly, the matter should be remanded to the trial court for a computation of its damages. The order appealed from should be modified, by reversing so much thereof as affirms the dismissal of [Loral's] claim and, except as so modified, affirmed.

The order [is] affirmed. [The majority prevailed by a vote of 4 to 3; a dissenting opinion argued that Loral's failure to seek out alternative suppliers other than those it had used in the past raised an issue of fact as to whether Loral had acted reasonably.]

Merry Gentleman, LLC v. George and Leona Productions, Inc.

United States District Court, Northern District of Illinois, 2013.
2013 WL 4105578.

FEINERMAN, DISTRICT JUDGE. Merry Gentleman, LLC, alleges that Michael Keaton and his loan-out company, George and Leona Productions, Inc., whose presence in this suit will be ignored for ease of exposition, breached their obligations under the parties' contract for directing services for the motion picture, *The Merry Gentleman.* Keaton has moved to dismiss the complaint under FRCP Rule 12(b)(6). . . .

Merry Gentleman, a production company, produced *The Merry Gentleman,* a motion picture that Michael Keaton directed and in which he starred. On February 1, 2007, Keaton entered into both an acting services agreement and a directing services agreement with Merry Gentleman. This case does not concern the acting services agreement. The directing services agreement is governed by Illinois law.

One of Keaton's responsibilities under the directing services agreement was to deliver a "first cut" of the film. During the film's shooting in Chicago in March and April 2007, Keaton declined the services of an editor who could review the daily film footage with him. Nor did Keaton use the editing facilities that Merry Gentleman had set up for him in Santa Monica, California, after shooting concluded, electing instead to go fly-fishing for a period of weeks in Bozeman, Montana. Merry Gentleman responded by setting up editing facilities in Bozeman, which Keaton used periodically, leaving the selection and editing together of the "best scenes" to subordinates.

Keaton submitted his first cut of the film to Merry Gentleman behind schedule, in August 2007. Merry Gentleman found the first cut "unsatisfactory," a sentiment with which Keaton agreed. At Keaton's request, Merry Gentleman allowed him to make a second cut; at the same time, and without Keaton's knowledge, Merry Gentleman worked to prepare its own cut with the intention of ultimately proceeding with whichever turned out to be the better version. Ultimately, Merry Gentleman chose to submit its own cut, rather than Keaton's second cut, to the Sundance Film Festival.

In November 2007, Sundance selected *The Merry Gentleman* to be premiered at its largest theater, the Eccles Theatre, a prestigious opportunity often portending commercial success. Upon learning of the selection and without notifying Merry Gentleman, Keaton approached Sundance personnel and informed them that unless Sundance screened his version of the film, he would not appear at the festival. Wishing to have Keaton present, Sundance notified Merry Gentleman that the film would not be shown unless Keaton appeared. At that point, Merry Gentleman had invested over $4 million in the film.

The impasse was resolved with Merry Gentleman and Keaton signing a Settlement Agreement and Release ("Release") on December 14, 2007, in which Merry Gentleman agreed that Keaton's version of the film would be shown at Sundance. In addition, Merry Gentleman and Keaton released "any and all claims" against the other "arising from or relating to any Contracts in respect of or relating to the Picture, the provision or performance of directing . . . by [Keaton] . . . up to the date of this Agreement." Both parties also agreed to comply with their obligations under their existing directing services agreement. The Release is governed by Illinois law.

After the Release was executed, Keaton was responsible for preparing the film for both Sundance and commercial release, a responsibility that entailed duties such as cleaning up the cut, sound and color correction, and music selection. Keaton chose music for the Sundance screening that exceeded the pre-determined budget, and when Merry Gentleman noted that the music selections were not within budget, Keaton insisted that his selections were "in" and refused any further discussion. Keaton also refused to cooperate with key members of the production and marketing teams with whom he had disagreements.

Keaton's cut premiered at Sundance on January 18, 2008. Despite Merry Gentleman's intention to release the film during the 2008 Christmas season, production delays pushed the release date back to May 2009. And although the film was well received by critics, including Roger Ebert, its U.S. box office was less than $350,000. On April 23, 2009, Keaton made a promotional appearance on ABC's *Good Morning America* in which he wore sunglasses and looked away from the screen during the showing of a clip of the film, and stated that he "ha[dn't] even seen [the film] for a while" after being asked by host Robin Roberts about the plot.

Merry Gentleman filed this suit nearly four years later, on April 10, 2013, alleging that Keaton breached the directing services agreement in several respects throughout the parties' relationship and that those breaches delayed the film's release, increased costs, and harmed the film's prospects for commercial success. . . .

Keaton argues that the portions of the complaint concerning events occurring before December 14, 2007, the Release's effective date, fail to state a viable contract claim because the Release bars any claims arising from pre-Release conduct. Merry Gentleman anticipated this defense in the complaint, which alleges that the Release is invalid because it lacks consideration and also because it was the product of duress. The question here is whether the facts alleged by Merry Gentleman, with all inferences drawn in its favor, could show that the Release is invalid on either ground. Because the alleged facts make a viable case for duress, Merry Gentleman may proceed with its pre-Release claims.

Illinois law defines duress as "a condition where one is induced by a wrongful act or threat of another to make a contract under circumstances which deprive him of the exercise of his free will." Rissman v. Rissman,

213 F.3d 381, 386 (7th Cir. 2000). "Economic duress . . . is an affirmative defense to a contract," Bank of America v. 108 N. State Retail LLC, 928 N.E.2d 42, 57 (Ill. App. 2010), and exists where "the conduct of the party obtaining the advantage [is] shown to be tainted with some degree of fraud or wrongdoing," but not where "consent . . . is secured merely through hard bargaining positions or financial pressures." Krilich v. Am. Nat. Bank & Trust Co. of Chicago, 778 N.E.2d 1153, 1162 (Ill. App. 2002).

Merry Gentleman contends that Keaton's pre-Sundance conduct—his threat to effectively boycott the festival unless his second cut was shown left Merry Gentleman with no practical choice but to enter into the Release, which provided not only that Keaton's second cut would be shown, but also that Merry Gentleman would release any pre-Release breaches by Keaton. This lack of practical choice, Merry Gentleman maintains, constitutes the kind of duress that invalidates the Release. Keaton acknowledges Merry Gentleman's allegation that he breached the directing services agreement by directly approaching Sundance to "seize artistic control over the promotion of the film." However, he argues that "an alleged breach by Keaton of the Directing Agreement cannot constitute duress under Illinois law because [Merry Gentleman] made no effort to use the remedies afforded by the courts to address the alleged breach." Keaton's position, in other words, is that the Release cannot have been the product of duress because Merry Gentleman could have sued Keaton for his pre-Sundance conduct rather than enter into the Release.

It is true that duress ordinarily involves "some probable consequences of the threat for which the remedy for the breach afforded by the courts is inadequate." Kaplan v. Keith, 377 N.E.2d 279, 281 (Ill. App. 1978). That said, "a remote possibility of litigation as an alternative to settlement" does not "always scotch[ ] a claim of duress." Rissman, 213 F.3d at 386. The Seventh Circuit in *Rissman* described a hypothetical example of duress that strikes close to home for purposes of this case:

> Illinois . . . applies a functional approach under which opportunistic exploitation of options that contracts were designed to foreclose equals duress. The party that performs first incurs sunk costs, which the other may hold hostage by demanding greater compensation in exchange for its own performance. The movie star who sulks (in the hope of being offered more money) when production is 90% complete, and reshooting the picture without him would be exceedingly expensive, is behaving opportunistically.

Id. at 386–87. *Rissman* took note of an older Ninth Circuit case finding duress where, after a fishing vessel reached a remote location, the crew refused to work until they were promised double wages. Id. at 387 (citing Alaska Packers' Ass'n v. Domenico, 117 F. 99 (9th Cir. 1902)). The crew's conduct constituted duress, the Seventh Circuit explained, because "the remote location and lack of an alternate crew had enabled the sailors to behave opportunistically" and because "[n]o one would have thought that the owner's ability to file a lawsuit could have helped; the fishing season would be over before the case could be adjudicated, and the seamen might have been judgment-proof anyway." Id.

The facts alleged by Merry Gentleman would allow the conclusion that a pre-Sundance suit by Merry Gentleman against Keaton, while certainly a possibility, was not a feasible alternative under the circumstances. Keaton's threat to not appear at Sundance unless Merry Gentleman agreed to allow his second cut to shown—an agreement memorialized in the Release—could be found opportunistic within the meaning of the duress doctrine in light of Merry Gentleman's allegations, assumed true at this stage, that: (1) Keaton understood that "Sundance officials wished to have [him] present at the premiere (both because of his name recognition and because Sundance is known as a director's festival)"; (2) by the time Sundance selected the film, Merry Gentleman had already invested more than $4 million in the film's production; (3) "[h]aving a film selected to premiere at Sundance, particularly in the Eccles Theatre, is a highly coveted opportunity often leading to substantial commercial success"; and (4) there were only two months between Sundance's offer in November 2007 to show *The Merry Gentleman* and the scheduled premiere in January 2008. On this factual predicate, Keaton's actions could be found akin to the hypothetical actor's conduct in *Rissman* and the sailors' conduct in *Alaska Packers' Association.* Because Merry Gentleman was left with no practical choice but to relent to Keaton's demands, the Release could be found the product of duress and thus invalid under Illinois law. . . .

Smithwick v. Whitley

152 N.C. 369, 67 S.E. 913 (1910)

Plaintiff contracted in writing to purchase from defendant a tract of land containing not quite 14 acres, for $35 an acre, went into possession (without getting a deed) and began clearing it. Three years later defendant informed plaintiff that the deal was off. Shortly thereafter, plaintiff went to see defendant, who told him he could have the land for a price of $50 an acre. "After considerable talk," plaintiff paid the sum demanded "rather than lose the land," which he had worked for three years, ditching, fencing, and getting it into tillable condition. Defendant gave him a deed in return for the payment. In an action brought to recover the overpayment, *held*, a nonsuit ordered by the trial court was proper. The payment made to secure a deed was "voluntary." Duress exists only where the unlawful act of another has deprived one of free will. Plaintiff could have sued in equity for specific performance when defendant demanded a higher price. [Is there anything here suggesting that plaintiff would have been hard-pressed to make effective use of its legal remedies against breach, or that defendant knew that to be the case? Compare an illustration given by Rest.2d, Contracts § 175: "A, with whom B has left a machine for repairs, makes an improper threat to refuse to deliver the machine to B, although B has paid for the repairs, unless B agrees to make a contract to have additional repair work done. B can replevy the machine, but because he is in urgent need of it and delay would cause him heavy financial loss, he is induced by A's threat to make the contract. B has no reasonable alternative, A's threat amounts to duress, and the contract is voidable by B."]

Wolf v. Marlton Corp.

57 N.J.Super. 278, 154 A.2d 625 (1959)

The Wolfs, husband and wife, contracted to buy land in a subdivision that Marlton was developing and to pay $24,500 for a house to be built by Marlton on the land. Marlton's plan for developing the subdivision was to combine the sale of lots and the building of houses. The Wolfs made a down payment of $2,450. Another $2,450 was to be paid when their house was "closed in," but by that time marital difficulties led them to request a cancellation of their contract and repayment of the $2,450 they had paid. Marlton's agent proposed to return only $1,450; Mr. Wolf demanded $2,000. According to Marlton's agent, Wolf stated that unless this was agreed to he would go through with the purchase and then resell to "an undesirable purchaser," so that this "will be the last tract that you will ever build in New Jersey and it will be the last house that you will sell in this tract." Marlton eventually sold the house to another person. In an action by the Wolfs to recover their full $2,450 deposit, *held*, it was error for the trial court to hold Marlton in default for its refusal to go forward with the contract in face of this threat. There was no physical violence exerted or threatened by Wolf, but a distinction depending on the kind of pressure exerted carries little weight. "Duress is tested, not by the nature of the threats, but rather by the state of mind induced thereby in the victim." It is true that once plaintiffs bought the house they had a legal right to sell to whomever they wished, but "where a party for purely malicious and unconscionable motives threatens to sell such a home to a purchaser, specially selected because he would be undesirable, for the sole purpose of injuring the builder's business, fundamental fairness requires the conclusion that his conduct in making this threat be deemed 'wrongful' as the term is used in the law of duress." The case was remanded for the trial judge to determine whether the threat was made, whether Marlton's manager believed it would be carried out, and whether his will was thereby overborne.

NOTE: AN "IMPROPER" THREAT

The *Marlton* court said that the Wolfs had a "legal right" to sell to whomever they wished, yet, in the end, their conduct was deemed "wrongful." Statements to the effect that "it is not a breach of contract to threaten to do something you have a right to do" are seen often. In a contractor's suit to declare a settlement agreement null and void, Stewart M. Muller Constr. Co.

v. New York Tel. Co., 40 N.Y.2d 955, 390 N.Y.S.2d 817, 359 N.E.2d 328 (1976), the court said:

> The order of the Appellate Division should be affirmed. A contract may be voided on the ground of economic duress where the complaining party was compelled to agree to its terms by means of a wrongful threat which precluded the exercise of its free will. [Citing Austin Instrument v. Loral Corp.] Here, plaintiff alleged that the settlement agreement was induced by defendant's threat to terminate their earlier contract. The amended complaint and the affidavit in opposition to the motion to dismiss fail to allege that the defendant was not within its contractual rights in threatening to exercise the termination clause contained in the contract. Rather, it appears that the defendant, in the context of contractual dispute, preserved its rights by following the letter of the termination clause, while at the same time seeking an accommodation with the financially hard-pressed plaintiff. In view of the explicit provisions of the termination clause, which gave defendant the right to cancel the contract upon an architect's certificate of substantial breach, there is no possibility that the plaintiff could present evidence which would establish that the defendant's threatened cancellation was in excess of its contractual rights and, hence, was wrongful. The only reasonable inference that can be drawn from the complaint and the affidavits is that the plaintiff is unable to prevail.

Consider also the following passage from Dawson, Economic Duress—An Essay in Perspective, 45 Mich. L. Rev. 253, 283–288 (1947):

> If it can be assumed that the object of relief for duress is to cancel out advantages secured by superior bargaining power, the whole group of duress cases takes on a new perspective. The objective of ensuring the freedom of the individual will, so frequently proposed in the nineteenth century cases, becomes on this analysis an incidental or at most a subsidiary objective. More important, the concentration of the modern cases on the distinction between legal and illegal means seems misdirected, a survival from an earlier period in which duress doctrines were merely an adjunct of the law of crime and tort.
>
> It is indeed this concentration on distinctions between legal and illegal means which has chiefly arrested the modern development of the law of duress. No single formula has achieved so wide a circulation in the duress cases as the statement that "It is not duress to threaten to do what there is a legal right to do." Certainly no other formula is anything like so misleading. Its vice lies in the half-truth it contains. For an enormous range of conduct is included in the class of acts that there is a "right" to do (and therefore, under this formula, to threaten). At one extreme are various types of severe injury and oppression that narrowly escape the sanctions of the law of crime and tort. At the opposite extreme are the types of pressure that are specifically provided by organized legal agencies, for the very purpose for which they are used (e.g., the remedies of

> civil litigation). Somewhere between these extremes must be classed all those multiplied forms of economic pressure by which the exchange of goods and services is accomplished in an individualist society. Without doubt such forms of pressure are normally permissible, and it is the essence of economic individualism to subject their use to a minimum of external regulation. From this it by no means follows that the effects of pressure exerted in particular cases will always escape judicial scrutiny. Doctrines of duress are intended to raise precisely the question whether it is "rightful" to use particular types of pressure for the purpose of extracting an excessive or disproportionate return. Over the whole range of conduct to which this question applies, it is plain that the tests of the criminal law or a damage remedy can no longer determine the limits of relief for unjust enrichment. The insight of Holmes cut through to the central distinction: "When it comes to the collateral question of obtaining a contract by threats, it does not follow that, because you cannot be made to answer for the act, you may use the threat."

A typical case of duress in early law was a deed of land executed by a grantor to secure release from imprisonment or to forestall a threat of serious bodily harm. In the eighteenth century, the concept was extended to include the kind of economic duress that consisted of a wrongful seizure or detention of personal property. This extension began with Astley v. Reynolds, 2 Strange 915 (1732), which is cited and distinguished in Hackley v. Headley, infra p. 858. "Duress of goods" is now well established as a ground for rescission and restitution. Another type of relievable duress, developed in the nineteenth century, is the refusal of a public utility, endowed by law with a monopoly of a service (transportation, gas, electric power), to supply the service unless paid a sum exceeding the authorized rate. Both duress of goods and refusal of service by public utilities have the same feature that helped to open up remedies in cases of violence to the person: the conduct, actual or threatened, is independently wrongful by the law of tort. For a collection of the early American cases on duress by physical compulsion distinguished from duress by threat, see United States for Use of Trane Co. v. Bond, 322 Md. 170, 586 A.2d 734 (1991).

The Chancery had for some time given relief analogous to that provided by the law courts through the doctrine of duress. Undue influence, a notion developed originally in equity, involved not economic pressure but, as we have seen, personal ascendancy over individuals weakened by age, illness, or mental deficiency. The Chancery's solution was rescission of the transaction procured through undue influence, with restitution of any gains thereby secured. There was, and is, considerable overlap between undue influence and abuse of "confidential" relations, in which the securing of unfair advantages by one party from the other is often called "constructive fraud" (see Jackson v. Seymour, supra p. 529). With the fusion of law and equity, the barriers between common law duress and the various equity doctrines have been broken down. The ultimate result of this intermixture is still uncertain.

The legal system faces the challenge of policing misbehavior without at the same time thwarting contract renegotiations that are mutually beneficial and on which parties may subsequently rely. The material that follows examine some of the doctrines that have emerged. The first case begins with the legal duty rule, the idea that contract modifications need to be supported by consideration to be enforceable.

Levine v. Blumenthal

Supreme Court of New Jersey, 1936.
117 N.J. L. 23, 186 A. 457.

HEHER, J. By an indenture dated April 16th, 1931, plaintiff leased to defendants, for the retail merchandising of women's wearing apparel, store premises situate in the principal business district of the city of Paterson. The term was two years, to commence on May 1st next ensuing, with an option of renewal for the further period of three years; and the rent reserved was $2,100 for the first year, and $2,400 for the second year, payable in equal monthly installments in advance.

... [D]efendants adduced evidence tending to show that, in the month of April, 1932, before the expiration of the first year of the term, they advised plaintiff that "it was absolutely impossible for them to pay any increase in rent; that their business had so fallen down that they had great difficulty in meeting the present rent of $175 per month; that if the plaintiff insisted upon the increase called for in the lease, they would be forced to remove from the premises or perhaps go out of business altogether;" and that plaintiff "agreed to allow them to remain under the same rental 'until business improved.'" While conceding that defendants informed him that "they could not pay the increase called for in the lease because of adverse business conditions," plaintiff, on the other hand, testified that he "agreed to accept the payment of $175 each month, on account." For eleven months of the second year of the term rent was paid by defendants, and accepted by plaintiff, at the rate of $175 per month. The option of renewal was not exercised; and defendants surrendered the premises at the expiration of the term, leaving the last month's rent unpaid. This action was brought to recover the unpaid balance of the rent reserved by the lease for the second year—$25 per month for eleven months, and $200 for the last month.

The District Court found, as a fact, that "a subsequent oral agreement had been made to change and alter the terms of the written lease, with respect to the rent paid," but that it was not supported by "a lawful consideration," and therefore was wholly ineffective.

The insistence is that the current trade depression had disabled the lessees in respect of the payment of the full rent reserved, and a consideration sufficient to support the secondary agreement arose out of these special circumstances; and that, in any event, the execution of the substituted performance therein provided is a defense at law, notwithstanding the want of consideration. The principle invoked is applied in Long v. Hartwell, 34 N.J.L. 116. . . . It is said also that, "in so far as the oral agreement has become executed as to the payments which had fallen due and had been paid and accepted in full as per the oral agreement," the remission of the balance of the rent is sustainable on the theory of gift, if not of accord and satisfaction. . . .

It is not suggested that the primary contract under consideration was of a class which may not lawfully be modified by parol. . . . The point made by respondent is that the subsequent oral agreement to reduce the rent is *nudum pactum*, and therefore created no binding obligation.

It is elementary that the subsequent agreement, to impose the obligation of a contract, must rest upon a new and independent consideration. The rule was laid down in very early times that even though a part of a matured liquidated debt or demand has been given and received in full satisfaction thereof, the creditor may yet recover the remainder. The payment of a part was not regarded in law as a satisfaction of the whole, unless it was in virtue of an agreement supported by a consideration. Pinnel's Case, 5 Coke 117a; 77 Eng.Rep. 237; Fitch v. Sutton, 5 East. 230; Foakes v. Beer, 9 App.Cas. 605. . . . The principle is firmly imbedded in our jurisprudence that a promise to do what the promisor is already legally bound to do is an unreal consideration. . . . It has been criticized, at least in some of its special applications, as "mediaeval" and wholly artificial—one that operates to defeat the "reasonable bargains of business men." . . . But these strictures are not well grounded. They reject the basic principle that a consideration, to support a contract, consists either of a benefit to the promisor or a detriment to the promisee—a doctrine that has always been fundamental. . . . It is a principle, almost universally accepted, that an act or forbearance required by a legal duty owing to the promisor that is neither doubtful nor the subject of honest and reasonable dispute is not a sufficient consideration. . . .

Yet any consideration for the new undertaking, however insignificant, satisfies this rule. Coast Nat'l Bank v. Bloom, 113 N.J.L. 597, 174 A. 576. For instance, an undertaking to pay part of the debt before maturity, or at a place other than where the obligor was legally bound to pay, or to pay in property, regardless of its value, or to effect a composition with creditors by the payment of less than the sum due, has been held to constitute a consideration sufficient in law. The test is whether there is an additional consideration adequate to support an ordinary contract, and consists of something which the debtor was not legally bound to do or give. . . .

The cases to the contrary either create arbitrary exceptions to the rule, or profess to find a consideration in the form of a new undertaking which in essence was not a tangible new obligation or a duty not imposed by the lease, or, in any event, was not the price "bargained for as the exchange for the promise," and therefore do violence to the fundamental principle. They exhibit the modern tendency, especially in the matter of rent reductions, to depart from the strictness of the basic common law rule and give effect to what has been termed a "reasonable" modification of the primary contract. . . .

So tested, the secondary agreement at issue is not supported by a valid consideration; and it therefore created no legal obligation. General economic adversity, however disastrous it may be in its individual consequences, is never a warrant for judicial abrogation of this primary principle of the law of contracts.

It remains to consider the second contention that, in so far as the agreement has been executed by the payment and acceptance of rent at the reduced rate, the substituted performance stands, regardless of the want of consideration. This is likewise untenable. Ordinarily, the actual performance of that which one is legally bound to do stands on the same footing as his promise to do that which he is legally compellable to do. . . . This is a corollary of the basic principle. Of course, a different rule prevails where *bona fide* disputes have arisen respecting the relative rights and duties of the parties to a contract, or the debt or demand is unliquidated, or the contract is wholly executory on both sides. Anson on Contracts (Turck Ed.) 240, 241.

It is settled in this jurisdiction that, as in the case of other contracts, a consideration is essential to the validity of an accord and satisfaction. . . . Judgment affirmed, with costs.

McDevitt v. Stokes

174 Ky. 515, 192 S.W. 681 (1917)

Plaintiff's petition alleged that he, "a driver of great skill and experience," was employed by Shaw, owner of the mare Grace, to drive Grace in the Kentucky Futurity, one of the most noted races in the United States for trotting horses, that was to occur in 1910 in Lexington, Kentucky. The petition alleged that defendant Stokes owned a large stock farm near Lexington on which he bred horses, and that Stokes owned the sire, dam, and two brothers of Grace, so that her winning the race would entitle him to $300 from the purse for the race and would greatly increase the value of these four relatives of Grace. The petition then alleged that Stokes promised plaintiff $1,000 if he would drive Grace to victory in the Futurity, that plaintiff did so, and that Stokes had paid him only $200 and owed him an $800 balance, for which plaintiff sued. The court held that the defendant's demurrer was properly sustained. Plaintiff was already legally and morally bound by his contract with Shaw to perform the service called for by defendant's promise. To hold that he would not have won the race with Grace, if Stokes had not promised to pay him the $1,000, would be to say that he would have been recreant to his duty, an inference that the petition does not justify. Plaintiff incurred no detriment and the benefit to Stokes was purely incidental, one to which he was already entitled.

COMMENT: THE LEGAL-DUTY RULE

The view of the *Blumenthal* court was stated as long ago as 1602, when Coke reported a dictum (it was no more than this) in Pinnel's Case, 5 Coke Rep. 117a: "It was resolved by the whole court, that payment of a lesser sum on the day in satisfaction of a greater, cannot be satisfaction for the whole, because it appears to the judges that by no possibility, a lesser sum can be a satisfaction to the plaintiff for a greater sum: but the gift of a horse, hawk, robe, etc., in satisfaction is good. For it shall be intended that a horse, hawk, robe, etc., might be more beneficial to the plaintiff than the money, in respect of some circumstance, or otherwise the plaintiff would not have accepted it in satisfaction." But Coke, serving as a judge 12 years later, quoted himself—again in strong dicta—to precisely the opposite effect, and the King's Bench before that had found consideration in a benefit to the creditor in securing the payment without court action. Reynolds v. Pinhowe, Cro.Eliz., 429 (1595). The inability of the parties to discharge a money debt through part payment was not finally settled in England until the House of Lords decision in Foakes v. Beer, L.R. 9 A.C. 605 (1884). Altogether, then, although it was a distinct reversal of much earlier authority, during the nineteenth century it came to be widely accepted in this country that consideration doctrines preclude an effective accord and satisfaction through part payment of "matured and liquidated" money debts. The sweeping effect of this limitation on contract modifications is summarized in J. Dawson, Gifts and Promises 210 (1980):

> After the House of Lords had spoken in 1884, the generalization swept all before it and became an immutable principle of the common law, engraved on a tablet. Any performance that was already due under an existing obligation was erased—deleted—as a permissible subject of new agreement. . . . Thus, within the limits of the obligation their agreement had created, the parties had destroyed their own power to contract.

The legal-duty rule—often described as the doctrine of Foakes v. Beer—extends far beyond money debts for which part payment is made or promised. We shall see more of it in the materials ahead, including the problem of contract adjustments prompted by unexpected or changed circumstances. The court's account in Levine v. Blumenthal reflects standard solutions, both as to the effects of the rule where it does apply and as to the means by which it can be escaped. Prepayment, payment at a different place, or probably payment to a different person are variations from the preexisting duty that would alter the result. Payment in whole or in part with something other than money would do the same—e.g., if Levine had been willing to take a coat or a dress from Blumenthal's stock. And what if Blumenthal could show an "honest" dispute with Levine as to how much rent was due?

Section § 89 of the Restatement, Second, states:

> A promise modifying a duty under a contract not fully performed on either side is binding
>
> (a) if the modification is fair and equitable in view of circumstances not anticipated by the parties when the contract was made; or
>
> (b) to the extent provided by statute; or
>
> (c) to the extent that justice requires enforcement in view of material change of position in reliance on the promise.

How would *Blumenthal* come out if § 89 applied? One court embraced § 89 as "the proper rule" because it "not only prohibits modifications obtained by coercion, duress, or extortion but also fulfills society's expectation that agreements entered into voluntarily will be enforced." Angel v. Murray, 113 R.I. 482, 322 A.2d 630 (1974).

Statutes modifying the doctrine found in the principal case are fairly common, which is to say that the subject has generated a substantial history of legislative intervention. The most important development by far is § 2–209(1) of the UCC, which provides: "An agreement modifying a contract within this Article needs no consideration to be binding." While the Official Comment indicates that this sweeping language is intended to free all "necessary and desirable modifications" from the "technicalities which at present hamper" them, it goes on to declare that modifications must meet the test of good faith imposed by the Code. You should study the Comment for the guidance it provides on the meaning of "good faith" in this context.

Is there a parallel between the approaches taken in Restatement, Second § 89 and UCC 2–209(1)? In Roth Steel Products v. Sharon Steel Corp., 705 F.2d 134 (6th Cir. 1983), an often-cited decision applying 2–209(1) in a modification setting, it was observed that the Code's general obligation of "good faith" requires inquiries into (1) the parties' "subjective honesty" and (2) the "justification" for the decision to seek a modification. In applying these tests, will it matter if the reason for a party's requesting a modification rests in circumstances the party should have "anticipated" when the contract was made? Had the Code applied in *Levine* (a lease of real estate, not a sale of goods), is there much doubt about the outcome under § 2–209(1)?

As to "modifying" transactions outside the reach of the UCC, the statutory solutions vary somewhat. Some representative examples are provided below.

California Civil Code § 1524 (West 2007). "Part performance of an obligation, either before or after a breach thereof, when expressly accepted by the creditor in writing, in satisfaction, or rendered in pursuance of an agreement in writing for that purpose, though without any new consideration, extinguishes the obligation." [This provision is copied in Montana (Code Ann. § 28–1–1403 (2003)); North Dakota (Cent.Code § 9–13–07 (2005)); and South Dakota (Codified Laws Ann. § 20–7–4 (1995)).]

Michigan Comp. Laws § 566.1 (1996). "An agreement hereafter made to change or modify, or to discharge in whole or in part, any contract, obligation, or lease, or any mortgage or other security interest in personal or real property, shall not be invalid because of the absence of consideration: Provided, That the agreement changing, modifying, or discharging such contract, obligation, lease, mortgage or security interest shall not be valid or binding unless it shall be in writing and signed by the party against whom it is sought to enforce the change, modification, or discharge." [Written agreements for "receipts, releases and discharges" are effective without other consideration in Alabama (Code § 12–21–109 (1995)), and Tennessee (Code Ann. § 24–7–106 (2000)).]

Virginia Code Ann. § 11–12 (2001). "Part performance of an obligation, promise or undertaking, either before or after a breach thereof, when expressly accepted by the creditor in satisfaction and rendered in pursuance of an agreement for that purpose, though without any new consideration, shall extinguish such obligation, promise, or undertaking." [Does this differ significantly from the California provision quoted above? Substantially the same result as in Virginia is reached, with wide variations in language, in Georgia (Code Ann. § 13–4–103 (1982)), Maine (Rev. Stat. Ann. tit. 14 § 155 (2003)), and North Carolina (Gen. Stat. § 1–540 (2000)).]

Schwartzreich v. Bauman-Basch, Inc.

231 N.Y. 196, 131 N.E. 887 (1921)

In August 1917, Bauman-Basch and Schwartzreich signed a contract by which Bauman agreed to employ Schwartzreich, and he agreed to work full-time, as a designer of coats and wraps, at a salary of $90 a week for one year starting November 22, 1917. Schwartzreich testified that he told Bauman in October that he had received an offer of $110 a week from another firm, and said: "Will you advise me as a friendly matter what to do?" Schwartzreich stated that Bauman said nothing at the time but the next day came to him and said: "I will give you $100 a week and I want you to stay with me." Bauman's version of the conversation was that Schwartzreich said he wanted to leave, since he had been offered $115 a week, and that Bauman replied: "I cannot get a designer now, and, in view of the fact that I have to send my sample line out on the road, I will give you a hundred dollars a week rather than to let you go." On October 17, Bauman and Schwartzreich signed a new employment contract providing a wage of $100 a week. Schwartzreich surrendered to Bauman his copy of the original contract with the signatures torn off. Schwartzreich worked for Bauman-Basch until December, when he was discharged. *Held*, judgment for plaintiff Schwartzreich for damages affirmed. The parties to a contract can rescind it by mutual consent. They can then proceed to make a new contract in which their mutual promises are consideration for each other. "The same effect follows . . . from a new contract entered into at the same time the old one is destroyed and rescinded by mutual consent. . . . [T]he time of rescission, whether a moment before or at the same time as the making of the new contract, is unimportant. . . . There is no reason that we can see [why] both transactions [cannot] take place at the same time."

QUESTIONS

(1) The authorities leave no doubt that the *Schwartzreich* court correctly stated the premise from which it proceeded, that the parties to a bilateral contract neither has performed may rescind it by mutual agreement. Still, if consideration is required for the modification or discharge of a contract, how is it that the agreement to rescind is effective?

(2) The Restatement, Second, in comment accompanying § 89, approves the result in *Schwartzreich* but not the court's reasoning. Why can't two things the parties are perfectly free to do—rescind an old agreement and make a new one—"take place at the same time"?

One court has given this answer: "[W]here an alleged rescission is coupled with a simultaneous re-entry into a new contract and the terms of that new contract are more favorable to only one of the parties, doubt is created as to the mutuality of the agreement to rescind the original contract. . . . Moreover, this exception [to the new-consideration requirement] is based on circular logic because the validity of the new agreement depends upon the rescission while the rescission depends upon the new agreement." McCallum Highlands v. Washington Capital Dus, Inc., 66 F.3d 89 (5th Cir. 1995).

Universal Builders, Inc. v. Moon Motor Lodge, Inc.

Supreme Court of Pennsylvania, 1968.
430 Pa. 550, 244 A.2d 10.

EAGEN, J. This appeal is from a final decree of the [trial court] sitting in equity. Plaintiff asked the court to set aside a real estate conveyance as a violation of the Fraudulent Conveyance Act, 39 P.S. §§ 351–363, to declare void a supplemental agreement allegedly induced by fraud, and to grant plaintiff a money decree for work done under both the supplemental agreement and the basic contract as well as for loss of profits and punitive damages. Defendant denied that there was fraud involved in either the real estate conveyance or the supplemental agreement, denied that it owed plaintiff any sum under the basic contract and supplemental agreement, claimed a set-off for uncompleted work and counterclaimed for delay damages. The court below refused the request for a reconveyance under the Fraudulent Conveyance Act, refused to declare the supplemental agreement void, dismissed plaintiff's claims for lost profits and punitive damages, denied defendant a set-off for uncompleted work, dismissed the counterclaim for delay damages and decreed that defendant should pay plaintiff $127,759.54 (the balance due on the basic contract price together with extras) plus interest. Defendant appeals.

. . . On August 16, 1961, the plaintiff, Universal Builders, entered into a written contract with the defendant, Moon Motor Lodge, for the construction of a motel and restaurant in Allegheny County. The contract provides, inter alia, that all change orders must be in writing and signed by Moon and/or the Architect and that all requests for extension of time must be made in writing to the Architect. The contract specifications also required that a certain proportion of a re-inforcing substance be used in the building walls. The masonry sub-contractor failed to use the specified proportion. When this defect was discovered, Moon magnified its importance, withheld from Universal a progress payment to which [it] was entitled, threatened to expel Universal from the job and thereby induced Universal to enter into the supplemental agreement. The supplemental agreement, dated March 27, 1962, provides that Universal will pay Moon $5000 as damages for the absence of the re-inforcing material, that Universal will perform certain additional work at no additional cost to Moon, that the date for completion of the project is extended from April 1, 1962, to July 1, 1962, and that liquidated damages at a specified rate per day will be assessed for delay.

Universal substantially completed performance on September 1, 1962, and left the construction site on October 1. After filing this suit, Universal went into bankruptcy. The trustee prosecuted this action and won a final decree in the lower court. . . .

First Moon submits that the chancellor erred in not enforcing the contract provision that extras would not be paid for unless done pursuant to a written, signed change order.

Unless a contract is for the sale of goods, see the [UCC] § 2–209(3), as amended, 12A P.S. § 2–209(2), it appears undisputed that the contract can be modified orally although it provides that it can be modified only in writing. . . . Construction contracts typically provide that the builder will not be paid for extra work unless it is done pursuant to a written change order, yet courts frequently hold that owners must pay for extra work done at their oral direction. See generally Annot., 2 A.L.R.3d 620 (1965). This liability can be based on several theories. For example, the extra work may be said to have been done under an oral agreement separate from the written contract and not containing the requirement of a written authorization. 3A Corbin on Contracts, § 756 (1960). The requirement of a written authorization may also be considered a condition which has been waived. 5 Williston on Contracts § 689 (3d ed. 1961).

On either of the above theories, the chancellor correctly held Moon liable to pay for the extras in spite of the lack of written change orders. The evidence indicates that William Berger, the agent of Moon, requested many changes, was informed that they would involve extra cost, and promised to pay for them. In addition, Berger frequently was on the construction site and saw at least some of the extra work in progress. . . . [H]e was a keen observer with an extraordinary knowledge of the project in general and the contract requirements in particular. Thus it is not unreasonable to infer that he was aware that extra work was being done without proper authorization, yet he stood by without protesting while the extras were incorporated into the project. Under these circumstances there also was an implied promise to pay for the extras.

C.I.T. Corp. v. Jonnet, 419 Pa. 435, 214 A.2d 620 (1965), does suggest that such non-written modifications are ineffective unless the contract provision requiring modifications to be in writing was first waived. That case, however, is misleading. Although it involved a contract for the sale of movable bar and restaurant equipment, which is a contract for the sale of "goods" controlled by the [UCC], it overlooks that legislation, in particular § 2–209, which provides:

> ["(1) An agreement modifying a contract within this Article needs no consideration to be binding.]
>
> "(2) A signed agreement which excludes modification or rescission except by a signed writing cannot be otherwise modified or rescinded but except as between merchants such a requirement on a form supplied by the merchant must be separately signed by the other party.
>
> "(3) The requirement of the Statute of Frauds section of this Article (Section 2–201) must be satisfied if the contract as modified is within its provisions.
>
> "(4) Although an attempt at modification or rescission does not satisfy the requirements of subsection (2) or (3) it can operate as a waiver.
>
> "(5) A party who has made a waiver affecting an executory portion of the contract may retract the waiver by reasonable notification received by the other party that strict performance will be required of any term waived, unless the retraction would be unjust in view of a material change of position in reliance on the waiver."

From subsection (5) it can be inferred that a provision in a contract for [goods] that the contract can be modified only in writing is waived, just as such a provision in a construction contract is waived, under the circumstances described by Restatement of Contracts § 224 (1932), which provides:

"The performance of a condition qualifying a promise in a contract within the Statute [of Frauds or in a contract containing a provision requiring modifications to be in writing (§ 407)] may be excused by an oral agreement or permission of the promisor that the condition need not be performed, if the agreement or permission is given while the performance of the condition is possible, and in reliance on the agreement or permission, while it is unrevoked, the promisee materially changes his position."

Obviously a condition is considered waived when its enforcement would result in something approaching fraud. 5 Williston on Contracts § 689 (3d ed. 1961). Thus the effectiveness of a non-written modification in spite of a contract condition that modifications must be written depends upon whether enforcement of the condition is or is not barred by equitable considerations, not upon the technicality of whether the condition was or was not expressly and separately waived before the non-written modification.

In view of these equitable considerations underlying waiver, it should be obvious that when an owner requests a builder to do extra work, promises to pay for it and watches it performed knowing that it is not authorized in writing, he cannot refuse to pay on the ground that there was no written change order. Focht v. Rosenbaum, 176 Pa. 14, 34 A. 1001 (1876). When Moon directed Universal to "go ahead" and promised to pay for the extras, performance of the condition requiring change orders to be in writing was excused by implication. It would be manifestly unjust to allow Moon, which misled Universal into doing extra work without a written authorization, to benefit from nonperformance of that condition. . . . [T]here was sufficient evidence to establish the amount of Universal's claim for extras and that there was not sufficient evidence to establish Moon's set-off claim for uncompleted work. The decree of the lower court therefore was correct, except insofar as it failed to allow Moon's counterclaim for delay damages, as before indicated, for the period from July 1, 1962, to September 1, 1962.

3A A. Corbin, Contracts

§ 753 (1960)

"[W]e have seen that a promise can become enforceable by reason of other factors than a bargained-for exchange. . . . We need not be surprised, therefore, to find that a promisor can sometimes turn his conditional duty into an unconditional one by a 'waiver' of the condition, without any consideration therefor. . . . A condition of a promisor's duty can be eliminated by a mere voluntary expression of his willingness to waive it, if its performance does not constitute a material part of the agreed equivalent of the promise and its nonperformance does not materially affect the value received by the promisor. . . .

"In order to illustrate the kind of condition that [cannot] be voluntarily waived, let us suppose the following case: A contracts to erect a building for B, and the latter promises to pay $10,000 therefor after completion. . . . [The] completion of the building, substantially according to plans and specifications, is by construction of law a condition of B's duty to pay the price. Suppose that B should, without consideration, agree to waive this condition and to pay $10,000 to A without getting any building whatever. It is believed that no court would enforce this promise of B to pay $10,000 for nothing. A promise to make a gift of $10,000 would not be enforced, if no antecedent building contract had been made. One can not 'waive' himself into a duty to make a gift of the money. And the fact that a building contract had formerly been made is not a good reason for reaching a different result, when the waiver eliminates the building and causes the new promise to be, in substantial part at least, the promise of a gift." [As Corbin noted many times (e.g., 3A A. Corbin § 752), "if the question is asked whether a 'waiver' can be legally effective if it is not accompanied by a 'consideration,' it cannot be answered without knowing what it is that is being 'waived' and what is the mode in which the 'waiver' is being attempted."]

Nassau Trust Co. v. Montrose Concrete Prod. Corp.

56 N.Y.2d 175, 451 N.Y.S.2d 663, 436 N.E.2d 1265 (1982)

"The [court below] erred in failing to distinguish between an oral agreement that purports to modify the terms of a prior written agreement and an oral waiver by one party to a written agreement of a right to require of the other party certain performance in compliance with that agreement. . . . Modification of the terms of a [contract] requires consideration except when a statute . . . dispenses with the need for consideration when a writing [exists]. Neither waiver [nor estoppel] rests upon consideration or agreement. A modification, because it is an agreement based upon consideration, is binding according to its terms and may only be withdrawn by agreement. . . . While estoppel requires detriment to the party claiming to have been misled, waiver requires no more than the voluntary and intentional abandonment of a known right which, but for the waiver, would have been enforceable. . . . A waiver, to the extent that it has been executed, cannot be expunged or recalled[,] . . . but, not being a binding agreement, can, to the extent that it is executory, be withdrawn, provided the party whose performance has been waived is given notice of withdrawal and a reasonable time after notice within which to perform[.]"

Cole Taylor Bank v. Truck Ins. Exch.

51 F.3d 736 (7th Cir. 1995)

"Unlike modification of a contract, the efficacy of a waiver of a contractual right is generally not thought to require special tokens of reliability, such as a writing, consideration, reliance, judicial screening, or a heightened standard of proof. . . . What is more, a waiver of contractual rights can be implied as well as express—implied from words or actions inconsistent with the assertion of those rights. . . . Yet all that waiver means, when it is carefully defined, is the intentional relinquishment of a right. . . . [T]he courts have not been indifferent to the danger of [one party's] self-serving testimony that the other party to the contract waived a right that the contract had conferred on him. In some cases they have required proof of reliance on the alleged waiver, in effect converting the doctrine of waiver into the harder-to-prove doctrine of estoppel. . . . [Other courts] require[ ] that an alleged waiver either have induced reliance or that it be *clearly* inferable from the circumstances. . . . The fact that the courts have not converged on a blanket general requirement of reliance, consideration, a writing, a heightened standard of proof, or other means of assuring the reliability of questionable evidence may reflect the inherent implausibility of offers to prove 'bare' waiver in a contractual setting. Unless the right waived is a minor one . . ., why would someone give it up in exchange for nothing? If something is given in return, there is consideration."

Quigley v. Wilson

474 N.W.2d 277 (Iowa Ct.App. 1991)

In 1980, Quigley sold his farm "on contract" to the Wilsons, husband and wife, who made the annual installment payment of $7,000 plus interest until 1985, when they assigned the contract to Hatfield. Sometime prior to February 1986, Hatfield returned the farm to the Wilsons, informing them that he could not make the payments. The Wilsons then met with Quigley, telling him that they, too, were unable to make the yearly payments, another of which was due March 1. After negotiations, Quigley agreed to change a number of the contract's original terms, including a reduction of the price from $210,000 to $120,500 and the annual payments from $7,000 to $1,562, plus interest. These changes were written up in a new contract prepared by Quigley's lawyer and signed by Quigley and the Wilsons on March 7, 1986. The Wilsons thereafter made all payments due under the 1986 contract. In 1988, Quigley who had been in a nursing home since 1985, established a voluntary conservatorship appointing his two children as "co-conservators" for him. The co-conservators then filed suit against the Wilsons seeking a declaratory judgment that they were in default under the 1980 contract, because the 1986 contract was unenforceable for lack of consideration, Quigley's lack of mental competency, fraud, and undue influence. The trial court found for the Wilsons on all plaintiffs' claims (some of which were tried separately before a jury) and ruled the 1986 contract enforceable. This judgment was affirmed on appeal.

The trial judge had stated that the 1986 contract "appeared to constitute a waiver" within the meaning of an earlier Iowa case, In re Guardianship of Collins, 327 N.W.2d 230 (Iowa 1982). In *Collins*, the seller under a land contract, despite advice not to alter the bargain, agreed to eliminate the interest requirement altogether and to reduce the period of the buyer's payments from 24 to 12 years. A conservator of the seller, appointed after execution of the new agreement, sued to declare that agreement unenforceable for lack of consideration (mental incompetence was also alleged, but not proved). The Iowa Supreme Court found the agreement to be a "valid waiver," saying: "[W]e have long held that contract rights can be waived. . . . The essential elements [of a waiver] are the existence of a right, actual or constructive knowledge of it, and an intention to give it up. No consideration is required. Nor is prejudice necessary."

After quoting this language from *Collins*, the *Quigley* appellate court said: "The distinguishing factor [in *Collins* is that] the vendor simply made a unilateral decision to waive her right to interest so each payment made by the buyer went entirely toward principal, whereas Quigley and the Wilsons renegotiated a new price and payment schedule. . . . [I]t could be said that Quigley waived the $89,500 difference between the original price of $210,000 and the amended price of $120,500. However, it is difficult to describe the changing of a payment schedule providing for annual payments of $7,000 plus interest to one providing for annual payments of $1,562 plus interest, along with the changing of the due date for a balloon payment from March 1, 1988, to March 1, 1996, as simply a waiver of payments. Additionally, the amendment provides for changes in the insurance requirements and allows for sale of the mobile home on the property.

"These changes constitute more than the seller abandoning a contractual right arising from a contract. They create new and different obligations to be performed by the buyer. We therefore limit waiver to situations where a party to a contract abandons a right that party has under a contract. We categorize situations where contracting parties incur different duties and obligations from those in their original contract as modifications.

"Therefore, we do not find [a waiver here], but rather a modification which normally require[s] consideration. . . . We [further] find [this] case an appropriate circumstance for the adoption of the Restatement's position [on modifications resting on circumstances not anticipated, § 89]. The unanticipated circumstances were the drastic decrease in the value of the land[1] coupled with the seller's concern about tax repercussions from reacquiring the land and the fact the Wilsons had not received any income from the farm for the previous year. Additionally, the new agreement followed negotiations lasting over a period of time, the document was written by the seller's attorney, the trial court found the reduced price was roughly the fair market value of the property at the time the re-negotiations occurred, and the buyers had already paid $58,000 toward principal on the original contract and the balance of the new contract price was $62,500. Additionally, we find it significant that the jury found Quigley was competent when he entered the 1986 agreement and the trial court found no undue influence or fraudulent misrepresentation involved in the agreement. These factors lead us to find this is a situation where it is appropriate to find the modification fair and equitable and does not require proof of additional consideration." [This decision was affirmed per curiam by the Iowa Supreme Court, 474 N.W.2d 277 (1991).]

NOTE: FINALIZING CONTRACT DISPUTES

Sometimes an agreement to modify a contract is made midstream, at a time when neither party has done what the bargain requires. At other times, trouble arises only after the party who was required to perform first—typically a provider of services or goods—has completed performance. The "trouble" usually takes the form of disagreement over the amount the "paying party" owes the "performing party." Such disputes more often than not end in a settlement agreement. The question now before us is what happens when the settlement is challenged or otherwise becomes derailed. Again, a settlement agreement, like a modifying agreement, is itself a contract, subject to the ordinary contract defenses.

---

1 [There occurred a dramatic fall in the market value of midwestern farm land during the first half of the 1980s, 40 to 50 percent in some places.—Eds.]

Hackley v. Headley

Supreme Court of Michigan, 1881.
45 Mich. 569, 8 N.W. 511.

COOLEY, J. Headley sued Hackley & McGordon to recover compensation for cutting, hauling and delivering in the Muskegon River a quantity of logs. . . . The contract was in writing, and date[d] August 20, 1874. Headley agreed thereby to cut on specified lands and deliver in the Muskegon river the next spring 8,000,000 feet of logs[,] [which] were to be measured or scaled by a competent person to be selected by Hackley & McGordon, "and in accordance with the standard rules or scales in general use on Muskegon lake and river," and the expense of scaling was to be mutually borne by the parties.

[Two issues were in dispute. One related to the food supplied the scaler. The court rejected evidence offered by Hackley that it was the custom "on the Muskegon river" for jobbers like Headley to assume the whole cost of maintaining scalers, concluding that the scaler's board was to be shared equally by the parties. The other dispute related to the scale that would be used to measure logs. The "Scribner rule" was the scale generally used at the time the contract was made, but by the time the logs were cut and delivered the scale in general use was the "Doyle scale," by which the amount Headley would be entitled to would be reduced by some $2,000. The court concluded that the scale contemplated must have been that in common use when the scaling was done, because the scalers would be third parties whom they would expect to use whatever scale was standard at that time.]

The question of duress[,] in obtaining the discharge, remains. The paper [the defendants claim was given in settlement] reads as follows:

> Muskegon, Mich., August 3, 1875.
>
> Received from Hackley & McGordon their note for four thousand dollars, payable in thirty days, at First National Bank, Grand Rapids, which is in full for all claims of every kind and nature which I have against said Hackley & McGordon.
>
> Witness: Thomas Hume.
> John Headley.

Headley's account of the circumstances under which this receipt was given is [this:] On August 3, 1875, he went to Muskegon . . . from his home in Kent county, for the purpose of collecting the balance which he claimed was due him under the contract. The amount he claimed was upwards of $6200, estimating the logs by the Scribner scale. He had an interview with Hackley in the morning, who insisted that the estimate should be according to the Doyle scale, and who also claimed that he had made payments to others amounting to some $1400 which Headley should allow. Headley did not admit these payments, and denied his liability for them if they had been made. Hackley told Headley to come in again in the afternoon, and when he did so Hackley said to him: "My figures show there is 4260 and odd dollars in round numbers your due, and I will give you $4000. I will give you our note for $4000." To this Headley replied: "I cannot take that: it is not right, and you know it. There is over $2000 besides that belongs to me, and you know it." Hackley replied: "That is the best I will do with you." Headley said: "I cannot take that, Mr. Hackley," and Hackley replied, "You do the next best thing you are a mind to. You can sue me if you please." Headley then said: "I cannot afford to sue you, because I have got to have the money, and I cannot wait for it. If I fail to get the money today, I shall probably be ruined financially, because I have made no other arrangements to get the money only on this particular matter." Finally he took the note and gave the receipt, because at the time he could do nothing better, and in the belief that he would be financially ruined unless he had immediately the money that was offered him, or paper by means of which the money might be obtained.

If this statement is correct, the defendants not only took a most unjust advantage of Headley, but they obtained a receipt which, to the extent that it assumed to discharge anything not honestly in dispute between the parties, and known by them to be owing to Headley beyond the sum received, was without consideration and ineffectual. But was it a receipt obtained by duress? That is the question. . . . The circuit judge was of opinion that if the jury believed the statement of Headley they would be justified in finding that duress existed. . . .

Duress exists when one by the unlawful act of another is induced to make a contract or perform some act under circumstances which deprive him of the exercise of free will. It is commonly said to be of either the person or the goods of the party. . . . It is not pretended that duress of the person existed in this case; it is if anything duress of goods, or at least of that nature, and properly enough classed with duress of goods. Duress of goods may exist when one is compelled to submit to an illegal exaction in order to obtain them from one who has them in possession but refuses to surrender them unless the exaction is submitted to.

The leading case involving duress of goods is Astley v. Reynolds, 2 Strange, 915. The plaintiff had pledged goods for £20, and when he offered to redeem them, the pawnbroker refused to surrender them unless he was paid £10 for interest. The plaintiff submitted to the exaction, but was held entitled to recover back all that had been unlawfully demanded and taken. This, say the court, "is a payment by compulsion: the plaintiff might have such an immediate want of his goods that an action of trover would not do his business. . . ." The principle of this case was approved [in] Ashmole v. Wainwright, 2 Q.B. 837[,] [which] was a suit to recover back excessive charges paid to common carriers who refused until payment was made to deliver the goods for the carriage of which the charges were made. There has never been any doubt but recovery could be had under such circumstances. Harmony v. Bingham, 12 N.Y. 99. . . . So if illegal tolls are demanded, for passing a raft of lumber, and the owner pays them to liberate his raft, he may recover back what he pays. Chase v. Dwinal, 7 Me. 134. . . .

But where the party threatens nothing which he has not a legal right to perform, there is no duress. . . . When therefore a judgment creditor threatens to levy his execution on the debtor's goods, and under fear of the levy the debtor executes and delivers a note for the amount, with sureties, the note cannot be avoided for duress. Wilcox v. Howland, 23 Pick. 167. . . .

In what did the alleged duress consist in the present case? Merely in this: that the debtors refused to pay on demand a debt already due, though the plaintiff was in great need of the money and might be financially ruined in case he failed to obtain it. It is not pretended that Hackley & McGordon had done anything to bring Headley to the condition which made this money so important to him at this very time, or that they were in any manner responsible for his pecuniary embarrassment. . . . The duress, then, is to be found exclusively in their failure to meet promptly their pecuniary obligation. But this, according to the plaintiff's claim, would have constituted no duress whatever if he had not happened to be in pecuniary straits; and the validity of negotiations, according to this claim, must be determined, not by the defendants' conduct, but by the plaintiff's necessities. The same contract which would be valid if made with a man easy in his circumstances, becomes invalid when the contracting party is pressed with the necessity of immediately meeting his bank paper. But this would be a most dangerous, as well as a most unequal doctrine; and if accepted, no one could well know when he would be safe in dealing on the ordinary terms of negotiation with a party who professed to be in great need. . . .

These views render a reversal of the judgment necessary, and the case will be remanded for a new trial. . . .

[Headley prevailed before a jury in the new trial following remand, and the case was again taken to the Supreme Court of Michigan. This time Headley did not urge duress, but "took the ground that [the payment of the $4,000 and the giving of the receipt] operated to prove that there was no [binding] compromise at all," because defendant "well knew his firm was indebted in a much larger sum and acted in bad faith and set up claims which he knew were unfounded," all of which resulted in the giving of a receipt which was "without valid consideration." The court agreed, saying: "[W]hen one of the parties to a transaction sets it up against the other as an effective compromise, the latter may hinder it from operating in that sense and with that force by showing that his opponent acted unfairly or oppressively and asserted claims which he knew to be void of right with the design of getting the terms which were nominally assented to." 50 Mich. 43, 14 N.W. 693 (1883).]

Capps v. Georgia Pacific Corp.

253 Or. 248, 453 P.2d 935 (1969)

The complaint alleged that, with defendant's approval, plaintiff had searched for and found a lessee of industrial property owned by defendant, that defendant signed with this lessee a 20-year lease of the property for a total rent of $3,040,000, and that defendant therefore owed plaintiff a commission of five percent of this sum, plus one-half of one month's rent, or a total commission of $157,000, but that defendant had paid him only $5,000, leaving a balance owed of $152,000. Defendant filed a general denial and, as an affirmative defense, submitted to the court a release given by plaintiff in return for the $5,000 payment. Plaintiff's reply alleged that, when he had requested payment of his commission, defendant knew that because of his adverse financial situation plaintiff was in danger of losing his home immediately by mortgage foreclosure, and of losing other personal property by repossession, and that defendant also knew that plaintiff had no other source of funds. Plaintiff further alleged that defendant's agent informed him that, even though he was entitled to the sums he demanded, he would receive nothing unless he signed the release, since defendant had "extensive resources and powerful and brilliant attorneys," who could and would prevent him from recovering more in any later legal proceeding. Plaintiff then alleged that he was deprived of the free exercise of his will and was forced to sign a release of his valid claim for $157,000 for "the grossly inadequate sum" of $5,000. Defendant's demurrer to this reply was sustained by the court.

Held, reversed. Defendant's answer setting up the signed release was defective for failing to allege that the claim released was "either unliquidated or otherwise in dispute." As to duress, in early decisions, of which Hackley v. Headley was a leading example, dire financial circumstances, of which the other party took advantage, were held to provide no basis for a finding of duress. More recent cases, though often conflicting, seem to take a different view. "[W]e conclude that the better rule is one which allows the statement of a duress cause or defense such as plaintiff has pleaded here to be tried on its facts."

Denecke, J., concurred only in the result. Though conceding that "[t]his seems to be as strong a case [for] economic duress as can be made," he nevertheless urged that it would be "judicially unwise" to hold these allegations to constitute duress. "[A] substantial number of business transactions today have these same basic ingredients." A majority of the business community, while not approving such conduct, do not believe it to be enough to avoid an otherwise binding legal obligation, especially because the party asserting duress "will usually be an unfortunate and unsuccessful party opposing a fortunate and successful party." This could "cause the trier of fact to find the facts to fit the result." Other grounds for relief are available and more desirable. On these facts, it would be much better to rest the result on the recognized doctrine that a release given for payment of a sum less than the amount acknowledged to be owing fails for a "lack of consideration."

NOTE: IDENTIFYING DURESS

Duress can take many forms, ranging from old-fashioned violence to the person to threats of criminal prosecution or a simple lawsuit for damages. The question raised by Hackley v. Headley (and by Capps v. Georgia Pacific Corp.) is whether the withholding of a performance due under an existing contract can constitute duress where the opposite party is in need, and is known to be in need, of the performance. If one simply were to tabulate the decisions involving a withheld performance on one side and the pressure of circumstances—usually financial—on the other, it is quite probable that the views expressed in Hackley v. Headley still would be found to represent the prevailing view. Financial difficulty by itself will not justify setting aside a settlement. What is it about standard tests of duress that produce such results? One court has said: "The adverse effect on the finality of settlements and hence on the willingness of parties to settle their contract disputes without litigation would be great if the cash needs of one party were alone enough to entitle him to a trial on the validity of the settlement." Selmer Co. v. Blakeslee-Midwest Co., 704 F.2d 924 (7th Cir. 1983).

NOTE: LEGAL DUTY APART FROM CONTRACT

On occasion, a promise of compensation is made to a public official, who, by virtue of the position held, already owes a duty to the general public (and thus the promisor) to perform the acts or services that are the reason for the promise. It is agreed everywhere that a bargain by a public official to obtain additional benefits for performing regular duties is unenforceable as against public policy. Still, the scope of a legal duty that is noncontractual in origin may be uncertain (consider the "legal" duties of public utilities, fiduciaries, spouses, or citizens generally). Is the legal duty in fact owed to the promisor? If it is not, performance of the duty is presumably consideration for a promise, even though concerns about public policy remain.

Denney v. Reppert

Court of Appeals of Kentucky, 1968.
432 S.W.2d 647.

MYRE, SPECIAL COMMISSIONER. The question [is] which of several claimants is entitled to an award for information leading to the apprehension and conviction of certain bank robbers. Since the learned judge of the Pulaski Circuit Court correctly set out the facts and the law[,] we are affirming the judgment entered in accordance thereto and are adopting, in substance, the written opinion of the circuit judge as the opinion of this court.

On June 12th or 13th, 1963, three armed men entered the First State Bank, Eubank, Kentucky, and with a display of arms and threats robbed the bank of over $30,000. Later in the day they were apprehended by State Policemen Garret Godby, Johnny Simms and Tilford Reppert, placed under arrest, and the entire loot was recovered. Later all of the prisoners were convicted and Garret Godby, Johnny Simms and Tilford Reppert appeared as witnesses at the trial.

The First State Bank of Eubank was a member of the Kentucky Bankers Ass'n which provided and advertised a reward of $500 for the arrest and conviction of each bank robber. Hence the outstanding reward for the three bank robbers was $1,500. Many became claimants for the reward and the Kentucky State Bankers Ass'n being unable to determine the merits of the claims asked the circuit court to determine . . . who was entitled to receive the reward or share in it. All of the claimants were made defendants in the action.

At the time of the robbery the claimants Murrell Denney, Joyce Buis, Rebecca McCollum and Jewell Snyder were employees of the First State Bank and came out of the grueling situation with great credit and glory. Each one of them deserves approbation and an accolade. They were vigilant in disclosing to the public and the peace officers the details of the crime, and in describing the culprits, and giving all the information that they possessed that would be useful in capturing the robbers. Undoubtedly, they performed a great service. . . .

The first question [is] whether the employees of the robbed bank are eligible to receive or share in the reward? The great weight of authority answers in the negative. In re Waggoner, 47 S.D. 401, 199 N.W. 244 (1924) states the rule thusly: "To the general rule that, when a reward is offered to the general public for the performance of some specified act, such reward may be claimed by any person who performs such act, is the exception of agents, employes and public officials who are acting within the scope of their employment or official duties." . . .

In Stacy v. State Bank of Ill., 4 Scam., Ill., 91 (1842), it was held that a director of a bank was not entitled to share in the reward offered by the bank for the arrest of a robber because it was his duty as a director to further the best interests of the bank, and apprehending one who had robbed the bank was in the best interest of the bank. . . .

At the time of the robbery the claimants Murrell Denney, Joyce Buis, Rebecca McCollum, and Jewell Snyder were employees of the First State Bank. They were under duty to protect and conserve the resources and moneys of the bank, and safeguard every interest of the institution furnishing them employment. Each of these employees exhibited great courage, and cool bravery, in a time of stress and danger. The community and the county have recompensed them in commendation, admiration and high praise, and the world looks on them as heroes. But in making known the robbery and assisting in acquainting the public and the officers with details of the crime and with identification of the robbers, they performed a duty to the bank and the public, for which they cannot claim a reward.

The claims of Corbin Reynolds, Julia Reynolds, Alvie Reynolds and Gene Reynolds also must fail. . . . [T]hey gave valuable information to the arresting officers[,] [but] they did not follow the procedure as set forth in the offer of reward in that they never filed a claim with the Kentucky Bankers Ass'n. . . . A claimant of a reward must comply with the terms and conditions of the offer of reward. Miles v. Booth, 287 Ky. 246, 152 S.W.2d 577 (1941).

State Policemen Garret Godby, Johnny Simms and Tilford Reppert made the arrest of the bank robbers and captured the stolen money. All participated in the prosecution. At the time of the arrest, it was the duty of the state policemen to apprehend the criminals. Under the law they cannot claim or share in the reward and they are interposing no claim to it.

This leaves the defendant, Tilford Reppert the sole eligible claimant. The record shows that at the time of the arrest he was a deputy sheriff in Rockcastle County, but the arrest and recovery of the stolen money took place in Pulaski County. He was out of his jurisdiction, and was thus under no legal duty to make the arrest, and is thus eligible to claim and receive the reward. In Kentucky Bankers Ass'n v. Cassady, 264 Ky. 351, 94 S.W.2d 622, it was said: "It is . . . well established that a public officer within the authority of the law to make an arrest may accept an offer of reward or compensation for acts or services performed outside of his bailiwick or not within the scope of his official duties."

The claimant Tilford Reppert was present with Garret Godby and Johnny Simms at the time of the arrest and all cooperated in its consummation. The claimant Tilford Reppert personally recovered the stolen money. He recovered $2,000 more than the bank records show was stolen. This record does not reveal what became of the $2,000 excess.

It is manifest from the record that Tilford Reppert is the only claimant qualified and eligible to receive the reward. . . . [H]e is entitled to receive payment of the $1,500 reward now deposited with the Clerk of this Court.

The judgment is affirmed.

Board of Comm'rs of Montgomery County v. Johnson

126 Kan. 36, 266 P. 749 (1928)

Everett Bible killed a man in Kansas and fled the state, a fugitive from justice. Montgomery County, Kansas, and the State of Kansas had offered rewards for the arrest of Bible, totaling $500. Four months later, Bible drove up to a diner operated by Johnson in Tulsa, Oklahoma, purchased lunch, and drove away without paying for it. Johnson armed himself, chased and caught up with Bible, who shot at Johnson; Johnson returned the fire; they clinched, scuffled, and fell to the ground. Both had hold of Johnson's gun; Bible, partly on top of Johnson, was trying to bend Johnson's arm around so that when the gun discharged it would shoot Johnson. At that point, Crabaugh and Hamilton, constables in the district, and Hopkins, a special deputy sheriff, drove up, separated, and arrested the two wrestlers. If they had not intervened, Johnson would probably have been killed or severely injured. The $500 reward was paid into court to await the outcome of a suit brought to determine who was entitled to the rewards. The lower court concluded that all four claimants, Johnson and the three officers, were entitled, each to receive one-fourth. *Held*, affirmed. There was no law in Oklahoma requiring constables or deputy sheriffs to arrest fugitives from justice from other states. (The court did not comment on Johnson's assertion that, at the time of the arrest, the officers did not know Bible was a fugitive.) Johnson tackled Bible first, but if the other three had not intervened his arrest would not have occurred.

In re Estate of Lord

93 N.M. 543, 602 P.2d 1030 (1979)

In 1974, the decedent, a widow then 64 and suffering from cancer, lived alone on a ranch. According to Lord, a claimant against her estate, in October 1974 the decedent entered into an oral agreement with Lord whereby she agreed to devise to him her entire estate, if he would agree to marry her and to "be a loyal, faithful husband" and "take care of her like a husband would" until her death. Lord and the decedent were married on November 21, 1974. The following day, the decedent executed a will devising $10,000 to Lord and the bulk of her estate to her sister, Hughes, the plaintiff. Lord contends that he fulfilled his part of the oral agreement by caring for decedent until her death in 1977. Plaintiff Hughes sought formal probate of decedent's will; Lord urged specific performance of the oral agreement. *Held*, the oral agreement is void as against public policy; there was no error in excluding all evidence of it. This court adheres to the view that "a contract whereby one spouse agrees to pay the other spouse for his or her care, which is part of the other's duties as a spouse, is against public policy and void." It is the state's policy "to protect the marriage institution" by "not encourag[ing] spouses to marry for money." Lord's contention that this agreement is distinguishable because of "extraordinary services, far beyond the normal duties any spouse owes to the other," is unconvincing. There is nothing exceptional or extraordinary about one spouse utilizing his or her particular skills or aptitudes to assist the other spouse in times of trouble. (No mention was made of lack of consideration.)

[A year later, the New Mexico court found no breach of a reconciliation contract when a husband failed to keep promises—"to refrain from infidelity, be a faithful and providing husband, and to submit to counselling"—given in return for his wife's promise to forbear prosecution of a divorce action she had commenced. The court said: "[A] promise to do what a party is already obligated by contract or law to do is not consideration for a promise made in return. . . . [Here,] appellee promised to do no more than what he was already obligated to do as a husband. There was no mutuality of contract and therefore no breach. Further, we [have] previously held that nuptial contracts which attempt to alter the legal relations of the parties [are] 'void for want of consideration, or against public policy.' . . . It is the policy of this State to foster and protect the marital institution. See In re Estate of Lord, 93 N.M. at 544, 602 P.2d at 1031." Hurley v. Hurley, 94 N.M. 641, 615 P.2d 256 (1980).]

SECTION 3. SCRUTINY OF LIMITED COMMITMENT

INTRODUCTORY NOTE

In a number of environments—franchising and employment among the most conspicuous—the parties enjoy a long-term relationship and often plan on it continuing, even though the duration of the contract itself may be unspecified, even quite limited. For example, in the employment setting the background common-law rule in this country is a contract at will: In the absence of agreement to the contrary, the employer or the worker can end the relationship unilaterally—for any reason or no reason at all. In recent decades, however, we have seen legislative (and sometimes judicial) interventions into the employment relationship as well as others in which the parties have long-term relationships but only limited legal commitments to each other. In reading the materials that follow, you should consider the extent to which it makes sense to have legal obligations that are so out of step with the ordinary expectations of the parties (e.g., studies show that vast numbers of employees working under indefinite-term contracts do not understand the full meaning of "at will") and whether it makes sense to develop doctrines—such as implied duties of good faith or fair dealing—to bring the two more in alignment with each other.

COMMENT: THE FRANCHISED DEALER AND THE LAW

In Corenswet, Inc. v. Amana Refrigeration, Inc., 594 F.2d 129 (5th Cir. 1979), Judge John Minor Wisdom expressed doubt that "public policy frowns on any and all contract clauses permitting termination without cause." Nearly 40 years earlier, in Bushwick-Decatur Motors v. Ford Motor Co., 116 F.2d 675 (2d Cir. 1940), another federal court rejected a terminated dealer's claim in a suit involving an equally broad termination clause ("at any time at the will of either party by written notice to the other"). Judge Clark explained why the automobile manufacturer, by giving notice, had ended its obligations under the contract:

> With a power of termination at will here so unmistakably expressed, we certainly cannot assert that a limitation of good faith was anything the parties had in mind. Such a limitation can be read into the agreement only as an overriding requirement of public pol-

> icy. This seems an extreme step for judges to take. The onerous nature of the contract for the successful dealer and the hardship which cancellation may bring him have caused some writers to advocate it, however; and an occasional case has seized upon elements of overreaching to come to such a result on particular facts. . . . But, generally speaking, the situation arises from the strong bargaining position which economic factors give the great automobile manufacturing companies: the dealers are not misled or imposed upon, but accept as nonetheless advantageous an agreement in form bilateral, in fact one-sided. To attempt to redress this balance by judicial action without legislative authority appears to us a doubtful policy. We have not proper facilities to weigh economic factors, nor have we before us a showing of the supposed needs which may lead the manufacturers to require these seemingly harsh bargains.

Judge Clark in 1940, like Judge Wisdom in 1979, was not prepared to promote "mutuality" by the means made available by conventional contract doctrines. The point to be stressed is that courts, especially federal courts, can no longer follow the course of abstention recommended by these judges. That is because courts today are called upon to apply a considerable body of legislation, state and federal, involving various aspects of the franchise system, including general antitrust and unfair trade practices statutes.

It is in the automobile industry that the dealer-franchise has been most widely used and most extensively studied, but of course its importance reaches far beyond that industry. In the early years of franchising autos, it soon became clear that the formal separation between franchisor and franchisee achieved in legal analysis did not correspond with the interdependence that existed in fact. The franchisor's interests would ordinarily lead it to press its retailers to expand sales. But the facilities of the particular franchisee might be limited, and expansion might be costly or beyond the franchisee's means. Not surprisingly, clauses reserving an unlimited power of cancellation became common. They were reinforced by clauses requiring the franchised dealer to provide "satisfactory sales performance" or "best efforts," either of which would be tested by the franchisor's "satisfaction." Since the impact of such controls was for the most part one-sided, tensions and conflict arose.

Efforts began in the 1930s to provide controls through state legislation. By 1964, statutes had been passed in 40 states, most commonly requiring both manufacturers and retailers to be licensed to sell automobiles within the state, setting up administrative procedures for mediation of disputes, and authorizing cancellation of licenses of manufacturers found to have acted unfairly or to have used undue coercion. In some states, sanctions enforced by courts were provided, perhaps even injunctions. By 1980, only a few states lacked legislation focusing directly upon the automobile manufacturer-dealer relationship. A provision found in many states (e.g., Delaware, Massachusetts, Rhode Island) simply declares that "it shall be unlawful directly or indirectly to impose unreasonable restrictions" on the motor vehicle dealer or franchisee respecting a wide range of matters, including "right to renew" and "termination." The various provisions, including restrictions on franchise termination, are collected in Note, State Motor Vehicle Franchise Legislation: A Survey and Due Process Challenge to Board Composition, 33 Vand. L. Rev. 385 (1980). See also Briley, Franchise Termination Litigation: A Comparative Analysis, 16 U. Tol. L. Rev. 891 (1985).

After extensive public hearings, Congress in 1956 passed the Automobile Dealers' Day in Court Act, which provided a damage remedy for losses sustained by an automobile dealer through the failure of a manufacturer to act in "good faith" in performing or in terminating (including not renewing) the dealer's franchise. "Good faith" was defined as acting "in a fair and equitable manner toward each other so as to guarantee the one party freedom from coercion or intimidation by the other party." A proviso was then added that "recommendation, endorsement, exposition, persuasion, urging or argument" would not constitute lack of good faith.

How wide was the range of inquiry that courts were directed to undertake under tests so open-ended as "good faith" and "a fair and equitable manner," and on what sources could courts draw to give these phrases content? Take an imaginary example—a successful dealer, who for 25 years has shown superior salesmanship, is served with a notice of cancellation in order to make room for the child of a high company executive. The displaced franchisee may (or may not) be able to salvage some of its considerable investment in quite specialized facilities. Is the termination in "good faith"? Look back to the key words quoted in the last paragraph and underline "*so as to*" after "fair and equitable manner." The legislative history of the Day in Court Act has much in it to show that this phrasing was chosen deliberately. At any rate, it is now just about settled (after some hesitation) that in the conduct that can amount to "bad faith" for the purposes of the federal damage remedy, coercion or intimidation will be an essential element. Would you have it otherwise?

Legislative efforts, both state and federal, were of course not limited to the automobile industry. There developed a wide assortment of state enactments designed to regulate both franchise relationships in general and franchising in specific types of goods—e.g., petroleum products, beer and wine. These statutes impose a variety of restraints on franchisors, which are collected and discussed in Annot., 67 A.L.R.3d 1299 (1975). An example of parallel action at the federal level is the Petroleum Marketing Practices Act 15 U.S.C. § 2801, which Congress enacted in 1978 in order to balance the perceived unequal bargaining power between oil companies and their dealers. More generally, in 1987 the National Conference of Commissioners on Uniform State Laws drafted and recommended for adoption the Uniform Franchise and Business Opportunities Act (7A U.L.A. 77), which mainly imposes on the parties a duty of "good faith" in the performance and enforcement of the franchise agreement. It does not call for a "good cause" rule on terminations.

In short, courts are now cabined by statutes in resolving franchise disputes. The whole subject has become quite specialized, prompting separate courses in the law schools. For the typical franchise litigation, see The Original Great American Chocolate Chip Cookie Co., Inc. v. River Valley Cookies

Ltd., 970 F.2d 273 (7th Cir. 1992), involving claims under both a federal act and the Illinois Franchise Disclosure Act. To be sure, there remain some painful questions as to how far the courts should go, and by what means, in enforcing the legislative mandate. But one point seems settled. The mandate under the typical franchise act is that franchisors deal with their franchisees in "good faith." What does that mean when the contract states that "either party may terminate this Agreement upon 90 days' written notice"? Again, a party may always stand on rights given by the contract. When the contract is unquestionably terminable at will, it is not easy to find that a general duty of good faith read into every franchise arrangement authorizes a judicial inquiry into the motives for exercising the contractual right. So the duty of good faith created by a franchise act seems no more powerful as a trumping device than the common law and UCC versions of the good faith duty. Something more, perhaps opportunistic or otherwise improper efforts to escape contractual obligation, is likely required.

Sheets v. Teddy's Frosted Foods, Inc.

Supreme Court of Connecticut, 1980.
179 Conn. 471, 427 A.2d 385.

PETERS, J. [The issue] is whether an employer has a completely unlimited right to terminate the services of an employee whom it has hired for an indefinite term. The plaintiff, Emard H. Sheets, filed a complaint that as amended alleged that he had been wrongfully discharged from his employment as quality control director and operations manager of the defendant, [who] responded with a motion to strike the complaint as legally [in]sufficient. The plaintiff declined to plead further when that motion was granted. . . .

Since this appeal is before us pursuant to a motion to strike, we must take the facts to be those alleged in the plaintiff's complaint as amended, and must construe the complaint in the manner most favorable to the pleader. . . . The complaint alleges that for a four-year period, from November 1973 to November 1977, plaintiff was employed by defendant, a producer of frozen food products, as its quality control director and subsequently also as operations manager. . . . [He] received periodic raises and bonuses. In his capacity as quality control director and operations manager, plaintiff began to notice deviations from the specifications contained in defendant's standards and labels, in that some vegetables were substandard and some meat components underweight. These deviations meant that defendant's products violated the express representations contained in [its] labeling; false or misleading labels in turn violate the provisions of Gen. Stat. § 19–222, the Conn. Uniform Food, Drug and Cosmetic Act. In May of 1977, plaintiff communicated in writing to defendant concerning the use of substandard raw materials and underweight components in defendant's finished products. His recommendations for more selective purchasing and conforming components were ignored. On November 3, 1977, his employment [was] terminated. Although the stated reason for his discharge was unsatisfactory performance of his duties, he was actually dismissed in retaliation for his efforts to ensure that defendant's products would comply with the applicable law relating to labeling and licensing.

The plaintiff's complaint alleges that his dismissal was wrongful in three respects. He claims that there was a violation of an implied contract of employment, a violation of public policy, and a malicious discharge. . . . [T]he claim of malice has not been separately pursued, and we are asked to consider only whether he has stated a cause of action for breach of contract or for intentionally tortious conduct. On oral argument, it was the tort claim that was most vigorously pressed, and it is upon the basis of tort that we have concluded that the motion to strike was granted in error.

The issue before us is whether to recognize an exception to the traditional rules governing employment at will so as to permit a cause of action for wrongful discharge where the discharge contravenes a clear mandate of public policy. In addressing that claim, we must clarify what is not at stake in this litigation. The plaintiff does not challenge the general proposition that contracts of permanent employment, or for an indefinite term, are terminable at will. . . . Nor does he argue that contracts terminable at will permit termination only upon a showing of just cause for dismissal. Some statutes, such as the Conn. Franchise Act, Gen. Stat. §§ 42–133e through 42–133h, do impose limitations of just cause upon the power to terminate some contracts; see § 42–133f; but the legislature has recently refused to interpolate such a requirement into contracts of employment. See H.B. No. 5179, 1974 Sess.[3] There is a significant distinction between a criterion of just cause and what the plaintiff is seeking. "Just cause" substantially limits employer discretion to terminate, by requiring the employer, in all instances, to proffer a proper reason for dismissal, by forbidding the employer to act arbitrarily or capriciously. See Pierce v. Ortho Pharm. Corp., 166 N.J.Super. 335, 399 A.2d 1023, 1026 (1979). By contrast, the plaintiff asks only that the employer be responsible for damages if the former employee can prove a demonstrably *improper* reason for dismissal, a reason whose impropriety is derived from some important violation of public policy.

The argument that contract rights which are inherently legitimate may yet give rise to liability in tort if they are exercised improperly is not a novel one. Although private persons have the right not to enter into contracts, failure to contract under circumstances in which others are seriously misled gives rise to a variety of claims sounding in tort. See Kess-

[3] Some statutes of course expressly forbid retaliatory discharge. See, e.g., Public Acts 1979, No. 79–599, and 29 U.S.C. § 660(c)(1) (1976), which is discussed in Marshall v. Whirlpool Corp., 593 F.2d 715 (6th Cir. 1979), cert. granted, 444 U.S. 823 (on other grounds).

ler & Fine, "Culpa in Contrahendo," Kessler & Fine, "Culpa in Contrahendo," 77 Harv.L.Rev. 401 (1964). The development of liability in contract for action induced by reliance upon a promise, despite the absence of common-law consideration normally required to bind a promisor; see Restatement (Second), Contracts § 90 (1973); rests upon principles derived at least in part from the law of tort. See Gilmore, The Death of Contract 8–90 (1974). By way of analogy, we have long recognized abuse of process as a cause of action in tort whose gravamen is the misuse or misapplication of process, its use "in an improper manner or to accomplish a purpose for which it was not designed." Varga v. Pareles, 137 Conn. 663, 667, 81 A.2d 112, 115 (1951) . . . .

It would be difficult to maintain that the right to discharge an employee hired at will is so fundamentally different from other contract rights that its exercise is never subject to judicial scrutiny regardless of how outrageous, how violative of public policy, the employer's conduct may be. Cf. Gen. Stat. § 31–126 (unfair employment practices). The defendant does not seriously contest the propriety of cases in other jurisdictions that have found wrongful and actionable a discharge in retaliation for the exercise of an employee's right to: (1) refuse to commit perjury; . . . (2) file a workmen's compensation claim; . . . (3) engage in union activity; . . . (4) perform jury duty. . . . While it may be true that these cases are supported by mandates of public policy derived directly from the applicable state statutes and constitutions, it is equally true that they serve at a minimum to establish the principle that public policy imposes some limits on unbridled discretion to terminate the employment of someone hired at will. See Blades, "Employment at Will vs. Individual Freedom: On Limiting the Abusive Exercise of Employer Power," 67 Colum.L.Rev. 1404 (1967) . . . . No case has been called to our attention in which, despite egregiously outrageous circumstances, the employer's contract rights have been permitted to override competing claims of public policy, although there are numerous cases in which the facts were found not to support the employee's claim. . . .

The issue then becomes the familiar common-law problem of deciding where and how to draw the line between claims that genuinely involve the mandates of public policy and are actionable, and ordinary disputes between employee and employer that are not. We are mindful that courts should not lightly intervene to impair the exercise of managerial discretion or to foment unwarranted litigation. We are, however, equally mindful that the myriad of employees without the bargaining power to command employment contracts for a definite term are entitled to a modicum of judicial protection when their conduct as good citizens is punished by their employers.

The central allegation of the plaintiff's complaint is that he was discharged because of his conduct in calling to his employer's attention repeated violations of the Conn. Uniform Food, Drug and Cosmetic Act. This act prohibits the sale of mislabeled food. . . . The act, in § 19–215, imposes criminal penalties upon anyone who violates § 19–213; subsection (b) of § 19–215 makes it clear that criminal sanctions do not depend upon proof of intent to defraud or mislead, since special sanctions are imposed for intentional misconduct. The plaintiff's position as quality control director and operations manager might have exposed him to the possibility of criminal prosecution under this act. The act was intended to "safeguard the public health and promote the public welfare by protecting the consuming public from injury by product use and the purchasing public from injury by merchandising deceit. . . ."

It is useful to compare the factual allegations of this complaint with those of other recent cases in which recovery was sought for retaliatory discharge. In Geary v. United States Steel Corp., [456 Pa. 171, 319 A.2d 174 (1974)], in which the plaintiff had disputed the safety of tubular steel casings, he was denied recovery because, as a company salesman, he had neither the expertise nor the corporate responsibility to "exercise independent, expert judgment in matters of product safety." By contrast, this plaintiff . . . did have responsibility for product quality control. Three other recent cases in which the plaintiff's claim survived demurrer closely approximate the claim before us. In Trombetta v. Detroit, Toledo & Ironton R. Co., 81 Mich.App. 489, 265 N.W.2d 385 (1978), a cause of action was stated when an employee alleged that he had been discharged in retaliation for his refusal to manipulate and alter sampling results for pollution control reports required by Michigan law. There as here falsified reports would have violated state law. In Harless v. First Nat'l Bank in Fairmont, 246 S.E.2d 270 (W.Va. 1978), an employee stated a cause of action when he alleged that he had been discharged in retaliation for his efforts to ensure his employer's compliance with state and federal consumer credit protection laws. There as here the legislature had established a public policy of consumer protection. In Pierce v. Ortho Pharm.Corp., 166 N.J.Super. 335, 399 A.2d 1023 (1979), the plaintiff was entitled to a trial to determine whether she had been wrongfully discharged for refusing to pursue clinical testing of a new drug containing a high level of saccharin; the court noted that the plaintiff's status as a physician entitled her to invoke the Hippocratic Oath as well as state statutory provisions governing the licensing and the conduct of physicians. There as here the case might have been dismissed as a conflict in judgment.

In the light of these recent cases, which evidence a growing judicial receptivity to the recognition of a tort claim for wrongful discharge, the trial court was in error in granting defendant's motion to strike. The plaintiff alleged that he had been dismissed in retaliation for his insistence that defendant comply with the requirements of a state statute. . . . We need not decide whether violation of a state statute is invariably a prerequisite to the conclusion that a challenged discharge violates public policy. Certainly when there is a relevant state statute we should not ignore the statement of public policy that it represents. For today, it is enough to decide that an employee should not be put to an election whether to risk criminal sanction or to jeopardize his continued employment.

There is error and the case is remanded for further proceedings.

COTTER, C.J. (dissenting). I cannot agree that, on the factual situation presented to us, we should abandon the well-established principle that an indefinite general hiring may be terminated at the will of either party without liability to the other. . . . The majority by seeking to extend a "modicum" of judicial protection to shield employees from retaliatory discharges instead offers them a sword with which to coerce employers to retain them in their employ. In recognizing an exception to the traditional rules governing employment at will[,] . . . the majority is necessarily led to the creation of an overly broad new cause of action whose nuisance value alone may impair employers' ability to hire and retain employees who are best suited to their requirements. Other jurisdictions which have recognized a cause of action for retaliatory discharge have done so on the basis of a much clearer and more direct contravention of a mandate of public policy. . . .

In contrast, the purposes of the statute the majority would rely on . . . can only be considered as, at most, marginally affected by an allegedly retaliatory discharge of an employee who observed the supposed sale of shortweight frozen entrées and the use of [substandard] vegetables. A retaliatory discharge in the present case would not necessarily thwart or inhibit [the Act's] purpose of protecting the consumer. The plaintiff, if he desired to protect the consumer, could have communicated [his concerns], even anonymously, to the commissioner of consumer affairs. . . . [T]he plaintiff need not have jeopardized his continued employment. There is no indication that the plaintiff has either, before or after his discharge, informed or even attempted to inform the commissioner of consumer protection of violations the plaintiff claims. . . . Unlike those cases where an employer allegedly discharged employees for engaging in union activities or filing workmen's compensation claims and the discharge itself contravened a statutory mandate, [here] the discharge itself at most only indirectly impinged on the statutory mandate.

Consequently, the majority seemingly invites the unrestricted use of an allegation of almost any statutory or even regulatory violation by an employer as the basis for a cause of action by a discharged employee hired for an indefinite term. . . . [T]he majority is creating an open-ended arena for judicial policy making and the usurpation of legislative functions. To base this new cause of action on a decision as to whether an alleged reason for discharge "is derived from some important violation of public policy" is not to create adequate and carefully circumscribed standards for this new cause of action but is to invite the opening of a Pandora's box of unwarranted litigation. . . .

Moreover, this is policy making that the Connecticut legislature recently declined to undertake. In 1974, the General Assembly considered and rejected a bill which would have provided that "[a]ny employee [including private sector employees] hired for an indefinite term, may be dismissed only for just cause or because of the employer's reduction in work force for business reasons." H.B. No. 5179, 1974 Sess. [T]he bill's sponsor gave examples of the kind of discharges he intended the bill to cover: discharges for overlooking violations of building codes or for campaigning for the wrong political party. . . . Thus, "just cause" in the overwhelmingly rejected 1974 bill was meant to encompass the kinds of retaliatory discharge that the majority approves as a new cause of action. Furthermore, the most recent legislature enacted a statute protecting "whistle blowing" state employees; Public Acts 1979, No. 79–599; and in Public Acts 1979, No. 153, addressed the problem of retaliatory dismissals of building officials. The legislature is thus adopting appropriate remedies for certain types of retaliatory discharges at its own considered pace. . . . In these circumstances, this court should consider itself precluded from substituting its own ideas of what might be wise policy. . . .

Finally, it should be reiterated that the minority of jurisdictions which have created a cause of action for retaliatory discharges have done so with caution. . . . It is because the majority abandons that caution and for the reason that the factual situation before us does not demonstrate a "wrongful discharge where the discharge contravenes a clear mandate of public policy" that I feel compelled to dissent.

[Another justice joined the dissent; the vote was 3 to 2.]

QUESTION

Suppose, at a trial after remand, plaintiff requested the following jury instruction: "As a matter of law, if you find for the plaintiff, Emard Sheets, you may award him such damages as are attributable to the amount of salary and fringe benefits he would have made had he continued to work at Teddy's Frosted Foods, minus any amounts which Mr. Sheets earned during the period from the date of discharge until the date of this trial. You may, in addition, compensate Mr. Sheets for his complete injury by awarding him such damages as are attributable to any mental distress caused by the termination of his employment." Would the court commit reversible error by giving this instruction?

Price v. Carmack Datsun, Inc.

109 Ill. 2d 65, 485 N.E.2d 359 (1985)

Defendant, an auto dealer, had a group health-insurance plan for employees. Plaintiff, a sales representative for defendant, was hospitalized following an automobile accident which left him with serious injuries and $7,000 in medical expenses. When plaintiff returned to work three months later, defendant asked whether he intended to submit a claim under the health-insurance plan and sought to discourage him from doing so. Three days later, plaintiff told defendant of his intention to file a claim. Defendant then discharged plaintiff, who brought suit alleging that the health-insurance provisions of the Illinois Insurance Code reflect a "public policy" against the discharge of employees for filing such claims. A jury found for plaintiff and awarded him $5,525 in compensatory damages and $2,762 in punitive damages.

On appeal, the court held that plaintiff failed to state a cause of action in tort for retaliatory discharge. An exception to the at-will doctrine is made in Illinois only when the discharge violates a "clearly mandated public policy." While that term is imprecise, a survey of cases elsewhere shows that "a matter must strike at the heart of a citizen's social rights, duties, and responsibilities before the tort will be allowed." This court has approved a cause of action for a discharge in retaliation for filing a workers' compensation claim and for furnishing police with information regarding possible criminal conduct of a fellow employee. But here "the matter is one of private and individual grievance rather than one affecting our society," and plaintiff's reliance on the health-care provisions of the Insurance Code is unavailing. "The entire insurance industry . . . is a regulated industry. The Insurance Code regulates all types of insurance and all policies issued are required to have State approval. It should be noted, too, that the Code was designed to govern operations of insurance companies, not insureds, such as defendant. The filing of a claim under a policy of insurance is pursuant to an individual contract between the insurer and the insured. We consider that the discharge of an employee for filing a claim under a policy in which he is a beneficiary does not violate a clearly mandated public policy."

NOTE: THE PUBLIC'S POLICY

What is the "public policy" rule of the *Sheets* and *Price* cases designed to protect? It is clear that a great majority of states have adopted the public-policy "exception" to the at-will doctrine, and that a recurring theme in the cases is the "public-private" dichotomy observed in Price v. Carmack Datsun. Still, in most places the exception is viewed as "narrow" or "limited." Discharged at-will employees suing for tort damages in California must show that the public interests they seek to vindicate are "tethered to fundamental policies delineated in constitutional or statutory provisions." Gantt v. Sentry Ins., 1 Cal. 4th 1083, 4 Cal. Rptr. 2d 874, 824 P.2d 680 (1992). The Connecticut court, in later applications of *Sheets*, has stressed that, absent unusual circumstances, "we will interfere with a personnel decision only if it implicates an explicit statutory or constitutional provision, or judicially conceived notion of public policy." Daley v. Aetna Life & Cas. Co., 249 Conn. 766, 734 A.2d 112 (1999). In Illinois, as *Price* suggests, absent a firing for refusing to violate a statute or to act illegally, courts are likely to find the requisite "mandate of public policy" in only two settings: a discharge stemming from an employee's pursuit of a worker's compensation claim or from an employee's reporting of unlawful or improper conduct. Russ v. Pension Consultants Co., 182 Ill. App. 3d 769, 538 N.E.2d 693 (1989). Separating a "private" concern from a matter of "public policy" is perhaps most difficult in the latter situation, where, as in *Sheets*, the basis for the discharge is alleged to be "whistleblowing" in some form. Should such cases turn on the entity to whom plaintiff reported workplace activity (firm management rather than public or law-enforcement officials), or on a characterization of what plaintiff reported (actual criminal activity distinguished from co-workers' shoddy performance or questionable practices)? See, e.g., Belline v. K-Mart Corp., 940 F.2d 184 (7th Cir. 1991), where a dissenter complained that "[i]t is easy for a jury to mistake a pest, a busybody, for a champion of the law." Is that a persuasive reason for narrowing the exception?

New York's highest court, in Murphy v. American Home Products Corp., 58 N.Y.2d 293, 461 N.Y.S.2d 232, 448 N.E.2d 86 (1983), refused to recognize either a common-law tort theory based on abusive or wrongful discharge ("the Legislature has infinitely greater resources and procedural means to discern the public will") or the implied covenant of "good faith" that perhaps seven or eight states have carried over to the at-will cases. In rejecting plaintiff's urging of an implied covenant of "good faith" in employment contracts, the court reaffirmed but distinguished Wood v. Lucy, Lady Duff-Gordon, stressing that the implied obligation in that case was "in aid and furtherance of other terms of the agreement." A dissenterargued that the "same reasoning that reads into an output contract the requirement that the manufacturing plant continue to perform in good faith" requires reading the good-faith obligation into employment contracts which are only "impliedly," not expressly, terminable at will.

A useful survey of common law doctrines used to erode the at-will rule can be found in Note, Implied Contract Rights to Job Security, 26 Stan. L. Rev. 335 (1974). Although both tort and contract theories have provided a basis for judicially-created exceptions, the most successful technique appears to be the tort claim that a discharge violates some "mandate of public policy."

McDonald v. Mobil Coal Producing, Inc.

Supreme Court of Wyoming, 1991.
820 P.2d 986.

GOLDEN, J. This employment termination case comes before the court on appellee Mobil Coal Producing's motion for rehearing. In our previous decision, McDonald v. Mobil Coal Producing, Inc., 789 P.2d 866 (Wyo. 1990) (*McDonald I*), we ruled that summary judgment in favor of the appellees must be reversed and the case remanded for further proceedings. The five justices of this court rendered a total of four opinions, including a special concurrence and two separate dissents. Following our decision, we granted Mobil's petition for rehearing to review and clarify our earlier decision.

The relevant facts are more fully set out in *McDonald I*. [In brief, McDonald worked at Mobil's Caballo Rojo mine as a technician in the preparation plant, from August 1987 until June 1988, when he "resigned" his position following rumors that he had sexually harassed a female coworker. McDonald contended that his resignation in fact was a "dismissal," resulting from a meeting with three company officials including the mine superintendent, who told him he had "the choice of either resigning or being fired." McDonald's suit challenging his dismissal named Mobil Coal and the three company officials as defendants.]

After the trial court granted summary judgment against him, [McDonald] appealed to this court, claiming breach of contract based on the terms of his employee handbook. . . . A plurality of this court rejected the [claim] that Mobil's handbook constituted a valid contract sufficient to modify the terms of McDonald's at-will employment. . . . However, a different plurality reversed summary judgment and remanded for a determination of whether the principle of promissory estoppel applied to the facts of this case.

Justice Golden, specially concurring, rejected the application of promissory estoppel, stating that he would have remanded to resolve the ambiguity in the effect of the disclaimer contained in Mobil's employee handbook. Justice Cardine, dissenting, found the disclaimer effective to assure there was not an employment contract. . . . Justice Thomas, also dissenting, agreed with Justice Cardine, noting that he could see no difference between [viewing] the handbook as creating a contract and finding it to be a binding promise under the doctrine of promissory estoppel.

We reaffirm our earlier decision reversing summary judgment and remanding this case for further proceedings. We hold that a question of material fact exists concerning whether the employee handbook and Mobil's course of dealing with appellant modified the terms of appellant's at-will employment.

. . . Mobil claims that it effectively disclaimed any employment relationship other than at-will. McDonald argues Mobil objectively manifested its intent to modify the initial at-will contract with the employment manual and by its course of dealing. We examine both [claims].

The Federal District Court of Wyoming explored the issue of effective contract disclaimers in Jimenez v. Colorado Interstate Gas Co., 690 F.Supp. 977 (D.Wyo. 1988). The plaintiff's employer had adopted standard operating procedures relating to cause for termination. The employer had inserted a disclaimer in these procedures to the effect that they did not constitute terms of a contract. The court stated that for a disclaimer to be effective it must be conspicuous and whether it was conspicuous was a matter of law. Where the disclaimer was not set off in any way, was placed under a general subheading, was not capitalized, and contained the same type size as another provision on the same page, it was not conspicuous.

We adopt the rule in *Jiminez* that disclaimers must be conspicuous to be effective against employees and that conspicuousness is a matter of law. The trial court erred in its statement that there was no requirement that the disclaimers be conspicuous. We examine the disclaimers in this case to see whether they were sufficiently conspicuous to be binding on appellant.

The application form which Craig McDonald signed on July 20, 1987, contained the following disclaimer:

> READ CAREFULLY BEFORE SIGNING
>
> I agree that any offer of employment, and acceptance thereof, does not constitute a binding contract of any length, and that such employment is terminable at the will of either party, subject to appropriate state and/or federal laws.

The MCPI Employee Handbook which he received [after starting work at the mine] contained the following disclaimer, located on its first page, which we reproduce in full to show the context in which [it] was made:

> WELCOME
>
> Mobil Coal Producing Inc., Caballo Rojo Mine, is proud to welcome you as an employee. We believe you will find safety, opportunity and satisfaction while making your contribution to Mobil's growth as a major supplier of coal. This handbook is intended to be used as a guide for our nonexempt mine technicians and salaried support personnel, to help you understand and explain to you Mobil's policies and procedures. It is not a comprehensive policies and procedures manual, nor an employment contract. More detailed policies and procedures are maintained by the Employee Relations supervisor and your supervisor. While we intend to continue policies, benefits and rules contained in this handbook, changes or improvements may be made from time to time by the company. If you have any questions, please feel free to discuss them with your supervisor, a member of our Employee Relations staff, and/or any member of Caballo Rojo's Management. We urge you to read your handbook carefully and keep it in a safe and readily available place for future reference. Sections will be revised as conditions affecting your employment or benefits change.
>
> Sincerely, R.J. Kovacich
> Mine Manager
> /s/ Caballo Rojo Mine

The circumstances surrounding this disclaimer are nearly identical to those of the *Jiminez* case. [It] was not set off by a border or larger print, was not capitalized, and was contained in a general welcoming section of the handbook.

Additionally, the disclaimer was unclear as to its effect on the employment relationship. For persons untutored in contract law, such clarity is essential, as stated [by the] New Jersey Supreme Court[:]

> It would be unfair to allow an employer to distribute a policy manual that makes the workforce believe that certain promises have been made and then to allow the employer to renege on those promises. What is sought here is basic honesty: if the employer, for whatever reason, does not want the manual to be capable of being construed by the court as a binding contract, there are simple ways to attain that goal. All that need be done is the inclusion in a very prominent position of an appropriate statement *that there is no promise of any kind by the employer contained in the manual; that regardless of what the manual says or provides, the employer promises nothing and remains free to change wages and all other working conditions without having to consult anyone and without anyone's agreement; and that the employer continues to have the absolute power to fire anyone with or without good cause.*

Woolley v. Hoffmann-La Roche, Inc., 99 N.J. 284, 309, 491 A.2d 1257, 1271 (1985), [modified,] 101 N.J. 10, 499 A.2d 515 (1985). No explanation was given in the disclaimer that Mobil did not consider itself bound by the terms of the handbook. Instead, McDonald would have been led to draw inferences from the handbook language: that it was intended to be a guide, and that Mobil intended to continue the policies, benefits and rules contained in the handbook. The same paragraph which disclaimed a contract also informed McDonald that he could discuss "any questions" he might have with his supervisor, employee relations staff and management and urged him to read the handbook carefully and to keep it in a safe and readily available place.

The trial court erred in finding that the disclaimer was conspicuous. We hold that the attempted disclaimers in the employee handbook and in the employment application were insufficiently conspicuous to be binding on McDonald.

In our earlier opinion, [we] stated:

> Following [Mobil Coal Producing, Inc. v. Parks, 704 P.2d 702 (Wyo. 1985)], Mobil revised its handbook. The most significant revision was the addition of a statement that the handbook was not an employment contract. A contract exists when there is a meeting of the minds. Mobil's express disclaimer demonstrates that it had no intention to form a contract.

McDonald I, 789 P.2d at 869.

The above quotation could be interpreted as importing an unduly subjective element into contract analysis. See Pine River State Bank v. Mettille, 333 N.W.2d 622, 630 n. 6 (Minn. 1983). However, we did not mean to say that a contract could not be formed where one party somehow lacked "subjective intent" but nevertheless proceeded as if there were a contract.

Under the "objective theory" of contract formation, contractual obligation is imposed not on the basis of the subjective intent of the parties, but rather upon the outward manifestations of a party's assent sufficient to create reasonable reliance by the other party. . . That Mobil did not subjectively "intend" that a contract be formed is irrelevant, provided that Mobil made sufficient intentional, objective manifestations of contractual assent to create reasonable reliance by McDonald. . . .

We must determine whether there is a genuine issue of material fact concerning Mobil's objective manifestations of assent to contract. The disclaimers figure in this analysis, as do the remainder of the handbook provisions and Mobil's course of dealing with McDonald.

The handbook informed McDonald that "individual consideration on employee-supervisor matters provides the best method for satisfying the employees' and the Company's needs" which could not be improved on by union representation. Mobil stated that it planned to provide, inter alia, "free and open communications" and stated that "on those rare occasions when differences cannot be resolved, we have a Fair Treatment Procedure that affords an employee the opportunity to be heard, without fear of reprisal." Union representation, the handbook stated, is unnecessary for employees to enjoy job security or consistent treatment.

The manual stated that Mobil recognized a "fundamental obligation" to its employees to "give helpful consideration when an employee makes a mistake or has a personal problem with which we are asked to help." The handbook outlined a procedure for presenting a problem or complaint which an employee might have. The manual also set forth a progressive discipline schedule for cases in which the employee broke the company rules or failed to meet a reasonable standard of conduct and work performance. This five-step schedule could be disregarded by the company at its discretion.

The "welcoming" section, quoted above, stated that Mobil intended to continue policies, benefits and rules contained in the handbook and that changes or improvements could be made from time to time by the company. The inference favorable to McDonald is that Mobil would follow the rules unless changed, and that since they had not been changed, Mobil was bound by them.

When McDonald went to his supervisor over the rumors that he had heard, he was told that he should "just do his job and not worry about what had been said." McDonald alleges that Mobil's course of conduct led him to believe that Mobil would follow the handbook procedures concerning the complaint of his co-employee.

Examining the handbook provisions cited above and Mobil's course of dealing with McDonald on the rumor of accusation and his termination, we find ambiguity as to whether Mobil manifested intent to modify the at-will employment to an employment which could be terminated only for cause. Mobil made numerous statements which could be construed as promises to McDonald concerning communication with him and Mobil's disciplinary procedures. Mobil's handbook stated that individual consideration and open communication would be an effective substitute for unionization. All of these manifestations could suggest to a reasonable person that Mobil intended to make legally-binding promises. . . .

The meaning and effect of this employment contract, a mixed question of law and fact, remains unresolved. Therefore, we must reverse summary judgment on the contract issue. The case is remanded to the trial court for determination of whether the employee handbook and Mobil's course of dealing with McDonald modified the employment relationship from one terminable at will to one terminable only for cause.

MACY, J. (concurring). I specially concur. In *McDonald I*, we stated that genuine issues of material fact existed as to the effect, if any, the representations made by Mobil in its handbook had upon an otherwise at-will employment relationship. The Court went on to state in *McDonald I* that those issues were (1) whether Mobil should have expected McDonald's reliance upon the procedures outlined in the handbook, (2) whether McDonald's reliance was reasonable, and (3) whether Mobil's termination procedures should have been enforced to avoid injustice.

. . . Even if the employment handbook was ambiguous, Mobil's course of conduct clearly demonstrated that Mobil intended to make legally binding promises concerning Mobil's employment termination procedures and that Mobil certainly led McDonald to rely upon the termination procedures outlined in the handbook. [Thus,] the only question which should be resolved on remand is whether Mobil's termination procedures should have been enforced to avoid an injustice; i.e., whether Mobil should have been estopped from firing McDonald without cause.

THOMAS, J. (dissenting). I persist in my vote to affirm the trial court in this case. Like Justice Cardine, in whose dissent I join, I am at a loss to understand what more Mobil Coal Producing, Inc. could do to make it clear to an employee that he was entering into an employment-at-will arrangement. I am satisfied that this was an employment-at-will. That relationship was not modified by the handbook. . . .

. . . [T]he fact of that specific employment-at-will arrangement serves to distinguish this case from [*Jimenez*]. There are other distinguishing facts. The employee handbook, in this instance, was not adopted and issued after the time that McDonald was employed. It is difficult for me to understand how it could amend, or could in some manner have changed, the clear employment-at-will that was documented. In *Jimenez*, there was no separate document articulating an employment-at-will, and the court was dealing only with the factors of employment plus the existence of a handbook. While it might be appropriate to emphasize in an employee's handbook, that was issued without a separate document articulating the employment arrangement, the caveat explaining that the handbook is not an employment contract, that requirement is far less imperative when one recognizes that the handbook was generally available to [Mobil's] employees. After the handbook already had been published and issued, McDonald signed a document that provided that the "employment is terminable at will." Under these circumstances, the subsequent delivery of the handbook simply did not make any difference.

In my opinion, this case strikes the death knell for employment-at-will in Wyoming. It says, in effect, that even though there is a clear statement by the employee that the relationship with the employer is an employment-at-will, after the employment commences, the employer cannot engage in any dialogue with the employee about the conditions and circumstances of the employment. If any such dialogue occurs, it will be considered to have amended the arrangement in such a way that the question of employment must be submitted to a jury. I lack the imagination to visualize any situation in which dialogue about the conditions and circumstances of the employment would not occur and, consequently, it is hereafter impossible to have an employment-at-will in Wyoming.

CARDINE, J. (dissenting, with whom Thomas, J., joins). I continue my dissent . . . for the reasons previously stated. *McDonald I*, 789 P.2d 866, 871 (Wyo. 1990) (Cardine, C.J., dissenting). This opinion after rehearing merely informs Mobil of additional requirements for effective disclaimer. If Mobil should in the future satisfy these requirements, can it assume that this court will give effect to its disclaimer—or should Mobil eliminate its employee handbook? Perhaps the answer will only come with more litigation.

In *McDonald I*, the court reversed summary judgment on the basis of promissory estoppel. Despite the disclaimer in the handbook, the court said McDonald could recover if he could demonstrate that it was reasonable to rely upon the promises contained in the handbook and if enforcement of the promises was the only way to avoid an injustice. 789 P.2d at 870. The court held that no contract was formed because there was no meeting of the minds in forming a contract. . . . Now, upon rehearing, the court holds that if it was reasonable to rely upon promises in the handbook, then a contract was formed. This opinion states a contract is formed by "outward manifestations of a party's assent sufficient to create reasonable reliance by the other party." . . . A promise is not a contract. But this court now says the making of a promise alone reasonably relied upon by another creates an enforceable contract.

. . . It is clear from the disclaimer that Mobil never intended to make a contract. There was never a meeting of the minds nor was there a valid consideration. There was no contract. That is why this court in *McDonald*

I rested its decision to reverse upon the doctrine of promissory estoppel. I would affirm the decision of the trial court.

Kari v. General Motors Corp.

79 Mich. App. 93, 261 N.W.2d 222 (1977)

Plaintiff, an engineer employed by defendant from 1955–1972, was "separated" from the company when he attempted to return to work following an extended leave of absence. Plaintiff brought suit to recover separation pay allegedly guaranteed by defendant's employee handbook. The handbook, entitled "Working with General Motors," had been issued to plaintiff at the time of his initial employment. A section termed "Separation Allowance" read in part:

> A Separation Allowance Plan has been established for the benefit of salaried employe[e]s laid off or separated from the payroll under certain circumstances. The primary purpose of this Plan is to provide a source of income to eligible employe[e]s beyond the date of their layoff or separation. The inclusion of a schedule of separation allowances in this booklet, together with the conditions governing their payment, however, is not intended nor is it to be interpreted to establish a contractual relationship with the employe[e]. . . .

Additional language appeared on the last page of the handbook, italicized and outlined in red:

> The contents of this handbook are presented as a matter of information only. While General Motors believes wholeheartedly in the plans, policies and procedures described here, they are not conditions of employment. General Motors reserves the right to modify, revoke, suspend, terminate, or change any or all such plans, policies, or procedures, in whole or in part, at any time, with or without notice. The language used in this handbook is not intended to create, nor is it to be construed to constitute, a contract between General Motors and any one or all of its employe[e]s.

Plaintiff contended that the handbook's separation-allowance provision constituted an offer which he had accepted by working for defendant. *Held*, summary judgment for defendant affirmed; as a matter of law, no contract existed. The theory that an employer's communications to employees may constitute an offer to contract is sound. But the offer must contain a promise, "communicated in such a manner . . . that [the promisee] may justly expect performance and may reasonably rely thereon." This is not a situation where an employer adopts a policy of severance payments as a part of a drive to attract employees. Here, the handbook "clearly evinced an intention *not* to create an offer capable of acceptance"; the communication was "couched in disclaimers." It is difficult to imagine what defendant could have done, short of not mentioning the severance plan, to prevent it from being read as an offer. "An employee reading this language . . . should realize that further negotiations . . . are necessary to create a contract for severance pay."

Dore v. Arnold Worldwide, Inc.

Supreme Court of California, 2006.
39 Cal. 4th 384, 46 Cal. Rptr. 3d 668, 139 P.3d 56.

WERDEGAR, J. . . . Plaintiff Brook Dore was employed with an advertising agency in Colorado as a regional account director specializing in automobile accounts. In late 1998, Dore discussed with his employer the possibility of relocating to the employer's Los Angeles office.

In 1999, Dore learned that a management supervisor position was available in the Los Angeles office of defendant Arnold Worldwide, Inc., formerly known as Arnold Communications, Inc. (hereafter AWI). Dore interviewed with several AWI officers and employees. According to Dore, he was never told during the interview process that his employment would be terminable without cause or "at will." Dore alleges he was told that AWI had landed a new automobile account and needed someone to handle it on a long-term basis. He also was told that, if hired, he would "play a critical role in growing the agency," that AWI was looking for "a long-term fix, not a Band-Aid," and that AWI employees were treated like family. Dore alleges he learned that the two people previously holding the position for which he was being considered had been terminated for cause—one for committing financial indiscretions, the other because his work had not satisfied a client. Dore states that AWI offered him the management supervisor position by telephone in April 1999, and he orally accepted.

Later that same month, Dore received a three-page letter from Sharon McCabe, senior vice-president of AWI, dated April 6, 1999 (AWI's letter), purporting to "confirm our offer to join us as Management Supervisor in our Los Angeles office" and to state "[t]he terms of this offer." AWI's letter then listed, in bullet-pointed sections, a commencement date, compensation details, and various benefits (including reimbursement of relocation expenses, parking at the AWI offices, various types of insurance, expense reimbursement, and vacation).

AWI's letter also stated: "You will have a 90 day assessment with your supervisor at which time you will receive initial performance feedback. This assessment will also be the time that you will work with your supervisor to set objectives against which you will be evaluated at the time of your annual review. After your assessment is complete, you and your supervisor will have the opportunity to discuss consideration for being named an officer of Arnold Communications."

In a separate paragraph central to the present dispute, AWI's letter stated: "Brook, please know that as with all of our company employees, your employment with Arnold Communications, Inc. is at will. This simply means that Arnold Communications has the right to terminate your employment at any time just as you have the right to terminate your employment with Arnold Communications, Inc. at any time."

AWI's letter requested that Dore sign and return the letter signifying his acceptance of these employment terms. Dore read and signed the letter.

AWI terminated Dore's employment in August 2001. Thereafter, Dore sued AWI and a related entity, Arnold Worldwide Partners (AWP). . . .

Dore alleges that AWI, by various oral representations, conduct, and documents, led him reasonably to understand there existed between AWI and himself an implied-in-fact contract that provided he would not be discharged from his employment except for cause. AWI contends that its oral representations, conduct, and documents could not reasonably have raised any such understanding in Dore. . . .

Dore acknowledges that a clear and unambiguous at-will provision in a written employment contract, signed by the employee, cannot be overcome by evidence of a prior or contemporaneous implied-in-fact contract requiring good cause for termination. But he contends this rule cannot govern here because AWI's letter neither constitutes nor contains a clear and unambiguous agreement that his employment would be terminable without cause. . . .

The Court of Appeal below agreed with Dore that AWI's letter, signed by Dore, was not clear and unambiguous with respect to cause for termination. Notwithstanding the letter's statement that "your employment with Arnold Communications, Inc. is at will," the court reasoned, by going on to define the term "at will" to mean that AWI had the right to terminate Dore's employment "at any time," AWI impliedly relinquished the right to terminate Dore without cause. We disagree. . . .

We disagree with Dore that the verbal formulation "at any time" in the termination clause of an employment contract is per se ambiguous merely because it does not expressly speak to whether cause is required. As a matter of simple logic, rather, such a formulation ordinarily entails the notion of "with or without cause." . . .

That the phrase "at any time" is not in itself ambiguous with respect to cause for termination does not preclude the possibility that AWI's letter, when considered as a whole, contains ambiguity on the topic. . . .

In this case, the trial court recognized that the presumption of at-will employment . . . can be overcome by an express or implied agreement to the contrary. Nevertheless, the court ruled that because the express written contract—i.e., AWI's letter—controls, it need not consider whether Dore's proffered extrinsic evidence establishes the existence of an earlier implied agreement to terminate only for cause.

The Court of Appeal, in reaching the contrary conclusion, relied primarily on the fact that AWI's letter, after stating that Dore's employment is "at will," defines "at will" in a manner that refers expressly only to the duration of the contract (i.e., as meaning "that Arnold Communications has the right to terminate your employment at any time") and does not state explicitly whether cause is required. The Court of Appeal also relied on evidence extrinsic to the letter, in particular, that AWI required Dore to sign a post-employment noncompetition and nondisclosure agreement.

The trial court's ruling was correct. The language of the parties' written agreement is unambiguous. AWI's letter plainly states that Dore's employment with AWI was at will. Indeed, as the trial court observed, Dore admitted as much and further admitted that he "read, signed, understood and did not disagree with the terms of the letter." Even the Court of Appeal acknowledged that the term "at will" when used in an employment contract normally conveys an intent employment may be ended by either party "at any time without cause." Although AWI's letter also states that AWI would provide Dore a "90 day assessment" and "annual review," these provisions, in describing AWI's employee evaluation schedule, neither expressly nor impliedly conferred on Dore the right to be terminated only for cause.

That AWI's letter went on to define at-will employment as employment that may be terminated at any time did not introduce ambiguity rendering the letter susceptible of being interpreted as allowing for an implied agreement that Dore could be terminated only for cause. In defining at-will employment, AWI used language similar to the language the Legislature used in our statutory provision. Labor Code section 2922 says that an "employment, *having no specified term*, may be terminated at the will of either party on notice to the other." (Italics added.)

. . . For the parties to specify—indeed to emphasize—that Dore's employment was at will (explaining that it could be terminated at any time) would make no sense if their true meaning was that his employment could be terminated only for cause. Thus, even though AWI's letter defined "at will" as meaning "at any time," without specifying it also meant without cause or for any or no reason, the letter's meaning was clear.

Nor did Dore's proffered extrinsic evidence render AWI's letter ambiguous concerning whether he could be terminated only for cause. As noted, Dore declared that he was told his role would be "critical" because AWI "needed a long-term fix" of certain problems and wanted Dore to "build a relationship" with an important new client. He also testified that he learned in interviews that some people at AWI had been employed there for long periods and he was assured the company had a family atmosphere. Even if credited, such evidence would not support an inference that Dore reasonably understood AWI's letter as consistent with a promise not to terminate him without cause. "When a dispute arises over the meaning of contract language, the first question to be decided is whether the language is 'reasonably susceptible' to the interpretation urged by the party. If it is not, the case is over." Southern Cal. Edison Co. v. Superior Court (1995) 37 Cal.App.4th 839, 847, 44 Cal.Rptr.2d 227.

We conclude, in sum, that AWI's letter contained no ambiguity, patent or latent, in its termination provisions. Accordingly, we agree with the trial court that no triable issues of fact exist with respect to Dore's causes of action for breach of contract and breach of the implied covenant of good faith and fair dealing. . . .

SECTION 4. STANDARDIZED TERMS, UNCONSCIONABLE INEQUALITY, AND GOOD FAITH

INTRODUCTORY NOTE

We have seen a number of instances in which one or more printed forms entered into the making of a contract. The classic use of preprinted writings is of course the "battle of the forms," where a form is sent by one party to the other and answered by the other's own form. Our concern now is not an exchange of forms (and the problems addressed through UCC 2–207), but the situation where one party simply signs, or acquiesces in, the standard form prepared and presented by the other—the much-maligned "contract of adhesion" that is infected with a take it or leave it quality. Most transactions between businesses and consumers fall into this pattern, as do a great many contracts between businesses. Accordingly, the recurring question is whether a party should be prevented from enforcing a term of a contract because the term is "buried in the fine print" and was not "freely negotiated."

Although our principal interest remains the "assent" analysis of traditional contract law, we will see that the talk in the cases in this section shifts often to "unconscionability" and "public policy." This is not surprising, since it is difficult to isolate the "assent problem" from the larger "fairness problem" that results from an imbalance of some sort, including boilerplate one-sidedness.

The starting point in the interpretation of fine-print terms in form contracts is the common law "duty to read." A Florida case, Allied Van Lines, Inc. v. Bratton, 351 So. 2d 344 (Fla. 1977), illustrates the reasoning commonly employed:

> May an interstate shipper avoid the legal consequences of a limitation of liability contained in a Bill of Lading issued by a carrier and signed by the shipper, on the ground that the shipper did not read the document and therefore did not assent to its provisions? . . . It has long been held in Florida that one is bound by his contract. Unless one can show facts and circumstances to demonstrate that he was prevented from reading the contract, or that he was induced by statements of the other party to refrain from reading the contract, it is binding. No party to a written contract in this state can defend against its enforcement on the sole ground that he signed it without reading it. . . . [Here, we are not] dealing with a situation where a shipper signed a Bill of Lading under the mistaken belief that it was not a contractual document at all. . . . In

> the [two cases] before us, there is no evidence of misrepresentation as to the character of the documents signed. Both shippers knew they were signing a contract. [One] simply did not read the documents furnished or even ask questions about the Bill of Lading. [The other's] situation is different, however, for she sought information, was misled by the carrier's agent as to available [insurance] coverage, and was prevented from exercising her right to choose adequate coverage. . . . [T]he legal consequences of the contract [she signed] may be avoided.

Observe that the "duty to read," like the "duty to speak" encountered earlier, appears rooted in the idea that action or inaction "with reason to know" results in a preclusion of sorts, a foregoing or waiver of the privilege of objecting to legal consequences. A good discussion of the formal approach indicated by the traditional rule can be found in Calamari, Duty to Read—A Changing Concept, 43 Fordham L. Rev. 341 (1974).

Yet the duty to read, like most legal generalizations, depends ultimately on circumstances; the duty may be raised or lowered, even extinguished. Take, for example, the ordinary transaction litigated in Agricultural Ins. Co. v. Constantine, 144 Ohio St. 275, 58 N.E.2d 658 (1944).

Bova parked her car on defendant's parking lot one morning, left her keys in the ignition as the attendant instructed her, and was given a "ticket." When Bova returned about 3 p.m., defendant could not locate the car on the lot. It was found by the police three days later, in a damaged condition, and returned to Bova. Plaintiff, having insured the car, paid $155 for the repairs and sued defendant to recover that amount. Defendant's answer alleged that the car had been removed from the lot by an unknown person, without the knowledge or consent of defendant's employees, and that on the ticket given to Bova was "printed in clear, legible type" the following:

> No attendant on duty after regular closing time. Cars left after closing hour at owner's risk. This station will endeavor to protect the property of its patrons, but it is agreed that it will not be liable for loss or damage of cars, accessories or contents, from whatever cause arising.

Plaintiff's evidence showed that Bova had parked her car on defendant's lot an average of twice a week for a period of five to six years, that she had always left the keys in the ignition as instructed, and, though given a ticket in the form described by defendant, she had never read it. At the conclusion of plaintiff's evidence, the trial court directed a verdict for defendant on the basis of the "not-liable-for-loss" provision on the ticket. This judgment was reversed by the court of appeals, and defendant appealed. Ohio's highest court agreed that the trial court's judgment was properly reversed. In considering the legal relations of Bova and the defendant, that court concluded:

(1) Since the attendant assumed control over and custody of the Bova automobile, defendant became a bailee rather than a mere lessor of a parking space.

(2) Under the "great weight of authority," a ticket like that given Bova was "a mere token for identification," and the terms on it limiting liability

did not become a part of the bailment contract, "at least in the absence of anything to indicate that the bailor assented to the conditions before delivering the property to the bailee." There was no evidence of Bova's assent. Her mere retention of the ticket was not enough, since she had no knowledge of the conditions on the ticket. Defendant should have called her attention to the printed terms.

(3) Even if Bova had assented to the exculpation clause, she would not have been bound by it since an attempt by a bailee for hire to relieve itself of liability for its negligence, "in the course of a general dealing with the public," is "contrary to law and against public policy."

Does it appear that defendant was attempting to take advantage of the special vulnerabilities of people like Bova (i.e., operating at the edges of fraud)? One court has noted that "perhaps most of us are blind when confronted by a parking receipt with disclaimers of liability on the back." Northwestern Nat'l Ins. Co. v. Donovan, 916 F.2d 372, 378 (7th Cir. 1990).

Weisz v. Parke-Bernet Galleries, Inc.

67 Misc. 2d 1077, 325 N.Y.S.2d 576 (N.Y. Civ. Ct. 1971)

At auctions conducted by defendant in May of 1962, Dr. Weisz purchased, for $3,348, a painting listed in the auction catalog as the work of "Raoul Dufy," and David and Irene Schwartz paid $9,360 for a painting also listed as Dufy's work. Later, as a result of a district attorney's investigation, all parties learned that the paintings in question were forgeries, of little value. When defendant denied any legal responsibility, Weisz and the Schwartzes sued to recover the prices paid for the paintings, alleging that defendant's catalog presentation constituted an express warranty of authenticity. Defendant relied on a "disclaimer" set forth in its catalog:

> The Galleries has endeavored to catalogue and describe the property correctly, but all property is sold "as is" and neither the Galleries nor its consignor warrants or represents, and they shall in no event be responsible for, the correctness of description, genuineness, authorship, . . . or condition of the property, and no statement contained in the catalogue or made orally at the sale or elsewhere shall be deemed to be such a warranty or representation, or an assumption of liability.

This disclaimer was positioned on a preliminary page of the catalog, entitled "Conditions of Sale" in large print, under which appeared 15 paragraphs running a page and a half in length (the disclaimer was paragraph 2), in print somewhat smaller in size than that used in most of the catalog. Following the "Conditions" pages came an index of the works to be auctioned, listed alphabetically by the name of the artist, with catalog numbers provided. The balance of the catalog consisted of over 80 pages setting forth a black-and-white reproduction of each painting and descriptive material about the artist and the work. At both auctions, the procedure followed by defendant was simply to announce at the outset that "the auction is subject to the conditions of sale"; no reference to the disclaimer or other "conditions" was made.

A jury having been waived, the trial judge first concluded that Dr. Weisz had no knowledge of the "conditions of sale." Nor could he be charged with knowledge, since, in the circumstances, a reasonable bidder on defendant's impressive premises would not expect that a catalog "overwhelmingly devoted to descriptions of works of art" would also disclaim liability for the accuracy of the very information provided. To bind Dr. Weisz, defendant must do "considerably more" by way of notice. The Schwartzes, on the other hand, knew of the disclaimer; the question, then, is whether "the language of disclaimer relied upon as a bar to the action should be deemed effective for that purpose." The judge ruled the disclaimer ineffective, saying:

> Parke-Bernet expected that bidders at its auctions would rely upon the accuracy of its descriptions, and intended that they should. [It] is an exceedingly well-known gallery, linked in the minds of people with the handling, exhibition, and sale of valuable artistic works and invested with an aura of expertness and reliability. The very fact that Parke-Bernet was offering a work of art for sale would inspire confidence that it was genuine. . . .
>
> The wording of the catalogue was clearly designed to emphasize the genuineness of the works to be offered. . . . After reassuring the reader that Parke-Bernet endeavored to catalogue the works of art correctly, there follow highly technical and legalistic words of disclaimer in a situation in which plain and emphatic words are required. And this provision, in light of the critical importance to the buyer of a warning that he may not rely on the fact that a work attributed to an artist was in fact his creation, is in no way given the special prominence that it clearly requires. The language used, the understated manner of its presentation, the failure to refer to it explicitly in the preliminary oral announcement at the auction, all lead to the conclusion that Parke-Bernet did not expect the bidders to take the disclaimer too seriously or to be too concerned about it. I am convinced that the average reader of this provision would view it as some kind of technicality that should in no way derogate from the certainty that he was buying genuine artistic works, and that this was precisely the impression intended to be conveyed.

[The judgments for the plaintiffs in the *Weisz* case were reversed by the Appellate Term of the New York Supreme Court, in part on the ground that defendant's catalog "gave [a] leading and prominent place, in its prefatory terms of sale, [to] a clear, unequivocal disclaimer of any express or implied warranty or representation of genuineness of any paintings." In addition, the situation itself—a public auction of paintings whose value depended upon "the degree of certainty with which they could be authenticated"—required that plaintiffs act "with the caution of one in circumstances abounding with signals of *caveat emptor*." 77 Misc. 2d 80, 351 N.Y.S.2d 911 (1974).]

COMMENT: FORM "CONTRACTS"

It has been observed that ours is not an economy "in which the terms of every transaction, or even of most transactions, are individually dickered; even when they are, standard clauses are commonly incorporated in the final contract, without separate negotiation of each of them." Northwestern Nat'l Ins. Co. v. Donovan, 916 F.2d 372, 377 (7th Cir. 1990). Many of the same ideas reappear in the following discussion by Karl Llewellyn, The Common Law Tradition 362–363 (1960), including the impulse to economize in carrying out repetitive transactions:

> I know of few "private" law problems which remotely rival the importance, economic, governmental, or "law"-legal, of the form-pad agreement, and I know of none which has been either more disturbing to life or more baffling to lawyers.
>
> The impetus to the form-pad is clear, for any business unit: by standardizing terms, and by standardizing even the spot on the form where any individually dickered term appears, one saves all the time and skill otherwise needed to dig out and record the meaning of variant language; one makes check-up, totaling, follow-through, etc., into routine operations; one has duplicates (in many colors) available for the administration of a multidepartment business; and so on more. The content of the standardized terms accumulates experience, it avoids or reduces legal risks and also confers all kinds of operating leeways and advantages, all without need of either consulting counsel from instance to instance or of bargaining with the other parties. Not to be overlooked, either, is the tailoring of the crude misfitting hand-me-down pattern of the "general law" "in the absence of agreement" to the particular detailed working needs of your own line of business—whether apartment rentals, stock brokerage, international grain trade, installment selling of appliances, flour milling, sugar beet raising, or insurance. It would be a heart-warming scene, a triumph of private attention to what is essentially private self-government in the lesser transactions of life or in those areas too specialized for the blunt, slow tools of the legislature—if only all businessmen and all their lawyers would be reasonable.
>
> But power, like greed, if it does not always corrupt, goes easily to the head. So that the form-agreements tend either at once or over the years, and often by whole lines of trade, into a massive and almost terrifying jug-handled character; the one party lays his head into the mouth of a lion—either, and mostly, without reading the fine print, or occasionally in hope and expectation (not infrequently solid) that it will be a sweet and gentle lion.

After giving some of the reasons why standardized forms may have terms that seem one-sided, Llewellyn added that it was no less vital to note that:

> [W]here, as with the overseas grain contracts or the Pacific Coast dried fruit contracts or the Worth Street Rules on textiles,

two-fisted bargainers on either side have worked out in the form a balanced code to govern the particular line or trade or industry, there is every reason for a court to assume both fairness and wisdom in the terms, and to seek in first instance to learn, understand, and fit both its own thinking and its action into the whole design. Contracts of this kind (so long as reasonable in the net) are a road to better than official-legal regulation of our economic life; indeed, they tend to lead into the setting up of their own quick, cheap, expert tribunals.

Llewellyn then described the methods by which courts, when troubled by unfairly one-sided terms, "construed" language to mean the opposite of what it obviously was saying, to find inconsistencies so that troublesome clauses could be treated as cancelled out, even to reject particular clauses as counter to the purposes of the transactions they served. He criticized such techniques for providing invitations to form-writers to "recur to the attack" and try again, as failing to give guidance by marking out the minimum decencies for particular transaction-types, and (being "tools of intentional and creative misconstruction") as seriously embarrassing efforts to find the true meaning of wholly legitimate clauses. "Covert tools are never reliable tools." Llewellyn then discussed the possibilities of finding statutory solutions (especially through provisions like UCC 2–302), but concluded that in our system an approach through statute was dubious, uncertain, likely to be awkward and spotty in its results. The "true answer," he said, was obvious.

The answer, I suggest, is this: Instead of thinking about "assent" to boiler-plate clauses, we can recognize that so far as concerns the specific, there is no assent at all. What has in fact been assented to, specifically, are the few dickered terms, and the broad type of the transaction, and but one thing more. That one thing more is a blanket assent (not a specific assent) to any not unreasonable or indecent terms the seller may have on his form, which do not alter or eviscerate the reasonable meaning of the dickered terms. The fine print which has not been read has no business to cut under the reasonable meaning of those dickered terms which constitute the dominant and only real expression of agreement. . . .

The queer thing is that where the transaction occurs without the fine print present, courts do not find this general line of approach too hard to understand; . . . nor can I see a court having trouble, where a short memo agrees in due course to sign "our standard contract," in rejecting an outrageous form as not being fairly within the reasonable meaning of the term. The clearest case to see is the handing over of a blank check: no court, judging as between the parties, would fail to reach for the circumstances, in determining whether the amount filled in had gone beyond the reasonable.

Why, then, can we not face the fact where boiler-plate is present? There has been an arm's-length deal, with dickered terms. There has been accompanying that basic deal another which, if not on any fiduciary basis, at least involves a plain expression of confidence, asked and accepted, with a corresponding limit on the powers granted: the boiler-plate is assented to en bloc, "unsight, unseen," on the implicit assumption and to the full extent that (1) it does not alter or impair the fair meaning of the dickered terms when read alone, and (2) that its terms are neither in the particular nor in the net manifestly unreasonable and unfair. Such is the reality, and I see nothing in the way of a court's operating on that basis, to truly effectuate the only intention which can in reason be worked out as common to the two parties, granted good faith. And if the boiler-plate party is not playing in good faith, there is law enough to bar that fact from benefiting it. We had a hundred years of sales law in which any sales transaction with explicit words resulted in two several contracts for the one consideration: that of sale, and the collateral one of warranty. The idea is applicable here, for better reason: any contract with boiler-plate results in two several contracts: the *dickered* deal, and the collateral one of *supplementary* boiler-plate.

Rooted in sense, history, and simplicity, it is an answer which could occur to anyone.

KARL N. LLEWELLYN
1893–1962

Motors and Chrysler to recover damages for her personal injuries; her husband joined in the action, seeking recovery of consequential losses. Both claims were based on an alleged breach of an implied warranty of merchantability imposed by the Uniform Sales Act. The defense relied on a contractual disclaimer of the warranty, which the Sales Act would permit. The disclaimer in question appeared on the back of the sales contract, among 8½ inches of fine type, consisting of 10 separate paragraphs and 65 lines. It purported to limit liability for breach of any warranty to replacement of defective parts within 90 days of the sale or before the car had been driven 4,000 miles, whichever period was shorter.

The sales contract was a one-page printed form, front and back. Most of the print on the front was twelve-point type. Near the bottom of the front, above the signature lines, the type became smaller, different in style, and more difficult to read. The following paragraphs appeared there:

> The front and back of this Order comprise the entire agreement affecting this purchase and no other agreement or understanding of any nature concerning same has been made or entered into, or will be recognized. . . .
>
> I have read the matter printed on the back hereof and agree to it as a part of this order the same as if it were printed above my signature. I certify that I am 21 years of age, or older, and hereby acknowledge receipt of a copy of this Order.

Henningsen testified that he did not read these two paragraphs or any of the printed material on the back of the form. This evidence was not contradicted and defendants did not contend that any of these provisions were called to Henningsen's attention.

From a judgment for plaintiffs, the defendants appealed. The opinion of Justice Francis fills 60 pages in the official report; it has been severely edited here.]

FRANCIS, J. . . . The terms of the warranty are a sad commentary upon the automobile manufacturers' marketing practices. Warranties developed in the law . . . to protect the ordinary consumer who cannot be expected to have the knowledge or capacity or even the opportunity to make adequate inspection of mechanical instrumentalities, like automobiles, and to decide for himself whether they are reasonably fit for the designed purpose. . . . But the ingenuity of the Automobile Manufacturers Association [AMA], by means of its standardized form, has metamorphosed the warranty into a device to limit the maker's liability. . . .

[W]hat effect should be given to the express warranty in question which seeks to limit the manufacturer's liability to replacement of defective parts, and which disclaims all other warranties, express or implied? . . . [W]e must keep in mind the general principle that, in the absence of fraud, one who does not choose to read a contract before signing it, cannot later relieve himself of its burdens. . . . And in applying that principle, the basic tenet of freedom of competent parties to contract is a factor of importance. But in the framework of modern commercial life and business practices, such rules cannot be applied on a strict, doctrinal basis. The conflicting interests of the buyer and seller must be evaluated realistically and justly, giving due weight to the social policy evinced by the Uniform Sales Act, the progressive decisions of the courts engaged in administering it, the mass production methods of manufacture and distribution to the public, and the bargaining position occupied by the ordinary consumer in such an economy. This history of the law shows that legal doctrines, as first expounded, often prove to be inadequate under the impact of later experience. . . .

The traditional contract is the result of free bargaining of parties who are brought together by the play of the market, and who meet each other on a footing of approximate economic equality. In such a society there is no danger that freedom of contract will be a threat to the social order as a whole. But in present-day commercial life the standardized mass contract has appeared. It is used primarily by enterprises with strong bargaining power and position. "The weaker party, in need of the goods or services, is frequently not in a position to shop around for better terms, either because the author of the standard contract has a monopoly (natural or artificial) or because all competitors use the same clauses. His contractual intention is but a subjection more or less voluntary to terms dictated by the stronger party, terms whose consequences are often understood in a vague way, if at all." Kessler, "Contracts of Adhesion—Some Thoughts About Freedom of Contract," 43 Colum.L.Rev. 629, 632 (1943). . . .

The warranty before us is a standardized form designed for mass use. It is imposed upon the automobile consumer. He takes it or leaves it, and he must take it to buy an automobile. No bargaining is engaged in with respect to it. In fact, the dealer through whom it comes to the buyer is without authority to alter it; his function is ministerial—simply to deliver it. The form warranty is not only standard with Chrysler, but, as mentioned above, it is the uniform warranty of the [AMA] . . . .

The gross inequality of bargaining position occupied by the consumer in the automobile industry is thus apparent. There is no competition among the car makers in the area of the express warranty. Where can the buyer go to negotiate for better protection? Such control and limitation of his remedies are inimical to the public welfare and, at the very least, call for great care by the courts to avoid injustice through application of strict common-law principles of freedom of contract. Because there is no competition among the motor vehicle manufacturers with respect to the scope of protection guaranteed to the buyer, there is no incentive on their part to stimulate good will in that field of public relations. Thus, there is lacking a factor existing in more competitive fields, one which tends to guarantee the safe construction of the article sold. . . .

Although the courts, with few exceptions, have been most sensitive to problems presented by contracts resulting from gross disparity in buyer-seller bargaining positions, they have not articulated a general principle condemning, as opposed to public policy, the imposition on the buyer of a skeleton warranty as a means of limiting the responsibility of the manufacturer. They have endeavored thus far to avoid a drastic departure from age-old tenets of freedom of contract by adopting doctrines of strict construction, and notice and knowledgeable assent by the buyer to the attempted exculpation of the seller. . . . Accordingly to be found in the cases are statements that disclaimers and the consequent limitation of liability will not be given effect if "unfairly procured"; . . . if not brought to the buyer's attention and he was not made understandingly aware of it; . . . or if not clear and explicit. . . .

The rigid scrutiny which the courts give to attempted limitations of warranties and of the liability that would normally flow from a transaction is not limited to the field of sales of goods. Clauses on baggage checks restricting the liability of common carriers for loss or damage in transit are not enforceable unless the limitation is fairly and honestly negotiated and understandingly entered into. If not called specifically to the patron's attention, it is not binding. It is not enough merely to show the form of a contract; it must appear also that the agreement was understandingly made. . . . The same holds true in cases of such limitations on parcel check room tickets, . . . and on storage warehouse receipts; . . . on automobile parking lot or garage tickets or claim checks; . . . as to exculpatory clauses in leases releasing a landlord of apartments in a multiple dwelling house from all liability for negligence where inequality of bargaining exists, see Annot., 175 A.L.R. 8 (1948) . . . .

It is true that the rule governing [many of] the limitation of liability cases . . . is generally applied in situations said to involve services of a public or semi-public nature. Typical, of course, are the public carrier or storage or parking lot cases. . . . But in recent times the books have not been barren of instances of its application in private contract controversies. . . . Basically, the reason a contracting party offering services of a public or *quasi*-public nature has been held to the requirements of fair dealing, and, when it attempts to limit its liability, of securing the understanding consent of the patron or consumer, is because members of the public generally have no other means of fulfilling the specific need represented by the contract. Having in mind the situation in the automobile industry as detailed above, . . . there would appear to be no just reason why the principles of all of the cases set forth should not chart the course to be taken here.

It is undisputed that [the dealer] with whom Henningsen dealt did not specifically call attention to the warranty on the back of the purchase order. The form and the arrangement of its face, as described above, certainly would cause the minds of reasonable men to differ as to whether notice of a yielding of basic rights stemming from the relationship with the manufacturer was adequately given. The words "warranty" or "limited warranty" did not even appear in the fine print above the place for signature. . . .

But there is more than this. Assuming that a jury might find that the fine print referred to reasonably served the objective of directing a buyer's attention to the warranty on the reverse side, and, therefore, that he should be charged with awareness of its language, can it be said that an ordinary layman would realize what he was relinquishing in return for what he was being granted? Under the law, breach of warranty against defective parts or workmanship which caused personal injuries would entitle a buyer to damages even if due care were used in the manufacturing process. Because of the great potential for harm if the vehicle was defective, that right is the most important and fundamental one arising from the relationship. Difficulties so frequently encountered in establishing negligence in manufacture in the ordinary case, make this manifest. . . . Any ordinary layman of reasonable intelligence, looking at the phraseology, might well conclude that Chrysler was agreeing to replace defective parts and perhaps replace anything that went wrong because of defective workmanship during the first 90 days or 4,000 miles of operation, but that he would not be entitled to a new car. It is not unreasonable to believe that the entire scheme being conveyed was a proposed remedy for physical deficiencies in the car. *In the context* of this warranty, only the abandonment of all sense of justice would permit us to hold that, as a matter of law, the phrase "its obligation under this warranty being limited to making good at its factory any part or parts thereof" signifies to an ordinary reasonable person that he is relinquishing any personal injury claim that might flow from the use of a defective automobile. Such claims are nowhere mentioned. . . .

The task of the judiciary is to administer the spirit as well as the letter of the law. . . . [P]art of that burden is to protect the ordinary man against the loss of important rights through what, in effect, is the unilateral act of the manufacturer. . . . From the standpoint of the purchaser, there can be no arms length negotiating on the subject [of warranties]. Because his capacity for bargaining is so grossly unequal, the inexorable conclusion which follows is that he is not permitted to bargain at all. . . .

Public policy is a term not easily defined. Its significance varies as the habits and needs of a people may vary. It is not static and the field of application is an ever increasing one. A contract, or a particular provision therein, valid in one era may be wholly opposed to the public policy of another. . . . Public policy at a given time finds expression in the Constitution, the statutory law and in judicial decisions. In the area of sale of goods, the legislative will has imposed an implied warranty of merchantability as a general incident of sale of an automobile by description. The warranty does not depend upon the affirmative intention of the parties. It is a child of the law; it annexes itself to the contract because of the very nature of the transaction. . . . The judicial process has recognized a right to recover damages for personal injuries arising from a breach of that warranty. The disclaimer of the implied warranty and exclusion of all obligations except those specifically assumed by the express warranty signify a studied effort to frustrate that protection. True, the Sales Act authorizes agreements between buyer and seller qualifying the warranty obligations. But quite obviously the Legislature contemplated lawful stipulations (which are determined by the circumstances of a particular case) arrived at freely by parties of relatively equal bargaining strength. The lawmakers did not authorize the automobile manufacturer to use its grossly disproportionate bargaining power to relieve itself from liability and to impose on the ordinary buyer, who in effect has no real freedom of choice, the grave danger of injury to himself and others that attends the sale of such a dangerous instrumentality as a defectively made automobile. . . . [W]e are of the opinion that Chrysler's attempted disclaimer of an implied warranty of merchantability and of the obligations arising therefrom is so inimical to the public good as to compel an adjudication of its invalidity. . . . The principles that have been expounded as to the obligation of the manufacturer apply with equal force to the separate express warranty of the dealer. . . .

[W]e conclude that the disclaimer of an implied warranty of merchantability by the dealer, as well as the attempted elimination of all obligations other than replacement of defective parts, are violative of public policy and void. . . . [T]he judgments in favor of the plaintiffs and against the defendants are affirmed.

NOTE

At the time of *Henningsen*, three manufacturers made substantially all of the cars sold in the United States, and they entered an explicit agreement to provide the same warranty and to require their dealers to do the same. Indeed, the minutes survive from the meeting in which this agreement was discussed and voted upon. The 4,000-mile warranty that was to persist until the 1960s was put in place in the 1930s. See Fed. Trade Comm'n, Report on the Motor Vehicle Industry at 56–57 (1939). Does the existence of an agreement among the manufacturers to limit the warranties they offered change the way you look at the case?

The UCC replaced the Sales Act in New Jersey some three years after *Henningsen* (most of our state legislatures did the same by the 1960s). Hence, today, and nearly everywhere, considerable "public policy" relating to the sale of goods, including warranty creations and disclaimers and limitations on remedies, is to be found in the UCC. Take a look at §§ 2–314, 2–315, 2–316, 2–719, and 2–302. In the excerpt immediately below, Professor Grant Gilmore provides some broad outlines of the story as it was unfolding in the middle of the last century. The seller's warranty liability was only a part of a larger story. The major tort development he notes, the move to strict liability for personal injuries caused by an allegedly defective product, was in fact accelerated shortly after *Henningsen* was decided. See Restatement of Torts, Second § 402A.

The full picture of the overlap between warranty and tort law, and the question whether one is preemptive of the other, must await courses in Commercial Law and Products Liability. The summary of Superwood Corp. v. Siempelkamp Corp., below, suggests a principal means of ensuring that the UCC governs ordinary commercial disputes. Much depends on the type of loss asserted—personal injury, property damage (the product itself, or other property), or business harms (contract interests). Observe that the UCC attempts to take account of such differences, e.g., §§ 2–318, 2–715(2), 2–719(3). On the "conspicuousness" of warranty exclusion in form contracts, a representative application of § 2–316 can be found in Sierra Diesel Injection Serv. v. Burroughs Corp., 890 F.2d 108 (9th Cir. 1989).

Grant Gilmore, Law, Logic and Experience

3 How. L. J. 26, 40–41 (1957)

"In most social or economic relationships there is an active party and a passive party, an enterprising party and a party who merely receives—which is, we are told on authority, less blessed. Over the past hundred years—to go no further back—we have experienced a curious shift of attitude toward the relative merits of action and passivity. Our forefathers were, on the whole, tender toward the party who acted: it was better to do than to do nothing; action should be encouraged; and, since action is dangerous, the actor should be protected from the incidentally harmful consequences of his socially useful activity. The risks, therefore, should fall on the passive party. We have, even in our own generation, made great strides toward reversing that position. Ethically, we feel, the weak should be protected against the strong, and the full consequences of his actions should be visited on the head of whoever dares to act.

"In politics and government—if a private law man may poach for a moment on the public law domain—we may see an illustration of what we are saying in the downfall of laissez-faire and the rise of the welfare state, not to mention our current passion for security—political, economic and social. We seek protection and stability and status—which means, in an overliteral sense to be sure, the right to stand still wherever we are. . . .

"It has been a commonplace of legal scholarship that one of the great ground-swells of movement in the nineteenth century was from status to contract—from the protection of rights of property and ownership to the protection of rights of contract. It is easy to see how this should have happened as wealth multiplied and an aristocratic society gave way to its pushing, aggressive, dynamic successor. I suggest that the ground-swell carried an undercurrent with it and that, as the great wave recedes, we are being caught in the undertow. The next half century may well record a reverse movement.

"In the crucial business of allocating commercial and social risks we have already gone a long way toward reversing the nineteenth century. In tort we follow a banner which bears the strange device: liability without fault—although we soften the impact on the innocent tortfeasor by various schemes of insurance and compensation. In contract we have broken decisively with the nineteenth century theory that breach of contract was not very serious and not very reprehensible—as Justice Holmes once put it: every man is 'free to break his contract if he chooses'—from which it followed that damages for breach should be held to a minimum. Today we look on breach of contract as a very serious and immoral thing indeed: never, I dare say, in our history have the remedies for breach been so easily available to the victim, or the sanctions for breach so heavy against the violator—who will be, in most cases, the active or enterprising party. The continuing increase in seller's warranty liability is merely one illustration of what has been going on all along the contract front.

"I assume—although I will not attempt to prove, if indeed I could—that what has been going on, alike in our public law theories of the state and in the obscure and dusty corner of the private law attic which we have visited this afternoon [the obligation imposed on a seller of goods for their quality], reflects a great swing in our fundamental ethical concepts—a swing which, at a still further remove, reflects, if it did not inspire, the later stages of the industrial, economic and technological revolution of the past two hundred years. As I suggested, nothing can ever be explained—but the perspective is a spacious one."

Superwood Corp. v. Siempelkamp Corp.

311 N.W.2d 159 (Minn. 1981)

A press plaintiff had purchased from defendant failed and could not be repaired. Plaintiff sued in a federal district court, alleging claims in negligence, strict tort, breach of warranty, and breach of contract, and asking for $600,000 in damages for lost profits and damage to the press itself. After ruling that the contract and warranty claims were barred by the statute of limitations, the federal court certified questions of "uncertain" state law to the Supreme Court of Minnesota: "1. Is the manufacturer of defective equipment (a press) . . . liable in negligence to the user of the equipment damaged in its property and business? 2. Is the manufacturer of defective equipment (a press) strictly liable in tort to the user of the equipment damaged in its property and business by the product defect?" The Minnesota court answered both questions in the negative, saying: "The U.C.C. clarifies the rights and remedies of parties to commercial transactions. For example, there are specific provisions covering warranties, [§ 2–314]; warranty disclaimers, [§ 2–316]; liability limitations, [§ 2–719]; and notice provisions, [§ 2–607]. The recognition of tort actions in the instant case would create a theory of redress not envisioned by the legislature when it enacted the U.C.C. Furthermore, tort theories of recovery would be totally unrestrained by legislative liability limitations, warranty disclaimers and notice provisions. To allow tort liability in commercial transactions would totally emasculate these provisions of the U.C.C. . . . We, however, do not [believe] that the U.C.C. was intended to preempt the entire area of products liability. Strict products liability developed in large part to fill gaps in the law of sales with respect to consumer purchasers. . . . Limiting the application of strict products liability to consumers' actions or actions involving personal injury will allow the U.C.C. to satisfy the needs of the commercial sector and still protect the legitimate expectations of consumers. . . . [W]e hold that economic losses that arise out of commercial transactions, except those involving personal injury or damage to other property, are not recoverable under the tort theories of negligence or strict product liability."

[Observe that the court's distinction between physical harms to person or property and commercial harms is based on the traditional thinking that separates contract from tort (contract liability rests on obligations undertaken by bargain, tort liability on duties imposed by law). The function of the "economic loss" doctrine, a judicially-created rule of case law, is to confine remedies for contract-type losses—the "inadequate value" that results from a failure of performance—to the well-developed remedies of contract law featured in this book. The problems, and divisions, in applying the doctrine are collected in Fox & Loftus, Riding the Choppy Waters of East River: Economic Loss Doctrine Ten Years Later, 64 Def. Couns. J. 260 (1997).]

Richards v. Richards

Supreme Court of Wisconsin, 1994.
181 Wis. 2d 1007, 513 N.W.2d 118.

ABRAHAMSON, J. . . . The circuit court granted summary judgment to Monkem Co., the defendant, dismissing the complaint with prejudice. It held that the form signed by Jerilyn Richards, the plaintiff, was an exculpatory contract that was not void or unenforceable as contrary to public policy. It further held that the plaintiff's claim for injuries suffered while riding as a passenger in a truck operated by Leo Richards, her husband, and owned by Monkem Co., her husband's employer, was clearly within the contemplation of the parties at the time the exculpatory contract was executed. The circuit court thus foreclosed the plaintiff's claim as a matter of law [and the] court of appeals affirmed. . . . [We reverse].

. . . An examination of the principles underlying the determination of the validity of exculpatory contracts leads us to the conclusion that the form is an unenforceable exculpatory contract due to a combination of three factors. None of these factors alone would necessarily invalidate the release; however, taken together . . . the contract is void as against public policy. . . .

In February 1990, Leo Richards was hired by Monkem Co. as an over-the-road truck driver. Shortly thereafter, the plaintiff and her husband discussed the possibility of her riding as a passenger with him. Before the plaintiff could accompany her husband, however, Monkem required that she sign a form entitled "Passenger Authorization," and she did so on or about May 22, 1990.

The "Passenger Authorization" form used by Monkem appears to have two purposes. First, it served as the Company's authorization to the passenger to ride in a company truck. Second, it serves as a passenger's general release of all claims against the Company. The language of release attempts to transform the "Passenger Authorization" form into an exculpatory contract relieving Monkem and all of its affiliated companies, partnerships, individuals and corporations (as well as others) from any and all liability for harm to the person signing the form. . . . The form reads as follows:

Passenger Authorization

Date: 5/22/90

Full and final release covering all claims or rights of action of every description past, present or future.

I/we being of lawful age, for myself/ourselves, my/our heirs, administrators, executors, successors, and assigns, hereby fully and forever release an[d] discharge the said Monkem Co., Inc., and all affiliated, associated, or subsidiary companies, partnerships, individuals or corporations and all other person, firms, and corporations, and their heirs, administrators, executors, successors, and assigns from any and all actions, causes of actions, claim and demands of whatsoever kind or nature on account of any and all known and unknown injuries, losses, and damages by me/us or my/our property sustained or received while a passenger in any and all equipment, vehicles, or while located on any/all Monkem Co., Inc./Joplin Hiway, Inc. property.

It is expressly understood and agreed that this release is intended to cover and does cover not only all now known injuries, losses and damages, but any future injuries, losses and damages not now known or anticipated, but which may later develop or be discovered, including all the effects and consequences thereof.

Permission is granted by Monkem Co., Inc. for *Jerilyn Richards* to be a passenger in Monkem Co., Inc./Joplin Hiway Inc./Burlington Motor carrier leasing vehicle unit number *42424* for a period starting *6/1/90* and ending 9/1/90. This permission is given only upon full understanding of the above release and is accepted and executed and acknowledged by signature of the person below:

Absolutely no driving privileges

Signed /s/ L. J. Richards
Driver Signature

Signed /s/ Jerilyn Richards
Passenger Signature

/s/ C. L. McCarley
C.L. McCarley, Director of Risk Mgt.

On June 14, 1990, plaintiff accompanied her husband on one of his scheduled trips. When the truck, negotiating a left curve, overturned, plaintiff was pinned inside the vehicle. The injuries she sustained as a result of this accident are the basis for the current lawsuit.

The principles applicable to the determination of the validity of exculpatory contracts were recently set forth in Dobratz v. Thomson, 161 Wis.2d 502, 468 N.W.2d 654 (1991), which incorporated, explained, and elaborated on the principles set forth in several earlier cases. See, e.g., Discount Fabric House v. Wisconsin Tel. Co., 117 Wis.2d 587, 345 N.W.2d 417 (1984) (contract releasing liability of telephone company for negligent omission of ad from yellow pages); Arnold v. Shawano Co. Agr. Socy., 111 Wis.2d 203, 330 N.W.2d 773 (1983) (contract releasing liability of race track to driver), overruled on other grounds; Merten v. Nathan, 108 Wis.2d 205, 321 N.W.2d 173 (1982) (contract releasing liability of horseback riding school to pupil); and College Mobile Home Park & Sales v. Hoffmann, 72 Wis.2d 514, 241 N.W.2d 174 (1976) (contract releasing liability of landlord to tenant).

. . . Exculpatory contracts are not favored by the law because they tend to allow conduct below the acceptable standard of care applicable to the activity. Exculpatory contracts are not, however, automatically void and unenforceable as contrary to public policy. . . . Rather, a court closely examines whether such agreements violate public policy and construes them strictly against the party seeking to rely on them. [*Merten*],108 Wis.2d 205.

In determining whether an exculpatory agreement [is] void, courts recognize that public policy is not an easily defined concept. The concept embodies the common sense and common conscience of the community. Public policy is that principle of law under which "freedom of contract is restricted by law for the good of the community." [*Merten*, 108 Wis. 2d at 213.] In [*Dobratz*,] 161 Wis.2d 502, 520, a unanimous court, striking down an overly broad release, stated that "this court will not favor an exculpatory contract that is broad and general in its terms."

In reviewing an exculpatory agreement for violation of public policy, a court attempts to accommodate the tension between the principles of contract and tort law that are inherent in such an agreement. The law of contract is based on the principle of freedom of contract; people should be able to manage their own affairs without government interference. Freedom of contract is premised on a bargain freely and voluntarily made through a bargaining process that has integrity. Contract law protects justifiable expectations and the security of transactions. The law of torts is directed toward compensation of individuals for injuries resulting from the unreasonable conduct of another. Tort law also serves the "prophylactic" purpose of preventing future harm; tort law seeks to deter certain conduct by imposing liability for conduct below the acceptable standard of care. . . .

Applying these principles[,] we conclude that the exculpatory contract at issue is void as against public policy. In this case, the public policy "of imposing liability on persons whose conduct creates an unreasonable risk of harm" outweighs the public policy of "freedom of contract." [*Merten*], 108 Wis.2d at 215. Accordingly we conclude that it would be contrary to public policy to enforce the exculpatory language in Monkem Co.'s "Passenger Authorization" form. A combination of three factors in this case leads us to this conclusion.

First, the contract serves two purposes, not clearly identified or distinguished[:] . . . (1) the Company authorizes the passenger to ride in a Company truck, and (2) the passenger releases the Company and others from liability. This dual function, however, is not made clear in the title of the contract; the form is designated merely as a "Passenger Authorization." The written terms clearly state that the document is a release of liability. A person signing a document has a duty to read it and know the contents of the writing. . . . Nevertheless it is not reasonably clear to the signer of a form entitled "Passenger Authorization" that the document would in reality be the passenger's agreement to release the Company (and others) from liability. Rather the title "Passenger Authorization" implies that only the Company is making the concessions and only the Company is bound. We conclude that [this] release should have been conspicuously labelled as such to put the person signing the form on notice. Moreover, to prevent confusion under these circumstances, the passenger's release of the Company from liability should have been carefully identified and distinguished from the Company's authorization for a passenger to ride along. Identifying and distinguishing clearly between those two contractual arrangements could have provided important protection against a signatory's inadvertent agreement to the release.

Second, the release is extremely broad and all-inclusive. It purports to excuse intentional, reckless, and negligent conduct not only by the Company but by another entity (Joplin Hiway, Inc.) and by all affiliated, associated, or subsidiary companies, partnerships, individuals, or corporations, and all other persons, firms or corporations. Further, although the passenger's release is combined with the Company's authorization to the plaintiff to ride in a specified Company vehicle during a specified period, the release does not refer to an injury the plaintiff may sustain while riding as a passenger in the specified Company vehicle during the specified time period. It purports to release the Company from liability for any and all injury to the plaintiff while the plaintiff is a passenger in any vehicle (not necessarily one owned by the Company) at any time and while the plaintiff is on any and all Company property at any time. The release, unlike the authorization, is not limited to a specified vehicle or to a specified time period. Had the Company intended that it be released from liability to the plaintiff while she was riding with her husband in the Company truck during the period the Company authorized, that is not what the release says. The very breadth of the release raises questions about its meaning and demonstrates its one-sidedness; it is unreasonably favorable to the Company, the drafter of the contract. . . .

Third, this contract is a standardized agreement on the Company's printed form which offers little or no opportunity for negotiation or free and voluntary bargaining. . . . [W]hen the Company forwarded the form to plaintiff its cover letter did not advise her that the document was a release of all claims and did not advise her of the legal significance attached to her signing of the document. The employee handbook advised employees that Company authorization was needed for a passenger to ride along but did not advise employees that the passenger would have to release all claims against the Company.

The fact that a release is printed in a standardized form is not, by itself, enough to invalidate it. However, the plaintiff's lack of an opportunity for discussing and negotiating the contract is significant when considered with the breadth of the release. If her plans to ride with her husband were to go forward, the plaintiff simply had to adhere to the terms of the written form. While the Company had the time and resources to draft the provisions and plan their effect, the plaintiff did not. Had the plaintiff been afforded the opportunity to negotiate a release, she might have declined to release the Company from liability for intentional or reckless actions or the driver's negligence, or from liability for its defective equipment. Because the Company probably derives some benefit from allowing family members to join drivers on the road, such as improving employee morale, the Company might not necessarily have rejected such proposals out of hand.

As we have said, none of these factors alone would necessarily have warranted invalidation of the exculpatory contract. [But here] a combination of these factors demonstrate that adherence to the principle of freedom of contract is not heavily favored. The principle of tort law, to compensate persons for injuries resulting from unreasonable conduct of another, prevails. Accordingly, . . . the document contravenes public policy and is void and unenforceable. The decision of the court of appeals is reversed and the cause remanded for proceedings not inconsistent with this opinion.

[The vote was 4 to 3. The dissenters disagreed with each of the reasons given by the majority, as well as their application "in combination."]

NOTE

As *Richards* illustrates, it is not unusual for courts to associate form contracts with inequality of bargaining power. We shall see more of this. For now, it should be enough simply to direct attention to some of the main issues. The overriding question would seem to be whether excessive one-sidedness built into fine-print forms raises problems that, on balance, are a mismatch for the assent doctrines of general contract law. Even if it were feasible for courts to conduct evidentiary hearings on issues of relative market power and overall bargaining fairness, case-by-case and form-by-form, the finding of imbalance does not itself dictate a conclusion of impaired assent. Persons and firms no doubt sign form contracts for any number of reasons, including a desire to act quickly and inexpensively and a wish to be unburdened by a mass of detail (mainly nonperformance terms) that probably will never come up. Perhaps the test of fine-print terms should be "externalized," that is, turned away from the parties themselves, at least to the extent of viewing superior bargaining power as primarily a matter to be observed, and taken note of, not probed. Look again at the court's approach in *Richards*. Has conventional "assent analysis" been removed altogether?

Woollums v. Horsley

Court of Appeals of Kentucky, 1892.
93 Ky. 582, 20 S.W. 781.

HOLT, C.J. In August, 1887, the appellant, John Woollums, was living upon his mountain farm of 200 acres in Bell County. He was then about 60 years old, uneducated, afflicted with disease disabling him from work, owned no other land, and very little personal property. He knew but little of what was going on in the business world. . . . He moved in a small circle.

At this time the appellee, W.J. Horsley, who was then a man of large and varied experience in business; who was then buying mineral rights in that locality by the thousands of acres, and who was evidently familiar with all that was then going on and near at hand in the way of business and development in that section, through his agent entered into a contract with the appellant, which was signed by the latter only, by which he sold to Horsley all the oils, gases and minerals in his land, with customary mining privileges, for 40 cents per acre, and obligated himself to convey the same by general warranty deed, free of dower claim or other incumbrance, when the purchase money was paid, to-wit; one-half in three months and the balance in four months from the first payment, or as soon as the deed should be made, three dollars of it, however, being then paid.

It is suggestive upon the question of the then value of the purchase, and as regarded by Horsley, that his agent, who made it, was to get $80 for his pay, or as much as Woollums was to receive for all he sold. . . .

The purchase money was not paid as stipulated, but the reason given is that it was a sale of the minerals by the acre, and the quantity of land was not known and Woollums refused to survey it. Nothing appears to have transpired between the parties until the summer after the trade, when Horsley demanded a deed. He says he sent his agent to do so before that time, but it does not appear he did so.

In December, 1888, this suit was brought for a specific performance of the contract. The main defense is that it was procured through undue advantage, and under such circumstances that, in equity, its performance should not be decreed. . . . The specific execution of the contract was ordered. Considering all the circumstances, and the rule applicable in such a case, the judgment should not be upheld.

There is a distinction between the case of a plaintiff asking a specific performance of a contract in equity, and that of a defendant resisting such a performance. Its specific execution is not a matter of absolute right[,] but of sound discretion in the court. It requires less strength of case on the side of the defendant to resist the bill, than it does upon the part of the plaintiff to enforce it. If the court refuses to enforce specifically, the party is left to his remedy at law.

Thus a hard or unconscionable bargain will not be specifically enforced, nor, if the decree will produce injustice or under all the circumstances be inequitable, will it be rendered. In other words, a court of equity will not exercise its power . . . to enforce a claim which is not, under all the circumstances, just as between the parties, and it will allow a defendant to resist a decree, where the plaintiff will not always be allowed relief upon the same evidence.

A contract ought not to be carried into specific performance unless it be just and fair in all respects. When this relief is sought ethics are considered, and a court of equity will sometimes refuse to set aside a contract, and yet refuse its specific performance. Story says: "Courts of equity will not proceed to decree a specific performance where the contract is founded in fraud, imposition, mistake, undue advantage, or gross misapprehension; or where, from a change of circumstances or otherwise, it would be unconscientious to enforce it." (2 Story's Equity, § 750a.). . . .

The appellee testifies that he did not know anything as to the mineral value of this land when the contract was made; but it is evident he had a thorough knowledge of the value of lands generally in that section, and of the developments then in progress or near at hand. All this was unknown to the appellant. . . . [H]is land was valuable almost altogether in a mineral point of view. While it is not shown what it was worth at the date of the contract, yet it is proven to have been worth in April, 1889, $15 an acre, and that this value arises almost altogether from its mineral worth; and yet the appellee is asking the enforcement of a contract by means of which he seeks to obtain all the oil, gas, and minerals, and the virtual control of the land, at 40 cents an acre. The interest he claims under the contract is substantially the value of the land. Equity should not help out such a harsh bargain.

The appellee shows pretty plainly, by his own testimony, that when the contract was made he was advised of the probability of the building of a railroad in that locality in the near future. His agent, when the trade was made, assured the appellant that he would never be bothered by the contract during his life time. He was lulled in the belief that the Rip Van

Winkle sleep of that locality in former days was to continue; and the grossly inadequate price of this purchase can only be accounted for upon the ground that the appellant was misled and acted under gross misapprehension.

The contract was not equitable or reasonable, or grounded upon sufficient consideration, and no interest has arisen in any third party. A court of equity should, therefore, refuse its specific enforcement but the [appellee] should have what was in fact paid, with its interest; and when this is done his petition should be dismissed.

Judgment reversed, and cause remanded for proceedings consistent with this opinion.

QUESTION

It appears that John Woollums was not much of a traveler, so that any suit against him for damages would probably have to be brought in Kentucky, in the county of his residence. Would you have advised Horsley to bring such an action?

Kleinberg v. Ratett

252 N.Y. 236, 169 N.E. 289 (1929)

Plaintiffs contracted to buy a lot in the village of Mt. Kisko, paying down $2,000. The contract called for a deed warranting the title to be free of all encumbrances, except a specified mortgage. At closing, plaintiffs refused to perform on the ground that a stream of water, contained in a 24-inch pipe laid four feet underground, crossed the lot from south to north. One block to the south it was "a living stream of water" across open fields; after crossing the lot that plaintiffs had contracted to buy, it passed through a culvert under a village street and resumed its flow as an open brook. There was no evidence that the stream's course in crossing defendant's lot, encased in pipe, had been altered, lowered, or lifted in any way following the making of the contract. The court concluded that such a subterranean water course was not an encumbrance, since nature was responsible for it, though the owners of land above and below had the right to have the stream continue with an undiminished flow. Plaintiffs proved that they were unaware of the existence of the stream at the time of the contract and that defendant was silent on the subject. Plaintiffs sued for restitution of their $2,000 down payment; defendant, by answer, prayed for specific performance. *Held*, since there was no showing of fraud, plaintiffs could not have rescission. But since they were ignorant of the underground water course, and defendant was well aware of it, great hardship would result through specific performance. While the court could not grant rescission, it would "stay its hand" and refuse specific performance.

NOTE

What factors distinguish Kleinberg v. Ratett from Jackson v. Seymour, supra p. 529, where, you will recall, a vendor who had failed to establish her claim of fraud was nevertheless granted rescission?

The Court of Appeals of New York reads the *Kleinberg* decision as establishing that "the rules of law governing mistake as related to specific performance differ from those governing rescission for mistake." Da Silva v. Musso, 53 N.Y.2d 543, 444 N.Y.S.2d 50, 428 N.E.2d 382 (1981). Do you understand what the court means by this statement? The question of rescission for unilateral mistake was presented in the *Elsinore* case, p. 641, where it was concluded: "Under the circumstances, the 'bargain' for which the board presses . . . appears too sharp for law and equity to sustain." It is quite common for the courts in such cases to ask whether enforcement of the agreement would be "unconscionable." Is it surprising to find the same question asked where a defense of unilateral mistake is made in a suit for specific performance? The cases suggest not. E.g., Bailey v. Musumeci, 134 N.H. 280, 591 A.2d 1316 (1991).

The tactic of discretionary refusal of specific performance goes far back in New York legal history. As early as 1824, Chief Justice Savage, urging such a refusal in his dissenting opinion in Seymour v. Delancy, 3 Cow.(N.Y.) 445, provided a most candid statement of what was behind this evasive device: A court of equity granting specific performance "must act *ex rigore*, and cannot weigh the equities of the parties; whereas a jury, in a Court of law, can mitigate the damages according to equity and good conscience. It seems, indeed, paradoxical, to send parties from a Court of Equity to a Court of Law, to obtain equity; but it arises from the peculiar construction and practice of the Courts."

COMMENT: DENIAL OF EQUITABLE RELIEF

1. The "Cleanup" Principle

In a well-known American decision, Marks v. Gates, 154 F. 481 (9th Cir. 1907), a written agreement made in 1903 provided that defendant Gates would convey to plaintiff a 20 percent interest in any property Gates might thereafter acquire in Alaska. The agreement was under seal and recited that Gates had received $1 "in consideration." Two years later, plaintiff sued for specific performance of the agreement, alleging that in fact $1,000 cash and the cancellation of a debt of $11,225 had been given as consideration for the promise and that defendant, since signing the agreement, had acquired Alaska holdings worth $750,000 (mainly mining claims), all of which entitled plaintiff to a decree ordering defendant to transfer property having a value of at least $150,000. The trial court sustained a demurrer to the complaint, on the ground the contract sued on was too "unjust and inequitable" to warrant the relief sought. This decree was affirmed on appeal. The court said:

> A contract may be valid in law and not subject to cancellation in equity, and yet the terms thereof, the attendant circumstances,

and in some cases the subsequent events, may be such as to require the court to deny its specific performance. . . . The contract [here] had, when it was made, no reference to any property then owned by the contracting parties, or even to property then in existence. It did not obligate Gates ever to go to Alaska or to acquire property there. It bound him during his lifetime to transfer to the appellant a one-fifth interest in all property of every description that he might acquire in Alaska by whatever means, . . . property of which neither party could know even approximately the value. It was a bargain made in the dark. . . .

Courts of equity have often decreed specific performance where the consideration was inadequate. . . . But where the consideration is so grossly inadequate as it is in the present case, and the contract is made without any knowledge at the time of its making . . . of the nature of the property to be affected thereby, or of its value, no equitable principle is violated if specific performance is denied, and the parties are left to their legal remedies, if any they have. . . .

The facts presented [here] are not such as to entitle the court to retain the case for the assessment of such damages as the appellant may have sustained for breach of the contract. A court of equity will not grant pecuniary compensation in lieu of specific performance unless the case presented is one for equitable interposition such as would entitle the plaintiff to performance but for intervening facts, such as the destruction of the property [or] the conveyance of the same to an innocent third person.

The possibility mentioned in Marks v. Gates, of retaining the case for assessment of damages after refusal of specific performance, rests on the so-called "cleanup" principle, sometimes called the principle of "completeness." This is an idea that goes far back in Chancery history and has much to recommend it still. The usual statement of the principle is that when an equity court acquires jurisdiction of a case, it will proceed to give whatever remedies are needed for a complete and final disposition of the issues raised. The clearest case for invoking the principle is one in which equitable relief is awarded and decision of the equity issues compels the court to receive evidence, and decide disputed issues, as to claims that would be clearly "legal" by historical tests. E.g., Turley v. Ball Associates Ltd., 641 P.2d 286 (Colo. Ct. App. 1981). In a suit for specific performance of a contract, the defendant's breach may already have caused damage; in an injunction action against trespass or nuisance, the past tort may have caused injuries that will not be indemnified merely by enjoining defendant's wrongful acts for the future. The arguments for awarding damages in the equity suit may not be so clear where, for some reason especially appealing in an "equity" context, all equitable relief is refused. Yet there is abundant authority for giving damages *in lieu of* equitable relief, instead of as a supplement to such relief. See, e.g., Ferguson v. Green, 266 Ark. 556, 587 S.W.2d 18 (1979); Fran Realty, Inc. v. Thomas, 30 Md. App. 362, 354 A.2d 196 (1976); Charles County Broadcasting Co., Inc. v. Meares, 270 Md. 321, 311 A.2d 27 (1973). The same reasons of convenience, the same desire to save time, money, and duplicated effort, can operate in this latter situation, if to decide the equity case it has been necessary to receive most of the evidence and consider most of the issues that can arise in awarding damages.

In all of these situations, the main obstacle to awarding damages in the equity suit will be the constitutional guarantees of jury trial. See, e.g., Bourne & Lynch, Merger of Law & Equity Under the Revised Maryland Rules: Does it Threaten Trial by Jury? 14 U. Balt. L. Rev. 1 (1984). It is assumed that the award of damages will be by the equity judge, without the aid of a jury. This is essential if the main purpose of avoiding duplicated effort is to be served, since the judge in the equity case will normally have heard the case with no jury present. Still, the constitutional guarantees of jury trial are not a conclusive deterrent to complete relief in equity. They presuppose a historical test, and use of the cleanup principle goes far back in time, before our American constitutions were adopted, even thought of. It can therefore be argued that the right to jury trial guaranteed by our constitutions was always qualified by the power of equity courts to administer legal relief as an incident to, or in lieu of, equitable relief, in cases properly brought in equity. Then, too, it has long been true that a trial court has considerable discretion to try legal and equitable issues separately, despite connections between the two, thereby safeguarding rights to a jury on legal issues. Quigley v. Wilson, 474 N.W.2d 277 (Iowa Ct. App. 1991).

The cleanup principle presents a peculiar dilemma in the cases just considered. Indeed, it is the defendant who is in a dilemma, proving a wide disparity of values to defeat specific performance and then, if sued at law, forced to prove the opposite in order to reduce any liability in damages. Levin, Equitable Cleanup and the Jury, 100 U. Pa. L. Rev. 320 (1951), discusses these and related questions. The case of Medtronic, Inc. v. Intermedics, Inc., 725 F.2d 440 (7th Cir. 1984), is also helpful on the limitations of the cleanup principle.

On the whole, the federal cases have been conservative in their use of the cleanup principle, in order to preserve rights to jury trial. There is other authority, not only in federal but in state decisions, employing the test stated in Marks v. Gates—was the obstacle to specific performance some fact intervening since the transaction took place, or even since the bill in the case was filed? This approach is most likely explained by the broader rule that a plaintiff, in order to get any legal relief from an equity court, must first show a good case in equity (else one could bypass the law court and litigate a purely legal claim in equity).

2. The Effects of Withholding Equitable Relief

The requirements of good faith and fairness found in the specific performance cases are applied in a great variety of equitable actions. They derive from the premise, historically accurate, that equitable remedies are exceptional and supplementary, so that denying equitable relief in a particular case does not necessarily, or entirely, defeat the claim asserted. History also played a part in creating a large deposit of "good conscience" and morality in the standard doctrines of equity, even in those areas where, like the express trust, equitable remedies are not merely a supplement to common law remedies but are for practical purposes exclusive.

We shall not have much to do with such special equity doctrines as "unclean hands" or "laches." Both lead to a denial of equitable relief without purporting to outlaw the transaction for the purposes of legal remedies. "Unclean hands" is an extension of illegality and operates on equity plaintiffs who have engaged in criminal, immoral, or unfair conduct in the transaction in question. Laches is a law-French term best translated as "laxness." It describes a delay in suing or in asserting rights, often a delay far short of the statutory period of limitation. It is usually close to estoppel in the sense that the delay has induced reliance and prejudice to an opponent, though the reliance factor is not indispensable if the delay has been prolonged.

There are, of course, other doctrines that lead to a denial of equitable relief, without any attempt to preclude a remedy at law. The technique of discretionary refusal of equitable remedies is, in short, well known and widely used. In most situations where the technique is used the same question arises—how effective is it?

An early study by Frank & Endicott, Defenses in Equity and "Legal Rights," 14 La. L. Rev. 380 (1954), produced an interesting conclusion. The authors took 350 reported cases in which equitable relief was refused, not for adequacy of the legal remedy, but for some reason of "conscience," hardship, soiled hands, or laches. The cases covered a wide range of tort and contract claims. The authors then wrote to the lawyers for the unsuccessful litigants to find out what had happened next. They received 56 responses, none of which reported success in a later action at law. In only two cases were later law actions even brought. In the authors' words, "in every instance equitable defeat was total defeat." The most multifarious reasons made plaintiffs' counsel decide against a second try. In some cases, the reasons for dismissal of the equity suit were phrased in the special vocabulary of equity, but counsel considered the risk too great that "unclean hands" might prove to be illegality, or equitable fraud might be legal fraud—in other words, that law and equity might in fact coincide in their results despite different formulations. In one case it was held that the dismissal in equity was res judicata, a bar to a later action at law. It should be noted in passing that the risk from res judicata is increased by the cleanup principle, which makes it proper for the equity court to retain the case for legal relief. If "cleanup" is proper, a decree of dismissal which fails to specify the grounds of dismissal can often be interpreted as an adjudication of both legal and equitable issues.

From a sample of only 56 cases, no firm conclusions could be drawn, as the authors conceded. But they raised some further questions. They suggested, first, that the finality of the dismissals from equity had the virtue in all but two of the cases studied of settling the issues without further litigation. They then suggested that there may be "judicial self-deception" in denying an equitable remedy in the belief that a legal remedy remains; "if without that mistaken belief [the judge] might have given judgment for the plaintiff, then serious injustice is done." The authors also suggested that if the special equity defenses were "bodily and overtly taken out of the cloud of conscience and transferred to law," plaintiffs in equity would not lose anything substantial and "the conscious responsibility" of judges might thereby be increased. Instead of a "bodily transfer" of these special equity doctrines to courts of law, would it be better if the equity doctrines themselves were eliminated or reduced in scope?

Waters v. Min Ltd.

Supreme Judicial Court of Massachusetts, 1992.
412 Mass. 64, 587 N.E.2d 231.

LYNCH, J. This case arises from a contract between Gail A. Waters (plaintiff) and "the DeVito defendants"[2] (defendants), whereby the plaintiff was to assign her annuity policy having a cash value of $189,000 to the defendants in exchange for $50,000. The plaintiff brought suit to rescind the contract on the ground of unconscionability. Defendant Min Ltd. counterclaimed seeking declaratory relief and specific enforcement of the contract. [The trial] judge, sitting without a jury, found for the plaintiff, ordered that the annuity be returned to the plaintiff on repayment of $18,000 with interest, and dismissed the counterclaim of Min Ltd. . . . We now affirm.

. . . The plaintiff was injured in an accident when she was twelve years old. At the age of eighteen, she settled her claim and, with the proceeds, purchased the annuity contract in question from the defendant Commercial Union Ins. Co. When the plaintiff was twenty-one, she became romantically involved with the defendant Thomas Beauchemin, an ex-convict, who introduced her to drugs. Beauchemin suggested that she sell her annuity contract, introduced her to one of the defendants, and represented her in the contract negotiations. She was naive, insecure, vulnerable in contract matters, and unduly influenced by Beauchemin. The defendants drafted the contract documents with the assistance of legal counsel, but the plaintiff had no such representation. At least some portions of the contract were executed in unusual circumstances: i.e., part of the contract was signed on the hood of an automobile in a parking lot, part was signed in a restaurant. The defendants agreed to pay $50,000 for the annuity policy which would return to them as owners of the policy $694,000 over its guaranteed term of twenty-five years, and which had a cash value at the time the contract was executed of $189,000.

Beauchemin acted for himself and as agent of the defendants. For example, the defendants forgave a $100 debt of Beauchemin as deposit

---

[2] The judge referred to the defendants Min Ltd., Cube Ltd., David A. DeVito, Robert A. DeVito, and Michael D. Steamer, collectively as "the DeVito defendants" because their identities and roles were not made clear at trial. The plaintiff originally agreed to assign her rights and interest in a certain annuity policy to Cube Ltd., which later transferred all its interest in the annuity to Min Ltd. David A. DeVito is president of Cube Ltd. Michael D. Steamer is business manager of Min Ltd. Robert A. DeVito conducted negotiations with the plaintiff regarding the annuity policy.

for the purchase of the annuity policy. From a subsequent $25,000 payment, the defendants deducted $7,000 that Beauchemin owed them.

Based on the foregoing, the judge found the contract unconscionable. . . . The defendants argue that the evidence does not support the finding that the contract was unconscionable or that they assumed no risks and therefore that the contract was oppressive. . . . The doctrine of unconscionability has long been recognized by common law courts in this country and in England. . . . "Historically, a [contract] was considered unconscionable if it was 'such as no man in his senses and not under delusion would make on the one hand, and as no honest and fair man would accept on the other.' Hume v. United States, 132 U.S. 406[, 411,] (1889), quoting Earl of Chesterfield v. Janssen, 38 Eng.Rep. 82, 100 (Ch. 1750). Later, a contract was determined unenforceable because unconscionable when 'the sum total of its provisions drives too hard a bargain for a court of conscience to assist.' Campbell Soup Co. v. Wentz, 172 F.2d 80 (3d Cir. 1948)." . . .

The doctrine of unconscionability has also been codified in the [UCC], G.L. c. 106, § 2–302,[3] and, by analogy, it has been applied in situations outside the ambit of the code. See, e.g., Zapatha v. Dairy Mart, 381 Mass. 284, 408 N.E.2d 1370 (1980) (termination clause in franchise agreement not considered unconscionable); Commonwealth v. DeCotis, 366 Mass. 234, 316 N.E.2d 748 (1974) (extraction of resale fees for no rendered services deemed unfair act or practice under G.L. c. 93A, § 2[a]). . . . As explained in Bronstein v. Prudential Ins. Co., 390 Mass. 701, 459 N.E.2d 772 (1984), "[in *Zapatha*] the court applied statutory policy to common law contract issues, which, for centuries have been within the province of this court." Accordingly, although we are not here concerned with a sale of goods or a commercial transaction, *Zapatha* is instructive on the principles to be applied in testing this transaction for unconscionability.

Unconscionability must be determined on a case-by-case basis, with particular attention to whether the challenged provision could result in oppression and unfair surprise to the disadvantaged party and not to allocation of risk because of "superior bargaining power." *Zapatha*, 381

---

[3] General Laws c. 106, § 2–302, reads as follows:

"§ 2–302. Unconscionable Contract or Clause.

"(1) If the court as a matter of law finds the contract or any clause of the contract to have been unconscionable at the time it was made the court may refuse to enforce the contract, or it may enforce the remainder of the contract without the unconscionable clause, or it may so limit the application of any unconscionable clause as to avoid any unconscionable result.

"(2) When it is claimed or appears to the court that the contract or any clause thereof may be unconscionable the parties shall be afforded a reasonable opportunity to present evidence as to its commercial setting, purpose, and effect to aid the court in making the determination."

The standards of determining a contract unconscionable set forth in G.L. c. 106, § 2–302, are the same standards expressed in Restatement (Second) of Contracts § 208 (1981). "The issue is one of law for the court, and the test is to be made as of the time the contract was made." Zapatha v. Dairy Mart, Inc., 381 Mass. 284, 408 N.E.2d 1370 (1980).

Mass. at 292–293, 408 N.E.2d 1370. Courts have identified other elements of the unconscionable contract. For example, gross disparity in the consideration alone "may be sufficient to sustain [a finding that the contract is unconscionable]," since the disparity "itself leads inevitably to the felt conclusion that knowing advantage was taken of [one party]." Jones v. Star Credit Corp., 59 Misc.2d 189, 298 N.Y.S.2d 264 (N.Y.Sup.Ct. 1969). . . . High pressure sales tactics and misrepresentation have been recognized as factors rendering a contract unconscionable. . . . If the sum total of the provisions of a contract drive too hard a bargain, a court of conscience will not assist its enforcement. *Campbell Soup Co.*, supra at 84.

The judge found that Beauchemin introduced the plaintiff to drugs, exhausted her credit card accounts to the sum of $6,000, unduly influenced her, suggested that the plaintiff sell her annuity contract, initiated the contract negotiations, was the agent of the defendants, and benefited from the contract between the plaintiff and the defendants.[4] The defendants were represented by legal counsel; the plaintiff was not. . . . The cash value of the annuity policy at the time the contract was executed was approximately four times greater than the price to be paid by the defendants. For payment of not more than $50,000 the defendants were to receive an asset that could be immediately exchanged for $189,000, or they could elect to hold it for its guaranteed term and receive $694,000. . . . [T]he judge could correctly conclude the contract was unconscionable.

The defendants assumed no risk and the plaintiff gained no advantage. Gross disparity in the values exchanged is an important factor to be considered in determining whether a contract is unconscionable. "[C]ourts [may] avoid enforcement of a bargain that is shown to be unconscionable by reason of gross inadequacy of consideration accompanied by other relevant factors." 1 A. Corbin, Contracts § 128, at 551. . . . See In re Estate of Vought, 76 Misc.2d 755, 351 N.Y.S.2d 816 (N.Y.Sur.Ct. 1973) (assignment of interest in spendthrift trust for $66,000 under provisions which guaranteed assignees ultimate return of $1,100,000). We are satisfied that the disparity of interests in this contract is "so gross that the court cannot resist the inference that it was improperly obtained and is unconscionable." In re Estate of Vought, at 760, 351 N.Y.S.2d 816.

The defendants also argue that the judge erred in failing to require the plaintiff to return the full amount paid by them for the annuity.[5] The judge's order was consistent with his findings that Beauchemin was the

---

[4] These latter two findings were grounds enough for the judge to rescind the contract. See 1 H.C. Black, Rescission of Contracts § 32 (2d ed. 1929), and cases cited. The plaintiff relied on Beauchemin to represent her in the contract negotiations. Accordingly, he was obligated to act on her behalf and in her interest. Instead, he acted in his own self-interest and caused benefits to inure to himself by having his debts forgiven and requiring he be named beneficiary of the annuity policy.

[5] The defendants paid $18,000 cash after deducting $7,000 for a debt which was owed to them by Beauchemin. The remaining $25,000 due on the contract was never paid.

agent of the defendants, and that the plaintiff only received $18,000 for her interest in the annuity.

QUESTION

If the plaintiff in *Waters* had not mentioned unconscionability, but relied exclusively on the tort of fraud, would the result have been any different?

Williams v. Walker-Thomas Furniture Co.

United States Court of Appeals, District of Columbia Circuit, 1965.
350 F.2d 445.

WRIGHT, CIRCUIT JUDGE. Appellee, Walker-Thomas Furniture Co., operates a retail furniture store in the District of Columbia. During the period from 1957 to 1962 each appellant in these cases purchased a number of household items from Walker-Thomas, for which payment was to be made in installments. The terms of each purchase were contained in a printed form contract which set forth the value of the purchased item and purported to lease the item to appellant for a stipulated monthly rent payment. The contract then provided, in substance, that title would remain in Walker-Thomas until the total of all the monthly payments made equaled the stated value of the item, at which time appellants could take title. In the event of a default in the payment of any monthly installment, Walker-Thomas could repossess the item.

The contract further provided that "the amount of each periodical installment payment to be made by (purchaser) to the Company under this present lease shall be inclusive of and not in addition to the amount of each installment payment to be made by (purchaser) under such prior leases, bills or accounts; and all payments now and hereafter made by (purchaser) shall be credited pro rata on all outstanding leases, bills and accounts due the Company by (purchaser) at the time each such payment is made." The effect of this rather obscure provision was to keep a balance due on every item purchased until the balance due on all items, whenever purchased, was liquidated. As a result, the debt incurred at the time of purchase of each item was secured by the right to repossess all the items previously purchased by the same purchaser, and each new item purchased automatically became subject to a security interest arising out of the previous dealings.

On May 12, 1962, appellant Thorne purchased an item described as a Daveno, three tables, and two lamps, having total stated value of $391.10. Shortly thereafter, he defaulted on his monthly payments and appellee sought to replevy all the items purchased since the first transaction in 1958. Similarly, on April 17, 1962, appellant Williams bought a stereo set of stated value of $514.95.[1] She too defaulted shortly thereafter, and appellee sought to replevy all the items purchased since December, 1957. The Court of General Sessions granted judgment for appellee. The [D.C.] Court of Appeals affirmed, and we granted appellants' motion for leave to appeal to this court.

Appellants' principal contention, rejected by both the trial and the appellate courts below, is that these contracts, or at least some of them, are unconscionable and, hence, not enforceable. . . . [T]he [D.C.] Court of Appeals explained its rejection of this contention as follows:

> Appellant's second argument presents a more serious question. The record reveals that prior to the last purchase appellant had reduced the balance in her account to $164. The last purchase, a stereo set, raised the balance due to $678. Significantly, at the time of this and the preceding purchases, appellee was aware of appellant's financial position. The reverse side of the stereo contract listed the name of appellant's social worker and her $218 monthly stipend from the government. Nevertheless, with full knowledge that appellant had to feed, clothe and support both herself and seven children on this amount, appellee sold her a $514 stereo set.
>
> We cannot condemn too strongly appellee's conduct. It raises serious questions of sharp practice and irresponsible business dealings. A review of the legislation in the District of Columbia affecting retail sales and the pertinent decisions of the highest court in this jurisdiction disclose, however, no ground upon which this court can declare the contracts in question contrary to public policy. We note that were the Maryland Retail Installment Sales Act, Art. 83 §§ 128–153, or its equivalent, in force in the District of Columbia, we could grant appellant appropriate relief. We think Congress should consider corrective legislation to protect the public from such exploitive contracts as were utilized in the case at bar.

We do not agree that the court lacked the power to refuse enforcement to contracts found to be unconscionable. In other jurisdictions, it has been held as a matter of common law that unconscionable contracts are not enforceable. While no decision of this court so holding has been found, the notion that an unconscionable bargain should not be given full enforcement is by no means novel. In Scott v. United States, 79 U.S. (12 Wall.) 443, 445, 20 L.Ed. 438 (1870), the Supreme Court stated:

> . . . If a contract be unreasonable and unconscionable, but not void for fraud, a court of law will give to the party who sues

[1] At the time of this purchase her account showed a balance of $164 still owing from her prior purchases. The total of all the purchases made over the years in question came to $1,800. The total payments amounted to $1,400.

> for its breach damages, not according to its letter, but only such as he is equitably entitled to. . . .

Since we have never adopted or rejected such a rule, the question here presented is actually one of first impression.

Congress has recently enacted the Uniform Commercial Code, which specifically provides that the court may refuse to enforce a contract which it finds to be unconscionable at the time it was made. The enactment of this section, which occurred subsequent to the contracts here in suit, does not mean that the common law of the District of Columbia was otherwise at the time of enactment, nor does it preclude the court from adopting a similar rule in the exercise of its powers to develop the common law for the District. . . . In fact, in view of the absence of prior authority on the point, we consider the congressional adoption of § 2–302 persuasive authority for following the rationale of the cases from which the section is explicitly derived. Accordingly, we hold that where the element of unconscionability is present at the time a contract is made, the contract should not be enforced.

Unconscionability has generally been recognized to include an absence of meaningful choice on the part of one of the parties together with contract terms which are unreasonably favorable to the other party. Whether a meaningful choice is present in a particular case can only be determined by consideration of all the circumstances surrounding the transaction. In many cases the meaningfulness of the choice is negated by a gross inequality of bargaining power.[7] The manner in which the contract was entered is also relevant to this consideration. Did each party to the contract, considering his obvious education or lack of it, have a reasonable opportunity to understand the terms of the contract, or were the important terms hidden in a maze of fine print and minimized by deceptive sales practices? Ordinarily, one who signs an agreement without full knowledge of its terms might be held to assume the risk that he has entered a one-sided bargain. But when a party of little bargaining power, and hence little real choice, signs a commercially unreasonable contract with little or no knowledge of its terms, it is hardly likely that his consent, or even an objective manifestation of his consent, was ever given to all the terms. In such a case the usual rule that the terms of the agreement are not to be questioned should be abandoned and the court should

---

7 Inquiry into the relative bargaining power of the two parties is not an inquiry wholly divorced from the general question of unconscionability, since a one-sided bargain is itself evidence of the inequality of the bargaining parties. This fact was vaguely recognized in the common law doctrine of intrinsic fraud, that is, fraud which can be presumed from the grossly unfair nature of the terms of the contract. See the oft-quoted statement of Lord Hardwicke in Earl of Chesterfield v. Janssen, 28 Eng. Rep. 82, 100 (1751):

> [Fraud] may be apparent from the intrinsic nature and subject of the bargain itself; such as no man in his senses and not under delusion would make. . . .

And cf. Hume v. United States, 132 U.S. at 413, 10 S.Ct. at 137, where the Court characterized the English cases as "cases in which one party took advantage of the other's ignorance of arithmetic to impose upon him, and the fraud was apparent from the face of the contracts."

consider whether the terms of the contract are so unfair that enforcement should be withheld.

In determining reasonableness or fairness, the primary concern must be with the terms of the contract considered in light of the circumstances existing when the contract was made. The test is not simple, nor can it be mechanically applied. The terms are to be considered "in the light of the general commercial background and the commercial needs of the particular trade or case." Corbin suggests the test as being whether the terms are "so extreme as to appear unconscionable according to the mores and business practices of the time and place." 1 Corbin, Contracts § 128 (1963). We think this formulation correctly states the test to be applied in those cases where no meaningful choice was exercised upon entering the contract.

Because the trial court and the appellate court did not feel that enforcement could be refused, no findings were made on the possible unconscionability of the contracts in these cases. Since the record is not sufficient for our deciding the issue as a matter of law, the cases must be remanded to the trial court for further proceedings.

So ordered.

DANAHER, CIRCUIT JUDGE (dissenting). The [D.C.] Court of Appeals obviously was as unhappy about the situation here presented as any of us can possibly be. [It] concludes: "We think Congress should consider corrective legislation to protect the public from such exploitive contracts as were utilized in the case at bar."

My view is thus summed up by an able court which made no finding that there had actually been sharp practice. Rather the appellant seems to have known precisely where she stood.

There are many aspects of public policy here involved. What is a luxury to some may seem an outright necessity to others. Is public oversight to be required of the expenditures of relief funds? A washing machine, e.g., in the hands of a relief client might become a fruitful source of income. Many relief clients may well need credit, and certain business establishments will take long chances on the sale of items, expecting their pricing policies will afford a degree of protection commensurate with the risk. Perhaps a remedy when necessary will be found within the provisions of the "Loan Shark" law, D.C.Code §§ 26–601 et seq. (1961).

I mention such matters only to emphasize the desirability of a cautious approach to any such problem, particularly since the law for so long has allowed parties such great latitude in making their own contracts. I dare say there must annually be thousands upon thousands of installment credit transactions in this jurisdiction, and one can only speculate as to the effect the decision in these cases will have. . . .

[It is reported that the case was settled following remand, with Walker-Thomas dropping all claims and paying Williams the fair value of the items it had taken from her. Dostert, Appellate Restatement of Unconscionability: Civil Legal Aid at Work, 54 A.B.A.J. 1183 (1968).]

NOTE

The cross-collateralization clause in the contract Williams signed gave Walker-Thomas a security interest in the stereo and all the other furniture she bought from it over the years. To understand the case, one has to understand the work the clause is doing. Some readers of the case are left with the impression that the clause gives Walker-Thomas the right to keep all of the property in the event of default even if its value exceeds what it is owed. This is wrong. A secured creditor has no right to keep collateral in the event of default. As long as the debtor insists, the seller is obliged to sell the property and return any surplus of the sale proceeds to the debtor. So something else must be at work in such clauses.

A distinctive feature of debtor-creditor law suggests a reason for the cross-collateralization clause. Those in the position of Walker-Thomas—those who are owed money and who have sued and reduced their claim to judgment—can reach most of a debtor's property without relying on any particular term in the contract. A cross-collaterization clause does nothing to increase the pool of assets available to satisfy the debt. Some property, however, is sufficiently important to the debtor that the law puts it presumptively beyond the reach of creditors. Such assets are "exempt" from creditor levy. Creditors can reach them only if the debtor grants a security interest in them at the time he or she borrows. Williams's household furniture was such "exempt" property. The cross-collateralization clause therefore enabled Walker-Thomas to reach assets that it otherwise could not.[2] Does this clause make the use of fine print especially suspect? Once the law protects certain assets from the reach of creditors, it would seem to follow that the debtor's waiver of such a right ought to be deliberate and knowing.

One can take this argument a step further. How can we ever be confident that the waiver is a deliberate and knowing one? Can there ever be a fully informed waiver on the floor of an inner-city furniture store? In a mass market, credit transactions are so routine that requiring that a cross-collateralization be disclosed conspicuously, or made the subject of explicit negotiation, may not be enough. Such logic is a justification for making cross-collateralization clauses, such as the one in cases such as *Walker-Thomas*, an unfair credit practice. This was done in the 1980s. See 16 C.F.R. §§ 444.1–444.5.

---

[2] A secured creditor also has a right to repossess in the event of a default without first going to court, provided the repossession can be done without a breach of the peace. As "breach of the peace" includes any unauthorized entry into a private home, this right, while relevant when the collateral is a car parked on the street, has little relevance when the collateral is household furniture.

Shapiro, Courts, Legislatures, and Paternalism

74 Va. L. Rev. 519, 534–538 (1988)

"In the sphere of contract, the judicial decisions most likely to be paternalist in their motivation, at least in substantial part, are those in which a contract term is imposed or invalidated despite the contrary intention of the parties. Even these outcomes may be substantially induced by a desire to achieve a greater measure of efficiency or a fairer distribution of resources. But I agree with those who find the notions of unfair overreaching and unequal bargaining power in these cases (and to a lesser extent, some uses of the notions of coercion and duress) proxies for the idea that one of the contracting parties simply did not know what was in his own best interest. . . .

"For present purposes, the important point is that in a wide range of human activity—even those touching sensitive moral nerves—the courts are reluctant to invoke common law principles to invalidate private choice. And despite the charter granted to the courts by the Uniform Commercial Code's unconscionability provision [§ 2–302], such decisions remain especially rare in the realm of commercial and consumer sales. The landmark decisions declining enforcement of written provisions—decisions like Henningsen v. Bloomfield Motors, Inc., and Williams v. Walker-Thomas Furniture Co.—are beginning to stand out in the casebooks as curiosities. . . .

"Indeed, the *Williams* case, which cast doubt on the validity of a particularly troublesome credit arrangement in an installment sale of consumer goods to a person on welfare, was far from clear about the basis of the holding: was it the procedural irregularities suggested by the record, the unfairness of the arrangement, or some combination of both? To the extent that procedural irregularities (such as lack of adequate notice of the nature and impact of the arrangement) lay at the root of the holding, it can hardly be classified as paternalist. To the extent that the court's true goal was substantive but was dressed in procedural clothing, the decision may underscore even reformist judges' unwillingness to take an openly paternalist stance. Finally, to the extent that the opinion reveals a paternalist readiness to invalidate a credit arrangement that a consumer was willing to enter in order to get the goods she wanted, that readiness has not met with universal approval. . . .

"For the most part, then, courts are still reluctant—at least when acting without legislative guidance or mandate—to interfere with sales agreements that people apparently regard as in their interests, even though if the world were a better and fairer place, they might not have to enter such bargains.[71]

---

[71] It might be argued that some basic contract doctrines, like consideration and the unenforceability of certain oral agreements, as well as certain remedial rules like that against punitive damage clauses, are paternalist to the extent that they interfere with private preferences. While not denying the presence of a paternalist ingredient in the mix, I believe that the primary explanation for these doctrines lies elsewhere, and that the heavy going that some of them have encountered in recent years may be due to an effort to rid them of their paternalist aura.

The statute of frauds, for example, has been riddled with exceptions designed to permit enforcement of agreements when the evidentiary hazards are reduced by such events as part performance. The [UCC] has gone so far as to take an agreement for the sale of goods outside the statute if its existence is admitted in litigation (voluntarily or under compulsion). See U.C.C. § 2–201(3)(b) (1978). As for the doctrine of consideration, I think it reflects the view that in the

Outside the realm of sales transactions, there are some significant developments that may have paternalist roots—for example, the judicial imposition of limitations on employment at will in employment contracts, and of a warranty of habitability in landlord-tenant relations. To the extent that employment at will contracts and warranty of habitability provisions involve the filling of gaps that the parties have left open, and are free to change, these developments can perhaps best be explained as prompted by motives of efficiency and redistribution. To the extent that the judicially imposed limitations are not subject to waiver, the paternalist explanation seems more natural, though not inevitable. Yet it is significant that the spread of limitations on employment at will has not been unrestrained, and that the warranty of habitability is widely reinforced by housing code provisions that impose criminal penalties on landlords who fail to meet minimum standards. . . .

"The problem of analyzing the degree to which paternalist ideas have affected the common-law doctrines governing private agreement is complicated by the inroads that tort law has made on areas traditionally reserved for contract. But these inroads do not in the main appear to be the result of paternalist prompting. The most dramatic change in tort law in this century—the emergence of strict product liability—is supported by powerful arguments for economic efficiency. Moreover, even in the midst of all this change, courts remain reluctant to override a clearly expressed intention to sell a product 'as is,' warts and all, or to hold a manufacturer liable for dangers that the buyer should have understood when he bought the product."

Orcilla v. Big Sur, Inc.

California Court of Appeal, 2016.
244 Cal. App. 4th 982.

PREMO, J. . . . The Orcillas are Filipino, and English is their second language. Virgilio is unable to work due to a 2004 medical diagnosis. In 2006, Teodora contacted Quick Loan Funding, Inc. (Quick Loan), about refinancing the Property. She did so in response to marketing materials she had received from the company. After speaking with a Quick Loan agent, Teodora applied to refinance the Property for $525,000. At the Quick Loan agent's recommendation, Teodora did not include Virgilio on the loan application. Teodora told the agent she could not afford the loan modification because the monthly payments would be more than her monthly income, but she eventually accepted the agent's false representation that she could afford the loan modification.

On May 9, 2006, Teodora obtained a $525,000 real property loan from Quick Loan. She alone executed an adjustable-rate note (the Note), in which she promised to repay the loan at an initial interest rate of 8.99 percent. The Note provided that the interest rate would be variable after

vast majority of cases, the unbargained-for promise is not a reliable indicator of the promisor's intent to tie himself to the mast. After all, a promisor can find the necessary rope by transferring property outright, or even by a declaration of trust.

two years and would never exceed 14.99 percent. The Note further provided that Teodora's initial monthly payments would be in the amount of $4,220.49. (In 2005 and 2006, Teodora's monthly income was less than $3,000 and Virgilio did not work.)

[The loan soon fell into default. There was a modification of the mortgage in 2008 and further communications and miscommunications between the Orcillas and various financial intermediaries. The lender declared a default, the Orcillas were displaced, and the property was eventually sold.

The Orcillas then sought to set aside the sale. To do this, they needed to show, as a threshold matter, that the contract itself was unconscionable.]

Unconscionability generally is a legal question we review under the de novo standard. "Unconscionability has procedural and substantive aspects," both of which must be present for a court to refuse to enforce a contract based on unconscionability. Abramson v. Juniper Networks, Inc. (2004) 115 Cal.App.4th 638, 655, 9 Cal.Rptr.3d 422 (*Abramson*); Armendariz v. Foundation Health Psychcare Services, Inc. (2000) 24 Cal.4th 83, 114, 99 Cal.Rptr.2d 745, 6 P.3d 669 (*Armendariz*). Courts use a " 'sliding scale' " approach in assessing the two elements, such that "the more substantively oppressive the contract term, the less evidence of procedural unconscionability is required to come to the conclusion that the term is unenforceable, and vice versa." *Armendariz*, 24 Cal.4th at 114.

Procedural unconscionability concerns the manner in which the contract was negotiated. Abramson, 115 Cal.App.4th at 656. "Absent unusual circumstances, evidence that one party has overwhelming bargaining power, drafts the contract, and presents it on a take-it-or-leave-it basis is sufficient to demonstrate procedural unconscionability and require the court to reach the question of substantive unconscionability, even if the other party has market alternatives." [Lona v. Citibank, N.A. 202 Cal.App.4th 89, 109, 134 Cal.Rptr.3d 622 (2011) (*Lona*).]

As to both the original loan and the 2008 modification, the Orcillas allege they have limited English fluency and education and that the loan documents were on standard, preprinted forms in English. These allegations are sufficient to allege at least some measure of procedural unconscionability.

As noted, the *degree* of procedural unconscionability present is relevant to the enforceability inquiry. The relevant factors in assessing the level of procedural unconscionability are oppression and surprise. Abramson, 115 Cal.App.4th at 656. "The oppression component arises from an inequality of bargaining power of the parties to the contract and an absence of real negotiation or a meaningful choice on the part of the weaker party." Id. That the loan documents were on standard, preprinted forms suggests the Orcillas had no role in negotiating their terms. "The component of surprise arises when the challenged terms are hidden in a prolix printed form drafted by the party seeking to enforce them." Id. The Orcillas do not allege that any of the key terms of the loans, such as the monthly payment or the interest rate, were hidden in fine print. Thus, they do not allege the element of surprise is present. Based on the foregoing, we conclude the Orcillas have alleged a low degree of procedural unconscionability. . . .

"Substantive unconscionability pertains to the fairness of an agreement's actual terms." Pinnacle Museum Tower Assn. v. Pinnacle Market Development, LLC 55 Cal.4th 223, 246, 145 Cal.Rptr.3d 514, 282 P.3d 1217 (2012). As our Supreme Court has explained, the unconscionability doctrine "ensures that contracts, particularly contracts of adhesion, do not impose terms that have been variously described as 'overly harsh,' 'unduly oppressive,' 'so one-sided as to shock the conscience', or 'unfairly one-sided.' All of these formulations point to the central idea that the [substantive] unconscionability doctrine is concerned not with 'a simple old-fashioned bad bargain,' but with terms that are 'unreasonably favorable to the more powerful party.' " Sonic-Calabasas A, Inc. v. Moreno, 57 Cal.4th 1109, 1145, 163 Cal.Rptr.3d 269, 311 P.3d 184. (2013). Thus, substantive unconscionability exists where a provision is both "one-sided" and there is no justification for its one-sidedness.

The Orcillas maintain that the disparity between the monthly loan payments and their income indicates that the loan and loan modification were overly harsh and one-sided. We agree that the allegation that the monthly loan payments exceeded the couple's income by more than $1,000 is sufficient to allege substantive unconscionability.

In sum, we conclude the Orcillas have alleged that the original loan and the loan modification were unconscionable and unenforceable, such that the trustee's sale of the Property enforcing them was illegal. Accordingly, the Orcillas adequately allege the first element of their cause of action to set aside the trustee's sale. . . .

[The court went on to find that the Orcillas also adequately pled the other elements needed to set aside the sale.]

COMMENT: REGULATION OF UNFAIR TERMS

There is a further dimension of unconscionability. Every jurisdiction in this country has some form of unfair and deceptive trade practices or consumer protection act. The various types of statutes, a fair number of which were inspired by the Federal Trade Commission Act (15 U.S.C. § 45(a)–(m) (1982)), are collected and examined in Comment, Consumer Protection: The Practical Effectiveness of State Deceptive Trade Practices Legislation, 59 Tul. L. Rev. 427 (1984), and Leaffer & Lipson, Consumer Actions Against Unfair or Deceptive Acts or Practices: The Private Uses of Federal Trade Commission Jurisprudence, 48 Geo. Wash. L. Rev. 521 (1980). Perhaps as many as 15 to 20 of the state acts specifically include "unconscionable" practices or contract provisions among the "fraudulent or illegal" activities reached by the legislation. The telling feature of a number of these statutes is the alternative to private litigation that is added—a suit by a public agency, upon a consumer complaint, to obtain injunctive relief against objectionable business practices. See, e.g., State v. Avco Fin. Serv. of New York, 50 N.Y.2d 383, 429 N.Y.S.2d 181, 406 N.E.2d 1075 (1980). The main point here is that common law and UCC approaches to unconscionability have been expanded, and that, in general, much of the law of consumer protection is currently the work of statutes and not common law doctrines. These developments, and the issues they raise, are usually treated in courses in Commercial and Consumer Law.

Development by the courts of more potent tools for dealing with oppression, accomplished typically through the use of printed-form contracts, parallels the efforts of legislatures and, to some extent, of private associations, to reach the same goal. Several of the techniques developed merit brief mention.

(1) **Compulsory contracts.** The capacity for coercion by a supplier of essential goods and services is obviously increased if the supplier has available the option not to deal at all. That option was surely implicit in general common law principles of contract. In a number of areas, however, modern statutes eliminate or greatly restrict it. Utility companies—deemed "quasi-public" in character, like common carriers—are required to provide service on a nondiscriminatory basis to all who request it. Insurance companies writing types of insurance that consumers are legally required to carry (for example, automobile liability coverage) may be required to underwrite any standard risk and to share with other insurers the underwriting of high-risk applicants. Modern civil rights legislation, applicable to enterprises ranging from restaurants to landlords, has also expanded the scope of compulsory contracts.

Of course, government compulsion to make the more powerful party deal is of limited benefit to the weaker party if the more powerful party has the sole discretion to determine the substantive terms of the required contract. This fact has led in a number of instances to substantial legal control over the terms of the contracts themselves. To cite one example, the Restatement (Second) of Torts, § 763 declares that utilities are under a duty to contract "on proper terms" with those who seek service. This flexible standard of fair terms, derived from decisional law, is buttressed by modern statutory schemes of regulation. A utility company, for example, will be assured a reasonable rate of return on its investment, but a public regulatory commission must approve the rates the utility charges to realize that return. Even insurance companies that are under no legal duty to make contracts are commonly required to use, in policies they do issue, provisions set wholly or in substantial part by statute or administrative regulation.

(2) **Prohibited terms.** Despite the basic theme of "freedom of contract," we have encountered numerous judicially-developed restraints on what the parties may agree to, or, at the least, on what courts will enforce.

In some instances, proscriptions will have been developed with sufficient certainty to take on the appearance of firm legal rules—for example, the distinction between valid liquidated damages clauses and unenforceable penalties. In others, the denial of legal effect to a clause may be grounded on a judicially-perceived "public policy." The cases cover a vast range of consensual activity, from the gambling question in *Cobaugh* (p. 392) to the exculpation question in *Richards* (p. 903) to surrogacy in *Baby M* (p. 805). In the end, this ill-defined and thus highly pliable defense, when successful, amounts to a judicial determination that private choice should be overridden by social ends. Moreover, contract terms that are unenforceable because "against public policy" merge imperceptibly into terms deemed "illegal." Illegality is a complex concept, applied case-by-case and often with scant guidance as to its scope. We cannot explore it fully here, but must rest on a caution that illegality is a basis for invalidating entire contracts or only selected provisions, and that the standard may be created by the legislature, the courts, or possibly administrative authorities. Furthermore, illegality can have a variety of legal effects, particularly on the question of relief in restitution.

(3) **Requirements of form.** Even if a contract provision is not prohibited or denied legal effect, it may have such severe and perhaps unanticipated consequences for one of the parties that special care is warranted to assure that the term is brought to the attention of the party who would be disadvantaged. We saw in Chapter 3 that at least some of the doctrines on mutual assent impose requirements of form, by denying legal effect to clauses or terms that would escape the notice of normally-attentive readers. Such requirements may achieve much greater specificity and inflexibility in statutes. For example, UCC 2–316 requires that if the implied warranty of merchantability is to be excluded or modified, the language must mention "merchantability" and, if written, must be "conspicuous."

(4) **Balancing the standard form.** One of the most attractive techniques for preserving the advantages of printed forms, while avoiding their potential for misleading and oppressing, involves private, not official, action. Parties regularly operating in a particular trade or business, perhaps organized in a trade association, may devise standard forms that fairly balance the interests of all the parties. A good example from commercial history is the Worth Street Rules, which were developed by a number of associations representing all interests in the cotton industry. Another is the standard agreement between an owner and a general contractor developed by the American Institute of Architects. The mere fact that a trade association has developed the form does not, of course, assure its fairness. A standard listing agreement prepared by a board of realtors may serve only to aggregate tendencies toward over-reaching. The best assurance of fairness and balance arises when the process that gave rise to the form itself is itself unbiased. This can happen when there is negotiation or bargaining between the groups whose transactions will be structured by the form, when an impartial third group whose interests are not centrally involved in the transaction prepares the form, or when the parties to the negotiations are equally likely to be on either side of the transaction

---

SECTION 5. UNCONSCIONABILITY, FRAUD, AND ARBITRATION

Brower v. Gateway 2000, Inc.

Supreme Court of New York, Appellate Division, 1998.
246 A.D.2d 246, 676 N.Y.S.2d 569.

MILONAS, J. Appellants are among the many consumers who purchased computers and software products from defendant Gateway 2000 through a direct-sales system, by mail or telephone order. As of July 3, 1995, it was Gateway's practice to include with the materials shipped to the purchaser along with the merchandise a copy of its "Standard Terms and Conditions Agreement" and any relevant warranties for the products in the shipment. The Agreement begins with a "NOTE TO CUSTOMER," which provides, in slightly larger print than the remainder of the document, in a box that spans the width of the page: "This document contains Gateway 2000's Standard Terms and Conditions. By keeping your Gateway 2000 computer system beyond thirty (30) days after the date of delivery, you accept these Terms and Conditions." The document consists of 16 paragraphs[;] paragraph 10 of the agreement, entitled "DISPUTE RESOLUTION," reads as follows:

> Any dispute or controversy arising out of or relating to this Agreement or its interpretation shall be settled exclusively and finally by arbitration. The arbitration shall be conducted in accordance with the Rules of Conciliation and Arbitration of the International Chamber of Commerce. The arbitration shall be conducted in Chicago, Illinois, U.S.A. before a sole arbitrator. Any award rendered in any such arbitration proceeding shall be final and binding on each of the parties, and judgment may be entered thereon in a court of competent jurisdiction.

Plaintiffs commenced this action on behalf of themselves and others similarly situated for compensatory and punitive damages, alleging deceptive sales practices in seven causes of action, including breach of warranty, breach of contract, fraud and unfair trade practices. In particular, the allegations focused on Gateway's representations and advertising that promised "service when you need it," including around-the-clock free technical support, free software technical support and certain on-site services. According to plaintiffs, not only were they unable to avail themselves of this offer because it was virtually impossible to get through to a technician, but also Gateway continued to advertise this claim notwithstanding numerous complaints and reports about the problem.

. . . Gateway moved to dismiss the complaint based on the arbitration clause in the Agreement. Appellants argued that the arbitration clause is invalid under UCC 2–207, unconscionable under UCC 2–302 and an unenforceable contract of adhesion. Specifically, they claimed that the provision was obscure; that a customer could not reasonably be expected to appreciate or investigate its meaning and effect; that the Int'l Chamber of Commerce ("ICC") was not a forum commonly used for consumer matters; and that because ICC headquarters were in France, it was particularly difficult to locate the organization and its rules. To illustrate just how inaccessible the forum was, appellants advised the court that the ICC was not registered with the Secretary of State, that efforts to locate and contact the ICC had been unsuccessful and that apparently the only way to attempt to contact the ICC was through the United States Council for Int'l Business, with which the ICC maintained some sort of relationship.

In support of their arguments, appellants submitted a copy of the ICC's Rules of Conciliation and Arbitration and contended that the cost of ICC arbitration was prohibitive, particularly given the amount of the typical consumer claim involved. For example, a claim of less than $50,000 required advance fees of $4,000 (more than the cost of most Gateway products), of which the $2,000 registration fee was nonrefundable even if the consumer prevailed at the arbitration. Consumers would also incur travel expenses disproportionate to the damages sought, which appellants' counsel estimated would not exceed $1,000 per customer in this action, as well as bear the cost of Gateway's legal fees if the consumer did not prevail at the arbitration; in this respect, the ICC rules follow the "loser pays" rule used in England. Also, although Chicago was designated as the site of the actual arbitration, all correspondence must be sent to ICC headquarters in France.

The IAS court dismissed the complaint based on the arbitration clause. . . . We agree with the court's decision and reasoning in all respects but for the issue of the unconscionability of the designation of the ICC as the arbitration body.

First, the court properly rejected appellants' argument that the arbitration clause was invalid under UCC 2–207. . . . [A]s the court correctly concluded, the clause was not a "material alteration" of an oral agreement [under UCC 2–207(2),] but, rather, simply one provision of the sole contract that existed between the parties. That contract, the court explained, was formed and acceptance was manifested not when the order was placed but only with the retention of the merchandise beyond the 30 days specified in the Agreement enclosed in the shipment of merchandise. Accordingly, the contract was outside the scope of UCC 2–207.

[In omitted passages, this conclusion was rested on the rationale of ProCD, Inc. v. Zeidenberg and Hill v. Gateway 2000, Inc., supra pp. 446–453. The court, addressing "the realities of conducting business in today's world," including the "cash now, terms later" transaction, approved in full the lower court's embrace of the contract-formation analysis found in those decisions. Hence there was no "battle of the forms" here, only a sole contract "proposed" and "effectual" as a whole.]

Second, with respect to appellants' claim that the arbitration clause is unenforceable as a contract of adhesion, in that it involved no choice or negotiation on the part of the consumer but was a "take it or leave it" proposition[,] we find that this argument, too, was properly rejected. Although the parties clearly do not possess equal bargaining power, this factor alone does not invalidate the contract as one of adhesion. . . . [W]ith the ability to make the purchase elsewhere and the express option to return the goods, the consumer is not in a "take it or leave it" position at all; if any term of the agreement is unacceptable to the consumer, he or she can easily buy a competitor's product instead—either from a retailer or directly from the manufacturer—and reject Gateway's agreement by returning the merchandise (see, e.g. Carnival Cruise Lines v. Shute, 499 U.S. 585, 593–594 . . .). The consumer has 30 days to make that decision. Within that time, the consumer can inspect the goods and examine and seek clarification of the terms of the agreement; until those 30 days have elapsed, the consumer has the unqualified right to return the merchandise, because the goods or terms are unsatisfactory or for no reason at all.

While returning the goods to avoid the formation of the contract entails affirmative action on the part of the consumer, and even some expense, this may be seen as a trade-off for the convenience and savings for which the consumer presumably opted when he or she chose to make a purchase of such consequence by phone or mail as an alternative to on-site retail shopping. That a consumer does not read the agreement or thereafter claims he or she failed to understand or appreciate some term therein does not invalidate the contract any more than such claim would undo a contract formed under other circumstances. . . . We further note that appellants' claim of adhesion is identical to that made and rejected in Filias v. Gateway 2000, Inc., an unreported case brought to our attention by both parties that interprets the same Gateway agreement (No. 97C 2523 [N.D.Ill., January 15, 1998]). . . .

Finally, we turn to appellants' argument that the IAS court should have declared the contract unenforceable, pursuant to UCC 2–302, on the ground that the arbitration clause is unconscionable due to the unduly burdensome procedure and cost for the individual consumer. The IAS court found that while a class-action lawsuit, such as the one herein, may be a less costly alternative to arbitration (which is generally less costly than litigation), that does not alter the binding effect of the valid arbitration clause contained in the agreement. . . .

As a general matter, under New York law, unconscionability requires a showing that a contract is "both procedurally and substantively unconscionable when made" (Gillman v. Chase Manhattan Bank, 73 N.Y.2d 1, 10, 537 N.Y.S.2d 787, 534 N.E.2d 824). That is, there must be "some showing of 'an absence of meaningful choice on the part of one of the parties together with contract terms which are unreasonably favorable to the other party' [citation omitted]" (Matter of State of New York v. Avco Fin. Serv., 50 N.Y.2d 383, 389–390, 429 N.Y.S.2d 181, 406 (N.E.2d

1075)). The *Avco* court took pains to note, however, that the purpose of this doctrine is not to redress the inequality between the parties but simply to ensure that the more powerful party cannot "surprise" the other party with some overly oppressive term.

As to the procedural element, a court will look to the contract formation process to determine if in fact one party lacked any meaningful choice in entering into the contract, taking into consideration such factors as the setting of the transaction, the experience and education of the party claiming unconscionability, whether the contract contained "fine print," whether the seller used "high-pressured tactics" and any disparity in the parties' bargaining power (*Gillman,* at 10–11, 537 N.Y.S.2d 787, 534 N.E.2d 824). None of these factors supports appellants' claim here. Any purchaser has 30 days within which to thoroughly examine the contents of their shipment, including the terms of the Agreement, and seek clarification of any term therein. The Agreement itself, which is entitled in large print "STANDARD TERMS AND CONDITIONS AGREEMENT," consists of only three pages and 16 paragraphs, all of which appear in the same size print. Moreover, despite appellants' claims to the contrary, the arbitration clause is in no way "hidden" or "tucked away" within a complex document of inordinate length, nor is the option of returning the merchandise, to avoid the contract, somehow a "precarious" one. . . .

With respect to the substantive element, . . . we do not find that the possible inconvenience of the chosen site (Chicago) alone rises to the level of unconscionability. We do find, however, that the excessive cost factor that is necessarily entailed in arbitrating before the ICC is unreasonable and surely serves to deter the individual consumer from invoking the process. . . . Barred from resorting to the courts by the arbitration clause in the first instance, the designation of a financially prohibitive forum effectively bars consumers from this forum as well; consumers are thus left with no forum at all in which to resolve a dispute. In this regard, we note that this particular claim is not mentioned in the *Hill* decision, which upheld the clause as part of an enforceable contract.

While it is true that, under New York law, unconscionability is generally predicated on the presence of both the procedural and substantive elements, the substantive element alone may be sufficient to render the terms of the provision at issue unenforceable. . . . Excessive fees, such as those incurred under the ICC procedure, have been grounds for finding an arbitration provision unenforceable or commercially unreasonable. . . .

In the *Filias* case previously mentioned, the [court] stated that it was "inclined to agree" with the argument that selection of the ICC rendered the clause unconscionable, but concluded that the issue was moot because Gateway had agreed to arbitrate before the American Arbitration Association ("AAA") and sought court appointment of the AAA pursuant to Federal Arbitration Act (9 U.S.C. § 5). The court accordingly granted

Gateway's motion to compel arbitration and appointed the AAA in lieu of the ICC. Plaintiffs in that action (who are represented by counsel for appellants before us) contend that costs associated with the AAA process are also excessive, given the amount of the individual consumer's damages, and their motion for reconsideration of the court's decision has not yet been decided. While the AAA rules and costs are not part of the record before us, the parties agree that there is a minimum, non-refundable filing fee of $500, and appellants claim each consumer could spend in excess of $1,000 to arbitrate in this forum.

Gateway's agreement to the substitution of the AAA is not limited to the *Filias* plaintiffs. Gateway's brief includes the text of a new arbitration agreement that it claims has been extended to all customers, past, present and future (apparently through publication in a quarterly magazine sent to anyone who has ever purchased a Gateway product). The new arbitration agreement provides for the consumer's choice of the AAA or the ICC as the arbitral body and the designation of any location for the arbitration by agreement of the parties which "shall not be unreasonably withheld." It also provides telephone numbers at which the AAA and the ICC may be reached for information regarding the "organizations and their procedures."

As noted, however, appellants complain that the AAA fees are also excessive and thus in no way have they accepted defendant's offer (see, UCC 2–209); because they make the same claim as to the AAA as they did with respect to the ICC, the issue of unconscionability is not rendered moot, as defendant suggests. We cannot determine on this record whether the AAA process and costs would be so "egregiously oppressive" that they, too, would be unconscionable. . . . Thus, we modify the order on appeal to the extent of finding that portion of the arbitration provision requiring arbitration before the ICC to be unconscionable and[,] [vacating that portion of the arbitration agreement,] remand to Supreme Court so that the parties have the opportunity to seek appropriate substitution of an arbitrator pursuant to the Federal Arbitration Act (9 U.S.C. § 1 et seq.), which provides for such court designation of an arbitrator upon application of either party, where, for whatever reason, one is not otherwise designated. . . .

All concur.

Sphere Drake Ins. Ltd. v. All Am. Ins. Co.

United States Court of Appeals, Seventh Circuit, 2001.
256 F.3d 587.

EASTERBROOK, CIRCUIT JUDGE. Who pays losses incurred on seven insurance policies is a subject of dispute. All American Insurance underwrote the policies. Contracts apparently representing the agreement of Sphere Drake Insurance to reinsure these risks are in All American's files—but Sphere Drake denies that it has agreed to any such reinsurance. A broker called Euro International Underwriting ("EIU") wrote the reinsurance on Sphere Drake's behalf. EIU had actual authority to represent Sphere Drake, but only up to an annual limit of risks. According to Sphere Drake, EIU exceeded this limit when agreeing to reinsure All American's policies. Moreover, Sphere Drake contends, All American knew that EIU had gone over the top, so that EIU had neither actual nor apparent authority. The parties appear to agree that if this defense prevails then Sphere Drake need not pay; they also agree on the extent of Sphere Drake's liability if EIU had power to bind it. What they do not agree on is which tribunal has the authority to decide the extent of EIU's authority as Sphere Drake's agent.

Sphere Drake wants the dispute resolved in court—federal court in particular, because the parties are of diverse nationalities. All American contends that the parties have agreed to arbitrate. It relies on the language in the short form agreements (called slip policies) that EIU signed. The parties concentrate on one particular slip policy, which agrees to reinsure workers' compensation risks. . . .

All American contends that this policy contains two arbitration clauses. First, the last paragraph of the "General Conditions" section says that "[t]he Arbitration contract shall also be governed by the law and jurisdiction of the state of Illinois, U.S.A." This use of the definite article, All American insists, establishes that Sphere Drake has agreed to arbitrate. Second, the initial paragraph of "General Conditions" says that the reinsurance follows "all terms clauses and conditions on the original contract"; because the Unicare policy has an arbitration clause, this follow-form slip policy also requires arbitration. Sphere Drake disputes both of these contentions and adds a defense: even if EIU plastered the papers with arbitration clauses that can't kick Sphere Drake out of court on the question whether EIU was its agent. To arbitrate the agency issue, Sphere Drake insists, would be circular, for arbitration is proper if and only if EIU indeed could bind Sphere Drake. . . .

Having concluded that the "General Conditions" section incorporates the arbitration agreement in the Unicare policy, we can bypass other disputes and cut straight to the question whether EIU's authority is arbitrable. Recall that Sphere Drake and All American would not ask the arbitrator to resolve anything except whether they have a reinsurance agreement in the first place—a question that depends entirely on EIU's authority to bind Sphere Drake. This dispute seems to us covered by the principle that courts, rather than arbitrators, usually determine whether the parties have agreed to arbitrate. . . . EIU agreed to the slip policy, but whether EIU spoke for Sphere Drake is debated. If All American produced a policy purportedly signed by Sphere Drake's CEO, but evidence showed that a clerk at All American had forged the signature, then Sphere Drake would not have to arbitrate (or pay); why would it be different if EIU lacked authority to speak for Sphere Drake? Section 2 of the

Federal Arbitration Act, says that an arbitration agreement "shall be valid, irrevocable, and enforceable, save upon such grounds as exist at law or in equity for the revocation of any contract." An agent's lack of authority is a ground that prevents the enforcement "of any contract"; does it not follow that judges must determine whether the agent had authority?

According to All American, Prima Paint Corp. v. Flood & Conklin Mfg. Co., 388 U.S. 395 (1967), supplies a negative answer. *Prima Paint* holds that, unless the arbitration clause excludes such disputes, an arbitrator resolves a claim of fraud in the inducement. This means, All American believes, that all disputes about contract *formation* go to arbitrators; only disputes about the scope of arbitration clauses . . . are resolved in advance by courts. That is, we suppose, a possible reading of *Prima Paint*. . . . But it is not a plausible reading, for it would disregard the principle that arbitration is contractual. Unless the parties agree otherwise, they are entitled to have courts resolve their disputes. The parties in *Prima Paint* did agree otherwise and promised to have the arbitrator resolve "[a]ny controversy or claim arising out of *or relating to* this Agreement" (emphasis added), the broadest possible clause. Whether one party defrauded another during the negotiations for the agreement "related to" that agreement. There was no doubt that the arbitration agreement (and the contract of which it was a part) had been signed; both sides knew what they were getting. A claim of fraud in the inducement—which boils down to "we wouldn't have signed this contract had we known the full truth about our trading partner"—supposes that the unhappy party did agree, but now wishes it hadn't. If a claim of "we wish we hadn't agreed" could be litigated, even when the arbitration clause is so broad, this would move a good portion of contract disputes back to court and defeat this part of the agreement at the outset, for it is easy to cry fraud. *Prima Paint* thought it important that no one argued that the arbitration clause was itself the result of fraud; that enabled an arbitrator to resolve defenses to enforcement of the contract without calling into question the arbitrator's own authority to act.

Fraud in the inducement does not negate the fact that the parties actually reached an agreement. That's what was critical in *Prima Paint*. But whether there was *any* agreement is a distinct question. [Chastain v. Robinson-Humphrey Co., 957 F.2d 851 (11th Cir. 1992),] sensibly holds a claim of forgery must be resolved by a court. A person whose signature was forged has never agreed to anything. Likewise with a person whose name was written on a contract by a faithless agent who lacked authority to make that commitment. This is not a defense to enforcement, as in *Prima Paint*; it is a situation in which no contract came into being; and as arbitration depends on a valid contract an argument that the contract does not exist can't logically be resolved by the arbitrator (unless the parties agree to arbitrate this issue after the dispute arises). It was possible to arbitrate in *Prima Paint* without circularity; in forgery and agency cases, by contrast, the arbitrator's authority to resolve the dispute would depend on one particular answer to that very dispute. Only a court can break that circle. Disputes about the adequacy of consideration (or some other formation issues) would be closer questions, for a contract without consideration represents an *agreement*. Lack of consideration has historically made the promise unenforceable in court, but parties may be able to create contracts that the public tribunals do not enforce yet private tribunals will enforce. Nonetheless, we have held, a claim of missing consideration will be heard by a court and, if the agreement is not supported by consideration, the dispute will not be sent to arbitration. If this is so, then the treatment of a contract signed by a person who lacks authority follows directly. . . .

Sphere Drake may be required to arbitrate if and only if EIU had authority to bind it to these reinsurance contracts. If EIU *did* have authority, then there appears to be no further dispute that needs to be resolved, by judge or arbitrator. Accordingly, the judgment is affirmed (there will be no arbitration unless some additional issue for private dispute resolution surfaces later in the case) and the case is remanded with instructions to resolve the parties' only real dispute: the extent of EIU's authority.

Rent-A-Center v. Jackson

Supreme Court of the United States, 2010.
561 U.S. 63, 130 S.Ct. 2772.

SCALIA, J. . . . On February 1, 2007, the respondent here, Antonio Jackson, filed an employment-discrimination suit . . . against his former employer in the United States District Court for the District of Nevada. The defendant and petitioner here, Rent-A-Center, West, Inc., filed a motion under the [Federal Arbitration Act] to dismiss or stay the proceedings, and to compel arbitration. Rent-A-Center argued that the Mutual Agreement to Arbitrate Claims (Agreement), which Jackson signed on February 24, 2003 as a condition of his employment there, precluded Jackson from pursuing his claims in court. The Agreement provided for arbitration of all "past, present or future" disputes arising out of Jackson's employment with Rent-A-Center, including "claims for discrimination" and "claims for violation of any federal . . . law." It also provided that "[t]he Arbitrator, and not any federal, state, or local court or agency, shall have exclusive authority to resolve any dispute relating to the interpretation, applicability, enforceability or formation of this Agreement including, but not limited to any claim that all or any part of this Agreement is void or voidable."

Jackson opposed the motion on the ground that "the arbitration agreement in question is clearly unenforceable in that it is unconscionable" under Nevada law. Rent-A-Center responded that Jackson's unconscionability claim was not properly before the court because Jackson had expressly agreed that the arbitrator would have exclusive authority to resolve any dispute about the enforceability of the Agreement. It also disputed the merits of Jackson's unconscionability claims. . . .

The FAA reflects the fundamental principle that arbitration is a matter of contract. Section 2, the "primary substantive provision of the Act," Moses H. Cone Memorial Hospital v. Mercury Constr. Corp., 460 U.S. 1, 24, 103 S.Ct. 927, 74 L.Ed.2d 765 (1983), provides:

> A written provision in . . . a contract evidencing a transaction involving commerce to settle by arbitration a controversy thereafter arising out of such contract . . . shall be valid, irrevocable, and enforceable, save upon such grounds as exist at law or in equity for the revocation of any contract. 9 U.S.C. § 2.

The FAA thereby places arbitration agreements on an equal footing with other contracts, and requires courts to enforce them according to their terms. Like other contracts, however, they may be invalidated by "generally applicable contract defenses, such as fraud, duress, or unconscionability."

The Act also establishes procedures by which federal courts implement § 2's substantive rule. Under § 3, a party may apply to a federal court for a stay of the trial of an action "upon any issue referable to arbitration under an agreement in writing for such arbitration." Under § 4, a party "aggrieved" by the failure of another party "to arbitrate under a written agreement for arbitration" may petition a federal court "for an order directing that such arbitration proceed in the manner provided for in such agreement." The court "shall" order arbitration "upon being satisfied that the making of the agreement for arbitration or the failure to comply therewith is not in issue." *Ibid.*

The Agreement here contains multiple "written provision[s]" to "settle by arbitration a controversy," § 2. Two are relevant to our discussion. First, the section titled "Claims Covered By The Agreement" provides for arbitration of all "past, present or future" disputes arising out of Jackson's employment with Rent-A-Center. Second, the section titled "Arbitration Procedures" provides that "[t]he Arbitrator . . . shall have exclusive authority to resolve any dispute relating to the . . . enforceability . . . of this Agreement including, but not limited to any claim that all or any part of this Agreement is void or voidable." The current "controversy" between the parties is whether the Agreement is unconscionable. It is the second provision, which delegates resolution of that controversy to the arbitrator, that Rent-A-Center seeks to enforce. Adopting the terminology used by the parties, we will refer to it as the delegation provision.

The delegation provision is an agreement to arbitrate threshold issues concerning the arbitration agreement. We have recognized that parties can agree to arbitrate "gateway" questions of "arbitrability," such as whether the parties have agreed to arbitrate or whether their agreement covers a particular controversy. This line of cases merely reflects the principle that arbitration is a matter of contract. An agreement to arbitrate a gateway issue is simply an additional, antecedent agreement the party seeking arbitration asks the federal court to enforce, and the FAA operates on this additional arbitration agreement just as it does on any other. The additional agreement is valid under § 2 "save upon such grounds as exist at law or in equity for the revocation of any contract," and federal courts can enforce the agreement by staying federal litigation under § 3 and compelling arbitration under § 4. The question before us, then, is whether the delegation provision is valid under § 2.

There are two types of validity challenges under § 2: "One type challenges specifically the validity of the agreement to arbitrate," and "[t]he other challenges the contract as a whole, either on a ground that directly affects the entire agreement (*e.g.,* the agreement was fraudulently induced), or on the ground that the illegality of one of the contract's provisions renders the whole contract invalid." *Buckeye,* 546 U.S., at 444, 126 S.Ct. 1204. In a line of cases neither party has asked us to overrule, we held that only the first type of challenge is relevant to a court's determination whether the arbitration agreement at issue is enforceable. See Prima Paint Corp. v. Flood & Conklin Mfg. Co., 388 U.S. 395, 403–404, 87 S.Ct. 1801, 18 L.Ed.2d 1270 (1967). That is because § 2 states that a "written provision" "to settle by arbitration a controversy" is "valid, irrevocable, and enforceable" *without mention* of the validity of the contract in which it is contained. Thus, a party's challenge to another provision of the contract, or to the contract as a whole, does not prevent a court from enforcing a specific agreement to arbitrate. "[A]s a matter of substantive federal arbitration law, an arbitration provision is severable from the remainder of the contract." *Buckeye,* 546 U.S., at 445, 126 S.Ct. 1204; see also *id.,* at 447, 126 S.Ct. 1204 (the severability rule is based on § 2).

But that agreements to arbitrate are severable does not mean that they are unassailable. If a party challenges the validity under § 2 of the precise agreement to arbitrate at issue, the federal court must consider the challenge before ordering compliance with that agreement under § 4. In *Prima Paint,* for example, if the claim had been "fraud in the inducement of the arbitration clause itself," then the court would have considered it. 388 U.S., at 403–404, 87 S.Ct. 1801. "To immunize an arbitration agreement from judicial challenge on the ground of fraud in the inducement would be to elevate it over other forms of contract," *id.,* at 404, n. 12, 87 S.Ct. 1801. In some cases the claimed basis of invalidity for the contract as a whole will be much easier to establish than the same basis as applied only to the severable agreement to arbitrate. Thus, in an employment contract many elements of alleged unconscionability applicable to the entire contract (outrageously low wages, for example) would not affect the agreement to arbitrate alone. But even where that is not the case—as in *Prima Paint* itself, where the alleged fraud that induced the whole contract equally induced the agreement to arbitrate which was part of that contract—we nonetheless require the basis of challenge to be directed specifically to the agreement to arbitrate before the court will intervene.

Here, the "written provision . . . to settle by arbitration a controversy," 9 U.S.C. § 2, that Rent-A-Center asks us to enforce is the delegation provision—the provision that gave the arbitrator "exclusive authority to resolve any dispute relating to the . . . enforceability . . . of this Agreement." The "remainder of the contract," *Buckeye, supra,* at 445, 126 S.Ct. 1204, is the rest of the agreement to arbitrate claims arising out of Jackson's employment with Rent-A-Center. To be sure this case differs from *Prima Paint, Buckeye,* and *Preston,* in that the arbitration provisions sought to be enforced in those cases were contained in contracts unrelated to arbitration—contracts for consulting services, check-cashing services, and "personal management" or "talent agent" services. In this case, the underlying contract is itself an arbitration agreement. But that makes no difference. Application of the severability rule does not depend on the substance of the remainder of the contract. Section 2 operates on the specific "written provision" to "settle by arbitration a controversy" that the party seeks to enforce. Accordingly, unless Jackson challenged the delegation provision specifically, we must treat it as valid under § 2, and must enforce it under §§ 3 and 4, leaving any challenge to the validity of the Agreement as a whole for the arbitrator. . . .

The District Court correctly concluded that Jackson challenged only the validity of the contract as a whole. Nowhere in his opposition to Rent-A-Center's motion to compel arbitration did he even mention the delegation provision. Rent-A-Center noted this fact in its reply: "[Jackson's response] fails to rebut or otherwise address in any way [Rent-A-Center's] argument that the Arbitrator must decide [Jackson's] challenge to the enforceability of the Agreement. *Thus, [Rent-A-Center's] argument is uncontested.*"

The arguments Jackson made in his response to Rent-A-Center's motion to compel arbitration support this conclusion. Jackson stated that "the *entire agreement* seems drawn to provide [Rent-A-Center] with undue advantages should an employment-related dispute arise." (emphasis added). At one point, he argued that the limitations on discovery "further suppor[t] [his] contention that the *arbitration agreement as a whole* is substantively unconscionable." (emphasis added). And before this Court, Jackson describes his challenge in the District Court as follows: He "opposed the motion to compel on the ground that the *entire arbitration agreement,* including the delegation clause, was unconscionable." (emphasis added). That is an accurate description of his filings.

As required to make out a claim of unconscionability under Nevada law, he contended that the Agreement was both procedurally and substantively unconscionable. It was procedurally unconscionable, he argued, because it "was imposed as a condition of employment and was nonnegotiable." But we need not consider that claim because none of Jackson's substantive unconscionability challenges was specific to the delegation provision. First, he argued that the Agreement's coverage was one sided in that it required arbitration of claims an employee was likely to bring—contract, tort, discrimination, and statutory claims—but did not require arbitration of claims Rent-A-Center was likely to bring—intellectual property, unfair competition, and trade secrets claims. This one-sided-coverage argument clearly did not go to the validity of the delegation provision.

Jackson's other two substantive unconscionability arguments assailed arbitration procedures called for by the contract—the fee-splitting arrangement and the limitations on discovery—procedures that were to be used during arbitration under *both* the agreement to arbitrate employment-related disputes *and* the delegation provision. It may be that had Jackson challenged the delegation provision by arguing that these common procedures *as applied* to the delegation provision rendered *that provision* unconscionable, the challenge should have been considered by the court. To make such a claim based on the discovery procedures, Jackson would have had to argue that the limitation upon the number of depositions causes the arbitration of his claim that the Agreement is unenforceable to be unconscionable. That would be, of course, a much more difficult argument to sustain than the argument that the same limitation renders arbitration of his factbound employment-discrimination claim unconscionable. Likewise, the unfairness of the fee-splitting arrangement may be more difficult to establish for the arbitration of enforceability than for arbitration of more complex and fact-related aspects of the alleged employment discrimination. Jackson, however, did not make any arguments specific to the delegation provision; he argued that the fee-sharing and discovery procedures rendered the *entire* Agreement invalid.

Jackson's appeal to the Ninth Circuit confirms that he did not contest the validity of the delegation provision in particular. His brief noted the existence of the delegation provision, but his unconscionability arguments made no mention of it. He also repeated the arguments he had made before the District Court, that the "entire agreement" favors Rent-A-Center and that the limitations on discovery further his "contention that the arbitration agreement as a whole is substantively unconscionable." Finally, he repeated the argument made in his District Court filings, that under state law the unconscionable clauses could not be severed from the arbitration agreement. The point of this argument, of course, is that the Agreement *as a whole* is unconscionable under state law.

Jackson repeated that argument before this Court. At oral argument, counsel stated: "There are certain elements of the arbitration agreement that are unconscionable and, under Nevada law, which would render the *entire arbitration agreement* unconscionable." And again, he stated, "we've got both certain provisions that are unconscionable, that under Nevada law render the *entire agreement* unconscionable . . ., and that's what the Court is to rely on." . . .

We reverse the judgment of the Court of Appeals for the Ninth Circuit.

NOTE: UNCONSCIONABILITY AND ARBITRATION

The Supreme Court's cases on arbitration have generated intense academic scrutiny. For an excellent example, David Horton, Arbitration About Arbitration, 70 Stan. L. Rev. 363 (2018). Quite apart from the benefits of resolving the merits of a single dispute before a judge and jury rather than an arbitrator, the ability to litigate a dispute may allow a class action. By being able to insist on arbitration, a large firm may be able to avoid large liabilities (and substantial attorney's fees) when the harm arising from any individual incident is small.

Sphere Drake and *Rent-a-Center* suggest a sharp distinction between whether a party entered into an agreement at all and whether a contract that contains an arbitration clause is unconscionable. Someone who never signs a contract does not have to put the issue of whether she signed the contract to an arbitrator, but someone who claims that a contract is unconscionable must. But how watertight is this distinction? Presumably, Judge Easterbrook would allow someone to argue before a judge that she signed the contract only because the other party held a gun to her head. How exactly is a contract that is procedurally and substantively unconscionable different? If I did not exercise my free will when I signed the contract, how can I be bound by any of its terms? And if I am not, how can I be said to have agreed to *any* clause in the contract, including the arbitration clause?

CHAPTER 7

THE RIGHTS AND DUTIES OF NONPARTIES

SECTION 1. THIRD PARTY BENEFICIARIES

Lawrence v. Fox

Court of Appeals of New York, 1859.
20 N.Y. 268.

Appeal from the Superior Court. . . . On the trial [below], it appeared by the evidence of a bystander, that one Holly, in November, 1857, at the request of [Fox], loaned and advanced to him $300, stating at the time that he [Holly] owed that sum to [Lawrence] for money borrowed of him, and had agreed to pay it to him the then next day; that [Fox] in consideration thereof, at the time of receiving the money, promised to pay it to [Lawrence] the then next day. . . . [Fox] moved for a nonsuit, upon [several] grounds, viz.: . . . that the agreement by [Fox] with Holly to pay [Lawrence] was void for want of consideration, and that there was no privity between [Lawrence] and [Fox]. The court overruled the motion, and the [jury] found a verdict for [Lawrence] for the amount of the loan and interest, $344.66, upon which judgment was entered; from which [Fox] appealed to the Superior Court, at general term, where the judgment was affirmed, and [Fox] appealed to this court. . . .

H. GRAY, J. . . . [I]t is claimed that notwithstanding [Fox's] promise was established by competent evidence, it was void for the want of consideration. It is now more than a quarter of a century since it was settled by the Supreme Court of this State . . . that a promise in all material respects like the one under consideration was valid; and the judgment of that court was unanimously affirmed by the Court for the Correction of Errors. Farley v. Cleaveland, 4 Cow., 432; 9 id., 639. In that case one Moon owed Farley and sold to Cleaveland a quantity of hay, in consideration of which Cleaveland promised to pay Moon's debt to Farley; and the decision in favor of Farley's right to recover was placed upon the ground that the hay received by Cleaveland from Moon was a valid consideration for Cleaveland's promise to pay Farley, and that the subsisting liability of Moon to pay Farley was no objection to the recovery.

The fact that the money advanced by Holly to [Fox] was a loan to him for a day, and that it thereby became the property of [Fox], seemed to impress [Fox's] counsel with the idea that because [Fox's] promise was not a trust fund placed by [Lawrence] in [Fox's] hands, out of which he was to realize money as from the sale of a chattel or the collection of a debt, the promise although made for the benefit of [Lawrence] could not enure to his benefit. The hay which [Moon] delivered to [Cleaveland] was not to be paid to Farley, but the debt incurred by Cleaveland for the purchase of the hay, like the debt incurred by [Fox] for money borrowed, was what was to be paid.

That case . . . puts to rest the objection that [Fox's] promise was void for want of consideration. [There,] the promise was not only made to Moon but to the plaintiff Farley. In this case the promise was made to Holly and not expressly to [Lawrence]; and this difference between the two cases presents the question . . . as to the want of privity between [Lawrence and Fox]. As early as 1806 it was announced by the Supreme Court of this State, upon what was then regarded as the settled law of England, "That where one person makes a promise to another for the benefit of a third person, that third person may maintain an action upon it." Schermerhorn v. Vanderheyden (1 John R., 140), has often been reasserted by our courts and never departed from. . . .

The same principle is adjudged in several cases in Massachusetts. . . In Hall v. Marston, [17 Mass. 575 (1822)], the court say: "It seems to have been well settled that if A promises B for a valuable consideration to pay C, the latter may maintain assumpsit for the money;" and in Brewer v. Dyer, [61 Mass. 337, 337 (1851)], the recovery was upheld, as the court said, ". . . not upon the ground of any actual or supposed relationship between the parties as some of the earlier cases would seem to indicate, but upon the broader and more satisfactory basis, that the law operating on the act of the parties creates the duty, establishes a privity, and implies the promise and obligation on which the action is founded." . . .

But it is urged that because the defendant was not in any sense a trustee of the property of Holly for the benefit of the plaintiff, the law will not imply a promise. I agree that many of the cases where a promise was implied were cases of trusts, created for the benefit of the promiser. Felton v. Dickinson, 10 Mass., 189, and others that might be cited are of that class; but concede them all to have been cases of trusts, and it proves nothing against the application of the rule to this case. The duty of the trustee to pay the *cestuis que trust*, according to the terms of the trust, implies his promise to the latter to do so. In this case the defendant, upon ample consideration received from Holly, promised Holly to pay his debt to the plaintiff; the consideration received and the promise to Holly made it as plainly his duty to pay the plaintiff as if the money had been remitted to him for that purpose, and as well implied a promise to do so as if he had been made a trustee of property to be converted into cash with which to pay. The fact that a breach of the duty imposed in the one case may be visited, and justly, with more serious consequences than in the other, by no means disproves the payment to be a duty in both. The principle illustrated by the example so frequently quoted (which concisely states the case in hand) "that a promise made to one for the benefit of another, he for whose benefit it is made may bring an action for its breach," has been applied to trust cases, not because it was exclusively applicable to those cases, but because it was a principle of law, and as such applicable to those cases.

It was also insisted that Holly could have discharged the defendant from his promise, though it was intended by both parties for the benefit of the plaintiff, and therefore the plaintiff was not entitled to maintain this suit for the recovery of a demand over which he had no control. It is enough that the plaintiff [Holly?] did not release the defendant from his promise, and whether he could or not is a question not now necessarily involved; but if it was, I think it would be found difficult to maintain the right of Holly to discharge a judgment recovered by the plaintiff upon confession or otherwise, for the breach of the defendant's promise; and if he could not, how could he discharge the suit before judgment, or the promise before suit, made as it was for the plaintiff's benefit and in accordance with legal presumption accepted by him, Berly v. Taylor, 5 Hill 577, until his dissent was shown.

The cases cited, and especially Farley v. Cleaveland, establish the validity of a parol promise; it stands then upon the footing of a written one. Suppose the defendant had given his note in which, for value received of Holly, he had promised to pay the plaintiff and the plaintiff had accepted the promise, retaining Holly's liability. Very clearly Holly could not have discharged that promise, be the right to release the defendant as it may. No one can doubt that he owes the sum of money demanded of him, or that in accordance with his promise it was his duty to have paid it to the plaintiff; nor can it be doubted that whatever may be the diversity of opinion elsewhere, the adjudications in this State, from a very early period . . . have established the defendant's liability; if, therefore, it could be shown that a more strict and technically accurate application of the rules applied, would lead to a different result (which I by no means concede), the effort should not be made in the face of manifest justice.

The judgment should be affirmed.

JOHNSON, C.J., DENIO, SELDEN, ALLEN and STRONG, JJ., concurred. JOHNSON, C.J. and DENIO, J., were of opinion that the promise was to be regarded as made to the plaintiff through the medium of his agent, whose action he could ratify when it came to his knowledge, though taken without his being privy thereto.

COMSTOCK, J. (dissenting). The plaintiff had nothing to do with the promise on which he brought this action. It was not made to him, nor did the consideration proceed from him. If he can maintain the suit, it is because an anomaly has found its way into the law. . . . In general, there must be privity of contract. The party who sues upon a promise must be the promisee, or he must have some legal interest in the undertaking. [Here], it is plain that Holly, who loaned the money to the defendant, and to whom the promise in question was made, could at any time have claimed that it should be performed to himself personally. He had lent the money to the defendant, and at the same time directed the latter to pay the sum to the plaintiff. This direction he could countermand, and if he had done so, manifestly the defendant's promise to pay according to the direction would have ceased to exist. The plaintiff would receive a benefit by a complete execution of the arrangement, but the arrangement itself was between other parties, and was under their exclusive control. If the defendant had paid the money to Holly, his debt would have been discharged thereby. So Holly might have released the demand or assigned it to another person, or the parties might have annulled the promise now in question, and designated some other creditor of Holly as the party to whom the money should be paid. It has never been claimed, that in a case thus situated, the right of a third person to sue upon the promise rested on any sound principle of law. . . .

The cases in which some trust was involved are also frequently referred to as authority for the doctrine now in question, but they do not sustain it. If A delivers money or property to B, which the latter accepts upon a trust for the benefit of C, the latter can enforce the trust by an appropriate action for that purpose. Berly v. Taylor, 5 Hill 577. If the trust be of money, I think the beneficiary may assent to it and bring the action for money had and received to his use. If it be of something else than money, the trustee must account for it according to the terms of the trust, and upon principles of equity. There is some authority even for saying that an express promise founded on the possession of a trust fund may be enforced by an action at law in the name of the beneficiary, although it was made to the creator of the trust. Thus, in Comyn's Digest [B.15], it is laid down that if a man promise a pig of lead to A, and his executor give lead to make a pig to B, who assumes to deliver it to A, an assumpsit lies by A against him. The case of The Delaware & Hudson Canal Co. v. The Westchester County Bank, 4 Denio 97, involved a trust because the defendants had received from a third party a bill of exchange under an agreement that they would endeavor to collect it, and would pay over the proceeds when collected to the plaintiffs. A fund received under such an agreement does not belong to the person who receives it. He must account for it specifically; and perhaps there is no gross violation of principle in permitting the equitable owner of it to sue upon an express promise to pay it over. Having a specific interest in the thing, the undertaking to account for it may be regarded as in some sense made with him through the author of the trust. But further than this we cannot go without violating plain rules of law. In [this] case there was nothing in the nature of a trust or agency. The defendant borrowed the money of Holly and received it as his own. The plaintiff had no right in the fund, legal or equitable. The promise to repay the money created an obligation in favor of the lender to whom it was made and not in favor of any one else. . . . The judgment of the court below should therefore be reversed, and a new trial granted.

GROVER, J., also dissented.

COMMENT: THE USES OF LEGAL CATEGORIES

The opinions in this famous case deserve study, not only for the points of view they adopt on the Lawrence-Holly-Fox triangle, but also as samples of nineteenth century legal analysis. To be sure, the debate within the court showed concern for practical problems. Judge Comstock, for example, foresaw serious inconvenience through overlap and conflict between the claims of Lawrence and Holly against Fox. Looming larger than such considerations, however, was the question whether the solution was ordained by some "plain rules of law," ascertainable by reason (at least lawyers' reason) derived from basic premises of the legal order itself. If so, judges might naturally disregard the intentions of the contracting parties or any calculus of social gains and losses. This larger question can be framed by asking whether Judge Comstock's dissent rests on some such "plain rules of law," that is, fundamental conceptual objections to allowing a person who is not a party to a contract to sue under it as a "beneficiary." It was of course a relative novelty for the common law to allow nonparties to enforce a contract.

In fact, as we shall see in Seaver v. Ransom, the next case, the difficulties Comstock identified in permitting an action by Lawrence against Fox made enough impression on his contemporaries that there followed for decades a sharp retreat from the sweeping propositions asserted by the majority in Lawrence v. Fox. Only in the twentieth century did the claims of third party beneficiaries advance again on a broad front.

The great nineteenth century effort to organize and systematize legal doctrine deserves respect, however much it may now seem misdirected in details. Similar efforts were made in Western Europe, for similar reasons and with similar results on lawyers' thinking. Certainly it would be too much to say that these efforts have now been wholly abandoned. Lawyers, like others dealing with large bodies of knowledge, must have the means to organize at ascending levels of generality. Perhaps the major shift of attitudes can best be described by saying that the broad movements of opinion in the twentieth century and beyond have exposed the multiple purposes that a legal order must serve, making the internal consistency of the rules themselves merely one of the values to be measured against many others.

When the claims of third party beneficiaries began to be asserted on a broad scale, they placed a considerable strain on legal categories. There were several modes of analysis that would almost (though not quite) fit the assertion of third-party rights in a contract, as the opinions in Lawrence v. Fox reveal. The labels and classifications that have been used most often are described here, in the form of variations on that case.

(1) Holly takes from his wallet three $100 bills, hands them over to Fox and says, "Take these and use them to pay Lawrence the $300 I owe him." Fox takes the three bills and uses them to make a payment on his own overdue debt at the corner saloon. Is this a misapplication of funds deposited for a special purpose, or something that sounds still more serious, a breach of *trust*? In Lawrence v. Fox, the statement of facts might almost permit one to say so, for the statement was that "at the time of receiving the money, [Fox] promised to pay it to the plaintiff [Lawrence] the next day." If Fox really did

QUESTION

The results in illustration 19 obviously rest on the belief that, in the circumstances stated, recognition of beneficiary rights in B and C would not be appropriate. Why should this be so?

Pierce Assocs. v. Nemours Found.

865 F.2d 530 (3d Cir. 1988)

"The intent to confer a third party beneficiary benefit is to be determined from the language of the contract. . . . The language of a contract, however, cannot be divorced from the context in which it is written. Here, we are dealing with a general contract and a subcontract in the construction industry. Typically when major construction is involved an owner has neither the desire nor the ability to negotiate with and supervise the multitude of trades and skills required to complete a project. Consequently, an owner will engage a general contractor[,] [who] will retain, coordinate and supervise subcontractors. The owner looks to the general contractor, not the [subs], both for performance of the total construction project and for any damages or other relief if there is a default in performance. Performance and payment of damages are normally assured by the bond of a surety on which the general contractor is principal and the owner is the obligee. The [general], in turn, who is responsible for the performance of the [subs], has a right of action against any [sub] which defaults. Performance and payment of damages by a [sub] are normally assured by the bond of a surety on which the [sub] is principal and the [general] is the obligee.

"Thus the typical owner is insulated from the [subs] both during the course of construction and during the pursuit of remedies in the event of a default. Conversely, the [subs] are insulated from the owner[,] [who] deals with and, if necessary, sues the [general], and the [general] deals with and, if necessary, sues the [subs]. These typical construction relationships have long been recognized [quoting 4 A. Corbin, Contracts § 779D]. . . . [Courts have] referred to the 'buffer zone' which a general contract creates between the owner and a subcontractor. . . . There is nothing to prevent a departure from the typical pattern, and . . . a contractor and subcontractor may agree to [extinguish the buffer zone by conferring] upon an owner rights which are enforceable directly against the [sub]. However, an intent to do so must be found in the contract documents."

Anderson v. Fox Hill Village Homeowners Corp.

Supreme Judicial Court of Massachusetts, 1997.
424 Mass. 365, 676 N.E.2d 821.

LYNCH, J. The plaintiff appeals from summary judgment for the defendant entered in her claim for damages arising from a slip and fall caused by an icy condition on property under the control of the defendant. [We] affirm the judgment.

The following facts are not in dispute. . . . The defendant is a tenant of property used as a retirement community in Westwood. Its lease states in part:

> Tenant agrees to be solely responsible for maintaining the Premises and the Improvements and each and every part thereof in good condition throughout the term of this Lease, reasonable wear and use only excepted and agrees without limitation to:. . . (iv) *promptly remove snow and ice from all driveways and walkways* (emphasis added).

The plaintiff worked at Clark House, a skilled nursing facility, located on the premises. On December 9, 1990, while getting out of her automobile, she slipped and fell on a patch of ice in the Clark House parking lot. The defendant did nothing to remove the ice prior to that morning.

On appeal the plaintiff claims that she was entitled to recover on two theories. First, the plaintiff argues that she was an intended third-party beneficiary of the lease. Alternatively, the plaintiff argues that the defendant assumed a duty greater than that imposed under tort principles to remove the snow and ice promptly, and negligently failed to do so.

The judge correctly ruled that the plaintiff was not an intended third-party beneficiary under the lease. Choate, Hall & Stewart v. SCA Servs., Inc., 378 Mass. 535, 392 N.E.2d. 1045 (1979). In order to prevail under this theory the plaintiff must show that the defendant and the lessor intended to give her the benefit of the promised performance. [See Rest.2d,] Contracts § 302 (1981). We look at the language and circumstances of the contract for indicia of intention. *Choate*, at 545–547, 392 N.E.2d 1045. The intent must be clear and definite. . . .

Under the lease the defendant assumed sole responsibility for operation and maintenance of a retirement complex.[3] There is no indication, express or implied, that any obligations were imposed for the benefit of employees of the nursing facility. Compare Rae v. Air-Speed, Inc., 386 Mass. 187, 435 N.E.2d 628 (plaintiff and her decedent intended beneficiary of contract between employer and insurer to obtain insurance); *Choate*, supra (named creditor intended beneficiary of contract with indemnity clause). In these circumstances the plaintiff is no more than an incidental beneficiary and cannot recover under the lease. . . .

Neither can the plaintiff recover in tort. As a general rule, there is no duty by a landowner to remove a natural accumulation of snow or ice.

---

[3] The "Background and Purpose" section of the lease reads, in pertinent part, as follows:

"Whereas, concurrently herewith, Landlord has conveyed to Tenant all of Landlord's right, title and interest in and to the improvements on said parcel, except for the building containing a 70-bed skilled nursing facility and the land under said improvements and building. . . ."

Sullivan v. Brookline, 416 Mass. 825, 626 N.E.2d 870 (1994). . . . However, the plaintiff argues that the defendant assumed a greater duty than that imposed under the common law because the defendant agreed "promptly [to] remove snow and ice from all driveways and walkways."

We have held that a landlord, who agrees in a lease to remove snow and ice and negligently fails to perform that duty, may be liable to his tenant. Falden v. Gordon, 333 Mass. 135, 128 N.E.2d 778 (1955). . . .

We have also concluded that one who assumes a duty under contract "is liable to third persons not parties to the contract who are foreseeably exposed to danger and injured as a result of its negligent failure to carry out that obligation." Parent v. Stone & Webster Eng'g Corp., 408 Mass. 108, 556 N.E.2d 1009 (1990), quoting Banaghan v. Dewey, 340 Mass. 73, 162 N.E.2d 807 (1959). See [Rest.2d,] Torts § 324A (1965). Thus, a defendant who contracted to design and build an electric power plant was liable to a utility company employee injured as a result of the defendant's negligent performance of the contract. Parent v. Stone & Webster Eng'g Corp., supra. Similarly, a defendant who agreed to maintain an elevator in a safe condition was liable to third persons injured as a result of the negligent failure to carry out that obligation. Banaghan v. Dewey, supra. In those cases, the contract created a relationship between the defendant and third parties, by reason of which the law recognized a duty of reasonable care in the performance of the obligation, that supported a tort action.

However, failure to perform a contractual obligation is not a tort in the absence of a duty to act apart from the promise made. . . . See Redgrave v. Boston Symphony Orchestra, Inc., 557 F.Supp. 230 (D.Mass. 1983) ("a breach of contract is not, standing alone, a tort as well"). "Although the duty arises out of the contract and is measured by its terms, negligence in the manner of performing that duty as distinguished from mere failure to perform it, causing damage, is a tort." Abrams v. Factory Mut. Liab. Ins. Co., 298 Mass. 141, 10 N.E.2d 82 (1937). This view is endorsed by a leading authority on tort law: "Tort obligations are in general obligations that are imposed by law on policy considerations to avoid some kind of loss to others. They are obligations imposed apart from and independent of promises made and therefore apart from any manifested intention of parties to a contract or other bargaining transaction. Therefore, if the alleged obligation to do or not to do something that was breached could not have existed but for a manifested intent, then contract law should be the only theory upon which liability would be imposed." W. Prosser & W. Keeton, Torts § 92, at 656 (5th ed. 1984).

To conclude that tort liability exists solely because the defendant did not perform a contractual duty to remove snow and ice would give rise to a common law duty which we repeatedly have declined to impose on landowners. As we indicated in Sullivan v. Brookline, supra at 827, 626 N.E.2d 870, . . . "under Massachusetts law, landowners are liable only for injuries caused by defects existing on their property and . . . the law does not regard the natural accumulation of snow and ice as an actionable property defect, if it regards such weather conditions as a defect at all."

Judgment affirmed.

H.R. Moch Co. v. Rensselaer Water Co.

Court of Appeals of New York, 1928.
247 N.Y. 160, 159 N.E. 896.

CARDOZO, C.J. The defendant, a water works company[,] made a contract with the city of Rensselaer for the supply of water during a term of years. Water was to be furnished to the city for sewer flushing and street sprinkling; for service to schools and public buildings; and for service at fire hydrants, the latter service at the rate of $42.50 a year for each hydrant. Water was to be furnished to private takers within the city at their homes and factories and other industries at reasonable rates, not exceeding a stated schedule. While this contract was in force, a building caught fire. The flames, spreading to the plaintiff's warehouse near by, destroyed it and its contents. The defendant according to the complaint was promptly notified of the fire, "but omitted and neglected after such notice, to supply or furnish sufficient or adequate quantity of water, with adequate pressure to stay, suppress or extinguish the fire before it reached the warehouse of the plaintiff, although the pressure and supply which the defendant was equipped to supply and furnish, and had agreed by said contract to supply and furnish, was adequate and sufficient to prevent the spread of the fire to and the destruction of the plaintiff's warehouse and its contents." By reason of the failure of the defendant to "fulfill the provisions of the contract between it and the city of Rensselaer," the plaintiff is said to have suffered damage, for which judgment is demanded. A motion, in the nature of a demurrer, to dismiss the complaint, was denied at Special Term. The Appellate Division reversed by a divided court.

. . . The complaint, we are told, is to be viewed as stating: (1) A cause of action for breach of contract within Lawrence v. Fox, 20 N.Y. 268; [and] (2) a cause of action for a common-law tort, within MacPherson v. Buick Motor Co., 217 N.Y. 382, 111 N.E. 1050. . . .

(1) We think the action is not maintainable as one for breach of contract.

No legal duty rests upon a city to supply its inhabitants with protection against fire. Springfield Fire & Marine Ins. Co. v. Village of Keeseville, 148 N.Y. 46, 42 N.E. 405. That being so, a member of the public may not maintain an action under Lawrence v. Fox against one contracting with the city to furnish water at the hydrants, unless an intention appears that the promisor is to be answerable to individual members of the public as well as to the city for any loss ensuing from the failure to fulfill the promise. No such intention is discernible here. On the contrary, the contract is significantly divided into two branches: one a promise to the city for the benefit of the city in its corporate capacity, in which branch is included the service at the hydrants; and the other a promise to the city for the benefit of private takers, in which branch is included the service at their homes and factories. In a broad sense it is true that every city contract, not improvident or wasteful, is for the benefit of the public. More than this, however, must be shown to give a right of action to a member of the public not formally a party. The benefit, as it is sometimes said, must be one that is not merely incidental and secondary. . . . It must be primary and immediate in such a sense and to such a degree as to bespeak the assumption of a duty to make reparation directly to the individual members of the public if the benefit is lost. The field of obligation would be expanded beyond reasonable limits if less than this were to be demanded as a condition of liability. A promisor undertakes to supply fuel for heating a public building. He is not liable for breach of contract to a visitor who finds the building without fuel, and thus contracts a cold. The list of illustrations can be indefinitely extended. The carrier of the mails under contract with the government is not answerable to the merchant who has lost the benefit of a bargain through negligent delay. The householder is without a remedy against manufacturers of hose and engines, though prompt performance of their contracts would have stayed the ravages of fire. "The law does not spread its protection so far." Robins Dry Dock & Repair Co. v. Flint, 275 U.S. 303.

So with the case at hand. By the vast preponderance of authority, a contract between a city and a water company to furnish water at the city hydrants has in view a benefit to the public that is incidental rather than immediate, an assumption of duty to the city and not to its inhabitants. . . . Such with few exceptions has been the ruling in other jurisdictions. . . . Page, Contracts, § 2401. An intention to assume an obligation of indefinite extension to every member of the public is seen to be the more improbable when we recall the crushing burden that the obligation would impose. . . . The consequences invited would bear no reasonable proportion to those attached by law to defaults not greatly different. A wrongdoer who by negligence sets fire to a building is liable in damages to the owner where the fire has its origin, but not to other owners who are injured when it spreads. The rule in our State is settled to that effect, whether wisely or unwisely. . . . If the plaintiff is to prevail, one who negligently omits to supply sufficient pressure to extinguish a fire started by another, assumes an obligation to pay the ensuing damage, though the whole city is laid low. A promisor will not be deemed to have had in mind the assumption of a risk so overwhelming for any trivial reward.

The cases that have applied the rule of Lawrence v. Fox to contracts made by a city for the benefit of the public are not at war with this conclusion. Through them all there runs as a unifying principle the presence of an intention to compensate the individual members of the public in the event of a default. For example, in Pond v. New Rochelle Water Co., 183 N.Y. 330, 76 N.E. 211, the contract with the city fixed a schedule of rates to be supplied not to public buildings but to private takers at their homes. In Matter of Int'l Ry. Co. v. Rann, 224 N.Y. 83, 120 N.E. 153, the contract was by street railroads to carry passengers for a stated fare. In Smyth v. City of N.Y., 203 N.Y. 106, 96 N.E. 409, and Rigney v. N.Y.C. & H.R.R.R. Co., 217 N.Y. 31, 111 N.E. 226, covenants were made by contractors upon public works, not merely to indemnify the city, but to assume its liabilities. These and like cases come within the third group stated in the comprehensive opinion in Seaver v. Ransom, 224 N.Y. 233, 120 N.E. 639. The municipality was contracting in behalf of its inhabitants by covenants intended to be enforced by any of them severally as occasion should arise.

(2) We think the action is not maintainable as one for a common law tort.

"It is ancient learning that one who assumes to act, even though gratuitously, may thereby become subject to the duty of acting carefully, if he acts at all" (Glanzer v. Shepard, 233 N.Y. 236, 135 N.E. 275). . . . The plaintiff would bring its case within the orbit of that principle. The hand once set to a task may not always be withdrawn with impunity though liability would fail if it had never been applied at all. A time-honored formula often phrases the distinction as one between misfeasance and nonfeasance. Incomplete the formula is, and so at times misleading. Given a relation involving in its existence a duty of care irrespective of a contract, a tort may result as well from acts of omission as of commission in the fulfillment of the duty thus recognized by law (Pollock, Torts [12th ed.], p. 555; Kelly v. Met. Ry. Co., 1895, 1 Q.B. 944). What we need to know is not so much the conduct to be avoided when the relation and its attendant duty are established as existing. What we need to know is the conduct that engenders the relation. It is here that the formula, however incomplete, has its value and significance. If conduct has gone forward to such a stage that inaction would commonly result, not negatively merely in withholding a benefit, but positively or actively in working an injury, there exists a relation out of which arises a duty to go forward (Bohlen, Studies in the Law of Torts, p. 87). So the surgeon who operates without pay is liable, though his negligence is in the omission to sterilize his instruments (cf. Glanzer v. Shepard, supra); the engineer, though his fault is in the failure to shut off steam (Kelly v. Met. Ry. Co., supra); the maker of automobiles, at the suit of some one other than the buyer, though his negligence is merely in inadequate inspection (MacPherson v. Buick Motor Co., 217 N.Y. 382, 111 N.E. 1050). The query always is whether the putative wrongdoer has advanced to such a point as to have launched a force or instrument of harm, or has stopped where inaction is at most a refusal to become an instrument for good. . . .

The plaintiff would have us hold that the defendant, when once it entered upon the performance of its contract with the city, was brought into such a relation with every one who might potentially be benefited through the supply of water at the hydrants as to give to negligent performance, without reasonable notice of a refusal to continue, the quality of a tort. . . . We are satisfied that liability would be unduly and indeed indefinitely extended by this enlargement of the zone of duty. The dealer in coal who is to supply fuel for a shop must then answer to the customers if fuel is lacking. The manufacturer of goods, who enters upon the performance of his contract, must answer, in that view, not only to the buyer, but to those who to his knowledge are looking to the buyer for their own sources of supply. Every one making a promise having the quality of a contract will be under a duty to the promisee by virtue of the promise, but under another duty, apart from contract, to an indefinite number of potential beneficiaries when performance has begun. The assumption of one relation will mean the involuntary assumption of a series of new relations, inescapably hooked together. . . . "The law does not spread its protection so far" (Robins Dry Dock & Repair Co. v. Flint, supra.) . . . What we are dealing with at this time is a mere negligent omission, unaccompanied by malice or other aggravating elements. The failure in such circumstances to furnish an adequate supply of water is at most the denial of a benefit. It is not the commission of a wrong. . .

The judgment should be affirmed with costs.

Doyle v. South Pittsburgh Water Co.

414 Pa. 199, 199 A.2d 875 (1964)

Plaintiffs' complaint alleged that the destruction of their home by fire would have been averted if the local fire department could have obtained water from fire hydrants, of which there were at least five, in the immediate neighborhood of the house. The complaint also alleged that defendant Water Co. had contracted with the city of South Pittsburgh to provide water for these fire hydrants, "for the sole purpose" of fighting fires in the vicinity of plaintiffs' home. The complaint further alleged that defendant had negligently allowed the water in the hydrants to freeze, had failed to inspect the hydrants, had failed to maintain sufficient pressure or repair inoperative valves or notify plaintiffs or the fire department that the hydrants were inoperative. *Held*, the complaint stated a cause of action in negligence. Defendant gained nothing by "the elusive debating dialectic" that it was the fire and not the lack of water that destroyed the house. The case fell squarely within the rule that "where a party to a contract assumes a duty to the other party to the contract, and it is foreseeable that a breach of that duty will cause injury to some third person not a party to the contract, the contracting party owes a duty to all those falling within the foreseeable orbit of risk of harm." As to the opinion of Judge Cardozo in H.R. Moch v. Rensselaer Water Co., "it must be stated, with some regret, that at this point Homer nodded," for Judge Cardozo, "without apparently intending to do so, contradicted what he had said" in MacPherson v. Buick Motor Co., 217 N.Y. 382, 111 N.E. 1050 (1916). Once he recognized that the city was guilty of a "negligent omission," the "breach of duty" required for negligence was conceded.

"The argument that to insure safety to the public would entail great expense is, and should no longer be, a defense where a duty to life, limb and property is inherent. Depressing as the reflection may be, it is true nevertheless that the absence of financial responsibility for negligence is to encourage further negligence. To announce to water companies throughout the Commonwealth that no species of indifference on their part, no negligence, no matter how gross, will call for pecuniary answerability is to invite progressive inattention and indifference to protection against the scourge of flame and incendiary invasion." [The result here is not typical; tort claims against water companies usually fail.]

NOTE

Who should have the right to sue—that is, what remedies should be available—when a contract designed to effectuate a government-initiated program is breached?

The problem of the *Moch* case (and the cases digested above) is dealt with by the Restatement of Contracts, Second.

Restatement of Contracts, Second

§ 313. Government Contracts

(1) The rules [on contract beneficiaries] apply to contracts with a government or governmental agency except to the extent that application would contravene the policy of the law authorizing the contract or prescribing remedies for its breach.

(2) In particular, a promisor who contracts with a government or governmental agency to do an act for or render a service to the public is not subject to contractual liability to a member of the public for consequential damages resulting from performance or failure to perform unless

(a) the terms of the promise provide for such liability; or

(b) the promisee is subject to liability to the member of the public for the damages and a direct action against the promisor is consistent with the terms of the contract and with the policy of the law authorizing the contract and prescribing remedies for its breach.

The situations described in subsection (2) are designed to conform to the classification of beneficiaries in § 302 ("intended" and "incidental," the former comprehending the definitions of donee and creditor beneficiaries in § 133 of the first Restatement). Does subsection (2) adequately bring into focus the policy considerations relevant in determining the existence of enforceable rights in a member of the public? In the view of one court, such determinations are "much like the question whether a particular federal statute creates an implied right of action in favor of its beneficiaries." Price v. Pierce, 823 F.2d 1114 (7th Cir. 1987) (applicants for subsidized housing not third-party beneficiaries of contracts between developers and state housing agency). The Restatement, Second, in a comment accompanying § 313, states that the factors which may make inappropriate a direct action against the promisor include "arrangements for governmental control over the litigation and settlement of claims, the likelihood of impairment of service or of excessive financial burden, and the availability of alternatives such as insurance."

Sovereign Bank v. BJ's Wholesale Club, Inc.

United States Court of Appeals, Third Circuit, 2008.
533 F.3d 162.

MCKEE, CIRCUIT JUDGE. . . . These consolidated appeals involve two law suits that arose from the theft of credit card information from the computer files of a prominent retailer. Visa U.S.A., Inc., is a corporation, comprised of an association of financial institutions, which operates a credit card payment system known as "Visa." Sovereign Bank and the Pennsylvania State Employees Credit Union ("PSECU") are both members of the Visa network. Sovereign and PSECU have a Membership Agreement with Visa that allows them to issue Visa cards to their respective customers and members. Within the Visa network, Sovereign and PSECU are referred to as "Issuers," which means that they issue Visa cards to cardholders pursuant to the contracts they enter into with them.

Fifth Third Bank is also a member of the Visa network, and it also has a Membership Agreement with Visa. Within the network, Fifth Third is referred to as an "Acquirer," which means that Fifth Third enters into contractual relationships with businesses that agree to accept Visa cards as payment for their goods and services ("Merchants"). Acquirers process those transactions on behalf of the Merchants. BJ's Wholesale Club, Inc., is a Merchant. Accordingly, Fifth Third and BJ's have entered into a Merchant Agreement. Although Merchants participate in the Visa network, they are not members. Only financial institutions are eligible for membership. Therefore, Merchants have no contractual relationship directly with Visa.

Every time a cardholder uses a Visa card to pay a Merchant for goods or services, the Issuer, Acquirer and Merchant must interact to process and complete the transaction. The Merchant's computer scanners first "read" the "Cardholder Information" contained in the magnetic stripe on the back of Visa cards as they are swiped through the familiar terminal at the checkout. The Merchant then sends the pertinent account information through the Visa network to the Issuer. The Issuer reviews the Cardholder Information and, assuming the card is valid with sufficient available credit, the Issuer authorizes the transaction, and so notifies the Merchant. Upon receiving that notification, the Merchant completes the transaction with the cardholder, and then forwards the receipt to the Acquirer who pays the Merchant pursuant to their agreement. The Acquirer then notifies the Issuer that payment has been received, and the Issuer pays the Acquirer and charges the cardholder.

Visa has created an extensive set of "Operating Regulations" to both govern and facilitate transactions involving Visa cards. Those Regulations address virtually every aspect of the Visa payment system, and impose both general and specific requirements on participants in the network.

The disputes in these appeals center on certain security regulations including the Cardholder Information Security Program ("CISP"). The CISP provisions apply to Issuers and Acquirers and include broad security requirements intended to protect Cardholder Information. Those requirements include a prohibition against retaining or storing the data encoded in the familiar magnetic stripe on the back of credit cards, *i.e.*, Cardholder Information, after a consumer transaction is completed.

One provision of the Operating Regulations, entitled "Enforcement," defines procedures by which Visa can enforce compliance with the Operating Regulations. That provision expressly allows Visa to take specified remedial actions against Members who do not comply with the Operating Regulations, including levying fines and penalties. Enforcement actions can be appealed to Visa's Board of Directors, but the Board's decision is final. The Operating Regulations give Visa, and only Visa, the right to interpret and enforce the Operating Regulations, and only Visa can determine whether a violation of the Operating Regulations has occurred.

The Operating Regulations also impose extensive security requirements on Issuers and Acquirers. Section 2.3 of the Operating Regulations requires Issuers and Acquirers to ensure that their agents, service providers and Merchants comply with the Operating Regulations.

The Visa Operating Regulations also include comprehensive provisions for resolving disputes between Visa members. These provisions allow members to challenge disputed charges through "chargeback" and representment procedures, in accordance with risk allocation judgments made by Visa. Disputes about the use of these procedures are resolved by arbitration.

Finally, the Operating Regulations also include "Compliance" provisions that apply when a Member's violation of a Regulation causes a financial loss to another Member who cannot be made whole by resorting to chargeback or representment. For example, a loss resulting from fraudulent charges using stolen data is allocated to the Issuer. However, the Issuer may use the Compliance proceedings to shift that loss to the Acquirer if it resulted from the Acquirer's violation of an Operating Regulation. The Compliance provisions do not eliminate any rights a Member may have to pursue any legal remedies that may otherwise be available.

Pursuant to their Membership Agreements with Visa, all Members of the Visa network . . . agree to be bound by the Operating Regulations. In addition, before an Acquirer can enter into a Merchant Agreement with a Merchant, the Acquirer must first determine that the Merchant will abide by the Operating Regulations. Given the importance attached to uniform compliance, an Acquirer's initial determination is deemed insufficient. Rather, an Acquirer must agree to ensure continued compliance with the Operating Regulations. Finally, the Acquirer must have a Merchant Agreement with each of its Merchants. The Merchant Agreements may generally contain whatever extraneous provisions the Acquirer and Merchant agree upon, but, the Agreement must, at a minimum, contain the provisions of Section 5.2 of the Operating Regulations. These disputes involve § 5.2.h.3.b. That subdivision prohibits a Merchant from retaining or storing Cardholder Information after an Issuer authorizes a transaction. Like all Visa Members, Fifth Third's predecessor agreed to be bound by the Visa Operating Regulations and By-Laws, which are incorporated by reference into the Membership Agreement.

The seeds that sprouted this litigation were sewn in February 2004, when Visa identified a potential compromise of electronically stored Cardholder Information pertaining to certain Visa cards issued by Sovereign, PSECU and other financial institutions. Electronic data on some credit cards had been copied and used to fraudulently obtain goods and services after cardholders had used the cards at various BJ's stores. Visa responded by issuing a "CAMS alert" to potentially affected Issuers. Such CAMS alerts notify Visa members that Cardholder Information may have been compromised. The CAMS alert here notified the Issuers that Visa cards which had been properly presented for payment at BJ's stores from July 2003 through February 2004 had been compromised and could be used to make fraudulent purchases.

Sovereign responded to the February 2004 alert by cancelling some Visa cards and issuing new Visa cards to the affected cardholders. Sovereign claims that the fraud was only possible because BJ's improperly retained and stored the Cardholder Information from its customers' cards instead of deleting the data immediately after a sales transaction was completed, as required by Visa Operating Regulation § 5.2.h.3.b. In Sovereign's view, BJ's failure to comply with the requirements of § 5.2.h.3.b. breached a duty owed to Sovereign. Sovereign further contends that Fifth Third failed to comply with the Operating Regulations by failing to ensure that BJ's complied with § 5.2.h.3.b.

According to Sovereign, BJ's failure to delete the Cardholder Information magnetically stored in Visa cards, and Fifth Third's failure to ensure that BJ's complied with § 5.3.h.3.b, allowed the unauthorized and fraudulent use of Cardholder Information. Sovereign maintains that it was legally obligated to reimburse its cardholders for the resulting fraudulent charges, and that it incurred expenses, and lost income and fees from doing so. This purportedly included the costs of issuing replacement cards to Cardholders (in an effort to mitigate further losses), and loss of goodwill of its customer base. . . .

Sovereign's breach of contract claim is based on a third-party or intended beneficiary theory and depends, in part, upon whether Fifth Third and Visa intended to give Sovereign enforceable rights under their separate contract even though Sovereign is not a party to it. Ultimately, the district court converted Fifth Third's motion for reconsideration into a motion for summary judgment and ordered the parties to conduct discovery on the third-party beneficiary issues, *i.e.,* whether Fifth Third's contractual obligation to Visa to comply with the Visa Operating Regulations was intended to benefit Issuers like Sovereign. . . .

Historically, under Pennsylvania law, "in order for a third party beneficiary to have standing to recover on a contract, both contracting parties must have expressed an intention that the third party be a beneficiary, and that intention must have affirmatively appeared in the contract itself." Scarpitti v. Weborg, 609 A.2d 147, 149 (Pa. 1992). Sovereign appropriately concedes that it is not an express third-party beneficiary of the Visa-Fifth Third Member Agreement. However, in *Scarpitti,* the Pennsylvania Supreme Court adopted § 302 of the Restatement (Second) of Contracts. That provision allows an "intended beneficiary" to recover for breach of contract even though the actual parties to the contract did not express an intent to benefit the third party. . . .

Under § 302, Sovereign's contract claim depends on whether the "recognition of a right to performance" in Sovereign "is appropriate to effectuate the intentions of" both Visa and Fifth Third in entering into their member agreement and whether "the circumstances indicate that" Visa (the promisee) "intend[ed]" to give Sovereign "the benefit of the promised performance."

[T]he district court converted Fifth Third's Rule 12(b)(6) motion to dismiss to a motion for summary judgment and ordered limited discovery. The ensuing discovery included production of numerous documents as well as the deposition of Visa's designated representative, Alex Miller. Fifth Third relies in part on Miller's testimony that he was not aware that Visa intended to create a direct right of enforcement under the Operating Regulations among Members and he has never seen a document that would allow a Member "to step into Visa's shoes under its contract with other members" and enforce the Operating Regulations. Miller testified in part as follows:

> [T]he core purpose of the Operating Regulations is to set up the conditions for participation in the system, to set up the rules and standards that apply to that ultimately for the benefit of the Visa payment system, the members that participate in it and

> other stakeholders such as cardholders, merchants, and others who may participate in the system as well.

Fifth Third further contends that Miller also made it clear that the Operating Regulations' prohibition against retaining Cardholder Information, which Fifth Third claims was enacted long after it entered into its agreement with Visa, was not to benefit any *individual* member or *class* of members. Rather, according to Miller:

> [t]he purpose of the CISP program . . . is to maximize the value to the Visa system as a whole. That can include the protection of any entity that may be involved in the use or—or handling of cardholder data, so it's to protect a cardholder, the privacy of their information, to protect their confidence in using the Visa system, to protect issuers, to protect acquirers, to protect merchants; and by creating a system that protects cardholder data, generally it's to maximize the usage and value of the Visa payment system for all of those participants. . . .

Fifth Third contends that Miller's deposition testimony clearly shows that the intent of the Operating Regulations, and more particularly the prohibition on Merchant retention of Cardholder Information, is to benefit the Visa system as a whole and not Sovereign or any particular Issuer in particular. Accordingly, Fifth Third argues that it is entitled to summary judgment on Sovereign's breach of contract claim.

Sovereign responds that there is a genuine issue of material fact as to Visa's intent which precludes summary judgment. Sovereign notes that in August 1993, Visa wrote a memorandum entitled "Retention of Magnetic-Stripe Data Prohibited." The memorandum described a new section of the Operating Regulations prohibiting the storage of magnetic-stripe data, *i.e.,* Cardholder Information. It read in part as follows:

> To protect the Visa system and Issuers from potential fraud exposure created by databases of magnetic-stripe information, Section 6.21 has been revised. Effective September 1, 1993, the retention or storage of magnetic stripe data subsequent to the authorization of a transaction is prohibited. Acquirers are obligated to ensure that their merchants do not store the magnetic-stripe information from Visa Cards for any subsequent use.

Sovereign contends that this August 1993 memorandum shows that Visa understood and clearly intended that Issuers such as Sovereign (and PSECU) would obtain direct benefits from the requiring members to ensure that magnetic-stripe data was not retained.

Sovereign further contends that other evidence obtained from Visa shows that Visa expressly understood and intended that the prohibition would provide direct benefits to Issuers and that the type of harm suffered by Sovereign was specifically intended to be avoided by compliance with the prohibition. Visa published an on-line article entitled "Issuers and Acquirers Are At Risk When Magnetic-Stripe Data Is Stored," in

May 2003. The article stated that the CISP "was established to preclude a compromise that could lead to the duplication of valid magnetic-stripe data on counterfeit or altered cards," because such a data compromise "impacts Issuers, Acquirers, cardholder goodwill and the integrity of the payment system." Sovereign submits that this article is additional evidence that the prohibition against retaining Cardholder Information contained in the magnetic strip was intended to directly benefit Issuers. . . .

In order to be an intended beneficiary of the Visa-Fifth Third Member Agreement, Sovereign has the burden of producing, *inter alia,* sufficient evidence that Visa intended to give it the benefit of the Fifth Third's promise to Visa to ensure that BJ's complied with the provision of the Member Agreement prohibiting Merchants from retaining Cardholder Information. We believe that Sovereign met that burden.

We do not, however, regard the May 2003 on-line article entitled "Issuers and Acquirers Are At Risk When Magnetic-Stripe Is Stored" as indicative of an intent to benefit a particular Issuer such as Sovereign or PSECU. That article simply states the reason for the prohibition against retention of Cardholder Information, *viz.,* a data compromise that could result from storage of magnetic-stripe data "impacts Issuers, Acquirers, cardholder goodwill, and the integrity of the system." However, we do believe that Visa's August 1993 memorandum, entitled "Retention of Magnetic-Stripe Data Prohibited," and Miller's "core purpose" deposition testimony raise a genuine issue of material fact regarding the intent of the Visa and Fifth Third Member Agreement. That was sufficient to preclude the grant of summary judgment on Sovereign's breach of contract claim.

In his deposition, Miller testified that the core purpose of the Operating Regulations was to benefit the Visa system and "the members that participate in it." Admittedly, any indication of an intent by Visa to specifically benefit Issuers is arguably undermined by Miller's references to "other shareholders such as cardholders, merchants and others who may participate in the system as well." Nonetheless, his testimony clearly suggests an intent by Visa to benefit Issuers. An argument to the contrary is tantamount to claiming that since Visa intended to benefit everyone who was part of the Visa system, it did not specifically intend to benefit anyone. However, the fact that it intended to benefit several Members or classes of Members does not negate the possibility that it intended to benefit individual Issuers such as Sovereign.

Moreover, as recited earlier, the August 1993 memorandum provides, in relevant part: "To protect the Visa system and *Issuers* from potential fraud exposure *created by databases of magnetic-stripe information* . . . . Acquirers are obligated to ensure that their merchants do not store the magnetic-stripe information from Visa Cards for any subsequent use." (emphasis added). Thus, the memorandum clearly states that Acquirers must act to protect Issuers by ensuring that their Merchants do not retain Cardholder Information. Accordingly, the August 1993 memorandum is sufficient evidence by itself to create a genuine issue about whether Visa intended to give Sovereign the benefit of Fifth Third's promise to Visa to ensure BJ's compliance with the provisions of the Visa-Fifth Third Member Agreement. Therefore, we will reverse the district court's grant of summary judgment to Fifth Third on the breach of contract claim and remand for further proceedings on that claim. . . .

Restatement of Contracts, Second

§ 311. Variation of a Duty to a Beneficiary

(1) Discharge or modification of a duty to an intended beneficiary by conduct of the promisee or by a subsequent agreement between promisor and promisee is ineffective if a term of the promise creating the duty so provides.

(2) In the absence of such a term, the promisor and promisee retain power to discharge or modify the duty by subsequent agreement.

(3) Such a power terminates when the beneficiary, before he receives notification of the discharge or modification, materially changes his position in justifiable reliance on the promise or brings suit on it or manifests assent to it at the request of the promisor or promisee.

(4) If the promisee receives consideration for an attempted discharge or modification of the promisor's duty which is ineffective against the beneficiary, the beneficiary can assert a right to the consideration so received. The promisor's duty is discharged to the extent of the amount received by the beneficiary.

NOTE

The first Restatement of Contracts, in §§ 142 and 143, distinguished between creditor and donee beneficiaries as concerns the power of the contracting parties to alter or terminate rights under the beneficiary contract. The rights of the donee beneficiary were deemed to vest at once upon the making of the contract; there was no vesting of creditor beneficiary rights until there was reliance on the contract by that nonparty. The Second Restatement, in § 311 set out above, discards the distinction, treating all intended beneficiaries alike. The Reporter's Note to § 311 states that "[t]he weight of authority is opposed to a distinction between donee beneficiaries and creditor beneficiaries with respect to the power of promisor and promisee to vary" duties owed third parties, and that the authorities support termination of that power "by either assent or reliance by the beneficiary." Accordingly, the power to vary duties is made to turn "primarily on the terms of the promise." Some courts continue to follow the rule that the rights of the donee beneficiary vest indefeasibly at the time of the contract. See, e.g., Biggins v. Shore, 523 Pa. 148, 565 A.2d 737 (1989) ("Restatement (Second) [§ 311] affords no greater freedom of contract than exists [under Pennsylvania's indefeasibility rule]; if [the parties] do not intend to convey an [irretrievable] benefit, they need merely say so in the contract").

SECTION 2. ASSIGNMENT AND DELEGATION

INTRODUCTORY COMMENT

The power of creditors to make effective transfers of rights created by contract developed late in our legal history, and the development has encountered many obstacles. Assignees, like third party beneficiaries, are strangers to the contract. Both have caused lawyers much strain and discomfort, as was almost bound to occur with strangers who arrived late at a supposedly well-organized feast. In theory, the claims of assignees might appear even more troublesome than the claims of third party beneficiaries, for with assignees one cannot use the ready explanation that both contracting parties agreed that the third party was to receive the benefit of the promised performance. The assignee usually steps in without the debtor's consent, often against the debtor's wish. To explain how this can occur requires some basic rethinking of postulates, and basic rethinking is apt to come only after social needs have been clearly demonstrated.

Similar difficulties were encountered in the development of Roman law, where obligations were understood to be intensely personal relations between particular people. Whether obligations arose through consent (i.e., contract) or through delict (tort), their personal nature made it difficult for Roman lawyers to conceive of simple substitution of a different creditor by the unilateral act of an assignor. Yet, as was true in medieval English law, there were certain situations for which it was necessary to make provision. One was the creditor who died leaving an uncollected claim arising from contract. Another was the surety who had paid the principal's debt and then sought an assignment of the rights of the paid-off creditor against the principal debtor. But such scattered instances did not produce a general theory authorizing assignments. The nearest approach to a generalized technique in classical Roman law was that employed for centuries by the English common law—the assignee became an agent (in Roman terms, was given a "mandate") with a power to sue in the assignor's name. But, until very late in Roman law, the agency (mandate) was fully revocable, so that it was most incomplete as a device for the transfer of rights.

The concept used by common lawyers to describe rights created by contract was the French legal phrase "chose in action." This is an essentially negative term, meaning a right enforceable only by action and in no way connected with ownership, custody, or use of an identified physical asset. The term encompasses an enormous diversity of human relationships, and this has been one of the difficulties in constructing an intelligible theory. It includes, for example, tort claims of all kinds. The drag produced by this extensive coverage may be illustrated by the fact that even now claims for personal torts, unconnected with specific property, are generally not assignable.

Why should they be? What needs are served by opening up commerce in damage claims for personal injuries or defamation? Might not such commerce cause positive harm in fomenting litigation by persons having no connection with the injured party? Doubts of this kind have operated to restrict the assignability of various kinds of personal claims. Even today, when assignability has become a familiar feature of many types of choses in action, much can depend on the kind of chose in action it is.

It may also be that the early lawyers had difficulty visualizing the process by which rights unconnected with a tangible thing could be effectively transferred. There would be no cow or horse to be handed over, no twig or clod of earth that could be given as a symbol. But, fairly early, lawyers began to develop the notion that an owner out of possession could transfer an ownership interest, a mere right of action, without physical delivery of the asset itself, and surely it was not too great a stretch to extend this notion more broadly. Indeed, the incapacity of early lawyers to corporealize the incorporeal has been greatly over-stressed by modern writers. Medieval lawyers were perfectly capable of imagining ownership of disembodied interests—ownership of an office, the right to appoint a parson to a church, rights to services in homes or in fields, rights to be paid annuities, to collect tolls from passersby, or to occupy a front seat at the King's coronation. The difficulty was that at the point when lawyers were ready to formulate broader theories for explaining transfers of "rights of action," their thinking became confused. They mixed the question of assignments with the problem of fomented litigation, which was dealt with by the rules against "maintenance" and "champerty."

Maintenance in modern law is the supporting or promoting of another's litigation; champerty is the same, plus an agreement to share the proceeds. Both may have been crimes under the early common law; they were certainly made crimes by a series of statutes that began in the fourteenth century. To understand the problem, one must imagine a society in which central governments were weak and power was dispersed through an aristocracy that was often turbulent. The favor and support of powerful persons and their armed retainers were much sought after, especially by those who quarrelled with their neighbors. Maintenance, with or without profit-sharing, was a constant threat to the administration of justice, especially during the civil wars of the fifteenth century. Even after the power of the central government was rebuilt under the Tudors, the problem survived. Coke, in the early seventeenth century, revived memories that were not yet stale when he expressed his approval of the rule that "no possibility, right, title nor thing in action shall be granted or assigned to strangers, for that would be the occasion of multiplying of contentions and suits, of great oppression of the people, and chiefly of terre-tenants, and the subversion of the due and equal execution of justice." Lampet's Case, 10 Coke Rep. 48a, 77 Eng. Rep. 994.

The rules against maintenance and champerty have been greatly modified since the time of Coke, though they have not disappeared. Legal aid societies escape the penalties of maintenance because of their charitable purpose in aiding needy persons. A person who has an interest to assert can conduct litigation on behalf of others, pay all the expenses, and share in the proceeds. But if a person's only interest is in securing an agreed share in the proceeds of a claim belonging to another, the arrangement will ordinarily be illegal; under the law of most states, any purported assignment of a right to sue will be ineffective. Most of the problems of champerty and maintenance now arise in connection with arrangements for lawyers' services. A contingent-fee contract between lawyer and client would probably be valid in every state, even though it gives a share in the proceeds to the lawyer in the event of success. But if the lawyer under a contingent contract agrees, in addition, to pay the costs of litigation, this may well suffice to make the whole contract illegal. Ambulance chasers who actively promote litigation and pay others to bring them business are not only subject to discipline by bar association committees, but are subject independently, in some states at least, to criminal penalties also. Though the sanctions are now much diluted and the scope of the offense much narrowed, there remain some areas in which profit-making through promoting litigation of other persons' claims is still strongly disapproved.

It should be evident that there was some confusion of thought in the identification of assignments with maintenance or champerty. The obvious purpose of an assignment was to create an interest in the assignee, which that person would then assert. The law courts, however, were not consistent in the policies they asserted. Even before the time of Coke, in one large group of cases the courts had admitted that an assignee of a claim for money acquired a power of attorney to sue in the name of the assignor—where the assignment was in settlement of a debt already owed the assignee by the assignor. The assignee in such a case was not charged with maintaining another's quarrel; by taking the assignment for the protection of self-interest, the assignee had become a party to the quarrel. This kind of reasoning could readily have been extended to the case of an outright purchaser who paid cash or other consideration for an assignment of the claim. Indeed, in one isolated case in 1590, a law court so held, using again the theory that the assignee had a power of attorney to sue in the assignor's name. Penson v. Hickbed, Cro. Eliz. 70, 78 Eng. Rep. 427. But this case was not followed until almost a century had elapsed. There were certain exceptions: assignments by and to the Crown, and transfers of contract rights to executors or administrators on the death of a contract creditor. But, on the whole, the common law courts stood their ground until the eighteenth century. Even the concession that an assignee might have a power of attorney was limited to the case of assignment in satisfaction of an antecedent debt.

The date when the Chancery first began to intervene is not clear. Perhaps it responded quite early to the appeals of individual merchants who had purchased mercantile debts. It was not until the seventeenth century, apparently, that the Chancery began regularly to protect the assignee against the assignor's attempts to defeat the assignment. In the eighteenth century, such relief became a standard feature of Chancery jurisdiction, for even after the power-of-attorney technique became broadly available in law actions, it had the major defect of any simple agency theory: the agency was revocable by the death, the bankruptcy, or the repudiation of the principal (assignor), even though revocation might be a breach of the duty the assignor owed to the assignee. It was not until 1787 that the King's Bench achieved the position, already reached by the Chancery, that the bankruptcy of the assignor did not destroy or impair the assignee's right under an assignment made before the bankruptcy. Winch v. Keeley, 1 T.R. 619, 99 Eng. Rep. 1284.

This long-delayed response of the law courts was partly due, no doubt, to a desire to meet the Chancery's competition. But the courts must have been influenced also by the example of free transferability supplied by such mercantile instruments as the bill of exchange and the promissory note. These instruments had been evolved by "the custom of merchants," a body of rules applied in the trading communities of Europe through special courts and through self-regulation by the merchants themselves. The absorption of the custom of merchants into the common law began in the sixteenth century, through decisions that allowed the rules of custom to be proved as facts and then applied as governing norms in common law actions. The process of absorption was gradual and involved much more than the principle of assignability of contract rights. The bill of exchange and promissory note were important devices, much used in trade, and their most prominent feature was that the holder's right was highly transferable. If the promise expressed in the instrument satisfied certain strict requirements of form, a transferee could acquire better rights than the transferor had enjoyed. The instrument, in other words, was "negotiable," and if transferred before maturity, for value, to a "holder in due course" (i.e., a purchaser in good faith), most of the defenses that would be available to the promisor against the promisee-transferor would be excluded as against the good-faith purchaser. As to the bill of exchange (a modern analogue is the bank check), the common law before 1700 had gone a long way in absorbing the rules of negotiability developed by the law merchant. A statute passed in 1704 achieved similar results for promissory notes. The full-scale adoption of the law merchant by the common law owed much to the influence of Lord Mansfield in the second half of the eighteenth century. If so much could be accomplished through negotiable instruments, the lawyers must have seen the anomaly of denying protection to other kinds of assignees.

This section examines contract rights that, through defects of form or for other reasons, are not negotiable under contemporary rules of commercial law. The rules for negotiable instruments form a special and complex subject, now governed by the UCC, that must be postponed to a later course.

Assignees of nonnegotiable choses do receive some aid from statutes, whose popularity began in the nineteenth century, requiring that actions be brought in the name of "the real party in interest." This procedural requirement dispenses with the form of suit by the assignee in the assignor's name.

Langel v. Betz

Court of Appeals of New York, 1928.
250 N.Y. 159, 164 N.E. 890.

POUND, J. Plaintiff, on August 1, 1925, made a contract with Irving W. Hurwitz and Samuel Hollander for the sale [to them] of certain real property. This contract the vendees assigned to Benedict, who in turn assigned it to Isidor Betz, the defendant herein. The assignment contains no delegation to the assignee of the performance of the assignor's duties. The date for performance of the contract was originally set for October 2, 1925. This was extended to October 15, 1925, at the request of the defendant, the last assignee of the vendees. The ground upon which the adjournment was asked for by defendant was that the title company had not completed its search and report on the title to the property. Upon the adjourned date the defendant refused to perform. The vendor plaintiff was ready, able and willing to do so, and was present at the place specified with a deed, ready to tender it to the defendant who did not appear.

The plaintiff as vendor brought this action against the defendant assignee for specific performance of the contract [and] has had judgment therefor.

The question is: "Can the vendor obtain specific performance of a contract for the sale of real estate against the assignee of the vendee, where the assignee merely requests and obtains an extension of time within which to close title?" Here we have no novation, no express assumption of the obligations of the assignor in the assignment and no demand for performance by the assignee.

The mere assignment of a bilateral executory contract may not be interpreted as a promise by the assignee to the assignor to assume the performance of the assignor's duties, so as to have the effect of creating a new liability on the part of the assignee to the other party to the contract assigned. The assignee of the vendee is under no personal engagement to the vendor where there is no privity between them. . . . The assignee may, however, expressly or impliedly, bind himself to perform the assignor's duties. This he may do by contract with the assignor or with the other party to the contract. It has been held, Epstein v. Gluckin, 233 N.Y. 490, 135 N.E. 861, that, where the assignee of the vendee invokes the aid of a court of equity in an action for specific performance, he impliedly binds himself to perform. . . . "He who seeks equity must do equity." The converse of the proposition, that the assignee of the vendee would be bound when the vendor began action, did not follow from the decision in that case. On the contrary, the question was wholly one of remedy rather than right and it was held that mutuality of remedy is important only so far as its presence is essential to the attainment of the ends of justice. This holding was necessary to sustain the decision. No change was made in the . . . rule for the interpretation of an assignment of a contract.

A judgment requiring the assignee of the vendee to perform at the suit of the vendor would operate as the imposition of a new liability on the assignee which would be an act of oppression and injustice, unless the assignee had, expressly or by implication, entered into a personal and binding contract with the assignor or with the vendor to assume the obligations of the assignor.

It has been urged that the probable intention of the assignee is ordinarily to assume duties as well as rights and that the contract should be so interpreted in the absence of circumstances showing a contrary intention. . . . [The] Restatement of Contracts (§ 164) proposes a change in the rule of interpretation of assigned contracts[:] . . .

"(1) Where a party to a bilateral contract which is at the time wholly or partially executory on both sides, purports to assign the whole contract, his action is interpreted, in the absence of circumstances showing a contrary intention, as an assignment of the assignor's rights under the contract and a delegation of the performance of the assignor's duties.

"(2) Acceptance by the assignee of such an assignment is interpreted, in the absence of circumstances showing a contrary intention, as both an assent to become an assignee of the assignor's rights and as a promise *to the assignor to assume the performance of the assignor's duties.*"

This promise to the assignor would then be available to the other party to the contract. Lawrence v. Fox, 20 N.Y. 268. . . . The [Restatement's] proposed change is a complete reversal of our present rule of interpretation as to the probable intention of the parties. It is, perhaps more in harmony with modern ideas of contractual relations than is "the archaic view of a contract as creating a strictly personal obligation between the creditor and debtor," Pollock on Contracts (9th ed.), 232, which prohibited the assignee from suing at law in his own name and which denied a remedy to third party beneficiaries. "The fountains out of which these resolutions issue" have been broken up if not destroyed, Seaver v. Ransom, 224 N.Y. 233, 120 N.E. 639, but the law remains that no promise of the assignee to assume the assignor's duties is to be inferred from the acceptance of an assignment of a bilateral contract, in the absence of circumstances surrounding the assignment itself which indicate a contrary intention.

With this requirement of the interpretation of the intention of the parties controlling, we must turn from the assignment to the dealings between the plaintiff and the defendant to discover whether the defendant entered into relations with the plaintiff whereby he assumed the duty of performance. The assignment did not bring the parties together and the request for a postponement differs materially from the commencement of an action in a court of equity, whereby the plaintiff submits himself to the jurisdiction of the court or from a contractual assumption of the obligations of the assignor. If the substance of the transaction between the vendor and the assignee of the vendee could be regarded as a request on the part of the latter for a postponement of the closing day and a promise on his part to assume the obligations of the vendee if the request were granted, a contractual relation arising from an expression of mutual assent, based on the exchange of a promise for an act might be spelled out of it; but the transaction is at least as consistent with a request for time for deliberation as to the course of conduct to be pursued as with an implied promise to assume the assignor's duties if the request were granted. The relation of promisor and promisee was not thereby expressly established and such relation is not a necessary inference from the nature of the transaction. . . .

Plaintiff contends that the request for an adjournment should be construed (time not being the essence of the contract) as an assertion of a right to such adjournment, and, therefore, as a binding act of enforcement, whereby defendant accepted the obligations of the [assignor]. Here again we have an equivocal act. There was no demand for an adjournment as a matter of right. The request may have been made without any intent to assert a right. It cannot be said that by that act alone the assignee assumed the duty of performance. Furthermore, no controlling authority may be found which holds that a mere demand for performance by the vendee's assignee creates a right in the complaining vendor to enforce the contract against him. . . . That question may be reserved until an answer is necessary.

[Judgment] reversed and the complaint dismissed.

Restatement of Contracts, Second

§ 328. Interpretation of Words of Assignment; Effect of Acceptance of Assignment

(1) Unless the language or the circumstances indicate the contrary, as in an assignment for security, an assignment of "the contract" or of "all my rights under the contract" or an assignment in similar general terms is an assignment of the assignor's rights and a delegation of his unperformed duties under the contract.

(2) Unless the language or the circumstances indicate the contrary, the acceptance by an assignee of such an assignment operates as a promise to the assignor to perform the assignor's unperformed duties, and the obligor of the assigned rights is an intended beneficiary of the promise.

Caveat:

The Institute expresses no opinion as to whether the rule stated in Subsection (2) applies to an assignment by a purchaser of his rights under a contract for the sale of land.

NOTE

Langel v. Betz purported to reserve decision on the question whether the assignee's "assertion of a right" under the contract could amount to an assumption of the vendee's obligations. In Kunzman v. Thorsen, 303 Or. 600, 740 P.2d 754 (1987), another vendor's suit for specific performance against the vendee's assignee, the court took the view that "a claim of the contract's benefits"—e.g., taking possession of the land, making payments directly to the vendor, and "behaving generally" like a party to the original contract—creates a presumption that the assignee intended to assume the duties the contract imposes. In evaluating such a test, consider whether assignments of land-sale contracts are likely to be broadly worded and whether, in the usual case, the parties' intentions at the time of the assignment are likely to be unclear.

Section 328 of the Restatement, Second follows the phrasing of UCC 2–210(4), which governs when the contract assigned is for the sale of goods. New York, it seems, remains out of line with the position taken in the second Restatement (and the UCC) on the construction of an assignment of simply "the contract." E.g., A.C. Assocs. v. Metropolitan Steel Indus., 1989 WL 1111034 (S.D.N.Y. 1989) (citing *Langel* in support of "settled rule" that, absent contrary indication, "the mere assignment of a contract is an assignment of rights . . . and not of the assignor's duties and liabilities"). The second Restatement's caveat to § 328(2) is based on the views expressed in Langel v. Betz, which, said the restaters in 1981, represents the overwhelming weight of authority in the land-contract cases. If § 328 offers a defensible approach to the interpretation of "assignments" in general, are you satisfied that land contracts should be treated differently? Is the explanation that an assignment by a purchaser (vendee) under a land contract is the practical equivalent of a sale "subject to" any mortgage on the land?

Herzog v. Irace

Supreme Judicial Court of Maine, 1991.
594 A.2d 1106.

BRODY, J. Anthony Irace and Donald Lowry appeal from an order entered by the Superior Court affirming a District Court judgment in favor of Dr. John P. Herzog in an action for breach of an assignment to Herzog of personal injury settlement proceeds[1] collected by Irace and Lowry, both attorneys, on behalf of their client, Gary G. Jones. Irace and Lowry contend that the District Court erred in finding that the assignment was valid and enforceable against them. . . .

Gary Jones was injured in a motorcycle accident and retained Irace and Lowry to represent him in a personal injury action. Soon thereafter,

[1] This case involves the assignment of proceeds from a personal injury action, not an assignment of the cause of action itself.

Jones dislocated his shoulder, twice, in incidents unrelated to the motorcycle accident. Dr. Herzog examined Jones's shoulder and concluded that he needed surgery. . . Jones was unable to pay for the surgery and in consideration for the performance of [it], he signed a letter dated June 14, 1988, written on Dr. Herzog's letterhead stating:

> I, Gary Jones, request that payment be made directly from settlement of a claim currently pending for an unrelated incident, to John Herzog, D.O., for treatment of a shoulder injury which occurred at a different time.

Dr. Herzog notified Irace and Lowry that Jones had signed an "assignment of benefits" from the motorcycle personal injury action to cover the cost of surgery on his shoulder and was informed by an employee of Irace and Lowry that the assignment was sufficient to allow the firm to pay Herzog's bills at the conclusion of the case. Dr. Herzog performed the surgery and continued to treat Jones for approximately one year.

In May, 1989, Jones received a $20,000 settlement in the motorcycle personal injury action. He instructed Irace and Lowry not to disburse any funds to Dr. Herzog indicating that he would make the payments himself. Irace and Lowry informed Herzog that Jones had revoked his permission to have the bill paid by them directly and indicated that they would follow Jones's directions. Irace and Lowry issued a check to Jones for $10,027 and disbursed the remaining funds to Jones's other creditors. Jones did send a check to Dr. Herzog but the check was returned by the bank for insufficient funds. . . .

Dr. Herzog filed a complaint in District Court against Irace and Lowry seeking to enforce the June 14, 1988 "assignment of benefits." . . . The court entered a judgment in favor of Herzog finding that the June 14, 1988 letter constituted a valid assignment of the settlement proceeds enforceable against Irace and Lowry. Following an unsuccessful appeal to the Superior Court, Irace and Lowry appealed to this court. . . . [W]e will set aside trial court findings based solely upon documentary evidence and stipulated facts only if clearly erroneous. . . .

An assignment is an act or manifestation by the owner of a right (the assignor) indicating his intent to transfer that right to another person (the assignee). Shiro v. Drew, 174 F.Supp. 495, 497 (D.Me. 1959). . . . [T]he assignor must make clear his intent to relinquish the right to the assignee and must not retain any control over the right assigned or any power of revocation. The assignment takes effect through the actions of the assignor and assignee and the obligor need not accept the assignment to render it valid. Palmer v. Palmer, 112 Me. 149, 153, 91 A. 281, 282 (1914). Once the obligor has notice of the assignment, the fund is "from that time forward impressed with a trust; it is . . . impounded in the [obligor's] hands, and must be held by him not for the original creditor, the assignor, but for the substituted creditor, the assignee." Id., at 152, 91 A. 281. After receiving notice of the assignment, the obligor cannot lawfully pay the amount assigned either to the assignor or to his other creditors and if the obligor does make such a payment, he does so at his peril because the assignee may enforce his rights against the obligor directly.

Ordinary rights, including future rights, are freely assignable unless the assignment would materially change the duty of the obligor, materially increase the burden or risk imposed upon the obligor by his contract, impair the obligor's chance of obtaining return performance, or materially reduce the value of the return performance to the obligor, and unless the law restricts the assignability of the specific right involved. See Restatement (Second) Contracts § 317(2)(a) (1982). In Maine, the transfer of a future right to *proceeds* from pending litigation has been recognized as a valid and enforceable equitable assignment. McLellan v. Walker, 26 Me. 114, 117–18 (1896). An equitable assignment need not transfer the entire future right but rather may be a partial assignment of that right. *Palmer*, 112 Me. at 152, 91 A.281. . . .

Relying primarily upon the Federal District Court's decision in *Shiro*, 174 F.Supp. 495, a bankruptcy case involving the trustee's power to avoid a preferential transfer by assignment, Irace and Lowry contend that Jones's June 14, 1988 letter is invalid and unenforceable as an assignment because it fails to manifest Jones's intent to permanently relinquish all control over the assigned funds and does nothing more than request payment from a specific fund. We disagree. The June 14 letter gives no indication that Jones attempted to retain any control over the funds he assigned to Dr. Herzog. Taken in context, the use of the word "request" did not give the court reason to question Jones's intent to complete the assignment and, although no specific amount was stated, the parties do not dispute that the services provided by Dr. Herzog and the amounts that he charged for those services were reasonable and necessary to the treatment of the shoulder injury referred to in the June 14 letter. Irace and Lowry had adequate funds to satisfy all of Jones's creditors, including Herzog, with funds left over for disbursement to Jones himself. Thus, this case simply does not present a situation analogous to *Shiro* because Dr. Herzog was given preference over Jones's other creditors by operation of the assignment. Given that Irace and Lowry do not dispute that they had ample notice of the assignment, the court's finding on the validity of the assignment is fully supported by the evidence and will not be disturbed. . . .

Dinslage v. Stratman

105 Neb. 274, 180 N.W. 81 (1920)

Frank Stratman lived with, and was in debt to, his mother, Thresa, for loans totaling $1,400, the indebtedness not being evidenced by any note or other writing. A granddaughter, Tracey Dinslage, also lived with Thresa, who very much wanted the young child to remain with her. Thresa told those around her (including Tracey's father) that if Tracey continued to live with her until she reached the age of 18, or until Thresa died, whichever first occurred, Tracey would be given $1,000. Later Thresa, with witnesses present, told her son Frank to pay Tracey $1,000 of the $1,400 debt he owed, when Tracey became of age or at Thresa's death. Upon Thresa's death some five months later, Frank paid $1,000 to John Dinslage, Tracey's father, for her. In an action by the administrator of Thresa's estate to recover the $1,400 debt from Frank, it was held that Thresa had made an effective assignment to Tracey and that the payment by Frank for Tracey's benefit discharged that much of the debt. The court said: "[T]here was no promissory note or other documentary evidence of the $1,400 debt, and, consequently, there was nothing tangible that could be delivered by Thresa Stratman to anyone. The whole thing rested in parol. The only thing that could be done by her was to direct her debtor to pay $1,000 of the money to Tracey, instead of to herself. It is conclusively established by the evidence that she gave that direction. Hence, she did everything that was in her power to divest herself of the title to the chose in action, and invest Tracey with it. . . . To hold otherwise would be to say that there can be no delivery of a chose in action unless it is accompanied by delivery of written evidence of it, and this would be absurd. . . . [I]t is inconceivable that [Thresa] had any other notion than that the gift was absolute[;] her direction to [Frank] settled the matter beyond recall," amounting in law to "a sufficient constructive delivery."

NOTE

One of the attributes of ownership is the power to dispose. If the asset to be transferred is a contract right, cases such as *Herzog* and *Dinslage* raise generally the question whether lack of formality renders the transfer ineffective. After all, an assignment is at bottom a present transfer of a right by the owner to another (distinguished from a contract, which is a promise of future performance). It may be gratuitous or for value. The statement found in Lone Star Cement Corp. v. Swartwout, 93 F.2d 767 (4th Cir. 1938), is representative of much authority: "No particular phraseology is required to effect an assignment, and it may be either in oral or written form; but the intent to vest in the assignee a present right in the thing assigned must be manifested by some oral or written word or by some conduct signifying a relinquishment of control by the assignor and an appropriation to the assignee." Yet, as the Restatement provision displayed below suggests (Rest.2d § 332), a gratuitous assignment remains revocable unless the formal requisites of a valid gift are met. We must therefore talk of the common law's traditional tests of "intention" and "delivery," of "stripping the donor of dominion over the thing given." *Dinslage* serves as a reminder of the many problems in applying the time-worn property test of delivery, rooted in gifts of chattels (visible things), to a vast array of intangibles. How would you characterize the test of "delivery" applied in that case?

The Second Restatement, § 324 on the essentials of an assignment, generally adopts the *Lone Star Cement* approach quoted above, but with the qualification that a statute or a contract may alter the requirements for an effective assignment. The statute of immediate importance is of course the UCC, and it preempts much of the law of assignments. Still, the common law of assignment generally remains effective despite a state's adoption of the Code. This means that even though the Code now governs many transactions (in particular assignments of obligations that fall within the definition of, "accounts receivable" within the meaning of Article 9), the common law of assignment continues to apply to transactions outside the scope of the UCC.

Restatement of Contracts, Second

§ 332. Revocability of Gratuitous Assignments

(1) Unless a contrary intention is manifested, a gratuitous assignment is irrevocable if

(a) the assignment is in a writing either signed or under seal that is delivered by the assignor; or

(b) the assignment is accompanied by delivery of a writing of a type customarily accepted as a symbol or as evidence of the right assigned.

(2) Except as stated in this Section, a gratuitous assignment is revocable and the right of the assignee is terminated by the assignor's death or incapacity, by a subsequent assignment by the assignor, or by notification from the assignor received by the assignee or by the obligor.

(3) A gratuitous assignment ceases to be revocable to the extent that before the assignee's right is terminated he obtains

(a) payment or satisfaction of the obligation, or

(b) judgment against the obligor, or

(c) a new contract of the obligor by novation.

(4) A gratuitous assignment is irrevocable to the extent necessary to avoid injustice where the assignor should reasonably expect the assignment to induce action or forbearance by the assignee or a subassignee and the assignment does induce such action or forbearance. . . .

Lojo Realty Co. v. Isaac G. Johnson's Estate, Inc.

253 N.Y. 579, 171 N.E. 791 (1930)

This question was certified to the Court of Appeals: "Could plaintiff have specific performance where it is the assignee of the contract and a valid assignment has been executed by plaintiff's assignor when the contract contains no prohibition against assignment, but on the contrary contains the following clause, to wit: 'The stipulations aforesaid are to apply to and bind the heirs, executors, administrators, successors and assigns of the respective parties,' and the contract does not state that the purchaser's bond and mortgage must be delivered at the closing?" The court answered: "We interpret the [question] as propounding an inquiry whether specific performance may be granted to an assignee of such a contract as is pleaded in the complaint if he has failed to tender a bond executed by his assignor. So interpreting it, the answer must be 'no'."

P/T Ltd. II v. Friendly Mobile Manor, Inc.

79 Md. App. 227, 556 A.2d 694 (Md. Ct. Spec. App. 1989)

"The UCC, [in contrast with the weight of authority at common law,] provides that duties as well as rights pass under the assignment unless there are circumstances or language to the contrary. . . . There is, at least historically, a logical basis for the distinction [made for the sale of goods]. Originally, assignments of contracts were either not permitted or were frowned upon. When A contracts with B, he bargains for B's performance, not C's. But if the contract is one of performance of service by A in exchange for payment of money by B, it is of little consequence to B whether he pays the money to A or to C, provided he gets what he bargained for, A's performance. Correspondingly, so long as he is paid for his work, it little matters to A whether he performs the same duties for the benefit of B or C. Consequently, the law eventually came to accept the notion of assignment of benefits while still rejecting the proposition that one could assign his duties, i.e., foist off on the promisee someone else's work, craftsmanship, reliability, skill, etc., in place of his own. Most contracts for sales of goods, however, involve obligations that can be performed by C just as well as A or B. Unless the goods are unique, they may be supplied by C as well as B; unless A is relying on B's credit, payment by C should be just as satisfactory as payment by B. And if the contract is of such a peculiar nature that substitution of C for B would be prejudicial to A, A may by appropriate contract provision prevent the assignment of either benefits or duties. For example, if the sale is on credit, A may object to B's assignment to C of the duty to pay. Or, if A's obligation is to supply all the goods of a certain type that B needs, A may be very reluctant indeed to permit C, whose needs may be totally different, to be substituted for B. But, here again, the UCC [in § 2–210(2) and (3)] establishes rules to apply in the absence of a manifestation of a contrary intent."

Macke Co. v. Pizza of Gaithersburg, Inc.

Court of Appeals of Maryland, 1970.
259 Md. 479, 270 A.2d 645.

SINGLEY, J. The appellees and defendants below, Pizza of Gaithersburg, Inc.; Pizzeria, Inc.; The Pizza Pie Corp., Inc. and Pizza Oven, Inc., four corporations under the common ownership of the same [three] individuals as partners or proprietors (the Pizza Shops) operated at six locations in Montgomery and Prince George's Counties. The appellees had arranged to have installed in each of their locations cold drink vending machines owned by Virginia Coffee Service, Inc., and on 30 December 1966, this arrangement was formalized at five of the locations, by contracts for terms of one year, automatically renewable for a like term in the absence of 30 days' written notice. A similar contract for the sixth location, operated by Pizza of Gaithersburg, Inc., was entered into on 25 July 1967.

On 30 December 1967, Virginia's assets were purchased by The Macke Co. (Macke) and the six contracts were assigned to Macke by Virginia. In January, 1968, the Pizza Shops attempted to terminate the five contracts having the December anniversary date, and in February, the contract which had the July anniversary date.

Macke [sued] each of the Pizza Shops for damages for breach of contract. From judgments for the defendants, Macke has appealed.

The lower court based [its] result on two grounds: first, that the Pizza Shops, when they contracted with Virginia, relied on its skill, judgment and reputation, which made impossible a delegation of Virginia's duties to Macke; and second, that the damages claimed could not be shown with reasonable certainty. These conclusions are challenged by Macke.

In the absence of a contrary provision—and there was none here—rights and duties under an executory bilateral contract may be assigned and delegated, subject to the exception that duties under a contract to provide personal services may never be delegated, nor rights be assigned under a contract where *delectus personae* was an ingredient of the bargain.[1] 4 Corbin on Contracts 865 (1951). . . . Crane Ice Cream Co. v. Terminal Freezing & Heating Co., 147 Md. 588, 128 A. 280 (1925), held that the right of an individual to purchase ice under a contract which by its terms reflected a knowledge of the individual's needs and reliance on his credit and responsibility could not be assigned to the corporation which purchased his business. . .

The six machines were placed on the appellees' premises under a printed "Agreement-Contract" which identified the "customer," gave its place of business, described the vending machine, and then provided:

> "TERMS
>
> "1. The Company will install on the Customer's premises the above listed equipment and will maintain the equipment in good operating order and stocked with merchandise.
>
> "2. . . .This equipment shall remain the property of the Company and shall not be moved from the location at which installed, except by the Company. . .
>
> "4. The Customer will exercise every effort to protect this equipment from abuse or damage.
>
> "5. The Company will be responsible for all licenses and taxes on the equipment and sale of products.

---

1 Like all generalizations, this one is subject to an important exception. [Article 9 of the UCC] makes ineffective a term in any contract prohibiting the assignment of a contract right: i.e., a right to payment. Compare Restatement, Contracts § 151(c) (1932).

"6. This Agreement-Contract is for a term of one (1) year from the date indicated herein and will be automatically renewed for a like period, unless thirty (30) day written notice is given by either party to terminate service.

"7. Commission on monthly sales will be paid by the Company to the Customer at the following rate:. . . ."

The rate provided in each of the agreements was "30% of Gross Receipts to $300 monthly[,] 35% over [$]300," except for the agreement with Pizza of Gaithersburg, Inc., which called for "40% of Gross Receipts."

We cannot regard the agreements as contracts for personal services. They were either a license or concession granted Virginia by the appellees, or a lease of a portion of the appellees' premises, with Virginia agreeing to pay a percentage of gross sales as a license or concession fee or as rent, . . . and were assignable by Virginia unless they imposed on Virginia duties of a personal or unique character which could not be delegated. . . .

The appellees earnestly argue that they had dealt with Macke before and had chosen Virginia because they preferred the way it conducted its business. Specifically, they say that service was more personalized, since the president of Virginia kept the machines in working order, that commissions were paid in cash, and that Virginia permitted them to keep keys to the machines so that minor adjustments could be made when needed. Even if we assume all this to be true, the agreements with Virginia were silent as to the details of the working arrangements and contained only a provision requiring Virginia to "install . . . the above listed equipment and . . . maintain the equipment in good operating order and stocked with merchandise." We think the Supreme Court of California put the problem of personal service in proper focus a century ago when it upheld the assignment of a contract to grade a San Francisco street:

"All painters do not paint portraits like Sir Joshua Reynolds, . . . nor do all writers write dramas like Shakespeare or fiction like Dickens. Rare genius and extraordinary skill are not transferable, and contracts for their employment are therefore personal, and cannot be assigned. But rare genius and extraordinary skill are not indispensable to the workmanlike digging down of a sand hill or the filling up of a depression to a given level, or the construction of brick sewers with manholes and covers, and contracts for such work are not personal, and may be assigned." Taylor v. Palmer, 31 Cal. 240 at 247–248 (1866).

. . . Moreover, the difference between the service the Pizza Shops happened to be getting from Virginia and what they expected to get from Macke did not mount up to such a material change in the performance of obligations under the agreements as would justify the appellees' refusal to recognize the assignment, Crane Ice Cream Co. v. Terminal Freezing & Heating Co., supra. . . .

We find . . . apposite [a case which was] not cited by the parties. In The British Waggon Co. & The Parkgate Waggon Co. v. Lea & Co., 5 Q.B.D. 149 (1880), a lessor of railway cars, who had agreed to keep the cars "in good and substantial repair and working order," made an assignment of the contract. . . . When [the assignee of the lessor] sued for rent, [the] court held that the lessee remained bound under the lease, because there was no provision making performance of the lessor's duty to keep in repair a duty personal to it or its employees.

. . . Modern authorities [establish] that, absent provision to the contrary, a duty may be delegated, as distinguished from a right which can be assigned, and that the promisee cannot rescind, if the quality of the performance remains materially the same. . . . In cases involving the sale of goods, the Restatement rule respecting delegation of duties has been amplified by [UCC] § 2–210(5), . . . which permits a promisee to demand assurances from the party to whom duties have been delegated. . . .

As we see it, the delegation of duty by Virginia to Macke was entirely permissible under the terms of the agreements. . . .

Having concluded that the Pizza Shops had no right to rescind the agreements, we turn to the question of damages. [The court rejected the lower court's conclusion that damages could not be proved with reasonable certainty.]

Judgment reversed as to liability; judgment entered for appellant for costs, on appeal and below; case remanded for a new trial on the question of damages.

QUESTION

Suppose that on March 1, A agrees to sell and B to buy a particular automobile for $15,000, payment, delivery of possession, and transfer of title all to occur on April 1. Would an assignment on March 15, by B to C of the right to receive the automobile, be valid? Would an assignment on March 15, by A to D of A's right to receive $15,000, be valid?

Crane Ice Cream Co. v. Terminal Freezing & Heating Co.

147 Md. 588, 128 A. 280 (1925)

Defendant Terminal had supplied ice to Frederick, an ice cream manufacturer, under a three-year contract in which defendant undertook to supply Frederick's requirements of ice up to a total of 250 tons a week. Frederick promised not to buy ice from any other source (except in excess of the 250-ton maximum) and to pay $3.25 a ton on the Tuesday following the week in which ice was delivered. On the expiration of this contract, a new contract for an additional three years (with the same terms) was agreed to by the parties. Less than a year after the new contract was signed, Frederick sold his plant, equipment, good will, "rights" and "contracts" to the Crane Ice Cream Co., a corporation engaged in the ice cream business on a large scale in Pennsylvania and Maryland. The Crane Co. indicated to defendant Terminal its willingness to pay cash for all ice delivered under the contract, but defendant refused to deliver any ice whatever and notified Frederick that the contract was at an end.

The trial court's order sustaining a demurrer to Crane's complaint for damages was affirmed by the Court of Appeals. The contract made by defendant Terminal was with an individual whose character, credit, and resources had been tried and tested by defendant. Frederick's requirements of ice were variable, but defendant had learned what they were. Defendant had also acquired confidence in the stability of Frederick's enterprise, his competence in commercial affairs, and his probity, personal judgment, and financial responsibility. The contract called for an extension of credit that might continue for as many as eight days after ice had been delivered. If the Crane Co. found it more profitable to do so, it could supply the plant purchased from Frederick with ice it had purchased in Philadelphia, or it could concentrate its purchases and buy the maximum of 250 tons a week from defendant, thus imposing on defendant a greater obligation than had been anticipated. Moreover, Frederick had evidently attempted to transfer not only his rights but also the performance of his duties, so that the assignment was in itself a repudiation of his duties. Defendant could not be required to accept the performance of a stranger in place of that due from an individual whom it knew and on whom it had relied.

Seagull Energy E & P, Inc. v. Eland Energy, Inc.

Supreme Court of Texas, 2006.
207 S.W.3d 342.

MEDINA, J. . . . Seagull Energy E & P, Inc. is a lessee and operator of two offshore oil and gas leases in the Gulf of Mexico near the Texas coast—Blocks 828 and 831, Mustang Island Area. In 1994, Eland Energy, Inc. purchased an interest in both leases, acquiring a 1. 09375% interest in Block 828 from General Atlantic Resources, Inc. and a 9. 41719% interest in Block 831 from UMC Petroleum Corporation. As the new owner, Eland expressly assumed certain rights and responsibilities under two offshore operating agreements, each applicable to its respective block. Both agreements designated Seagull as the operator and were essentially the same. They provided that Eland and the other lessees were to share the cost of operations in proportion to their respective interests, and that Seagull, as operator, was to exploit the minerals and collect the operating costs from the other lessees.

In July 1996, Eland sold its interest in these leases to Nor-Tex Gas Corporation, also assigning to Nor-Tex its rights and obligations under the operating agreements. Not long thereafter, Nor-Tex failed to reimburse Seagull for its share of operating costs, and Seagull sought these costs from Eland as an interest owner. Eland, however, refused to pay because it no longer owned an interest in the leases.

Seagull then sued Eland and Nor-Tex for breach of the operating agreement. . . .

This dispute . . . turns on whether the parties to the operating agreement expressly agreed upon the consequences that should follow an assignment of one's interest to a third party. . . .

Our primary concern when interpreting a contract is to ascertain and give effect to the intent of the parties as that intent is expressed in the contract. . . .

Eland focuses on several provisions that connect its obligation to reimburse the operator for costs and expenses to its participating interest, which is in turn based on its ownership in the lease. The pertinent provisions define participating interest and allocate costs and expenses in proportion to these interests as follows:

> Article 2
>
> Definitions . . .
>
> 2.10 *Participating Interest.* The respective percentage of participation of each Party electing to participate in each of the operations conducted hereunder, including the production of Oil and Gas, based on ownership in the Lease. . . .
>
> Article 8
>
> *Expenditures*
>
> 8.1 *Basis of Charge to the Parties.* Operator shall pay all costs and each Party shall reimburse Operator in proportion to its Participating Interest. . . .
>
> Article 14
>
> *Abandonment and Salvage*
>
> 14.1 *Platform Salvage and Removal Costs.* When the Parties owning a platform mutually agree to dispose of such platform, it shall be disposed of by the Operator as approved by such Parties. The costs, risks, and net proceeds, if any, resulting from such disposition shall be shared by such Parties in proportion to their Participating Interests. . . .
>
> 14.4 *Abandonment Operations Required by Governmental Authority.* Any well abandonment or platform removal required by governmental authority shall be accomplished by Operator with the costs, risks, and net proceeds, if any, to be shared by the Parties owning such well or platform in proportion to their Participating Interests.

Eland concludes from these provisions that its obligation to reimburse the operator continued only so long as it owned a participating interest. Once it assigned its interest, it was, according to Eland's interpretation, released from any continuing obligation to the operator for future costs or expenses.

Eland, however, reads far too much into these provisions. Nowhere do they mention the subject of release or the consequences which are to follow the assignment of a working interest. These subjects are, however, mentioned elsewhere in the agreement.

For example, section 15.1, entitled "Withdrawal," permits a party to withdraw from the agreement by assigning its interest to the other parties, while section 14.3, entitled "Assignment of Interest," provides that a party desiring to abandon a well shall assign its interest to the non-abandoning parties. Moreover, Article 26 pertains generally to the subject of assignment, providing that the "[a]greement shall be binding upon and inure to the benefit of the parties and their respective heirs, successors, representatives and assigns" and providing further that any assignment be made subject to the operating agreement. But like the cost allocation provisions on which Eland relies, none of these provisions deals specifically with the present circumstances. The operating agreement simply does not explain the consequences of an assignment of a working interest to a third party. Thus, we disagree with Eland that the parties expressly agreed that an assignment of a working interest was to operate as a novation, effectively ending any further obligation of the assignor under the operating agreement.

Generally speaking, a party cannot escape its obligations under a contract merely by assigning the contract to a third party. Thus, as a general rule, a party who assigns its contractual rights and duties to a third party remains liable unless expressly or impliedly released by the other party to the contract.

Even when the contract does not expressly provide for the consequences resulting from the assignment of one's interest, the contract's subject or other circumstances may indicate that obligations were not intended to survive assignment. For example, the *Restatement of Property* provides that "[w]hether a promise respecting the use of land of the promisor will continue to bind the promisor after he has ceased to have an interest in the land with respect to which the promise was made depends upon the intention manifested in the making of the promise." Restatement of Property: Servitudes § 538. The comment notes that "[s]uch promises are often of such a character that they can be satisfactorily performed only by the possessor of the land affected." As an example, the *Restatement* suggests that a promise to maintain a dam on one's property to provide a certain water level for a neighbor would cease upon the conveyance of the land. Eland does not argue that this contract's subject or circumstances imply that it should be released of its obligations after assignment. Even if it were to argue this, it is not apparent why Eland would not have been able to fulfill its obligations under the operating agreement even after the transfer of its interest in the underlying lease.

Because the operating agreement did not expressly provide that Eland's obligations under the operating agreement should terminate upon assignment and Seagull did not expressly release Eland following the assignment of its working interest, we reverse the court of appeals' judgment and render judgment for Seagull as the trial court did.

NOTE: DELEGATION UNDER THE UCC

Would the outcome of the *Crane* case now be different under UCC 2–210(2)? Note the Official Comment to that subsection.

Recall that the court in *Macke Co.* stated that the common law rules on delegation of duties have been "amplified" by UCC 2–210(5). That subsection provides that a nonassigning party to a contract for the sale of goods "may treat any assignment which delegates performance as creating reasonable grounds for insecurity and may without prejudice to his rights against the assignor demand assurances from the assignee (§ 2–609)."

Also, the *Macke Co.* court's reference to the "Restatement rule respecting delegation of duties" was based on § 160(3) of the first Restatement, which was phrased in terms of whether a delegee's performance would "vary materially" from the delegor's performance. In the Restatement, Second, the phrasing of the rule on delegation of performance of a duty is somewhat different. Section 318(2) provides: "Unless otherwise agreed, a promise requires performance by a particular person only to the extent that the obligee has a substantial interest in having that person perform or control the acts promised." This is the approach taken in UCC 2–210.

The question of delegation under UCC 2–210 was before the court in Sally Beauty Co. v. Nexxus Products Co., 801 F.2d 1001 (7th Cir. 1986), where Nexxus had contracted with Best for the exclusive distribution of its hair products in a specified area. When Best was acquired by and merged into Sally Beauty, a wholly-owned subsidiary of a major Nexxus competitor, Nexxus cancelled the distribution contract. This cancellation was not a breach, said the court:

> The UCC recognizes that in many cases an obligor will find it convenient or even necessary to relieve himself of the duty of performance under a contract, see Official Comment 1, UCC 2–210 ("[T]his section recognizes both delegation of performance and assignability as normal and permissible incidents of a contract for the sale of goods."). The Code therefore sanctions delegation except where the delegated performance would be unsatisfactory to the obligee: "A party may perform his duty through a delegate unless otherwise agreed to or unless the other party has a substantial interest in having his original promisor perform or control the acts required by the contract." UCC 2–210(1). Consideration is given to balancing the policies of free alienability of commercial contracts and protecting the obligee from having to accept a bargain he did not contract for. . . .
>
> In the exclusive distribution agreement before us, Nexxus had contracted for Best's "best efforts" in promoting the sale of Nexxus

> products. UCC § 2–306(2) states that "[a] lawful agreement by either buyer or seller for exclusive dealing in the kind of goods concerned imposes unless otherwise agreed an obligation by the seller to use best efforts to supply the goods and by the buyer to use best efforts to promote their sale." This implied promise on Best's part was the consideration for Nexxus' promise to refrain from supplying any other distributors within Best's exclusive area. . . . It was this contractual undertaking which Nexxus refused to see performed by Sally. . . .
>
> [We hold] that the duty of performance under an exclusive distributorship may not be delegated to a competitor in the market place—or the wholly-owned subsidiary of a competitor—without the obligee's consent. . . . [S]uch a rule is consonant with the policies behind § 2–210, which is concerned with preserving the bargain the obligee has struck. Nexxus should not be required to accept the "best efforts" of Sally Beauty when those efforts are subject to the control of [its competitor.] It is entirely reasonable that Nexxus should conclude that this performance would be a different thing than what it had bargained for.

COMMENT: CONTRACTUAL PROHIBITION OF ASSIGNMENT

In Allhusen v. Caristo Constr. Corp., 303 N.Y. 446, 103 N.E.2d 891 (1952), a general contractor's agreement with a painting subcontractor included this prohibitory provision: "The assignment by the [Subcontractor] of this contract or any interest therein, or of any money due or to become due by reason of the terms hereof without the written consent of the [General Contractor] shall be void." The sub, without the general's consent, later assigned to a third party the "right to moneys due and to become due" under the painting contract. The contract itself was not assigned. When the assignee sued to recover monies allegedly due and owing for work done by the sub, the general invoked the anti-assignment clause. The Court of Appeals agreed that the assignee's complaint must be dismissed, saying:

> [W]hile the courts have striven to uphold freedom of assignability, they have not failed to recognize the concept of freedom to contract. . . . We have [here] a clause embodying clear, definite and appropriate language, which may be construed in no other way but that any attempted assignment of either the contract or any rights created thereunder shall be "void" as against the obligor. One would have to do violence to the language here employed to hold that it is merely an agreement by the subcontractor not to assign. . . .

The approach taken in *Allhusen* has many followers, including courts that have explicitly adopted the Second Restatement's formulation, in § 322, of the "ineffective term" principle (prohibition gives "a right to damages for breach [but] does not render the assignment ineffective"). See, e.g., Bel-Ray Co. v. Chemrite Ltd., 181 F.3d 435 (3d Cir. 1999).

The language of Justice Holmes in Portuguese-American Bank v. Welles, 242 U.S. 7 (1916), has been quoted often. After stating that a promisor's undertaking ordinarily may be defined as narrowly as the promisor wishes, Holmes said (242 U.S. 11):

> But when [the promisor] has incurred a debt, which is property in the hands of the creditor, it is a different thing to say that as between the creditor and a third person the debtor can restrain his alienation of that, although he could not forbid the sale or pledge of other chattels. When a man sells a horse, what he does, from the point of view of the law, is to transfer a right, and a right being regarded by the law as a thing, even though a res incorporalis, it is not illogical to apply the same rule to a debt that would be applied to a horse.

In the case before Holmes, the obligor (the City of San Francisco) had not objected to the assignment, unlike the obligor defendant, the general contractor, in the *Allhusen* case. The city in Holmes' case was perfectly willing to pay whoever was entitled to the money, and the contest was for priority between two successive assignees. It is generally agreed that a contractual prohibition of assignment by the creditor will seldom have any bearing on this issue, since priority between successive assignees is rarely a matter of concern to the debtor. See Gilmore, Security Interests in Personal Property § 7.8 (1965).

Some of the reasons why debtors might desire to protect themselves by contract provisions that prohibit assignments by their creditors have been explained by Professor Gilmore (vol. I, § 7.6):

> Prohibitions of assignment have their principal commercial use in the case of obligors who have large numbers of creditors to deal with. There are public authorities, federal, state and municipal, dealing with contractors. There are prime or first-tier contractors dealing with subcontractors. There are manufacturers dealing with suppliers of raw materials, component parts or sub-assemblies. There are banks dealing with holders of bank obligations. There are insurance companies dealing with policy holders. It is easy to understand why obligors so situated are loath to be required to recognize claimants other than those they originally dealt with. Where thousands and tens of thousands of claims are involved, the mere bookkeeping, if transfers must be recognized, becomes an expensive item. . . . When many claims are to be paid, it is inevitable that mistakes will be made, and if the obligor pays the wrong person he still owes the money to the rightful claimant. . . . Beyond clerical error and routine mistake, there is the problem of deciding whether an assignment is valid, under the law of some state or of a foreign country. Finally, under the normal rule of assignment law, the obligor will not be able to make set-offs against the assignee on account of claims or defenses against the assignor which arise after the obligor has received notification of the assignment. Quite naturally the obligor would prefer to avoid the fuss, the bother, the cer-

> tainty of mistake, the duty of deciding difficult and obscure questions of law and the possibility of losing rights to resist payment. He therefore writes into his contract, letter of credit or insurance policy a clause to prohibit assignments made without his consent.

The author then observed that public authorities, especially the federal or a state government, by virtue of legislation can refuse consent to be sued by strangers and are not controlled in this respect by ordinary rules of private law. He found that the *Allhusen* case had been qualified and its effects obscured by later decisions (vol. I, § 7.9), but, in its application to privately-created debts, he rejected the decision in any event (vol. I, § 7.6):

> The position taken here is in favor of the unrestricted and unrestrictable alienability of contract rights. . . . On propositions of so fundamental an order belief is instinctive and irrational, not logical or reasoned. Freedom of contract cuts both ways: to the freedom of a debtor to restrict or prohibit transfer of claims against him may be opposed the freedom of a creditor to transfer rights whose value may be attested by the fact that a transferee is willing to pay for them or lend money on their security. The social and economic utility of permitting creditors to transfer rights is believed to outweigh the utility of permitting obligors to forbid the transfer. That one utility outweighs the other lies beyond demonstration or proof.

This is pretty clearly the view adopted by the Uniform Commercial Code. See UCC 9–406(c). As the comment notes, "[t]he policies underlying the ineffectiveness of contractual restrictions under this section build on common-law developments that essentially have eliminated legal restrictions on assignments of rights to payment as security and other assignments of rights to payment such as accounts."

The passage previously quoted from Gilmore describes some of the administrative burdens and legal risks of "account debtors" who have many creditors to keep track of. Under traditional common-law rules, debtors are required to pay the assignee, not the original creditor, after notice of the assignment. This means that account debtors must identify assignees correctly—and even decide at their own peril the validity of the assignments asserted. Risks of this kind may be reduced by the requirements of § 9–406, that the notification to the account debtor must "reasonably identify the rights assigned," and that the assignee, if requested by the account debtor, must furnish "reasonable proof" of the assignment (if the proof is not furnished the debtor is left free to pay the assignor).

NOTE: THE ASSIGNMENT OF FUTURE RIGHTS

The leading case of Taylor v. Barton-Child Co., 228 Mass. 126, 117 N.E. 43 (1917), provides the common law view on the assignability of rights not yet in existence. At issue in that case was the enforceability of a wholesaler's assignment of "future book accounts," that is, sums to be earned in the future from transactions occurring in the course of business. The court said:

> The crucial question is whether the assignment of book accounts which are to come into existence in the future in connection with an established business, will be enforced [by the assignee] in equity. . . . It is a well recognized principle . . . that a man cannot sell or mortgage property which he does not possess and to which he has no title. . . . There can be no present transfer of property not in existence, or of property not in the possession of the seller to which he has no title. . . .
>
> There is an exception at the common law to the effect that one may sell that in which he has a potential title although not present actual possession. The present owner might sell the wool to be grown upon his flock, the crop to be harvested from his field or the young to be born of his herd, or assign the wages to be earned under existing employment. . . . That [principle] has never been carried so far as to include the case at bar. The catch of fish expected to be made upon a voyage about to begin cannot be sold. . . . There can be no sale of the wool of sheep, the crop of a field or the increase of herds not owned but to be bought, and there can be no assignment of wages to be earned under a contract of employment to be made in the future. . . . Practical difficulties of no small consequence would be encountered in the operation of the contrary doctrine. . . . Merchants and manufacturers well might acquire a considerable credit upon the supposed strength of book accounts which later might turn out to have been assigned long before they came into existence. A door would be opened for the accomplishment of fraud in business.

Legislation, most notably Article 9 of the UCC, has reduced dramatically the role of the common law in disputes over the assignment of future claims. As for developments apart from the Code, the treatment of the subject of wages is representative of legislative action in general.

The court in Taylor v. Barton-Child Co. stated that one might "assign the wages to be earned under existing employment," but that "there can be no assignment of wages to be earned under a contract of employment to be made in the future." This was essentially the view at common law: unless wages related to existing employment or an existing contract of employment, they were not assignable. As one court explained it, "an assignment of wages expected to be earned in the future, and not based upon an existing contract, engagement, or employment, is [an attempt] to assign something which exists in expectancy only. In such a case it is apparent that there is nothing to assign. The expectancy may never become a reality." Metcalf v. Kincaid, 87 Iowa 443, 54 N.W. 867 (1893).

Most of our states have enacted statutes regulating the assignment of wages and salary. Policy considerations only vaguely reflected in the common law rules are brought sharply into focus by such acts. A few fairly common provisions in this legislation are worth noting. (1) The statutes frequently distinguish between assignments given to secure small loans and those given for other purposes, the former being more stringently regulated.

(2) The assignment is commonly required to be in writing, sometimes in accord with a statutory form, and signed by the assignor personally. (3) If the assignor is married, the spouse may also be required to sign. (4) A valid assignment is commonly limited to only a part of the wages earned—a designated percentage or the amount in excess of a specified nonassignable sum. (5) The assignment is usually limited in duration, the permissible periods varying up to three years. (6) In order to protect the employer against competing claims, prompt notice of the assignment is frequently required. Some states also make wage assignments ineffective unless the employer consents. (7) Recordation of the assignment is sometimes required to give the assignee priority over subsequent, attaching creditors of the assignor.

The court in Taylor v. Barton-Child Co. noted an additional aspect of the problem of enforcing assignments of future rights—the prospect that equity courts might enforce a mortgage of property not yet acquired. In fact, from early times, there is in the equity cases a strong propensity in favor of enforcing contracts to give security interests in identified assets. The case of Holroyd v. Marshall, 10 House of Lords Cases 191, 11 Eng. Rep. 999 (1862), gives an example. It involved an attempted transfer, not of choses in action, but of chattels not yet owned by the owner of a textile factory. Owing a debt of £5,000, the owner transferred, by way of mortgage, machinery and equipment he then owned; he also covenanted to transfer all machinery, implements, and fixtures that he should in the future place in his factory while the mortgage debt was unpaid. Machinery thereafter acquired was attached by one of his creditors, but the House of Lords affirmed an equity decree establishing the priority of the mortgage as to after-acquired assets. Lord Westbury said:

> It is quite true that a deed which professes to convey property which is not in existence at the time is as a conveyance void at law, simply because there is nothing to convey. So in equity a contract which engages to transfer property, which is not in existence, cannot operate as an immediate alienation merely because there is nothing to transfer. But if a vendor or mortgagor agrees to sell or mortgage property, real or personal, of which he is not possessed at the time, and he receives the consideration for the contract, and afterwards becomes possessed of property answering the description in the contract, there is no doubt that a court of equity would compel him to perform the contract, and that the contract would, in equity, transfer the beneficial interest to the mortgagee or purchaser immediately on the property being acquired. This, of course, assumes that the supposed contract is one of that class of which a court of equity would decree the specific performance. If it be so, then immediately on the acquisition of the property described the vendor or mortgagor would hold it in trust for the purchaser or mortgagee, according to the terms of the contract. For if a contract be in other respects good and fit to be performed, and the consideration has been received, incapacity to perform it at the time of its execution will be no answer when the means of doing so are afterward obtained.

To be sure, the relief given in such cases depends on an "equity" that arises as a byproduct of specific performance (that is to say, the contract in question must meet some version of the "inadequacy" test, so that the result can be explained, as *Holroyd* explains it, as specific performance). The question, of course, is whether the doctrine applied in *Holroyd* should be carried over to assignments of nonexistent rights. The doctrine has been so extended by our courts, from an early date. See, e.g., Field v. City of New York, 6 N.Y. 179 (1852), where the equity court recognized the primacy of the claim of the first assignee, as against the assignor and subsequent assignees, under an attempted assignment which covered claims not yet in existence and which therefore had no present effectiveness. The court explained: "There was indeed no present, actual, potential existence of the thing to which the assignment or grant related, and therefore it could not and did not operate *eo instanti* to pass the claim which was expected thereafter to accrue to [the assignor] against the [obligor]; but it did nevertheless create an equity, which would seize upon these claims as they should arise, and would continue so to operate until the object of the [assignment] agreement was accomplished." Some courts gave another explanation that was a clear short-circuit: that the agreement itself creates an "equitable lien."

In many instances, courts must confront a contest between an assignee and other creditors of the assignor. Having an equitable lien does not itself ensure that the assignee will enjoy priority. How exactly the assignee fares in that battle must await a course in secured transactions. In any event, the modern common law's generally favorable attitude toward the assignment of rights to arise in the future is captured in the provisions of Restatement, Second § 321. In a word, the assignee has rights in court against the assignor only to the extent that contractual remedies are available to enforce a promise to assign.

Homer v. Shaw

Supreme Judicial Court of Massachusetts, 1912.
212 Mass. 113, 98 N.E. 697.

[Shaw was the general contractor for the construction of a section of the Tremont Street subway in Boston. Lancaster was a subcontractor who agreed to do certain excavating and mason work, as well as the erection and riveting of iron work for this section. Lancaster began work on June 1, 1896, but on June 13, in need of funds, he applied to Homer, plaintiff in this action, for money. Homer advanced $1,010.83 to Lancaster under an agreement that Lancaster would give him half the profits of his work. About June 27, Lancaster gave Homer as security a written assignment of the sums due and to come due to him under his contract with defendant. This assignment was sent to defendant and accepted by him in writing. On July 20, Lancaster wrote defendant: "Owing to my peculiar financial circumstances it will be impossible for me to go on with the iron work on the subway and shall have to give the job up." Defendant met with Lancaster the same day, and it was agreed, at defendant's request, that Lancaster would complete the work he had agreed to do, that defendants would pay debts Lancaster had already incurred for labor and material, would advance the money needed in the future for labor and material, and would pay Lancaster personally $25 a week until the job was done. Defendant testified that his original contract was entirely rescinded and that he assumed entire responsibility for payments for labor and materials, though he did agree that if Lancaster completed the work to defendant's satisfaction, and "got rid of the plaintiff's claim and any other claims and suits," he would pay Lancaster the difference between the cost of completing the job and the contract price of $6 a ton. An auditor to whom the case was referred found that "this new arrangement was in effect a rescission of the original contract and the substitution of a new and radically different one for it, and that the rights of the plaintiff under his assignment did not extend to the sums payable to Lancaster after this date." Plaintiff, alleging that Lancaster had completed the work, asked for rulings that the new contract between defendant and Lancaster was merely a change in the terms of payment, that defendant owed no duty to pay Lancaster's employees, and that after accepting the assignment he (defendant) could not deprive plaintiff of his rights under it. The trial judge refused these rulings and gave judgment for defendant.]

BRALEY, J. The defendant's liability upon acceptance of the assignment depended upon the assignor's performance of his contract to transport, erect and paint the steel work required for a section of a subway which the defendant was building in accordance with the plans and specifications of the transit commissioners. If not fully performed the entire contract price although payable in monthly instalments never became due, or if before completion the assignor by reason of his inability to go on, voluntarily abandoned the work, he could not recover for work and labor already performed and furnished. Homer v. Shaw, 177 Mass. 1, 58 N.E. 160. . . . [A]fter the assignor entered upon the performance of the contract he informed the defendant, that owing to the failure of the plaintiff to advance money, which apparently he had agreed to furnish, he would be unable to complete the work as his workmen had not been paid, and if their wages remained in arrears they would leave his employment. The evidence, if no further action had been taken by the parties, and performance of the work had ceased, would have warranted a finding, that, the assignor having repudiated or abandoned his contract before the first instalment of the contract price became payable, the defendant would not have been indebted to the plaintiff. Homer v. Shaw, 177 Mass. 1, 58 N.E. 160; Bowen v. Kimbell, 203 Mass. 364, 89 N.E. 542. . . . But without any ostensible change the assignor remained in charge of the work until completion, and the plaintiff contends under the substituted declaration, that the money thereafter received should be considered as earned under the original contract. The assignor needed immediate financial assistance, and if the defendant might have advanced the money which the evidence shows he furnished to enable him to pay his employees, yet if he had done so the plaintiff's assignment would have been given priority over the loan. Buttrick Lumber Co. v. Collins, 202 Mass. 413, 89 N.E. 138.

The parties, while they could not modify to his prejudice the terms of the contract assigned without the plaintiff's consent, or by a secret fraudulent arrangement deprive him of the benefit of the assignment, were not precluded from entering into a new agreement if performance by the assignor had become impossible from unforeseen circumstances. Eaton v. Mellus, 7 Gray 566, 572. . . . It consequently was a question of fact upon all the evidence for the presiding judge before whom the case was tried without a jury to decide whether upon facing the exigencies of changed conditions the parties mutually agreed to a cancellation, and thereupon in good faith an independent contract was substituted, by the terms of which the defendant undertook to furnish sufficient funds to pay the workmen the wages then due, and their future wages as they accrued, while the assignor was to receive a weekly salary for his personal services of supervision. The refusal to comply with the plaintiff's request for findings, and the general finding for the defendant manifestly show his conclusion to have been that the first contract was treated as having been rescinded, and the plaintiff had no enforceable claim against the defendant under the assignment. . . . The plaintiff's requests for rulings in so far as they were not given were rightly refused, and the exceptions must be overruled. So ordered.

SECTION 3. TORTIOUS INTERFERENCE WITH CONTRACT

We began this book with Oliver Wendell Holmes' observation that, at common law, a legally enforceable promise gives its maker a choice between keeping the promise or paying a compensatory sum. From this perspective, it would seem the person who induces another to breach a contract could not commit a tort. Doing what the law entitles one to do is not a civil wrong. Advising someone to do it would not seem to be either. (Both may be the acts of Holmesian "bad men," but this is not relevant as far as the law is concerned.) Indeed, from the perspective of Holmes' heir—Richard Posner—there are times when the person who chooses to pay damages is an efficient breacher. Far from being morally reprehensible, the breach is affirmatively desirable; the person who induces the breach of contract is even doing affirmative good.

In the first chapter of the book, however, we saw that there are times when equity intervenes to take away the option not to perform. The paradigm case is Lumley v. Wagner. A performer with extraordinary skills, even if she cannot be forced to keep her promise, can be enjoined from working any place else. So too there are times when a court will allow an action against someone who induces a breach of contract. The leading case again grew out of the contract between Benjamin Lumley and Johanna Wagner.

This time the defendant is the impresario who persuaded Wagner to sing at his theater instead.

Lumley v. Gye

Court of Queen's Bench, 1853.
[1843–1860] All ER Rep 208.

CROMPTON, J. [The plaintiff Lumley alleged that Wagner had agreed to sing at his opera house, but the defendant Gye] maliciously procured her to depart out of the employment of [Lumley]; whereby she did depart out of the employment and service of [Lumley]; whereby damage was suffered by [Lumley]. It was said, in support of the demurrer, that it did not appear in the declaration that the relation of master and servant ever subsisted between [Lumley] and Miss Wagner; that Miss Wagner was not averred . . . to have entered upon the service of [Lumley]; and that the engagement of a theatrical performer, even if the performer has entered upon the duties, is not of such a nature as to make the performer a servant within the rule of law which gives an action to the master for the wrongful enticing away of his servant. It was laid down broadly, as a general proposition of law, that no action will lie for procuring a person to break a contract, although such procuring is with a malicious intention and causes great and immediate injury. The law as to enticing servants was said to be contrary to the general rule and principle of law, to be anomalous, and probably to have had its origin from the state of society when serfdom existed and to be founded upon, or upon the equity of, the Statute of Labourers. It was said that it would be dangerous to hold that an action was maintainable for persuading a third party to break a contract unless some boundary or limits could be pointed out; that the remedy for enticing away servants was confined to cases where the relation of master and servant, in a strict sense, subsisted between the parties; and that, in all other cases of contract, the only remedy was against the party breaking the contract.

Whatever may have been the origin or foundation of the law as to enticing of servants, and whether it be, as contended by the plaintiff, an instance and branch of a wider rule, or, as contended by the defendant, an anomaly and an exception from the general rule of law on such subjects, it must now be considered clear law that a person who wrongfully and maliciously, or, which is the same thing, with notice, interrupts the relation subsisting between master and servant by procuring the servant to depart from the master's service, or by harbouring and keeping him as servant after he has quitted it and during the time stipulated for as the period of service, whereby the master is injured, commits a wrongful act for which he is responsible at law. I think that the rule applies wherever the wrongful interruption operates to prevent the service during the time for which the parties have contracted that the service shall continue: and

I think that the relation of master and servant subsists, sufficiently for the purpose of such action, during the time for which there is in existence a binding contract of hiring and service between the parties. I think that it is a fanciful and technical and unjust distinction to say that the not having actually entered into the service, or that the service is not actually continuing, can make any difference. The wrong and injury are surely the same whether the wrongdoer entices away the gardener, who has hired himself for a year, the night before he is to go to his work, or after he has planted the first cabbage on the first morning of his service; and I should be sorry to support a distinction so unjust, and so repugnant to common sense. . . .

. . . In deciding this case . . ., I wish by no means to be considered as deciding that . . . in no case except that of master and servant is an action maintainable for maliciously inducing another to break a contract to the injury of the person with whom such contract has been made. It does not appear to me to be a sound answer to say that the [actionable] act in such cases is the act of the party who breaks the contract; for that reason would apply in the acknowledged case of master and servant. Nor is it an answer to say that there is a remedy against the contractor and that the party relies on the contract; for, besides that reason also applying to the case of master and servant, the action on the contract and the action against the malicious wrong-doer may be for a different matter; and the damages payable for such malicious injury might be calculated on a very different principle from the amount of the debt which might be the only sum recoverable on the contract. Suppose a trader, with a malicious intent to ruin a rival trader, goes to a banker or other party who owes money to his rival, and begs him not to pay the money which he owes him, and by that means ruins or greatly prejudices the party: I am by no means prepared to say that an action could not be maintained, and that damages, beyond the amount of the debt if the injury were great, or much less than such amount if the injury were less serious, might not be recovered. . . .

Without however deciding any such more general question, I think that we are justified in applying the principle of the action for enticing away servants to a case where the defendant maliciously procures a party, who is under a valid contract to give her exclusive personal services to the plaintiff for a specified period, to refuse to give such services during the period for which she had so contracted, whereby the plaintiff was injured.

I think, therefore, that our judgment should be for the plaintiff.

NOTE

Lumley v. Gye leaves a number of questions open. While the *Lumley* doctrine grows out of the law governing master and servant, it has been applied in many contexts, perhaps most notably in Pennzoil's multi-billion dollar action against Texaco for interfering with its contract to buy part of Getty Oil. See Texaco, Inc. v. Pennzoil, Co., 729 S.W.2d 768 (Tex. App. 1987). But identifying when redress is available has proved elusive. If a party to a contract is free to choose whether to perform or breach and pay damages, then why should it be a tort for someone to persuade that person to exercise one of the choices the law gives? Should this tort be available only if a right of specific performance exists against the breacher of the underlying contract? And what exactly does the *Lumley* court mean when it refers to "malice"? Is it enough that the defendant acted with knowledge of the contract? The next case explores these questions and also examines the way the doctrine has expanded over time to include not only interference with an existing contract, but also situations in which a person deliberately acts to prevent a contract from coming into being in the first instance.

Della Penna v. Toyota Motor Sales, U.S.A., Inc.

Supreme Court of California, 1995.
11 Cal. 4th 376, 45 Cal. Rptr. 2d 436, 902 P.2d 740.

ARABIAN, J. . . . John Della Penna, an automobile wholesaler doing business as Pacific Motors, brought this action for damages against Toyota Motor Sales, U.S.A., Inc., and its Lexus division, alleging that certain business conduct of defendants both violated provisions of the Cartwright Act, California's state antitrust statute, and constituted an intentional interference with his economic relations. The impetus for Della Penna's suit arose out of the 1989 introduction into the American luxury car market of Toyota's Lexus automobile. Prior to introducing the Lexus, the evidence at trial showed, both the manufacturer, Toyota Motor Corp., and defendant, the American distributor, had been concerned at the possibility that a resale market might develop for the Lexus in Japan. Even though the car was manufactured in Japan, Toyota's marketing strategy was to bar the vehicle's sale on the Japanese domestic market until after the American roll-out; even then, sales in Japan would only be under a different brand name, the "Celsior." Fearing that auto wholesalers in the United States might re-export Lexus models back to Japan for resale, and concerned that, with production and the availability of Lexus models in the American market limited, re-exports would jeopardize its fledgling network of American Lexus dealers, Toyota inserted in its dealership agreements a "no export" clause, providing that the dealer was "authorized to sell [Lexus automobiles] only to customers located in the United States. [Dealer] agrees that it will not sell [Lexus automobiles] for resale or use outside the United States. [Dealer] agrees to abide by any export policy established by [distributor]."

Following the introduction into the American market, it soon became apparent that some domestic Lexus units were being diverted for foreign sales, principally to Japan. To counter this effect, Toyota managers wrote to their retail dealers, reminding them of the "no-export" policy and explaining that exports for foreign resale could jeopardize the supply of Lexus automobiles available for the United States market. In addition, Toyota compiled a list of "offenders"—dealers and others believed by Toyota to be involved heavily in the developing Lexus foreign resale market—which it distributed to Lexus dealers in the United States. American Lexus dealers were also warned that doing business with those whose names appeared on the "offenders" list might lead to a series of graduated sanctions, from reducing a dealer's allocation to possible reevaluation of the dealer's franchise agreement.

During the years 1989 and 1990, plaintiff Della Penna did a profitable business as an auto wholesaler purchasing Lexus automobiles, chiefly from the Lexus of Stevens Creek retail outlet, at near retail price and exporting them to Japan for resale. By late 1990, however, plaintiff's sources began to dry up, primarily as a result of the "offenders list." Stevens Creek ceased selling models to plaintiff; gradually other sources declined to sell to him as well.

In February 1991, plaintiff filed this lawsuit against Toyota Motors, U.S.A., Inc., alleging both state antitrust claims under the Cartwright Act and interference with his economic relationship with Lexus retail dealers. At the close of plaintiff's case-in-chief, the trial court granted Toyota's motion for nonsuit with respect to the remaining Cartwright Act claim (plaintiff had previously abandoned a related claim—unfair competition—prior to trial). The tort cause of action went to the jury, however, under the standard . . . instructions applicable to such claims with one significant exception. At the request of defendant and over plaintiff's objection, the trial judge modified . . . the basic instruction identifying the elements of the tort and indicating the burden of proof[,] to require plaintiff to prove that defendant's alleged interfering conduct was "wrongful."[1]

The jury returned a divided verdict, nine to three, in favor of Toyota. [Della Penna] appealed. In an unpublished disposition, the Court of Appeal unanimously reversed the trial court's judgment, ruling that a plaintiff alleging intentional interference with economic relations is not required to establish "wrongfulness" as an element of its prima facie case, and that it was prejudicial error for the trial court to have read the jury an amended instruction to that effect. The Court of Appeal remanded the case to the trial court for a new trial; we then granted Toyota's petition for review and now reverse.

Although legal historians have traced the origins of the so-called "interference torts" as far back as the Roman law, the proximate historical impetus for their modern development lay in mid-19th century English common law. . . .

The opinion in [Lumley v. Gye] dealt, of course, with conduct intended to induce the *breach* of an *existing* contract, not conduct intended to prevent or persuade others *not to contract* with the plaintiff. That such an interference with *prospective* economic relations might itself be tortious was confirmed by the Queen's Bench over the next 40 years. In Temperton v. Russell, 1 Q.B. 715 (1893), a labor union, embroiled in a dispute with a firm of builders, announced what today would be called a

---

[1] The standard instruction governing "intentional interference with prospective economic advantage," . . . describes the essential elements of the claim as (1) an economic relationship between the plaintiff and another, "containing a probable future economic benefit or advantage to plaintiff," (2) defendant's knowledge of the existence of the relationship, (3) that defendant "intentionally engaged in acts or conduct designed to interfere with or disrupt" the relationship, (4) actual disruption, and (5) damage to the plaintiff as a result of defendant's acts. The modification sought by defendant and adopted by the trial court consisted in adding the word "wrongful" in element (3) between the words "in" and "acts." The trial court also read to the jury *plaintiff's* special jury instruction defining the "wrongful acts" required to support liability as conduct "outside the realm of legitimate business transactions. . . . Wrongfulness may lie in the method used or by virtue of an improper motive."

secondary boycott, intended to force a resolution of the union's grievances by pressuring suppliers of the builder to cease furnishing him construction materials. A failure to comply with the union's boycott demands, suppliers were warned, would result in union pressure on those who bought *their* supplies not to deal with *them*.

One such supplier of the builder, Temperton, sued the union's leadership, alleging that his business had been injured by breaches of supply contracts and the refusal of others to do business with him, all as a result of the union's threats. A unanimous Queen's Bench upheld the jury's verdict for the plaintiff, reasoning in part on the authority of *Lumley*, that in the words of Lord Esher, the Master of the Rolls, "the distinction . . . between the claim for inducing persons to break contracts already entered into . . . and . . . inducing persons not to enter into contracts . . . can [not] prevail." (*Temperton*, at p. 728.)

"There was the same wrongful intent in both cases, wrongful because malicious," Lord Esher wrote. "There was the same kind of injury to the plaintiff. It seems rather a fine distinction to say that, where a defendant maliciously induces a person not to carry out a contract already made with the plaintiff and so injures the plaintiff, it is actionable, but where he injures the plaintiff by maliciously preventing a person from entering into a contract with the plaintiff, which he would otherwise have entered into, it is not actionable." (*Temperton*, at p. 728.)

As a number of courts and commentators have observed, the keystone of the liability imposed in *Lumley* and *Temperton* to judge from the opinions of the justices, appears to have been the "malicious" intent of a defendant in enticing an employee to breach her contract with the plaintiff, and damaging the business of one who refused to cooperate with the union in achieving its bargaining aims. While some have doubted whether the use of the word "malicious" amounted to anything more than an intent to commit an act, knowing it would harm the plaintiff, Dean Keeton, assessing the state of the tort as late as 1984, remarked that "[w]ith intent to interfere as the usual basis of the action, the cases have turned almost entirely upon the defendant's motive or purpose and the means by which he has sought to accomplish it. As in the cases of interference with contract, any manner of intentional invasion of the plaintiff's interests may be sufficient if the purpose is not a proper one." (Prosser & Keeton on Torts (5th ed. 1984) § 130, p. 1009.)

It was, legal historians have suggested, this early accent on the defendant's "intentionality" that was responsible for allying the interference torts with their remote relatives, intentional torts of a quite different order-battery, for example, or false imprisonment. More than one account of the rise of the tort has relied on Lord Bowen's statement in an interference with contract case that "intentionally to do that which is calculated in the ordinary course of events to damage, and which does, in fact, damage another in that person's property or trade, is actionable if done without just cause or excuse." (Mogul Steamship Co. v. McGregor, Gow & Co., 23 Q.B.D. 598, 613 (1889)).

One consequence of this superficial kinship was the assimilation to the interference torts of the pleading and burden of proof requirements of the "true" intentional torts: the requirement that the plaintiff need only allege a so-called "prima facie tort" by showing the defendant's awareness of the economic relation, a deliberate interference with it, and the plaintiff's resulting injury. By this account of the matter—the traditional view of the torts and the one adopted by the first Restatement of Torts—the burden then passed to the defendant to demonstrate that its conduct was *privileged*, that is, "justified" by a recognized defense such as the protection of others or, more likely in this context, the defendant's own competitive business interests.

These and related features of the economic relations tort and the requirements surrounding its proof and defense led, however, to calls for a reexamination and reform as early as the 1920's. . . .

Calls for a reformulation of both the elements and the means of establishing the economic relations tort reached a height around the time the Restatement Second of Torts was being prepared for publication and are reflected in its departures from its predecessor's version. Acknowledging criticism, the American Law Institute discarded the prima facie tort requirement of the first Restatement. A new provision, § 766B, required that the defendant's conduct be "improper," and adopted a multifactor "balancing" approach, identifying seven factors for the trier of fact to weigh in determining a defendant's liability. The Restatement Second of Torts, however, declined to take a position on the issue of which of the parties bore the burden of proof, relying on the "considerable disagreement on who has the burden of pleading and proving certain matters" and the observation that "the law in this area has not fully congealed but is still in a formative stage." (See Rest.2d of Torts (1965 ed.), Introductory Note, ch. 37, pp. 5–6.) In addition, the Restatement Second provided that a defendant might escape liability by showing that his conduct was justifiable and did *not* include the use of "wrongful means." *Id.*, §§ 768–771. . . .

In searching for a means to recast the elements of the economic relations tort and allocate the associated burdens of proof, we are guided by an overmastering concern articulated by high courts of other jurisdictions and legal commentators: The need to draw and enforce a sharpened distinction between claims for the tortious disruption of an *existing* contract and claims that a *prospective* contractual or economic relationship has been interfered with by the defendant. Many of the cases do in fact acknowledge a greater array of justificatory defenses against claims of interference with prospective relations. Still, in our view and that of several other courts and commentators, the notion that the two torts are analytically unitary and derive from a common principle sacrifices practical wisdom to theoretical insight, promoting the idea that the interests invaded are of nearly equal dignity. They are not.

The courts provide a damage remedy against third party conduct intended to disrupt an existing contract precisely because the exchange of promises resulting in such a formally cemented economic relationship is deemed worthy of protection from interference by a stranger to the agreement. Economic relationships short of contractual, however, should stand on a different legal footing as far as the potential for tort liability is reckoned. Because ours is a culture firmly wedded to the social rewards of commercial contests, the law usually takes care to draw lines of legal liability in a way that maximizes areas of competition free of legal penalties.

A doctrine that blurs the analytical line between interference with an existing business contract and interference with commercial relations *less* than contractual is one that invites both uncertainty in conduct and unpredictability of its legal effect. The notion that inducing the breach of an existing contract is simply a subevent of the "more inclusive" class of acts that interfere with economic relations, while perhaps theoretically unobjectionable, has been mischievous as a practical matter. Our courts should, in short, firmly distinguish the two kinds of business contexts, bringing a greater solicitude to those relationships that have ripened into agreements, while recognizing that relationships short of that subsist in a zone where the rewards and risks of competition are dominant.

Beyond that, we need not tread today. It is sufficient to dispose of the issue before us in this case by holding that a plaintiff seeking to recover for alleged interference with prospective economic relations has the burden of pleading and proving that the defendant's interference was wrongful "by some measure beyond the fact of the interference itself." Top Service Body Shop v. Allstate Ins. Co. 582 P.2d 1365, 1371 (1978). It follows that the trial court did not commit error when it . . . require[d] the jury to find that defendant's interference was "wrongful." And because the instruction defining "wrongful conduct" given the jury by the trial court was offered by plaintiff himself, we have no occasion to review its sufficiency in this case. The question of whether additional refinements to the plaintiff's pleading and proof burdens merit adoption by California courts—questions embracing the precise scope of "wrongfulness," or whether a "disinterested malevolence," in Justice Holmes's words, American Bank & Trust Co. v. Federal Reserve Bank 256 U.S. 350, 358 (1921), is an actionable interference in itself, or whether the underlying policy justification for the tort, the efficient allocation of social resources, justifies including as actionable conduct that is recognized as anticompetitive under established state and federal positive law—are matters that can await another day. . . .

We hold that a plaintiff seeking to recover for an alleged interference with prospective contractual or economic relations must plead and prove as part of its case-in-chief that the defendant not only knowingly interfered with the plaintiff's expectancy, but engaged in conduct that was wrongful by some legal measure other than the fact of interference itself. . . .

Eldridge v. Johndrow

Supreme Court of Utah, 2015.
345 P.3d 553.

DURHAM, J. . . . Appellees Joseph and Lindsey Eldridge are the owners and operators of Harrison Companies, LLC, and Harrison Companies Property Management, LLC. Through these limited liability companies, the Eldridges manage residential property and provide various other services for wealthy homeowners in Summit County. Because providing these services means taking responsibility for clients' homes, the Eldridges' success depends a great deal on their reputation.

Appellant David Johndrow is a former friend and client of the Eldridges who used to recommend their services to his friends and other associates in the area. But the friendship lasted only a year. Lindsey Eldridge accused Mr. Johndrow of attacking her at a restaurant, and Mr. Johndrow accused the Eldridges of spreading false rumors and stealing his mobile phone. The once amicable relationship gave way to threats of legal action.

The action Johndrow actually took, however, did not involve a lawsuit. Instead, he "turned [the matter] over" to an "investigative team," which discovered various embarrassing facts about the Eldridges: liens, a foreclosure, an old felony conviction, and unflattering news reports from before they moved to Utah. Mr. Johndrow threatened that if the Eldridges refused to retract their accusations and compensate him for the allegedly stolen phone, he would have to protect his "credibility" by revealing what he had found to the people to whom he had recommended the Eldridges. When the Eldridges did not accede to his demands, he emailed embarrassing information to "at least nine" of the Eldridges' institutional clients and communicated it verbally to a number of their individual clients.

The Eldridges sued, asserting several theories of liability: tortious interference with economic relations, tortious interference with prospective economic relations, defamation, false light, and intentional infliction of emotional distress. The tortious interference theories each rested on two separate allegations: first, that by defaming the Eldridges, Mr. Johndrow had interfered with their economic relations through an improper means; and second, that because Mr. Johndrow's only goal was to hurt the Eldridges' business, he had interfered with their economic relations in pursuit of an improper purpose.

After preliminary discovery, Mr. Johndrow moved for summary judgment on the tortious interference claims, the defamation claim, and the false light claim. The district court concluded that the information Johndrow had disseminated was "at least substantially true" and "not susceptible to a defamatory interpretation." It therefore granted summary judgment on the defamation and false light claims. Further, because the "improper means" basis for tortious interference liability depended on Johndrow's alleged defamation of the Eldridges, the court granted summary judgment on the tortious interference claims insofar as they were based on improper means.

However, the district court denied summary judgment on the tortious interference claims insofar as they were based on allegations of improper purpose. Mr. Johndrow had argued that the court should follow the *Restatement* and hold that the communication of "truthful information," regardless of purpose, cannot constitute tortious interference. Restatement (Second) of Torts § 772(A) (1979). But the court relied on our decision in *Pratt v. Prodata, Inc.,* which explicitly rejected the Restatement's truth defense in the context of improper-purpose claims. 885 P.2d 786, 790 (Utah 1994). Correctly concluding that the reconsideration of *Pratt* was a matter for a higher tribunal, the court denied summary judgment with respect to the Eldridges' improper-purpose claims. . . .

The Eldridges' remaining tortious interference claims depend on the allegation that Mr. Johndrow interfered with their economic relations for an improper purpose. This improper-purpose doctrine was adopted in *Leigh Furniture & Carpet Co. v. Isom:* "[I]n order to recover damages [for tortious interference], the plaintiff must prove (1) that the defendant intentionally interfered with the plaintiff's existing or potential economic relations, (2) *for an improper purpose* or by improper means, (3) causing injury to the plaintiff." 657 P.2d 293, 304 (1982) (emphasis added). The *Leigh Furniture* court made clear that "improper purpose (or motive, intent, or objective) will support a cause of action for intentional interference with prospective economic relations even where the defendant's means were proper." Id. at 307. . .

If we were convinced that the improper-purpose doctrine served important public purposes, we would uphold it despite its weak basis in precedent. But our conviction is the opposite: improper purpose, in the absence of any improper means, should not be a basis for tortious interference liability.

As our decisions have recognized, determining the predominant purpose behind a defendant's actions raises significant evidentiary problems. Because this inquiry is necessarily fact-intensive, appellate review has been limited, and little case law has developed to guide courts' and juries' work. The improper-purpose doctrine thus requires trial courts and juries to make decisions that are effectively without guidance.

This vagueness does more than lead to unpredictable verdicts. It also fails to give parties adequate notice of their rights and duties. If improper-purpose liability became commonplace, it would have a chilling effect on legitimate, socially beneficial competitive practices. Worse, it would chill speech, discouraging the free spread of information and opinion.

For these reasons, among others, other states have increasingly limited or rejected improper-purpose liability. In addition to supporting our arguments against improper-purpose liability, this trend further weakens the authority on which *Leigh Furniture* was based. With both contemporary authority and our own reasoning opposed to improper-purpose liability, we conclude that it should be rejected. . . .

Anger and even malice are commonplace human emotions, and it would be neither possible nor desirable to treat every angry or malicious action as a tort. Even a tort allowing liability whenever a defendant maliciously interfered with a plaintiff's economic relations would be unwise. As *Leigh Furniture* recognized, such a tort would interfere with "much competitive commercial activity, such as a businessman's efforts to forestall a competitor in order to further his own long-range economic interests." *Leigh Furniture & Carpet Co. v. Isom*, 657 P.2d 293, 307 (Utah 1982).

Leigh Furniture sought to foreclose this possibility by requiring plaintiffs to show not merely that an improper purpose was present, but that it predominated over legitimate motivations. Yet even so, it recognized that there were "[p]roblems inherent in proving motivation or purpose" and cautioned against overuse of the improper-purpose prong. *Id.* . . . .

Because improper-purpose findings are so dependent on fact-finders' personal sympathies, and so insulated from appellate review, the outcome of an improper-purpose suit becomes unpredictable as soon as any evidence of improper purpose is introduced. This is a problem not merely because it may lead to unjust outcomes in individual cases, but because it makes it impossible for private parties to understand their rights and duties under tortious interference law.

Under the improper-purpose prong as it has developed, a business owner could be sued for undercutting his competitor's prices if he held a grudge against her. An investor in a Ponzi scheme might be sued for exposing the scheme if she did so with enough malice towards her swindlers. And a customer leaving angry reviews online might receive a response to her complaints via service of process.

It is of course likely that few juries would find a predominantly improper purpose in any of these cases, but that is beside the point. The mere risk that a jury might find liability, coupled with the low bar the claims need to clear in order to reach a jury in the first place, could become a substantial deterrent to socially beneficial speech and conduct if improper-purpose suits became common. . . .

We agree with Justice Stewart's *Pratt* concurrence that tortious interference law needs flexibility to deal with the new and creative methods people might invent to inflict gratuitous economic harm on each other. But we disagree that improper-purpose liability is the best way to maintain this flexibility. As we explained above, because of the improper-purpose rule's highly fact-dependent character, the doctrine hinders rather than promotes case-by-case efforts to adapt the common law to solve contemporary problems. . . .

The better approach is to encourage further development of the improper-means prong. . . . Neither has our improper-means jurisprudence since *Leigh Furniture* set precise boundaries that will prevent courts from recognizing new sorts of improper means when they arise.

Further development of the improper-means prong is therefore possible, and it has a great advantage over developing the improper-purpose prong. Unlike findings of improper purpose, findings of improper means will not depend solely on defendants' state of mind. They will thus allow for more careful appellate review, leading to a better defined and more predictable tortious interference jurisprudence. . . .

Although we reject our past doctrine that improper purpose is sufficient grounds for tortious interference liability, this does not mean that defendants' motives and intent are entirely irrelevant to tortious interference claims. We wish to make clear that defendants' motivation is still relevant to tortious interference claims in two ways.

First and more obviously, tortious interference remains an intentional tort. . . .

Second, defendants' motivation will often be relevant to the improper means prong of the *Leigh Furniture* test. For example, a plaintiff might bring a tortious interference suit alleging that the defendant's improper means of interference was an abuse of judicial process. In order to adjudicate that claim, a court would have to determine whether the defendant used a legal process "primarily *to accomplish a purpose* for which it is not designed." [*Gilbert v. Ince*, 981 P.2d 841, 845 (Utah 1999) (emphasis added).] This is only one of many possible claims in which the propriety of a particular means will depend in part on the defendant's reasons for employing it.

In such cases, however, it will never be the defendant's motivation by itself that leads to liability. Abuse of process is an improper means not because the defendant bore the plaintiff ill will; it is an improper means because those who avail themselves of the legal system's coercive powers have a duty to do so for legitimate legal reasons. A person who violates this duty, with the intent to hinder someone's economic relations, is liable for whatever damages result from that improper act.

On the other hand, a person who violates no legal duties, infringes no one's rights, and commits no wrongful action can never be held liable for malice alone. . . .

For the foregoing reasons, we conclude that in the absence of any improper means, an improper purpose is not grounds for tortious interference liability. We therefore overrule *Pratt v. Prodata*, 885 P.2d 786 (Utah 1994). We also disavow all dicta in *Leigh Furniture & Carpet Co. v. Isom*, 657 P.2d 293 (Utah 1982), that would allow liability based solely on an improper purpose. In order to win a tortious interference claim under Utah law, a plaintiff must now prove "(1) that the defendant intentionally interfered with the plaintiff's existing or potential economic relations, (2) . . . by improper means, (3) causing injury to the plaintiff." Id. at 304.

The Eldridges' tortious interference claims fail the second prong of this test: they have failed to produce evidence of an improper means. The district court's denial of summary judgment on the tortious interference claims is therefore reversed, and the matter is remanded for further action consistent with this opinion. . . .

J.D. Edwards & Co. v. Podany

United States Court of Appeals, Seventh Circuit, 1999.
168 F.3d 1020.

POSNER, CHIEF JUDGE. A company had a contract to sell computer services. The buyer broke the contract, but the seller's suit, a diversity suit governed, so far as substantive issues are concerned, by the law of Illinois, is not against the buyer; it is against a consulting firm (and a former employee of the firm) that advised the buyer and was responsible for the buyer's decision to break its contract with the seller. The defendants are accused of having committed the tort of deliberately inducing a breach of contract. This is a mysterious tort. It seems to give the victim of a breach of contract two remedies, where one—a suit for breach of contract against the party who broke the contract—ought to suffice. But in some cases, of which this is not one, the contract breaker is insolvent; and in others, the third party could have avoided the breach of contract at a lower cost than the contract breaker. This may be such a case; SNE, the party that broke the contract, did so on the advice of a consultant who purported to be a specialist in the field of business and computer systems.

In any event, whether the provision of a remedy in tort for inducing a breach of contract is wise is not for us to decide. It is a settled part of the law of Illinois. Nor is there any doubt that the plaintiff made out a prima facie case. The only issue is whether the jury was justified in rejecting, en route to awarding the plaintiff $2.3 million in damages, the defense to inducing breach of contract that is called the "consultant's privilege," or more commonly the privilege of "honest advice." This is the privilege of a consultant, or other advisor, to offer good-faith advice to a client without fear of liability should the client act on that advice to the harm of a third person, in this case the plaintiff.

The privilege resembles the rule in defamation law that where there is a duty to speak, a defamatory utterance, if made in good faith and not disseminated any further than necessary, is privileged. A consultant is hired to give advice. Often the advice is painful, because firms frequently turn to consultants when they are in trouble or when they want to do something that hurts and want to spread the blame a bit. The consultant's advice may lead to downsizing, layoffs, outsourcing, and countless other perturbations, including, as here, contractual terminations. It would cast quite a large, dark cloud over the consulting business if consultants could be hauled into court for having given advice that in hindsight could be characterized as having been ill-advised, ill-informed, or otherwise negligent. The consultant's privilege cuts off this possibility. But it is not absolute. It is a qualified privilege, like qualified immunity as distinct from absolute immunity in the law of public officers' torts.

It is qualified in two ways. First, it is limited to advice given within the scope of the consultant's engagement. If a consultant hired to advise the client, a fast-food chain, on selecting a new telephone system suggested that the client terminate its fast-food franchisee in Oshkosh because the franchisee was serving soggy doughnuts, and the suggestion was adopted, the consultant could not set up the consultant's privilege in defense of the franchisee's suit for interference with contract. Not having been hired to advise on the client's franchise system, the consultant would have no contractual duty to render frank and fearless (or indeed any) advice on the subject.

Second, if the consultant does not give honest advice—if he uses his engagement to hurt other people exclusively for his own benefit (or out of dislike of his victim) rather than for the benefit of his client—he forfeits the privilege. If solely to feather his own nest, and without believing that (or caring whether) he is helping his client, he causes the client to break a contract to the detriment of the other party to the contract, he is liable for inducing the breach.

Both limitations on the consultant's privilege, scope and good faith, are in issue here. The defendants argue that there was insufficient evidence to justify the jury's rejecting the privilege on either ground. The argument fails, as we can show largely just by recounting the facts, viewed as favorably to the plaintiff, the winner in the district court, as the record will permit.

SNE—the client and contract breaker—manufactures windows. It hired J.D. Edwards & Co., the plaintiff, to supply software for a project that SNE called PBS (for "Primary Business System") and that involved streamlining SNE's business and obtaining the computer support necessary for the streamlining. SNE rejected another company's software called BPCS because BPCS lacked a "configurator," which is a program that facilitates custom manufacturing. While the transition to PBS was under way, there was a reorganization that made SNE one of three divisions of a corporation headed by Gary Massel. Enter the defendants, Randy Podany and Mercer Management Consulting, Inc. Massel knew Podany, an employee of Mercer, and asked him to do what is called in the consulting trade a "sniff test"—a very quick, light review—of PBS. The fee was $10,000. After "sniffing" for a day (concretely, meeting with the PBS managers and reviewing relevant documents), Podany advised Massel that the basic approach that SNE had taken to streamlining its business, that of "reengineering in parallel," and the leading role that it had assigned to J.D. Edwards, were unsound. Reengineering in parallel means defining the company's business needs and *at the same time* obtaining the necessary computer support or other technical support. Podany is not a software expert and neither he nor his company had been retained to select software or offer a critique of the contract with J.D. Edwards. His advice had been sought at the business level. But reengineering in parallel is an example in consultant-speak of a "systems concept" and thus fell within the scope of Podany's (and Mercer's) engagement.

Podany also advised Massel to stop installing J.D. Edwards' software. The plaintiff argues that this advice was outside the terms of the engagement and so outside the protection of the consultant's privilege, but we disagree. If reengineering in parallel was a mistake and (as Podany urged) the definition of SNE's business needs should precede the installation of any software, it followed that the installation should be halted; and making this explicit did not carry the consultant's advice outside the boundaries of the privilege. To hold that it did would simply lead consultants to insist on very broad terms of engagement. That, or make them too timid. If a surgeon discovered a cancerous polyp on the patient's colon while performing an appendectomy, we wouldn't want him to refuse to remove the polyp because he feared exceeding the scope of his engagement. There might be medical reasons for him to decline to remove it; it might be beyond his competence; but if it were within his competence, we would want him to act because the patient if he could be consulted would want him to act. Similarly, if a consultant discovers a problem that is outside the strict terms of his engagement but within the range of his competence, the client would want him to bring the problem to the client's attention without fear of being sued should the solution involve the termination of a contract. So likely is this to be what the client would want that we can assume, just as in the surgical case, that it is an implied term of the engagement.

Podany, however, went further than merely advising Massell to stop installing J.D. Edwards' software. He ordered the SNE executive in charge of implementation of the contract with J.D. Edwards to stop paying Edwards. This went well beyond his original engagement, but the engagement had been enlarged by Massel, who had directed everyone in his company to "have all computer related purchases approved by Randy [Podany]." Podany's stop-payment orders were within the implied scope of this new engagement.

The problem with the defendants' assertion of the consultant's privilege is not that Podany exceeded the scope of their engagement; it is that a reasonable jury could find that he acted in bad faith. Podany knew very little about the software that was being supplied by J.D. Edwards. The only software program he was familiar with was—BPCS. So he maneuvered to replace Edwards' software with BPCS, even though BPCS lacked a configurator, which SNE had wanted. The reason he gave was that the only one of Massel's three divisions that was able to provide Massel with timely and accurate financial data had BPCS, and he ascribed the division's success in this regard to BPCS. But he did not attempt to trade off this advantage against the disadvantage, for SNE, that BPCS lacked a configurator. He arranged things so that BPCS would be selected without a fair comparison with J.D. Edwards' software. And, what is critical—for mistakes do not void the consultant's privilege—he did all this in order to land himself a lucrative job with SNE's parent as director of information services. And having done so he procured further engagements of his former employer, Mercer. During the 18 months that he remained employed by SNE, he earned $370,000 and Mercer billed SNE $1.6 million. But BPCS was a flop; it was never successfully installed in SNE. One reason it was a flop was that it lacked a configurator.

If Podany was simply a fool, and got SNE to replace J.D. Edwards' software with BPCS because he ignorantly believed that the latter really was superior for SNE's needs even though it lacked a configurator, he and his employer would be sheltered from liability by the consultant's privilege. They would be, indeed, securely within the core of the privilege. But if Podany's only object was to enrich himself—and Mercer—the privilege is forfeited. Here we pause to observe that the parties have not tried to distinguish Mercer's liability from Podany's. It has been understood that they sink or swim together. Podany was acting to further Mercer's interests as well as his own, thus making Mercer liable for Podany's intentional tort under the doctrine of respondeat superior.

In pointing to Podany's motives, we do not make the mistake of confusing bad faith with greed. A consultant might be in consulting purely for the money, but as long as he made his money by offering honest advice within the scope of his employment, his private motives would be irrelevant. It is when a consultant decides to make money by rendering dishonest advice (or going outside the terms of his engagement) that he loses the protection of privilege and assumes the usual liabilities.

Podany denied any such ulterior motive. But his credibility was impeached, and the jury was not required to believe him. His lack of credibility, like pretext in a discrimination case, combined with circumstantial evidence to justify the jury in finding bad faith. A plaintiff cannot win just by putting the defendant on the stand and asking the jury to disbelieve him. But if there is other evidence of liability, then unconvincing denials by the defendant can help persuade the jury that the plaintiff's story is true. The other evidence in this case included the fact that, after rejecting the concept of reengineering in parallel and on the basis of that rejection halting the implementation of the contract with J.D. Edwards, Podany had SNE install BPCS on the same basis—that is, in parallel with the specification of SNE's needs. The justification for rigging the software selection process to assure the selection of BPCS—the only software he could work with—that he offered (the success of BPCS in generating prompt and accurate financial information for another division) was inadequate given BPCS's lack of a configurator, which SNE had deemed essential. He misrepresented the relative cost of the two software packages. He pronounced the J.D. Edwards software a "piece of shit" without knowing enough about it to have an opinion. Of course all these things could have been innocent mistakes. But the more, and the more egregious, a consultant's mistakes, the less innocent they are likely to be. And when on top of this the defendants' efforts to show that they were innocent (maybe negligent, but not deliberate) foundered, there was enough to justify a reasonable trier of fact in rejecting the defense of privilege. That doesn't mean that the jury was right in this case. But its decision was not so unreasonable as to warrant reversal.

INDEX

References are to Pages